THE ARCHAEOLOGY
OF ISRAELITE SAMARIA
Volume II

HARVARD SEMITIC MUSEUM PUBLICATIONS
Lawrence E. Stager, General Editor
Michael D. Coogan, Director of Publications

HARVARD SEMITIC STUDIES
Jo Ann Hackett and John Huehnergard, editors

23. *Syriac Manuscripts: A Catalogue*	Moshe H. Goshen-Gottstein
24. *Introduction to Classical Ethiopic*	Thomas O. Lambdin
25. *Dictionary of Old South Arabic*	Joan C. Biella
27. *The Songs of the Sabbath Sacrifice*	Carol Newsom
28. *Non-Canonical Psalms from Qumran:*	
A Pseudepigraphic Collection	Eileen M. Schuller
29. *The Hebrew of the Dead Sea Scrolls*	Elisha Qimron
30. *An Exodus Scroll from Qumran*	Judith E. Sanderson
31. *You Shall Have No Other Gods*	Jeffrey H. Tigay
32. *Ugaritic Vocabulary in Syllabic Transcription*	John Huehnergard
33. *The Scholarship of William Foxwell Albright*	Gus Van Beek
34. *The Akkadian of Ugarit*	John Huehnergard
35. *Features of the Eschatology of IV Ezra*	Michael E. Stone
36. *Studies in Neo-Aramaic*	Wolfhart Heinrichs, Editor
37. *Lingering over Words: Studies in Ancient Near Eastern*	
Literature in Honor of William L. Moran	
Tzvi Abusch, John Huehnergard, Piotr Steinkeller, Editors	
38. *A Grammar of the Palestinian Targum Fragments*	
from the Cairo Genizah	Steven E. Fassberg
39. *The Origins and Development of the Waw-Consecutive:*	
Northwest Semitic Evidence from Ugaritic to Qumran	Mark S. Smith
40. *Amurru Akkadian: A Linguistic Study, Volume I*	Shlomo Izre'el
41. *Amurru Akkadian: A Linguistic Study, Volume II*	Shlomo Izre'el
42. *The Installation of Baal's High Priestess at Emar*	Daniel E. Fleming
43. *The Development of the Arabic Scripts*	Beatrice Gruendler
44. *The Archaeology of Israelite Samaria: Early Iron Age*	
through the Ninth Century BCE	Ron Tappy
45. *A Grammar of Akkadian*	John Huehnergard
46. *Key to* A Grammar of Akkadian	John Huehnergard
47. *Akkadian Loanwords in Biblical Hebrew*	Paul V. Mankowski
48. *Adam in Myth and History: Ancient Israelite*	
Perspectives on the Primal Human	Dexter E. Callender Jr.
49. *West Semitic Vocabulary in the Akkadian Texts from Emar*	Eugen J. Pentiuc
50. *The Archaeology of Israelite Samaria, Volume 2:*	
The Eighth Century BCE	Ron E. Tappy

THE ARCHAEOLOGY OF ISRAELITE SAMARIA

Volume II
The Eighth Century BCE

by

Ron E. Tappy

EISENBRAUNS
Winona Lake, Indiana
2001

THE ARCHAEOLOGY OF ISRAELITE SAMARIA
Volume 2

by
Ron E. Tappy

Copyright © 2001
The President and Fellows of Harvard University

Printed in the United States of America

Library of Congress Cataloging-in-Publication Data

Tappy, Ron E.
    The archaeology of Israelite Samaria / by Ron E. Tappy.
      p. cm. — (Harvard Semitic studies ; no. 44 [v. 1]; no. 50 [v. 2])
    Includes bibliographical references and index.
      Contents: I. Early iron age through the ninth century BCE. II. Eighth century BCE.
    ISBN 1-55540-770-6 (v. 1)
    ISBN 1-57506-916-4 (v. 2)
      1. Samaria—Antiquities. 2. Excavations (Archaeology)—West Bank—Samaria. 3. West Bank—Antiquities. I. Title. II. Series.
DS110.S3T37 1992
933—dc20   92-32945
                                                          CIP

The paper used in this publication meets the minimum requirements of the American National Standard for Information Sciences—Permanence of Paper for Printed Library Materials, ANSI Z39.48-1984.∞™

To
my wife,
Connie,
and my daughter,
Madeleine Rose

אֱלֹהִים מוֹשִׁיב יְחִידִים בַּיְתָה

ACKNOWLEDGMENTS

Scholarship is, by definition, an interpersonal activity; that it cannot be achieved in isolation bequeaths to us the grandest legacy of the entire enterprise. Anyone who takes up serious research will quickly recognize two extraordinary rewards for the effort. First, one has the privilege of encountering a company of scholars whose previous works have touched on the subject at hand in some direct or indirect way. Though many of these individuals now dwell among us only through the insights and ideas they committed to paper long ago, their writings retain the power to introduce us over and over as if for the first time to their memory and to the world they knew. Second, there is the pleasure of interacting with a myriad of current scholars, curators, and administrators whose combined interests and disciplines allow a new investigation to amass preliminary data, assume a logical trajectory, and evolve into a finished statement. In my attempts to learn more about the archaeology of the Israelite capital at Samaria, the numerous meetings and steady assistance that I have gained from my intellectual forbearers and my contemporary colleagues alike have constantly brought me the richest rewards that research can offer.

In addition to the individuals already recognized in *The Archaeology of Israelite Samaria*, Volume I, I would like to acknowledge those colleagues who have taken the time to read and review that initial work. I believe that their observations and comments have helped to strengthen the present study in many ways. Once again, I am extremely grateful to the officers and staff of the Palestine Exploration Fund in London, England, who not only gave me free and unfettered access to primary excavation data stored in that venerable institution but who also repeatedly assisted me in my search for materials germane to the Fund's early work at Samaria. Without their many kindnesses shown to me during my visits to London and their permission to reproduce and publish excerpts and drawings from the archives of the PEF, I could not have completed this investigation. Particularly, I would like to thank Jonathan Tubb, Rupert L. Chapman III, and Felicity Cobbing for their generous assistance on behalf of the PEF.

Through a program under the direction of Professor Nathan O. Hatch, the Pew Charitable Trusts provided a Research Fellowship in support of the first major phase of writing devoted to this project during the academic year 1997-1998. I cannot overstate the role that this award played during the formative stages of this manuscript. I would like to extend particular thanks to Mr. Michael S. Hamilton, Program Coordinator, for his constant encouragement during those early days of my work and for his assistance during the fellowship competition. I am also grateful to the members of the fellowship review committee for their decision to support a proposal in archaeology.

At Pittsburgh Theological Seminary, I recognize the faithful support that my work has received from the administration, my faculty colleagues, and my students. In the autumn of 1999, a Faculty Development Grant that allowed a pivotal period of research in London gave a timely boost to the entire project and particularly to the chapter dealing with the ivory fragments and glass inlays from Samaria. The generous patronage of the late G. Albert Shoemaker and the continuing support and interest shown by Ms. Mercedes Shoemaker in the archaeological program at Pittsburgh Seminary have made my appointment and research at this institution possible. I have also benefited greatly both from the practical support of Mr. William R. Jackson, Sr., and Mr. William C. Pettit of Pittsburgh and from the many conversations on a variety of archaeological topics that I have had with these two gentlemen. I owe a great debt to Ms. Kathy Anderson for her meticulous proofreading and reference checks for each and every footnote that appears in this book.

I am honored once again to have this volume appear in the Harvard Semitic Studies series of the Harvard Semitic Museum Publications. Both Lawrence E. Stager, General Editor, and Michael D. Coogan, Director of Publications, have facilitated this opportunity and have helped guide the manuscript through the publication process. Throughout this procedure, James Eisenbraun has also proved immensely helpful. For his discerning comments and thoughtful directions I am most grateful.

Finally, I must return to the interpersonal nature of research. As knows every author—especially those who have labored to produce a large-scale work—no one sacrifices more time and energy and, on occasion, suffers in more profound ways during the process of research than the author's own family. The road to Samaria has seemed a long one. Yet I have had the pleasure of knowing that, despite the sacrifice, my wife, Connie, and my daughter, Madeleine, have taken each step of that journey with me. Connie has, in fact, already read and commented on the entire manuscript. But at no time have these two companions sought personal recognition, gain, or reward for their commitment to my project. I could not travel the road to Samaria or anywhere else without them, and it is to them that I dedicate this book.

CONTENTS

Acknowledgments vii

Contents ix
List of Figures xiv
List of Tables xvii
List of Abbreviations xix

Preface xxix

INTRODUCTION

    I. Modern Attempts to Excavate Samaria: Achievements and Problems 1

    II. Samaria *in situ*: An Interface of Geology, Geography, and History 4

CHAPTER I — POTTERY PERIOD 4-4a:
Remains of Prosperity and Expansion in the Early Eighth Century BCE?

    I.   Introduction 11

    II.   Pottery Period 4 14
        Part A. House Floors — Rooms *g*, *h*, *j*, *k*, *n* 16
            1) Stratigraphic Detail 20
                a. Rooms *g*, *h*, and *j* 20
                    [i]   120.121.19.126 20
                b. Rooms *h* and *k* 27
                    [i]   125.144 27
                c. Room *h* 37
                    [i]   125.144 37
                    [ii]   147.145.151.136 37
                    [iii] 155.151.136.147 37
                    [iv] 120.121.19.126 40
                    [v]   122.125.19.121 40
                d. Room *j* 43
                    [i]   North of Test Trench 2 43
                    [ii]   E Strip; North of Test Trench 2 43
                    [iii] 120.121.19.126 48
                    [iv] 509.126 48
                e. Room *k* 55
                    [i]   Between Test Trench 2-Test Trench 3 55
                    [ii]   E Strip; Between Test Trench 2-Test Trench 3 55
                    [iii] 125.144 58
                f. Room *n* 58
                    [i]   502.503 58

        2) Pottery Analysis 66
            a. Bowls (6:1-7) 67
            b. Cooking Pots (6:25-30, 32-40) 77
            c. Jars (6:8, 12, 14-18) 88
            d. Holemouth Jars (6:19-24) 102
        3) Evaluation and Summary 107

    Part B. North Courtyard 114
        1) Stratigraphic Detail 117
            a. 86.2.88 117
            b. 86.2.88.E 117
            c. 86.2.88.W 117
            d. 86.2.88.E; W of 104 117
        2) Pottery Analysis 124
            a. Cooking Pots (6:31) 124
            b. Jars (6:9-11, 13) 124
        3) Evaluation and Summary 129

    Part C. Courtyard 131
        1) Stratigraphic Detail 135
            a. 325.304 135
        2) Pottery Analysis 144
            a. Jars (6:19) 144
        3) Evaluation and Summary 144

    Part D. Casemate Repair Deposit 145
        1) Stratigraphic Detail 149
            a. 504.508.509.510 149
        2) Pottery Analysis 153
            a. Bowls (7:1-5) 153
            b. Cooking Pots (7:6-8) 159
            c. Jars (7:9) 161
        3) Evaluation and Summary 164

    Pottery Period 4: Conclusions 166

CHAPTER II — POTTERY PERIOD 5: *Remains of the Last Israelite Occupation?*

   I.   Introduction 175

  II.   Pottery Period 5 182
    Part A. House Floors — Rooms *hk, j, n* 184
        1) Stratigraphic Detail 186
            a. Rooms *hk/hq* 186
                [i]   125.144 — Room *hk* 186
                [ii] West of 124 — Room *hq* 190
                [iii] E Strip; Between Test Trench 2–Test Trench 3 — Room *hk* 197
            b. Room *j* 202
                [i]   509.126 202
            c. Room *n* 206
                [i]   502.503 206

Contents

        2) Pottery Analysis 207
            a. Cooking Pots (8:6-7) 209
            b. Jars (8:1-2, 5, 8) 211
            c. Holemouth Jars (8:3-4) 217
        3) Evaluation and Summary 220

    Pottery Period 5: Conclusions 222

CHAPTER III — POTTERY PERIOD 6: *Remains of an Ephemeral Historical "Period"?*

    I.   Introduction 227

        Excursus — Establishing a Ceramic Control Group through Comparative Stratigraphic
             Analysis of Selected Northern Sites 230

    II.   Pottery Period 6 252
        Part A. Leveling Contemporary with Wall 573 254
            1) Stratigraphic Detail 257
                a. North of 551 257
                b. 513.514 261
            2) Pottery Analysis 265
                a. Bowls (9:1-3) 266
                b. Cooking Pots (9:10-18) 277
                c. Jugs and Juglets (9:4, 6-7) 281
                d. Decanters (9:5) 287
                e. Braziers (9:8-9) 291
            3) Evaluation and Summary 294

        Part B. Pit *i* 296
            1) Stratigraphic Detail 299
                a. 122.125.19.121 299
                b. 122.126(?).19.121 299
            2) Pottery Analysis 301
                a. Bowls (10:1-14) 302
                b. Cooking Pots (10:26-27) 319
                c. Jars (10:25) 322
                d. Jugs and Juglets (10:15-16, 21-24) 324
                e. Decanters (10:17-20) 337
            3) Evaluation and Summary 341

    Pottery Period 6: Conclusions 347

CHAPTER IV — POTTERY PERIOD 7: *Remains of the Assyrian Siege?*

    I.   Introduction 351

    II.   Pottery Period 7 354
        Part A. Deposits Overlying House Floors in Rooms *e, f, g, hk, hq, j, kq,* and *l* 355
            1a) Stratigraphic Detail: Single-feature Segments 359
                a. Room *e* 359

Contents

        [i] 19.51.14.20 359
    b. Room *hk* 365
        [i] 122.125.19.121 365
        [ii] 125.144 365
    c. Room *l* 367
        [i] 504.503.509.508 367
  1b) Stratigraphic Detail: Multiple-feature Segments 375
    a. 120.121.19.126 376
        [i] Rooms *e*, *f*, *g*, and *kq* 376
    b. 509.126 381
        [i] Rooms *f*, *j*, and *l* 381
    c. W of 124 383
        [i] Rooms *hq* and *kq* 383
2) Pottery Analysis 390
    a. Bowls (11:1-9, 11-23, 36) 391
    b. Cooking Pots (11:32) 414
    c. Jars and Jar Stands (11:24-27, 29-31, 33, 35) 416
    d. Jugs and Juglets (11:28, 34) 425
    e. Lamps (11:10, 37) 430
3) Evaluation and Summary 433

Pottery Period 7: Conclusions 435

CHAPTER V — THE SAMARIA IVORIES:
A Case Study in Theory, Method, and Outcome

I.   Introduction 443

II. The Archaeo-Historical Context of the Samaria Ivories 444
Part A. Spatial Distribution of Published Ivories: Overview 446
  1) Stratigraphic Detail 452
    a. Principal Findspots 452
        [i]   19.51.14.20 (N. & S.) — Room *e* 452
        [ii] 49.26.25 — Room *hq* 464
        [iii] W of 124 — Rooms *hq* and *kq* 468
    b. Miscellaneous Findspots 478
        [i]   E 207 — Shrine (or Tomb?) 478
        [ii]   12.27.14.13 — Room *e* 478
        [iii] 19.12.20 — Room *e* 478
        [iv] 9.21.31 — Northern Slope 479
        [v]   North of Wall 20 — Northern Slope 479
        [vi] 120.121.19.126 — Room *g* 483
        [vii] 125.144 — Rooms *h*/*hk* 483
        [viii] E Strip.E Half — Rooms *k*/*hk* 485
        [ix] 507.503.504.505 — Room *l* 487
        [x]   Hellenistic Robber Trench — Backfill/Room *l* 487

  2) Evaluation and Summary 490

The Samaria Ivories: Conclusions 491

Excursus — A Comment on the Spatial Distribution of the Samaria Ostraca:
Horizontal Axis 496

CHAPTER VI — ISRAEL AND ASSYRIA:
A Summary of Relations during the Iron Age II

I. Introduction 505

II. Samaria's Entanglement with Assyria 507
    Part A. Early Encounters 507
        1) Shalmaneser III: 853, 841 BCE 507
        2) Adad-nirari III: 796 BCE 516

    Part B. The Western Campaigns and Inscriptions of Tiglath-pileser III 529
        1) Introduction to Phases A.4 and S.5 529
        2) The West: Phase I (743-738 BCE) 531
        3) The West: Phase II (734-732 BCE) 542

    Part C. Israelite Sovereignty: The Final Years 558
        1) Shalmaneser V: 727-722 BCE 558
        2) Sargon II: 720, 716 BCE 563

Israel and Assyria: Conclusions 575

CHAPTER VII — CONCLUDING REMARKS:
The City and Region of Samaria beyond the Iron Age 581

Appendixes 585
    Appendix A: Findspots for Published Stratified Pottery (Periods 4-7) 587
    Appendix B: Findspots for Published Stratified Fragments of Ivory 591
    Appendix C: Findspots for Published Stratified Israelite Ostraca 599
    Appendix D: Neo-Assyrian Literary References to the Northern Kingdom of Israel 601
    Appendix E: Published Stratified Pottery Representing Periods 4-7 612
Bibliography 617
Indexes 651
    Biblical References 651
    Apocrypha 652
    General Index 653

LIST OF FIGURES

Introduction

1. Overview of Summit Excavations: Harvard University, Joint Expedition, and Soundings by F. Zayadine 2
2. Major Sites and Roadways in the Region of Samaria 6
3. General Area of the "Dimorphic Zone" in Israel 8

Chapter I — Pottery Period 4

4. Published "Period III" Top Plan 14
5. Published "Period IV" Top Plan 15
6. Published Section EF 19
7. Auxiliary Section A: Segments *N of TT2* and *Btw TT2-TT3* 21
8. Auxiliary Section B: Segments *Btw TT2-TT3*; *125.144*; *122.125.19.121* 24
9. Auxiliary Section C: Layers West of Wall 120 (in Room *g*) 25
10. Segment *125.144* 33
11. Segment *125.144*: Supplement 36
12. Field-drawn Top Plan for Area around Pit *i* 38
13. Segment *North of Test Trench 2*: Section down Center of East Strip 45
14. *North of Test Trench 2*: Supplement No. 1 — Section along South Edge of Area 46
15. *North of Test Trench 2*: Supplement No. 2 46
16. *North of Test Trench 2*: Supplement No. 3 46
17. The Summit Strip System: Location of Excavated Areas 49
18. Horizontal Locations of Selected Stratified Segments 51
19. Segment *509.126* 53
20. Field Sketch of Unphased Top Plan Relating to Segment *502.503* 59
21. Configuration of Walls and Pavements in the Vicinity of Rooms *r* and *n* 61
22. Restricted Field Sketch No. 1 from Segment *502.503* 65
23. Restricted Field Sketch No. 2 from Segment *502.503* 65
24. Composite Top Plan for North Courtyard Area: BP I-II, III, IV 116
25. Segment *Series 86.2.88* 118
26. Segment *Series 86.2.88*: Supplement No. 1 — E and W of Wall 95 120
27. Segment *Series 86.2.88*: Supplement No. 2 — Section on Line of 99 121
28. Top Plan of Summit Strip Qg: Approximate Location of Segment *325.304* 133
29. Local Plan of Summit Strip Qg: Architectural Relationships of Wall 325 134
30. Segment *325.304*: Section West of Wall 325 134
31. Segment *325.304*: Section West of 316 135
32. Portion of Published Section GH Relevant to Segment *325.304* 136
33. Section West of Foundation Trench 336 136
34. Area Around Robber Trench 333 137
35. Area Around Robber Trench 372 138
36. Depositional History in the Vicinity of RT 333 and RT 372 138
37. Summit Strip Qg: Segments *325.304, 364.337.363, 313.306, 302.304* 139
38. Segment *504.508.509.510*: Top Plan of Coordinate Walls 148
39. Segment *504.508.509.510*: Local Deposits West of Wall 504 150
40. General Topography of Rock West of Palace Area 168

Chapter II — Pottery Period 5

41. Published "Period V" Top Plan 184
42. Field Section Relating to Segment *West of 124* 191
43. Segment *West of 124*: Field Section South of Wall 125 192
44. A: Stratigraphic Correlations between Segments *W of 124* and *Btw TT2–TT3* 198
45. B: Stratigraphic Correlations between Segments *W of 124* and *Btw TT2–TT3* 198
46. C: Stratigraphic Correlations between Segments *W of 124* and *Btw TT2–TT3* 199
47. D: Stratigraphic Correlations between Segments *W of 124* and *Btw TT2–TT3* 199
48. Segment *509.126* 203
49. Segment *North of Test Trench 2* 205

Chapter III — Pottery Period 6

50. Published Section CD: Segments *North of 551* and *513.514* 255
51. Segment *North of 551* 258
52. Segment *North of 551*: Supplement 259
53. Segment *513.514* 262
54. Segment *513.514*: Supplement 263
55. Segment *North of 514* 264

Chapter IV — Pottery Period 7

56. Published BP V Top Plan (including Architecture Related to PP 7) 356
57. Segment *19.51.14.20* 360
58. Portion of Published Section GH @ 445°–467° N 361
59. Segment *19.51.14.20*: Southern Sector 363
60. Segment *504.503.509.508* — Top Plan No. 1 368
61. Segment *504.503.509.508* — Top Plan No. 2 369
62. Segment *504.503.509.508* 370
63. Segment *504.503.509.508*: Supplement 371
64. Segment *509.126* 373
65. Segment *502.500.503* 374
66. Segment *504.508.509.510* 375
67. Segment *120.121.19.126* — Room *g* 378
68. Location of Wall 124 and the Segment *West of 124* 384
69. Segment *W of 124* — South of Walls 56 and the 125 Series 385
70. Section South of Wall 125 387
71. *W of 124* and other Segments 388

Chapter V — The Samaria Ivories

72. The Strip System: Location of Principal Ivory-bearing Areas (Qc, Qd, Qf, Qk, Qn) 449
73. Plan of Summit Strip Qc, Segment *19.51.14.20*, and Published Section GH 452
74. Segment *19.51.14.20* — *North and South* 454
75. Partial Plan of Summit Strip Qc: Coordinate Walls *12.27.14.13* in Segment *19.51.14.20.N* 459
76. Field Section Showing a Portion of Room *12.27.14.13* 460
77. Wall 12 from Room *12.27.14.13* 463
78. Partial Plan of Summit Strip Qc: Segment *49.26.25*, Layer II (Room *hq*) 467

79.	Lateral Section South of and Parallel to Wall 125	471
80.	Hollowed Stone Set into *W of 124*, Layer VI	474
81.	Room *9.21.29.30* — Stratification under Wall 21	480
82.	Section of Trench North of Wall 20	482
83.	*East Strip: South Half* — Section .50 m West of 129	486
84.	Plan of the Ostraca House	497
85.	Section through the Ostraca House and Superimposed Layers	500

LIST OF TABLES

Chapter I — Pottery Period 4

1. Horizontal + Vertical Dimensions of PP 4 Stratigraphy 13
2. Correlation of Extant Sections and Courtyard Rooms North of 450° N, East of 638° E 19
3. Analysis of Architecture Presented in *SS I*, Pl. VII, Section EF 22
4. Abridged Stratigraphic Summary of Segment *509.126* 50
5. Abridged Stratigraphic Summary of Segment *502.503* 63
6. Distribution of PP 4-4a Ceramic Forms Published from House Floors (Rooms *g-k, n*) 66
7. Provenance Data: PP4 Bowls from Area Labeled "House Floors" 68
8. Provenance Data: PP4 Cooking Pots from Area Labeled "House Floors" 77
9. Provenance Data: PP4 Jars from Area Labeled "House Floors" 89
10. Provenance Data: PP4 Holemouth Jars from Area Labeled "House Floors" 103
11. Distribution of PP 4-4a Ceramic Forms in Local Stratigraphy of House Floors (Rooms *g-k, n*) 108
12. Provenance Data: PP4 Jars from Area Labeled "North Courtyard" 125
13. Distribution of PP 4-4a Ceramic Forms in Local Stratigraphy of North Courtyard
    (Segment Series *86.2.88* . . .) 130
14. Provenance Data: PP4 Jars from Area Labeled "Courtyard" 144
15. Provenance Data: PP4 Bowls from Area Labeled "Casemate Repair Deposit" 153
16. Provenance Data: PP4 Cooking Pots from Area Labeled "Casemate Repair Deposit" 159
17. Provenance Data: PP4 Jars from Area Labeled "Casemate Repair Deposit" 161
18. Distribution of PP 4-4a Ceramic Forms in Local Stratigraphy of the Casemate Repair Deposit 165

Chapter II — Pottery Period 5

19. Horizontal + Vertical Dimensions of PP 5 Stratigraphy 183
20. Stratigraphic Correlations Relating to Rooms *hk, hq,* and *kq* 201
21. Distribution of PP 5 Ceramic Forms Published from House Floors (Rooms *hk, j, n, hq*) 208
22. Provenance Data: PP5 Cooking Pots from Area Labeled "House Floors" 209
23. Provenance Data: PP5 Jars from Area Labeled "House Floors" 211
24. Provenance Data: PP5 Holemouth Jars from Area Labeled "House Floors" 218
25. Distribution of PP 5 Ceramic Forms in Local Stratigraphy of House Floors
    (Rooms *hk, j, n, hq*) 220

Chapter III — Pottery Period 6

26. Horizontal + Vertical Dimensions of PP 6 Stratigraphy 253
27. Provenance Data: PP6 Bowls from the Leveling Contemporary with Wall 573 266
28. Spectrographic Analysis of "Samaria Ware" Fragment Discovered at Samaria 274
29. Spectrographic Analysis of "Samaria Ware" Fragment Discovered at Megiddo 275
30. Provenance Data: PP6 Cooking Pots from the Leveling Contemporary with Wall 573 277
31. Provenance Data: PP6 Jugs and Juglets from the Leveling Contemporary with Wall 573 281
32. Provenance Data: PP6 Decanter from the Leveling Contemporary with Wall 573 288
33. Provenance Data: PP6 Braziers from the Leveling Contemporary with Wall 573 292
34. Distribution of PP 6 Ceramic Forms in Local Stratigraphy of Leveling Associated
    with Wall 573 295

35.	Provenance Data: PP6 Bowls from Pit *i*	303
36.	Attributes of Ware and Surface Treatment on PP 6 Bowls from Pit *i*	304
37.	Provenance Data: PP6 Cooking Pots from Pit *i*	319
38.	Provenance Data: PP6 Jar from Pit *i*	322
39.	Provenance Data: PP6 Jugs and Juglets from Pit *i*	324
40.	Summary of Attributes for Iron I-II Juglets	332
41.	Provenance Data: PP6 Decanters from Pit *i*	338
42.	Distribution of PP 6 Ceramic Forms in Local Stratigraphy of Pit *i*	342
43.	The Pottery Group Ascribed to Pit *i*: Summary of Analysis	345
44.	Comparative Stratigraphy of Major Northern Sites in and around the Samaria-Jezreel Valley Area	347

Chapter IV — Pottery Period 7

45.	Horizontal + Vertical Dimensions of PP 7 Stratigraphy	354
46.	Provenance Data: PP7 Pottery from Segment *120.121.19.126*	377
47.	Stratigraphic Summary of Layers *West of 124*	389
48.	Distribution of PP 7 Ceramic Forms Published from Debris Reportedly Covering the BP V House Floors	390
49.	Provenance Data: PP7 Bowls from the Putative Destruction Debris Covering the BP V Floors	392
50.	Provenance Data: PP7 Jars & Jar Stands from the Putative Destruction Debris Covering the BP V Floors	417
51.	Provenance Data: PP7 Jugs & Juglets from the Putative Destruction Debris Covering the BP V Floors	426
52.	Provenance Data: PP7 Lamps from the Putative Destruction Debris Covering the BP V Floors	430
53.	Distribution of PP 7 Ceramic Forms in Local Stratigraphy of House Floors (Rooms *e-g*, *hk*, *hq*, *j*, *kq*, *l*)	434
54.	Excavated Segments Relating to PP 7: Synopsis of Local Stratigraphy	436

Chapter V — The Samaria Ivories

55.	Ivory-bearing Loci and Ivory Distribution	447
56.	Concentrations of Ivory and Glass Fragments: Horizontal Axis	448
57.	Concentrations of Ivory and Glass Fragments: Vertical Axis	451
58.	Summary of Segment *19.51.14.20–North*	456
59.	Abstract of Selected Levels: Summit Strip Qc	461
60.	Stratigraphic Summary of Layers *West of 124*	469
61.	Summary of Walls Relating to Segment *West of 124*	470
62.	Spatial Distribution of Ostraca: Horizontal Axis	496

Chapter VI — The Assyrian Entanglement

63.	Historical Inscriptions Relating to the Reign of Adad-nirari III of Assyria	517
64.	Historical Entries in the Eponym Chronicle	518
65.	Tiglath-pileser III: Summary and Context of Military Activities in the West (Phase I)	532
66.	Tiglath-pileser III: Political Entities in the Tribute List from 738 BCE	538
67.	Eponym Chronicle Entries: 734-732 BCE	549

LIST OF ABBREVIATIONS

I. Samaria: Excavation Reports

HES I	G. A. Reisner, C. S. Fisher, and D. G. Lyon. *Harvard Excavations at Samaria, 1908-1910*, Volume I. Text. Harvard Semitic Series. Cambridge, MA: Harvard University Press, 1924.
HES II	G. A. Reisner, C. S. Fisher, and D. G. Lyon. *Harvard Excavations at Samaria, 1908-1910*, Volume II. Plans and Plates. Harvard Semitic Series. Cambridge, MA: Harvard University Press, 1924.
SS I	J. W. Crowfoot, K. M. Kenyon, and E. L. Sukenik. *The Buildings at Samaria*. London: Palestine Exploration Fund, 1942.
SS II	J. W. and G. M. Crowfoot. *Samaria-Sebaste 2: Early Ivories from Samaria*. London: Palestine Exploration Fund, 1938.
SS III	J. W. Crowfoot, G. M. Crowfoot, and K. M. Kenyon. *Samaria-Sebaste III: The Objects*. London: Palestine Exploration Fund, 1957.

II. Periodicals and Serials

AAA	Annals of Archaeology and Anthropology, University of Liverpool
AASOR	Annual of the American Schools of Oriental Research
ADAJ	Annual of the Department of Antiquities of Jordan
AfO	Archiv für Orientforschung
AJA	American Journal of Archaeology
AJSL	American Journal of Semitic Languages and Literature
APEF	Annual of the Palestine Exploration Fund
ʿAtîqôt	Journal of the Israel Department of Antiquities
AUSS	Andrews University Seminary Studies
BA	The Biblical Archaeologist
BASOR	Bulletin of the American Schools of Oriental Research
BBSAJ	Bulletin of the British School of Archaeology in Jerusalem
BIA	Bulletin of the Institute of Archaeology, University of London
BIES	Bulletin of the Israel Exploration Society [Hebrew]
BMB	Bulletin du Musée de Beyrouth, Paris
CT	Cuneiform Texts from the British Museum
FRLANT	Forschungen zur Religion und Literatur des Alten und Neuen Testaments
HTR	Harvard Theological Review
IEJ	Israel Exploration Journal
JANES	The Journal of the Near Eastern Society of Columbia University
JEA	Journal of Egyptian Archaeology
JHS	Journal of Hellenic Studies
JNES	Journal of Near Eastern Studies

JPOS	Journal of the Palestinian Oriental Society
LA	Liber Annuus
MDOG	Mitteilungen der Deutschen Orient-Gesellschaft
NABU	Nouvelles Assyriologiques Brèves et Utilitaires
PEFQ(S)	Palestine Exploration Fund Quarterly (Statement)
PEQ	Palestine Exploration Quarterly
QDAP	Quarterly of the Department of Antiquities in Palestine
RB	Revue Biblique
RLA	Reallexikon der Assyriologie
SAA	State Archives of Assyria
TA	Tel Aviv, Journal of the Tel Aviv University Institute of Archaeology
VT	Vetus Testamentum
WdO	Die Welt des Orients
ZDPV	Zeitschrift des deutschen Palästina-Vereins

III. Other Publications

ABC	A. K. Grayson. *Assyrian and Babylonian Chronicles.* Texts from Cuneiform Sources, A. Leo Oppenheim, ed. (Locust Valley, NY: J. J. Augustin Publisher, 1975).
ABL	R. F. Harper. *Assyrian and Babylonian Letters* (London and Chicago, 1892-1914).
AD	G. Smith. *Assyrian Discoveries: An Account of Explorations and Discoveries on the Site of Nineveh, During 1873 and 1874.* New York, 1875.
ʿAfula	M. Dothan, "Excavations at ʿAfula," *ʿAtîqôt* 1 (1955) 19-70 [English Series].
Aharoni-Amiran	Y. Aharoni and R. Amiran, "A New Scheme for the Sub-Division of the Iron Age in Palestine," *IEJ* 8 (1958), 171-84.
AHw	W. von Soden. *Akkadisches Handwörterbuch.* Weisbaden, 1981.
ʿAi	J. A. Callaway, "The 1966 ʿAi (et-Tell) Excavations," *BASOR* 196 (1969), 2-16.
ʿAi [JM-K]	J. Marquet-Krause. *Les Fouilles d'Ay (et-Tell).* Paris, 1949.
AIS I	R. E. Tappy. *The Archaeology of Israelite Samaria, Vol. I: Early Iron Age through the Ninth Century BCE.* Harvard Semitic Studies 44. Atlanta, GA: Scholars Press, 1992.
Amiran	R. Amiran. *Ancient Pottery of the Holy Land.* Jerusalem: Masada, 1969.
ANET	J. B. Pritchard, ed. *Ancient Near Eastern Texts Relating to the Old Testament.* Princeton, NJ: Princeton University Press, 3rd ed. 1969.
Antiquities	Josephus, *Jewish Antiquities*, Vol. VII, R. Marcus, translator; Vol. VIII, R. Marcus and A. Wikgren, translators and editors. Cambridge, MA: Harvard University Press, 1943 and 1963.
APTJ	R. E. Hendrix, P. R. Drey, and J. Bjørnar Storfjell. *Ancient Pottery of*

	Transjordan: An Introduction Utilizing Published Whole Forms, Late Neolithic through Late Islamic. Berrien Springs, MI: Institute of Archaeology/Horn Archaeological Museum–Andrews University, 1996.
ARAB I-II	D. D. Luckenbill. *Ancient Records of Assyria and Babylon*, Vols. I-II. Chicago, 1926.
AS II	E. Grant. *ʿAin Shems Excavations, 1928-1929-1930-1931*, Part II. Haverford, 1932.
AS IV	E. Grant and G. E. Wright. *ʿAin Shems Excavations, Part IV: The Pottery (plates)*. Haverford, 1938.
AS V	E. Grant and G. E. Wright. *ʿAin Shems Excavations, Part V (text)*. Haverford, 1939.
AS—PEFA	D. Mackenzie, "Excavations at Ain Shems (Beth-Shemesh)," *Palestine Exploration Fund Annual* II. Manchester, 1912-1913.
Ashdod I	M. Dothan and D. N. Freedman, "Ashdod I: The First Season of Excavations, 1962," *ʿAtîqôt* 7 (1967).
Ashdod II-III	M. Dothan, "Ashdod II-III: The Second and Third Seasons of Excavations, 1963, 1965, Soundings in 1967 (Text; Figures and Plates)," *ʿAtîqôt* 9-10 (1971).
Ashdod IV	M. Dothan, "Ashdod IV," *ʿAtiqot* 15 (1982).
ʿAtlīt	C. N. Johns, "Excavations at Pilgrims' Castle, ʿAtlīt (1933): Cremated Burials of Phoenician Origin," *QDAP* 6 (1937) 121-52.
ʿAtlīt—Cemetery	C. N. Johns, "Excavations at ʿAtlīt (1930-1931): The South-Eastern Cemetery," *QDAP* 2 (1933) 41-104.
Azor [1]	M. Dothan, "Excavations at Azor," *IEJ* 11 (1961), 171-75.
Azor [2]	M. Dothan, "The Excavations at Azor, 1960," *BIES* 25 (1961), 224-30 [Hebrew].
BANE	G. E. Wright, ed. *The Bible and the Ancient Near East: Essays in Honor of W. F. Albright*. New York, 1961.
Beersheba I	Y. Aharoni, ed. *Beer-Sheba I. Excavations at Tel Beer-Sheba, 1969-1971 Seasons*. Tel Aviv, 1973.
Beersheba II	Z. Herzog, *Beer-Sheba II: The Early Iron Age Settlements*. Tel Aviv, 1984.
Beersheba—TA	Y. Aharoni, "Excavations at Tel Beer-Sheba, Preliminary Report of the Fifth and Sixth Seasons, 1973-74," *TA* 2 (1975), 146-68.
Bethel	W. F. Albright and J. L. Kelso. *The Excavation of Bethel (1934-1960)*, in *AASOR* 39. Cambridge, MA, 1968.
Beth-Shan II	G. M. Fitzgerald. *Beth Shan II, The Four Canaanite Temples of Beth Shan: The Pottery*. Philadelphia, 1930.
Beth-Shan, James	F. W. James. *The Iron Age at Beth-Shan*. Philadelphia, 1966.
Beth-Shan, Oren	E. D. Oren. *The Northern Cemetery of Beth-Shan*. Leiden, 1973.
Beth-Shan, Yadin	Y. Yadin and S. Geva. *Investigations at Beth Shean, The Early Iron Age Strata*, in Qedem 23 (1986).
Bikai, BASOR	P. M. Bikai, "The Late Phoenician Pottery Complex and Chronology," *BASOR* 229 (1978), 47-67.
Byblos II	M. Dunand. *Fouilles de Byblos*, Vol. II. Paris, 1954.

Abbreviations

CAD	*The Assyrian Dictionary*, I. J. Gelb et al., ed. Chicago: University Press/Oriental Institute, 1956- .
CAH	J. Boardman, I. E. S. Edwards, N. G. L. Hammond, and E. Sollberger, eds. *The Cambridge Ancient History*, Vol. III/1, Second Edition. Cambridge, Eng.: Cambridge University Press, 1982.
Carmel	P. L. O. Guy, "Mt. Carmel, An Early Iron Age Cemetery Near Haifa, Excavated September 1922," *BBSAJ* 5 (1924), 47-55.
Chambon	A. Chambon. *Tell el-Farʿah I, L'Âge du Fer*. Paris, 1984.
Chapman	S. V. Chapman, "A Catalogue of Iron Age Pottery from the Cemeteries of Khirbet Silm, Joya, Qrayé and Qasmieh of South Lebanon," *Berytus* 21 (1972) 55-194.
CMHE	F. M. Cross, *Canaanite Myth and Hebrew Epic*. Cambridge, MA: Harvard University Press, 1973.
Corinth, XII	G. R. Davidson. *Corinth, XII: The Minor Objects*. Princeton: American School of Classical Studies at Athens, 1952.
CPP	J. G. Duncan. *Corpus of Dated Palestinian Pottery*. London, 1930.
Deir ʿAllā	H. J. Franken. *Excavations at Tell Deir ʿAllā*. Leiden, 1969.
Dibon	A. D. Tushingham, "The Excavations at Dibon (Dhībân) in Moab, The Third Campaign 1952-53," *AASOR* 40 (1972).
EAEHL	M. Avi-Yonah and E. Stern, eds. *Encyclopedia of Archaeological Excavations in the Holy Land*, Vols. I-IV. Jerusalem, 1975-1978.
ʿEin Gev	B. Mazar, M. Dothan, and I. Dunayevsky, "ʿEin Gev Excavations in 1961," *IEJ* 14 (1964), 1-49.
En-Gedi	B. Mazar, T. Dothan, and I. Dunayevsky. *En-Gedi, The First and Second Seasons of Excavations, 1961-1962*. *ʿAtiqot* 5. Jerusalem, 1966.
Forsberg	S. Forsberg. *Near Eastern Destruction Datings as Sources for Greek and Near Eastern Iron Age Chronology: Archaeological and Historical Studies, The Cases of Samaria (722 B.C.) and Tarsus (696 B.C.)*. Uppsala, 1995.
Franken	H. J. Franken. *In Search of the Jericho Potters: Ceramics from the Iron Age and from the Neolithicum*. Amsterdam, 1974.
Gerar	W. M. F. Petrie. *Gerar*. London, 1928.
Gezer	R. A. S. Macalister. *The Excavation of Gezer*, Vols. I-III. London, 1912.
Gezer I	W. G. Dever, H. D. Lance, G. E. Wright. *Gezer I*. Jerusalem, 1970.
Gezer II	W. G. Dever, et al. *Gezer II*. Jerusalem, 1974.
Gezer III	S. Gitin. *Gezer III, A Ceramic Typology of the Late Iron II, Persian and Hellenistic Periods at Tell Gezer*. Jerusalem, 1990 (see also *Gitin*).
Gezer IV	W. G. Dever, et al. *Gezer IV*. Jerusalem, 1986.
Gezer Gateway	J. S. Holladay, Jr., "Red Slip, Burnish, and the Solomonic Gateway at Gezer," *BASOR* 177/178 (1990), 23-70.
GGP	J. N. Coldstream. *Greek Geometric Pottery: A Survey of Ten Local Styles and Their Chronology*. London, 1968.
Gibeah	L. A. Sinclair, "Archaeological Study of Gibeah (Tell el-Fûl)," *AASOR* 34-35 (1960), 5-52.

Abbreviations

Gibeah, Albright	W. F. Albright, "Excavations and Results at Tell el-Fûl (Gibeah of Saul)," *AASOR* 4 (1924).
Gibeon	J. B. Pritchard. *Winery, Defenses, and Soundings at Gibeon*. Philadelphia, 1964.
Gibeon Cemetery	J. B. Pritchard. *The Bronze Age Cemetery at Gibeon*. Philadelphia, 1963.
Giloh	A. Mazar, "Giloh: An Early Israelite Settlement Site Near Jerusalem," *IEJ* 31 (1981), 1-36.
Gitin	S. Gitin. An Abstract of "A Ceramic Typology of the Late Iron II, Persian, and Hellenistic Periods at Tell Gezer." Ph.D. diss., Hebrew Union College, Cincinnati, 1979.
Halif	A. Biran and R. Gophna, "An Iron Age Burial Cave at Tel Ḥalif," *IEJ* 20 (1970), 151-69.
Hazor I	Y. Yadin, et al. *Hazor I*. Jerusalem, 1958.
Hazor II	Y. Yadin, et al. *Hazor II*. Jerusalem, 1960.
Hazor III-IV	Y. Yadin, et al. *Hazor III-IV*. Jerusalem, 1961.
Hazor V	A. Ben-Tor, et al. *Hazor V*. Jerusalem, 1997.
Herodotus, *History*	A. D. Godley, trans. *Herodotus*. Cambridge, MA: Harvard University Press, 1946.
Holladay	J. S. Holladay, Jr. "Ninth and Eighth Century Pottery from Northern Palestine." Th.D. diss., Harvard University, 1966.
IDB—1	G. A. Butterick, ed. *The Interpreter's Dictionary of the Bible*, Vol. 1. Nashville, 1962.
Inscriptions	A. H. Layard. *Inscriptions in the Cuneiform Character, from Assyrian Monuments*. London, 1851.
ITP	H. Tadmor. *The Inscriptions of Tiglath-pileser III King of Assyria, Critical Editions, with Introductions, Translations and Commentary*. Jerusalem, 1994.
Jericho	E. Selling and C. Watzinger. *Jericho, Die Ergebnisse der Ausgrabungen*. Leipzig, 1913.
Jericho II	K. M. Kenyon, et al. *Excavations at Jericho II. The Tombs Excavated in 1955-8*. London, 1965.
Jezreel-1	D. Ussishkin and J. Woodhead, "Excavations at Tel Jezreel 1990-1991: Preliminary Report," *TA* 19 (1992) 3-56.
Jezreel-2	D. Ussishkin and J. Woodhead, "Excavations at Tel Jezreel 1992-1993: Second Preliminary Report," *Levant* 26 (1994) 1-48.
Jezreel—Zimhoni	O. Zimhoni, "The Iron Age Pottery from Tel Jezreel—An Interim Report," *TA* 19 (1992) 57-70.
KAI	H. Donner and K. Röllig. *Kanaanäische und aramäische Inschriften*, Vols. I-III. Wiesbaden: Otto Harrassowitz, 1962-1964.
Kheleifeh	G. D. Pratico, "Nelson Glueck's 1938-1940 Excavations at Tell el-Kheleifeh: A Reappraisal," *BASOR* 259 (1985), 1-32.
Kheleifeh—Pratico	G. D. Pratico. *Nelson Glueck's 1938-1940 Excavations at Tell el-Kheleifeh: A Reappraisal*. ASOR Archaeological Reports No. 3. Atlanta, GA: Scholars Press, 1993.

KTP	P. Rost. *Keilschrifttexte Tiglath-pilesers III, I: Einleitung, Transscription und Ubersetzung, Worterverzeichnis mit Commentar*; *II: Autographierte Texte.* Leipzig, 1893.
Lachish II	O. Tufnell, et al. *Lachish II, The Fosse Temple.* London, 1940.
Lachish III	O. Tufnell, et al. *Lachish III, The Iron Age* (Text and Plates). London, 1953.
Lachish IV	O. Tufnell, et al. *Lachish IV, The Bronze Age.* London, 1958.
Lachish V	Y. Aharoni. *Investigations at Lachish: The Sanctuary and the Residency.* Tel Aviv, 1975.
Lachish-1	D. Ussishkin, "Excavations at Tel Lachish — 1973-1977, Preliminary Report," *Tel Aviv* 5 (1978) 1-97, Pls. 1-33.
Lachish-2	D. Ussishkin, "Excavations at Tel Lachish 1978-1983: Second Preliminary Report," *Tel Aviv* 10 (1983) 97-175, Pls. 1-44.
Lachish—Zimhoni	O. Zimhoni, "Two Ceramic Assemblages from Lachish Levels III and II," *TA* 17 (1990) 3-52.
Lapp and Lapp	P. W. Lapp and N. Lapp, "Iron II—Hellenistic Pottery Groups," in *The 1957 Excavation at Beth-Zur*, by O. R. Sellers, R. W. Funk, J. L. McKenzie, P. and N. Lapp. *AASOR* 38 (1968).
M. & Y. Aharoni	Aharoni, M. and Y. Aharoni, "The Stratification of Judahite Sites in the 8th and 7th Centuries B.C.E.," *BASOR* 224 (1976) 73-90.
Madeba	G. L. Harding, "An Iron Age Tomb at Madeba," *PEFA* 6 (1953), 27-47; and "The Tomb of Adoni Nur in Amman," *PEFA* 6 (1953) 48-75.
Magnalia Dei	F. M. Cross, et al., eds. *Magnalia Dei, The Mighty Acts of God: Essays on the Bible and Archaeology in Memory of G. Ernest Wright.* New York, 1976.
MBA	Y. Aharoni and M. Avi-Yonah. *The Macmillan Bible Atlas.* New York: Macmillan, 1977.
Megiddo I	R. S. Lamon and G. M. Shipton. *Megiddo I.* Chicago, 1939.
Megiddo II	G. Loud. *Megiddo II.* Chicago, 1948.
Megiddo Cult	H. G. May. *Material Remains of the Megiddo Cult.* Chicago, 1935.
Megiddo, Davies	*Cities of the Biblical World: Megiddo.* Cambridge, Eng.: Lutterworth, 1986.
Megiddo Ivories	G. Loud. *The Megiddo Ivories.* Chicago, 1939.
Megiddo, Shipton	G. M. Shipton. *Notes on the Megiddo Pottery of Strata VI-XX.* Chicago, 1939.
Megiddo Tombs	P. L. O. Guy. *Megiddo Tombs.* Chicago, 1938.
Megiddo Water	R. S. Lamon. *The Megiddo Water System.* Chicago, 1935.
MPP-1	L. T. Geraty, et al., eds. *Madaba Plains Project 1: The 1984 Season at Tell el-ʿUmeiri and Vicinity and Subsequent Studies.* Berrien Springs, MI: Andrews University, 1989.
MPP-2	L. G. Herr, et al., eds. *Madaba Plains Project 2: The 1987 Season at Tell el-ʿUmeiri and Vicinity and Subsequent Studies.* Berrien Springs, MI: Andrews University, 1991.
Munshara	F. Zayadine, "*Une Tombe du Fer II a Samarie-Sébaste*," *RB* 75 (1968), 562-85.

NEAEHL	E. Stern, ed. *The New Encyclopedia of Archaeological Excavations in the Holy Land*, Vols. 1-4. Jerusalem, 1993.
OEANE	E. M. Meyers, ed. *The Oxford Encyclopedia of Archaeology in the Near East*, Vols. 1-5. New York, 1997.
PCC	P. W. Lapp. *Palestinian Ceramic Chronology, 200B.C.-A.D.70*. ASOR Publications of the Jerusalem School, Archaeology: Volume III. New Haven: ASOR, 1961.
Philistines	T. Dothan. *The Philistines and Their Material Culture*. New Haven, 1982.
III R	Sir H. Rawlinson. *Cuneiform Inscriptions of Western Asia*. London, 1870 (copied by G. Smith).
Rabud	M. Kochavi, "Khirbet Rabûd = Debir," *TA* 1 (1974) 2-32.
Ramat Raḥel I	Y. Aharoni, et al. *Excavations at Ramat Raḥel I. Seasons 1959 and 1960*. Rome, 1962.
Ramat Raḥel II	Y. Aharoni, et al. *Excavations at Ramat Raḥel II. Seasons 1961 and 1962*. Rome, 1962.
RCOT	K. Kenyon. *Royal Cities of the Old Testament*. New York, 1971.
Rawlinson IIIR	Sir H. Rawlinson. *Cuneiform Inscriptions of Western Asia*. London, 1870.
Saʿidiyeh 1	J. N. Tubb, "Tell es-Saʿidiyeh: Preliminary Report on the First Three Seasons of Renewed Excavations," *Levant* 20 (1988) 23-88.
Saʿidiyeh 2	J. N. Tubb, "Preliminary Report on the Fourth Season of Excavations at Tell es-Saʿidiyeh in the Jordan Valley," *Levant* 22 (1990) 21-42.
Sarepta	J. B. Pritchard. *Sarepta: A Preliminary Report on the Iron Age*. Philadelphia, 1975.
Sargons II	A. Fuchs. *Die Inschriften Sargons II. aus Khorsabad*. Göttingen, 1994.
SCE, IV.2	E. Gjerstad. *The Swedish Cyprus Expedition*, Vol. IV. Part 2. Stockholm, 1948.
Shiloh, Buhl	M.-L. Buhl and S. Holm-Nielsen. *Shiloh: The Danish Excavations at Tell Sailun, Palestine, in 1926, 1929, 1932, and 1963. The Pre-Hellenistic Remains* in Publications of the National Museum, Archaeological-Historical Series 1, Vol. 12. Copenhagen: The National Museum of Denmark, 1969.
Shiloh, Kjaer	Kjaer, "The Excavation of Shiloh, 1929," *JPOS* 10 (1930), 87-174.
Stager	L. E. Stager, "Shemer's Estate," *BASOR* 277/278 (1990), 93-107.
STP	R. D. Barnett and M. Falkner. *The Sculptures of Assur-naṣir-pal II (883-859 B.C.), Tiglath-pileser III (745-727 B.C.), Esarhaddon (681-669 B.C.), from the Central and South-West Palaces at Nimrud*. London, 1962.
STT	O. R. Gurney and J. J. Finkelstein. *The Sultantepe Tablets I*. London, 1957; and O. R. Gurney and P. Hulin. *The Sultantepe Tablets II*. London, 1964.
Sukas I	P. J. Riis. *Sūkās I: The North-East Sanctuary and the First Settling of Greeks in Syria and Palestine*. Publications of the Carlsberg Expedition to Phoenicia 1. København: Kommissionær, Munksgaard, 1970.

Taʿanach	W. E. Rast. *Taanach I, Studies in the Iron Age Pottery*. American Schools of Oriental Research, 1978.
TAH	R. W. Hamilton, "Excavations at Tell Abu-Hawām," *QDAP* 4 (1935), 1-69.
Tarsus III	H. Goldman. *Excavations at Goezlü Kule, Tarsus III*, Princeton, 1963.
TBM I	W. F. Albright. *The Excavation of Tell Beit Mirsim, Vol. I: The Pottery of the First Three Campaigns*, in *AASOR* 12. New Haven, 1932.
TBM II	W. F. Albright. *The Excavation of Tell Beit Mirsim, Vol. II: The Bronze Age*, in *AASOR* 17. New Haven, 1938.
TBM III	W. F. Albright. *The Excavation of Tell Beit Mirsim, Vol. III: The Iron Age*, in *AASOR* 21-22. New Haven, 1943.
TBM-Greenberg	R. Greenberg, "New Light on the Early Iron Age at Tell Beit Mirsim," *BASOR* 256 (1987), 55-80.
T. ʿAmal	S. Levy and G. Edelstein, "Cinq années de fouilles à Tel ʿAmal (Nir David)," *RB* 79 (1972), 325-67.
T. ʿEitun	G. Edelstein and Y. Glass, "The Origin of Philistine Pottery Based on Petrographic Analysis," in *Excavation and Studies: Essays in Honor of S. Yeivin*, Y. Aharoni, ed. Tel Aviv, 1973 [Hebrew].
T. ʿEton	O. Zimhoni, "The Iron Age Pottery of Tel ʿEton and Its Relation to the Lachish, Tell Beit Mirsim and Arad Assemblages," *TA* 12 (1985), 63-90.
T. Esdar	M. Kochavi, "Excavations at Tel Esdar," *ʿAtîqôt* 5 (1969), 14-48 [Hebrew series].
T. Farʿah-RB [58]	R. de Vaux, O.P., "La troisième campagne de fouilles à Tell el-Farʿah près Naplouse," *RB* 58 (1951), 393-430; 566-90.
T. Farʿah-RB [59]	R. de Vaux, O.P., "La quatrième campagne de fouilles à Tell el-Farʿah, près Naplouse," *RB* 59 (1952), 551-83.
T. Farʿah-RB [62]	R. de Vaux, O.P., "Les fouilles de Tell el-Farʿah, près Naplouse," *RB* 62 (1955), 541-89.
T. Ḥalaf IV	M. F. von Oppenheim and B. Hrouda. *Tell Halaf IV: Die Kleinfunde aus historischer Zeit*. Berlin, 1962.
T. Kedesh	E. Stern and I. Beit Arie, "Excavations at Tel Kedesh (Tell Abu-Qudeis)," *TA* 1973, 93-116 [Hebrew].
T. Keisan	J. Briend et J. B. Humbert. *Tell Keisan (1971-1976)*. Paris, 1980.
T. Masos	W. Fritz and A. Kempinski. *Ergebnisse der Ausgrabungen auf der Ḥirbet el Masas (Tel Masos), 1972-1975*. Wiesbaden, 1983.
TN I	C. C. McCown. *Tell en-Naṣbeh I*. Berkeley, 1947.
TN II	J. C. Wampler. *Tell en-Naṣbeh II: The Pottery*. Berkeley, 1947.
TN—Cistern	J. C. Wampler, "Three Cistern Groups from Tell en-Naṣbeh," *BASOR* 82 (1941) 25-43.
T. Qasîle [1]	A. Mazar, *Excavations at Tell Qasile, Part One, The Philistine Sanctuary: Architecture and Cult Objects*, in Qedem 12 (1980).
T. Qasîle [2]	A. Mazar, *Excavations at Tell Qasile, Part Two, The Philistine Sanctuary: Various Finds, the Pottery...*, in Qedem 20 (1985).
T. Qasîle [BM]	B. Maisler (Mazar), "The Excavations at Tell Qasîle, Preliminary Re-

	port," *IEJ* 1 (1951), 61-76; 125-40; 194-218.
T. Qiri	A. Ben-Tor, Y. Portugali, et al., *Tell Qiri: A Village in the Jezreel Valley, Report of the Archaeological Excavations, 1975-77*, in Qedem 24 (1987).
T. Sippor	A. Biran and O. Negbi, "Tel Ṣippor," *IEJ* 16 (1966), 160-73.
T. Yoqneʿam [1]	A. Ben-Tor and R. Rosenthal, "The First Season of Excavations at Tel Yoqneʿam, 1977: Preliminary Report," *IEJ* 28 (1978) 57-82.
T. Yoqneʿam [2]	A. Ben-Tor, Y. Portugali, and M. Avissar, "The Second Season of Excavations at Tel Yoqneʿam, 1978: Preliminary Report," *IEJ* 29 (1979) 65-83.
T. Yoqneʿam [3]	A. Ben-Tor, Y. Portugali, and M. Avissar, "The Third and Fourth Seasons of Excavations at Tel Yoqneʿam, 1979 and 1980 [given as 1981 in the article's title]: Preliminary Report," *IEJ* 33 (1983) 30-54.
Tyre	P. M. Bikai. *The Pottery of Tyre*. Warminster, 1978.
Ugaritica II	Claude F.-A. Schaeffer. *Ugaritica II: Nouvelles Études Relatives aux Découvertes de Ras Shamra, Tome* V. Paris: Librairie Orientaliste Paul Geuthner, 1949.
War	Josephus, *The Jewish War*, Books I-II, H. St. J. Thackery, translator. Cambridge, MA: Harvard University Press, 1997.
WHJP	A. Malamat, ed. *The World History of the Jewish People*, Vol. IV/1. Jerusalem, 1979.
Wightman, *Myth*	G. J. Wightman, "The Myth of Solomon," *BASOR* 277/278 (1990), 5-22.
Wright	G. E. Wright, "Israelite Samaria and Iron Age Chronology," *BASOR* 155 (1959), 13-29.
Yoqneʿam I	A. Ben-Tor, M. Avissar, and Y. Portugali. *Yoqneʿam I: The Late Periods*. Jerusalem: The Institute of Archaeology at Hebrew University and the Israel Exploration Society, 1996.

IV. Miscellaneous

B-o-R	(Cypro-Phoenician) Black-on-Red Ware
BP	"Building Period" at Samaria
cm	centimeter
EBA	Early Bronze Age
Fl	Floor
FT	Foundation Trench
km	kilometer
l (or L)	locus (or layer)
LBA	Late Bronze Age
m	meter
mm	millimeter
MBA	Middle Bronze Age
Occ Deb	Occupational Debris

Abbreviations

PEF	Palestine Exploration Fund, London
PP	"Pottery Period" at Samaria
RM	Rockefeller Museum, Jerusalem
RT	Robber Trench ("Ghost Wall")
TT	Test Trench
W	Wall
YRP	Yoqneʻam Regional Project
↔	$x \leftrightarrow y$ (deposit x correlates to deposit y)

PREFACE

This study represents the conclusion to my broader investigation into the Iron Age levels and materials published as a result of the work of the Joint Expedition to Samaria from 1932 to 1935. This portion of my analysis focuses on Pottery Periods 4-7 and follows upon an earlier book that addressed Pottery Periods 1-3. Thanks to the preservation of numerous unpublished field sections and the generosity of the officers of the Palestine Exploration Fund in allowing me the freedom to study and to publish them, I can offer not only a *typologically* based but also a *stratigraphically* based reassessment of the history of this important site. This approach complements the one taken recently in reevaluations of other sites that have assumed a strong role in traditional interpretations of the history and archaeology of Iron Age Israel (e.g., see J. Balensi's preface to her reassessment of Tell Abu-Hawam in *BASOR* 257 [1985], 65).

The prodigious length of the discussion that results from such a method stems from the need to analyze not only the primary data themselves (i.e., the actual stratigraphy and the material remains) but also a series of full-scale reports in which a number of scholars have already processed and interpreted those data against certain field and research strategies current during their actual excavation of the site. Thus one must constantly move between primary and secondary levels of analysis. Each level carries its own set of complexities and requires a full discussion to understand it in its own right and to ascertain and study the dialectic between the two levels.

At no point have I intended this study to present simply a catalogue of ceramic forms or even a detailed comparative ceramic analysis. Rather, a complete reconstruction of the depositional history of Samaria holds a central place in my research method. If there is one aspect that can claim more value than the artifact itself, it is, in my judgment, the context from which excavators removed that piece of material culture (see the comments in *AIS-I*, 2). Intrasite comparative stratigraphic study, though enhanced considerably by solid pottery analysis, can itself contribute much to the understanding of the history of a site. Furthermore, it must serve as the basis for all intersite stratigraphic comparisons. Therefore, I shall pursue as full a debris-layer analysis as possible for every excavated segment at Samaria, even when the segment in question eventually contributed only a meager number of vessels or fragments to the final report (e.g., PP 4, Segment *325.304*).

A pursuit of the holistic goals mentioned above inevitably results in a lengthy study with long chapters devoted to each ceramic and historical period. For this situation I will offer no apologies; ultimately, it stems from the valued place that tight stratigraphic analysis assumes in my overall philosophy regarding archaeological method and theory. In this volume, my treatment of the depositional history at Samaria consumes even more space than the related portion of my study in *AIS-I*. Because the present volume aims to complete an overall investigation into the archaeology of the Israelite period at Samaria and to place this broad period into a larger, more complete historical and archaeological context, the discussion takes up not only the local deposits from which published pottery came but also most of the later deposits as well.

I have maintained certain styles of formatting to assist in navigating a course through the materials presented here. First, I have designed the Table of Contents, chapter divisions, and section headings to allow the reader to select the relevant portions of the narrative quickly and to proceed directly to them rather than having to wade through the entire text to find material of special interest. Second, I have, for purposes of practicality, retained all notes at the foot of each page to help facilitate quick referencing during the detailed stratigraphic and ceramic analyses. Third, the footnote format itself is designed to provide ready access to basic bibliographic data rather than to supply a coded reference that requires the reader to turn to the end of the chapter or book for full details. Fourth, because of the numerous drawings and cross-references between them, I sometimes repeat a figure either for the sake of convenience or when some new feature (such as the plotting of a published section) is added to a former figure. Fifth, whenever possible I have supplied a metric scale for the previously unpublished drawings presented here. Though Kenyon did not record a scale on many of her field sketches, she frequently (though not always) used a ratio of 2 cm : 1 m on those for which she did provide a scale. I suspect that this same formula may apply to at least some of the drawings that bear the notation "scale not recorded."

The appendixes at the end of the book serve as the backbone of the entire study. But the primary data presented there at times proved quite elusive and required a great deal of detective work to track down. I have now corrected all entries in accordance with the original stratification cards written and maintained by Ms. Grace M. Crowfoot. Private letters found in the archives of the PEF in London confirm Ms. Crowfoot's role in this endeavor and even reveal times at which Dame Kenyon herself wrote to request information contained on the cards from her colleague, "G. M. Crowfoot." These cards, then, seem to hold the authoritative documentation of the provenance data for both the pottery and the ivories. I have collated the information contained in various field registries with that appearing on these cards.

Finally, I note that when a large amount of data becomes available on a single subject, or when a writer invests a great deal of time to a particular subject, the temptation is strong to allow that topic to gravitate slowly but steadily to the center of all related research. In the case of an archaeological site, it can easily become the sole yardstick by which the excavator or commentator assesses all other sites and historical events of the past. In my judgment, this very phenomenon has clouded much research, and Kenyon's own ground breaking work at Samaria ultimately proved no exception. I have, therefore, attempted to deal honestly and accurately with both the archaeological and historical data presented here. I have tried not to smooth over the archaeological challenges that the site itself and the British excavations have bequeathed to us. Similarly, I have periodically reminded myself to refrain from making more of Samaria than it actually was. This need for caution and an evenhanded interpretation arose especially in Chapter VI, where I desired to see this city as much from an Assyrian point of view as from the perspective of the Samarians themselves or through the lens of the biblical writers. As a consequence, this study has not attempted to portray Samaria as the center of the Assyrian plan or empire, mainly because I do not believe it ever claimed this role. In this vein, I might note that, once Shalmaneser V and Sargon II succeeded in their protracted siege against this regional capital and resettled various foreign populations there, references to "Omri-land," "Samaria," "Israel," or "Israelite" virtually disappear from the Assyrian sources in the last decade of the eighth century and the succeeding seventh century BCE. That the governor at Samaria served as the eponymate for the year 690 BCE stands as the exception that only underscores this phenomenon.

R. E. Tappy
Pittsburgh
August, 2001

INTRODUCTION

I. Modern Attempts to Excavate Samaria: Achievements and Problems

Harvard University initiated the archaeological exploration of Samaria under the leadership of Gottlieb Schumacher (1908) followed by George Andrew Reisner and architect Clarence Fisher (1909-1910). Focusing on the western half of the summit, these excavations revealed much of the Israelite royal palace and, immediately to its west, a sizable storeroom complex. The latter feature became known as the Ostraca House due to the discovery inside of dozens of laconic shipping dockets (known as the Samaria Ostraca) recording the transfer of various commodities (primarily wine and oil) from outlying villages to the capital during the reigns of Jehoash and Jeroboam II in the first half of the eighth century BCE.

A consortium of institutions, mostly from England and Israel, renewed excavations at Samaria from 1932 to 1935. John Winter Crowfoot directed this so-called Joint Expedition, and Kathleen M. Kenyon, who supervised all work in the royal quarter, introduced to the project new techniques of debris-layer analysis, which she and Sir Mortimer Wheeler had refined at sites in England. After exposing a north-south section across the entire summit east of the earlier excavations by Schumacher and Reisner (fig. 1), Kenyon concluded that the pottery found there provided crucial evidence that justified a redating of the stratigraphic history and ceramic traditions at other Iron II sites in Palestine, such as Megiddo and Hazor. Not only did her published reports become the new standard for understanding this period at Samaria and in Palestine generally, but Aegean archaeologists soon correlated their chronologies to Kenyon's framework for Samaria.

Though the rock surface yielded clear signs of Early Bronze Age I occupation, most of the material remains pointed to Iron Age cultures. The date of the earliest Iron Age settlement, however, proved problematic. Kenyon interpreted 1 Kgs 16:24 as precluding any occupation of the site prior to Omri's reign. From there, she outlined eight major building phases (Periods I-VIII), with Periods I-VI spanning from Omri to the fall of Samaria to Assyria in 722-720 BCE. Additionally, the Kenyon construct argued that new ceramic traditions accompanied each new building phase. But other scholars proposed maintaining a distinction between the ceramic and architectural developments at Samaria, with the earliest Iron Age pottery providing evidence of pre-Omride occupation.

The resulting controversy stemmed mainly from differences in archaeological method and interpretation. Whereas Kenyon dated floor levels based on the material

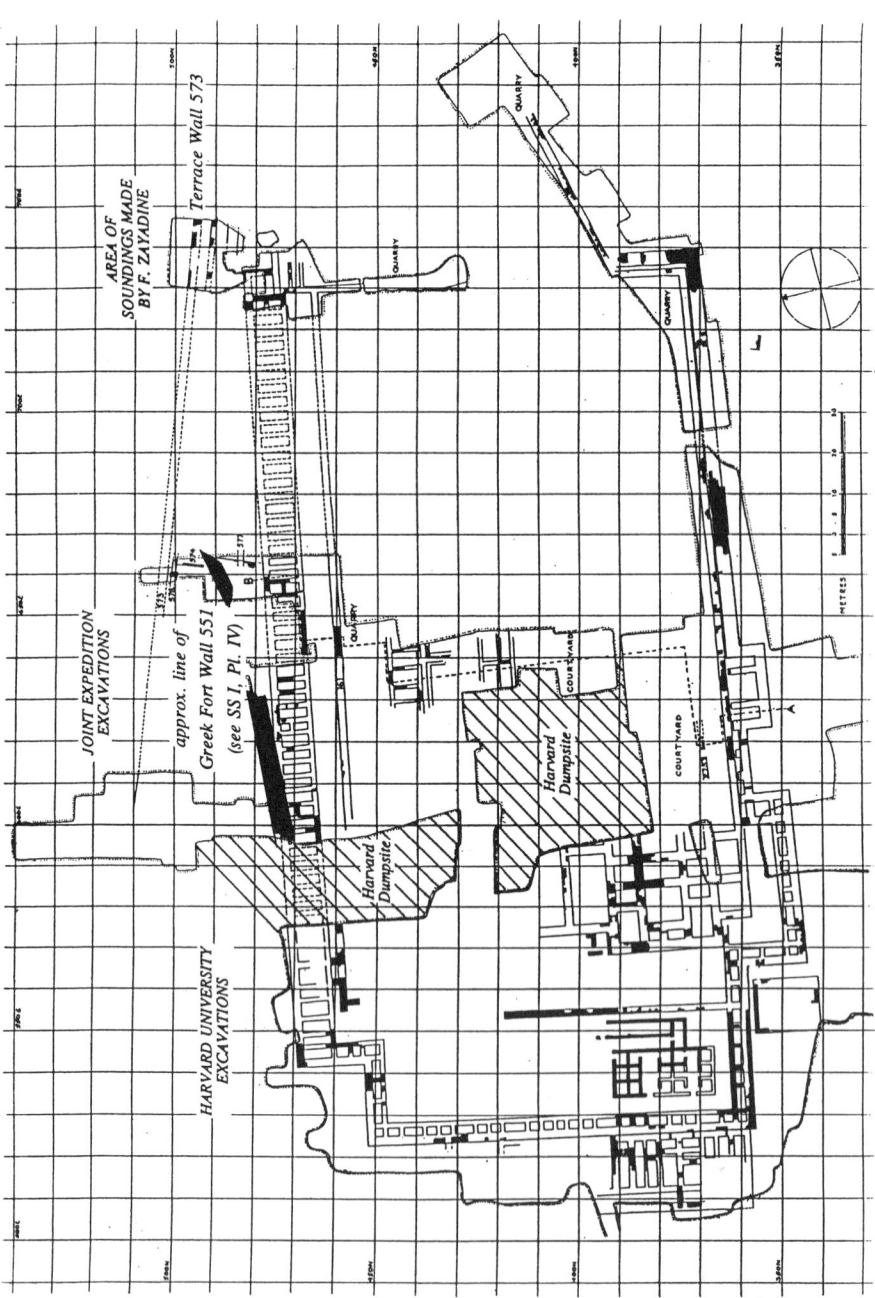

Overview of Summit Excavations:
Harvard University, Joint Expedition, and Soundings by F. Zayadine
(adapted from *SS I*, Pl. II)

fig. 1

found beneath them (sometimes by as much as several depositional layers), George Ernest Wright and others dated surfaces according to the material found lying directly on them. Each method addresses different aspects of chronology. While Kenyon's system offers the earliest possible date of a surface's construction, Wright's approach identifies the span of time the floor was actually used. Recent reevaluations of the Samaria evidence, from both ceramic and stratigraphic starting points, have confirmed an Iron Age I occupation of the site but have shown (with Kenyon) that this phase lacked any monumental architectural features. Instead, installations either resting on or cut into the rock surface seem to indicate the presence of a modest family estate that produced oil and wine already during the late pre-monarchic era. The text of 1 Kgs 16:24 in no way precludes this conclusion.

Unfortunately, much of the pottery and other materials published from the Samaria excavations came from disturbed or secondary contexts, such as backfill recovered from foundation trenches. As a result, many fewer stratigraphically secure archaeological data are available from the city for the ninth century BCE than Kenyon's official report implied. Without further field work at Samaria, therefore, one cannot rely on this evidence alone when establishing or adjusting chronologies at other sites in Israel or the Aegean world. Though many rightly proclaimed at the publication of the reports from Samaria that they represented a new standard in archaeological accounting, scholars must now temper this enthusiasm with the observation that Kenyon published only 140 fragments of pottery to support the historical and chronological reconstructions for all of Pottery Periods 4-7. This astonishing fact obviously falls short of today's standards for reporting and helps to exacerbate the many problems that have plagued attempts to gain a clear view of the historical events surrounding the final decades of the Kingdom of Israel. Since the time span in question takes in the final years of the city's life under Israelite rule, these years have remained a subject of discussion and debate, a situation owing largely to this constricted exposure to the archaeology of the site, the limited repertoire of materials published from the field work, and, as much as any other single factor, the failure of the authors to include in their final reports the kind of primary excavation and provenance data needed to test their proposed historical reconstruction. Those who have undertaken investigations into these events from the point of view of the extant textual sources have encountered their own set of historical adversities. Whatever collaboration the future brings must, in my judgment, include a sound knowledge of the depositional history of Samaria. To this end I have dedicated both *AIS-I*[1] and the present study.

---

[1] R. E. Tappy, *The Archaeology of Israelite Samaria, Volume I: Early Iron Age through the Ninth Century BCE*. Harvard Semitic Studies 44 (Atlanta, GA: Scholars Press, 1992) (hereafter, *AIS-I*).

II. Samaria *in situ*: An Interface of Geology, Geography, and History

Around 884 BCE, Omri transferred his political capital to the city of Samaria, located near the center of the Northern Kingdom of Israel (32°17′ latitude x 35°12′ longitude).[2] Situated 56 km (35 mi) north of Jerusalem and west of the Ephraimite watershed, its summit rose to a height of 430 m above sea level and overlooked the main coastal road (דֶּרֶךְ הַיָּם in Is 8:23) connecting Egypt and the Southern Kingdom of Judah with the Jezreel Valley and northern routes to Phoenicia and Damascus. The site's biblical names, *Šāmîr* (Judg 10:1-2) and, somewhat later, *Šōmərôn* (1 Kgs 16:24, et passim), mean "watch" or "watchman." Both designations stem from an original **qātil* participle and reflect successive changes in the pronunciation of that verb form (**šāmir-v —> *šōmir —> šōmēr*). The name of the site's earliest recorded private owner, *Šemer*, represents a secondary nominal formation of this verbal antecedent,[3] regardless of the impression that some, including Kenyon, have received from the ordering of names in 1 Kgs 16:24. Omri either retained the old name (Shomron) that Shemer's kin had already assigned to their patrilineal estate, or he used an archaic form of the consonantal root of the name "Shemer" to pay adequate respect to the former owner of the hill, while simultaneously hinting at an earlier etiology for the name of the new capital. Aharoni has suggested that perhaps both Shemer and Omri may have held lineage connections to the tribe of Issachar and that Shemer's genealogical roots may trace back specifically to the clan of Shimron.[4] Interestingly, Omri would not represent the only figure from that region to become king at Samaria since, according to 1 Kgs 15:27 and 16:8, both Baasha and Elah before him had come from "the House of Issachar" (note the lineage of the earlier judge Tola, in Judg 10:1; see n. 4).

Though never explicitly delineated in the Hebrew Bible, the region of Samaria included mainly the mountainous territories south of Lower Galilee and the Jezreel Valley (i.e., below the Mount Carmel–Mount Gilboa line), west of the Beth-Shan and Jordan River Valleys, and east of the Sharon and Acco Plains. According to biblical traditions, the southern border fluctuated with the political vicissitudes between north and south (1 Kgs 14:30; 15:16ff.; 2 Chron 13:19) until King Asa of Jerusalem established it in the area between Bethel and Mizpah (Tell en-Naṣbeh), both of which served henceforth as border stations. The sons of Joseph, Manasseh and Ephraim (Josh 16:1-4), became the eponymous ancestors for Israelite tribes occupying this north-central hill country region, but Ephraim emerged as the dominant tribe early on, and consequently

---

[2] For an earlier version of this discussion, see R. E. Tappy, "Samaria," pp. 1155-59 in *Eerdman's Dictionary of the Bible*. D. N. Freedman, A. C. Myers, and A. B. Beck, eds. (Grand Rapids, MI: Eerdmans, 2000).

[3] *AIS-I*, 68-69, n. 185.

[4] Y. Aharoni, *The Land of the Bible* (rev. ed.; Philadelphia: Westminster, 1979), 333-34; also B. Mazar, "The House of Omri," *Eretz-Israel* 20 (Yadin Volume, 1989), 215-19. For other connections between the Ephraimite hill country and Issachar, Asher, and Machir/Manasseh, see Aharoni, pp. 243-44. Mazar suggested that Omri descended from the Tola family, who constituted Issachar's most important clan.

the entire area took on his name (compare Gen 48:14). Later, under the political influence of Omri, the territory assumed the same name as the capital city of "Samaria" (1 Kgs 13:32 notwithstanding). Still, some eighth-century Judahite prophets preserved a distinction between region and city by referring both to Ephraim, with its ties to the House of Joseph, and to Samaria, in relationship to the broader Kingdom of Israel (Is 7:9; 9:8-9; Mic 1:5; compare Am 3:12 and 6:1 vs. 6:6).

Shechem, the first Canaanite city mentioned in Egyptian writings about military activity (MBIIA tomb inscription of Khu-sebek), quickly became the religious and political hub of Samaria because it controlled a crucial pass between the centrally located mountains of Ebal and Gerizim. One may, therefore, speak of "North Samaria," the area north of Shechem, which correlated roughly with the tribe Manasseh (Josh 17:7-10), and "South Samaria," the territory south of Shechem, which basically represented tribal Ephraim (Josh 16:5-10; fig. 2). These areas reveal different geological formations which helped determine patterns of settlement. The mountains of South Samaria were formed primarily of hard, uplifted, Cenomanian limestone and rose to greater heights (3,000 ft.) than the ranges north of Shechem. This area lacked a topographical complement to the western Shephelah and eastern wilderness areas of Judah to the south. Rather, deeply cut drainage systems on both sides of the southern Ephraimite watershed made access to it more difficult and restricted travel to primary ridge routes, which followed a long exposure of chalk stretching longitudinally between eastern and central Samaria. That the Book of Joshua failed to provide a list of cities for Ephraim, unlike other tribal territories, may reflect the difficulties encountered in settling this area. Once populated, however, terrace farmers made good use of the shallow but fertile *terra rosa* soil produced by the deteriorating rock formations.

By contrast, North Samaria presented a more variegated geological portrait as the Ephraim arch declined toward the northern valleys. Uplifted strata of Cenomanian limestone dominated the eastern sector of this area, while an even harder Eocene limestone base (which decomposed into a less-than-fertile brown forest soil) characterized the central portion of North Samaria from Gilboa to Ebal and Gerizim. The so-called chocolate soil that Kenyon encountered in the earlier levels of Israelite stratigraphy very likely represented the natural matrix of earth that overlay the rock surface[5] and that distinguished itself from the churned up, imported soils deposited on the site artificially. West of these areas, a mixture of limestones (Cenomanian and Turonian) and Senonian chalks, which had experienced more moderate degrees of faulting, combined to facilitate the establishment of a local and regional network of roadways that prompted denser settlements and made for greater communication and trade. Here the principal roads either followed the Naḥal Shechem to the coastal route or proceeded northward through the Dothan Valley to Jezreel and points farther north and east. Though initially forested throughout, the entire region of Samaria underwent significant

---

[5]For example, compare *SS III*, 99, and *AIS-I*, 73-76, fig. 14, Layers XIV and XVII; note also Stager's comments in "Shemer's Estate," *BASOR* 277/278 (1990), 101 (hereafter, *Stager*).

THE ARCHAEOLOGY OF ISRAELITE SAMARIA

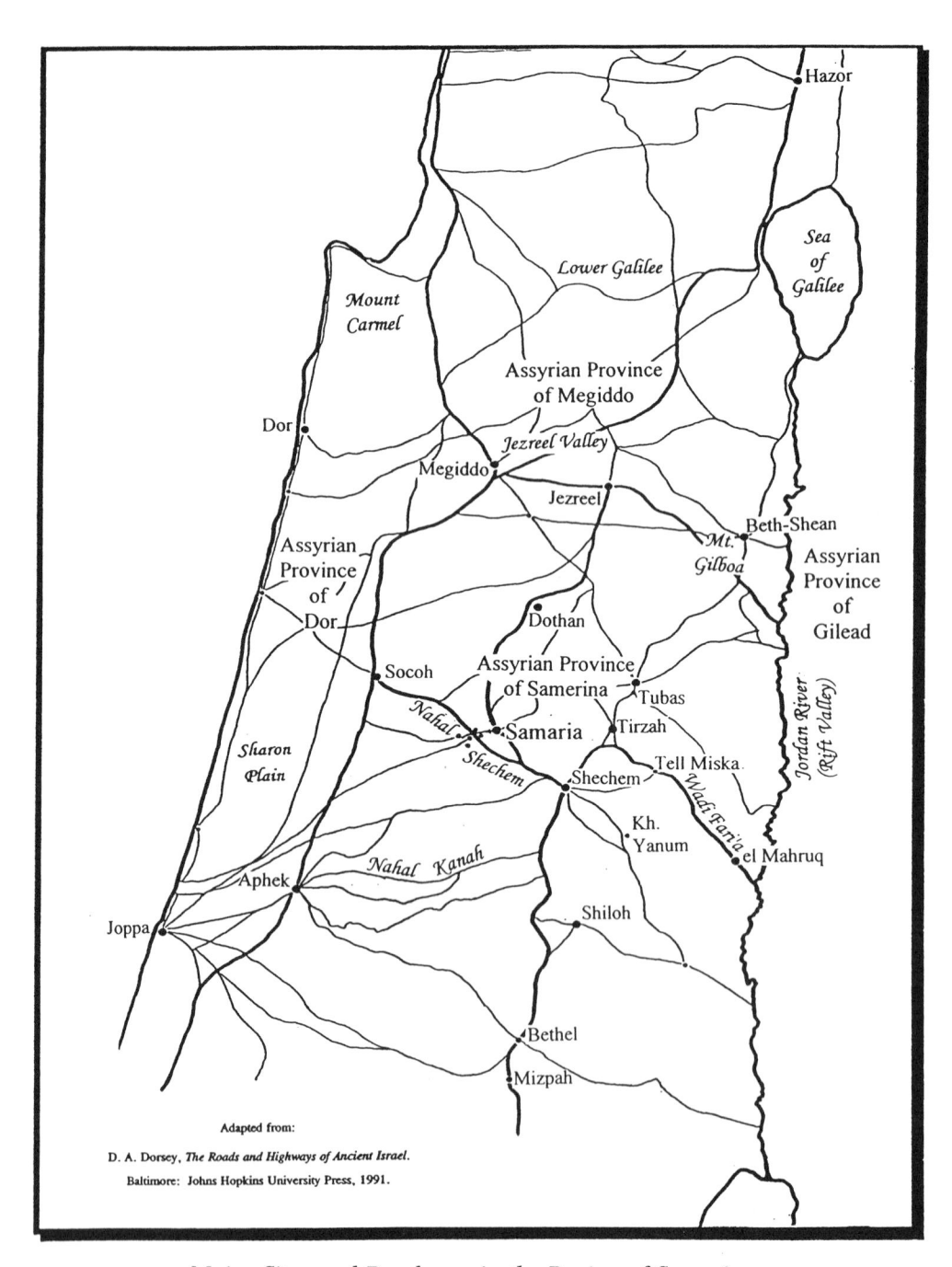

Major Sites and Roadways in the Region of Samaria
(adapted from D. Dorsey, 1991:back cover)

fig. 2

ecological change resulting from intense deforestation as the area absorbed large numbers of inhabitants starting in the early Iron Age (Josh 17:14-18).

Here, in the cradle of Israelite civilization, settlement patterns of the Iron Age resemble those of the Early Bronze Age I (3500-3100 BCE) and Middle Bronze Age IIA (2000-1800 BCE).[6] In all three phases, survey data seem to suggest that peoples spread generally from east to west and north to south. Those who see the Iron Age highland population emerging only from processes of deurbanization among the Canaanite city-states of the western lowlands must reckon with the *longue durée* aspect of this apparent pattern of migration.[7] In Iron Age I, a mixture of sedentary settlements and interspersed, seasonal campsites lay mainly in the dry forest ecozone just east of the watershed, where rainfall averaged approximately 200-400 mm annually (fig. 3). Both the nature of sites surveyed and their concentration in this particular zone point to a localized, dimorphic, socio-economic base in which pastoralists and agriculturists existed in a symbiotic relationship.[8]

The main approach to the central hill country of Samaria from the east lay in the deeply faulted Wadi Farʿah, which ascended toward Tell el-Farʿah (biblical Tirzah) from el-Mahruq in the Rift Valley south of the fords of the Jordan River at Adam (fig. 2). During Iron Age I, this main road turned south from Tirzah and continued to Shechem. A secondary road diverged from it just prior to reaching Tirzah (at Tell Miska) and led directly to Shechem from the northwest end of the Wadi Farʿah, thereby avoiding the craggy Wadi Beidan. A string of more than a dozen Iron Age I-II sites along these routes attests to their maintenance and use in both periods. This eastern access to Shechem served mainly North Samaria, while another Iron I route linking Shiloh and the Jordan River Valley served South Samaria. The latter passageway has yielded few Iron Age II remains, reflecting developments associated with the nascent monarchy in Jerusalem and the demise of Shiloh as a cultic and political center (see the reflections on this in Jer 7:12-15; 26:4-5; Ps 78:56-67). Instead, a new road followed a

---

[6]I. Finkelstein, "The Emergence of Israel: A Phase in the Cyclic History of Canaan in the Third and Second Millennia BCE," pp. 150-78 in *From Nomadism to Monarchy: Archaeological and Historical Aspects of Early Israel*. I. Finkelstein and N. Na'aman, eds. (Jerusalem: Israel Exploration Society, 1994); see especially pages pp. 153ff.

[7]For a description of historical change from the perspective of *la longue durée*, see (among numerous other writings) F. Braudel, "La longue durée," *Annales Economies Sociétés Civilisations* 13 (1958), 725-53. For a full explanation of Braudel's historical method, see idem, "History and the Social Sciences," pp. 25-54 in *On History* (Chicago: University of Chicago Press, 1980) and for an application of the method to historical studies see idem, *The Mediterranean and the Mediterranean World in the Age of Philip II, Volume I* (New York: Harper and Row, 1972). For the usefulness of the basic approach to archaeological interpretation, see I. Hodder, "The Contribution of the Long Term," pp. 1-8 in *Archaeology as Long Term History* (Cambridge, Eng.: Cambridge University Press, 1987).

[8]The most detailed study of the "dimorphic society" remains that of Michael Rowton in a series of 16 articles based on his exploration and analysis of regions in Mesopotamia (see M. Rowton, "Dimorphic Structure and Topology," *Oriens Antiquus* 15 [1976], 17, n. 4 for bibliographic information relating to the following 15 studies).

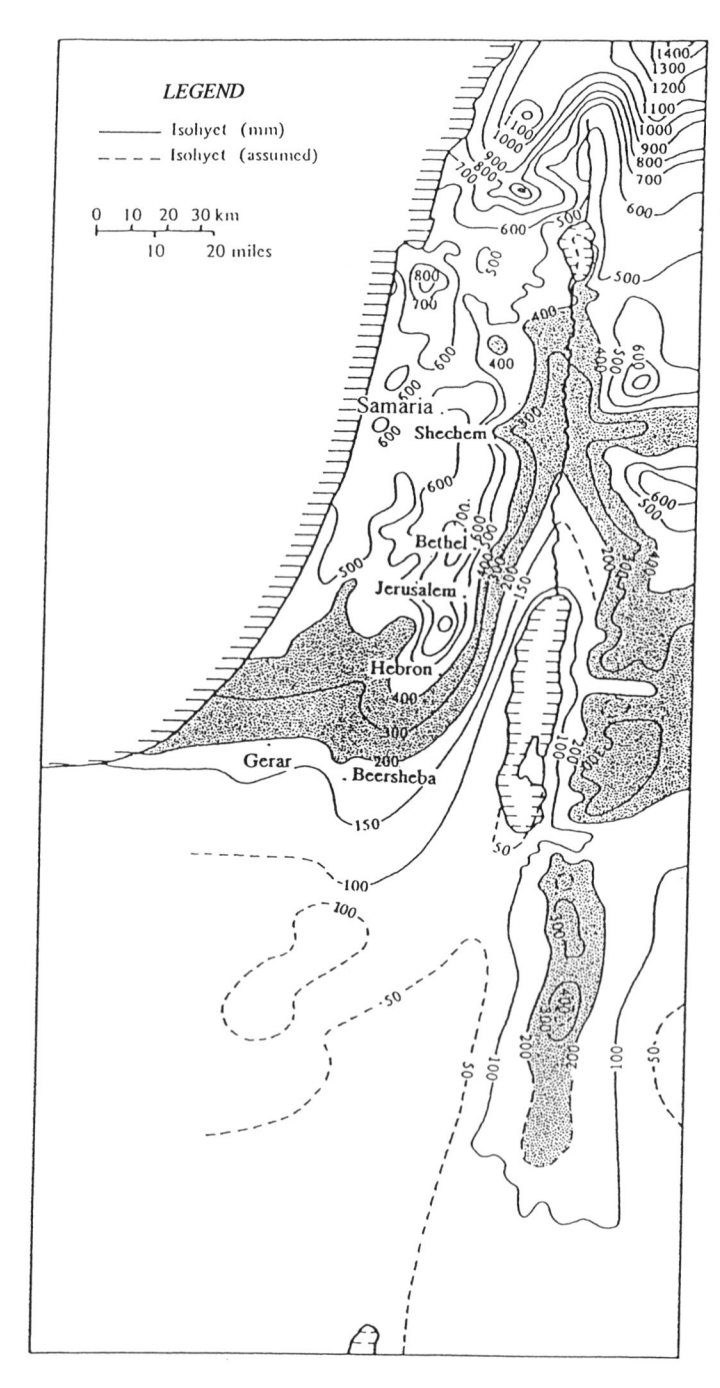

General Area of the "Dimporhic Zone" in Israel
(adapted from E. Orni and E. Efrat, 1976:145)

fig. 3

more northerly course from the valley area east of Shiloh and proceeded along the Ephraim-Manasseh border through Khirbet Yanun (biblical Janoah?; Josh 16:6-7) to Shechem.

By the time the population spread west in Iron Age II, highland society had become more complex in its political and economic structure. Numerous settlements of a more uniform character (with virtually no ephemeral campsites) appeared on the seaward slopes of Samaria and survived or thrived there as part of a much larger network of trade, while locally a new type of dimorphism resided in the symbiosis between capital and countryside. A look at the gazetteer for the clan holdings appearing in the Samaria Ostraca shows that, by the first half of the eighth century BCE, Samaria lay in the center of a tight constellation of towns and family owned estates,[9] many of which undoubtedly resembled in character the site of Shomron during its pre-royal days. Early Iron Age II chronologies for the late tenth and early ninth centuries are not yet archaeologically secure enough in this region to determine precisely how many of these settlements arose as a result of Solomon's administrative districts (1 Kgs 4:7-8) and how many came about through Omri's economic programs and demands. But clearly these sites both served the capital city at Samaria and participated in interregional trade, if only by offering auxiliary services such as overnight lodging and animal care to passing caravans. In this way, they facilitated trade between the highland centers and the main coastal route leading north to Phoenicia or northeastward through the Jezreel Valley past Hazor to Damascus. The close spatial distribution of these new western settlements indicates that not all represented mere caravan stops; rather, many of these villages bolstered their own local economies by producing and trading commodities such as wine and oil (Samaria Ostraca).

Omri's shift of the region's political center from Tirzah west of the watershed to the city of Samaria (biblical Shomron) in the early ninth century, then, prompted significant demographic and economic change throughout the region. Few Iron I sites had existed in this area (e.g., Khirbet Kabuba, Khirbet el-Babariya, Khirbet Kusein es-Sahel, Khirbet Qarqaf, Khirbet ed Duweir; see fig. 2, west of Samaria), and they had all remained quite small and very near Shemer's family estate, the site of the future capital city (1 Kgs 16:24). But Iron II western expansion of rural villages left a footprint of settlements that has allowed the identification of at least 11 lateral and local roadways connecting the highlands in the Samaria-Shechem area with the lucrative trade moving along the coastal route. Most notable among these routes were: (1) those that connected the villages of South Samaria to the major center at Aphek via the lateral valley systems north of Shiloh (Naḥal Kanah); and (2) those that utilized the more northerly Naḥal Shechem to link the highland towns of North Samaria to Socoh by intersecting the coastal route just south of the southwest entrances to the strategic Jezreel Valley. Undoubtedly, both Socoh and Aphek became trading stations or clearing houses for goods and commodities produced by or transported through the matrix of

---

[9] See Y. Aharoni and M. Avi-Yonah, *The Macmillan Bible Atlas* (rev. ed.; New York: Macmillan, 1977), 87, Map no. 137.

highland villages leading down from the Israelite capital and other large centers situated at higher elevations (Samaria, Tirzah, Tubas, Tappuah, Dothan, Shechem).

Omri's choice of Shomron as his new capital, then, not only freed him from the baggage of earlier political and military associations but kept his administrative infrastructure in or near the nucleus of a vast, new network of economic activity. Ironically, as I shall show, world developments in the latter area would eventually lead to the total collapse of Israelite hegemony over both Samaria and its outlying countryside.

Chapter I

POTTERY PERIOD 4

*Remains of Prosperity and Expansion
in the Early Eighth Century BCE?*

I. Introduction

When I began my study of Pottery Period 4, I frequently encountered apparent errors made in the recording of findspots and artifacts. Discrepancies existed both within the unpublished field notes and between these notes and the published report. By way of illustration, *SS III*, Fig. 6 presented 41 fragments of pottery (with 6:5 subsuming two entries) in support of Kenyon's "Periods IV-IVa" and, of these, recording discrepancies attended no fewer than 17 entries (41.5%).[1] These mistakes sometimes involved relatively straightforward and soluble details, such as the precise name of a coordinate (e.g., *Between TT2-TT3* vs. *E Strip, Btw TT2-TT3*). Other occurrences, however, touched on critical but more obscure data not as easily checked, such as the exact local layer which yielded a particular findspot (Layer VII vs. Layer VIII) or even the identification of the larger architectural feature from which the excavators removed a certain ceramic fragment (Room *g* vs. *j*, *j* vs. *n*, *h* vs. *l*). Some of these dubious entries involved more than one such detail so that seven questions emerged pertaining to coordinates[2] while eight related to local layers[3] and four involved distinct architectural features.[4] I have checked each of the 17 questionable entries mentioned above for Fig. 6 against the information recorded originally by Grace Crowfoot on the handwritten stratification cards in London; to the best of my knowledge, all data presented in Appendix A are now correct in every aspect.[5]

Besides this pottery group, *SS III*, Fig. 7 presented nine additional fragments as further support for Kenyon's conclusions regarding her "Period IV," and similarly equivocal data entries existed for six of them (66.7%).[6] Between Figs. 6 and 7, then,

---

[1] *SS III*, Fig. 6:5 (two fragments), 7, 9, 11-12, 17-18, 21-22, 24-26, 33, 35, 37, 39.

[2] *SS III*, Fig. 6:5, 7, 9, 17, 25, 33, 35.

[3] *SS III*, Fig. 6:5 (two fragments), 9, 11, 22, 26, 37, 39.

[4] *SS III*, Fig. 6:12, 18, 21, 24.

[5] I have also located stratification cards for every item in *SS III*, Figs. 7-11 and corrected many questionable entries there.

[6] *SS III*, Fig. 7:3 and 4 were transposed in the published report. According to field notebook *Sabastya Qn*

26 of 50 items (52%) claimed dubious entries in the fieldbooks or published reports, or both. I have categorized and flagged each suspicious recording found within the Samaria documentation, whether in original field notes or the published report, in Table 1 and Appendix A, though both inherently become a bit less wieldy due to the multiple sigla involved.

Another factor cast even greater doubt on the reliability of the major pottery group published in support of Kenyon's "Period IV." Of the 41 fragments presented in *SS III* Fig. 6, 11 items (26.83%) were plainly marked as discards in the field notes and pre-publication pottery notes (see Appendix A, second column).[7] The excavators had also hatched through another three entries in their unpublished records,[8] a likely indication that they intended to discard these pieces as well. This would raise the total percentage of fragments once marked for discard but later used as evidence for a distinct archaeo-historical period in the life of Samaria to 34.15% for Fig. 6 alone. Retrieval of over a third of one's published material from an erstwhile pottery dump hardly instills confidence in any of the conclusions reached regarding the historical phase in question even though a certain number of those conclusions may, in fact, be historically accurate despite the faulty database used in their support. In this situation, the historical probability of virtually all the excavators' published opinions must remain in doubt. One can only wonder how the hiatus between the close of excavations (1935) and the publication of the pottery (1957), during which time World War II had a significant negative effect on London, might relate to some of the problems outlined here.[9] At any rate, for the sake of accuracy I shall note each recording discrepancy and/or each originally discarded pottery fragment when it appears below in my discussion of the stratigraphy and pottery.

(Rockefeller Museum, Jerusalem), both 7:5 and 7:8 received the registry number 5256. Basic scribal errors seem to have occurred in the recording of the registry numbers for 7:6 (No. 5257 according to the stratification cards found in the PEF vs. No. 4257 in the Rockefeller Museum's records and in *SS III*, 118) and 7:9 (Reg. No. 4924 = Rockefeller Museum; No. 4927 in *SS III*, 118). Finally, I had to assume that 7:6 and 7:8 came from the same Local Layer (V) as the other fragments in this group, though the field notes did not make this clear.

[7] *SS III*, Fig.6:5 (two fragments), 7, 17-19, 22, 24-25, 33, 35.

[8] *SS III*, Fig. 6:20-21, 23.

[9] Note, for comparison, that R. A. S. Macalister and J. G. Duncan appear to have recovered at least 27 Egyptian-style, dome-shaped weights from Jerusalem (13 of which displayed inscriptions and the characteristic "loop sign") during their excavations there between 1923 and 1925, though none of these items actually appeared in their official report (see J. G. Duncan, *Digging up Biblical History*, Vol. II [London: Society for Promoting Christian Knowledge, 1931], 216 and 218). Apparently, many of these artifacts went to the Palestine Exploration Fund in London, where only 16 of them survived World War II. Today, the Institute of Archaeology at the University of London maintains this diminished collection of valuable weights (see A. Eran, "Weights and Weighing in the City of David: The Early Weights from the Bronze Age to the Persian Period," pp. 204-56 in *Excavations at the City of David IV*, D. T. Ariel and A. de Groot, eds. *Qedem* 35 [Jerusalem: The Hebrew University, 1996], 215).

PP 4: INTRODUCTION 13

	Horizontal Axis	Vertical Axis = Local Layers	Coordinates	No. of published sherds/vessels ( ) = No. marked for discard
Figure 6	House Floors: Room *g*	Wall 136	120.121.19.126	1
	Room *h*	IVa	125.144	1
		IX	147.145.151.136	1
		IX	155.151.136.147	1 (1)a
		Wall 151 (157?)	120.121.19.126	1
		Va	122.125.19.121	1b
		ratio of apparent discards to group - 1:5 (20%)		
	Room *j*	IX	North of TT2	2
		IXr	(E Strip?); N of TT2	1 (1)
		IXb	120.121.19.126	1 (1)a
		X	509.126	1
		ratio of apparent discards to group - 2:5 (40%)		
	Room *k*	VII, VIII	Between TT2-TT3	3 (1)
		VII	(E Strip?); Btw TT2-TT3	4 (4)c
		IVa.y, Vy	125.144	1 (1)c
		ratio of apparent discards to group - 6:8 (75%)		
	Room *n*	Xa, XI, XIa, XIa.b, XII, XIIa.b	502.503	15 (1-4?)a
		ratio of apparent discards to group - 4:15 (26.6%)		
	Resurfacing (PP 4a?): Room *h*	IVx.z	125.144	1
	North Courtyard	V, VIe	86.2.88.E	2
		IV(h?)	86.2.88.W	1
		V	86.2.88.E; W of 104	1
		IV	86.2.88	1
	Courtyard	IX	325.304	1 (1)
		ratio of apparent discards to group - 1:1 (100%)		
Figure 7	Casemate Repair Deposit	V	504.508.509.510	9

Horizontal + Vertical Dimensions of PP 4 Stratigraphy[10]
Table 1

---

[10] We will address discrepancies in Kenyon's recording system as we come to them in the ensuing discussion. Here we have flagged them along the right side of Table 1 as follows:

a = Disagreements between field records and published report:
    i) Fig. 6:18 (155.151.136.147, Layer IX) — *SS III* assigns to Room *l* vs. Room *h*
    ii) Fig. 6:24 (120.121.19.126, Layer IXb) — *SS III* assigns to Room *n* vs. Room *j*
    iii) Fig. 6:21 (502.503, Layer XIIa.b) — *SS III* assigns to Room *g* vs. Room *n*

b = Though the fieldnotes did not assign this jar rim fragment to a particular architectural feature, they identified it as belonging to "early Period VI." In the published report, however, Kenyon located its findspot in Room *h* and dated it to her "Period IV."

c = *SS III*, Fig. 6:5 encompassed two fragments with separate registry numbers (see Appendix F) and yielded a sum of 41 (vs. 40) sherds published in this group. Our percentages relate to 41 items.

II. Pottery Period 4

To facilitate the stratigraphic and ceramic discussion of Kenyon's "Periods IV-IVa," I have extracted the relevant data from Appendix A and reorganized them in Table 1 in a way that provides a complete list of the PP 4 findspots and groups together the various stratigraphic coordinates which relate to a particular architectural feature (such as Room g, h, etc.) or construction activity (such as repairs along Casemate Wall 556). Only one excavation segment (that identified by the coordinates *120.121.19.126*)

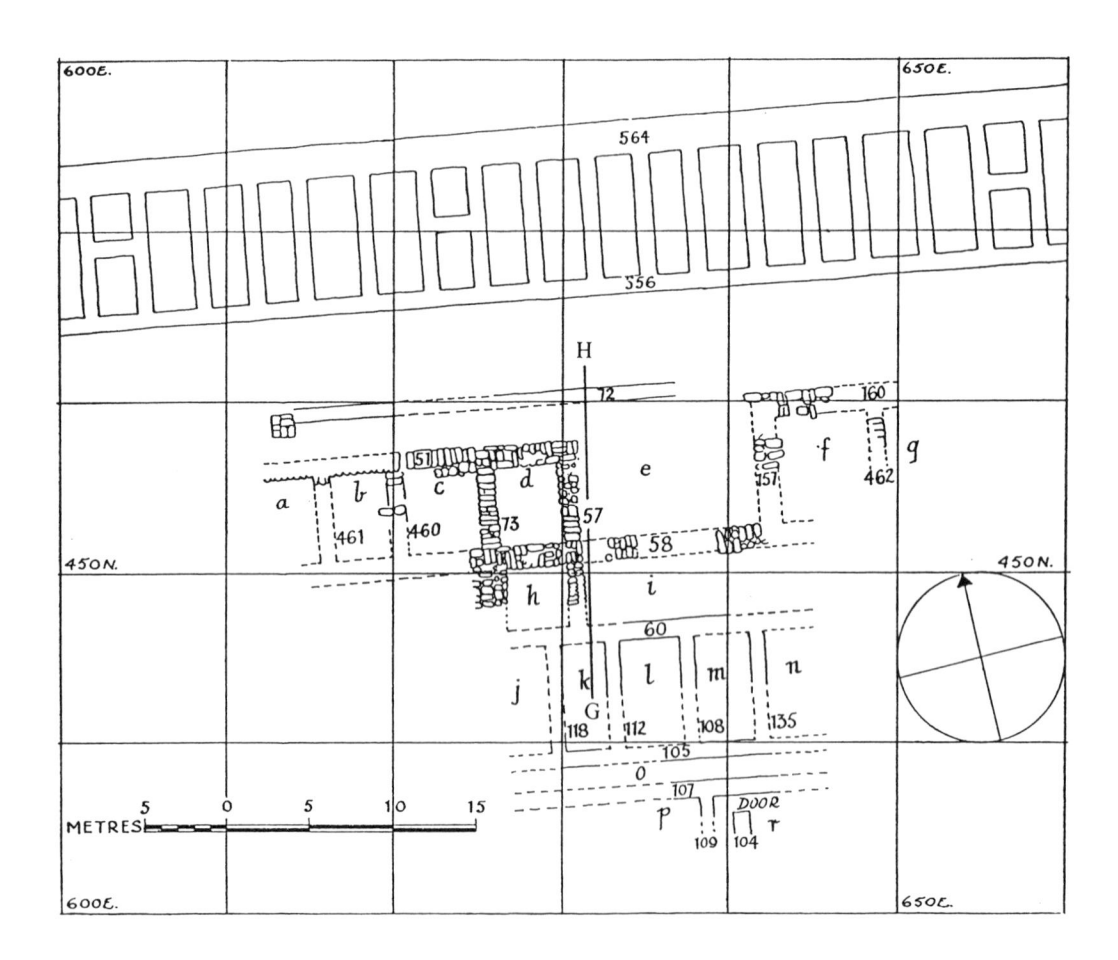

Published "Period III" Top Plan
(adapted from *SS I*, Fig. 47 and *Fieldbook Qc-g*, 58a)

fig. 4

PP 4: INTRODUCTION

clearly ran through more than one feature (Rooms *g*, *h*, *j*).[11] Table 1 also lists the number of fragments and whole or near-whole vessels which the excavators published from each locus, outlines the local stratigraphy (by layer) of the various loci, and marks parenthetically the number of original discards ultimately published from each architectural feature.

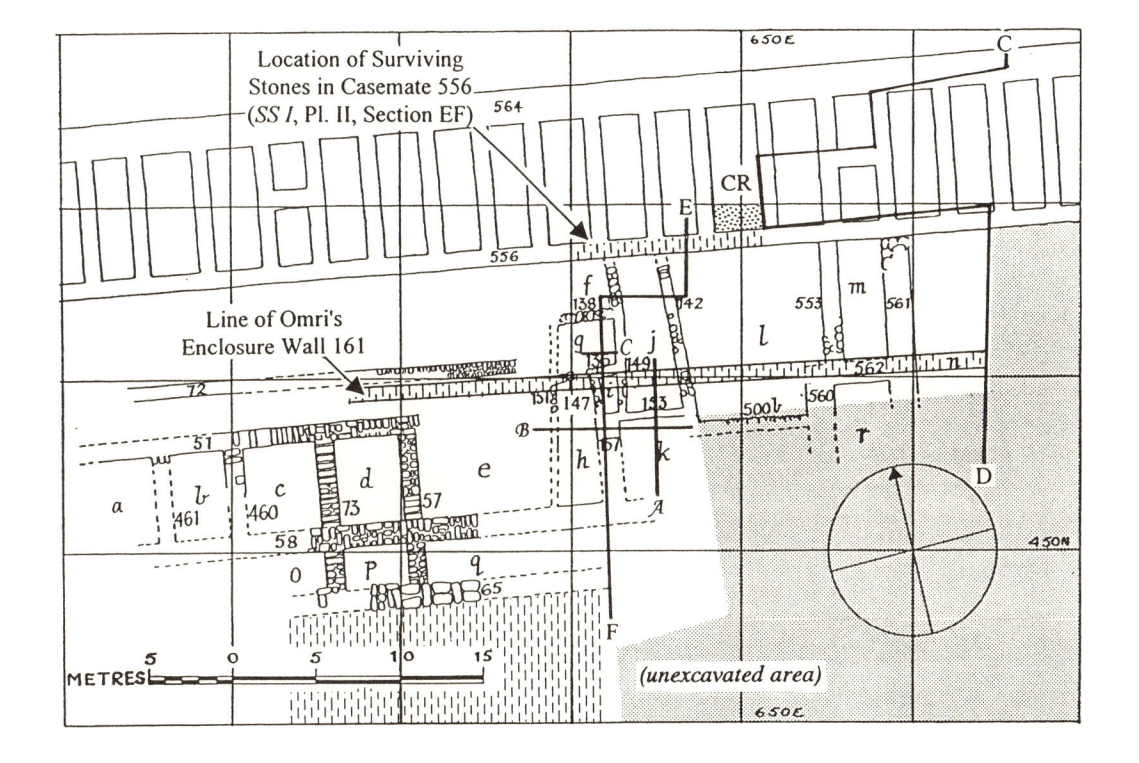

Published "Period IV" Top Plan
(adapted from *SS I*, Fig. 48)[12]

fig. 5

---

[11] The base fragment listed in Table 1 as "IVa.y, Vy – 125.144" under Room *k* (= Q 2373 in *SS III*, Fig. 6:5a) most likely came instead from Room *h*. By the completion of the published report, Kenyon mistakenly assigned it to Room *k* apparently due to a notation in field registry *Sabastya Qn, 1935* (Rockefeller Museum) which stated that the rim fragment from *Btw TT2-TT3*, Room *h* (= Q 2374 in *SS III*, Fig. 6:5b) came "possibly from bowl of base 2373." The two fragments in question do not seem, however, to have derived from the same locus.

[12] I have adapted the published version of this plan by (1) plotting the locations of published Sections CD and EF, (2) plotting the locations of various subsidiary sections that relate in some way to Segment *120.121.19.126* (see my Auxiliary Sections in figs. 7-9); and (3) indicating the points at which Omri's original Enclosure Wall 161 ran beneath the walls of the northern complex rooms assigned to BP IV in the excavation report.

Part A. House Floors — Rooms *f, g, h, j, k, n*
(*SS I*, Figs. 48-49; Pl. VII — Sections CD, EF)
(*SS III*, Fig. 6:1-8, 12, 14-18, 20-30, 32-40)

According to the final report, the east-west series of rooms labeled *a, b, c, d,* and *e* (partially destroyed) and assigned to Building Period III continued in use during Kenyon's "Period IV" (see figs. 4-5; I have included the BP III Phase Plan here for comparative purposes). This conclusion, based strictly on stratigraphic observations, will emerge later as an important factor contributing to the difficulty in distinguishing the pottery groups PP 3 and PP 4 as evidence of truly distinct ceramic phases at the site.[13] During Building Period IV, alterations occurred in the architecture situated both south and east of these reused rooms; all the stratified ceramic material published in the final report for this period came from the additions made to the east.

To the south of Rooms *a-e*, the BP III series of rectangular rooms labeled *j-n, p, r* and the associated Corridor *o* went out of use in BP IV. According to the official BP III Phase Plan (fig. 4), the excavators had identified this complex of rooms only by a series of robber trenches in the area; no actual architectural remains were found there. The northernmost wall shared by these rooms (Wall 60) was now replaced by a new wall (65) immediately to its north (at approximately 447-48° N) that thereby reduced the longitudinal area inside Rooms *p-q* (which now superceded *h* and *i*). These two truncated spaces nevertheless continued in BP IV as Rooms *o-p-q*, though the final report presented no pottery from this area. Interestingly, to the south of Wall 65 "a floor of pounded limestone was laid down over the area . . . , sealing the remains of the [BP III] walls and the [BP III] trenches from which they had been removed" (see hatched area on fig. 5).[14] It seems curious, then, that no pottery from either the "Period III" deposits sealed by this new floor or the "Period IV" occupational debris found lying on this surface (or, for that matter, from inside the relatively well-preserved Rooms *c, d,* and *p* to the immediate north) appeared in the final report to corroborate the dating and interpretation of key features found in this area. And given Kenyon's principle of dating a floor level by materials found *beneath* it, it seems even more surprising that the final report presented no material culture recovered from the local layers situated immediately below this BP IV limestone floor since this sealing would certainly have protected a series of secure, primary findspots.[15] Instead, the

---

[13] Due to numerous recording errors and formidable stratigraphic challenges (particularly regarding BP III Rooms *c-d*), I cast serious doubts in an earlier study on the overall integrity of Kenyon's "Period III" as a rubric used in the final report to represent both a distinct building phase and a distinct ceramic phase at Samaria (see *AIS-I*, 145ff.). I shall return to this problematic subject in my conclusions to PP 4. (See especially Kenyon's statement cited in *AIS-I*, 209, n. 269.)

[14] *SS I*, 105.

[15] The Robber Trench relating to Wall 65 and the BP IV deposits south of that wall appears at the southernmost end (right side) of published Section EF (see *SS I*, Pl. VII). As is the case with all the published sections, the depositional history of BP IV is presented in non-detailed blocks of deposits (see EF) overlying the Robber Trench for BP I Wall 60 and the layers associated with that wall. A more exact pic-

report speculates only that this new surface represents a northward extension of the main courtyard which lay farther south in the royal compound and which now "extended right up to wall 65," though the two surface remnants were separated by a distance of 40 m and an elevation variation of .75 m and though no direct stratigraphic connection between the two presented itself.

Neither could the excavators establish a stratigraphic relationship between this sealed area and the disturbed one from which they, in fact, did retrieve their assemblage of published pottery, namely the new complex of small, rectilinear though somewhat irregularly designed rooms to the northeast of the earlier Rooms *a-e*. These purportedly new BP IV rooms were labeled *f, g, h, j, k, l, m, n*, and *r* (see fig. 5). The horizontal exposure of this area extended southward at best to the northern face of lateral Wall 500b,[16] and thereby hardly revealed the interior portion of Room *r*. More important, the area excavated east of 635° longitude and both north and south of 450° latitude—i.e., the eastern extension of Room *q* plus Rooms *h* and *k*—appeared quite heavily disturbed, with only a few traces of robber trenches left remaining. Rooms *g* through *k* formed a rough quadrangle around the stone-lined Pit *i*, which was set into the now partially destroyed BP III Wall 157 (= the western wall of BP III Room *f*).[17] The report noted that none of these rooms seemed well built. The foundations of the thin (less than .60 m), shallowly set walls barely extended below the floor levels in each chamber, and the walls themselves consisted in crudely laid field stones of varying shapes and sizes, all reinforced by smaller rocks forced into the crevices between the stones.[18] As I shall explain later, the poor caliber of construction throughout this area belies its utilitarian, service-oriented function and helps to distinguish it from the well-planned and better-built units to the west (Rooms *a-d, o-q*).

In short, one can see two distinct clusters of north courtyard buildings which exhibit markedly different manifestations of quality in both their design and work-

---

ture of the local layers within the "Period IV" deposit is desirable but not offered in the official report. It appears, however, that here one sees another rather thick deposit of imported fill serving as the base for the new surface laid south of Wall 65. Moreover, the original stratigraphic relationship of the local layers to the wall itself cannot be determined with certainty since the robber trench subsequently broke that connection. Finally, according to Kenyon, Wall 60 remained in use throughout her "Periods I-III" (see the final Phase Plans, *SS I*, Pl. VIII = BP I-II, and *SS III*, Fig. 47 = BP III), when Wall 65 replaced it. One may assume, then, that the material from inside the Robber Trench of Wall 60, which Kenyon has labeled "Period I," should in fact belong to BP IV, i.e., to the period in which the wall was removed and the resulting trench backfilled. Similarly, the materials taken from the backfill of RT 65 belong to a phase *later* than BP IV.

[16] According to the limits of excavation shown on *SS I*, Pl. II, this wall appears to have fallen outside the area exposed (I have allowed for this in my adaptation of the Top Plan in fig. 5).

[17] The stratigraphic correlations for this pit remain extremely ambiguous. No surface ever sealed the pit, and Kenyon concluded that it continued in use through her "Period VI." And though it was filled with midden-like rubbish, Kenyon drew nearly two-thirds of her representative ceramic sample for PP 6 from it (see Chapter IV below for a detailed discussion of this problem).

[18] *SS I*, 104-05.

manship. A swathe of considerable disturbance covered the area between the two complexes, obscuring their exact spatial and functional relationship in antiquity.

The pottery sample representing Kenyon's "Period IV" came from roughly two limited areas within this shabby complex of rooms: first, the quadrangle of Rooms *g*, *h*, *j*, *k* (55.9% of the published assemblage), and second, a small portion of the more easterly Room *n* (44.1%; see fig. 5 for the location of these areas). The Joint Expedition excavated eleven individual segments[19] distributed over these five rooms, and I have defined each segment by the coordinates listed in Table 1.

The pottery-bearing loci of the first area named above, i.e., the *g-h-j-k* complex, ran directly over the line established by Omri's original Enclosure Wall 161 and followed later by BP III Wall 160 (I have indicated the path of these walls in my fig. 5; see also *SS I*, Pl. VII, Section EF). Table 1 shows that, in terms of the quantity of material eventually published from this cluster of north courtyard chambers (excluding momentarily Room *n*), Room *h* constitutes the most significant area. By contrast, the pottery group assigned to Room *k* (which actually contributed more pieces to the final report than did *h*) stands out as the potentially least reliable collection since 75% of the vessels published from here were tagged as discards in the original field registry. Taken together, these two BP IV rooms (*h* and *k*) now overlay most of what the excavators had called Room *f* on their BP III plan. Yet the final report states that "in *f* the Period IV level was below that of Period III, and indeed of Period I."[20] This would seem to indicate that the construction activities of BP IV destroyed all earlier deposits in this area—i.e., that the foundations and basal layers of Rooms *h* and *k* penetrated all the way to bedrock—though that is not the way it appears on either the published Phase Plan for BP III (where Rooms *f* and *g* remain clearly visible; fig. 4) or the final sections for this area (where a thick "Period I" deposit appears immediately south of Walls 161/160, i.e., in the area of Room *f*; compare Sections EF and AB). The necessity of clarifying the local stratigraphy inside Rooms *h* and *k*, then, will become central not only for a discussion of the putative historical phase called "Period IV-IVa" but for the successive phase as well, since these chambers extended southward into the area then covered by the BP V Room *hk* (see Chapter II, fig. 41 below).

Fortunately, one published section (EF) and three unpublished field sections (which I have labeled Auxiliary Sections A, B, and C) bearing upon this area remain available to help guide us through the following stratigraphic analysis. Two of these sections (EF and Auxiliary A) follow longitudinal courses through this complex of rooms, while the others (Auxiliary B and C) record lateral cuts across the area. I have plotted the lines taken by each section on the Top Plan in fig. 5. The drawings convey individual rooms as outlined in Table 2.

---

[19]This assumes that a difference existed between *N of TT2* and *E Strip*; *N of TT2*; likewise with *Btw TT2-TT3* and *E Strip*; *Btw TT2-TT3*.

[20]*SS I*, 103.

PP 4: INTRODUCTION

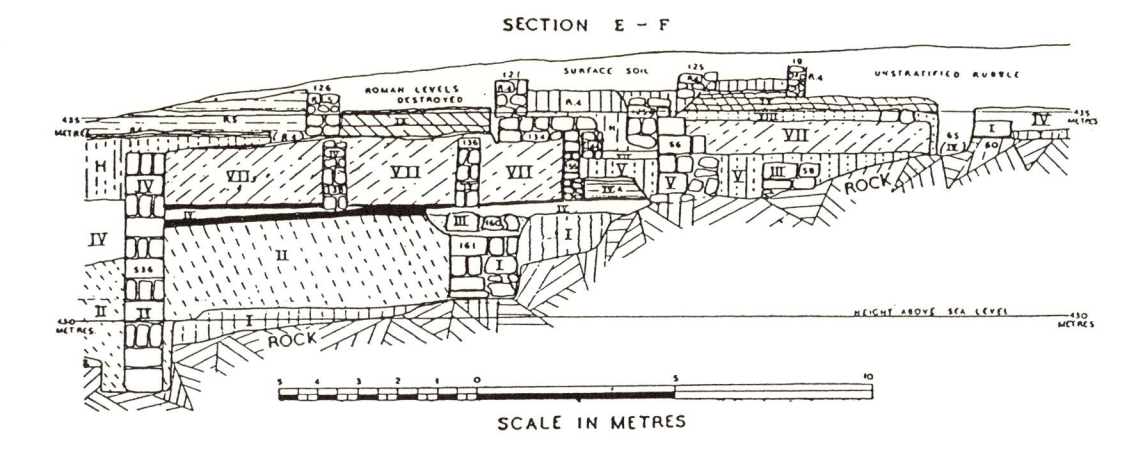

Published Section EF
(adapted from *SS I*, Pl. VII)
<— N S —>
View toward East

fig. 6

Since these sections relate to the rooms in various combinations and usually proceed through portions of two or more chambers,[21] and since the first cluster of chambers addressed (*g, h, j*) involves all four sections, it seems prudent to present the drawings together at this point and to cite them when appropriate as the discussion of each room progresses. In addition, detailed comments on the depositional history and ceramic yields of earlier layers in several segments already encountered in the environs

Section EF	⇒ Rooms *g* and *h* (plus later Room *hk*)
Auxiliary Section A	⇒ Rooms *j* and *k* (plus later Room *hk*)
Auxiliary Section B	⇒ Rooms *h* and *k* (plus later Room *hk*)
Auxiliary Section C	⇒ Room *g*

*Correlation of Extant Sections and
Courtyard Rooms North of 450° N, East of 638° E*
Table 2

---

[21] Published Section EF ⇒ Rooms *g* and *h* (and the subsequent *hk* in Kenyon's "Period IVa"); Auxiliary Section A (*North of Test Trench 2*) ⇒ Room *j* and *k* (later *hk*); Auxiliary Section B ⇒ Rooms *h* and *k* (later *hk*); Auxiliary Section C ⇒ apparently Room *g*, though this is not entirely clear.

of these rooms have appeared in a previous work and will often facilitate the present discourse on the BP IV architecture.[22]

1) Stratigraphic Detail

a. Rooms *g–h–j* (Published Section EF; Auxiliary Sections A, B, and C)

[i] 120.121.19.126

As noted earlier, examination of this segment will require data from more than one architectural feature since it proceeded through at least three of the rooms in this complex (*g*, *h*, *j*). Though my usual method will entail the collection and presentation of the various excavated segments according to the single structure with which they were associated, it seems logistically prudent to treat the details surrounding *120.121.19.126* collectively, particularly since the three rooms involved lay contiguous to one another and effectively formed one structural unit. My full discussion of *120.121.19.126*, therefore, appears here, and additional remarks made later under Room *h* or *j* will hark back to these initial comments.[23]

As reported in my previous work relating to this area,[24] the Joint Expedition located its Segment *120.121.19.126* in Summit Strip Qk at approximately 636-42° E x 456-60+° N.[25] Here the publication of "Period IV" materials focused mainly on Wall 136 which ran between Rooms *g* and *h* and, more specifically, on the doorway in the western half of that wall which connected the two rooms. The robber trench for the western extent of Omri's Wall 161 began here. This area, then, lay just west of published Sections AB and EF (both of which show the truncated remains of Wall 161 at 642° E x 459-60° N) and east of published Section GH (whose baulk crossed the Robber Trench of Wall 161 about 7 m farther west, at ca. 635° E). The fieldbooks did not fully present the stratigraphy of *120.121.19.126* in section (see fig. 9). In her field notes, however, Kenyon correlated the earliest layers found here with those excavated in the adjacent segment labeled *N of TT2*, which she did record in a field section.[26]

---

[22] Consult the appropriate sections of *AIS-I* for the following segments: *120.121.19.126* = *AIS-I* 105-06 (PP 2); *North of TT2* = *AIS-I* 21-23 (PP 1), 104-05 (PP 2); *509.126* = *AIS-I* 19-21 (PP 1), 104-05 (PP 2); *Between TT2-TT3* = *AIS-I* 43-46 (PP 1), 147-49 (PP 3).

[23] I shall also consider simultaneously the two areas (Rooms *h* and *k*) on which Segment *125.144 may* have touched (see n. 11 above).

[24] See *AIS-I*, 105-06.

[25] As with other segments, the numerals used to designate this area refer to the remains of specific walls that the excavators discovered, though the walls in question do not always relate to the historical period under discussion. For example, Walls 121, 19, and 126 (and presumably also 120, though it does not appear in section) relate historically to large private buildings located in the area adjoining the Late Roman temple complex, i.e., to Kenyon's "R.4" period in the 4th cent. CE, and not to BP IV/PP 4 as it may seem. See *SS I*, Pl. VII, Section EF.

[26] For relevant fieldnotes, see *Fieldbook Qk-l-m*, 2a-3, 28a-31; stratigraphic summaries, 2a, 3a, 28a.

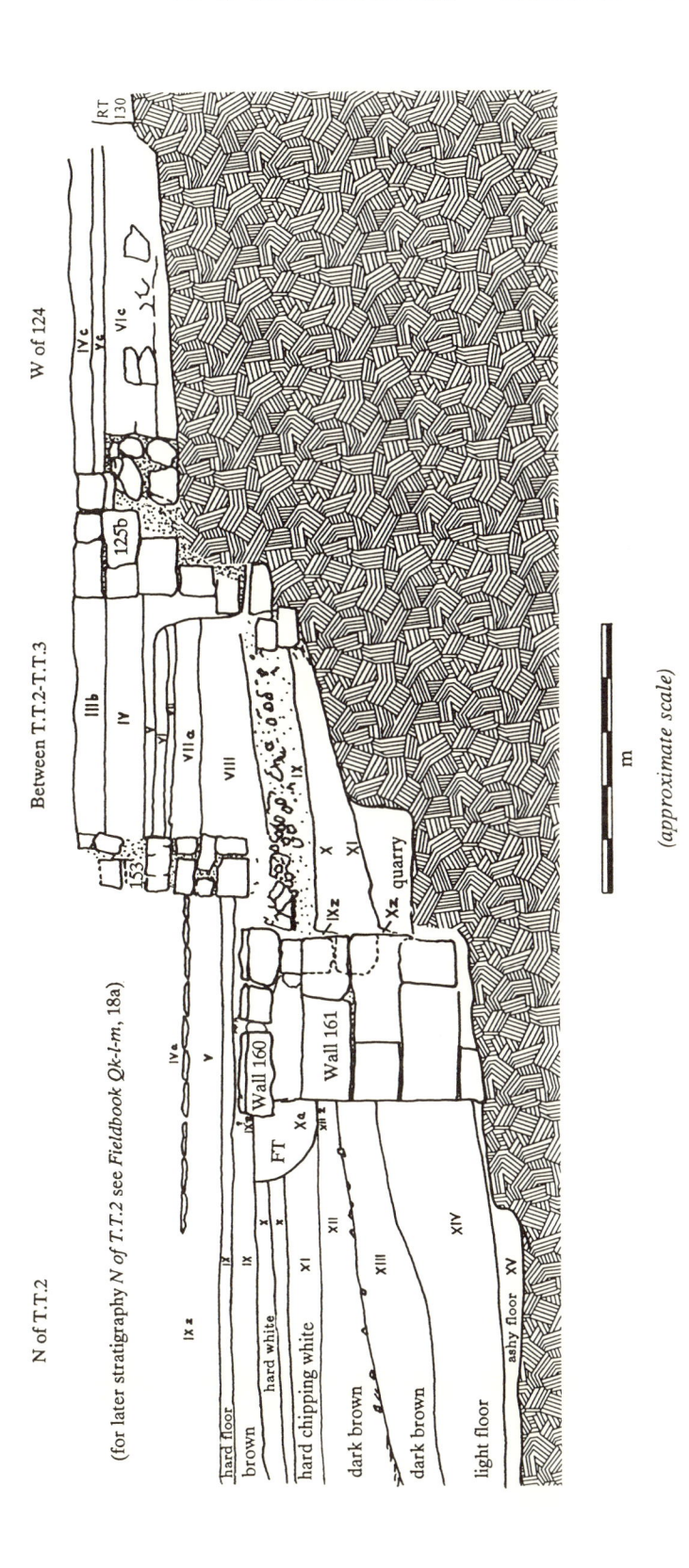

Auxiliary Section A:
Segments N of TT2 and Btw TT2-TT3
<— N S —>
View toward East

fig. 7

For comparative purposes, I have again included this information exactly as Kenyon sketched it in the field, adding only a few descriptive headings to identify the relevant features or segments (= Auxiliary Section A; fig. 7).

Although the deposits shown in this field drawing (at approximately 645° E) ran parallel and close to those of the official Section EF at 642° E, various discrepancies between the two necessitate an orientation to their precise locations on the BP IV top plan and to the architectural features which they present. The field-drawn section lay roughly three meters east of Section EF and extended from the approximate position of the robber trench associated with Wall 58 northward to Wall 153 (= area of Room *k*; see fig. 5). From there, it followed Layer IX further north through Room *j* but did not continue as far north as Casemate Wall 556. As shown in fig. 7, Layer IX overran and sealed the remains of the earlier, ninth-century BCE Walls 161 and 160 beneath this room. Similarly, published Section EF began just inside the northern casemate system (Wall 556) but extended slightly farther south, to the Robber Trench of Wall 65. From north to south (i.e., E to F), the following relevant walls and spaces are visible:

a) Inner face of casemate Wall 556 (mislabeled as 536) to Wall 138[27] (compare Section AB) = Room *f* (?)
b) Wall 138 to Wall 136 = Room *g*
c) Wall 136 to Wall 153[28] = Room *h*/Pit *i*
d) Walls 155/153 to Wall 58 = Room *h*[29]
e) RT 58 to Wall 65 = disturbed area south of Room *h*, east of Room *q*

Analysis of Architecture Presented in
SS I, Pl. VII, Section EF

Table 3

As I have shown elsewhere, Segment *120.121.19.126* contained no counterpart to Kenyon's suggested "Period I" floor level in *N of TT2*, i.e., to Layer XIV.[30] In fact,

---

[27] Despite the right angle that the published plans in *SS I*, Pl. VII show in this section, the drawing itself does not include the remains of Wall 149 or the robber trench of Wall 142.

[28] Though Kenyon identified this feature only as Wall 155 in Section EF, it stands in the area where Wall 153 must have existed. Judging from the published section, it appears that Wall 155 represents a later, somewhat narrower structure built on the truncated remains of a broader, unlabeled wall with a "Period IVa" deposit abutting it. I believe this latter feature depicts Wall 153.

[29] Now no traces of BP III Wall 157 remain visible, and it appears that most of the deposits from "Period IV" Room *h*, and even "Period IVa" Room *hk*, have also succumbed to the construction of BP V Wall 56 and the rooms both north and south of it.

[30] See *AIS-1*, 105-06.

Layers XI-XV in fig. 7 represent the first substantial deposits of imported fill dumped north of Wall 161 and, as such, they reflect construction activities from the time of Ahab, not the raising of an earlier floor level as Kenyon suggested.

The excavators understood Layer IX in Segment *120.121.19.126* generally as the "floor of small Isr[aelite] rooms" and, observing that it postdated (i.e., overlay) the truncated Wall 160, they assigned it to their "Period IV."[31] The field notes enumerate two subdeposits related to IX. First, Layer IXa comprised the material actually used to block the doorway between Rooms *g* and *h* in Wall 136. Though Kenyon suggested in the notes that this blockage occurred either in her "Period IIIa" or in "Period IV," her published top plans place it subsequently in "Periods IVa-V."[32] Second, Layer IXb received the label "Wall 136." Pottery from this segment attributed to Wall 136 (*SS III*, Fig. 6:1) and Layer IXb (*SS III*, Fig. 6:24), then, appear to derive from one and the same locus.

On published Section EF, Layer IX seals completely the truncated remains of BP III Wall 160 and continues southward (toward the summit) until it encounters the rise in bedrock at the base of Wall 56. The upper portion of the layer seems to run up to the southern face of Casemate Wall 556 (mislabeled in Section EF as Wall 536) and, to the south, up to the faces of both Wall 138 and Wall 136. This seems to confirm Kenyon's top plan which depicts the floors of Rooms *f* and *g* as contemporary with these walls. Farther south, Wall 153 (beneath 155) seems not to have had much of a foundation trench but to have rested on the top of Layer IX, which thickens slightly as it proceeds southward beneath this wall.[33]

In the corresponding field section from *N of TT2*, the portrait of the depositional history in this area differs from that just outlined in Section EF. This depiction (through Room *j*) divides Layer IX more specifically into two distinct deposits, both of which received the same identifying label, "IX." The field notes describe the earlier portion as a darkish makeup beneath the new floor; this undoubtedly corresponds to the level labeled "brown IX" in fig. 7, a level which contained mainly PP 4 pottery. The lower, heavy black line on Kenyon's Section EF must signify the bottom elevation of this makeup. This brown base enveloped the stub of Wall 160. One also sees that both the subfloor makeup and the compacted matrix of the surface itself (designated by the upper, heavy black line in Section EF) lap up against the northern face of Wall 153 without a trace of a foundation trench. This indicates that the ancient builders set the wall first and then laid the constituent layers of the floor around it, covering even the first course of the wall. The basal and surface portions of Layer IX, then, represent the

---

[31] In her stratigraphic summary, Kenyon originally placed general Layer IX in her "Period III" (with a correction to IV) and Wall 160 to "Period II" (without correction). See *Fieldbook Qk-l-m*, 3a.

[32] See *SS III*, Figs. 48-50.

[33] See n. 28 above. Once again, potential discrepancies exist within the field records as they pertain to the separate identifications of Walls 153 and 155. It remains unclear whether these designations, in fact, represent two distinct walls or whether two identifying numerals were assigned to the same wall. Compare Wall 153 on my fig. 6 with Wall 155 on fig. 8.

floor level in Room *h*/Pit *i*. The micro-stratigraphy south of Wall 153, in Segment *Btw TT2-TT3*, also receives greater detail in the field section than it did in Section EF; I shall address this area below (see Room *k*).

Because another section in *Fieldbook Qk-l-m* intersected laterally the area just described, I shall introduce it here as well and return to it below as appropriate (fig. 8). This section ran roughly parallel to and just south of Walls 161 and 153, at ca. 456/57° N, and extended east-to-west from ca. 647° E to 638° E (see fig. 5). The importance of this stratigraphic record for Kenyon's "Period IV, IVa and V" lies in its outline of both

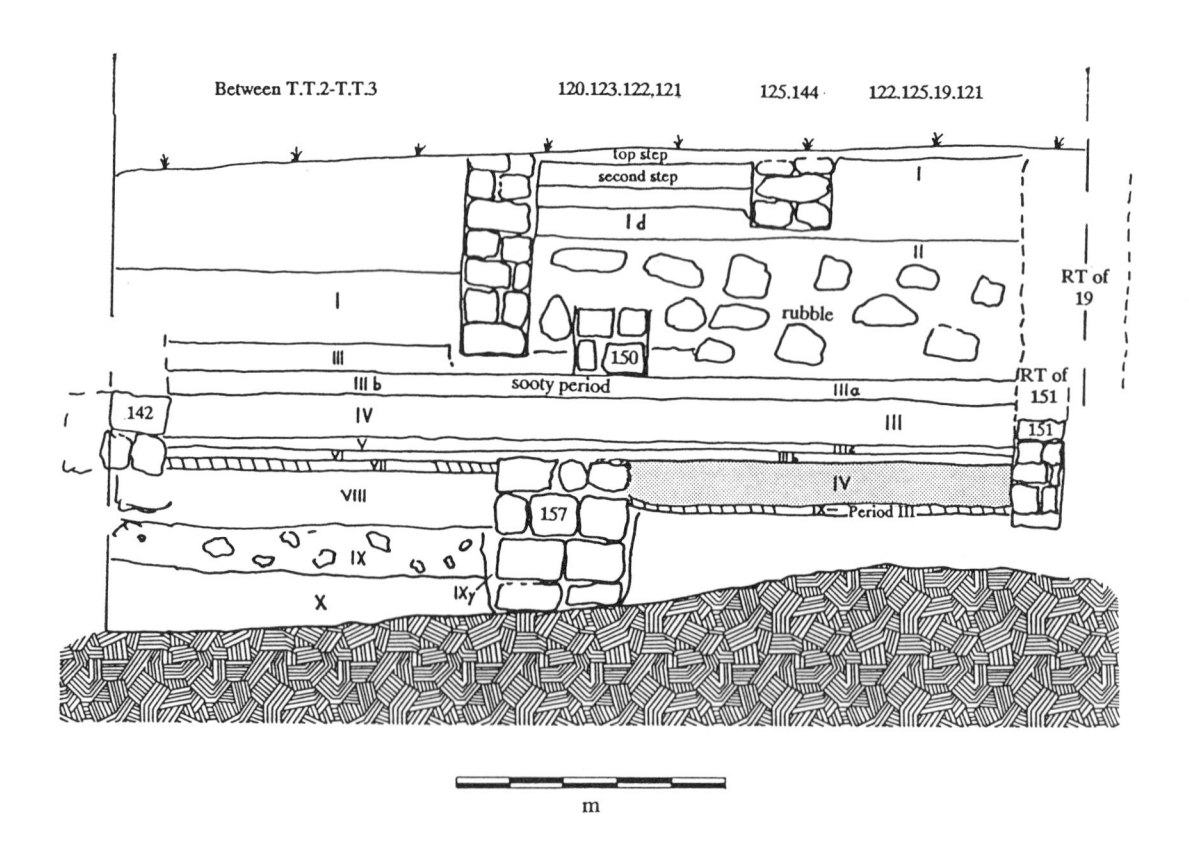

Auxiliary Section B:
Segments Btw TT2–TT3; 125.144; 122.125.19.121
< — E W —>
View toward South

(running parallel to and just south of Wall 161 @ ca. 456/57° N;
the section extends east-to-west from ca. 647°-638° E)

fig. 8

the local deposits remaining in Rooms *h* and *k* (situated immediately west and east of Wall 157, respectively) and the depositional history in the subsequent Room *hk*, from a time when Wall 157 was already out of service. I shall return to this material below in separate discussions of those rooms. Here it will suffice to note that the floor levels indicated by Layer VII in Room *k* and Layer IX in Room *h* appear to represent the first living surfaces established there (other than the use of the rock surface itself during the Iron Age I occupation by the ancestral estate of Shemer). These levels (VII; IX) belonged originally to Walls 142 and 151, respectfully, and served during a time when Wall 157 was still in use (= Kenyon's "Period IV").

Finally, to underscore the general disturbance which existed throughout this area (note that most of the rooms are defined only by robber trenches), I have included a previously unseen field drawing which apparently depicts the deposits in Room *g*[34] (Auxiliary Section C; fig. 9). The section stretched westward from the robber trench of Wall 149, which established the boundary between Rooms *g* and *j* (see the plan in fig.

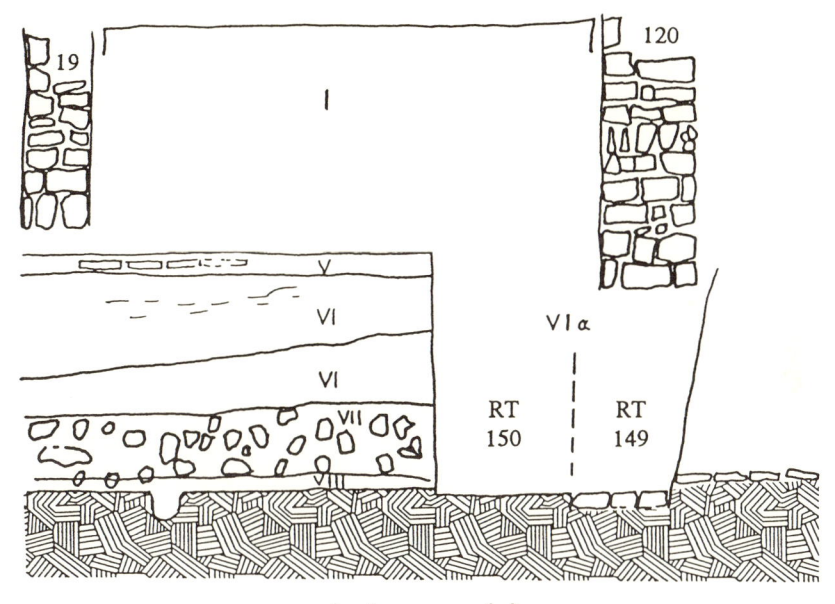

(scale not recorded)

Auxiliary Section C: Layers West of Wall 120 (in Room g)
<— W E —>
View toward North
fig. 9

---

[34]*Fieldbook Qk-l-m*, 29a. I have not, however, succeeded in locating either of the later walls (197 or 120) shown here on any published section or plan to corroborate this placement.

5 above). Besides this plundering, the removal of Wall 150 also destroyed substantial portions of the original deposits in this room. Moving west from RT 149, however, one sees a number of interesting features in this area. First, a carved pocket or basin appears in the bedrock, similar to those seen at various points in the courtyard south of these rooms and which reflect pre-Omride activities at the family estate of Shemer.[35] According to a laconic statement in their field records,[36] it seems that the excavators also recovered traces of a burnt plaster floor beneath the succeeding Layer VIII.[37]

Overlying this area of rock, Layer VIII comprised a "middenish layer" approximately .20 m thick, followed by the rubble-filled matrix of Layer VII.[38] Next one sees at least two successive deposits of additional, cleaner fill beginning with an unnamed layer and followed by Layer VI. The final report did not include PP 4 materials from any of these deposits, even though they provided a smooth, level building surface for the floor made of hard yellow matrix and labeled Layer V.[39] The substantial amount of fill required here resulted from the fact that the natural rock surface had already begun to decline sharply toward the north side of the site (in the area between Walls 58 and 153, in Room *k*; note the topography of the rock in fig. 7); the importance of this fact will become apparent later in this study. The floor of Layer V did not cover the entire room, and a heavy deposit of fill which apparently contained some burned material covered it. Kenyon stated:

> the hard yellow level V found n[o]t to be present on S[outh] side/sh[oul]d have seen it before. As far as can be seen, really all one level for top 1.50 m., [with] sloping streaks of black.[40]

Though the field drawing proved rather faint in this area, the floor level of Layer V appears to have contained a row of flat paving stones across most of its surface. The section incorporated similar stones from an otherwise undelineated deposit east of RT 149, in what would constitute Room *j*. According to Kenyon's published top plans, it seems likely that these floor levels originated in her "Period V" (see *SS III*, Figs. 48-

---

[35]Compare *AIS-I*, fig. 14, p. 74, and the discussion on pp. 72-73, 77-78; for further evidence that such surface carvings and pits extended into this area north of 450° N, see *SS III*, 92, Fig. 46. Stager has successfully plotted all such installations that remain traceable in the literature produced by the excavation and has shown that they derive from the early Iron Age, not from the Early Bronze Age as Kenyon believed (*Stager*, 93-107).

[36]*Fieldbook Qk-l-m*, 28.

[37]Though this is not shown on the field section, the notes later refer to it as Layer IX.

[38]In her field notes, Kenyon included a Layer VIIa between these two deposits, at the level where she first began to run out of the rubble of VII and encounter mainly the midden of VIII (*Fieldbook Qk-l-m*, 28).

[39]Recall Kenyon's method of dating a floor level by the materials found beneath it.

[40]*Fieldbook Qk-l-m*, 28.

50; compare also fig. 7 above, *N of TT2*, between Layers IVa and V). Judging from fig. 9 above, the same imported soil with inclusions of apparent destruction debris mentioned above not only covered the floor and paving stones of Layer V, but also filled the breaches created by Robber Trenches 149 and 150.[41] If both of these observations prove correct, then these walls were destroyed or robbed sometime after Period V. Commenting on the temporal relationship between this matrix of fill and the architecture around it, however, Kenyon concluded that

> The filling of this room is really diff[erent] on W. [and] on E. sides, [therefore] the room was apparently filled [with] the streaky soot [and] hard yellow soil *before* the E. wall was robbed (RT 149). This is suggested by the fact that on the E. side, a hard yellow filling, similar to the yellow parts of VII, etc., is cut through on line of the paving stones V of N. of T.T.2. The yellow filling must [therefore] have been there *before* the paving stones were also cut through, or the wall against wh[ich] they ended removed. This last is the most prob[able].[42]

It seems clear, then, that the complex of shabbily built rooms north of 450° N and east of 640° E failed to present the excavators with many secure, primary stratigraphic contexts. Two factors contributed to this situation. First, these chambers overlay the area where the rock surface of the site dropped significantly and erratically down the northern slopes. This prompted the need to utilize considerable amounts of imported fill to achieve suitable building levels in this area. Second, as witnessed in the numerous robber trenches throughout this vicinity, this complex succumbed to heavy disturbance by the end of "Period IV." Those events which essentially destroyed Rooms *e* and *q*, situated west-southwest of this complex, also impinged upon the enclosures and walls (such as 136) throughout Segment *120.121.19.126*.

b. Room *hk* (Published Section EF; Auxiliary Sections A and B)

[i] 125.144

As with Segment *120.121.19.126* above, I will consolidate Rooms *h* and *k* in my coverage of Segment *125.144*, since it possibly touched upon both areas (see again nn. 11 and 23 above).[43] To facilitate this analysis, I shall return to the three auxiliary sections presented above in figs. 7-9 before taking up some new, previously unpublished data available in section.

---

[41] Comments made in the field notes confirm this reading.

[42] *Fieldbook Qk-l-m*, 29 (my emphasis).

[43] Data relating to this segment appear in *Fieldbook Qk-l-m* as follows: field section drawings, pp. 33a and 49a (compare also 40a); excavation notes, pp. 33-35, 48, and the upper portion of 49; stratigraphic summary of local layers, pp. 48a and the lower half of 49.

α. Auxiliary Sections A and B (figs. 7-8)

Before proceeding, I should establish once again the exact location of Auxiliary Section B[44] on the BP IV Top Plan (fig. 5). While the series of sections presented in the official report for Summit Strip Qk generally assumed a N-S orientation, the excavators cut this short section laterally in an E-W direction. It nearly perfectly bisected the portion of Section EF shown in the final report, crossing it at 457° N, or immediately south of Wall 153 (below 155). As seen in fig. 8, the section records the deposits in Rooms *h* and *k*, from Wall 142 on the east (near the point at which it forms a corner with Wall 500b)[45] to just beyond Wall 151 on the west. The segment labeled *Between TT2–TT3* lay east of Wall 157 and south of Wall 153, in Room *k* (compare figs. 7 and 13). One can see, therefore, that the expedition delineated segment *125.144* mainly to the west of Wall 157, in Room *h*, though a small portion of it extended beyond that wall into Room *k* as well.[46] I have indicated this situation also in Table 1 above.[47]

As I have demonstrated elsewhere, "the notes summarizing the layers presented here show numerous corrections in which the period assignments originally given to each layer were later raised by one period, so that material initially interpreted as 'Period II' became associated instead with 'Period III,' and so on."[48] These interpretative adjustments, apparently made after the close of excavations, were not retrojected onto the original field section, where Layer IIIb remained in "Period V," Layer VII in "Period III," and so on.[49]

The following observations emerge, nevertheless, upon a close examination of fig. 8. In Kenyon's "Period IV," Room *k* occupied the area immediately east of Wall 157, while Room *h* lay immediately west of it. According to the published top plans, ancient workers built Wall 157 in BP III, setting it directly on the rock surface. As

---

[44] See fig. 8 above, plus the comments on pp. 24-25. One may refer also to *AIS-I*, 44, fig. 9. This section came from *Fieldbook Qk-l-m*, 40a; compare p. 18a (presented as fig. 13 below).

[45] As indicated on the Top Plan in fig. 5, this locus lay very near the eastern limits of the excavation area south of 460° N.

[46] G. M. Crowfoot's stratification card for the fragments in Fig. 6:5 includes the following notation regarding the specific layers in question: "N.B. These levels, 125.144 IVa.y, Vy, and Btw T.T.2 and T.T.3 VII and VIII are really the same, only divided by a later wall."

[47] The field record indicating that segment *125.144* did extend into Room *k* appears somewhat problematic in that the local layer in question (Layer IVa.y) seems to stop at Wall 157 on the field section, i.e., it seems limited to Room *h*.

[48] *AIS-I*, 45; also 21, n. 4. Compare *Fieldbook Qk-l-m*, 14a-15a, 18, 40-41.

[49] As noted in my earlier study, "The level of dark soil which comprised Layer VIII seems to have initiated the series of adjustments presented here, for it is the first layer to show such changes in interpretation. The notebooks describe it as 'Period IV [from III] makeup, or just poss[ibly] Period III [from II] filling associated [with] wall 160.' In terms of the pottery found here, Kenyon's notes seem to indicate a strong mixture of pieces typifying her 'Periods III-IV.' Another nearby note, however, states that the layers from VIII through X (inclusive) yielded pottery 'almost entirely I'" (*AIS-I*, 45, nn. 93-95).

expected, various leveling operations had taken place in this area prior to this construction, and the foundation trench deposit IXy shows that the lower courses of Wall 157 cut several preexisting deposits of this fill material (Layers IX and X to the east; below Layer IX to the west). Kenyon recorded the following observations relating to these features:

> The plaster floor IX def[initely] runs right up to 157, [and] in fact makes a concave moulding against it. The face of 157 is plastered, [and] is in direct line [with] 147, wh[ich] orig[inally] was cont[inued] on this face. At time of construct[ion] of 155, 157 was broken down to below level of IIIb, except on line of 155, where a cross section of it was incorporated in [IIIb (?)] .... W of 157 are no floor levels beneath IX, while to E of it are none below IIIb (VII) wh[ich] crossed broken top of this wall. This area was [therefore] n[o]t included in house till its second period, at any rate S of RT 153. Prob[able] that the pit in 147.136.150.155 was cut in the thickness of Wall 157, [and] dates fr[om] 2nd period.[50]

Thus, Layer VIII constitutes the first deposit east of 157 (in the area of Room *k*) which actually belongs with the wall itself and, as such, represents a fresh dumping of fill designed to raise the floor level of Layer VII (*Btw TT2-TT3*) to an acceptable, level elevation. Westward, in Room *h*, workers laid the floor's surface (Layer IX) directly on the earlier fill without adding to the latter. In general, Room *h* required less fill than Room *k* due to the rise in bedrock beneath the former (west of Wall 157). Though both surfaces (Room *k*, Layer VII and Room *h*, Layer IX) retained their "Period III" designations on the field section, Kenyon's field notes emended that assignment to "Period IV."

The natural summit, then, sloped downward in the area east of Wall 157. Previously cited sections from both the published and unpublished collection show that the rock surface also began its dramatic descent in the areas north of Wall 58[51] and, more noticeably, in the spaces further north beyond lateral Walls 153 and 500b.[52] In other words, the complex of well-built Rooms *a-d* and *o-q* represent construction

---

[50] *Fieldbook Qk-l-m*, 48. From this description, one may also presume that Wall 147 represented the western enclosure of Pit *i*. I have added this identification to the BP IV Top Plan in fig. 5. That the 157 portion of this wall exhibited a plaster facing indicates that it served originally in the complex of rooms reserved for official activity (i.e., Rooms *a-e* and areas eastward). Judging from the fairly (though not exact) spacing of the longitudinal walls that separated these rooms (from west to east, Walls 461, 460, 73, and 57), it seems that Wall 157 would have defined the *eastern* limit of Room *f* rather than the western boundary of it as Kenyon shows it in her BP III plan (fig. 4 above). The room which she labeled *e* in that plan was likely bisected by a longitudinal wall that succumbed to later construction activities in this area.

[51] This area correlates to the descending rock surface just north of Wall 60 in the north-south Sections AB and EF (*SS I*, Pl. VII).

[52] See deposits north of Wall 58 in fig. 6 above (= *SS I*, Section EF); also the area north of Walls 125b and 153 in Auxiliary Section A, fig. 7 above.

activities immediately beyond the northernmost extent of the highest and most serviceable level summit rock. Beyond that point, the cluster of irregularly built Rooms *f-k* sat above a descending surface and required ever increasing amounts of fill to achieve a level building platform and to stabilize the structures that sat above this area of rock. The importance of this seemingly mundane observation will become apparent in my Evaluation and Summary below.

In the subsequent phase of building activity in this area, it appears that Wall 157 went out of service, allowing Rooms *h* and *k* to become one chamber. The deposits overlying the truncated 157 in fig. 8 show a series of hard surfaces[53] and correlate well with those presented in a section from Segment *Btw TT2-TT3*, situated immediately to the east (compare this area in fig. 7). The field notes described Layer V in *Btw TT2-TT3* as a "good hard level" which was believed to have represented "Period V" (corrected from IV).[54] The excavators assigned the "hard floor" of Layer VI and the "hardish yellow level" of Layer VII, both of which were cut by Wall 125b, to "Periods IVa-IV," respectively (both corrected from "Period IIIa" and "IIIb"). They understood Layer VIIa, in turn, as the "Period IV" makeup for Layer VII.

Returning to Segment *125.144*, it is important to note that all of these deposits overlaid Layer IV and its associated deposits; i.e., one should not equate Layer IV in Room *h* with Layer IV in Room *k*.[55] The stratigraphic summary in *Fieldbook Qk-l-m* described Layer IV, Room *h* (*125.144*) as a "soft dark level contemp[orary with] Wall 155" and assigned it to "Period IVa."[56] This appears to represent another deposit of secondary fill which likely consisted in the brown forest soil produced by the deterioration of Eocene limestone formations found in the general area of Samaria. In other places, Kenyon sometimes referred to this soil type as "chocolate soil." The subdeposit labeled Layer IVx.z. represents a noteworthy lens subsumed by this layer of fill and

---

[53] Layers V-VI east of the line of Wall 157; Layers IIIa-IIIb west of that line.

[54] On these emendations to the field notes, see *AIS-I*, 21, n. 4. In *Fieldbook Qk-l-m*, 1a, Kenyon explains her notation system as it relates to the stratigraphic analysis in the field notes as follows: (1) an upper case "P." + Roman numeral placed at the beginning of a line in the stratigraphic summary sheets indicates the *period* to which she assigned a particular deposit, based on stratigraphic evidence; all such notations in the summaries were reassessed and corrected as needed at the close of excavations in 1935; (2) an underscored upper case "P." or lower case "p." + Roman numeral placed at the end of a given stratigraphic entry indicated the *pottery phase* found in that particular layer. It is important to note that not all these entries were corrected in 1935. While the handwritten field notes, which serve as the basis of this study, may primarily represent preliminary field observations, they have, in the interest of accuracy and clarity, received final assessment in the light of the full results of the excavation. As the basis of the official reports, then, these notes should exhibit close agreement with the data and conclusions published therein.

[55] In light of this, a further recording mistake may attend the association of another fragment from a subdeposit of Layer IV in Segment *125.144* (*SS III*, Fig. 6:5a) with Room *k*. It may actually belong to Room *h* since, according to the field section, Layer IV in *125.144* does not appear to have extended east of Wall 157.

[56] *Fieldbook Qk-l-m*, 48a.

described as a "black patch" of soil. The field records left nearly all the sublayers (i.e., Layers IV-t, w, w.z, x, z) associated with this deposit, however, in "Period IV," including the soft dark earth of Layer IVa, which yielded the jar rim presented in *SS III*, Fig. 6:15. This becomes significant because (1) the final report contained only two fragments of pottery taken from this segment of Room *h* (6:14-15); (2) these fragments came from the sublayers IVa and IVx.z;[57] and (3) one of these sherds (No. 14), which Kenyon believed came from a so-called Hippo jar (but see pp. 93-94 below), represents the sole piece of stratified evidence offered in support of Kenyon's "Period IVa" as an historical phase distinct from "Period IV."

Curiously, the official report states only that 6:14 came from a "new floor" added above the original surface of this room.[58] This laconic description remains ambiguous since, according to her usual methodology, Kenyon would have taken the sherd from the deposits found *beneath* this repaving. As a result, questions remain regarding the exact nature of the findspot: was it a matrix of imported fill used as makeup for this purportedly new floor? was it actually part of the occupational debris (shaded layer in fig. 8) resting just above the original floor of Room *h*? how extensive was the resurfacing? etc. Though I cannot enjoy certainty in my conclusions since neither the field sections nor the published ones plotted the locations of the sublayers associated with Layer IV, I may suggest with confidence that the blackened patch which yielded 6:14 (sub-Layer IVx.z) does not point to a general destruction of the area since several *ṭabunîm* were located in the vicinity (see below). Furthermore, the field notes admit that other related subdeposits, such as IVa.y-Vy from which the excavators recovered *SS III* Fig. 6:5, "prob[ably] included" some soil and materials from the Late Roman quarry assigned to "Period R4."[59] In short, though the depositional history here seems to present an area of closely laid surfaces, descriptions of individual findspots still leave some doubt as to their stratigraphic reliability.

Above Segment *125.144*, Layer IV, the excavators encountered the main series of packed surfaces just mentioned. All these floors clearly overran the defunct Wall 157 and, as a result, reflected the combining of former Rooms *h* and *k* into a new, elongated chamber called Room *hk* (see *SS I*, Fig. 49 = "Period IVa"). The earliest of these floor levels, Layer IIIb, sealed Layer IV but was itself cut by Wall 125b. The field notes assigned this floor level to "Period IVa," understood it as contemporary

---

[57] The designation "IVa" appears in the handwritten pottery records and in Kenyon's stratigraphic summary in *Fieldbook Qk-l-m*, 48a.

[58] *SS III*, 113.

[59] *Fieldbook Qk-l-m*, 49. These quarrying activities impinged on other local segments as well, such as along the southern edge of *North of TT2*. In this process, the Romans robbed the eastern end of Wall 125b, and quarried the entire section south of there. Kenyon observed that "the filling [throughout this area] is obviously the levels excavated in mining the quarry, and contains pottery of all periods down to fairly late ribbed, and also small frags. of burnt ivory fr[om] the ivory level cut through. Wall 129 (R.4; 4th century CE), the stylobate for a colonade, . . . , is immed[iately] past the quarry" (*Fieldbook Qk-l-m*, 12a).

with the addition of Wall 155 (see fig. 10 below), and correlated it to Layer VI in Segment *Btw TT2-TT3* (compare figs. 7-8).

Kenyon associated the succeeding Layer IIIe(?)[60] with *Btw TT2-TT3*, Layer V, and ascribed both to her "Period V" (corrected from IV). In her field notes, she recorded this layer as "*one of several* levels making up III, above IIIb . . . ."[61] While the depiction of this layer in fig. 8 resembles an actual floor level, then, one must leave open the likelihood that the deposit comprises simply the bottommost striations of the fill material visible in the thicker layers above it (Layers III in Segment *125.144* and IV in *Btw TT2-TT3*). According to Kenyon, the latter functioned together with Wall 125b. Finally, as indicated on fig. 8, Layer IIIa comprised a sooty deposit overlying III (= *Btw TT2-TT3*, Layer IIIb) and belonged, according to Kenyon, in "Period VII."

β. New Stratigraphic Evidence (figs. 10-11)

My research uncovered two additional field sections which relate directly to Segment *125.144*. The preceding discussion has already incorporated walls which appear only on these drawings (e.g., Walls 125b and 155). The principal drawing (fig. 10) proves useful in two ways. First, it helps to corroborate my stratigraphic analysis of deposits from earlier periods (I-III), particularly in the areas north and south of Omri's Enclosure Wall 161. In fact, this section contains even more detail than previous ones in that it clearly distinguishes between Layers X and XI as they extend away from the south face of 161. Northward from 161, this section subdivides the hard white chipping recorded only as Layer XI in fig. 7 into two distinct deposits, Layers XI and XIa. At any rate, this section confirms my earlier suggestion that no floor level existed in this area prior to those layers cut by the foundation trench for Wall 160 (i.e., Layers X-XI).

Second, this drawing also provides new data important to my analysis of "Period IV" levels. It depicts the deposits lying on a north-south axis not only in Room *hk*, but extending through Pit *i* and into Room *g*. I have added the appropriate identifying labels to the original drawing. Two of the three walls germane to this discussion appear actually to rest on the remains of earlier ones. Toward the south end of the section, Wall 125b[62] was built over Wall 56 as indicated on published Section EF. North

---

[60]Kenyon's handwritten label for this deposit was small and difficult to read. She appears, however, to have called it IIIc, or possibly IIIe. At any rate, I mislabeled it as IIIa in *AIS-1*, 44, fig. 9; I have made the necessary correction in fig. 8 above.

[61]*Fieldbook Qk-l-m*, 48a (my emphasis).

[62]Once again, Kenyon's choice to utilize a wall from this numerical series as a main coordinate for Israelite levels at the site seems curious, since both Wall 125b and, more certainly, Wall 125 belong to much later periods of occupation. Even Wall 144 (visible immediately south of the upper remains of Wall 155 in *SS I*, Pl. VII, Section EF) belongs no earlier than Israelite "Period VII." A notation in *Fieldbook Qk-l-m*, 33-34, states that this wall "rests *about* on III of *125.144*" and that there "seems to be a face in the middle" of it which "belongs to a Wall 155." It suggests further that "the back of this wall [i.e., 144] w[oul]d have been destroyed" (my emphasis). The segment designation *125.144*, then, seems somewhat anomalous within the purview of Israelite history.

PP 4: HOUSE FLOORS — STRATIGRAPHY

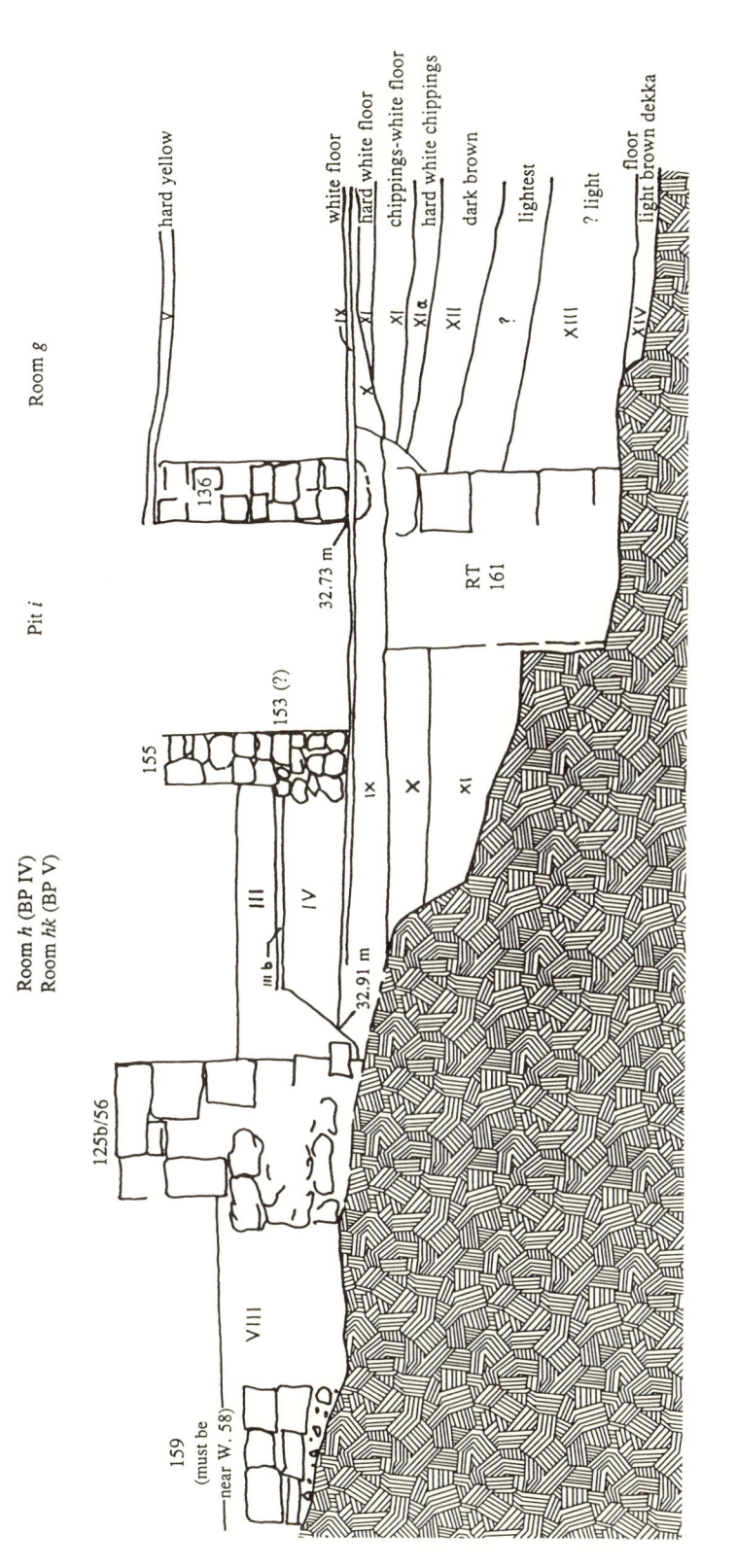

Segment 125.144
(compare figs. 7-8)
<— S N —>
View toward West

fig. 10

of that point, two possibilities exist for understanding the feature labeled Wall 155. First, the more regularly constructed upper portion represents a rebuild over an earlier, somewhat cruder Wall 153. Section EF shows this difference in the quality of the offset upper and lower sections of this structure but does not provide separate identification numbers for them.

The other conceivable interpretation of this wall would suggest that the irregular courses of stones on the lower, southern face of 155 represent simply the subterranean support system covered by the fill of Layer IV. As expected, the superstructure from the floor level of Layer IIIb upward became more regular. Kenyon seemed to prefer this reading of the stratigraphy here when she wrote that

> It is clear that 155 on this side [i.e., the lower south face] cannot have belonged to the plaster floor V, [since] bottom .50 m. is v[ery] rough indeed. It seems that the floor level was ruined [?] .50 m., and that Wall 147 [was] broken down to sufficient depth to be covered by this floor. This floor is the level IIIa [b?; unclear] wh[ich] is cut by 125b., so that the soft level IV belongs to 155.[63]

This observation notwithstanding, the ancient workers must have constructed Wall 155 over or very near the area where Wall 153 appears on the plan shown in fig. 5, given the location of the section itself and the relative positions of the identifiable features on it.[64] I have, therefore, chosen to label the lower portions of this structure "Wall 153 (?)." This decision seems congruent with the utilization of nearby Wall 56 as a base for the succeeding 125b, a situation which is more apparent in both the field notes and published sections. In short, I believe that the bottom four to five courses of Wall 155 belonged originally to Wall 153, and that the latter feature functioned with the hard, plaster floor of Layer V on which it sat. Figure 8 would also seem to confirm Kenyon's suggestion that Pit *i* first existed in BP IV and that it remained open as the deposits built up around it. Its basal level was apparently not raised, for example, with the addition of fill (IV) and a new floor (IIIb) to the south of 153/155.

Questions do exist, however, regarding the excavators' interpretations of several important layers in this area. Both Wall 136 and Wall 155 rested on the surface of Layer V, a "hardish white floor beneath IV."[65] Level V correlates to Layer IX in Segment *120.121.19.126* above. The elevations recorded at the bases of Wall 125b (32.91 m) and Wall 136 (32.73 m) confirm that this floor sloped gradually (.18 m) toward the

---

[63] *Fieldbook Qk-l-m*, 34. On p. 35, she added that Wall 151, which was "present beneath III, [was] broken down too" (see the western extent of the section presented in fig. 8 above). Elsewhere, Kenyon seemed to express a different opinion by noting that she cleared Wall 144 to the face of 155, which belonged to 136—a feature contemporary with the plastered floor.

[64] Similarly, Wall 159 on the southernmost extent of this section must have rested very near or on the remains of former Wall 58 (compare again fig. 5, and the relative positions of architectural features on published Section GH, *SS I*, Pl. VII).

[65] *Fieldbook Qk-l-m*, 33.

north as it proceeded from Room *hk* into Pit *i*. But the fact that this surface was "apparently broken by 125b, wh[ich] at this level is offset slightly,"[66] confirms that this wall is stratigraphically later than the surface, with a *terminus post quem* of no earlier than "Period V."[67] Since the substantial deposits of fill that abut both the northern (Layer III[68]) and southern (Layer VIII) faces of 125b represent the first and only layers presented in fig. 10 contemporary with that wall, any floor level that belonged with it has disappeared. Between Walls 125b/56 and 155/153 on fig. 8, then, only Layers IIIb-V could possibly belong to BP IV, even though the original area inside Room *hk* would have extended to the southernmost point of the section.

A further complication, however, attends these particular deposits. As noted, Kenyon understood the cut on their southern end to represent the Foundation Trench for Wall 125b/56. Of Layer IV she wrote, "[it] sh[oul]d prob[ably] be free fr[om] F.T., but n[o]t abs[olutely] cert[ain]."[69] This admission increases the likelihood of the contamination of Layer IV as well as the BP IV resurfacing in Layer IIIb, which the FT of 125b/56 also cut.[70] Moreover, the field entry for June 12, 1933, recorded:

> In 125.144, quarter of F.T. of 125b cut away. It looks however that [there] is another floor level IIIa [b?] wh[ich] is [a] v[ery] g[oo]d one, .25 m. below III (included with it in digging, wh[ich] sealed off Layer IV, wh[ich] was broken by 125b.[71]

Thus it appears that the excavators failed to distinguish the materials found in or on floor level IIIb from those contained in the subsurface makeup of IV. And since they were also uncertain as to whether or not they had kept any of this material free from the later foundation trench deposit, the entire area unfortunately takes on a secondary character for purposes of interpretation.

From the field notes, one also learns that the floor level of IIIb revealed more striations than either the published or private sections present. On the 15th of June, 1933, the workers cleared this "v[ery] g[oo]d hard floor, [which consisted in] two layers close together, wh[ich] obviously present (?) replastering of this floor. = Level VI of *Between TT2-TT3*."[72]

---

[66] *Fieldbook Qk-l-m*, 33.

[67] Kenyon, therefore, correctly placed Wall 56 on her "Period V" Top Plan in *SS III*, 107, Fig. 50.

[68] The field records indicate as well that this deposit appeared "rather soft against the wall."

[69] *Fieldbook Qk-l-m*, 33.

[70] Compare also the remarks to this effect for both IIIb and IV in the entry for June 19, 1933, in *Fieldbook Qk-l-m*, 48. Recall my earlier observation that materials from various subdeposits of Layer IV apparently included intrusions from later quarrying activity in this area.

[71] *Fieldbook Qk-l-m*, 33.

[72] *Fieldbook Qk-l-m*, 35.

Another previously unpublished though less detailed field section offers some corroboration for this situation. This drawing concentrated on the local stratigraphy against the north face of Wall 125b (fig. 11).[73] From this one sees that another deposit appears to have existed between Layers IIIb and IV. It seems likely that these resurfacings represent the sub-Layers IIIa and IIIb and that, by the time of the final report, they

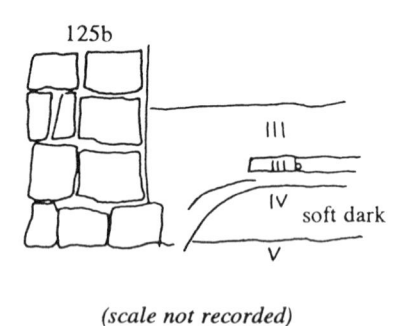

Segment 125.144: Supplement
<— S N —>
View toward West

fig. 11

were treated as one deposition and were referred to sometimes as IIIa and other times as IIIb.[74] In the matching portion of Auxiliary Section A above (fig. 7, north of 125b), these levels received the designations Layers VI and VII. Finally, Wall 125b seems to have had its footing set immediately on the rock, with the BP IV floor of Layer V running away from the sloping bedrock at that point and continuing over the increasingly heavy fills to the north.

Finally, I should reiterate that the burnt and sooty patches scattered throughout these layers do not seem to indicate a general destruction of these rooms. Rather, I can point again to several *tābunîm* found here, such as the one discovered beneath Wall 150 upon its removal (fig. 8). According to the field notes, this wall "rested on sooty earth [and] poss[ibly] burnt ivory of Layer IIIb" (which Kenyon correlated to VI in

---

[73] *Fieldbook Qk-l-m*, 33a.

[74] Hence one sees the occasionally suggested corrections [made in brackets] of IIIa to IIIb in my quotations from Kenyon's field notes above. Given the sequence in which the excavators would have encountered these floors, one might suppose that Layer IIIa represents the upper (i.e., later) resurfacing, while IIIb points to the earlier one. Yet this is not the way in which these closely spaced deposits seem to be labeled on fig. 11. I might, however, note Kenyon's tendency to renumber levels from the earliest to the latest (as in "Period I" = Omri, "Period II" = Ahab, and so on).

120.121.19.126, discussed above).[75] The field notes contain mention of another *ṭabûn* in the area around Wall 125b/56, saying that it "seems to be in IIIa, resting on III."[76] With the removal of Wall 155 to its juncture with Wall 157, the workers encountered a possible third *ṭabûn* also associated with Layer IIIa.z which lay nearer Wall 155 than 125b/56.[77] Stratigraphically, these (and presumably other) cooking installations seem to relate mainly to the later stages of BP IV. On the horizontal axis, they cluster around Pit *i* and help to confirm its function as a kitchen midden and not a latrine as Kenyon suggested (see Chapter III, Part B below).

c. Room *h* (Published Section EF; Auxiliary Section B)

[i]   **125.144**

(See the full discussion under Rooms *h-k* above, § b.i)

[ii] **147.145.151.136**
[iii] **155.151.136.147**

This portion of my study will treat these two segments together since their numerical identifications are quite close. (Except for Walls 145 and 155, the same basic set of walls serves to identify each segment; but see n. 25 above.)[78] From these coordinates, it seems clear that the area in question lay in the northernmost portion of Room *h*, to the west of Pit *i*, where the chamber narrowed slightly as it approached the doorway to Room *g* in Wall 136. In addition, Layer IX in each of these segments yielded the pottery eventually published from this area, suggesting that the respective findspots may share a similar matrix and perhaps even an overall context. I should note that the architecture of this segment existed in an area that presented the excavators with a "terrible muddle of walls and misc[ellaneous] stones . . . ,"[79] and this may account for some of the variance in recording numbers assigned to the features found here. The following crudely drawn top plan of the area (fig. 12) confirms the density of architectural features in the area around Pit *i* (i.e., inside 640° E x 460° N).

From this plan, one can identify all the walls listed as coordinates in the present segment except for Wall 145. Most of these structures, which I have darkened for easier location, lay beneath the walls of Segment *120.121.19.126*, discussed above.[80]

---

[75] *Fieldbook Qk-l-m*, 34.

[76] *Fieldbook Qk-l-m*, 34.

[77] *Fieldbook Qk-l-m*, 48.

[78] The field notes also associate Segment *155.151.136.147* with Segment *150.155.147.136* (though the former area is often variously labeled *147.155.151.136* [or 156?]). See *Fieldbook Qk-l-m*, 35, 47.

[79] *Fieldbook Qk-l-m*, 32.

[80] The field notes confirm this with such statements as "beneath 19 found to be another Wall 151, wh[ich] prob[ably] belongs to 136 . . ." (*Fieldbook Qk-l-m*, 32).

In addition, the drawing confirms that the line of earlier Walls 161 (BP I; Omri) and 160 (BP III; Jehu) passed beneath the northern part of Pit *i*, just as it appears in section in fig. 10 and in my addition to the plan in fig. 5. These last two drawings, together with *SS I*, Pl. VIII, also establish the fact that the few stones which actually remained from Wall 161 lay precisely in this spot below Pit *i* (situated along 460° N and just east of 640° E). One curious aspect of the field plan involves the eastern limit of Room *j*

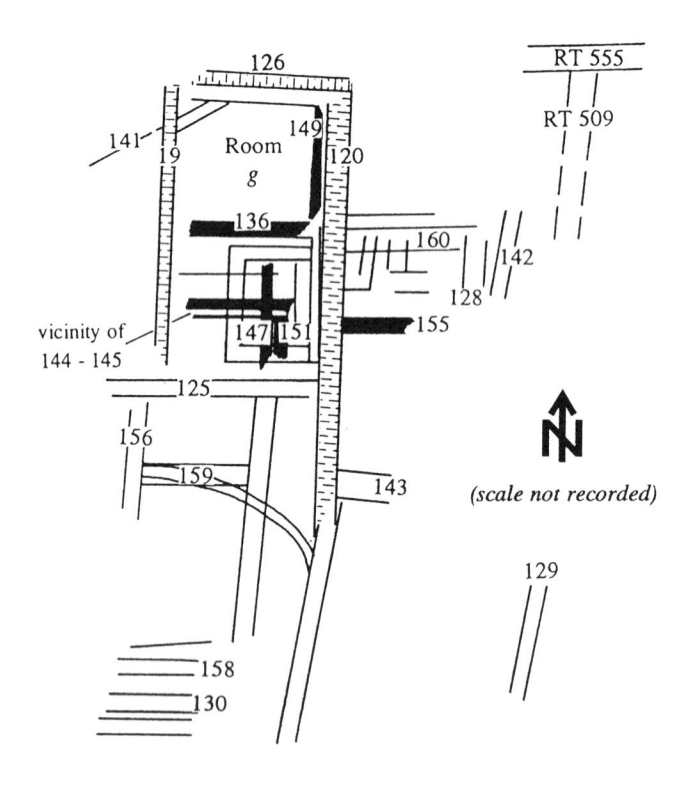

Field-drawn Top Plan for Area around Pit i[81]

fig. 12

established by Wall 142. Here this feature assumes a different orientation from that seen in the published plan of *SS III*, 104, Fig. 48, running northeast to southwest rather than northwest to southeast.

To facilitate my discussion of the depositional history in these segments, I can return to both Auxiliary Section A in fig. 7 and the new field section presented in fig.

---

[81] *Fieldbook Qk-l-m*, 1a. For a continuation of this plan in areas to the east (including Rooms *l*, *m*, and *n*), see fig. 20 below and the discussion of Room *l* in Chapter VI, fig. 61.

10 above, the details of which did not appear in the final report.[82] The latter drawing confirms that Walls 136 and 155 lay in the vicinity of the line taken by Omri's original Wall 161, which was only partly robbed out in this particular area. Allowing for the reverse orientations of figs. 7 and 10, one can also see that Wall 155 of the present segment existed in the same proximity to 161 as did Wall 153 (compare published Section EF). This provides additional confirmation for my conclusion above that 153 comprises the roughly built lower courses of 155 visible in fig. 10. One may assume, then, that Walls 153 and 155 are roughly equivalent, and that each feature, in turn, served as the southern boundary of Room/Pit *i*. As such, they ran basically parallel to Wall 136 on the northern side of Room/Pit *i* (see top plan in fig. 5), just as they appear in section.

As one may expect, the depositional history in 147.145.151.136 and 155.151.136.147 follows closely that already seen in contiguous segments. A black, sooty Layer IIIr (= IIIa in *125.144*, and IIIb in *Btw TT2-TT3*; fig. 8) extended over the "broken top" of Wall 151.[83] The continuation of this deposit to Wall (153)155 received the label "IIIf"; it both ran against the uppermost courses on the north side of that wall and continued over its top.[84] Because of earth which had fallen into this area from above during the course of excavations, the field notes indicate the possibility of intrusive elements here within the rubbish pit itself, where the soot lay against the northern face of 155.[85] The notes also state that Layer III followed this level, though Kenyon included none of this local stratigraphy from inside the pit in her field section presented in fig. 10.

The stratigraphic summary of 147.145.151.136 and its companion segment also commented on the hard, white plaster floor of Layer IX which extended up to Walls 155 and 136, and which Kenyon correctly assigned to BP IV. Though Wall 155 rested on IX, 136 went just below the surface, which then ran "right up to it."[86] The excavators also detected several subdeposits here. Layer IXa contained "stones belonging to [the] mouth of [the] pit, above the level of [the] top of 161, presumably belonging to the period of the little rooms."[87] The clearance of the plaster floor in the area over Wall 157 (= Layer IXz) "unfortunately" included materials from the foundation trench of that wall (compare fig. 8), although Kenyon later thought that this material "sh[oul]d be pure."[88]

In addition, the expedition found on further examination that the robber trench of Omride Wall 161 had impinged upon the deposits around 157 and that the workers

---

[82] *Fieldbook Qk-l-m*, 47a.

[83] *Fieldbook Qk-l-m*, 32-33.

[84] *Fieldbook Qk-l-m*, 35 and 47.

[85] *Fieldbook Qk-l-m*, 47a-47.

[86] *Fieldbook Qk-l-m*, 47.

[87] *Fieldbook Qk-l-m*, 47.

[88] Compare the field notes from *Fieldbook Qk-l-m*, 47a and 47.

had failed to distinguish between the two. The plaster surface of IX, however, sealed all these remains. Layer X comprised the white chippings immediately below IX and undoubtedly reflects construction activities relating to the latter feature. Finally, the records describe Layer XI as a "hard level" of "Period I filling belonging to 161, but [with] R.T. of 161 unfort[unately] included."[89] Because of this potentially lowered *terminus ante quem* for the overall deposit, Kenyon ultimately assigned all of XI to her "Period IV." Later on, it will become important to note again that the broken portion of 161 lay right against a rock scarp which abutted its southern face, and that the debris of deconstruction concluded "exactly at the scarp."[90]

In light of the preceding evidence, it becomes apparent that the heaviest of the black, sooty levels postdates the occupational life of the plaster floor in Layer IX and the makeup (Layer IV) and new surface of Layer IIIb, together with all associated walls. This burnt material lay one or more levels above the truncated remains of longitudinal Walls 151, 157, 142 (fig. 8)[91] and of cross Walls 153/155 and 136 (fig. 10). This charred deposit, then, seems either to have covered this area as the result of the destruction of the poorly built rooms themselves or as a significant fill level imported to this space from another area that did suffer destruction sometime around the final days of the architecture of BP IV. Later on, I shall explain why I favor the latter scenario (see Evaluation and Summary below).

[iv] 120.121.19.126

See the full discussion of this segment under Room *g* above (§ a.i). The Joint Expedition recovered and published a cooking pot rim of the notched variety (*SS III*, Fig. 6:39) from just south of the intersection of Walls 136 and 151, in Room *h*. The precise findspot, or local layer, was listed as Wall 151 (mislabeled Wall 157 in the field books at the Rockefeller Museum in Jerusalem). One may assume, therefore, that the fragment came from a deposit found lying against the eastern face of Wall 151 or perhaps from within the wall itself.

[v] 122.125.19.121

Judging from the location of Walls 19, 122, and 125 on the plan in fig. 12, it is clear that this segment pertains to the same general area in Summit Strip Qk as have those discussed to this point, namely, the northern extent of Room *h* and inside Pit *i* (see the western side of Auxiliary Section B, fig. 8). Still, this portion of the excavation deserves a brief commentary and stratigraphic analysis for several reasons. First,

---

[89] *Fieldbook Qk-l-m*, 47a.

[90] *Fieldbook Qk-l-m*, 47.

[91] And presumably Wall 147 as well, at the western border of Pit *i*.

they help clarify a rather obtuse aspect in Kenyon's method of recording. It is only at this point that the field records provide information allowing the reader to place chronologically many of the architectural features which Kenyon has routinely utilized as segment coordinates for Israelite deposits. For example, the stratigraphic summary for this area assigns a Hellenistic date to Wall 134 and reveals that Walls 19 and 120 belong in the R_3 Period, while Walls 123 and 125[92] relate to the later R_4 era. It becomes clear that Kenyon's method of locating even very early deposits on their horizontal plane often involved keying off specific architectural units from much later historical periods which were encountered early on in the process of excavation. Thus she frequently utilized Hellenistic-to-Late Roman wall numbers to place Israelite deposits. Initially, this approach is misleading; once understood, however, it becomes a simple annoyance.

Second, notes from this segment relate the excavators' first encounter with Pit *i*, a feature that came to assume a central place in the final, official publication of pottery from this area north of the main courtyard.[93] Though only a single fragment from the PP 4 group (*SS III*, Fig. 6:12) derived from deposits associated with Layer Va of this pit, I will show later that a large cache of diverse ceramic forms taken from this same layer and dated to PP 6 appeared in *SS III*, Fig. 10:1-27. Besides these pieces, Kenyon identified one additional fragment (*SS III*, Fig. 11:25) by means of the coordinates *122.125.19.121* and assigned it to the PP 7 levels of Room *hk*.

Third, since much of what the field notes record here derived from later periods, details from descriptions of this segment will help to outline the stratigraphic relationship between the black, sooty deposits described above and the layers which followed immediately upon them. Such data will prove beneficial in accessing both the cause and the date of the burning of this material.

On May 25, 1933, workers cut a trench through an area of rubble adjacent to Segment *120.121.19.126* (see above). Their efforts exposed "a good number of stones running north from Wall 125."[94] Though, according to subsequent notations, these stones at first showed no definite arrangement, their removal revealed an even larger mass of intentionally laid stones which stretched from 125 to Wall 134 slightly to the north. This prompted Kenyon to suggest that they possibly comprised a wall which ran alongside 125; she labeled this putative feature Wall 146 (see fig. 12). At any rate, these stones rested "on [and] in a mixed sooty [and] yellow level (cf. E. end of *120.121.19.126*)," which received the layer designation "IId.y." and a tentative dating in "Period VII(?)."[95] The Hellenistic Wall 134, which ran parallel to and just south of

---

[92] Wall 125 appears to have rested near the southernmost limits of Summit Strip Qk. Farther to the south, one enters Summit Strip Qm (compare fig. 12 and *AIS-I*, 16, fig. 3 = *SS III*, p. xv).

[93] See the comments in *SS I*, 108, which refer to the pottery from this midden deposit as "the most important evidence" from the complex of buildings under discussion.

[94] This paraphrase of Kenyon's note in *Fieldbook Qk-l-m*, 4, obviates her many abbreviations.

[95] *Fieldbook Qk-l-m*, 5.

Israelite Wall 136 (on the north side of Pit *i*; compare figs. 5 and 12) also sat on this matrix of sooty-yellow soil.

By June 6, 1933, laborers began clearing the hard, yellowish trench deposit of Layer III from beneath Wall 134 and found that it ran at least from Wall 144 to Wall 136. During this operation, they left strips of soil intact against the faces of the walls, a vital step toward accessing later on the presence or absence of foundation trench cuts. The following day, the removal of Layer III continued to a depth of 1.50 m, with the last half meter yielding a mixed matrix which combined the softer, darker soil with harder yellow earth and some burnt material. Kenyon labeled the strip of this material—which ran against Wall 144—"Layer IIIy" and noted that the wall appeared to have been built *into* this preexisting level, although she could not detect a clear foundation trench for it.[96] The excavators, then, appear to have experienced their first encounter with a mixed matrix containing burnt material in Layer III of Segment *122.125.19.121*, particularly in the basal striations of that level. In fig. 8 above, these descriptions appear to correspond well to Layers III-IIIb in *Btw TT2-TT3* and IIIa in *125.144 + 122.125.19.121*, with the thick rubble deposit containing the large stones visible above the last two segments mentioned.

Beneath Layer III and to the west of Wall 147, they recovered a good plaster floor which correlated to Layer IX of *120.121.19.126* (compare Layer V on fig. 8).[97] East of 147 (inside the area of Pit *i*), however, they did not find this floor; instead, they cleared approximately one additional meter of the softer, darker fill deposit[98] and labeled it Layer IV. This fill inside the rubbish pit contained an abundance of pottery and appeared to the excavators to belong to their "Period VI."[99]

To the east of Wall 147 (i.e., the western perimeter of Pit *i*), the possible mouth of a cistern appeared. It measured ca. 1.5 m in diameter, and contained a soft and "rather middenish" filling (Layer Va) with much pottery, the bulk of which Kenyon assigned to PP 6 (*SS III*, Fig. 10, though much greater detail concerning the specific findspot appears in Appendix A). Regrettably, Kenyon did not record the depositional history of the local stratigraphy inside the pit on the field section presented in fig. 10 above, between Walls 153 and 136. The sooty deposits which overran these and other Israelite walls (listed above), however, appear to relate to the mixed debris encountered in Segment *122.125.19.121*, Layers III-IIIa (and their affiliated subdeposits), i.e., in levels which the excavators encountered immediately beneath a series of Hellenistic walls, with at least one of those walls (144) having been set in the debris.

At least two possibilities present themselves concerning the depositional history of these layers and features. They include either the elapse of a relatively short incre-

---

[96]*Fieldbook Qk-l-m*, 5.

[97]*Fieldbook Qk-l-m*, 32.

[98]I.e., below level IX of *120.121.19.126*.

[99]*Fieldbook Qk-l-m*, 5a.

ment of time or the passing of a longer period with relatively minimal occupation of the site between the original deposition of the charred, mixed matrix and the construction activities of the early Hellenistic period. This situation opens both the *terminus ante quem* of the sooty levels and the historical circumstances surrounding their deposition in this area to further scrutiny.

d. Room *j* (Auxiliary Section A — fig. 7)

Since the center of Room *j* lay on the excavator's grid near 645° E x 460° N, this chamber also overlay the section of Omri's enclosure wall (161) which was only partially disturbed or left virtually intact following BP I-II (see *SS I*, Pl. VIII for the wall remains at 641-47° E x 459-61° N; compare fig. 5 above). The deposits in this room, then, rested just east of the stratigraphy shown in published Sections AB and EF, both of which bisected this surviving portion of Omri's wall near 642° E, i.e., just west of Wall 149 which Room *j* shared with *f*, *g*, and *i*.

[i] North of Test Trench 2
[ii] E Strip; North of Test Trench 2

For the following analysis, I shall return to Auxiliary Section A, fig. 7; an additional drawing sketched in the field but not published will also help to elucidate the local stratigraphy in these closely related segments (fig. 13).[100] As observed earlier (n. 59), quarrying activities during the Late Roman period destroyed virtually all primary stratigraphic contexts in the area south of Room *j* and to the easternmost limits of the excavation. These mining operations impinged upon the southern edge of the segment labeled *North of TT2*, among others. Kenyon was able to discern that Wall 129 (R.4), which served as the stylobate for a colonnade, lay immediately past the quarry on the east.[101] From fig. 12 above, one can see that at least the entire area from the eastern stub of Wall 125b to the 129 fragment suffered considerably under these ancient excavations. One wonders whether this realization alone dissuaded Kenyon and her supervisors from pursuing any work further to the east. Not only did the fills used by the Romans to cover various sectors of their completed work reveal pottery from virtually every earlier period, they also yielded fragments of burnt ivory. Since this quarrying occurred above the natural rock scarp located inside the line of Omride Wall

---

[100] The full body of field notes pertaining to these segments appears in *Fieldbook Qk-l-m*, 12-15, with records relating to the northern half of this area continuing on 16-19, 36-38, and 40-41, while those for the southern half proceed on 24-27. My following comments on the depositional history of this area are based on information recorded in these pages. Various related sections appear on 12a, 13a, 16a, 18a, 40a (= my fig. 8), and 41a (= my fig. 7). Stratigraphic summaries are provided on 16a-17a and 19a.

[101] *Fieldbook Qk-l-m*, 12a.

161 (i.e., basically south of BP IV Wall 153 in Room *j*), one may assume that many of these ivories came from contiguous loci situated originally on the highest part of the royal compound, in Rooms *a-e* and *o-q* and their eastward continuations.

The new section just mentioned, which presents a longitudinal slice through the center of the "eastern strip" of both *North of TT2* and *Btw TT2-TT3*,[102] vividly depicts the effects of this quarrying activity upon this area. As a complement to my Auxiliary Section A (fig. 7), this drawing helps to clarify the depositional history north and south of the line taken by Wall 153. To the north, one enters the space of Room *j*, while south of 153 (*Btw TT2-TT3*) one can see the partial remains in Room *k* before encountering the area of Roman digging.

North of Test Trench 2, levels I and II derive from the R.4 (fourth century CE) and R.3 (late second century CE) periods, respectively. While the very thin layer of II might possibly have comprised a floor, the thicker (1.20 m) and harder Layer I was interpreted as a possible road surface. The latter deposit covered the entire area and appears to have impinged on Layer II approximately 1.8 m inside the southern portion of the much earlier Room *j* (i.e., north of RT 153).

Levels III, IV, V, and VI encompass the deposits central to this discussion. The hard, white matrix of Layer III rested only .15 m beneath the R.3 floor of II. Kenyon understood III as a compacted floor level likely dating to her early post-Israelite "Period VIII." While it appears to have maintained a relatively uniform thickness in both fig. 13 and the supplementary section in fig. 14,[103] another rather limited drawing[104] from this segment (fig. 15) shows that, at least in places, it filled in significant gaps in the filling beneath it (IIIa and III B = softer areas on the east and west sides of III, respectively, which Kenyon assigned to her "Period VII"). Similarly, yet another field sketch (fig. 16[105]) seems to suggest that the soil of IIIa also served to backfill holes previously dug in certain portions of this segment.

Beneath III lay a deposit which apparently filled another, rather deep hole and whose description resembles closely that already seen for certain levels in nearby segments (e.g., *125.144*, IIIa; *147.145.151.136* + *155.151.136.147*; *122.125.19.121*, III; compare below, *Btw TT2-TT3*, III-IIIb). Layer IV comprised a mixture of hard and soft soils plus appreciable quantities of burned materials. Perhaps more importantly, one learns that portions of it also yielded fragments of burnt ivories. But a notation that the removal of this layer "cert[ainly] included some of R.T. 149 ... [and] of R.T. 152"[106] precludes us from pressing an early date for this material since, accord-

---

[102] I shall, therefore, utilize this section again in considering the depositional history of Room *k* below and of Room *hk* in Chapter II.

[103] *Fieldbook Qk-l-m*, 12a. This section apparently ran along or very near the north face of Wall 153.

[104] *Fieldbook Qk-l-m*, 13a.

[105] *Fieldbook Qk-l-m*, 16a.

[106] Several other subdeposits of this level also became mixed with potential contaminants during the process of excavation. As examples, Layer IVa.x. included materials from the foundation trenches or

PP 4: HOUSE FLOORS — STRATIGRAPHY

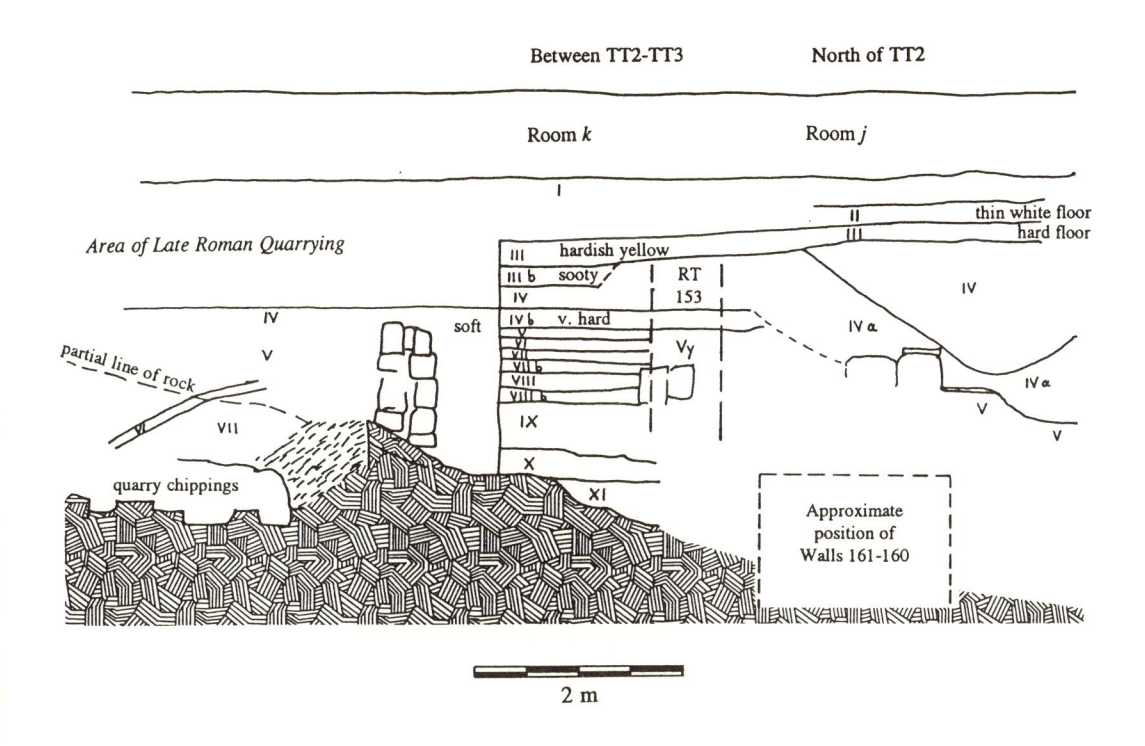

Segment North of Test Trench 2:
Section down Center of East Strip
<— S N —>
View toward West

fig. 13

ing to Kenyon's published top plans, Wall 149 continued in use at least through BP V.[107] In her field notes, she placed general Level IV in "Period VII," yet labeled the mixed matrix itself variously as "Period V" or "Period VII" filling.[108] Though distinguishable from IV, the soft soil into which the hole/pit had originally cut (Layer IVa) was also viewed as "Period VII" leveling material.

Walls 148 (BP V) and 140 (?); IVa.z. mixed with foundation trench material from Wall 120 (R.3 period); and IVz possibly included remains from the foundation deposits of Wall 120 (R.3 period). See *Fieldbook Qk-l-m*, 17a.

[107] See *SS III*, Figs. 48 (BP IV), 49 (BP IVa), and 50 (BP V), on pp. 104, 106, and 107, respectively. Though the dating of Wall 152 remains unclear to us, it has not entered Kenyon's discussion of these periods and therefore seems to postdate them altogether. Judging from the plan in fig. 12 above, it apparently ran immediately north of and parallel to Omri's old Enclosure Wall 161 and along the same line taken by the BP IV-V Wall 136.

[108] She even thought that the softer, whitish soil derived from her "IVa" (*Fieldbook Qk-l-m*, 16a).

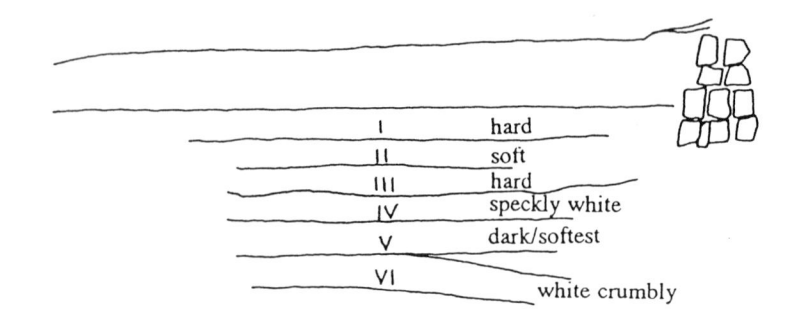

	I	hard
	II	soft
	III	hard
	IV	speckly white
	V	dark/softest
	VI	white crumbly

(scale not recorded)

North of Test Trench 2: Supplement No. 1
Section along South Edge of Area
<— E W —>
View toward South
fig. 14

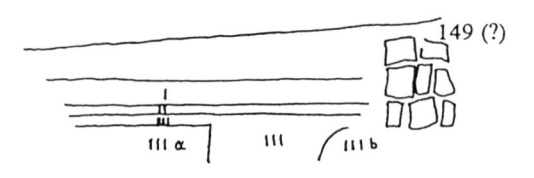

(scale not recorded)

North of Test Trench 2: Supplement No. 2
<— E W —>
View toward South
fig. 15

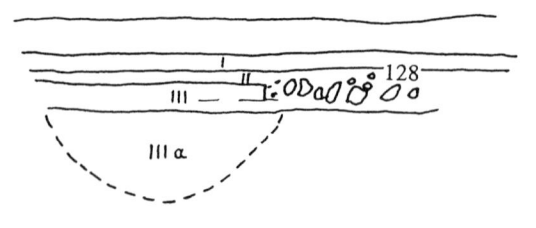

(scale not recorded)

North of Test Trench 2: Supplement No. 3
<— N S —>
View toward East
fig. 16

Layer IVa.b. should have constituted the most valuable and carefully excavated subdeposit associated with general Level IV, inasmuch as it came from the "bottom of IVa" where it rested directly on the paving of Layer V and was noted as a "pure" (i.e., undisturbed and cleanly excavated) accumulation.[109] In other words, this appears to have incorporated dependable occupational debris from a surface sealed by flat paving stones (see *N of TT2* in fig. 7). One must wonder why the final report failed to include pottery from such a covering, particularly since so many of the other subdeposits associated with either general Level IV or V were admittedly contaminated (e.g., see n. 106). The same holds true for Layer Vy, or that part of the paved surface itself which lapped up against Wall 153 and which also received the designation "pure."

Instead, Kenyon held scrupulously to her prevailing method and theory by choosing to publish only a limited number of fragments[110] (one of which was marked for discard) recovered from Layers VI (relabeled IX to correspond to other areas, as in fig. 7 above[111]) and VI/IXr, i.e., from the subfloor makeup (IX) including that portion of it which ran up to the "hole"[112] of Wall 161 (IXr). As I have shown elsewhere, such a ceramic corpus can succeed only in helping to establish a *terminus post quem*, or construction date, for the paved surface lying immediately above. In situations such as these, the retrieval, analysis, and publication of significant quantities of cultural remains from the primary, occupational debris lying on the stones themselves, or even found lodged between them in the upper striations of the surface base, is fundamental to establishing a firm chronology—not only for the layer in question but for contiguous or nearby ones as well.[113]

In the earlier levels below Layer IX (X-XV), even greater amounts of fill represent efforts by the laborers of King Ahab (BP II) to raise a suitable building level outside Omri's original Enclosure Wall 161. The northern extension of the section in fig. 7 relates to these projects, which have received full attention in my earlier work.[114] In short, I can reiterate that, whereas Kenyon saw a series of five floor levels in these deposits, my analysis demonstrates that no such feature existed here prior to the hard, white Layer X, with its subfloor makeup and construction debris lying in XI.

---

[109] *Fieldbook Qk-l-m*, 17a.

[110] *SS III*, Fig. 6:8, 16, 33.

[111] Kenyon proceeded to label all levels below this one consecutively, starting from IX. Consequently, the record of local stratigraphy in segment *North of TT2* omits completely the designations "VII" and "VIII."

[112] I assume this refers to a partial robber trench.

[113] In her summary notes for this area, Kenyon not only specifies certain blocks of subfloor makeup as "pure" (even though they, by definition, very likely represent imported fills of highly qualified chronological worth), but she also sometimes assigns the term to deposits whose general integrity is admittedly compromised (e.g., Layer IXx = "Prob. pure, but poss. disturbed by R.T. 150"; Layer IXz [see fig. 7] = "Prob. pure, but where paving V gone"; etc.).

[114] *AIS-I*. For the appropriate pages, see *North of TT2* listed under "Segments" in the General Index, p. 293.

This floor and the massive fills beneath it abutted the nicely dressed, once exposed northern face of Wall 161 and helped to compensate for the erratic, undulating rock of the northern slopes. In the succeeding BP III (mid-to-late ninth century BCE), the construction of Wall 160, which utilized the truncated 161 as a subterranean base, cut this floor and undoubtedly had a new surface laid up to its northern face. This putative floor, however, has disappeared forever, inasmuch as the present Layer IX overruns and seals the remains of 160 and, therefore, must postdate it.

Finally, I may suggest that several valuable, albeit negative, observations have begun to emerge from the findings thus far. First, the relative proximity of the late Israelite (or perhaps very early post-Israelite) remains to those from significantly later phases of occupation (Kenyon's R.3 and R.4 periods) is striking. Had any additional Israelite levels existed in this area, they appear to have succumbed to Late Roman excavation and leveling activities. Second, it seems clear that, to this point in my investigation, we have not encountered a single fragment of ivory that might possibly have derived from a primary stratigraphic context. Third, those fragments which have received mention seem, on the basis of stratigraphy, not to have reached their final resting place until well after the close of the Israelite period. And fourth, unless one can establish a reliable ceramic sequence for the levels involved, it will remain difficult to refine the relative dating, to say nothing of the absolute dating, of their deposition.

[iii] 120.121.19.126

For the depositional history of this segment, see again the discussion under Room *g* above. The final report included a rim fragment from an apparent holemouth jar (*SS III*, Fig. 6:24) among its listing of pottery taken from stratified contexts. The excavators recorded this fragment as having come from Room *j*, Layer IXb.

[iv] 509.126

Two factors justify my extending only brief treatment to this segment of summit excavations. First, this general area has already received extensive review in my previous work on this subject;[115] I shall need simply to reiterate a few main details here. Second, though I took issue with many points of Kenyon's interpretation of the earliest depositional history in this segment (from XIII down to XVI), I remain in basic agreement with her understanding of the succeeding floor levels stemming from the early eighth century BCE.

Segment *509.126* takes us momentarily from Summit Strip Qk and into Qn (fig. 17), slightly further east and north of the other rooms discussed in this portion of my study.[116] It comprised part of a general area identified in the fieldbooks as *North*

---

[115] See especially *AIS-I*, 19-21, 37-43, and 104-05.

[116] I shall return to Strip Qn once more when I address the depositional history in Segment *502.503*, Room *n* below.

PP 4: HOUSE FLOORS — STRATIGRAPHY

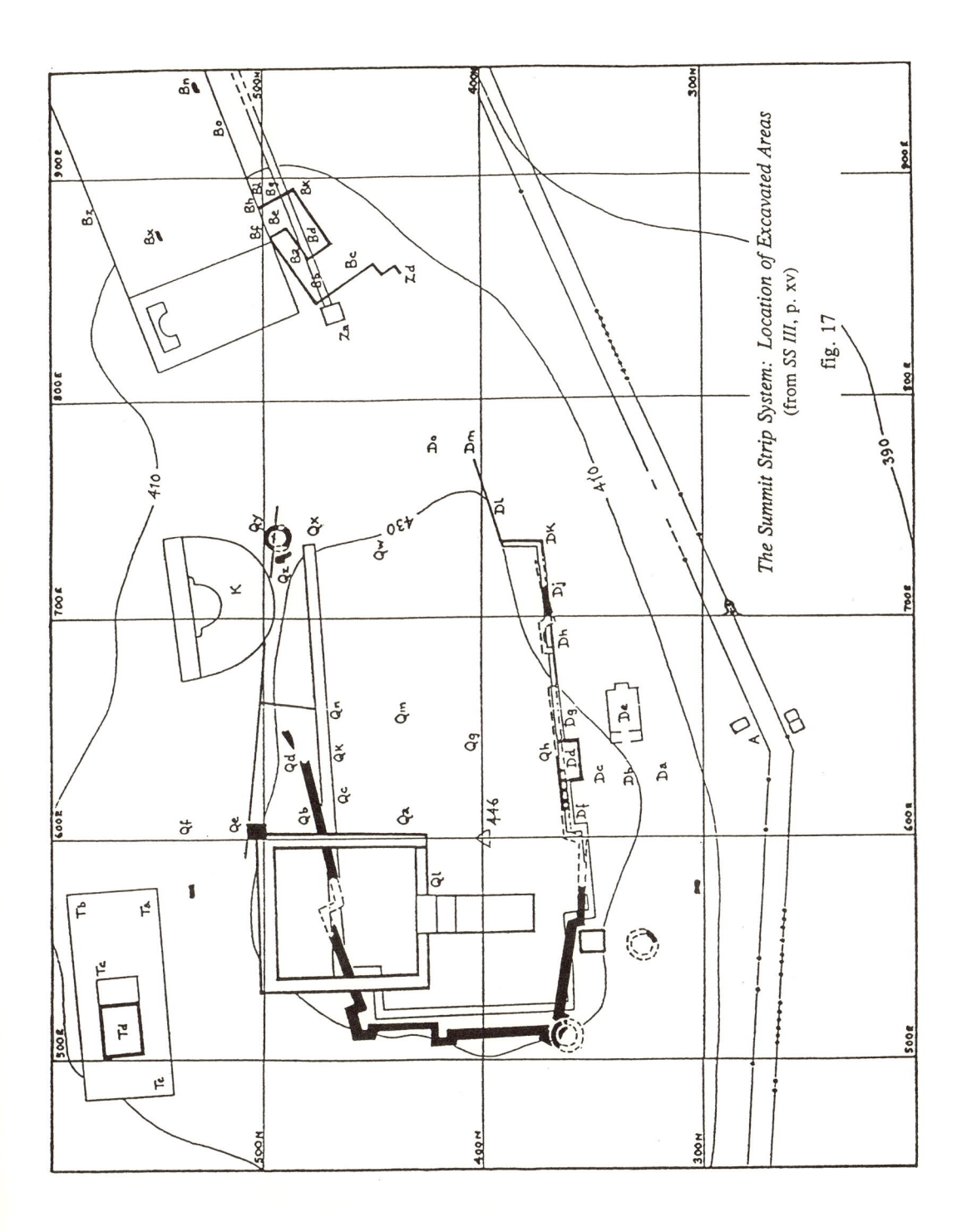

The Summit Strip System: Location of Excavated Areas
(from SS III, p. xv)
fig. 17

of 161[117] and extended from the inner face of the Casemate System (Wall 556) southward towards the summit at approximately 650° E (δ in fig. 18; compare also *SS I*, Pl. VII, south of Wall 556 on Sections EF[118] and GH, and just north of Wall 503 on CD for the published blocks of local stratigraphy found here). This locale, then, appears to have extended to very near the western edge of RT 553, whose original wall had served as the boundary between Rooms *l* and *m* (see the plan in fig. 5).[119] But this rumples an interesting wrinkle, for the field records unanimously assign the single PP 4 fragment published from this segment to Room *j*. Indubitably, one of two viable options must account for this apparent discrepancy. First, Segment *509.126* simply extended further west along the inner face of Casemate Wall 556 than the field notes make clear. Or second, the oblique orientation of Wall 142 stands in need of correction from a NNW approach to 551 to a NNE or ENE course as it, in fact, appears on the field plan fig. 12 (see my prior comments on p. 38 above). This would transfer a considerable portion

General Level	Kenyon's Proposed Dating	Description
XII-XVI	PP 1-2	(pre-eighth century)
XI	PP 2	Period II floor
X	PP 4	Period IV floor. Xa. Ditto E. of 142
IX	PP 5	Paving stones. Period V floor. IX. Contemp. floor E. of 142
VIII	PP 7	IIa.f. . . . Period VII debris overlying Period V floors
IIa.	PP 7-8	Floor sealing IIa.f. Apparently contains H[ellenistic] pottery, but this poss. a mistake
VI, V	Hellen.	G[reek] F[ort] W[all] period filling of robbed casemates
IV	R.3	Poss. contemp. [with] 537 ("Rm. I" = Sev[eren Period])
IIb., with II	R.5	Floors associated [with] 538 and 639 . . .
Ib. with I	R.5	Floors assoc. [with] 511 = 512, Layer A+, n[o]t found over rest of area. Coin of House of Constantine.

Abridged Stratigraphic Summary of Segment 509.126

Table 4

---

[117] For a description of this area, see *AIS-I*, 19.

[118] Mislabeled 536 on this section, though correctly assigned to BP II. By observing the stratigraphic position and apparent date of Wall 126 (R.5 Period), a coordinate for this segment, one will also notice again the use of much later architectural features as designations for Israelite phases.

[119] *Fieldbook Qn (Vol. II)*, 11a, diagrams the local stratigraphy on either side of this robber trench. I present these sectional data, together with a field-drawn top plan of the area, in conjunction with Room *l* of PP 7 (see Chapter IV, fig. 65).

PP 4: HOUSE FLOORS — STRATIGRAPHY

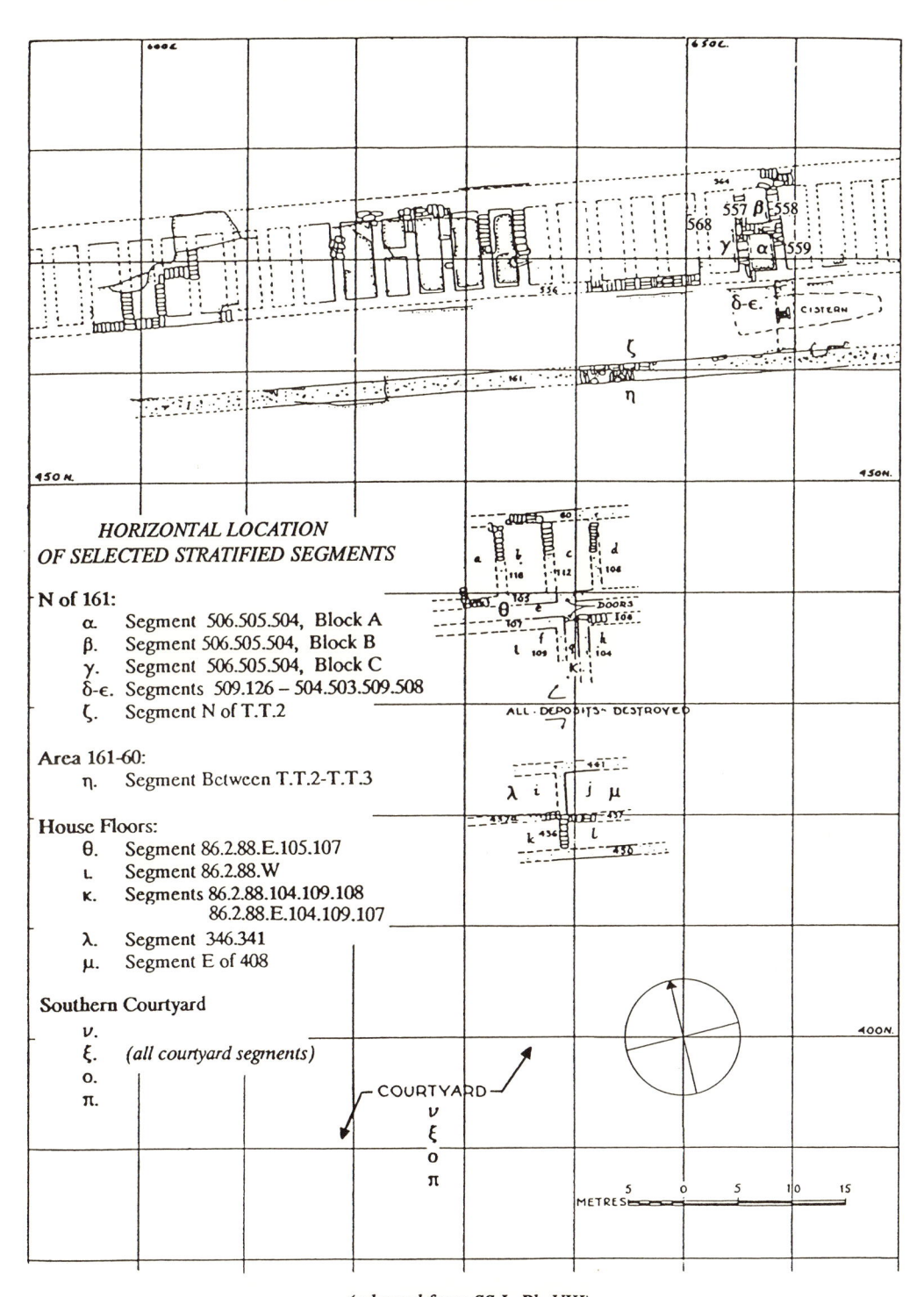

HORIZONTAL LOCATION
OF SELECTED STRATIFIED SEGMENTS

N of 161:
- α. Segment 506.505.504, Block A
- β. Segment 506.505.504, Block B
- γ. Segment 506.505.504, Block C
- δ-ε. Segments 509.126 – 504.503.509.508
- ζ. Segment N of T.T.2

Area 161-60:
- η. Segment Between T.T.2-T.T.3

House Floors:
- θ. Segment 86.2.88.E.105.107
- ι. Segment 86.2.88.W
- κ. Segments 86.2.88.104.109.108
  86.2.88.E.104.109.107
- λ. Segment 346.341
- μ. Segment E of 408

Southern Courtyard
- ν.
- ξ. (all courtyard segments)
- ο.
- π.

(adapted from SS I, Pl. VIII)

fig. 18

of Room *l* to Room *j* instead, bringing the latter chamber at least closer to the vicinity in which the excavators seem to have plotted Segment *509.126*.

The field records contain extensive notes on the excavation of this segment,[120] including an additional, abridged version of the stratigraphic summary section that bears repeating here (Table 4)[121] in conjunction with a field section which appeared in my earlier work on this area (fig. 19).[122]

I believe, with Kenyon, that Layers IX (including the paving stones) and X represent those deposits which relate best to developments during the early eighth century BCE.[123] The very hard white floor (XI), together with its rather loosely compacted makeup (upper portion of XII), reflect Ahab's northward extension of the royal courtyard outside the original limits established by Omri's Enclosure Wall 161. As I reported earlier:

> We can conclude only that no floor level existed in this area below that designated by Kenyon's Layer XI in [fig. 19] . . . . Unfortunately, our view of the exact relationship of the latter to Wall 556 has been obliterated on both sides by Robber Trench 556. If it was originally laid against Wall 556, then it likely belonged to King Ahab. On the other hand, if Wall 556 cut this floor as well, its construction could conceivably be assigned to Omri. Our analysis of the underlying stratigraphy together with the narrowness of the Robber Trench to the south of this wall (which leaves Layer XI intact very near the face of the wall) prompt us to choose the former scenario and to suggest that the living quarters of King Omri's palace compound did not extend north of his Enclosure Wall 161.[124]

---

[120] *Fieldbooks Qn (Vol. I)*, 34-38 and *(Vol. II)*, 102-06; the stratigraphical summary appears in *Vol. I*, 35a and 37a-38a. Sections relating directly or indirectly to this segment appear in *Vol. I*, 11a-12a, 32a, 34a, and in *Vol. II*, 102a, 103a, 105a.

[121] For this laconic summary, see *Fieldbook Qn (Vol. II)*, 104a. I have emended the list only to include the chronology proposed by Kenyon.

[122] Taken from *Fieldbook* Qn (Vol.II), 105a. Compare *AIS*-I, 20, fig. 5. For further detail of the counter stratigraphy north of Wall 556, see *AIS-I*, 38, fig. 8a.

[123] Kenyon's suggested correlations for the levels presented in Table 4 appear as follows:
    Level II   ↔ *504.503.509.508*, I
    Level IIa.   ↔ *120.121.19.126*, V (?)
    Level IVb.   ↔ *W. of 537*, IV
    Level Vt.   ↔ *N. of 555*, V
    Level Vx.   ↔ *Between 509 and 544*, V
    Level VIII   ↔ *504.503.509.508*, Va
    Levels IX-IXa. ↔ *504.503.509.508*, VI
    Level X   ↔ *120.121.19.126*, IX and *504.505 (503?).509.508*, VII
    Level XI   ↔ *N. of TT2*, X
    Level XIII   ↔ *N. of TT2*, XII

[124] *AIS-I*, 41-42.

PP 4: HOUSE FLOORS — STRATIGRAPHY

paving
yellow floor X IX
brown
very hard white
XI
Strip Qk
← - - - - - -
N of T.T.2
crumbly white

XII

XIII
light brown

Wall 161
← - - - - - -
building line

building line
XIV a white chips

light brown
XIV
white chips
XIV b
original floor
light red brown clayey
white chips
XV
building debris

red soil + broken rock
probably natural
XVI
XIV b.z.
FT 556

V

RT 556

VI

556

white chips

2 m

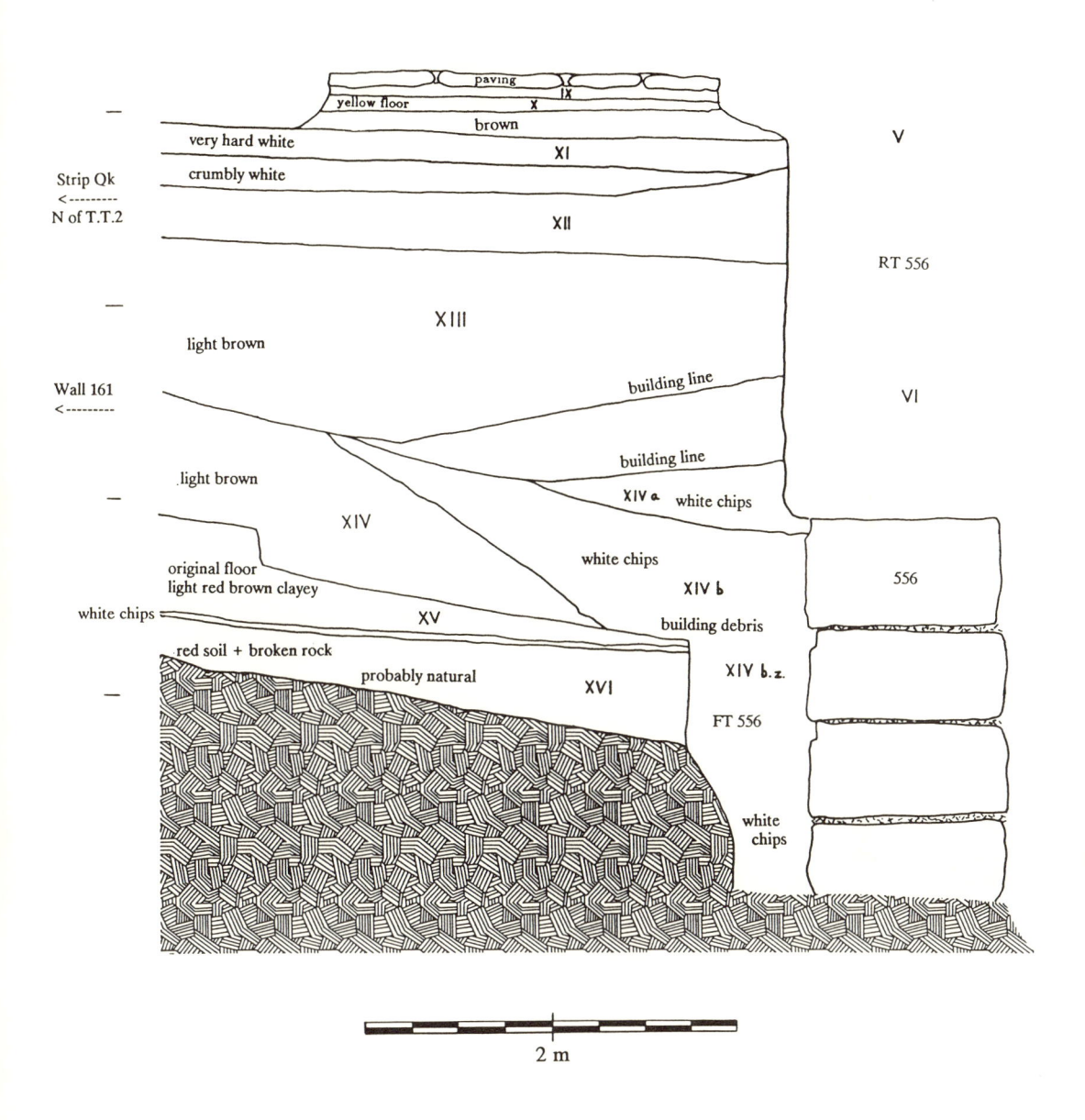

Segment 509.126
<— S N —>
View toward West

fig. 19

The lower (i.e., stratigraphically earlier) portion of the "crumbly white" Layer XII, then, represents the final leveling activity laid against (or poured from) the southern face of Wall 556 by Ahab's laborers. Though a later robber trench broke the layer's direct stratigraphic connection to that wall, one can still see that it thickened and angled upward as it approached the wall—similar to most of the other so-called "building lines." Upper Layer XII, however, does not reflect leveling *fill*; rather, it provided the actual subfloor makeup for surface XI, the first living surface contemporaneous with the new, grand casemate system. When it went out of use, an additional though conservative quantity of brown fill (unnumbered in Kenyon's section, fig. 19) was poured over the area to serve as a base for a new decca floor level of yellowish composition, Layer X. This comprises the level from which the workers recovered the fragment published in *SS III*, Fig. 6:32 under PP 4. This dating seems correct since both this layer and its brownish foundation correlate nicely with Layer IX in *N of TT2*, which overran, sealed, and therefore postdated the BP III Wall 160 (traditionally ascribed to King Jehu).

Subsequent to this, another light, crumbly packing (actually = Layer IXa) served as a base supporting a nicer floor of paving stones laid east of Wall 142 (Layer IX).[125] Though RT 556 in fig. 19 again destroyed the stratigraphic connection between this surface and nearby walls, comparative stratigraphic analysis in *N of TT2* (fig. 7) confirms that these stones constituted at least the second significant resurfacing of Room *j* following BP III (Wall 160). One sees here a series of presumably closely dated floor levels; a comprehensive analysis of the full ceramic sequence recovered from these levels, however, remains critical to rendering them "datable" and, thereby, to establishing the most probable historical circumstance for their construction. This makes it all the more surprising, then, that so little pottery from this area actually reached the final report. Ceramic and stratigraphic analyses must always complement one another, and the absence of a suitable database in either case will hamstring success in the other. In the publications from Samaria, it is usually the meager quantity and equivocal loci of the published ceramic assemblage that most depreciates the historical reconstructions.

Two final points concerning Segment *509.126* merit highlighting. First, the stratigraphic proximity of the late Israelite levels to those of the late Hellenistic or, more often, of the late Roman periods seems striking. The noticeable dearth of material remains from the intervening centuries has presented itself consistently in the north courtyard segments studied thus far. Second, the field notes pertaining to this field of excavation contain only minimal—or virtually no—mention of appreciable deposits of charcoal or burnt material and, more important, not a word relating to the discovery of

---

[125] Another field section recovered from Kenyon's unpublished notes both confirms this interpretation of these layers and, at the same time, raises further questions. Since this cut seems to relate to the NW corner of Room *l*, however, I will discuss it fully at that point in my study (see Ch. IV, PP 7, *509.126*). For now, it will suffice to compare the earliest local stratigraphy depicted in that drawing south of Robber Trench 555 with levels IX-XI from *N of TT2* (fig. 7) and IX-XII from *509.126* (fig. 19).

ivory fragments (quantifiable or not) here. The relative closeness of *509.126* to the other segments discussed in this part of my study heightens the disparity. It seems clear, at this point at least, that the ivories reveal a rather localized spatial distribution, and that the complex of poorly built rooms situated behind Rooms *a-e* and *o-q* constitute their dominant context. Within that context, nearly all the findspots lay in late Roman fillings rather than in secure, primary levels from the Iron Age II period.

e. Room *k* (Auxiliary Sections A and B — figs. 7-8)

[i] Between Test Trench 2–Test Trench 3
[ii] E Strip; Between Test Trench 2–Test Trench 3

As with the nearby segment *N of TT2*, the principal section data for these areas come once again from fig. 13 above, with the center portion of fig. 7 and the eastern half of fig. 8 providing supplementary information. Using the relative locations of architectural features on both figs. 7 and 10, I have emended fig. 13 to indicate the horizontal position of Walls 161/160, which I shall occasionally cite as points of reference.[126] In light of the stratigraphy recorded for segment *Btw TT2-TT3* south of Wall 153 on the various available sections, one must assume that the local Layers VI, VII and VIIa on the field section of fig. 7 correspond to the block of deposits labeled "[Period] IVa" on Kenyon's Section EF. By extension, one should perhaps equate Layer VIII on the field section with the southernmost extension of "[Period] IV" on the published section, though this remains uncertain.

From fig. 13, one sees clearly that even though the Late Roman quarrying activity approached the complex of poorly built rooms presently under consideration and, in fact, impinged heavily on its southernmost extension, a 1.5 meter-wide strip of deposits lying just inside Room *k* on the south side of RT 153 escaped the plunder and remained basically intact. The stratigraphic summary of these layers in the field notes[127] also provided correlations between these and other deposits from adjacent segments; when appropriate, I have entered these analogies in my notes by means of the equation $X \leftrightarrow Y$ (as in n. 123).

The uppermost level recorded for this area coalesces nicely with the latest stratum in the adjacent segment *N of TT2*. The thick, hard surface of Layer I, with generous quantities of soft, ribbed ceramic forms from the Late Roman period (R.4 phase), once again extends over the entire segment. But the thinner, white surface of Layer II which lay beneath this deposit in *N of TT2* presents itself here as a substantial rubble covering resulting from the robbing of multiple walls (134 and/or 142) in the area during the slightly earlier R.3 period.

---

[126] As with all the other sections presented in this study, I have also added various identifying labels to fig. 13.

[127] *Fieldbook Qk-l-m*, 14a-15a.

Following this, I once again come directly to the hard, yellowish level III,[128] which likewise overran and sealed RT 153 and extended over the entire area, including the vicinity of *N of TT2* to the north. The upper portions of this layer, however, exhibited signs that it had also suffered moderate disturbances during the plundering processes which had claimed the stones of various walls in the area. Records indicate that the workers continued to recovered a few samples of pink and buff ribbed ware at these elevations. The next earlier layer, which received the sublayer designation IIIb even though it appears on fig. 7 as a distinct deposit, emerges as a pivotal correlation in one's comparative analysis of the local stratigraphy. This 1.15 meter-thick deposit, which also revealed signs of disturbance, yielded a blanket of sooty soil which contained fragments of burnt ivory. In both consistency and content, then, this matrix seems quite consonant with Layer IIIa in segment *125.144*.[129]

Though RT 153, as depicted in fig. 13, destroyed the exact stratigraphic relationship between this deposit and the actual Wall 153, the corresponding level in *125.144*—only slightly further east near the juncture of Rooms *h* and *k*—appears to run up against the south face of Wall 153, indicating possible contemporaneity (fig. 10). Even so, other portions of this layer seem to have suffered under the robbing of related walls; for example, sub-Layer IIIy shows evidence of robber trench cuts near the southwestern corner of Wall 142. The R.4 quarry area had affected still other parcels of this layer adversely (IIIz). This general disturbance notwithstanding, however, Layer IIIb provides a clear analogue to deposits located elsewhere on the northern summit. Kenyon assigned both III and IIIa to her "Period VII."

Beneath this rested the compacted, yellowish fill of Layer IV[130] which, despite Kenyon's note that it seemed contemporary with Wall 125b,[131] appears clearly cut by that wall on fig. 10. Kenyon placed this deposit in "Period V" (corrected from "Period IV"). It is instructive to note that sub-Layer IVa denoted a series of paving stones positioned "in and on" IV, while IVt signified the continuance of these stones in the eastern half of the segment, where they supported the base of Wall 148.[132] One turns immediately to parallel notations regarding paving stones associated with *N of TT2*, Layer IVa in fig. 13 and, more directly, to the graphic presentation of this companion level in fig. 7, where the preserved stones run directly over the old line of Wall 161. These stones appeared, ultimately, to be resting on a "g[oo]d hard level" called Layer V,[133] or more specifically the striation labeled Vx.

---

[128]*Btw TT2-TT3*, III ↔ *120.121.19.126*, V.

[129]Compare also *N of TT2*, IV ↔ *120.121.19.126*, V.

[130]*Btw TT2-TT3*, IV ↔ *125.144*, III.

[131]*Fieldbook Qk-l-m*, 14a.

[132]A nearby notation equates this feature with Wall 137.

[133]*Btw TT2-TT3*, V ↔ *125.144*, IIIe (or c?).

Immediately beneath this surface lay another apparent floor, Layer VI.[134] As shown by fig. 7, this level represents the first in a block of deposits which clearly pre-date the construction of Wall 125b and the backfilling of its foundation trench with Layer V. Kenyon dated this floor to "Period IVa" and the next surface beneath it (Layer VII) to her "Period IV." She correctly observed that the latter deposit represented the earliest floor level traceable in this area, since Layer VIIa comprised its subfloor makeup and Layer VIII yielded a thicker covering of dark colored fill. As shown in Table 1 (p. 13), the seven fragments of pottery published from *Btw TT2-TT3* proper and its *East Strip* complement[135] derived from the floor itself (Layer VII) and the darker, imported fill (Layer VIII) positioned two levels beneath it. Mysteriously, however, all but one of these ceramic pieces were marked as discards in the early records, and the single specimen that was not so marked (*SS III*, Fig. 6:3) represented the only one that derived from Layer VIII, i.e., from the imported fill rather than from the living surface two layers above it. Clearly, something seems amiss here, but the logic of it remains impenetrable.

All the deposits just mentioned (Layers VI-VIII) ran up to and met the south face of Wall 153, which served as the dividing line between *N of TT2*/Room *j* to the north and *Btw TT2-TT3*/Room *k* to the south. Yet it remains difficult to access the stratigraphic relationship between the dark fill of Layer VIII and the brown subfloor makeup of Layer IX in the segment *N of TT2* (see fig. 7). They appear to blend together somewhere beneath Wall 153, which had its base set into and on both levels without a trace of a foundation trench.

Finally, the three stratigraphically earlier levels visible in fig. 7 for segment *Btw TT2-TT3* are quite consistent with the deepest levels presented in fig. 13. All these deposits—from the rubble of IX to the darker, more compacted fill of X[136] and the whitish accumulation in XI found lying directly on the rock—reflect developments from Iron Age I through BP I-III in the ninth century BCE. I have treated each layer in detail in my previous study.

As a postscript to my discussion of the segments excavated in the area of Test Trench 2, I may add that if the hard white resurfacings in Layer X of *N of TT2* (fig. 7) represent, as I have suggested, living floor levels from the time of Ahab, then the compact matrix of Layer IX which rested atop them—and which overran and sealed the remains of the late ninth-century BP III Wall 160—should represent the first living surface from the early eighth century BCE.[137] In the adjacent segment *Btw TT2-TT3*, the

---

[134]*Btw TT2-TT3*, VI ↔ *125.144*, IIIb.

[135]*SS III*, Fig. 6:6, 7, 17, 25, 35 from Layer VII; Fig. 6:3 from Layer VIII. Another fragment, 6:5a, was curiously attributed in the notes to both VII and VIII.

[136]Kenyon's correlations associated *125.144*, Layer VI, with both of these deposits.

[137]If, in agreement with Kenyon, Wall 160 correctly belonged to the period of King Jehu (BP III), then no associated surfaces from that time remain in this area. I make this observation, however, under the assumption that Layer Xa in *N of TT2* (see fig. 7) correctly represents 160's foundation trench that cut through Ahab's floors, which were not then repaired. Layer Xa could, on the other hand, easily point to

earliest eighth-century floors consist in Layers VII and VI, in that stratigraphic sequence. And on all sections, one can see again that these small rooms, unimpressive in their design and construction, rested above areas where the rock surface dropped sharply toward the north. Figures 5, 8, and 11, in particular, demonstrate that this steep and unwieldy descent of the bedrock began already several meters inside (i.e., south of) Wall 153, on a course which aligns quite well with the rock scarp charted by Reisner further to the west, along a lateral course at roughly 437°N and from 559°-578° E,[138] where it disappeared beneath one of two summit dump sites utilized by the Harvard project.

[iii] 125.144

(See the discussion under Room *hk* above; § b.i.).

f. Room *n* (Published Section CD)

[i] 502.503

Thus far, my discussion has focused on the complex of rather poorly constructed rooms situated between 638°-650° E and 453°-466° N. To the east of this complex, in Summit Strip Qn, the second area from which the excavators drew many of their published fragments (Room *n*) ran as far as 670° E according to the final report, though only its westernmost Wall 561 appears on the official BP IV Phase Plan (at 658°-660°) and, as I have mentioned earlier, the site plan in *SS I*, Pl. II marks the eastern limits of the excavation area at roughly 665° E (compare fig. 5).

Several roughly sketched top plans from the field notes help to situate Room *n* on the horizontal axis in this area, while various other field drawings supplement the presentation of the relevant blocks of vertical stratigraphy seen in published Section CD. First, an unphased plan of the entire area spanning from the western edge of Room *j* eastward through the exposed portion of Room *n* appears in fig. 20.[139] The location of westerly walls associated with Rooms *g* and *j* (Nos. 138, 149 [both of which I have added to this drawing], 142, and 553) amply demonstrates the cohesion between this new plan and fig. 12; in addition, it serves as a starting point for matching the rele-

---

a robber trench that severed the stratigraphic relationship between the double Layer X (which Jehu could have reused) and Wall 160 (which he built) at a later time. Finally, a caveat: the fact that Kenyon construed both Xz and IXz as foundation cuts for Wall 160 on its south side (even though the section portrays them as stratigraphically disparate cuts) makes the much wider (ca. 75 cm) counter breach in Xa resemble, to my eyes, robbing activities more than the residue of construction.

[138] In Reisner's grid plan, this laterally oriented northern scarp appears in Grids F7, G7, and H7. I shall address what I will call the "western scarp," the beginnings of which are traced longitudinally in Grid G7, later in this study, when I assess the overall significance of the summit topography to the city planning of Samaria.

[139] Adapted from *Fieldbook Qn (Vol. I)*, 7a.

PP 4: HOUSE FLOORS — STRATIGRAPHY

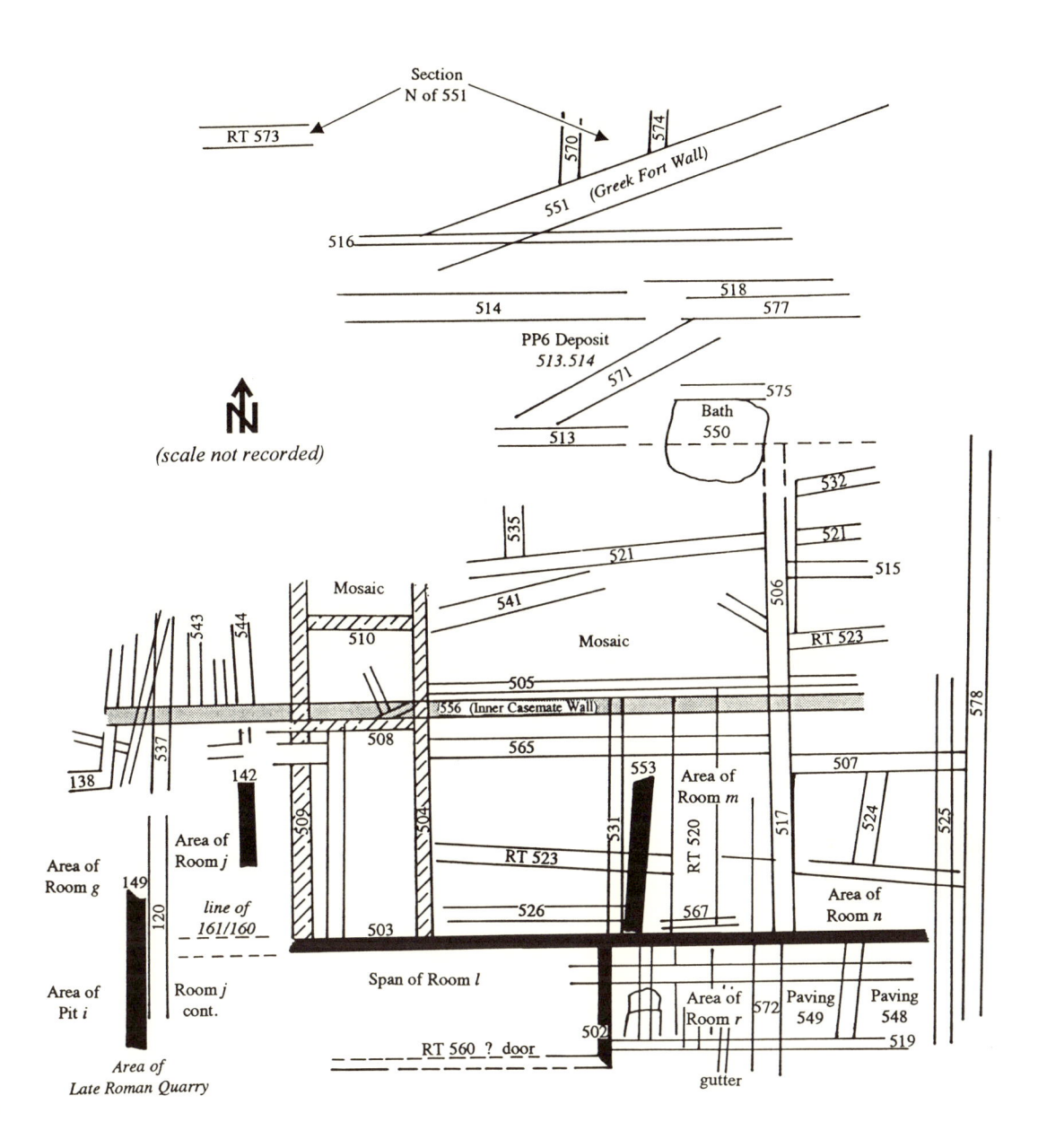

Field Sketch of Unphased Top Plan Relating to Segment 502.503
fig. 20

vant features of the more easterly Room *n* with Kenyon's illustration of them in her published drawings.

Toward this end, one can move across this plan from west to east and detect where the partially remaining portions of Wall 149 divide Room *g/i* from *j*, where 142 separates *j* from *l*, and where 553 distinguishes *l* from *m*.[140] Plotting two other important walls, however, proves more difficult. First, the feature which differentiated Rooms *m* and *n*, Wall 561, remains unclear on this plan. Yet it undoubtedly rested below or near Wall 517 since the collation of fig. 20 with another, limited field sketch confirms that Pavement 549 lay immediately east of both the contemporaneous 561 and the later 517 (see fig. 21[141]). Second, the line establishing the southern border of Room *m* (Wall 562), also not completely evident in Kenyon's draft, must have run basically beneath Wall 503, since fig. 5 shows that 562 and Omri's 161 assume virtually the same course at this point, and since Section CD indicates that 503 actually sat in the robber trench of 161.

The southeastern corner of fig. 20, then, constitutes the focus of discussion for Segment *502.503*.[142] The field notes reflect a depositional history for this area very similar to that seen already in Room *j*, Segment *509.126*. That is, the pattern of late Israelite levels mixed with Hellenistic and Roman intrusions continues here in Room *n*. The excavators reported a very significant deposit of fill to the east of Wall 561 (in Room *n*) which went "right down to rock," "was clear all over the room," and included the backfill of multiple robber trenches in the area.[143] These strata appear only in Kenyon's typical "block" format on the extreme southern side of *SS I*, Pl. VII, Section CD. Presumably, one of these trenches represented the line of the original summit Enclosure Wall 161, which had extended through this area during BP I in roughly an E-W direction just above 450° N and which was filled by Wall 503 in the Roman period. Judging from this published section,[144] it seems that the PP 4 material presented in *SS III* came only from a limited area just south of the line established originally by 161, precisely in the area where Pavements 548 and 549 appear in fig. 20 (compare fig. 5).[145] North of this point, Kenyon assigned a comparable fill deposit to her "Period II" and saw only a very thin "Period IV" layer above it. At a much later

---

[140] As with field drawings presented earlier in this study, I have emended Kenyon's original plan only slightly by darkening these walls and, for the sake of reference, labelling the rooms appropriately.

[141] *Fieldbook Qn (Vol. II)*, 89a.

[142] The following references relate to this segment: daily field notes = *Fieldbook Qn (Vol. I)*, 39-43 and *Qn (Vol. II)*, 79-82, 111; stratigraphic summary = *Qn (Vol. I)*, 39 and *(Vol. II)*, 82a, 111a, and the bottom half of 111; germane field sections = *Qn (Vol. I)*, 39a, 40a, 41a, 42a, and *(Vol. II)*, 80a, 81a.

[143] *SS III*, 112.

[144] The line represented by this drawing marks the easternmost extent of the excavations inside the northern casemate system (except for some work at the very NE corner of the compound) by the Joint Expedition (*SS I*, Pl. II; *AIS-I*, fig. 1).

[145] I.e., at roughly 660°-664° E x 458°-460° N.

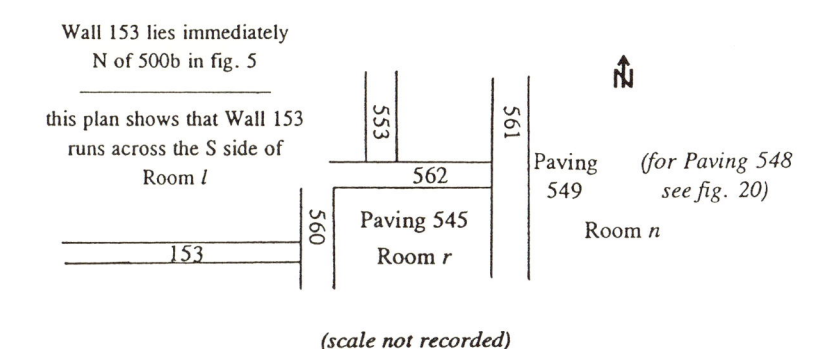

Configuration of Walls and Pavements in the Vicinity of Rooms r and n

fig. 21

time, the Herodian Wall 503 used bedrock as a foundation and thereby cut all deposits in this area.

The deposits were not as neatly stacked in chronological succession, however, as they might appear in the conglomerated blocks of layers on Section CD. Though the latest stratigraphy, Layers I-III, stems from the Late Roman period (R.4), many subdeposits, particularly those used to backfill foundation or robber trenches, yielded appreciable quantities of late Israelite pottery (e.g., Layers IIa, IIb, IIx, III). The fieldbooks recorded that the massive filling of the so-called "Greek Fort Wall" (Layer IV)—a fill which Kenyon also included in the Hellenistic period itself—contained Hellenistic pottery mixed with *mid*-Israelite fragments as well as considerable amounts of soot.[146] Unless an Israelite occupation on the steep northern slopes can be established more clearly, it seems reasonable to suppose that the Greeks and Romans simply gathered their fill material on the summit itself, from whatever debris remained of Israelite and the apparent meager post-Israelite occupations.

Couched within the striations associated with Pavement 545 in Room *r* (Layer IVy) and the level of hard soil beneath them (Layer IVa), at least four subdeposits were lowered to the Hellenistic period by the excavators due to their observation in these layers of pottery dating from the late Israelite and early post-Israelite phases (PP 6 and 8; Layers IVc, IVc.a, IVd, and IVd.a).[147] Layers VI-VII and their various subdeposits, which comprised the debris lying above Pavings 248-249, received dates in

---

[146]The presentation of these deposits in section appears in *Fieldbook Qn (Vol. I)*, 41a. Since these and other "late" levels fall beyond the chronological purview of this study, I have chosen not to include the drawing itself.

[147]See the appropriate section in *Fieldbook Qn (Vol. I)*, 42a-43a.

Kenyon's "Period VII."[148] An interesting note which accompanies this level states that the matrix comprised:

> hardish soil [with a] stretch of hard yellow on top, wh[ich] overlies paved area at W. end. Does not seem to be quite [the] same W. of [this] vert[ical] block, where stones look more like broken wall than paving, as E. of it, where is clearly paving.[149]

Kenyon related the sublevels of VIII to the robbing of Wall 161 and the filling of the resultant trench with soil imported from the construction of the Greek Fort Wall; consequently, they reflect further activities during the Hellenistic period.[150] According to the pottery notations which accompany the stratigraphic summaries, these fillings again contained some material from PP 4 while most of the fragments recovered there came from PP 8.

As attested in Table 1, the levels of principal concern for Pottery Periods 4-5 consist in Layers IX-XIII. A roster of these layers appears in Table 5.

In separate drawings, which Kenyon herself labeled "sketches,"[151] two sections—apparently cut perpendicularly to one another—only partially relate the local stratigraphy beneath Pavings 549 and 548 in Room *n* (figs. 22-23). Since these sections display an extremely limited horizontal breadth, and since they must lie in the area between Wall 561 and the edge of the excavations (roughly along Section CD), I may presume that they reflect limited findings from narrow trenches cut through the floors of Room *n*.

Using the field notes as a guide,[152] I can make the following observations regarding the deposits that were assigned to "Period IV" mainly on the basis of the pottery removed from them. Kenyon interpreted Layer XIa to represent the basal portion of a BP IV paving in this area (see fig. 23). The field records indicate that the excavators encountered this hardish brown earth ca. 50 cm below Pavement 548. After coming upon a relatively thin streak of blackish earth approximately 1 m into this deposit (labeled "soot" on fig. 23), the apparent continuation of the brown matrix became Layer XIa.b, "tho[ugh it was] prob[ably] all [the] same." Judging from field notes and fig. 23, then, the substantial block of soil(s) associated with general Layer XI

---

[148] One should note that Layers VII and VIIa.b.—i.e., *some* of the debris overlying these pavements—apparently contained some sooty deposits over Pavements 248 and 249 (*Fieldbook, Qn [Vol. I]*, 39, and *[Vol. II]*, 111a).

[149] *Fieldbook Qn (Vol. I)*, 39.

[150] See the appropriate section in *Fieldbook Qn (Vol. II)*, 80a.

[151] Since she rarely appended this notation to her other field drawings, this seems to imply that these particular sketches were not necessarily drawn to scale and that one cannot establish with certainty their exact proximity to Wall 561.

[152] Here I rely primarily on *Fieldbook Qn (Vol. II)*, 80-82 and 111. All quoted material comes from those pages, and I shall cite specific page numbers in parentheses when appropriate.

PP 4: HOUSE FLOORS — STRATIGRAPHY

General Level	Kenyon's Proposed Dating	Description
IX	PP 5	Paving stones 549
IXa	PP 5	Paving stones 548[153]
X	PP 5	Light coloured [with] soot beneath, makeup of Per. V floor, beneath 249
Xa	PP 5	Makeup of Per. V floor; beneath 248
XI	PP 4	Hard brown, basis of Per. IV paving 249a
XIa	PP 4	[same]
XIa.b.	PP 4	Sooty }
XIIa.	PP 4	Hardish } = Period IV filling of
XIIa.b.	PP 4	Stones } Robber Trench 161
XIIb.	PP 4	Stones }
XIII	PP 4	Level beneath Per. IV robbing of RT 161, and beneath (?) stones of 553
XIIIz.	R.4	F.T. 503a

Abridged Stratigraphic Summary of Segment 502.503

Table 5

alone proved nearly 2 m thick. If one includes the .5 m-thick deposit of Layer Xa, one sees roughly 2.5 m of accumulation separating Pavement 548 from the latest striations of Layer XIIa. Elsewhere, however, Kenyon indicated that only "*c.* 1.50 m below 548 a decca floor [was] reached sloping down to [the] E. = XIIa" (see again fig. 23, noting also the horizontal plane on fig. 20). A degree of incongruity, therefore, seems to attend the depths recorded for the various levels in this segment. At any rate, the clearance of XIIa continued to a layer of rough stones, entered in the notes as Layer XIIa.b.

In the corollary section presented in fig. 22, it becomes apparent that well beneath Pavement 549 the excavators found a similar strip of rather compact, greyish-yellow soil, which they labeled Layer XII, and a few stones lying immediately beneath this; they became XIIb. (These stones apparently represent the complement to XIIa.b just mentioned beneath Pavement 548.) The notes add that these layers were "apparently all one fill" and, more specifically, that Layer XII appeared to represent "either [a] F.T. or R.T. of [the] cont[inuation] E. of [BP III Wall] 160."

---

[153] Stone pavings 549 and 548 extended east from Wall 561 across the southern area of Room *n*, while a similar paving, 545, lay west of 561 in Room *r*.

Further below the stones of XIIa.b and XIIb, and *beneath* the robbing of Wall 161 (= Omri's original Enclosure Wall!), another rather hardish level appeared (Layer XIII) which sloped down to the east, just as some of the subsequent deposits have done (see above). Kenyon also ascribed this layer to BP IV/PP 4. (For the sake of convenience, I have entered the approximate location of the line of 161-160 on the western side of fig. 20.) When the workers cleared this deposit below the stones of 549a (see fig. 22), they retrieved at least one fragment of black glazed ware, which Kenyon assumed came from Robber Trench 553 situated near the edge of this general area. Actually, the plans in figs. 5 and 20 show that RT 553 lay some 6-to-7 meters northwest of this pavement, at the westernmost border of the putative BP IV Room *m*.

As indicated in Table 5, Kenyon's stratigraphic summary sheets associated all deposits earlier than Layer Xa with her "Period IV," including even Layer XIII which rested beneath the robbing of BP I Wall 161. Importantly, she also interpreted the following layers as the "Per. IV filling of R.T. 161": the sooty streak above XIa.b; Layer XIa.b itself; the hardish earth of XIIa; and the miscellaneous stones of both XIIa.b and XIIa (compare fig. 23). The two successive deposits (Layers XI and XIa) distinguished themselves by comprising, according to Kenyon, the subpaving makeup for Pavement 249a.[154] In this scenario, then, the break between two significantly different historical activities (i.e., the plundering of Wall 161 and the laying of pavement 249a) occurs precisely at the thin, unlabeled striation of soot running through XIa and XIa.b in fig. 23. But neither Kenyon's own description of the layers involved nor the sectional data appear to support this distinction. Moreover, I have only just pointed out that Kenyon herself saw the depositional history portrayed in the *XIa—sooty striation—XIa.b* sequence as "probably all the same." I believe that the nearly three meters' worth of layers in this general area represent thick accumulations of fill deposits which, according to published Section CD, extended down to bedrock (see also p. 60, n. 143).

One may also wonder, based on fig. 22, whether enough intact stones survived to merit taking Locus 549a as a clear, paved level that once covered a rather widespread area east of Wall 561. The official report contained the curious attestation that "this area was sealed by a stone paving, of which only a few stones remained."[155] Taken at face value, this remark seems self-contradictory. I interpret it to mean that (1) the excavators believed a layer of paving stones to have sealed the deposits beneath it *at some point in antiquity* and (2) they observed that the seal was broken already in antiquity. Therefore one may expect both derived and intrusive forms among the yield of ceramic fragments from Room *n*. Undoubtedly, the former elements result because the layer comprised a deposit of imported fill with an open *terminus post quem* and the latter situation exists because a significant breach in the stone sealing above the layer had

---

[154] I remain a bit perplexed at the apparent recording of the various pavements as 248, 249, and 249a in the field notes but as 548, 549, and 549a on the field sections.

[155] *SS III*, 112.

PP 4: HOUSE FLOORS — STRATIGRAPHY

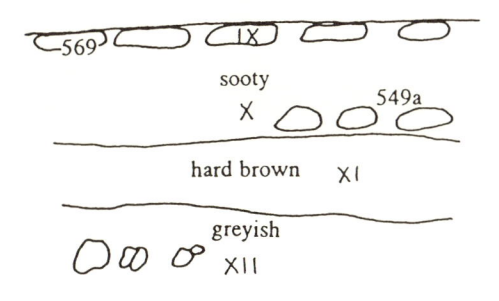

(scale not recorded)

Restricted Field Sketch No. 1 from Segment 502.503
<— E W —>
View toward South
fig. 22

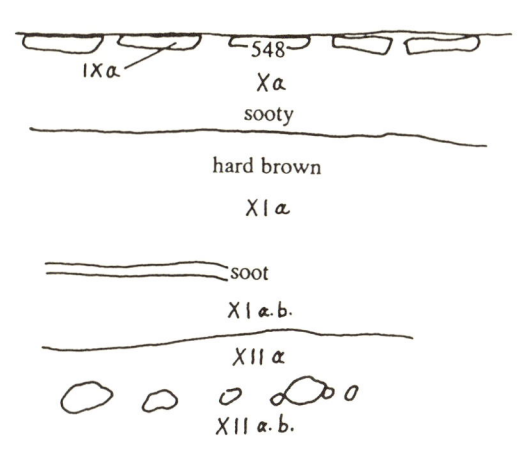

(scale not recorded)

Restricted Field Sketch No. 2 from Segment 502.503
<— N S —>
View toward East
fig. 23

occurred already at some point in the past, creating a potentially open *terminus ante quem* at that time. Either situation can severely bias a pottery sample if left undetected, and both need clarification in any comparative ceramic analysis, particularly since the final report presented more fragments and vessels from this single room than from any other in support of its "Period IV" (15 fragments from Layers Xa, XI, XIa, XIa.b, XII, and XIIa.b in figs. 22-23; compare the entry for Room *n* in Table 1).

The significance of these observations and hesitations looms large in light of the fact that nearly 43% of the total PP 4 ceramic repertoire derives from Segment *502.503* in Room *n*. I shall turn next to an analysis of the complete repertoire of pottery published not only from Room *n* but from all the rooms and segments discussed thus far.

2) Pottery Analysis

The largest single assemblage of pottery published in support of Kenyon's "Period IV-VI" derived from the preceding collection of rooms situated north of the main courtyard.[156] The overall group contained 35 fragments from four types of vessels, and a spatial analysis of their distribution appears as follows:

	bowls	cooking pots	jars	holemouth jars	TOTAL
Room *g*	1	-	-	1	2
Room *h*	1	1	4	-	6
Room *j*	-	2	2	-	4
Room *k*	5	2	1	-	8
Room *n*	1	10	-	4	15
TOTAL	8	15	7	5	35

Distribution of PP 4-4a Ceramic Forms
Published from House Floors (Rooms g-k, n)

Table 6

A number of observations emerge from these data. First, the published report presented a relatively limited number of forms and individual fragments taken from this area. A thorough ceramic record should, at minimum, include several plates of vessels recovered from multiple loci *within each room*. Second, all the pottery recovered from these rooms reflect basic, utilitarian vessels. The final report made no mention of forms such as bottles, flasks, pyxides, chalices, goblets, amphoriskoi, etc.; neither did it include examples of clear imported goods, whether from Cypriot, Cypro-Phoenician, or Assyrian origins. The range of vessels reported, then, fits well within an area containing a number of *ṭābunîm*, which I noted from various loci in Rooms *g-k* above.

---

[156]This group constituted 68.6% of the fragments presented in *SS III*, Figs. 6-7.

Third, of the five rooms considered, Room *n* contributed the greatest number of fragments to the final repertoire (15 of 35 pieces, or nearly 43% of the total group). This resulted mainly from the apparent concentration of cooking pots in that area (rims came from 10 individual specimens which, in turn, comprise 66.6% of all the cooking pots published from these chambers). Speaking more generally, I might add that the cooking pot emerges as the largest single class of vessel recovered from these areas (15 of 35 total pieces, or 42.8%). Room *n* also contained 4 of the 5 holemouth jars taken from the two complexes of rooms (80%). On the other hand, most of the other jar forms came from Room *h* (57%), where one of the fragments exemplified the only piece published in support of Kenyon's subphase labeled "Period IVa" (*SS III*, Fig. 6:14). Room *k* yielded most of the better-preserved bowls (62%). Fourth, the northern alcoves in the cluster of shabby rooms (*f-g-h-j-k*) were less well-represented in the published ceramic corpus. Room *j* contributed two rims each from cooking pots and jars, while relatively little pottery came from Room *g* and none derived from Room *f*.

In light of the foregoing remarks, the BP IV rooms north of the main courtyard appear to typify an area utilized mainly for food processing. The large ratio of cooking pots and holemouth jars in relation to other vessel types, the presence of multiple *ṭabunîm*, and the irregular design and thin-walled construction of the architecture all seem congruent with this conclusion. The entire vicinity strikes one as a service related area, not a precinct of royal activity. Yet one must acknowledge that the restricted overall repertoire of pottery published from these rooms forces nearly any interpretation to remain open to both question and later adjustment. Only the excavators themselves knew whether or not the range of forms and wares included in their official report accurately reflected the real, overall classification and distribution of pottery types recovered from these areas. That fact notwithstanding, I may add that the distribution of vessel types will, in fact, change when I move to findspots located beyond the range of these rooms, i.e., to loci situated both in the Northern Courtyard/Courtyard to their south and inside the casemate chambers to their north. For example, the percentages of cooking pots and holemouth jars will decrease significantly in those areas, indicating that I have likely moved outside the so-called service area (see Table 8 and my further conclusions at the end of this chapter).

I shall now offer an evaluation of the fragments retrieved from these north courtyard rooms and assigned to each class of vessel.

a. Bowls

The official report included eight whole or near-whole bowls recovered from local deposits in four of these rooms. The following information (Table 7), taken from Appendix A, will assist my navigation through certain inconsistencies in the records pertaining to these vessels and will facilitate my discussion generally.

SS III Published Figure	Registry No. (* = marked for discard)	Provenance				
		Strip	Coordinates	Feature	Local Layer
6:1	Q 5271	Qk	120.121.19.126	Room *g*	Wall 136
6:2	QX 53	Q(x)-k	147.145.151.136	Room *h*	IX
6:3	QX 61	Q(x)-k	Btw TT2-TT3	Room *k*	VIII
6:4	Q 4571	Qn	502.503	Room *n*	XII
6:5a	*Q 2373	Qk	125.144	Room *k/h*?	IVa.y, Vy
5b	*Q 2374	Qk	▶Btw TT2-TT3	Room *k*	VII, VIII
6:6	QX 55	Q(x)-k	Btw TT2-TT3	Room *k*	VII
6:7	*Q 2548d	Qk	▶Btw TT2-TT3	Room *k*	VII

Provenance Data:
PP4 Bowls from Area Labeled "House Floors"

Table 7

These data reveal that three of the eight vessels were marked as discards in the early records (Nos. 5a, 5b. 7). This may have resulted from the fact that the excavators remained unsure of the specific locus designations for these particular pieces. Kenyon's handwritten, prepublication draft of the pottery section in *Samaria-Sebaste III*[157] lists bowl Nos. 5b and 7 (earmarked with ▶) as having come from the Segment *Between Test Trench 2-Test Trench 3*, and the stratification cards (which I believe originated with Ms. Grace Crowfoot) seem to confirm this assignment for No. 7.[158] A parallel copy of the pottery notes found in the Rockefeller Museum, however, stipulates that at least No. 5b (and possibly also 7) actually derived from the area labeled more specifically "E. Strip, Btw TT2-TT3."[159]

Similarly, while Kenyon's prepublication manuscript ascribed entry No. 5a to Room *k*, one should perhaps credit it instead to the contiguous Room *h*, immediately west of *k* (see n. 46 and the related discussion above). This incongruity may have resulted ostensibly from the collection of a widespread "sherd scatter" involving both chambers and the eventual restoration of bowl No. 5 from those fragments. The fact that both the notes and final report assign the two items presented in Nos. 5a and 5b to four different local layers in two separate, though stratigraphically related, segments may support this suggestion.[160] Still, this reasoning would seem to require the credible

---

[157]This manuscript is currently stored in the Palestine Exploration Fund, London, England.

[158]G. M. Crowfoot's stratification card notes describe No. 7 as "discarded and taken to England."

[159]See the field registry titled *Sabastya, Qn, 1935*. These notes appear quite ambiguous concerning the locus for No. 7. All sources agree, however, in assigning Nos. 3 and 6 simply to *Btw TT2-TT3*.

[160]Otherwise, how can a single sherd have come from two distinct deposits, as appears the case with both 5a (Layers IVa.y. *and* Vy) and 5b (VII *and* VIII)? In fact, *Sabastya Qn, 1935* (Rockefeller

strength of a relatively secure findspot for the sherds involved. Our stratigraphic analysis has already shown, however, that these fragments derive from secondary fillings, with some deposited only in much later periods (e.g., Layer Vy, which "probably included some of [the R.4] quarry").[161]

Working without the aid of detailed stratigraphic data such as those presented above, Holladay recognized the broad chronological range of the bowls presented under PP 4 and, as a result, readily excluded them from his corpus of reliably located materials. He suggested that the spectrum of attributes which they exhibited bore witness to "a very mixed origin for these materials."[162] On grounds of typology alone, he tentatively classified the bowls into three chronologically disparate phases of ceramic tradition: an early group, dating from ca. 860 or 840 BCE (Nos. 3 and 6); a middle group, from the late ninth century, 840-810 BCE (No. 4); and a late group, which "extended down to a time near or past the mid-eighth century" (Nos. 1 and 2).[163] Interestingly, he made no mention of Nos. 5a, 5b, or 7. Though he could not have known it at the time, these represent the three entries marked as discards in at least one of the field registries and the ones for which even the excavators and registrars themselves had recorded variable loci for the original findspots.

On the basis of the collective attributes shown by these vessels, I offer a classification scheme which resembles that of Holladay, without duplicating it. One may divide the PP 4 bowls into the following typologically related groups: Nos. 1 and 2; Nos. 4 and 5; and Nos. 6 and 7 (also possibly No. 3). Though my system generally favors Holladay's, I can present a few additional comments regarding the dating of the various groups outlined. Let me begin with the observation that the vessels in many of these categories appear to continue the ceramic traditions of earlier pottery periods at Samaria and elsewhere. Even though the majority of these fragments came from fill deposits, it remains crucial to establish as precise a chronological range for the vessels as possible in order to arrive at a viable *terminus ante quem* for the filling activity and, by extension, a likely date for the end of the functional life of the rooms in which the fills were found. If the latest materials recovered from the fills date to the early eighth century, for example, then the rooms and surfaces which those deposits covered certainly went out of use sometime prior to that period. The justification for this discussion of admittedly secondary contexts comes also from the fact that the depositional history within this general area of rooms bears heavily on the interpretation of the important and much discussed corpus of ivory fragments, for which Samaria has remained so famous.

Museum) indicates that Q 2374 (= No. 5b) itself actually consisted of at least two fragments, 2374a and 2374b, and it designates both sherds as "discards." G. M. Crowfoot's notes on the stratification card for No. 5b offer confirmation: "N.B. one fragment of the rim from Level VII, other from Level VIII."

[161] *Fieldbook Qk-l-m*, 49. Kenyon's R.4 period dates to the fourth century CE.

[162] J. S. Holladay, Jr., "Ninth and Eighth Century Pottery from Northern Palestine" (Th.D. diss., Harvard University, 1966), 131 (hereafter, *Holladay*).

[163] *Holladay*, 130, nn. 114-16.

Our first group includes two examples of the straight-sided, shallow bowls (Nos. 1 and 2) which resemble—in details of form, ware, and surface treatment—a vessel assigned to Pottery Period 2 in *SS III*, Fig. 3:3. These saucers display a reddish (No. 1) to creamy (No. 2) buff colored ware, with a smooth red slip inside and an irregular slip on the exterior. They have relatively wide, flat, string-cut bases and simple rim-form modes which at times can manifest a slight thickening on the exterior (as in No. 2). Though Wright concluded that these dishes entered the mainstream of

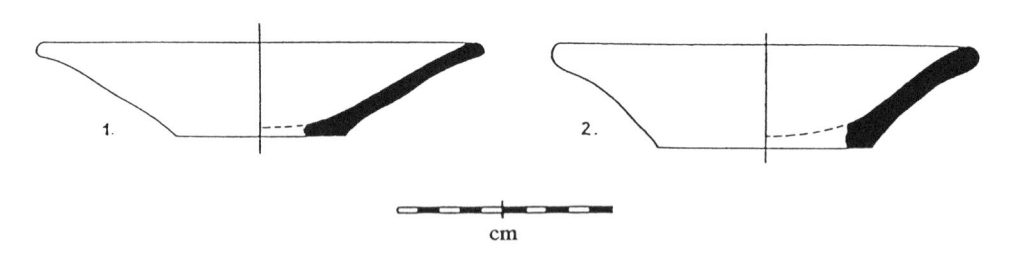

SS III, Fig. 6:1-2

ceramic tradition only from the latter half of the ninth century on, he believed that their origins slightly predated that period.[164] Various problems with his supporting evidence, however, militated against that position.[165] Holladay, in turn, too quickly accepted Wright's inclination and placed the parallel from PP 2 (Fig. 3:3) in his 870-840 BCE period without offering corroborating examples.[166] He also placed the PP 2 specimen in his "Type Bp" group of "platter bowls" and thought of it as "probably a cheap version" of the PP 3 bowl series presented in *SS III*, Fig. 4:13-19.[167] All this seems questionable. The PP 2 dish shows a diameter of only 17 or 18 cm (not enough to merit calling it a "platter"), while all the putative PP 3 descendants exceed 22 cm in top width.[168] Further, the base forms, rims, and often the sidewalls themselves differ in the PP 3 group.[169] Importantly, many items within the PP 3 assemblage revealed a coarser ware, a darker red slip, and an absence of burnishing (at least for *SS III*, Fig. 4:13-16), all of which would indicate an earlier date for them than for *SS III*, Fig. 3:3, from PP 2.

---

[164] G. E. Wright, "Israelite Samaria and Iron Age Chronology," *BASOR* 155 (1959), 27 (hereafter *Wright*).

[165] For example, he cited as a parallel an example from Hazor, Stratum VII, and mistakenly assigned it to Stratum VIII (see *AIS-I*, 114, n. 36).

[166] *Holladay*, Fig. 6:I.

[167] *Holladay*, 189.

[168] The present PP 4 bowls show diameters of roughly 21 cm (No. 1) and 19 cm (No. 2).

[169] For a full discussion of these PP 3 platters, see *AIS-I*, 184-90.

PP 4: HOUSE FLOORS — POTTERY

The PP 4 examples in *SS III*, Fig. 6:1-2, then, actually provide closer parallels to the PP 2 bowl than do the PP 3 vessels cited by Holladay. In fact, a good illustration of this style bowl does not appear in the plate of figures for PP 3; one sees only a possible prototype, with dirty buff ware and pinkish slip on both the interior and exterior, in *SS III*, Fig. 4:13. While the style of *SS III*, Fig. 6:1-2 may have appeared in the latter half of the ninth century, it seems to have flourished primarily during the middle two quarters of the eighth century BCE. Parallels from Hazor–Stratum V, Megiddo–Stratum III, Tell el-Farʿah (N)–Niveau II (compare examples from Chambon's Niveau VIId), and Yoqneʿam–Stratum 4[170] confirm this later dating.[171] Judging from these bowls, then, one cannot date the associated fills from which they came in Rooms *g* and *h* much earlier than the second or even third quarters of the eighth century BCE. Finally, I should reiterate here Reisner's observation that many of the Israelite ostraca found in the western sector of the summit compound appeared on sherds from bowls of this general type.[172] In this vein, I note that although Holladay dated the PP 2 dish in *SS III*, Fig. 3:3 between 870 and 840 BCE, he placed the similar PP 4 examples in his late group (from 750 BCE on).[173] I agree that *SS III*, Fig. 6:1 and 2 both represent basic eighth-century traditions. They amply demonstrate that simplicity in form does not necessarily imply an earlier rather than later date.

The second group of PP 4 bowls which share a chronological and morphological relationship (*SS III*, Fig. 6:4-5) comprises two thin-walled, carinated forms with ring bases and everted or outwardly splayed rims. These bowls, especially No. 5, reflect advances made on the series seen in PP 3, *SS III*, Fig. 4:10-12.[174] In the PP 4 group, the walls are thinner, the clay better levigated, and the ring- or pedestal base has both shortened and narrowed to a kind of hollowed, disc-like form. Item 4 exhibits a rather low riding carination, while No. 5 shows a carination so sharp that it actually results in a very shallow, smoothed groove just above it. In No. 4, the sidewall above the point of carination thickens toward the top and ends in a slightly angular, incut type of bevelled rim.[175] Good late ninth to early

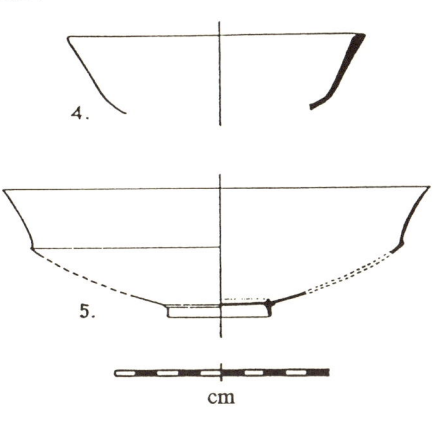

SS III, Fig. 6:4-5

---

[170]*T. Yoqneʿam* [2], Fig. 8:1 (Areas A3, A4, and B2).

[171]See the discussion and full references in *AIS-I*, 114-15. Compare also the close parallel from the late Iron Age II at Tell en-Naṣbeh (*TN II*, Pl. 68:1549).

[172]*AIS-I*, 115, n. 43.

[173]*Holladay*, 130, n. 116.

[174]See *AIS-I*, 181-84 for a comparative analysis of these forms.

[175]Compare the nonstratified example in *SS III*, Fig. 14:8, from S Tombs 107, though the upper

eighth-century parallels for this rim-form mode are available from Tell el-Farʿah (N),[176] Shechem[177] and Gezer.[178] As far as I can tell, however, the complete black (carbonized) ware of this Samaria exemplar remains quite rare. The upper sidewall of No. 5 continues to narrow toward a simple, pointed rim profile. Another Gezer rim from the Iron IIC period offers the best parallel for this style.[179] As noted in the excavation report from Samaria, the very fine, pinkish ware of No. 5 most distinguishes it from earlier samples exhibiting similar forms.[180] This vessel represents one of the most impressive pieces within the entire assemblage of PP 4 pottery. It is regrettable, therefore, that recording ambiguities cloud its original provenance. For the present, I may conclude that the evolution which this bowl displays in both form and ware beyond antecedent types at Megiddo,[181] Taʿanach,[182] and Tell en-Naṣbeh[183] in the north, and at Lachish,[184] Beth-Shemesh,[185] and Tell Beit Mirsim[186] in the south—not to mention the advances over earlier pieces from Samaria itself, as in Fig. 4:12 (PP 3)—precludes placing this item any earlier than the mid-eighth century BCE.[187] Yet I believe the antecedents for this stylish but angular form may extend back to the older cyma-style bowl.[188] Entry No. 4, on the other hand, likely belongs to a slightly earlier

---

sidewall displays a more uniform thickness than that seen on the PP 4 bowl. See also Fig. 17:4 (from a disturbed area of Summit Strip Qk), which exhibits a similar form though with thicker walls.

[176]*Chambon*, Pl. 57:5-7; compare also 58:12 (all from Niveau VIId).

[177]See *Holladay*, Fig. 13:B, from Locus 1641 at Shechem.

[178]*Gezer II*, Pl. 33:28 (Field II, Strata 6A-5B/A = late ninth to early eighth centuries BCE). This particular vessel came from the "disaggregated destruction debris" of Locus 2118 (see p. 117) and may, therefore, belong to the earlier part of that time span.

[179]See *Gitin*, Pl. 24:2 (Field VII, Stratum V = Iron Age IIC period, spanning primarily the late eighth and seventh centuries BCE).

[180]*SS III*, 115, which draws a comparison to the rim profile seen in *Megiddo I*, Pl. 28:93a (Stratum V).

[181]*Megiddo I*, Pl. 24:56 (Strata IV-III). For a possible morphological prototype at this site, see *Megiddo I*, Pl. 28:93a (labeled Strata V-IV), though all other attributes (brown ochre ware; blue-black core; dark red wash; hand + wheel burnishing) predate and differ considerably from those seen on the Samaria bowl.

[182]*Taʿanach*, Figs. 45:1; 46:4; 48:1-14 (Period IIB).

[183]*TN II*, Pl. 54:1217.

[184]*Lachish III*, Pl. 98:571-575.

[185]*AS-II*, Pl. XXXII:64, 68 (Iron I); *AS-IV*, Pl. LXIII:23-27 (Iron II; Nos. 23 and 25 appear considerably deeper), though none of these near-parallels even approaches the quality and craftsmanship apparent in the Samaria exemplar.

[186]*TBM I*, Pls. 64:9, 16; 65:5, 7-8 (Stratum A).

[187]See my conclusions regarding the related PP 3 forms in *AIS-I*, 184.

[188]One can see the possible evolutionary relationship in late Iron I-early Iron II samples such as *AS-IV*, Pl. LXIII:11 and 12.

PP 4: HOUSE FLOORS — POTTERY

period, possibly even near the close of the ninth century BCE (though one may also compare the rim-form mode and continuous burnishing techniques of No. 4 with a mid-eighth-century piece from Ta'anach[189]).

Perhaps the earliest samples among the PP 4 group of bowls include Nos. 6 and 7. Both stem from a tradition of round-sided bowls with flat or rounded bases and relate typologically to a class of vessel seen in my previous analysis of both Pottery

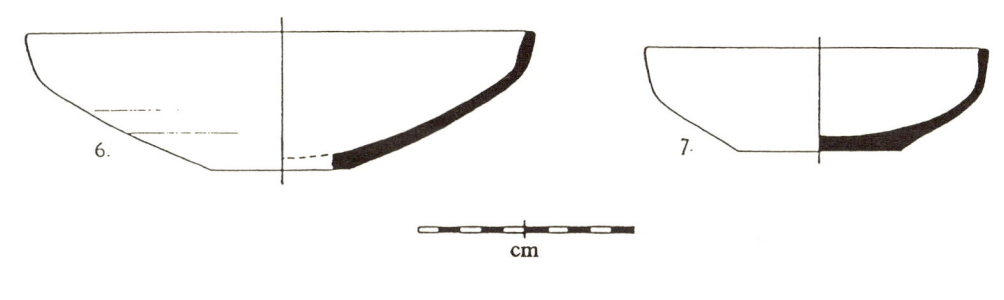

SS III, Fig. 6:6-7

Periods 2 and 3 (compare *SS III*, 3:10 and 4:4 with 6:6; also 4:3, 5 with 6:7). Traits that distinguish these bowls from other Iron I-Iron II transitional forms include:

> their more rounded sides and rounded (vs. inturned) rim forms [contrast the slightly inturned rims on *SS III*, Figs. 3:1 and 4:1-2 from PP 2-3, as well as 7:3 from PP 4, with Fig. 7:3 from PP 4]. The curvature of the sidewalls appears smooth and completely non-angular. It is usually strongest in the upper one-third of the body but does not develop into full carination.... These bowls have simple, rounded rims, occasionally with a thickened or bulbous top ... [No. 7]. On some vessels, the upper walls bend in slightly, producing a mildly inverted stance.[190]

Judging from the descriptions provided in the official pottery report, only an advance in firing techniques seems to differentiate these PP 4 bowls from their antecedents in PP 3. This produced a harder, ringing ware as over against the coarser ware seen in PP 3; the PP 3 sampling, however, actually exhibits thinner sidewalls than do the vessels from PP 4. Otherwise, the color of the basic material appears the same in both phases (light reddish-brown to purplish-red), and both groups show the presence of limestone grits. Apparently neither the PP 3 nor the PP 4 examples exhibited techniques of burnishing,[191] and Kenyon herself observed the similarity in form between *SS*

---

[189]*Ta'anach*, Fig. 74:4, from Period IV, dated to 750-732 BCE.

[190]*AIS-I*, 175.

[191]Kenyon noted that some of the form parallels that she drew for these Samaria vessels exhibited traces of burnishing, whereas the Samaria group did not (e.g., see her description of *SS III*, Fig. 4:4 and the parallel from Lachish). A causal relationship may exist between the increased use of this new, harder

III, Fig. 6:7 (PP 4), and the earlier group from PP 3.[192] A good Iron I parallel in form, though with burnishing, is available from Tell Qiri in the western Jezreel Valley.[193]

Kenyon's remarks that the PP 3 bowls differ from those of later periods in their ware, shape, and "sharp-cut bases,"[194] then, remains generally unpersuasive. Morphologically, the PP 3-4 forms are quite compatible, and the bases of *SS III*, Fig. 6:6-7 (especially 7) appear just as sharply cut as any of their PP 3 predecessors. Only a single attribute relating to ware (appreciable hardness) actually distinguishes *SS III*, Fig. 6:6-7 (and Fig. 3:10 of PP 2[195]) from slightly earlier members of the same basic class.[196] According to Kenyon, bowls of this hard, ringing ware appeared but remained relatively rare in PP 4, and became common only in PP 6.[197] As a larger group, all these vessels relate as well to Iron Age I trends seen in *SS III*, Fig. 1:2 (PP 1)[198] and elsewhere,[199] and may also bear some affiliation to the earlier cyma forms. While parallels for the double ring base of *SS III*, Fig. 3:6 (PP 2) remain difficult to locate,[200] a well preserved bowl from tenth-century levels at Beth-Shan shows that this style sometimes appeared on vessels similar to No. 6.[201] These early variants may extend down as far

---

ware and the decline or lack of burnishing that had become so popular during the tenth century BCE.

[192] *SS III*, 115.

[193] *T. Qiri*, Fig. 15:1 (Area D, Stratum VIII).

[194] *SS III*, 109.

[195] See the discussion in *AIS-I*, 112-13. Holladay also noted the comparison between 6:6 and 3:10 (see *Holladay*, 130, n. 114 and Fig. 23:D).

[196] Consequently, I can refer the reader to the parallels cited in my comparative analysis of this style bowl in *AIS-I*, 175-78. In terms of form alone, I may also note the similarities between Fig. 6:7 and the bar-handle bowl from PP 1 shown in *SS III*, Fig. 1:3, though the latter exhibits a slightly more flattened rim-form mode which resulted in a slight inner and outer lip. Unlike 6:7, the PP 1 entry also showed a thick, purple-red interior slip with continuous ring burnishing and an irregularly applied slip and burnishing technique on the exterior.

[197] *SS III*, 115.

[198] See my comments in *AIS-I*, 81-82 and 175, nn. 79-80.

[199] For example, compare *SS III*, Fig. 6:6 and *Beth-Shan*, James, Fig. 59:4 (Lower Level V = tenth century BCE down to Shishak's invasion), though the latter has a smaller diameter and the stance of the sidewall above the break is vertical-to-inverted as opposed to slightly everted.

[200] See my earlier comments in *AIS-I*, 118-19.

[201] *Beth-Shan*, James, Fig. 59:10 (Lower Level V); compare Fig. 19:1 from Block B-2, though this is called a "disk base" in the narrative (p. 64). For further corroborating evidence from Samaria itself, though from a nonstratified context, see *SS III*, Fig. 17:1-3, a small group of fine ware bowls, which Kenyon believed represented the only clearly early (PP 1-2) pottery of all that published in her "General List" (*SS III*, 134). A ring base coupled with an unusually thick bottom gives another bowl (?) from Al Mina, Syria, a similar look (see J. du Plat-Taylor, "The Cypriot and Syrian Pottery from Al-Mina, Syria," *Iraq* 21 [1959], 80, Fig. 6:41). For a possible later variant of the double-ring base, see E. N. Lugenbeal and J. A. Sauer, "Seventh-Sixth Century B.C. Pottery from Area B at Heshbon," *AUSS* 10 (1972), Pl. X:549. According to the authors (p. 60), "sherd 549 is the only double step-cut base in the

PP 4: HOUSE FLOORS — POTTERY

as the Iron I-Iron II transition,[202] and their PP 4 descendants do not seem to belong much later than the mid-ninth century BCE.[203]

I now turn, finally, to *SS III*, Fig. 6:3. Holladay places this saucer/platter, together with the one shown in *SS III*, Fig. 7:3, in his 860 or 840 BCE group, i.e., among the earliest exemplars of pottery published from PP 4. The form exhibits a ring base, slightly bowed sidewalls of uniform thickness, and a simple, rounded rim form that is unaltered by tapering, in- or outcutting, flattening, etc. Its reddish- to purplish-brown ware and sizable, white limestone inclusions are consonant with attributes of other forms stemming from this period. The form bears a close resemblance to another from PP 3 seen in *SS III*, Fig. 4:13, except that the sidewalls of 6:3 flex outward slightly more and the ware is once again darker (red to purple versus a softer fabric of a dirty buff color). Figure 6:3 also represents a clear advance over the narrower and pudgier PP 2 saucer bowl attested in Fig. 3:2.[204] Good, early morphological parallels—though with solid, disc-like bases—appear in the south at Beth-Shemesh[205] and in the north at Beth-Shan.[206] As shown by the descendant Iron Age IIB-C forms from Tell en-Naṣbeh,[207] the rim on this style bowl eventually came to display a flattened, outcut mode which produced a bevelled edge around the top.

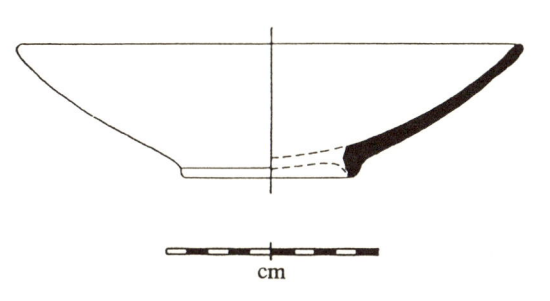

SS III, Fig. 6:3

Clearly, the chronological and morphological range of the bowls published as representatives of PP 4 speaks to the very mixed nature of the deposits which yielded

---

corpus. (The drawing is rather unclear; looked at from the bottom this base has a small central disk around which are two further ridges or rings.)"

[202] *AIS-I*, 178.

[203] Holladay seemed to take the similar, though later, bowl presented in *Hazor II*, LXXIX:6 (Stratum VB) "as either accidental of the end-product of another developmental tradition" (*Holladay*, 198). Several differences distinguish the Hazor piece from the Samaria bowls under discussion: e.g., the former is deeper, displays a ring base and a slightly more pointed edge on the rim, and shows a smooth red slip on the exterior walls, over the rim, and down to the break in the interior sidewall. Overall, he concluded that this class of bowl represents "a fairly distinctive, but chronologically unhelpful (?) vessel-form mode possibly having its floruit in the period ca. 840-810 B.C." (*Holladay*, 198).

[204] Though Kenyon labeled both Figs. 3:2 and 6:3 "saucer bowls," the latter displays a significantly broader diameter (nearly 24 cm vs. 17 cm for 3:2) and appears shallower (judging from the depth-to-diameter ratio) than the PP 2 bowl. Consequently, one should perhaps refer to 3:2 as a "saucer *bowl*" and to 6:3 as a "saucer *plate* or *platter*" to preserve their distinction in the literature.

[205] *AS-II*, Pl. XXXIII:3 (Iron Age I).

[206] *Beth-Shan*, James, Fig. 63:3 (Upper Level V; tenth century BCE).

[207] *TN II*, Pls. 59:1354 and 68:1561 (the latter also has a flat vs. ring base).

them. These forms appear to span the better part of a century, and their basic, utilitarian nature precludes us from thinking of them as possible heirlooms which were intentionally preserved. The latest samples belong in the mid-eighth century BCE, if not later still (Nos. 1-2). The first of these fragments (No. 1) came from Wall 136, or perhaps from the deposit used to block a doorway which once passed through that structure (see p. 20 above). As I have shown, the blockage remained of uncertain date; Kenyon assigned it variously to BP III, IV, and V. The partitioning off of Room *g* from Room *h*, then, may have occurred as late as the third quarter of the eighth century BCE. The workers recovered the second late specimen (No. 2) from a hard, white, plaster floor level (Layer IX) in Room *h*. Collectively, this evidence seems to suggest a functional life for these rooms somewhere in middle two quarters of the eighth century.

SS III, Fig. 6:5a-b, which I assigned to my "middle group," may belong to this same general time period. Despite the quality in ware and design, it remains difficult, on stratigraphic grounds, to utilize this piece in my chronological considerations. The questionable number of fragments actually represented by the entry, the muddled recording of its original provenance (comprising multiple layers in two separate rooms), and the admission that its context (or at least one of them) likely included contaminating soil and materials from Late Roman quarrying activity (see p. 31), force us regrettably to eliminate this impressive piece from further consideration.

The earliest bowls discussed above (Nos. 3, 6, 7) derived from a series of closely laid deposits in Room *k*. Beneath the hard surface and paving stones of Layer V (pp. 57-58) lay at least two earlier floors surfaces, Layers VI (assigned by Kenyon to BP IVa) and VII (BP IV). Layer VIII comprised the dark, leveling fill beneath the last level. As shown in Table 7, bowl Nos. 6 and 7 were associated stratigraphically with the earliest of the floors in this room, Layer VII. Another early specimen (No. 3) came from the fill beneath that surface. (Again, dubious recording data for another fragment from the item of fine ware just mentioned—No. 5b—compromise any conclusion which I might draw from it here.) Unsettling questions regarding the eventual use of apparently discarded fragments cast a further pall over the credibility of these entries. It appears, however, that at least one early fragment survives from the fill beneath the first floor level recorded in Room *k* (No. 3) and one early fragment from the floor matrix itself (No. 6). This hardly constitutes adequate evidence on which to base historical interpretation and, in my judgment, the earliest floor level in Room *k* could conceivably range in date from mid-to-late ninth to early eighth centuries BCE.

To this point, the scanty evidence available to us (without further field exploration) may indicate that some of the earliest deposits in Room *k*—levels which historically belong with the eastward continuation of the series of nicer Rooms *a-d* (see fig. 5)—became mixed in the process of excavation and the ensuing reports with later historical phases in Rooms *g* and *h*. Given the *terminus ante quem* of the latest materials thus far assigned to BP IV, however, one cannot reliably date this complex of rooms much earlier than the mid-eighth century BCE.

PP 4: HOUSE FLOORS — POTTERY

b. Cooking Pots

This class of vessel dominates the PP 4 assemblage taken from the two clusters of rooms situated north of the main courtyard and thereby tends to corroborate my conclusion that this general vicinity functioned mainly as a food preparation area. Two-

SS III Published Figure	Registry No. (* = marked for discard)	Strip	Coordinates	Feature	Local Layer
6:25	* Q 2328a	Qk	▶ Btw TT2-TT3	Room *k*	VII
6:26	Q 5058	Qn	502.503	Room *n*	XI?/XIIa.b
6:27	Q 5061	Qn	502.503	Room *n*	XIa
6:28	Q 5059	Qn	502.503	Room *n*	XII
6:29	Q 5060	Qn	502.503	Room *n*	Xa
6:30	Q 5054	Qn	502.503	Room *n*	Xa
6:32	Q 5066a	Qn	509.126	Room *j*	X
6:33	* Q 2532	Qk	» N of TT2	Room *j*	IXr
6:34	Q 5056	Qn	502.503	Room *n*	XI
6:35	* Q 2328b	Qk	▶ Btw TT2-TT3	Room *k*	VII
6:36	Q 5055	Qn	502.503	Room *n*	Xa
6:37	Q 5065	Qn	502.503	Room *n*	XI (XIa?)
6:38	Q 5057	Qn	502.503	Room *n*	XI
6:39	Q 5062	Qk	120.121.19.126	Room *h*	Wall 151(?)
6:40	Q 5063	Qn	502.503	Room *n*	XIa

Provenance Data:
PP4 Cooking Pots from Area Labeled "House Floors"

Table 8

thirds of the fragments presented came from the putative Room *n*, situated to the east of the complex of irregularly built chambers which yielded the collection of bowls discussed above (*g-h-j-k*). Otherwise, Room *h* produced only one rim fragment, while Rooms *j* and *k* yielded two each. The four sherds which did not derive from any of these rooms appeared either in the area to their south, in the segment labeled *North Courtyard* (*SS III*, Fig. 6:31), or from inside the casemate chambers to their north (*SS III*, Fig. 7:6-8; see the appropriate sections below for my comments on these two groups). Because of the relative size of this overall group, I have once again opened my analysis by presenting the primary data pertaining to the individual findspots (see Table 8; compare Appendix A).

At this point, it seems judicious to organize my treatment of these cooking pots according to the individual rooms in which they were found. Once my comparative analysis allows me to reach conclusions on typological grounds, I shall conclude my discussion by regrouping the fragments according to their form. Following a brief review of the evolution of cooking pot forms at other sites, then, my comments will proceed from Room *h* to Rooms *j* and *k*, then finally to Room *n*. First, I can note from Table 8 that three entries claim both dubious information regarding their provenance coordinates (▸/») and notations designating them as discards (*). That this situation attends both pieces taken from Room *k* effectively removes this chamber from the discussion. Room *j* will also exist under a shadow of suspicion, since the same holds true for one of the two fragments found there.

Though most cooking pots appear with burned-out bottoms, the Late Bronze Age—Iron Age evolution of their shoulders and rims remains quite traceable, making them good diagnostic indicators for chronological considerations.[208] I have outlined the developments in the form of this vessel elsewhere;[209] here, I need only reiterate the basic sequence. The everted, triangular rims with rounded lip of the LBA[210] become noticeably inverted near the outset of the Iron Age.[211] During the course of the twelfth and eleventh centuries BCE, this basic rim form elongated but maintained its outer, lower flange.[212] The outside face of this elongated style generally gave a slightly concave, or "grooved," appearance (which resulted from simply pinching the flat rim), though it could also remain flat at times and exhibit either an inverted or virtually erect stance.[213] In the eleventh century particularly, the rounded lip on the rim often maintained a relatively sharp or pointed edge.[214] In addition, cooking pots at many sites in both the north and south began to display the use of handles during this same period.[215]

---

[208] For insightful comments regarding some practical aspects behind the shape of cooking pots and the fabric used to manufacture them, see M. M. E. Vilders, "Some Remarks on the Production of Cooking Pots in the Jordan Valley," *PEQ* 125 (1993), 149-56, esp. 150-53. See also G. M. Crowfoot's seldom cited but fascinating, firsthand investigation of the morphology and manufacturing techniques of modern cooking pots in Kufr Lebbad, Sinjil, Balata, Jeba, Nablus, and other villages in the district around Samaria (G. M. Crowfoot, "Pots, Ancient and Modern," *PEQ* [October, 1932], 179-87).

[209] *AIS-I*, 31-34, 60-62, 82-83, 119-121, 160. The numerous examples cited there help corroborate the following brief survey.

[210] E.g., see *Taʿanach*, Fig. 2:1-8 (Period IA Cuneiform Tablet Building).

[211] Transition types appear in *Taʿanach*, Fig. 14:11-13 (Period IB Drainpipe Structure), on their way to the Iron I variations seen in Figs. 29:1-5 (Period IIA), 49:1-3 (Period IIB Cultic Structure), 66:8-35 (Period IIB Cistern 74).

[212] E.g., *T. Qasîle* [2], Fig. 23:8-15 (Stratum XI); *Beth-Shan*, James, Fig. 2:2 (Locus 1094); *Hazor III-IV*, Pl. CCIX:1-12 (Stratum IX).

[213] *TAH*, 7, Fig. 10 (Stratum III); *Megiddo II*, Pl. 85:13-16 (primarily Stratum VI); etc.

[214] See *AIS-I*, 83 (and notes) for numerous examples from Taʿanach, Tell Keisan, Tell Beit Mirsim, Gibeah, Tell Abu Hawām, Beth-Shemesh, Megiddo, Hazor, Beth-Shan, Lachish, Afula, Tel Mevorakh, and Deir ʿAllā.

[215] *Megiddo II*, Pl. 85:12 (Stratum VI; with somewhat unique horizontal handles); *Tell Keisan*, Pl. 77:2 (Stratum 9c); *Gezer I*, Figs. 26:9, 21 (Field I, Stratum 3); 27:1 (Field I, Stratum 4); 35:15 (Field I, Stratum 7) and 21, 24 (Field I, Stratum 8); *Gezer II*, Figs. 29:30 (Field II, Stratum 9?); 30:7 (Field II,

Sometime in the mid-to-late tenth century, a popular new rim-form mode—a shorter version of the concave, flanged rim—became the leading form until its displacement by a thickened, notched variety in the mid-ninth century BCE (at most sites generally by 840 BCE).[216] This hallmark type effectively replaced completely the older, flanged-style rim during the mid-to-late ninth century. It continued as the normative mode in the eighth century and, in fact, for the duration of the Iron Age II period, though it declined in Judah during the latter half of the seventh century BCE.[217]

The excavators recovered the rim fragment in *SS III*, Fig. 6:39, from Room *h*. The field records remain ambiguous, however, as to whether its original findspot related to a deposit associated with Wall 151 or with Wall 157.[218] These features basically defined the western and eastern borders of Room *h*, respectively, and both had invasive robber trenches associated with them. Though Kenyon did not provide the diameter of the vessel's mouth, this example undoubtedly represents the open, shallow-type cooking pot with its short, inverted rim with a thickened and rounded interior side and a squared notch on its outer side. It constitutes perhaps the clearest example I have shown thus far of Aharoni's and Amiran's "Late Shallow Type" bowl, which appeared throughout the country around 840 BCE. Good parallels appear at virtually all sites, including Hazor,[219] Megiddo,[220] Ta'anach,[221] Tell Yoq-

SS III, Fig. 6:39

Stratum 9); *AS-IV*, Pl. 59:17; 62:31, 36 (all Stratum III); *T. Masos*, Pls. 145:8; 149:3; 175:4 (Stratum II).

[216] For the notched variety, see *Hazor I*, Pls. LV:1-10 (Stratum V); LXXII:1-5 (Strata V-IV); *Hazor II*, Pls. LXIX:4-19 (Stratum VI); LXXXV:1-12 (Stratum VA). See also the discussion of this so-called Late Shallow Type in *Aharoni-Amiran*. The preceding, short triangular rim with flange then became known as the "Early Shallow Type" of cooking pot.

[217] M. & Y. Aharoni, 76. Even so, this style continued in use among the southern coastal sites throughout the Iron IIC period (see the comments and references to Ashdod in *T. Qasîle* [2], 109, n. 9).

[218] The field registry stored at the Rockefeller Museum in Jerusalem (*Sabastya Qn, 1935*) associates it with Wall 157; on the other hand, Kenyon's hand-written, prepublication draft of *SS III* (from the PEF in London) assigns it to Wall 151.

[219] *Hazor III-IV*, Pls. CCXV:7 (Stratum VII = late ninth century); CLXXXIV:6, 9 (without handles), 13 (no handles), 14 and CCXX:23 (Stratum VI = early eighth century; compare CLXXXIV:7 and 10 for the flattened interior lip); CCXXVII:11 and CCXXXI:6 (Stratum VA = mid-eighth century). Compare also *Hazor II*, Pl. LXXIX:20 (Stratum VB). As seen from this corpus, this style usually appeared with handles. *Hazor II*, Pl. LXIX:18 (Stratum VI) shows a variant form, with the underside of the groove or notched area appearing convex versus concave.

[220] *Megiddo I*, Pl. 39:1, 3, 5-6, 8, 12 (the last two parallel nicely the smooth, interior groove situated just below the bulbous inside lip) (Strata IV-I).

[221] *Ta'anach*, Fig. 76:6-7 (Period V = early seventh century BCE).

neʿam,[222] Tell Qasîle,[223] and Ashdod.[224] Some of these rims became so squat that they essentially lost their distinctive outer flange.[225] The early excavators at Megiddo cited this style cooking pot as an illustration of "the strong cultural continuity that was characteristic of Megiddo from Solomonic times to at least the beginning of Stratum I."[226] Though their cultural interpretation seems overstated, the observation does speak to the ubiquitous nature of this rim form during the Iron II period, with a *terminus post quem* of around 840 BCE.[227]

Rim Nos. 32 and 33 came from Room *j*, just to the northeast of *h*, from Layers X and IXr, respectively. As noted, wary recording data for the latter fragment may help explain why either the excavators or the museums involved in the excavations (PEF or Rockefeller) at some point designated it as a discard. The former piece (No. 32, in like manner, represents the only sherd published for PP 4 from Segment *509.126*, and questions surround the precise relationship of this area to Rooms *j* and *l* (see my discussion on pp. 50-52 above). If, as suggested, the segment and the fragment both belong to Room *j*, then Layer X appears to have constituted a BP IV floor level dating to the early eighth century.[228] Rim No. 33 appears to derive from the imported fill of subfloor makeup (see pp. 47-48), a context for which the *terminus post quem* must remain open. Typologically, however, No. 32 seems to predate No. 33. Yet both fragments could easily reflect late tenth- to mid-ninth-century transitional types, with their flanges pushed upward but not yet squared into a true notch. Entry No. 32 maintains a rather pointed lip and concave outer face,[229]

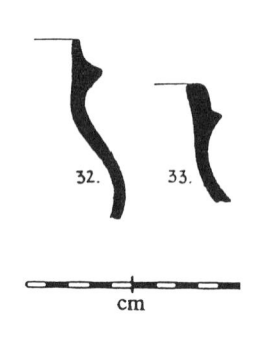

SS III, Fig. 6:32-33

---

[222]*T. Yoqneʿam* [1], Fig. 11:15 (with handles; from levels tentatively dated to the ninth-eighth centuries BCE). Compare also *T. Yoqneʿam* [3], Fig. 12:1 (Area A, Stratum 10 = ninth-eighth centuries); Fig. 10:4 (Area A, Stratum 9, tentatively dated to the seventh century BCE).

[223]*T. Qasîle* [2], Fig. 56:7-11 (Stratum VII). The interior lip on this type sometimes, though rarely, appears quite flattened, as in Fig. 56:13 (also Stratum VII; compare *Hazor III-IV*, Pl. CLXXXIV:10 [Stratum VI]).

[224]*Ashdod II-III*, Fig. 55:5-6 (esp. No. 5) (Area D, Strata 2-1).

[225]See *Gezer II*, Fig. 32:36 (Field II, Stratum 6A). Holladay referred to this style as a "rolled-rim cooking pot with gentle carination" (*Gezer II*, 66 and n. 104), though his suggested parallels are not always apt ones. *Gezer II*, Fig. 35:20 (Field II, Stratum 4) offers another basic comparison to No. 39 from Samaria, but one in which the potter has not cut the notch quite as sharply.

[226]*Megiddo I*, 172.

[227]A very nice parallel from Samaria itself appears under the description "small one-handled jug" in *HES I*, Fig. 160:7.

[228]See fig. 19; also p. 52, n. 123 for stratigraphic correlations relating to this surface.

[229]Compare the early pot from *T. Qasîle* [2], Fig. 24:17 (Stratum XI, ca. 1100-1050 BCE).

PP 4: HOUSE FLOORS — POTTERY

while No. 33 displays a thickened upper lip with flattened top and a tool-cut upper flange.[230] Other parallels at Tell el-Farʿah (N) capture well this progression from flanged, triangular rims to the more squat, notched variety.[231]

Supposedly, *SS III*, Fig. 6:25 and 35 both came from Layer VII of the Segment *Between TT2-TT3* in Room *k*; I have, however, already noted the tremendous ambiguity which manifests itself in the records concerning these items. Entry No. 25 exhibits an upright, elongated, triangular rim with a flat outer face. This rim-form mode, together with those whose outer face displays only a slightly convex profile, occasionally bears incised potter's marks of various styles (particularly at sites located in the western Jezreel Valley—northern Sharon Plain region).[232] This rim strongly resembles another specimen from Pottery Period 1, *SS III*, Fig. 1:20, though it slightly exceeds the latter specimen in overall length (3 cm vs. 2.5 cm). Still, the many parallels which I have elsewhere cited for the PP 1 fragment apply here as well.[233] Some of the earliest Iron I examples of this erect, pointed-rim style are available from Beth-Shan;[234] corroboration for this early appearance has come more recently from across the Jordan River, at Tell es-Saʿidiyeh.[235] In the south, samples from Lachish[236] and Beth-Shemesh[237] confirm that

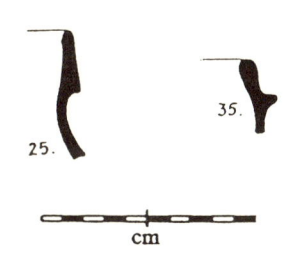

***SS III*, Fig. 6:25, 35**

---

[230]*AS-IV*, Pl. LXIII:29 (Stratum IIb, Room 75), though this example from Beth-Shemesh is more inverted and the top of the outer flange is not as trimmed as on the Samaria fragment.

[231]Compare *T. Farʿah-RB* [62], Fig. 19:5 (compare also the rim on the large bowl in No. 14) and Fig. 19:4, albeit with handles (all from Niveau intermédiaire, Période 3 = mid-ninth century BCE).

[232]Virtually all marked cooking pots belong to Aharoni's and Amiran's "Early Shallow Type," and at Qiri most marked rims dated to the tenth century, with only a few earlier examples (*T. Qiri*, 123). For obvious reasons, the notch that developed in the mid-ninth-century rims rendered them less suitable for inscribing. See *T. Yoqneʿam* [1], Fig. 12:1-4; *T. Yoqneʿam* [3], Fig. 12:13-14 (Area A, Stratum 11 = tenth century BCE); see also the related notes and parallels on p. 53. For a full discussion of this phenomenon, see *T. Qiri*, 224-35; compare also p. 74, Photos 24-25; p. 77, Fig. 12:1-9.

[233]See *AIS-I*, 82-83. This rim also bears a likeness to *SS III*, Fig. 3:13 and 17, though these PP 2 attestations appear slightly concave on their outer faces. *T. Qiri*, Fig. 16:4 (Area D, Stratum VIII) provides an excellent morphological parallel from the Iron Age I period.

[234]*Beth-Shan*, James, Fig. 50:12 (Stratum VI = twelfth century BCE).

[235]*Saʿidiyeh 1*, Fig. 20:1, 4 (Area AA, Stratum XII = late twelfth century BCE).

[236]*Lachish III*, Pl. 104:685 (from Tomb 120, late tenth century BCE). One should note that this tomb contained mixed contents resulting from a later phase of reuse. This situation necessitates that I distinguish between contiguous contexts labeled "Tomb 120-Burials" (late tenth century BCE) and "Tomb 120-Ossuary" (late seventh-early sixth centuries BCE; see *Lachish III*, 194-96). Though similar examples of this rim type sometimes appeared close to contexts assigned generally to Lachish Levels III-I, the official report noted that nearly all of these derived from "disturbed groups or open areas" and suggested that their true horizon lay in Levels VI-IV (*Lachish III*, 310).

[237]*AS-IV*, Pl. LXIII:32 (Stratum II, Room 334 = Iron Age IC-II).

this mode continued at least to the Iron I-Iron II transition period. Though the bottom of the triangular rim and the rounded groove beneath it likely functioned to provide a place to insert the fingers when lifting this vessel by its rim, even this vertical-rim style sometimes appears with handles added.[238]

Rim No. 35, with its rounded and somewhat thickened upper rim or lip and its flange pushed up to a horizontal position, postdates the previous fragment from Room k. A striking similarity exists between this mode and those seen previously in *SS III*, Fig. 3:19 and 26 (= PP 2), though No. 19 there displays a slightly more upright posture. These rims clearly approach the notched-rim style which typifies the mid-ninth-century "Late Shallow Type," a fact which both Wright[239] and Holladay[240] have correctly observed, but the technique of their manufacture continues to differ from that new style. As an example from Cistern 74 at Ta'anach confirms,[241] these rims were stretched up, then folded over on the exterior of the vessel as far down as the neck groove, with the rounded tip of the clay then pushed upward to shape the horizontal flange. The thickened upper rim which resulted, then, was achieved by a process of folding rather than pinching the fabric. An excellent mid-ninth-century parallel comes from Hazor,[242] while mid-to-late tenth-century antecedent forms appear in the reports from Ta'anach[243] and Tell Qasîle.[244]

The remainder and bulk of the cooking pot fragments presented in *SS III*, Fig. 6, came from a single segment excavated in Room n, namely *502.503*. The individual loci ranged from general Layer X to Layer XII, including various sub-deposits (Xa, XIa, XIIa.b). The recorded data pertaining to these items seem reliable, relatively speaking. The principal uncertainty centers on whether No. 26 derived from Local Layer XIa.b or XIIa.b, a question beyond solution at this point. Both appear to constitute secondary deposits of fill material. Categorized broadly, Nos. 26-30 and 38 demonstrate several variations on the elongated, flanged class of rim, while Nos. 34, 36-37, and 40 tend toward the subsequent, "grooved" or notched variety.

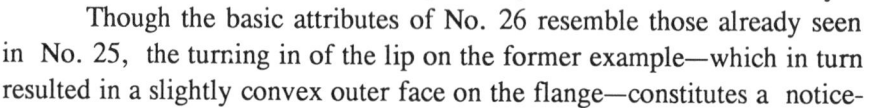

Though the basic attributes of No. 26 resemble those already seen in No. 25, the turning in of the lip on the former example—which in turn resulted in a slightly convex outer face on the flange—constitutes a notice-

SS III, Fig. 6:26

---

[238]Compare *T. Keisan*, Pl. 55:1 (Niveau 8). Rims often assume a more inverted stance when handles are present.

[239]See his comments regarding *SS III*, Fig. 3:25 and 26 in *Wright*, 21-2, n. 24; I have included Fig. 3:19 in this same category (*AIS-I*, 121).

[240]*Holladay*, 130, n. 114 and Fig. 61:N from Locus 1047 at Shechem.

[241]*Ta'anach*, Fig. 66:15 (Period IIB).

[242]*Hazor II*, Pl. LVII:4 (Stratum VIII).

[243]*Ta'anach*, Figs. 49:2 (Period IIB Cultic Structure) and 53:2, 4 (Period IIB, Cistern 69 deposit).

[244]*T. Qasîle* [2], Fig. 54:19 (Stratum IX).

able difference. Good parallels in the north from Ta'anach[245] and in the south at Lachish[246] confirm a tenth-century date for the overall class. Similar examples appear in reports from Afula,[247] Shechem,[248] 'Ai,[249] Tell Qasîle,[250] Gezer,[251] Beth-Shemesh,[252] and Tel Masos,[253] to name but a few. Nos. 27 and 28 appear very similar in design, though the lower barb on the former is cut rather more sharply. Together, they continue the tradition of the outer fold on the rim seen in Pottery Period 2, *SS III*, Fig. 3:16. Tell Qasîle[254] and Gezer[255] provide good comparisons for the overall class, while the early report from Megiddo[256] contains a particularly useful parallel for No. 28. A comparable rim from late eleventh-century levels at Tell Keisan appears with rather thick handles attached.[257] Though also similar, No. 29 has a somewhat thicker and more inverted rim, and the barb beneath the outer fold has been smoothed into a grooved pattern. In addition, the curvature of the upper sidewall or shoulder arcs in a more convex pattern than do those on Nos. 26-28. These features suggest a reasonably later date for this piece, perhaps nearer the mid-ninth century BCE. One may compare concurrent trends at Tell Qasîle[258] and apparently later ones at Tell 'Amal.[259]

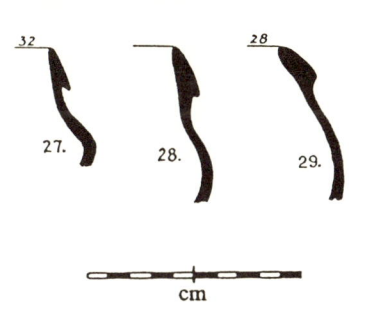

SS III, Fig. 6:27-29

---

[245]*Ta'anach*, Fig. 66:28 (Period IIB, Cistern 74 deposit).

[246]*Lachish III*, Pl. 104:693 (Locus 120; see n. 230 above).

[247]*'Afula*, Fig. 12:6, 8.

[248]See *Holladay*, Fig. 63:D (Locus 1645).

[249]*'Ai* [JM-K], Texte, 228; Atlas, Pl. LXXVII:1843.

[250]*T. Qasîle* [2], Fig. 33:15, 18 (Stratum IX).

[251]*Gezer II*, Fig. 29:29 (Field II, Stratum 9?).

[252]*AS-IV*, Pl. LXIII:31 (Stratum II, Room 315).

[253]*T. Masos*, Fig. 131:14.

[254]*T. Qasîle* [2], 44:28 (Stratum X).

[255]*Gezer IV*, Fig. 45:20 (Field VI, Stratum 4B/A = late eleventh-early tenth centuries), though this example appears slightly more inverted.

[256]*Megiddo I*, Pl. 40:16 (Strata V-IV, and earlier).

[257]*T. Keisan*, Pl. 63:1 (Niveau 9a/b).

[258]*T. Qasîle* [2], Fig. 55:8 (Stratum VIII).

[259]*T. 'Amal*, Fig. 7:9 (Niveaux I-II). The curvature of the upper sidewall appears slightly higher on this example. The date of these levels remained somewhat uncertain: "Il n'est donc pas possible de dater avec précision les niveaux I et II. La majeure partie de la céramique est typique du VIIIe siècle, et le reste, du VIIe siècle avant J.—C." (*T. 'Amal*, 328).

The cooking pot with subtly inverted, rounded rim seen in *SS III*, Fig. 6:30 seems to have developed alongside similar jug and bowl rims during the Iron Age I period.[260] The relatively narrow diameter of its mouth (only 18 cm compared to the usual 28-32 cm for the typical pot) prompts us to refer to this form as a cooking jug, though this same rim mode also occurred from its inception on full-sized pot forms.[261] The ratio of width to depth on the Samaria example would undoubtedly have given this vessel the appearance of a rather tall piece of kitchen crockery when compared to the usual pot style. Here, the body is globular rather than carinated. Despite its apparent Iron I origins, this form shows a functional life that spanned the tenth and extended into the ninth and eighth centuries BCE.[262] This style cooking jug (or jar) appears at number of sites, though never with great frequency at any given location. Yet, despite its broad chronological and relatively sparse numerical distributions, the tradition clearly had its period of greatest use (at least in the north) during the early-to-mid tenth century BCE.[263]

SS III, Fig. 6:30

The final rim amongst my "early group" from Room *n* appears in *SS III*, Fig. 6:38. It bears a strong resemblance to No. 31, recovered from the *Northern Courtyard* (see below), to an earlier specimen with handles from Pottery Period 1 (*SS III*, Fig. 1:21),[264] and, to a lesser extent, to a fragment from Pottery Period 2 (*SS III*, Fig.

---

[260] Compare *T. Qasîle* [2], Fig. 14:22 (Stratum XII = ca. 1150-1100 BCE) for a compatible jug rim, and Figs. 17:16, 22 (Stratum XII), 27:13 (Stratum XI), and 45:22 (Stratum X) for the cooking pot version; see Fig. 26:11 (Stratum XI) for a cooking jug. For the same on a deep bowl, see *Megiddo I*, Pl. 29:110 (Strata V-IV) and, from its nearby satellite site, *Taʿanach*, Fig. 42:1-2, 4 (Period IIB Cultic Structure), though the outside, lower edge of the rim fold is smoother on the exemplar from Samaria. Compare also the style of krater rim seen in *T. ʿAmal*, Fig. 14:10 (Niveau IV).

[261] Compare *Megiddo I*, Pl. 40:20 (Stratum V); *T. Yoqneʿam* [3], Fig. 12:10 (Area A, Stratum 11).

[262] *Gezer I*, Fig. 35:15 (Field II, Stratum 7 = early tenth century); *TN II*, Figs. 47:987, 994; 50:1072 (Iron II/ninth century); *TAH*, p. 22, No. 80 (Stratum III = tenth or early ninth century); *T. Qasîle* [2], Fig. 55:8 (Stratum VIII); *Megiddo I*, Pls. 5:118-119 (Strata III-II = through Iron IIC); 29:110 (Strata V-IV = down to late ninth century, with more inverted rim-form mode); *Hazor III-IV*, Pls. CCXLVII:24 (Stratum VII = late ninth century) and CLXXXIII:1 (Stratum VI = late ninth-early eighth century). For another late Iron I-Iron II series, see the examples classified as "CP Group IV: Cooking Jars" in *T. Qiri*, 143, Fig. 34; for a new assessment of Amiran's typology and distribution of cooking pots, see pp. 183-84; compare also the form labeled "storage jar" in Fig. 9:5 (Area D, Stratum VI).

[263] Compare similar, though not always exact, samples from *Taʿanach*, Figs. 21:5 (Period IIA = 1020-960 BCE); 42:1-4; 43:4 (though less inverted); 50:1 (all Period IIB = 960-918 BCE); *Megiddo I*, Pl. 20:115 (Stratum V); *Megiddo Tombs*, Pl. 39:14 (Tomb 37); *T. Yoqneʿam* [3], Fig. 12:10 (Area A, Stratum 11); *T. Qiri*, Figs. 13:2 (Area D, Stratum VIIA); 17:1 and 3 (Area D, Stratum VIIIA+B); 22:12 (Area C, Strata VA+B); 34:3-4 (Area D, Strata VIIIA and VIIA, respectively); *Beth-Shan*, James, Pl. 60:2 (Lower Level V); *Beth-Shan II*, PL. XLVI:17; *T. ʿAmal*, Figs. 9:5 and 8; 14:10 (Niveau IV); *T. Esdar*, Fig. 5:7; and passim.

[264] For a full discussion of the latter, see *AIS-I*, 60-62.

3:28).²⁶⁵ The sharply inverted stance, the rounded and even plump upper rim or lip, and the persistent flange which is now slightly pushed up, combine to help us locate a functional life for this style securely in the mid-eleventh to the mid-tenth centuries BCE, with its heaviest concentration falling in the latter part of that period (see the many parallels cited in *AIS-I*).²⁶⁶ Later exemplars of this mode, which overlap only slightly with the incipient notched variety of rim, generally have a more pronounced groove around the interior face of the rim.²⁶⁷ Otherwise, the tenth-century BCE date for this rim is secure enough to raise some caution against Holladay's intimation that it belongs only, or even mainly, in the mid-ninth century BCE.²⁶⁸

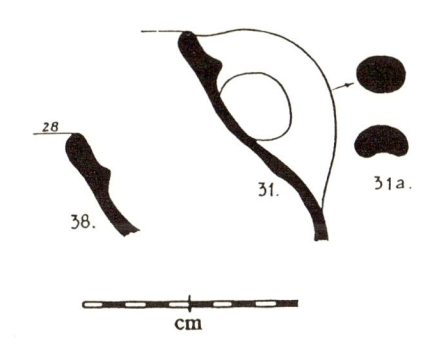

SS III, Fig. 6:31, 38

The thickened, nailhead lip profile, smooth exterior groove, and lower single ridge help identify No. 34 as a later development in the sequence of cooking pot forms. Rims with multiple ridges appear over the course of the eighth century, particularly on closed, globular cooking pot forms (with a more vertical rim stance) from sites in Judah, and are replaced by a single protruding ridge (in thinner, more metallic ware) sometime around the mid-seventh century BCE.²⁶⁹ Trends toward this style rim manifest themselves on other vessel types as well, as seen in antecedent pitcher rims from tenth-century Tell el-Farʿah (N)²⁷⁰ and krater rims from ninth- and eighth-century levels at sites like Hazor and Megiddo²⁷¹ (com-

SS III, Fig. 6:34

---

²⁶⁵See *AIS-I*, 119-21. Generally, the PP 4 rim appears a bit thicker than the one in 3:28.

²⁶⁶A rather close parallel from Transjordan, though with external flange not quite as pushed up, dates tentatively to the late tenth or very early ninth centuries BCE (*Saʿidiyeh 1*, Fig. 11:26 [Area AA, Stratum IX]). Other comparative data from this site, however, may indicate a slightly earlier appearance of this form in that region, since some samples there apparently date to the late twelfth century (Fig. 20:2-3, 5 [Area AA, Stratum XII]). At the time of this publication from Saʿidiyeh, the ceramic chronology remained open to revision in anticipation of more detailed study of the pottery excavated thus far.

²⁶⁷*Hazor II*, Pl. LVII:6 (without handles; Stratum VIII), 15 (with handles; presumably also Stratum VIII, but see the comments in *Hazor II*, 8-9).

²⁶⁸*Holladay*, 130, n. 114; further, many of the rims to which he appeals for relative data provide less than apt comparisons (e.g., see the examples in Fig. 63B-E).

²⁶⁹M. & Y. *Aharoni*, 76 and Figs. 2:4; 3:4. The single-ridge mode typifies many jug and decanter forms of the period as well.

²⁷⁰*Chambon*, Pl. 48:7 (Niveau VIIb), though the incipient nailhead is everted above the ridge.

²⁷¹For examples, compare *Hazor II*, Pl. LVI:3, 4, and 6 (Stratum VIII); *Hazor III-IV*, Pl. CCXXVII:4 (Stratum VA); *Megiddo II*, Pl. 28:88 (Strata IV-III). The flattened, nailhead rim-form mode, with or

pare also the jar rim in *SS III*, Fig. 6:14, but with the nailhead turned out rather than in). An even earlier possible prototype, for this cooking-pot rim appears at Beth-Shan,[272] though with the nailhead pushed downward to create a more prominent groove on the interior face of the rim area.[273] Another good tenth-century parallel from Tell Qasîle helps reveal the nascent trend toward this nailhead design,[274] as does a specimen from Beth-Shemesh in the south.[275] In short, I take this rim style to represent a somewhat elongated variation on the earlier notched rim-form mode, with the lengthening of the latter creating the smooth exterior groove seen on the example from Samaria.

Rim No. 36 displays a strongly inverted, rounded lip above a similar style ridge on the exterior face of the rim. This style tends toward those from the mid-ninth century and later, but without the squared, tool-cut notch above the ridge or flange. Adequate parallels are available from, among other sites, Hazor,[276] Lachish,[277] Tell Beit Mirsim,[278] and Tell en-Naṣbeh.[279] As nearly all these parallels show, when this pot appeared with handles they usually extended from ridge to shoulder as against the earlier style (tenth century—compare No. 31) which reached from lip to shoulder.[280]

No. 37 represents a slightly thicker, shorter variation on the form of No. 35; both point to the transition from the inverted, rounded rims (often with handles) of the tenth century to the more notched styles current from the mid-ninth century on. Good late ninth-century parallels from Hazor[281] speak to the expected overlap between these two modes during this transition period. Once again, when these early Iron II forms utilize

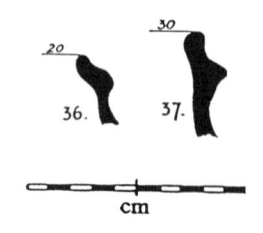

SS III, Fig. 6:36-37

---

without the lower ridge, seems particularly common on kraters. See also the similar, though not exact, krater rim from late tenth-century levels at Tell Qiri (*T. Qiri*, Fig. 28:3, Area A, Stratum VIII).

[272]*Beth-Shan*, James, Fig. 66:10 (Upper Level V). Compare the inverted cooking pot rim in *Chambon*, Pl. 53:1 (Niveau VIIb).

[273]Compare also *TN II*, Pl. 47:1002.

[274]*T. Qasîle* [2], 52:3 (Stratum IX); given the exterior design seen on the left side of this vessel, I believe the lower ridge is not apparent enough in the section to the right. The depiction in *T. Qasîle* [2], Fig. 27:14 (Stratum XI) also resembles certain attributes of No. 34, though with the stance of the nailhead portion above the ridge more erect than inverted.

[275]*AS-IV*, Pl. LXIII:37 (Stratum IIa or b).

[276]*Hazor III-IV*, Pl. CCXXIV:3-4 (Stratum VB).

[277]*Lachish III*, Pl. 93:442.

[278]*TBM I*, Pl. 56:2 (late Stratum A2; see comments on pp. 81-2).

[279]*TN II*, Pl. 47:107.

[280]See the photographs in *TBM I*, Pl. 35:3-5.

[281]Note especially *Hazor III-IV*, Pl. CCXLVIII:7 (Stratum VII).

handles, they generally display a ridge-to-shoulder rather than rim-to-shoulder placement.

In like manner, rim No. 40 also reflects the rim-form mode characteristic of the mid-to-late ninth century. It bears witness to the changeover from the short, triangular flanged style to the notched variety, derived by pushing the outside lower barb of the flange upward (and eventually trimming the top of it to form the more squared notch). Many parallels from multiple sites survive for this style, as at Hazor,[282] Tell el-Far'ah,[283] Tell Yoqne'am,[284] and—for one example from the south—Beth-Shemesh.[285]

SS III, Fig. 6:40

As with the group of bowls discussed above in conjunction with Rooms *g-k*, the repertoire of cooking pot forms recovered from Room *n* shows an extended chronological range. The time period reflected in these materials, however, generally predates that represented by the bowls. This may seem to suggest an earlier functional life for Room *n* than for the complex of later rooms (*f-k*) west of it. Yet the nature of the depositional history in the area from which the excavators removed the ceramic corpus proves problematic. As shown in my stratigraphic analysis above (pp. 60ff.), the vicinity in which Segment *502.503* lay revealed multiple robber trenches, including a backfilled cut from the plundering of Omri's original Enclosure Wall 161. I believe that the PP 4 assemblage of cooking pots came from immediately south of the line of RT 161, while north of that point a thick BP II fill covered the area. Though some of the rim fragments (Nos. 27, 34, 37, 38, and 40) came from basal layers associated with the putative BP IV Paving 249 (which itself showed significant breaches in many places), others derived from fill deposits serving as makeup for what Kenyon believed represented BP V surface levels (Nos. 29, 30, 36). Yet these rims range in date from the eleventh to the mid-ninth century (except, perhaps, for the later No. 34). While I had earlier anticipated finding both derived and intrusive elements in the material culture retrieved from these layers, it appears now that the bulk of the corpus comprises derived items located in various secondary fills. As a result, I can once again say only that the *terminus post quem* of these rooms must remain open. Further, the latest cooking pots published from the fills in Room *n* preclude dating its construction and use much earlier than the eighth century BCE.

---

[282]*Hazor II*, Pl. LVII:14, 17, 18-19 (Stratum VIII).

[283]Compare *T. Far'ah-RB* [62], Fig. 19:4 (Niveau intermédiaire, Période 3 = mid-ninth century BCE), albeit with handles from rim to shoulder.

[284]*T. Yoqne'am* [3], Fig. 10:6 (with handles; Area A, Stratum 9, tentatively dated slightly later, to the late eighth or even early seventh centuries BCE).

[285]*AS-IV*, Pl. LXIII:38 (Stratum IIb, Room 249), also with handles from rim to shoulder and with the former flange a bit more rounded.

As a result of my comparative analysis for these rims, I may suggest the following temporal sequence for the overall PP 4 group, recognizing that some of the Iron Age IIA styles likely extended throughout the Iron II period: eleventh-tenth centuries BCE = No. 25; late eleventh-tenth centuries = Nos. 31, 38; tenth century = Nos. 26-30; late tenth to mid-ninth centuries = Nos. 32-33, 35; mid-to-late ninth century = Nos. 36-37, 39-40; eighth into seventh centuries = No. 34. This overview will subsequently serve as a basis for examining additional cooking pot fragments which Kenyon assigned to Pottery Periods subsequent to PP 4 at Samaria.

c. Jars

The excavators recovered a group of seven jar rim fragments from two principal areas within the rooms discussed above: five sherds derive from Rooms h and/or k (*SS III*, Fig. 6:12, 14-15, 17-18), while two came from Room j (Fig. 6:8, 16). They also recovered similar pieces from various sectors of the courtyard, and I shall treat those items under the appropriate sections to follow. Besides variations in the rim- and neck-form modes reflected in this series, the jars plainly divide themselves as well into two subgroups based on the diameter of their mouths. The first group includes a series of "closed" forms displaying openings of less than 11 cm (Nos. 8-12, 14). The rims of the second set, however, belong to wider-mouth vessels whose openings range between 23 and 28 cm. These fragments appear to present us with a set of "open" forms; otherwise, the overall diameter of the complete vessel would, in certain cases, have had to exceed 56 cm.[286] This attribute alone, then, may require that I reclassify certain of these pieces in categories other than jars. At least, any analysis of the form and function of the vessels represented here must take into account the noticeable variations in their diameters. The specific findspots for these remains appear in Table 9 below. Within this group, I have earmarked (with †) the single fragment published by Kenyon in support of her "Period IVa" (*SS III*, Fig. 6:14).

The rims in this group that indicate a vessel mouth diameter of 11 or fewer centimeters belong primarily to the well-attested class of ovoid- or oval-shaped store jars with either short or high necks (despite Kenyon's reference to No. 14 as a "hippo jar"). The dimensions, weights, and capacities of both the short- and high-necked jars, as well as a third subtype with a so-called button base, appear roughly the same: ca. 53-60 cm in height; maximum diameter of 31-35 cm; maximum capacity of ca. 25 liters; and an empty weight ranging from 7 to 10 kilograms.[287] Such attributes, as well as differences in ware, help to distinguish these storage jars from the taller and wider (though not much heavier) hippo forms with an average capacity of 68 liters.

---

[286] For the technical distinction between closed and open forms, see my discussion of holemouth jars below, specifically n. 393.

[287] Y. Alexandre, "The 'Hippo' Jar and Other Storage Jars at Hurvat Rosh Zayit," *TA* 22 (1995), 80.

PP 4: HOUSE FLOORS — POTTERY

SS III Published Figure	Registry No. (* = marked for discard)	Provenance Strip	Coordinates	Feature	Local Layer
6:8	QX 44	Q(x)-k	N of TT2	Room *j*	IX
6:12	QX 42	Q(x)-k	122.125.19.121	Room *h* (?)	Va
† 6:14	QX 76	Q(x)-k	125.144	Room *h*	IVx.z
6:15	QX 45	Q(x)-k	125.144	Room *h*	IVa
6:16	QX 41	Q(x)-k	N of TT2	Room *j*	IX
6:17	*Q 2328c	Qk	▶ Btw TT2-TT3	Room *k*	VII
6:18	*Q 2377	Qk	155.151.136.147	Room *h* (*l* ?)	IX

Provenance Data:
PP4 Jars from Area Labeled "House Floors"

Table 9

This first category of vessel mentioned above includes rim No. 8, which appears to represent a short neck variant of *SS III*, Fig. 3:32 from Pottery Period 2. Both forms display short-to-medium height necks with an inwardly slanting posture, rims that are slightly thickened both internally and externally, and rounded or smoothed upper lips. The shorter neck on No. 8 emerges as the main feature distinguishing it from the PP 2 antecedent just mentioned. Otherwise, they both consist of a hard, reddish-brown ware which contains appreciable quantities of limestone grit.

In an earlier examination of related forms, I showed that the high-necked versions of these early simple storage jars date primarily to the eleventh and tenth centuries BCE, and that it remains difficult to trace them through the ninth century in secure findspots.[288] Related exemplars with shorter necks,[289] on the other hand, postdate this parent group only slightly, appearing sometime during the mid-ninth century and continuing, in variable guises, through most of the Iron II period.[290]

SS III, Fig. 6:8

---

[288]See *AIS-I*, 35-36 (for *SS III*, Fig. 1:17 = PP 1) and 121-22, 141-42 (regarding *SS III*, Fig. 3:31-32 = PP 2). In his dissertation, Holladay noted that "the last *reasonably*-securely dated examples" of this style occur in Stratum VIII at Hazor (*Holladay*, 213; emphasis added).

[289]E.g., *SS III*, Fig. 1:18 (*AIS-I*, 63-65) and 3:33-34 (*AIS-I*, 121).

[290]For more recent confirmation of the sequence I suggested for the high- and short-necked jars, see again Y. Alexandre, *TA* 22 (1995), 80-81.

Adequate parallels from Hazor,[291] Tell Qiri,[292] Megiddo,[293] Taʿanach,[294] Tell en-Naṣbeh,[295] and Tell Qasîle[296] help establish the *terminus post quem* for the style seen in No. 8 to the mid-ninth century. Within this northern purview, a specimen from Beth-Shan, Upper Level V, provides a possible transition form toward this shorter, inwardly inclined rim.[297] In the south, compare the slightly later examples at Gezer,[298] Beersheba,[299] and Lachish.[300] These data also adequately demonstrate the many subtle nuances in form which this family of jars encompasses. As I have shown in my stratigraphic analysis above, Layer IX in Room *j*, Segment *North of Test Trench 2*, consisted in a secondarily deposited matrix of dark brown fill (see fig. 13).

While the rim-form mode on No. 12 may resemble, in certain respects, that just seen on fragment No. 8 (in that both its interior and exterior edges appear thickened as a result of flattening from above), the fragment indicates a much taller neck, a strong, outward inclination of the upper neck and rim, and a relatively rough face on the inner wall of the neck. The pale, drab ware once again exhibited a hard consistency and held observable inclusions, some noted as large, of limestone grit. Its closest companion within the Samaria corpus appears in *SS III*, Fig. 11:26,[301] though it shows clear affinities to 11:27 (and possibly even 28) as well (assigned to PP 7). Though this rim appears to stem from traditions incipient in the late tenth-early ninth centuries BCE,[302] the closest parallels point to the eighth and

SS III, Fig. 6:12

---

[291]*Hazor I*, Pls. L:30 (Stratum VII; with a slightly more bulbous rim); LXXII:10-11 (Strata V-IV); *Hazor III-IV*, Pl. CLXXXV:16 (Stratum VI; with rim flattened in and oblique, outward slant).

[292]*T. Qiri*, Fig. 13:6 (Area D, Stratum VII = Iron II).

[293]*Megiddo I*, Pl. 14:71 (Strata IV-I; with stance of neck slightly more erect).

[294]*Taʿanach*, Fig. 87:1 (Period VIB; though with incipient ridge at the mid-neck level).

[295]*TN II*, Pls. 15:251-52 (good parallels for mouth diameter), 247 (rim more rounded); 16:266 (very good parallel for form, ware, and mouth size).

[296]*T. Qasîle* [2], Figs. 43:1 (Stratum X); 52:14 (Stratum IX); 57:4 (Stratum VII; with lip pinched up in center).

[297]*Beth-Shan*, James, Fig. 64:5.

[298]*Gezer III*, Figs. 12:2-3 (Field VII, Stratum 6B); 23:4 (VII/5B-A). Contrast the tall-neck variant with more bulbous rim in 26:15 (VII/5A).

[299]*Beersheba I*, Pl. 79:9 (Stratum II).

[300]*Lachish V*, Pl. 48:14 (Level II).

[301]Kenyon apparently wanted to disassociate 6:12 from 11:26, for she stated in the final report that vessels like 11:26 were common in PP 7 and that they "appear[ ] in VI, but not in IV" (*SS III*, 128). Yet similarities in form (described above), ware (hard, drab or reddish, grey at the break, and with limestone inclusions), and type (tall-necked store jar) amply corroborate my comparison of the two.

[302]Compare the form of the decorated piece in *Hazor II*, Pl. LII:20 (Stratum IX). Its origins may lie even earlier; compare *Taʿanach*, Figs. 4:6 (Period IA) and 11:2 (Period IB).

seventh centuries for its primary existence (starting around the time of Hazor, Stratum VI, and extending through Gezer, Field VII—Stratum 5A). Late reflexes of this style, however, continue even into the Hellenistic period. Working parallels, though not perfect ones, are seen at northern sites such as Hazor,[303] Megiddo,[304] Tell Keisan,[305] Tell Yoqneʿam,[306] Taʿanach,[307] Tell Qasîle,[308] and Gezer.[309]

Though it remains difficult to speak with certainty on this piece, then, I believe that it best fits the profile of a high-, straight-necked conical jar with splayed upper neck and rim. The reports from Tell ʿAmal[310] and Tell en-Naṣbeh[311] both provide a nice series of related whole forms. Using these groups as reference points, I shall suggest later that this rim very likely relates to the same family of conical jars as *SS III*, Fig. 6:15, taken from Room *h*. A similar assemblage of so-called "goblets" appears in the report from Tell Keisan.[312] Gitin is correct in assigning the overall form and ware

---

[303] *Hazor II*, Pl. LIX:8 (Stratum VIII); *Hazor III-IV*, Pls. CCXVI:1 (Stratum VI; note the rippled inner neckwall). This rim seems distantly related to both much earlier (*Hazor III-IV*, Pl. CCXIII:1 [a Stratum XI painted jug]) and much later (*Hazor III-IV*, Pl. CXC:9 [store jar from Stratum II]) traditions at Hazor.

[304] *Megiddo I*, 21:123 (Stratum V; with a similar small neck opening).

[305] *T. Keisan*, Pl. 44:2 (Niveau 5; showing an outer neck ridge).

[306] *T. Yoqneʿam* [3], Fig. 13:1 (Area A, Stratum 11). For another possible late reflex of this Iron II style, compare *T. Yoqneʿam* [3], Fig. 7:15 (Area A, Stratum 6; = table amphora, with a slight concavity in the outer face of the rim, from the Hellenistic period).

[307] *Taʿanach*, Fig. 62:4 (but with shorter, bowed neck; taken from the Cistern 74 deposit, which was thought to represent mainly Period IIB). Compare the jug rim (thickened on interior side only) and neck in Fig. 39:2, though an even better jug rim match comes from much earlier, Period IA levels (Fig. 4:6). The resemblance that No. 12 holds both to this early jug form from Taʿanach and to the Iron IIC conical jar forms gives the impression that it belongs either very early in the Iron Age or very late.

[308] *T. Qasîle* [2], Fig. 44:14-15 (Stratum X).

[309] *Gezer III*, Fig. 26:14, 32 (Field VII, Stratum 5A = seventh-sixth centuries BCE). These rims tend toward an exterior lip only; the mouth diameter of No. 14 appears much closer to the Samaria example than that of the larger No. 32. In his identification of the latter fragment, Gitin wonders whether it might actually represent a stand rather than a jar form.

[310] *T. ʿAmal*, Fig. 18:1-4, from Tombs III, VI, V, and IV, respectively (No. 1 provides the best parallel for No. 12 from Samaria in every respect; note its tall, straight neck with slight ribbing effect on the interior wall, its outwardly splayed rim that is thickened on both sides and flattened on top). These tombs undoubtedly contained a mixed repertoire of goods. The report states: "Cinq autres tombes creusées dans la terre également apparues au locus 20 . . . à l'intérieur des niveaux III et IV. L'étude stratigraphique ne permet pas de déterminer de quel niveau elles datent. . . . Du point de vue céramique, notons quatre petites jarres (une par tombe) placées en offrande près des ossements . . . et une carafe (decanter) lustrée en sa partie supérieure" (p. 341). Neither these conical jars nor the decanter can stem from the tenth century BCE; the group seems more at home in a seventh-century context.

[311] *TN II*, Pl. 27:444-451. Note that at least No. 451 exhibits the rippled effect on the interior neckwall, much like that seen on the exemplar from Samaria. Compare also the example recovered from Cistern 370 at Tell en-Naṣbeh and presented in *TN—Cistern*, Fig. 2:x231.

[312] *T. Keisan*, Pl. 37:10, 10a-b, and especially 10c (Niveau 5 = 720-650 BCE).

of this vessel type primarily to the post-733 BCE ceramic horizon.[313] In light of this observation, the semblance which No. 12 holds to certain Assyrian forms becomes more readily apparent and quite significant. The tall, straight neck and splayed upper wall and rim, in particular, resemble motifs common in late Assyrian pottery recovered in large quantities from such places as Fort Shalmaneser.[314] Though the tombs mentioned above from Tell ʿAmal may have experienced a primary use sometime during Niveaux III-IV (tenth century BCE), the excavators commented on the conical jars found in them by noting that "Ce type de céramique est connu dans la culture assyrienne du VIIe siècle avant J.-C."[315] Identical jars from Tell Ḥalaf (Guzana/Gozan), located at the headwaters of the Khabur River, provide nice examples from the geographical center of the Israel—Assyrian contacts during this late Iron II period.[316] In short, I shall assign to rim No. 12 a working chronological range from the late eighth through most of the seventh centuries BCE.[317]

I believe this time span fits well the stratigraphic context from which the excavators removed this rim. As observed in my review of the depositional history in Segment *122.125.19.121*, this fragment represents the only PP 4 exemplar associated with Layer Va of Pit *i*. Beyond this, the large cache of late, mixed ceramic traditions

---

[313]*Gezer III*, 144. See also the small but convincing comparanda of materials cited there.

[314]For the prevalence of the general form among late Assyrian pottery, compare the following vessel-types presented in J. Oates, *Iraq* 21 (1959): small drinking vessels, called *istikans*, Pl. XXXVI:37, 40; chalice necks and rims in Pl. XXXVII:57; at least the morphology of certain fine, thin Palace Ware beakers, as in Pl. XXXVII:60, 62; a tradition of high-necked jars, in Pls. XXXVIII:97-99 and XXXIX:101. Though this pottery group derives mainly from the period of the collapse of Nimrud and the conquest of the fortress itelf, i.e., the late seventh century BCE (ca. 612 BCE), the basic design traits mentioned here began in Assyria already sometime shortly after the mid-eighth century BCE. See also J. Lines, *Iraq* 16 (1954), Pl. XXXVIII:2, 4-6. Here I must stress that my comparison involves only general morphological traits; the ware on these Assyrian vessels—particularly the pale, grey-green clay that typifies the Palace Ware—differs significantly from the Samaria piece. Other Assyrian vessels cited above, such as the non-Palace Ware *istikans* and chalices, often appear in either a buff or reddish fabric similar to the local wares in Israel.

[315]*T. ʿAmal*, 341.

[316]E.g., *T. Ḥalaf IV*, Tafel 56:15.

[317]See *Amiran*, Pl. 83 for additional, though nuanced, parallels from Hazor, Beth-Shan, Megiddo, Gezer, Beth-Shemesh, Tell Beit Mirsim, Tell el-Farʿah (S), and Amman in Transjordan. On the latter examples, recovered from the tomb of Adoni-Nur, one should not allow Gitin's statement that "It is likely that Type 16 [= conical jars in his classification system] is a local copy of a form common in Ammonite pottery ... and in neo-Assyrian pottery" (*Gezer III*, 144) to sway us to believe that this vessel-type can claim any origins in the territory of Ammon. Amiran stresses that even those forms which appear in that region "belong to Assyrian ceramics" (*Amiran*, 297; e.g., Pl. 101:28 = Pl. 83:16, though the former shows a painted rim while the latter does not). All the specimens cited in my study imitate an *Assyrian* form but appear to be locally made. Admittedly, however, certain of these jars may also share local prototypes dating from as early as the tenth century BCE (compare *T. Farʿah-RB* [58], Fig. 10:10 [Niveau 3, Locus 162]; *T. Farʿah-RB* [62], Fig. 16:10 [Niveau 3, Locus 418]; *Megiddo I*, Pl. 19:113-114 [Stratum V]; *Munshara*, Fig. 1:3-6, for similar two-handled jars with straight, simple rims, recovered from a tomb near Samaria; etc.).

presented in *SS III*, Fig. 10:1-27 came from this same layer. Since most of these materials will prove to derive from the late eighth and seventh centuries (Kenyon herself placed them in PP 6), it seems unreasonable to suppose that Fig. 6:12 embodies the only "early" piece in the entire locus.

According to Kenyon, *SS III*, Fig. 6:14 "comes from a floor of Period IVa . . . , and is the earliest rim sherd found of the so-called 'Hippo' jar,"[318] implying that the widest diameter of the vessel occurs just above the base rather than at the midpoint or upper sector of the sidewalls. Though not a true "hippo" form,[319] this ovoid- or oval-shaped jar with ridged neck represents a predominantly northern tradition which appears only sporadically in the south.[320] Though nuanced, antecedent versions may survive from the late tenth century BCE,[321] solid parallels for this sherd concentrate in the late ninth and first three quarters of the eighth centuries.[322] By the mid-to-late seventh century, only vestigial, degenerate forms persisted.[323] Similar rim forms also appear during the Iron II period on the taller "sausage jar," as shown by samples from Beth-

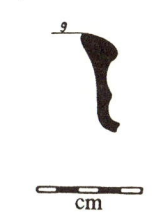

SS III, Fig. 6:14

---

[318]*SS III*, 115.

[319]See similar comments by Gitin (*Gezer III*, 122) and Alexandre (*TA* 22 [1995], 84). Alexandre's study has now shown that, although the true hippo form (see p. 88 for details) also belongs almost exclusively to the Israelite-Phoenician regional cultures, it displays a more limited lifespan than the ovoid- or oval-style jars, appearing primarily during the second half of the tenth century BCE and generally lasting only until the destruction levels resulting from Shishak's campaign (though perhaps slightly later at the fort of Hurvat Rosh Zayit). Consequently, A. Mazar has called this jar a *fossil directeur* for the north Israelite culture of the tenth century BCE (A. Mazar, *Levant* 29 [1997], 162).

[320]Note the comments regarding "regionalism" as it relates to this basic type in *T. Qiri*, 187. For possible parallels from the south, see (in chronological order, from earliest to latest), *TN II*, Pl. 18:303-311, and note especially 303-05 (ninth-seventh centuries BCE); *Gibeon*, Figs. 45:7; 39:25 (Levels 4 and 1 = eighth and seventh centuries BCE); *Lachish III*, Pl. 94:481 (Level III) and 480 (Level II); Bethel in *AASOR* 39, Pls. 67:1; 66:14-15 (sixth century BCE).

[321]*Gezer III*, Fig. 9:8 (Field VII, Stratum 7A), though this piece appears much more strongly inverted and exhibits a rim profile that is squat and rather thick compared to the Samaria fragment. *Hazor II*, Pls. LI:18-19 (Stratum X), with a narrow mouth diameter; LII:23-24 (Strata X-IX); *Hazor III-IV*, Pls. CLXXVI:10-12 (Stratum IXB); CLXXIX:14-15 (Stratum IXA). See also *T. ʿAmal*, Fig. 8:5-9 (Niveau III = second half of tenth century), with No. 7 providing a good example of a high, vertical neck mode; an even better parallel (bearing an inscription) from this site appears in Fig. 5 (p. 336) and also dates to the tenth century BCE (Niveaux IV-III). *T. Yoqneʿam* [3], Fig. 13:4 (Area A, Stratum 11 = late tenth-early ninth centuries BCE).

[322]*Gezer III*, Fig. 12:4-5 (Field VII, Stratum 6B); *Hazor I*, Pls. L:34 (Stratum VII); LXIV:6 (grey ware), 7 (pink ware) (Stratum V); *Hazor II*, Pls. LX:1-7 (Stratum VIII); LXV:4 (Stratum VII); LXXI:10-18, with No. 12 reflecting a globular-body style; LXXV:14 (Stratum V); *Hazor III-IV*, Pls. CCXVI:4 (Stratum VII), 6-7 (Stratum V); CCXVIII:1, 6 (Stratum VII); CCXIX:23-24 (Stratum VI); CCXXIX:7 (Stratum VA); *Megiddo I*, Pl. 15:76 (Strata IV-II); *Taʿanach*, Figs. 94:1-2 (Periods III-IV); the 810-760/745 BCE Ceramic Period at Shechem, in *Holladay*, Figs. 78:A-B, E, H; 80:B'-M; 81:D, though with slightly concave top of rim; *T. Qiri*, Fig. 13:8 (Area D, Stratum VII).

[323]E.g., *Gezer III*, Fig. 26:13 (Field VII, Stratum VA); *T. Qasîle* [2], Fig. 57:1 (Stratum VII).

Shan.³²⁴ I may refine somewhat the classification of these rims based on their comparative heights, the erect versus inverted stance of their necks and rims, and the placement of the ridge relative to the shoulder and upper rim areas. Generally speaking, the neck and rim zone decreases in height beginning, perhaps, by the mid-ninth century BCE, but certainly by the closing decades of that century. As this occurs, the ridge itself gravitates more toward the juncture of the shoulder and neck rather than remaining higher up at the midpoint of the neck and, together, these features tend to incline inward.³²⁵

The examples presented from PP 7 at Samaria seem to combine various elements of this evolutionary process (see *SS III*, Fig. 11:24-25). Of these later pieces, No. 24 provides the best parallel at Samaria itself for 6:14, though the former has already begun to lose some of the interior thickening of the rim. On the basis of these comparisons, then, I date No. 14, with its ridged neck and rim that is thickened both internally and externally, in the mid-to-late ninth-century BCE range. This style appears to hark back to store jar Type SJ I/c in the Yoqneʿam Regional Project.³²⁶ There (the western Jezreel Valley region), however, similarly profiled rims appear to have faded numerically already by the tenth century BCE.³²⁷ Though its precise stratigraphic location remains quite unclear (see my full discussion on pp. 30-31 and n. 57 above), the fragment appears to derive from a "black patch" of soil that constituted part of Layer IV, i.e., the deposit of brown forest soil poured against Wall 155.³²⁸

Various features of both No. 15 and No. 16 in the PP 4 jar series once again evoke comparisons to the class of conical vessels just discussed under rim No. 12. There, I indicated that certain entries in the conical series published from Tell ʿAmal and Tell en-Naṣbeh bear an initial strong resemblance to No. 15.³²⁹ After arriving at this comparison independently, I noticed that Wampler had drawn a similar analogy between Tell en-Naṣbeh rim No. 454 and assorted remnants of conical jars recovered from Summit Strip 1, Cistern 7, during the

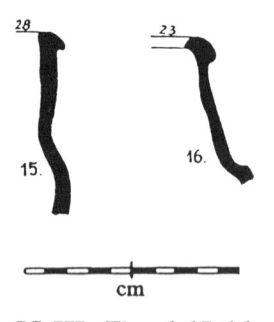

SS III, Fig. 6:15-16

---

³²⁴*Beth-Shan*, James, Fig. 70:3, 5 (Level IV).

³²⁵See Gitin's comments on this evolution and his separation of examples according to these criteria in *Gezer III*, 120-21.

³²⁶See *T. Qiri*, 144; Fig. 35:4, though with a taller neck wall than the Samaria fragment. Note also the remark on p. 189 that this rim-form mode appears to embody a "good chronological indicator." Compare *T. Yoqneʿam* [3], Fig. 13:4 (Area A, Stratum 11 = tenth century BCE).

³²⁷*T. Qiri*, 187.

³²⁸*Fieldbook Qk-l-m*, 48a.

³²⁹The following exemplars from those sites prove most applicable here: *T. ʿAmal*, Fig. 18:1 and 4, from Tombs III and IV, respectively; *TN II*, Pl. 27:454.

Harvard Excavations at Samaria and presented in their early reports.[330] Though the upper necks on the Harvard fragments seem to splay outward more than the entry in *SS III*, Fig. 6:15, they all appear to share the tool-trimmed notch beneath their exterior lips.[331] Reisner summarized the morphology of his fragments as a "pitcher (without handle?)" and described the ware as "drab or gray ware, reddish when hard burnt, greenish when soft burnt."[332] The latter description may, in fact, point to Assyria as the point of origin for this piece.[333] Figure 6:15 at Samaria exhibited "reddish buff ware, [and] a mass of grits."[334]

But the single attribute which militates most against this putative identification, however, concerns the unusually wide mouth (28 cm) which Kenyon has ascribed to No. 15. This is not in keeping with typical conical jug forms. But neither does it seem congruent with the fairly standard mouth or neck openings attested in the various classes of storage jars. While this rim form resembles that seen on various other classes of vessels over the Iron Age II and Persian periods,[335] the overall mouth size of this vessel favors most the category of kraters which entered the mainstream of ceramic tradition during the late ninth to mid-eighth centuries BCE. Apt comparisons are available from Hazor,[336] Tell Keisan,[337] Tell Qiri,[338] and Tell en-Naṣbeh.[339] Earlier prototypes for this krater style may come from late tenth-century levels at Tell

---

[330] See *TN II*, Appendix A, pp. 79-80, for references to *HES I*, 290, Fig. 167:5 and *HES II*, Pl. 65:b (fragment pictured in the upper right). For representative descriptions and drawings of the pottery group recovered from Cistern 7, see *HES I*, 289-93, Figs. 165-71. The vessels shown here seem to range from late Iron Age II (see the sausage jars, various pitchers, carinated bowl forms, etc.) to the Hellenistic (perhaps even Roman) era (compare the ribbed bowls, black-glazed lamps, and the recorded but not drawn fragment of Red-Figured Ware).

[331] To the examples cited by Wampler, add *HES I*, Fig. 167:5.

[332] *HES I*, 290, description No. 5.

[333] Compare the descriptions of wares/fabrics used in late Assyrian pottery given in the following studies: J. Lines, *Iraq* 16 (1954), 164-67; P. S. Rawson, "Palace Wares from Nimrud—Technical Observations on Selected Examples," *Iraq* 16 (1954), 168-72; J. Oates, *Iraq* 31 (1959), 130-46.

[334] *SS III*, 115.

[335] Compare, for example, the following forms from Field VII in *Gezer III*: jug rim in Fig. 19:5 (Stratum 6A = mid-eighth century); amphora fragment with waisted neck Fig. 29:19 (Stratum 4 = Persian/fifth-fourth centuries); and the cooking pot with handles in Fig. 31:11 (Stratum 4 = Persian/fifth-fourth centuries). The shoulders and sidewalls on all these types, however, seem to bulge out beneath the neck in a more rounded form than on No. 15.

[336] *Hazor I*, Pl. LVII:16 (Stratum V; ca. 21 cm); *Hazor II*, Pl. LXVIII:7 (Stratum VI; ca. 23 cm); *Hazor III-IV*, Pl. CCXLVII:23 and 25 (Stratum VII; ca. 14 and 33 cm, respectively).

[337] *T. Keisan*, Pl. 28:9 (Niveau 4 = second half of seventh century; ca. 15 cm); this krater provides a good rim parallel but shows more rounded shoulders and sidewalls.

[338] *T. Qiri*, Fig. 22:10 (Area C, Stratum V = late eighth-early seventh centuries; ca. 23.5 cm).

[339] *TN II*, Pl. 3:37 (ca. 28 cm; again, this presents a good parallel from the shoulder up, but the shoulder itself and the sidewall appear more rounded).

Qasîle[340] and Tell Qiri;[341] for early neck and shoulder parallels, one may compare the slender conical jar from Tell el-Farʿah (N).[342]

To sum up, I suggest that No. 15 fits best in Gitin's high-necked, globular-shaped amphora group (Type 90B).[343] While an earlier, decorated subtype of this family appeared in the mid-eighth century, the undecorated variety (such as Samaria's No. 15), often with an outwardly slanting neck, belongs primarily in the seventh (or even early sixth) century. Whether one should, with Gitin, consider the overall class to reflect "a degenerate imitation of earlier amphorae of Cypriote Bichrome II and Cypro-Geometric II Ware groups of the 10th and 9th centuries B.C." remains open to discussion.[344] In fact, the form seems related to another, taller rim with neck ridge recovered from an early cistern deposit at Samaria (*SS III*, Fig. 2:4).[345] In any case, the utilization of similar rim-form modes on the conical jars, goblets, kraters, jugs, amphora, and even certain decanters,[346] demonstrates the versatility of this style during the Iron Age II period.[347] Though this Samaria fragment may derive from an amphora and not a conical jar, then, both styles seem to have flourished during the same general period in Iron Age IIC. The subdeposit of fill from which the excavators recovered this rim (Segment *125.144* of Room *h*, Layer IVa), then, likely dates no earlier than this time.

Though solid comparative data for *SS III*, Fig. 6:16 remain rather meager, the fragment does enjoy one nearly perfect parallel from mid-to-late eighth-century BCE

---

[340] *T. Qasîle* [2], Fig. 53:8 (Stratum IX; ca. 29 cm).

[341] *T. Qiri*, Fig. 29:5 (Area A, Strata VIII-IX; ca. 28 cm). Note that the rim is more flattened on top and does not exhibit the tool trimming beneath its outer lip.

[342] *Chambon*, Pl. 61:15 (Niveau VIIb). The mouth diameter, however, is much smaller than that recorded for the Samaria fragment.

[343] *Gezer III*, 206-07.

[344] The styling of No. 15 resembles only somewhat the parallels cited from *Megiddo I*, Pl. 22:127; *Megiddo II*, Pl. 89:7; and *T. Farʿah-RB* [62], Fig. 19:2. Similarly, the observation that many of the putative Cypro-Phoenician predecessors "come from cremation cemeteries," and the suggestions that they might have served to hold ashes and, therefore, may relate to "a specific ethnic practice associated with Phoenician culture" (*Gezer III*, 207), raise for consideration an extremely intriguing and provocative set of historical connections and grisly rites (e.g., child sacrifice; compare 2 Kgs 17:17) for late eighth- and seventh-century BCE Samaria that require much additional study for corroboration.

[345] See my discussion of this piece and its general context in *AIS-I*, Excursus I, 219-27, especially 225-26, where I also recognized possible late Iron I, Phoenician traditions behind this style vessel.

[346] *Hazor II*, Pl. C:32 (Stratum IV). Once again, the mouth size of this vessel obviously does not agree with the measurement given for *SS III*, Fig. 6:15.

[347] These fragments may reflect hybrid vessels that incorporated foreign influences from different areas. As noted above, Gitin has pointed to Cypro-Phoenician traits in such rims. I have suggested that several of the so-called jar fragments in the PP 4 group also betray early tendencies toward Assyrianizing techniques. Given recent data from excavations and surveys in the north, particularly from sites in the Jezreel Valley region, one no longer has to restrict the beginnings of this local imitation of Assyrian styles to the late eighth and seventh centuries BCE (i.e., postfall of Samaria; compare Amiran's position in *Amiran*, 272-75). Results from the Yoqneʿam Regional Project have shown that such borrowing of ceramic traditions began in Israel already during the ninth century BCE (see the comments of A. Ben-Tor and

PP 4: HOUSE FLOORS — POTTERY

Gezer.[348] These rims belong to yet another subgroup of ovoid- or oval-shaped jar, with its tall, inwardly slanted neck and rim that is rounded and externally thickened but pinched or slightly pulled inward to form a tapered point. Unfortunately, hardly any of the sidewall below the juncture of neck and shoulder has survived. Yet the subtle channel which circumnavigates this vessel at this point, together with the shoulder which *appears* to drop again rather quickly after leaving the neck (compare No. 15), may seem once again to argue for placing this rim in the group of conical jars discussed under rim Nos. 12 and 15 above. Further, the wavy interior face of the neckwall (compare No. 12) also seems to echo a trait familiar to a conical jar. A related but distant typological parallel from Tell en-Naṣbeh[349] would appear to offer supporting evidence for this identification. The wide mouth (23 cm) of No. 16, the fact that most conical jar necks assume a more vertical or outwardly splayed posture, and the strong parallel from Gezer, however, dissuade us from opting for that reading.

Assuming, then, that this piece belongs to an ovoid-style jar rather than a conical one, one can ascertain its evolutionary strain—albeit poorly attested—from the late tenth century through the Iron Age II period.[350] Besides citing many of these parallels, Gitin has also shown that this form represents primarily a northern tradition, especially prior to the mid-eighth century BCE.[351] The Samaria piece seems most at home in the mid-(to-late) eighth century BCE. The expedition retrieved it from the same stratigraphic environment as No. 8 above, that is, a context of secondary, subfloor makeup beneath Layer IX in the Segment *North of TT2* (compare figs. 7 and 13[352]).

SS III, Fig. 6:17 displays a relatively thin-walled construction, a high, straight neck rounded outwards to a strongly everted rim with an overhanging, sharp lower

---

Y. Portugali in *T. Qiri*, 203).

[348] *Gezer III*, Fig. 15:13 (Field VII, Stratum 6A). Though Gitin terminates Stratum 6A (General Stratum VI) at ca. 750 BCE, A. Mazar extends this local level to the close of the century based on the presence in it of complete *LMLK* jars (A. Mazar, *Levant* 29 [1997], 162, n. 8).

[349] *TN II*, 27:461.

[350] Compare the following: *late tenth century*: *T. Qiri*, Fig. 17:1 (Area D, Stratum VIII); *Beth-Shan*, James, Fig. 64:5 (Upper Level V); *early ninth century*: ʿEin Gev, Fig. 8:2 (Stratum III); *mid-ninth century*: *Gezer III*, Fig. 12:3 (Field VII, Stratum 6B); *late ninth century*: *Hazor I*, Pl. L:35 (Stratum VII; though this rim maintains a more triangular shape, with an obliquely outcut rim); *early-to-mid eighth century*: *Hazor II*, Pl. LXXI:5-7 (Stratum VI; also compare these examples with *SS III*, Fig. 6:10-11); *Gezer III*, Fig. 15:13 (cited above); *late eighth century*: *Hazor II*, Pl. XC:8-11 and *Hazor III-IV*, Pl. CCXXIX:1-3 (Stratum VA; again, close to Nos. 10-11 from Samaria); *late seventh-early sixth centuries*: *Gezer III*, Fig. 26:15 (Field VII, Stratum 5A); compare also *SS III*, Fig. 12:23 (PP 8).

[351] In *Gezer III*, 141, Gitin cites suggested parallels from Stratum B2 at Rabud (*Rabud*, Fig. 7:12); Gibeon, Level 3 (*Gibeon*, Fig. 40:9); Beersheba II (*Beersheba I*, Pl. 57:5); Tomb 7 at Beth-Shemesh (*AS—PEFA*, Pl. XLIX); Gibeon, Level 1 (*Gibeon*, Figs. 39:21; 43:17); and Lachish, Level II (*Lachish III*, Pls. 95:483 and 96:528). The dates for some of these levels, such as the last one, seem to support the revised chronology for Gezer VI recognized in n. 348.

[352] As noted in my consideration of the stratigraphy in this segment (p. 47), one must remember that Kenyon relabeled Layer VI in fig. 13 as "Layer IX" in order to correspond to the floor and makeup levels jointly designated "Layer IX" in fig. 7.

flange,³⁵³ and buff ware with red-painted decoration running horizontally around the neckwall and vertically down over the rim. Though these distinctive attributes would seem to provide good diagnostic indicators for comparative studies, satisfactory parallels for this fragment remain difficult to locate. Since the report did not provide the minimum diameter (i.e., the width of the neck or mouth orifice) of the original vessel, a question arises as to whether one should see this rim as part of a jar (with Kenyon), or a jug,³⁵⁴ decanter,³⁵⁵ vase,³⁵⁶ or some other vessel type. As recent systematic typologies of Iron Age rims from both northern and southern sites have shown, most *jar* rims remain rather erect in stance or tend to lean inward during these periods, particularly when they also claim a high neck.³⁵⁷ A noticeable exception to this general rule consists, once again, in the high-necked, conical-shaped jar with a strongly everted, flanged rim. The best parallels for this type from excavated jar groups come from late Iron II levels at Gezer³⁵⁸ and a cistern deposit at Tell en-Naṣbeh.³⁵⁹ Neither of these vessels, however, display the sharp, lower flange seen on the Samaria fragment. For this attribute, the best comparison is found on another form from Tell en-Naṣbeh which also shows a closely spaced series of small ridges on the neck below the rim.³⁶⁰ One can see, then, that

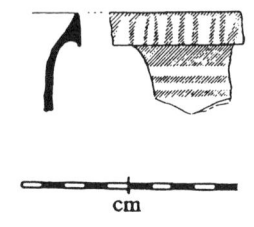

SS III, Fig. 6:17

---

³⁵³Similar attributes also appear in the north on some much later jug rims from the Early Roman period (compare *T. Qiri*, Fig. 1:30).

³⁵⁴Compare the painted jug with overhanging, bevelled rim in *SS III*, Fig. 22:5 from a nonstratified context (Z Deep Pit; on typological grounds, Kenyon associated this piece with her PP 3 group). Though some earlier Iron Age jugs maintain an everted or outturned rim and neck, they still do not strike the same kind of profile as No. 17. Compare *Taʿanach*, Figs. 6:7, 15 (Period IA); 11:2-3 (Period IB); 58:4-6, 19 (Period IIB).

³⁵⁵Compare *Beth-Shan*, James, Fig. 71:13-14 (Level IV), which provide good parallels for the buff colored ware and red rim decoration on the Samaria fragment. As these examples show, however, decanter necks typically display a ridge at or near their midpoints.

³⁵⁶Compare the upper neck and rim on the so-called "vase" form in *TBM I*, Pl. 71:4 (Stratum A2). This vessel type, which Albright believed represented "a class of imported vases" (*TBM I*, 87, § 120), exhibits "long, graceful necks and two double-handles." As *TBM I*, Pl. 37:17-18 shows, the necks of these vessels would tend to break just above the handles and would not, therefore, show the characteristic ridging seen on most decanters. Unlike the Samaria rim, the Tell Beit Mirsim vase showed a "creamy white slip, highly burnished." Albright suggested, in typical laconic style, that this piece reflected an attempt to imitate similar forms in alabaster from New Kingdom Egypt (even though it came from Stratum A2).

³⁵⁷For jar rims, compare the detailed analyses in *T. Qiri*, 144-45, 184-89; *Gezer III*, 47-51, 119-46.

³⁵⁸*Gezer III*, Pl. 26:14 (Field VII, Stratum 5A).

³⁵⁹*TN—Cistern*, Fig. 2:x231 (Cistern 370, dated roughly to the seventh century BCE—see p. 31; two *LMLK* impressions were also found in this cistern group). Compare also *TN II*, Pl. 27:447-48 (see p. 13, § 66).

³⁶⁰*TN II*, Pl. 27:450 = "fine texture; lt brown surface; wet-smoothed. H. 60mm." (p. 142). In his report on the pottery, Wampler concluded that this general class of jars "had some representation in the

PP 4: HOUSE FLOORS — POTTERY

these exemplars from Gezer and Naṣbeh date mainly from the seventh and early sixth centuries BCE, and that their harder, red or reddish-brown fabric simultaneously distinguishes them from the buff-colored ware of No. 17 and allies them more closely with the fragments presented in *SS III*, Fig. 11:26-27 (PP 7).[361] The ware and decoration of No. 17 provide clues that this piece belongs to an earlier phase of ceramic tradition.

Until clearer comparisons emerge, I propose a comparison between this decorated rim from Samaria and several traditions of ring-based jugs from regions farther to the north, in southern Phoenicia. Though *exact* comparisons once more remain elusive, near-parallels occur there among the so-called Red-Painted Ware, Bichrome Ware, and Neck-Decorated Ware groups[362] for both the form and decoration of No. 17. These jugs typically display ring bases, globular bodies with painted, vertical circles, handles attached from lower shoulder to lower neck, and strongly everted rims that are (a) simple, (b) square-cut (i.e., similar to No. 17 but without the sharp, lower flange), or (c) drooping.[363] The last two styles most approximate the rim on No. 17, and the "drooping" outer lip of the "c group" may relate to the sharp flange that protrudes downward on the Samaria fragment.[364]

The upper-neck decoration on these forms regularly involves a broad red band immediately beneath the everted rim, with two (or three) narrower bands/lines in red or black below the band.[365] Besides these regularly spaced horizontal bands and lines, these jugs often include indeterminant red strokes on the handle and/or rim (sometimes on the interior, other times on the exterior, or on both).[366] The Samaria fragment

---

late preexilic period but did not become common until later. That they are types of frequent occurrence in the 6th cent. B.C., the present information warrants, although it does not indicate a complete history. However, they are probably LI and Hellen. types" (p. 13).

[361] While the clay and form of these exemplars may resemble better the attributes of Fig. 6:12, the fineness of their ware and overall construction do, in fact, remind us more of No. 17.

[362] See the extensive catalogue in *Chapman*, 57-90.

[363] E.g., **simple everted** = *Chapman*, Fig. 6:185; **square-cut** = Fig. 6:33, 178; **drooping** = Fig. 6:40-41. A fourth class of rims, the "stilted thickened rim," maintains a vertical rather than everted stance (e.g., *Chapman*, Fig. 7:32, 175-76).

[364] Chapman saw the drooping rims of the Neck Decorated Ware as "perhaps illustrating a half-way stage between the square-cut rim and the mushroom lip" (*Chapman*, 75). The latter style appears in Palestine already by the final quarter of the eighth century and extends into the seventh century, especially at sites with a strong Phoenician character, such as Akhziv (see the discussion in *Amiran*, 272-73; Pl. 92). For selected examples of mushroom rims, see *SS III*, Figs. 25:1, 3-4, 7, 9, 13; 26:7; *Megiddo I*, Pls. 1:38 (?; Stratum III); 3:78-79 (Strata II and III, respectively); *Megiddo II*, Pl. 91:4 (Stratum IV; Bikai reassigns this vessel to Stratum III, in *Tyre*, 35); *Hazor I*, Pl. LXXXVIII:5 (Stratum VA); *Ashdod I*, Fig. 37:23; *Tyre*, Pls. I:3; V:14-17, 19-23; VI:4 (from Strata III-I).

[365] Compare, for example, *Chapman*, Fig. 5:193 (Bichrome Ware with buff clay with red lines on neck and handle; from Joya); Fig. 6:33, 42 (Bichrome Ware with broad, red band and three black lines on the upper neck; from Khirbet Silm); etc.

[366] E.g., see Chapman's descriptions of the following selected entries: No. 54, pp. 71-72; No. 194, p. 72; No. 57, p. 73 (Fig. 5:57); No. 43, p. 83 (Fig. 8:43); etc.

clearly carries this motif, at least on the exterior face of the rim (Kenyon did not indicate whether or not they continued over the lip and onto the interior face).

If these comparisons prove correct, one should locate the origin of this fragment late in the Iron Age I period or, perhaps better, near the Iron I-Iron II transition (late tenth–early ninth century). Jugs with similarly painted necks (sometimes *only* the neck is decorated) appear then at sites like Hazor,[367] Mount Carmel Tomb VII,[368] Tell Abu-Hawām,[369] and Megiddo.[370] From the eighth century, compare an example from Ashdod.[371] My earlier investigation discussed a similar jug with buff ware and red-black decoration (*SS III*, Fig. 5:1).[372] Though Kenyon assigned this piece to PP 3, I concluded that it belonged to the period of Omride rule at Samaria and that it reflected the strong ties between Israel and Phoenicia during that time. To the comparative data cited mainly from within Israel in that study, I can now add the close parallel between 5:1 and jugs from Khirbet Silm and Joya, both east of Tyre.[373]

At Tyre itself, the tradition is attested in the late ninth and the eighth centuries BCE, as Bikai's "Jug Type 8."[374] The ninth-century exemplar from Tyre (Fig. XX:2) provides an especially good parallel for the strokes of red decoration on the outer face of the rim, as displayed on the Samaria piece. Another excellent comparison from Stratum IX at Hazor predates this only slightly.[375] In light of the foregoing observations, and until better comparative data emerge, I assign a tentative date of early ninth century BCE to *SS III*, Fig. 6:17.[376] As shown in my stratigraphic analysis above, this

---

[367] *Hazor III-IV*, Pl. CCCLV:13 (Stratum XB) = red ware; vertically burnished like the Phoenician antecedents; with bichrome decoration; possibly also Pl. CCXIII:1 (Stratum IX). Compare the more elaborately decorated example in Pl. CLXXVI:6 (Stratum IXB). For descendant forms, see *Hazor II*, Pl. LVIII:28 (Stratum VIII); *Hazor I*, Pl. LII:22 (Stratum VI).

[368] P. L. O. Guy, "Mount Carmel, An Early Iron Age Cemetery near Haifa, Excavated September 1922," *BBSAJ* 5 (1924), 47-55, Pl. III:27.

[369] *TAH*, No. 67 (nonstratified).

[370] *Megiddo Tombs*, Pl. 66:20 (Tomb 73, assigned to the Early Iron Age but, as Bikai notes, "the same (disturbed) tomb yielded a Cypriote Red on Black I [III] Ware juglet" — *Tyre*, 62, n. 130); *Megiddo II*, Pls. 75:13; 81:22 (Stratum VI; the latter shows an additional horizontal band enclosed by two lines on the body rather than the vertical, concentric circles — compare *SS III*, Fig. 22:5, from the "Z Deep Pit," which Kenyon correlated to PP 3); for descendant forms, see *Megiddo II*, Pl. 91:4 (Stratum IV) = mushroom lip; *Megiddo I*, Pl. 3:79 (Stratum III).

[371] *Ashdod I*, Fig. 37:23 (Area D, Stratum 3b-3a).

[372] *AIS-I*, 191-94.

[373] *Chapman*, Fig. 8:43, 189.

[374] *Tyre*, 37-40; Pls. XIV:2-5 (with everted cut rim); 6 (with stilted thickened rim; Stratum IV = to ca. 740 BCE); XX:2 (and 3?; with everted cut or, perhaps, drooping-style rim; Stratum VIII = to ca. 800 BCE). See also Bikai, *BASOR* 229 (1978), Fig. 3:3-4.

[375] *Hazor III-IV*, Pl. CCVIII:45.

[376] I believe that rims and ridges on certain later jars, such as the conical form cited from Tell en-Naṣbeh in n. 307, might actually have developed from these earlier traditions, with the closely-spaced ridges just below the neck providing the counterpart to the former painted bands/lines. Similar rim-form modes

PP 4: HOUSE FLOORS — POTTERY

important sherd came from Layer VII of the segment labeled *(E. Strip?), Between TT2-TT3*, in Room *k*. This findspot appears secure; Layer VII comprises the earliest surface traceable in this area (see figs. 7, 8, and 13),[377] and successive floor levels—including the later paving stones of Layer V—sealed it. Clearly, then, the Joint Expedition seems to have encountered a floor from the Omride era beneath Room *k*. Though Kenyon assigned this level to her "Period IV," it more likely belongs to BP I or II. Finally, I must note that this very important jar rim eventually received the inexplicable designation of "discard" (see Table 9).

SS III, Fig. 6:18 belongs to a category of ovoid-shaped jars exhibiting vertical, short, simple rims, and virtually no necks. Gitin has given this class of jars, including the various subtypes, full treatment under his Jar Types 1A-D.[378] As explained there, the earliest antecedents of this form appear in the mid-tenth through the ninth centuries BCE, with drooping shoulders that slope obliquely away from the rim area.[379] During the course of the eighth century BCE, this vessel type shows several distinct developments. First, a so-called pressure bulge appears on the interior lower rim area[380]—a result of the force exerted there from setting the rim into the neck opening. Second, the body's becoming more ovoid in shape helps to create a "high pronounced shoulder."[381] By the close of the eighth century, as the form trails off into the seventh and early sixth centuries,[382] the rim shortens even further and the body acquires a more pointed base. Jar Types 472 and 469 from Lachish adequately portray these changes.[383]

SS III, Fig. 6:18

---

occur much later, on various pitchers from the Hellenistic period (see *HES I*, Fig. 177:7b-c; the jug in 177:11a may even represent a very degenerate vestige of this old, Iron Age tradition).

[377] My fig. 7 shows that this floor abutted a surviving section of Wall 153 (and therefore likely coexisted with it), but that it was cut by Wall 125b (and therefore predated it). Further, fig. 13 suggests that the robber trench associated with 153 cut Layer VII. Finally, fig. 8 shows that the surface was probably also contemporary with Walls 142 (on the east side of Room *k*) and 157 (on the room's west side). For the relative locations of these features on the horizontal plane, see fig. 5. If this fragment provides an accurate reading regarding the date of this floor, then the data cited here imply that the Joint Expedition failed to sort out the earliest phases of architecture in this very complicated area north of the main courtyard. Otherwise, the floor would have to belong in BP IV or later, with *SS III*, Fig. 6:17 comprising an *ex-situ*, derived element from earlier phases. (See my further comments below, in the Evaluation and Summary of Part A.)

[378] *Gezer III*, 119-20.

[379] *Hazor III-IV*, Pls. CLXXII:14 (Stratum XB); CLXXIX:11 (Stratum IXA); *Megiddo I*, Pl. 20:119 (Stratum V).

[380] E.g., *Gezer III*, Pl. 17:3 (Field VII, Stratum 6A).

[381] *Gezer III*, 119.

[382] *Gezer II*, Pl. 37:14 (Field II, Stratum 3) may embody a late reflex of this form, with flattened outer rim-wall, from the Persian period.

[383] *Lachish III*, Pl. 94:472 (which "seemed to be confined to tell Level III" — *Lachish III, Text*, 313), and 469 (which characterized Level II).

The best overall parallel for rim No. 18 comes from mid-ninth-century BCE levels at Gezer,[384] though some variations do exist between the two specimens. The lip of the Gezer fragment is bent slightly inward, and this bend helps to create a smooth channel around the interior wall of the rim. This same groove appears on No. 18, though its simple, rounded rim remains more vertical in stance. Differences also exist in the curvature of the shoulders and the angle at which they meet the lower rim. These observations notwithstanding, I have not found a better parallel for the rim itself, and I therefore date this piece between the late ninth and early-to-mid-eighth centuries BCE. Related rims from the eighth century sometimes show a ridge on their lower, exterior wall. Since this Samaria fragment apparently comprised part of the actual matrix of the hard, white plaster floor of Layer IX in Segment *155.151.136.147*, Room *h* (see figs. 7 and 10 above), it helps establish a date for this surface in the early or mid-eighth century BCE, at the earliest.

d. Holemouth Jars

The distinctive fragments in *SS III*, Fig. 6:19-24 present a series of relatively immaterial variations on a developed form of the folded-rim holemouth jar. The findspots germane to the sample in question appear in Table 10 below.[385]

Contra Kenyon, I have included rim No. 19 in this group, primarily on grounds of its form (compare No. 24) and buff-colored ware (see Nos. 20-24), while I recognize that the latter attribute exhibits a harder texture than it does on the other members of the PP 4 assemblage. A notation in Holladay's study[386] suggests that he also sees a valid comparison between at least Nos. 19 and 24; in his overall typology, however, he interprets these forms as a category of kraters rather than of holemouth jars.[387] As Table 10 indicates, fragment No. 19 derives from an area of the summit that I shall

---

[384]*Gezer III*, Pl. 12:7 (Field VII, Stratum 6B).

[385]The presentation of these fragments in *SS III*, 115, creates a false impression regarding their individual findspots by listing the registration numbers in sequential order as follows: "20-24. Q5211, Q5212, Q5213, Q5214, QX54." Based on G. M. Crowfoot's original stratification cards, I have successfully collated each entry in *SS III*, Fig. 6:20-24 with its proper registration number and provenance data (see Appendix A and Table 10).

[386]*Holladay*, 130, n. 114.

[387]*Holladay*, 208. Some ninth- and eighth-century krater rims do, in fact, exhibit a more pronounced groove beneath the outer rim area similar to that seen on No. 23 (for example, the comparable though not exact parallel in *T. Yoqneʻam* [3], Fig. 11:11 (Area A, Stratum 10). Others from that same period show a single groove in the top of the rim very similar to No. 19 and resembling No. 24 (e.g., *Gitin*, Pl. 24:20 [Field VII, Stratum 5]; *Saʻidiyeh 1* Fig. 7:1 [Area AA, Stratum VII]). This indentation may have functioned to receive a lid on both the krater and holemouth forms (though relatively few lids have appeared in the archaeological record; see *Holladay*, 208). Otherwise, the groove beneath the plain, flattened rim, or the everted rim on earlier jars, may have served as a channel in which to stretch a cord around the neck before tying it above a lump of clay pressed into the mouth of the vessel (see the note concerning this technique in *Beth-Shan*, James, 228).

PP 4: HOUSE FLOORS — POTTERY

SS III Published Figure	Registry No. (* = marked for discard)	Provenance		
		Strip	Coordinates	Feature	Local Layer
6:19	* Q 2267	Qg	325.304	Courtyard	IX
6:20	* Q 5213	Qn	502.503	Room *n*	XII (?)
6:21	* QX 54	Q(x)-k	120.121.19.126	Room *g* (*n*?)	IXb
6:22	? Q 5214	Qn	502.503	Room *n*	XIa
6:23	? Q 5212	Qn	502.503	Room *n* (*g*?)	XIIa.b
6:24	? Q 5211	Qn	502.503	Room *n*	XIa

Provenance Data:
PP4 Holemouth Jars from Area Labeled "House Floors"

Table 10

address below, namely, the excavated segment labeled simply *Courtyard*. Because of its close ceramic affinity with the holemouth rims recovered from the rooms north of the main courtyard, I shall include my comments regarding its form here but leave its precise stratigraphic context to the appropriate discussion to follow.

Unhappily, Table 10 also amply demonstrates that the overall chronological worth of these rims ultimately seems quite compromised for two primary reasons. First, conflicting data once again appear in the field notes and published report concerning either the specific feature (Nos. 21, 23) or the local layer (No. 20) from which excavators recovered certain fragments (see n. 385). Second, one must recognize, perhaps more disconcertingly, that at least half (and perhaps *all*) the pieces presented here carry notations in the field registries designating them as discards. As already reported, I have remained unable to clarify the exact origin of these notations[388] or to penetrate the logic of Kenyon's having eventually utilized such fragments as primary evidence in her historical reconstruction.

In many respects other than stance, these rims (particularly Nos. 20-24) resemble the specimen published under Pottery Period 2 in *SS III*, Fig. 3:35.[389] They are folded and flattened into a triangular, flanged form similar to that seen on many Iron I cooking pots (compare No. 25 above).[390] Following this, in the early-to-mid-ninth

---

[388]That is, I cannot tell with certainty whether the decision to discard these fragments occurred in the field—at the point of recovery or during a subsequent pottery reading—or some time later, perhaps during the post-excavation analysis of materials at either the PEF or the Rockefeller Museum (or both).

[389]See my discussion in *AIS-I*, 122-24. For a parallel to 3:35, compare *Chambon*, Pl. 45:11 (Niveau VIIb); *T. Yoqneʿam* [3], Fig. 13:3 (Area A, Stratum 11 = tenth century BCE).

[390]*Megiddo I*, 11:55-56 (Strata IV-I). While the former example relates best to the triangular form of cooking pot rim, the latter one harks back to rim modes well established for tenth-century BCE cooking pots (such as those seen in *SS III*, Fig. 1:19, 21, 24 [PP 1] and Fig. 6:31, 38 [PP 4]).

century, they are bent inward to a strongly inverted stance (as in Fig. 3:35) or even to a horizontal position to produce a broad, flat rim like those seen here.[391] There is essentially no neck between the rim and body of this vessel type. The body itself, which usually varies from between 30 to 35 cm in height,[392] most often assumes either a cylindrical or a baggy, sack-like shape, which, at least according to a strict, form-

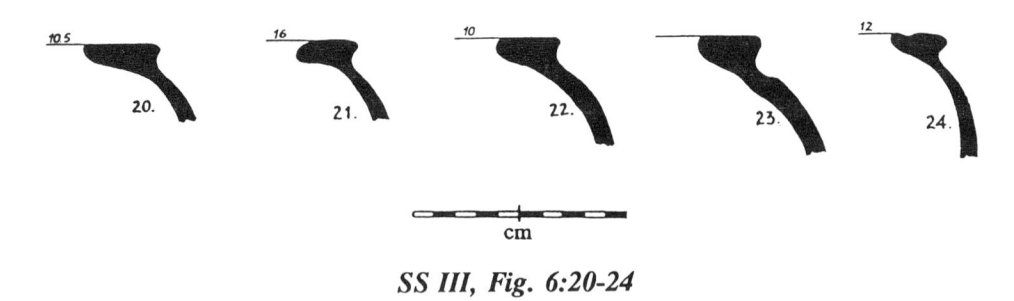

SS III, Fig. 6:20-24

based paradigm, remains "open" in its upper body and rim-form modes.[393] Because the holemouth category cannot base itself on rim stance alone, then, various early reports correctly classified vessels with both everted and inverted rims under this rubric.[394] Kenyon's important observation that the earlier Iron II bodies displayed somewhat of a shoulder, while the later Iron II sidewalls tended to drop "more vertically from the rim" generally proves correct, but not consistently so.[395] Though it does not, therefore, provide a criterion for a close dating of an overall corpus, this attribute does seem to represent a carryover from earlier jars with deeply grooved necks and everted rims

---

[391] Compare *Gitin*, Pl. 18:1-2 (Field VII, Stratum 6A, from the succeeding late ninth-mid/late eighth centuries BCE). They do not, however, always appear as nicely rounded as these Samaria examples (contrast *T. Yoqneʿam* [3], Fig. 12:2 [Area A, Stratum 10]).

[392] *TBM I*, 79, § 103.

[393] Analysts have sometimes automatically considered the holemouth jar a "closed" form due to its inward-pointing rim mode (at least by the Iron Age II period). The stance of the rim alone (inverted vs. everted), however, does not determine the "open" or "closed" nature of a vessel. A closed form occurs only when the diameter inside its minimum opening (i.e., the mouth or neck) measures less than 50% of the maximum diameter of its body (e.g., most jars and jugs; see *APTJ*, 28-29). If the minimum diameter proves greater than 50% of the maximum diameter, the vessel is considered an "open" form (e.g., all bowls). The wide-open shape of the holemouth jar, then, emerges as a principal criterion distinguishing it from most other types of jars (which, generally speaking, constitute closed forms).

[394] E.g., see *TBM I*, Pls. 33:1-4 and 52:1-9, 12-13 (Stratum A); also § 103; *Megiddo I*, Pl. 20:116-18 (Stratum V); also p. 166, § 40, which describes Nos. 117-18 as the "possible predecessors of the entire holemouth group."

[395] *SS III*, 116. Contrast, for example, the entries in *AS-IV*, Pl. LXV:18-19 and 21-33 from Stratum II with LXV:34 from the earlier Stratum III. (Incidentally, some of the rims shown in this plate seem to have been presented in an entirely wrong stance; consider LXV:4-7, 9-12, which may actually reflect a mixture of late Iron II holemouth and krater rims). But note as well the mixed forms in *Gitin*, Pl. 26:23-27 versus 28-31 (Field VII, Stratum 5/sub-4); also Pl. 16:7 versus 18:1 (Stratum 6A) and 15:2 (Stratum 6B).

(as seen in groups of "handleless jars" from Beth-Shan[396] and Hazor[397]); it may also bespeak a certain consanguinity with Iron I cooking pot forms that show carination in the upper half of the body.[398]

The chronology of the examples just cited (particularly from Megiddo) also serves as evidence for the incipient appearance of holemouth jars as early as the late tenth century BCE. At that time, rims typically displayed one of two forms: (1) a sharply everted but relatively smooth curvature without being pressed down into a fold;[399] (2) folding, with a central ridge produced by pinching or molding the fold itself.[400] Numerous examples of these forms recovered from successive levels at Hazor and elsewhere attest to the fact that they maintained a strong tradition through the early and mid-ninth century BCE.[401] Though these styles persisted in limited numbers in even later contexts,[402] a new, smoother form of rim began to replace them by the mid-to-late ninth century BCE.[403] A flattened and horizontal top often typified the new style (see Nos. 20, 22-23),[404] which was also eventually pushed down even farther so that the edge of the rim actually slanted inward, as in No. 21 from Samaria.[405] In my

---

[396] *Beth-Shan*, James, Fig. 40:1-14 (Upper Level V).

[397] *Hazor II*, Pl. LXI:1-2 (Stratum VIII); still, one can also see the transition to more grooved (or "ribbed") flat rims with vertical sidewalls (LXI:14).

[398] That is, many of these holemouth rims resemble late Iron I cooking pot rims that have been bent down from an inverted to a completely flat (horizontal) position and which have had their sidewalls straightened out to a vertical stance below the point of carination.

[399] Besides the references in the preceding note, see, for example, *Chambon*, Pl. 45:10 (Stratum VIIb).

[400] E.g., *Gitin*, Pl. 9:3-6 (Stratum VIIA = late tenth century); 12:12 and 15:2 (VIB); *Hazor II*, Pl. LIX:1-2 (Stratum VIII). Compare also the tenth-century series of rims on the so-called "handleless jars with pointed bases" in *Beth-Shan*, James, Fig. 40:1-14 (Upper Level V). Albright also believed that holemouth jars could exhibit either rounded or pointed bottoms (see *TBM I*, 79, § 103).

[401] E.g., *Hazor II*, Pl. LXI:1-2, 4-10, 12 (Stratum VIII). The numbers of these early styles, however, declined noticeably during the second half of the ninth century (compare Hazor Stratum VII and comments by the excavators themselves on the sharp curtailment in the production of these rims in Strata VI-V [*Hazor II*, 28]; compare also *Gitin*, Pl. 12:12 [Stratum VIB]; *Chambon*, Pl. 45:15 [Niveau VIId] and 19 [Niveau VIIe]).

[402] E.g., *Chambon*, Pl. 45:15, 19 (Strata VIId-e).

[403] E.g., *Gezer II*, Pl. 32:2, 7 (Field II/Stratum 6A); *Hazor I*, Pl. XLVII:26 (Stratum VIII); *Hazor II*, Pl. LXV:8 with an undercutting of the fold (Stratum VII). Compare the late ninth-century example from Shechem, also with undercutting, in *Holladay*, Fig. 88:C.

[404] Compare the PP 4 examples from Samaria (Fig. 6:20, 22-24) with those in *Gitin*, Pl. 12:11 (Stratum VIB; note the relationship of Nos. 11-12); *TBM I*, Pl. 33 (Stratum A); and, from later on, *Hazor II*, Pl. CI:18 (Stratum IV); *Chambon*, Pl. 45:21 (Stratum VIIe); etc. From the late ninth century on, these broad, flat rims were sometimes grooved or "ribbed" on top, as in Samaria PP 5 (Fig. 8:4); *Megiddo I*, Pl. 11:57 (Strata IV-I); *Gitin*, Pl. 16:6-7 (Stratum VIA); and *Chambon*, Pl. 45:20 (VIIe). Some Iron II krater rim modes followed these same patterns, e.g., *Gezer II*, Pl. 35:2-3 (Field II/Stratum 4); *Hazor III-IV*, Pl. CLXXXIII (Stratum VI).

[405] See n. 391 and, from slightly later, *Gezer II*, Pl. 33:20 (Field II, Stratum 5B-A), 35:13, 15? (Field

earlier study, I concluded that *SS III*, Fig. 3:35 (PP 2) represented an interim, "transitional stage when the rims were folded and smoothed but not yet flattened or slanted down."[406] Consequently, I suggested that this rim, though stratigraphically associated with PP 2, belonged in the PP 3 or PP 4 group from a typological standpoint, along with a good parallel from Megiddo.[407]

The preceding overview sharpens at least two points pertaining to the PP 4 holemouth group. First, Kenyon's observation that, at Samaria, "only two examples of holemouth jars occurred in Periods I and II, while they were extremely common in IV on,"[408] does not, in light of a broader comparative analysis, necessarily support her corollary claim that holemouth jars "came into use about 800 B.C."[409] The antecedent members of this class appeared around a century earlier.[410] Second, while appropriate comparative data indicate a chronological range for this vessel type that may span the mid-to-late ninth, eighth, and seventh centuries BCE, the PP 4 corpus itself surely derives from the second half of that period (i.e., mid-eighth to mid- or late seventh centuries BCE). If I cannot place the slanted form in *SS III*, Fig. 3:35, with its *soft* buff colored ware, any earlier than the ninth or even early eighth centuries BCE,[411] then the PP 4 rims presented here surely follow upon the trends reflected in that piece. Both their general morphology (including the horizontal rims and relatively narrow mouths—only about 10 cm for Nos. 20 and 22) and their buff ware typify mainly the mid- or even late-eighth century BCE. The wider mouth (16 cm) and inward slanting rim of No. 21 likely appeared by the late eighth to early seventh centuries. Finally, the grooved specimens in Nos. 19 (exhibiting a much *harder* ware[412]) and 24 developed

---

II, Stratum 4). Also, *TN II*, Pls. 19:322 (with handles); 25:402, 404 (with a more pointed inside edge), 406; 26:422-23, 432.

[406] *AIS-I*, 123.

[407] *Megiddo I*, Pl. 11:55 (Strata IV-I). I noted as well that "by this time, holemouth jars were generally more scarce in the North than they were in the South where a wide range of rim forms is attested (see Amiran, *Pottery*, 241)."

[408] *SS III*, 107.

[409] *SS III*, 116.

[410] Recall the early examples cited from Megiddo, Gezer, and Tell Farʿah (N). See *AIS-I*, 123, n. 94, regarding the general absence of this class from the Period IIB assemblage at Taʿanach and the suggested sporadic occurrence of holemouth forms in the tenth century BCE.

[411] *AIS-I*, 123 (note the possible late tenth-century antecedent form from Tel Yoqneʿam in n. 389 above). See *Megiddo I*, Pl. 11:55-56 (Strata IV-I). Compare also a similar holemouth rim in *T. Yoqneʿam* [3], Fig. 10:7 (Area A, Stratum 9), which seems truly transitional in that it exhibits an inward posture but maintains its rather pointed lip and flange (as against *SS III*, Fig. 3:35, whose features appear more rounded).

[412] Though the ware of this jar from Samaria appeared noticeably harder to Kenyon (*SS III*, 115), it maintained its buff color (compare *SS III*, 21:9 [nonstratified], with buff-to-greyish fabric) while comparable jars, here and elsewhere, were appearing in a hard, reddish ware (see *SS III*, 11:29 [PP 7]). By the mid-seventh century BCE, red ware predominated. (See also n. 510 below regarding Fig. 6:19.)

ostensibly during the course of the Iron IIB-C periods, when ridged-rim holemouth jars were more common in both Judah and the southern coastal areas.[413] Even then, however, some excellent parallels for the single-grooved style of No. 19 appear alongside the ridged specimens in the south.[414] This prompts us to reject Holladay's conclusion that the rim mode of 19 provides an excellent horizon marker for deposits that occur "only for a very limited period of time around the mid-ninth century."[415] The style generally seems to have entered the mainstream of ceramic tradition sometime later on. One may place it anywhere in the second half of the eighth or the first half of the seventh centuries BCE.[416]

The findspots for these holemouth rims (excepting No. 19, which I discuss below) emerged from the same general area and local stratigraphy as did those for the cooking pot fragments treated above, namely Layers XIa (No. 22 and 24), XIIa.b (No. 23), and XII (No. 20) in Segment *502.503*. As my stratigraphic analysis has shown, these deposits seem to comprise substantial fillings of "imported" (even if from nearby areas just farther south on the summit) soils. Since the *terminus post quem* must, by definition, remain open for such contexts, it is not surprising to see derived materials from previous phases of occupation in this secondary matrix. Once again, however, the latest ceramic traditions found mixed with these earlier forms allow us to establish a somewhat firmer *terminus ante quem* for the overall deposit and, by extension, a *terminus post quem* (or construction date) for the stone pavings numbered 548 and 549 (figs. 22-23). In view of this, rims 19 and 24 argue for a conservative date in the very late eighth or, more probably, seventh centuries BCE for the deposition of these layers. This conclusion harmonizes well with that reached concerning other pottery groups (bowls; cooking pots) analyzed above. It will, in turn, bear significantly on my historical reconstruction later in this study.

3) Evaluation and Summary

The overall distribution of the various pottery groups taken from Rooms *g-k* and, farther to the east, from the putative "room" in area *n*, appears in Table 11 below.

---

[413] For the latter, see *T. Qasîle* [2], Fig. 57:7-13 (Stratum VII); also p. 110, and the references in n. 16. See also *Gitin*, Pl. 16:6-7 (Field VII, Stratum 6A, which extends to the late eighth century BCE).

[414] E.g., *Gezer III*, Pl. 45:8 (Iron II); see also Pl. 26:29-30 (Field VII, Stratum V/sub-IV), for the appearance of this (mainly northern—see *Gezer III*, 131) variant among the more numerous ridged style. Compare the specimen from Cistern 370 at Tell en-Naṣbeh (ca. 700-586 BCE) in *TN—Cistern*, Fig. 4:X175; also *TN II*, Pl. 26:434-36. Gitin has suggested that similar rims "loosely dated" to the late fourth century BCE at Gibeah (Tell el-Fûl) more likely belong to the seventh century (*Gezer III*, 131; see *Gibeah*, Pl. 23:9-11). Note also *Gibeon*, Fig. 39:2 (Gibeon 1); *Lachish III*, Pl. 95:492; and *En-Gedi*, Fig. 21:4 (Stratum V).

[415] *Holladay*, 208. Holladay himself acknowledges that his supporting evidence from Shechem and Samaria (Fig. 6:19) does not derive from "stratigraphically acceptable loci."

[416] To the sample of rims cited (from the south) in n. 307, add *Megiddo I*, 11:56 (Strata IV-I).

	bowls	cooking pots	jars	holemouth jars	TOTAL
Rooms *g-h-j*					
120.121.19.126					
Wall 136 *(g)*	1	-	-	-	1
IXb *(j)*	-	-	-	1	1
Wall 151/157? *(h)*	-	1	-	-	1
Rooms *h-k*					
125.144					
IVa.y; V *(k/h?)*	1	-	-	-	1
IVx.z *(h)*	-	-	1	-	1
IVa *(h)*	-	-	1	-	1
Room *h*					
147.145.151.136					
IX	1	-	-	-	1
155.151.136.147					
IX	-	-	1	-	1
122.125.19.121					
Va	-	-	1	-	1
Room *j*					
North of TT2					
IX	-	-	2	-	2
E Strip-N of TT2					
IXr	-	1	-	-	1
509.126					
X	-	1	-	-	1
Room *k*					
Btw TT2-TT3					
VIII	1	-	-	-	1
VII	1	-	-	-	1
E Strip-Btw TT2-TT3					
VII; VIII	1	-	-	-	1
VII	1	2	1	-	4
Room *n*					
502.503					
Xa	-	3	-	-	3
XI	-	2	-	-	2
XIa	-	3	-	2	5
XIa.b	-	-	-	-	-
XII	1	1	-	1	3
XIIa	-	-	-	-	-
XIIa.b	-	1	-	1	2
XIIb	-	-	-	-	-
XIII	-	-	-	-	-
TOTAL	8	15	7	5	35

Distribution of PP 4-4a Ceramic Forms in Local Stratigraphy of House Floors (Rooms g-k, n)

Table 11

For the most part, the published report presents us with a mixed assemblage of ceramic fragments that show a chronological range from the mid-tenth to the early or even mid-seventh centuries BCE. This situation results from the fact that many, though not all, of the PP 4 materials come from imported deposits of secondary fill undoubtedly raked down into this area from erstwhile accumulations atop the rock scarp to the south. Still, such observations do not render these artifacts chronologically useless as Holladay suggests.[417] The most homogeneous pottery groups derive from Room *k* and, to a lesser extent, Room *n*. In light of my detailed presentation above of the local stratigraphy and specific findspots associated with each chamber, I need only add a few summary comments here. The remarks will follow the organization of Table 11; that is, I shall begin with the excavated segments that touch upon two or more rooms (Segments *120.121.19.126* and *125.144*) and then proceed to the mixed groups recovered from Rooms *h* and *j* proper before turning finally to the more compatible materials from Rooms *k* and *n*.

Segments *120.121.19.126* + *125.144*. Segment *120.121.19.126*, which extended through Rooms *g, h,* and *j*, yielded three pieces of (published) ceramic evidence: a straight-sided bowl with simple rim (*SS III*, Fig. 6:1); a flat, single-grooved holemouth jar rim (Fig. 6:24); and a notched rim from the Late Shallow Type cooking pot (Fig. 6:39). Of these three pieces, the cooking pot fragment likely entered the mainstream of ceramic tradition first (ca. mid-ninth century BCE). Though an incipient tradition of holemouth jar was already under way during that time, the particular style of rim seen here only appeared as much as a century later. Still, all three forms could easily have coexisted during the mid-to-late eighth century.

The report associates two of the entries, namely the bowl and the cooking pot rim, with specific architectural features. First, excavators apparently found the bowl lodged in the makeup of Wall 136. Judging from the presentation of this vessel in the final report, it comprised a whole form. It seems somewhat curious to find an intact item such as this in the meager remains (see fig. 5) of this thin partition wall between Rooms *g* and *h*. Whatever the reason behind its location (which could hardly have comprised a foundation deposit), this bowl likely came from the late blockage of the one-time doorway through that wall. Consequently, it helps to date the addition of that impediment to the mid-eighth century BCE.

Second, though the cooking pot rim seems to have emerged from a similar situation, uncertainty in the records as to whether it was associated with Wall 151 or Wall 157 precludes us from drawing firm conclusions based on this fragment. I have mentioned that, whichever wall actually provided its final locus, the chronological range of this piece does not necessarily stand in discord with that of the bowl. As indicated earlier, the field notes equated "Layer IXb," from which the holemouth jar fragment came, with "Wall 136." Their equation suggests that both this rim and the bowl were simply used as packing debris in the closing of the gap in this wall. Yet so many

---

[417]See his comments in *Holladay*, 130-31.

potential recording discrepancies plague the holemouth jar fragment that any further comment seems unjustified.

The lateral segment *125.144* ran through Rooms *h* and *k* and also contributed only three fragments to the published repertoire: one sherd assigned to the fine ware bowl in *SS III*, Fig. 6:5a, and the two store jar rims in Fig. 6:14-15. As I have shown, problems of nearly every kind attend the bowl fragment published as No. 5a. Here I need only add that, though the paired fragments seem compatible from a morphological point of view, the base and upper sidewall of Fig. 6:5 are not actually connected. Kenyon assumed that they belong together. One should recall that, according to the field records, multiple fragments of this bowl were recovered from two different rooms. Further, the notes present an impossible situation by assigning the *single* fragment published as No. 5a to *two* distinct local layers. There is now no way of knowing to which portion of the vessel (base or sidewall) the stratigraphic data entered for No. 5a might relate. While I believe that this bowl dates no earlier than the mid-eighth century, then, I hesitate to base any further historical conclusions on it.

Though Kenyon claimed that jar rim No. 14 came from a BP IVa "floor level," and offered it as the only ceramic evidence supporting her proposed "Period IVa," I have shown that it actually derived from a lens of blackish soil that comprised part of a deeper filling poured against Wall 155. Neither the stratigraphic context nor this solitary sherd, then, constitutes adequate evidence for declaring a distinct archaeological or historical subphase in the area of Room *h*. The rim in *SS III*, Fig. 6:15, with its rounded but very narrow shoulder, belongs to a globular-shaped amphora from the seventh century BCE. As such, it likely represents an intrusion into this otherwise mid- to-late eighth-century BCE context. The actual stratigraphic context of the findspot consisted in a deposit of fill material (Layer IVa, Room *h*).

Room *h*. The three fragments taken from segments relating only to this room also date to the eighth century BCE (*SS III*, Fig. 6:2, 12, 18). The thick-sided bowl (Fig. 6:2) and a simple store jar rim (Fig. 6:18) comprise the two earlier pieces; their chronological range spans from the early to the mid-eighth century. Together, these fragments help to corroborate a mid-eighth-century date for the plaster floor level (Layer IX, Segments *147.145.151.136* + *155.151.136.147*) that directly overruns the truncated remains of Omride Wall 161 and the fill levels which Ahab subsequently poured against that wall (see fig. 10). Once again, I see no intervening deposits between these BP I-II layers and the actual subfloor makeup for the BP IV surface in Level IX. Ahab's extension of Omri's courtyard north of Wall 161, then, appears to have produced the only floor levels commissioned in this area by a royal figure prior to the second or third quarter of the eighth century BCE.

The third sherd taken from Room *h* exemplifies the high-necked conical jar fragment with splayed rim. It postdates the previous two items and belongs either in the last quarter of the eighth century or in the seventh century BCE. Its stratigraphic context explains its later date. It came from Layer Va of Segment *122.125.19.121*. In fig. 8, I presented a lateral section that the excavators cut through this segment. Layer Va does not appear there, however, because it actually lay just north of that cut, in the area of Pit *i* (see fig. 5 for the relative horizontal positions of Auxiliary Section B and Pit *i*). Though Kenyon did not delineate the local stratigraphy within this pit, my fig. 10 shows its approximate location relative to other nearby architectural features. It is not surprising, then, to find this later vessel, with its similarity to Assyrian forms, in a deposit that saw continued use just before and after the fall of Samaria in 722/21 BCE. In this vein, it proves noteworthy that a relatively large cache of PP 6 material (*SS III*, Fig. 10:1-27) came from this very same layer inside the pit. I shall return to this locus, then, with additional detail when I examine that pottery group in Chapter III, Part II.B, below.

Room *j*. The two jar fragments in *SS III*, Fig. 6:8 and 16 came from the matrix of the hard surface in Segment *N of TT2*, Layer IX, presented in Auxiliary Section A (fig. 7). While the first of these rims appears to belong to the mid-to-late ninth century BCE, the second one stems from types used during the mid-to-late eighth century. Another "early" specimen—namely, the late tenth- to mid-ninth-century cooking pot rim in Fig. 6:33—surfaced in Layer IXr, the subfloor makeup imported to prepare the area for the surface of Layer IX. Arguably, this evidence once again places the first sure floor level to succeed Ahab's BP II surfaces in the mid-eighth century BCE at the earliest. The open *terminus post quem* of the levelings beneath the floor clearly account for the derived elements from older traditions reaching back to the tenth and ninth centuries BCE.

The exact same picture emerges for the cooking pot rim fragment in *SS III*, Fig. 6:32, which again reflects styles current mainly in the period between the late tenth and mid-ninth centuries. As shown in fig. 19, this sample came either from a yellowish floor level or from its makeup, both of which deposits received the designation "Layer X" on the field section. The earlier dating of this fragment suggests that it likely belongs to the basal layers of the surface or to the leveling fill beneath it. This BP IV surface surely correlates to Layer IX in *N of TT2* and, as figs. 7 and 19 both demonstrate, it lay sandwiched between a layer of paving stones and the intact portions of the hard floor used from the time of Ahab (BP II).[418] The deposits that yielded the PP 4 materials, then, occur stratigraphically *earlier* than the paving and *later* than the BP II floors. Moreover, they comprise virtually the only accumulations separating the paving from the BP II levels built by Ahab in the mid-ninth century BCE. If the yellowish floor of Segment *N of TT2*, Layer X, represents the interior surface of Room *j*, then one should place the functional life of that chamber roughly in the third quarter of the eighth century BCE. This same dating seems to apply to the depositional history in Room *h* and to the alterations to Wall 136 between Rooms *g* and *h*.

Room *k*. Chronologically speaking, the seven fragments representing three vessel types (bowls, cooking pots, and store jars) published from Room *k* manifest the most homogeneous collection of PP 4 pottery. Yet, as Table 1 discloses, this assem-

---

[418] For the dating of the latter feature, see *AIS-I*, 19-21 and 37-42.

blage also contained the highest percentage of discarded fragments (75%) of any ceramic group from this period. The field records assign all these pieces to one of two local layers (VII or VIII) in the segment labeled *Between Test Trench 2-Test Trench 3* (*SS III*, Fig. 6:3, 6) or, sometimes more specifically, in the *Eastern Strip* of that segment (*SS III*, Fig. 6:5b, 7, 17, 25, 35). Except for bowl fragment No. 5b, this entire group dates securely to the mid-ninth century BCE on typological grounds. As explained in my stratigraphic analysis above, Auxiliary Section A (fig. 7) shows that Layer VII emerges as the earliest floor level laid down in this area and that Layers VIIa and VIII, situated beneath that floor, constitute thicker depositions of imported fill. As seen with the surface levels discussed in Rooms *h* and *j* above, this floor was followed by a series of paving stones (designated sub-Layer IVa) found resting both "in and on" Layer IV. But unlike those other surfaces, this one in Room *k* was apparently not preceded by an earlier floor. Rather, the pottery readings show that Layer VII itself likely constitutes the living surface of Ahab's ninth-century designs. Virtually every fragment published from the fill of Layer VIII (*SS III*, Fig. 6:3) or, more important, from the actual matrix of Layer VII itself (*SS III*, Fig. 6:6, 7, 17, 25, 35) points directly to a mid-ninth-century BCE setting. Of these pieces, only the cooking pot rim seen in No. 25 may stem from the late tenth or early ninth century; but that in no way alters the overall picture. The one fragment that clearly derives from the fill of Layer VIII (discounting for the moment the very problematic entry in No. 5b[419]) supports a *terminus post quem* (or construction date) for the associated floor of Layer VII in the mid-ninth century BCE.

Further, fig. 8 clarifies that both Layers VII and VIII do not postdate Wall 157; rather, they appear contemporary with it. The layers addressed in Rooms *h* and *j* above correlate to deposits later than the VII-VIII sequence presented in this section. Wall 157 served originally as the continuation of the ninth-century chambers *a-d*; its affiliation with Rooms *g-k* is completely secondary. Kenyon, in fact, includes this feature on her BP III Top Plan (fig. 4), but one may conclude that 157 originated slightly earlier still, during the days of King Ahab. It rests on bedrock and cuts only accumulations of fill debris, and this dating is supported by the pottery taken from the first floor level associated with the wall (*Btw TT2-TT3*, Layer VII). The same argument cannot be forwarded, however, with regard to the later Wall 153 for, alas, the cut made by Robber Trench 153 (see fig. 13) has destroyed the exact stratigraphic relationship between these features (Wall 157 and Layers VII-VIII) and 153.

Finally, I note that fig. 7 confirms that, north of the line of Wall 153, the mid-eighth-century makeup and floor levels (Layer IX) plus the subsequent paved surface rested at lower elevations than did the original ninth-century surface south of that wall (namely, Layer VII). In this regard, I have stressed that the inclination of the bedrock

---

[419] Once again, the records reveal uncertainty over whether this discarded sherd from a fine ware bowl originated in the area *Btw TT2-TT3* or in the *East Strip* portion of that segment, and whether it appeared in Layer VII or in Layer VIII. In any event, the piece seems intrusive in this general context.

drops to a slight degree east of Wall 157 but to a dramatic one north of it. In fact, the steep pitch of the rock in this area evoked comment from Kenyon herself in the field notes.[420] Later in this study, the gradient and relative elevations of the floor levels laid in this area will help inform my suggested portrait of the summit of Samaria during the closing years of Israelite rule in the middle two quarters of the eighth century BCE. I believe the final report has misappropriated Levels VII and VIII in Room *k* to BP IV and that it has conflated them with later deposits from the mid-eighth century.

Room *n*. Aside from one bowl fragment that likely dates from the late ninth or early eighth centuries BCE (*SS III*, Fig. 6:4), Segment *502.503* in the area of "Room" *n* yielded two disparate groups of rather homogeneous pottery. First, a series of cooking pot rims shows variations both on the elongated, flanged style (Fig. 6:26-30, 38) from late Iron I-early Iron II traditions and on the notched, so-called Late Shallow Type from the mid-ninth century on (Fig. 6:34, 36, 37, 40). Intermingled in the same layers that produced these finds, however, was an assemblage of mid-eighth to mid-seventh-century holemouth jar rims (Fig. 6:20, 22-24). Though each collection exhibits consistency within its ranks, the intergroup chronological disparities are noticeable; as much as a century separates the cooking pots from the jars.

I have discussed the complex depositional history of this area above. As a result, I can now draw this discussion to a close by correlating information in figs. 22-23 with data in Tables 5 and 11 and by ultimately arriving at the following conclusions. First, Kenyon herself acknowledged that Layer Xa, which yielded three cooking pot fragments from late tenth- or early ninth-century traditions (Fig. 6:29, 30, 36), comprised subfloor makeup for a BP V paved surface. In similar fashion, Layer XI also represented basal deposits supporting levels paved with a kind of flagstone. Though Kenyon placed the latter accumulation in her "Period IV," it also belongs in BP V together with its subdeposit in Layer XIa, which contained a mixture of three mid-ninth-century cooking-pot fragments (Fig. 6:27, 37, 40) and two holemouth rims from the late eighth to early seventh centuries (Fig. 6:22, 24). Second, I return to the fact that the excavators tied the earlier deposits in *502.503* to the robbing of Wall 161 and the subsequent backfilling of the resultant trench (Layers XIa.b through XIIb). Finally, I suggest that, though these levels also produced a mixture of ninth-century cooking-pot rims and eighth-century holemouth fragments, it is the latest elements in these layers—namely, the series of holemouth rims—that provide the *terminus post quem* for the plundering of Wall 161. In this light, Omri's original Enclosure Wall 161 seems to have maintained some sort of functional life until the mid-eighth century BCE, at least in the northeastern quadrant of the royal compound, east of 660° E.

As a result of this extensive investigation into the rooms north of the main courtyard, I propose to place the remains associated with BP IV activities no earlier than the mid-eighth century BCE, i.e., to a time later than Kenyon's suggested dating

---

[420]*Fieldbook Qk-l-m*, 35.

in the opening years of that century (around 800 BCE[421]). Since the material culture that survives from a given period generally stems from the closing years of that era,[422] I believe that BP IV relates to the last half of the rule of Jeroboam II and possibly to the years immediately following his reign.

Several important points have emerged concerning the depositional history of layers exposed from this period. First, though occasional lenses of blackish or sooty soil appear, the relatively meager quantities of this type of matrix do not point to destruction levels associated with large scale military activity against the city. Second, my discussion of these layers also becomes important for what it has not included, namely, appreciable amounts of ivory fragments. Though most of the ivories came from this same area, particularly from the vicinity of Rooms *h* and *k*, they emerged from stratigraphically later deposits, whose nature I shall address in the following chapters of this study. Third, the levels ascribed to BP IV lie in a close stratigraphic sequence and are ensconced squarely between relatively clear floor levels from the mid-ninth century BCE and the paved surfaces that appear, at this point, to belong to BP V. Fourth, though similar pavings also appear east of the substantial Wall 561—in the area assigned to Room *n* (see fig. 5)—the evidence does not support seeing yet another "room" in this vicinity. The size and configuration of Walls 560-561-562 bear a greater resemblance to a perimeter system around the inner compound area than to either the official rooms (such as Chambers *a-d*) or the ordinary, utilitarian rooms (as in *g-k*) located to the west. The stone pavings east of 561 might just as easily represent an open-air piazza. Fifth, the depositional history relating to these levels consistently shows, across this entire area, a stratigraphic juxtapositioning of late Israelite layers and levels from the considerably later Hellenistic and Roman periods, without appreciable accumulations from the intervening years. Finally, as Kenyon noted in the published report, "the building changes [in BP IV] are fairly considerable, but not more so than those between both earlier and later periods. In every case, *further excavation of the site is necessary* to show whether the rebuildings are local or not."[423]

Part B. North Courtyard
(*SS I*, Pl. VII — Section GH)
(*SS III*, Fig. 6:9-11, 13, 31)

This area comprised a new courtyard floor made of hard-pounded limestone and laid over the now defunct rooms south of 445° N[424] (see *AIS-I*, 17, fig. 4 = *SS I*, Pl. VIII; compare Pl. VII, Section GH[425]). These rooms and their associated corridors had

---

[421] *SS I*, 105.

[422] See *AIS-I*, 5, n. 8.

[423] *SS I*, 105 (emphasis added).

[424] *SS III*, 113.

[425] Published Section AB also passed through this area, but it included only the earliest layers (mainly

served the north courtyard area since the early building activities of Omri and Ahab (BP I-II). The act of now paving them over reflects an apparent expansion of the "inner" or main courtyard northward without having to move back any of the main perimeter walls.

Figure 24 traces the various phases of building activity in the area of the northern courtyard. Resting south of the group of irregularly built rooms discussed in Part A above, the BP I-II (and III) complex of rooms[426] maintained the latitudinal Wall 60 as its northernmost boundary. The functional life of the more northerly and larger series of BP I-II rooms and corridors (*a-h*) continued in BP III (now labeled *j-n* in fig. 5),[427] while an annex of more squarish alcoves (BP III *a-i*) was added to the NE. These latter chambers were exposed along a 35 x 10-meter span situated just above 450° N and extending from 615° E to nearly 650° E. During BP IV, this set of spaces remained[428] and the much less impressive Rooms *f-k* were added behind them, together with Rooms *l* and *m* to the east. Room *r* (and possibly *n*) appears, in both design and quality of construction, to conform better with the surviving BP III suite *a-e* than with the new BP IV cluster in *f-k*.

Given the width of BP IV longitudinal Wall 561 (ca. 1.8 m) relative to the walls of all the other structures in the area, including even the better-built ones, and given the apparent lack of perpendicular walls to the east of 561,[429] I believe that it may have functioned as the eastern perimeter of the courtyard rather than as the starting point of yet another new room. As a perimeter wall, 561 would have served as the counterpart to the longitudinal wall seen on Reisner's plans farther west—between the Ostraca House and royal palace—a wall that exhibits a similar width.[430] If so, the area designated "Room *n*" may, in fact, constitute not another enclosed chamber but rather the beginnings of a large, paved piazza extending east from the inner compound toward the main city gate area. The eastern limits of the excavation area, however, preclude us from corroborating this suggestion. A pattern of planning similar to that which Biran has shown to have existed at Tel Dan during the ninth and eighth centuries BCE would accord well with the plan of the capital itself.[431] Since the leveling of this surface along

---

BP I-II) found just above the natural rock surface.

[426] Labeled α-η on *SS I*, Pl. VIII (*AIS-I*, fig. 4).

[427] See *AIS-I*, 54, n. 115. The southern complex of BP I-II rooms (*i-l*) apparently went out of service in BP III, somewhat earlier than their northern counterparts.

[428] Chambers *h* and *i* were narrowed slightly as BP IV Wall 65 became their new southern boundary. As *SS I*, Pl. VII, Section GH reveals, Wall 65 was built against the northern face of its BP III predecessor, Wall 60, and thereby usurped some of the earlier space inside the rooms it served.

[429] Wall 562, which adjoins 561 perpendicularly from the west, served only Rooms *m* and *r* ; i.e., it did not continue eastward beyond the line of 561.

[430] Unfortunately, not enough intact stones remain from Wall 561 to permit a comparison of construction techniques.

[431] See A. Biran, *Biblical Dan* (Jerusalem: Israel Exploration Society and Hebrew Union College—Jewish Institute of Religion, 1994), 235ff., Figs. 200 and 206.

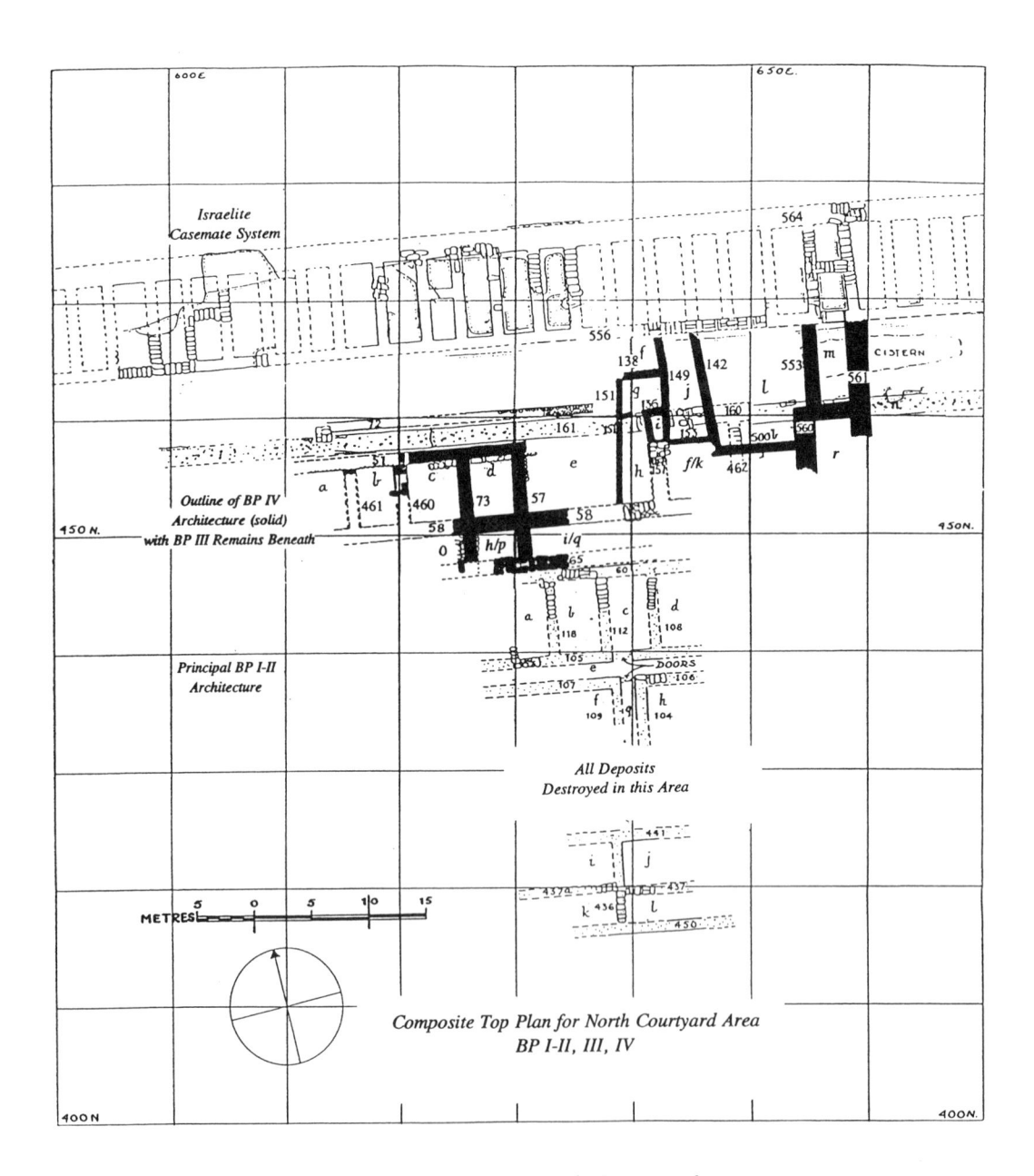

*Composite Top Plan for North Courtyard Area:
BP I-II, III, IV*

fig. 24

460° N involved raking deep fillings into the area from the rooms to the west, the large number of utilitarian, food-processing vessels (a cache of cooking pots and holemouth jars published in *SS III*, Fig. 6:20-23, 26-30, 34, 36-38, 40, plus the bowl in 6:4) appeared in a rather mixed matrix.

The present group of coordinates (i.e., the *86.2.88* . . . series) takes us back to the southernmost sector mentioned above, i.e., to the stretch of thick, compacted courtyard surface lying roughly between 635°-640° E and 435°-445° N. The field of excavation included this area as part of the southern reaches of its Summit Strip Qc (which apparently continued south only to about 430° N).[432] Kenyon's published Top Plan for BP IV, however, reflects a virtual absence of any traceable architectural features here (see fig. 5 above). My previous investigation showed that the earliest levels in this vicinity actually preserved a number of secure, primary, stratigraphic findspots related to BP I.[433] Published pottery comprising the PP 4 corpus, on the other hand, consists mainly in a few jar rim fragments recovered from fills beneath new, eighth-century BCE courtyard levels (*SS III*, Fig. 6:9-11, 13; the final report also included one cooking pot rim, Fig. 6:31). A portrait of the local stratigraphy from this and later phases of Israelite occupation follows and complements my earlier discussion in *AIS-I*.

1) Stratigraphic Detail

    a. 86.2.88
    b. 86.2.88.E
    c. 86.2.88.W
    d. 86.2.88.E, W of 104

Though I shall treat the following coordinates as an overall group, I will distribute my comments throughout the individual subsegments as appropriate, since the field notes themselves distinguish between these component areas in their stratigraphic summaries.[434] I shall begin with material recorded as simply *86.2.88*.

In approaching these coordinates, it behooves us to recall a section presented in my previous study from *Fieldbook Qc-g* (fig. 25).[435] The strata presented here concentrate on the area just south of 440° N, that is, around the BP I-II corridor walls 105 and 107 in fig. 24. I have recently collated data from two new field sections (figs. 26-27), one of which (No. 27) displays the same north-south orientation as fig. 25, while

---

[432] An outline of the parameters of Strip Qc is provided in *SS II*, 3.

[433] See the segments marked with an asterisk in *AIS-I*, 18, Table 1.

[434] The relevant narratives for these segments appear in *Fieldbook Qc-g*, 8, 11-13, 18-19, 55, and 63 (field notes pertaining to *86.2.88*); 56, 58-59 (field notes for *86.2.88.E*); 57, 61-62, 65-66 (field notes for *86.2.88.W*); 8a, 11a-12a (stratigraphic summary of *86.2.88*); 56a (stratigraphic summary of *86.2.88*); 57a, 61a (stratigraphic summary for *86.2.88.W*); 11a, 59a, 63a (field sections depicting *86.2.88.E*); 66a (field section relating to *86.2.88.W*); 58a (top plan for general area).

[435] *Fieldbook Qc-g*, 63a. This section first appeared in *AIS-I*, 55, fig. 11.

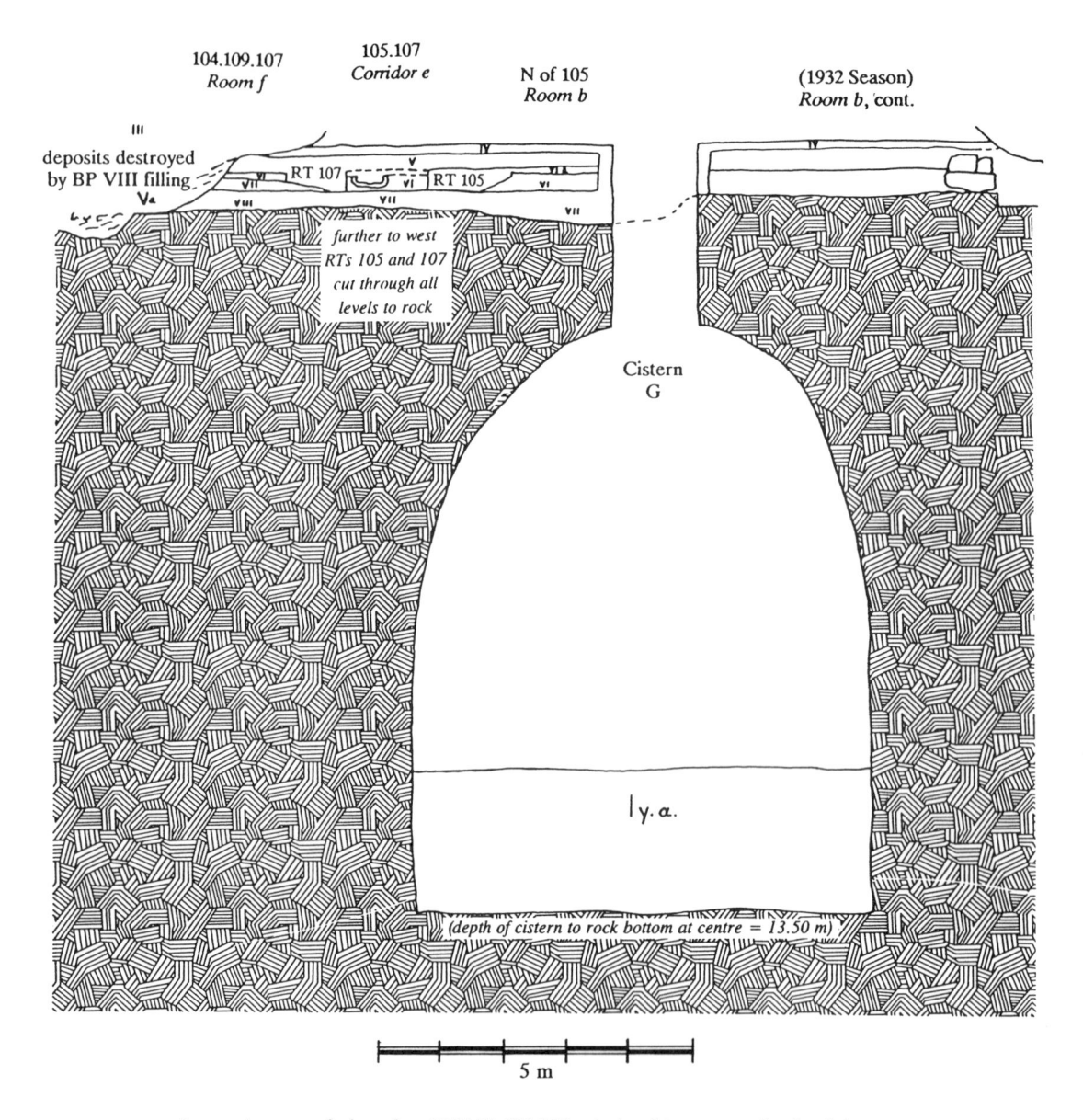

104.109.107   105.107
Room f   Corridor e   N of 105   (1932 Season)
                               Room b   Room b, cont.

deposits destroyed
by BP VIII filling

RT 107   RT 105

further to west
RTs 105 and 107
cut through all
levels to rock

Cistern
G

ly. a.

(depth of cistern to rock bottom at centre = 13.50 m)

5 m

(approximate scale based on RT 105–RT 107 relationship, not on depth of cistern)

Segment Series 86.2.88
<— S N —>
View toward West

fig. 25

the other reflects an east-west cut across this area. The former delineates the continuation of the deposits to the immediate north of fig. 25, into the spaces occupied successively by BP I-II Rooms *a-d* and BP III Rooms *k-n* (compare fig. 5). One can locate the latter drawing along the course of Section GH by using the later Robber Trench 98 as a reference.[436]

It is noteworthy that the layers in fig. 26 reveal a slightly different depositional history from those seen already further north in the BP IV Rooms *g-k*. While the seemingly ever present remains from the Roman period appear here as expected (Layers I, Ia, plus at least 22 additional subdeposits),[437] previously unencountered deposits of the so-called chocolate soil[438] lay beneath these levels (Layers IIa-II; figs. 26-27). The principal difference between these accumulations and those recovered north of BP IV Wall 58 lies in the fact that the field descriptions of this chocolate soil seem to indicate that it was basically 'pure', i.e., not riddled with mixed yellowish soil and striations of soot. The excavators found only a thin layer of "mixed chocolate" (labeled Layer IIa) at the elevation where II met the Late Roman materials. It also seems possible that IIa might have contained elements from the occupational debris associated with the surface lying beneath it.

Neither do the records concerning these chocolate deposits reflect the presence of ivory fragments among any of the loci excavated here, even though the excavators reported in *SS II* that "the strip where [they] made the richest haul of ivories was called Qc."[439] When considering the archaeological context of these most impressive artifacts, then, it is important to remember that their locations lay further north on the horizontal plane of that strip, in stratigraphy situated above Omri's original Enclosure Wall 161 where the shabbily built complex of BP IV rooms (*g-k*) came to exist. I shall return to the implications of this fact in my Conclusions to PP 4 below.

Layer IIIb rested immediately below II, while Layer III contained the principal makeup for II (figs. 26-27). The field notes do not comment in detail on the distinction—whether it involved mainly color, consistency, or contents—that apparently

---

[436]On the horizontal axis for this area, Wall 98 lay roughly half way between the BP I-II (III) Walls 60 and 105, at roughly 443° N (see *AIS-I*, 17, fig. 4).

[437]Level I in fig. 26 comprised a Late Roman (R.4) plaster floor covering most of the southern area of Summit Strip Qc in the fourth century CE; Level Iy.a, representing a breach in I, designated a cistern mouth not sealed by any deposit; Level II revealed a floor of beaten earth situated approximately 1.10 m below I. Sub-Layer IIb (to the immediate right of RT 95 on fig. 26) referred to a rubbish pit which, like the cistern, was found "cutting down fr[om the] top" (i.e., based on the rendering in fig. 26, presumably from the top of the Roman period Layer Ia, perhaps even I). The field notes record that pink- and buff-colored ribbed ceramic forms appeared throughout both layers (*Fieldbook* Qc-g, 8a). Finally, Layers IIIb.a and IIIb indicated still other points at which rough stones had broken the chocolate soil of II. Clearly, then, the stratigraphy of the later floor levels in this segment was hampered by multiple intrusions.

[438]This likely points to the brown forest soil that results from the deterioration of Eocene limestone formations found throughout the region around the city of Samaria (see Introduction).

[439]*SS II*, 2.

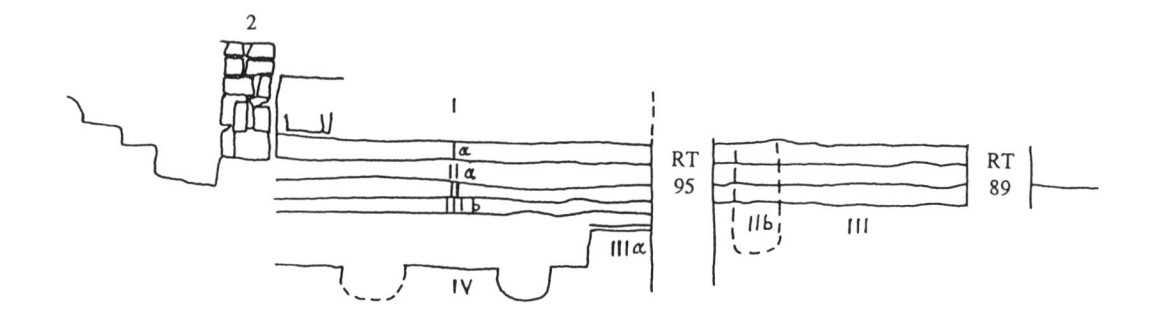

(scale not recorded)

Segment Series 86.2.88:
Supplement No. 1 — E and W of Wall 95
<— E W —>
(orientation uncertain)

fig. 26

existed between these two related deposits; they do add, however, that the excavators effectively removed them *en masse*. Based on her reading of the pottery, Kenyon assigned both the chocolate level and its makeup to her "Period VIII," with the latest of these layers (the mixed deposit of IIa) possibly extending into Period IX.[440] As I have found so often, however, the published repertoire failed to include any of the ceramic materials from these levels. Similarly, the field notes provide only a laconic description of Layer IVa (fig. 27) by saying that it comprised the "bottom of III" and by placing it in "Period VIII."[441]

According to Kenyon, the partial remains of still another floor level (Layer IIIa) appeared below the layers just discussed, though it was "n[o]t present everywhere" (one may note, for example, its absence from fig. 27). Based on her observations of a ceramic assemblage that she described as "P[ottery] Period VI + Isr[aelite],"[442] Kenyon dated this accumulation to "VIIa," i.e., to a nascent PP 7. She also associated two circular pits that cut into Layer IV with the deposit of IIIa and even labeled them

---

[440]Kenyon did not use the designation "Period IX" frequently; I presume that it reflects a kind of transitional phase between her Period VIII and the Hellenistic/Roman levels that followed. On a second matter of interest, the field notes at this point also indicate that sub-Layer IIb, a rubbish pit that cut down from the very top of the deposit, contained soft buff-colored ribbed ware and some mosaic tesserae (*Fieldbook Qc-g*, 11a).

[441]*Fieldbook Qc-g*, 12a.

[442]*Fieldbook Qc-g*, 11a.

'IIIa' as well. Her rendering of these features in fig. 26, however, seems to suggest that the depositional history of these pits developed according to the following sequence, from earliest to latest: the two pits cut into the pre-existent Layer IV; Layer IIIa subsequently filled and covered the pits; Layer III then cut IIIa across the area of the pits. It seems likely, therefore, that these pits would have yielded mixed remains associated with level IV as well as with IIIa and III, with the last two perhaps serving as both the fills and the makeup for the chocolate colored surfaces above. At the south extension of fig. 25, where BP VIII building activities heavily disturbed earlier layers, the excavators recorded the bottom portion of III as Layer IVa.

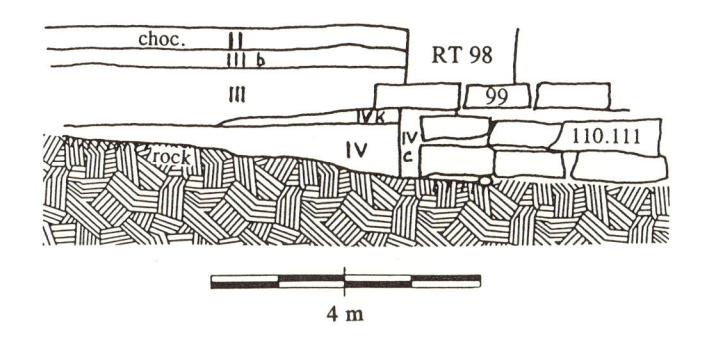

Segment Series 86.2.88:
Supplement No. 2 — Section on Line of 99
<— S N —>
View toward West

fig. 27

As reported in *AIS-I*,[443] Kenyon assigned Layer IV, which sealed the area south of the rooms mentioned in my introduction to this segment, to her "Period IV" courtyard floor (here, one can collate fig. 25 to 26-27).[444] This compacted surface showed signs of destruction along the southernmost edge of the excavation area. The interpretation of the next earliest deposit, Layer V (seen only on fig. 25), proves somewhat ambivalent, stating that it represented "the makeup of IV, or another floor (orig[inal] one) on same phase, sealing the walls of early Isr[aelite] buildings."[445] In either case, it appears to have filled and sealed Robber Trench 107 and to have sealed Robber Trench 105. This situation may indicate that the plunderings of these two walls were

---

[443] *AIS-I*, 54-58.

[444] A summary of these layers appears in *Fieldbook Qc-g*, 12a, 56a.

[445] *Fieldbook Qc-g*, 12a.

not concurrent events; rather, they were rather separated by a (brief) hiatus.[446] I believe this deposit likely served as the makeup for IV and that both were laid down in the same period[447]—either BP III or IV. A more detailed description of the consistency, color, and contents of these layers would have enabled us to make a better determination as to the most likely time when this occurred.

Since at least two fragments of published pottery assigned to PP 4 came from deposits associated with Layer VI, I include for the sake of convenience my description of the earlier levels from this area presented in fig. 25:

> The soft, darkish soil of Layers VI (in areas *104.109.107* + *105.107*) and VIb (*N of 105*), taken to contain the remains of the "Period III" floor (compare *SS I*, PL. VII, Section GH), were "associated w[ith] alterations to [the] original Israelite walls" 105 and 107. In the segment *N of 105*, the deposit labeled VI proper was equated with Layer VII in *104.109.107* and interpreted as the "Period I" floor level. Here it consisted of a "thick layer of decca, and below [it the] dark earth = VII" [*Fieldbook Qc-g*, 59].
>
> Beneath this fairly level surface and lying directly on the rock, a band of homogeneous matrix received the layer designations VIII in segment *104.109.107* and VII in *105.107* + *N of 105*. Though in their final analysis the excavators recognized these two "layers" as one and the same, some confusion persisted regarding whether to construe them as "Period I" makeup or as the "original floor" itself. In either case, the PP 1 pottery seen in the final report derived from this layer and, according to Kenyon's reading of the stratigraphy, the entire area presented itself devoid of any "Period II" remains. Interestingly, the notebooks record that in *104.109.107* (= Room *f*) Layer VII lay only .10 m beneath VI, and that it sloped down to the north and showed no signs of having been cut by the line of Wall 107.[448]

The depositional history reviewed above does not differ in any significant way from that presented in the field notes for the other segments listed in the *86.2.88* series (*86.2.88.E*; *86.2.88.W*; *86.2.88.E–W of 104*). As I have noted elsewhere, the designations *E* and *W* seem to refer to deposits situated on either side of Wall 95 (see fig. 26), a feature which appears prominently in the notebook records for the general area of *86.2.88*.[449]

---

[446]If so, the fill in RT 105 requires a separate layer designation.

[447]In the segment *N of 105*, excavators recovered two ovens surrounded by the matrix of Layers IV-V. These installations "rested on VI [presumably Kenyon's VId], slightly breaking it" (*Fieldbook Qc-g*, 59).

[448]*AIS-I*, 56.

[449]See *AIS-I*, 147-48. For example, *86.2.88.E of 95* and *86.2.88.W of 95* received their own stratigraphic summaries in *Fieldbook Qc-g*, 56a (*East*), 57a and 61a (*West*). I presume, therefore, that fig. 26 exhibits a lateral orientation, though it remains uncertain whether the drawing is presented from east-to-west or vice-versa (due mainly to my lack of success in locating RT 89 in either the published sections or the field notes).

The final report published five fragments of pottery from these interrelated segments, with none of the specimens marked as discards. Except for the pottery presented in *SS III* from Room *g* and the suggested PP 4a resurfacing of Room *h*, each of which contributed only one sherd to the published repertoire, the small ceramic group from *86.2.88...* emerges as the only one in *SS III*, Fig. 6 to have remained untainted by the eventual reliance on originally discarded fragments (recall my discussion in the Introduction to this chapter). Moreover, as Table 1 above reveals, the single fragment from Room *g*—though not marked for discard—was apparently found lodged in Wall 136 and therefore may comprise a scrap of secondary construction debris.

The five fragments removed from these segments, then, deserve close scrutiny in my Pottery Analysis below. The distribution of this group, which consists primarily in rim fragments from various styles of jars, appears as follows (presented by layer, from earliest to latest): *86.2.88.E (of 95)* yielded rim fragments from a cooking pot (Fig. 6:31) and a jar (Fig. 6:9) recovered from Layer VIe, described as "= V in filling of R.T. 105"; *86.2.88* added another jar rim (Fig. 6:10) from Layer VI; *86.2.88.E-W of 104* contributed still another jar fragment (Fig. 6:13) from Layer V; and *86.2.88.W* contained the jar rim (Fig. 6:11) taken from Layer IV (or IVh?). From the preceding analysis of the stratigraphy, one can see that at least two of these findspots possibly rested in a primary (or relatively secure) stratigraphic context. First, Layer VI *may* represent the BP I-II floor level associated with Walls 105 and 107. Second, Layer IV appears to denote the next preserved living surface, which means that it likely stems from BP III or BP IV. Layer V, on the other hand, comprised a fill layer imported to the area after the robbing of Walls 105 and 107. Finally, Layer VIe appears from the notes to correlate directly to that part of V which actually lay inside the trench created by the removal of Wall 105 (see my comments in nn. 446-47).

Within this list of findspots, the most difficult one to locate with certainty remains that attributed to Layer VI. The question centers on which particular portion of VI (as seen in fig. 25) Kenyon intended. If she meant Layer VI in the area north of RT 105, then it would seem to derive from Omri's original limestone floor, perhaps resurfaced by his son Ahab. If, on the other hand, this designation "VI" should relate to the accumulation depicted in *104.109.107*[450] and/or *105.107*, then the deposit might reflect the actual occupational debris found lying immediately on top of that floor. In this case, it would belong to the *final* phases of the floor's functional life, which could have extended easily into the early-to-mid-eighth century BCE.[451]

---

[450] "Though Kenyon interpreted Layer VI of *104.109.107* as her 'Period III' floor, the dark color and soft consistency of the soil suggests rather than this is occupational debris and not a new surface" (*AIS-I*, 147).

[451] For my earlier recognition of this problem, see the discussion in *AIS-I*, 147-48, where I recognized that the floor might easily have continued in use through the reign of Jehu. On the likelihood that material recovered from such a surface usually reflects the closing years/days of activity there, see *AIS-I* 5, n. 8.

2) Pottery Analysis

a. Cooking Pots

The final report contained only a single cooking pot fragment recovered from Segment *86.2.88.E* in the North Courtyard area. The rim mode attested on the piece in *SS III*, Fig. 6:31, belongs to the same ceramic tradition and chronological range as No. 38, except that 31 appears with handles. I need not reiterate the full discussion given under Part A., Room *n* above, and in my earlier study of the pottery recovered from this general area.[452] The form is clearly at home in the mid-eleventh to mid-tenth centuries BCE, with its greatest concentration falling toward the end of that time span. The presence of this early piece among the putative PP 4 assemblage receives quick explanation from the fact that it derives from a secondary deposit of debris imported to backfill the robber trench created by the plundering of Wall 105 (Layer VIe). This filling occurred in the mid-to-late eighth century BCE, when the inhabitants abandoned the long-used courtyard levels constructed in the ninth century and began laying new ones. The stratigraphic context and historical circumstance, then, explain why this early style cooking-pot fragment appeared in the same local layer as a much later jar rim (see No. 9 below).

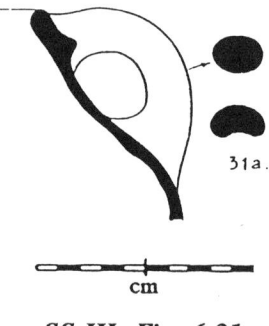

SS III, Fig. 6:31

b. Jars

The Joint Expedition recovered a small group of jar rims from the collection of segments ascribed to *86.2.88...*, in Summit Strip Qc. This ceramic lot remained relatively free of recording discrepancies, and none of its members received the designation "discard." Stratigraphic data for each findspot appear in Table 12.

Rim Nos. 9-11 represent further permutations (primarily with regard to the slope of the neck) in the ovoid-shaped storage jar with externally thickened rim. As Gitin's study has demonstrated, this basic vessel form spawned more subtypes than any other kind of jar.[453] While all the rims show basic triangular sections with rounded edges, fragment Nos. 9 and 11 display short

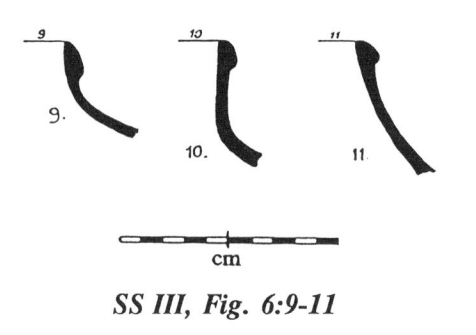

SS III, Fig. 6:9-11

---

[452]*AIS-I*, 60-62, 119-121.

[453]Compare the roster of Iron II types and subtypes in *Gezer III*, 47-51.

SS III Published Figure	Registry No. (none marked for discard)	Provenance		
		Strip	Coordinates	Feature	Local Layer
6:9	QX 30	Q(x)-c	▷86.2.88.E	N Courtyard	VIe
6:10	QX 43	Q(x)-c	86.2.88	N Courtyard	IV
6:11	QX 40	Q(x)-c	86.2.88.W	N Courtyard	IVh
6:13	QX 46	Q(x)-c	86.2.88.E/W-104	N Courtyard	V

Provenance Data:
PP4 Jars from Area Labeled "North Courtyard"

Table 12

and high versions, respectively, of necks that are inwardly inclined. Entry No. 10, on the other hand, presents a high, straight neck with a stance that leans very slightly outward. Though these rims belong to the same general class of vessel as No. 8, the absence of internal rim thickening distinguishes them from that variant. The band or collar, created by the external thickening, around No. 9 appears slightly wider than the others, while the more bevelled rim No. 11 slants outward to a greater degree and thereby forms a more noticeable outer lip. These exemplars generally consist in a hard fired reddish-brown to grey ware (No. 10 = buff ware) with inclusions of (sometimes large) limestone grits. In terms of surface treatment, Kenyon recorded a slip only on Nos. 9 (drab) and 10 (buff).

Holladay dates this PP 4 subgroup "to a time near or past the mid-eighth century."[454] Though Gitin basically concurs with this placement, he correctly recognizes that one should find the prototypes for this style in the ninth century, possibly even in the first half of that era.[455] Nuances in the rim-form mode constitute the principal attribute that allows us to distinguish between these antecedent forms and later exemplars. In the eighth century, the rim "is rounded, drawn up from the neck and down over it, so the rim only appears on the exterior side of the neck."[456] Prior to this period, rims display greater internal thickening[457] and, following the eighth century, they become more bulbous and assume a position on top of the neck. Holladay indi-

---

[454]*Holladay*, 130 and n. 116.

[455]*Gezer III*, 140. Compare *Beth-Shan*, James, Fig. 64:5 (Upper Level V); *'Ein Gev*, Fig. 8:2 (Level III). From the second half of the ninth century, Gitin cites *Hazor I*, Pl. L:35 (Stratum VII). Similar though thicker collars with more rounded upper lip appear also in Iron I contexts (e.g., *T. Qasîle* [2], Fig. 30:6, Stratum XI).

[456]*Gezer III*, 140.

[457]Holladay suggests that *Hazor II*, Pl. LIX:8 represents a transitional form linking this early rim style to the externally thickened, eighth-century mode (*Holladay*, 213).

cates that the tendency toward slight internal thickening continues down even to the 760 BCE jars but generally disappears by the 733 BCE horizon.[458]

A good morphological parallel from late eighth-century levels at Hazor suggests that form No. 9 may represent a distant descendant of the bulging, "hippo" body form and that it likely dates to the last quarter of that century.[459] Comparisons for No. 10 from Hazor,[460] Beth-Shan,[461] Megiddo,[462] Keisan,[463] Tell Qiri,[464] Tell en-Naṣbeh,[465] Beth-Shemesh,[466] and Lachish[467] suggest a range of dates for this piece in the mid-to-late eighth century BCE.

Exact parallels for rim No. 11 remain difficult to locate.[468] With its swooping neck- and upper side-walls, however, it appears to follow No. 10 in the chronological series, though not by much.[469] In fact, this form, with its plain, sloping neck and hard, red-brown ware with white grits,[470] bears a strong resemblance to the primary jar type

---

[458] *Holladay*, 214. In his study, he acknowledged that since this "slight nuance falls within the range of drawing error, it is perhaps best not to make too much of it." Gitin's subsequent, more detailed analysis, however, suggests that this subtle distinction in rim form provides a viable criterion for refined dating.

[459] *Hazor I*, Pl. LVII:((Stratum V). Admittedly, the Hazor piece shows a more noticeable bend at the juncture of the neck and shoulder. The full hippo form disappeared around the close of the tenth century BCE (see n. 319 above).

[460] *Hazor II*, Pl. Pls. LIX:3, 5-6 (Stratum VIII); LXXI:7 (Stratum VI), with painted decoration; XC:8-13 (Stratum VA), though with the exterior juncture between neck and shoulder slightly more trimmed than on the Samaria fragment; *Hazor III-IV*, Pl. CCXXIX:2-4 (Stratum VA).

[461] *Beth-Shan*, James, Fig. 34:8 (Level IV).

[462] *Megiddo I*, Pl. 10:37-38 (Stratum III; with more globular body form).

[463] *T. Keisan*, Pl. 51:4 (Niveau 7 = 900-850 BCE).

[464] *T. Qiri*, Fig. 13:5 (Area D, Stratum VII)—a short-necked variant.

[465] *TN II*, Pl. 14:241-46.

[466] *AS-IV*, Pls. LXV:1-3; LXVIII:16 (Stratum IIC = sixth century BCE), though with neck walls flexed or bowed inward a bit more.

[467] *Lachish III*, Pl. 95:486 (seventh-sixth centuries); compare also Pl. 96:528.

[468] The best comparison comes from *TBM III*, Pl. 13:3 = photo in Pl 68:1 (Stratum A2). Note Albright's comments on the paucity of adequate parallels in *TBM III*, 145, § 146. See also *TN II*, Pl. 19:314. These later forms, with increased upper-body diameter, may hark back to a tradition of similar but svelte jars dating as early as the tenth century BCE (compare *Ta'anach*, Fig. 30:3, Period IIB).

[469] Compare *Hazor III-IV*, Pl. CLXXXV:15 (Stratum VI); *Megiddo I*, Pl. 16:82 (Stratum III); *TN II*, Pl. 19:314 (which embodies probably the best overall parallel); compare *TN II*, Pl. 22:357 for a suggested body form that likely accompanied this rim.

[470] Attention to the fabric (hard-fired but not well levigated) is important here. Zimhoni has noted that the reddish-brown ware with white grits seen on the *LMLK* jars from Lachish actually "differs from that of the rest of the Level III vessels, assuring their [the *LMLK* jars] identification even when they bear no impressions" (*Lachish*–Zimhoni, 15). Samaria rim No. 10 also seems congruent with many of the *LMLK* neck and rim forms (particularly in its straighter neck mode), but its buff colored ware and slip ultimately distinguish it from the standard material used in the *LMLK* tradition. Compare the following forms in Zimhoni's study to *SS III*, Fig. 6:10-11 — Fig. 8:4 (from Level III: Group IIIA, *LMLK* storage

used in conjunction with the royal *LMLK* seal impressions.[471] Though the rim itself on the Samaria piece appears slightly more "rolled" than the usual simple rim on many of the *LMLK* jars, both Tufnell[472] and Aharoni[473] cited this exact style (using the exemplar from Tell Beit Mirsim) as a good comparison to the *LMLK* vessels from Lachish.[474] The appearance of this "*LMLK*-like" jar at Samaria, then, may point to an unusual circumstance, since the true *LMLK* jars—though similar in many respects to other ovoid forms from the north—occur primarily in assemblages from the south.[475] But interestingly, Tufnell also noted that this style jar and a certain group of bowls at Lachish (her Class B.13[476]) seemed akin to a series of bowls published from PP 7 at Samaria (*SS III*, Fig. 11:1-6; see Ch. IV below). This observation, in turn, prompted her to wonder whether the jars "were made by potters trained in a northern school who moved south after the fall of Samaria in 720 B.C.?"[477] Recently, Tushingham has pursued that thesis further by arguing that the two-winged solar disk represented the royal symbol of Judah, and thus appears on jars originating there, while the four-winged scarab constituted an Israelite (i.e., northern) symbol placed on jars manufactured there.[478] This hypothesis, however, requires much greater substantiation and I

---

jars); 12:2; 14:1 (from Level III: Group IIIB, "*LMLK*-like" jars). The last citation seems particularly close in form and ware to Fig. 6:11 at Samaria. As for the buff ware of No. 10, I may note an apparent association with the gritty, "light brown to yellowish" clay of the *LMLK* look-alikes at Lachish (see again Zimhoni's study, p. 19). It is important to note that though the *LMLK* royal seal impressions still occur only in the late eighth century, *LMLK*-style jars begin already in the ninth century (see, among other recent studies, A. M. Maeir, "The Philistine Culture in Transformation," in *Settlement, Civilization and Culture*, A. M. Maeir and E. Baruch, eds. [Ramat-Gan: Bar-Ilan University, 2001], Fig. 10:1).

[471] See Tufnell's Class S.7a, Type 484 in *Lachish III*, Pl. 95:484; *Lachish III, Text*, 315-16. For the exact rim-form parallel, see especially the unstamped jar cited from Tell Beit Mirsim in n. 324.

[472] See *Lachish III, Text*, 316, for the reference to *TBM III*, Pl. 13:3 (compare n. 468) together with *TBM I*, Pl. 52:10-11, which show the simpler rim-form mode.

[473] M. & Y. Aharoni, 83.

[474] Further, Zimhoni has described the *LMLK* rim mode as a "thickened ring-like rim [that] protrudes slightly outwards, sometimes inwards" (*Lachish*-Zimhoni, 15). This description seems also to work nicely for rim No. 11 in the PP 4 series from Samaria.

[475] M. & Y. Aharoni, 83, asserts that "this type of jar is typical of the south *only*" (emphasis added).

[476] *Lachish III, Text*, 277-79.

[477] *Lachish III, Text*, 316.

[478] A. D. Tushingham, "New Evidence Bearing on the Two-Winged *LMLK* Stamp," *BASOR* 287 (1992), 61-65. Tushingham also observed that excavations have recovered only the two-winged stamp "in the nuclear city of Jerusalem, viz., the southeast hill and the Temple Mount," and that occurrences of the four-winged impression are limited to "the walled Mishneh on the western hill" (pp. 63-64). Interestingly, this western "suburb" of old Jerusalem would likely have constituted the area of principal settlement for the refugees entering from the north during and after the fall of Samaria in 722/21 BCE. If, as he argues, the origin of the four-winged scarab design lay in the Northern Kingdom, the events of the late eighth century provided ample historical opportunities for this motif to migrate south and mix with similar, local traditions there (a point that Tushingham fails to emphasize). Working earlier on and with a limited database, Ussishkin had already begun to notice differences between the two types of royal

cannot accept it as a viable conclusion at this time. At any rate, one can safely place all these rims (9-11) in the mid-to-late eighth century BCE.

Although No. 9 (together with the cooking pot fragment in *SS III*, Fig. 6:31) comes from a locus that yielded secondary materials (Layer VIe), rims 10 (Layer VI) and 11 (Layer IV or IVh) likely derive from primary contexts that may give us clues to the historical sequence in this area. The stratigraphic and ceramic data presented above combine to suggest that No. 10 represents the latest class of materials still knocking about on the reused original courtyard levels, while the findspot of No. 11 associates itself with the next preserved living surface discovered here. The close dating of these two rims, then, indicates that the northern courtyard did not receive its new paving much before the mid-to-late eighth century BCE. With so few ceramic data available, greater precision in dating remains difficult to ascertain.

In the final report, Kenyon included rim No. 13 in her assemblage of jar forms; the fragment almost certainly belongs, however, to a deep, carinated krater in which the potter has rolled the uppermost sidewall into a bulbous rim with rounded lip and left the interior of the rim itself hollow. Both the rim-form mode and the diameter of the mouth (28 cm) support this identification.[479] This technique of rim making seems related to Gitin's Types 88 and 89A,[480] though the Gezer reports do not contain a perfect parallel for this piece from Samaria. According to Gitin, the rolled bulbous rim mode and rounded carination typifies assemblages dating from the late ninth to mid-eighth centuries only.[481] Yet these rims actually seem to reflect the early Iron Age II development of an older trend of krater manufacture—one in which the rolled rim remains hollow. The best sequence of this Iron I style is available from Taʿanach, where such rims range from Period IA (1200-1150 BCE) through Period IIB (960-918 BCE).[482] I may refer as well to the C I/a class of late Iron I

SS III, Fig. 6:13

---

stamps and their affiliation or nonaffiliation with private seals (D. Ussishkin, "Royal Judean Storage Jars and Private Seal Impressions," *BASOR* 223 [1976], 12). I must, however, stress that No. 11 bore no seal impressions of any kind and that the putative connection between this style jar and Judaean traditions rests solely on a tentative comparative ceramic analysis, not on grounds of epigraphy or political history.

[479]Similarly rolled, Iron II jar rims generally show either ridging on the exterior of the roll, taller necks, and narrower mouths (compare *TN II*, Pls. 1:3-5, 11; 2:13, 21, 27). For a taller neck below an Iron I rolled jar rim, see *Taʿanach*, Fig. 4:1 (Period IA).

[480]See *Gezer III*, Pl. 204-06 for full descriptions and suggested parallels.

[481]As examples from within the Gezer corpus, he appeals to *Gezer III*, Pls. 13:22 and 21:5 (Field VII, Strata 6B and 6A, respectively).

[482]*Taʿanach*, Figs. 1:8, 9 (roll not completed), 10 (Period IA, Cuneiform Tablet Building); 4:10 (Period IA, Twelfth-Century House); 7:1-2, 3 (with a closed hollow), 4-5 (Period IA); 16:1-2, 5 (Period IB); 22:8 (Period IIA); 28:4 (Period IIA); and 63:6, 9, 11 (Period IIB). Compare also Fig. 89:1, from Period IA. Only a few examples of this style came from periods later than the tenth century (see Fig. 70:3, from Period III = 875-800 BCE, with the rounded break in the upper sidewall so high that the krater profile resembles a double roll; Figs. 72:5 and 74:2 (Period IV = 750-732 BCE). A comparison of these cita-

kraters with circular rim profile from Tell Qiri.[483] Judging from the Hazor reports, which appear virtually devoid of convincing comparisons, this style did not enjoy much popularity in the far north. Most of the parallels that Rast cites in the Taʿanach report show rims that have been rolled so tightly as to close their central hollow space.[484]

In sum, the best jar rim parallel for No. 13 occurs on an Iron II fragment from Tell en-Naṣbeh[485]; accepting the recorded diameter of the Samaria vessel as correct, however, leads us to ascribe this rim to the late Iron Age I (tenth-century) krater family. The distinction may rest on the different profiles of the upper sidewalls: on the jar from Naṣbeh, the wall slopes down from the rim in a convex arc; on the krater, however, the wall above the point of carination appears more convex, as on *SS III*, Fig. 6:13. Moreover, the earlier Iron I kraters with rolled, hollow rims from Taʿanach generally display a noticeably high carination, while those from the latter part of Iron Age I (Periods IIA-B = tenth century) show a lower point of carination similar to that of No. 13. The appearance of a possibly early krater fragment in this area is not surprising, however, since it clearly derives from a secondary stratigraphic context, namely, Layer V, which comprises the imported soil/debris used to backfill RT 107 and to level off the area above the former Walls 105-107 (see fig. 25).

3) Evaluation and Summary

Provenance data for the meager assemblage of pottery published from the area of the North Courtyard appear in Table 13. As noted in my introductory comments to this portion of the summit, the construction of a new BP IV courtyard floor achieved a slight northern expansion of that open-air surface without having to relocate any of the major perimeter walls. The establishment of the grand casemate system under Ahab had already enlarged the royal compound to its greatest feasible area, given the difficult terrain of the surrounding slopes. Little evidence remains, however, to suggest that Ahab pursued his plan in order to gain additional building space *inside* the compound perimeter, particularly on the north side of the site. That is, while floor levels were extended north of Omri's original Enclosure Wall 161, the excavations identified virtually no remains of buildings or rooms in the new space between 161 and Ahab's

---

tions to the descriptions and examples in the corpus of *Gezer III* will reveal that, by the ninth and eighth centuries BCE, the rolled rim appears closed (i.e., not hollow)—almost ball-shaped—and rests on top of the upper sidewall; it occurs mainly on smaller kraters of the period, as in *Megiddo I*, Pl. 27:87 (Stratum III), and *Hazor II*, Pl. LXXXIII:4 (Stratum VA); see Rast's supporting comments in *Taʿanach*, 43.

[483] *T. Qiri*, 146, 194, and Fig. 38:11 (Area C, Stratum VIII). The report states that this rim mode "is a good chronological indicator for Iron I. C I is not the most frequent Iron I form, but its profile shows a definite peak during Stratum IX; by the tenth century it was in decline. The form is never very frequent in any of the later Iron II levels at Yoqneʿam" (p. 194).

[484] *Taʿanach*, 12. *Megiddo Tombs*, Pl. 73:13 (from Tomb 1090; see p. 126, Fig. 155, and p. 142) represents the only real exception among his citations.

[485] *TN II*, Pl. 2:13.

	bowls	cooking pots	jars	holemouth jars	TOTAL
North Courtyard					
86.2.88					
86.2.88.E					
86.2.88.E, W of 104					
86.2.88.W					
IV	-	-	1	-	1
IV(h?)	-	-	1	-	1
V	-	-	1	-	1
VIe	-	1	1	-	2
TOTAL	-	1	4	-	5

Distribution of PP 4-4a Ceramic Forms
in Local Stratigraphy of North Courtyard
(Segment Series 86.2.88 . . .)

Table 13

Casemate Wall 556.[486] As shown in the BP I-II Top Plan in *SS I*, Pl. VIII, the only real installation traced in this area consists in a rather large cistern with multiple mouths. Given the political vicissitudes of the times at Tirzah, the former capital of the Northern Kingdom, the implementation of Omri's original city plan must have required a punctual, if not expeditious, completion. Yet his basic design would prove quite enduring by lasting for over a century. Ahab's elaboration on the blueprint appears to have focused more directly on the need for defense than on an apotheosis of personal or royal capabilities; that is, the addition of the casemate system stemmed from and satisfied practical goals more than symbolic or psychological ones. It not only provided a stalwart city wall around the site, but it also established a nearly 7-meter-wide buffer zone between the inner face of that wall (Casemate Enclosure 556) and the central area of courtyard activity.

My readings of both the stratigraphy and the pottery from this area prove harmonious. Two fragments derive from a primary context involving Layer IV (see fig. 25), or the actual matrix of the new courtyard floor laid in this area (*SS III*, Fig. 6:10-11). These two store jar rims originated in the mid-to-late eighth century BCE; consequently, they help substantiate that this resurfacing of the northern courtyard occurred in conjunction with the construction of the service rooms (*g-k*) located immediately further north. From the subfloor makeup in Layer V, the excavators recovered a sherd from an earlier, late tenth-century style jar or, as I have suggested, a deep krater (*SS*

---

[486] I now adjust my earlier view that Ahab, in fact, dismantled Wall 161 during the construction of the casemate system (see *AIS-I*, 164).

III, Fig. 6:13). That materials from the Iron I-Iron II transition period appear in the bedding for this mid-eighth-century surface again indicates that such debris remained readily available in nearby areas (probably on the summit itself). Renovations inside the royal compound following the Omride period apparently had not swept the area clean or buried all the remains from that earlier phase. The ancient builders poured the filling of Layer V into this space following the robbing of BP I-II Walls 105 and 107; the soil actually filled the trench left over from the plunder of 107. Finally, one sees that even though Layer VI might actually represent a previous floor level in this area (perhaps even from the time of Omri or Ahab), the subdeposit VIe comprised merely the backfill in Robber Trench 105. As expected, derived elements appear in this matrix, such as the late eleventh- or tenth-century BCE cooking-pot fragment in *SS III*, Fig. 6:31. One finds mixed with this pottery, however, later forms, such as the mid-eighth-century jar rim in Fig. 6:9.

Collectively, these data place the filling of RT 105 (Layer VIe), the filling of RT 107 in conjunction with the leveling of the area above both trenches (Layer V), and the laying of the new courtyard floor (Layer IV) in the middle years of the eighth century BCE. And, once again, virtually no trace of any significant depositional history appears between these layers and the original floor level from the mid-ninth century BCE (fig. 25).

Part C. Courtyard
    (*SS I*, Pl. VII — Section GH)
    (*SS III*, Fig. 6:19)

Within the area of the main, open-air courtyard situated east of the palace precinct, I have already noted both the strip of pounded limestone floor that lay immediately south of Wall 65 in Summit Strip Qc (fig. 5) and the larger, possible continuation of that surface farther to the south in Summit Strip Qg. I mentioned that, according to the official report from the excavation, these floor levels overran and sealed the truncated walls and robber trenches of BP III but that the report itself contained no pottery found lying on, in, or beneath the northernmost section of the courtyard just south of Wall 65. Neither could the excavators establish a direct stratigraphic connection between the two parts of the surface—parts separated by more than 40 meters on the horizontal plane and as much as 75 cm in elevation. By extension, this means that the historical relationship between the more southerly parcel of courtyard floor and the BP IV buildings discussed above had to remain open for the excavators.[487] A strong comparison between the ceramic assemblages associated with those buildings and the courtyard would normally provide the best evidence linking the two.

When one comes to the more southerly strip of courtyard, however, one finds that the only BP IV segment exposed here (labeled *325.304*) contributed just a single

---

[487] *SS III*, 113.

ceramic fragment to the published PP 4 corpus (a holemouth rim from *SS III*, Fig. 6:19, marked in the notes as a discard).[488] Despite its meager donation to the assemblage of pottery, however, this segment emerges as an important one because it lies in the central part of what would likely have constituted a principal area of outdoor activity and because the stratigraphic sequence here seems particularly well preserved (due largely to the more regular surface of the bedrock as over against the erratic areas outside the northern scarp and the steep pitch of the northern slopes).[489] As my discussion of this segment progresses, it will also afford us an opportunity to offer several comments relating the principles that underlie my own method and theory.

Before proceeding to the stratigraphic details of this area, I can now plot the horizontal location of *325.304* more exactly, thanks to several plans and sections contained in the field notes.[490] First, a rather crudely drawn and unphased top plan of the area of Summit Strip Qg relating generally to this particular segment appears in fig. 28.[491] By cross-referencing these data to those on the published Section GH (see fig. 32 below), one can synchronize the following series of walls and trenches on both drawings (moving from north to south, and darkened on the plan): W. 324; W. 323; RT 372; RT 333; RT 377; RT 376; and RT 363. (As I shall show momentarily, both the field plan and the published section failed to include another robber trench, 371, which lay south of Wall 323.) I have also located and darkened another, longitudinal wall on the plan whose identification number served as a coordinate for this segment, namely Wall 325. As confirmed in a second plan (fig. 29),[492] this feature formed a 90° right angle[493] with (and was therefore contemporary with) Wall 323. Later, the foundation trench for another longitudinal wall (316), which ran parallel to and east of 325, cut the line taken by 323.[494]

---

[488] Yet the final report states that "from the pottery it is fairly certain that it [the southern courtyard] was contemporary with them [the northern buildings]" (*SS III*, 113).

[489] The stratigraphy of Segment *325.304* also provided a valuable point of reference for PP 1 deposits recovered from adjacent or nearby segments but not recorded in field sections in the notebooks (*AIS-I*, 73).

[490] For data pertaining to this segment, see *Fieldbook Qc-g*, 28-29, 40, 50, 68-70 (field notes); 29a, 40a (stratigraphic summary); 28a, 33a, 34a, 50a, 67a, 69a (field sections); 20a (unphased to plan of Strip Qg).

[491] *Fieldbook Qc-g*, 20a.

[492] *Fieldbook Qc-g*, 28a.

[493] The field notes presented this simple drawing with no compass orientation. My depiction is based on the apparent relationship between 325 and 323 seen in the plan of fig. 28. I have maintained the standard of placing North at the top of the drawing; Kenyon appears to have done the opposite in her rendering of these walls in *Fieldbook Qc-g*, 28a. I might add that she did, in fact, provide compass directions for fig. 28 below, and there she reversed normal procedures by placing South at the head of the diagram.

[494] This plan clarifies the reverse impression given by fig. 28, namely that 323 cut 316.

PP 4: COURTYARD — INTRODUCTION

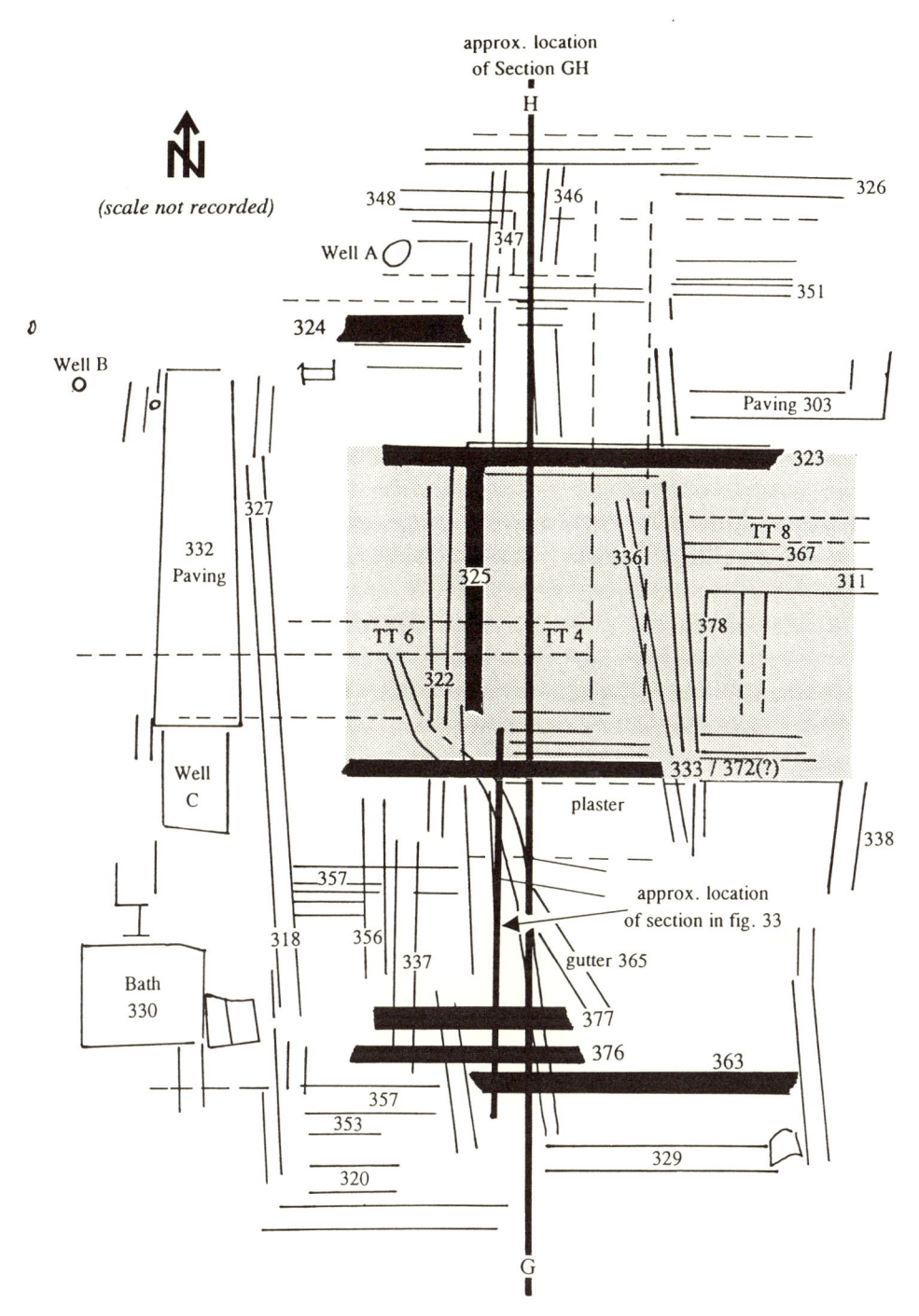

Top Plan of Summit Strip Qg
Approximate Location of Segment 325.304

fig. 28

Local Plan of Summit Strip Qg:
Architectural Relationships of Wall 325

fig. 29

Moreover, two field sections relating to this plan show (1) that Wall 325 lay just east of Walls 322 and 304 (fig. 30; with 304 constituting the other coordinate for this segment), and (2) that Segment *325.304* extended mainly south of Wall 323 (fig. 31).[495] In short, the excavators seem to have located their Segment *325.304* immedi-

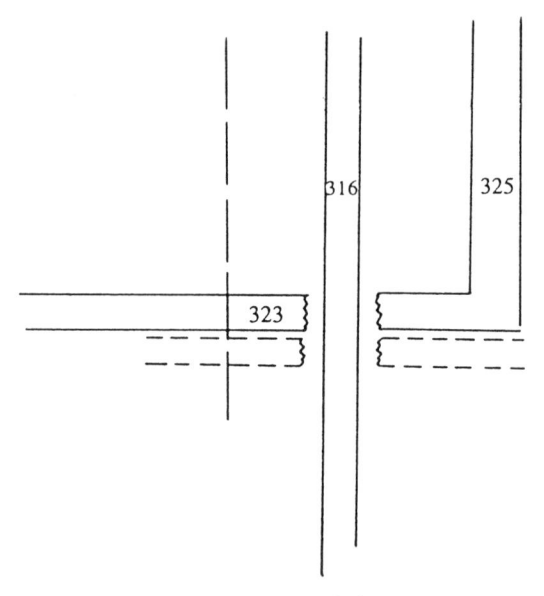

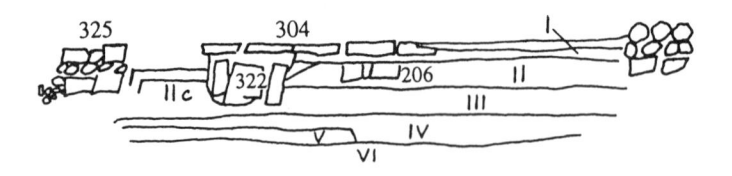

(scale not recorded)

Segment 325.304:
Section West of Wall 325
<— E W —>
View toward South

fig. 30

---

[495] Both of these sections appeared in *Fieldbook Qc-g*, 28a.

ately east of published Section GH (presented below, fig. 32; here, "east" implies "toward the reader"), in the area south of Wall 323 (fig. 31) and north of Robber Trench 333 (see fig. 34 below). I have shaded this portion of the plan presented in fig. 28. The official Section GH (*SS I*, Pl. VII) appears to have followed a course along a north-south axis just west of both 316 and 325, as I have suggested in each of the above plans.

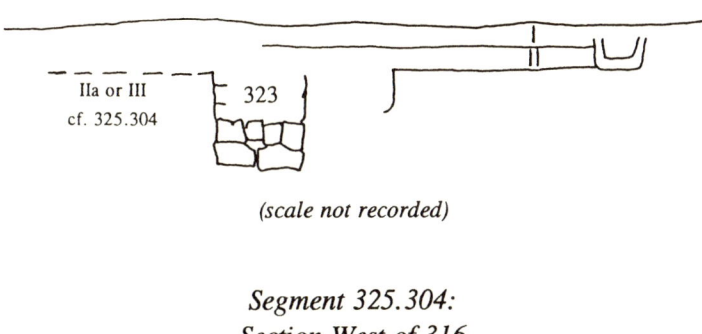

(scale not recorded)

Segment 325.304:
Section West of 316
<— S N —>
View toward West

fig. 31

1) Stratigraphic Detail

a. 325.304

To facilitate my comparative stratigraphic analysis, I am including here the portion of published Section GH that relates directly to Segment *325.304*.[496] The significant area lies between Robber Trench 339 on the south and Wall 324 on the north. Except for RT 339, one can collate all the major features seen on this section with those highlighted in some manner on the top plan in fig. 28. In fig. 37 below, I shall show that yet another robber trench (371) lay between RT 372 and Wall 323; neither the field plan nor the published section included this trench. The complete diagram of Section GH, available in the final report, also shows that no Israelite levels later than those of BP IV remained in the courtyard area south of the portion presented here. There, very thick deposits (nearly 1.5 m) from the late Hellenistic period covered the entire area, including the quarries cut into the rock surface near the south edge of the summit. Judging from Section GH, nothing but natural overburden eventually covered this block of layers; no signs of Roman activity appeared there. Accordingly, then, the oblique cut through the Roman levels seen near the center of fig. 32 — directly above

---

[496]*SS I*, Pl. VII.

136   THE ARCHAEOLOGY OF ISRAELITE SAMARIA

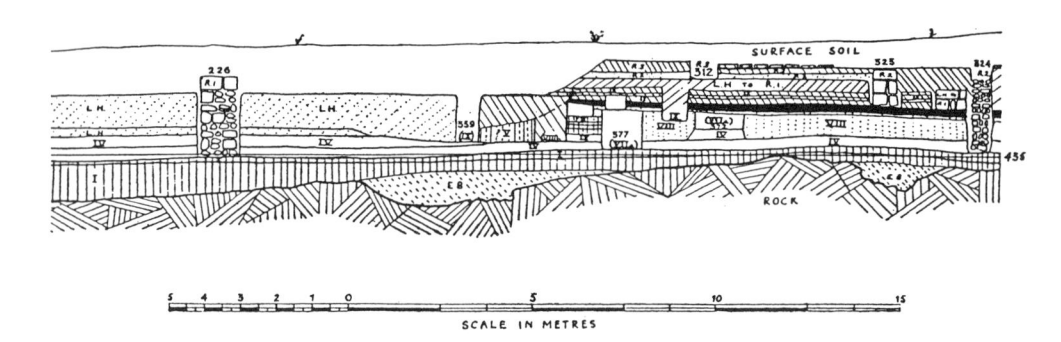

Portion of Published Section GH Relevant to Segment 325.304
<— S N —>
View toward West

fig. 32

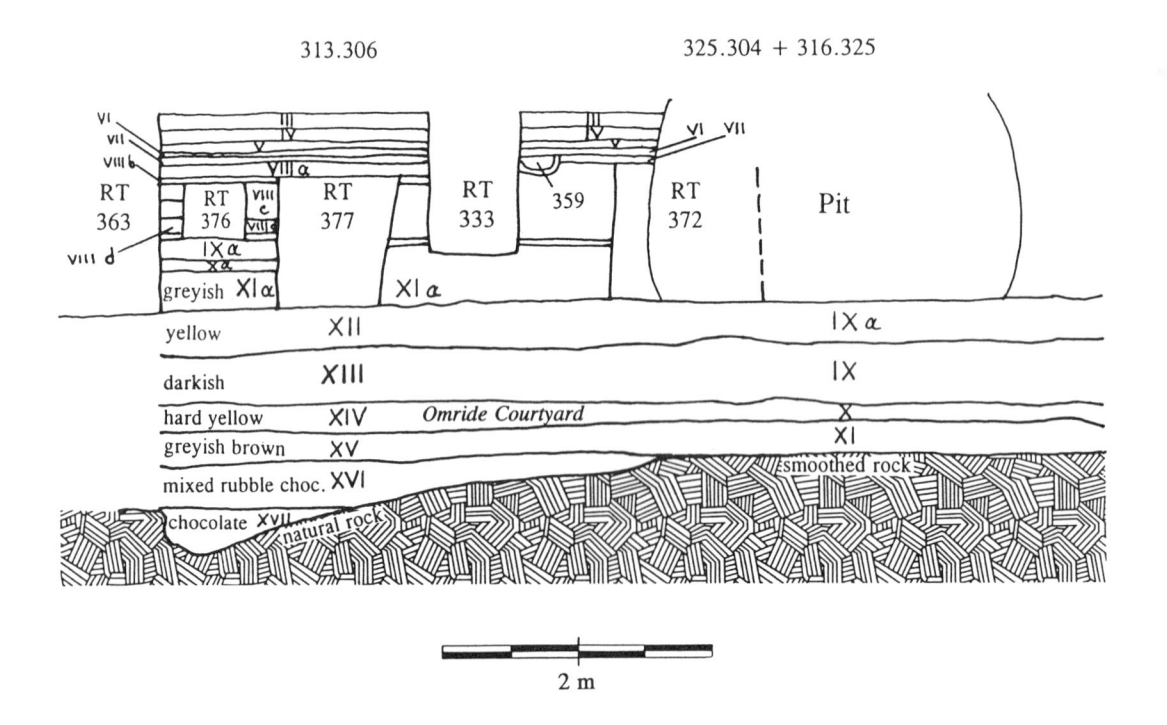

Section West of Foundation Trench 336
<— S N —>
View toward West

fig. 33

Robber Trenches 363 and 376 (see fig. 33)—represents the southernmost extent of summit remains from that period.

The Joint Expedition also trimmed and recorded a sectional cut (fig. 33)[497] west of the foundation trench for Wall 336 (shaded on fig. 28 above) and apparently east of Wall 325, which provided a coordinate reference for this segment.[498] I have indicated the approximate location of this section on fig. 28. This diagram provides a nearly complete portrait of the depositional history in Segment *325.304* and reveals the presence of a major intrusion: a pit that cut through every deposit above Layer IXa and into the northern portion of that area. Further, one sees that Segment *325.304* lay above an area of summit rock that had been artificially smoothed, perhaps already from activities during the Iron Age I occupation of the site by the ancestral kin of Shemer (1 Kgs 16:24). Immediately south of *325.304*, the natural rock began its gradual descent into the southernmost of two surface depressions in the summit area.[499] As evidenced here, I have terminated the lateral area of Segment *325.304* just inside the northern edge of Wall/Robber Trench 333. Though presented with a reverse orientation, another field-drawn section corroborates this decision (fig. 34).[500] Still another section includes the layers found in the immediate vicinity of Robber Trench 372[501] and thereby incor-

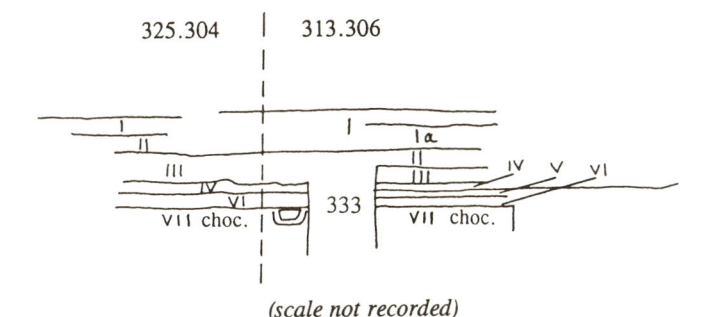

(scale not recorded)

Area Around Robber Trench 333

<— N S —>

View toward East

fig. 34

---

[497] *Fieldbook Qc-g*, 67a.

[498] I should stress here that I reproduced the top plan in fig. 28 exactly as Kenyon had drawn it, i.e., without any apparent scale. On the section I present in fig. 33, however, Kenyon did indicate the scale of the drawing (2 cm = 1 m). Without further data, one should therefore utilize the latter diagram when assessing the spatial relationships of architectural features (such as the actual distance between Robber Trenches 363-376-377 and 333-372; the two groups are much closer on the section than they appear on the plan).

[499] See *AIS-I*, 75-76.

[500] *Fieldbook Qc-g*, 33a.

[501] *Fieldbook Qc-g*, 50a.

porates Level IX, which yielded the holemouth rim fragment published in *SS III*, Fig. 6:19. I might also note that the official Section GH again failed to include a significant architectural feature, this time the stones of Wall 332, set into Layers V-VIIa just to the north of RT 372. Finally, the field notes partially recorded the vicinity of both RT 333 and RT 372 in another abridged section (fig. 36).[502] I have included this drawing not just for the sake of completeness but because of slight variations in the stratigraphic detail.

One can also place all the depositional history seen in these smaller sections in a larger context by harking back to the main diagram of courtyard deposits first presented in *AIS-I* (fig. 37).[503]

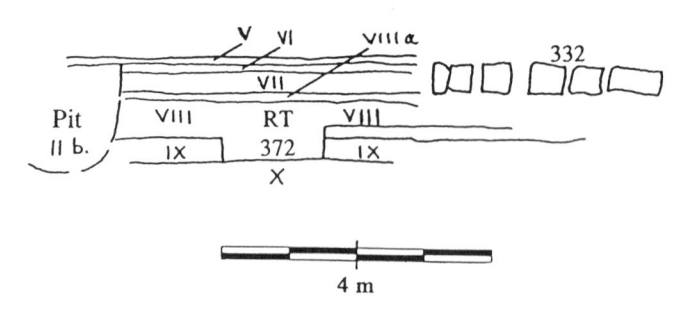

Area Around Robber Trench 372
<— S N —>
View toward West
fig. 35

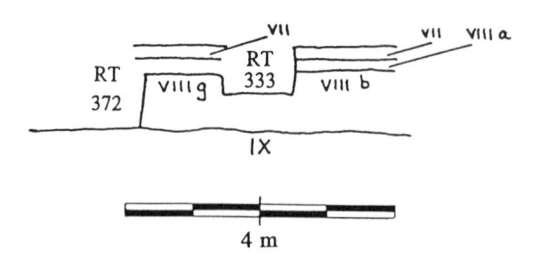

Depositional History in the Vicinity of RT 333 and RT 372
<— N S —>
View toward East
fig. 36

---

[502]*Fieldbook Qc-g*, 67a.

[503]See fig. 18. This section appears in the field records of *Fieldbook Qc-g*, 69a.

PP 4: COURTYARD — STRATIGRAPHY

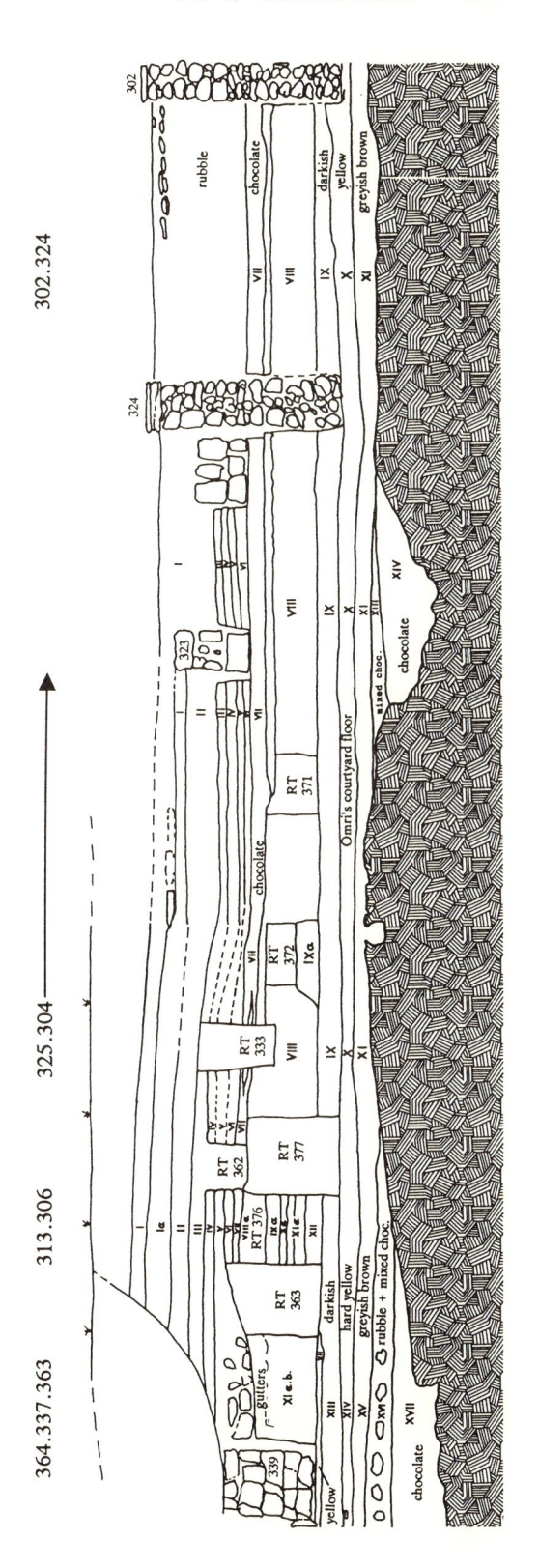

Summit Strip Qg
Segments 325.304, 364.337.363, 313.306, 302.304
<— S N —>
View toward West

fig. 37

Before describing the nature of the most relevant layers shown in the various sections above, I should note the differences in the way these diagrams depict certain deposits and features. While not all of these variant recordings impinge on the level of central concern here (Layer IX), a brief mention of some of them will serve to underscore the sorts of discrepancies that inevitably creep into the necessary and crucial act of recording field observations. While I realize, of course, that the foregoing sections derive from different locations and that they were, therefore, never intended simply to duplicate the *exact* same stratigraphic field, I may suggest that their courses lay close enough to each other that some of the disparity may point to actual errors in the record keeping. The discrepancies seem to center on the series of robber trenches and the stratigraphic relationship of each trench to the layers around it. Proceeding always from north to south, I can at least offer the following observations (in addition to the variations already cited):

a. Robber Trench 371 appears on fig. 37 but not on published Section GH;
b. fig. 33 shows a large pit to the immediate north of RT 372; the pit cut down to the top of Layer IXa; it is nowhere depicted on figs. 35 or 37;
c. in the area of the pit on fig. 35, one sees the bottom courses of an apparently later wall (352), which clearly cut into Layer VII and probably VIIIa as well; this wall is also missing from fig. 37 and Section GH;
d. in fig. 37, a nondescript deposit overruns RT 372 from the north; in fig. 33, another unidentified layer appears to continue over the trench from the south, while fig. 35 indicates that the substantial fill of Layer VIII (on the south) also filled the trench itself;
e. yet again, fig. 36 suggests that both 372 and 333 were backfilled at the same time and with the same imported fill;
f. fig. 33 (and possibly also fig. 37) indicates that, following RT 372, Levels III, IV, V, VI, and perhaps even VII (at least on fig. 33) were cut by an unidentified intrusion, in contrast to fig. 35 and Section GH;
g. importantly, Layer IXa underlies RT 372 in both figs. 33 and 37 as well as in Section GH[504];
h. in two of the sections just cited (fig. 37 and Section GH), the horizontal scope of Layer IXa is limited to the area immediately beneath the robber trench; in fig. 33, on the other hand, IXa comprises a rather thick accumulation that spans the entire southern courtyard area;
i. fig. 34 confirms the majority opinion that the "chocolate" soil of Layer VII ran up to RT 333 on both the north and south sides;
j. however, the drain or gutter labeled 359 rests on the north side of RT 333 in

---

[504] One must bear in mind that the Roman numerals on the published sections reflect *periods*, not layer designations. One can see from Section GH, then, only that RT 372 sits atop a deposit from "Period IV." Without the unpublished data from the field notebooks, however, one cannot know from this diagram either the specific identification number of that deposit or even whether the deposit actually reflects a "block" of several successive local accumulations.

fig. 33 but, apparently on the south side in fig. 34 (though it remains unlabeled in the latter instance);

k. also, Layer III actually fills RT 333 in fig. 34, but it is cut by it in figs. 33 and 37;

l. instead, Layer III fills RT 362 in fig. 37 (and possibly on GH, though this remains unclear);

m. both fig. 37 and GH place this robber trench (362) directly above RT 377, while fig. 33 omits it altogether;

n. rather, in fig. 33 Layer VIIIa overruns and seals RT 377, contra fig. 37 and GH;

o. one must assume that the matrix of Layer XIa to the immediate north of RT 377 truly matches the yellowish (?) XIa south of 377, even though it is placed at roughly the same elevation of IXa to the south (and may therefore represent a simple metathesis in recording);

p. either way, fig. 37 labels this entire block north of 377 "Layer VIII";

q. the breach made by RT 376 appears narrower in fig. 33 than it does in fig. 37, where it stretches from 377 all the way southward to 363; in Section GH, RT 376 abuts 363 to its south but not 377 to its north;

r. RT 363 cuts Layers III-XIa in fig. 33 versus VI-XII in fig. 37;

s. finally, Layer XII beneath Robber Trenches 363 and 377 (fig. 33; Segment *313.306*) comprises the southern extension of Layer IXa beneath RT 372 (Segment *325.304*), while it appears as a relatively thin layer restricted to the south of RT 363 in fig. 37, where Layer XIII seems to complement Layer IX (not IXa) further north.[505]

Though this recitation of discrepancies does not undercut any stratigraphic analysis that I may pursue in this (or any other) section, it does raise the strong caveat that one must always read every excavation report critically. It also brings up the question of which section should stand as most authoritative. My response holds that no single section can assume preeminent status; one should consider each in the context of all the others. I do, however, give a slight edge to the sections drawn in the field at or near the point of excavation as over against the published version, which represents a composite drawing produced much later. Having said this, I may reiterate a basic premise that undergirds this entire investigation, namely, that one can justifiably attribute different degrees of authority to field sections versus field notes. The latter are, admittedly, very preliminary sketches—sometimes no more than intuitive guesses—which the excavator has every right to alter as she or he finalizes the interpretation of field work. The stratigraphic relationships portrayed in sections, on the other hand, are more fixed at the point of discovery. That is to say, if a certain feature cuts (and therefore postdates) a given layer on the day of their excavation, that same stratigraphic relationship should still exist at the point of publication, regardless of how much time passes in the

---

[505] In fact, Kenyon herself specifies this correlation (Segment *313.306*, Layer XIII ↔ Segment *325.304*, Layer IX) in her stratigraphic summary of *313.306*, Fieldbook *Qc-g*, 43a.

interim. From my point of view, then, discrepancies between sections and plans pose a greater problem than differences that one may detect between field records and the narrative of the final report.

Based on the sections presented above and on the pottery recovered from each level, Kenyon concluded that Layers I[506] and II-III represented floor levels from the Late Roman (R.3) and Late Hellenistic-early Roman (R.1) periods, respectively. She also argued that the succession of three underlying levels reflected a series of surfaces from her "Period IX," with Layer IV described simply as a "floor," Layer V as a "g[oo]d hard plaster floor," and Layer VI as a "rather chocolaty" floor.[507] Notes related to the pottery associated with these surfaces[508] indicate that most of the fragments resembled those assigned to PP 6.

Layers VII and VIII were assigned to "Period VIII" and, according to the notebooks, yielded pottery from PP 6 (= Layer VII) and PP 8 (= Layer VIII). The fact that Kenyon saw so much "Period VIII" pottery in layers that were physically (i.e., spatially) and stratigraphically (i.e., temporally) earlier than many others which produced "Period V-VI" wares speaks to the multiple disturbances that run throughout *325.304* and all surrounding segments. The chocolate soil of Layer VII rested on a thin deposit immediately beneath it (Layer VIIIa), and then on the actual makeup of the chocolate (Layer VIII). Layer IXa, in turn, comprised the "bottom of [the] Period VIII filling."[509] I have already noted the questions that arise concerning the lateral extent of this deposit.

Layer IX, from which the workers removed the fragment in *SS III*, Fig. 6:19, emerged as a darkish level that seems congruent with Layer XIII south of RT 377 (figs. 33 and 37). The principal question that surrounds this deposit centers on whether one or more intrusive robber trenches cut into its matrix (as on figs. 35 and 37 plus Section GH) or whether it remained a sealed, primary context (as in fig. 33). The preponderance of evidence seems to suggest the former situation. The sectional data stand in greater agreement on the relationship between IX and that which lay beneath it. This layer covered a substantial portion of the hard, yellow courtyard surface laid down originally by King Omri. It is not surprising, then, that Kenyon recorded finding pottery from both PP 1 and PP 4 (corrected from 3) in this layer.[510] This remark may

---

[506]Layer I ↔ Segment *313.306*, Layer Ia.

[507]*Fieldbook Qc-g*, 29a. Layer V ↔ Segment *W. of 318*, Layer II.

[508]Recall that, in Kenyon's general methodology, "associated with" usually means "located in the makeup found beneath the surface."

[509]*Fieldbook Qc-g*, 40a.

[510]*Fieldbook Qc-g*, 40a. In fact, G. M. Crowfoot noted on her stratification card for Fig. 6:19 that this fragment appeared "with EB ware" but that it was "probably I—not EB." She added further that the ware of No. 19 seemed "much harder than the usual I ware."

also speak to the extended functional life of this courtyard. Though I can expect that most of the material culture recovered from IX came from a time near the end of the courtyard's life, I may also surmise that some pottery or heirlooms from the already distant past may have maintained a presence in the courtyard area even to its final days.

Layer IX, then, likely presents us with very mixed contents, ranging from possible occupational debris from the mid-ninth century to sundry objects that entered the locus as part of the imported fill to further intrusions as a result of the robber trenches that seem to have cut the deposit. In keeping with her principles of dating levels, of course, Kenyon did not consider Layer IX as occupational debris, but only as makeup contributing to "a raising of the level of the original southern courtyard."[511] This makeup, according to her, "consisted of approximately 25 cms. of darkish earth, with a surface of 25 cms. of pounded limestone with a very hard surface."[512] One problem with this restricted interpretation, particularly in the area of Segment *325.304*, stems from the lack of any trace of a new surface itself. As figs. 33 and 37 and even Section GH show, Layer IX appears rather to represent only one in a series of substantial fillings poured across the old courtyard floor. The best evidence for the actuality of a new Israelite surface in this area would appear to reside in the close sequence of layers situated between RT 363 and RT 377 and below 376 (= Segment *313.306*). But *Samaria-Sebaste III* offered only a single fragment of pottery from this segment (Fig. 3:31 = PP 2), and it came from the greyish-brown makeup sealed beneath Omri's original floor (Layer XV).[513] The stratigraphic summary of deposits in that segment, however, contained the following descriptions: Layers XII-XIIa = yellow floor (with affiliated pottery assigned to PP 4);[514] Layer XIa = hard, grey floor (pottery from PP 3); Xa = greyish clay (pottery from PP 3-4); and IXa = hard white level beneath Gutter 376. In addition, Kenyon added a note explaining Layers VIIIa-XIa as "remains of later Israelite levels (Period IVa) denuded away elsewhere,"[515] a point which precludes speculation as to the lateral extent of these surfaces. Though the reference to BP IVa as a *late* phase of Israelite occupation may at first seem somewhat incongruous with Kenyon's overall interpretive scheme, it may prove more accurate than expected as I proceed to examine "Periods V-VII" in the following chapters.

Judging from the evidence of the sections, then, the exact number of major repavings of the Israelite courtyard—or whether a repaving ever occurred—must remain open to question. Within Segment *325.304* itself, the next clear surface appears in the thick, chocolate Layer VII attributable to the early post-Israelite period ("Period VIII"), perhaps during the Babylonian or Persian empires.

---

[511] *SS III*, 113.

[512] *SS III*, 113.

[513] For further comments on this jar fragment and its general context, see *AIS-I*, 141-42.

[514] *Fieldbook Qc-g*, 43a. This summary also drew the following correlation: Layers XII-XIIa ↔ Segment *325.304*, Layer IXa.

[515] *Fieldbook Qc-g*, 42a.

2) Pottery Analysis

a. Jars

SS III Published Figure	Registry No. (* = marked for discard)	Provenance Strip	Coordinates	Feature	Local Layer
6:19	*Q 2267	Qg	325.304	Courtyard	IX

Provenance Data:
PP4 Jars from Area Labeled "Courtyard"

Table 14

SS III, Fig. 6:19 comprises the only fragment of pottery recovered and published from this *Courtyard* area. Though Kenyon included it in her general category of jars, I have argued that it belongs more specifically in the series of holemouth jar rims seen in Nos. 20-24. I therefore added it to my earlier discussion of the pottery associated with the house floors north of the courtyard area (see Part A above).

This particular holemouth rim came from Layer IX of Segment *325.304*, a relatively thick deposit of darkish soil found lying directly over Omri's original courtyard surface. I have just shown in my discussion of the depositional history in this area that this layer might likely have contained both occupational debris from the courtyard itself (most likely from a period of reuse subsequent to the days of Omri) and mixed elements that entered the locus as fill. Since, primarily on the basis of its form, I dated No. 19 within a range of mid-to-late eighth to the seventh centuries,[516] it would appear that the original courtyard level maintained a functional life at least as late as the middle part of the eighth century, if not later. One fragment from a holemouth jar, however, clearly presents us with a deficient data base and precludes us from speculating further on issues pertaining to chronology or the historical activity in this area.

SS III, Fig.6:19

3) Evaluation and Summary

Segment *325.304* emerges as somewhat of an enigma. Despite several positive characteristics mentioned at the outset of my treatment of this area, the overall

---

[516] My classification and dating of this rim receive confirmation in Gitin's detailed analysis of his Type 10B holemouth form in *Gezer III*, 130-32.

stratigraphic reliability of the deposit ultimately seemed uncertain. In any event, the official excavation report myopically included only a single rim of a holemouth jar from this segment in its published repertoire (*SS III*, Fig. 6:19). This piece comes from a comparatively thick pouring of fill that covered the original courtyard surface laid by the workers of King Omri roughly a century earlier, in the ninth century BCE. Evidence of a putative repaving of this specific courtyard area in the mid-eighth century, however, remains somewhat elusive on the extant sections, published and unpublished. The only other ceramic documentation in the final report consists in a cyma bowl (*SS III*, Fig. 1:1) and two krater rims (*SS III*, Fig. 1:11 and 14) recovered from the actual matrix of the original, yellowish courtyard surface (Layer X) and the grey bedding beneath it (Layer XI; see fig. 37). All three pieces were assigned to Pottery Period 1. While these fragments helped to anchor the date of that first courtyard to the Omride era, the present holemouth rim could not have appeared long before the mid-eighth century, and it may even come from a half century or more later. Without clear traces of a new courtyard paving that correlates to the surviving levels in the North Courtyard area and to the resurfacings in the house rooms farther north, one cannot show (as I have with other layers discussed thus far) that this apparent mid-eighth-century accumulation also lies closely sandwiched between floor levels dating to the mid-ninth and mid-to-late eighth centuries. Still, that the deposit clearly lies immediately above the level of Omri's original courtyard once again suggests a long functional life for the latter feature.

Throughout my presentation of the local stratigraphy in Segment *325.304*, I have taken the opportunity to address not only the difficulties one encounters in the unpublished records relating to this central area, but also various issues of method and theory generally. In this vein, it seems somewhat peculiar that the report presented neither additional stratigraphy nor pottery from BP V-VII; in this area, the narrative proceeds from BP IV to BP VIII. Kenyon says only that PP 8 included two centuries worth of ceramic traditions.[517] Thus, if PP 4 relates directly to the mid-eighth century BCE, then PP 8 should take us immediately to the mid-sixth century, or near the end of the Persian rule. Plainly, a comprehensive publication should have incorporated the depositional history and samples of material culture from Pottery Periods 4, 5, 6, and 7 in Segment *325.304* and in the adjacent *313.306*, where possible traces of a new courtyard paving may survive.

Part D. Casemate Repair Deposit
(*SS I*, Pl. VII — Sections CD, EF)
(*SS III*, Fig. 7:1-9)

My look at the final segment of excavation that contributed materials to the published PP 4 repertoire takes us back to the northern edge of the summit, to a deposit

---

[517] *SS III*, 129.

recovered from 648°–651° E x 469° N (Segment *504.508.509.510*[518]). I have located this area on the plan in fig. 5 by means of the notation "CR," for Casemate Repairs. Kenyon believed this area stemmed from restorations made to the grand casemate system and, on the basis of the pottery found there, she "confidently" assigned the group to PP 4 even without detecting a single stratigraphic connection to anything else in that period.[519] The final report also states that "a new floor was apparently added inside the casemates at this period . . . , but only a very small portion survived, and no examples from it are figured."[520]

Though several published sections passed near this area (Sections AB, CD, and EF[521]), none of them provides a clear presentation of the stratigraphic block in question. Section AB restricts itself to earlier levels (BP I-II), while CD depicts only a very limited BP IV deposit inside the casemate system (north of Wall 505, which dates from the Late Roman period; R.4a). Section EF provides the best, though still inadequate, insight into the specific location of these layers. On that drawing, one can locate the inner Casemate Wall 556 (mislabeled 536; see n. 526 below), with its lower courses assigned to BP II and its upper ones to the purported rebuild during BP IV. One can also see extending northward from the inside face of 556 a block of stratigraphy attributed to this same period, with BP II remains beneath it and Hellenistic ones overlying it.[522] Working from the excavation's unpublished notes and drawings, I can now provide greater detail for this area.[523]

In keeping with her general procedures, Kenyon once again utilized a series of much later walls as the coordinates for Segment *504.508.509.510*. These walls comprised a rather large building that ran directly over the Israelite casemate system in the Late Roman period. We have, in fact, already encountered these features in fig. 20 above (where I identified them by means of hachures),[524] and in my study of Pit *i* and

---

[518]For unpublished data pertaining to this segment, see *Fieldbook Qn (Vol. I)*, 30-33 (notes); 30, 33a (stratigraphic summary); 31a-32a (field sections); and 6a-7a (field plans).

[519]*SS III*, 113.

[520]*SS III*, 113.

[521]*SS I*, Pl. VII.

[522]Elsewhere along the north face of Casemate Wall 556, Hellenistic construction activities involving deep fills apparently cleared all earlier deposits down to bedrock (compare the northern extension of Section GH).

[523]This segment lay just inside the casemate area immediately to the west of Wall 568 in a location adjacent to a series of chambers discussed at length in *AIS-I*, 17, fig. 4 (see also the indexed pages relating to Segments *506.505.504, Blocks A-C*).

[524]Several differences appear in a comparison of the two plans. For example, northern Wall 513 spans a greater distance in fig. 38 than in fig. 20—it actually intersects longitudinal Walls 504 and 517 and nearly meets Wall 509 on the west; the Mosaic room in the northwest corner of the building is virtually complete in fig. 38 but almost totally destroyed in fig. 20; interior Wall 505 merely connects 504 and 517 in fig. 38, while it extends east of 517 in fig. 20; and, on the south side, the short longitudinal Wall 502 simply abuts the longer, lateral Wall 519 in fig. 38 but extends slightly beyond 519 and forms a 90°

Rooms g and j to the west-southwest of this Roman structure and Room n to the east-southeast of it. A supplementary plan concentrating only on the Roman building itself appears on the following page in fig. 38.[525]

Published Section CD conveniently displays the position of this building above the old Israelite wall system. In a comparison to the plan in fig. 38, one sees that the walls situated at or near the outside perimeter of this structure (Wall 503 on the south and 513 on the north) used either the rock surface itself or the remains of earlier, well-built walls as their foundations. Interestingly, the Romans set the base of Wall 503 precisely on the line taken by Omri's original Enclosure Wall 161 over a millennium earlier. At least 13 subterranean courses from 503 cut through thick Hellenistic and Israelite levels, including the paving stones associated with Room n (compare CD and fig. 20 above). Yet the trench into which the Roman engineers built 503 displays evenly cut sides that remain regular and uniformly close to the faces of the wall itself from top to bottom. Generally, this characteristic typifies a foundation trench more than robbing activity. The appearance of the trench suggests that the plundering of Wall 161 occurred much earlier than the Roman period and that the location of 503 at this very spot was a serendipitous one.

In this light, it seems uncanny that an apparent load-bearing wall on the north side of the Roman building (Wall 513) utilized the truncated remains of the BP II outer Casemate Wall 564 as its base (see Section CD, where 564 is apparently mislabeled 504[526]). But the subterranean courses and the trench into which they were set display the same regular features as those of Wall 503 to the south. Moreover, judging from Section CD, the great cut that sweeps obliquely away from the top, southern corner of Wall 564 clearly seems to date the robbing of this wall to the Hellenistic period. With the perimeter walls well founded on bedrock or on solid, ashlar blocks set on bedrock, the Romans could rest their interior wall (505) in nothing more than Hellenistic fill. Yet, had its foundation trench continued downward until reaching bedrock, it too would have landed virtually on the same footing created originally for inner Casemate Wall 556, as CD makes clear. Using parallel broken lines, I have indicated on the plan in fig. 38 the approximate locations where the casemate features 564 and 556, as well as the original Enclosure Wall 161, lay beneath Segment *504.508.509.510*. The main

---

left angle with 500 in fig. 20. Since these sketches represent nothing more than roughly drawn, unphased field plans, I must reiterate that they were likely not intended to demonstrate perfectly the spatial or temporal relationships between features and that, therefore, one should refrain from overly interpreting the differences noted above.

[525] *Fieldbook Qn (Vol. I)*, 6a.

[526] As I have shown, 504 signifies a wall associated directly with the Late Roman structure now under discussion. Both fig. 20 and fig. 38 corroborate this conclusion. Wall 504, then, certainly did not belong to BP II, as Kenyon has it on Section CD. There seems no recourse but to suggest that she has inadvertently mislabeled 564 as 504. (Compare the relative positions of Walls 556 and 564 on *SS I*, Pl. II.) Similarly, the draftsman for Section EF appears to have mislabeled the inner Casemate Wall 556 as 536.

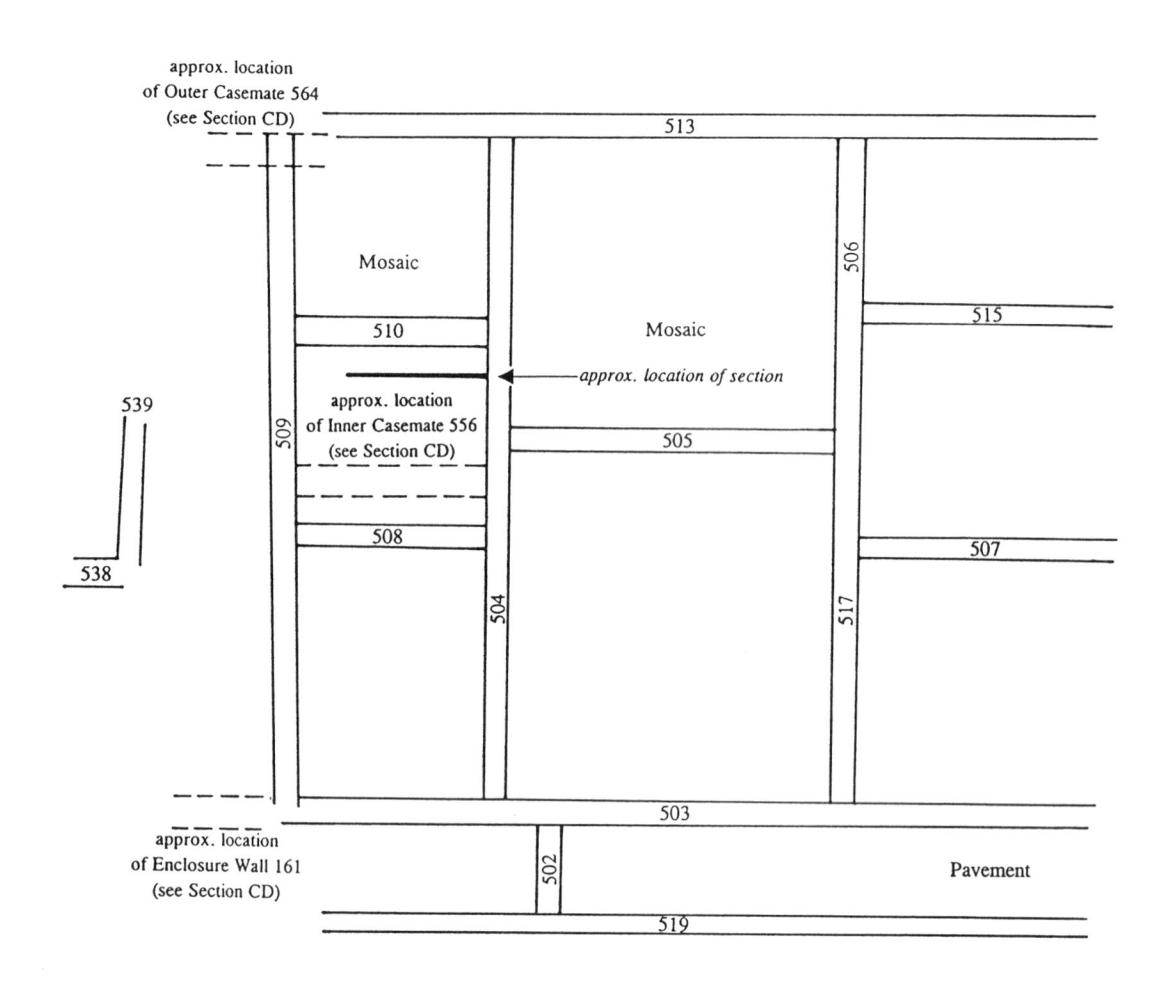

148   THE ARCHAEOLOGY OF ISRAELITE SAMARIA

Segment 504.508.509.510
Top Plan of Coordinate Walls

fig. 38

walls of the Late Roman building, then, assumed courses almost identical to the earliest series of city walls on the north side of the royal compound.

Several plausible suggestions emerge from these observations. First, most of the robbing of Israelite walls in the north courtyard area, including the BP I Enclosure Wall and the BP II casemate system, occurred during the Hellenistic period. Second, virtually no intervening deposits appear between the Israelite and Hellenistic levels in any segment of excavation in the north courtyard area, and particularly north of casemate Wall 556, where the post-Israelite "chocolate" layer ended. Unless the Hellenistic plunderers actually swept away all the debris churned up by their activities, which seems unlikely, relatively little occupation appears to have occurred at the site between these two major stratigraphic periods. An alternate approach involves a considerable lowering of the dates for "Periods IV-VIII," which would bring the settlement history that they reflect chronologically closer to the Hellenistic period. I shall assess the viability of this option later in this study. Third, I may presume with some certitude that the Romans would have made good use of the stones remaining from Hellenistic structures built in this area. One now sees that at least some of those stones derived originally from Israelite structures, which implies that the Romans now placed them in tertiary use. Given the incredible scope of Roman construction activity at this site, which even received the emperor's name (Sebaste), the supply of ready-made stones proved inadequate. To satisfy the demands of these projects, Roman quarries were opened across a significant portion of the north courtyard area (partly seen in fig. 20 above). But to reach and extract the new rock, they had to displace enormous amounts of natural and artificial accumulations that had amassed on the summit. Toward this end, they proceeded to strip the surviving Hellenistic features bare and to mine rock from the highest elevations of the summit, i.e., above the lateral scarp that ran across this area. To access the upper summit, they scraped the northernmost courtyard levels down over the scarp and thereby filled and leveled the breaches that they themselves had created. Unfortunately, many of these fillings appear to have subsumed the contents of the so-called Israelite Ivory House. Consequently, they, too, derive from contexts that are secondary, at best, and likely tertiary in nature.

1) Stratigraphic Detail

a. 504.508.509.510

Besides the plan presented in fig. 38 above, the field notebooks provided the section presented in fig. 39, which portrays the depositional history in a 3-meter-long strip west of the foundation trench for Wall 504.[527] (I have indicated the approximate location of this section on fig. 38 above.) This trench clearly cut each of the layers presented here, with the possible exception of Layer V, which yielded all the fragments from five bowls, three cooking pots, and one jar seen in *SS III*, Fig. 7.

---

[527] *Fieldbook Qn (Vol. I)*, 32a.

The stratigraphy appears relatively straightforward in this section, with only a few wrinkles occurring in levels from the Israelite period. Kenyon designated two layers as "I" on this diagram and even appears to have used this numeral in reference to a third deposit. The stratigraphically latest of these revealed a level of hardish earth that was "broken in parts"[528] and "not present all over [the] area."[529] Since most of the pottery associated with this layer derived from the Hellenistic period, Kenyon concluded that the matrix may reflect an erstwhile floor level from that time. The first

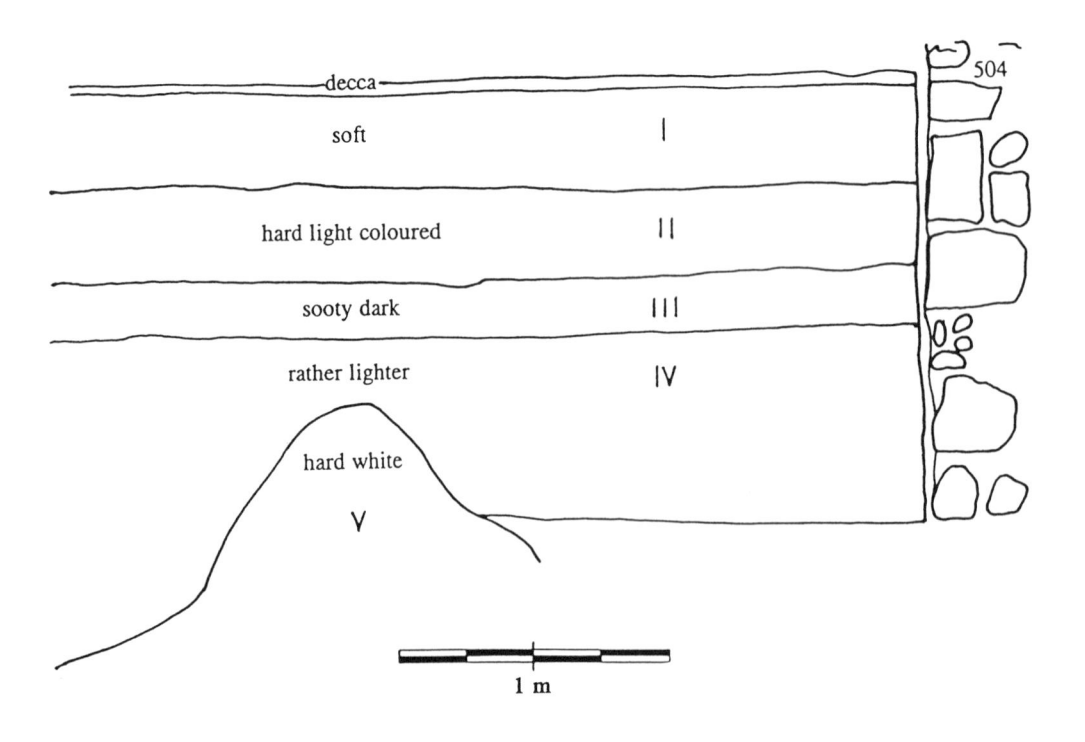

Segment 504.508.509.510:
Local Deposits West of Wall 504
<— W E —>
View toward North

fig. 39

"Layer I" that actually appears on the section comprised a "hard decca level" assigned to the very Late Roman period (Kenyon's R.4 or even R.5 phase). The sublayers

---

[528] *Fieldbook Qn (Vol. I)*, 30.

[529] *Fieldbook Qn (Vol. I)*, 33a.

excavated with this level yielded ceramic specimens ranging from late Hellenistic forms to red and grey ribbed vessels. Kenyon provided the following comment on this surface:

> Dekka floor, [but] n[o]t v[ery] g[oo]d surface. This may n[o]t go right up to small stones on top of 510, wh[ich] [are] set back fr[om] lower part of bigger stones, [and] I seems to stop on their line.[530]

The soft matrix found lying beneath this surface (and also labeled I) likely represents the subfloor makeup.

Level II contained a deposit of hard earth that was distinct from the decca floor above but that did not appear to reflect an earlier surface. Kenyon also assigned it to her R.4 period, though she recorded the pottery yield as Hellenistic in character. Layer II seems, therefore, to comprise part of the Hellenistic levels which the Romans scraped down into this area from points slightly farther south on the summit. Ultimately, Kenyon believed that II actually served as an extension of I.

Immediately beneath these Late Roman levels, the excavators encountered two rather thick deposits of Hellenistic fill. Layer III contained a soft, black matrix while IV consisted in a lighter soil which evinced sooty subdeposits (as in Layer IVa, not delineated in fig. 39). Sub-Layer IVb comprised the same mixture of hard and soft soils that spread farther out and covered the areas of the earlier casemate walls. Kenyon concluded that these levels stemmed from the massive fills associated with the robbing of the Israelite casemate system and the backloading of trenches dug for the so-called Greek Fort Wall.

Two facts pertaining to these Hellenistic levels merit attention at this point. First, it is interesting that, according to both the plan in *SS I*, Pl. II and the section in Pl. VII, EF, a lateral portion of the inner Casemate Wall 556 survived in this exact area (stretching for roughly 10 m, from 641° E to 651/652° E). In fact, the Segment *504.508.509.510* deposit under consideration appears to have lain against the inside (i.e., northern) face of that wall. Perhaps the Greek designers left this section of wall here, where the drop of the rock scarp was deep and the topography of the rock below quite steep and erratic, to serve as a subterranean "sleeper wall" to help retain and stabilize the enormous quantities of loose fill entering the area.[531] Second, the records again uniformly mention the presence of soft black, burnt, or sooty deposits *only* in these layers from the Hellenistic period. As I have consistently shown, the field notes do not connect matrix of this sort with either earlier or later depositions. The depositional history of the adjacent alcove to the north, identified as Segment *504.510.509* in the field notes, further corroborates this picture. There, Hellenistic levels III, IIIb, and

---

[530]*Fieldbook Qn (Vol. I)*, 30.

[531]I have commented elsewhere on the apparent use of such "sleeper walls" along this same area north of the rock scarp (e.g., *AIS-I*, 205).

IIIe yielded thick sooty deposits,[532] unlike both the later Roman Level I and the earlier, hard, white Israelite Layer IV. I may note as well that the bulk of the ivories recovered from this site were also extremely charred or burnt and came from areas situated ca. 16 meters south-west of this deposit (primarily Rooms *h* and *k*), in layers I have correlated to this same period of activity.

Finally, the Joint Expedition exposed and removed an undulating layer of hard, white composition (Layer V) and a level of darkish soil (Layer VI[533]), both of which they found lying immediately below the Hellenistic levels. Noting that the pottery here was "all IV," Kenyon assigned this deposit to "Period IV" and described it as the "remains of casemate filling, contemp[orary with] a repair."[534] The ceramic assemblage in *SS III*, Fig. 7, came entirely from the bulging Layer V visible in fig. 39. Though initially one might presume this to represent a prime example of imported fill material, its irregular contours, color, and composition (a matrix of hard, white detritus) resemble more the sort of construction debris that resulted both from artificially shaping the rock surface[535] and from dressing the ashlar blocks of the original casemate walls. If the latter applies here, the overall value of the pottery group contained in the deposit rises somewhat, since the assemblage would relate more directly to local rather than possibly distant activities (in locations from which builders would have transported the residue secondarily to this locus). We encountered levels of this same nature in adjacent chambers of the casemate system already in my earlier study of this area.[536]

I may conclude my stratigraphic analysis of this segment with the observation that, in the mosaic-covered alcove to the immediate north of this room (see fig. 38), Kenyon assigned the level that best correlates to Layer V (namely, Layer IV in Segment *504.510.509*) to her "Period II" rather than to IV. This assignment should prompt

---

[532] *Fieldbook Qn (Vol. I)*, 26a.

[533] The field section in fig. 39 did not include this local deposit. While I may presume that it lay to the east (and perhaps west?) of Layer V, below the basal portion of Layer IV, I cannot state this with certainty.

[534] *Fieldbook Qn (Vol. I)*, 33a. In comparison with this interpretation, note Z. Herzog's intimation that the ancient builders had, from the first, filled the Casemate System with earth, apparently to strengthen the city's enclosure (Z. Herzog, "Fortifications," *OEANE* 2, 325). His comment elsewhere (p. 320) that the filled casemate chambers "served as structural foundations" similar to the so-called *Kastenmauer* of Anatolia and North Syria finds no basis in the Iron Age remains from Samaria; yet, my discussion above clearly shows that, later on, Roman engineers did utilize the filled casemates as "foundation boxes" beneath their large building projects.

[535] All Iron Age (and probably Early Bronze Age) occupants of this site had pursued this practice in some form or the other, whether by cutting relatively small pits or cups into the surface (as I have shown in the pre-Omride period; see both *AIS-I*, 69, and *Stager*, 93-107) or preparing a squared foundation trench for the lower courses of various walls (e.g., compare the bases of 161, 556, and 564 on all the published sections: AB; CD; EF; and GH).

[536] See the discussion of Segments *506.505.504* and *558.556.557.559* + *558.559.564.557* in *AIS-I*, 24-25 and 26-27, figs. 7a-7b.

one to undertake a close examination of the pottery group removed from Layers V-VI in Segment *504.508.509.510* to discern whether any conspicuous changes in the overall attributes of that assemblage should, in fact, point to a time period later than BP II in the mid-ninth century BCE. Given the similar appearance of construction deposits on the summit from throughout the Israelite period, it appears that any permutation toward post-PP 3 attributes in the ceramic record would provide a better basis on which to reassign these levels to BP IV (from BP II) than either the higher elevation of the findspots or traceable changes in the construction of the casemate wall itself—changes that the team apparently did not detect.

2) Pottery Analysis

As noted in my stratigraphic analysis above, the pottery reviewed here came from an area inside the casemate chamber located north of Room *l*, at 650° E and immediately south of 470° N (see "CR" for *Casemate Repairs*, fig. 5). Though the final report acknowledged that this locus "cannot be dated stratigraphically, since there is no direct evidence connecting this repair with any of the main building periods," it noted that "the ware however is exactly similar to that of Period IV elsewhere both in what it includes and in what is not present."[537] As often happens in the report, it remains unclear whether Kenyon intended her reference to "ware" to relate to the actual fabric used in the manufacture of the vessels or to the form of the fragments presented.

a. Bowls

SS III Published Figure	Registry No. (none marked for discard)	Strip	Coordinates	Feature	Local Layer
7:1	Q 4881	Qn	504.508.509.510	Casemate	V
7:2	Q 4876	Qn	504.508.509.510	Casemate	V
7:3	Q 5254	Qn	504.508.509.510	Casemate	V
7:4	Q 5255	Qn	504.508.509.510	Casemate	V
7:5	[no registry number in the published report; this rim likely came from the same locus as the other fragments in this group]				

Provenance Data:
PP4 Bowls from Area Labeled "Casemate Repair Deposit"

Table 15

---

[537]*SS III*, 117 (see also n. 618 below).

A series of five bowl rims from this casemate repair locus appeared in the final report. None of these pieces were marked as discards and, except for entry No. 5, no other recording discrepancies attended the data describing their specific findspot. Though I could find no registry number for rim No. 5, it surely must belong to the same local layer as the other members of this group. Four of these bowls display a rather hard, reddish-buff ware with noticeable grits. Specimens 1 and 2 have red slip inside and out, while No. 4 shows a buff slip. Numbers 1 and 5 exhibit signs of good, continuous burnishing. Bowl No. 4 consists in hard, grey, ringing ware with larger white grits than most of the other samples include.

Bowl No. 1 displays a ring base, rather thick ware, upper sidewalls smoothly curved into a vertical stance (with the curvature gradual enough not to constitute carination), and a flat rim whose outer thickening forms an exterior ledge. Kenyon drew an apt comparison of it to Lachish bowl class B.7.[538] At that site, "the bowl types which make up this group are among the most characteristic.... They are also very closely confined within certain [chronological] limits."[539] Samples representing this class appear in tomb contexts dating to around 850 BCE (Tombs 224 and 1004) and predominate the assemblage of bowls in another tomb from 800 BCE (Tomb 1002); on the tell itself, this style was dominant in Level III but did not appear in Level II.[540] In the slightly earlier Tomb 218 (dated to the late tenth century BCE), which yielded a large assemblage of bowl forms, only two sherds appeared from this particular class. These data indicate that, at Lachish at least, this style effectively entered the mainstream of ceramic tradition during the course of the ninth century BCE,[541] but it flourished primarily during the early eighth century and disappeared entirely by the seventh century BCE.

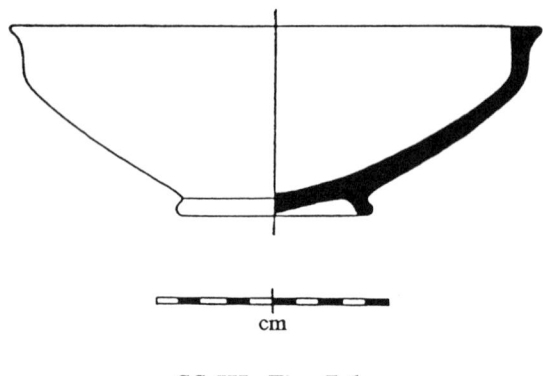

SS III, Fig. 7:1

This chronological picture is borne out at other sites, such as Tell en-Naṣbeh,[542]

---

[538]*Lachish III*, Pl. 79:48 (Tomb 224).

[539]*Lachish III*, Text, 273.

[540]*Lachish III*, Text, 50, 273.

[541]In the north, compare *Hazor I*, Pls. XLVII:10 (Stratum VIII); XLIX:12 (Stratum VII); *Hazor II*, Pls. LIV:9, 13-14 (Stratum VIII); LXIII:16, 18 (Stratum VII).

[542]*TN II*, Pl. 55:1257-1258, with a lower break in the sidewalls. Compare Pl. 56:1286, with a thickened but more rounded rim-form mode, and 56:1291, with the rim tipped slightly downward toward the outside. See also W. F. Badè, *Some Tombs of Tell en-Naṣbeh Discovered in 1929* (Berkeley, 1931), Pl. XIV:1164, from Tomb 3.

PP 4: CASEMATE REPAIR DEPOSIT — POTTERY

Beth-Shemesh,[543] Gezer,[544] Hazor,[545] Megiddo,[546] and Yoqneʿam.[547] At Taʿanach, incipient or prototypical forms appear already by the late tenth century, but they do not seem to continue in great numbers into the ninth or eighth centuries BCE.[548] Back at Megiddo, another ancestral form also appeared in the late tenth century BCE though its rim was thickened to an internal ledge as well as to an external one.[549] In the Jezreel Valley region, bowls with similar ledged rims appear with either rounder upper bodies (Bowl Group B/IIf) or a high-set carination (Bowl Group BIII/f).[550] In short, this bowl appears at a number of sites but never in great quantities.[551] Though a possible late tenth-century BCE prototype appears in the report from Keisan,[552] this rim mode appears to date mainly from the mid-ninth to early eighth centuries BCE in the north;[553] overall, however, the vessel type seems slightly more common in the south.[554]

---

[543] *AS-IV*, Pl. LXVI:4, 5 (Stratum IIb). These bowls resemble *SS III*, Fig. 7:1 by exhibiting a reddish-brown ware with small grey grits, and No. 4 also shows red slip and burnishing on both its interior and exterior. In *AS-V*, 137, Grant and Wright stated this style bowl proved "typical of the last phase of Stratum II." But, as Tufnell noted, this statement included rims that fall outside the specific type considered here (see *Lachish III, Text*, 273).

[544] *Gezer III*, Pls. 13:10; 14:18; 15:7 (Field VII, Stratum 6B), with inside corner of rim slightly rounded; at Gezer, these mid-ninth-century exemplars typically revealed a dark red slip and wheel burnishing on the interior and over the rim.

[545] *Hazor I*, Pls. XLIX:6-7, 13 (Stratum VII, but continuity in VI-V; see p. 20); LIII:14 (Stratum V), with thicker walls and slightly inturned rim; *Hazor II*, Pls. LXVI:8 (Stratum VI); LXXXI:15; LXXXII:11 (Stratum VA).

[546] *Megiddo I*, Pl. 24:29-31, shallower variants in 34-35 (these bowls range primarily from Strata IV-II). Pl. 24:39 presents the same basic form, but on a deeper bowl with a bar handle and the rim slightly inturned (again, assigned to Stratum IV, with intrusions detected in V).

[547] *T. Yoqneʿam* [3], Fig. 11:6 (Area A, Stratum 10 = eighth [possibly also late ninth] century BCE). This report classified this bowl under the rubric "Samaria Ware" (p. 51).

[548] Compare *Taʿanach*, Figs. 23:3; 44:5; 93:2 (all Period IIB).

[549] *Megiddo II*, Pl. 89:9 (Stratum VA). The report described the appearance of this bowl as follows: "pink-buff, numerous white grits, dark red wash and irregular burnish inside and over rim to shoulder; badly burned inside." Compare *Hazor II*, Pl. XCII:26 (Stratum VA).

[550] *T. Qiri*, 145. Compare *T. Yoqneʿam* [3], Fig. 11:6 (Area A, Stratum 10) (rounded upper body) and *T. Qiri*, Fig. 37:18 (carinated upper body). Also *T. Qiri*, Fig. 10:5 (Area D, Stratum VII); 37:17, with ledged rim slightly thickened on the interior as well.

[551] The form seems curiously absent at such sites as Tell Keisan.

[552] *T. Keisan*, Pl. 66:11a (Niveau 9a-b). Compare *Hazor II*, Pl. LII:7 (Stratum IX).

[553] Holladay placed it slightly later, "to a time near or past the mid-eighth century" (*Holladay*, 130 and n. 116). While the evidence from Lachish and other southern sites may support this conclusion for that area, documentation from the north suggests that these bowls lean toward the early side of that chronological mark (e.g., *Hazor III-IV*, Pl. CCXII:22 = Stratum IX).

[554] Gitin described this piece from Samaria as the only whole example of its kind attested in the north (*Gezer III*, 190). Northern exemplars tend to show a flattened rim that manifests both an exterior and an

In addition to bowl No. 1, Holladay also placed Fig. 7:2 in the mid-eighth-century ceramic group.[555] It displays bowed or somewhat rounded sidewalls with no carination, a flat base, and a straight, outcut rim form. Though Holladay compared this specimen to two bowls from Hazor,[556] I might observe that, while these bowls do display flat bases, their rims appear slightly less outcut and they both are "decorated" with a red band around the rim or, perhaps in the case of the example from *Hazor I*, with a red slip that extends over the rim only. The Samaria bowl bore a red slip over the entire interior and exterior surfaces. A similar form, with a light brown interior and exterior slip, also comes from Stratum VB at Hazor.[557] It remains somewhat ironic that this innocuous-looking bowl claims so few good parallels. The closest comparisons seem to have more bend in their sidewalls,[558] a more noticeable carination in the lower one-third of their body,[559] or a slightly modified rim-form mode.[560] A slightly wider version of this style comes from Tell en-Naṣbeh.[561] Still, the best available witnesses to this type seem to cluster around the period of Stratum V at Hazor.[562]

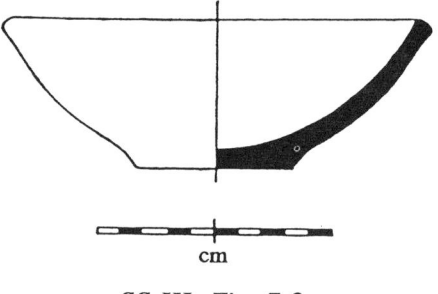

SS III, Fig. 7:2

Holladay placed the wide, shallow saucer of "hard grey ringing ware" in *SS III*, Fig. 7:3, between 860 and 840 BCE, i.e., slightly earlier than the previous bowls. His corpus of primary comparative data, however, consisted in the platter in *SS III*, Fig. 4:19 (PP 3) and the saucers in Figs. 4:13 (PP 3) and 6:3 (PP 4).[563] None of these comparisons seem all that apt, but they are perhaps no less so than the relationship Kenyon proposed between this piece and the saucer bowl with flat base and flaring rim in *SS III*, Fig. 13:2 (from S Tomb 103). Bowl No. 3 does not belong to the platter family, as a comparison between its diameter (20 cm)

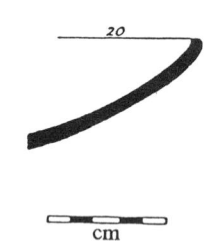

SS III, Fig. 7:3

---

interior ledge, as in *Hazor II*, Pl. LXXIX:5 (Strata VIII-VB); LXXXI:29 (Stratum VA).

[555] Holladay, 130, n. 116.

[556] *Hazor I*, Pl. LXVI:11 (Stratum V); *Hazor II*, Pl. LXXXI:13 (Stratum VA).

[557] *Hazor III-IV*, Pl. CCXXII:7.

[558] *Hazor II*, Pl. LXXX:17 (Stratum VA).

[559] *Hazor II*, Pl. LXXX:4 (Stratum VA).

[560] *Hazor II*, Pl. LXXX:20 (Stratum VA); *Hazor III-IV*, Pl. CCXXII:19 (Stratum VB).

[561] *TN II*, Pl. 59:1354.

[562] *Hazor II*, Pl. LXXXI:13 (Stratum VA). Note especially *Hazor III-IV*, Pl. CCXXVI:3 (Stratum VA), for the best overall morphological comparison, though with grey-buff versus reddish buff ware.

[563] Holladay, 130, n. 114. See *SS III*, 118 for the description of ware quoted above.

and that of Fig. 4:19 (approximately 31 cm) reveals. If anything, its thin walls and its simple, rounded lip that has been smoothed gently inward make an analogy to *SS III*, Fig. 4:1 and the deeper 4:2 (both from PP 3) a better one. While I need not repeat the corpus of parallels cited in my earlier treatment of the PP 3 bowls,[564] I can ultimately support Holladay's dating of No. 3, though it could easily belong slightly earlier still, somewhere in the late tenth to early ninth centuries BCE.[565]

Despite its simplicity in form, exact parallels also prove elusive for the coarse, gritty saucer bowl No. 4. Its buff ware and buff slip seem typical of late ninth-century BCE vessels. Similar straight-sided bowls with ordinary flat bases and simple, rounded rims appear in meager numbers at Megiddo,[566] Taʿanach,[567] and (on much wider forms) Keisan.[568] One may also compare an exemplar from Tell en-Naṣbeh.[569] Within the Samaria corpus itself, this form seems most akin to *SS III*, Fig. 3:3 from PP 2 and Fig. 6:1 from PP 4, and I therefore assign it to the same general period, namely the late ninth to mid-eighth centuries BCE.

SS III, Fig. 7:4

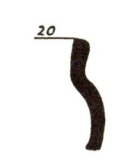

Finally, the rim type seen in Fig. 7:5 calls to mind the "cyma" profile seen on numerous bowls coming out of the Late Bronze Age and extending throughout the Iron Age I period, until they finally begin to fade in number during the late tenth century BCE. Unlike the other bowl types just discussed, this class enjoys numerous parallels at other sites. This familiar cyma form displays a soft, rounded carination in the upper one-third of the sidewalls together with an erect or even everted simple rim form mode. Between these two features lies a smooth groove. Below the rounded or carinated shoulder, the lower sidewalls slope inward strongly, usually to a ring base. I have given full treatment to another early Cyma Bowl from Samaria in *AIS-I*.[570] While most of the morphological attributes described above are standard on

SS III, Fig. 7:5

---

[564] *AIS-I*, 173-75.

[565] I also note a morphological similarity to much later bowl forms described as Eastern Terra Sigillata I in *Gezer III*, 89-90, Pl. 33:17. The fabric and surface treatment, however, differ considerably in this later tradition.

[566] *Megiddo I*, Pl. 24:40-41 (Strata IV-II), though the ware among this class of bowl was typically greenish-brown in color (see p. 168-69, § 56).

[567] *Taʿanach*, Fig. 65:9 (Period IIB).

[568] *T. Keisan*, Pl. 31:3 (Niveau 4 = seventh century BCE). Note that, here, the roughness on the exterior walls seems to relate to a series of ridges; though the Samaria drawing displays a similar characteristic, Kenyon commented only on the coarseness of the bowl, not on the presence of ridges.

[569] *TN II*, Pl. 68:1549, with a slightly modified base form. (Note p. 176, where the author states that the range of this bowl extended from the Late Bronze Age into the Late Iron Age.)

[570] *AIS-I*, 80-81. Again, I refer the reader to the citations given there to establish a chronological range for this vessel type; I need not repeat them here.

the cyma form, variations do often occur in the rim mode itself. Such variations are seen the presence or absence of handles, in the types of handles employed when they do appear, and in the various surface treatments applied to these bowls.[571] Yet these differences in detail have not provided substantial data to allow the clarification of firm subtypes. More generally, A. Mazar has suggested dividing these bowls into two groups based on their relative diameters.[572] The first group ranges from 15-25 cm in maximum width, while the second, larger assemblage runs from 25-35 cm in diameter. With its mouth opening of 20 cm, the Samaria example seen here falls squarely in the corpus of smaller cyma bowls.

While bowls from the same general class as Fig. 7:5 appear more widely attested than other forms in this Casemate group (Nos. 2 and 4 particularly), Kenyon noted in the published report that "these bowls . . . were not common" at Samaria.[573] Though she also recognized the association that Figs. 7:5 and 14:1-1a hold to the family of cyma bowls, her corollary suggestion that this type lasted throughout the Iron Age II period remains untenable.[574] The *terminus ante quem* for the functional life of the true cyma family falls somewhere in the late tenth century BCE.[575]

---

[571] Regarding the last attribute mentioned, note, for example, that at Tell Qasile bowls from Stratum XII often show a white slip (but not red), those from Stratum XI increasingly show red slip (but not white) with some burnishing and decoration (usually black concentric circles or red and black bands on an unslipped surface), and those from Stratum X show predominantly red slip and burnishing (with black decoration continuing in certain examples). Beyond Tell Qasile, the red slip and burnishing appear less frequently. It is noteworthy, then, that this exemplar from Samaria displays a "good burnish" (*SS III*, 118) over its buff ware (no recorded slip). In this vein, another specimen from an unstratified context in E 207 (*SS III*, Fig. 14:1a) proves even more significant in that it shows the typical buff ware but with a burnished red slip on the interior and over the rim. (See also other exemplars, enumerated under *SS III*, Fig. 14:1-1a, from E 207 and S Tombs 103 that display various combinations of red slip and burnishing.)

[572] *T. Qasîle* [2], 39.

[573] *SS III*, 146.

[574] This portion of her argument rests on a comparison drawn to the bowl presented in *Megiddo I*, Pl. 28:89, which may extend from Stratum IV to Stratum II at that site but which, in fact, is not a good example of a cyma bowl in the first place. Better examples of cyma bowls appear from that particular site in *Megiddo I*, Pls. 30:114-115; 31:158 (Stratum V) and in *Megiddo II*, Pls. 71:25 (Strata VII-VIA), with flat base; 74:6, 8 (Stratum VIB); 78:12 and 84:18 (Stratum VI); 89:14; 90:11 (Stratum VA-IVB), in other words, from levels dating to the tenth century and earlier periods.

[575] Regarding the ceramic corpus from Gezer Field VII, Gitin noted that "the cyma-shaped bowl is an uncommon form in the Corpus, appearing only in the 7th-6th century B.C. ceramic horizon" (*Gezer III*, 199). But his suggested examples from Gezer (*Gezer III*, Pls. 27:27 and 45:15) and elsewhere (Tell Beit Mirsim, Tell en-Naṣbeh, etc.) represent, at best, late, degenerate variants of a basic class of bowls that had disappeared much earlier.

PP 4: CASEMATE REPAIR DEPOSIT — POTTERY

b. Cooking Pots

SS III Published Figure	Registry No. (none marked for discard)	Provenance		
		Strip	Coordinates	Feature	Local Layer
7:6	Q 5257	Qn	504.508.509.510	Casemate	V(?)
7:7	Q 4880	Qn	504.508.509.510	Casemate	V
7:8	Q 5256	Qn	504.508.509.510	Casemate	V(?)

Provenance Data:
PP4 Cooking Pots from Area Labeled "Casemate Repair Deposit"

Table 16

The final report presented three cooking-pot fragments from the area of the putative repairs to the Casemate Wall. On the whole, these three rims add nothing remarkable to the assemblage of cooking-pot sherds already discussed for *SS III*, Fig. 6:25-40. The stratigraphic information pertaining to these rims appears in Table 16 above.

Rim No. 6[576] belongs in a class that developed alongside the notched styles starting in the early-to-mid-ninth century BCE and that continued throughout the Iron II period. Rather than displaying the usual groove or notch on its outer face, this rim is folded and smoothed into a rounded collar (Kenyon's "Class D" cooking-pot rim[577]). Though Kenyon wrote that "the shape of this pot is not known,"[578] I can point to a near perfect parallel from Beth-Shemesh[579] that displays a more substantial portion of its sidewall to verify that: the pot retained a high, smooth carination; it lacked any groove or undercutting of the rim above the point of carination (unlike *SS III*, Fig. 6:30 and 30:25); it appeared with two handles attached from the rounded rim collar to just above the carinated sidewalls; and it presented a deep rather than shallow form. In terms of form, ware, and thickness of walls, this rim most resembles the fragment assigned to PP 6 in *SS III*, Fig. 9:13.[580] While this style

SS III, Fig. 7:6

---

[576]The registration number assigned to No. 6 in *SS III*, 118 is 4257. G. M. Crowfoot's stratification cards, however, correct the entire 4250-4268 series of registration numbers to 5250-5268, respectively. My Appendix A and Table 16 present the proper number for this piece, 5257.

[577]*SS III*, 189.

[578]*SS III*, 189.

[579]*AS-IV*, Pl. LXIV:18 (Sub-strata IIb-c).

[580]Unlike this comparison, the parallels that Kenyon draws between Figs. 7:6 plus 9:12, 17 and 30:25

does not appear in numerous quantities, adequate parallels from Hazor[581] and Beth-Shan,[582] among other sites, justify dating this piece somewhere in the late ninth or early eighth centuries BCE, though the origins of these parallels extend back to the tenth century.[583] Antecedent collar rims appear as early as Iron Age I on both jars and kraters.[584] In the south, four-handled bowls with very similar rims appear frequently in the eighth century but diminish in number during later years.[585]

Fragment No. 7 seems to represent a variant form of the short, triangular rims common in Iron Age I levels at many sites. It finds good late tenth- to early ninth-century BCE parallels in the north at Beth-Shan,[586] where relatively close jar forms are also available.[587] The slight concavity in the outer face of the short rim fold and the angle of the lip and flange relative to the curvature of the upper sidewall give this rim a rather unusual, barbed appearance. Incipient examples of this style from Iron I (eleventh to early tenth centuries BCE) levels at Tell Qasîle,[588] Tell Keisan,[589] and Beth-Shemesh,[590] together with the Beth-Shan evidence, leads me to place this piece just before or near the Iron I-Iron II transition. It may actually represent a late descendant from the deeply undergrooved, prominent flanges from the Late Bronze Age II and the very early Iron Age I cooking pots.[591] I could not locate satisfactory

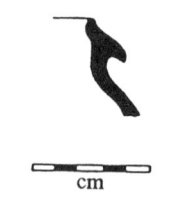

SS III, Fig. 7:7

(*SS III*, 189) are not apt ones for a variety of reasons.

[581]*Hazor I*, Pl. LVIII:7 (Stratum IV); *Hazor II*, Pl. LXIX:21 (Stratum VI); compare the krater rim in Pl. LXIV:3, 5 (Stratum VII; by the next level, these collar rims become more inverted, as in Pl. LXVII:10 and 11, until they are virtually horizontal and resemble the holemouth jar series; see Pl. LXVIII:4). Compare also Pl. LXXXIII:6, with the collar slightly trimmed at its bottom (Stratum VA).

[582]*Beth-Shan*, James, Fig. 69:2 (with thinner walls and undercut rim) and 3 (Level IV).

[583]Compare *T. Qasîle* [2], Fig. 47:4 (Stratum X); *T. Farʿah-RB* [59], Fig. 6:17 (Niveau III), though thickened both internally and externally.

[584]Compare the jar form in *T. Qasîle* [2], Fig. 14:27 (Stratum XII); for kraters, see *Megiddo I*, Pl. 32:161, 163, and particularly 166 (Stratum V); *Taʿanach*, Figs. 42:1-2; 43:2 (Period IIB); *T. Keisan*, Pl. 65:9 (Niveau 9a-b). Note also the continuing tradition on kraters among the examples cited from Hazor in n. 581 above. For this style on early cooking pots, see the reference to a tenth-century example from Tell Qasîle in n. 583.

[585]See the examples cited from Arad, Lachish, Tell Beit Mirsim, Tell en-Naṣbeh, Beersheba, and Beth-Shemesh in *M. & Y. Aharoni*, 76.

[586]*Beth-Shan*, James, Figs. 66:9 (Upper Level V); 69:21 (unstratified; Level IV).

[587]*Beth-Shan*, James, Fig. 64:4, 7.

[588]*T. Qasîle* [2], Figs. 27:20 (Stratum XI); 44:25; 45:14 (Stratum X); 54:20 (Stratum IX).

[589]*T. Keisan*, Pls. 63:1a, 7-8 (Niveau 9a-b); 77:1b (Niveau 9c).

[590]*AS-IV*, Pl. LXII:26, 28.

[591]See *Hazor I*, Pls. LXXXIX:4; CVII:1-7 (LB II); *Hazor III-IV*, Pls. CCI:14 (Stratum XII); CCXCII:6 (Stratum 1B = LB II).

comparisons much beyond the mid-ninth century BCE.[592]

Rim No. 8 represents a hybrid of *SS III*, Fig. 6:26 (with its turned in, rounded lip) and 37 (with its flange pushed up but not yet trimmed toward a notch as in 6:35). This mixed form, then, likely belongs in the late tenth or, more likely, in the early-to-mid-ninth century BCE. I need not reiterate parallels here.

SS III, Fig. 7:8

c. Jars

The Joint Expedition published only a single jar rim fragment from the area inside the repaired casemate chamber. Unlike the bowls and cooking pots recovered from this locus, this jar rim becomes an interesting piece not only because it provides a solid chronological indicator but because it might also furnish some interesting insights into trade relations between Israel and Phoenicia during and immediately following the closing years of the Northern Kingdom. Data pertaining to its findspot appear as follows:

SS III Published Figure	Registry No. (not marked for discard)	Provenance		
		Strip	Coordinates	Feature	Local Layer
7:9	Q 4927	Qn	504.508.509.510	Casemate	V

Provenance Data:
PP4 Jars from Area Labeled "Casemate Repair Deposit"

Table 17

This fragment derives from a class of jars traditionally known as "sausage jars,"[593] though others have suggested calling them "crisp ware storage jars"[594] or simply "cylindrical storage jars."[595] The principal characteristics of this vessel type include short rims manifested in variant forms (simple; thickened and ridged; folded

---

[592]See *Hazor III-IV*, Pl. CCVII:16 (Stratum X); *Hazor II*, Pl. LVII:6, 10, 12 (Stratum VIII), though the pointed flanges are already tending to rise upward toward the notched rim of the Late Shallow Type pots.

[593]*Amiran*, 241-42, Pls. 81-82.

[594]E.g., Bikai's Types 4-7, which she describes as belonging to the same family of jars exhibiting a long, "torpedo" or "sausage" shape (*Tyre*, 46-47).

[595]S. Geva, "Archaeological Evidence for the Trade Between Israel and Tyre?" *BASOR* 248 (1982), 69-72.

triangular; or bulbous),[596] the virtual absence of any neck, high and angular shoulders (often incised with concentric circles),[597] long body, and pointed base. Two small, crudely made handles generally appear just below the shoulders, and analysts have questioned their actual function. The impracticality of lifting these vessels (especially when full) by such cursory handles leads me to speculate that they served more as anchor points for rope ties during their transport via land or sea to trade destinations such as Hazor and Tyre (see below).

SS III, Fig. 7:9

The body of this vessel can assume either a relatively slender shape, with its tall sidewalls appearing slightly concave, or "waisted," in the vessel's midsection,[598] or a fully developed form, with a wider girth and sidewalls that drop straight down from the shoulder.[599] Geva has suggested that these two styles reflect two standard capacities used in Iron Age II Israelite exporting: 16 liters for the first type, and 24 liters for the second.[600] Judging from the juncture angle of its shoulder and sidewall, the fragment from Samaria belongs to the latter category. The ware of these jars is usually hard-fired and buff to pink or reddish-yellow in color—attributes which Bikai describes rather poetically as "crisp brittle ware usually with a light surface bloom."[601] This clay proves lighter in weight than the reddish-brown or purplish matrix used in other, contemporary vessels, including various classes of storage jars. This fact, coupled with the relatively thin section and thin base exhibited by these jars, prompted Geva to surmise that potters attempted to achieve a lighter overall weight for this rather large jar.[602] But even smaller forms, such as bowls, often utilize this same basic fabric. While the issue of weight may have constituted a concern, then, both the clay of choice and the styling seen in these store

---

[596]For externally thickened, plain, and ridged examples, see *Hazor II*, Pl. LXXIII:11, 15, 16; for seventh- and sixth-century BCE versions of simple, squat, plain rims, see *Hazor II*, Pl. XC:5-7; XCI:1-2, 5; *Gezer III*, Pl. 26:19; for the more bulbous style, see *Hazor II*, Pl. LXXIII:17 and *Gezer III*, Pl. 16:5. Another style, "with its unique combination of knob rim, short neck and slightly curved shoulder, only appears in the 7th/6th century B.C. ceramic horizon" (*Gezer III*, 125).

[597]In fact, the original drawing of this fragment on the stratification cards maintained by G. M. Crowfoot shows several ridges or incised circles just below the midpoint of the shoulder on No. 9. These rings appear only faintly in the section drawn in *SS III*, Fig. 7:9. Also from the published report, compare Fig. 21:4.

[598]E.g., *Megiddo I*, Pl. 16:79-80 (Strata III-I).

[599]E.g., *Hazor II*, Pl. XCI:9-11 (Stratum VA).

[600]S. Geva, *BASOR* 248 (1982), 72.

[601]*Tyre*, 46.

[602]Geva, *BASOR* 248 (1982), 70. She found that "the weight of a complete jar (empty) is about three-fourths that of a similar jar made of the usual darker brown-red clay."

jars may simply have proven more amenable to the high-firing processes used in their manufacture.

Though the true sausage-style store jar appears only in the late ninth century and becomes predominant in the eighth century BCE, earlier, tenth-century ancestral forms appear in the north at sites such as Megiddo.[603] The form clearly represents mainly a northern tradition,[604] though it does occur in the south, albeit somewhat sporadically.[605] It appears at Hazor[606] but not at many other inland sites far to the north. The form remains quite rare in Judah[607] and is completely absent from Transjordan.[608] Its most concentrated geographical distribution occurs in Israel and the northern coastal areas, particularly Phoenicia.[609] The chronological distribution of this jar type at Tyre proves informative. Bikai reports that in Strata III-II at Tyre (dated to the last third of the eighth century BCE[610]), this general class of storage jar contributes over 80% of all storage jar rims recovered. In the preceding mid-eighth-century Stratum IV, this type proved uncommon; moreover, the few fragments that did appear there could easily represent intrusions.[611] Neutron Activation Analysis underscored the dissimilarity

---

[603] See *AIS-I*, 64-65 for my comments regarding Jar Type 119 from Megiddo, Stratum V.

[604] E.g., *Megiddo I*, Pls. 14:72 (Strata IV-III); 16:79-81 (Strata IV-I); 15:78; 17:83. *Beth-Shan*, James, Figs. 70:1 (unstratified) and 37:7; 70:3 (Level IV); 128:2 = photograph (Level IV).

[605] Compare *Lachish III*, Pls. 95:489; 96:530. The parallels cited in *Lachish III, Text*, 314, also demonstrate the relatively later dates of the southern attestations. *Ashdod II-III*, Figs. 38:2, 3; 42:4, 6; 57:8-9 (Area D, Strata 3, 3b, 2); *Gezer II*, Pl. 36:7(?) and 16 (Field II, Stratum 4). Compare also the report from Tell en-Naṣbeh, where the ovoid and/or "hippo" styles continue to dominate the assemblage.

[606] *Ninth century BCE* = *Hazor II*, Pl. LX:9-10 (Stratum VIII); *Hazor III-IV*, Pl. CLXXX:19-20, 23 (Stratum VII); *early eighth century BCE* = *Hazor I*, Pl. LXV:13 (Stratum VI); *Hazor II*, Pls. LXXII:1-9 (Stratum VI); LXXIII:1-17 (Stratum VI); *Hazor III-IV*, Pl. CLXXXVI:11-12, 15, 17-19 (Stratum VI); *mid-eighth century BCE* = *Hazor I*, Pls. LVII:9-11 (Stratum V; No. 9 constitutes a nice comparison to the fragment from Samaria); LXIV:8 (Stratum V; = another good form parallel for the Samaria piece); *Hazor II*, Pls. LXXV:15 (Stratum V); LXXIX:24-25 (Stratum VB); XC:1-4 (Stratum VA); XCI:1-16 (Stratum VA); CVII:12 (Stratum VA); *Hazor III-IV*, Pls. CLXXXIX:22 (Stratum V); CCXXIX:9-13 (Stratum VA); CCXXX:28-29 (Stratum VA); CCLIII:1 (Stratum V); CCCLIII:10-11, 13-14 (photographs); *late eighth century BCE* = *Hazor II*, Pl. CI:9-10, 12-15 (Stratum IV).

[607] The typical store jar of the south during this period maintains a more ovoid-shaped body with carinated shoulders, a straight rim, no neck, and a thickened base. For examples, see *TBM I*, Pls. 52:14; 53:3 (Stratum A); Lachish Jar Types 472 (Level III) and 469 (Level II). See also the discussion in *M. & Y. Aharoni*, 83.

[608] Note its conspicuous absence from the discussion in *APTJ*, 170-202.

[609] From Phoenicia, see *Byblos II*, 279, No. 9384, Fig. 309:9384 (Levels VI-X); *Sarepta*, Fig. 23:17(?), 18-20 (Stratum D1, late ninth and eighth centuries); Al Mina (J. du Plat-Taylor, "The Cypriot and Syrian Pottery from Al-Mina, Syria," *Iraq* 21 [1959], 62-92, Fig. 4:2).

[610] *Tyre*, 67.

[611] Bikai, *BASOR*, 48. Compare also *Tyre*, Pls. II-IV, and Bikai's summary statements on p. 57. Note that the rim on the Samaria fragment (Fig. 7:9) most closely matches Bikai's type SJ 5, seen in Pl. II:5, 7, 9, (for waisted bodies) and Pls. II:11 and III:6 (for the fullbodied variety similar to the example from Samaria). Also, while the sausage-jar family at Tyre included Bikai's types SJ 4, 5, 6, and 7, more rims

between fragments from these jars and those from other types found at Tyre, including "all Cypriot compositional groups."[612] Geva has convincingly argued that the sausage jars originated in Israel and functioned as containers for agricultural products exported from there to Tyre.[613] Interestingly, the swell in the appearance of these "Israelite" trade vessels from around 732 BCE to the close of the eighth century BCE coincides with the dominance of Assyria along the northern coast and in the Ephraimite hill country. The persistent, or even increased, trade between Samaria and Tyre during a period of dramatically waning political fortunes in the former area may represent the result of Assyrian rather than Israelite policies and management.

This scenario fits well with Assyria's apparent strategy to gain control over an entire trade route by dominating its terminus, in this case Tyre. Importantly, these data also relate to the distribution of this style jar at Hazor. As seen in n. 606, the appearance of this vessel of trade at Hazor was concentrated in Strata VI-V, i.e., in the early eighth century down to approximately 732 BCE. It seems, then, that a noticeable shift in Samaria's trading allegiance—from Israelite Hazor to Phoenician Tyre—occurred following the establishment of Assyrian dominance in the hinterland of Israel by Tiglath-pileser III during the 730s BCE.[614] For the next two decades, the flow of at least certain goods ran out of Israel and directly to the Phoenician coastal cities of Sidon[615] and Tyre and, subsequently, by water to Cyprus.[616]

3) Evaluation and Summary

Despite her inability to establish a stratigraphic connection between various key levels on the summit itself, Kenyon offered a two-pronged interpretation regarding the casemate ceramic group presented in Figure 7 of *SS III*: (1) the pottery "came from a deposit contemporary with a rebuilding of part of the casemate walls"; (2) these materials stem from the same time period as all the other PP 4 items published in the final report because the ware appears "exactly similar" to that witnessed in the stratified corpus of PP 4 goods.[617]

---

from SJ 5 appeared there than from any other subtype (245 of 463 = nearly 53%; see p. 47).

[612] See the brief report by A. M. Bieber, Jr., in *Tyre*, 88-90.

[613] S. Geva, *BASOR* 248 (1982), 69.

[614] The close form parallels cited for No. 9 both from Stratum V at Hazor (n. 606) and from Bikai's Type SJ 5 (n. 611) indicate that this particular jar might have functioned on either side of this permutation in Samaria's trading patterns. Due to the questionable stratigraphic nature of the local layer that yielded this fragment (see fig. 39 and my Stratigraphic Detail, p. 152), comparative ceramic analysis such as this must provide the basis for any suggested dating of the rim.

[615] G. Contenau, "Mission archéologique à Sidon (1914)," *Syria* 1 (1920), 108-54, Fig. 27.

[616] *SCE, IV.*2, Fig. XLIV:11 (Period IV) = Plain White IV Ware of the Cypro-Archaic Period I; compare also Figs. LVI:28-29; LXII:3 = Plain White V and VI Ware of the Cypro-Archaic Period II.

[617] *SS III*, 117.

If, as I have already noted (p. 153), Kenyon's use of "ware" embodies a reference to the *form* of the vessels involved, then one may seriously question these conclusions.[618] The collection of bowls, and certainly the cooking-pot fragments, in *SS III*, Fig. 7:1-8 tend to favor an earlier date for the deposition of Layer V in Segment *504.508.509.510*, perhaps sometime in the mid-ninth century BCE. Though ancestral forms related to the apparent sausage jar rim (Fig. 7:9) also arise in the late ninth century, I acknowledge that this particular piece likely reflects a later tradition from the second half of the eighth century BCE. I have noted that Tyrian exemplars of this vessel type concentrate in the final three decades of that century and that they prove quite uncommon beforehand. Still, this would not necessarily preclude a ninth-century date for the deposition of Layer V inside the casemate system. As fig. 39 shows, the stratigraphic nature of this accumulation certainly seems to allow for some contamination by intrusive elements. Moreover, even if the sausage rim does not represent such a contaminant, it cannot singularly anchor the entire deposit to PP 4 generally or, more specifically, to a date in the late eighth century. It may simply anticipate the Israelite use of these jars in its economic trade with Tyre. In this case, it would belong somewhere in the late ninth-mid-eighth centuries BCE, when the evidence from Hazor confirms a heavy use of this jar form within Israel.

Finally, one must remember that, due to Kenyon's method of trenching through a given area, one sees these putative repairs to the casemate system only in a portion of one chamber. Inherently, this limited exposure cannot allow one to speculate on the

	bowls	cooking pots	jars	holemouth jars	TOTAL
Casemate Repair Deposit					
504.508.509.510 V	5	3	1	-	9
TOTAL	5	3	1	-	9

Distribution of PP 4-4a Ceramic Forms in Local Stratigraphy of the Casemate Repair Deposit
Table 18

---

[618] Kenyon's statement appears to refer to the form rather than the fabric of these vessels. The latter, in fact, displays a significant range of traits even within this limited ceramic group from the casemate chamber: reddish-buff ware with red slip; course buff ware with buff slip; buff-to-pinkish ware with no slip; buff ware with no slip but with burnishing; hard grey ware; purplish ware; and brown ware (see *SS III*, Fig. 7, pp. 117-18). "Ware" constitutes an awkward term, the meaning of which varies depending on the speaker; archaeologists should not employ it without clarifying precisely what they intend to convey.

causes of the disrepair in the first place: they might derive just as easily from a localized accident or natural erosion as from military activity. This limitation results primarily from one's inability to see the lateral extent of the damage and from the limited sample of ceramic traditions published from the area that was, in fact, exposed (see Table 18 on the preceding page).

Pottery Period 4: Conclusions

This extended analysis of BP IV allows me to explore three new areas of interest that will receive greater attention as the study progresses. These subjects are interconnected; each lays the groundwork for that which follows. First, an overall portrait has begun to emerge regarding the nature and layout of the summit generally and, within that area, of the royal compound itself. I will provide a working description of the city's plan and suggest specific functions for certain sectors of the site. Second, as a result of this new understanding of the area inside the grand casemate system, I can broach the subject of the archaeological and historical context of the impressive collection of ivory fragments recovered mainly north of the courtyard area. Third, the nature of the findspots from which the ivories came will lead me to some brief comments on the method and theory that guided Kenyon's work on the summit.

Though I have many more segments and three additional ceramic periods to examine in my study, one can already begin to understand certain primary characteristics of the site that helped to shape both the design and function of the summit area. The following comments will bring into sharper focus the summit topography and its importance for understanding the conceptual, or philosophical, roots of the city.

Both the longitudinal and lateral rock scarps that we now know encircled at least the western and northern perimeters of the summit emerge as central elements in this discussion. It is important to note first that, according to Reisner's early reports, these scarps represent planned and artificially constructed features, not natural ones. Further, one must begin again with King Omri, for it now appears that the city plan his engineers implemented at the site persisted as a master blueprint throughout the Israelite occupation and beyond. In Reisner's words,

> In the subsequent [i.e., post-Omride] periods the rock was often scarped to receive facing walls or cut away to give better foundations, but never so thoroughly as in the Omri period. One can safely say, therefore, that this elaborate rock scarping marks the area, and to a large extent determines the plan, of the original Omri structure.[619]

Reisner's published plans locate the juncture of the two core formations mentioned above just north of his lateral Section EF, in Grids G-H 7.[620] That the longitu-

---

[619]*HES I*, 94.

[620]*HES-II*, Plan 5. For a graphic depiction of the lateral scarp, compare the portion of Reisner Section

dinal scarp continued southward from there at least as far as the Israelite Palace area is confirmed by another laterally oriented drawing, namely, Reisner Section GH, Grid G 12, in which one sees a vertical drop of nearly three meters between the palace and the Ostraca House. West of this ledge, however, the rock rose again slightly in the area just beneath the Ostraca House (Section GH, Grids D-E-F). According to Reisner Plan 5, the floor of the chamber situated in the northwest corner of the palace, i.e., Room 10, showed an elevation of 436.02 m above sea level, while the pavement in Room 13 immediately west of the palace and scarp lay at only 432.63 m, or 3.39 m beneath the upper edge of the scarp. But in the area labeled 419, at the easternmost wall of the Ostraca House, the rock swelled again to 434.03 m, i.e., to an elevation only 1.99 m below the top of the main scarp (representing a 1.4 m rise over the initial dropoff behind the palace; see fig. 40).

This pattern matches the topography of the summit farther north, in the area where the western and northern scarps meet. Here, Reisner Section AB assumes a longitudinal orientation and shows that, beyond the ledge which runs laterally through Grid 7, the rock surface also dropped approximately 3.6 m toward the north. Only 5 m west of that point, the rock once again rose slightly to within 2.1 m of the top of the scarp (reflecting a 1.5 m rise from the initial drop).[621] Both the foot pool excavated in Grid G 5 and the drain leading away from the Ostraca House in C 5 and E 6-11, then, were set into the rock base on the lower level, and both exhibit similar elevations (433.47 m for the pool and 433.04 m for the drain at Grid E 7).

On the southern edge of the summit, the Harvard excavations located a similar east-west mantle in Grids L-M 14.[622] Other preliminary evidence appears to confirm the presence of this rock ledge,[623] which seems to run roughly parallel to its counterpart on the north side of the compound area.[624] The situation along the eastern sector of the summit (especially from 665° E to 730° E on Kenyon's plan[625]), however, remains somewhat uncertain due to much less extensive exploration of that area.

EF presented in Plan 11. (To draw clear distinctions between sections published by the Harvard Excavations and those resulting from the work of the Joint Expedition, I shall always use the formulae "Reisner Section *X-X*" and "Reisner Plan *X*" in reference to items belonging to the former group.)

[621] Reisner's team traced this vertical scarp through GH 7, recorded that it rose to "nearly 4 m. in height," and concluded that it "could be safely identified as the northern side of the palace . . ." (*HES-I*, 93).

[622] *HES-I*, 94.

[623] Compare the southernmost extensions of Reisner Section C-D (*HES II*, Plan 4, Grid D 15) and Kenyon's Section AB in *SS I*, Pl. VII, (the south end of which corresponds roughly to Reisner Grid N 15).

[624] Compare the scarp lines in Grids G-H 11 and L-M 14 on Reisner Plan 5.

[625] *SS I*, Pl. II. Reisner's excavations, of course, did not approach this area, and Kenyon's method of trenching exposed only limited spaces.

General Topography of Rock West of Palace Area
Section on Line of GH, Grids D12 – J12

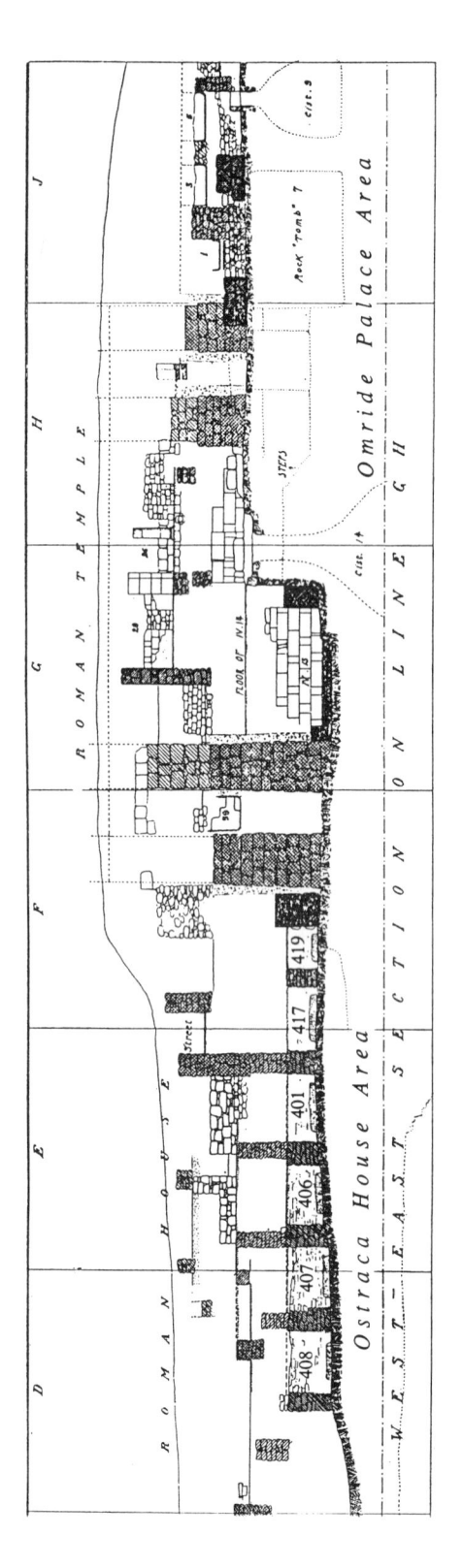

(horizontal scale: each grid = 10 m)

(G. E. Reisner, *HES II*, Plan 4)

<— W E —>

fig. 40

In short, the topography of the excavated portion of the summit revealed a rather abrupt and steep drop around the entire northern, western, and probably southern perimeters of the central compound area.[626] According to Reisner, "when the plan of [Omri's palace] had been determined upon and its site marked out, the rock outside its area was quarried away along the exterior lines of the building, leaving a solid core of rock with a perpendicular scarp, as a base for the structure."[627] This quarrying activity undoubtedly supplied many of the raw materials utilized in the construction of features such as the original Enclosure Wall 161 and, later, Ahab's Casemate System. On the basis of the data just presented, however, I believe that this massive rock foundation covered an area somewhat larger than that occupied by the palace alone. Reisner's own plans show the palace building covering only about half of the western portion of the shelf, from G-K 14 to G-K 11 (with an attached court in H-K 10-11), and the Joint Expedition failed to show definitively that the palace extended much farther east than 600° E (= Reisner's Grid K). The palace itself, then, occupied only the southwest quadrant of this rock plateau. This platform, whether created artificially or naturally, distinguished what one may call the "central summit" from the "peripheral summit." Though, as I have shown, the lower level rock swelled slightly as it proceeded westward from the central summit, it regained only about 41% of the elevation of the higher shelf. Further west, beyond the Ostraca House, the rock stepped its way down in smaller but regular increments until its more dramatic decline to the valley floor over 150 m below.[628]

This split-level character of the summit provided a rectilinear dais of solid rock measuring roughly 72 m in width on its western side and 93.5 m in length along its northern horizontal axis (and likely the southern axis as well). It rose an average of 3.5 m above the bedrock surrounding it. The area of this central summit covered only about .67 hectares and certainly would not have provided adequate living space for many more than 200 individuals. Rather than supporting common domestic areas,[629] the platform effectively constituted a quarterdeck designed to accommodate only the principal housing (main palace) and activity areas (northern buildings and main courtyard) of the royal family and their immediate attendants. While the intimation by Kenyon that the 232 "young men of the governors of the districts" mentioned in 1 Kgs 20:15 actually resided inside the summit compound may have some basis in historical fact, this group of residents alone would have taxed the city's available space. Kenyon's further insinuation that the 7,000 others alluded to in that same verse also

---

[626]I.e., from Reisner Grid G 7 southward to G 14; on the north side, from G 7 eastward to Kenyon's grid starting at 670° E x 460° N; on the south, from Reisner Grid G 14 eastward at least through L-M 14.

[627]*HES-I*, 93.

[628]Compare *HES II*, Reisner Plan 4-Section GH and Reisner Plan 13.

[629]Even the excavations down the northern slopes outside Casemate Wall 564, on the so-called Middle Terrace (in the general vicinity of 660° E; compare *SS I*, Pl. II), produced only meager architectural elements (e.g., fragments of Walls 573, 574, 577, and 578) that did not appear to exemplify the remains of a domestic quarter.

lived within the precincts of the compound takes one well beyond the pail of historical probability.[630] Moreover, her apparent belief that the 27,290 "Samarians" whom Sargon II claims to have deported[631] all lived inside the city itself, and her statement that "at its zenith" the Israelite city could have held up to 30 or 40 thousand citizens,[632] remain—together and individually—utterly unrealistic.[633]

This understanding of the physical setting of the Israelite capital enables me to bring the city planning into sharper focus than previous studies have achieved. First, it is important to realize that Omri's royal compound was actually limited to the "central summit" area, i.e., to the space atop the rock mantle itself. It also seems possible that the concept of a casemate enclosure around this principal compound originated already in BP I with King Omri, not with his son Ahab. Here one may compare Rooms 620, 622, and 623 in the northwest corner of Reisner's plans with Rooms *a-e* on the drawings of the Joint Expedition. These chambers, I believe, may reflect an early, efficacious "casemate" system regardless of whether the chambers functioned as store rooms or as dwelling places for humans. This "city wall" system originally included both the wall situated east of Ostraca House and Omri's Enclosure Wall 161 (followed by Wall 160) on the north. To the east, the relatively substantial longitudinal Wall 561 likely served as the eastern border of the central summit compound (at least in the early-to-mid-eighth century BCE, or BP IV, if not from the earlier BP I).[634] Either too little of this structure actually remains or excavations have revealed too little of it to evaluate its function with precision, however. Yet one sees that this wall basically aligns with the western wall that separated the Ostraca House from the palace area.

If further excavation in the eastern sector of the summit proves this theory true, then Wall 561 would essentially have divided the summit area roughly in half, with a bit more area to the west of the wall to accommodate the palace precinct itself. The space to the east of Wall 561 remains virtually unexcavated. In fact, one may ask whether 561, 562, and 560 constituted part of an original eastern "casemate" system built by Omri. A comparison with the chambers around the pool area, located in the

---

[630] *SS I*, 1. In fact, her reasoning allows for at least 14,000 occupants of Samaria already during the time of Ahab—including not only the 7,000 Israelites mentioned in 1 Kgs 20:15 but "at least an equal number of non-Israelites, Syrian merchants, craftsmen, priests and others connected with the court and government" (*SS I*, 1-2). The verse itself, however, in no way implies that either the 232 squires or the 7,000 people dwelt regularly inside the compound at Samaria.

[631] See the annalistic record in *ARAB II*, p. 2, § 4.

[632] *SS I*, 2.

[633] In fact, I believe that the entire area inside the grand Casemate System (covering ca. 19,600 m², or 1.96 hectares) could have comfortably provided for no more than around 500 individuals. (I might note that Herr's recent calculation of the area inside the palace compound arrived at an even smaller space of 178 x 89 meters, or 15,842 m² = 1.58 hectares. See L. G. Herr, "The Iron Age II Period: Emerging Nations," *BA* 60 [1997], 137.)

[634] Crowfoot himself apparently sensed this possibility (see his plan in *SS II*, 3; compare G. Barkay, "The Iron Age II-III," in *The Archaeology of Ancient Israel*, A. Ben-Tor, ed. [New Haven: Yale University Press, 1992], 319, Fig. 9.15).

north-northwest corner of the city in Reisner's plan, appears striking. It seems possible, therefore, that the so-called "central summit" might itself have always had a casemate type enclosure, even from the days of Omri, and that Ahab's BP II system really constituted an imitation of his father's original city plan, albeit on a much grander scale and with a much more impressive style of ashlar construction.

Only in BP II did the exterior casemate system, commissioned by Omri's son and successor, Ahab, come to constitute the main city wall. From its origins as a royal center, then, the actual compound remained considerably smaller than is usually recognized; it incorporated only the palace, a few complexes of rooms around the periphery, and a large open courtyard (recall, though, that hardly any of the more easterly section of the summit has been exposed). To date, no excavation has revealed the presence of a clear domestic quarter meant to accommodate common citizens anywhere on the site. Though the BP II casemate system did, in fact, increase the overall area of the summit, one does not see a great deal of quality architecture in the summit strips around the central rock mantle, particularly in the zone north of the line of Omri's BP I Enclosure Wall 161. The irregularly planned, thin-walled rooms (*g-k*) of BP IV provide a case in point. It appears, therefore, that only ancillary, service rooms of various sorts existed in the perimeter spaces surrounding the actual royal compound situated atop the rock shelf. The erratic decline of the bedrock outside this central compound required substantial deposits of fill even to obtain level building sites. Elevations here never seem to have approached those of the upper summit. In this vein, I should note that an eastward extension of the northern, lateral scarp line seen on Reisner's Plan 5 (Grids G-H 7) would place the continuation of this ledge directly beneath the northern sectors of Rooms *a-e* and *h-k* as seen on Kenyon's site plan.[635]

Along the northern edge of the rock scarp, a series of well-built, official (i.e., "royal") BP IV buildings (Rooms *a-d, o-q*) helped to separate the palace and courtyard from the service rooms farther north (Rooms *g-k*). Though they sat on the lower level rock, Rooms 13 and 81-83, immediately west of the palace (see Reisner Plan 5[636]), may have functioned in much the same way, i.e., to define the western extent of the "royal" compound proper. In this regard, I may draw attention once again to Reisner Rooms 620-623 and the nearby Pool 621.

From this overview, then, one sees that the planners of the official, or "central," compound designed it around a topographical feature of the site, i.e, a raised platform on the very summit. This platform appears naturally formed at certain points and artificially created at others. Even though the city expanded beyond these limits already during the Israelite period, the expansion and subsequent use of this area (at least during the early eighth century BCE) seems to have added mainly flanking areas used primarily for service-related activities, such as storage (Ostraca House), food

---

[635] *SS I*, Pl. II; see also the BP IV Top Plan presented in fig. 5 above.

[636] Kenyon's site plan in *SS I*, Pl. II omits this group of chambers.

processing (Rooms g-k[637]), and the like. Within this design, all the architecture relating to the summit itself centered on the king and his family. Precious little (if any) trace remains of residential, domestic quarters inside the city walls, such as those seen at Beersheba, or at the outlying royal cities of the north, such as Megiddo and Hazor. The designers and builders of Samaria set it apart as the seat of royal administration and power.[638]

Interestingly, some of the best known discoveries at Samaria came from the peripheral, service-related zones around the central compound. It seems logical that excavations have recovered at least one hundred shipping dockets (the Samaria Ostraca) in one of these areas west of the Israelite palace. Yet the well known ivory fragments also apparently came from a similar zone on the north side of the royal courtyard. Though the retrieval of such finely crafted luxury items from what basically represents a kitchen area seems somewhat puzzling at first, one must remember that the ivories stem from contexts that are clearly secondary to that vicinity. The levels that yielded them appear to have been scraped down over the scarp as part of later construction fill designed to level up the areas of sloping rock.

Judging from Kenyon's published Section GH,[639] the depositional history associated with Wall 56 will prove crucial to locating precisely the findspots of the famous ivories since they apparently came from thick deposits of soil laid against both the northern and southern faces of that wall. But this structure appears quite enigmatic. While the aforementioned section assigns the wall itself to Israelite "Period III," Kenyon ascribed the layers that abut it and that supposedly yielded the ivories to the "Early Hellenistic" period.[640] From the unpublished field records and sections, I have shown elsewhere that, in fact, this wall cut the BP III levels and therefore must post-date them.[641] Further, one can see now that two walls actually seem to have existed here; that is, builders set the base of Wall 56 in the deteriorated remains of the wall that cut the BP III deposits (see fig. 10). Stratigraphically (i.e., temporally) speaking, this removes the functional life of Wall 56 even further from BP III and the ninth century than previously thought. Moreover, both the wall and the stratigraphy around it

---

[637] I base this description of these rooms on their moderately impressive architecture, the clear utilitarian nature of the pottery found in them (including large caches of cooking pots, holemouth jars, etc.), the multiple ṭābunîm placed in them, etc.

[638] This should prompt us all to realize the need for more field exploration of both the slopes around the site and the outlying countryside—for example, at the sites/estates named in the Samaria Ostraca. In the effort to understand royal and urban centers such as Samaria and Megiddo, one cannot neglect the smaller, satellite sites. The tendency of earlier scholars to concentrate their efforts solely on the urban centers, or to separate these cities from the countryside that surrounded them, has resulted in mistakes at both the theoretical and methodological levels.

[639] SS I, Pl. VII.

[640] Kenyon's "E.H." designates the levels that predate the Hellenistic Fort Wall, i.e., the period from the late third to early second centuries BCE.

[641] AIS-I, 150-58, 165-66; figs. 20-21.

appear quite different in Section EF. And although it is assigned to BP III in Section GH, another published drawing (Section EF) ascribes it to BP V. Similarly, this feature does not appear on any phase plan prior to the one belonging to BP V (*SS III*, Fig. 50).[642]

It is important to note that, according to all available plans and sections, Wall 56 rested between Wall 58 (the southern boundary of Rooms *a-e* in fig. 5 above) and the line of Omri's original Enclosure Wall 161. That is to say, it overlay BP III/IV Rooms *a-e* and ran along the very edge of the lateral scarp described above. Though the natural rock had already begun to descend south of this wall (i.e., on the side facing the summit), its greatest decline occurred north of this structure (see published Section EF). Two observations become clear regarding the findspots for the bulk of the ivories: (1) they appear to have come from rather thick layers of either imported fill or destruction debris that cover the area north of Wall 56; (2) the deposition of these levels occurred sometime later than BP IV, which I have dated to the mid-eighth century BCE. It remains for me to determine as best I can the extent, or even the presence or absence, of the putative Assyrian destruction level so often associated with the end of Israelite rule at Samaria. I shall address this issue as I proceed to Building Periods V through VII.

This leads me to close this portion of my study with an observation regarding Kenyon's system of so-called Test Trenches. One must remember that, while the published top plans seen in the final report appear in chronological order (i.e., BP III, then BP IV, etc.), the excavators actually encountered them generally in the reverse sequence (i.e., IV, then, III, etc.). Since the series of "official rooms" (*a-e*) appears in plans for both BP III and BP IV, the report should contain data which adequately phase the levels inside these important rooms and which demonstrate that the BP III levels did, in fact, prove stratigraphically distinct from those belonging to the BP IV reuse of those same rooms. Unfortunately, the published report did not allow me to explore these areas. As I have shown, Kenyon's discussion of "Period IV-IVa" touched on neither the stratigraphy of those rooms nor the ceramics found in them. Still, she argued that the greatest break in ceramic tradition for the entire Israelite period falls between PP 3 and PP 4.[643]

---

[642] See *AIS-I*, 148, n. 6. The phasing of the walls that supposedly comprised Rooms *a-d* remains very ambiguous. Confusion surrounds not only Wall 56, but Walls 51, 57, and 58 as well (see Room *d* in fig. 5 above). My previous investigation revealed that Walls 51, 56, and 57 *cut* the BP III floor levels and therefore must postdate them. As for Wall 58, I have shown that the Top Plan in *SS I*, Fig. 47 ascribes it to "Period III," while Section GH assigns it to "Period V" (see *AIS-I*, 146-58, 163-67, 206-12). In fact, the overall design of the so-called Ivory House, which Rooms *a-e* represented for Kenyon, falls into question as a result of such stratigraphic uncertainties. This is particularly true for Room *d*, i.e., for the eastern portion of the building that lay near the area heavily disturbed by later building projects, Roman quarrying, etc. It seems, perhaps, ironic that Room *d* should epitomize these stratigraphic disputes since, according to *SS I*, Pl. VIII and *SS III*, Figs. 47-50, it constitutes the most complete and best preserved architectural unit recovered from the Israelite period by the Joint Expedition.

[643] *SS I*, 105. Kenyon appeared hesitant to associate this perceived break with a major historical event.

This seems a bold statement, when in fact the whole of her so-called Period III and Period IV loci may actually constitute two subphases of a single period. Given my earlier analysis of Kenyon's "Period III," together with the fact that now in BP IV all the published evidence derives from the series of poorly constructed rooms (*g-k*) north of Rooms *a-e* or from the courtyard area south of *a-e*, it becomes apparent that Kenyon's "Period III" turns out to represent the most nebulous phase of all.[644] All of my stratigraphic analyses in this chapter have confirmed that the long period of time between the rule of the House of Omri and BP IV receives only sparse documentation in the final report.

Turning to "Periods IV-IVa," I have shown that, while the local stratigraphy reveals some closely datable floor levels, one must ask whether this provides sufficient evidence to justify identifying an entirely new, distinct historical period. If so, one should see observable and significant changes in the overall material record, particularly in the various ceramic traditions associated with each new surface. Clearly, Kenyon's report failed to supply that information. Instead, she offered only a single rim fragment (*SS III*, Fig. 6:14) in support of her "Period IVa." Further, as I have elaborated in detail, a substantial portion of the overall PP 4 group carries the designation "discard" in the unpublished notes. What apparently emerges from this area, then, is simply a series of resurfacings that reflect only subphases of a single period of activity at the site. The main differences that turn up among the published ceramic pieces have more to do with the nature of their stratigraphic context (primary loci versus secondary, fill deposits) than with a momentous historical change. Archaeological periods do not always correlate directly to historical ones. The putative "Period IVa," then, represents merely a subphase of BP IV, not a separate archaeological or historical "period."

In light of the principles of dating adhered to by Kenyon (whereby she assessed floor levels by the material found beneath them rather than on them), her use of the term "Period" for the various historical phases at the site (traceable through distinct trends in the ceramic and building industries) proves inherently deceptive, inasmuch as the term refers (for Kenyon) only to a relatively short span of construction activity.[645]

---

[644] In this vein, it proves significant that the ceramic analysis in the final report posited two major breaks in tradition: first, between PP 1-2 and PP 3; second, between PP 3 and PP 4-6. The net effect of these suggestions involves isolating the pottery of PP 3 from all other groups attested during the Israelite period. According to this interpretation, then, the PP 3 assemblage apparently did not seem to fit into the overall ceramic history associated with the Israelite period. My ceramic analysis of the PP 3-4 groups (for PP 3, see *AIS-I*, Chapter III) has demonstrated both the mixed nature of the vessels included in them and points at which each assemblage does, in fact, stem from earlier ceramic traditions in the north.

[645] See the astute comments addressing this semantic problem in *Forsberg*, 18.

Chapter II

POTTERY PERIOD 5

Remains of the Final Israelite Occupation?

I. Introduction

As I have shown, the official excavation reports that resulted from the work of the Joint Expedition in 1932-1934 and the British Expedition in 1935 typically exhibit a great deal of certainty regarding the chronology of nearly all phases of occupation at Samaria. Within this context of confidence, the two dates most highly touted as fixed beyond any reasonable doubt consisted in the *terminus post quem* of BP I and the *terminus ante quem* of BP V, i.e., the points that presumably bracket off the Israelite occupation of the site. According to Kenyon, the former marker belongs to the purchase of the virgin site by King Omri and his inauguration of Israelite occupation and royal building projects there. I have assessed the viability of this thesis in an earlier work.[1] The second inviolable chronological peg relates directly to the alleged "extensive destruction"[2] of the city by the Assyrians in 722/21 BCE. In her publication of BP V, Kenyon argued that the structures of the so-called Period V House "were the latest ones of the Israelite period on the north side of the summit"[3] and that both they and the Rubbish Pit *i* met their destruction "at the end of the eighth century" during the Assyrian assault (which she dated to around 720 BCE).[4]

The assurance with which Kenyon espoused this date for the termination of her "Period V" seems based not only on the convenient correlation with a well-known historical event that supposedly receives attestation in both archaeological and written records, but also on the underlying assertion that the loci that yielded the PP 5 goods lay in clearly datable, primary, stratigraphic contexts. Indirect evidence of Kenyon's confidence in the secure nature of these findspots comes from a private response written to P. J. Riis concerning the chronology of a group of Attic Middle Geometric II fragments found at Samaria, mainly in Summit Strips Qk and Qn. J. W. Crowfoot had initially realized that "all these sherds except No. 5 came from adjoining strips but *from*

---

[1] *AIS-I*.

[2] *SS III*, 199.

[3] *SS I*, 107.

[4] *SS I*, 108.

deposits in a disturbed area which were labeled respectively Period V, Period VII, Hellenistic and Late Roman!"[5] Notwithstanding the poor stratigraphic context, he ultimately dated the fragments on comparative typological grounds "to the middle of the eighth century, to the reign that is of Jeroboam II."[6] In her communique to Riis, however, Kenyon wrote:

> The result so far therefore is that all the [MG II] sherds traced are from disturbed fill. But you can take it that if Mrs. Crowfoot says one of the sherds came from V, this was information I gave her and therefore one of the sherds was in *undisturbed stratification.*[7]

Though these comments generally follow Crowfoot's assessment of the situation surrounding the Attic MG II sherds from Samaria, they take one important exception regarding the reliability of levels belonging specifically to "Period V." The stratigraphic credibility of these layers, according to Kenyon, remains beyond reproach.

Following Kenyon's publication of the objects from Samaria in 1957, virtually all scholars working at sites in Syria-Palestine acquiesced to both her evaluation and suggested terminal date for the depositional history of "Period V" by placing the actual occupational phase of this period in the decades immediately preceding the Assyrian destruction of Samaria, though within a slight range of tentative dates that included 745 BCE,[8] 735 BCE,[9] 735/732 BCE,[10] and 732 BCE[11] (see *AIS-I*, Appendix B). Just as quickly, the proposed correlation between the Assyrian siege and the end of BP V received widespread acceptance and use by archaeologists working in the Aegean as well as in the Levantine world. For example, J. N. Coldstream argued decidedly to place the end of the MG II period in the mid-eighth century "since the dating of Period V at Samaria to the early eighth century is generally accepted."[12]

Back within Israel, Holladay went even further and declared that Pottery Period 5 represented one of three occupational phases at Samaria to which "*absolute dates* may

---

[5] *SS III*, 212 (emphasis added).

[6] *SS III*, 212.

[7] *Sukas I*, 146 (emphasis added).

[8] W. F. Albright, "Recent Progress in Palestinian Archaeology: Samaria-Sebaste III and Hazor I," *BASOR* 150 (1958), 21-25, especially p. 23.

[9] *Wright*, 20-22. Also, G. E. Wright, "The Archaeology of Palestine," pp. 73-112 in *The Bible and the Ancient Near East: Essays in Honor of William Foxwell Albright*, G. E. Wright, ed. (Garden City, NY: Doubleday, 1961), see esp. p. 100 (hereafter, *BANE*).

[10] Y. Yadin, "Ancient Judean Weights and the Date of the Samaria Ostraca," *Scripta Hierosolymitana* 8 (1961), 24.

[11] O. Tufnell, "Hazor, Samaria, and Lachish," *PEQ* 91 (1959), 105.

[12] *GGP*, 309. Like other archaeologists, Coldstream here appears to refer to the actual occupational phase of BP V rather than to its ending date.

be assigned."[13] He appealed to three factors as the basis for placing PP 5 precisely at 735 BCE. First, he accepted that BP V represented a single phase of building activity. Since this phase lacked any secondary refloorings or remodelings similar to those Kenyon had suggested for "Periods IV-IVa,"[14] Holladay reasoned that one could not raise the date of PP 5 too much prior to the events of the *final* years of Israelite occupation at the site. Second, and on the other hand, he observed that the "midden-like filling of Pit *i* . . . [gave] evidence that occupation at the site continued for a least a short time *after* the laying of the Period V floors."[15] Though these single phase structures could not predate the Assyrian destruction by much time, then, they did precede that event by at least a decade or so. Finally, he attempted to marshal support for this dating by correlating the levels that Kenyon excavated north of the courtyard with layers exposed over two decades earlier by Harvard University in the area of the so-called Ostraca House.[16]

In framing this correlation, Holladay based his reasoning on the following suppositions: (1) the findspots of the Israelite ostraca lay "scattered about on the living floor of several rooms" in the Ostraca House and in black debris lying on the courtyard outside the storeroom; (2) the latest floor level belonging to the Israelite period subsequently sealed the entire area; (3) the dates of the ostraca confirm that this uppermost Israelite floor "*probably* accompanied the larger general rebuilding [in] Period V"; and, (4) this rife refurbishing of the summit "*probably* followed the *general destruction* involved in the assassination of Pekahiah by Pekah."[17] According to Holladay, PP 5 therefore belonged in the early days of the interregional Syro-Ephraimite conflict. The "warfare or catastrophe" that led to the scattering of the ostraca, however, seems to have resided in the inner-capital competition for the throne between Pekahiah and Pekah.

One can see that, during the course of his argument, Holladay makes multiple, untested assumptions that further archaeological and textual research should have informed. For example, what data exist to corroborate a "general destruction" of Samaria stemming from the Pekahiah–Pekah rivalry? The account in 2 Kgs 15:8-31 tersely relates a series of political assassinations; nothing in the text indicates explicitly that any of these regnal shifts involved widespread conflagration across the entire site. Holladay also assumes that the functional life of Pit *i* ended during the Assyrian

---

[13]*Holladay*, 60 (emphasis added). Holladay included PP 3 (pp. 60-65), PP 5 (pp. 65-67), and the deposit in Pit *i* (pp. 67-69) in his category of precisely datable Pottery Periods at Samaria.

[14]I believe the data presented in Chapter I cast doubt on the viability of Kenyon's proposed subphasing of BP IV.

[15]*Holladay*, 66-67 (emphasis added).

[16]The artificial shaping of the western summit (see below), the general stratigraphic portrait displayed in this area, the absence of any direct stratigraphic connection between the layers exposed by Harvard and those revealed by the Joint Expedition, and the recording method used by Reisner to track the progress of his work all combine to make any proposed stratigraphic correlation difficult to verify.

[17]*Holladay*, 67 (my emphases).

destruction in 722/21 BCE. I shall present, however, additional stratigraphic evidence that suggests one should lower the *terminus ante quem* of the pottery group recovered from this feature. The leveling operations that truncated the upper section of this pit, then, may not relate to the initial Assyrian occupation at all. Still other, more tacit, conjectures lie behind Holladay's proposal. In this vein, his argument that the BP V floor levels must predate slightly the Assyrian destruction of the site presumes both that the inhabitants who occupied those surfaces had to be Israelites and that the Assyrians did, in fact, ultimately destroy the site to end that brief occupational phase. Holladay himself apparently sensed the tentative nature of the data available to substantiate such a refined reconstruction, for he gives ground almost immediately on his claim of an "absolute date" for PP 5 by introducing that period with the statement that it can receive a "reasonably secure date."[18]

Interestingly, it seems that at this point in the debris-layer analysis of remains from Samaria Holladay upholds the principle of dating floor levels by the material found beneath them more than Kenyon herself does. Yet he does not use the matrix resting just beneath the BP V surface to arrive at a date for it; rather, he relies on the ostraca that, according to his understanding, actually lay *in the occupational debris found on the next earliest surface* (presumably = BP IV) in the area. Because Kenyon, on the other hand, appealed primarily to the allegedly heavy destruction debris covering the BP V floor to date that surface, one comes finally to a kink in her overall chronological strategy. Up through BP IV, her method has endorsed the dating of floor levels by the materials found beneath them. To establish now the chronology of the BP V surface by the destruction debris *overlying* that feature and assigned to PP 7, and by the latest (PP 6) pottery found in Pit *i*, ignores entirely the depositional history situated *between* the BP IV and BP V levels. In other words, Kenyon arrived at a chronological framework for the functional life and destruction of the BP V building primarily through analysis of pottery and debris associated with that structure but assigned to PP 6-7.[19] In the final report, Kenyon states that the levels beneath the BP V house simply did not yield enough pottery to allow chronological judgments of any kind.[20] This claim seems quite unlikely. Holladay's suggested correlation between floor levels north of the courtyard and layers associated with the Ostraca House attempts to avert this lacuna in Kenyon's methodology without the benefit of a direct stratigraphic connection between the two areas in question.

More recently, an entirely new (and hitherto overlooked) proposal concerning the chronologies of BP V and PP 5 has come to light. A detailed study by S. Forsberg strongly challenges the traditional view, which sees a viable and detectable Assyrian destruction of Samaria around 722/21 BCE.[21] He argues, instead, that none of the most

---

[18]*Holladay*, 65-66.

[19]*SS I*, 108; *SS III*, 120.

[20]*SS I*, 108.

[21]*Forsberg*, 19-50.

significant areas of excavation, including not only the BP V building north of the courtyard but also the Israelite palace and Ostraca House, reveals signs of a conflagration by fire that stems from the period in which the Assyrians assumed control of the site. His analysis of a small corpus of PP 7 artifacts recovered from the destruction remains that overlay the BP V rooms prompted Forsberg to lower the terminal date of this complex to sometime during the third quarter of the seventh century, i.e., to the period when Assyria was losing rather than establishing its grip on Samaria as a provincial capital. He also astutely notes the complicating fact that "the [presumed] conflagration debris was nowhere found *in situ*,"[22] indicating that the context encountered by archaeologists already postdates the actual event that produced the destruction remains in the first place. Forsberg argues further that written evidence from both biblical and cuneiform written sources corroborate his interpretation of the archaeological evidence. I shall address the textual portion of my analysis in greater detail in Chapter VI below. The broad range of archaeological issues raised by Forsberg's investigation, however, leads us to interact with those conclusions from this point in my investigation through the discussion relating to PP 7 (Chapter IV).

Forsberg's provocative study contains much to commend itself, though it requires tighter ceramic and both local- and comparative-stratigraphic controls. For example, principal components of his position consist in the dating of the pottery group associated with Terrace Wall 573 at Samaria, the beginning and terminal dates of Megiddo Stratum III, and the correlation that each of these holds to the general PP 6 ceramic group at Samaria. Difficulties arise in the interpretation of each of these areas, however.

The foundation filling of Wall 573 contained pottery forms from PP 4 as well as examples of thin, hard-ware vessels that appear beneath the floors of the BP V building but that become more common during PP 6. As a result, Kenyon left open the question of whether the construction of 573 dated to the building of the BP V house or to its destruction, supposedly in 722/21 BCE. Ultimately, however, she tentatively placed Wall 573 in BP VI in light of its ceramic affiliation with the latest vessels in Pit *i*, by writing:

> It is important to notice the difference in the stratigraphic evidence with regard to this rubbish pit filling. It is the pottery *in use* with the Period V building presumably down to its destruction, and therefore different in significance from that beneath its floors, which dates to its original building.[23]

To decide this issue, Forsberg appeals to a segment of wall exposed much later (mid-1960s) during a small scale project under the direction of F. Zayadine.[24] Results

---

[22]*Forsberg*, 50.

[23]*SS I*, 108.

[24]F. Zayadine, "Samaria-Sebaste. Clearance and Excavations (October 1965-June 1967)," *ADAJ* 12 (1967), 77-80.

of these clearance operations reasonably suggested that the wall fragment found between 700° and 710° E represented the eastward extension of Kenyon's Wall 573. Zayadine dated the pottery taken from the foundation trench of this feature to the late eighth century BCE and noted that the group included a rim fragment from an apparent Assyrian-style bowl. Forsberg extrapolated from this that "the building of" Wall 573 dated to a time during the Assyrian occupation of the site and that the corollary ceramic group in Pit *i* also postdated the alleged conquest of the site in 722/21 BCE. Further, because the latest pottery in Pit *i* seems to relate to the final use of the larger building, Forsberg suggested that the BP V house itself mainly served the inhabitants of the site during the Assyrian occupation rather than those who resided there shortly before that event.[25]

Yet the proposed connection between the wall discovered by Zayadine and Kenyon's 573 remains without clear stratigraphic support. Even if the two segments belong together, one must note that Zayadine described his portion as a "later addition" to 573, a fact that may easily account for the presence of an Assyrian bowl in its foundation. Forsberg's argument here seems to rely too heavily on this single bowl fragment. But this sherd cannot singularly date either Wall 573 or Zayadine's Wall *c* because one cannot assume that Assyrian imports or the "Assyrianizing" of local forms began only after 722/21 BCE. Assyrian contact with the Northern Kingdom in general and Samaria in particular antedates that period by many years. Moreover, Kenyon observed elsewhere that the PP 6 ceramic groups (including those of Pit *i*) may well have been contemporary with those of PP 5, and that the earliest specimens recovered from the pit actually predate the BP V House.[26] Judging from the report, this pit does not seem to present a clearly stratified arrangement of pottery forms, but rather a very heterogeneous group of vessels found distributed throughout a single, mixed matrix. Moreover, the apparent post-destruction leveling of the "Period VII" debris truncated the upper section of the rubbish pit and made it impossible to establish a firm *terminus ante quem* for its functional life or for the overall pottery group it originally contained.

The second main pillar of Forsberg's position concerning the chronology of the BP V House rests on the close resemblance that Kenyon herself drew between the pottery of "Period VI" at Samaria and that of Megiddo Stratum III.[27] Two main ceramic groups provide the basis of the stratigraphic correlation, namely, jugs with trefoil mouths[28] and the so-called water decanters.[29] The chronological distribution of both vessel-types seems most concentrated in Stratum III at Megiddo. The precise dating of

---

[25] *Forsberg*, 19-20.

[26] *SS III*, 119-20.

[27] See the discussion in *SS III*, 203-06.

[28] As in *SS III*, Fig. 10:15-16, which Kenyon related to Jug Types 83, 85, 88, and 89 at Megiddo (*SS III*, 202-03).

[29] See *SS III*, Fig. 10:17, which Kenyon correlated to Megiddo Types 99 and 100 (*SS III*, 203).

this level at Megiddo, then, becomes the central issue but remains somewhat problematic and ambiguous (see below and also Chapter III). Here I need only sketch out the general role that Megiddo III assumes in Forsberg's argument.[30]

According to Forsberg, the Assyrians destroyed Megiddo Stratum IV, not III as once thought. Stratum III, in fact, represents the Assyrian rebuild of the city following their initial occupation. Rather than establishing a province in the region of Megiddo under Tiglath-pileser III sometime around 733 BCE, the Assyrians waited to do that until the latter stages (i.e., the activities of Sargon II, not Shalmaneser V) of their conquest of the capital at Samaria. During the interim (where Holladay places Samaria PP 5), Forsberg says that the destroyed city of Stratum IV actually lay in a "state of desolation and decay"[31] for some time prior to the rebuild in III. He nowhere offers an historical explanation for this putative occupational gap between the destruction of Stratum IV and the later occupation of III by the Assyrians.

Against the higher chronology originally proposed by the excavators of Megiddo for Stratum III,[32] and the lower beginning date subsequently suggested by Kenyon,[33] Forsberg recommends a further lowering of the dates for this level, to a period spanning from the 730s or 720s BCE to 650 BCE or slightly later still. After affirming the general principle that the pottery recovered from any given stratum dates primarily to the closing years of that level,[34] Forsberg places the assemblage from Megiddo Level III around 650 BCE (or perhaps even slightly later). As a result, he suggests that one should date the Megiddo III–Samaria PP 6 correlation to this same general time period, and certainly no earlier than 700-675 BCE. Consequently, the terminal date of BP V (which, as I have indicated, is basically set by the PP 6 pottery found in Pit *i* and the foundation deposits of Wall 573) postdates Assyria's initial occupation of Samaria and may even belong as late as the mid-seventh century BCE.

From this brief overview, one sees that a central question focuses on the actual date of the occupational phase of BP V. Judging from the positions presented here, this level reflects either the final Israelite control of the site and terminates during the clash of 722/21 BCE (Kenyon; Holladay), or it represents the main period of Assyrian occupation and belongs in the very late eighth and the seventh centuries BCE

---

[30]The main discussion of this topic appears in *Forsberg*, 21-24.

[31]*Forsberg*, 23. He holds that this view "is now generally recognized" (p. 22).

[32]Ca. 787-650 BCE in *Megiddo I*, 62. Elsewhere, others have placed the termination of Megiddo Stratum IV in the late ninth century and have seen Stratum III as spanning the better part of the first three quarters of the eighth century before succumbing to the Assyrians, who proceeded to rebuild the city in Stratum II (e.g., *Aharoni-Amiran*, 177 and 183).

[33]Ca. 750-650 BCE (*SS III*, 204). Recall from my discussion in *AIS-I* that Kenyon attempted to lower the entire chronological framework of Iron Age II Megiddo based on her interpretation of the Pottery Periods at Samaria.

[34]See my comments in *AIS-I*, 5, n. 8. But note that this general rule, as articulated by Albright, refers mainly to the intact or reparable vessels, not to stray, miscellaneous fragments that may appear in a deposit.

(Forsberg). I shall return to the issues involved in this discussion in my Evaluation and Summary after first presenting the local stratigraphy and ceramic assemblage from this period. In light of the widespread significance of the issues involved, I shall afford the stratigraphy a comprehensive discussion, even for those segments that ultimately contributed only a few ceramic fragments to the official report (e.g., Segment *W of 124*).

II. Pottery Period 5

The publication of materials ascribed to Pottery Period 5 once again highlights two recurring tendencies in the final report, both of which render the confidence exuded by the authors and proponents of *SS I-III*, as well as alternative proposals such as Forsberg's, difficult to assess critically. First, the official report provides an astonishingly limited corpus of goods to represent this time period. In fact, this portion of the publication presents only eight ceramic fragments: five jars and three cooking pot rims, according to Kenyon's classification. I shall suggest that one of the putative cooking pot fragments (*SS III*, Fig. 8:8), in fact, constitutes a sixth jar rim; I shall also treat separately the holemouth rims portrayed in *SS III*, Fig. 8:3-4. Second, the report lacks a clear correlation between the loci from which the published pottery came and the area of the summit that actually reveals the most significant building activity. Despite stating that the principal deposits associated with "Period V" related to floors in the reconstructed building covering 443°-458° N x 606°-644° E[35] (i.e., mainly Rooms *o, h, q, hq, kq* and *s*; see the hatched area in fig. 41 below), the report failed to include a single ceramic fragment from that 570 m² area. Instead, it placed six of the eight published pieces in Room *hk*, which represents the surviving portions of the now constricted and combined BP IV chambers *h* and *k* (*SS III*, Fig. 8:1-5, 8). (Later, I shall correct this published distribution by showing that one vessel came from Room *hq*.)

To this meager group, the report added only two cooking pot rims recovered separately from beneath stone pavings in Rooms *j* and *n* (*SS III*, Fig. 8:6-7). In other words, Kenyon continued to focus on the paltry perimeter architecture, situated in what we can now understand as a northern "service area," as opposed to presenting the stratigraphy and material culture retrieved from the new series of substantial rooms built on the central summit along the northern edge of the lateral rock scarp. Except for a single observation drawn in the previous chapter regarding the logic of having items such as shipping dockets emerge from an unofficial, service sector (see our comments regarding the Samaria Ostraca on p. 172), the wisdom of this choice would remain impenetrable. It seems reasonable to surmise that the appearance of ivory fragments in the late (post-Israelite) levels overlying the northern portions of Rooms *h* and *k* lured the excavators and publishers back to this vicinity despite the fact that these layers represented mainly secondary deposits of fill debris raked down into this area from atop

---

[35] *SS III*, 118.

the rock shelf to the south. Ultimately, however, I believe that even this suggestion cannot adequately justify either the virtual monopoly that Room *hk* commands in the final report or the total neglect of the better-constructed and more extensively-preserved chambers situated immediately west of that area. Despite the understandable initial attraction during the course of excavation to the area that yielded abundant quantities of ivory, the authors would surely have also recognized by the time of publication the value of the pottery groups and depositional history in more the westerly series of rooms, particularly since that area yielded the largest number of ivory fragments (see n. 36 below).

	Horizontal Axis	Vertical Axis = Local Layers	Coordinates	No. of published sherds/vessels (No. marked for discard)
Figure 8	House Floors:			
	Room *hk*	III, IIIo	125.144	4
		V	E Strip; Btw TT2-TT3	1 (1)
	Room *hq*	VIII	West of 124	1
	Room *j*	IX	509.126	1
	Room *n*	IX	502.503	1

Horizontal + Vertical Dimensions of PP 5 Stratigraphy

Table 19

In keeping with the approach used in the previous chapter, I have once again extracted the relevant data from Appendix A and reorganized them in Table 19 to facilitate my stratigraphic and ceramic discussion of Kenyon's "Period V." These data not only provide a complete list of the PP 5 findspots and group together the various stratigraphic coordinates that relate to a particular architectural feature (such as Room *hk*), but they also give the number of fragments the excavators published from each locus as well as the local stratigraphy (by layer) of the various loci. In addition, I have identified the one discarded sherd that Kenyon ultimately published (*SS III*, Fig. 8:4 taken from *E Strip; Between TT2-TT3*). Within this pottery group, the primary difficulties involve efforts to determine precisely from which local layer or sublayer the excavators recovered a given fragment (see the column labeled "Vertical Axis").

Part A. House Floors — Rooms *hk/hq, j, n*
(*SS I*, Fig. 50; Pl. VII — Sections CD, EF)
(*SS III*, Fig. 8:1-8)

As fig. 41 demonstrates, only a few changes occurred between BP IV and BP V in the complex of rooms discussed in the previous chapter. First, stone pavings appear in Room *j* and in the putative Room *n*. Second, Pit *i* now appears subdivided to include a very small alcove at its southern end, and only a remnant of Room *h* remains immediately west of the pit. Finally, a new wall (145) apparently now replaces Wall 153 in Kenyon's "Period IVa" plan (*SS I*, Fig. 49). Relative to other building projects

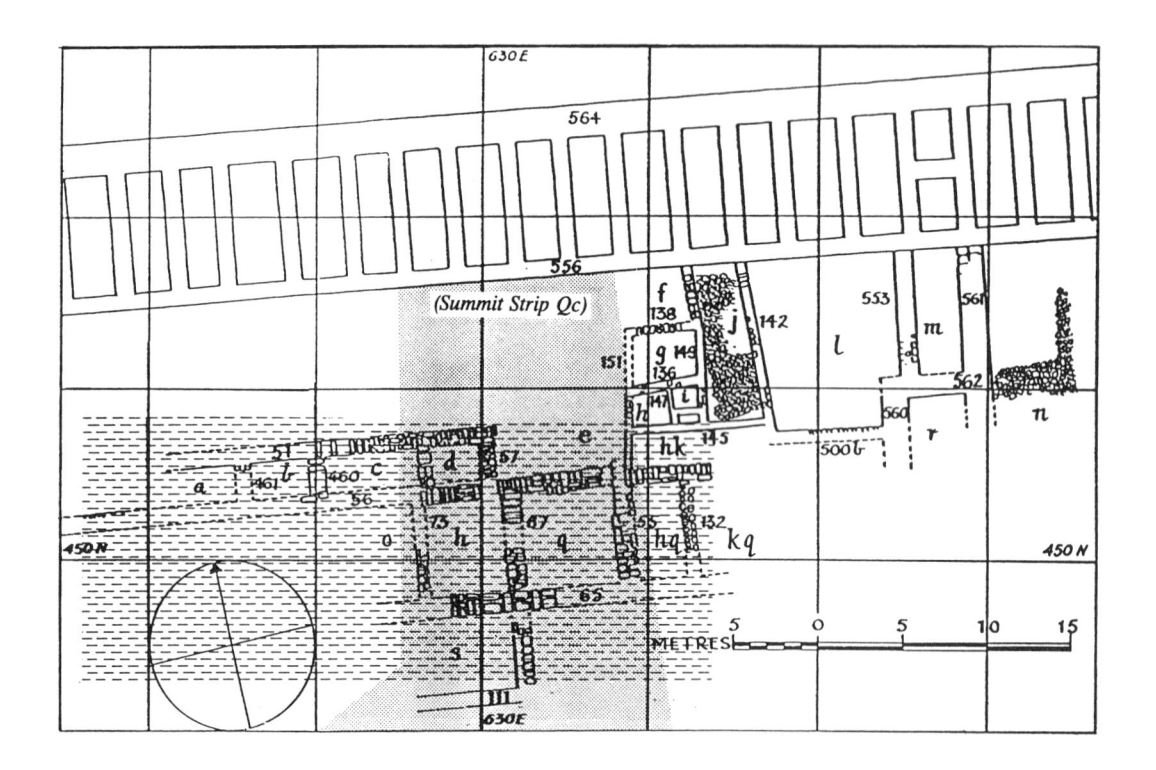

Published "Period V" Top Plan
(adapted from *SS I*, Fig. 50)[36]

fig. 41

---

[36]I have adapted the published version of this plan (1) by placing horizontal hachures over the area that constituted the primary tract of new construction in BP V (443°-458° N x 606°-644° E), and (2) by shading the relative location of Summit Strip Qc (roughly north of 430° N and between 625°-639/40° E, excluding Rooms *f-i* and *hk*, which lie in Strip Qk). According to the final reports, Summit Strip Qc yielded "the richest haul of ivories" (*SS II*, 2-3). The excavators failed, however, to present in these published reports any of the pottery recovered from this vicinity.

that appear on the summit at this time, however, these modifications seem quite insignificant. Judging from Kenyon's "Period IVa" plan (*SS I*, Fig. 49), Wall 153 had actually already separated out the combined areas of Rooms *h* and *k*, and Pit *i* already showed the inner partition sometime prior to BP V. The only truly new alterations to these rooms, then, consist in the stone pavings in Rooms *j* and *n*.

More prominent changes in the architectural layout of the summit manifest themselves in an entirely new series of well-built rooms to the south and west of the area just mentioned (Rooms *o, h, q, hq, kq,* and *s* on fig. 41). These new chambers now subsumed the southern half of the BP III-IV Rooms *a-d*, overran the disturbed area labeled *e*, and continued eastward to take in as well the southern half of Room *hk*. The new Wall 56 set the northern boundary of these rooms roughly in the middle of *a-d*.[37] A former BP IV wall, 65, which had constituted the southern border of chambers *o-p-q*, now separated the new chambers (*o-kq*) from an apparent matching set of spaces to their south (see Room *s*).

It is important to note that Wall 65 seems to run along the very northern edge of the rock shelf, which delineated the "central summit" area, assuming that the lateral scarp shown in the area excavated by the Harvard team (see Reisner Plan 5, Grids G-H 7) continued at roughly the same angle across the northern axis of the summit. Judging from published Section EF, the ancient engineers even appear to have set its base immediately below the scarp and may have bonded the lower courses of the wall to the northern face of the natural rock shelf, which, in turn, served as a buttress for the foundation of this feature. I believe further that the location of Wall 65 at this crucial juncture helps account for the extra strengthening of it by means of a more advanced construction technique (note the so-called "header–stretcher" sequence of ashlar blocks) than that utilized in most of the other walls, which merely delineate the individual rooms and typically exhibit a simple series of straight headers. If floor levels in the rooms north of 65 approached the same elevation as those in Room *s* and other areas situated atop the rock mantle, then one should expect to find larger quantities of fill beneath these surfaces. If one does not encounter substantial fillings beneath the floors of the BP V buildings, then one may safely assume that these peripheral structures again rested in the shadow of the elevated features on the central summit. Within this context, then, the location and construction of Wall 65 provided a rock-solid line against which to backfill a significant area. Unfortunately, Kenyon's final report does not provide adequate elevation readings for the various rooms exposed during the excavations. It seems likely, however, that the reinforced Wall 65 served as the final feature directly anchored to the north-central summit, to which the builders could bond the inherently less stable walls that overran the declivity of rock further north and whose foundations were set into or surrounded by deeper deposits of fill.

---

[37] I have noted the stratigraphic difficulties and recording discrepancies that attend the phasing of this feature in Chapter I, pp. 32-34 and 172-73 plus nn. 67 and 642.

It is not coincidental, then, that Wall 65 lies contiguous to the line of the BP I Wall 60 (see *SS I*, Pl. VII, Sections EF and GH plus Pl. VIII), which constituted the northernmost extent of construction activities in Omri's original city plan. Omri and his immediate successors utilized only the central rock shelf; even the space between the northern scarp and his Enclosure Wall 161 remained undeveloped during the mid-to-late ninth century BCE. Not until BP III did a series of rooms (*a-d*) appear immediately north of the central summit area (i.e., beyond the lateral scarp) and, if not already in BP III, their BP IV-V descendants attached themselves to Wall 65 and depended on it for their mooring to the architecture of the main summit (compare figs. 4-5 in Chapter I above with fig. 41 below). The impressive utilization of ashlar, header-stretcher masonry, then, delineates the northern boundary of the royal compound proper during most of the eighth century BCE (BP IV-V). Even in Judah, where the technique appears much less frequently, it typically serves to demarcate a royal quarter.[38] Depending on the lateral extent of the series of BP V rooms north of 65, the narrow exposure of these structures may in fact bear witness to a kind of inner casemate arrangement enclosing the north courtyard area.

Before proceeding to my analysis of the BP V stratigraphy, I must reiterate my surprise at learning that not a single scrap of ceramic evidence from these new rooms appears in the final report from Samaria. The value of understanding the local stratigraphy in this area becomes exceptionally clear against the realization that, according to *SS II* and the published Section GH in Pl. VII of *SS I*, fragments of burnt ivory first appeared in later (Early Hellenistic) fills, which covered the northern half of this complex.[39] A full view of the stratigraphic relationship between earlier Israelite levels and all subsequent depositional history in this area would have proved helpful.

1) Stratigraphic Detail

a. Rooms *hk/hq* (Published Section EF; figs. 8 and 10)

[i] 125.144 — Room *hk*

As shown in the previous chapter, Segment *125.144* lay on a section that the excavators cut laterally through the northern half of Rooms *h* and *k*,[40] which are now

---

[38] E.g., see the masonry used in the gate leading to the royal quarter south of the Temple area in Jerusalem, as reported in E. Mazar, "Royal Gateway to Ancient Jerusalem Uncovered," *BAR* 15/3 (1989), 38-51. More recently, L. Herr has noted that this type of ashlar construction also appears at Lachish, but added that it rarely occurs elsewhere in the south "probably because royal buildings outside Jerusalem and Lachish were infrequent" (L. Herr, "The Iron Age II Period: Emerging Nations," *BA* 60 [1997], 144).

[39] I.e., north of the BP IV Wall 58 and over the truncated Wall 56. See again the comments surrounding nn. 438-39 and on p. 173 in Chapter I, in addition to fig. 41 and n. 36 above. Refer also to my full discussion of the archaeological context of the ivories in Chapter V below.

[40] I can set the location of this segment in the *northern* portion of these rooms since both Wall 142 and Wall 151 remain visible in fig. 8 above. As the phase plans in figs. 5 and 41 show, the southern end of

combined into a single, elongated but narrow chamber (for its horizontal location, see the section line labeled B on fig. 5).[41] Further, fig. 8 shows that, while another segment (*Btw TT2–TT3*) related mainly to the eastern portion of this vicinity (i.e., to the former Room *k*), *125.144* aligned itself mainly with the more westerly space inside the previous Room *h* (compare fig. 10). Half of the meager group of published PP 5 fragments[42] derive from *125.144* in the western sector of Room *hk* situated just inside Summit Strip Qk (fig. 41).

It is important to remember that a series of chronological revisions appears in the field notes but not on the field sections that relate to layers excavated in this area.[43] These changes adjusted Kenyon's initial assessments upward by one period, i.e., layers and material originally assigned to "Period II" were transferred to "Period III," and so on. As a result, Kenyon ultimately associated the first floor levels in Rooms *h* and *k* (*125.144*, Layer IX and *Btw TT2–TT3*, Layer VII, respectively, in fig. 8) with BP IV rather than with BP III, as the labeling continues to indicate on the section. These surfaces provide the first signs of building activity in this area immediately north of the rock plateau that I have called the "central summit." This picture helps confirm my observation that the space between the northern scarp and the Casemate System remained undeveloped until the eight century BCE.[44] An apparently new surface, which Kenyon assigned to "Period IVa," ran directly over the BP IV floor in Room *k* (*Btw TT2–TT3*, Layer VII) and rested on an additional padding of leveling fill in Room *h* (*125.144*, Layer IIIb). Because the PP 4 pottery published from Segment *125.144* came from layers or sublayers other than IIIb (Table 1), it remains difficult to substantiate Kenyon's phasing of these levels. This new surface provides the only possible stratigraphic corroboration for her proposed subphasing of BP IV into "Period IV" and "Period IVa"; the single fragment of PP 4a pottery published from the blackish sub-Layer IVx.z (*SS III*, Fig. 6:14) certainly does not constitute adequate evidence of a distinct new phase of activity in this area.

Following closely upon the purported BP IVa floor, another surface also overran the now defunct Wall 157 and extended over both Room *h* (*125.144*, Layer IIIe[45]) and Room *k* (*Btw TT2–TT3*, Layer V) in fig. 8. In the final report, the excavators understood this surface to represent the sole BP V floor in this area. As noted in my introduction to BP V, Holladay seized on the single-phase nature of this construction to argue for a relatively brief lifespan for BP V as over against BP IV, which showed a

---

142 barely entered the area of chambers *h* and *k*.

[41] For appropriate references to *Fieldbook Qk-l-m* regarding daily field notes, stratigraphic summaries, and section drawings relating to Segment *125.144*, see Chapter I, 27, n. 43.

[42] See the jars in *SS III*, Fig. 8:2, 3, 4, 8.

[43] See Chapter I, 28, nn. 48-49.

[44] This excludes, of course, Omri's ninth-century Enclosure Wall 161, which traversed this otherwise undeveloped area.

[45] See Chapter I, 32, n. 60.

putative resurfacing. Both the stratigraphic and ceramic evidence available from this segment, however, remain too limited to address the relative lengths of occupation for these surfaces. Further, Kenyon herself observed in the original field notes that Layer IIIe actually comprises "*one of several* levels making up III, above IIIb."[46] While this thin deposit may, in fact, depict a distinct floor level, it seems that it may just as easily represent the bottommost striations of the thicker filling resting above it (see Layers III in Segment *125.144* and IV in *Btw TT2-TT3*). Either way, Kenyon's unpublished notation appears to undercut the argument that this surface clearly exhibited no "refloorings."

The multiple striae of Layer IIIe on fig. 8 must relate to the Layer IIIb that extends southward from Wall 155 on fig. 10, though the latter once again appears in section as a single layer (and thereby militates against Kenyon's separation of BP IV and BP IVa). Also, one may note again from fig. 10 that Wall 125b clearly cut both these thin bands of matrix and the thicker fill deposit beneath them (Layer IV). The field notes record that the other end of floor level IIIb, however, "abs[olutely] def[initely] runs up to 155."[47] This means that the substantial deposits of fill seen on either side of 125b (Layer III to the north and Layer VIII to the south) represent the earliest and, in fact, the only deposits in fig. 10 contemporary with that structure. Further, these data indicate that any floor level originally associated with that wall or with ivory fragments recovered from this area (see Kenyon's notation concerning burnt ivory in published Section GH) had disappeared already during antiquity.

Without additional primary data, then, one must assume that Kenyon's proposed BP V floor level consists of the following layers from Segment *125.144*: Layer IIIe in the western half of fig. 8 (= former Room *h*); and Layer IIIb in fig. 10 (between Walls 125b and 155). As seen on both of these sections, a relatively thick deposit of soil overlay this floor. Kenyon labeled this accumulation simply "Layer III" and dated it to her "Period V" (which she corrected from "Period IV"). Judging from the stratigraphic summary sheets found in the fieldbooks, this upward revision seems to have resulted from the presence of some "hard, ringing wares" among the pottery recovered from this layer, though most of the fragments actually impressed Kenyon as belonging to PP 4.[48] The notes describe Layer III as "a hard yellow level" that correlates directly with Layer IV farther east in the Segment *Btw TT2–TT3*. This latter layer (IV) continued eastward to the place where the robbing of Wall 125b began,[49] i.e., to a point that is not plotted on the available sections. Though the matrix of Level III appears more compact than preceding fills, the overall thickness of the deposit (*ca.* .4 m) precludes one from viewing this accumulation as yet another floor level, as a natural accumulation of

---

[46] *Fieldbook Qk-l-m*, 48a (emphasis added).

[47] *Fieldbook Qk-l-m*, 48.

[48] *Fieldbook Qk-l-m*, 48a.

[49] *Fieldbook Qk-l-m*, 34.

soil, or as pure occupational debris left on the BP V surface below. It seems, instead, to represent a densely packed filling spread across the entire area of Room *hk*. I may add that the subsequent robber trenches associated with the BP V Walls 142 and 151 appear to cut the fill and sooty debris in *W of 124*, Layers III-IIIa, and in *Btw TT2-TT3*, Layers IV-IIIb-III, a situation that further strengthens the correlation of these layers and walls. The plundering ceased at the elevation at which the diggers encountered the harder soil of Layer III/IV.

Two published PP 5 fragments—the jar shoulder and handle in *SS III*, Fig. 8:2, and the neck and rim of another jar in Fig. 8:5—derive from this concentrated filling. The portion of III that actually ran up to the face of Wall 155 received the designation IIIo, and two additional jar rims (including another possible holemouth specimen in Fig. 8:3 as well as the simple rim in Fig. 8:8) came from that sublayer. Though few details appear concerning the composition of this matrix and the rationale for assigning a separate layer number to the soil close to Wall 155, Kenyon noted that the deposit "sh[oul]d be pure" and that the pottery taken from it again included hard ringing wares along with PP 4 fragments. Still, she concluded that the group "may be [Period] VI."[50] As noted above, by dating the BP V floor according to the materials found lying above it, Kenyon departs at this point from her usual method of establishing the construction date for a given surface by means of the remains situated beneath it.

Layers IIIa (*125.144*) and IIIb (*Btw TT2-TT3*), which consisted in sooty earth with possible inclusions of burnt ivories,[51] overlay the compacted fill of Layer III and also appear to have extended across the full interior space of Room *hk*. These levels are visible only in fig. 8, though the field notes indicate that IIIa crossed over the truncated top of Wall 155 in fig. 10. The notes also record that Wall 150 "rested on" this sooty layer and therefore agree with the portrayal in fig. 8. Though Kenyon assigned this debris to her "Period VII," she did not offer a phasing for Layer III beneath it. One may presume, however, that the latter belongs either to "Period VI" (since it is sandwiched between the BP V floor in Layer IIIe and the PP 7 sooty debris of Layer IIIa) or also to "Period VII" together with IIIa above it. The noticeable evenness of this sooty deposit suggests that it, in addition to Layer III, reflects an intentional leveling operation designed to cover the breadth of Room *hk* sometime after the end of the room's functional life.

The point of primary interest here is that Layers III and IIIb represent deliberate, level fills laid down directly over the BP V surface. Little or no hiatus appears to have occurred between the abandonment of the floor and the filling activities. Whatever occupational debris remained on the BP V surface at the time of its covering undoubtedly became mixed into the basal striations of fill. Judging from the layer designations in the unpublished field notes, none of the PP 5 fragments actually published from Segment *125.144* appears to derive from *in situ* occupational material;

---

[50] *Fieldbook Qk-l-m*, 48a.

[51] *Fieldbook Qk-l-m*, 34.

rather, the excavators seem to have recovered the four pieces mentioned above from the yellowish fill of Layers III and IIIo. The report failed to include any pottery from the sooty level IIIb (assigned to PP 7), even though it apparently yielded fragments of burned ivory. It remains impossible to know precisely how much soot appeared in this layer. I have already noted the presence of several *ṭābunîm* in this area, and one can imagine that regular cleanings of such features over a period of two or more decades would result in an appreciable amount of ashy debris scattered about the immediate vicinity, particularly if it functioned merely as a service area located on the periphery of the main royal precinct as I have suggested.

[ii] West of 124 — Room *hq*

This segment takes my investigation into an area new to both *AIS-I* and the present study.[52] Though the fragments listed in the pottery registries assign this tract to Room *hk*, its exact location within that space remains difficult to determine with precision, mainly because Kenyon constantly refers to walls (including Wall 124 itself) that she nowhere discusses in the narrative or draws in the sections and plans of the published report.[53] Though it shows no clear compass orientation or scale, an unpublished field section that comprises part of the material which relates to this segment does, however, help us at least situate *W of 124* in the area south of the superimposed series of walls numbered 56–125a–125 and included on published Section EF (fig. 42; compare fig. 7).[54] As a complement to this information, fig. 7 above shows that *W of 124*

---

[52] The following references in *Fieldbook Qk-l-m* relate to this segment: daily field notes = pp. 10-11, 20-23, 44-46; stratigraphic summary = 10a-11a, 20a-22a; field sections = 10a, 22a, 23a, and 46a.

[53] Examples of such features, in addition to various phases of the key Wall 124 (Kenyon places 124 itself in the Roman.4 Period, fourth century CE), include the following: Walls 124a (R.3 = late second century CE), 124b (?); 125b ("Period V," though nowhere visible on the BP V plan; moreover see my comments below); 130 (?, though Robber Trench 130 seems variously dated to "Period IV," the Late Hellenistic, and the Herodian periods); 132E (LH = late second century BCE); 132W ("Period V," though nowhere visible on the BP V plan); 133 (?); and 156 ("Period III," though nowhere visible on the plan). See my further comments on p. 20, n. 25 in Chapter I. Walls 125 (R.4 = fourth century CE) and 125a (Late Hellenistic = late second century BCE) do, however, appear on published Section EF. Since Section EF appears to bisect Wall 125a and 125 (as well as the earlier 56 and 58) perpendicularly, one may presume an E-W orientation for these features and a location for them somewhere in the later stratigraphy situated just south of Pit *i*. Moreover, since neither the walls themselves nor their robber trenches appear on Sections EF or, a bit further west, GH, one must assume that the excavators encountered actual traces of these features in a very limited area, perhaps only above the earlier Room *hk*, and that Late Hellenistic and/or Roman leveling operations have completely erased any trace of these structures farther to the west; the area to the east of Room *hk* lay beyond the field of excavation.

[54] *Fieldbook Qk-l-m*, 10a. Though this conglomeration of walls, starting with 56, assumes the same general orientation as the BP IV Wall 58 (fig. 5), the latter structure lay approximately 3-3.25 m farther south from the line of 56-125. A comparison of the relative courses of 58 and 56 on the plans in figs. 5 and 41, respectively, at 450° N x 630° E establishes this distance. It also allows us to name the otherwise unidentified robber trench that partially appears at the very southern end of fig. 7. Remains of Wall 58, then, do not impinge on those of the 56-125 series.

PP 5: HOUSE FLOORS — STRATIGRAPHY

lay south of these walls and extended toward the summit area. Though Kenyon did not specifically identify Wall 125b on published Section EF, this new field section also confirms my earlier conclusion that 125b constitutes a stratigraphically later rebuild on the remains of Wall 56 (see fig. 10 above and the discussion surrounding it as well as my phasing of walls in fig. 7). With the lack of other published drawings (sections or plans) to clarify the relative locations of nearby walls (such as 130 or 133), these data provide the only available anchor for plotting this segment.

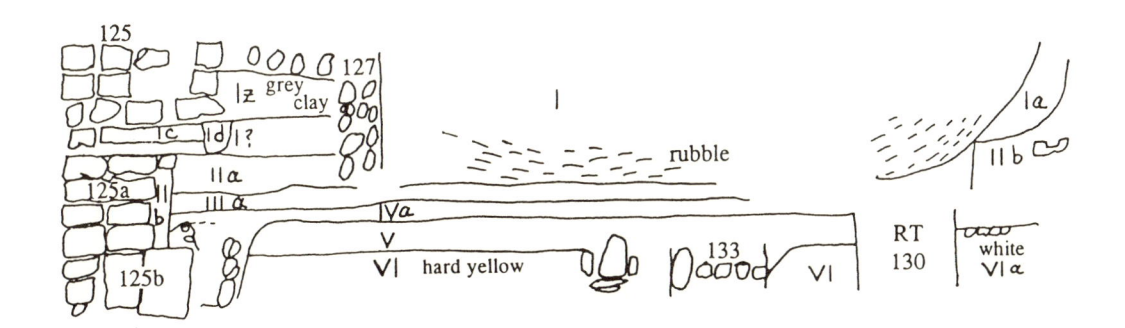

Field Section Relating to Segment W of 124
(no compass orientation or scale available from the field notes)[55]
<— S N —>
View toward West (?)

fig. 42

While fig. 7 helps to establish Segment *W of 124* on a horizontal axis south of Walls 125b/56, the depositional history presented in that drawing does not include the local Layer VIII, which yielded the well-preserved jar in *SS III*, Fig. 8:1. For a fuller view of the vertical axis in this area, I may refer to another previously unpublished field section that may provide some assistance in this matter (fig. 43, next page).[56]

Though helpful in plotting the general location of *W of 124* on both the horizontal (cultural) and vertical (chronological) planes, then, these data nevertheless collectively raise the question of whether this segment actually lay inside Room *hk* or somewhere just to the south of it, in either *hq* or *kq*. The principal fact that begs the question resides in the physical proximity of Wall 56 to the later rebuild in 125b (compare figs.

---

[55]My suggested orientation is based on a possible correlation between the cutting of Layers V-VI here and similar trench deposits in nearby segments (e.g., *Btw TT2–TT3* in fig. 7; *125.144* in fig. 10). But see also n. 67 below. Regarding scale, one may note that in many of Kenyon's field drawings, 2 cm = 1 m. I have provisionally adopted that ratio here, without direct evidence that we should.

[56]*Fieldbook Qk-l-m*, 46a.

7, 10, and Section EF). Now that new information has proved this association correct, and accepting that *W of 124* runs south from Wall 125 as indicated in fig. 43, one sees that both the section in fig. 7 and the plan in fig. 41 imply that this segment lay outside the parameters of Room *hk* somewhere within the better constructed rooms to its immediate south. Additional information presented below will corroborate this impression and will show more specifically that the layers of this segment lay on either side of Wall 132, which separated Room *hq* from *kq*.

Another factor which suggests that *W of 124* lies outside the confines of Room *hk* pertains to the sequence of historical periods represented in the strata of this segment. In my earlier discussion of BP IV Rooms *g, h, j,* and *k,* I showed that remains

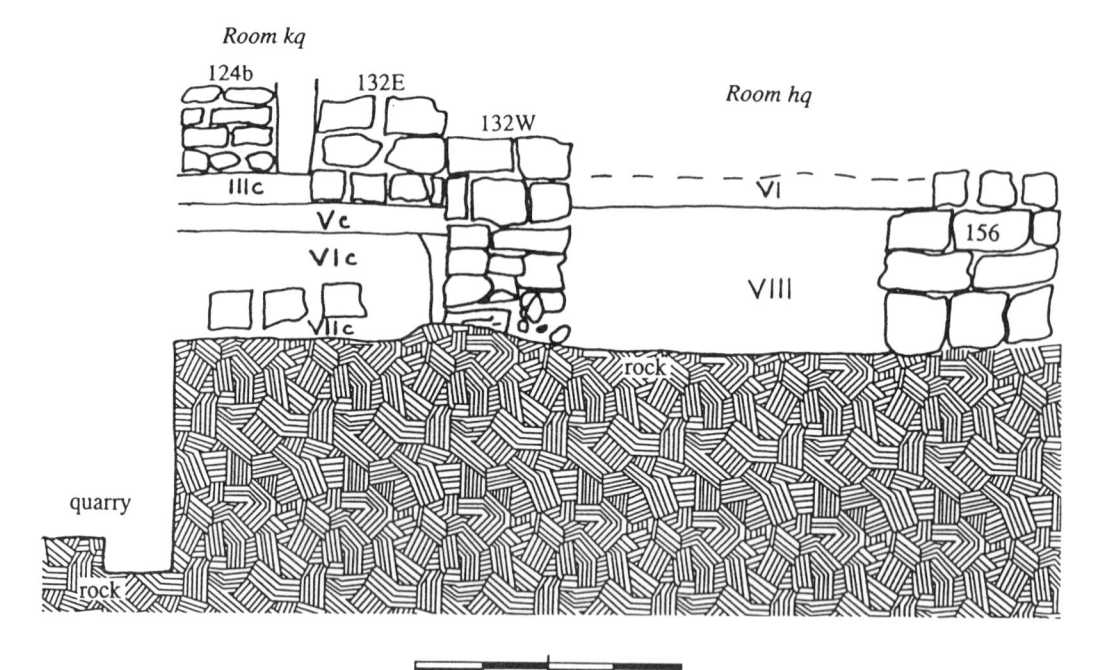

Segment West of 124: Field Section South of Wall 125
<— E W —>
View toward South

fig. 43

from the Late Hellenistic and Roman periods consistently lay directly over Israelite levels from the mid-to-late eighth century BCE. Kenyon's stratigraphic summary of layers situated *W of 124*, on the other hand, reveals substantial deposits from intervening phases of occupation, including "Periods VII-IX."[57] In fact, "Period VII" emerges

---

[57] My count reveals the following deposits recorded in the stratigraphic summaries: **Period VII** = 3 layers, 6 sublayers; **Period VIII** = 3 layers, 10 sublayers; **Period IX** = 6 layers, 14 sublayers.

as a transitional phase in these levels. At certain points, remains from VII appear intermingled with those from "Periods VIII and IX,"[58] while, at other times, they mix with materials from BP IV and V. By using fig. 7 from Chapter II and figs. 42-43 above as references, I may outline the depositional history encountered in this segment as follows (excluding the myriad of layers and sublayers not depicted on those drawings).

In an effort to present these deposits in their proper sequential order (from latest to earliest), let us begin with fig. 42.[59] To the immediate right (north?) of the 125-125a-125b series of walls, one sees a hard floor level, Layer Ic, that runs beneath Wall 125 (R.4 Period = late fourth century CE) and seals Wall 125a (Late Hellenistic Period = late second century BCE). Opposite a small pocket that broke into these materials (Layer Id), there appeared the remains of another surface (Layer Ig), which Kenyon thought was originally contemporary with the Late Hellenistic Wall 125a. But as fig. 42 shows, any possible stratigraphic connection has disappeared due to the laying of Ic,[60] which overrides the stump of Wall 125a. Juxtaposed to the remaining courses of this wall, one can detect some trench backfill in Layer IIb. Kenyon understood this feature as the *foundation* trench for Wall 125a (see further comments below). In any event, the trench clearly cuts, and therefore postdates, Layer IIa as well as the .15 m-thick IIIa, to which Kenyon assigned the curious datings of "Period VIII" and "Period IX," respectively, mainly on the basis of the pottery types found in them. Stratigraphically speaking, one would expect a reverse chronological ordering of these two deposits.

Kenyon remained somewhat uncertain in her interpretation of fig. 42's Layer I, the thick pocket of heterogeneous matrix located to the right of the conglomeration of levels and wall fragments just mentioned. The field section does not reflect the fact that the local stratigraphy in this area actually consisted of several levels, including an uppermost layer of soil, a middle scattering of rubble, and a lower strip of harder earth. Kenyon believed that the last deposit, labeled Layer II, represented a continua-

---

[58] Several sheets titled "Notes on Levels. Samaria Excavations, 1931-5. Q area (Summit)" appeared among the unpublished documentation recovered in the PEF during my investigation. These pages contain descriptions of "Periods VIII and IX" as follows: **Period VIII** = "Beneath a layer of chocolate coloured soil on the top of the hill. The laying down of this was preceded by a considerable destruction of Israelite deposits in this area, in parts down to rock, thus involving all levels back to Period I. The pottery from these deposits was incorporated in the thick filling beneath the chocolate soil. The pottery ranged from the seventh to possibly the early fifth centuries B.C."; and **Period IX** = "Remains of a house on the summit dating from the fifth to the early third centuries B.C." Since these data sheets were found loose among the records and exhibited no pagination, I cannot cite exact bibliographic references for them.

[59] I have gleaned this information mainly from Kenyon's own stratigraphic summaries, for which references are given in n. 52 above. The layers presented here seem to relate to those depicted to the immediate south of Wall 56/125b-125a, and below 125, in published Section EF; there, they are assigned to "Periods VII, VIII, and IX."

[60] Kenyon's analysis assumes that Ic is, in fact, unrelated stratigraphically to Ig, though she classified both as floor levels. Without additional details pertaining to the precise composition and consistency of these levels, it remains difficult to judge whether or not they originally functioned together.

tion of Layer IIIa mentioned above. As a working chronology, the layers in this pocket were also assigned to "Period IX," i.e., to sometime during the fifth to early third centuries BCE.

Layer IVa represents another .15 m-thick deposit, which Kenyon described as "covering 125b"—a wall she wanted to designate as "Period V." This seemingly jumbled layer deepens into a trench formation as it approaches the walls to its left and, therefore, prompts us to believe that the entire deposit contained a matrix used for leveling and backfilling operations rather than for a new living surface across this area. After filling the (foundation?) trench, then, this deposit likely served as the subfloor makeup for level IIIa and, subsequent to that, IIa.

A question remains, however, as to which architectural feature these layers originally belonged. While they seem to postdate Wall 125b (note that the foundation trench does not appear to extend to the bottom courses of this structure, and floor levels IIIa and IIa actually overlap the surviving top courses), they must predate Wall 125a if, in fact, Kenyon is correct in her interpretation that the cut enclosing Layer IIb comprises the *foundation* trench for that wall. In this scenario, several subphases of occupation must have transpired between the periods in which 125b and 125a were used, i.e., between "Period V" (Wall 125b) and the Late Hellenistic period (Wall 125a). The only other viable option involves associating Levels IIa, IIIa, and IVa with 125a and viewing the cut in IIb as part of a later robber trench rather than an original foundation deposit. In light of the miscellaneous, loose stones that remain visible in the trench portion of this layer, the deposit may represent the robber trench of 125b rather than the foundation of 125a. At any rate, I can only suggest that whether or not IVa corresponds to Wall 125a, the layer clearly seems stratigraphically later than the construction and use of Wall 125b. Moreover, though Kenyon assigned 125b to her "Period V," my discussion of Segment *125.144* above and the section presented in fig. 10 both suggest that this feature cut the BP V surfaces in this general vicinity and therefore *post*-dates that era.

Below Layer IVa in fig. 42, one encounters the "poorly consolidated, light-colored Layer V, which contained a good deal of clay." Layer V seems to represent another substantial filling, and Kenyon believed that it "probably" also dated to her "Period VIII" (somewhere between the seventh and early fifth centuries BCE). Some 25 cm below this deposit lay a level described as a "hard floor . . . [which] crosses [the] broken top of 125b,"[61] though that crossing is not apparent in fig. 42. Kenyon assigned this putative surface to "Period VII" in the seventh century BCE.

Turning to fig. 43, one observes the following sequence of layers. Layer IIIc, containing mixed soot and hard yellow soil, lies beneath the late second-century CE Wall 124b. Though this layer shows a matrix very similar to that seen earlier in Segment *125.144* (Layers IIIa-III, fig. 8), it seems to abut the eastern face of the bottom

---

[61] *Fieldbook Qk-l-m*, 21a.

course of Wall 132E, which Kenyon dated to the Late Hellenistic period (late second century BCE).

The excavators understood the next earliest level, Layer Vc, as a BP V floor. Accordingly, Kenyon attributed Wall 132W, which this layer abuts, to "Period V" as well. On her BP V top plan (fig. 41), this wall divides Room *hq* from *kq*, and therefore it stands as further evidence supporting my earlier suspicion that at least a portion of Segment *W of 124* actually extended south of Room *hk*, even though the pottery records and final report associate it with that chamber alone. This 20 cm-thick floor was laid against the east face of 132W after the founding of this wall had cut Layer VIc, which seems to reflect a substantial deposit of subfloor fill even though Kenyon describes it as a "Period IV" floor beneath Vc. Given the portrayal of VIc in fig. 43, this interpretation seems unlikely. Three dressed blocks of stone lay near the bottom of Layer VIc, and the field notes describe the soil under them (Layer VIIc) as lying "beneath poss[ible] Period I or II wall beneath VIc."[62] This supposition also seems unlikely, since the BP I-II plan in *SS I*, Pl. VIII shows no longitudinal wall north of 450° N in the generally undeveloped area lying off the shelf of the central summit. Rather, the stones may easily have fallen to their point of discovery during the robbing either of the southern section of Wall 132 or of the lateral Wall 65 (see fig. 41). These deposits all lay east of Wall 132, i.e., in the vicinity of Room *kq*, and the massive disturbance created by Roman quarrying activities appears on the eastern side of the section.

To the west, in Room *hq*, the thick deposit of Layer VIII lay against that face of Wall 132W.[63] Kenyon assigned VIII to "Period V" (corrected by her from IV), though the pottery readings included in the field notes indicate that it yielded primarily PP 1 and PP 4 fragments. Since this level constitutes the only "Layer VIII" presented in any of the drawings that relate to the Segment *W of 124*, I must assume that this deposit represents the local layer that yielded the jar form in *SS III*, Fig. 8:1.

Though Layer IX does not appear on this section, the notes indicate that it consisted in a "soft, dark level" situated beneath VIII, probably comprised part of VIII, and also belonged to BP V. Again, however, the pottery readings reveal "early Israelite-ish" forms. These pottery readings do not necessarily support Kenyon's understanding of the three stones east of Wall 132W as a remnant from BP I or II, since the levels in question represent secondary fill deposits that must retain an open *terminus post quem*. Moreover, the alleged architectural feature represented by these stones does not appear on any published drawing.

Finally, I can add that the layers just mentioned seem to correlate well with the few levels from *W of 124* that appear in fig. 7. This situation results from the

---

[62] *Fieldbook Qk-l-m*, 22a.

[63] Actually, the field notes record that the subdeposits VIIIw, x, y, and z comprise the soil that rested directly against the wall.

excavators' having cut the lateral (east-west) section in fig. 43 through the layers situated south of and parallel to Wall 125 on fig. 7. Here, Layers IVc, Vc, and VIc correspond directly—in composition, consistency, and thickness—to those seen east of Walls 132E and W in fig. 43. Only the latest of these deposits received variant identification numbers in the respective areas (IVc in fig. 7 vs. IIIc in fig. 43). I just outlined the association between the soot and yellowish earth of IIIc and the Late Hellenistic Wall 132E.[64] In the field notes, Kenyon described IVc (fig. 7) as "Wall 132E, [and] earth mixed up [with] it, *including ivories.*"[65] She incorporated this deposit into her "Period IX" remains from a fifth-to-early third-century BCE house constructed on the summit. Since this accumulation abuts the south face of Wall 125b without being cut by that feature (fig. 7), it may help provide the clearest reading on the date of that structure. Yet, as before, the excavators believed that Layer Vc, which also appears to run up against 125b, represents a floor beneath Wall 132E; they placed it in BP V, though the pottery again showed "mainly early" vessel-types with some additional PP 4 forms. Since these levels presumably represent fills poured against the lower courses of 125b, it is no surprise to find earlier pottery forms among their contents. Given the nature of the context, however, this pottery cannot put the same early date on the wall itself. Finally, Layer VIc was assigned to "Period IV" and construed as yet another floor level beneath Vc. On the basis of information relating to fig. 43, I have added the stratum number VIIc to fig. 7 in the soil situated beneath several more large stones and lying directly on bedrock.

To close the discussion of this segment, I offer two final observations. First, I have shown that the builders of Wall 125b fashioned it over the truncated remains of BP V Wall 56. I have added an identifying label for the latter feature on fig. 7 (compare fig. 10). Consequently, the suggestion may follow that the large stones resting in the basal portions of Layer VIc on figs. 7 and 43 simply represent discarded material from the plundering of Wall 56,[66] not a previously neglected wall from BP I or II, as Kenyon suggested. I have noted that her top plan for those early periods shows no such wall in this area beyond the central summit plateau. If my suggestion is accurate, then the deposition of these stones as well as the matrix surrounding them postdates BP V. The layer emerges as yet another example of leveling fill, this time associated with the robbing of 56 and the construction of 125b. Second, both Layers Vc and IVc overrun the stump of 56 and abut the southern face of 125b (fig. 7). Therefore, these layers apparently belong with Wall 125b, which Kenyon attempted to include in BP V (though it nowhere appears on the phase plan for that period) but which I have shown once again to postdate that period (recall fig. 10). Even though the field notes placed Wall

---

[64] As shown in fig. 43, one must draw a stratigraphic (temporal) distinction between the apparent BP V Wall 132W, founded directly on bedrock, and the contiguous but later Wall 132E, which rests on one meter of debris.

[65] *Fieldbook Qk-l-m*, 21a (emphasis added).

[66] They might also stem from the construction of this wall.

125b and Layer Vc in "Period V," they ascribed Layer IVc to "Period IX," which dates sometime during the late fifth to the early third centuries BCE. The suggestion that over three centuries separate Wall 125b and Layer Vc from Layer IVc in fig. 7 remains untenable. I believe that the only likely BP V level that lies west of 124 in fig. 7 consists in Layer VIIc, which directly overrides the rock surface. All subsequent deposits appear later than BP V and may postdate the entire Israelite period.

It seems clear, at least, that the deposition of two of the principal ivory-bearing loci in the Segment *W of 124* (Layer IIIc/IVc) occurred sometime after the close of Israelite administration of the site, and perhaps a considerable time later. Kenyon herself dated the locus from the fifth to the early third centuries BCE. Moreover, the mixed composition of the matrix (soot and yellowish soil) that yielded the fragments prompts us to treat this locus as secondary leveling fill transferred to this area from some other location, probably farther onto the summit itself. (See Chapter V for a fuller discussion of these topics.)

[iii] East Strip; Between Test Trench 2–Test Trench 3 — Room *hk*

We have already encountered this segment in my treatment of the BP IV levels in Room *k* (Chapter I, 55-58). My figs. 7 and 13 confirm that this exposed area lay immediately north of Wall 56 (125b) and just south of Wall 153, i.e., precisely in the eastern half of Room *hk* (= the space taken up by the former Room *k*; see the plan in fig. 41). A clear record of the depositional history in this segment appears in the central portion of fig. 7 and in the eastern half of fig. 8; one may also compare the "section down the center of the east strip" presented in fig. 13. Because this stratigraphy received such detailed treatment in the previous chapter, I need only add some brief, descriptive comments regarding the layers that rested in closest proximity to Layer V, from which came the holemouth rim fragment in *SS III*, Fig. 8:4. Following these remarks, I shall highlight some probable correlations between these layers and those just discussed in the excavated Segment *W of 124*.

Starting with the view of Segment *Btw TT2–TT3* presented in fig. 7, one can see that the deposits of principal concern include Layer V and the two stratigraphically later levels in IV and IIIb. The formation of V, which clearly cut VI-VIII, confirms only that the levels in V-IIIb postdate the BP IV-IVa floors and fills; it does not independently tell us how much later than the BP IV deposits these layers might date. Layer V comprised a 14 cm-thick, hard floor level that deepens into an apparent foundation deposit against the north face of Wall 125b. The compacted, yellowish fill of Layer IV rested above this surface. Kenyon placed both of these levels in her "Period V." As I noted earlier, the excavators found a series of presumed paving stones associated with these two levels. Lying atop this fill, the partially disturbed matrix of Layer IIIb contained appreciable quantities of sooty soil and ivory fragments.

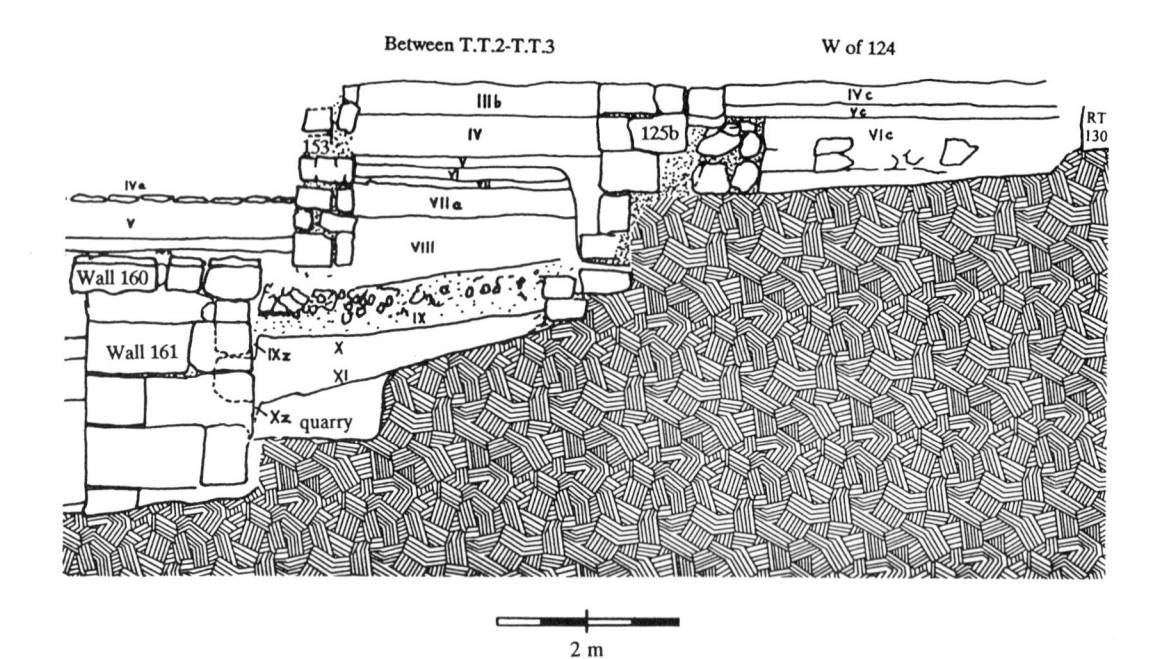

fig. 44

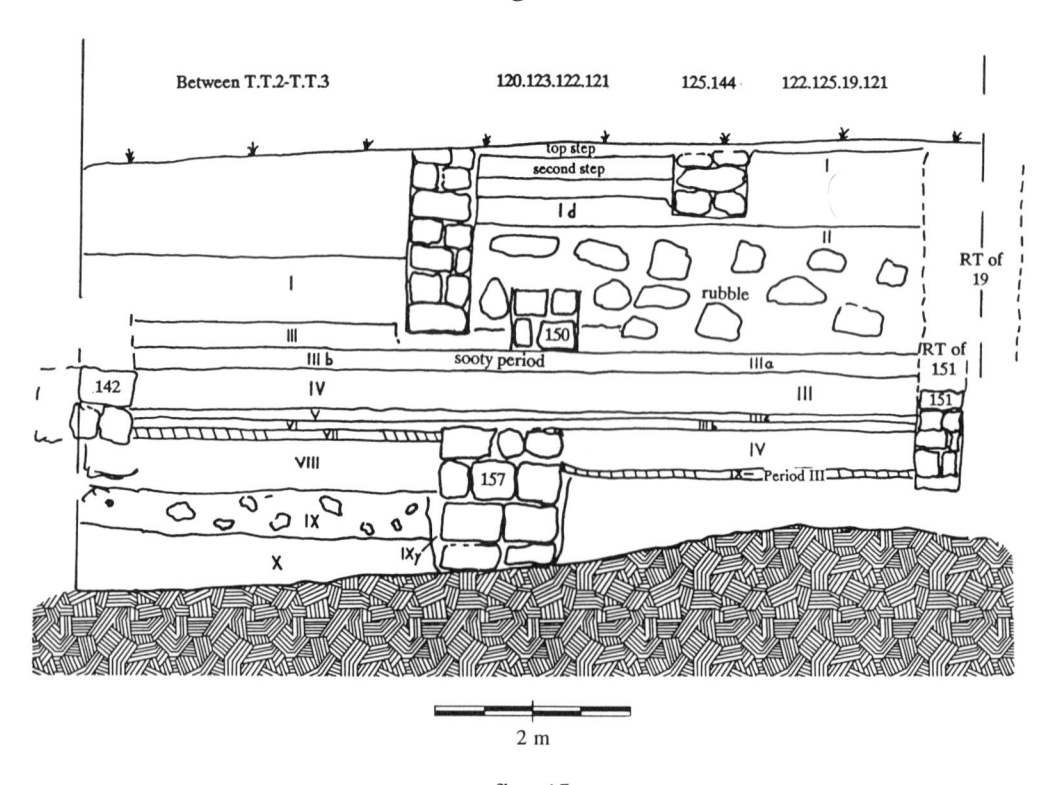

fig. 45

PP 5: HOUSE FLOORS — STRATIGRAPHY

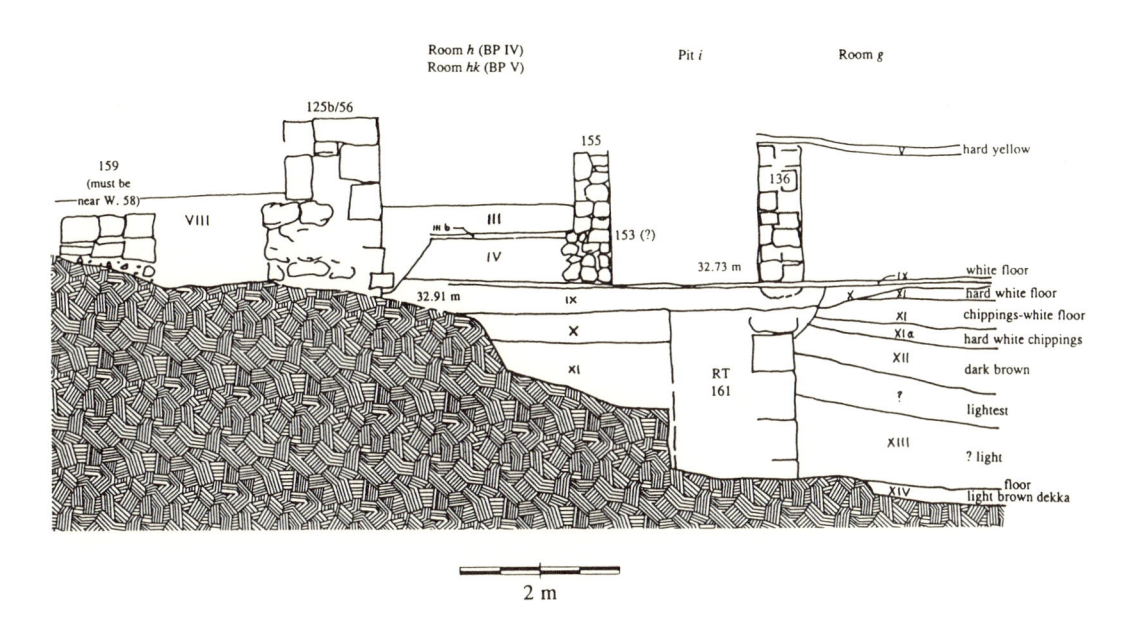

fig. 46

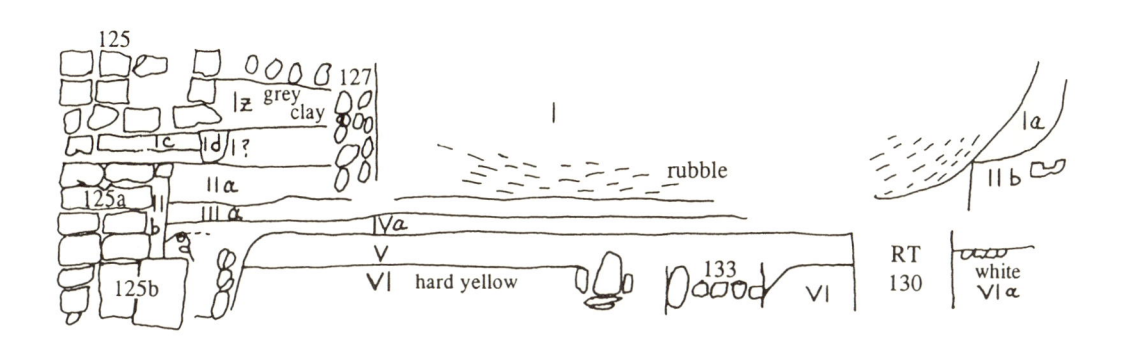

(scale not recorded)

fig. 47

Stratigraphic Correlations between Segments W of 124 and Btw TT2–TT3

To aid in the presentation of suggested stratigraphic correlations for these layers, I have repeated the most relevant portions of figs. 7, 8, 10, and 42, and have focused on the strata that abut the north face of Wall 125b (see figs. 44-47 on the preceding pages). For greater clarity in my comparisons, I have also harmonized the compass orientations of these drawings by reversing the course of fig. 7/44 to match the south-to-north (from left-to-right) direction of figs. 10/46 and 42/47. Among these four sketches, only fig. 8/45 exhibited a lateral orientation.

Even a cursory perusal of figs. 44, 46, and 47 reveals a similar portrait in two respects. First, in light of the north-south axis along which these sections were cut, one sees that Wall 125b represents a lateral (east-west) feature running through the area somewhere between Rooms *hk* and *hq/kq* to the south. Judging from fig. 41 above, I may suggest that this feature actually appears as the unmarked northern boundary of *hq/kq*. This segment of wall seems slightly offset from the main branch of Wall 56 to the west; moreover, it exhibits a rather unique style of construction in which workers laid the blocks side-by-side along the wall's northern face (toward Room *hk*) but end-to-end across its entire southern face (toward Rooms *hq* and *kq*). From the available sectional data, I believe that Wall 125b actually represents a repair of or rebuild on the broken remains of an earlier wall, namely 56 (note the offset lower courses in figs. 44 and 46). This identification would also help to explain my earlier observation that some of the excavated segments associated with 125b appear to lie in Room *hk* (*125.144; E Strip, Btw TT2–TT3*) while others belong in the *hq/kq* chambers (*W of 124*). Finally, it identifies the loose or displaced stones in Layers VIc (fig. 44), IVa (fig. 47), and possibly VIc (fig. 43) in the Segment *W of 124*.

Second, a strikingly similar trench cut appears against the basal courses of the northern face of Walls 56/125b (see especially figs. 44 and 46; it remains less clear on 39d that this cut extends to the bottom courses of stone or that it lies on the northern vs. southern face of 125b).[67] These sectional data must relate directly to Kenyon's published statement that the BP V Wall 56 "has a very clear foundational trench cutting through the floor levels of Periods IV and IVa to the north of it, while to the south . . . the earlier floors were cleared to rock."[68] Though it remains difficult to determine whether this breach represents a foundation deposit or a later robber trench, I believe it likely points to the foundation cut made for the construction of Wall 125b. If so, the following conceivable scenario emerges (compare the plans in figs. 5 and 41 with the above sections throughout this discussion). The establishment of the poorly-built, BP IV service rooms (*j-k*) north of the central summit platform involved the raising of lateral Wall 153 (relabeled "145" on the BP V plan). The associated floors and ensuing occupational debris seen in Segment *Btw TT2–TT3*, Layers VII-VI, respectively, ran from the south face of that structure and over some deposits of fill (VIIa and

---

[67] If the trench truly lay on the *north* side of 125b, then *W of 124* seems to have extended across this series of walls (given the location of this segment in fig. 7). Otherwise, the trench constitutes the southern counterpart to the foundation deposits seen in figs. 7 and 10.

[68] *SS I*, 106.

A. *Foundation trench and first leveling fill associated with 125b*

Btw TT2-TT3	(fig. 44)	Layer V; "good, hard level"; 14 cm thick
	(fig. 45)	Layer V; same
W of 124	(fig. 47)	Layer IVa; same; 15 cm thick
	(fig. 45)	Layer IIIe/(c?); same

B. *More substantial fillings poured against 125b*

Btw TT2-TT3	(fig. 44)	Layer IV; compacted, yellowish matrix with random (paving?) stones
	(fig. 45)	Layer IV
W of 124	(fig. 47)	Layer IIIa; hardish level; 15 cm thick
	(fig. 45)	Layer III

(Compare fig. 46, *125.144*, Layer III, in relation to both A and B above)

C. *Additional leveling including destruction debris*

Btw TT2-TT3	(fig. 44)	Layer IIIb; sooty, with fragments of ivory
	(fig. 45)	Layer IIIb; same
W of 124	(fig. 44)	Layer IVc; same; dated by Kenyon to "Period IX"; possibly should include Layer Vc as well
	(fig. 45)	Layer IIIa; same
	(fig. 47)	Layer IIa; described by Kenyon as "hard floor, cut by 125a," the first part of which seems unlikely; 25 cm thick[69]

Stratigraphic Correlations Relating to Rooms hk, hq, and kq

Table 20

VIII) until it reached the rising rock surface and continued to the north face of Wall 58[70] (fig. 44). Later, during BP V, workers set Wall 56 on a shoulder of declining rock located only ca. 2-2.5 m south of 153. Unfortunately, only deteriorated remains of 56 survived in the form of offset field stones and blocks beneath the north side of 125b in figs. 44 and 46. Floor levels associated with this wall virtually disappeared. When 56 weakened, or even collapsed (perhaps due to its precarious location on the edge of the rock shoulder exacerbated by mediocre construction techniques), the better-built 125b replaced it. After clearing away the BP V surface and penetrating the underlying BP IV floors and fills, the builders extended the northern face of this new structure over the edge of the rock shoulder for greater support, as best seen in fig. 44. They

---

[69]It is hard to imagine a 25 cm-thick floor level inside Room *kq* when the main, outdoor courtyard (which stretched across the entire central summit area south of this complex) maintained an average thickness of only 20 cm (see *AIS-I*, 75, and fig. 14).

[70]For the relative locations of Walls 56 and 58, see n. 54 above.

subsequently poured Layers V (*Btw TT2–TT3*; fig. 44), III (*125.144*; fig. 46), and IVa (*W of 124*; fig. 47) against the wall during the initial stages of backfilling and leveling in the area.

This proposed reconstruction of events again raises the question of whether levels thought to represent the earliest BP V surface in the Segments *Btw TT2–TT3* and *W of 124* (= Layers V in figs. 44-45 and IIIe in fig. 45, respectively)[71] actually depict a distinct floor level or the bottom striations of a later fill (see my discussion of *125.144* above). The deposit might well postdate BP V altogether. Since Layers V, IV, and IIIb (*Btw TT2–TT3*), together with Vc and IVc (*W of 124*), clearly run up against the two faces of Wall 125b,[72] the *terminus ante quem* of the pottery groups removed from these levels should help determine the construction date for that structure. With only one sherd (labeled "discard") published from Layer V in *Btw TT2–TT3* for all of PP 4-7, however, one cannot comment definitively on the date for these features.

In sum, I at least can suggest the stratigraphic correlations presented in Table 20, based on the sections reviewed above. Without further primary data, however, many of the proposed associations and questions raised above must remain open to discussion.

b. Room *j*

[i] 509.126

This segment of the excavations has received detailed coverage already in *AIS-I* and in Chapter I of the present work.[73] In those discussions, I plotted the precise location of this segment and noted the issue of whether it relates mainly to Room *j* or Room *l*. The field notes assign all pottery taken from this area to Room *j*, and the same holds true now for the flanged cooking pot rim from PP 5 seen in *SS III*, Fig. 8:7.

In my earlier treatment of the local stratigraphy relating to *509.126*, I summarized the basic information in Table 4 (p. 50; for the sake of convenience, I again present the sectional data in fig. 48). These data seem rather straightforward in their presentation of three successive floor levels laid across this segment. The earliest of these (Layer XI) exhibits a hard, white matrix and reflects Ahab's extension of the courtyard north of his father's Enclosure Wall 161. Though the outdoor courtyard now ran all the way to the grand Casemate System, I have already noted the continued absence of any significant building project in this area beyond the central summit.

---

[71] Since these layers seem to run against Walls 142 and 151 in fig. 45, it would help to know how long those features remained in use at the site, i.e., whether they lasted long enough to overlap the construction of 125b. With the information available to us at this time, however, it appears impossible to settle this issue.

[72] If, according to Kenyon's interpretation, Layer V belongs to BP V, then the lowest courses of stone in the wall depicted in fig. 44 must still comprise part of Wall 56, not 125b.

[73] See pp. 48-55 above and the reference to *AIS-I* on p. 48, n. 115.

PP 5: HOUSE FLOORS — STRATIGRAPHY

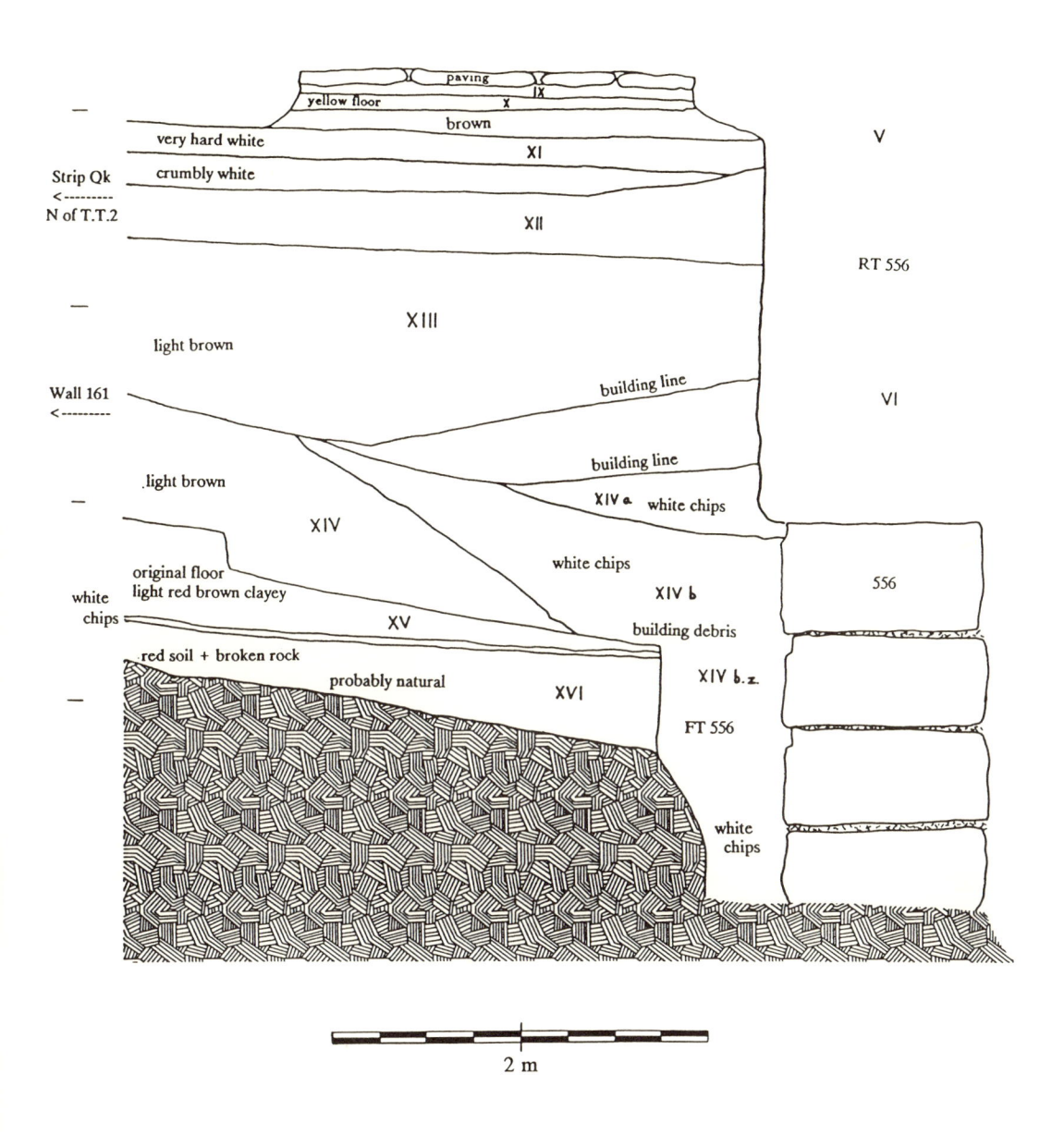

Segment 509.126
(formerly fig. 19)
<— S N —>
View toward West

fig. 48

Beneath a subfloor makeup of crumbly white material (unlabeled on fig. 48), one encounters deep deposits of fill, which the builders poured against the lower courses of the inner Casemate Wall 556. Though the lateral extent of these massive fillings remains undetermined, owing to the Joint Expedition's excavation method of trenching through a given area, one may assume that the deposits continued along the entire northern edge of the site, where the pitch of the declining rock was steepest (see *HES II*, Plan 13). One can assume from the sheer amount of soil required by this operation that the workers obtained at least some of the material from locations outside the main summit area. Layers XIII, XIVa, and XV yielded a mixed assemblage of Iron Age I-early Iron Age II pottery traditions. Though this portrait typifies assemblages removed from fill deposits, it nevertheless confirms the presence of a pre-Omride occupation at the site (see *AIS-I*).

Another surface of hard, yellowish soil (Layer X) and the softer, brownish makeup beneath it (unlabeled) ran just above the floor level used by Ahab. Layer X yielded the PP 4 bowl fragment published in *SS III*, Fig. 6:4, which fragment I placed in the very late ninth or possibly early eighth century BCE (a date that puts the construction of the floor itself sometime later).

Finally, I come to the light-colored, crumbly packing of Layer IX, which supports a series of flat, paving stones above it. Throughout the stratigraphy here, one has seen both thin strips (e.g., between Layers XV and XVI) and more substantial layers (XIVa-b; XII; sub-XI; and IX) of this loosely compacted, white material. This matrix surely derives from the limestone chips and small particle residue produced by extensive quarrying activities in the area from BP I on.[74] These deposits give the logical impression that the ancient workers not only artificially shaped the rock surface itself but that they mined and dressed the ashlar blocks used in the various building phases on-site as often as possible. These thin deposits of crumbly, white chippings from the extraction and shaping of the *nari* limestone ashlars[75] appear only in summit

---

[74] During the Harvard Excavations at Samaria, Reisner succeeded in identifying several of these quarries along the terraces south of the summit, in Reisner Plan 5, Grids H 15, H-J 18, J 13, and M 16. These areas revealed both single stones and groups of blocks left in various stages of removal by the ancient quarrymen (see *HES I*, 96, and *HES II*, Pl. XVb-c). One may compare the hallmark signs of ashlar extraction recorded in *HES I*, 96, Figs. 18-19 with identical bedrock cuts depicted at the southern end of Kenyon's Section GH (*SS I*, Pl. VII). On the north side of the summit, the rock surface that served as the footing for Omri's Enclosure Wall 161 and Ahab's Casemate Walls 556-564 undoubtedly received artificial shaping through mining activities in those areas (compare the squared or stepped look of the rock beneath these walls on all sections published by the Joint Expedition; see also my comments in Chapter III, pp. 255-57 regarding the topography of the bedrock visible in published Section CD).

[75] *Nari* consists in a hard caliche that forms over limestone or, more often, chalky rock, particularly in areas of Israel that receive 300-600 mm of rain annually. Though builders both before and after the Iron Age preferred the harder Turonian (*meleke* or *mizzi ḥelū*) or Cenomanian (*mizzi ahmar* or *mizzi yahudi*) limestones, construction crews working during the Iron Age consistently chose *nari* for their stone masonry (see Y. Shiloh and A. Horowitz, "Ashlar Quarries of the Iron Age in the Hill Country of Israel," *BASOR* 217 [1975], 37-48). Though the hill of Samaria is mostly formed of Senonian *ka'akula*, a "white indurated chalk with red hematitic stains" (see the reference to Gill below), the ashlars used in the

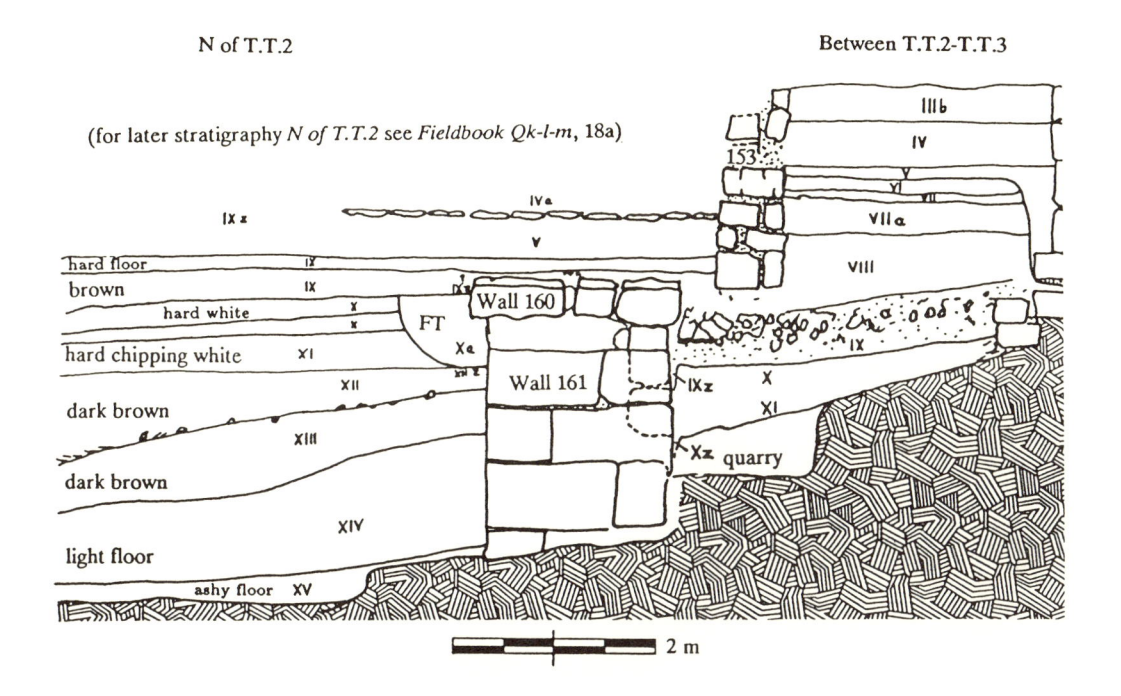

Segment North of Test Trench 2
(portion of former fig. 7)
<— S N —>
View toward West

fig. 49

levels associated with BP I-II; after that time, either buildings or deep fills covered the crown rock and forced the workers to mine their raw material from locations situated on the lower terraces or even somewhere off the site. The unwieldiness of the latter prospect also explains the heavy robbing activities in all subsequent building periods; simply stated, it proved easier to plunder the summit than to quarry at a distance and transport tons of blocks from the lode up the slopes to the construction site.

From the two latest floor levels recorded in this segment, one sees that the final report unfortunately included only a single fragment of pottery from each phase (Fig. 6:32 from Layer X, and Fig. 8:7 from Layer IX). As a result, the chronological framework for this segment must rely far more on intersegment stratigraphic correlations

---

Palace, Wall 161, Casemate System, Eastern Gate, and Terrace Wall (573?) consisted exclusively in *nari* limestone (Shiloh and Horowitz, 39, n. 8). For the age and description of these various stone formations in the hill country regions of Israel and Judah, see D. Gill, "The Geology of the City of David and its Ancient Subterranean Waterworks," pp. 1-28 in *City of David Excavations, 1978-1985, Vol. IV: Various Reports*, D. T. Ariel and A. de Groot, eds. Qedem 35 (Jerusalem: The Hebrew University, Institute of Archaeology, 1996), esp. pp. 2-4.

than on a fine-tuned ceramic analysis. Comparisons with deposits in Segment *N of TT2* prove especially helpful in this regard (see figs. 48-49; I have reversed the orientation of 40b to match that of 40a). Sectional data relating to this segment show the relevant layers as they run south and lie against the northern face of Wall 153,[76] while those from *509.126* trace their northern extension to the Casemate System. The intermediate floor level in *509.126* relates directly to Layer IX in *N of TT2*. Since the latter overran and sealed the remains of BP III Wall 160, I can suggest that these levels postdate the reign of Jehu and belong sometime in the first half of the eighth century BCE. Layer IX and the paving stones of *509.126* correspond, in turn, to the stones and Layer V in *N of TT2* and should date to the second half of the eighth century BCE or possibly later still. No ivory fragments or burned, sooty deposits appear in these levels.

c. Room *n* (Published Section CD)

[i] 502.503

Because of the detailed coverage given this segment in Chapter I above,[77] I need now deal only with the specific layer that yielded the single fragment of pottery published from this room with the PP 5 group (*SS III*, Fig. 8:6). Though Kenyon sought to identify this area, which lay between Wall 561 and the easternmost limit of the excavation at 665° E, as yet another enclosed "room," I have suggested that it may actually represent an open-air piazza east of the main courtyard area. Two phenomena jeopardize the chronological integrity of materials treated thus far from the space east of Wall 561: the presence of multiple robber trenches and deep fills that reportedly extended down to bedrock throughout most of the area. Two unpublished sketches of narrow test trenches cut into this area partially record the depositional history that rested beneath stone Pavings 548 and 549 (see Table 5 and figs. 22-23).

As recorded in Table 11 (p. 108), the PP 4 group was distributed among nearly all the thick fill deposits situated beneath Paving 548 (three fragments from Layer Xa, five from XIa, and two from XIa.b). A similar situation attended the levels below Paving 549 (two fragments from Layer XI, three from XIII), though no pottery came from the heavy, sooty Layer X found immediately beneath the stone floor. In other words, these fillings contributed nearly half of the total PP 4 ceramic assemblage presented in the final report. Now, in PP 5, only one of the eight published pieces—a cooking pot rim—comes from Layer IX, which apparently represents the earthen matrix packed between the stones of Paving 549. Kenyon departed from her usual method of dating floor levels by the pottery found beneath them[78] in deciding decided not to pub-

---

[76] See fig. 5; in her BP V phase plan, Kenyon renumbered this wall "145" (compare fig. 41).

[77] I described its horizontal location on pp. 58-61 and the vertical stratigraphy on pp. 62-66; plans are provided in figs. 20-21, while sectional data appear in figs. 22-23.

[78] As in the material published from Layer XI to help date the putative pavement labeled 549a.

lish any material from the sooty, subpaving makeup in Layer X below the stones of 549. The ceramic tradition reflected in the single sherd from Layer IX, then, must help us identify (if only tentatively, because of the limited evidence) a date for the functional life of this surface. Unfortunately, this fragment constitutes the only direct evidence now available that relates to this issue. The fact that the official report failed to include any pottery from layers on or above these stones ultimately forces us to rely on the PP 4 group—which came mostly from fill levels beneath Pavement 548 (10 of 15 pieces)—in hopes of establishing a *terminus post quem*, or construction date, for 549.

As I have shown, the preceding PP 4 assemblage consisted of two main vessel-types, which stemmed from markedly different periods of use. On the one hand, a large collection of cooking-pot rims dated from the late eleventh to the early or mid-ninth centuries BCE. The other group, a series of holemouth jar fragments, belonged at least in the latter part of the eighth century BCE. The stratigraphic distribution of these forms once again corroborates my understanding of these layers as substantial deposits of secondary fill material. For example, specimens from the "early group" often appeared in the latest local stratigraphy (e.g., the cooking pot rims in *SS III*, Fig. 6:29, 30, and 36, from Layer Xa immediately beneath Paving 548), while late ceramic forms turned up in stratigraphically earlier levels (e.g., the holemouth rims in Fig. 6:21 and 22, from Layers XIIa.b and XII, respectively). One should expect these sorts of inverted spatial and chronological relationships when dealing with deposits of backfill.[79] Despite multiple recording errors in the field notes that pertain to these layers and fragments, and despite the fact that much of the pottery carried the designation "discard," the latest ceramic styles in the overall group collected from beneath the stone pavings should provide a reasonable *terminus post quem* for the construction of those surfaces (even though the latest forms rested several layers beneath both the surfaces and the other levels that bore earlier forms). The general chronological range of the PP 4 group has already raised the question of whether or not these pavings (at least in "Room" *n*) truly belong in the Israelite period proper (i.e., pre-722 BCE). It seems possible that they reflect Assyrian activity.

2) Pottery Analysis

The corpus of pottery published in support of PP 5 should strike anyone as surprisingly small, particularly in view of Kenyon's belief that this phase represents the point at which Israelite control of the site finally succumbed to Assyrian domination in the wake of a massive conflagration. Most of the few pieces presented in the PP 5 group derived from one primary location in the collection of service rooms situated

---

[79] Given Reisner's excavation method in the Summit Strip system across the western sector of the compound (in which Summit Strip 1 served as the on-site dump for discarded soils and materials removed from Summit Strip 2, which in turn received debris from Summit Strip 3, and 3 from 4, and so on), reverse stratigraphy such as that just described would likely constitute a formidable problem to any attempted further excavation in that important area.

north of the main courtyard, namely, Room *hk*, which yielded five of the eight fragments published; Rooms *j* and *n* contributed one additional sherd each. Despite the pottery registry data that restrict all the finds to these particular rooms (as does *SS III* itself), however, one fragment likely derives from the better-built Room *hq*, which belonged to a new series of chambers attached to the central summit by means of the sturdy Wall 65. The overall group contained only jars and cooking pots, and the utilitarian nature of these vessels further substantiates my suggestion that these rooms functioned in a service-related capacity, probably that of food processing. The spatial distribution of the individual forms appears as follows:

	bowls	cooking pots	jars	holemouth jars	TOTAL
Room *hk*	-	-	3	2	5
Room *j*	-	1	-	-	1
Room *n*	-	1	-	-	1
Room *hq*	-	-	1	-	1
TOTAL	-	2	4	2	8

*Distribution of PP 5 Ceramic Forms
Published from House Floors (Rooms hk, j, n, hq)*

Table 21

Although but one[80] of the PP 5 entries derive from the same general areas that yielded the PP 4 group (Rooms *hk*, *j*, and *n*), the narrative in which Kenyon discusses the dating of BP V virtually ignores this pottery and instead rests its case on two different loci that remained stratigraphically disconnected from each other and from the main building activity on the summit: rubbish Pit *i* and a foundation deposit associated with a short section of Wall 573.[81] Yet Kenyon's official report on the pottery itself contained no actual PP 5 materials from either of these findspots; everything published from these areas appeared under PP 6.[82] I shall treat the assumptions made concerning these features in my Evaluation and Summary below and in Chapter III. Here I note only that the extremely abbreviated space devoted to the materials actually published

---

[80] Depending on how far south of Wall 125b the section in fig. 43 lay, all of the PP 5 fragments may come from areas associated with BP IV in the report. This possibility results from the fact that the northern half of *hq* overlay the southern portion of the former *h* and *k* spaces.

[81] See the discussion in *SS I*, 106-110.

[82] *SS III*, Fig. 9:1-18 (= massive leveling associated with Wall 573); Fig. 10:1-27 (= Pit *i*).

under "Period V" in the pottery volume (*SS III*) stands in curious discord with the historical significance attached to this Israelite–Assyrian transition in the earlier report on the stratigraphy (*SS I*).

a. Cooking Pots

This single vessel-type dominated the PP 4 assemblage published from the two clusters of rooms situated north of the main courtyard, particularly the putative "room" in the area labeled *n*. The PP 5 group adds two additional fragments to the collection, and the primary data that pertain to their individual findspots appears as follows:

SS III Published Figure	Registry No. (not marked for discard)	Provenance			
		Strip	Coordinates	Feature	Local Layer
8:6	Q 5215	Qn	502.503	Room *n*	IX
8:7	Q 5216	Qn	509.126	Room *j* (*n*?)	IX

Provenance Data:
PP5 Cooking Pots from Area Labeled "House Floors"

Table 22

Though the specific attributes of these two rims vary slightly, both belong to Kenyon's Class A category.[83] In her description of this group, Kenyon observed:

> In general pots in this class have a wide mouth and collared rim, the rim usually has a sharp edge and is slightly undercut; the body is shallow with the usual rounded base; the profile may be rounder ... or angular .... As far as our evidence goes these pots had no handles.... The type may be taken as present from Period I-VI, though it was not recorded from Period III.[84]

Rim No. 6 continues the elongated flanged tradition. It exhibits a flat outer face with a deep, rounded groove beneath the sharpened flange and a simple, rounded lip. A shallower groove appears below the lip on the inner face of the folded flange. This pot has an exceptionally wide mouth at a diameter of 36 cm, and its collar is so strongly inverted that the angle of its outer face exceeds even that of the vessel's upper

---

[83] *SS III*, 187-89; Fig. 30:10-14, with No. 14 (from E 207) showing the closest rim stance to the inverted PP 5 exemplars.

[84] *SS III*, 187 and 189.

shoulder. The last characteristic, more than any other, distinguishes this fragment from antecedent members of the same family that show only tendencies toward this form.[85] Even as late as the Iron I-Iron II transition, similar rims remain somewhat less inverted and often show a slight concavity on the outer face while developing the sharper flange that overhangs the upper shoulder wall.[86] Already by the tenth century BCE, some of these rims had a tool-cut groove placed in their outer faces[87] and, in this attribute, emerge as harbingers of the ninth-century notched-rim types. This basic style appears with subtle variations in form throughout the tenth and early ninth centuries BCE.[88] The strongly inverted rim also seems akin to those seen on some bag-shaped jars from the tenth century.[89]

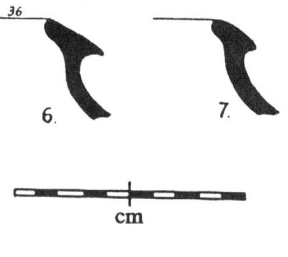

SS III, Fig. 8:6-7

Although the companion fragment in Fig. 8:7 reflects the same basic features as No. 6, it exhibits a shortened flange (or "collar," in Kenyon's terminology), which, in turn, somewhat diminishes the depth of the groove beneath it. In addition, the sidewalls of this exemplar appear thicker, and the outer face of the flange is not quite as flattened as that on No. 6. I believe the shorter rim suggests that this specimen slightly postdates the longer form in No. 6,[90] though earlier, antecedent forms are again available from the Iron I period.[91]

---

[85]As stratified examples of her Class A rim, Kenyon cites the following entries: ***PP I*** = Fig. 1:20, 22; ***PP II*** = Fig. 3:15-16; ***PP IV*** = Fig. 6:26-28; ***PP VI*** = Fig. 9:10 (see *SS III*, 189). Close scrutiny of these suggested parallels, however, sets Fig. 8:6-7 somewhat against the Class A group by revealing the uniquely inverted rim-form mode of these two fragments. *SS III*, Fig. 7:7 (PP 4), for example, seems a closer cousin to these PP 5 rims, except for its slightly concave outer face. Prototypes for this style may actually extend as far back as the Late Bronze Age II-early Iron I periods, as witnessed in *Hazor II*, Pl. CXIX:11 and *Taʿanach*, Fig. 17:11 (Period IB Cuneiform Tablet Building).

[86]Compare examples in *T. Qasîle* [2], Figs. 25:14 (Stratum XI) and 44:25 (Stratum X); *Gezer III*, Pls. 7:21 (Field VII, Stratum VIII); 8:21 (Field VII, Stratum VIIB); *Taʿanach*, Figs. 66:7, 14 (Period IIB); *T. Qiri*, Fig. 29:11 (Area A, Strata VIII-IX); *AS-IV*, Pl. LXIII:31 (Stratum IIa); *T. Keisan*, Pl. 63:7-9 (Niveau 9a-b); 77:1, 1a-c (with concave outer face), and 2d (with a more erect stance; all Niveau 9c).

[87]E.g., *T. Qasîle* [2], Fig. 45:14 (Stratum X); *T. Keisan*, Pl. 81:8 (Niveau 10-11), with a small notch trimmed near the lip.

[88]Compare *T. Qasîle* [2], Fig. 54:22 (Stratum VIII); *Beth-Shan*, James, Fig. 69:6 (Level IV).

[89]Compare examples from *Beth-Shan*, James, Figs. 40 and 64:4, 7 (all Upper Level V). Also some later, Iron II bowl forms seem to retain this basic rim style, while having their upper sidewalls curve in rather than out from the rim "collar" (*T. Keisan*, Pls. 30:3-4 [Niveau 4]; 41:3 [Niveau 5]).

[90]Though exact parallels remain difficult to locate, compare similar traditions in *AS-IV*, Pl. LXIII:39 (Stratum IIa-b), for a more angular version, with the upper sidewall dropping more vertically to the point of carination; *Hazor I*, Pl. XLVIII:1 (Stratum VIII), with concave outer face; *Hazor II*, Pl. LXVII:13 (Stratum VI), for a comparable later ninth- or early eighth-century krater rim.

[91]E.g., *Hazor III-IV*, Pl. CCI:12, 16 (Stratum XII); *Gezer III*, Pl. 5:25 (Stratum IXA) and 5 (Stratum IXB), both from Field VII; *AS-IV*, Pl. LXII:26 (Stratum III).

Holladay correctly recognized these rims as early ninth-century forms.[92] As such, they are hardly among the latest pottery associated with the so-called BP V House. In fact, their early date and stratigraphic contexts combine to demonstrate again the necessity of maintaining an open *terminus post quem* for secondary vs. primary deposits. Each of these fragments derives from such layers. First, No. 6 comes from Segment *502.503*, Layer IX, in Room *n*. As I have shown in fig. 22, this matrix represents the soil packed in around the stones of Pavement 549. Though I had hoped that No. 6, the single sherd published from this level, would assist me in determining more precisely the date of this floor level, it appears instead that it speaks only to the secondary nature of the packing used by the ancient workers. A similar situation attends the findspot for No. 7, though this fragment comes from Room *j*. As shown in fig. 48, Layer IX of Segment *509.126* also relates to a late, stone paving that extended as far north as the inner Casemate Wall 556 (compare the plan in fig. 41). Here, however, the layer in question does not comprise part of the actual floor packing, but rather the loosely concentrated, imported makeup that lay beneath the stones.

From the stratigraphic record alone, one sees that the functional life of these stone surfaces cannot date as early as the ninth century BCE. The correlations drawn between these areas and other, somewhat better-documented segments have confirmed this much. Unfortunately, the only two PP 5 fragments published from Rooms *j* and *n* (*SS III*, Fig. 8:6-7) represent simply derived elements in the makeup of late Iron II floor levels and possess virtually no chronological value at all for one's historical reconstruction. As I shall demonstrate, these two stray sherds constitute the only "early" ceramic traditions in the PP 5 group. Because of their respective contexts, they certainly cannot settle the question of whether the construction of the overriding stone floors occurred prior to or following the events of 722/21 BCE. Stratigraphic analysis, however, places them in the late eighth or even the seventh century BCE.

b. Jars

SS III Published Figure	Registry No. (none marked for discard)	Strip	Coordinates	Feature	Local Layer
8:1	Q 2535	Qk	West of 124	Room *hk?/hq*	VIII
8:2	QX 104	Q(x)-n	125.144	Room *hk*	III
8:5	QX 91	Q(x)-n	125.144	Room *hk*	III
8:8	QX 97	Q(x)-n	125.144	Room *hk*	IIIo

Provenance Data:
PP5 Jars from Area Labeled "House Floors"
Table 23

---

[92]Holladay, 131.

The final pottery report presented five fragments presumed to have derived from jars in its PP 5 repertoire (*SS III*, Fig. 8:1-5). This group incorporated two holemouth rims (Nos. 3-4), which I shall treat separately in the following section. In addition to the remaining three items, I include here another, rather small rim sherd which seems likely to belong to a jar form (Fig. 8:8), though Kenyon listed this piece as a cooking pot rim. The specific findspots for this collection appear in Table 23 above (see also Appendix A). Please note that I have corrected both the published registry number and, by extension, the line of provenance data ascribed to entry No. 5.[93]

The near-whole jar in Fig. 8:1 exhibits an elongated, bag-shaped body, uniform sidewalls that narrow toward high shoulders, two handles drawn from shoulder to upper body, a short neck with lower ridge, and a simple, rounded rim form that splays slightly outward.[94] The unusual body-form mode, with its widest diameter coming near the rounded base of the vessel, constitutes the most diagnostic feature of this jar. It also sets this piece apart from virtually every other style of jar that dates to the 733-722 BCE horizon, all of which tend to taper from shoulder to base rather than vice versa.[95] Kenyon described this entry rather tersely as a "small storage jar, imperfect, brownish ware," and assigned its findspot to Room *hk*.[96] While ancestral members of this jar class, either with or without handles, may occur as early as the late tenth-early ninth centuries,[97] the tradition seems more directly related to the many oval-shaped or archaized-"hippo" style store jars of the eighth century BCE.[98] The overall style of this vessel,

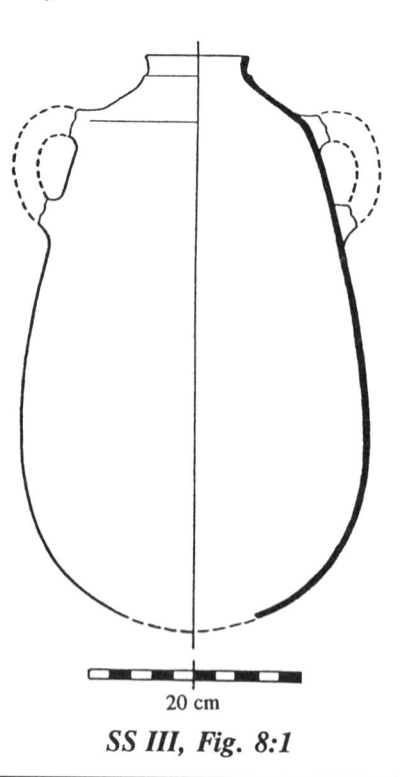

SS III, Fig. 8:1

---

[93]In her published report, Kenyon transposed the registry numbers cited for items 4 and 5 in Fig. 8. Since the pottery annotations in *SS III* failed to provide any provenance data beyond the registry number, this error remained undetected until my study of Grace Crowfoot's original stratification cards in London. These more primary records show that Fig. 8:4 actually received the registration number Q 2327 and that it derived from the segment called *E Strip, Btw TT2-TT3*. Entry No. 5, on the other hand, was registered as QX 91 and came from Segment *125.144*.

[94]Compare *SS III*, Fig. 21:2, from S Tombs 103.1.

[95]See Holladay's corpus of 733-722 BCE forms in *Holladay*, Figs. 76-78.

[96]*SS III*, 118.

[97]Compare *Hazor III-IV*, Pls. CCXI:3 (Strata X-IX); CCXIX:23 (Stratum VI), without handles.

[98]*Gezer III*, Pl. 18:4 (oval) and 5 ("hippo") (Stratum VIA). Compare *Megiddo I*, Pl. 20:120-21, and p. 168 § 50, for possible historical antecedents. Note that although Gitin classified the Gezer example in Pl. 18:5 as a hippo jar, he correctly recognized it as "an uncommon hybrid form" whose related (actually

however, seems clearly to postdate all these examples. In his report from Tell en-Naṣbeh, Wampler recognized that the chronologically significant bag-shaped body does not appear there prior to the seventh century BCE and that its floruit may fall slightly later still.[99] Similar body forms, with variant rim styles, from seventh- and sixth-century contexts at Tell en-Naṣbeh,[100] Lachish,[101] and Tell Jemmeh[102] seem to confirm this judgment.[103] Following this period, the form seems to have enjoyed a fairly long, albeit nuanced, history.[104] The fact that at Tell en-Naṣbeh whole or near-whole examples of this jar appeared only in cistern deposits dating from 750 to 587/586 BCE[105] suggests that this jar functioned primarily in the collection and transportation of water.[106] Unlike the broader shoulders and narrower base of other jars, the wider, rounded base and lower center of gravity claimed by this tradition provided greater comfort and better balance when carrying this style jar on one's head.

Though Kenyon assigned the findspot for this jar to Room *hk*, along with most of the other members of the PP 5 group, my stratigraphic analysis has demonstrated that it derives instead from Room *hq* to the south. The section in fig. 43 shows further that it came from a substantial fill deposit that lay directly on the bedrock surface (Segment *W of 124*, Layer VIII). Concerning this exact area, the final report states that, south of Wall 56 (see fig. 41),

> the earlier floors were cleared to rock, and the lowest existing floor sealed both

---

ancestral) forms reveal a "limited popularity and distribution" (*Gezer III*, 122). Alexandre's subsequent study of various storage jar traditions in the north confirmed these intuitive comments (see nn. 287, 290, 319, and 459 in Chapter I). The last work has also shown that the *Megiddo I* report incorrectly subsumed all ridge-necked jars under the "hippo" category.

[99] *TN II*, 9-10.

[100] *TN II*, Pls. 14:239; 17:295; 18:303, 311-312; probably also 13:233 and 15:256. Later exemplars of this basic form often display horizontally-rilled bodies, as in Pls. 21:352 and 22:360, while Pl. 22:356 shows a series of smooth interior grooves. According to the report, the earliest of these jars derives from the latter half of the seventh century BCE.

[101] *Lachish III*, Pl. 94:481 (with a more pronounced outer thickening of the rim and a slightly less elongated body).

[102] *Gerar*, Pl. 42:13-15. (For the identification of Tell Jemmeh with ancient Yurza and not Gerar, see Chapter IV, 399, n. 146.)

[103] Though only rim fragments appear in his report, see also Gitin's dating of his jar Type 17, which displays a sack-shaped body with everted rim and medium high neck (*Gezer III*, Pl. 26:4-5 = Stratum VA, seventh-sixth centuries BCE).

[104] For late, bag-shaped body forms on jars from the Jezreel Valley area, see *T. Yoqneʿam* [3], Fig. 8:1 (ribbed) and 2 (Hellenistic period). For the late history of this general vessel-type, see Petrie's comments in *Gerar*, 19.

[105] *TN II*, 9.

[106] In this vein, it likely represents the primary ancestor of the Hellenistic water jars presented in *HES I*, 298, fig. 175.

the foundation offset of 56 and the broken top of the Periods III and IV wall 58.[107]

Judging from fig. 43, this "lowest existing floor" must comprise part of Layer VI (situated above VIII) or else it does not appear in the drawing at all. In any event, if this new surface seals the area, as Kenyon suggests, it seems unlikely that the jar in Fig. 8:1 represents an intrusion into the fill of Layer VIII. One must, therefore, lower the date of deposition for this subfloor fill to the seventh century BCE and, in turn, the *terminus post quem* (or construction date) of the floor above it to a time well after the Assyrian occupation of Samaria.[108]

The handle and shoulder fragment in entry No. 2 comes from Layer III of Segment *125.144*, which does, in fact, belong to Room *hk*. The sidewall on this vessel appears considerably thicker and more uneven than on the previous jar, and Kenyon described the handle as "well-made" and "oval in section."[109] The lower handle approaches the sidewall in a graceful, downward curve, while the upper part goes more directly into the body above the line of the shoulder break. These attributes, coupled with the appreciable size of the apparently functional handle, the drab-to-red vs. hard-fired, reddish-yellow ware, and the slightly less-than-angular shoulder, suggest that this fragment belongs with an oval or ovoid store jar, not a so-called sausage jar (see my description of the latter on pp. 161-64 above). The curvature of the sidewall, which would place the vessel's widest diameter at its midsection or lower, further supports this identification. The fact that the shoulder is high and pronounced yet not sharply angular combines with the other characteristics of this fragment to argue for a date in the mid-to-late eighth century BCE. Morphological comparisons at such sites as Hazor and Gezer[110] confirm this dating. Still, it seems clear that the form continued into seventh-century levels, when the rim becomes somewhat shortened, the body becomes more squat, and the shoulder moves slightly higher, as attested in examples from Megiddo,[111]

SS III, Fig. 8:2

---

[107] *SS I*, 106. (This quotation completes that begun in n. 68 above.) Recall my suggestion that the offset reflects the construction of two distinct walls, 56 + 125b, not a mere foundation platform for Wall 56.

[108] See Holladay's discussion of the creation and nature of the "smaller sherds" that often emerge from substantial deposits of imported fills (*Holladay*, 27, n. 57). The principle he espouses there may hold true generally. Yet contra his statement that "it would be indeed remarkable if S.S. III fig. 8:1 were from an imported fill!," this nearly complete jar derived from just such a secondary context, as now confirmed through my presentation of previously unpublished sectional data.

[109] *SS III*, 118.

[110] *Hazor III-IV*, Pls. CLXXXVI:14 (Stratum VI); CCXXIX:5 (Stratum VA); *Gezer II*, Pl. 33:3 (Field II, Strata 6A-5B/A); see the lowered dating of 6A on p. 97, n. 348 above.

[111] *Megiddo I*, Pl. 15:74 (Strata III-II) and 76 (Strata IV-II).

PP 5: HOUSE FLOORS — POTTERY

Lachish,[112] Bethel,[113] Tell Beit Mirsim,[114] Ashdod,[115] and so on.

Though close parallels for this form remained rather scare at the publication of *Megiddo I*, the report notes that "as yet unpublished evidence from Samaria, where a number of rims and shoulder fragments of hippo jars have been found, indicates a MI distribution for these vessels over the north of Palestine at least."[116] Subsequent evidence seems to confirm this initial reading (though the jars involved are not likely true hippo forms; see n. 98 above) and allows us to place this fragment in the late eighth (or possibly even early seventh) century BCE. Unfortunately, the stratigraphic context that yielded this sherd (Segment *125.144*, Layer III) leaves us unable to refine this suggested chronological range due to the fact that it constitutes another secondary fill deposit (compare figs. 8 and 10). That this filling runs directly against the face of Wall 125b, however, combines with other evidence cited in this study to suggest once again a date sometime in the seventh century for this building activity and, very likely, for the robbing of the BP IV-V Walls 142 and 151.

The neck- and rim-form modes seen on No. 5[117] closely resemble those already discussed at length in my treatment of *SS III*, Fig. 6:12 from the PP 4 ceramic group. (I need not repeat the full discussion and numerous parallels cited there.) The tall, straight neck with splayed upper wall and rim, the hard, thin ware, and the diameter of the mouth opening (9 cm) clearly justify a comparison of this piece with the PP 4 exemplar taken from Pit *i*. The nearest morphological ancestors within local ceramic traditions once again seem to hark back to various styles of the ovoid store jar used from the late tenth through the eighth centuries BCE.[118] But the ware appears much thicker on these vessel-types, and they usually do not exhibit a full, light-colored slip as on this PP 5 rim.[119] Such features indicate a

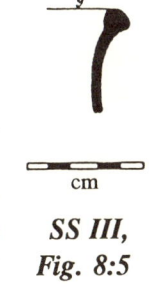

SS III, Fig. 8:5

---

[112]*Lachish III*, Pl. 94:469, 472. Note also that the position of the fingerholes in the handles (especially of 472) match those on the Samaria example. Tufnell recorded that Type 472 seemed confined to Level III but that Type 469 continued into Level II. The later forms exhibit a more pointed base, which has obviously not survived on the Samaria fragment.

[113]*Bethel*, Pl. 66:13 (sixth century BCE).

[114]*TBM I*, Pl. 53:2, 5 (Stratum A). See also pp. 79-80, § 104.

[115]*Ashdod II-III*, Figs. 6:1 (Area A, Str. 6); 48:4 (D; 3b); 57:6, 7 (D; 2-1); 95:1-7 (K; 6-5).

[116]*Megiddo I*, 167, § 42.

[117]In Appendix A, I have indicated some uncertainty regarding the registry number for this fragment. Judging from the private notes and pottery registries, the published report seems to have transposed the numbers for 8:4 and 8:5, which should appear as Q 2327 and Qx 91, respectively. Otherwise, the actual description of each item remains correct in the official report, i.e., only the registry numbers are reversed.

[118]See, for example, *Megiddo I*, Pl. 22:130 (V); *Hazor III-IV*, Pls. CCXVI:1 (Stratum VI); CCXXIX:1 (Stratum VA); *Hazor II*, Pl. LXXV:13 (Stratum V), also with grey ware but no slip.

[119]The jar just cited from Megiddo displays traces of a dark red wash on its exterior surface. The Hazor jars generally show a brownish ware, often with multicolored, gritty inclusions.

later date for this rim; in fact, Kenyon herself commented on the general lateness of the ware. I believe, therefore, that the collective attributes witnessed on this fragment reflect the influence of Assyrian designs current in the late eighth and the seventh centuries and manifested in the conical goblets and jars yielded by other sites, such as Tell 'Amal,[120] Tell Keisan,[121] and Tell en-Naṣbeh,[122] all of which show varying degrees of Assyrian contact but not all of which suffered destruction by the Assyrians.[123] In this vein, I may point out that, to date, scholars have discussed Assyrian cultural and artistic influence at Samaria mainly in relation to the ivories, not with regard to the pottery. That the excavation report rarely attempts to identify Assyrianizing motifs among the latter facies of culture seems quite inexplicable given the strong presence and ultimate control of the site and region that most historical reconstructions ascribe to this imperial power. While one perhaps should not expect to find a strong foreign influence in the design of basic, utilitarian goods (e.g., cooking pots), the more unique forms such as these conical jars and various classes of bowls (including *SS III*, Fig. 6:5 = PP 4; 10:8-10 = PP 6) often bear witness to the transfer of ideas and technologies (in this case, for the design and manufacture of locally-made ceramic imitations) as well as to the actual exchange of finished pottery or the commodities contained therein.

The lack of a complete form in entry No. 8 hampers a full typology for this piece. Kenyon believed this neckless, squat rim belongs to a certain style of cooking pot. Yet her comparisons to forms in *SS III*, Figs. 11:32 (PP 7) and 30:26 (nonstratified) are not apt from a morphological point of view, though the three fragments exhibit the same general grey ware with shining calcite grits. The comparison to the still later, globular cooking pot in Fig. 12:10 (PP 8) proves a much better one, and while this PP 5 rim may stem from that type of vessel, it may just as easily belong to a late Iron II family of jars. Either way, this sherd seems at home in the very late eighth or seventh century BCE. Good parallels from the seventh century appear in both Israel[124]

SS III, Fig. 8:8

---

[120]See p. 91, n. 310 for references.

[121]*T. Keisan*, Pl. 37:10, 10a-c (Niveau 5 = 720-650 BCE).

[122]*TN II*, Pl. 27:448. See also *TN—Cistern*, Fig. 2:x231 (Cistern 370, dated to "the latter half of the Middle Iron Age with some extension into the sixth century B.C." [p. 26], i.e., 700-586 BCE [p. 31]).

[123]E.g., Tell en-Naṣbeh reveals no signs of destruction during the Iron II period; still, excavators have recovered 87 *LMLK* impressions from this site, and I believe they relate directly to an anticipated Assyrian encroachment in the late eighth century BCE.

[124]*T. Keisan*, Pls. 25:2-3; 26:2-3; 27:7, 9-9a (all Niveau 4); *Megiddo I*, Pl. 13:69 (Strata IV-II). At Tell Qiri in the Jezreel Valley, the excavators commented that the low-necked storage jar tradition there showed an apparent association with other sausage-shaped and sharp-shouldered jar forms; *T. Qiri*, Fig. 9:8 (Area D, Stratum VI); 36:3; p. 144. See also *Hazor II*, Pl. LXXV:15 (Stratum V), from Locus 144, which yielded a mixture of late eighth- and seventh-century pottery; Gitin recognizes that item No. 15 belongs to a post-eighth-century tradition (*Gezer III*, 124).

and Judah[125] and also at various coastal sites, such as Tell Qasîle[126] and Ashdod.[127] These comparisons suggest that this piece may well belong to a sausage jar or to a late Iron II store jar with a stump base; the apparently drooping shoulder on the Samaria fragment possibly favors the latter. While the ware of entry No. 2 differs from that seen in this fragment, the morphology of the two items seems quite compatible. Variations on this form continue into the Persian and Hellenistic periods as well.[128] I acknowledge, however, that, unlike the grey ware of No. 8, the fabric used in most of these jar parallels ranges from a brownish color to various shades of red.

Whether a remnant from a jar or cooking pot, then, this fragment comes from the same basic stratigraphic context that yielded other late Iron II pieces, including those in Fig. 8:2-4. My earlier stratigraphic analysis showed that Layer IIIo in Segment *125.144* comprised part of a heavy fill layer poured over the BP V floor in that area. The overall context failed to produce satisfactory evidence to confirm a massive destruction of this area. Unfortunately, the report did not include any pottery from the later leveling, which incorporated a sooty fill (Layer IIIa, fig. 8). But even if this blackish matrix derived from either local or wholesale destruction, not from the multiple *tabunîm* found in the general area, one must reckon with the fact that a substantial deposit of pure fill separated the BP V floor from the sooty soil. Moreover, a heavy destruction would have produced chunks of charred debris, not just sooty soil. Yet in this area, the report uses the latter description exclusively.

c. Holemouth Jars

Provenance data for the two holemouth rim fragments not discussed in the preceding section appear in Table 24 below. Once again I refer the reader to n. 93 for stratigraphic information regarding entry No. 4.

Chronologically speaking, the ceramic traditions reflected in these holemouth rims follow both the horizontal, flattened forms (*SS III*, Fig. 6:20-23) and the single-grooved style (Fig. 6:19, 24) seen already in BP IV. Holladay notes that the BP V exemplars "are ubiquitous in seventh century deposits."[129] Specimen No. 3 displays an open,[130] 32 cm-wide mouth. Though the inside lip of its rim maintains a flat, horizon-

---

[125] *TBM I*, Pl. 53:2 (Stratum A); A. Mazar, "Iron Age Fortresses in the Judaean Hills," *PEQ* (1982), Fig. 14:19; *Lachish V*, Pl. 49:18-19 (Level II); compare *Gezer III*, Pl. 26:19 (Jar Type 5C; Field VII, Stratum VA).

[126] *T. Qasîle* [2], Fig. 56:18-20 (Stratum VII).

[127] *Ashdod II-III*, Fig. 57:6-7 (D; 2-1); compare the forms cited in n. 115 for *SS III*, Fig. 8:2.

[128] Compare *Taʿanach*, Figs. 80:5 (Period VIA); 83:2 (Period VIB); *T. Keisan*, Pl. 7:3a (Niveau 2); *Gezer III*, Pl. 28:11-12 (Jar Types 119B and 122A; Field VII, Stratum IV).

[129] Holladay, 131, n. 119.

[130] For a definition of "open" vs. "closed," see p. 104, n. 393 in Chapter I.

SS III Published Figure	Registry No. (* = marked for discard)	Provenance			
		Strip	Coordinates	Feature	Local Layer
8:3	QX 90	Q(x)-n	125.144	Room *hk*	IIIo (s?)
8:4	*Q 2327(?)	Qk	E Str, Btw TT2-TT3	Room *hk*	V

Provenance Data:
PP5 Holemouth Jars from Area Labeled "House Floors"

Table 24

tal position similar to its immediate predecessors, the outer portion develops a thickened, slightly molded triangular ledge. A rim from a late seventh-century context at Tell Qasîle compares favorably to this exterior part of this fragment, though its inside section tips downward slightly.[131] Other, albeit nuanced, versions of this thickened rim with an outside ledge appear at Tell en-Naṣbeh[132] and Beth-Shemesh.[133]

The double-grooved (triple-ridged) rim presented in Fig. 8:4 emerges as the most typical style of seventh-century BCE holemouth rims. Though the incipient form may appear as early as the mid-eighth century,[134] other parallels from sites such as Megiddo,[135] Tell en-Naṣbeh,[136] Gezer,[137] Lachish,[138] Tell Beit Mirsim,[139] and Beersheba[140] confirm that the seventh-to-early sixth centuries cover the primary lifespan for

---

[131] *T. Qasîle* [2], Fig. 57:15 (Stratum VII).

[132] *TN II*, Pls. 25:413, 415, 418, 420; 26:424.

[133] *AS II*, Pl. XXXIV:10, 17, 20. *AS IV*, Pl. LXV:22 (Stratum IIb) may represent an antecedent form. See also the rim from Beth-Shemesh IIc reviewed in *M. & Y. Aharoni*, Fig. 5:8.

[134] See *Gezer III*, Pl. 16:6 (Field VII, Stratum VIA). These sidewalls exhibit a more vertical stance than the later example from Samaria (see below).

[135] *Megiddo I*, Pl. 11:57 (Strata IV-I).

[136] *TN II*, Pl. 23:383-84; see p. 40, § 60 for a dating of these rims to the seventh and sixth centuries BCE. Compare *TN—Cistern*, Fig. 2:x92, x238 (from Cistern 370, also dated to this same time period; pp. 26 and 31).

[137] *Gezer III*, Pl. 23:3 (Field VII, Stratum VB/VA).

[138] *Lachish III*, Pl. 90:392, belonging to Tufnell's Class S.12. This class appeared near the end of city Level III and in Level II, when it succeeded the flattened, horizontal, nonridged type attested only in Level III (e.g., *SS III*, Fig. 6:20; *Lachish III, Text*, 318). For other examples of rims with two-to-three ridges, see *Lachish III*, Pl. 97:546-47, 549-51, 553, and 555 (547, 553, and 555 provide the best rim-to-sidewall parallels for the Samaria fragment).

[139] *TBM I*, Pl. 52:1 (where the sidewall drops directly beneath the ridged rim) and 7 (Stratum A).

[140] *Beersheba I*, Fig. 58:26 (Stratum II) = *M. & Y. Aharoni*, Fig. 4:8.

this style. In contrast to fragment No. 3, whose sidewalls drop down more directly from the rim, the walls of this jar bulge out from the rim, producing a more barrel-shaped body. Recently published vessels from Lachish Level II not only show good rim and sidewall parallels for this piece but also confirm that this tradition sometimes displays handles attached to the upper wall just below the rim and a ring base rather than a simple, round one.[141] As many of my citations demonstrate, the rim also often includes an outer ridge, which results in a small, bevelled ledge around the rim. In most of these instances, the rim itself maintains a more obliquely inverted posture.[142]

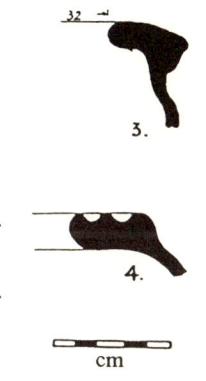

SS III, Fig. 8:3-4

The first of the holemouth rims (No. 3) published from PP 5 came from the same deposit that produced the jar fragment in entry No. 8, i.e., Segment *125.144*, Layer IIIo. Though this level shows a deposit of secondary fill, I have already shown that it ran against the face of Wall 125b (fig. 10) and therefore very likely belongs in the seventh century BCE (its deposition at least clearly postdates the BP V layers).

Now that I have corrected errors relating to the registry numbers assigned to Fig. 8:4-5 (n. 93), one sees that the second holemouth rim came from Layer V in the Segment *Btw TT2-TT3*, situated in the eastern half of Room *hk* (fig. 41). Kenyon identified this level as a post-BP IV floor and assigned it to her "Period V." I, however, would leave open the possibility that this deposit (whether an actual floor or simply compacted fill) dates to a slightly later time contemporary with the construction of Wall 125b in the seventh century BCE. This suggestion is based on the following observations (in addition to the results of my ceramic analysis): Layer V lies very near the elevation at which the BP IV-V Walls 153/145 (fig. 7) and 142-151 (fig. 8) suffered from plundering activities; and the field sections maintain no distinction between this putative floor and the foundation trench fill poured against the north face of Wall 125b (fig. 7). These facts may indicate that the entire layer represents only construction and leveling operations and not a living surface. The apparent cutting of this level (fig. 13) by Robber Trench 153 indicates that the dismantling of this feature occurred shortly after the construction of 125b. In short, I believe that sometime during the early-to-mid-seventh century BCE, the section of BP V Wall 56, which originally formed the northern boundary of Rooms *hq* and *kq* (fig. 41), fell into disrepair (whether or not by intentional destruction). Wall 125b represents the subsequent rebuild of this structure. These repairs also at least partially renovated the former service area to the north by

---

[141]*Lachish*—Zimhoni, Figs. 31:5; 32:2 (Level II); see the comments on p. 44. Compare *Lachish III*, Pl. 95:492. Though handles also sometimes occur on vessels that bear the plain rim, Tufnell acknowledges that the specimens with ridged rims and handles succeed that group and belong mainly in the seventh and early sixth centuries BCE (*Lachish III, Text*, 317). For other handles with a ridged rim but somewhat less barrel-shaped body, see *TN II*, Pl. 66:1492.

[142]E.g., *T. Qasîle* [2], Fig. 57:7-13 (Stratum VII).

removing Walls 151, 153, and 142 (listed west to east). The truncation of the upper courses of Pit *i* probably also occurred at this time. Thus it remains questionable whether Layer V in *Btw TT2–TT3* actually depicts a surface and whether it belongs in BP V. Rather, it seems contemporary with the building of Wall 125b. No clear signs remain of a heavy conflagration associated with any of these alterations. The earliest fragments of ivory appear two levels (both artificially deposited) above Layer V, in Layer III (compare Layer IVc in *W of 124*, fig. 7).

3) Evaluation and Summary

The overall distribution of the published PP 5 ceramic items recovered primarily from Room *hk* but also from Rooms *hq, j,* and *n* appears in Table 25. Within this small assemblage, only the two cooking-pot rims constitute early (i.e., ninth-century BCE) pieces. Both derive from secondarily deposited levels in Rooms *j* (Fig. 8:7) and *n*

	bowls	cooking pots	jars	holemouth jars	TOTAL
Room *hk*					
125.144					
III	-	-	1	1	2
IIIo	-	-	1	1	2
V	-	-	1	-	1
Room *j*					
509.126					
IX	-	1	-	-	1
Room *n*					
502.503					
IX	-	1	-	-	1
Room *hq*					
West of 124					
VIII	-	-	1	-	1
TOTAL	-	2	4	2	8

*Distribution of PP 5 Ceramic Forms
in Local Stratigraphy of House Floors (Rooms hk, j, n, hq)*

Table 25

(Fig. 8:6); together, these sherds constitute the only fragments published from those areas. Unfortunately, such remains serve only to remind us of the open *terminus post quem* that deposits of this nature must claim. In the case at hand, they merely indicate that the construction date(s) of the pavings in the rooms mentioned occurred sometime after the first half of the ninth century BCE. Since this ceramic evidence cannot help in further refining the historical chronology for this area, one must rely more on available stratigraphic clues.

The other stratified PP 5 evidence includes a small collection of jar fragments that clearly belong in the seventh century BCE or slightly later. Perhaps the most chronologically important piece among this lot is the near-whole entry in *SS III*, Fig. 8:1. Yet this relatively well-preserved vessel also came from a level of secondary fill (see n. 108). Moreover, the combined results of my stratigraphic and ceramic analyses have shown that the oldest surviving floor level in Room *hq* (south of 56/125b) dates to the seventh century BCE at the earliest.

Before presenting my concluding remarks for BP V, I can draw several important, preliminary observations from the investigation thus far. First, from the depositional history and material culture included in the published reports, it appears that both the events near the close of the Syro-Ephraimite conflict (ca. 732 BCE, when Tiglath-pileser III deposed Pekah as Israelite king and installed Hoshea as puppet king) and in 722/721 BCE (when Shalmaneser V and Sargon II established full Assyrian control over the capital itself) transpired with minimal destruction of Samaria. If this is *not* true, then the evidence for a wholesale conflagration of the main courtyard and service area north of the courtyard remains obscured in records never published and no longer available.

Second, as Forsberg noted, the final report holds that the pottery of PP 5 "could not be distinguished from that of the Period VI deposits."[143] I can now add to this observation the fact that Kenyon elsewhere indicated that "the pottery of Period IV can only be differentiated from that of Period VI by the types of wares [i.e., forms] which it does not include, so that when both are present, that of Period VI cannot be separated out."[144] Ultimately, then, one recognizes that virtually none of the pottery encountered and published after PP 3 proves adequate for phasing either archaeological or historical events much beyond the close of the ninth century BCE. My detailed investigation into the depositional history and ceramic traditions assigned to BP V have attempted to overcome this dilemma by bringing to the discussion previously unpublished sectional data that relate to the local stratigraphy and by subsequently identifying the most chronologically valuable findspots and pottery fragments situated within that stratigraphy.

Third, the fact that previous ceramic and historical studies have not enjoyed full access to these data has forced a tentative handling of the facts. For example, I have noted that Holladay's study introduces PP 5 with the claim that "absolute dates" are attainable for that period.[145] But he quickly scales back his optimism by promising

---

[143] *Forsberg*, 20. The author refers here to comments made in *SS I*, 108.

[144] *SS III*, 120.

[145] *Holladay*, 60.

only a "reasonably secure date" for this phase.[146] Still later, he must rather grimly state:

> Although accepted in Chapter II as a chronologically meaningful and stratigraphically secure ceramic group, dating down to ca. 735 B.C., subsequent comparison with the abundant 733-722 B.C. Horizon materials tends to cast doubt upon the integrity of at least one of these loci.[147]

The locus in question was Room *hk*, which produced the greatest share—62.5 %—of the entire PP 5 group. Thus Holladay's ceramic studies alone forced him ultimately to conclude that if several of the putative PP 5 items in fact belong to the period leading up to the Assyrian occupation of the site, then they must "witness the only pre-722 B.C. appearance of certain vessel ware-form modes,"[148] a prospect he holds as unlikely.[149] Moreover, he had no way to inform his comparative pottery analysis with precise data pertaining to the findspots for the individual pieces he considered. Thus he apparently was unaware of the stratigraphic relationship between Walls 56 and 125b, or between either of those features and the floors of BP V, or that at least the one near-whole vessel (Fig. 8:1) came from the better-built Room *hq* and not from the service alcove in *hk*, etc. Still, he astutely recognized that, on the whole, the materials of the PP 5 published corpus "fly in the face of all other stratigraphically significant data from the third quarter of the eighth century."[150] I believe my work confirms those observations stratigraphically as well as through additional ceramic analysis and thereby raises the need for a critical reassessment of the declining years of Israelite control over the city of Samaria.

Pottery Period 5: Conclusions

In her popular account of the royal cities in ancient Israel, Kenyon draws on the biblical text in 2 Kgs 17:23-24 to describe the "wholesale transference of populations [that] was basic to Assyrian policy"[151] during the late eighth century BCE. She goes on to say that, based on her excavations at Samaria,[152] "the archaeological record is equally eloquent of the *complete destruction* of the capital city."[153] Because, according

---

[146] Holladay, 65.

[147] Holladay, 131.

[148] Holladay, 131.

[149] Holladay, 131, n. 119.

[150] Holladay, 131.

[151] K. Kenyon, *Royal Cities of the Old Testament* (New York: Schocken, 1971), 132 (hereafter *RCOT*).

[152] See *SS III*, 199, for her description of an "extensive destruction" of the city by Sargon II.

[153] Kenyon, *RCOT*, 133 (emphasis added).

to the final report, the buildings presented in fig. 41 depict "the latest ones of the Israelite period on the north side of the summit,"[154] these structures should bear the traces of this pervasive Assyrian assault. Yet close examination of the local stratigraphy and published finds associated with these rooms raises important new questions regarding the nature of the transfer of civil authority from Israelite to Assyrian leadership.

Given the complexities of the depositional history encountered by the Joint Expedition in the area north of the main courtyard, challenges to achieving a tenable reconstruction of events surrounding this imperial takeover arose almost immediately. The excavation report indicates that the floor levels associated with the rooms in this area remained intact only north of Wall 65. Leveling operations for a thick layer of "chocolate" soil, dated to the sixth or fifth century BCE, had subsequently destroyed both the BP V floors and most earlier ones south of 65.[155] According to the final report, a considerable deposit of destruction debris overlay the few surviving floors. Thus far, however, this claim remains unsubstantiated. Further, according to Kenyon's own published statements, the various levels beneath the floors of the BP V House yielded only a meager quantity of pottery. In fact, the assemblage recovered from there proved so limited that the excavators could not even determine with reasonable certainty whether or not Wall 573 on the northern terrace—where the backfill and leveling contemporary with the wall yielded considerable remains—existed at the same time or later than the buildings situated around the central summit area. They tentatively concluded that it may have constituted either the very last defensive structure built by the Israelites—presumably to protect the main approach road which curved around the northern side of the site before turning south to the entrance gate located on the east side of the summit[156]—or one of the earliest phases of Assyrian construction ordered by Sargon II.[157] Neither option reflects an area of domestic housing.[158]

That the latest phase of Israelite Samaria (which the excavators, in the normal course of their work, would have encountered first) basically produced random pottery groups without clear architectural associations (Pit *i* and the massive leveling around Wall 573) on the one hand, and significant architecture without appreciable quantities of datable pottery (the BP V House), on the other hand, perhaps helped to determine the controversial method by which Kenyon proceeded to date all earlier floors according to the material situated beneath them and thereby to arrive at a series of construction dates rather than Israelite occupational phases. Here in BP V, however, Kenyon felt forced to date the functional life of the architecture by the latest pottery found not below the surviving BP V floors, but in the multiphased (at least BP IV-V-VI) Rubbish Pit *i*, which she ultimately designated as "Period VI." Yet I must point out that one

---

[154] *SS I*, 107.

[155] *SS III*, 107.

[156] In *RCOT*, 133, Kenyon mistakenly places this gate on the west side of the summit.

[157] Mistakenly identified as Sargon III in *RCOT*, 132.

[158] See Chapter I, 169-71, n.629.

cannot know the absolute latest pottery from this installation, inasmuch as late Iron Age building activities (by the Assyrians or some other group) shaved off the uppermost courses of the pit and, presumably, the pottery it enclosed. Consequently, there exists no fail-safe way of determining how long the pit may have continued in use, of classifying through comparative studies the latest ceramic assemblage it originally contained, or of establishing the precise stratigraphic relationship of the pit and pottery to the surrounding rooms of BP V. Much will depend on the ceramic analysis of the goods recovered and eventually published from the leveling associated with Wall 573 (*SS III*, Fig. 9) and the Pit *i* pottery (*SS III*, Fig. 10), both of which appear in PP 6 and neither of which maintained a stratigraphic connection to the other. Similarly, the filling around Wall 573 had no such connection to any part of the BP V House.

In the meantime, my analysis of BP V has already raised questions that will continue as I next consider PP 6-7. I have shown, for example, that the few ceramic fragments published from loci beneath the BP V house floors seem to postdate the Israelite-Assyrian political transition around 722/721 BCE (e.g., note *SS III*, Fig. 8:1, found in a fill deposit beneath the floor of Room *hq*). This observation provides a preliminary indication that both the rooms and the pit belong to a period of occupation following Israel's loss of hegemony over the city. Further consideration of the remains from both PP 6 (supposedly the latest Israelite pottery) and PP 7 (the Assyrian destruction debris that reportedly overlay the entire area) must, therefore, determine the date of the alleged conflagration and, by extrapolation, the period of use for the BP V House discussed here.

For the moment, I make several observations that will assume a greater role in my investigation as it continues. First, no apparent destruction level directly overlies the BP V floors presented thus far from Rooms *hq*, *hk*, *j* and *n* (or from *g* and *h* in BP IV). Second, the sooty layers that did appear in those areas, and that contained fragments of burnt ivory, always lay one or more levels above the BP V floors (as in figs. 7, 8, 13, and 39). Third, it does not appear thus far that ivory fragments were found south of the line of BP IV Wall 58 (fig. 5). If further research confirms this impression, it will help to assign at least the horizontal spread of these artifacts to an area overriding the earlier BP III-IV Rooms *a-e*. The question of whether or not that spread extended into or above the later BP V Rooms *o, h, q, hq,* and *kq* (Forsberg entertained the belief that they did not) will receive attention in Chapter V below. As I have indicated earlier, the fragments that appear in the service rooms farther north (*hk, j*) would have arrived there secondarily as part of the displaced soils raked or carried down[159] from the outer ring of official rooms encircling the central summit area. Fourth, one should note the limited number of floor levels traceable in the buildings north of the main courtyard over a rather extended period of time (BP I-V, which range from the

---

[159] The lack of clear elevation readings for the various floor levels constitutes one of the major shortcomings in the reports of the Joint Expedition. In contrast, relative elevation data effectively comprise the only stratigraphic information presented in the earlier Harvard reports.

second quarter of the ninth century through the eighth century BCE). The earliest of these surfaces dates to Ahab (BP II),[160] while the next belong, in turn, to BP IV[161] and BP V.[162] In other words, over the course of nearly 175 years, one sees only three main floors laid in this area (though undoubtedly many localized patchings and thin resurfacings occurred on each one over that span of time). Unless, in an unlikely sequence of events, the workers involved in each new Israelite building phase completely destroyed the preceding floors before laying the new one,[163] this situation speaks clearly to the continued use of such features by successive generations of kings. These widely separated stratigraphic markers and the growing recognition of the resilience of many Iron II ceramic traditions (in which specific forms may last a very long time and may considerably overlap styles that appear both before and after them) pose serious challenges to pottery analysts as they deal with materials either from Samaria or elsewhere.[164] At a minimum, one must recognize that long-standing living surfaces will likely yield somewhat of a mixture of forms, chronologically speaking.[165] Such cases warrant against mooring one's archaeological dating to transitions in a regnal list or to other known historical watersheds.

Finally, as I turn toward an examination of Pottery Periods 6 and 7, I may continue my assessment of the positions represented by Holladay and Forsberg—positions which I introduced at the beginning of this chapter. Whereas Holladay initially voiced great optimism concerning his ability to locate homogeneous pottery groups for BP V and to arrive at a rather narrow date for them, I demonstrated in my Evaluation and Summary above that he effectively undermined his own position later in the same study. His academic integrity merits applause, for it renders quite vulnerable his overarching thesis that the BP V House belongs in the brief period between 732 and 722 BCE and that the subsequent destruction debris published as PP 7 clearly derives from

---

[160] E.g., Segment *N of TT2*, Layer X (fig. 7); Segment *509.126*, Layer XI (fig. 19); etc.

[161] E.g., Segment *N of TT2*, upper Layer IX (fig. 7); Segment *509.126*, Layer X (fig. 19); etc.

[162] E.g., Segment *N of TT2*, paving stones between Layers IVa and V (fig. 7); Segment *509.126*, similar stones above Layer IX (fig. 19).

[163] This scenario seems unlikely simply by virtue of the fact that several phases of Israelite floors do, in fact, remain in most areas. It may be, however, that extremely heavy post-Israelite fills in other areas have removed nearly every trace of earlier surfaces that once existed there (e.g., see in fig. 37 the open-air courtyard to the south of these rooms, where, except for the space between RT 363 and RT 377, no surfaces remain between Omri's original courtyard level and the thick, chocolate deposit of the sixth or fifth century BCE).

[164] See A. Mazar's recent comments, which call for future ceramic studies "based on seriation and quantitative analysis, isolation of homogeneous assemblages belonging to a short time span, and the correlation of these assemblages with current, preferably calibrated, ^{14}C dates" (A. Mazar, *Levant* 29 [1997], 162). Regarding overlapping ceramic traditions within the pottery industry of a given culture or region, note Mazar's appeal to T. L. McClellan's concept of a "battleship curve" to depict the rise and gradual tapering off of specific forms.

[165] In this regard, see P. J. Riis's critique of G. E. Wright's interpretive methods in *Sukas I*, 148, n. 602.

an Assyrian conquest.[166] Forsberg, on the other hand, argued for the lowering of the PP 5-7 assemblages *en masse* to a time well beyond 722 BCE and for associating them with Assyrian Samaria during the middle decades of the seventh century. As already noted, one of the pillars upon which his suggestion rests consists in an allegedly strong correlation between Samaria PP 6 and Megiddo Level III. A comprehensive appraisal of this proposed connection, however, will involve not only a proper dating of Megiddo III but also a general consideration of the Iron II chronology at that site in light of the recent, strong debate over the placement of levels traditionally assigned to the tenth century BCE. I shall withhold that assessment until my introduction to PP 6 for the following reasons: (1) my determinations will bear on the chronology of PP 6-7 as well as PP 5; (2) the small size of the PP 5 group relative to the number of items presented in PP 6 justifies a delay in order to incorporate as much comparative data as possible; (3) Forsberg's proposed chronology rests mainly on his evaluation of two series of Megiddo jugs (i.e., decanters, and jugs with trefoil mouths) that he compares to PP 6 specimens at Samaria; and, from a more practical point of view, (4) the discussion will undoubtedly grow to a length unsuited to this conclusion of PP 5.

I can say, however, that my initial foray into BP V offers tentative support for the views held by Forsberg. Even before considering the PP 6 corpus of forms taken from Pit *i* and the leveling against Wall 573 on the northern slopes, I demonstrated that the small PP 5 group (which actually relates in one way or another to the surviving floors inside the BP V building) seems to date no earlier than the very late eighth and, perhaps mainly, the first half of the seventh centuries BCE. I may add that, to this point, my analysis has intentionally made rather minimal use of parallels from Megiddo in anticipation of a fuller assessment of Forsberg's suggestions. Instead, I have compared and contrasted materials from a number of other sites that represent each of the regional ceramic cultures (northern Israel; Judah; Phoenicia; southern coastal plain area).[167] In the following chapter, I shall return to the role that Megiddo III might play in relation to PP 5-6 at Samaria as part of my treatment of the relevant background issues.

---

[166] I shall return to his proposals concerning levels associated with the Ostraca House below in Chapter V.

[167] The sites appealed to in this chapter include: Hazor, Megiddo, Yoqneʿam, Tell Qiri, Taʿanach, Tell ʿAmal, Beth-Shan, Bethel, Tell en-Naṣbeh, Gezer, Beth-Shemesh, Lachish, Tell Beit Mirsim, Tell Jemmeh, Beersheba, Tell Keisan, Tell Qasîle, Ashdod, and others. Moreover, I have employed multiple citations from each of the sites (e.g., 23 listings spread over three references to Tell Keisan).

Chapter III

POTTERY PERIOD 6

Remains of an Ephemeral Historical "Period"?

I. Introduction

In the previous chapter, I outlined the primary stratigraphic problems inherent in the excavation and recording of BP V, cited earlier studies that, despite their original intent, failed to substantiate a credible (much less absolute) date for the PP 5 assemblage, and showed that Kenyon understood the limited "Period V" repertoire as indistinguishable from the collection in PP 6. Consequently, if the items presented in the PP 6 group exhibit a significant correlation to the pottery of Megiddo III, as Forsberg suggests, then the PP 5 corpus may also easily belong to that same period. My initial analysis of the PP 5 materials generally indicated a later date—namely, the last quarter of the eighth and the early seventh centuries BCE—for most of the pieces than others have previously recognized. It remains now to assess the proposed correlation between Samaria PP 5-6 (and 7) and Megiddo Stratum III. As this effort first involves situating Megiddo III chronologically and historically, it behooves us to survey closely the other Iron Age II levels at this site against the backdrop of a recent challenge to the traditional, tenth-century dating of Stratum VA-IVB.

In a provocative exchange of views presented in separate articles, I. Finkelstein and A. Mazar have outlined the major arguments for and against (respectively) lowering Megiddo Stratum VA-IVB from the tenth century into the ninth century BCE.[1] The multifarious issues involved will not only affect the archaeological interpretation of sites throughout the country but will shape (or reshape) one's understanding of history during the Iron Age II period generally. Since Finkelstein and Mazar have presented their respective positions so concisely (see n. 1), I need not reiterate the many details of the discussion they have launched. For present purposes, I shall instead offer only a few remarks concerning this debate before reviewing the depositional history at several key sites in an attempt to draw my own conclusions regarding the best dating of Megiddo III.

---

[1] For the principal references, see I. Finkelstein, "The Archaeology of the United Monarchy: an Alternative View," *Levant* 28 (1996), 177-87; A. Mazar, "Iron Age Chronology: A Reply to I. Finkelstein," *Levant* 29 (1997), 157-67. For another critique of Finkelstein's theory, see A. Zarzeki-Peleg, "Hazor, Jokneam and Megiddo in the Tenth Century B.C.E.," *TA* 24 (1997) 258-88.

Both Finkelstein and Mazar have focused their discussion on issues that relate to the higher end of Iron Age chronology, i.e., to the Iron Age I period and the United Monarchy.[2] Finkelstein holds that "the crucial question is whether the archaeology of the United Monarchy stands on solid ground."[3] Concluding that it does not, he suggests that "strata which were dated before to the tenth century should possibly be redated to the late-tenth or ninth century BCE."[4] At the center of these strata stands Megiddo VA-IVB. It is important to remember that, despite the generally used language of "tenth century" vs. "ninth century," the actual time difference separating the positions of Finkelstein and Mazar consists in approximately half a century. That is to say, Finkelstein desires to lower the remains found in Megiddo VA-IVB from the years leading up to the invasion of Shishak (ca. 925 BCE) to the reign of Ahab, which began already sometime between 873 and 870.[5] If he is correct, one would presumably need to push down the dates of all the succeeding levels at Megiddo roughly 50 years, including the beginning dates for both IVA (from roughly 875 to 825, i.e., from Ahab to the last decade or so of Jehu's reign) and III (from 787, according to the excavators of Megiddo, or 750, vis à vis Kenyon's chronology, to 737 or 700 BCE).

Assuming momentarily that Megiddo III does, in fact, bear a connection to PP 5-6 at Samaria, one sees that a *terminus post quem* of roughly 737 would suit Holladay's (and Kenyon's) proposed dating of these Samaria periods, whereas a later date at the close of the eighth century fits well with Forsberg's slightly lower chronology for Samaria 5-6. It seems curious that the positions of both Kenyon and Holladay here require the *higher* date for Megiddo III, since earlier Kenyon had argued strongly for an overall lowering of the Megiddo chronology (in that case, particularly for Stratum VA-IVB).[6] The chronological framework she attempted to impose on the Megiddo strata three decades ago stands as a harbinger for the scheme now espoused by Finkelstein.[7] But Kenyon's blueprint for Megiddo rested almost entirely on her interpretation of the earliest deposits and ceramic groups discovered at Samaria, neither of which, one now sees, provides adequate support for her sweeping theory. As a result, even Finkelstein acknowledges the ineffectual nature of Kenyon's argument[8] and, conse-

---

[2]While Finkelstein concentrates on questions concerning the dating of Megiddo Stratum VA-IVB and whether or not it represents the United Monarchy, Mazar sees Finkelstein's proposed lower chronology for the Philistine settlement and the tradition of bichrome pottery as the root cause of their disagreement. In both cases, however, the chronology of Megiddo assumes an important, if not vital, role.

[3]Finkelstein, *Levant* 28 (1996), 177.

[4]Finkelstein, *Levant* 28 (1996), 179.

[5]See *AIS-I*, 254, Appendix B.

[6]Kenyon, "Megiddo, Hazor, Samaria and Chronology," *BIA* (University of London) 4 (1964), 143-56.

[7]One sees the similitude between Kenyon's early proposals regarding the Megiddo chronology and Finkelstein's resurrection and elaboration of them in the statement by the latter that "ironically, though their [in this case, Kenyon and G. J. Wightman] method was wrong, . . . some of their conclusions may have been right" (Finkelstein, *Levant* 28 [1996], 179).

[8]Finkelstein, *Levant* 28 (1996), 179.

quently, excludes from his proposal any appeal to data from Samaria.

A question arises, then, as to whether a lowering of Megiddo VA-IVB to the reign of Ahab while leaving Level III in the early-to-mid eighth century (or, with Rast, as early as the second half of the ninth century; see below) overly compresses the time span required by the intervening Level IVA. While Finkelstein and Mazar only treat layers that relate to the higher end of the Iron I-II chronological spectrum (Strata VI through VA-IVB), Forsberg's work on materials associated with the later years of that time frame led him to conclude that one should, in fact, also lower the date of Megiddo III and place it after the Assyrian takeover of Samaria rather than before that historical watershed. At first glance, this position may seem to favor Finkelstein's argument at the earlier end of the time line, at least where it concerns the chronology of Megiddo. Yet one must add that, since a comparative ceramic analysis of only certain pottery groups at Megiddo and Samaria formed the sole basis of Forsberg's investigation, the conclusions reached may not apply to the entire gamut of Israelite and Judahite sites in the Iron Age II period and, thereby, may not necessarily confirm Finkelstein's overall thesis of a missing, or largely diminished, tenth century. It may prove quite possible, even judicious, to lower the date of Megiddo III and leave the dating of Stratum VA-IVB relatively intact, i.e., in the period of Solomon. Within this general discussion, then, the issues that bear most directly on the interpretation of PP 5-6 at Samaria include: the dates (i.e., length) of the rather ambiguous Megiddo Stratum IVA; the historical occasion of the IVA-III transition; and the overall chronological range of Level III.

I shall attempt to settle these issues, at least insofar as they bear on the present study, by comparing the evidence from Megiddo with that from a limited number of other important sites in the general region. The two well-stratified and well-excavated, recorded, and reported sites of Tell Ta'anach and Tell Keisan assume a central place in the discussion. My general approach entails providing an overview of the depositional history of Iron II Megiddo and Ta'anach[9] and weaving into this basic fabric as many references to and citations from Keisan as seem justified. Since, in this context, Ta'anach provides the reference points by which I shall chart my course through the materials and layers at Megiddo, I shall award the smaller site primacy of place in this discussion.[10] Finally, I shall incorporate data from other regional sites such as Yoqne'am and Tell Qiri and conclude this section by addressing the problematic nature of both Jezreel and Tell Abu-Hawām. Because of its scope, then, I shall cast the remainder of this introduction in the form of an extended excursus designed to buttress the analysis and comparisons that follow.

---

[9]The remarks relating to Ta'anach first appeared in my PhD dissertation titled *Studies in the Archaeology and History of Israelite Samaria* and submitted to the Department of Near Eastern Languages and Civilizations at Harvard University in April 1990 (see the relevant sections in "Excursus III. Comparative Stratigraphy and Loci: Establishing a Ceramic Control Group," pp. 328-92).

[10]See my earlier comments regarding the effectiveness of this approach in *AIS-I*, 11-14. A. Ben-Tor has also realized both the necessity and the profitability of turning "the standard procedure of archaeological comparison . . . on its head" by dating the Megiddo materials according to the discoveries made at smal-

Excursus
Establishing a Ceramic Control Group
through Comparative Stratigraphic Analysis of Selected Northern Sites

Taʿanach. The publication of the Iron Age pottery by the Concordia-ASOR excavations at Tell Taʿannek (Taʿanach)[11] has indeed helped sharpen the ceramic picture for typologists working with late Iron I-early Iron II materials. In fact, the stratigraphic sequence at this site provided invaluable data that helped to define a secure, tenth-century BCE ceramic control group with which I compared many of the early vessels from Samaria on my way to confirming a pre-Omride occupation of that site (see *AIS-I*).

Although "the complete description of the stratigraphy on which [Rast's] study rests is scheduled for a separate publication,"[12] the conclusions arrived at in his ceramic analysis allowed him to outline seven strata or "periods" (IA, IB, IIA, IIB, III, IV, and V) that relate to the Iron Age I-II. The first four of these periods assumed a vital role in my earlier study and, despite much more meager remains, the final three may help facilitate the present discussion. The early periods receive brief descriptions here, inasmuch as the Concordia-ASOR volume has undertaken the cumbersome sorting through of loci in a search for the "best stratified examples of sequences discovered on the mound during the three seasons."[13] On the whole, the results of this process seem reliable. Periods IIB-III, however, will require a more detailed discussion. I shall commence this survey with a look at the last two levels of Canaanite occupation, since the Canaanite–Israelite transition at Taʿanach bears heavily on the questions currently surrounding the corollary phases at Megiddo.

Periods IA-IB **(ca. 1200-1150 and 1150-1125 BCE, respectively).** Described as two subphases of a single Iron I period,[14] these levels are taken up together in light of their close relationship. The main pottery-bearing structures of these levels consist in the following: (1) *The Cuneiform Tablet Building*, SW 5-1, 5-2, 6-1, 6-2 (Fig. 1-2, 15-17, 96b), wherein L.80 and 81 represent debris from the building's Period IA destruction level, while L.103, 104, 106, which comprise an ashy, burnt-brick matrix, reveal a

---

ler sites explored as part of the Yoqneʿam Regional Project, not vice versa (see *T. Qiri*, 212).

[11] W. Rast, *Taʿanach I: Studies in the Iron Age Pottery* (Cambridge, MA: ASOR, 1978; cited simply as *Taʿanach* throughout this study). For individual reports on earlier work and materials, see P. W. Lapp, "The 1963 Excavation at Taʿannek," *BASOR* 173 (1964), 4-44; "The 1966 Excavations at Tell Taʿannek," *BASOR* 185 (1967), 2-39; and "The 1968 Excavations at Tell Taʿannek," *BASOR* 195 (1969), 2-49. See also E. Sellin, *Tell Taʿannek: Denkschriften der Kaiserlichen Akademie der Wissenschaften in Wien, Philosophisch-historische Klasse 50* (Wien: Carl Gerold's Sohn, 1904). Lapp includes a succinct list of bibliographic references for Sellin's work in *BASOR* 173 (1964), 5 n. 4.

[12] *Taʿanach*, 1.

[13] *Taʿanach*, 1.

[14] *Taʿanach*, 1.

similar fate in Period IB; (2) *The Drainpipe Structure*, SW 2-25, 3-25 (Fig. 3, 9-14, 96a), with IA remains preserved in a pocket of destruction debris, L.45, and IB pottery in debris-containing L.44, 49, 59, 61, 62, 124, 158,* 160,* 162, 171, 180 and 186* (* produced the bulk of published pottery); (3) *The Twelfth-Century House*, SW 5-8 (Fig. 4-8, 96c [limited to IA[15]]), with the pottery that derives both from the early use of Room 3, which includes a *tabûn* L.155 (9 published pieces), and a pit just west of the *tabûn* (L.157; 11 pieces),[16] and from the later, remodeled phase of Room 3 with *tabûn* L.124 (9 pieces) and a pavement of large, flat stones (L.138; 9 pieces), when the dirt floor of Room 2 (L.153; 20 pieces) served as a courtyard.

These phases offer a well-stratified sequence, then, in addition to an adequate number of pottery-bearing loci situated in primary contexts. All the vessels published from the Canaanite occupation of Periods IA-B derive from these findspots. Rast interprets the disruptions at the end of IA as local in nature while he takes the destruction of IB as the result of an outside military attack.[17] He relates the latter more specifically to the Israelite-Canaanite battle of Judges 4-5, with the subsequent full occupation of the site by the Israelites not occurring until a century later. This hiatus will assume a pivotal position in relating the depositional history at Megiddo to that of Taʿanach.

Period IIA (ca. 1020-960 BCE). Period IIA "represented an initial, rather limited reuse of the mound [roughly corresponding to the reigns of Saul and David] following the gap after IB, and . . . occupation spread out over larger parts of the mound during Period IIB."[18] In general, IIA yielded disparate pockets of debris and little traceable stratigraphy. Israelite Taʿanach, therefore, seems to have begun rather slowly under the nascent monarchy. Loci 60 and 61 from Square SW 5-2 (Fig. 24) comprise the most reliable findspots of IIA. These two sections of brown-to-gray soil with decomposed brick lay on either side of Wall L.69, above Period IB loci of the Cuneiform Tablet Building and below clear IIB layers. Although Rast also supported the reliability of L.68 in Square SW 6-2 (Figs. 22-23), one should note that he describes this locus as a probable fill beneath a Period IIB floor[19] and should therefore treat it with some caution.

Period IIB (ca. 960-918 BCE). This level provided perhaps the most valuable material from the site. The focus of attention rests on the so-called *Cultic Structure*,

---

[15] A new house constructed here in the IB Period was poorly preserved with only a minimum yield of IB pottery remains (see Fig. 91:2,4).

[16] I could not determine from the *Taʿanach* volume alone whether this pit contained a sealed deposit; until the full publication of the site's stratigraphy appears, only the excavator knows for sure. But the pottery published from this locus appears homogeneous with that from other IA-IB loci and is therefore included here.

[17] *Taʿanach*, 15.

[18] *Taʿanach*, 17.

[19] *Taʿanach*, 17. Assuming these materials do, in fact, derive from properly sealed fill, they are certainly admissible under the rubric of "period" rather than "horizon" inasmuch as they should only contain elements earlier than the floor above, which sealed them.

SW 2-7 (Figs. 30-51). Sections of its walls as well as some of its cultic installations survive (Fig. 97a). The East-West Wall L.15 divided the building into areas designated Rooms 1 and 2. "The pottery came from within the well sealed destruction debris of the preserved rooms, the larger amount from Room 1,"[20] where the destruction layer reached a depth of 0.75 m and lay below a loose, Iron II fill (L.14). Similarly, a new, Iron II floor (L.25) sealed the destruction of Room 2.

Vessels from two cistern deposits have been associated with the Cultic Structure and published alongside it with seemingly sound reasoning. But the interpretation of both cisterns merit caution, given the large amount of published pottery taken from them (Figs. 52-69). The first, Cistern L.69, SW 2-8 (Figs. 52-54), yielded a fairly homogeneous lot of pottery typologically belonging to the horizon found in the Cultic Structure. Yet no direct stratigraphic connection to the latter could be established, and earlier excavations had destroyed the upper section of the cistern's shaft (similar to the situation attending the later Pit *i* at Samaria). The second, Cistern L.74, SW 6-2 (Figs. 55-69), revealed a functional life in at least three chronologically distinct periods (Late Bronze Age, Period IIB, Period VI [with the last one dating from 450 BCE on, when it served as a refuse pit]), and its stratigraphic connections to the Cultic Structure, while somewhat firmer than those of Cistern L.69, are still not the most desirable. Though the pottery repertoires from both cisterns paralleled that from the Cultic Structure, each also yielded vessels not found in it.[21]

The strong affinities demonstrated by Rast (and confirmed and expanded in my previous study, *AIS-I*) between the pottery of Taʿanach Period IIB and that of Megiddo Stratum VA-IVB remain beyond reproach.[22] It follows, then, that to accept either Kenyon's or Finkelstein's proposed redating of Megiddo VA-IVB to the ninth century BCE, one must place Period IIB at Taʿanach there as well. This unwarranted action, however, would inevitably ensconce a century-long occupational gap at Taʿanach squarely in the tenth century BCE, either by lowering the already recognized break between Canaanite IB and Israelite IIA or by creating a new hiatus as the result of lowering Israelite IIA-B but not Canaanite IA-B. These options would not only inexplicably interrupt or delay, respectively, the early Israelite occupation of the site, but they would also individually spawn an impossible situation relative to the domestic records of Pharaoh Shishak preserved in the Amon temple in Karnak[23] and to the stele

---

[20]*Taʿanach*, 23. The material here finds very close parallels with that from Megiddo VA, Tell el-Farʿah (N) Niveau III, and Tell Beit Mirsim B3 (see Lapp, *BASOR* 173 [1964], 37-39 and n. 59). Holladay has noted that these correlations strengthen "the attribution of each of these strata to the ca. 918 B.C. campaign of Shishak" (*Holladay*, 172).

[21]*Taʿanach*, 35-36, 36ff.

[22]Rast has made a strong case for the contemporaneity of this Cultic Structure with Building 10 and Locus 2081 from Megiddo Stratum VA-IVB.

[23]See Chicago Epigraphic Survey – *Reliefs and Inscriptions at Karnak*, III, *The Babastite Portal*. H. H. Nelson, field director (Chicago: University of Chicago Press, Oriental Institute, 1954); K. A. Kitchen, *The Third Intermediate Period in Egypt* (London: Warminster, 1973), 432-47.

he erected in the field at Megiddo.[24] Collectively, these items indicate that he attacked and destroyed both Taʿanach and Megiddo near the end of the third quarter of the tenth century. As stated in my introduction to *AIS-I*,[25] unless the Egyptian leader assaulted a phantom city at Taʿanach, the stratigraphic controls in recent field work there successfully close the door on any possible lowering of Period IIB and, by extension, also argue against moving the terminus of Megiddo VA-IVB later than ca. 925 BCE. While I acknowledge Finkelstein's observation that both Megiddo VIA and VA-IVB show destruction levels, the absence of a clear correlation between Taʿanach IIB and Megiddo VIA[26] precludes his additional suggestion that *either* Megiddo VIA *or* VA-IVB could easily stem from the activities of Shishak.[27] In short, it appears that Shishak either intentionally or accidentally falsified the Egyptian records concerning Taʿanach or that he actually confronted the city of Megiddo VA-IVB, not VIA, immediately following the sacking of Taʿanach IIB. At this point, it seems prudent to uphold the latter scenario.

One may feel inclined to argue that the limited, more rustic occupation of Taʿanach Period IIA would actually support the new portrait proposed for the Solomonic period, while the more extensive and impressive remains of IIB would concur well with the developed, royal culture of the ninth century BCE. But two further elements preclude the lowering of the Taʿanach levels based on this reasoning. The first item involves the appearance of red slip and burnishing as surface treatments applied to many of the vessels in Period IIB. In fact, Rast underscored both the presence and importance of these attributes in his summary of the Cultic Structure pottery group.[28] I have shown elsewhere that even a detailed statistical analysis of the important Gezer gateway assemblage failed ultimately to lower even by a few decades the incipient stages of slipping and burnishing at sites generally.[29] These treatments continue to

---

[24]*Megiddo I*, 60-61, Fig. 70. The fact that only a fragment of this battle monument appeared out of *situ* does not singularly undercut its historical worth. For that, one would have to demonstrate conclusively that someone brought the stele to Megiddo secondarily from another location, and this seems unlikely.

[25]See also my 1990 Harvard dissertation prior to this published study (reference in n. 9 above).

[26]Megiddo VIA corresponds instead to the preceding Taʿanach Period IIA and to Tell Qasile Stratum X, Tell Abu-Hawām Stratum IVB, Gezer Field II/Local Strata 8-7, Beth-Shemesh Stratum IIa, ʿAfula Stratum IIIA, Deir ʿAllā Phases E-H, etc.

[27]Finkelstein, *Levant* 28 (1996), 180. Though he states further that "several sites" reveal "two destruction horizons," either of which may belong to the invasion by Shishak, Finkelstein does not list those sites by name. The destruction of level VIA correlates better with conflagrations witnessed at other northern sites late in the eleventh century BCE (e.g., Tell Abu Hawām IV, Hazor XI, and Tell Keisan 9; compare also Tell Qasîle Stratum X, on the coast). Scholars see in these levels either a systematic northern campaign by David alluded to by the late editor of 2 Sam 8:3-12 (e.g., J. Balensi, "Revising Tell Abu Hawam," *BASOR* 257 [1985], 68) or signs of more localized, or perhaps regional, conflicts (e.g., W. G. Dever, "Tell Keisan," *OEANE* 3, 278).

[28]*Taʿanach*, 38.

[29]See my critique of Holladay's useful study in *AIS-I*, 234-44, especially 239-41.

characterize ceramic traditions from possibly the very late eleventh but mainly the tenth century BCE at sites across the country.[30] A lowering of the Taʿanach levels in question to the ninth century would unduly delay the *terminus post quem* for these techniques.

The final matter that militates against moving Taʿanach IIB to the time of Ahab involves the established functional life of the collared-rim storage jar.[31] The specimen presented from the Shishak destruction level at Taʿanach (Fig. 35:1) remains the latest securely dated example of this vessel type. To transfer Period IIB from the tenth to the ninth century would unilaterally shift the *terminus ante quem* for this style jar to the later period. At this time, such a move would lack the mandatory corroborating evidence.

Thus, on historical, stratigraphic, and ceramic grounds, the archaeology of the Iron I and the Iron I-II transition periods at Taʿanach argues strongly for retaining Period IIB in the tenth century BCE. By extension, these data favor keeping Megiddo VA-IVB there as well. As a result, any lowerings of subsequent levels at Megiddo will have to stand on their own merit, not on a repositioned VA-IVB.

Period III (ca. 875-800+ BCE). According to Rast's analysis, Period III represents roughly the period of the House of Omri through the relatively long reign of Jehu (i.e., the last three quarters of the ninth century). In light of the disturbed condition of remains above the IIB levels, the meager number of pottery groups obtained from these remains, and the problematic relationships between these ceramic groups and their contemporaneous architectural features,[32] a fine-tuned evolution for Period III vessel forms remains difficult to trace. In fact, here one might issue a general caution against pressing any of the evidence too far. Nonetheless, the following comments seem safe to offer.

One of the two main findspots for Period III consisted in the "well-defined context" of loose, dark soil, namely Locus 41 (Fig. 70). A locus stratigraphically below L.41 (= L.65) produced sherds from Periods I-IIA, while another stratigraphically above it (= L.40) yielded clear Iron II remains.[33] This should provide a *terminus post quem* of ca. 960 BCE (end of IIA) for L.41. In addition, Rast notes that although the Period III forms show "a definite continuity with those of Period IIB,"[34] they point as well to clear developments beyond the time of IIB.[35] This would lower the date for III

---

[30] See A. Mazar, *Levant* 29 (1997), 160.

[31] For a full discussion of this jar type, see *AIS-I*, 86-90. To the references cited there, I may now add the detailed study of the relevant Megiddo evidence by D. Esse in "The Collared Pithos at Megiddo: Ceramic Distribution and Ethnicity," *JNES* 51 (1992), 81-103.

[32] *Taʿanach*, 41.

[33] *Taʿanach*, 41.

[34] *Taʿanach*, 44.

[35] In this way, then, Taʿanach III seems to agree with the change that Aharoni and Amiran saw in the Megiddo IVA material (see *Aharoni-Amiran*). Though they held that this shift in ceramic tradition could

to ca. 925/918 BCE and later. Yet here, between 925/918 and 875, Rast leaves a gap in his suggested chronology (IIA-B = 1020-918; III = 875-800) that he fails to explain or comment on in the text. I believe that Locus 41 of Period III could at least partially fill this gap. Rast's comment elsewhere that the overlying material of L.40 also contained Period IIB sherds[36] would seem to support a slight raising of the date for L.41 to 925/18-875 BCE. It then represents a kind of transition phase wherein one witnesses the tapering off of IIA-B's profiled jug rim[37] and the continuation but also incipient decline of the Iron I bowed-rim jug.[38] Other traditions, such as the krater with overlapped rim,[39] continue at Megiddo in Strata IV and II.[40] In addition, the only cooking-pot rim published from Period III comes from L.41 (Fig. 70:6; see also 66:1-35 for IIB rims) and shows a development from the older elongated rim-form modes to the shorter rims that characterize Aharoni-Amiran's "Early Shallow Type." So while the materials from this locus may help fill the gap in ceramic traditions in the early ninth century BCE,[41] they also present forms that continue into subsequent levels—at least at sites located in the north.

Besides raising slightly the date of L.41, one should also leave open the possibility of extending the latter part of Period III[42] down into the early eighth century at least as far as the earthquake of ca. 765 BCE. This would help fill another gap (800-750 BCE) that Rast leaves without comment. Further, it would agree nicely with the general chronological range he ascribes to Period III, a range that extends from Samaria PP 2 through Hazor VIII into Megiddo's Stratum IV and that includes Deir ʿAllā Phases K-L in Transjordan.[43] The Northeast Outwork (NEO-2) shows good ceramic parallels with Hazor VIII but seems to outlive the latter and to continue alongside Megiddo IV, with some traditions even extending into Megiddo III.[44] The suc-

---

be placed precisely at ca. 840 BCE, I have found that not all vessel classes support this exact date. Thus, while I agree that the ninth century was likely a period of some change in pottery styles, the specific dating of this change remains undetermined. The situation requires additional research dealing with pottery from findspots that prove more secure than those from which the Samaria material came.

[36]*Taʿanach*, 18.

[37]*Taʿanach*, 42 and Fig. 70:2. Compare *Deir ʿAllā*, Phase K, Fig. 72:96.

[38]*Taʿanach*, 70:1; see 61:7-11 from Period IIB.

[39]*Taʿanach*, 70:3-4; see *Megiddo I* 28:89 (Stratum IV); *SS III*, 105 and Fig. 3:11 (PP2).

[40]*Megiddo I*, Pl. 28:89; see also p. 169, § 65. This rim form represents a descendant of Iron I traditions. Its absence from Stratum III seems somewhat curious.

[41]Note that Holladay commented on this change in his 860 BCE Horizon material, indicating that the change had already begun before then.

[42]This phase is represented by the "uncontaminated" but quantitatively limited Loci 3, 5, and 36 of the so-called Northeast Outwork, referred to as NEO-2; see *Taʿanach*, 41 (compare n. 44 below).

[43]*Taʿanach*, 42. Compare the bowl series in *Taʿanach*, Fig. 71:1-5 with that in *Megiddo I*, Pls. 24:56 and 25:67 (Strata IV-III).

[44]The facts that the pottery from this feature came from the "core of large stones and rubble fill inside"

ceeding Period IV at Taʿanach correlates well with Hazor V, which terminates around 732 BCE.

Here, then, ones sees a rather long period initially corresponding to Hazor VII-VI, when the political hold over the north country was lost to the Aramaeans and the pottery of Hazor differs from that of Taʿanach. This phase spans the relatively weak reign of Jehu through the first half of Jeroboam II's tenure in office, when greater regionalism in ceramic production might be an expected result of a weakened or recovering central government. During this period, the Taʿanach repertoire finds its best correlations in forms that appear in Stratum IV at nearby Megiddo[45] and show that this stratum might easily extend down to the mid-eighth century BCE even though Rast terminates it as early as the mid-ninth century BCE.[46] As Jeroboam II strengthened his governmental apparatus and expanded his military control northward, the kingdom came to enjoy enough wealth and a network of contacts to overcome some of the limitations of regionalism, and one once again sees a renewed correlation between the pottery of Taʿanach IV and Hazor V.[47]

The applicability of Taʿanach III's ceramic analysis may, then, be expanded slightly in both its upper and lower limits. The new range centers on the Samaria PP 3-4 transition and, if Rast can detect no such transition midway through the Taʿanach III material, it is undoubtedly due to the poor stratigraphy there during that phase. I should stress again that this same fact prompts me to offer my comments here merely as suggestions that require clarification from further work. I have already shown that Samaria PP 4 extends at least to the mid-eighth century; it may reach even to the 732 BCE horizon, though the limited database there once again forces caution in this regard.

Periods IV-V (ca. 750-732 and 700-650 BCE, respectively). Level IV is represented by Loci 36, 37 and 38a of Square SW 4-7, situated in "a single, black, ashy layer found over most of the east half of the square."[48] These loci lay stratigraphically above L.40 and 41, mentioned above, and find their best parallels in Hazor VA, with certain traditions continuing into Megiddo III. The character of the ashy layer indicates a possible destruction, and the excavators tentatively relate it to the Assyrian activities ca. 733/732 BCE.

NEO-2, that "only a handful of sherds turned up" here, and that the "stratified evidence on all sides of the exterior was destroyed by the tunnelling of the earlier excavations" (*Taʿanach*, 41) make it difficult to date this structure precisely; it may, in fact, belong to a later subphase of Period III than is currently recognized.

[45] E.g., for *Taʿanach*, Figs. 71:5, 71:2, and 70:3, compare (respectively) *Megiddo I*, Pls. 24:56; 25:67 (both range from Stratum IV to III; and 28:89 (Strata IV-II).

[46] See *Taʿanach*, 56, Table 2.

[47] The Period IV pottery presented in *Taʿanach*, Figs. 94-95 exhibits few parallels within the Megiddo assemblage. At Hazor, Stratum V represents the refurbished city following an earthquake midway through the reign of Jeroboam II; it suffered total destruction at the hands of Tiglath-pileser III in 733/732 BCE (compare *Hazor I*, 22-23; *Hazor II*, 36-37; 2 Kgs 15:29).

[48] *Taʿanach*, 41.

It appears that at least several decades, if not more, separate the remains of IV from the principal Period V findspot, namely, Locus 16 at the north end of SW 5-6. This area consists in "a pile of strewn rocks, probably from a demolished structure, embedded in fine, brown soil."[49] Since the stones had "fallen *on* a small hoard of pottery,"[50] one may presume that the vessels belong primarily with the brown soil and represent the ceramic traditions in use immediately before the destruction event. A *terminus post quem* for this phase in the very late Iron II period seems reasonable since the excavators found late Iron II fragments beneath it (in L.17) and a compact fill (L.14) with Persian pottery immediately above it.[51] Generally speaking, however, the Megiddo comparisons Rast draws for the Period IV and V groups at Taʿanach seem somewhat paradoxical inasmuch as many of the parallels cited for the Period IV materials begin only in Megiddo III,[52] while those for the subsequent Period V commence already in Megiddo IV.[53]

Though the remains of Periods IV-V appear quite modest when compared to those from earlier phases of occupation, the discernible lapse between IV and V emerges as an important indicator of the slow recovery of sites in the Jezreel Valley region following their fall to Assyria in 732 BCE. In this vein, one may compare the apparent time lag between Yoqneʿam Stratum 10 (late ninth to early eighth centuries) and Stratum 9 (late eighth through the seventh centuries).[54] Levels at Tell Keisan (see below) also bear witness to the gradual development of that site by the Assyrians during the final two decades of the eighth century BCE (Niveau 5) compared to their accelerated influence there during the seventh century (Niveau 4b-a). As I shall also explain, it seems possible that a similarly brief lull transpired between Megiddo IVA and the beginning of III. Farther north, another fleeting hiatus appears to separate

---

[49] *Taʿanach*, 41.

[50] *Taʿanach*, 41 (emphasis added).

[51] Rast understood Period V as "a resumption of occupation at Taanach during the times of Assyrian control in the north" (*Taʿanach*, 45). His concern that a date of ca. 700-650 BCE "might be contested" on the basis that sausage jars "do not appear much after the 732 Assyrian destruction" seems unnecessary in light of the chronological range established for this vessel type by Geva's subsequent study, "Archaeological Evidence for the Trade Between Israel and Tyre?" *BASOR* 248 (1982), 70.

[52] Note the chronological distribution of parallels from Megiddo cited for the Taʿanach jar rims (*Taʿanach*, Figs. 72:1-3; 73:2; 74:1), small krater with folded rim (Figs. 72:4-6; 74:2), bowls (Figs. 72:7; 73:3-6; 74:3-4), and cooking pots (Fig. 72:8-9).

[53] Note the distribution of Megiddo comparisons for Taʿanach's late Iron II storage jar with profiled rim (*Taʿanach*, Fig. 75:1, 3), jugs (Fig. 75:7-8), bowls (Fig. 76:2, 4), and cooking pots (Fig. 76:6-8). The fact that both the Taʿanach and Megiddo forms also relate to pieces from Samaria PP4-7 strengthens the extension of Megiddo IVA to the period of Assyrian activity in the north (compare *SS III*, Figs. 6:35, 37-40 [PP 4]; 9:17-18 and 10:27 [PP 6]; 11:24-25 [PP 7]).

[54] See *T. Yoqneʿam* [3], 31, Table 1; also 33-38. The latest Iron Age levels at Tell Qiri (Strata VI-V) lay too close to the surface of the site and were too badly damaged by recent construction to allow "meaningful stratigraphic analysis and comparison" for the Assyrian period there (see *T. Qiri*, 62-65 for Area D; 110 for Area C; 116 for Area A2; and 124 for Area F).

Hazor Stratum V (ca. 760-732 BCE) from level IV (from the close of the eighth century to 650 BCE).[55] The slow and rather uneven pattern of recovery witnessed in the Judaean Shephelah following the subsequent conquests of Sennacherib echoes the former situation in the north.[56] These stratigraphic breaks at major sites may speak to the overall attitude of Assyria toward its westernmost provinces, at least initially. This apparent laissez faire posture may reflect the preoccupation of Assyrian leaders and resources with the continuing military efforts required in areas to the north during the years following their 732-722 BCE conquests in Israel (see Chapter VI.III.C).

Megiddo. The strategic location of Megiddo made it an extremely important city, in geopolitical terms, during every stage of its existence. From early on, it was hoped that the results of excavations there would substantially fill the lacunae left in the framework of Iron II ceramic typology and chronology by earlier work completed at sites where the later Iron Age levels proved either too broadly defined (Tell Beit Mirsim) or simply too unreliable, stratigraphically speaking (Beth-Shemesh). But, by necessity, the published reports from Megiddo soon met with much correction from various scholars. Albright's reanalysis of large groups of pottery published in *Megiddo I* showed that the report's authors had failed to distinguish clearly enough the Solomonic Stratum IVB from the succeeding Stratum IVA.[57] Less than a decade later, with the appearance of *Megiddo II*, G. Ernest Wright's reworking of the material published there expanded the tenth-century BCE stratum at Megiddo by defining more precisely two phases (B-A) of Stratum V in the northern gateway area and by demonstrating the connection of the latter phase, VA, with Stratum IVB.[58] These and other revisions of the Megiddo stratification set in place the basic sequence that remains commonly accepted for most

---

[55] Yadin described Stratum IV as "an intermediate layer between the destruction of the Israelite Citadel and the setting up of the Assyrian Citadel in Stratum III" (*Hazor II*, 43). It represents a failed attempt by the surviving Israelite inhabitants to maintain an open, unfortified settlement at the site; ultimately, however, they appear simply to have abandoned it (*Hazor II*, 58-59). Though the pottery shows mixed traditions, certain forms from primary loci (such as the Assyrian bowl in *Hazor II*, Pl. XCVIII:44, and a late water decanter in Pl. C:32) help confirm this dating.

[56] On this recovery, see A. Mazar, "The Northern Shephelah in the Iron Age: Some Issues in Biblical History and Archaeology," pp. 247-67 in *Scripture and Other Artifacts: Essays on the Bible and Archaeology in Honor of Philip J. King*, M. D. Coogan et al., eds. (Louisville: Westminster/John Knox, 1994), esp. 260-63.

[57] W. F. Albright, "Review of *Megiddo I: Seasons of 1925-1934, Strata I-V*," *AJA* 44 (1940), 546-50. See idem, *The Archaeology of Palestine*, Revised Edition (Baltimore: Penguin, 1960), 123; and *TBM III*, 2.

[58] G. E. Wright, "Review of *Megiddo II: Seasons 1935-1939*," *JAOS* 70 (1950), 56-60; "The Discoveries at Megiddo," *BA* XIII (1950), 42; see also W. F. Albright, *TBM III*, 29, n. 10, and H. G. May, "A Review of *The Excavation of Tell Beit Mirsim, Vol. III: The Iron Age*," *JBL* 63 (1944), 191-95; B. Maisler (Mazar), "The Stratification of Tell Abū Huwâm on the Bay of Acre," *BASOR* 124 (1951), 25, where Mazar suggested dates slightly lower than those of Albright/Wright (VB to 985-945 and VA-IVB to 945-920).

areas on the mound, though, as I have elaborated above, the dating of particular strata within that sequence has now come under question.

The chronology of the gateway area along the northern side of the tell (Gate 2156) has remained the focus of considerable discussion,[59] while other scholars have begun to investigate matters such as the relationship between domestic and public architecture at the site.[60] But although the dating of certain specific areas remains in debate, the general stratification of Megiddo is agreed on.[61] Though the Iron Age levels and loci of primary concern here are stratigraphically later than Megiddo VA-IVB, I shall begin my overview slightly earlier to provide adequate background information.

Stratum VIA. This level contained the remains of a large city built of brick resting on stone foundations. The Area AA houses, large Building 2072[62] and other buildings (3012; 3021) showed signs of wide-scale destruction by fire, and the overlying debris contained a large number of vessels. Though the excavators originally believed this conflagration resulted from an earthquake,[63] others later argued that VIA suffered under the northern campaign launched by David shortly after he had wrested control of the coastal route from the hands of the Philistines.[64] More recently, Dever has suggested that this destruction reflects merely local or regional conflicts (see n. 27). At any rate, loci associated with Rooms 2068-2071 of Building 2072 seem quite reliable for use in dating comparable deposits at other sites.[65] Stratum VIA dates to the lat-

---

[59] E.g., Y. Shiloh, "Solomon's Gate at Megiddo as Recorded by Its Excavator, R. Lamon, Chicago," *Levant* 12 (1980), 69-76; D. Ussishkin, "Was the 'Solomonic' City Gate at Megiddo Built by King Solomon?" *BASOR* 239 (1980), 1-18; Y. Yadin, "A Rejoinder," *BASOR* 239 (1980), 19-23; V. M. Fargo, "Is the Solomonic City Gate at Megiddo Really Solomonic?" *BAR* 9/5 (1983), 8-13; G. I. Davies, *Megiddo* (Cambridge: Lutterworth Press, 1986), 78-92 (hereafter, *Megiddo*, Davies); G. J. Wightman, "The Myth of Solomon," *BASOR* 277/278 (1990), 5-22. Unfortunately, the last study bases its proposed downward revision of the Megiddo chronology mainly on the earliest Iron Age materials from Samaria; but see now my investigation in *AIS-I*.

[60] G. J. Wightman, "Megiddo VIA-III: Associated Structures and Chronology," *Levant* 17 (1985), 117-29; G. I. Davies, "King Solomon's Stables—Still at Megiddo?" *BAR* 20/1 (1994), 44-49.

[61] Subsequent to Wright's reassessment of the depositional history at Megiddo, Kenyon, Shiloh, and others have more recently affirmed his formulation of the single Solomonic(?) Stratum VA-IVB (see Kenyon, "Megiddo, Hazor, Samaria and Chronology," *BIA (University of London)* 4 [1964], 149-51; Y. Shiloh, "Elements in the Development of Town Planning in the Israelite City," *IEJ* 28 [1978], 46-49). Wightman has offered some fine tuning to the conflation of these two strata (Wightman, *Levant* 17 [1985], 117).

[62] The partly extramural position of Building 2072 prompted Wightman to suggest that it may have functioned as a gatehouse (*Levant* 17, 118).

[63] *Megiddo I*, 7.

[64] E.g., T. Dothan, *Philistines*, 80. See also the reference to Balensi in n. 27 above.

[65] See *Taʿanach*, 18.

ter half of the eleventh century BCE,[66] and its pottery appears quite congruent with the material from Stratum XI at Hazor and Tell Qasîle, Stratum X; it belongs near the end of a century-long occupational gap at Taʿanach (1125-1025 BCE; see below).

Stratum VB. This occupational phase represents a settlement rebuilt after the destruction of VIA and consists mainly of domestic structures. Stratum VB seems to reflect the earliest Israelite occupation of the site.[67] Again, the remains are sometimes meager[68] or indistinguishable from those of VA.[69] In Area B/CC, it became apparent that the houses of this layer suffered considerable damage from the laying of the foundations for the ensuing Palace 1723.[70]

Stratum VA-IVB. Stratum VA-IVB revealed an impressive city that also ended in destruction by fire. Cult Room 2081 in Area D/AA contained numerous objects in a homogeneous deposit well-sealed by the overlying debris (Locus 2081, interpreted as the forecourt of the central room,[71] plus L.2100, 2102, 2111, 2162). To the east of Area C/DD, Yadin excavated Palace 6000 and its associated structures[72] and recovered much pottery from loci in their destruction debris. Other loci in the debris of Building IA and Buildings 10 and 51[73] in Area C/BB also produced good quantities of reliably datable pottery (e.g., Loci 6, 7, 31, 33, 50, 52, 53).

As noted above, Rast has now strengthened the dating of remains from Building 10 by relating it on both stratigraphic and ceramic grounds to the so-called Cultic Structure of Taʿanach IIB.[74] Along the southern sector of the mound, Area B/CC revealed a large compound that included Palace 1723, the lime-paved Courtyard 1693, an enclosure Wall 1610 with Gateway 1567, and an administrative center designated by

---

[66] See Y. Yadin, "Megiddo of the Kings of Israel," *BA* 33 (1970), 66-96, esp. 93-95.

[67] Yadin, *BA* 33 (1970), 95; also G. E. Wright, *BANE*, 96.

[68] *Megiddo II*, 45, Area AA.

[69] *Megiddo II*, 116, Area DD.

[70] *Megiddo I*, 3, Fig. 5.

[71] *Megiddo II*, 44-45, Fig. 100, 102.

[72] Yadin, "Megiddo," *IEJ* 16 (1966), 278-80 and *IEJ* 17 (1967), 119-21; Yadin et al., "Megiddo," *IEJ* 22 (1972), 161-64. Stratigraphically, this structure lay above the Davidic remains of Stratum VB and below the northern stable/storehouse complex of IVA.

[73] For the important Building 10, see *Megiddo I*, Fig. 6, Squares P-13 and Q-13 and H. G. May, *Megiddo Cult*, 4-11 and Pl. 1. Most of the pottery derives from Rooms 6-7. See also Albright/Wright in *TBM III*, 29-30 n. 10 and *Holladay*, 156-58.

[74] Rast, *Taʿanach*, 25. Finkelstein holds the belief that Taʿanach IIB, Megiddo VB, and Tell Qasîle X-IX date, "in the framework of the prevailing chronology, . . . to the *early*-tenth century BCE . . . (Finkelstein, *Levant* 28 [1996], 182). While this is true of the last two sites mentioned, a crucial sticking point arises with Taʿanach IIB, which in fact dates to the late tenth century BCE (ca. 925 BCE). Finkelstein continues by stating that, according to his proposed Low Chronology, all these strata "should be dated from the late-tenth century, to *c*. 900 BCE." I have explained above why this suggestion seems untenable at this point.

the excavators as Building 1482.[75] All of these features accent Stratum IVB's expansion of VA. Both the southern Palace 1723 and Palace 6000 (which served as the focal point of the northern compound) were of the Syrian *bīt-hilāni* layout and revealed a construction in a Phoenician style that utilized large ashlar blocks. Houses built alongside these compounds likely served as part of a casemate system.[76] Again, reliable deposits of pottery were found in destruction levels associated with these areas.

In Area D/AA, the six-chambered Gate 2156 also belongs to this phase of construction at Megiddo. The date of this gate represents the only item questioned by Ussishkin in this reconstruction.[77] He proposes to connect Gate 2156 with the solid Wall 325 and argues that certain acknowledged "constructional peculiarities" of the overall structure—such as the fact that the wall and gate were not actually bonded to one another—receive explanation in the fact that the entire surviving structure presents merely subterranean, foundational architecture rather than the actual gatehouse itself. More recently, Davies has shown that the solid wall was, in fact, bonded into a subsequent Gate 500 (which the excavators assigned only to Stratum III but which belongs originally to Stratum IVA).[78] As a result, Gate 2156 should remain in the tenth-century composite Stratum VA-IVB. The solid, offsets-insets Wall 325 and Gate 500 appeared early on in the ninth-century Stratum IVA and continued into the early phases of Stratum III, i.e., into the final quarter of the eighth century BCE. The heavy destruction of Stratum VA-IVB resulted from Shishak's I campaign.[79]

It is significant for the present study that Kenyon did not accept this correlation but instead related Shishak to the destruction of Stratum VB[80] and thereby attempted to move VA-IVB closer to her suggested dates for Samaria PP 1-2. Yet she persistently retained a dating of 918 BCE for the destruction of Tell Abu Hawām Stratum III, in which the ceramic horizon closely resembles that of Megiddo VA-IVB.[81] In the attempt

---

[75] *Megiddo I*, 9-27. Building 1482 is associated with the other features named above via pavement 1647.

[76] This, of course, was Yadin's theory, although an established connection between the suggested casemate system and the city gate was unprovable in light of the destruction of evidence in the area wrought by Schumacher's trench cut in 1903-1905. Even though Ussishkin would lower the date of the gate to the ninth century BCE, he also allows for the incorporation of the houses into a casemate-style fortification system (Ussishkin, *BASOR* 239 [1980], 6).

[77] Ussishkin, *BASOR* 239 (1980), 7-17.

[78] *Megiddo*, Davies, 90-91. Wightman's diagram of layers and features at Megiddo maintains a stratigraphic distinction between Wall 325 and Gate 500 (Wightman, *Levant* 17 [1985], 126; on p. 118, he accepts the contemporaneity of Wall 325 and Gate 2156 proposed by Ussishkin). In fact, his proposed datings for both Gate 2156 (Stratum IVA) and Gate 500 (Stratum III) remain too low; the former belongs in VA-IVB, while the latter originated in IVA and continued into III. As noted above, Finkelstein now attempts to accept Wightman's conclusions while rejecting his methodology.

[79] This was first suggested by Albright in *TBM III*, 18 n. 6, 29-30 n. 10, 38 n. 14, etc., and, despite Finkelstein's recent proposals, it remains the widely accepted view.

[80] See Kenyon, *BIA* (1964) 151-52; idem, *RCOT*, 67.

[81] At least the earliest materials from Tell Abu Hawām III correlate well with those from Megiddo VA-

to support her own chronology at Samaria, then, Kenyon skewed the established chronologies of other important sites. I have shown above that Finkelstein's more recent suggestion to relate Shishak's campaign to the end of Megiddo Stratum VIA (vs. Kenyon's VB or the traditional VA-IVB) remains equally untenable on the basis of a comparative study of stratigraphy and ceramics.[82] Consequently, the suggested lowering of Megiddo VA-IVB cannot serve as an opening argument for lowering the date of later strata at Megiddo (such as Level III) to suit the chronological framework proposed by Forsberg.

Stratum IVA. As I have already noted, this level contained both Gateway 500 and the solid, offset-inset Wall 325 circling around the periphery of the tell. Just inside the northern section of Wall 325, a stable/storehouse compound was constructed over the earlier Palace 6000 in Area C/DD.[83] Complementing this complex, Stable/Storehouse 1576 appeared in the southern section of the city (Area A/CC) and partially covered the former administrative Building 1482. In Area D/AA, a group of buildings assumed a completely different orientation from those of preceding levels.[84] It is important to note that these public buildings now dominated the site; very little, if any, room remained for a proliferation or even a continuation of the domestic areas seen in the previous Stratum VA-IVB. (I shall return to this point in my Conclusion to PP 6 below.)

Reliable locus groups from this general stratum remain difficult to assemble from the *Megiddo I* report. The separation of III from IVA constitutes a related problem.[85] Though scholars once associated the end of IVA with the Aramaean conflicts of

---

IVB, Tell Keisan Niveau 8, Tell Qasîle IX, etc. (see J. Balensi and M.-D. Herrera, "*Tell Abou Hawam 1983-1984. Rapport préliminaire (Planches V-VI),*" *RB* 92 [1985], 103).

[82] One should also remember the close semblance of Megiddo VA-IVB and Hazor Stratum X. I may note that the latter site revealed at least five discernable destruction levels *prior to* the final massive depredation at the hands of Tiglath-pileser III in 732 BCE (Stratum V). Unless one places the earliest of these assaults at least in the late tenth century BCE, enough *known* historical pegs on which one might hang all the remaining catastrophes suffered by the people of Hazor simply do not exist (though this is not to associate X with the campaign of Pharaoh Shishak, who did not mention Hazor in his list of conquered cities). For this reason, I disagree with Kenyon's attempt to force the pottery of Stratum X into the ninth century so as to support her desired dating of the PP 1 material at Samaria. Instead, I keep for the present both the architecture and pottery of Hazor X and Megiddo VA-IVB in the tenth century BCE and accept their Solomonic origin.

[83] *Megiddo I*, 41-47, Fig. 49. Through some intuitive detective work, G. I. Davies has suggested the plausible theory that Solomon had, in fact, already commissioned a similarly designed but smaller series of stables in Stratum VA-IVB. The scant remains of this complex are situated beneath the southernmost units of the northern stables (Squares N 12-13). Comparable buildings at Beersheba, taken by the excavators there to represent store rooms and not stables, also revealed two successive phases in the tenth and ninth centuries BCE (see G. I. Davies, "Solomonic Stables at Megiddo After All?" *PEQ* 120 [1988], 130-41; idem, "King Solomon's Stables: Still at Megiddo?" *BAR* 20/1 [1994], 45-49).

[84] See *Megiddo II*, Fig. 389, Squares K-8, L-8 and L-9 vs. Fig. 388.

[85] See *Holladay*, 158-59; Wright, *BANE*, 98. In light of the dubious reliability of the findspots involved, I have attempted to include the chronological "range" given in the Megiddo reports for vessels I cite

ca. 815 BCE (compare 2 Kgs 13:3-7),[86] it may prove better to relate the end of IVA to the Assyrian activities during the third quarter of the eighth century BCE.[87] It appears likely that, leading up to the Assyrian presence in the area under Tiglath-pileser III, the city of Megiddo IVA had grown quite weak as the capital at Samaria, beset with political intrigue and a rapid succession of rulers due to political assassinations, waned in its power and control over the kingdom following the reign of Jeroboam II. Though remains of burnt wood and mudbrick appeared in the debris of Building 338 (the so-called Governor's Quarters in the eastern sector of the city, between the stable/storehouse complexes), Megiddo IVA may have succumbed to Assyrian control with minimal military intervention. Perhaps for this reason, neither the Assyrian annals nor the biblical account in 2 Kgs 15:29, both of which record this transfer of control, mention the name of Megiddo.[88] The scenario of a fledgling city that passed rather easily into the hands of a foreign power would also help to account for the somewhat ambiguous archaeological record pertaining to the IVA-III transition.[89]

Strata III-II. Against the stratigraphic disjunction that exists between Strata IVA and III, there is relative continuity from Stratum III to Stratum II. Both levels yielded primarily private architecture from a relatively peaceful period.[90] Stratum III, I now believe,[91] represents a transitional stage of rebuilding during the last quarter of the eighth century BCE after the fall of the capital at Samaria in 722/721.[92] As such, III very likely follows closely upon a brief gap (or at least a rather low profile occupation) during the years between the termination of Stratum IVA in 733/732 BCE and the actual beginning of III around 720 BCE or even slightly later still.[93] In this respect,

---

from these later levels as parallels to the Samaria material.

[86] See Wright, *BANE*, 99, Chart 9; also earlier, Albright, *TBM III*, 2 n. 1.

[87] Recently, A. Mazar has agreed that this level might easily extend to 733/732 BCE, though not because of a lower date for the preceding level in VA-IVB (A. Mazar, *Levant* 29 [1997], 161).

[88] Davies suggests that "Megiddo would probably be included in the general expression 'Galilee'" (*Megiddo*, Davies, 98). See also the comments and references in n. 99 below.

[89] Some historians have consequently suggested that Israel did not actually lose control of Megiddo during the campaign of Tiglath-pileser III against Aram-Damascus and Israel in 733-732 BCE, but only during the subsequent period of Assyrian conflict with Samaria in 722/721 BCE (e.g., H. Barth, *Die Jesaja-Worte in der Josiazeit* [Neukirchen-Vluyn, 1977], 143; I. Eph'al, "Israel: Fall and Exile," pp. 180-91, 341-43 in *WHJP*, Vol. IV/Part 1 [Jerusalem: Magness, 1979], 187; *Forsberg*, 22-24).

[90] *Megiddo I*, 83.

[91] The following position regarding the dating of Stratum III represents an adjustment to views expressed in my 1990 dissertation (see bibliography in n. 9 above; "Excursus III," 342).

[92] Albright's view that Stratum III followed closely on the late ninth-century Aramaean incursions and that one should ascribe it in the main to Jeroboam II no longer remains tenable in light of more recent ceramic studies (Albright, *TBM III*, 3 n. 1).

[93] On this date, note the following comment by the Megiddo excavators themselves: "Stratum IV appears to have been followed by a period of nonoccupation of *possibly two or three decades* . . . during which most of the IV structures fell into almost complete ruin" (*Megiddo I*, 62, emphasis added). Compare also

Forsberg seems correct in his overall thesis, which I have outlined above (pp. 178-82). During this interlude, the Assyrian presence at the site appears to have remained quite minimal. Albright's proposed date of 810-733 BCE for Stratum III, in which he referred "most of its pottery to the years 750-733 B.C.,"[94] requires a downward revision.

Certain of the city's earlier features appear to have continued in use during Stratum III, including City Wall 325, a remodeled, two-chambered form of Gateway 500, and the subterranean water access system. Judging from *Megiddo I*, Figs. 71-72 (Areas C/BB and A/CC, respectively), most of the space inside the enclosure wall was once again occupied by private dwelling areas. The Stratum IVA stable/storerooms were now defunct,[95] and a circular, stonelined Storage Pit 1414,[96] capable of holding roughly 12,800 bushels of grain, served the town's inhabitants. While this domestic character of the city marks a return to the situation that preceded Stratum IVA, the orthogonal layout of streets and building insulae[97] reflects a new, Assyrian-style city plan that differs from all previous Israelite ones. Further, the few public buildings that do appear (Bldgs. 1052, 1369, 1853)[98] lie on the northern side of the site in Area D/AA west of the gate, and they represent the clearest examples of Assyrian Courtyard Buildings seen in Israel. These structures, built on raised platforms with sloping support walls, undoubtedly functioned as the new administrative seat of the Assyrian governors of the Magiddu province.[99] Though these buildings were not destroyed by

---

n. 89 above.

[94] W. F. Albright, "Recent Progress in Palestinian Archaeology: Samaria-Sebaste III and Hazor I," *BASOR* 150 (1958), 23-24. See also idem, *TBM III*, 2f. See also n. 92 above.

[95] Portions of the walls from unit 404 in the northern complex, however, were now reused as part of a Stratum III structure (*Megiddo I*, 63, Figs. 49, 54, 71).

[96] *Megiddo I*, 66-68, Fig. 77.

[97] *Megiddo I*, 63.

[98] *Megiddo I*, Fig. 89. Wightman's argument that an early phase of Stratum III (called IIIB) predates the fall of Samaria to Assyria seems based mainly on a supposed early phase of Building 1052 that preceded two subsequent phases contemporary with Building 1369 (see the diagram in Wightman, *Levant* 17 [1985] 126). This putative phase of 1052, however, remains difficult to establish either stratigraphically or ceramically. In Area A/CC, Wightman applies the same two-phase argument to Building 1616. But again, even if both phases belong to Stratum III (the excavators left open the possibility that the first phase belonged to Stratum IV; *Megiddo I*, 69), the pottery and small finds recovered from the structure proved too meager to allow a fine-tuned chronology (*Megiddo I*, 68).

[99] See the comments of G. Barkay, "The Iron Age II-III," pp. 302-73 in *The Archaeology of Ancient Israel*, A. Ben-Tor, ed. (New Haven: Yale University Press, 1992), 351. Contrary to popular belief, the Assyrians may not have organized this province as early as the activities of Tiglath-pileser III, but only sometime during the closing years of the eighth century BCE or even the early seventh century BCE. Magiddu certainly existed by the time its governor, Itti-Adad-aninu, became the eponym of the year 679 BCE (see I. Eph'al, "Assyrian Dominion in Palestine," *WHJP*, Vol. IV/1 [1979], 284-86 and n. 37). Further, against the traditional view that the Assyrians established three provinces in the area of the former Northern Kingdom, Eph'al argues that this foreign power organized only two provinces, namely Magiddu and Samirina.

fire,[100] they unfortunately yielded only a moderate amount of material culture.

As noted, Stratum II represents a continuation rather than a rebuilding of Stratum III. The most significant addition consists in the 48 x 69 m "fortress," which partially overlay the old (Strata IVA-III) City Wall 325 on the eastern side of the site (facing the Jezreel Valley) and which functioned "presumably [as] the only military protection for an otherwise unfortified town."[101] The chronological range of dates for this stratum covers primarily the seventh century BCE. Inasmuch as the pottery recovered from any given level generally comes from the last decades of its existence,[102] the bulk of Stratum II materials likely falls somewhere in the last half of that period, i.e., from the time of Josiah's reign in Jerusalem. In 1974, on the eastern slopes below the fortress, A. Eitan exposed a building that revealed a thick, lime-plastered floor, walls 1.1 m thick, and a ceramic repertoire dating to the late seventh century BCE.[103]

As a result of this overview, I can now return to Forsberg's suggested dating of Megiddo III to the period following the destruction of Samaria in 722/721 BCE. In short, this proposal seems perfectly acceptable, though not on the basis of a lowered date for earlier levels such as VA-IVB. Recently, scholars (including Forsberg) have generally accepted this dating for Level III but have not provided detailed, corroborating evidence. My survey has shown that one should now place Megiddo III more specifically in the two decades following the fall of Samaria to Assyria in 722/721 BCE.

But while Forsberg is correct in placing this Megiddo stratum after the political event at Samaria, he seems to have extended its overall range too far into the seventh century BCE. In addition to the comparative stratigraphic analysis, study of the pottery and small finds from Megiddo confirms the chronology offered above. For example, various limestone palettes[104] found at the site very likely reflect the Assyrian presence

---

[100] The lack of a destruction layer associated with Stratum III provides another datum that favors placing this level during the Assyrian occupation rather than attempting to see in it the city that succumbed to the Assyrians in 733 or 732 BCE.

[101] *Megiddo II*, 83, Fig. 95. Ussishkin has recently questioned both propositions, namely, whether this structure actually overrode Wall 325 and whether it provided the only defenses for the city (Ussishkin, "Megiddo," in *OEANE* 3, 468).

[102] See Albright, *TBM III*, 2, n. 1.

[103] A. Eitan, "Notes and News: Megiddo," *IEJ* 24 (1974), 275-76. The excavators apparently found the pottery lying directly on the plaster floor; holemouth jar forms dominated the group. Remains from the Late Bronze Age appeared immediately beneath the building. Though the earlier American expedition had partially exposed this structure, the authors of the expedition's report omitted any discussion of it. Its location in Squares O-N, 16-17 is designated, however, on the lateral section cut through Area C/BB and presented in *Megiddo II*, *Text*, Fig. 416 (where it is erroneously assigned to Stratum IV).

[104] *Megiddo I*, Pls. 108-11; see also p. 122, Locus 261.

in this level. Further, an Assyrian-style cylinder seal[105] and multiple Egyptian seals[106] not only help to set the *terminus post quem* for Megiddo III sometime around 720 BCE, but they also combine to support Davies' view of rather congenial Assyro-Egyptian relations at the site during the years that immediately ensued.[107] A particularly significant seal impression[108] appeared on the handle of Jar Type 77, one of the late, degenerate forms of the earlier "hippo" jar.[109] This seal bore the prenomen of Pharaoh Shabaka, who reigned from ca. 713-700/698 BCE in the Nubian XXV Dynasty. It quite likely dates to the eve of Sennacherib's invasion into Israel in 701 BCE. Assyrian-style pottery occurs with clear parallels from Tell Jemmeh.[110] From Samaria, one recalls the greenish-yellow, steatite scarab from E 207 (which Kenyon correlated to PP 6) with a partially preserved cartouche above a falcon-headed griffin. The scarab may have belonged to this same Pharaoh or to his successor.[111]

To these onsite data, I may add further comparative evidence from Tell Keisan, Niveau 5, including ceramic parallels in most all categories of vessels.[112] While the official report from Keisan initially set the range of Niveau 5 from 720 to 650 BCE,[113] J.-B. Humbert later raised the *terminus ante quem* of this level slightly to ca. 700 BCE on the basis of Cypriot stratigraphy and chronology.[114] As with Megiddo III, a new, more organized town plan now appeared, and the transition to Niveau 4 (which extended through the seventh century BCE, as did Megiddo II) transpired without any

---

[105] *Megiddo I*, Pl. 66:2 (Stratum II).

[106] *Megiddo I*, Pl. 67:36, 39, 43-53 (Stratum III).

[107] *Megiddo*, Davies, 102, 104.

[108] *Megiddo I*, Pls. 41:11 and 115:4. This stamped jar fragment came from Locus 957 in Building 1601 (Square Q 6 in Figs. 72-73 = Area A), which yielded many rich findspots (see *Megiddo I*, 139).

[109] *Megiddo I*, Pl. 15:77. On the hippo form, see Chapter I, 93-94.

[110] E.g., *Megiddo I*, Pls. 9:7 (Stratum II = Assyrian jar/bottle), 12 (Stratum III = jar); 23:15 (Strata III-II = ribbed bowl).

[111] See *SS III*, 86, No. 5. For the suggested interpretation of the scarab, see A. Rowe, *A Catalogue of Egyptian Scarabs, Scaraboids, Seals and Amulets in the Palestine Archaeological Museum* (Cairo: Imprimerie de L'Institut Français d'Archéologie Orientale, 1936), 208, No. 886. For the confident association between E 207 and PP 6, see *SS III*, 120, 137-39.

[112] E.g., **bottles** = *Megiddo I*, Pl. 9:7; *T. Keisan*, Pl. 37; **jars** = *Megiddo I*, Pl. 10:42-43 and 11:58; *T. Keisan*, Pl. 45:1; **sausage-shaped storage jars** = *Megiddo I*, Pl. 16:79; *T. Keisan*, Pl. 47:2; **jar stands** = *Megiddo I*, Pl. 18:94; 34:1, 2, 4, 10, 12; *T. Keisan*, Pl. 45:1, 7-8, 12; **jugs** = *Megiddo I*, Pl. 10:39; *T. Keisan*, Pl. 44:2; **juglets** = *Megiddo I*, Pl. 1:11-13; *T. Keisan*, Pl. 43:8-8a; **cooking pots/jugs** = *Megiddo I*, Pl. 5:118-19; *T. Keisan*, Pl. 46:3; etc.

[113] *T. Keisan*, 27, 176-77. The latter reference related this level to Samaria PP 6-7, Megiddo III-II, Al-Mina VIII, and Tyre III, and added that "un autre élément caractérise le matériel de ce niveau: la présence de poterie assyrienne ou d'imitation assyrienne, fait qui peut s'expliquer à la lumière des événements historiques, lorsque l'on sait que la ville d'Akko a été conquise par Sennachérib en 701 et que depuis 701 les armées de Sargon avaient ouvert la région au commerce assyrien jusqu'en Égypte."

[114] J.-B. Humbert, "Tell Keisan," *NEAEHL*, 866-67.

traceable destruction level. As these periods progressed, both Keisan and Megiddo appear to have benefited from the trade network that Assyria maintained with Phoenicia.[115] Importantly, however, the fact that parallels between Megiddo III and Keisan 4 virtually disappear indicates that Megiddo III probably does not extend much (if at all) beyond the 700-675 BCE period.[116] Further, on the higher end of the chronology, one sees that, prior to the eight-decade-long occupational gap at Keisan (ca. 800-720 BCE), late ninth-century levels there relate only to Megiddo VI-IV; the official report cited no parallels from Stratum III for that time period. As a result of these data, I believe that the former view, which placed the beginning of Megiddo III in the late ninth century BCE,[117] remains too high by a considerable span of time. Moreover, the noticeable absence of comparative material from the Keisan report for Megiddo IVA further indicates that this level existed during the eighth-century hiatus at Keisan. In short, *while an eleventh-century BCE occupational gap at Ta'anach prevents us from lowering Megiddo Stratum VA-IVB out of the tenth century, an extended gap at Tell Keisan in the eighth century precludes one's raising Megiddo III to the pre-Assyrian period.*

Other sites in the Jezreel Valley excavated as part of the Yoqne'am Regional Project (YRP) confirm this chronological framework for Megiddo. A correlation exists between Megiddo III and Yoqne'am Strata 10-9 (late eighth through the seventh centuries BCE). Admittedly, the stratigraphic preservation of Levels VI-V at Tell Qiri remains poor and difficult to assess fully due to surface preparations for the construction of modern housing in the general area.[118] Yet, while the YRP excavators acknowledge that Megiddo Stratum III "dates to the period following the Assyrian conquest and is thus later than much of the pottery from the YRP sites,"[119] the report from Tell Qiri could cite a number of ceramic parallels from that stratum for various styles

---

[115] E.g., note the jug form in *Megiddo I*, Pl. 1:34 (Stratum III) and the jug/decanter in 3:78 (Stratum II). At Keisan, the Assyrian-style bottles begin to display necks and omphalos bases typical of Phoenician traditions (see J.-B. Humbert, "Tell Keisan," *NEAEHL*, 866).

[116] Because of the continuity between Strata III and II, it remains somewhat difficult to establish that transition date with certainty. The excavators themselves believed that Stratum III "had a much longer existence than II," and they placed the beginning of II "arbitrarily at 650 B.C." (*Megiddo I*, 87). Importantly, Forsberg's study appeared before Humbert made his slight upward adjustment in the chronology of Tell Keisan. So while Forsberg seems generally correct in his assessment of PP 6, he tends to lower the date of this repertoire and of Megiddo III a bit too far based on the earlier, uncorrected chronology for Keisan (e.g., see *Forsberg*, 24, n. 36; 25; et passim).

[117] E.g., *Aharoni-Amiran*, 183; also Rast in *Ta'anach*, 42 and 56, Table 2. Though his suggested *terminus post quem* for Megiddo III seems too high, Rast is correct in setting the closing date for Megiddo III at roughly 700 BCE and in associating Stratum II primarily with the seventh century.

[118] See *T. Qiri*, 54-55, Plans 8-9; for comments relating to Area D, see pp. 62-66, 208; for Area C, see 103-10; and for Area A2, see 116.

[119] *T. Qiri*, 212.

of cooking pots, storage jars, bowls, and kraters[120] that continued into the so-called Iron III levels at Qiri (Strata VI-V).

Finally, I must add that the site of Jezreel itself remains far too problematic to influence seriously comparative stratigraphic or ceramic studies at any other location. Recent excavations there by the British School of Archaeology in Jerusalem and Tel Aviv University appear to have revealed a rather large enclosure, with an outer perimeter measuring roughly 332 m x 184 m (roughly 17.5 acres) and an inner, enclosed space spreading over 45 dunams (11 acres). The greater complex incorporated a six-chambered gateway, a casemate wall system, and a fosse ranging from 8-12 m in width and 6 m in depth. In sheer size, then, this stronghold far exceeds the royal compound at Samaria, as my discussion of the latter in the conclusion to Chapter I above demonstrates. Though, preliminarily, the excavators take the Jezreel structure to have served as "a central military base for the royal Israelite army at the time of the Omride kings,"[121] the enclosed area proved so badly damaged or destroyed by later building remains, and the ceramic repertoire recovered apparently came from loci with such questionable stratigraphic value,[122] that the chronology suggested thus far rests entirely on presumed historical connections, not on firm archaeological data. It seems unlikely—short of the appearance of substantial new data—that Jezreel will ever command the archaeological integrity necessary to impose a chronological framework on other sites. That it was well excavated by seasoned professionals serves only to validate this statement.

In light of this situation, and despite the fact that Finkelstein mentions many other sites in his argument to adjust the chronology of Iron Age I-early Iron Age II downward, his focus on Jezreel seems somewhat surprising, particularly when set against a total neglect of other towns like Taʿanach. After attacking the credibility of the traditional dating for sites such Hazor and Megiddo, Finkelstein proclaims Jezreel in the north and Arad in the south as possible chronological "anchors."[123] Later, when discussing tenth-century (United Monarchy) strata in the northern part of Israel, he forwards the *half* unexpected claim that the identification of these levels "depends first and foremost on two sites: Megiddo and Jezreel."[124] After again discrediting the chronological reliability of Megiddo, however, Finkelstein offers only a short paragraph relating to Jezreel, saying that "*if* the great compound . . . was indeed built by Ahab and destroyed in the course of Jehu's *coup d'etat* . . . then Jezreel provides an

---

[120]*T. Qiri*, Table 5 (note that the Megiddo references cited here from Strata VII-V correspond to *Megiddo II* and those from Strata IV-III derive from *Megiddo I*, not vice versa as the caption itself indicates).

[121]D. Ussishkin, "Tel Jezreel," *OEANE* 3, 246.

[122]See *Jezreel*—Zimhoni, 69.

[123]Finkelstein, *Levant* 28 (1996), 180.

[124]Finkelstein, *Levant* 28 (1996), 182. Jezreel, of course, represents the "unexpected" part of this statement.

extremely important chronological clue."[125] Claiming further that "the excavators were apparently able to date a pottery assemblage to the mid-ninth century BCE"[126] and to show that it appears "*somewhat* similar to the pottery of Megiddo VA-IVB,"[127] Finkelstein essentially uses Jezreel to buttress his suggested lower dates for both Philistine ceramic traditions and the strata at Megiddo. But as already noted, the ceramic picture at Jezreel remains far from certain; preliminarily, it can "only be dated generally within the 10th to 9th centuries B.C.E."[128] At the moment, then, it appears very probable that this site supported a pre-Omride occupation just as Samaria did[129] and that the earliest Iron Age pottery from Jezreel can no more alter the Megiddo chronology to fit Finkelstein's proposal than the corresponding groups from Samaria PP 1-2 could to suit Kenyon's theories. Overall, Jezreel can offer little to no support for chronological (re-)evaluations of the early Iron II period generally or for the comparative stratigraphic and ceramic analysis of Megiddo III or Samaria 6-7 specifically.

While various excavations at Tell Abu-Hawām have produced a vastly larger corpus of materials than the Jezreel project, the stratigraphic sequence at Hawām also remains problematic. A revision of Hamilton's earlier work by Balensi and Herrera has shown that, following five distinct periods of Iron I occupation, an extended Stratum III spans the period from the tenth to the eighth centuries BCE.[130] Though some of the

---

[125] Finkelstein, *Levant* 28 (1996), 183 (emphasis added).

[126] Finkelstein, *Levant* 28 (1996), 180.

[127] Finkelstein, *Levant* 28 (1996), 183 (emphasis added).

[128] *Jezreel*—Zimhoni, 69. All the individual articles by Zimhoni cited in the present investigation have now appeared in a collection of reprinted ceramic studies titled *Studies in the Iron Age Pottery of Israel: Typological, Archaeological and Chronological Aspects* (Tel Aviv: Tel Aviv University/Institute of Archaeology, 1997). The interpretations offered there form the basis of Finkelstein's revised chronology for the Iron Age.

[129] If so, it seems curious that Jezreel does not appear in Shishak's city list. The Egyptian army turned east from Tirzah (Tell el-Farʿah [N]) and circled through the Beth-Shan Valley and back to the Jezreel Valley before turning southward again via Socoh. The march thereby circumnavigated the Ephraimite hill country around Samaria, so its absence from the list is not surprising; moreover, the site was, at that time, simply a small-scale family estate. But even if the tenth-century BCE occupation of Jezreel proves equally limited, its strategic location between Shunem and Taʿanach and near Megiddo would seem to place it directly in Shishak's path. The absence of Jezreel from this list prompted Aharoni to conclude, perhaps unnecessarily, that the site rose to prominence only under the Omrides (Y. Aharoni, *The Land of the Bible*, 327).

[130] The principal studies include: R. W. Hamilton, "Tell Abu Hawam. Interim Report," *QDAP* 3 (1934), 74-80; idem, "Excavations at Tell Abu Hawam," *QDAP* 4 (1935), 1-69; J. Balensi et M.-D. Herrera, "*Tell Abou Hawam 1983-1984. Rapport préliminaire (Planches V-VI),*" *RB* 92 (1985), 82-128; J. Balensi, "Revising Tell Abu Hawam," *BASOR* 257 (1985), 65-74; M.-D. Herrera and J. Balensi, "More about the Greek Geometric Pottery at Tell Abu Hawam," *Levant* 18 (1986), 169-71; M. D. Herrera, *Las Excavaciones de R. W. Hamilton en Tell Abu Hawam, Haifa. El Stratum III, Historia del Puerto Fenicio durante los Siglos X-VIII a. de C.* Ph.D. dissertation (Cantabria, 1990); J. Balensi, M.-D. Herrera, and M. Artzy, "Abu Hawam, Tell," *NEAEHL*, 7-14. For a reassessment of the earlier, Iron I levels, see J. Balensi, *Les fouilles de R. W. Hamilton à Tell Abu Hawam, Niveaux IV et V: dossier sur l'histoire d'un port Méditerranéen durant les âges du Bronze et du Fer (?1600-950 av. J.C.)* Ph.D. dis-

tenth-century material belongs with the principal Iron I level (Stratum IV), Building 27 provides a stratigraphic transition to the early part of Stratum III, called IIIA. Further, the ashy debris layer covering the Stratum IV Houses 44 and 36 also belongs to IIIA and provides additional confirmation of two distinct phases within the general Stratum III, with each phase showing "several discontinuous periods of construction."[131] The first (IIIA) involves a "quite active" city dating to "the latter part of the reign of Solomon" (tenth century BCE), while the second phase (IIIB) takes in "the whole of the Divided Monarchy"[132] (i.e., late tenth century down to the period of greatest Assyrian activity in the 730s and 720s). One must glean two important points from this information—points which, previous to this new framework, might have appeared in conflict with one another. First, Rast and others remain correct in their continued recognition of viable tenth-century parallels between Tell Abu-Hawām III and Megiddo VA-IVB/Taʿanach IIB.[133] Second, on its lower end, Stratum III at Hawām may also contain examples of the finer, thin-walled Samaria Ware (= Wright's *Samaria Ware B*; see below) that properly date to the eighth century BCE.

The Keisan report does not cite ceramic comparisons from Tell Abu Hawām for its tenth-century Niveau 8. Thus it seems that the Tell Abu Hawām III connections may have run mostly toward the Jezreel Valley area of Israel rather than toward the northern Israelite/Phoenician culture.[134] The rather restricted use of marked Iron Age cooking pots seems to support this suggestion. These items appeared in such great numbers in the Yoqneʿam Regional Project[135] that the excavators concluded that they represent "a phenomenon characteristic of the western part of the Jezreel Valley and the northern Sharon Plain, and [that their distribution was] centered in the immediate vicinity at

---

sertation (University of Strasbourg, 1980). The work of Balensi and Herrera actually builds on and expands much earlier studies by scholars who already recognized the need to adjust the dating of Stratum III (e.g., B. Maisler [Mazar], "The Stratification of Tell Abū Huwâm on the Bay of Acre," *BASOR* 124 [1951], 21-25; G. W. Van Beek, "The Date of Tell Abu Hawam, Stratum III," *BASOR* 138 [1955], 34-38). For the geomorphology of the site, see A. Raban and I. Galanti, "Notes and News: Tell Abu Hawam, 1985," *IEJ* 37 (1987), 179-81.

[131] J. Balensi, "Revising Tell Abu Hawam," *BASOR* 257 (1985), 69 and 73, n. 24.

[132] Balensi, *BASOR* 257 (1985), 69. See also J. Balensi et al., "Tell Abu Hawam," *NEAEHL*, 9-10. Hamilton had originally assigned a higher chronology to Stratum III, one that ranged from 1100 to 925 BCE (R. W. Hamilton, *QDAP* 4 [1935], 19, 69).

[133] Balensi and Herrera themselves acknowledge that "good parallels [with Tell Abu Hawām III] are to be found at Tyre IV-XIII, Sarepta C-D, Keisan 5, 8, Megiddo VA-IVB, Qasîle IX, etc." (M. D. Herrera and J. Balensi, *Levant* 18 [1986], 171, n. 10).

[134] This orientation would seem to suggest that the strongly mixed Israelite-Phoenician culture seen at Tell Abu Hawām came mainly on the heels of the tenth-century Stratum IIIA. In any case, Balensi's statement that "the absence of a casemate rampart or of any four-roomed houses makes it likely that Tell Abu Hawam was Phoenician rather than Israelite" (Balensi, *BASOR* 257 [1985], 69) remains speculative since neither of these features seems to represent a firm ethnic marker.

[135] *T. Qiri*, 224-35. This report cited examples from Qiri, Yoqneʿam, Tell Mevorakh, and Megiddo and referred to others from Dor, the Raqefet Cave, Ramat Hashofet, Qashish, and Shikmona.

Yoqneʿam."[136] At Qiri itself, marked pots were confined to the tenth-century BCE Stratum VII.[137] But the appearance of virtually identical incisions on cooking-pot rims of the "Early Shallow Type" in Stratum III at Tell Abu Hawām and on at least two samples from Tell Keisan[138] may expand on the tenth-century trade connections recognized by the YRP. At Samaria, marks or incisions on cooking pots rarely occurred, and, when they did, they generally appeared on handles in the form of finger impressions. Yet one pot with a folded rim-form mode bore two connected crosses on its outer collar.[139]

The late Iron II period of Assyrian occupation at Tell Abu Hawām remains somewhat unclear. According to the revised site chronology, a brief hiatus in occupation appears to have occurred near the outset of this phase.[140] If further research confirms this potentiality, one may see the same pattern here as that discussed above for other sites (Yoqneʿam, Keisan, Megiddo, Hazor, etc.). Balensi reports that, "since some of the available repertoire from Tell Abu Hawam has parallels in the stratified sequence at Tell Keisan (niveaux 5-4), the Stratum III occupation under investigation may have lasted until around 650 B.C."[141] But with the adjusted *terminus ante quem* of Keisan 5 now set around 700 BCE, it seems likely that Tell Abu Hawām III came to an end either before or around that time. I suggest terminating it, along with Megiddo IVA, with the Assyrian activity of 733/732 BCE.[142] The short gap at Hawām would then correspond to the period between 732 and 720 (or 700) BCE and would fit well the parallels cited in the Tell Keisan report between Keisan Niveau 4 and Tell Abu Hawām II (both = seventh century BCE), but not III.

Finally, a number of important conclusions have emerged from this extended discussion, all of which will inform the investigation to follow. First, not enough evidence currently exists to justify lowering Megiddo Stratum VA-IVB from the tenth century BCE. Second, on the lower end of the chronological spectrum, Megiddo III seems securely anchored to the period *following* the fall of Samaria in 722/721 BCE. This level should not, however, extend much beyond the close of the eighth century or the opening decade or so of the seventh century. Third, if future discussion should succeed in lowering VA-IVB, it must therefore do so by compressing the long and sometimes nebulous Stratum IVA rather than by also pushing it downward and by

---

[136] *T. Qiri*, 226. Compare *T. Yoqneʿam* [1], 78, Fig. 12:1-4.

[137] *T. Qiri*, 123.

[138] *T. Keisan*, 305, Pls. 92:24 (from Square C-6); 93:50 (surface find from Square H-3).

[139] *SS III*, Fig. 30:27; note as well the handles in Nos. 28-33. Kenyon noted that "those illustrated all came from Qz, from the uppermost black occupation level; they were so knocked about that it was impossible to tell the shape of the handle, much less that of the pot, and they may therefore really belong to an earlier period than is indicated by the find-spot" (*SS III*, 190).

[140] Balensi, *BASOR* 257 (1985), 69.

[141] Balensi, *BASOR* 257 (1985), 73, n. 26.

[142] Herrera and Balensi seem to support this chronology in *Levant* 18 (1986), 171.

lowering, in turn, Strata III-II as well. Fourth, the relatively smooth movement from Megiddo III to II (and Keisan 5 to 4) proves roughly contemporaneous with the very turbulent transition between Levels III and II at Lachish in the south. The failed siege of Jerusalem notwithstanding, the feats of Sennacherib throughout the lower Shephelah mark a new phase of Assyrian interests in Israel at large following years of preoccupation with insubordinate vassals to the north from 720 to 701 BCE (see the historical discussion in Chapter VI below). Fifth, if a significant correlation between the pottery of Samaria PP 6 (and/or 7) and Megiddo III emerges from the following analysis, then the depositional history associated with those ceramic groups at Samaria must also date to the postfall period of Assyrian occupation, not to the years of the Syro-Ephraimite conflict or to the ensuing reign of Hoshea.

II. Pottery Period 6

In approaching the published PP 6 repertoire, I must comment on the method and theory that informed Kenyon's work at this point and seek to clarify the nature of the ceramic group as a whole. Toward this goal, one should note that the official report uses the same Phase Plan for both BP V and VI[143] and that it also collapses the narrative discussion of these two "periods" into a single presentation.[144] The concept of "Period VI," therefore, emerges as somewhat of a misnomer, in the *historical* sense, inasmuch as the materials belonging to it were used primarily to mark the conclusion of BP V. Though one may associate the construction of Wall 573 on the northern terrace with some of the findspots presented below, Kenyon's use of the "Period" rubric does not, in this instance, incorporate a distinct, new phase of building or remodeling across a significant area of the summit, as it has in previous phases. But a paradox occurs in the realization that the vessels published in this assemblage do, in fact, constitute a "period" in the *ceramic* sense, i.e., they represent (according to Holladay's general definition of "ceramic period")

> materials deriving from imported fills or other sources where the individual items must be presumed to have accumulated over a period of time, and thus constitute a continuum of ceramic development, rather than a single cross section of the ceramic traditions of a specific time.[145]

This fact notwithstanding, Kenyon's approach involved treating these items as a "horizon" group, i.e., as

---

[143] *SS I*, 107, Fig. 50 = my fig. 41.

[144] *SS I*, 106-110.

[145] *Holladay*, 16, n. 36. See my previous discussion of terminology in *AIS-I*, 9-11.

PP 6: INTRODUCTION

materials primarily deriving from destruction layers, and presumably representing the ceramic corpus in use at one specific date.[146]

My stratigraphic analysis will reveal, however, that the specific PP 6 findspots lay in backfills and multiphased rubbish levels and that the collection as a whole consequently fails to provide an adequate example of a destruction horizon.[147] If such a level exists at Samaria, it must receive its only expression in the assemblage from PP 7.

The two principal deposits that yielded the PP 6 collection lay in Summit Strips Qn and, to its west, Qk. Kenyon described the former as a "levelling contemporary with Wall 573," while the latter received the label *122.125.19.121* (see the discussion below of the variant *122.126.19.121*). Relative to other published loci, both areas contributed an appreciable number of fragments to the final report.

	Horizontal Axis	Vertical Axis = Local Layers	Coordinates	No. of published sherds/vessels (None marked for discard)
Figure 9	Leveling Contemporary with Wall 573 (cleared only at North Casemate Wall 564, 660°E)	V, Va VI	North of 551 513.514	17 1
Figure 10	Pit *i* (undated latrine or rubbish pit)	V(?), Va Va	122.125.19.121 122.126(?).19.121	17 10

Horizontal + Vertical Dimensions of PP 6 Stratigraphy
Table 26

In keeping with my general approach, I have once again extracted the relevant data from Appendix A and reorganized them in Table 26 to facilitate my stratigraphic and ceramic discussion of Kenyon's "Period VI." These data group together the various stratigraphic coordinates related to each of the two excavated areas mentioned above. In addition, they give both the number of fragments the excavators published from each locus and the local stratigraphy (by layer) of the individual findspots. In contrast to the items in the previous ceramic groups, none of the sherds involved in this collection received the designation "discard" in the unpublished records.

---

[146]*Holladay*, 16, n. 36.

[147]Even if one could call this collection a "horizon," one would have to do so in light of the caveats discussed in *AIS-I*, 10.

Part A. Leveling Contemporary with Wall 573
(*SS I*, Fig. 50; Pl. II, Pl. VII — Section CD)
(*SS III*, Fig. 9:1-18)

According to *SS III*, all the examples published from this area "came from a big raising of level contemporary with wall 573 . . . [which] was only cleared in a trench 2 m wide between this wall and the northern casemate wall at c. 660 E."[148] Though no published section extended this far beyond the Casemate System, the drawing in Section CD comes closest to Wall 573 and reaches as far north as Wall 578, which ran virtually contiguous to the south face of 573 (see *SS I*, Pl. II). Judging from Section CD, more than one "BP" VI wall ran laterally across the northern slopes. These structures constituted a series of apparent retaining walls and included the features labeled 577, 578, and 573. Two longitudinal walls (574 and, as shown on figs. 20 and 61, 570) may have linked these various structures. The northernmost extension of Section CD seems to have run immediately west of Wall 574, and both lay at the eastern edge of the exposed trench. In my introduction to this study, I incorporated a general summit plan that shows the relative locations of these structures (p. 2; fig. 1). In addition, I have plotted on this drawing the segment of wall that F. Zayadine exposed in 1965 farther to the east (at 700°-710° E x 498° N).[149] Both he and Forsberg associate this wall segment with Kenyon's Wall 573 (see above, pp. 179-80). According to *SS I*, Pl. I, the Joint Expedition located another architectural fragment in the area just west of 600° E; it apparently belonged to either a wall or a building that the excavators also assigned to the Israelite period.[150]

As noted in my conclusion to PP 5, of the various features just named, Wall 573 became the focus of attention in the published report. Though Kenyon remained unable to date this structure precisely, she held open two tentative conclusions: (1) the wall reflects the final defensive structure constructed by the Israelites just inside the main approach road, which curved around the lower northern slopes as it proceeded toward the city gate at the east side of the summit; (2) the wall represents one of the first construction activities commissioned by Sargon II. Once again, the primary issue centers on whether the wall and associated deposits date from before or after the Assyrian takeover of the city.

The published Phase Plan for BP V-(VI)[151] does not extend far enough beyond the grand Casemate System to enable us to plot the location of either of the segments related to the filling poured against Wall 573 (*N of 551* and *513.514*). Besides harking

---

[148] *SS III*, 119.

[149] F. Zayadine, "Samaria-Sebaste. Clearance and Excavations (October 1965-June 1967)," *ADAJ* 12 (1967), 77-80.

[150] *SS I*, Pl. I places this wall at roughly 575°-580° E; according to Pl. II, however, the area of actual excavation lay more than 10 meters farther east, at ca. 591/592°-600° E.

[151] *SS III*, 107, Fig. 50.

back to the horizontal plane in fig. 20 for reference points, therefore, I am now including a portion of the published Section CD (fig. 50). On it, I have darkened the three relevant patches of PP 6 deposits found lying on or just above the bedrock north of outer Casemate Wall 564 (mislabeled as 504). To introduce the local stratigraphy discussed below, I shall examine this section by working my way northward from the Israelite Casemate System.

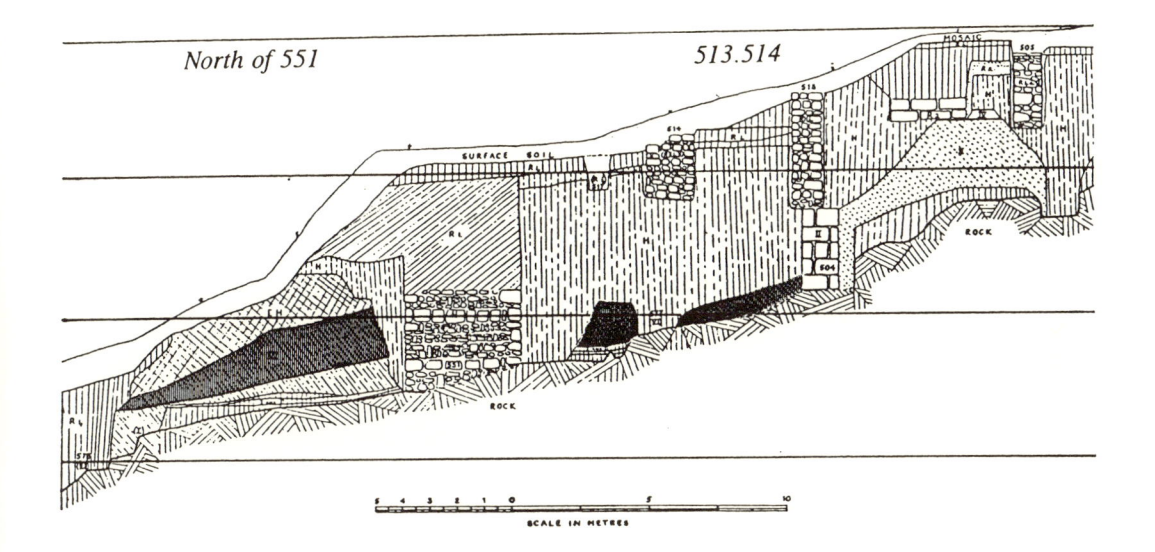

Published Section CD: Segments North of 551 and 513.514
(adapted from *SS I*, Pl. VII):

fig. 50

The area of Segment *513.514*[152] lay immediately beyond Casemate Wall 564. Here one sees that the plundering of Ghost Wall 577 cut through a surviving patch of PP 6 matrix; Section CD assigns the original wall to "Period VI," and a portion of its robber trench appears in the northeast quadrant of fig. 20. Most of this deposit lay directly on the rock surface. At one point, where the rock seems to step down, the microtopography of the surface seems to signal the presence of ancient mining activities similar to those already noted on the south side of the summit.[153] In these areas, distinctive rock cuttings provide a clear indication of the ancient extraction of raw materials used in the manufacture of ashlar blocks. This area comprises not only a construction site, then, but also a zone of mining activities. Both efforts would

---

[152] Once again, the walls used a coordinates for Israelite levels actually date from a much later period.

[153] See my comments in Chapter II, 204-05, nn. 74-75.

undoubtedly have produced appreciable quantities of whitish, loosely compacted limestone chippings.

Farther to the north, a major breach occurred in the continuation of the PP 6 deposit during the construction of the so-called Greek Fort Wall (labeled 551; hereafter GFW) in the Hellenistic period. As the name implies, the deposits of Segment *North of 551* lay on the downward slopes immediately beyond the outer face of this wall,[154] where one sees that the construction disturbed not only Israelite levels but some additional, early Hellenistic deposits that covered this area during the late third to early second centuries BCE. Subsequent to the completion of the large Fort Wall, a massive filling of imported soil covered the entire area, including the space inside the trench created by the dismantling of "Period VI" Wall 577 back in *513.514*. In some private papers bearing the title "Note on Levels. Samaria Excavations 1931-5. Q Area (Summit)," Kenyon describes this extremely deep deposit:

> Deposits contemporary with the construction of the Hellenistic Fort Wall. This included the filling of the large robber trenches made by the removal of part of the casemate walls, with material obtained by slicing off the highest deposits of the surrounding area, including a lot of Period VIII pottery. Objects from these deposits are in some cases marked G.F.W. Mid second century B.C.

From Section CD, one can also see that Herodian building operations (labeled "R.1," dated by Kenyon to ca. 30 BCE) later removed the upper courses of the GFW and backfilled the areas over the truncated remains and to their north. According to unpublished notes, these projects continued to rob and backfill sections of the Israelite Casemate System and to rake substantial amounts of earlier depositional history down from the higher summit area. Later still, in the fourth century CE (Period R.4), the construction of large, private buildings in the area adjoining the Roman temple involved "deep foundations cutting through earlier deposits, particularly the H[ellenistic] ones, and many of the objects from them originally came from the deposits through which they cut" (from "Note on Levels" mentioned above). This work penetrated all the way to bedrock and now removed the lateral Wall 578, which ran in juxtaposition to Wall 573 (see fig. 20) and which Section CD also assigns to Israelite "Period VI." North of the line established by Wall 513 of Segment *513.514* (this basically follows the line of the outer Casemate 564), no remains survive from between BP I/II and BP VI. Since the "Period VI" deposit seems originally to have overlaid this entire area (prior to the breaches made by Hellenistic and Roman construction activities), one must conclude either that no intervening Israelite levels ever existed here or that the deposition of the PP 6 layers themselves destroyed some previous accumulations. Without further evidence to the contrary, I am inclined to the former.

---

[154] See *SS I*, Pl. IV for the specific location of this feature (compare also fig. 20); I have plotted on fig. 1 (p. 2) the segments of this wall that the excavators recovered in the area outside the northern Casemate System.

This overview of the depositional history on the slopes north of the summit prepares us now to take up a presentation of the local stratigraphy in this area and to delineate the individual layers that comprise the composite "blocks" of debris seen in Section CD. I shall commence with Segment *N of 551*, since it yielded nearly all the PP 6 pottery published from this site of substantial leveling (*SS III*, Fig. 9:2-18).

1) Stratigraphic Detail

a. North of 551 (Published Section CD; figs. 5 and 20)

This segment[155] contributed all but the first fragment presented in *SS III*, Fig. 9. Of the 17 pieces included, 9 derived from Layer V, while 8 came from sub-Layer Va. As indicated in the preceding general discussion and confirmed in the unpublished field notes, only three main phases of activity appear in this segment, each with various associated sublevels: early Hellenistic (Layers I-IV); Israelite PP 6 (Layer V); and Israelite PP 1 (Levels VI-VIII).

Two unpublished field sections help clarify the local stratigraphy here. The first sketch (fig. 51 on the following page) correlates to the northernmost extension of Section CD, which depicts the last Israelite levels prior to encountering RT 578. This drawing relates primarily to the latest layers in this area and starts with the thick overburden bearing the "+" sign. Deposits receiving this designation yielded unstratified objects "contained either in surface soil or in a few cases from an area where from reasons of difficulty of digging etc., stratification could not be accurately observed" (from "Note on Levels"). Based on the presence of much buff-colored ribbed ware, Kenyon identified the layers beneath this level—from the lightish soil of I through the soft reddish-brown of II and the rubbly matrix of III to the soft, dark brown of IV—as belonging to the early Hellenistic period in the late third and early second centuries BCE. This means that they predated the construction of GFW 551.

The two trenches marked IVa and IVb provide our best reference points. The field notes describe the former as probably belonging to general Layer IV, and they add that it also likely included materials from RT 573. The latter trench fill (IVb) lay "in R.T. 573"[156] and continued to yield ribbed and late Roman pottery. Judging from the meager distance separating Walls 578 and 573 in *SS I*, Pl.II, and from the fact that IVb depicts RT 573, one may safely conclude that the first trench (IVa) represents RT 578. Curiously, while 573 apparently belongs to PP 6, Kenyon's notes assign 578 to "Period I." To assume the accuracy of this dating (and there remains no way to check it at this point) means that from the earliest days of the Omride period a lower perimeter wall encircled the northern side of the site, where the main approach road may have run.

---

[155]The unpublished narratives relating to *North of 551* appear in *Fieldbook Qn (Vol. II)*, 116-19 (field notes); 118a (stratigraphic summary); and 116a-117a (sectional data).

[156]*Fieldbook Qn (Vol. II)*, 118a.

258   THE ARCHAEOLOGY OF ISRAELITE SAMARIA

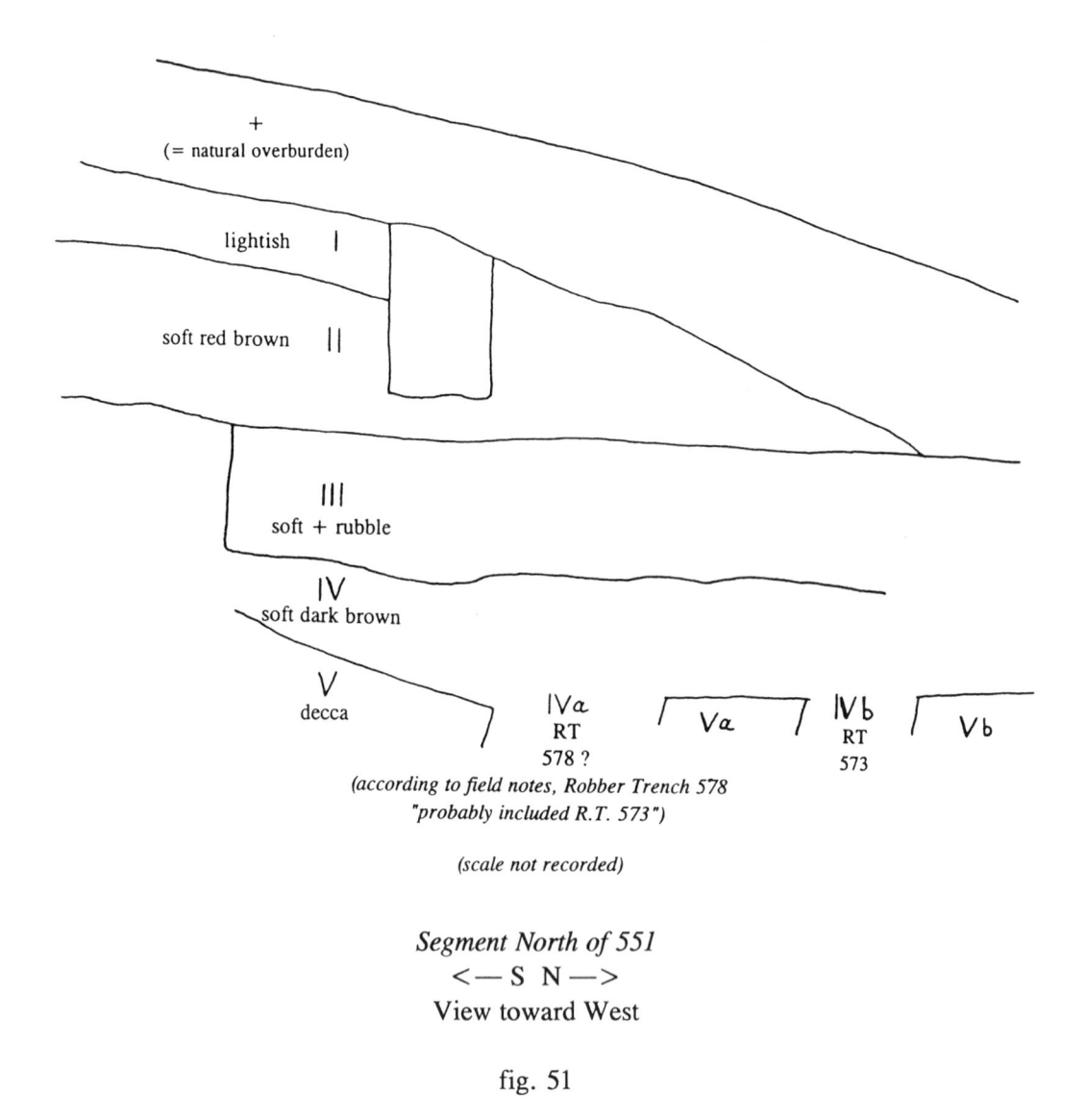

Segment North of 551
<— S N —>
View toward West

fig. 51

The field notes describe the "decca" soil of Layer V as "Period VI filling running up to 573."[157] While published Section CD traces this deposit only as far as RT 578, fig. 51 confirms that it continued northward to RT 573 as sub-Layer Va and even beyond that point as Vb.[158] While it seems quite logical to assume that this layer did, in fact, run up against the original Wall 573, I must note that the stratigraphic proof of that point vanished with the intrusion by the robber trench. While the pottery of Layers

---

[157] *Fieldbook Qn (Vol. II)*, 118a.

[158] In *Fieldbook Qn (Vol. II)*, 118a, the notes describe Va as "in R.T. 578, sealed by Vd, Period VI," and Vb as "part of R.T. 573 (L.R. [= 'Late Roman'])."

PP 6: LEVELING NEAR WALL 573 — STRATIGRAPHY

V, Va, and Vb belong to the PP 6 group, one cannot establish with absolute certainty the contemporaneity of this assemblage and Wall 573 using either fig. 51 or Section CD. Stated differently, there remains no way of knowing that the construction of the wall itself did *not* cut these deposits. I must, therefore, at least leave open the possibility that, in its original context, Wall 573 actually postdated the leveling seen in Section CD and, by extension, the PP 6 pottery group itself. In any event, it proves a risky method to date a given repertoire of materials by a *ghost* wall that not only lacks any stratigraphic connection to the main deposits on the summit of the site but that also had its link to the layers immediately around it destroyed by later plundering activities.

The second field section germane to the segment *N of 551* (fig. 52) dovetails with the previous one beginning with the soft, rubbly matrix of Layer III. As I have indicated on fig. 50, this lateral cut bisects the longitudinally oriented Section CD just

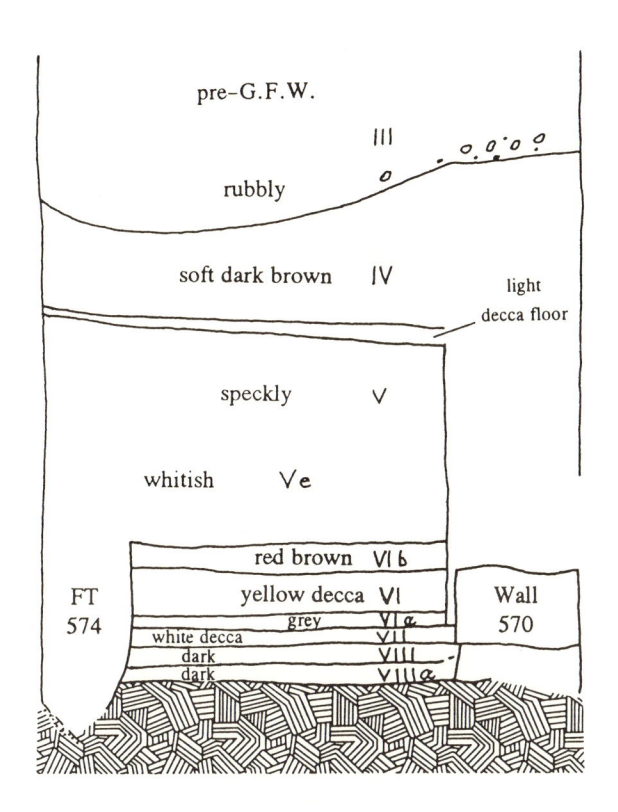

(scale not recorded)

Segment North of 551: Supplement
<— E W —>
View toward South

fig. 52

south of the point where fig. 51 lay. It depicts the depositional history situated between Walls 570 and 574 (at ca. 660°-662° E), both of which apparently ran vertically down the northern slopes and intersected Walls 578/573 (compare *SS I*, Pl. II; I have also identified this area on the plan in fig. 20). Beneath the rubbly III and the soft brown soil of IV (both again described as "pre 551"), fig. 52 better elucidates the earlier layers. While the field notes report that the rather thick, speckled Layer V represents the "Period VI filling running up to 573,"[159] I have already shown that an actual stratigraphic connection between this level and Wall 573 does not exist. The light, decca floor overrunning Layer V did not receive its own layer designation; however, Kenyon labeled the lower portion of V, which became whitish in color, sub-Layer Ve. It seems likely that these levels reflect a composite of construction debris (see my earlier comments) and leveling fill. Their deposition occurred stratigraphically later than the construction of Wall 574, since they form the backfill in the foundation trench for that feature, and stratigraphically earlier than the partial plundering of Wall 570, which cut through these deposits.

Resting at deeper elevations beneath these putative PP 6 remains, a series of closely spaced, thinner deposits appears. Curiously, Section CD records that the earliest of these levels date from "Periods I-II," while the succeeding ones come only from "Period I." This testifies to the often intermingled and inseparable nature of these two groups and to the fact that these layers likely represent accumulations from a pre-Omride occupation of the site (see *AIS-I* regarding both points). Resembling situations seen elsewhere on the summit, the earliest of these layers (the dark soil of Layer VIIIa) yielded pottery not only from PP 1 and 2 but from the Early Bronze Age as well. Since the published report failed to include any PP 1-2 fragments from this area, I cannot comment in detail on the ceramic traditions represented in these early layers; I can, however, note that the composition and consistency of the various levels seems to accord generally with the local stratigraphy presented from further up the slope, in the area of the Casemate System.[160] These layers may also have contained various intrusive elements, inasmuch as Layer VI ran up to RT 578 and the foundation trench of "Period VI" Wall 574 cut all the early levels visible in fig. 52.[161]

Finally, I may add that nowhere in the narratives related to the layers of this segment did the field notes mention deposits of burned debris or the presence of ivory fragments. This observation helps to circumscribe the distribution of this sort of material at the edge of the summit itself and, perhaps more importantly, to demonstrate the absence of apparent destruction levels in accumulations that may have existed right along the main approach road to the site. One might expect that a complete destruction of Samaria, as spoken of in the official report and related works, would surely have left

---

[159] *Fieldbook Qn (Vol. II)*, 118a.

[160] See, for example, *AIS-I*, 37-43, figs. 8a-b.

[161] The field notes indicate that the three primary levels (VI, VII, and VIII) possibly included materials from FT 574 (*Fieldbook Qn [Vol. II]*, 118a).

its traces along this vital approach to the main city entrance east of the royal compound.

b. 513.514 (Published Section CD; figs. 5 and 20)

A single PP 6 fragment (*SS III*, Fig. 9:1) may have come from the segment identified by the coordinates *513.514*.[162] Unlike the previous parcel, this area lay *inside* the line of the GFW 551, in a rather circumscribed space between lateral Walls 513 and 514 (I have delineated this small tract of excavation on fig. 20; see also published Section CD in fig. 50). Inasmuch as fig. 20 also shows that Wall 514 followed the same basic course as Wall 577, I can return to fig. 1 in my Introduction to locate this segment more precisely between the outer Casemate Wall 564 and Wall 577. In other words, Segment *513.514* lay immediately outside the Casemate System, whereas *North of 551* existed farther down the northern slopes and alongside the perimeter road leading around to the summit compound. I shall show the value of this datum in establishing further the northern limits of sooty soils, burned materials, and ivory fragments in the narrow field of excavations beyond the summit proper.

According to Kenyon's analysis, the depositional history in *513.514* reflects three main periods of activity: the Late Roman period (R.4 = fourth century CE); the Hellenistic period (mid-second century BCE); and disparate deposits from the Israelite period (PP 6 and PP 1).[163] The two available field sections record only the latest of these levels, i.e., the brownish earth of Layer V, which the excavators interpreted as a transitional deposit that yielded both Hellenistic and Late Roman remains (see figs. 53-54 on the following pages). For the sake of completeness, I also include sectional data for the area that extends northward from Wall 514 to just beyond Wall 516 (fig. 55), which crossed the path of the GFW 551 (see fig. 20). Here one can see the terracing of successive, subterranean retaining walls down the northern slopes, but the field drawing does not extend down to bedrock and therefore cannot help clarify the nature or extent of the artificial extraction of limestone from this area (see my earlier comments on this matter).

All the Late Roman levels appear yellowish in color and extend from the looser soil of Layer I (shown only on fig. 54) to the light clay of Layer IV. Level II appears to have run up against the northern face of Wall 513, while Layer III abutted both 513 and 514 to the north. Level II (= sub-Layer Iw) yielded the first traces of sooty material in this area. The field notes add that this "middenish-looking debris" partly lay beneath the overburden marked "+" (I have added this siglum to fig. 53) and may

---

[162] The stratification cards maintained by G. M. Crowfoot indicate that, like the other fragments in Fig. 9, this sherd may belong to Layer V of the segment labeled *North of 551*.

[163] *Fieldbook Qn (Vol. I)*, 69a and *(Vol. II)*, 137a.

513

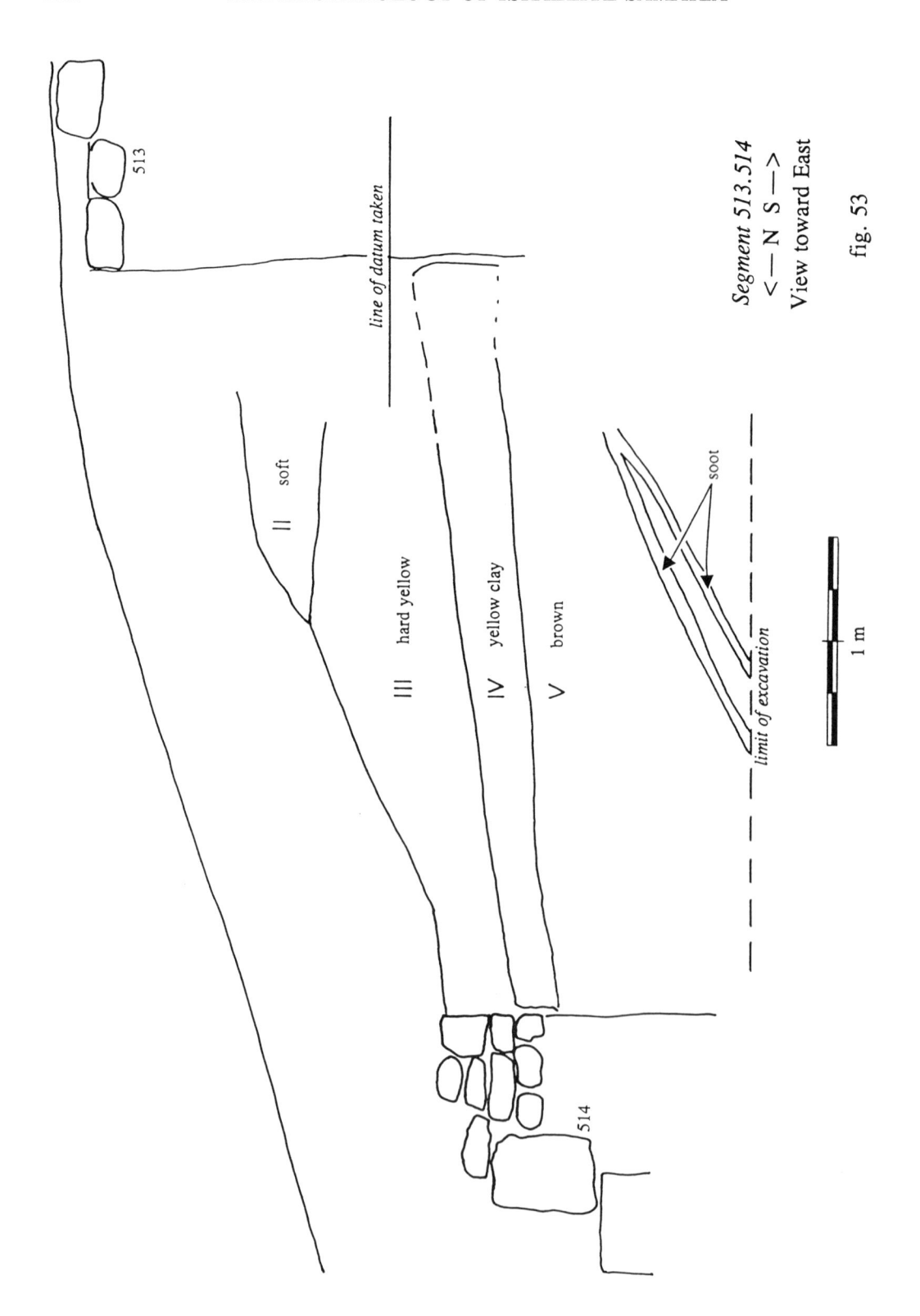

514

Segment 513.514
<— N S —>
View toward East

fig. 53

line of datum taken

II soft
III hard yellow
IV yellow clay
V brown

soot
limit of excavation

1 m

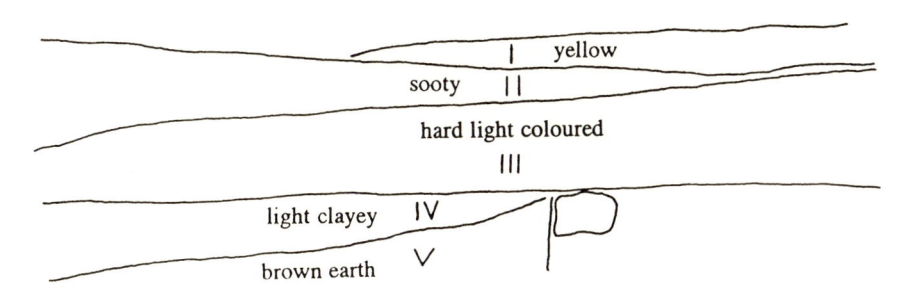

```
                    |  yellow
          sooty    ||
          hard light coloured
                   |||
   light clayey   IV
          brown earth  V
```

(scale not recorded)

Segment 513.514: Supplement
<— N S —>
View toward East
(presumed orientation; no compass direction provided in field notes)

fig. 54

have included some of it, since the slope of "+" actually cut into II.[164] Though the notes also state that the yellow clay of IV also ran up to Wall 513,[165] fig. 53 clearly shows that the foundation trenches of both 513 and 514 cut this deposit; consequently, these walls postdate that accumulation and, by extension, the brownish soil of Level I beneath it (though the sections do not present the latter stratigraphic relationship with such accurate detail).

Beneath to Layer II, significant quantities of burnt material did not appear until Layer V, taken by the excavators to comprise part of the massive fill poured against the Greek Fort Wall[166] (though V likely included some elements from the robber trench of Wall 541 to the south; see fig. 20). The same description applies to the "streaky, sooty" Layer VI, also from the Hellenistic period. Though the field sections did not identify these striations of burned debris specifically, I believe that they belong to the steeply-pitched accumulations of soot running beneath Layer V in fig. 53. Importantly, this drawing also shows that this debris does not form a consolidated deposit. Rather, a narrow band of this matrix appears, followed by additional brownish filling, in turn

---

[164] *Fieldbook Qn (Vol. I)*, 68. This statement presumes the presence of at least some artificially deposited stratigraphy in this material, since purely natural overburden would not, by definition, cut a preexisting layer. See p. 257 above for a description of the matrix marked "+."

[165] *Fieldbook Qn (Vol. I)*, 69a. On p. 68, however, the notes acknowledge that the construction of Wall 514 cut through Layer IV.

[166] The pottery readings from this layer also recognized some (apparently intrusive) forms from the Late Roman period.

followed by another streak of soot. This stratigraphic situation does not, then, reflect *in situ* destruction debris, but successive rakings of debris from earlier periods down over the northern slopes into a secondary locus, where it could serve a basic leveling material. It is important to remember as well that the notes record only charred soil from this segment, not the presence of ivory fragments, whose northernmost limits seem to lie on the summit inside the line of the former Israelite Casemate System.

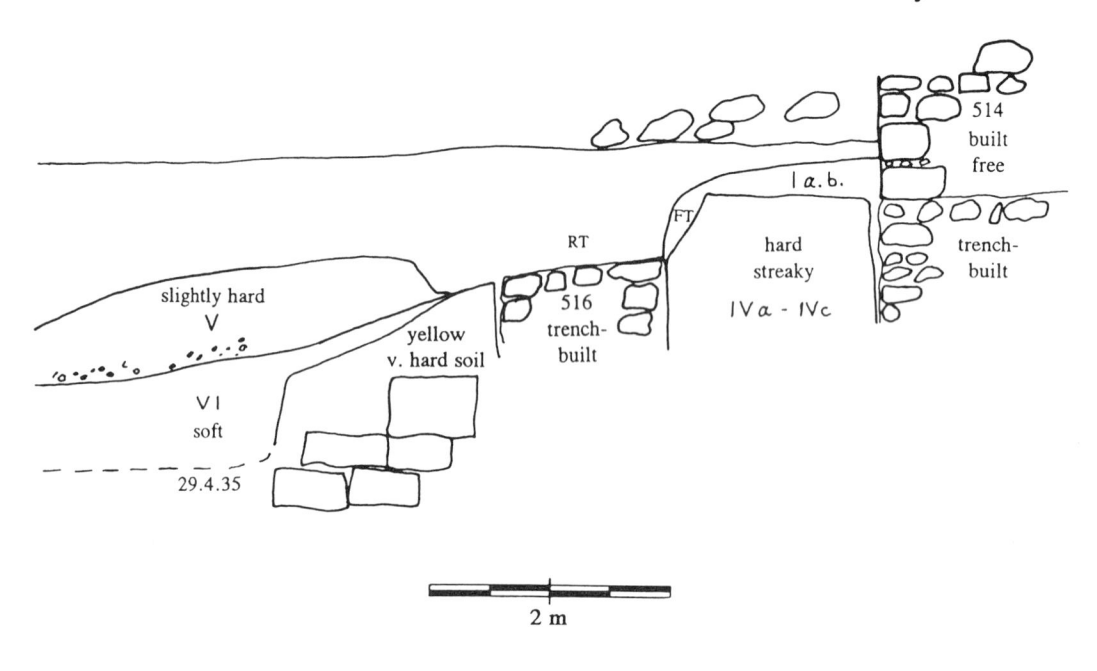

Segment North of 514 (north of fig. 53)
<— N   S —>
View toward East

fig. 55

Besides providing these stratigraphic insights, the Hellenistic Layer VI is important to this study because the only pottery fragment published from this segment derived from this particular local level (*SS III*, Fig. 9:1) and received an Israelite date. Assuming the accuracy of the Hellenistic dating for this general locus, then, this *complete* saucer bowl must either reflect a much later ceramic tradition or represent an intact intrusion into the deposit. Since, as I have shown, much of the matrix here came secondarily from the summit, the latter option seems entirely possible, though it is somewhat amazing that the bowl remained whole throughout the less-than-delicate act of backfilling this large area.

The stratigraphic summaries in the field notes for this area indicate that, beneath Layer VI and another Hellenistic fill deposit (VII), a light-colored matrix from two integrated layers (VIII-IX) actually represents Israelite "Period VI."[167] Further, the records state that these levels ran up to Wall 576 (which does not appear on any section or plan but which must lie somewhere in the vicinity of Wall 577 on Pl. II in *SS I*). The published report, however, did not incorporate any PP 6 fragments taken from these layers. Moreover, beneath these accumulations, the field notes include yet another layer (X), which ran beneath 576 and which Kenyon subsequently assigned to "Period I." But the field sections (e.g., fig. 53) indicate that in this area the excavations penetrated only to an elevation that yielded Hellenistic materials. While published Section CD does include a "Period VI" deposit beneath these later ones, it presents this material as lying directly on the bedrock in Segment *513.514* proper. One has to move north of 514 to see remains from PP 1-2 recorded on Section CD. At any rate, this bottommost deposit (Layer X) also apparently contained traces of sooty material, a situation which calls to mind the earliest material found lying directly on the bedrock just north of the Omride Enclosure Wall 161.[168]

2) Pottery Analysis

All but one (9:1) of the PP 6 fragments presented in *SS III*, Fig. 9 come from the composite Layer V-Va of the filling Kenyon treated as contemporary with the middle terrace Wall 573.[169] As shown above, however, one must temper the claims of contemporaneity between this deposit and the wall with the awareness that various robber trenches had broken the actual stratigraphic link between the two, at least in the areas depicted on the available sections. I should also reiterate that both the wall and the leveling near it are spatially removed from the main summit area and that the excavators could not establish any stratigraphic connection between them and accumulations within the compound itself. While the overall pottery group published from the fill deposit contained 18 fragments from five types of vessels, various styles of cooking pots comprised half the collection (*SS III*, Fig. 9:10-18). Since this entire assemblage comes from a downslope, secondary context containing remains originally situated along the northern periphery of the compound, the preponderance of utilitarian forms once again supports assigning a service related function (probably food preparation) to the rooms in that perimeter zone. It seems somewhat curious that the final report did not include any representative jar forms in this overall group.[170] Before moving to an analysis of the individual forms recovered from this area, I must note that the nature of the deposit itself inherently calls for an open *terminus post quem* for the

---

[167]*Fieldbook Qn (Vol. II)*, 137a.

[168]See *AIS-I*, 40, fig. 8c.

[169]But see n. 162.

[170]The scarcity of storage jars recovered from late Iron II levels at Yoqneʿam also elicited comment from the excavators there, though they presumed that this lacuna seems due to chance, as do I in the case of Samaria (*T. Yoqneʿam* [2], 83). An increased representation of jars appears in the layers associated with PP 7 at Samaria.

materials it contained. Consideration of the latest ceramic traditions reflected in the accumulation, however, may guide us in establishing a *terminus ante quem*, or latest possible date, for the overall pottery group. From this point, I may in turn extrapolate the *earliest* feasible date for the actual deposition of the surrounding matrix.[171]

a. Bowls

The final pottery report included three fragments of bowls in the ceramic assemblage recovered from the filling on the middle terrace. One of these items (Fig. 9:1) constitutes the only sherd in the entire repertoire for PP 1-7 published from Segment *513.514* (see n. 162). The specific findspots for this collection appear in Table 27 (compare Appendix A).

SS III Published Figure	Registry No. (none marked for discard)	Provenance		
		Strip	Coordinates	Feature	Local Layer
9:1 †	Q 4978	Qn	513.514	leveling	VI
9:2 †	Q 4976	Qn	North of 551	leveling	V
9:3	Q 5227	Qn	North of 551	leveling	Va

† = field register *Qn* lists only the published registry number without the other identifying data given here

Provenance Data:
PP6 Bowls from the Leveling Contemporary with Wall 573

Table 27

The saucer bowl in No. 1 displays relatively thick sidewalls that splay sharply outward, a simple, outcut rim mode that forms a beveled exterior edge around the opening, and a flat but very pronounced base. Rather than continuing directly in toward the base in a fashion typical of other flat-bottomed bowls (e.g., *SS III*, Figs. 1:5, 3:3, 4:2-5, 10:1-2), the outer, lower sidewalls of this vessel actually reverse their course to give the exterior basewalls an outward flare of their own. The outer profile of this base resembles that witnessed more frequently on ring-base forms. Three attributes, then, constitute the most important typological features of this bowl: the articulated base, the

---

[171] For this general standard of interpretation, see A. Walker, "Principles of Excavation," pp. 2-22 in *A Manual of Field Excavation: Handbook for Field Archaeologists*, W. G. Dever and H. D. Lance, eds. (New York: Hebrew Union College and The Jewish Institute of Religion, 1982), 5.

splaying (i.e., slightly arched vs. the more typical straight or convex) sidewalls, and the flattened, knife-cut rim. Besides describing the ware of this vessel as a "pale greyish buff" color,[172] the final report provided minimal comment regarding other characteristics of the fabric or the surface treatment.[173] Comparable regional parallels are available from Yoqne'am[174] and Megiddo.[175] The piece also seems related to but more stylish than various other Iron IIB examples from Beth-Shan.[176] Though Kenyon classified this item as a saucer bowl, it seems directly related to the slightly wider plate or platter form from late eighth-century BCE Tell el-Far'ah[177] and from an apparent seventh-century context at Tell en-Naṣbeh.[178] Numerous bowl specimens from late ninth and eighth-century BCE levels at Hazor seem directly related to this form but usually show slight variations, such as straighter sides, a more ordinary flat- or ring-base, and the like.[179]

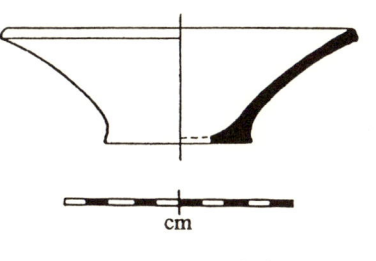

SS III, Fig. 9:1

Most of these citations fall within Gitin's categories of straight-sided bowls and plates (Type 62) from Field VII at Gezer.[180] The numerous exemplars that he cites in the extended discussion of this general class of bowls show a wide chronological and geographical distribution. Variations of the form range at least from the ninth through the seventh centuries BCE in Israel, Judah, Transjordan, Lebanon, Syria, Turkey, and

---

[172] *SS III*, 120.

[173] Kenyon does, however, seem to associate this vessel with ring-burnished bowls from other loci at Samaria.

[174] *T. Yoqne'am* [2], 83, Fig. 8:1 (Stratum 4 = Iron III, assigned to the eighth century BCE).

[175] *Megiddo I*, Pl. 24:40-42 (Strata IV-II), often with simple, rounded (vs. cut) rim.

[176] *Beth-Shan*, James, Figs. 26:8; 33:5; 67:12 (Level IV).

[177] Compare *Chambon*, Pl. 57:26 (Niveau VIId), with a more typical ring base.

[178] *TN—Cistern*, Fig. 4:x166 (Cistern 370 = 700-586 BCE), though with straighter sidewalls.

[179] Compare *Hazor I*, Pls. LXVI:29 (Stratum VIII), with a similar rim-form mode but showing a ring base; LIII:11 (Stratum V); LXXI:9 (Strata V-IV); *Hazor II*, Pls. LXVI:16 (Stratum VI); LXXX:40 and LXXXI:2-4 (Stratum VA), all with straighter sidewalls; a good transition form to this Samaria exemplar appears in *Hazor III-IV*, Pl. CLXXXI:36 (Stratum VI), though with ridged sidewalls (see also No. 35, with simple rim mode; compare *SS III*, Fig. 10:1, with similar sidewalls but with simple, rounded rim = PP 6 Pit *i*); CLXXXIX:2 (Strata VI-V); CCXIV:2 (Stratum VII); CCXIX:6-7 (Stratum VI); CCXXII:15 and CCXXIII:8 (Stratum VB), with simple rim but splayed walls; CCXXV:16 (Stratum VA); CCLI:7 (Stratum V), with straighter sidewalls but a good example of an outcut rim.

[180] *Gezer III*, 59, 182-85; Pls. 14:15 (Stratum VIB = mid-ninth century BCE); 24:8 (Stratum VB/VA = late eighth-seventh centuries BCE). They may also relate in various ways to the class of bowls with flaring sides (Gitin's Type 59; described in *Gezer III*, 58, 177-80), though many examples of this style display the flaring walls primarily above a point of sharp carination, as in *Gezer III*, Pl. 20:7 (Field VII, Stratum VIA).

Cyprus.[181] This class appears first in the north and enjoys its floruit there during the eighth century BCE, at the end of which time it begins to develop in appreciable numbers in the south. The shallower bowls tend to emerge during the latter half of this period (eighth-seventh centuries), and the color of the fabric tends to change from buff to reddish-brown following the eighth century BCE. While bowl No. 1 may belong to this general group, then, it distinguishes itself by means of its uniquely crisp lines and well-defined base, which bespeak an accomplished construction technique that seems more refined than most of the examples cited or alluded to above. As such, this bowl represents the ultimate expression of a style that may originate at Samaria among the mixed remains of PP 3, but that emanates particularly from PP 4 on.[182] Perhaps as a result, perfect parallels remain difficult to locate. The best form parallel from Samaria itself came from Summit Strip 4 (the area of the Ostraca House) during the Harvard Excavations.[183] While some of the comparative data cited above show that this well-made model might easily extend into the seventh century BCE, it likely belongs no earlier than the latter half of the eighth century BCE. It remains difficult, however, to locate the piece more precisely to a time either before or after the fall of Samaria around 722/21 BCE. As with all the other fragments in this PP 6 subgroup, the secondary stratigraphic context that yielded the bowl precludes one's ability to narrow this suggested dating range.

Though only a small sherd, the strongly inflected sidewall fragment in No. 2 represents one of the most stylish forms at Samaria to receive the so-called Samaria Ware treatment.[184] It displays the smooth, well-levigated buff ware with clean, bright red slip and the interior-exterior burnishing common to this technique. The lightness of this ware distinguishes it from similar fabrics used in Mycenaean Ware and the Terra Sigillata tradition.[185] Kenyon noted that the wheel burnishing often appears retouched by hand techniques, which results in a continuously smoothed, glossy surface that conceals virtually all burnishing lines. A wide, buff-colored

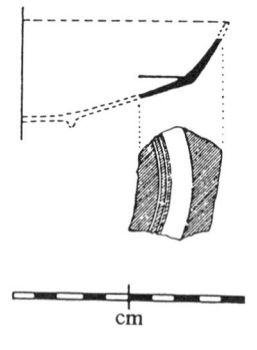

SS III, Fig. 9:2

---

[181]*Gezer III*, 184-85. For acceptable morphological parallels from south Lebanon, see *Chapman*, Fig. 24:240 (a Plain-Ware specimen from Joya) and Fig. 25:257 (a Bichrome Ware bowl, also from Joya).

[182]Compare the oblique parallels in *SS III*, Figs. 6:1-2 (PP 4); 10:1-3 (PP 6); see also Kenyon's comments on p. 120.

[183]*HES I*, Fig. 154:1 (Reg. No. 3482, apparently from subfloor makeup in Room 404 — see entry 13a on p. 277).

[184]The term "Samaria Ware" arose from the early discovery at Samaria of fine examples of this tradition; ironically, perhaps, the official report from this site itself hardly ever utilizes the term as a rubric to identify "the finest decorated ware of the Israelite period in Samaria" (*SS III*, 155). The closest Kenyon comes to establishing "Samaria Ware" as a technical ceramic class appears in her description of goods she associated with the Z Deep Pit, which lay southwest of the gate area located at the eastern edge of the compound (*SS III*, 134).

[185]*SS III*, 157. Kenyon described the ware as having a "biscuit-like feeling."

PP 6: LEVELING NEAR WALL 573 — POTTERY

band appears in reserve immediately below the point of inflection, followed by two closely incised circles. The profile of the fragment suggests an upper sidewall that thinned toward the top and ended in a simple, pointed rim mode. The wall proves thickest at the point of the external inflection, where it remains relatively smooth on its interior face. Beneath the break in its side angle, the wall quickly becomes rather thin as it proceeds toward the bottom of the vessel (which Kenyon has reconstructed as a ring-base form).

Kenyon suggested further that similar pieces seem to exhibit an initial buff slip. If her suggestion proves true, the sequence of surface treatment would have proceeded as follows: buff slip, complete burnishing, red slip, base slipped, bands left or trimmed[186] in buff reserve, a second wheel burnishing reworked afterward by hand, incision of concentric lines. From the point of view of morphology speaking, the Joint Expedition recovered only two whole or near-whole forms of Samaria Ware: a shallow, smoothly carinated bowl with slightly flaring upper walls and rim (*SS III*, Fig. 19:1), and a simpler design with "almost vertical walls and fantastically small ring base"[187] (*SS III*, Fig. 19:3). But sherd counts indicated that a third form, with wide, flat base and slightly bowed sidewalls that incline outward (compare *SS III*, Fig. 18:8), actually represents the most common type of Samaria Ware bowl found at the site.

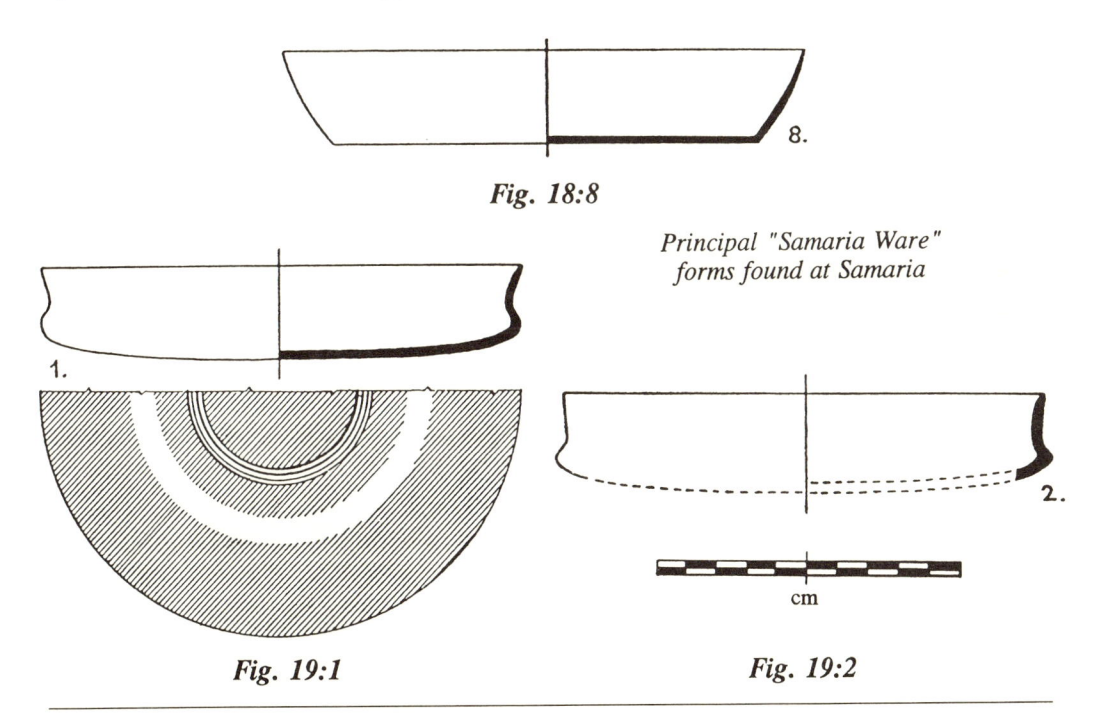

Fig. 18:8

Principal "Samaria Ware" forms found at Samaria

Fig. 19:1

Fig. 19:2

---

[186]Sukenik's suggestion that the entire bowl received a red slip, and that the bands were subsequently wiped clean, seems unlikely (*SS III*, 157).

[187]*SS III*, 157. I should note that, though the walls are generally straight, they do incline outward in their stance.

Though Aharoni and Amiran had already noted the presence of both the thick and thin varieties of Samaria Ware in Hazor Stratum VIII,[188] Wright formally proposed in 1959 a classification of two subtypes based on discernible differences in the techniques of slipping and burnishing used on each.[189] He called the heavier bowls of courser ware and darker red or reddish-brown slip *Samaria Ware A*, and he dated them to the mid-ninth century BCE on the basis of exemplars from Hazor VIII and, supposedly, Samaria PP 3 (but see n. 204 regarding the reference to PP 3). *Samaria Ware B* represented the thinner, more brightly-slipped bowls made of cleaner, smoother clay. This subgroup belonged, according to Wright, in the eighth century BCE, judging from parallels at Tell el-Farʿah (N) Niveau II, eighth-century fills at Shechem, Hazor VI-V, and Samaria PP 4-6. Finally, Wright noted that "differences between Wares A and B have to be noted from personal handling, unless future study can also discern datable and traceable differences in the form of the bowls."[190] Amiran subsequently concurred with Wright's assessment and presented separate plates of the thick- and thin-walled exemplars.[191]

Subsequent to these studies, analysts have noted various nuances in slip color and burnishing techniques.[192] Fragments at Samaria that resemble Fig. 9:2 show red bands on a buff surface on the interior of the bowl[193] and thereby appear as a photographic negative of the outside decorations. The recent report from Tell Qiri includes six different morphological types in the category of Samaria Ware.[194] But perhaps the most detailed presentation of this bowl class derives from Bikai's work at Tyre,[195] where eight categories of bowls comprise the broad collection of "Fine-Ware Plates." Though Bikai, who provides a working chronological range for each subgroup at Tyre, compares fragment No. 2 from Samaria to her Type 2, with its "flaring rim [and] a flat or slightly convex base,"[196] the Samaria piece seems to relate better to her Type 6.[197] The Tyrian Type 2, with its wide, flat base and outwardly leaning

---

[188] Their comments ultimately appeared in *Hazor II*, 12 (published in 1960).

[189] Wright, 22-24.

[190] Wright, 24, n. 28.

[191] *Amiran*, 207-12, Pl. 66 = eggshell-thin, Samaria Ware B; Pl. 67 = the thicker Samaria A specimens.

[192] Still, I hesitate to apply the term "Samaria Ware," at least in the strictest sense, to bowls with grey ware and black burnishing (such as those from *SS III*, Fig. 14:13; *Amiran*, Pl. 67:18; *Tyre*, Pl. XVI:10; see also *T. Qiri*, 201).

[193] *SS III*, 159, Fig. 19:6.

[194] *T. Qiri*, 148, Fig. 43:1-6. For the inclusion of other forms that appear relatively atypical of the traditional Samaria Ware (e.g., a hemispherical bowl with simple rim), see *Chapman*, Fig. 28:152-53, and the descriptions on pp. 137 and 139.

[195] See *Tyre* and Bikai, *BASOR* 229 (1978), 47-56.

[196] *Tyre*, 26 and n. 46.

[197] *Tyre*, 28, XV:1, 4, 7, 10, 11 (Stratum IV).

sidewalls, seems to correspond more directly to the third style of Samaria Ware bowl found at the Israelite capital (see my reference above to *SS III*, Fig. 18:8). Ironically, while this bowl class proved most common at Samaria, Bikai's Type 6 (to which Fig. 9:2 relates) represented the most popular variety at Tyre.[198] Moreover, Type 6 showed a fairly certain chronology at Tyre, where 71% of the group came from Stratum IV,[199] i.e., from the period leading up to 732 BCE. The simpler design of Type 2 succeeded it during Strata III-II, which spanned roughly the final two decades of the eighth century BCE.[200] Around 700 BCE, a variant with slightly higher sidewalls replaced, or perhaps joined, Type 2.[201]

One may draw several significant conclusions from these data. First, both Fine Ware Plate-Types 2 and 6 at Tyre fall within Wright's old *Samaria Ware B* group, with the thinner construction and better-levigated ware.[202] Judging from the relative chronological distribution of these types at Tyre, it seems that Type 6 slightly preceded Type 2. Since the design, construction, and ware of 6 seem to surpass those of 2,[203] the latter group appears as a final, almost degenerate phase of fine ware bowls and plates. Type 6, from around the third quarter of the eighth century BCE, reflects the heyday of the Samaria Ware tradition.[204] Second, the Samaria fragment presented in Fig. 9:2 belongs to a subgroup of Phoenician-style Samaria Ware (Fine Ware Plate Type 6 at Tyre) that made its way to Samaria but did not dominate the assemblage there. Kenyon and Bikai independently offered strikingly similar descriptions of this pottery when it appeared at their respective sites.[205] The tradition may well have originated from the pre-732 BCE period, and the small size of the fragment follows as a reflex of both its extremely thin ware and the fact that it derives from a context of

---

[198] Bikai's comment that "the carinated bowl which is so common at Samaria is rare at Tyre" (*Tyre*, 26) refers to the styles seen in *SS III*, Figs. 18:9-10 and 19:1-2, not to the tradition that lies behind Fig. 9:2.

[199] *Tyre*, 28.

[200] But see now Gitin's comments in *Gezer III*, 189, where he suggests that Type 2 very likely extended into the seventh century BCE.

[201] *Tyre*, 27, Table 4A.

[202] Bikai herself places Type 2 in this category (Bikai, *BASOR*, 229 [1978], 52).

[203] For example, the walls of Type 6 are even thinner than those of 2. In fact, Bikai described her Fine Ware Plate 6 as "the finest of the type which appeared in this excavation" (*Tyre*, 28).

[204] It seems unlikely that the thin-walled exemplars of Samaria Ware extend back into the ninth century BCE, as intimated by Kenyon in her description of the goods associated with the Z Deep Pit (which she desired to limit to PP 3). Though her comments regarding this rock-cut pit, which was situated beneath Byzantine house levels, provide rather sparse stratigraphic data, Bikai has concluded from the discussion that PP 6 materials overlay the pit area and could easily have become mixed with the contents of that feature (Bikai, *BASOR*, 229 [1978], 53). Kenyon's own comments in *SS III*, 124, seem to confirm Bikai's suspicion (see also the text relating to n. 523 below). Lowering the date of the Samaria Ware bowls in the Z Deep Pit has broad ramifications, including possible adjustments to the date of the colonization of Kition by the Phoenicians (see the comments in Bikai, *BASOR*, 54).

[205] Compare nn. 184-85 and 203.

secondary fill displaced from the higher summit area. Third, one can place the most common type of Samaria Ware found at Samaria itself in the closing decade or so of the eighth century based on parallels with Fine Ware Type 2 at Tyre. From the outcome of the Yoqneʿam Regional Project, I may add that the thin-walled, carinated bowl with pointed rim[206] also emerged as the most frequently attested Samaria Ware form at sites excavated in that survey.[207] Moreover, the results from Yoqneʿam itself indicate that the earliest examples of Wright's *Samaria Ware A* appear already in the tenth century BCE, a fact which Wright himself anticipated.[208]

This discussion leads me back to a point touched on in my introduction to this chapter (see *Excursus*, p. 250). Hamilton's recovery of buff-colored, red-slipped bowls from Stratum III at Tell Abu-Hawām can no longer provide an effective argument for raising the date for Wright's *Samaria Ware B* category. While the excavations at Hawām apparently yielded both the thick and thin varieties of this tradition, the report did not present them in drawing. Hamilton described the former group as "a coarser type of red-slip ware in which the section showed black in the centre."[209] In his description of the thinner types, he recorded that "on the most delicate fragments red and yellow are occasionally combined in alternate bands."[210] According to the report, the excavators recovered fragments (though only "a few pieces") of the thin-walled bowls from "on the pavement of rooms 13 and 14."[211] In 1978, Bikai expressed concern that "the occupation break at Tell Abu Hawam in any dating system covers the whole of the 8th and 7th centuries and part of the 6th."[212] Therefore, the apparent *Samaria Ware A* fragments assigned to Stratum III must, she surmised, stem from a previously unrecognized "transitory occupation" that occurred during some part of that gap. I have shown earlier, however, that the more recent work of Balensi and Herrera obviates this problem by correcting the overall range of Stratum III so that it extends to at least 732 BCE.[213]

Finally, much discussion has centered on the place of origin for this impressive ceramic tradition, with Samaria and some location in Phoenicia (probably Tyre) being the two principal candidates. Some scholars have raised strong resistance to the fact

---

[206]I.e., a style similar to *SS III*, Fig. 9:2 and Tyre Fine Ware Type 6 but dissimilar to *SS III*, Fig. 19:1-2 and Tyre Type 2.

[207]*T. Qiri*, 202.

[208]Compare the comments in *T. Qiri*, 202, and *Wright*, 24 (see the examples that he already cites from Hazor Strata X-IX, Tell Abu Hawām III, and Megiddo VA-IVB). See now also the survey of Samaria Ware forms in *Gezer III*, 180, 187-88.

[209]*TAH*, 7.

[210]*TAH*, 7.

[211]*TAH*, 7.

[212]Bikai, *BASOR*, 229 (1978), 53-54.

[213]Balensi, *BASOR* 257 (1985), 68-69.

that the overall group became a namesake of Samaria.[214] Though, even today, more sophisticated tests are required in order to establish a viable answer to this question, one may recall the seldom cited spectrographic analysis that the Joint Expedition performed on 15 ceramic and 5 clay samples from Samaria and surrounding areas.[215] Two of the pottery fragments tested included a Samaria Ware bowl with flat base (apparently of Type 2 at Tyre) from S Tomb 101 at Samaria, and a similar fine-ware bowl from Tomb 80C at Megiddo (*resembling* that seen in *Megiddo Tombs* Pl. 75:8). When compared to clay samples obtained from five locations,[216] the results appear as shown in Tables 28-29 below.

In a search for 29 elements, the test revealed traces (at varying levels)[217] of 22 elements in the sherds and/or clays. In Tables 28-29, I have reorganized Kenyon's data to highlight only the *differences* that became apparent between each of the Samaria Ware fragments and the five clay sources. Though this test involved an extremely limited sample of pottery, I may suggest the following observations from the results. All the soils tested contained traces of boron, none of which appeared in either pottery fragment. The bowl from Samaria displays the greatest compositional similarity to clay taken from the valley bed around the site. On the other hand, the Megiddo bowl shows a more significant compositional dissimilarity to the clays found at Samaria or in its immediate environs[218] than it does to the red ochre purchased in either Nablus or Jerusalem. On the whole, the makeup of the Megiddo fragment proved most congruent with the ochre from Jerusalem. These data led Kenyon to conclude that the wares of the two sherds "are not identical,"[219] a fact which may suggest different places of manufacture for these two Samaria Ware items. Until firmer evidence emerges to the contrary, it seems prudent to assume that no single location held a monopoly on the production and distribution of this impressive tradition of pottery—at least not during the period of its latest manifestation (late eighth and probably early seventh centuries

---

[214] E.g., note Katzenstein's exhortation that "it is high time they [Samaria Ware vessels] were called after their country of origin, that is 'Phoenician Ware'" (H. J. Katzenstein, *The History of Tyre* [Jerusalem: The Schocken Institute for Jewish Research, 1973], 148).

[215] *SS III*, 472.

[216] These locations include: clay from a valley bed at Samaria; clay from a summit bed at Samaria; a "red deposit from caves in rocks near Samaria"; "red ochre sold in Nablus"; and "red ochre sold in Jerusalem" (*SS III*, 472).

[217] The published report did not assign exact numerical values to the levels of each element found in a sherd or clay sample. Instead, the authors describe the presence of an element as follows: none (O); trace (T); moderate (M); and large (L). See *SS III*, 472.

[218] These clays typically contain four elements not found in the Megiddo vessel (silver, zinc, titanium, and boron). Similarly, the Megiddo sample contained the particular elements absent from the Samaria clays, such as potassium, phosphorus, and sometimes barium and strontium.

[219] *SS III*, 157.

CLAY SOURCE		TRACE ELEMENTS					
Samaria: valley bed	(+)	K	-	-	-	-	-
	(-)	-	-	-	B	-	-
Samaria: summit bed	(+)	K	-	Ti	-	-	-
	(-)	-	-	-	B	-	-
Caves near Samaria	(+)	-	-	-	-	Ba	Sr
	(-)	-	-	-	B	-	-
Nablus ochre	(+)	-	Zn	-	-	Ba	Sr
	(-)	-	P	-	B	-	-
Jerusalem ochre	(+)	-	Zn	-	-	-	-
	(-)	-	P	-	B	-	-

(+) = element traced in the Samaria fragment, but not in the test clays
(-) = element not traced in the Samaria fragment, but found in the test clays

K = potassium   Zn = zinc
P = phosphorus   Ti = titanium
Ba = barium   B = boron
Sr = strontium

Spectrographic Analysis of "Samaria Ware" Fragment Discovered at Samaria

Table 28

BCE, when Tyre FWP-Type 2 correlates to the most frequently attested form at Samaria).

The rim and sidewall fragment from the medium-sized bowl in No. 3 (p. 276) exhibits a rounded though apparently not carinated (or, rather, inflected) body wall[220] and a rim that is folded[221] outward and then undercut to form a very prominent lower flange. The continuing curvature of the sidewall results in a moderately inverted pos-

---

[220] At the site of Lachish, bowls with curved vs. angled sides predominated in the seventh-century BCE Tomb 106 (*Lachish III, Text*, 277).

[221] The term "folded rim" derives from Wampler's classification in *TN II*, 35, § 34. As Tufnell has noted, however, only by breaking the fragment can one establish with absolute certainty that the manufacturing technique involved an actual folding of the rim vs. a mere thickening of it. She suggests that, in some instances, "moulded" or simply "thickened" provide better descriptions of this style (see *Lachish III, Text*, 277).

CLAY SOURCE			TRACE ELEMENTS				
Samaria: valley bed	(+)	K	P	-	-	-	-
	(-)	Ag	Zn	Ti	B	-	-
Samaria: summit bed	(+)	K	P	-	-	-	-
	(-)	Ag	Zn	-	B	-	-
Caves near Samaria	(+)	-	P	-	-	Ba	Sr
	(-)	Ag	Zn	Ti	B	-	-
Nablus ochre	(+)	-	-	-	-	Ba	Sr
	(-)	Ag	-	Ti	B	-	-
Jerusalem ochre	(+)	-	-	-	-	-	-
	(-)	Ag	-	Ti	B	-	-

(+) = element traced in the Megiddo fragment, but not in the test clays
(-) = element not traced in the Megiddo fragment, but found in the test clays

K = potassium   Ag = silver
P = phosphorus   Zn = zinc
Ba = barium   Ti = titanium
Sr = strontium   B = boron

Spectrographic Analysis of "Samaria Ware" Fragment Discovered at Megiddo

Table 29

ture toward the 30 cm mouth and makes the point of widest diameter fall just below the flange area. The outward fold of the rim displays a slightly convex outer face that forms a collar around the vessel's orifice. Most antecedent members of this Iron II family that include similarly heavy collars generally have their (sometimes incipient) flange undercut to a lesser degree than this exemplar; they also frequently maintain more of an inward break in their upper sidewalls than that seen on this piece.[222] The fabric consists in a "soft creamy buff" clay with mostly small grits, and the surface of the fragment showed a "self slip."[223]

Though a good morphological parallel for the folded, flanged rim of entry No. 3 may emerge on a somewhat shallower bowl from Field VII at Gezer possibly as early

---

[222] For examples, see Bowl Types 50, 56, 57, and 71 in *Gezer III*, Pls. 20:20-21; 24:5; 25:7; 27:24 and 28, ranging from the mid-eighth into the early sixth centuries BCE.

[223] *SS III*, 121.

as the mid-ninth century BCE,[224] the fabric of this piece is more reddish in color than that of the Samaria fragment and thus indicates an earlier date for the Gezer bowl. Perhaps more important, the folded rim-form mode clearly proved atypical of all other styles apparent in the ninth-century BCE levels at Gezer.[225] This style rim reflects a tradition current primarily during the eighth and seventh centuries BCE. The inward slanting upper sidewalls, strongly articulated flange, and buff-color ware help place the Samaria fragment more precisely among similar elements of the late eighth and early seventh centuries BCE. Kenyon herself observed that this form first appears at Samaria in PP 6, but only infrequently, and that it seems to relate to styles common in the seventh century.[226] Ancestral variants from the pre-732 BCE period generally show a thicker construction, as at Beth-Shan,[227] Hazor,[228] and Tyre.[229] Adequate parallels from levels dating to the late eighth and the seventh centuries come from Hazor,[230] Megiddo,[231] Tell Keisan,[232] Tell el-Farʿah (N),[233] Tell en-Naṣbeh,[234] Tell Qasîle,[235] and, in the south, from Tell Beit Mirsim[236] and Lachish.[237] Similar rim styles wit-

SS III, Fig. 9:3

---

[224] *Gezer III*, Pl. 13:6 (Stratum VIB).

[225] *Gezer III*, 201, where Gitin commented that the folded rim on this piece "is either an aberrant or the earliest Corpus example of the folded rim technique."

[226] *SS III*, 121.

[227] *Beth-Shan*, James, Fig. 68:9 (good parallel for rim and angle of sidewall); 69:2 (slightly more bloated body form) and 7 (all Level IV). Some of these bowl rims also seem quite close to the cooking-pot fragments in *SS III*, Fig. 9:11 and 13, discussed below.

[228] *Hazor I*, Pl. LIV:1 (Stratum V); *Hazor II*, Pl. LXXXI:25 (Stratum VA); *Hazor III-IV*, Pl. CCXXXI:4 (Stratum VA).

[229] *Tyre*, Pl. X:29 (Stratum III).

[230] *Hazor II*, Pl. XCVIII:14 (Stratum IV), though with pinkish clay.

[231] *Megiddo I*, Pl. 27:84 (Strata IV-I), on a deep bowl. Compare also *Megiddo I*, Pl. 23:9 (Stratum III, with a groove cut into the outer face of the collar), and 18 (Strata III-II, without the undercut flange).

[232] *T. Keisan*, Pls. 40:6-6a; 41:3 (Niveau 5; compare also 41:5, with a severe flange with outer groove on the collar); see also p. 170, n. 57; the "int. légèrement lustré" and "ext. lustré" noted for Nos. 6 and 6a, respectively, may relate to the "self slip" that Kenyon saw on the Samaria example.

[233] *Chambon*, Pl. 54:8 (Niveau VIIe.1), with handles and "pâte rose à cœur gris . . . lustré à l'intérieur."

[234] *TN—Cistern*, Fig. 4:x24 (Cistern 370); *TN II*, Pl. 58:1330.

[235] *T. Qasîle* [2], Fig. 55:18, 21 (Stratum VII).

[236] *TBM I*, Pl. 61:15 (Stratum A).

[237] *Lachish III*, Pl. 101:629, 635, 638-39, 641, 643-44 (Level III) = variations on Tufnell's Bowl Type B.13. See also Chapter I, 127, n. 476 above. That Tufnell's survey associated the maximum occurrence of folded rim bowls with Samaria PP 7 (e.g., *SS III*, Fig. 11:1-7), Megiddo Stratum III, Tell el-Fûl Period III, Beth-Shemesh Stratum IIc, Lachish III-II, and Tell Beit Mirsim City Level A (*Lachish III*,

nessed on various large jars with wide bodies from Tell Beit Mirsim[238] indicate that this general tradition finds a cousin in seventh-century BCE holemouth forms.[239]

b. Cooking Pots

Half of the pottery group published from the leveling fill associated with Wall 573 consists in a varied series of cooking-pot rims (*SS III*, 9:10-18). All the fragments came from the segment *North of 551*, and adequate recording data existed for all but one of these items (see the provenance data and † in Table 30). The collection shows a rather wide range of styles typical of materials recovered from such secondary fill debris. Given the mixed ceramic traditions represented by these rims and their generally compromised context, I will combine my comments for the individual pieces into a single, collective discussion.

SS III Published Figure	Registry No. (none marked for discard)	Provenance			
		Strip	Coordinates	Feature	Local Layer
9:10	Q 5238	Qn	North of 551	leveling	V
9:11	Q 5236	Qn	North of 551	leveling	Va
9:12	Q 5237	Qn	North of 551	leveling	V
9:13	Q 5231	Qn	North of 551	leveling	V
9:14	Q 5239	Qn	North of 551	leveling	Va
9:15	Q 5233	Qn	North of 551	leveling	V
9:16	Q 5232	Qn	North of 551	leveling	Va
9:17	Q 5230	Qn	North of 551	leveling	Va
9:18 †	Q 4912	Qn	North of 551	leveling	Va

† = field register *Qn* contains no record of this fragment

Provenance Data:
PP6 Cooking Pots from the Leveling Contemporary with Wall 573

Table 30

The pots appear to belong to a medium-sized class of crockery in which the diameter of the mouth ranges from 27-30 cm; only Nos. 11-12 display smaller mouths of 20 and 18 cm, respectively.[240] The point of carination in the upper sidewall varies

---

Text, 278) corroborates my suggested dating of this Samaria fragment.

[238]*TBM I*, Pl. 52:2, 4 (Stratum A); *TBM III*, Pl. 13:2, 9 (Stratum A), and §§ 146-47.

[239]See nn. 226-27 for the further application of the nuance to Iron II cooking-pot forms.

[240]No measurements appeared for Nos. 10 and 15.

SS III, Fig. 9:10-18

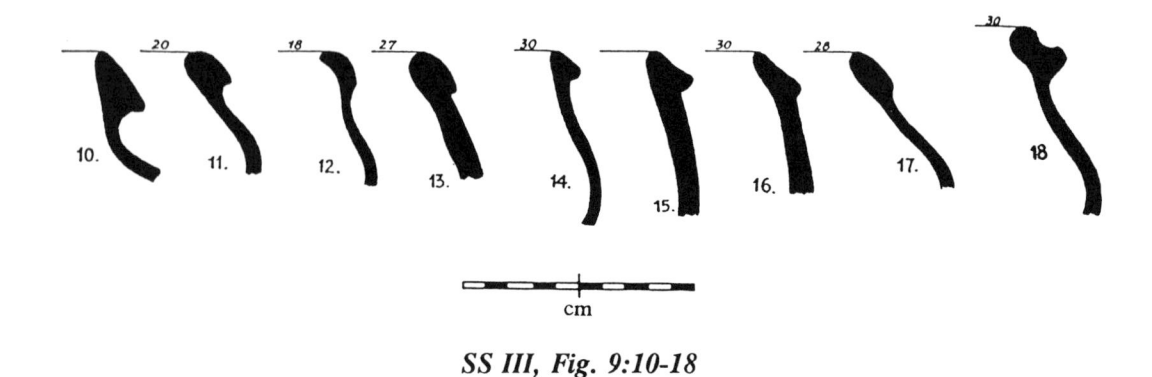

considerably among these forms. While some fragments maintain a relatively high carination (Nos. 10-11), others show this attribute closer to the midpoint of the vessel's body, where it results in a higher upper sidewall (Nos. 14, 18). Still other examples display sidewalls that fall more directly from the rim and suggest a body profile that made minimal use of carination (Nos. 13, 15-16). Though neither the published drawings nor the itemized descriptions mentioned the appearance of handles on any of these vessels, one should not entirely ignore the use of this feature on some of the traditions represented here (particularly those that show a more strongly inverted upper wall and rim, as in Nos. 11-13, 17).[241] The fabric generally appears brown to reddish-brown in color (Nos. 10-11, 14, 16-17), though two specimens showed a dark red ware (Nos. 12-13), while one ranged from grey to red in color (No. 15).

Excluding fragment No. 18, Kenyon offered the following comments on the group as a whole:

> The cooking pots, Nos. 10-17, are of a type which does not occur earlier, nor in E. 207. They may be the latest developments of the L.B. and E.I. I. type with a straight rim, but they are very much thicker in the rim, and usually shorter there also. The wall of the pot tends to be more vertical and less bulging.[242]

I presume that Kenyon's reference to the earlier "type with a straight rim" refers, in the main, to the elongated, flanged tradition common on the so-called Early Shallow Type of cooking vessel. If this assumption is true, I believe she is generally correct in her assessment cited above; only No. 18 shows any tendency toward the notched-rim of the "Late Shallow Type."

Judging from these observations, then, the prototypical roots of nearly all the forms presented here extend back at least as far as the Iron I-Iron II transition period. For example, the inverted rim seen in Fig. 9:10, with its flanged collar showing a flat

---

[241] Kenyon included Nos. 12-13 and 17 (along with Fig. 7:6 from PP 4) in her category of Class D cooking-pot rims, which she said probably belonged to deep pots with two handles (*SS III*, 189).

[242] *SS III*, 121.

outer face and simple, rounded lip, plus a rounded groove beneath the flange, seems to represent the earliest of the forms in this collection. A succession of adequate parallels from Tell Qasîle Stratum XI,[243] Beth-Shemesh Strata IIa-b,[244] and the late variant in Tyre Stratum II[245] demonstrates the extended lifespan of this tradition. Kenyon included No. 10 in her Class A Collared Rim cooking-pot variety, and noted that, while this style occurred from PP 1-6 (excluding 3),[246] one should regard it "as characteristic of our earlier periods."[247]

The thickened, rounded rims of Nos. 11 and 13 are quite similar,[248] but overall the fragments differ in two respects. No. 11 is rounded beneath the flange and maintains a high carination, while No. 13 displays a tool-trimmed lower flange and a thicker sidewall that drops more directly from the rim (compare *SS III*, Fig. 7:6 from PP 4, discussed in Chapter II above). A slightly more pronounced version of this style appears on several kraters from Hazor Strata VI and V; one may also compare the class of profiled krater rims with convex upper shoulder attested among the YRP sites.[249] Once again, however, the incipient tradition is seen on a piece from tenth-century BCE levels at Tell Qasîle.[250] No. 13 also seems to show some relationship to the medium-sized, red slipped bowls from Iron II levels at Gezer[251] and Hazor.[252] While the ancestral traditions behind several of these rims seem associated with early, deep bowl or cooking-pot forms, they eventually evolved into various late Iron II styles as well.

In addition to the krater-related rim just mentioned in No. 13, the somewhat narrower pot represented by rim No. 12 relates morphologically to both earlier[253] and later[254] rim-form modes. The short, flanged version of No. 14 has similarly early prototypes.[255] Though No. 15 displays a comparable rim-form mode, its thicker

---

[243] *T. Qasîle* [2], Fig. 25:14.

[244] *AS IV*, Pl. LXIII:31.

[245] *Tyre*, Pl. XII:27.

[246] *SS III*, 189.

[247] *SS III*, 191. Such comparative comments seem strange in light of Kenyon's previous statement that no style represented in Nos. 10-17 occurs before PP 6.

[248] See n. 227 above.

[249] *Hazor II*, Pls. LXVII:13 (Stratum VI); XCIV:10 (Stratum VA); *T. Qiri*, Fig. 38:13; p. 216.

[250] *T. Qasîle* [2], Fig. 44:28 (Stratum X).

[251] See *Gezer III*, Pl. 45:17, though without the trimming beneath the collar.

[252] *Hazor II*, Pl. LXXXIII:6 (Stratum VA).

[253] E.g., *T. Qasîle* [2], Fig. 14:23 (Stratum XII); *Megiddo I*, Pls. 31:153; 40:20 (Stratum V); *T. Keisan*, Pl. 64:2a (Niveau 9a-b); compare also the narrower, cooking jug in *Ta'anach*, Fig. 50:1 (Period IIB Cultic Structure).

[254] E.g., *Gezer III*, Pl. 27:27 (Field VII, Stratum VA); *Tyre*, Pl. XII:29, 32 (Strata II and III, respectively); see the krater in *T. Qasîle* [2], Fig. 56:2 (Stratum VII).

[255] *Ta'anach*, Fig. 42:3 (Period IIB); *T. Keisan*, Pl. 64:4c-d (Niveau 9a-b); *Hazor II*, Pl. LVII:9

sidewalls drop more directly from the flange area.[256] The slightly concave flange on No. 16 also has an upper sidewall that shows little sign of carination.[257] One may also compare the thickened rim with hardly any flange in entry No. 17 with various other bowls from Megiddo,[258] Ta'anach,[259] Tell en-Naṣbeh,[260] and Gezer,[261] among other sites. Generally speaking, the form recalls *SS III*, Fig. 6:29 from PP 4 (see the appropriate discussion in Chapter II). Also of interest here is Lugenbeal's and Sauer's description of a large class of either jar or "Holemouth Krater" rims from Heshbon (but these generally exhibit light tan or buff exteriors).[262] Kenyon cited Nos. 12, 13, and 17 in the published comments on her "Class D Rim with Rounded Collar"[263] and added that this type appeared less frequently and generally later in the Samaria series.[264] Judging from the available evidence, the overall chronological range for this tradition extends from the early ninth century into the seventh century BCE.

Finally, fragment No. 18 (which presumably derives from the same findspot as the other items in Table 30, though it lacks a clearly recorded provenance) exhibits a concave rim with rounded, thickened lip and thickened flange pushed upward to a more horizontal position.[265] As noted, this piece seems the closest to the notched rim forms, which appeared in the mid-ninth century BCE and continued through the Iron II period. Many variants of this tradition appear in levels that date to the ninth and eighth centuries BCE.[266] As the area above the "notch" shortened even more, the latter fea-

---

(Stratum VIII), with a similarly thin construction but with the outer flange slightly more pinched, as in No. 15; *T. Qasîle* [2], Fig. 54:22 (Stratum VIII).

[256] Compare *Hazor I*, Pl. LXXIV:20 (Stratum V); *Hazor II*, Pl. XCIV:2-3 (Stratum VA); *TN II*, Pl. 65:1484 (taken as an early Iron Age form with LBA connections; see § 59).

[257] Compare *Megiddo I*, Pl. 40:16 (Strata V-IV and earlier); *Lachish III*, Pl. 104:684, though the sidewall on No. 16 drops more directly from the rim; see also the rounded bowl in *Beth-Shan*, James, Fig. 69:1.

[258] *Megiddo I*, Pls. 31:156 (with upper wall and rim slightly less inverted than on the cooking pot from Samaria) and 32:166 (Stratum V).

[259] *Ta'anach*, Fig. 42:1-2 for good morphological comparisons, but again with a less inverted stance than that on the true cooking-pot form (Period IIB). Note also the discussion of the small krater with folded rim in *Ta'anach*, 43.

[260] *TN II*, Pl. 47:998.

[261] *Gezer III*, Pl. 24:12 (Field VII, Stratum VB/VA).

[262] E. N. Lugenbeal and J. A. Sauer, "Seventh-Sixth Century B.C. Pottery from Area B at Heshbon," *AUSS* 10 (1972), 50-52; compare Pl. VII:367 for the closest morphological parallel to No. 17 (and to No. 13). The authors cite *SS III*, Fig. 12:2, from PP 8.

[263] *SS III*, 189.

[264] *SS III*, 191.

[265] Compare CP Group II/b among the YRP sites (*T. Qiri*, 143).

[266] *Megiddo I*, Pl. 39:11 (Strata IV-I); *Hazor I*, Pl. LV:4, 6 (Stratum V); *Hazor II*, Pl. LXIX:6, 7, 9, 14 (Stratum VI); *Hazor III-IV*, Pls. CCXXIV:3-4 (Stratum VB); CCXXVII:20 (Stratum VA); *T. Qasîle* [2],

ture evolved into a mere groove around the top of the rim.[267]

In sum, I agree with Kenyon that this collection of cooking-pot fragments reflects various streams of tradition that derive from the basic elongated, flanged-style rim of the early Iron Age. In light of the heterogeneous nature of the rim and sidewall attributes, the group as a whole might easily span the ninth and eighth centuries BCE. The detailed rim typology worked out for the sites in the Yoqneʿam Regional Project incorporates three of these fragments (Nos. 10, 13, and 18) and confirms my dating.[268] Given the secondary nature of the archaeological context from which the excavators recovered these rims, however, it remains difficult to refine the dating of their original historical context to either the period before or immediately following the years of heaviest Assyrian activity in the region (ca. 734-720 BCE). From a strictly morphological point of view, most of these pieces could have originated during either phase. All things considered, they cannot, as a group, tighten any of the various chronologies suggested for the site. As indicated earlier, Kenyon noted only that these rims reflect an Iron II evolution of "L.B. and E.I. I." motifs; otherwise, she did not cite a single parallel for any of the fragments published from this stratified context.

c. Jugs and Juglets

The official report included three fragments that originated from different diagnostic points (rim and upper neck; upper body; lower body and base) on diverse styles

SS III Published Figure	Registry No. (none marked for discard)	Provenance		
		Strip	Coordinates	Feature	Local Layer
9:4 †	Q 5028	Qn	North of 551	leveling	V
9:6	Q 5226	Qn	North of 551	leveling	Va
9:7 †	Q 4977	Qn	North of 551	leveling	V

† = field register *Qn* lists only the published registry number without the other identifying data given here from unpublished stratification cards

Provenance Data:
PP6 Jugs and Juglets from the Leveling Contemporary with Wall 573
Table 31

Figs. 40:17; 43:18; 44:11, 13 (Stratum X); *Lachish III*, Pl. 93:442; *AS-IV*, Pl. LXIII:35 (Stratum II). Compare also Gezer cooking-pot Type 102, as in *Gezer III*, Pl. 22:4 (Field VII, Stratum VIA = mid-eighth century).

[267] *Hazor II*, Pl. LXIX:16 (Stratum VI); LXXXV:9 (Stratum VA).

[268] See *T. Qiri*, 216, Table 8 (PP 6 column). Note also that the Qiri rim types associated with *SS III*,

of jugs. The information in Table 31, taken once again from Appendix A, not only provides the basic provenance data for these items but indicates as well the presence of certain difficulties regarding the lack of records for two of the three entries. As I shall show, questions surrounding these two sherds appear to be interrelated.

Fragment No. 4[269] appears to depict a body sherd from a painted jug or jar tradition.[270] Only through G. M. Crowfoot's meticulously kept stratification cards could one learn that, along with the other pieces discussed in this section, this item derived from Layer V of the excavated segment identified as *North of 551*. The laconic description offered by Kenyon in the publication of this entry, however, remains somewhat anomalous in both its complete neglect of the painted decoration and its mention that "another similar *base* was found."[271] For the moment, then, I shall note only that band-painted jugs appear to precede similarly decorated jars in the pottery industries at other sites in the same regional culture as Samaria, such as Megiddo[272] and Taʿanach.[273] If the vessel represented by this fragment originated in the late eighth or the seventh century, then, it may belong to the jar family rather than to a tradition of jugs.

SS III, Fig. 9:4

The rim and upper neck fragment presented in No. 6 may arguably belong to one of two classes of jugs. The first group exhibits a long, concave neck (so that it curves outward toward the top) and a rim that assumes a vertical or slightly inverted stance and gives a flanged or notched profile similar to that seen already on many Iron

---

Fig. 9:10 (= Qiri designation *CP I: Triangular*), 13 (= *C II: Profiled*), and 18 (= *CP II: Pinched*), appear at a variety of northern sites from the Iron Age I period through the eighth century BCE (compare *T. Qiri*, 217, Tables 9-11).

[269]The data and pencil drawing originally recorded on the stratification card for this entry reveal that it actually consists of two joined fragments. The break runs diagonally through the broad center band of painting.

[270]The principal difference between the two categories lies in the fact that the jar was intended for storing (and transporting) while the jug was intended for pouring a given commodity. This difference in function manifested itself typologically in the design of the necks (generally shorter in jars) as well as the rims and lips (more frequently pinched on the jug) utilized on the two classes of containers. (For more typological details, see *APTJ*, 45-55.)

[271]*SS III*, 121 (emphasis added). See my further comments under entry No. 7 below.

[272]Band-painted jugs appear already in Stratum V (*Megiddo I*, Pls. 6:147, 149, 154; 7:163, 172-73) while similar jars belong primarily to Strata IV/III-I (*Megiddo I*, Pl. 9:30; 10:47; 11:48-52; 12:65). Compare the jar in *Hazor III-IV*, Pl. CCXXI:4 (Stratum VB) for a similar, though more closely spaced, pattern of bands drawn on the upper body of the vessel. The decoration of the jar in *Megiddo I*, Pl. 10:47 appears to resemble most closely the basic pattern seen on the Samaria fragment (i.e., a wide band with a slightly narrower one beneath it and two thin bands above it). Though the Megiddo jar clearly stems from a bichrome tradition, I cannot speak with certainty on the color scheme preserved on the Samaria entry, due to a lack of properly recorded information.

[273]*Taʿanach*, Fig. 58:14; 59:1-2, for band-painted jugs from Cistern 74, Period IIB.

PP 6: LEVELING NEAR WALL 573 — POTTERY

II cooking pots of the so-called Late Shallow Type.[274] From better-preserved examples of these jugs, one sees that this style typically maintained a globular body form with a ring base and a pinched rim that produced a spout set opposite a single handle, which generally extended from the rim (without arching above it) to the vessel's shoulder. Though the drawing in *SS III*, Fig. 9:6 does not make it apparent, this fragment did show the "trace of [a] handle springing from [the] rim."[275]

SS III, Fig. 9:6

A very closely related jug form bears all the attributes just mentioned but shows for the rim itself more of a cyma profile, in which the lip of the rim curves outward slightly.[276] The two classes are so closely related that analysts sometimes blur the distinctions between them.[277] It appears, however, that notched or flanged rims generally occur more frequently on jugs with wider necks than do their cyma counterparts, and that the upper handles of the former group tend to remain even with the lip of the rim rather than arching above that point, as they often do in the cyma class. Still, these observations constitute only general guidelines and cannot always distinguish the two styles dogmatically. Moreover, the mouth diameters of the wide-necked and narrow-necked families tend to overlap at around 9-10 cm. Since Kenyon measured the orifice on No. 6 at 10 cm, it remains difficult to tell from this single attribute to which style the fragment actually belongs. Further, the upper neckwall on No. 6 appears more everted, as in most narrow-necked, cyma types; yet a pushed-up flange (called a "stub-flange" in Gitin's terminology) assumes a more horizontal rather than angular position and clearly separates the upper neck and rim areas.[278] In short, the Samaria specimen may display mixed attributes that derive from both the cyma- and flanged-rim varieties of high-necked jugs, but it seems clearly to favor the latter tradition.

---

[274]Interestingly, Kenyon even cites this fragment later in the official report as an example of her Class B (collared with flange) cooking-pot rim (*SS III*, 189); she relates it to other fragments presented earlier in PP 1 (Fig. 1:19, 24), PP 2 (Fig. 3:20, 22, 29), and PP 4 (Fig. 6:31, 33, 35).

[275]*SS III*, 121. G. M. Crowfoot added the following description on her stratification card: "Hard ringing ware. Brownish surface, black break, red inside. Scattered w[ith] limestone grits."

[276]A good, side-by-side comparison of these two subtypes appears in *Gezer III*, Pl. 19:3 (cyma shaped rim) and 6 (with a short-flanged rim), both from Field VII, Stratum VIA (mid-eighth century BCE).

[277]For example, Gitin frequently notes the presence of a flange when describing rims actually classified in his cyma group (see *Gezer III*, 147-48). He also refers to the entry in *SS III*, Fig. 22:8 as a cyma type, though it seems very near the flanged form of the present PP 6 example. The major differences involve the respective fabrics (hard, well levigated, brownish in color, and with some grits for the PP 6 fragment vs. a red-slipped, soft, buff-to-grey ware for the piece in 22:8) and the fact that the PP 6 sample carries a slightly more pronounced notched effect on its rim flange.

[278]According to Gitin, the sharply angular version of rim (his Type 20C; see *Gezer III*, Pl. 19:6) currently appears only in the south (*Gezer III*, 147).

While one may trace the historical antecedents of both the flanged[279] and cyma[280] traditions back to the Iron I period and the Iron I-II transition, neither style rose to real prominence prior to the eighth century BCE, when the bodies gradually became slightly smaller in diameter and the necks/rims became slightly taller in height.[281] During that time, the cyma form appeared in both the north and the south, as shown by examples from Megiddo,[282] Beth-Shan,[283] and Lachish.[284] Roughly contemporaneous parallels for the flanged type are available from both before and after the 732 BCE and 722 BCE horizons at Hazor,[285] Megiddo,[286] Tell Qiri,[287] Tell en-Naṣbeh,[288] Gezer,[289] Beth-Shemesh,[290] Tell Beit Mirsim,[291] and Lachish,[292] among other sites. Tufnell noted that the majority of her Jug Type J.3 displayed pink, buff, or brown ware, and a medium to hard firing.[293] Gitin's analysis has assigned chronologi-

---

[279]Compare *Gezer III*, Pls. 9:10 (Field VII, Stratum VIIA = tenth century BCE); 12:15(?)-16 and 15:3 (VII, Stratum VIB = mid-ninth century); *Taʿanach*, Fig. 59:4 (Period IIB); *Hazor III-IV*, Pl. CCVIII:42 (Stratum IX); *ʿEin Gev* Fig 5:3 (Stratum III cooking jug). One may also note the morphological semblance of an earlier juglet tradition in Transjordan (*Saʿidiyeh 1*, Fig. 19:4; Area AA, Stratum XII, provisionally = late twelfth century BCE); in this regard, see as well *Dibon*, Fig. 1:7-8 (Iron Age pottery from the fill of the Nabataean Temple Podium).

[280]*Taʿanach*, Fig. 37:2 (Period IIB); *Hazor I*, Pl. L:20 (Stratum VII).

[281]See the comments in *Gezer III*, 146.

[282]*Megiddo I*, Pl. 3:73-74 (Strata IV-III).

[283]*Beth-Shan*, James, Fig. 37:6 (Level IV).

[284]*Lachish III*, Pl. 85:227 (Tomb 1002, associated with City Level III).

[285]*Hazor II*, Pls. LXX:17 (Stratum VI); XCVII:2, 4, 6, (Stratum VA); *Hazor III-IV*, Pl. CCXXIV:8 (Stratum VB); compare also a similar rim-form mode on a late eighth-century BCE juglet in *Hazor II*, Pl. C:10 (Stratum IV).

[286]*Megiddo I*, Pl. 2:72 (Stratum III).

[287]*T. Qiri*, Fig. 13:11 (Area D, Stratum VII). A spouted, Phoenician Ware jug from Yoqneʿam exhibits a similar rim mode but straighter sidewalls in *T. Qiri*, Fig. 43:15 (see p. 203 for comments regarding the meager appearance of Phoenician Ware in the YRP sites).

[288]See the "pitchers" in *TN II*, Pl. 32:559-60, 563; for the same style rim that continues the everted line of the upper neckwalls, see Pl. 33:583. Many of the jugs in Pls. 32-33 vacillate between the flanged and cyma traditions.

[289]See n. 277 above.

[290]*AS IV*, Pl. LXV:38 (with ridged interior and exterior neckwalls); LXVII:10 (interior neck slightly ridged, but a very good overall rim and neck parallel for Samaria 9:6). The latter citation comes from Cistern 25, assigned to Beth-Shemesh Stratum IIc near the end of the eighth century BCE.

[291]*TBM I*, Pl. 58:6; *TBM III*, Pl. 14:4 (all Stratum A).

[292]*Lachish III*, Pl. 85:213 (Tufnell's Jug Type J.2), 214-15, 218, and 227 (Jug Type J.3) (contexts associated with Level III). Gitin has questioned the typological consistency in Tufnell's Class J.3 and has reclassified certain items listed there (such as Fig. 85:227 cited in n. 284 above) in new categories (*Gezer III*, 147-48).

[293]*Lachish III*, Text, 288.

cal indicators to these traits, and placed the pinkish fabrics in the Iron I period (twelfth to tenth centuries), the buff-to-brown ware in Iron Age IIA and B (tenth to mid-ninth centuries), and the brownish-pink paste in the Iron IIB phase (mid-ninth through the eighth centuries BCE).[294] That the hard, ringing ware of No. 6,[295] with its brownish surface and reddish interior, seems to fall near the end of this sequence concurs with the best morphological parallels for this piece.[296] Generally, the fragment seems akin to other PP 6 pitcher forms presented in *SS III*, Fig. 10:15-16, though the rim of No. 6 does not continue the outward flare of the upper neck walls as it does in those specimens.

The small, elegant oil or perfume juglet presented in Fig. 9:7 exhibits a markedly squat, egg-shaped (vs. piriform) body with strongly arced sidewalls; a relatively heavy construction that thickens even more toward the bottom and base; sidewalls that are very smooth on the exterior but left somewhat irregular inside; and a narrow, split-ring base with a central, omphalos-like boss on both the inside and outside of the vessel's bottom. Unfortunately, the surviving fragment lacks its upper part, where the neck and rim modes and the placement of the handle(s) (if any) often provide the best diagnostic indicators for this general class of vessel. The preservation of the sidewalls extends high enough to show that the attachment of a handle, if one existed, occurred fairly high on the shoulder. The juglet appeared in buff ware with traces of both red slip and burnishing.

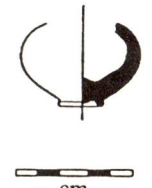

SS III, Fig. 9:7

Solid parallels bearing the collective attributes attested to by this compact vessel remain virtually impossible to find; similarly, I have encountered no other independent citation of this piece as a comparison for materials at other sites. The form—particularly the base—clearly distinguishes itself from the well-known series of squat, continuously burnished, black (and sometimes buff or brownish) perfume juglets with rounded or pinched, nob-like bases.[297] By far the best comparative evidence for the form, ware, and surface treatment of No. 7 comes from Megiddo Stratum III[298] and a

---

[294] *Gezer III*, 147.

[295] G. M. Crowfoot sensed the combination of a traditional form and a newer fabric when she noted on her stratification card that this vessel emerged "probably from reproducing the old soft ware jugs . . . in a hard ware."

[296] Neither nuance of this jug (with cyma- or flanged-rim) continues past the seventh century BCE, and exemplars from that time period continue to show the close similarity between the two styles (e.g., *Jericho II*, Fig. 257:3 [Tomb WH.1]; *Gibeon*, Fig. 47:20 [Area 17]; and *Bethel*, Fig, 84:3).

[297] See *TBM I*, Pl. 68:1-32, pp. 83-84, § 113. Compare *Megiddo I*, Pl. 2:47-54. This style spanned the long period from the close of the tenth century BCE through the seventh century BCE; the elongated, one-handled juglet gradually replaced it toward the end of that time.

[298] *Megiddo I*, Pl. 1:41-42 (Stratum III); 2:45 (Stratum III; one intrusive example found in Stratum II). Number 41 provides the best parallel for the base on the Samaria piece. The excavators there described the findspots for these juglets as "well grouped in Stratum III" (p. 161, § 8). The "analogous forms" in Types 43-45 (Pl. 2) begin already in Stratum IV and show different base-form modes (rounded and nipple-base).

contemporaneous juglet (albeit with round bottom) from Stratum IV at Hazor.[299] Ancestral forms for this tradition may appear in earlier levels at Tell el-Farʿah (N) and other sites.[300] These samples show a tall, narrow neck with a handle drawn from the midpoint of the neckwall to the shoulder. If the Samaria fragment, in fact, had this sort of structure, one may suggest that the heavy construction of the lower sidewalls and base helped to provide a lower center of gravity for the vessel, and thereby prevented it from constantly tipping over due to the narrowness of the base relative to the bulging sidewalls and to the higher-placed weight of the neck and handle. The closest on-site comparisons come from the putative shrine in Locus E 207, which Kenyon correlated with PP 6.[301] The fact that, in these exemplars, the lower handle was simply pressed against the shoulder may explain the apparent absence of any sign of this feature on the upper portion of stratified fragment No. 7. Another possible prototype for this style appears in Upper Level V at Beth-Shan.[302]

While this entry may well represent a true, though relatively rare, juglet tradition, I wish to leave open other possible explanations. Of the juglets just cited from E 207, Kenyon noted that they "came up with small amphorisci" like the one presented in *SS III*, Fig. 23:8.[303] It seems possible, then, that Fig. 9:7 may reflect a late style of amphoriskos such as that seen in Megiddo Stratum II.[304] Or perhaps better, the form

---

[299]*Hazor II*, Pl. C:2 (the report lists the ware for this piece simply as "unbaked clay"). Note also the somewhat more svelte example in *Hazor III-IV*, Pl. CCXXVIII:21 (Stratum VA).

[300]*T. Farʿah-RB* [59], p. 563, Fig. 6:4, with flat base (Niveau 3); the basic concept for this style juglet extends back even further at this site (*T. Farʿah-RB* [58], 425, Fig. 13:2). One should also possibly compare Tufnell's category of juglets in Class D.7a (*Lachish III, Text*, 302; compare *Megiddo I*, Pl. 5:126 = Strata V-IV), though these vessels generally show nipple, or "button," bases (but see *Lachish III*, Pl. 88:327) and have their handles incorporated into the upper sidewall rather than simply pressed against it as with most of the Samaria juglets. Also *TN II*, Pl. 41:802, with disc-like base; see p. 24, § 56 for a suggested progression from disc- to button-bases, and from there to the round-bottomed series of black juglets.

[301]See *SS III*, 23:6-7 (representing four additional specimens from E 207 and four others from Summit Strip Qn). For a similar form with bulging body (to nearly 7 cm compared to 6 cm on No. 7) but different base mode (flat vs. ring), see the so-called "handled jug" in *HES I*, 276, Fig. 153:7, where the "reddish yellow ware" may match closely the red slipped and burnished buff color ware of No. 7. Importantly, this exemplar represented at least four similar fragments that Reisner recovered from the subfloor levels in Ostraca House Room 117 in Summit Strip 4 (see figs. 85-86). Moreover, he noted that all these fragments comprised part of the corpus of ostraca discovered there (*HES I*, Fig. 153:7a = Ostracon No. 36 [presented on p. 236]; 153:7b = Ostracon No. 33 [p. 235]; 153:7c = Ostracon No. 22 [p. 234]; and 153:7d = Ostracon No. 34 [p. 236]). This observation helps to set the *terminus post quem* for these bloated juglet forms already in the early-to-mid eighth century BCE.

[302]*Beth-Shan*, James, Fig. 65:9, which shows a good fabric and body form parallel but a simple, disc-like base. Compare also the body forms in *Chambon*, Pl. 50:26 (Niveau VIIb), 28 (Niveau VIIc; with pointed base), 36 (Niveau VIIa), and 37 (Niveau VIIb; with a button base).

[303]*SS III*, 171.

[304]*Megiddo I*, Pl. 9:3, with a straight, flat base. Note that Amiran has reconstructed a considerably taller neck on this vessel than the one recommended by the excavators themselves (compare *Amiran*, Pl. 88:20).

may represent a relatively rare, specialized class of juglets, which some have unfortunately labeled "flasks" (a term that undoubtedly calls to mind the considerably larger pilgrim flask). These juglet-flasks comprise "very short-to-short jugs often characterized by their ovoid or lenticular bodies."[305] A late Iron II/early Persian level at Tell el-ʿUmeiri provides a possible example of this short-necked, spoutless form (though with thinner ware than No. 7),[306] which one might more appropriately call a "drop pot" type of vessel. If the comparison holds up, the fragment may relate in some way to the nuanced small jars with round or slightly pointed bottoms that are again concentrated in Megiddo Stratum III.[307] In any event, the form in No. 7 represents a freestanding vessel and does not belong to any of the subcategories of dipper juglets.

I should make one final observation regarding the listing of this item in the official report.[308] Kenyon's description of it recites verbatim the one given for the painted, upper body jar or jug fragment seen in entry No. 4 above (note † in Table 31). In my brief comments concerning that piece, I noted the anomalous reference in *SS III* to "another similar base" and suggested that the entire caption seemed misplaced. The exact repetition of the description here confirms my earlier suspicion. Since the recorded details pertain to the juglet form figured in No. 7 better than to the body sherd in No. 4, I conclude that the entry given for the latter item represents a mere dittography. The published report, then, omits any description of the decorated sherd in Fig. 9:4.

d. Decanters

Though decanters actually represent a subtype of short-to-tall jugs, typically with sharp, angular shoulders, their collective attributes prove distinct enough to merit placing these vessels in their own category. The Joint Expedition recovered and published only one clear decanter fragment from the stratified Segment *N of 551*. Data pertaining to its provenance appear in Table 32 below.

In 1932, when Albright presented the first report describing his work at Tell Beit Mirsim, he observed that "the water-decanter . . . is found all over central and southern Palestine, and is common at Jericho, Tell en-Naṣbeh, and many other sites." He added, however, that "our northern material is defective at present, owing to the paucity of relevant publications."[309] By the appearance of *TBM III* just over a decade

---

[305] See *APTJ*, 54-55; see the hypothetical form on p. 52, Fig. 27:flask, which seems particularly close to the morphology of *SS III*, Fig. 9:7.

[306] J. I. Lawlor, "Field A: The Ammonite Citadel," pp. 15-52 in *MPP-2*, L. G. Herr et al., eds. (Berrien Springs, MI: Institute of Archaeology/Andrews University, 1991), 25, Fig. 3.12:22 (Area A, Field Phase 3B).

[307] *Megiddo I*, Pl. 9:13-17. Compare also possibly *Hazor II*, Pl. LXXXVI:5-6 (Stratum VA, from the 732 BCE horizon).

[308] *SS III*, 121.

[309] *TBM I*, 82-83, § 111.

SS III Published Figure	Registry No. (not marked for discard)	Strip	Coordinates	Feature	Local Layer
9:5	Q 5225	Qn	North of 551	leveling	Va

Provenance Data:
PP6 Decanter from the Leveling Contemporary with Wall 573

Table 32

later (1943), the published assemblage in *Megiddo I*[310] had partially filled this northern gap and seemed to confirm Albright's earlier intuition that the decanter family appeared during the course of the ninth century BCE and survived throughout the eighth and seventh centuries but not into (at least not far into) the Persian period. Albright noted further that the rather ubiquitous southern decanter form, with its conical body slipped but burnished only on its upper portions to just beneath the shoulder keel, did not occur in the northern part of the country. There, a "related, but not identical," style differed in two significant aspects: it typically showed a double-ridged lip and a plain or thinly slipped surface treatment with no burnishing.[311]

Generally speaking, subsequent studies have identified the two principal categories of Iron Age II decanters as those forms which assume a vertical orientation by means of conical or sack-shaped bodies and those on which a more rounded body exhibits a greater horizontal orientation. The difference lies mainly in the location of the point of widest diameter, which falls closer to the base on the former group and at the midsection of the body on the latter class. Besides this distinction, variations in the rim-form mode and the fabric utilized in the manufacturing process have continued to help in the classification of these vessels. According to Amiran, the typical northern decanter displays a splayed or funnel-shaped upper neck and rim, the latter of which is deeply grooved to give the "double" rim appearance noted by Albright; its ware consists in a well-baked, metallic fabric, and the vessel frequently has a series of small grooves incised around its upper shoulder. By contrast, the southern variety most often reveals a "splayed and cut-off rim, and is usually made of 'fatty' ware, with a red slip."[312] More recently, Gitin's survey of this vessel class has supported and expanded on Amiran's work by demonstrating that the decanters with horizontally oriented bodies (and grooved rims) seem to occur primarily in the north from the ninth through the end

---

[310] See *Megiddo I*, Pl. 4:99-107, which, as Albright noted, "nearly all [came] from III (especially) and II, with only 4% stated to be from IV."

[311] *TBM III*, 148, § 152.

[312] *Amiran*, 259, 262.

of the eighth centuries BCE. According to Gitin, within the vertically oriented group (which usually shows variations on the splayed rim mode), the globular model appears sporadically in both the north and the south and also ranges from the ninth through the eighth centuries BCE. The sack-shaped version, on the other hand, "appears only in the south" and in Transjordan and derives primarily from succeeding contexts in the seventh and sixth centuries BCE.[313]

Judging from these descriptions, the decanter neck and proposed handle presented in *SS III*, Fig. 9:5 emerges as somewhat of a hybrid form, particularly if its body originally resembled the horizontally oval, almost spherical one seen in Fig. 10:17 (from Pit i).[314] Both specimens exhibit funneled or splayed upper necks, ridges positioned high on the neckwall and close to the rim, and a hard, thin red ware; in light of these duplicate traits, it seems reasonable to assume that the example in Fig. 9:5 also shared with 10:17 the bloated, horizontally oriented body just mentioned and that it included a series of incised lines around the virtually *keel*-less shoulder. These traits might easily make No. 5 a contemporary or close descendant of other decanters from eighth-century BCE levels at northern sites such as Hazor,[315] Megiddo,[316] and Beth-Shan.[317] Yet its splayed rim, thickened both internally and externally, may prove more prevalent among southern traditions[318] attested, for example, at Lachish,[319] Tell Beit Mirsim,[320] and the borderland site of Tell en-Naṣbeh.[321] A very close neck and

SS III, Fig. 9:5

---

[313] *Gezer III*, 154 (see the many citations given there in support of these lifespans).

[314] Compare the photograph in *SS III*, Pl. XVII:10. G. M. Crowfoot's stratification card for this piece included the following notation: "in shape identical with rim of Q 2480" (= *SS III*, Fig. 10:17). This relatively peculiar body form of 10:17 proves extraordinary among most all decanter types, whether they originated in the north or the south. One wonders whether a connection might exist with the "large cast" decanter with its anomalous, "egg-shaped" body recovered at Tell Beit Mirsim and described by Albright in *TBM III*, 130-31, § 132, Pl. 54A:6 (Stratum A; see 103, § 93 for the casting technique). The Samaria piece shows an even more bloated body form than the one from Tell Beit Mirsim.

[315] *Hazor I*, Pl. LXII:12 (Stratum V), though with light brown clay and a lower neck ridge.

[316] *Megiddo I*, Pl. 4:101-02 (Strata II and III, respectively). Compare also Jug Type 100, without the neck ridge but with the hard, metallic ware. The authors of the Megiddo report noted that "while there were relatively few examples from Strata I and IV, [these 'water decanters'] were found in profusion in III" (*Megiddo I*, 163, § 21).

[317] *Beth-Shan*, James, Fig. 71:12, 14 (Level IV).

[318] At least the grooved, double-rim seems to predominate in the north. The splayed rim was not common among the few decanters recovered from Samaria; Kenyon noted, to the contrary, that most of the specimens showed the grooved, double-rim style (*SS III*, 167).

[319] *Lachish*—Zimhoni, 44-47, Fig. 33:1-5.

[320] *TBM I*, Pl.59:1-6; *TBM III*, Pl. 16:6, 8 (all Stratum A). Most of the examples from this site display the flaring rim that is tapered or, in Gitin's terminology, "beaked" (see the Class 2 Decanter in *Gezer III*, 154).

[321] *TN II*, Pl. 39:733-44. This group incorporates a variety of rim forms, including thickened examples

rim parallel from the last site mentioned appears on a decanter whose body profile again reflects the southern regional pottery industry by assuming a sack-like, vertical posture.[322]

Several traits deserve greater attention in the classification of decanter necks and rims. First, the location of the neck ridge in relation to the rim seems significant, as it appears slightly higher in later examples.[323] Second, one should draw a distinction between ridges created by pinching the clay of the neckwall outward and those which result from joining a two-part neck, as the Samaria examples seem to display. In the latter variety, the upper neck and rim actually sit down in the slightly splayed lower neck, and the "ridge" derives from the somewhat wider diameter of the lower neck walls.[324] A close examination of the neck profiles (particularly from the exterior view vs. the sectional cut) from various forms reveals the different construction techniques.[325] In the end, consideration of all these factors leads us to suggest a date for *SS III*, Fig. 9:5 near the end of the eighth century BCE. As noted, this vessel (which appeared at Samaria only in meager numbers)[326] presents a rather mixed collection of attributes. While its rim form has a few close parallels in the pre 732 BCE period,[327] its comparatively squat, very rounded body and well-fired, metallic ware with blue-black core seem closest to an example from Megiddo II.[328]

Finally, I must comment on the function of decanters. Throughout the comparative literature, analysts use the term "water decanters" to identify this general class of vessel. Though this rubric may have come to denote a generic reference to a particular form, it obviously also implies a function, namely, the serving of water. But at least two complete decanters from the south that carry inscriptions on their shoulders correct this restricted view of the purpose of these vessels.[329] The first bears the phrase

---

(Nos. 734-35, 739-44), rims with tapered lips (No. 736-37), and even a grooved, double-rim mode (No. 733).

[322]*TN II*, Pl. 39:739 (compare Nos. 741-42 as well). As with this rim, the Samaria fragment in No. 5 has its rim slightly thickened both internally and externally. One should distinguish this technique from the tapered or "beaked" style seen in *TN II*, Pl. 39:736-37 and other representatives of Gitin's Class 2 decanter (a series in which he proposes to include *SS III*, Fig. 10:17; see *Gezer III*, 154).

[323]Compare, for example, the pre-732 BCE decanter in *Beth-Shan*, James, Fig. 71:14 with *SS III*, Figs. 9:5; 10:17, and *Lachish*—Zimhoni, Fig. 33:5 (Level II).

[324]Compare examples of Tufnell's jug classes J.8 (= her "water decanter") and J.7b in *Lachish III*, Pl. 103:665-66.

[325]For the true *ridged* neck, see *Megiddo I*, Pl. 4:99, 101, 105, 107; *TN II*, Pl. 39:735-36, 738, 741; *Lachish* — O. Zimhoni, *TA* 19 (1990) Fig. 33:3; on the coast, see *T. Qasîle* [2], Fig. 57:18 (Stratum VII); for the *joined* technique, see *TN II*, Pl. 39:739-40; *Lachish*—Zimhoni, *TA* 19 (1990) Fig. 33:5 (and both Samaria exemplars in 9:5 and 10:17); *T. Qasîle* [2], Fig. 57:16-17 (Stratum VII).

[326]*SS III*, 167.

[327]Note again *Beth-Shan*, James, Fig. 71:14 (Level IV).

[328]*Megiddo I*, Pl. 4:108, but with the typically northern "double-rim."

[329]A third decanter with an inscription from Lachish may provide further evidence of this use, though

lyḥzyhw yyn khl, meaning either "belonging to Yaḥzeyahu, wine of Koḥel"[330] or "belonging to Yaḥzeyahu, dark wine."[331] The second example, from Lachish Level II,[332] reads *yyn. ʿšn.* and likewise may indicate either the original provenance of the wine ("wine of ʿAshan") or the type of wine contained in the decanter ("strong wine," "vintage wine," or the like).[333] Regardless of whether one should read the final word in these inscriptions as a place name[334] or as an attributive adjective, the two direct references to *yyn* (which preserves the uncontracted diphthong typical of Judahite Hebrew) provide rare, empirical evidence that at least some vessels in this class functioned in the storage and serving of wine, not water. While Gitin is justified in his surprise that hardly any decanters appeared in the assemblages of Gezer and Ashdod,[335] then, his suggestion that "there may be some economic variable related to the contents of the decanter form which could explain this unusual distribution pattern" seems unlikely if, in fact, wine constituted the principal commodity involved. I do not mean to say, however, that wine service constituted the only function for the decanter family. Other, remarkably slender, exemplars from seventh-century BCE contexts might also have contained oils or perfumes.[336]

e. Braziers

Kenyon included two rim fragments from vessels she identified as braziers in the assemblage from the segment excavated *North of 551*. As indicated in Table 33 on the following page, recording difficulties attend both pieces. Still, the very presence of these items alongside the other sherds recovered from the filling inside Wall 573 proves quite important given the apparently limited life span of this vessel type near the end of the Iron Age II period. Unhappily, these forms are also some of the rarest and most enigmatic pieces in the entire PP 6 assemblage due to a virtual dearth of suitable parallels.

---

the reading is less clear (see *Lachish-1*, 88, Inscription XXX; Fig. 30 and Pl. 32:1-2).

[330] N. Avigad, "Two Hebrew Inscriptions on Wine-Jars," *IEJ* 22 (1972), 1-9.

[331] A. Demsky, "'Dark Wine' from Judah," *IEJ* 22 (1972), 233-34.

[332] *Lachish-1*, Fig. 26 and Pl. 27:1; see also *Lachish*—Zimhoni, 44-46, Fig. 33:1-2.

[333] See the discussion in *Lachish-1*, 83-84.

[334] See F. M. Cross, Jr., "Jar Inscriptions from Shiqmona," *IEJ* 18 (1968), 226-33.

[335] There was a similarly scant appearance of decanters at Samaria (n. 318). I may plausibly conclude from these distribution patterns that the presence or absence of the decanter does not correlate to the economic or political prestige of a given site. Samaria, of course, stood as the capital of Israel and then, apparently, as an Assyrian administrative center. During the zenith of the *Pax Assyriaca* (roughly 732-630 BCE), Gezer came to assume a similar role in the northern Shephelah (B. Brandl and R. Reich, "Gezer Under Assyrian Rule," *PEQ* 117 [1985], 41-54). Despite the decanter's unique, even attractive, shape, then, one perhaps should not exclude it from the general category of utilitarian vessels.

[336] E.g., see *Lachish*—Zimhoni, 46, Figs. 32:3; 34:1-7 (Level II); *Amiran*, 262, Photo 260; Pl. 89:4.

SS III Published Figure	Registry No. (not marked for discard)	\multicolumn{4}{c}{Provenance}
		Strip	Coordinates	Feature	Local Layer
9:8 †	Q 4979b	Qn	North of 551	leveling	V
9:9 ††	Q 4979a	Qn	North of 551	leveling	V

† = field register *Qn* lists only the published registry number without the other identifying data given here

†† = field register *Qn* contains no record of this fragment

Provenance Data:
PP6 Braziers from the Leveling Contemporary with Wall 573

Table 33

When one first encounters a line depiction of these fragments, it is perhaps natural to think immediately of the heavy bowl-like forms known as mortaria, particularly since this class arose during the late Iron Age II and continued into the Persian and Hellenistic periods. Yet closer scrutiny of the Samaria rims reveals two key points of dissimilarity between them and the mortaria. First, the morphology of the sidewall appears quite distinct from the typically round- or straight-sided walls of nearly all mortaria.[337] Second, the buff-colored ware of entries 8 and 9[338] departs from the usual brown or reddish-brown fabric seen on most mortaria, at least those from the late Iron Age II period.[339] By the same

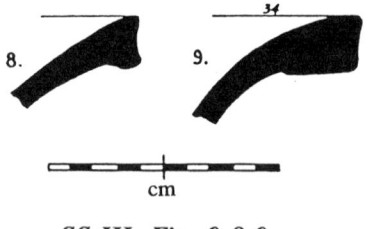

SS III, Fig. 9:8-9

token, the splay of the sidewalls and rims results in an opening whose diameter exceeds that typically displayed on most jar or pot stands.[340] Though some morphological

---

[337] Though examples abound, compare *Megiddo I*, Pl. 23:13-14, 17 (Strata III-I); also *T. Keisan*, Pls. 20:21 (Niveau 3); 31:6a (Niveau 4); and 45:5 (Niveau 5); *TN II*, Pl. 59:1357; *Gezer III*, Pl. 28:10 (Field VII, Stratum VA = seventh-sixth centuries BCE). These citations offer some of the closest possible parallels for No. 8, at least among the mortarium class. Most mortaria have sides whose exterior profile appears more convex, and many of them display substantial ridging down the outside of the walls.

[338] In *SS III*, Kenyon lists the color of the ware only for No. 9; G. M. Crowfoot's stratification card for Q 4979, however, identifies the same color clay for No. 8.

[339] See *Gezer III*, 211. By the Persian period, the ware of mortaria becomes reddish-yellow in color. Changes in clay consistency also occur between the Iron II and Persian periods: during the former phase, mortaria show a high density in clay and a low density in grits or other inclusions; the opposite situation exists by the Persian period.

[340] Compare the selected examples in *Megiddo I*, Pls. 34-35 (generally Strata IV-I); *TBM I*, Pl. 71:7-8, 10-13 (Stratum A).

similarity seems to exist between these fragments and a rather uncommon jar(?) form recovered from Hellenistic levels at Tell Keisan,[341] the divergent wares plus various uncertainties that stem from the scarcity of these "formes particulières de cols"[342] at Keisan preclude extending the analogy at this time.

Rather than opting for any of these comparisons, Kenyon appears correct in her identification of these items as fragments of braziers, even though she did not report any traces of charcoal or other organic substances inside the vessels; nor did any ventilation holes appear on the sherds (though one perhaps should not expect them this high on the vessel body). Given the thickness and concave arc (especially on No. 8) of the sidewalls, the affinity that Kenyon saw between these pieces and the whole or near-whole braziers yielded by Locus E 207 seems apt. For the sake of comparison, one should review the two specimens published in *SS III*, Fig. 28:1-2, even though they do not comprise part of the stratified sequence of ceramic traditions at Samaria. Each of the four rims displays its own peculiar form. In both the stratified examples (Nos. 8-9), the uppermost extension of the sidewall thickens into a heavy rim mode (perhaps formed by pressing the wall itself down and, in the case of No. 9, folding it back against the exterior face of the wall itself). The vertical outer face of the rims then received a slightly concave groove made, in all likelihood, by the potter's finger. Another subtle, finger-trimmed groove appears beneath the rim of No. 8 and results in an overhanging flange. The heavier rim in No. 9 exhibits a narrower, tool-trimmed groove on its underside, where the potter had pressed the folded sidewall back against itself. The rims in Fig. 28:1-2 also show finger-trimmed and tool-trimmed undergrooves, respectively. Yet neither rim has a concave groove in its outer face (which is sharply angled in 28:2) to make it resemble No. 8, and neither one appears as bulky and heavy as the form seen in No. 9 above.

Kenyon reported that the Joint Expedition retrieved at least 11 of "these strange brazier shapes"—10 from E 207 (correlated to PP 6) and one from the Z Deep Pit (thought to relate to PP 3, but see n. 204 above).[343] Stratified contexts in Summit Strips Qn, Qd, Qk, Dg,[344] yielded only rim fragments from similar vessels. All the samples exhibited buff ware, interior red slip that extended over the rim,[345] and (usually) traces of burnishing. The lower walls, which formed a kind of stand for the brazier, were pierced with either square or round openings, though none of the actual floors showed perforations of any kind.

---

[341] *T. Keisan*, Pl. 10:3, 5 (Niveau 2; note especially the rim profile on No. 3 at Keisan and No. 8 at Samaria; for Keisan No. 5 and Samaria No. 8, compare the severe splaying of the upper walls and rims).

[342] *T. Keisan*, 106.

[343] *SS III*, 183.

[344] For the location of these areas, see *SS III*, "Plan of the Sites," p. xv.

[345] These descriptions appear in *SS III*, 183, though on p. 121 Kenyon reports that the red slip appeared on the *outside* and over the rim of No. 8.

Adequate parallels for these remains prove difficult, if not impossible, to locate. The comparison Kenyon drew between 28:2 and an apparent brazier or censer from Lachish is an oblique one at best.[346] She reports no known parallels in Palestine for the extremely high-arching floor of 28:1.[347] Unfortunately, I cannot add anything to this paltry database. I can only suggest that the heavy construction of the rim and sidewall and the overall morphology of the class at large (e.g., the extremely high, ring-like base) may have grown out of various traditions of somewhat thinner, Iron II (late ninth-early eighth centuries BCE) plate/platter forms[348] and may also relate somehow to the rise of the mortaria during the late Iron II period. But even this statement remains speculative.

3) **Evaluation and Summary**

The overall distribution of the various pottery groups taken from the downslope areas situated between the outer Casemate Wall 564 and the lower terrace Wall 573 appears in Table 34 below. For the most part, the published report once again presents us with a somewhat mixed assemblage of ceramic fragments that span the ninth and eighth centuries and, at points, possibly extend into the very early seventh century BCE. This situation results directly from the nature of the deposits from which the excavators removed these pieces. The local stratigraphy here basically reflects bands of unconsolidated debris, which builders from a post-Israelite period pulled down from the northern summit area and incorporated into their large-scale leveling and backfilling operations. In light of my detailed presentation above of both the local stratigraphy and the related ceramic assemblage, I need only add my summary comments here.

As indicated in my discussion, Kenyon's interpretation relied on the contemporaneity of Wall 573 and the massive filling around it. But one can no longer remain dogmatic on this point, since both published Section CD and the available field drawings show that robber trench(es) broke the actual stratigraphic connection between the two entities. One cannot say with certainty, then, whether or not the deposits in question abutted Wall 573 (or were cut by it). Given the secondary nature of the deposit itself—apart from its temporal relationship to the terrace wall—the pottery group published in *SS III*, Fig. 9 represents a ceramic period and not a horizon, contra the way Kenyon employed the group in her interpretative framework.

---

[346]*Lachish III*, Pl. 90:389 (see photo in Pl. 72:21). This unusual vessel, made of gritty, pink ware, appeared with a group of miscellaneous pottery and objects in Cave 6024. Tufnell believed this "large, partly denuded" chamber first served as a dwelling place during the Early Bronze Age; later, during the early Iron I period, it apparently became a dwelling and workshop area for weavers (see *Lachish III, Text*, 250-52).

[347]See *SS III*, 183, for mention of "a much earlier clay 'fire box' found on Melos."

[348]Compare, for example, *SS III*, 4:16-18 (PP 3; note the similar ware and surface treatments, as described in *AIS-I*, 186-90); *TN II*, Pl. 68:1364-1365. Along these same lines, compare *Munshara*, Fig. 6:3-4; *T. ʿAmal*, Fig. 7:5-6 (Niveaux I-II). At Tyre, note certain examples of Bikai's Type 8 Plate (*Tyre*, Pl. XVIA:30, 32, 36; note that some appear to show a tendency toward concave outer sidewalls, though

	bowls	cooking pots	jugs & juglets	decanters	braziers	TOTAL
Leveling (573)						
513.514						
VI	1	-	-	-	-	1
North of 551						
V	1	4	2	-	2	9
Va	1	5	1	1	-	8
TOTAL	3	9	3	1	2	18

*Distribution of PP 6 Ceramic Forms
in Local Stratigraphy of Leveling Associated with Wall 573*

Table 34

Many of the forms seen here might easily derive from the late eighth-early seventh centuries BCE, i.e., from the earliest decades of Assyrian hegemony over the site. This group includes bowl Nos. 1 and 3, the decanter in No. 5, the juglet in No. 7, and the braziers of Nos. 8-9. The fragment of Samaria Ware presented in entry 2, on the other hand, may come from the period leading up to 732 BCE. The mixed series of cooking-pot rims (Nos. 10-18) displays perhaps the longest chronological range, since these pieces appear to represent mainly late variations on the flanged-style rim that cover the ninth and eighth centuries BCE. Though I cannot speak conclusively about the date of the layers that yielded these goods, I may reiterate that the latest pottery appearing here must guide us in suggesting the earliest possible date of deposition. With this principle in view, one sees that a date near the turn of the eighth century seems most reasonable; the parallels with Megiddo III help confirm this conclusion.

Finally, all the pottery in this group once again fits well with my suggested function for the northern courtyard perimeter as a food processing area. As indicated in the stratigraphic analysis above (pp. 260-61), the layers involved in this portion of my study also help to circumscribe the northern limits of the spatial distribution of ivory fragments. Segment *513.514* seems especially significant in this regard, since it lay farther up the northern slopes than *North of 551* and just outside the Israelite Casemate System. While *513.514* produced striations of charred soil, no ivory fragments appeared there. Importantly, Kenyon assigned Layer VI of this segment, from which she published only one bowl (Fig. 9:1), to the Hellenistic period.[349]

---

all display flat bases).

[349] The following entry appears in *Fieldbook Qn (Vol. I)*, 69a: "H[ellenistic]. VI. Streaky, sooty, all part of G. F. W. [= Greek Fort Wall] filling, but also R.T. 541."

Part B. Pit *i*
   (*SS I*, Fig. 50; Pl. II, Pl. VII — Section EF)
   (*SS III*, Fig. 10:1-27)

My examination of the second significant pottery group assigned to PP 6 takes us back inside the Casemate System, to the service area located around the northern periphery of the central compound in Summit Strip Qk. Kenyon claimed to have removed the entire assemblage published in *SS III*, Fig. 10:1-27 from two related layers (V-Va) in the same general locus, namely Pit *i*. As I have already shown, this pit rested near the center of the poorly built complex of Rooms labeled *f-g-h-j-k* (see fig. 5 for BP IV; fig. 41 for BP V; compare also the field-drawn plan in fig. 12). Most of the fragments came from Segment *122.125.19.121*, a designation that apparently takes in the pit and extends toward the south, where Wall 125 came to mark the southern boundary of the combined Rooms *h* and *k* in BP V. Ten of the pieces included in *SS III*, however, exhibit an alternate set of coordinates, ***122.126.19.121***.[350] If this designation is accurate and not a natural slip given the many closely-numbered walls that ran through this area,[351] it seems to indicate that these particular fragments derive from the area of the pit and slightly northward, toward the northernmost wall (138) of Room *g* (the course of Wall 126 lay contiguous to the north face of 138; see fig. 12).

Whether or not any of the materials presented in *SS III* came from areas outside and adjacent to Pit *i*, Kenyon ultimately attributed everything to this single feature, which she assigned to the "Period V house."[352] In the official report's second volume, which appeared in 1942,[353] Kenyon had already concluded that

> The most important evidence [relating to 'Periods V-VI'] comes from the rubbish pit at 457-460.5 N, 641-644 E. This . . . belonged originally to the Period IV house, but continued in use in the Period V house. In it was a great quantity of pottery identical with that in the filling contemporary with wall 573. . . . It is the pottery *in use* with the Period V building presumably down to its destruction, and [is] therefore different in significance from that beneath its floors, which dates to its original building.[354]

---

[350] *SS III*, Fig. 10:9-14, 24-27.

[351] No segment bearing the exact label *122.126.19.121* appears in any of the field notebooks, including *Fieldbook Qk-l-m*, which reports on the area around Pit *i* and Segment *122.125.19.121*.

[352] *SS III*, 119.

[353] Though this work actually constituted the second part of the full report, I have followed conventional practice in designating it *SS I*, since the monograph that actually preceded it in 1938 had appeared already under the title *Samaria-Sebaste 2: Early Ivories*. Hence, the latter book now generally receives the abbreviation *SS II*, while the 1942 publication of the architecture is called *SS I*, and the report that eventually presented the pottery and small objects in 1957 appears under the rubric *SS III*.

[354] *SS I*, 108.

In a reversal of her general methodology, then, Kenyon here chooses to accent a context of supposed occupational debris in an attempt to establish a *terminus ante quem* for a given "period," rather than concentrating (as she has up to now) on subfloor construction debris to set the *terminus post quem* for the phase in question (in this case, BP V). As part of this change in strategy, Kenyon devoted very little space to the pottery found beneath the floors of the so-called Period V House, and she justified this move by asserting that the levels there yielded hardly any fragments—only "a few sherds of . . . harder ware, including some fragments of water decanters."[355] Given the uncertainties surrounding the archaeological context of the somewhat anomalous pit (see below), one wonders why her modified method did not focus now on the true occupational debris resting directly *on* the BP V surfaces rather than on materials taken from a more stratigraphically spurious rubbish pit. At any rate, it seems curious that her principle of dating based on materials recovered from subfloor deposits has, according to Kenyon's presentation of it, functioned smoothly to this point but suddenly runs amok with regard to the BP V structures. She offers neither an archaeological nor an historical explanation for this apparent snag. But the resultant shift in methodology essentially omits the layers that were stratigraphically later than the floors of BP IV but earlier than those of BP V, as well as the deposits lying immediately on the BP V surfaces.

By the official publication in 1957 of the pottery and small objects from Samaria, Kenyon had expanded her understanding of the function of Pit *i*. In *SS III*, she wrote:

> It may have been either a rubbish pit or a latrine. No entrance was visible and since the walls were standing considerably above the level of the adjoining rooms, it must presumably have had an aperture on an upper floor, and its identification as a latrine is very probable.[356]

Stratigraphically speaking, she observed that the putative pit/latrine

> . . . was dug out of the middle of wall 157, with the edges of this wall rebuilt to form enclosure walls for the pit. . . . This pit was not sealed by any floor, and was apparently in use to the end of the occupation of the house. The Period VII debris which overlay the floors of the rest of the house *did not actually overlie* the pit, since the walls of the latter were standing to the top of the general level of this debris, and the filling inside it was level with the tops of the walls.[357]

The last sentence in this description raises serious doubt concerning Kenyon's desire to assign the same terminal date to the functional lives of both the pit and the BP V rooms

---

[355] *SS I*, 108.

[356] *SS III*, 120.

[357] *SS III*, 119-20 (emphasis added).

into which it was dug. At this point, numerous issues emerge and remain difficult to settle based on currently available information. From Kenyon's descriptions, it seems clear that the pit postdates the BP IV Wall 153; yet the installation is already included on the BP IV Phase Plan (see fig. 5). The report includes no discussion of a subdivision of the pit by the short, unidentified, transverse wall seen on the BP V Phase Plan (fig. 41). Moreover, this wall appears neither on the published Section EF nor on any unpublished field section (e.g., fig. 10). The fact that the uppermost courses of the pit stood at least as high in elevation as the destruction(?) level surrounding them and "considerably above the level of the adjoining rooms," and the observation that the debris clearly did not seal or even run partly across the open mouth of the pit, both seem to indicate a functional life for the pit that survived (or possibly even postdated altogether) the destruction event itself and the postdestruction leveling operation. Perhaps the most important datum relating to this feature consists in Kenyon's own acknowledgement that none of the destruction remains in question appeared *in situ*.[358] Instead, someone had apparently raked all this material into and across the general area at some point after the event (whether intentional or accidental) that produced the debris in the first place. In this manner, this level secondarily covered the now defunct service rooms but surrounded and left open the still serviceable pit. Finally, one can see from fig. 10 that a later floor level of hard, yellow matrix laid above the area of the former Room *g* ran up to the northern edge of the pit. This stratigraphic connection implies the contemporaneity of these two features. The identification and analysis of the latest ceramic traditions represented in both the pit (PP 6) and the encircling debris (PP 7) may help to determine approximately how long after the original creation of the debris the leveling and new flooring occurred.

In sum, the date more than the actual function of this pit becomes vitally important in Kenyon's chronology and historical reconstruction of the waning of Israelite sovereignty over Samaria. Yet she nowhere presents the contents of this feature in section. In my judgment, its location falls between the Walls 153/155 and, to the north, Wall 136 on published Section EF. Notwithstanding the fact that no local stratigraphy ever appears on any section presented in the final report, even the aggregated blocks of remains depicted on Section EF do not allow for material from PP 6 (or 5) in this space; an unusually thick (for the Israelite period) deposit from PP 7 seems to overlie directly that from PP 4. If, as Kenyon suggests, the multiphase pit functioned at least from PP 4 to PP 6 (and I have suggested perhaps even beyond this time), then surely the structure contained its own local depositional history. To justify using this pit as a lynch pin in dating the final years of Israelite control of the site, the report should have presented this history in quite some detail. As I shall show, even the unpublished data from the field ultimately fail to answer many of the questions raised here. Whatever the correct phasing of this unsealed structure, the fact that it lay "full of midden-like rubbish, which contained a large amount of pottery"[359] suggests that it served as a dump

---

[358] *SS III*, 125.

[359] *SS III*, 119-20.

site for broken and discarded vessels once used in the processing of food in this "kitchen" area on the northern edge of the central compound. Short of a scientific analysis of the "midden-like rubbish" (which, of course, is no longer possible) in addition to the pottery, I remain disinclined to view this feature as a latrine.

The surviving pit filling included at least nine seal impressions depicting a winged scarab and stemming from Dynasty XXII in Egypt, which lasted until ca. 712 BCE (against Kenyon's higher date of 720 BCE).[360] In addition, the excavators recovered yet another impression from the contents of the pit showing "a winged sphinx walking left." Kenyon dated this seal to the eighth or seventh century BCE. These seals help to confirm both a post-Israelite date for the deposition of at least a portion of the recoverable remains of the pit (to say nothing of its stratigraphically later but lost contents) and a certain period of peaceful Assyro-Egyptian contact at the site in the years following 722/721 BCE (as suggested above, pp. 245-46).

In presenting the scarabs, seals, and seal impressions from Samaria, J. W. Crowfoot commented on the overall relative number of impressions found there and on the fact that they appeared concentrated "in the area where most of the ivories were found."[361] These considerations led him to suggest that "a room was nearby in which the archives of the northern kingdom had been kept, a sort of chancery."[362] Though the excavations in this area unfortunately remained bereft of epigraphic finds that might confirm this thesis, the only obvious candidate for such an official building rests in the series of better-built rooms situated along the northern edge of the central rock plateau, in the area I have called the "central summit." Whether or not one should see the famous "Ivory House" as a royal chancery, Crowfoot's general scenario concurs well with my view that the support staff working in the shabbier complex of rooms around Pit *i* served the courtiers of Samaria in basic, utilitarian capacities (such as food preparation; recall the multiple *ṭābunîm* found here) and that much of the material remains discovered in those rooms (including certain pottery forms, the ivories, the seal impressions, and the like) first appeared there already in a secondary context.

1) Stratigraphic Detail

a. 122.125.19.121
b. 122.126(?).19.121 (Published Section EF; figs. 5, 8, 10, 20)

As previously indicated, these two sets of variant coordinates focus on the contents of Pit *i* but may also include some materials found immediately to the north and

---

[360] *SS III*, 108. Though most artifacts survive from near the end of the historical period in which they originated (see n. 102 above), these impressions may admittedly represent heirlooms saved from an earlier phase of Dynasty XXII. Hence they alone cannot establish a firm *terminus ante quem* for the context that yielded them at Samaria.

[361] *SS III*, 85.

[362] *SS III*, 85.

south of that feature. In fact, both the published and private reports placed the single ceramic fragment already encountered from this segment (an apparent Assyrian-style conical jar in *SS III*, Fig. 6:12) in Room *h* rather than in Pit *i*. This jar came from sub-Layer Va, as did many of the pieces published under PP 6 (*SS III*, Fig. 10:1-27, excluding No. 8, which came from general Level V). Since the jar came from the same local accumulation (Va) in the same locus (*122.125.19.121*) as the PP 6 group, it is not clear why Kenyon chose to publish the former item with the PP 4 materials. I have shown that, stylistically, the vessel likely belongs to the late eighth century BCE or even slightly later, i.e., to a period subsequent to BP IV.

It remains impossible to present or discuss the subphasing of deposits inside Pit *i* in adequate detail, since Kenyon nowhere disclosed them in section or in the narrative portion of her field notes or published report.[363] From her rather generic descriptions of the pit, however, one may conclude with confidence that the structure did not contain a homogeneous matrix or pottery assemblage; the repertoire published in *SS III*, Fig. 10, at least, does not present consistently contemporaneous forms. Because the final report included the conical jar fragment in PP 4, I have offered my summary of Segment *122.125.19.121* in an earlier discussion pertaining to Room *h* (Chapter I, 40-43, 110-11). As a result, I need only reiterate a few particulars at this point.

The location on the plan in fig. 12 of three of the coordinate structures named in the segment (Walls 122, 125, and 19) confirms that this segment relates to Summit Strip Qk (see also the western side of Auxiliary Section B, fig. 8). Data from this segment help to clarify the stratigraphic relationship between the black, sooty deposits found in this area and the layers that followed immediately upon them. As I have shown, the excavators first encountered a mixed matrix that included burnt material in Layer III, particularly in the basal striations of that level. These descriptions correlate well to Layers III-IIIb in *Btw TT2-TT3* and IIIa in *125.144 + 122.125.19.121* (see fig. 8). A thick deposit of rubble with some large stones appears above IIIa in the last two segments mentioned.

Clearance beyond the western wall of Pit *i* (Wall 147; see fig. 41) and beneath Layer III revealed a plaster floor, which Kenyon correlated to Layer IX of *120.121.19.126* (compare Layer V on fig. 8). On the opposite side of 147, i.e., inside the area of Pit *i*, no floor appeared. Rather, the workers encountered what they initially believed to represent a cistern mouth ca. 1.5 m in diameter. With the removal of approximately one additional meter of softer, darker fill, labeled Layer IV, the structure became known as Pit *i*. The field notes stipulate that the aforementioned filling contained an abundance of pottery and appeared to belong to "Period VI."[364] Besides the filling of Level IV, the structure yielded another soft and "rather middenish" deposit (Layer Va), which also contained much pottery. Kenyon assigned the bulk of this material to her "Period VI" and published a representative sample of ceramics

---

[363] My fig. 10 shows its approximate location relative to other nearby architectural features.

[364] *Fieldbook Qk-l-m*, 5a.

from it in *SS III*, Fig. 10:1-27. The field notes add that "a good deal of the pottery really belonging to Va was included with IIIb."[365]

Though she showed the northern and southern perimeter walls of Pit *i* (136 and 153/155, respectively) on the field section presented in fig. 10 above, Kenyon failed to detail the depositional history between or above these structures, i.e., in the area on which she based most of her chronological judgments relating to PP 6. From her notes, however, it appears that the sooty deposits that overran these and other Israelite walls correspond to the mixed debris encountered in Segment *122.125.19.121*, Layers III-IIIa (and their affiliated subdeposits). These materials lay immediately beneath a series of Hellenistic walls, one of which (144) actually rested in the debris. On this basis, I have suggested that either a relatively short increment of time or a longer period but with minimal occupation of the site separates the original deposition of the charred, mixed matrix from the early Hellenistic construction activities. These options seem to leave open the depositional date of the sooty levels as well as the historical occasion which gave rise to them.

2) Pottery Analysis

The items depicted in *SS III*, Fig. 10 reflect a situation similar to that seen for the preceding pottery group in Fig. 9. All but one of the fragments or vessels presented here derive from a single layer (Va) situated, this time, in Pit *i*. (The Assyrian-style bowl in Fig. 10:8 comes from a related deposit in the same locus labeled Layer V.) I may note two interesting facts concerning these materials. First, this assemblage represents the most diverse one, typologically speaking, published from Pottery Periods 4-6, from the point of view of both the overall group and each specific vessel class within the collection (compare, for example, the assortment of bowls). Second, it also contains the greatest proportion of whole or near-whole vessels. Not since the series of bowls and plates published from PP 3 (*SS III*, Fig. 4) has there appeared a selection of forms this well preserved.

The latter situation stems partly from the fact that the locus that yielded these vessels (or, as I shall show, *some* of the overall group) represents neither a true fill deposit nor a living surface. Rather, one may liken the contents of Pit *i* to those left in an isolated room or comprising part of a tomb group.[366] In such cases, the recoverable pottery may appear relatively intact or prove quite restorable. Yet a difference occurs in the fact that the pottery of tombs or serviceable rooms would have arrived there in a functional capacity. From Kenyon's description of Pit *i*, however, the goods taken from it appear simply to have been abandoned. When, for whatever reason, these vessels *passed out of use*, they were placed directly in Pit *i*. In this sense, the cache perhaps

---

[365] *Fieldbook Qk-l-m*, 32.

[366] See the discussion in *Holladay*, 26-30 and particularly nn. 55 and 57. Holladay also commented on the generally good preservation of the PP 6 items recovered from Pit *i* as compared to others published from PP 4 (Fig. 7:3-10), PP 5 (Fig. 8:2-8), and PP 6 (Fig 9) contexts (see *Holladay*, 27, n. 57).

bears a greater resemblance to a cistern deposit, which generally includes dropped or discarded items. Though one might expect smaller fragments from greater breakage in such a context, the cistern groups from Tell en-Naṣbeh[367] show that bowls, juglets, and thick-walled jars can sometimes survive reasonably well there.

The Samaria materials in Fig. 10 were neither discarded and kicked about on the surface prior to their deposition in Pit *i* nor poured into the structure as part of a deliberate fill. Once inside the pit, they apparently did not suffer from subsequent, heavy disturbances. The straight-sided saucer and plate forms, heavier pedestal bowls, jugs, juglets (see the black juglet in No. 24), coarse-ware jars, etc., that typify this group survived virtually intact in this stratigraphic environment. The thinner wares of Assyrian-style bowls (e.g., Nos. 9-10), Samaria Ware bowls (as in No. 11), and late decanter forms (Nos. 18-19), on the other hand, became quite vulnerable even under these relatively protected conditions; as a result, these types appear only in fragmentary form. But even here one sees that some thin-walled forms managed to survive quite well (compare the Assyrian bowl in No. 8, which incidentally derived from a different local layer from all the other pieces, and the decanter in No. 17).

If, as Kenyon recorded, essentially all these materials come from the same level inside the pit (Layer Va), one may expect them to emerge as a rather homogeneous group. As such, they would provide relatively good evidence for dating that section of the pit. A difficulty arises, however, in any attempt to relate that specific level to one or more of the surfaces or sub-surface fills found in the BP IV-VI/VII rooms around the pit. Moreover, one must bear in mind that these materials depict only a single cross-section of the overall contents of the pit. They cannot provide a *terminus ante quem* for the functional life of the pit since I have already shown that later leveling operations shaved off its uppermost courses (one cannot know how many). Ultimately, then, the partial destruction of the key locus and the nebulous connections between the various findspots inside that locus and the surrounding floors leave us with many unresolved questions of chronology.

In my opening comments to the evaluation of pottery in other groups, I have generally included a table outlining the distribution of ceramic forms across the various rooms and loci involved. Since the present group reportedly derives entirely from a single, isolated deposit (but see below), such a table of data becomes superfluous here.[368] I shall, therefore, proceed to an analysis of each particular class of vessel.

a. Bowls

The final pottery report included 14 examples of various style bowls retrieved from Pit *i*, including saucer bowls (Nos. 1-3), bowls with ring- or high-footed pedestal-

---

[367] See *TN—Cistern*, Figs. 2-4.

[368] The same situation holds true for the other pottery treated in this chapter (from the massive leveling near Wall 573; see above).

bases (Nos. 4-6), Assyrian motifs (Nos. 8-10), Samaria Ware forms (No. 11, and possibly 12), a bowl(?) with handles (No. 13), and one with a rilled upper sidewall (No. 14). The specific findspots for this collection appear in Table 35 (compare Appendix A).

SS III Published Figure	Registry No. (none marked for discard)	Provenance			
		Strip	Coordinates	Feature	Local Layer
intact forms:					
10:1	Q 2471	Qk	122.125.19.121	Pit *i*	Va
10:2	Q 2472	Qk	122.125.19.121	Pit *i*	Va
10:3	Q 2473	Qk	122.125.19.121	Pit *i*	Va
10:4	Q 2450	Qk	122.125.19.121	Pit *i*	Va
10:5	Q 2478	Qk	122.125.19.121	Pit *i*	Va
10:6	Q 2479	Qk	122.125.19.121	Pit *i*	Va
10:7	Q 2475	Qk	122.125.19.121	Pit *i*	Va
10:8	Q 2365	Qk	122.125.19.121	Pit *i*	V
small-size fragments:					
10:9	Q 2511	Qk	122.126.19.121	Pit *i*	Va
10:10	Q 2512	Qk	122.126.19.121	Pit *i*	Va
10:11	Q 2514	Qk	122.126.19.121	Pit *i*	Va
10:12	Q 2513	Qk	122.126.19.121	Pit *i*	Va
10:13	Q 2515	Qk	122.126.19.121	Pit *i*	Va
10:14	Q 2516	Qk	122.126.19.121	Pit *i*	Va

Provenance Data:
PP6 Bowls from Pit i

Table 35

As shown in this table of data, all the items listed here supposedly came from local Layer Va inside the pit, except for Fig. 10:8, which appeared in Layer V. I may remind the reader, however, that the use of both Walls 125 and 126 in the coordinate designations for this group may indicate that the field that yielded these vessels extended both slightly south (toward 125) and north (to 126)[369] of the actual pit area (see the discussion on pp. 299-301). It is immediately noticeable that the coordinates that include Wall 125 relate to the intact bowl forms (Nos. 1-8), while those involving Wall 126 pertain only to the fragments (Nos. 9-14) published as part of this series.[370]

---

[369]Wall 126 lay immediately north of Wall 138, which fixed the northern perimeter of Room *g* (see figs. 12 and 41).

[370]Note that the other items assigned to Wall 126 (Nos. 24-27) also include quite small fragments of cooking-pot rims (Nos. 26-27), which would typify the contents of a fill deposit. The fact that the black juglet of No. 24 and the thick-walled jar of No. 25 survived relatively intact does not mean that they

That is to say, from Pit *i* toward the central summit plateau, one encounters better-preserved pottery; from the pit away from the rock shelf, in areas that required deeper layers of fill to cover the declining slope, one sees a more fragmentary assemblage.[371] As Table 36 reveals, these two potential sub-groups of bowls also differ rather consistently in their wares and surface treatments. The intact forms (except for No. 8) dis-

SS III Published Figure	Ware Buff	Ware Red-Brown	Ware Grey	Red Slip (on interior, exterior, rim)	Burnishing
intact forms:					
10:1	+			+ (i)	
10:2	+			+ (i/e)	
10:3	+			+ (i)	
10:4	+			+	+
10:5	+			+ (i/e)	+
10:6	+			+ (i/e)	+
10:7	+			+ (r)	
10:8		+ (thin)			+ (1 band & incised lines)
small-size fragments:					
10:9		+			
10:10			+		
10:11		+ (thin)			
10:12		+ (thin)		+	
10:13	+ (thin)			+ (i/e)	(incised lines)
10:14	+ (thin)				+

Attributes of Ware and Surface Treatment on PP 6 Bowls from Pit i (SS III, Fig. 10:1-14)

Table 36

play a thicker construction of buff ware with red slip over the interior or on both the inside and outside of the form (the slip on No. 7 appears only on the rim). Within this group, those bowls with either a ring or footed base (Nos. 4-6) also exhibit signs of burnishing. The more fragmentary forms, on the other hand, appear in a much thinner ware of a red, reddish-brown, or grey color (1 specimen), and usually without any

---

could not come from such a churned up matrix for, as Holladay has noted, "a virtually intact black juglet or fairly substantial piece of a thick jar rim . . . might easily come under this heading" (i.e., the heading of "small sherds" deriving from displaced and redistributed fill; see *Holladay*, 27, n. 57).

[371] In my Evaluation and Summary below, I show that this general distribution of intact vs. fragmentary pottery proves true for the entire group of forms attributed to Pit *i*.

PP 6: PIT i — POTTERY

notation of burnishing. (It is doubtful that the buff-colored sidewall fragment with handle in No. 13 actually belongs in this assemblage of bowls.)

Such observations strengthen the likelihood that one should view these two coordinates as distinct from one another (and not as a simple misprint in the notes)[372] and that the materials associated with Wall 126 come, in fact, from the portion of Room *g* that lay north of the relatively protected confines of the pit and that consisted in a matrix of secondary, leveling fill. In this light, Kenyon's statement that the excavators retrieved all the items presented in Fig. 10 from *inside* Pit *i* seems unlikely. Instead, one must allow for the possibility that only those pieces attributed to Segment *122.125.19.121* actually come from the pit itself; those assigned to *122.126.19.121* belong to an entirely different stratigraphic context (and also possibly to a different ceramic horizon).[373] In my Evaluation and Summary below, I shall return to the fact that Kenyon nevertheless assigned virtually the entire group to a single layer, namely Va. Finally, this situation may also cast some doubt on Holladay's claim that "no serious questions can be raised about the essential homogeneity of the group" ascribed to Pit *i*.[374]

Entries 1-3 in Fig. 10 reflect a tradition of relatively plain bowls with straight or slightly flaring sidewalls, flat (often string-cut) bases, and rims that may assume either a simple, rounded form or display a slight thickening on the exterior. Members of this group can appear as either saucer (Nos. 1-2) or plate (No. 3) forms, a distinction that Kenyon does not draw. Though they generally lack signs of substantial burnishing (some plates show widely spaced burnish lines on the inside),

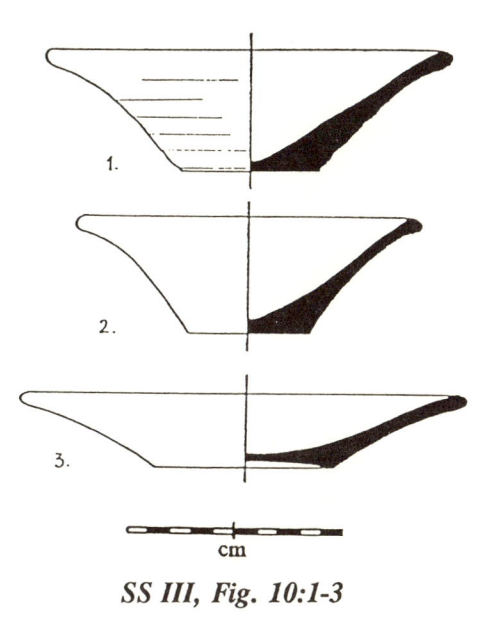

SS III, Fig. 10:1-3

---

[372] As I have indicated in Appendix A, the Field Register *Qn* lists only the published registry numbers and gives no additional identifying data for any fragment listed in Fig. 10. The provenance data I present in Appendix A, however, appear on G. M. Crowfoot's handwritten stratification cards and therefore derive from a reliable, primary source.

[373] Note again Kenyon's statement that "the Period VII debris which overlay the floors of the rest of the house did not actually overlie the pit, since the walls of the latter were standing to the top of the general level of this debris, and the filling inside it was level with the tops of the walls. Its [I assume this means the pit's] upper part would therefore have merely been removed in the clearing-up to which the debris belongs" (*SS III*, 120). Holladay has noted that this allows for the mixing of forms from different contexts already in antiquity (contra his statement cited in n. 374). Consequently, he proposed that only the "whole or mostly restorable pieces should be utilized" as part of his primary "Corpus" (*Holladay*, 68-69). Without knowing it, then, he relegated to secondary importance the fragments assigned specifically to *122.126.19.121*.

[374] *Holladay*, 68.

members of this class usually exhibit a red slip on both the interior and exterior (No. 2) or just on the inside (Nos. 1, 3), and the slip is sometimes wet-smoothed to give the impression of burnishing. Though at the appearance of *SS III* Kenyon understood the overall type "to be a northern one,"[375] subsequent classifications have shown that these bowls do, in fact, occur in the south but in appreciable numbers and in secure contexts starting only in the latter half of the eighth century BCE.[376] Their incipient use in the north predates this time, as demonstrated by examples from the late ninth and early eighth centuries BCE at sites such as Hazor,[377] Beth-Shan,[378] and Tell el-Farʿah (N).[379] The geographical distribution of this simple, functional design also includes Jordan, Lebanon, and Syria,[380] though it sometimes appears there with various nuances in ware, form, and surface treatment.[381]

Though antecedent forms of this group extend back into the ninth century BCE, the class as a whole rose to prominence during the course of the eighth century BCE and primarily during the latter part of that period. While they appear already in Stratum VII at Hazor, the reports from there noted that these bowls "are very common in Stratum VI, and actually predominate in Stratum V."[382] To the examples already cited, I may add others from both Hazor and Megiddo that date to the second half of the eighth century[383] and the eighth-seventh centuries BCE.[384] The flat base, thick walls,

---

[375] *SS III*, 113.

[376] *Gezer III*, 183.

[377] Compare *Hazor II*, Pl. LXIII:10 (Stratum VII. This piece appeared with other household wares in the West Room 138 of the Casemate Wall area; see the stratigraphic comments on p. 15); *Hazor III-IV*, Pls. CLXXX:4, 6 (Stratum VII); CLXXXI:26-30, 32-37 (Stratum VI).

[378] *Beth-Shan*, James, Figs. 26:8 (from Locus 92 in Block D-2, a room that overlay a Lower V series of walls; thus, this piece likely belongs to the Upper V level—see pp. 80-82 in James's report); 39:3 (Level IV); 67:8-9, 11-12 (Level IV).

[379] *T. Farʿah-RB* [59], Fig. 8:9-10 (Niveau 2). *Chambon*, Pl. 57:19-24, 27-28 (Niveau VIId).

[380] E.g., *Tyre*, 23-24, Plate Type 8, and Pls. X:4, 7 (Stratum III); XVI:18-38 (Stratum IV); XVIII:3 (Stratum V); and XIX:9-12 (Stratum VIII); these levels roughly span the period between 800 and 732 BCE. See also *Sareptah*, Figs. 17:14 (for the saucer style) and 18:24 (for the plate); for other examples from Khaldé, ʿAtlīt, and Cyprus, see *Tyre*, 23, nn. 20-22. See also *Gezer III*, 183.

[381] Compare, for example, *Chapman*, 128 and 166, Nos. 127-29; Fig. 25:127. These parallels from Khirbet Silm appear in orange-colored clay, show no slip, and display sidewalls that flare out slightly less than those on the Samaria exemplar. Other eighth-century examples from Israel also show a variety of wares beyond the buff-colored fabrics of the Samaria group (note the citations given from Stratum V at Hazor in *Holladay*, Fig. 8:G-H, J-X).

[382] *Hazor I*, 20. See Pls. XLIX:10 (Stratum VII); LI:12-13 (Stratum VI; the latter exemplar has ribbing on the external sidewall similar to No. 1 from Samaria, though the upper sidewalls flare out a bit more on the Hazor piece); LIII:11-12 (Stratum V). Compare also *Hazor II*, Pl. LXIII:10 and the comments on p. 17.

[383] *Hazor I*, Pls. LXVI:14; LXXI:6; *Hazor II*, Pl. LXXX:38-40; LXXXI:1-6, 8-13; see also the comments in *Hazor II*, 49 (and Pls. XX, XVXI).

[384] *Hazor II*, Pl. XCVIII:17-19 (Stratum IV, with light brown ware); *Hazor III-IV*, Pl. CLXXXIX:2

simple-rounded rim, and external ribbing of No. 1 closely resembles a heavy bowl ("mortier") from Niveau 4 (early seventh century BCE) at Tell Keisan.[385] The corpus of parallels attested at southern sites, such as Lachish,[386] Tell Beit Mirsim,[387] Beersheba,[388] and Jericho,[389] confirms that the small-to-medium sized saucer with straight or flaring sides and the wider plate variation also appear in that region mainly during the late eighth and the seventh centuries BCE.[390]

Generally speaking, then, the basic motif reflected in Nos. 1-3 seems to have originated in the north and to have spread to the south in the late eighth century. Though it continues into the seventh and even possibly the early sixth centuries BCE,[391] the tradition appears to have waned by the close of the Iron Age II period.[392] As the notes to my citations indicate, a shift

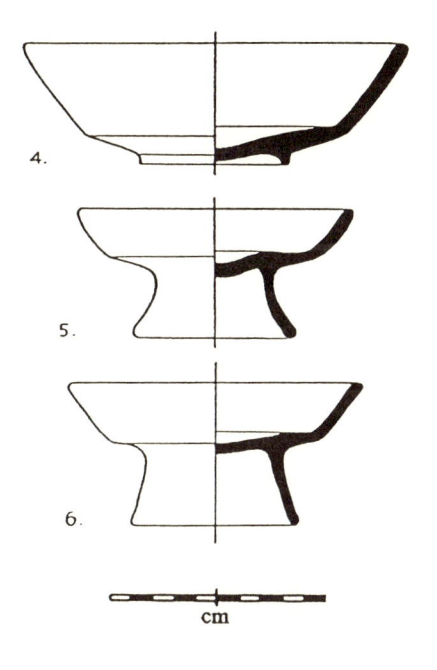

SS III, Fig. 10:4-6

(Stratum VI-V); *Megiddo I*, Pl. 24:40-44 (Strata IV/III-II).

[385]*T. Keisan*, Pl. 31:3. Such heavy, pronounced ribbing on these and other bowls may have served a functional as well as decorative purpose by providing a better grip for one lifting the fully loaded vessel (see Gitin's remarks concerning a different form in *Gezer III*, 179). For the continuation of this general motif, see the Persian period exemplar in *Gezer III*, Pl. 25:18 (Field VII, Stratum IV = early fifth century BCE).

[386]*Lachish III*, Pl. 80:63 (Bowl Type B.11, which most resembles the plate form of No. 3 at Samaria; Tufnell concluded that "the varieties grouped in Class B.11 . . . cannot [ ] be more than a decade or so earlier than the seventh century B.C."—*Lachish III, Text*, 275). One should also note the "straight-sided bowls without any moulding to the rim" in Tufnell's Class B.8 (I reject, however, her inclusion in this same group of the bowls with round or curved sides [Class B.4]; see *Lachish III, Text*, 258).

[387]*TBM I*, Pl. 65:28, 30; *TBM III*, Pl. 21:4-5 (all from Stratum A).

[388]*Beersheba I*, Fig. 74:3 (with brown ware and wheel burnish on the interior).

[389]*Jericho II*, Fig. 256:12 (with brown ware and wheel burnish on the interior).

[390]An antecedent form may appear in *AS-IV*, Pl. LXVI:9 (Stratum III), though the sidewalls do not flare outward as in the Samaria examples.

[391]Compare *En-Gedi*, Fig. 15:4 (Stratum V; with reddish-brown ware); *Ramat Raḥel I*, Fig. 28:5-6 and *Ramat Raḥel II*, Fig. 16:2, 10-13 (Stratum VA; with pink to reddish-brown ware and wheel burnished interior); and *TN II*, Pl. 68:1549, 1560-1561. At Tell en-Naṣbeh, Wampler noted the increased use of the plate form during the "Middle Iron" phases and expressed caution about appealing to the surface finish as a principle of classification (*TN II*, 41, § 70).

[392]At Megiddo, the style occurred in Strata IV-II but proved poorly attested in Stratum I (*Megiddo I*, 168, § 56).

toward the increased use of red or reddish-brown fabrics (as opposed to buff-colored clays) and wheel burnishing on the interior of the vessel seems to have occurred sometime during the late eighth century and to have continued into the seventh century BCE (see also n. 391). In the Yoqne'am Regional Project, plate forms similar to No. 3 show a dramatic rise in frequency during the latter part of the Iron II period.[393] At Samaria itself, Kenyon compared the plate in No. 3 to *SS III*, Fig. 6:1-2 (from PP 4) and added that the type proved common in PP 4 and PP 6, but not earlier.[394] A possible prototype for this emerging family may appear, however, in *SS III*, Fig. 4:13 (PP 3), though this specimen shows a ring- versus flat-base mode. Another similar form that Kenyon assigned as early as PP 2 seems, in fact, to represent an intrusion into those levels.[395]

Items 4-6 in Fig. 10 belong to a group of medium sized bowls of relatively thick construction[396] with simple, slightly rounded, flattened, or knife-cut rims (for the last style, compare *SS III*, 14:8 from S Tombs 107).[397] The inflection (not a true carination) of the sidewalls rides very low on the dish and may derive from a much earlier tradition in the Late Bronze Age.[398] Above this bend, the sides maintain straight walls that flare out so that the widest diameter of the vessel occurs at the rim and is generally twice that of the base element.[399] While these pieces continue the buff-colored ware of Nos. 1-3, their surface treatment reveals a red slip and burnishing on both the interior and exterior of the vessel. Though Nos. 4-6 relate to the same basic class, then, differences in their base forms prompt us to treat No. 4 apart from 5 and 6.

In his analysis of No. 4, Holladay appeals to a series of bowls recovered from Stratum VA of Area B at Hazor to place the group at large in his 733-722 BCE Horizon.[400] Yet, in his presentation of these carinated forms, Yadin instructs us to

---

[393] *T. Qiri*, 191 (see Bowl Group IV/b:Plate, in Fig. 38:2).

[394] *SS III*, 113. See Chapter I, 69-71 for my full discussion of Fig. 6:1-2.

[395] See *AIS-I*, 114-15. Both Aharoni and Amiran suspected this situation early on (*Hazor II*, 17).

[396] Gitin has observed that the majority of the numerous parallels for this class appear as whole forms (*Gezer III*, 178). This situation likely represents a reflex of the solid construction techniques used for these bowls.

[397] A close relative of this group displays an everted lip as part of the rim-form mode (e.g., *Gezer III*, Pl. 13:5 [Field VII, Stratum VIB]; Gitin notes that this form represents a relatively uncommon style that appears in the mid-ninth century BCE; p. 177).

[398] For Iron Age II expressions of this style, see *Hazor II*, 17, 54, and Pls. LXIII:27 and LXXX:25-28.

[399] Holladay noted that these bowls may appear more or less "open" (his Types Bst A and Bst B, respectively), depending on the flaring or vertical posture of their upper sidewalls (*Holladay*, 248).

[400] *Holladay*, Fig. 11:C, G-O, Q, S-T (entries P and R come from general Stratum V at Hazor). For the bulk of the Hazor references, see *Hazor II*, Pl. LXXX:2, 5-11, 13-14, 19, 21, 23. Several of these specimens seem securely dated, since they derive from the remains of a building covered by destruction debris (Locus 3100a) and from a sealed floor deposit (Locus 3067a).

refer to the discussion of materials published from Stratum VII in Area A.[401] There one learns the specific value of the base form as a diagnostic feature of these bowls for, at Hazor, the low ring base similar to that exhibited by No. 4 at Samaria "predominates in Stratum VII, in contrast to the characteristic disc-base of Strata VI-V."[402] This observation suggests an earlier date for the origin of the tradition reflected in No. 4. From a morphological point of view, the evidence from Samaria seems to confirm an earlier appearance of this general style. In this regard, I might note the red-slipped, hand-burnished exemplars made from a gritty, reddish-brown ware that typified the Samaria assemblage beginning already in PP 1-2.[403] Here one can also recognize the full series of these bowls, which manifest multiple rim selections but show bases quite similar to No. 4, from the tenth-century BCE Cultic Structure at Taʿanach.[404] Comparable examples from late ninth and eighth-century levels at Hazor,[405] Megiddo,[406] Tell el-Farʿah (N),[407] Lachish,[408] Beth-Shemesh,[409] and from a tomb group at Munshara near to Samaria,[410] help confirm this picture.

Gitin's detailed analysis arrives at the following evolution of base forms for this class of bowls. The earliest exemplars, beginning already in the tenth century BCE, show a footed ring base. This style lasts through the ninth and into the eighth centuries, as the above references demonstrate. Following the appearance of this base, a slightly raised flat or disc form emerges, though its floruit does not occur until the eighth century. While the basic, flat base first appears in the ninth century BCE, it also becomes most popular only during the second half of the eighth century.[411] The high-

---

[401] *Hazor II*, 54.

[402] *Hazor II*, 16.

[403] Note the variant forms in *SS III*, Figs. 4:11 (PP 3) and 17:4-5, (6-8?) (unstratified); see also Kenyon's comments on p. 151. Compare *HES I*, Figs. 156:11a-b and 161:17; Reisner recovered the last example of Iron II, Israelite pottery from the lower levels of Cistern 3 near the Roman Basilica. The original color of the ware used in the manufacture of Fig. 10:4 proved difficult even for the excavators themselves to determine. On her stratification card, G. M. Crowfoot recorded the following observations: "ware probably buff but much discoloured; red slip, traces of burnish—one side almost green with discoloration from damp." Crowfoot also noted the rim-to-rim diameter of this bowl at 19 cm.

[404] *Taʿanach*, Figs. 45:1-8; 46:1-17; 47:1-4. From an even earlier phase, compare *Megiddo II*, Pl. 89:10 (Stratum VA).

[405] *Hazor II*, Pl. LXIII:1-2 (Stratum VII). Prior to Stratum VII, the point of carination occurs slightly higher on the sidewall of these bowls, as in *Hazor II*, Pls. LIII:2-3 and LV:13 (Stratum VIII).

[406] *Megiddo I*, Pl. 24:31, 48 (Strata IV-II); also compare *Megiddo I*, Pls. 25:58; 28:96; 31:144 (from Strata V-III).

[407] *T. Farʿah-RB* [58], Fig. 11:1 (Niveau 2); *T. Farʿah-RB* [59], Fig. 8:6 (Niveau 2). Gitin places these specimens, which display the flat, incut rims, in the eighth century BCE (see *Gezer III*, 178).

[408] *Lachish III*, Pl. 79:9 (from Cave 1002).

[409] *AS IV*, Pl. LXVI:6, 11-12 (Stratum IIb).

[410] *Munshara*, Fig. 5:1-4. For Zayadine's dating of this tomb to ca. 800 BCE, see p. 567.

[411] Compare the appropriate examples in *TBM III*, Pls. 24-25 (Stratum A).

footed or pedestal base represents the least common form with the shortest life span and occurs primarily during the eighth century but wanes by the close of the third quarter of that period.[412] If, however, Holladay is correct in reassigning Locus 371 at Tell el-Farʿah (N) to Niveau III in the (early?) ninth century (as opposed to the succeeding Niveau II), the last category of base-form may have arisen earlier than Gitin allows.[413] While this would permit a higher *terminus post quem* for the styles seen in Nos. 5-6,[414] it remains clear that the high-footed tradition continued at Tell el-Farʿah (alongside the ring-base models) at least to the beginning of the last quarter of the eighth century BCE.[415]

The forms in Nos. 4-6, then, stand in a stream of ceramic development that extends back to the tenth and ninth centuries and that appears to dissipate during the course of the seventh century BCE and certainly by the close of the Iron II period.[416] The buff-colored ware helps to distinguish the Pit *i* exemplars from earlier specimens made of red or reddish-brown fabrics, and the simple, rounded or slightly tapered rims attested on these pieces lasted into the second half of the eighth century BCE, even though their inception (tenth century)[417] predates the flat, incut ones also used during the eighth century.

Finally, I may note that various nuances within this tradition seem closely related to elements in the so-called "Samaria Ware" group discussed above.[418] Yet while this specific form (particularly the high-footed type) seems well attested in Israel,[419] it did not appear in the far north at Hazor[420] and also proved relatively rare

---

[412] *Gezer III*, 180.

[413] Compare *T. Farʿah-RB* [59], Fig. 8:13 (published under Niveau II, but see *Holladay*, 120, n. 56).

[414] E.g., *Megiddo I*, Pl. 24:32 (Strata IV-II; again, the earlier pieces appear in brownish rather than buff-colored ware). Gitin mistakenly attributes Nos. 5 and 6 to the putative Israelite Shrine in Locus E 207 rather than to Pit *i* (*Gezer III*, 179).

[415] See the examples from Locus 151, Niveau II, in *T. Farʿah-RB* [58], Fig. 11:1, 3. Also *Chambon*, Pl. 58:12-20 (Niveau VIId).

[416] The specimen with outcut rim assigned to Stratum III in *Hazor I*, Pl. LXXVI:14 very likely belongs instead to the late tenth century BCE (see the remarks by Rast in *Taʿanach*, 32). The Megiddo reports noted that these bowls appeared primarily in Strata IV-II, "but they were poorly represented in Stratum I" (*Megiddo I*, 168, § 56). It suggests further that the style seen in Pl. 23:5-9 (often with more rounded sidewalls and profiled rim mode) may have displaced examples like Nos. 4-6 by Stratum I, i.e., by the late seventh-early sixth centuries BCE (see §§ 52 and 56).

[417] Note *Megiddo I*, Pl. 28:97-98 (Strata V-IV).

[418] See *SS III*, Pl. XVI:1-2.

[419] E.g., *T. Yoqneʿam* [1], 75, Fig. 11:4 (probably a traditional ring base) and 5 (pedestal base); *T. Qiri*, Fig. 43:7. See also the classification of No. 6 specifically in *T. Qiri*, 216.

[420] Compare the wide selection of "Samarian" bowls in *Hazor II*, Pl. LV (Stratum VIII) and note especially the comment that the high-footed variety "does not appear at all at Hazor, although it is common at Samaria" (*Hazor II*, 12).

at Tyre.[421] Moreover, the Samaria collection differs in certain key morphological respects from the tradition of red slip bowls at Al Mina, Syria.[422] While the forms seen in Nos. 4-6 may relate in some way to the Syrian red ware family, then, one should exercise caution in identifying them as imports from Phoenicia;[423] they might just as easily represent variant local or regional styles.

The last two specimens assigned to *122.125.19.121* (Nos. 7-8) exhibit differing attributes in both ware and surface treatment. The small, shallow bowl in No. 7 shows a rounded base and straight upper sidewalls with a near-vertical stance. Traces of red slip cover only the rim of this piece, where a slight tapering on the inside of the lip produced an inwardly beveled effect. This rather plain form seems akin to several related streams of bowl-making tradition attested during the Iron Age at many sites.[424] Yet it did not fully evolve into the true fine-ware styles, with their thinned upper sidewalls and tapered rim modes, that appear reminiscent of Samaria Ware and that typify the eighth and early seventh centuries BCE.[425] Thus while, on grounds of morphology, Holladay drew a somewhat apt comparison to a similar piece from Shechem,[426] the hard, ringing, well-levigated, and dark red-brown ware of the latter bowl clearly distances it from the Samaria specimen and resembles more closely the fragmentary items listed in Table 36 above. In fact, the nearest parallels for the buff-colored No. 7 derive from Megiddo Stratum III.[427] While the general style of this saucer, which displays "a light

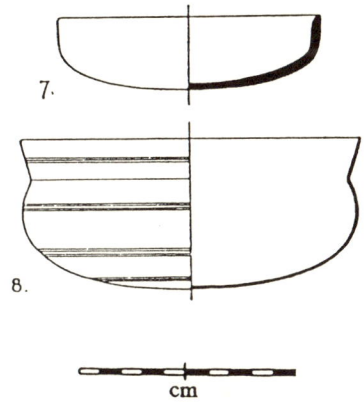

SS III, Fig. 10:7-8

---

[421] *Tyre*, 26.

[422] Compare Nos. 4-6 with those presented in J. du Plat Taylor, "The Cypriot and Syrian Pottery from Al-Mina, Syria," *Iraq* 21 (1959), 80, Fig. 6:10, 13, 15, 17.

[423] See Gitin's suggestions in *Gezer III*, 180.

[424] E.g., consider only the basic form with its many variations as seen in *TN II*, Pl. 53:1173; *Ta'anach*, Figs. 48:15-19 (Period IIB; with completely rounded sides or upper sidewalls that remain more everted); 64:5,7 (Period IIB; all these examples, however, appear in light red-to-reddish brown ware rather than in the later buff-colored fabric); *T. Keisan*, Pls. 55:9-9c (Niveau 8); 52:1-4 (Niveau 7); 41:11a (Niveau 5); 29:2, 5; 30:6; 35:8 (all Niveau 4); *Chambon*, Pl. 57:10 (Niveau VIIb; apparently with a variant base). Also compare my discussion of *SS III*, Fig. 4:9 (PP 3) in *AIS-I*, 159-60. For a slightly larger but related "hollow bowl" form made of reddish-brown ware and showing a red wash and burnishing on the interior and over the rim, see *HES I*, Fig. 156:13a.

[425] Compare *Gezer III*, Bowl Type 64A, Pls. 20:4 (Stratum VIA); 24:1 (Stratum VB/VA).

[426] *Holladay*, Fig. 5:A (Shechem, B60.VII.9.120.7425, from Locus 1622).

[427] *Megiddo I*, Pl. 24: 50 (of "burnt umber" ware) and especially 51 (of "brown ocher" ware). The latter ware might well approximate the buff-colored fabric of No. 7. *M I*, Pl. 24:51, then, provides the best parallel in terms of its constellation of attributes: morphology, ware, and surface treatment.

red wash inside and over the rim," ranged from Stratum IV to Stratum II at Megiddo,[428] the closest comparisons to No. 7 stem only from Stratum III, which yielded 11 such exemplars.[429] As a result, I may offer a slight but consequential downward adjustment to Holladay's statement that "stratified examples [of this bowl style are] confined to the third quarter of the eighth century."[430] Rather than restricting this piece (with Holladay) to the 733-722 BCE Horizon, then, one may easily place it in the final quarter of the eighth century and perhaps even slightly later still.

While Nos. 8-10 represent a series of thin-walled, Assyrian-style forms,[431] only No. 8 emerged relatively intact (see Table 36). As noted earlier, it also constitutes the only piece in this group (and, indeed, in the entire PP 6 repertoire) ascribed to Layer V in Segment *122.125.19.121* and not to the subdeposit Va. Holladay included No. 8 in his "miscellaneous" group of bowl forms, which he described as "all unique in one way or another, among the stratigraphically assured bowls, and probably should be ignored until further information is forthcoming."[432] Still, he added that it looks "suspiciously like" a seventh-century form. Its thin, hard-fired ware, rounded base, sidewalls, and shoulders, sharply everted neckwall, and simple rim mode certainly seem to support this reading. Moreover, the general motif of horizontal lines, ribs, or bands proves quite common on many classes of Assyrian-style pottery from the seventh century BCE.[433]

Entries 9-10 follow this same pattern but show a more rounded juncture between their shoulder and neck. The neck and lip of No. 9 both exhibit a strong, outward flare, while those of No. 10 are more simply everted (resembling No. 8) and thickened toward the top so that they end in a rounded, simple lip. Rather than a buff- or reddish-colored ware, however, No. 10 consists in a greyish clay (see parallels below). According to Holladay, these bowls "are, almost without question, 'Assyrian Bowls', although visual inspection would be required to confirm this."[434] Even without the benefit of firsthand observation, however, I may note several differences between the Palestinian exemplars and the true Palace Ware tradi-

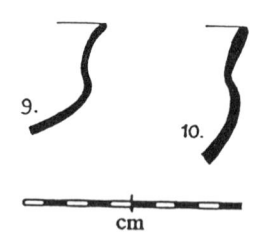

SS III, Fig. 10:9-10

---

[428]*Megiddo I*, 169, § 57.

[429]*Megiddo I*, 186-87.

[430]*Holladay*, 189.

[431]Recognition of this connection first came from Petrie during his work at Tell Jemmeh (see *Gerar*, 7 and 23-24; Pls. XLVIII, LXV), where he labeled the overall class "Assyrian Table Service."

[432]*Holladay*, 204; Fig. 41:G.

[433]Compare J. Oates, "Late Assyrian Pottery from Fort Shalmaneser," *Iraq* 21 (1959), Pls. XXXV (ring-based bowls); XXXVI:29 (open bowl with handles); XXXVII:59 (open bowl with lines resulting from a ribbed shoulder), 60, 64 (beakers), 68 (cup); XXXVIII:90 (bottle) and 91 (jar); from the Aqaba region, see *Kheleifeh*—Pratico, 41-43 and Pls. 27:10-11; 28:7-8; et passim.

[434]*Holladay*, 204.

tion from Assyria. First, the ware of the Assyrian forms consistently runs from grey-green to greenish-buff in color.[435] Many of the Samaria exemplars occur in red ware. Second, the Assyrian designs typically show taller neckwalls that flare out considerably more than on the Samaria bowls. In Assyria, the lip of the rim generally extends well beyond the point reached by the rounded shoulder carination.[436] Several of the examples cited in the previous note attest to the use of ring bases as well as simple rounded bottoms for this bowl family; one should not, therefore, necessarily assume a rounded base form for either No. 9 or 10 in the Samaria group.

Carinated forms similar to the Assyrian styles have appeared in the north in levels dating from the last quarter of the eighth century at Tell Keisan[437] to seventh-century deposits at Tell el-Farʿah (N) and Shechem.[438] The tradition reached both the Jezreel and Beth-Shan Valleys during this same time period[439] and also began a sparsely attested distribution down the southern coastal plain[440] and into the Shephelah.[441] The chronology for this style follows a similar pattern at Hazor, though here it may have begun slightly earlier in the eighth century[442] before also continuing into the seventh century BCE.[443] According to Amiran, "In all excavations it [i.e., this specific class of bowls] appears in strata of the period following the Assyrian conquest of Samaria, that is, after 721 B.C."[444] Within that same time frame, near-perfect parallels are available for No. 10 from both Tell Keisan, Niveau 4,[445] and Tell Qasîle, Stratum

---

[435] J. Oates, *Iraq* 21 (1959), 136.

[436] For both of these observations, compare J. Lines, "Late Assyrian Pottery from Nimrud," *Iraq* 16 (1954), Pl. XXXVII:7-9; J. Oates, *Iraq* 21 (1959), Pls. XXXV:20; XXXVII:59.

[437] *T. Keisan*, Pl. 37:11, 11a-e (Niveau 5).

[438] *T. Farʿah-RB* [58], 419, Fig. 12:1-4, 6 (Niveau 1). *Chambon*, Pl. 61: 1 (Niveau VIId), 2-11 (Niveau VIIe). L. E. Toombs and G. E. Wright, "The Fourth Campaign at Balâṭah (Shechem)," *BASOR* 169 (1963), Fig. 22:2, from Stratum VI. Note also the so-called Samarian bowl in *Hazor III-IV*, Pl. CCVIII:30, from Stratum IX(!).

[439] *T. Yoqneʿam* [3], Fig. 10:3 (Stratum 9); *T. ʿAmal*, 327, Fig. 7:3 (Niveau II), apparently from the very late eighth or the seventh century BCE. According to Levy's and Edelstein's preliminary report from ʿAmal, "il n'est donc pas possible de dater avec précision les niveaux I et II. La majeure partie de la céramique est typique du VIIIe siècle, et le reste, du VIIe siècle avant J.-C." (p. 328).

[440] Compare *T. Qasîle* [2], 109 and Fig. 55:26, 28 (Stratum VII); *Ashdod II-III*, Fig. 5:7 (Area A, Stratum 6; with a more pointed carination); 93:1-9 (Area K, Strata 6-5; these examples appear in a variety of ware colors); *Ashdod IV*, Fig. 26:1-2 (Stratum VII); *Gerar*, Pls. L:23m-n(?); LI:26w and 26x(?).

[441] These forms seem clearly related to Gitin's Bowl Types 73, 74, and 75 at Gezer, none of which proved very well attested there (see *Gezer III*, 197-99; Pls. 22:7—Stratum VB = late eighth to early seventh centuries BCE).

[442] *Hazor II*, Pls. LXVII:5 (Stratum VI); LXXX:25-27 (Stratum VA).

[443] *Hazor II*, Pl. XCVIII:44 (Stratum IV).

[444] *Amiran*, 291.

[445] *T. Keisan*, Pl. 29:14 (Briend and Humbert classified this piece as an "imitation de la 'Palace Ware'").

VII.[446] Although, based on the pottery from Hazor and more recently excavated sites in the Jezreel Valley, some have suggested that these bowls appeared slightly earlier (at least in the northern parts of the country) than the post-722 date offered by Amiran, the evidence remains sketchy and the issue unsettled.[447]

It appears, then, that the dissemination of this family spread from sites in the far north (Hazor; Keisan) into the northern valleys (Yoqneʿam; Qiri; ʿAmal) and to a few key sites in the Ephraimite hill country (Samaria; Tell el-Farʿah) before reaching some southern coastal sites and parts of the Shephelah.[448] Beyond this arena, some of this pottery seems even to have reached Tell el-Kheleifeh,[449] very likely by way of sites in Jordan such as Buṣeirah,[450] an Iron II administrative center in Edom (and perhaps the capital of Bozrah) situated just 4 km west of the King's Highway.

Though some have noted that "Les bols carénés . . . sont les formes assyriennes les plus répandues en Palestine en nombre et en distribution,"[451] it remains somewhat surprising that these bowls maintained such modest numbers at the sites mentioned in Israel. Virtually every excavation report comments on the relative scarcity of this form at each site, particularly at locations such as Gezer, which many believe served as a regional administrative center during the *Pax Assyriaca* (see n. 335).

---

[446]*T. Qasîle* [2], Fig. 55:27 (compare the "pale grey ware" of the Samaria exemplar with the "grey-yellowish clay [with] grey core" on the Qasîle bowl).

[447]*T. Qiri*, Fig. 203; Fig. 44:5. In the report from Qiri, Ben Tor asserts that the Assyrian or Assyrianizing forms recovered during the YRP argue for a *terminus post quem* for these bowls in a pre-conquest period (i.e., prior to 722/21 BCE). According to the discussion in *T. Qiri*, 203, the excavations at Yoqneʿam recovered only one such carinated bowl, and that from "below a Stratum 10 floor" (Stratum 10 is dated generally to the eighth century BCE). Yet the only bowl of this type presented in the preliminary report from Yoqneʿam itself was assigned to Stratum 9 and dated to the seventh century BCE (see n. 439 above). Moreover, at Qiri, only two such bowls appeared, with only one coming from a stratified context (Stratum VII, dated roughly to the ninth century BCE); but this item appeared to be an intrusion into that locus. At any rate, clearly one cannot retain the entire group in the 733-722 BCE Horizon as in *Holladay*, Fig. 41:B, C, G, though he elsewhere states explicitly that at least Nos. 9 and 10 represent "almost certain intrusions from the post-VI period" (*Holladay*, 68).

[448]A few examples of this general class also seem to have been used at Tell en-Naṣbeh, but the report from there seems uncertain regarding the dating of these items (*TN II*, 33-34, § 25; Pl. 54:1196-1197, and possibly a few other entries).

[449]*Amiran*, 300-01, Photo Nos. 328-29. G. D. Pratico, "Nelson's Glueck's 1938-1940 Excavations at Tell el-Kheleifeh: A Reappraisal," *BASOR* 259 (1985), Fig. 15:2-6 (hereafter, *Kheleifeh*). According to Pratico, "Assyrian" pottery and related forms (in local imitation) represent "the second largest horizon at the site, after the 'Negevite' wares" (p. 25). N. Glueck assigned all these items to Period IV, which spanned from "about the end of the eighth to the end of the sixth centuries BCE" (N. Glueck, "Tell el-Kheleifeh," *NEAEHL*, 869). For a wider selection of Assyrian-style pottery at Tell el-Kheleifeh, see *Kheleifeh*—Pratico, Pls. 25-27:11.

[450]C.-M. Bennett, "Excavations at Beṣeirah, Southern Jordan, 1973," *Levant* 7 (1975), Fig. 6:18. Though the pottery from Buṣeirah needs further study, it does not appear to extend back farther than the seventh century BCE (compare Bennett's comments on p. 3 of the article just cited with P. Bienkowski, "Buṣeirah," *OEANE* 1, 389).

[451]*T. Keisan*, 166.

Given the differences in ware and form cited above, it seems that many of these Assyrian-style bowls are actually locally-made imitations. If so, one must allow time for the original Assyrian style to take hold within the local cultures before being copied in the local red-colored ware. Since the imitations would naturally fall later in the chronological span attested to by the Assyrian prototypes themselves, they likely belong mainly to the seventh century BCE. Finally, a general consensus exists that sees all these forms as clay renditions of metal forerunners. This connection receives strength from a morphological comparison to the cache of around 150 bronze vessels, including many bowl forms, recovered by Layard in Room AB of the North-West Palace at Nineveh.[452]

The straight-sided, saucer bowl in entry No. 11, with its simple, somewhat tapered rim, perhaps receives its greatest distinction from its flat or slightly convex (vs. rounded) bottom.[453] This feature alone proves relatively scarce in the search for potential parallels. The point of inflection, which falls at or very near the base of this form, can display a rather strong, angular corner on its outer edge. This flat saucer belongs primarily to traditions current during the late eighth and seventh centuries BCE. Morphologically, it appears to relate directly to the latest phases of thin, hard-fired Samaria Ware, which I discussed extensively on pp. 268-77 above. In this vein, I might reiterate that this style emerged as the most common form of Samaria Ware recovered from the northern capital and that most of the specimens there displayed the expected series of concentric circles on their exterior bottom sides, though Kenyon did not record that attribute for No. 11.

SS III, Fig. 10:11

While the seeds of this tradition as a whole may extend back as far as the late tenth and ninth centuries, the few suggested parallels from that period generally display much more rounded lines than these late Iron II examples.[454] The emergent corpus of

---

[452]See A. H. Layard, *Discoveries in the Ruins of Nineveh and Babylon* (New York: G. P. Putnam and Co., 1853), 177-91, and note especially the bronze "cup" depicted on p. 190; J. Oates, *Iraq* 21 (1959), 132, 142 entry 59; M. E. L. Mallowan, "The Excavations at Nimrud (Kalḫu), 1949-1050," *Iraq* 12 (1950), 183, Pl. XXXII:2; *TN II*, 33-34, § 25; A. Chambon, "Far'ah, Tell-el (North): Late Bronze Age to the Roman Period," *NEAEHL*, 440; see *TN—Cistern*, 41, Fig. 12:x71, for a slightly later form recovered from Cistern 361 at Tell en-Naṣbeh that appears to preserve certain traits of this tradition and to parallel closely a bronze bowl yielded by a so-called Philistine tomb at Gezer (Grant and Wright dated the Gezer tomb to the Persian period; see *AS V*, 78); et passim.

[453]Compare *SS III*, Fig. 18:8 for the flat base and 18:6 for the convex style.

[454]E.g., compare *TAH*, 7, Fig. 9 (Stratum III); *Ta'anach*, Fig. 52:8 (Cistern 69, Period IIB), with an early example of concentric circles but a thicker, more rounded form; *TN II*, Pl. 53:1176, for slightly deeper bowls in thicker ware. In his report from Gezer, Gitin cited a possible early parallel from Locus 1163 at Beth-Shan, and, while James herself described this piece as "a flat-based, hard-ware bowl of the Samaria period V type," it again fails to match closely the later items from Samaria, though it may even represent some sort of antecedent member of the family (compare *Gezer III*, 187 and *Beth-Shan*, James, 69, Fig. 22:12). Moreover, that at least one hard-ware decanter also came from Locus 1163 suggests a possible range of ceramic periods here. James even noted that although the findspot yielded a significant quantity of pottery, "since so little of the walls survived, it is of rather doubtful diagnostic value" (p. 69).

Samaria Ware, then, seems to have adapted already existent ceramic forms; the tradition's novelty lies more in its newly combined patterns of surface treatment than in an innovative morphology. Other than a few scattered exemplars from later levels at sites located elsewhere in the north,[455] Samaria seems to have yielded the largest single collection of bowls in the style of No. 11.[456] Several good exemplars appeared in apparent seventh-century BCE tombs at ʿAtlīt, where the excavator understood both this saucer and the oenochoe jug form[457] as having clear Phoenician (vs. Cypriot) origins.[458] Though sparse in number, then, the available northern parallels help confirm a date for this entry at least in the late eighth and the seventh centuries BCE.[459] In some instances during this period, the basic design appears in very wide plate form made of hard but thicker red ware with burnishing.[460] In the south, the form seems most closely associated with Tufnell's Bowl Class B.9 at Lachish[461] and with Gitin's Type 64A, Variant 1 at Gezer.[462]

Perhaps more than any other single ceramic corpus, the late Iron II pottery from Tyre helps to refine the chronology of the style seen in No. 11. The evolution of forms

---

[455] Compare *Megiddo I*, Pl. 24:52 (Stratum III, though it consists of a thicker, greenish-brown ware and shows a less acute angle for the sidewalls); *Hazor I*, Pl. LXVII:24 (Stratum V; described as a "Samarian" bowl); possibly also *Hazor II*, Pl. LXXXII:16 (Stratum VA; described as a "Cypro-Phoenician" item); *T. Keisan*, 170-71, Pl. 40:12-12a (Niveau 5), where Briend and Humbert include this form among "la poterie phénicienne rouge lustrée"; *T. Farʿah-RB* [59], Fig. 8:11 (Niveau 2); *Chambon*, Pl. 61:25 (Niveaux VIId-e, in "pâte rose à coeur noir, fine et très cuite"); *Beth-Shan*, James, Fig. 67:13 (Level IV); from near Beth-Shan, *T. ʿAmal*, Fig. 7:2 (Niveaux II-I, likely from the late eighth and seventh centuries BCE; see n. 439 above).

[456] Kenyon indicates that this style bowl did not appear prior to PP 6 and E 207 (*SS III*, 123).

[457] See *SS III*, Figs. 10:15 and 22:7 and the discussion below. Compare also *SS III*, Fig. 5:5 and *AIS-I*, 196-97.

[458] *ʿAtlīt*, Figs. 6:2 (from Burial iv *a*); 10:2 (Burial x); 13:3 (Burial xiii *b*, with "concentric thumb-grooves underneath"). On the possible Phoenician (or even west-Phoenician Carthage, Sicily, or Sardinia) ties, see Johns's discussion on pp. 129-34, 135-38.

[459] In stating that all "stratified examples [are] confined to the third quarter of the eighth century," Holladay places *SS III*, Fig. 10:7 and 11 in the same typological category and accepts Kenyon's dating of each (*Holladay*, 189, Fig. 5:B, D).

[460] *Chambon*, Pl. 58:22 (Niveau VIIe, seventh century BCE). (I must correct Chambon's cross reference from *T. Farʿah-RB* [58], Fig. 8:9 to Fig. 12:8, Niveau 1). Though "La fin du niv. 1 reste incertaine" for de Vaux, his examination of the pottery allowed him "proposer 600 comme date extrême" (see *T. Farʿah-RB* [58], 429-30). Subsequent study of the evidence from the palace and gateway areas has allowed Chambon to subdivide this occupational phase into Niveau VIIe, extending from the last quarter of the eighth through the seventh centuries BCE, and Niveau VIIe-1, taking in a squatters settlement around the Iron II-Persian transition period (Chambon, *NEAEHL*, 440).

[461] *Lachish III*, Pl. 79:34 (from Tomb 106, dating to the first half of the seventh century BCE); *Lachish III*, Text, 274, where Tufnell confined this style to tell Level III and Tomb 106.

[462] *Gezer III*, 187-89. As examples of this category, see Pls. 20:4 (Stratum VIA, eighth century) and 24:1 (Stratum VB/VA, late eighth through seventh centuries BCE), but note again the more rounded bottoms and lower outside corners on these exemplars. (Compare also Pl. 24:2, Type 64B, with slightly nuanced sidewalls.)

there seems clear. The straight-sided, thin-ware bowls with convex bottoms appear to have emerged first, as they occur already in Tyre Strata V-IV.[463] In Strata III-II, similar bowls but now with flat or only slightly curved bottoms predominate. The sidewalls now flare out considerably and produce a rather wide diameter.[464] This same form continues in Stratum I, though now the angle of the sidewall relative to the base tightens to yield "a higher rim and a smaller diameter."[465] Comparatively speaking, the sidewall-to-base angle on the Samaria fragment proves quite acute and suggests strongly that this form belongs well into the seventh century BCE. The principal difference between the bowls from Samaria and those from Tyre consists in the ware. At Tyre, all such forms appeared in buff-colored clay and, usually, with a red slip covering at least the interior and extending over the rim if not the entire form. The hard-fired, thin-walled Samaria bowls, however, display a more reddish-brown ware and, for No. 11, Kenyon made no comment on any trace of slip or burnishing.

The Samaria entry in No. 12 also appears to stem mainly from this same general tradition of hard-fired, thinly constructed Samaria Ware, but it displays noticeably more rounded lines and a dark red slip overall. Perusal of the Stratum III assemblage from Megiddo provides an overview of both the morphological and chronological relationship between these two styles of bowl-making;[466] in Syria, the corpus of red-slipped bowls from Al Mina corroborates this comparison.[467] Still, the rounded body-mode seems to have originated earlier than the flat variety,[468] and prototypes appear already in appreciable numbers in, for example, the Cultic Structure at Ta'anach[469] in the north and various contexts at Lachish in the south.[470] These items, however, relate more directly to the PP 3 bowl presented in *SS III*, Fig. 4:9.[471] By the appearance of No. 12, the buff-colored ware of

SS III,
Fig. 10:12

---

[463] Bikai, *BASOR* 229 (1978), Fig. 3:9; Bikai's Fine-Ware Plate "Class 2: Type 1."

[464] Bikai, *BASOR* 229 (1978), Fig. 3:10, Bikai's "Class 2: Type 2."

[465] Bikai, *BASOR* 229 (1978), 52-54; Fig. 3:13, Bikai's "Class 2: Type 3." I cannot agree with Gitin's suggested placement of No. 11 in the group of bowls with wider mouths (see *Gezer III*, 187-88, bowl "Type 64A, Variant 1).

[466] Compare the juxtaposed forms in *Megiddo I*, Pl. 24:49-55.

[467] J. du Plat Taylor, "The Cypriot and Syrian Pottery from Al-Mina, Syria," *Iraq* 21 (1959), Fig. 6:1-3.

[468] Compare *Megiddo I*, Pl. 28:93B (Strata V-IV), with a tapered rim rather than the outcut mode on the Samaria piece; Pl. 31:143 (Stratum V) and the comments on p. 169, § 57. See also *Hazor III-IV*, Pl. CCVIII:24-25 (Stratum IX), with only a slight break in the sidewalls.

[469] *Ta'anach*, Fig. 48:15-19 (Period IIB), though these early exemplars typically show a tan-colored ware, red slip, and continuous burnishing on both the interior and exterior (*Ta'anach*, 33).

[470] Compare *Lachish III*, Pl. 81:88 (Tufnell's Bowl Class B.6; *Lachish III*, Text, 272-73).

[471] See *AIS-I*, 159-60.

the earlier bowls has become a hard, thin, red or reddish-brown fabric. The chronological distribution that I have outlined above agrees with Kenyon's observation that "bowls of this type [i.e., No. 12] appear first as a few rare sherds in IV, but are found in VI, and there were a number of fragments in E 207."[472] She noted further that at least one of these rounded forms displayed the same ware attributes as No. 11. Bowls with simple, thin rims and rounded bottoms appear fairly consistently throughout most of the Iron II period. But because this particular item lacked a "reserve base" and apparently showed no signs of burnishing (according to Kenyon's description), Holladay placed it late in the series, when, he says, typological degeneration had begun.[473]

There is, of course, no problem in extending the use of Samaria Ware beyond the closing date of Israelite control over the site. This attractive tradition might easily have appealed to the Assyrians and others as much as to Phoenicians and Israelites. In short, one must remember that even though the basic corpus may have originated principally in Phoenicia, it represents a *regional* ceramic industry, not an ethnic-specific one.

While the two bowl fragments in Nos. 13-14 also display a manufacture in thin ware, the buff color of the fabric differs from the hard, red ware of the previous examples. Still, the red slip on both the interior and exterior surfaces of No. 13 would have resulted in an appearance similar to the others in this group. Before the application of the slip occurred, this piece received at least two series of incised lines that encompassed the vessel at the level of its handles. This decoration, combined with the vessel's hard-baked, thin ware and red slip, produced an overall appearance very similar to that of the bowl in No. 8.

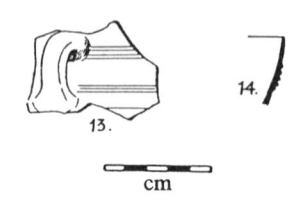

SS III, Fig. 10:13-14

Although it displays a fine, thin *buff*-colored ware similar to the preceding bowl, the rounded bowl with simple rim in No. 14 falls into the same general Iron Age II class as the red-ware vessel in No. 12 above. Judging from the contours of its surviving sidewall, however, entry No. 14 appears to represent a deeper version of the rounded bowl.[474] Typologically, its most interesting feature consists in a series of narrow grooves around its upper sidewall that resulted in a rilling effect. Several bowl forms from Tell el-Far'ah (N) provide the nearest parallels for this distinguishing trait.[475] One late ninth-century specimen from Shechem revealed a wider band of shal-

---

[472] *SS III*, 123.

[473] *Holladay*, 187, Fig. 1:Aa.

[474] From Tyre, compare the specimen in "golden-colored ware . . . [with] a thick red slip on the exterior only" in Bikai, *BASOR* 229 (1978), 52, Fig. 3:8. Here this bowl form seemed to flourish in Strata IX-VI, ranging from ca. 850 to 760 BCE.

[475] *T. Far'ah-RB* [58], 429, Fig. 11:9 (Locus 151, Niveau 2, dated by de Vaux to the eighth century BCE down to the fall of Samaria); *Chambon*, Pl. 61:23 (Niveau VIId, which Chambon places rather broadly in the ninth and eighth centuries BCE).

low grooves in the same location on the upper sidewall,[476] while another piece had a raised, unrilled band at that point.[477] Both *SS III*, Fig. 9:2 (also PP 6) and a series of bowls from Tell Keisan[478] attest to a connection between this rilling and the reserve bands left on other thin-walled Samaria Ware forms, including those resembling No. 11 above. On the basis of these few parallels in either form or decorative motif, and particularly those from Tell el-Farʿah (N), No. 14 might easily predate the fall of Samaria into Assyrian hands. Consequently, from a ceramic point of view, it may accompany or perhaps precede slightly the appearance of the Assyrian-style bowls published as Nos. 8-10 and certainly the late Samaria Ware form in No. 11. In fact, the *terminus post quem* for this tradition belongs in the latter half of the ninth century BCE.[479]

b. Cooking Pots

The Joint Expedition published only two examples of cooking-pot rims recovered from Pit *i*. Since the field notes assign these sherds more specifically to Segment *122.126.19.121*, I may reiterate that the small size of the two fragments proves consistent with other pieces yielded by that findspot (as opposed to the more intact goods taken from the locus labeled *122.125.19.121*). Data pertaining to the provenance of these two rim fragments appear as follows:

SS III Published Figure	Registry No. (not marked for discard)	Strip	Coordinates	Feature	Local Layer
10:26	Q 2509a	Qk	122.126.19.121	Pit *i*	Va
10:27	Q 2509b	Qk	122.126.19.121	Pit *i*	Va

Provenance Data:
PP6 Cooking Pots from Pit i

Table 37

---

[476]See *Holladay*, Fig. 2:A. (Note that Holladay erroneously identifies his Fig. 1:A as *SS III*, Fig. 10:5 rather than as the correct 10:14.)

[477]*Holladay*, Fig. 1:N, in a hard, ringing, grey ware with buff slip on the interior and over the rim and exterior band. Production of this raised band likely comprised the first step in preparing the vessel for the shallow, closely spaced, incised grooves that appear on other exemplars.

[478]*T. Keisan*, Pl. 40:12a-d (Niveau 5); see the comments and parallels on p. 171.

[479]For the basic form, compare *Hazor III-IV*, Pl. CLXXXI:17, 19 (Stratum VI), in pinkish, well-levigated clay with burnished red slip (exterior only on No. 17).

Cooking-pot entry No. 26 reflects an early Iron II variation on a basic tenth-century BCE style rim. The classic tenth-century form appears in *SS III*, Fig. 1:21 (PP 1).[480] On the present specimen, the potter has turned the once rounded, even bulbous, lip strongly outward and thereby produced a deeply concaved fold that he smoothed to a crescent shape. Within the PP 1-7 repertoire from Samaria, this rim seems most reminiscent of Fig. 3:29 from PP 2, though the latter appears to have a slightly thinner wall construction than No. 26. Though hardly any of the upper sidewall survived on this fragment, the general stance of that feature on Fig. 3:29 may suggest a rather low point of carination. At any rate, this pot does not approach the notched rim-form mode that characterizes Aharoni's and Amiran's so-called Late Shallow Type, despite its strongly protruding, horizontal flange. The vessel might easily have appeared without handles and as early as the first half of the ninth century BCE. Good parallels from late tenth- and ninth-century levels at Hazor confirm this assessment.[481]

Rim No. 27, on the other hand, shows an advance on the notched style of the "Late Shallow Type" cooking pot that appeared in the mid-ninth century BCE and continued well into the eighth century. Here, the area of rim above the notch is shortened from a flattening process that thickened both its internal and external edges. The resultant broad, rather blunt lip also customarily slants inward toward the mouth of the vessel. These attributes distinguish this mode from the sharper, triangular lips witnessed on both the Early and Late Shallow Types of bowls. In Kenyon's typology, this style would undoubtedly fall among her "Class Ċ" rims, i.e., with those showing a "thickened rim with flange, sometimes called thick ridged rim."[482] This distinctive, overall style typifies only the Iron Age II period. Though incipient trends toward this motif may appear already by the Iron I-Iron II transition period,[483] this rim mode does not extend far back into Iron Age I groups; rather, it increases in frequency as the basic, triangular form of Iron Age I declines in number.[484] Antecedent forms from the ninth and eighth centuries BCE typically show a more strongly incut lip,[485] an attribute

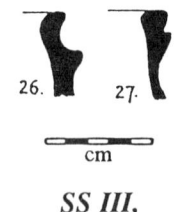

SS III,
Fig. 10:26-27

---

[480]For my discussion of this style, see *AIS-I*, 60-62. Compare *Taʿanach*, Fig. 53:4 (Period IIB).

[481]*Hazor III-IV*, Pls. CLXXX:10 (Stratum VII); CCXII:28 (Strata IX-X).

[482]*SS III*, 189. Compare Fig. 30:4-6, 20-24.

[483]Compare, for example, *Chambon*, Pl. 53:1 (Niveau VIIb = tenth century BCE), with a much less pronounced exterior notch. Though a possible relative of this same tradition, a later pot from Tell el-Farʿah (N) shows an incut-rim mode with a more flattened lip (Pl. 53:7, from Niveau VIId); see also *T. Farʿah-RB* [59], Fig. 9:1 (Niveau 2).

[484]Compare *Megiddo I*, Pls. 39 (forms common in Strata IV-I) and 40 (styles typical of Strata V-IV). Beyond this general statement, however, the Megiddo material proves of little value in refining the Iron II sequence of this style rim (see the discussion in *Megiddo I*, 172, § 76, and my caveat in n. 489 below).

[485]See again *Chambon*, Pl. 53:7 (Niveau VIIb); also *Hazor II*, Pl. LVII:26 (Stratum VIII); *Jezreel*—Zimhoni, 68, Fig. 9:1.

that appears to persist as late as the 732 BCE horizon on rims that are even more squat in profile than No. 27.[486] During its principal period of use in the late eighth and the seventh centuries BCE, however, this feature waned as the posture of the rim assumed a more vertical stance (as in No. 27).[487] In the Yoqʻneam Regional Project, this rim style appeared in quantity beginning only in Strata V-VI at Qiri (dated by Ben-Tor and Portugali to the "Iron III" period)[488] and in Stratum 10 at Yoqnʻeam itself.[489] At Taʻanach, this new brand of grooved rim rose to prominence in Period V, which the excavators dated to the period of Assyrian occupation from ca. 700-650 BCE.[490] Within the Samaria corpus itself, Holladay regarded this piece as one of several "almost certain intrusions from the post-VI period."[491]

Besides these two cooking-pot rims, Kenyon noted that two additional styles "were also found,"[492] presumably in Pit *i*. The report, however, drew its exemplars of these forms from its "General List" of nonstratified pottery presented in *SS III*, Fig. 30:10 (assigned to Summit Strip Qc) and 22 (recovered from E 207). Holladay understood the former piece as "unquestionably (early) ninth century!"[493] but it may predate even this period and seems to me to represent the oldest of the four modes discussed here. That fact notwithstanding, both 30:10 and 30:22 would seem quite at home in the PP 4 cooking-pot group treated earlier. Most of those pieces came from contexts of secondary fill[494] (compare *SS III*, Fig. 6:29 with 30:10, though the former

---

[486]*Hazor II*, Pl. LXXXV:1-2 (Stratum VA). For an even later example, see *Hazor II*, Pl. XCIX:22 (Stratum IV).

[487]See *ʻEin Gev*, Fig. 9:9 (Area A, Stratum II, dated earlier in the eighth century BCE). Morphologically related bowl rims, though sometimes bearing a more everted posture, appear in the 732 BCE horizon material at Hazor (*Hazor II*, Pls. LXXXII:3, 12; XCIII:7, 10; all from Stratum VA).

[488]*T. Qiri*, 5, 182. The authors of this report classified this style rim under their Type III, "Modelled" cooking pot and drew a comparison to *SS III*, Fig. 6:39, from PP 4 (*T. Qiri*, 216; compare pp. 79-80 and accompanying notes in Chapter I above).

[489]*T. Yoqneʻam* [2], Fig. 8:16 (= Stratum 4 in this preliminary report; the excavators subsequently redesignated it Stratum 10 in *T. Yoqneʻam* [3], 31). Compare *T. Qiri*, 217, Tables 9-11. One must, however, discount the insinuation in those tables that the style of No. 27 appeared already in quantity in Megiddo Stratum IV, since the report from Megiddo simply presents drawings of 12 general motifs that occurred in Strata IV-I at that site and makes no further effort to define a closer typology (see *Megiddo I*, Pl. 39). In fact, the authors of *Megiddo I* stated explicitly that they relied much less on these cooking-pot rims than on other types of pottery to establish their ceramic chronology at the site (p. 172, § 76). The Megiddo report, then, cannot stand as evidence of an early Iron II prominence for these or similar materials (see n. 484 above; but compare *Lapp and Lapp*, 66-67).

[490]*Taʻanach*, 44-45; Fig. 76:6-7 (these exemplars remain much more squat and inverted than the rim from Samaria); Table 2 on p. 56.

[491]*Holladay*, 68.

[492]*SS III*, 125.

[493]*Holladay*, 347, Fig. 60:F. (See Fig. 65:C for No. 22).

[494]See pp. 87-88 above. Also, a number of apparent recording errors attended this group (see Table 8 and pp. 77-78).

is more strongly inverted, and 6:39 with 30:22). Curiously, in both the published report and the handwritten field registry, Fig. 30:10 bears the same identification number (2215c) as the cooking-pot rim shown in Fig. 4:21 (from PP 3) and assigned to Layer VI of Segment *86.2.88.E* in Room *n*, which, in fact, does not lie within Summit Strip Qc. Moreover, the typescript copy of "Field Registry Qn, Sabastya 1935," stored in the Rockefeller Museum, records this fragment as yet another "*discard.*"

c. Jars

Kenyon included only one jar form among the published pottery assigned to Pit *i*. The relevant provenance data appear as follows:

SS III Published Figure	Registry No. (not marked for discard)	Strip	Provenance Coordinates	Feature	Local Layer
10:25	Q 2536	Qk	122.126.19.121	Pit *i*	Va

Provenance Data:
PP6 Jar from Pit i

Table 38

This jar represents the larger of the two intact pottery items assigned to Segment *122.126.19.121* (the small black juglet in entry No. 24 represents the other complete form recovered from this locus). This vessel falls in the category of tall storage jars (for this class, I accept a range in height from 25 to 75 cm), and its overall dimensions appear as follows: its height reaches 30 cm, while its diameter expands to approximately 21.25 cm at its widest point on the lower third of the body (measured from the exterior walls); finally, its mouth is just over 9 cm in width.

Since most Iron II store jars become narrower in the lower half of their bodies and carry some variation of profiled-rim mode, exact parallels for this entry remain difficult to trace. Within the published list of stratified pottery, this jar seems reminiscent of a slightly shorter (ca. 25 cm) specimen from the PP 5 assemblage (*SS III*, 8:1). The shoulder-, handle-, and general body-forms of these two vessels appear basically compatible, though the PP 5 jar consisted in an "imperfect, brownish ware" while the present example showed a "coarse creamy buff ware [with] red grits."[495] Kenyon also cross-referenced 8:1 and 10:25 to *SS III*, Fig. 21:2 and 3, respectively, both of which

---

[495]*SS III*, 118, 125.

came from nonstratified contexts in S Tombs 103 and 104; additional matches came from the Locus E 207. In addition to these comparisons, she also drew a connection between 10:25, 21:3, and the rim fragment from PP 4 presented in Fig. 6:18.

At Samaria, then, this style jar proves most at home in levels beginning in the mid to late eighth century BCE and continuing into the seventh century. This seems to concur with the admittedly sparse evidence from other sites, though some possible northern antecedents may appear in different fabrics already during the tenth and ninth centuries BCE.[496] Although adequate parallels remain equally difficult to locate in the south, this jar form relates best to those with plain-collared necks, curved shoulders, and ovoid bodies, as in Tufnell's Class S.4 at Lachish.[497] The official report described this group as consisting of "a fine pink paste, tempered with grits, . . . covered with a cream or buff slip" and dating primarily to tell Level II.[498]

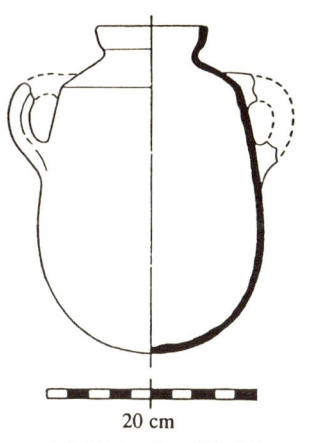

SS III, Fig. 10:25

Holladay placed No. 25 in his category of miscellaneous store jar forms[499] and limited his remarks to the style of its handles. His study shows that, apart from one or two examples at Shechem,[500] neither large, flat handles nor handles with double ribs typify the ninth or eighth centuries BCE. Rather, handles during this period consistently display either a single ridge (Holladay dubbed these "hogback" handles), an off-centered diamond design, or an oval-to-almond shape. Further, these motifs may occur "in apparently random interchange."[501] Though Kenyon did not present the handles of entry No. 25 in section, the drawing of the left handle leads me to conclude that they tend toward either Holladay's "hogback" style or the flatter design of a subsequent period. Within his corpus of forms, Holladay placed this jar in the 733-722 BCE ceramic horizon. Given the lack of adequate comparative data, any dating of this vessel

---

[496] Compare, for example, *Taʿanach*, Fig. 62:3 (Period IIB, Cistern 74). This example seems to anticipate the Samaria jar in both form and ware, though it displays droopier shoulders. For an even earlier comparison in form alone, see *Taʿanach*, Fig. 15:8 (Period IB, Cuneiform Tablet Building). See also *Jezreel*—Zimhoni, Fig. 6:19 (Room 118 in Area A) and *Jezreel*-1, 20.

[497] *Lachish III*, Pl. 94:478, 481 (with the latter bearing a profiled rim).

[498] *Lachish III, Text*, 314. Compare *TN II*, Pl. 18:303, with profiled rim and droopier shoulders; see also the rims (with more pronounced necks) in Pl. 17:288 and 294. The above description of No. 25 resembles in certain details that used in Zimhoni's presentation of a much larger, "coastal" storage jar that received sparse attestation in Level III at Lachish (*Lachish*—Zimhoni, 26, Fig. 17:1).

[499] *Holladay*, Fig. 90:A.

[500] See *Holladay*, Fig. 91:Aa and B, from Loci (Sub-)1739 and (Sub-)1748, respectively, both situated in a matrix of fill material. On grounds of morphology and stratigraphic context, then, Holladay deemed these fragments likely intrusions from Stratum IX_B or even X.

[501] *Holladay*, 216.

d. Jugs and Juglets

For these two pottery types, the final report of the Joint Expedition presented from Pit *i* two jugs (or "pitchers"), a series of three dipper juglets, and one so-called Black Juglet, named after the usual color of its ware and surface treatment. All these items appear as whole or near-whole vessels, and all but one derive from Segment *122.125.19.121*. This observation, once again, proves consistent with the pattern of high preservation already attested among other pottery recovered from this particular locus. Only the small Black Juglet in entry No. 24 comes from the alternate Segment *122.126.19.121*, which routinely yielded a corpus of materials in fragmentary condition. Earlier, however, I recognized that such compact, sturdily-built objects might easily survive intact even in a stratigraphic environment that saw the destruction of most of the larger goods around it.[502] Despite this one variation in segment coordinates, the report assigned all these goods to the same local layer, namely Va. Data pertaining to the findspots and registration of these vessels follow in Table 39.

SS III Published Figure	Registry No. (none marked for discard)	Provenance			
		Strip	Coordinates	Feature	Local Layer
jugs:					
10:15	Q 2481	Qk	122.125.19.121	Pit *i*	Va
10:16	Q 2483	Qk	122.125.19.121	Pit *i*	Va
juglets:					
10:21	Q 2489	Qk	122.125.19.121	Pit *i*	Va
10:22	Q 2487	Qk	122.125.19.121	Pit *i*	Va
10:23	Q 2488	Qk	122.125.19.121	Pit *i*	Va
10:24	Q 2508	Qk	122.126.19.121	Pit *i*	Va

Provenance Data:
PP6 Jugs and Juglets from Pit i

Table 39

---

[502] See n. 370 above; also Chapter II, n. 108. At Beth-Shan, James noted that "the Beisan stratification makes it plain that juglets have great powers of survival, as unbroken specimens of Iron Age forms are recorded in Roman and later loci, and in one extreme case an Early Bronze Age juglet was found in an Upper V locus, Fig. 31, 37" (*Beth-Shan*, James, 128).

PP 6: PIT i — POTTERY

In virtually every excavation or comparative ceramic analysis, jugs present a very heterogeneous class of goods from a typological point of view.[503] Even the two primary features that distinguish the jug from a jar form, namely, the jug's shorter height and the presence of a lip designed for pouring, can vary to a significant degree.

In this vein, one sees that although both items presented in *SS III*, Fig. 10:15-16 appear to represent descendants of the so-called oenochoe family of pitcher-jugs, they also attest to the many nuances in form that related jugs often exhibit. According to most form paradigms, both vessels fall into the category of "short jugs" (No. 15 appears just over 18 cm and No. 16 measures approximately 13.5 cm in height).[504] Both items have high necks that flare outward toward the top, but the neck on No. 16 narrows to a smaller diameter as it approaches the upper body. This tapering creates a much sharper break between the neck and shoulder. While No. 15 has incised lines on both its mid-neck and shoulder areas, No. 16 shows similar lines only at the same location on its neck;[505] through form alone, the strong break between neck and shoulder on No. 16 likely accomplishes what the lower set of decorative lines are themselves meant to signify on No. 15. Each jug has a single, oblong (in section) strap handle[506] that attaches from rim to shoulder, with its upper edge rising above the level of the rim (the

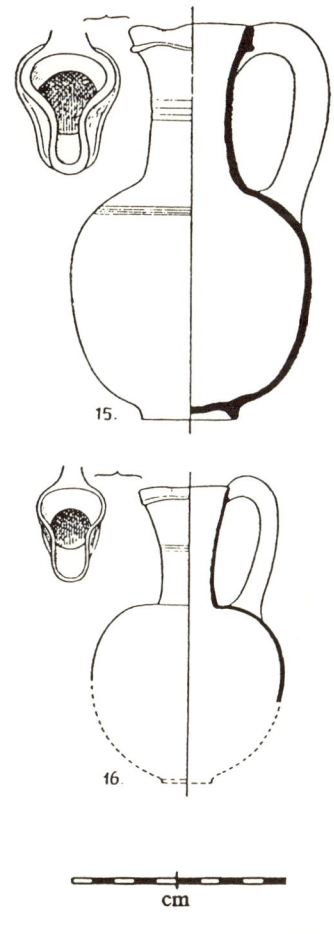

SS III, Fig. 10:15-16

---

[503] A quick comparison of the corpus catalogues presented in *Amiran*, *Holladay*, and *Gezer III* (assembled by S. Gitin) will verify this observation. Many excavators have faced this challenge in classifying the results of their field work. For example, A. Mazar notes in his report from Tell Qasîle that, among the non-Philistine material, "there are almost no two identical jugs, and they show a wide variety of shapes. Therefore, . . . the typological classification can only be in wide terms, on the basis of certain common features" (*T. Qasîle* [2], 61).

[504] See the conventions for these and other standard measurements in *APTJ*, 51.

[505] Judging from the drawn forms in *SS III*, Fig. 10:15-16 (and from the painted frontispiece for No. 15), the plate descriptions in both *SS III*, 124, and *Holladay*, Fig. 107:A-B, appear to reverse this attribute for these jugs by stating that No. 16 has lines on both its neck and shoulder, while No. 15 has them only on the neck.

[506] At Tyre, two types of handles occurred on red-slipped trefoil jugs, namely the strap handle and the double-strand variety (*Tyre*, 36-37, Table 7). The latter type appeared as double or twin handles on similar jugs at ʿAtlît, Hazor, and elsewhere (see *Chapman*, 166-67; *ʿAtlît*, Fig. 6:1 [Burial iv a]; *Hazor II*, 13).

handle of No. 16 springs higher than the one on 15). While both body forms are globular-shaped, their points of greatest diameter appear in the upper half of this feature. The curvature of the body wall on No. 16, however, indicates that its missing lower section was slightly more tapered than that of No. 15 and thus gave it somewhat of a piriform design. It seems likely that both vessels had ring bases, though Kenyon's proposed reconstruction of No. 16 seems almost disc-like. Both specimens display flanged-style rims with slightly everted inflections and with the flange itself pushed up to form a ridge that separates the rim from the neck area. The red-slipped, buff-colored ware of No. 15 is noticeably thicker than the red, unslipped (?), and apparently better-levigated fabric of No. 16.

The fact that an earlier vessel from PP 3 (*SS III*, Fig. 5:5)[507] may well belong to this same general class of oenochoe jugs demonstrates the range of possible diversity in their basic forms. In my previous treatment of the PP 3 piece, I noted that a reliable classification of this overall type remains in need of data from better-stratified contexts.[508] I also suggested that the oenochoe family began already during the ninth century BCE,[509] never appeared in appreciable numbers, and may reflect some degree of Phoenician influence on Iron II ceramic traditions.[510] More than the globular bodies, base- or handle-forms, the flanged rims and trefoil mouths of Nos. 15 and 16 emerge as their most distinguishing characteristics. Most other jugs possess rims that are simple, outcut, or thickened into a bulbous profile.[511] When the flanged motif occurs on early Iron II jugs (or jars), it often belongs to forms with shorter and wider necks and with mouths that remain round and without a pouring lip.[512] Further, a

---

[507]To my comparisons offered for this piece in *AIS-I* I should certainly add *Lachish III*, Pl. 86:241 (from Tomb 116), which helps to confirm my suggested mid-ninth-century date for this particular pitcher from Samaria). Tufnell believed that this elegant style represented "the earliest forms in the series" (*Lachish III, Text*, 290).

[508]*AIS-I*, 196-97.

[509]The best possible Iron I prototypes appear in *Megiddo II*, Pl. 75:3-4, 11, 12[?] (mostly from Stratum VI), and *T. Keisan*, Pl. 61:6 (Niveau 9a-b). Concerning this last piece, Humbert noted that "cette cruche unique offre un type particulier avec son col haut et évasé, sa panse globulaire et sa base en anneau. . . . Il est difficile de trouver un parallèl exact à cette cruche, mais on peut en rapprocher des cruches trouvées à Megiddo" (*T. Keisan*, 208; the reference to Megiddo aims at *Megiddo I*, Pl. 7:173, Stratum V, and *Megiddo II*, Pl. 75:9, Stratum VI). In addition to these, compare similar jugs from tenth-century levels at Tel ʿAmal near Beth-Shan (*T. ʿAmal*, Figs. 11:5,7 and 12:1 [all assigned to Niveau IV]). From even earlier still, note the general features of *T. Farʿah-RB* [58], Figs. 8:12-13 (Niveau 4); 13:2 (*Période* I); *T. Farʿah-RB* [62], Fig. 2:5 (from *Tombe* 16).

[510]To my observations regarding No. 5 in *AIS-I*, 197, n. 208, I should certainly now add *Chapman*, Figs. 26-27 and the discussion on pp. 166-68; also Tufnell's comments in *Lachish III, Text*, 290; and remarks by C. N. Johns in *ʿAtlīt*, 129-32, 135-38.

[511]E.g., note the pitchers in *TN II*, Pl. 31:539-51.

[512]E.g., see *T. Keisan*, Pl. 56:8 (Niveau 8); *AS-IV*, Pls. LXV:38 (Room 363, Stratum IIc); LXVII:10 (Cistern 25, Stratum IIc; on this example, the upper edge of the handle remains level with the rim); *TN II*, Pl. 18:301. Various other modified exemplars appear among the collection of pitchers in *TN II*, Pls.

smooth groove typically appears on the interior rim wall opposite the flange area on the outside. In short, most of the potential parallels better resemble the fragment published in *SS III*, Fig. 9:6, which I have assigned rather broadly to the eighth century BCE. Passable, though never perfect, comparisons come from Hazor,[513] ʿAtlīt,[514] Megiddo (see below), Tell el-Farʿah (N),[515] a tomb at nearby Munshara,[516] Tell en-Naṣbeh,[517] and, in the south, Lachish.[518] I may add that one likely parallel from Hazor Stratum VA not only resembles the ware (grey-buff clay with some grits) and surface treatment (red slip) of No. 15, but it also shows a set of four incised lines on both its mid-neck and shoulder area.[519] As on the Samaria pitcher, these lines are closely drawn on the shoulder and more widely spaced on the neck.[520] Two pitchers from Lachish displayed applied, knob-like features immediately below the lower handle attachment to the shoulder.[521] Tufnell interpreted these features as skeuomorphic representations of metal rivets. Others have similarly concluded that the overall design of the trefoil-mouthed

---

32-33. For other possible antecedent forms, see *Taʿanach*, 37:2 (Period IIB Cultic Structure) and 59:6 (Period IIB), with the former showing a pinched mouth. For a trefoil mouth, compare *Hazor II*, Pl. LVIII:14 (Stratum VIII); yet the bodies on these early exemplars often assume a much more bloated appearance than on the generally more svelt pitchers in Nos. 15-16.

[513] *Hazor II*, Pls. LXIV:19 (?), with simple rim (Stratum VII); LXX:17 (Stratum VI); LXXXVII:1-3 (all from Stratum VA and generally with trefoil mouths); XCVII:2 (Stratum VA, with pinched mouth). *Hazor III-IV*, Pl. CCXXIV:8 (Stratum VB), though with a slightly taller body form. See also the more recent *Hazor V*, Fig. III.39:24 (Stratum VI), with red slip and trefoil mouth but a handle that remains lower than the lip of the rim.

[514] *ʿAtlīt*, Fig. 16:4 (Burial xvii *b*, likely from the seventh century BCE). Compare also Fig. 6:1 (Burial iv *a*), with a different neck mode.

[515] *T. Farʿah-RB* [58], Fig. 11:14 (Niveau 2, which Chambon now says suffered destruction by fire at the hands of Sargon II in 721 BCE; A. Chambon, "Farʿah, Tell el- [North]," *NEAEHL*, 440). Compare also *Chambon*, Pl. 49:21 (Niveau VIId), with simple rim.

[516] *Munshara*, Figs. 1:7-8; 2:1-5 (mostly No. 4; Zayadine said that Nos. 1-5 "sont les plus communs"—p. 565); 3:1,8 (all examples from Chamber 1). Zayadine tentatively dated this tomb after PP 1-2 at Samaria and before Niveau 2 at Tell el-Farʿah, that is to say, roughly to the late ninth century BCE (*Munshara*, 567). It seems possible, however, that some items discovered there belong to a later period.

[517] *TN II*, Pls. 32:562-63 (again with handles rising only to rim level); 33:576 (with lines on the middle neck area but with an alternate rim form). These items belong to two series of pitchers recovered at Tell en-Naṣbeh for which the excavators found few good parallels and for which they had little information (see *TN II*, 16, §§ 6, 8).

[518] See Tufnell's comments and types in Jug Class J.6 (*Lachish III, Text*, 290-91).

[519] *Hazor II*, Pl. LXXXVII:21 (Area B). That Yadin included this item in his group of decanters underscores a likely close connection between these two classes of vessels (see *Hazor II*, 55); in this same vein, compare the jug and decanter (with shoulder grooves) in *Hazor III-IV*, Pl. CCXXIV:8-9 (Stratum VB). Though another Hazor exemplar lacks a handle, it displays a comparable neck, rim, and mouth as well as incised grooves on its shoulder (*Hazor III-IV*, Pl. CLXXXIX:17; Stratum V).

[520] Compare the specimen with only two lines in each location and a double-strand handle in *Lachish III*, Pl. 86:237.

[521] *Lachish III*, Pl. 86:232, 237.

oenochoe pitchers, at least the later ones, imitates metal (bronze) originals.[522]

Besides these two examples of oenochoe jugs from stratified contexts (albeit poor ones) at Samaria, Kenyon also included several similar items from nonstratified findspots (*SS III*, Fig. 22:7-9). While the bulkier exemplar, No. 8, derived from the Z Deep Pit, which Kenyon associated with PP 3, the other two jugs came from the E 207 locus purportedly affiliated with PP 6. If these stratigraphic correlations are correct (and one can argue this point),[523] then one can witness an evolution in design from the mid-ninth century to the late eighth century BCE. In the earlier period, the forms display a larger, heavier body, a flanged rim that does not continue the outward flare of the upper neck, and a trefoil mouth. By the late eighth century BCE, the tradition moves to a shallower but still bloated body, a taller neck form with greater outward flare, either incised lines or a sharp break at the body-neck juncture, variant rim modes (sometimes flanged) that now continue the outward inflection of the neck, and trefoil mouth. The corpus of stratified examples cited above from other sites supports this development. Incidentally, Kenyon noted that Fig. 22:7 "was the commonest jug on the site."[524]

The two attractive pitcher-jugs in *SS III*, Fig. 10:15-16 constitute one central strand of evidence in Forsberg's argument to link the PP 6 group with materials assigned to Megiddo Stratum III (the other thread of his suggestion ties in the globular-shaped decanter in entry No. 17, which I shall address below).[525] One certainly cannot gainsay his appeal to comparisons between the morphology of Nos. 15-16 (plus 22:7, 9) and the basic forms in the jug series published mainly from Stratum III at Megiddo.[526] In fact, these are the very ceramic correlations that Kenyon herself had drawn in 1957.[527] Moreover, both scholars have noted that, though some small fragments belonging to this jug form appeared (perhaps as intrusions) in the fillings associated with Megiddo IV, "the form is preponderantly a Stratum III form at Megiddo."[528] There exists general agreement, then, that these particular PP 6 jugs from Samaria bear

---

[522] E.g., G. L. Harding in Harding and Tufnell, "The Tomb of Adoni-Nur," *APEF* 6 (1953), 48-75; W. Culican, "Quelques aperçus sur les ateliers phéniciens," *Syria* 45 (1968), 275-93; *Amiran*, 272; see also Bikai's comments in *Tyre*, 61, n. 94.

[523] See n. 204 above.

[524] *SS III*, 168 (fragments from at least 26 individual specimens came from E 207 alone).

[525] *Forsberg*, 21.

[526] *Megiddo I*, Pl. 3:83, 86, 88-89. In the pottery report from Tyre (*Tyre*, 36), Bikai argued to classify these jugs into two subgroups, with the earlier one showing elongated, concave necks (as in *Tyre*, Pl. XX:1, from Stratum IX in the late ninth century BCE; and *Megiddo II*, Pl. 91:3, from Stratum IV) and with the later type changing to more conical-shaped necks (as in *Megiddo I*, Pl. *Megiddo I*, Pl. 3:83 and 85). Judging from these examples, however, the distinction is not a clear one (a fact which Bikai herself acknowledges); consequently, it cannot help refine the chronology for Nos. 15-16 at Samaria.

[527] *SS III*, 204 (within the context of the broader discussion of Megiddo Strata IV-III on pp. 201-04).

[528] *SS III*, 203. Forsberg also recounts the stratigraphic distributions of these jugs (and the decanter style of No. 17) at Megiddo (*Forsberg*, 21).

a distinct typological relationship to similar specimens from Megiddo III. Given the untrustworthy nature of the findspot at Samaria, the chronology of the Megiddo level becomes a central issue in any attempt to ascertain the proper historical associations of PP 6. While I shall revisit this concern in my Conclusions below, I believe that my comparative stratigraphical analysis at the outset of this chapter argues strongly for assigning the *terminus ante quem* of both Megiddo III and the mixed repertoire of Pit *i* at Samaria somewhere in the very late eighth or, perhaps better, in the first half of the seventh century BCE. The jug forms in entries 15-16 would not contradict this judgment.[529] In light of this date, the latest trefoil-mouthed jugs may have spread from Phoenicia into both Israel (e.g., Megiddo and Samaria) and Transjordan (Amman and Sahab) as part and parcel of Assyrian expansion.[530]

Before addressing entries 21-24 individually, I shall quickly note the morphological distinction claimed by No. 24. Its unique body and neck forms help to locate it in a class of *container-* rather than dipper-juglets (as in Nos. 21-23). A succinct comparison between the form and function of these two subgroups appears in the pottery report from Tell Qiri. Briefly, the greater bodies plus wider necks and mouths of the dipper class suggest that these vessels served to draw small quantities of liquid from a larger jar or to transfer liquids from one container to another. When not in use, this domestic juglet would likely have remained empty and, if traded, would have been transported that way. By contrast, the smaller, more squat body and narrower neck[531] and mouth of No. 24 have led many to infer that it functioned as a holder of "small quantities of some relatively expensive liquid, such as a special oil, perfume or drug."[532] In trading circumstances, greater interest would have focused on the contents of this juglet than on the vessel itself. Both the manufacturing technique and collective morphological attributes of this style juglet (see below) corroborate this suggestion. Yet I must add that any trade of this juglet and, by extension, whatever commodity it held, appears restricted to Israel. Bikai's study of the pottery from Tyre did not contain a single clear example of a Black

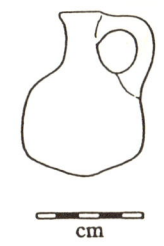

SS III,
Fig. 10:24

---

[529]In my judgment, then, this tradition might well extend later than the 733-722 BCE Horizons suggested in *Holladay*, 221. At Tyre, Bikai noted that the latest of these forms (her conical-necked variety) likely did not "enter the Phoenician repertoire until the eighth century." It seems to have flourished, however, at Al Mina, Khaldé, Akhziv, ʿAtlit, and in Punic contexts as far west as Spain during the seventh and even sixth centuries BCE (*Tyre*, 36; *Chapman*, 167).

[530]Compare again Harding's views in *APEF* 6 (1953), 48-75, for the suggestion that these forms represent local Ammonite products, with Tufnell's recognition of the strong Assyrian presence in Transjordan during the late eighth and early seventh centuries BCE (*Lachish III, Text*, 291).

[531]Necks were generally about the diameter of a common pencil (*TBM III*, 123-23, § 125).

[532]*T. Qiri*, 203-204. At Tell Beit Mirsim, Kelso and Thorley officially referred to these vessels as "Small Squat Black Perfume Juglets" (*TBM I*, 83, § 113; *TBM III*, 123, § 125).

Juglet;[533] neither did this vessel class travel to Cyprus, according to Ben-Tor and Hunt.[534]

Finally, dipper style juglets generally appear in significantly greater numbers than the Black Juglets at most northern sites.[535] At first thought, this may appear to result from the common, utilitarian function of dippers in contrast to the more specialized use of containers. But a closer look at the geographical distribution of the latter group undercuts this suggestion, for the Black Juglet appears in more impressive numbers at many sites in the south. At Lachish, for example, Tufnell described the black burnished juglet (her Class D.8, Type 309) and its typological antecedent (Type 322) as "the most common type of juglet at Tell ed-Duweir, for over a hundred examples of each are recorded."[536] Similarly, the excavators at Tell Beit Mirsim recorded dozens of exemplars of this form.[537] Excavation results from other southern towns (such as Beth-Shemesh) substantiate this heavy concentration in the assemblages of that area as opposed to the pottery industries of northern cultures. The real reasons for this skewed distribution will undoubtedly prove complex and will likely stem more from economic factors and issues of regionalism than from simple differences in function between dipper and container forms.

I shall elaborate further on the Black Juglet after offering some general comments on the group of dippers recovered from Pit *i*. Besides two specimens taken from layers associated with PP 1 (*SS III*, Fig. 1:7-8), the published repertoire of Israelite pottery has remained devoid of dipper juglets. In the PP 6 group, however, one sees three of them, all reportedly from Pit *i*, Segment *122.125.19.121*, Layer Va. In light of my previous extended discussion concerning this general vessel type,[538] I need not reiterate the many details here.

From their morphology alone, entries 21-23 show that they clearly predate the Black Juglet form in No. 24. These three specimens are more closely aligned with the dipper juglets just mentioned from PP 1. Traditionally, analysts have concentrated on the body-form mode when attempting to classify this vessel type.[539] According to this system of reckoning, the elliptical body with pointed base characterized the Late Bronze and earlier Iron I periods before giving way in the later Iron Age I to a more

---

[533]*Tyre*, 41-43, and the pottery plates mentioned there.

[534]*T. Qiri*, 204.

[535]E.g., at Qiri only 1 (unstratified) of 26 recovered juglets belonged to the container style, black juglet group; at Yoqneʻam, the ratio was 127 dippers to 5 containers (*T. Qiri*, 204).

[536]*Lachish III, Text*, 303.

[537]*TBM I*, Pl. 68:1-32 (Stratum A), "which form only a fraction of the specimens discovered" (83, § 113); *TBM III*, 123, §§ 125 and 158 (the latter reference describes the Black Juglet as excessively abundant, the "commonest" juglet form second only to elongated styles), Pls. 18:1-9; 70b:1-15.

[538]*AIS-I*, 65-68.

[539]E.g., see *Amiran*, 251-65; *T. Qasîle* [2], 70.

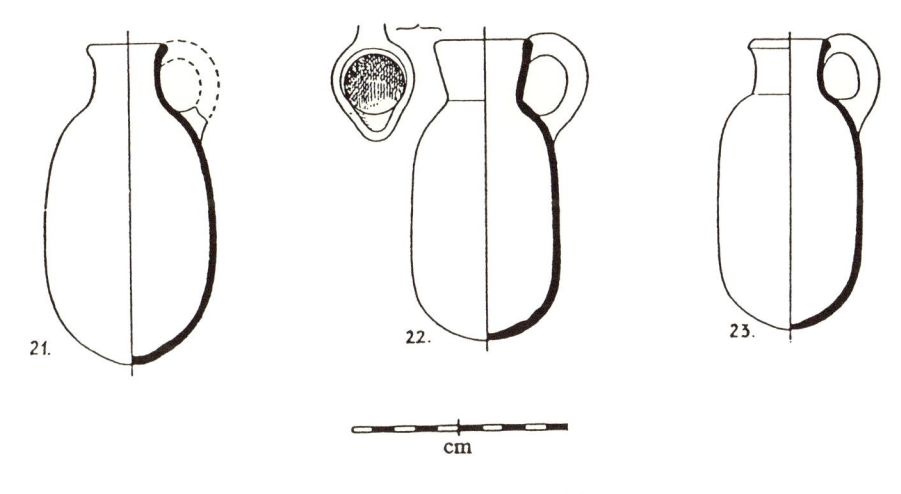

SS III, Fig. 10:21-23

sack-shaped body that widens toward its bottom (compare No. 21).[540] While the latter style continued through the tenth century BCE, a cylindrical body form and rounded rim displaced it shortly thereafter. More recent studies have begun to attach greater significance to the stance and width of the different neck styles than to the individual body forms.[541] Here the data seem to suggest that specimens with wider necks (compare No. 22) occur mainly in the ninth century BCE and precede slightly those with the narrower motifs (Nos. 21, 23) of the late ninth and eighth centuries BCE.[542] Yet regardless of the particular attribute that receives the greater focus, it remains difficult to arrive at anything more than a general categorization of the abundant nuances in style that manifest themselves across the spectrum of juglet forms.[543]

A summary of the most detailed description of Iron II juglets[544] appears in Table 40 on p. 332. This list demonstrates the variability of attributes exhibited by members of the juglet family. For example, No. 22 displays a body-form that appears somewhat cylindrical and that Kenyon herself described as "elongated."[545] The mouth, which the Samaria report characterizes as "pinched," certainly borders on the earlier trefoil style.[546] The neck tends toward the wider variety, the handle likely shows a

---

[540] E.g., see Juglet Types JT 1 and JT 2 at Tell Qasîle (*T. Qasîle* [2], 70).

[541] *Gezer III*, 155-57, Juglet Types 37 A-C and 38 A-B.

[542] See *Gezer III*, 160.

[543] A. Mazar comments on this difficulty (*T. Qasîle* [2], 70) and Gitin devotes an entire section to the possible reasons for this variety of specific attributes (*Gezer III*, 160).

[544] The basis of this summary appears in *Gezer III*, 160-61, and forms part of the larger discussion on pp. 155-65 in that same report.

[545] *SS III*, 125.

[546] Compare the notation in *SS III*, 125, with Gitin's comments in *Gezer III*, 156.

	CENTURY			
	10th	9th	8th	7th
ATTRIBUTE				
Body form	rounded	cylindrical	tall, slender	sack-shaped
Mouth form	trefoil	trefoil/pinched	pinched	rounded
Neck form:				
height	--	--	--	very short
inclination	--	inward	outward	outward
width	wide	wide/narrow	narrow	--
Handle form:				
section	round	round	thinner/oblong	--
Surf. Treatment:				
slip	dk.reddish	dk. reddish	bright lt. red	(rare)
burnishing	vert. w/slip	vert. w/slip	vert. w/slip	vert. w/o slip
Ware	--	buff	buff	harder/"salted"

Summary of Attributes for Iron I-II Juglets

Table 40

round section (though certainty remains difficult to achieve here given the laconic description in *SS III*),[547] and the outer walls contained traces of a red slip. Collectively, these traits argue for a ninth-to-early eighth-century BCE date for this specimen, notwithstanding the outward inclination of the neck walls. Perhaps as a result of lacking access to important stratigraphic details, Gitin leaves this form in the eighth century while citing a similar exemplar from Beersheba V that dates as far back as the tenth century BCE.[548]

Similar observations pertain to juglet No. 23, though here the rim, with its outwardly beveled edge, continues the inclination of the neck walls more than does the simple, rounded rim in No. 22. In addition, its slightly narrower neck and round mouth suggest that this specimen follows No. 22 in the overall evolution of juglet traditions.

---

[547] Similarly, one cannot draw firm conclusions from the ware of this vessel, since Kenyon described it as "greyish" but noted that it seemed discolored from exposure to considerable dampness (*SS III*, 125).

[548] *Gezer III*, 156 (compare *Beersheba—TA*, Fig. 5:11).

The juglet in entry No. 21, with its smooth juncture between upper shoulder and neck and a rounder body that attains its maximum diameter toward the bottom, seems clearly to antedate the elongated types in Nos. 22-23. Yet the base form has almost completed its evolution away from the pointed styles of the Iron Age I period. One may, as a result, place the origin of this specimen in the mainstream of ninth-century BCE ceramic traditions. Nos. 22-23, in turn, follow it during the late ninth or first half of the eighth century. Given their morphology, ware, and surface treatments, all three of these vessels might easily represent survivors from several decades before the waning years of Israelite control over Samaria in the 730s and 720s BCE.

Let us return now to the distinctive juglet in No. 24 (pictured on p. 329), which shows a black fabric beneath a surface treatment of black slip and a rather coarsely spaced, vertical burnishing. Since these vessels reflect an apparently poor (i.e., brief) firing process at low temperatures, it rather seems that their compact size, generally well-levigated clay (with occasional inclusions of limestone temper), and original satin-like surface combine to account for their ability to survive relatively intact in most stratigraphic contexts (see n. 502 above).[549] Though at least 13 similar forms emerged from nonstratified contexts at Samaria (mostly from the putative extramural shrine of Locus E 207),[550] Kenyon noted:

> This type is rare on the whole site, and this is the only example in a stratified position. On most E.I. II sites it is common down to at least the seventh century B.C., and is distinguished from the E.I. I types by the fact that the handle joins the neck at the rim, instead of below, as in the earlier ones.[551]

These statements lead me to comment further on at least three areas of interest related to the family of Black Juglets: their chronological distribution, diachronic changes in design, and geographical distribution.

On the whole, juglets made of a dark fabric covered with a dark slip (black, dark grey, or deep reddish) and showing signs of burnishing range at least from the tenth century to the close of the Iron Age II period.[552] Morphological analysis, however, reveals that these vessels fall broadly into two subgroups, which I shall call *Phase I* and *Phase II*. The earlier styles, located primarily in the tenth and ninth

---

[549]*TBM III*, 123, § 125.

[550]These areas included S Tombs 110 (1 similar juglet), Z Deep Pit (1), locus E 207 (9), Summit Strip Qd on the northern slopes of the site (1), and Summit Strip Dg just outside the summit's southern enclosure wall (1); see *SS III*, 169, Fig. 23:2. The concentration of this container-style juglet (10 of 14 total = 71.4%) in a tomb and a possible shrine setting supports my general understanding of its function relative to oils, ointments, various aromatics such as perfumes or spices, drugs, etc., as outlined above. In this regard, see the tomb corpus from nearby Munshara (*Munshara*, Fig. 7:1-11, as well as Zayadine's comments on p. 566).

[551]*SS III*, 125.

[552]One specimen from Tell el-Farʿah (N) suggests a possible *terminus post quem* for this general class already in the late twelfth or eleventh centuries BCE (*Chambon*, Pl. 50:36 = Niveau VIIa).

centuries BCE, have taller necks that flare outward toward the top, taller and more rounded bodies, round bases, and (as noted by Kenyon) handles that reach from the shoulder to the neck generally at or just above the midpoint.[553] (Possible Iron I prototypes differ in a number of aspects; for example, they consistently possess an alternate, small, flat base and show the dark-colored ware and slip only sporadically.)[554] This early phase of juglet appears in the north at Megiddo and other sites in the Jezreel Valley (e.g., Taʿanach; Yoqneʿam)[555] and at Tell Abu Hawām Stratum III.[556] In the south, sites such as Beth-Shemesh[557] and Lachish have yielded good exemplars of this phase.

Already during the course of the ninth century BCE,[558] however, the tradition begins to change toward a shorter, more squat body that often bulges out to a point of inward inflection on its lower half, a base that is pinched off to a nob- or nipple-like shape,[559] a noticeably shorter neck, and a rather overscale handle now drawn from rim (vs. neck) to shoulder.[560] Apparent transitional forms, with their necks and bases resembling Phase I but with the form and placement of their handles anticipating Phase II, are attested at several sites in the Jezreel Valley area.[561] Other intermediate types retain the Phase I handles but display the later, pointed or nob-like bases.[562]

---

[553] Adequate photographs of this style are available in *AS IV*, Pl. XLIV:31-32.

[554] *AS IV*, Pls. XXXVII:22-23, 27; LXI:36 (Stratum III; see *AS-V*, 139); *TN II*, Pl. 41:798-802; *Megiddo I*, Pl. 5:129 (blue-black ware) and 130 (burnt umber color; both specimens derive from Stratum V); *T. Farʿah-RB* [58], Fig. 10:2; *T. Farʿah-RB* [59], Fig. 6:3; *T. Farʿah-RB* [62], Figs. 16:5; 17:4 (all from Niveau 3).

[555] See *Taʿanach*, Fig. 40:4-6 (Period IIB Cultic Structure); *T. Qiri*, Fig. 40:19. At Yoqneʿam, "the only stratified examples of Black Juglets occurred in the tenth century" (*T. Qiri*, 204).

[556] *TAH*, 23, Pl. XIII:91 (from "F7, west of room at 11, by the top surviving course of the town wall").

[557] *AS IV*, Pls. XLIV:31-32; LXVI:30 (from Tomb 1).

[558] While Grant and Wright dated the outset of these changes to the ninth century BCE (*AS V*, 139), Wampler suggested that they were underway already during the late tenth century BCE on the basis of pottery groups from Tombs 5, 29, 32, and 54 from Tell en-Naṣbeh (*TN II*, 24-25, § 59, n. 67). As a general outline, then, it appears that the taller juglets with longer necks and lower handle attachments stem mainly from the Iron Age I period, while the shorter, less graceful forms with higher handle attachment characterize Iron Age II. For a ninth-century, Phase II form, see now *Hazor V*, Fig. III.33:12 (Area L, Stratum VII).

[559] E.g., *T. ʿAmal*, Fig. 13:16 (Niveau III = second half of the tenth century BCE).

[560] Holladay noted that the handle "is nearly at the rim" already by the 840 BCE ceramic horizon (*Holladay*, 218).

[561] *Megiddo I*, Pl. 2:50-51 (beginning in Stratum IV); *T. Qiri*, Fig. 40:18. See also *T. Farʿah-RB* [62], Fig. 19:10 (Niveau intermédiaire = ninth century BCE).

[562] *Megiddo I*, Pl. 5:124, 128 (Stratum V); *TN II*, Pl. 42:843-45. A nice pictorial presentation of this evolution of styles appears in *Amiran*, 263, Photos 262-64. Compare also *T. Farʿah-RB* [62], Fig. 17:3 (already in Niveau 3, with the not infrequent Iron I variation in ware, "terre blanchâtre").

While the basic, Iron Age II-style Black Juglet occurs in the north,[563] it proves much more common in the south,[564] as demonstrated in levels such as Beth-Shemesh IIb-c,[565] Lachish III-II,[566] Tell Beit Mirsim A2,[567] Beersheba II,[568] and Arad X-VIII.[569] A large corpus of Black Juglets published from Tell en-Naṣbeh displays the full range of forms,[570] as does a similar northern group from Tell el-Farʿah (N).[571] At Lachish, Juglet Type 309 (= No. 24) completely replaces its typological forerunners in the rooms of tell Levels III and II and in Tomb 106 (ca. 675 BCE) where, as noted above, excavators recovered hundreds of specimens of Black Juglets.[572] The principal period of use at this site for the late form of Black Juglet, then, falls after the demise of Israelite Samaria. Though Aharoni and others have questioned the reliability of some of the Level II findspots at Lachish,[573] evidence from elsewhere seems to support a seventh-century date for a significant number of the Black Juglets. At Tell en-Naṣbeh, for example, Wampler noted that these vessels "are fairly common . . . and almost without exception none are earlier than 700 B.C."[574] Albright recovered them in similar quantities from Stratum A2 at Tell Beit Mirsim.

As a group, the late eighth and early seventh-century Black Juglets of Phase II reveal a clear decline in workmanship. Their large handles, which are often "clumsily applied," seem out of proportion to the remainder of the body,[575] and their pinched-off, hand-smoothed (often carelessly so) bottoms generally appear off-center in relation to the remainder of the vessel. Kelso and Thorley reported finding no wheel-turned bottoms among this group, and they offered pointed remarks on the obvious haste with

---

[563] See *Megiddo I*, Pl. 2:49-56 (excluding No. 52, which reflects a Phase I type); *Hazor II*, Pl. LXXXVI:2-6 (in light-colored ware and with neither slip nor burnishing), and surely 16-19 (Area B, Stratum VA; Yadin observed that "these juglets are rare at Hazor"; p. 55).

[564] See *Amiran*, 263.

[565] *AS IV*, Pl. LXVI:36 (with a slightly altered rim-form).

[566] *Lachish III*, Pl. 88:309-13; 319-21; 323.

[567] *TBM I*, Pls. 18:4; 68:24.

[568] *Beersheba I*, Pl. 69:17 (Stratum II = the rebuilt administrative city of the late eighth century BCE). Though Kenyon believed this stratum preceded Lachish Level III, tighter ceramic controls now indicate that both suffered destruction during the Assyrian campaign of 701 BCE (see Z. Herzog, "Tel Beersheba," *NEAEHL*, 171).

[569] M. & Y. Aharoni, Fig. 3:14.

[570] *TN II*, Pls. 41:798-807, 810; 42:811-19, 842-53; 43:854-71. See also the comments on p. 24, § 59.

[571] *Chambon*, Pl. 50:7-8, 10-15, 17-27, 29-32, 34-35, 37 (Niveau VIIb = tenth century BCE); 50:28 (Niveau VIIc = early ninth century); 50:9, 16, 33 (Niveau VIId = late ninth to eighth centuries BCE).

[572] *Lachish III*, Text, 50, 303.

[573] M. & Y. Aharoni, 84.

[574] *TN II*, 25, § 61; Pl. 42:817-819.

[575] *Lachish III*, Text, 303.

which these items were made.[576] In fact, the other end of the juglet—the rim—received the greatest care in manufacture. Its gracefully flared mouth aided in the filling of the vessel, and its neat rim facilitated pouring only a drop or two at a time. In like manner, the handle-rim attachment appears smoothly and neatly made on top but often hurriedly and imperfectly secured below; like the base forms, the handles on late specimens more often than not prove out of alignment with the neck.[577]

In short, the style of Black Juglet seen in No. 24 represents a somewhat degenerate form and method. Its class was apparently mass-produced in a hurried, careless manner, sometimes from rather gritty clay. The potter snatched each juglet from a continuously spinning wheel, pinched its bottom sidewalls into a protruding nob, and quickly fired the product at low temperatures. Yet despite such signs of mass production, these juglets appear in relatively meager numbers, particularly in the north. The burnishing of their outer surfaces almost always looks irregular, and it sometimes appears only as perpendicular marks across the body. Complete and thorough burnishing rarely occurs. Even when the body shows this treatment, the neck and handles generally remain partially done; in many instances, their surfaces appear in a relatively poor state of preservation.[578]

In the late group of Black Juglets, therefore, one witnesses somewhat of a disjuncture between presumed *function* and *appearance*, though not necessarily between that function and the vessel's overall form. If, as frequently reported, this juglet served as a container for a precious or semiprecious commodity, one might have expected greater care in its manufacture and surface treatment. Moreover, the economic networks in which this class became involved reached only across regional lines within Palestine (and even there the form flourished mainly in the south). Current evidence does not indicate a diffusion through trade to either Phoenicia or Cyprus. At face value, none of this discussion seems in keeping with the traditional understanding (based on form alone) that this juglet held a valuable, luxury commodity. Such lack of congruity between manufacture and purported function suggests the need for a fuller study of the class at large (see n. 585 below).

To conclude, I may return to Kenyon's statement cited above. In it, she entertained the possibility that No. 24 (a member of my Phase II group) stems from the Assyrian occupation of Samaria during the last quarter of the eighth and the early seventh centuries BCE. Holladay's independent conclusion that this distinctive juglet

---

[576] *TBM III*, 97-98, § 82.

[577] See *TBM III*, 123, § 125 for a full discussion of the characteristics and manufacturing techniques mentioned here.

[578] Holladay has astutely noticed an apparent but previously undocumented change in ware starting in the early eighth century BCE. He calls this grainier fabric "black salty ware" and adds that the majority of the later juglets display this attribute (*Holladay*, 218). These observations may relate to Albright's earlier comments that the firing of these vessels had occurred at such low temperatures "that the clay in places had not baked, and the chemicals of the soil in which the juglets were found had reacted upon these unbaked spots until the clay had decomposed, leaving pit marks" (*TBM III*, 123, § 125).

very likely belongs to a post-PP 6 period further supports this interpretation.[579] While this evaluation appears correct, it remains unclear that the class as a whole persisted to the very close of the Iron Age II period in areas much beyond the heartland of Judah. This style juglet did not maintain a presence in the later assemblages of En-gedi, Ramat Raḥel, Tell Masos, Meṣad Ḥashavyahu, or Arad Strata VII-VI.[580] It did remain, as noted, in Tell Beit Mirsim Stratum A2[581] and in late Tomb groups associated with Stratum IIc at Beth-Shemesh.[582] While Albright dated the former context to the Babylonian destruction of the city and consequently asserted that this evidence "proves conclusively that [the Black Juglet] was still in use as late as the end of the seventh century,"[583] more recent studies have argued to reassign this level to the Assyrian activities of 701 BCE on both ceramic and epigraphic grounds.[584] Likewise, one sees that although both the architectural and ceramic sequences for Stratum IIc at Beth-Shemesh were originally quite muddled, an appreciable number of royal *LMLK* seal impressions appeared among the remains of this level. In addition, this fact strongly encourages a date for Level IIc at the turn of the eighth century BCE. Yet the Beth-Shemesh assemblage taken from Tomb 14, located on the northeast slope of the tell, seems to designate this context as the latest in the series of burials at this site, and the group may well belong as late as the Babylonian period in the early sixth century BCE.[585] Thus one may confidently place No. 24 at least in the early, post-Israelite phases of Assyrian Samaria in a period contemporaneous with Megiddo Stratum III (which yielded a concentration of this juglet class there), if not slightly later still.

Concerning the series of juglets taken from Pit *i*, then, I may conclude by stating that, if No. 21 represents the earliest of the four specimens seen in *SS III*, Fig. 10, then No. 24 stands out as the latest item in that group.

e. Decanters

Finally, the Joint Expedition published four additional vessels or fragments of vessels that represent decanters (*SS III*, Fig. 10:17-19) or decanter-like (10:20) forms.

---

[579]*Holladay*, 68. Still, in the plates accompanying his discussion, Holladay continued to include this piece (and the class in general) in the 733-722 BCE ceramic horizon (Fig. 97:J).

[580]M. & Y. *Aharoni*, 84.

[581]*TBM I*, Pl. 68:1-32; *TBM III*, Pl. 18:1-9.

[582]*AS IV*, Pls. XLVIII:11; LXVI:36 (both from Stratum IIc); LXVIII:4 (Tomb 14).

[583]*TBM I*, 83-84, § 113.

[584]Compare Y. Aharoni, *BASOR* 154 (1959), 35-39; D. Ussishkin, *BASOR* 223 (1976), 6-11; and O. Zimhoni in *T. ʿEton*, 82-84.

[585]*AS V*, 139; *Lachish III, Text*, 303; S. Bunimovitz and Z. Lederman, "Beth-Shemesh," *NEAEHL*, 251. Compare my comments in n. 550 regarding the concentration of Black Juglets in other tomb (and cultic?) groups from Samaria and Munshara. If further study shows that these forms functioned more in a context of funerary rites than in commercial trade, the very fact that they would not daily remain visible may account for their rather mediocre manufacturing and surface techniques.

According to the field registry, all four members of this group once again derive from the same local deposit in a segment (*122.125.19.121*) associated with Pit *i*.

SS III Published Figure	Registry No. (none marked for discard)	Provenance			
		Strip	Coordinates	Feature	Local Layer
10:17	Q 2480	Qk	122.125.19.121	Pit *i*	Va
10:18	Q 2485	Qk	122.125.19.121	Pit *i*	Va
10:19	Q 2484	Qk	122.125.19.121	Pit *i*	Va
10:20	Q 2486	Qk	122.125.19.121	Pit *i*	Va

Provenance Data:
PP6 Decanters from Pit i

Table 41

Because of my previous, extended discussion of the morphology and history of Iron Age II decanters,[586] I may refer the reader to that section without repeating the many details here. The rim, neck, and ware (hard, thin red fabric) of *SS III*, Fig. 10:17 most closely match the collective attributes of the decanter recovered from the leveling near Wall 573 (Fig. 9:5; see nn. 314-18 above), with the only difference centering on the slightly higher placement of the neck ridge on 9:5 (where it meets the very top of the handle attachment as opposed to the handle's midsection, as in 10:17). On the basis that the outer, lower edge of the rim appears slightly more "beaked" in 9:5 than in 10:17, James suggested that the former piece actually postdated the latter by a few years in the general evolution of decanter forms. In addition, she observed that this general style proves much more common at southern sites during the seventh century BCE, and she speculated that it may have appeared then under the influence of the Cypriot juglet with mushroom rim and lip.[587]

The neck ridges on the decanters published from Samaria range from high (i.e., slightly above the neck's midpoint, as in No. 17) to very high (see No. 19). All the clear decanter forms published from Pit *i* exhibit hard, thin, red (Nos. 17-18) or grey (No. 19) ware. Kenyon noted that none of the Samaria decanters displayed signs of burnishing and that the lack of this feature agreed with the comparative evidence at Tell el-Farʿah (N) and Megiddo.[588]

---

[586]See my treatment of *SS III*, Fig. 9:5, on pp. 287-91 above.

[587]*Beth-Shan*, James, Fig. 127-28; compare Fig. 71:12 (Level IV).

[588]*SS III*, 124 (the only decanter showing traces of burnishing came from Stratum II at Megiddo; *Megiddo I*, Pl. 4:101). She added that the southern exemplars "seem almost invariably to be burnished, and they are apparently not in the hard ware of the Samaria and Farʿah vessels."

SS III, Fig. 10:17-19

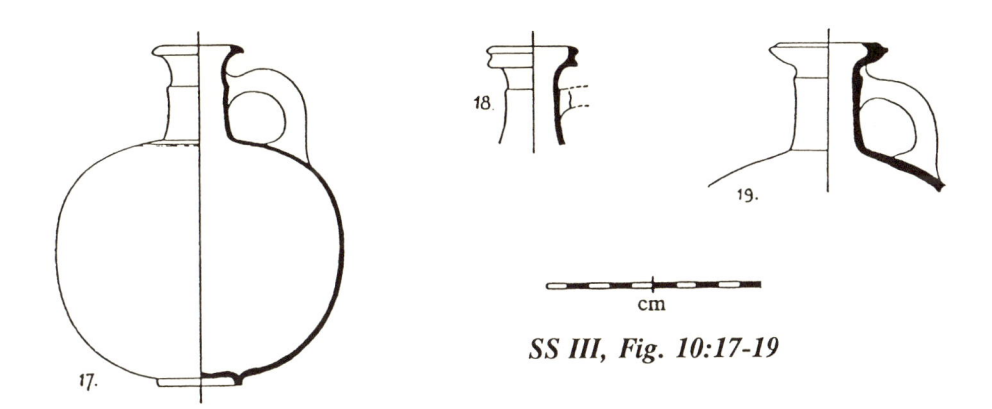

With its double-ridged, vertically oriented rim and lip, fragment No. 18 seems most representative of the classical northern traditions during the eighth and even early seventh centuries BCE. An excellent rim parallel derives from Stratum IV at Hazor.[589] This style actually dominated the Samaria group, as attested by the nonstratified examples published in *SS III*, Fig. 22:1-4. In this sense, then, both *SS III*, Fig. 9:5 and Fig. 10:17, with their splayed and thickened rims with slightly rounded, convex lips, exhibit motifs that are least at home among the regional pottery industries of the north. Kenyon thought that these two specimens marked "the first appearance of this type" at Samaria.[590] In a similar vein, 22:1-2 both reveal a movement toward a more sack-shaped body (with the widest diameter falling to the lower half of the body), a trait which Gitin restricted to decanter traditions in the south and in Transjordan during the seventh and sixth centuries BCE.[591] A parallel from Megiddo Stratum I provides an excellent comparison to 22:1 from Samaria[592] (and also to 22:2, though this example assumes a slightly more vertical orientation). Figure 10:17 represents the only published body-form that survived in a stratified context, and its very globular shape and complete lack of a shoulder keel clearly distinguish it from the types shown in Fig. 22.

Entry No. 20, which Kenyon may have identified correctly as a small jug and not a true decanter form, consists in a buff-colored ware with red slip; moreover, no clearly articulated neck ridge remains visible on the extant fragment. Though satisfac-

---

[589] *Hazor II*, Pl. C:17. This level dates from roughly 722 to 650 BCE. Compare also *Beth-Shan*, James, Fig. 71:7 (Level IV).

[590] *SS III*, 124.

[591] By the close of the Iron Age II period, some decanters slimmed down even further, became quite cylindrical in body-form, and lost their ring-bases altogether. Compare *SS III*, Fig. 12:22 (E 207); *Megiddo I*, Pl. 2:70 (Stratum II); *Beth-Shan*, James, 127 and Fig. 71:10 (unstratified; 71:11 reflects the movement toward this style, as does *Megiddo I*, Pl. 2:71-72).

[592] *Megiddo I*, Pl. 4:100; the report flags this variety as a "common type" that "occurred in practically every locus" (*Megiddo I*, 173, 176).

tory parallels remain difficult to find,[593] I accept this rim style at least as a possible harbinger of the decanter family;[594] its funnel-shaped neck with slight, external thickening, everted and outcut-rim mode, and its thicker, grittier, buff fabric help place this fragment among other late ninth- and early eighth-century materials. If future morphological comparisons corroborate this dating, entry No. 20 will reflect the period of incipient use of the decanter class generally.

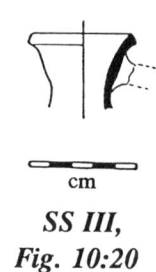

SS III, Fig. 10:20

As noted earlier, this decanter group represented one of the two principal components in Forsberg's suggested correlation between Samaria PP 6 and Megiddo Stratum III.[595] His appeal to *Megiddo I*, Pl. 4 (miscited as Pl. 3):99, 100, 106, and 109 as the best evidence by which to date the Samaria assemblage (particularly Fig. 10:17)[596] elicits several observations. First, such a general comparison fails to consider the subtle but typologically significant differences that exist within the Megiddo corpus and between it and the meager decanter group from Samaria. Second, only through a more detailed analysis of collective attributes can one begin to sort out the local decanter forms from those that may have arrived at northern sites from either the south or Transjordan. As I have shown, the specific form in Fig. 10:17 likely may have originated outside the northern kingdom. Third, Forsberg's correlation is not a new one. As with the red-slipped jugs from Megiddo, Kenyon herself already recognized that "the best comparable material comes from Megiddo (*M I*, pl. 4, 99-110), where the forms are very similar to those at Samaria" and that the deposition of the Megiddo decanters "is almost exclusively in Stratum III."[597] Further, she believed that the Samaria decanters in question emerged from ceramic traditions current during the late eighth century BCE. On the whole, she accepted that the principal decanter forms common in the north (at Megiddo, Samaria, and Tell el-Farʿah, North[598]) arose between 750 and 690 BCE, while the primary southern groups (from Tell Beit Mirsim,[599] Beth-

---

[593]Gitin relates this piece to *Gezer III*, Pl. 12:20 (from the mid-ninth-century BCE Stratum VIB) and to *Hazor II*, Pl. LVIII:17 (Stratum VIII), but neither reference provides an exact comparison inasmuch as they both display some degree of neck ridge (see *Gezer III*, 152). Still, the ware and surface treatment offer a close match for the Samaria rim. Compare also *Hazor II*, Pl. LXIV:23 (Stratum VII), with slight neck ridge and lower handle attachment to the neckwall.

[594]Holladay classifies this piece among the "globular decanters with 'wavy' neck and everted simple rim" of the late eighth century BCE (see *Holladay*, Fig. 102:A-D). Once again, however, none of the three suggested parallels from *Hazor II*, Pl. LXXXVII:11, 17, and 20 (Stratum VA) provide adequate comparisons.

[595]For the other strand of his argument, see my discussion of the red-slipped, oenochoe pitcher-jugs on pp. 325-29 above, with primary reference given to Forsberg on pp. 328-29.

[596]*Forsberg*, 21.

[597]*SS III*, 124, 203-04.

[598]*T. Farʿah-RB* [58], 11:23 (Niveau 2).

[599]*TBM I*, Pl. 59.

Shemesh,[600] and Lachish[601]) extended as late as 586 BCE.[602] Unfortunately, the Samaria report did not include any examples of decanters from the post-PP 6 group, though they apparently did appear in levels associated with that period.[603]

These views appear to contain nothing that would seriously militate against Forsberg's basic argument for a post-Israelite, early Assyrian origin for the Samaria decanters. Despite the exclusively late eighth- and seventh-century comparisons recognized by Kenyon herself, however, she asserted maintained her overall view of the depositional history and chronology at Samaria in her assertion that Fig. 22:2 from the Z Deep Pit (ascribed to PP 3) represents "a possibly earlier appearance" of this vessel class at Samaria.[604] Yet, immediately, she also had to compromise the credibility of that suggestion by noting the contaminated nature of the pit.[605] In other words, the findspot (Z Deep Pit) cannot in this case dictate the chronological range of all the pottery found within it; rather, the mixed ceramic corpus must define the nature and the functional dates of the context. Ultimately, it is the preponderance of available ceramic comparisons and not the irreproachable stratigraphic integrity of either Megiddo III or Samaria PP 6 that provides the best support for Forsberg's position.

3) Evaluation and Summary

Table 42 on the next page presents the overall distribution of the various ceramic items assigned to Pit *i* and published as part of the PP 6 group. Although the official report gave the impression that all these items came from a single locus inside the pit itself, namely, Local Layer Va (with only 10:8 ascribed to Layer V), the unpublished field notes and registry reveal that they derive from at least two apparently disparate tracts of excavation. One of these areas, labeled Segment *122.125.19.121*, may have included some portion of the pit, but the locus also extended south toward Wall 125 in Room *hk* and the higher rock of the summit plateau. The other site, Segment *122.126.19.121*, perhaps bore a similar relationship to the pit, though it stretched farther northward apparently through the area of Room *g* and toward Wall 126, where the rock continued to decline and where greater amounts of fill were required to level the area for building in later periods (see the published Section EF from *SS I*, Pl. VII, presented in fig. 6 above). I have already noted in detail the differences between these

---

[600] *AS IV*, Pl. XLV.

[601] *Lachish III*, Pl. 87.

[602] *SS III*, 124.

[603] On this observation, see also *Beth-Shan*, James, 127.

[604] *SS III*, 124. But see already nn. 204 and 523 above.

[605] For example, she acknowledges the presence of much later (very late seventh century BCE) items such as "a deep, narrow, cooking pot" presented in *SS III*, Fig. 30:8. I have already discussed, from a stratigraphic point of view, the dubious nature of the Z Deep Pit (see the preceding note for references).

	bowls	cooking pots	jars	jugs & juglets	decanters	TOTAL
Pit *i*						
122.125.19.121						
V	1	-	-	-	-	1
Va	7	-	-	5	4	16
122.126.19.121						
Va	6	2	1	1	-	10
TOTAL	14	2	1	6	4	27

Distribution of PP 6 Ceramic Forms
in Local Stratigraphy of Pit i

Table 42

two ceramic subgroups with respect to attributes such as ware and surface treatment. According to the data in Table 42, the excavators retrieved most of the published pottery from among the remains lying toward the summit (17 of 27 total pieces, or 63%). Generally speaking, this material appeared in a much better state of preservation than did the items recovered from the area north of the pit.[606] I may note further that most of the materials found in the debris stretching northward from the pit (8 of 10 entries attributed to Segment *122.126.19.121*) belonged to the later phases of ceramic traditions attested to by the overall group. Conversely, more of the goods encountered in the area between the pit and the summit displayed earlier motifs (10 of 17 entries in *122.125.19.121*). These observations endorse my conclusion that not all the vessels presented in *SS III*, Fig. 10 came from Pit *i*; rather, at least some of them seem to have derived from the surrounding leveling debris, which Kenyon assigned to her "Period VII."[607] And since the latest materials in these unconsolidated fill deposits span at least the first half of the seventh century BCE, the leveling activity itself must have occurred sometime after that point, not in the years 722/721 BCE.

---

[606] Compare again Table 36 above. The following picture emerges: Segment *122.125.19.121* = the whole or near-whole vessels in *SS III*, Fig. 10:1-8, 15-23 (with entries 18-20 appearing as large fragments of decanters); Segment *122.126.19.121* = the small-size fragments in *SS III*, Fig. 10:9-14, 24-27 (with only the juglet in No. 24 and the jar in No. 25 representing relatively intact forms).

[607] Concerning this fill, Kenyon wrote that "The Period VII debris which overlay the floors of the rest of the house did not actually overlie the pit, since the walls of the latter were standing to the top of the general level of this debris, and the filling inside it was level with the tops of the wall" (*SS III*, 120). Though the PP 6 repertoire reportedly represents the final stages of Israelite control over the site, such ambiguity between the PP 6 and PP 7 assemblages requires that I continue my study through PP 7 (as I do in the following chapter).

In summarizing this material, I may return to Kenyon's description of the general context that yielded this pottery (see her statements on pp. 296-97 above). Here, she understood the central installation in question as a rubbish pit located inside a house that stood during both BP IV and BP V. While she claimed that the pottery taken from the pit proved "identical" to the goods recovered from the fill associated with the northern terrace wall 573 (see *SS III*, Fig. 9), clear differences also exist between these two groups, including in the latter context the preponderance of thick, heavy bowls or braziers and cooking pots, which account for 61% of that published group. Moreover, I have shown in Part A of this chapter that the excavators remained unable to offer a clear, incontestable date for the 573 deposit. Certainly, therefore, one cannot date the final use of the house discussed in Part B on the grounds that the pottery left in Pit *i* resembles to some extent the fill material located near (but not always abutting) a stratigraphically disconnected perimeter wall (573) situated over 45 m downslope from the pit.

Kenyon argued further that the supposedly homogeneous pottery from Pit *i*, as well as the filling near Wall 573 that she effectively treated as *occupational debris*, differed in significance from the items found beneath the BP V floors, which she thought of as *construction debris*.[608] While the latter rubric is an apt one for its context, and while the materials associated with this locus might have provided a *terminus post quem* for the laying of the BP V floors (assuming those surfaces adequately sealed the deposits of makeup resting beneath them), one may question strongly the stratigraphic reliability of the two former ceramic groups associated with Pit *i* and Wall 573. Actually, there seems to exist very little difference between the Pit *i* pottery and the small repertoire recovered from beneath the BP V house floors. Though, according to Kenyon's final report, hardly any items appeared in these subfloor deposits (an unhappy circumstance for her preferred method of dating surfaces), she described the few sherds that did emerge there as showing a hard-fired ware and including at least some identifiable decanter fragments. Since this description matches closely the morphological and/or ware attributes of over 40% of the Pit *i* group,[609] the suggested distinctions between this collection and the subfloor pottery become quite murky at best. Moreover, any putative differences remain incalculable now owing to the absence of an adequate presentation of elements taken from the subfloor makeup.

As a consequence of these observations, I can hardly agree with Holladay that Pit *i* represents one of three contexts that can receive an *absolute date*.[610] After accepting Kenyon's ultimate designation of this pit as a latrine, Holladay speculates:

> its [i.e., the latrine's] apparent dimensions (*ca.* 1 x 2 m x ? m deep) indicate that
> it might not be totally adequate for such a long period without cleaning out. In

---

[608] *SS I*, 108.

[609] E.g., note the hard fabric of bowl Nos. 8-14 and the decanter forms in Nos. 17-20.

[610] Holladay, 67-68.

fact, we may assume with some degree of assurance that, in times of peace, it was regularly emptied by users of night soil, and therefore its major deposits most likely accumulated during the long period of siege [sic], when the fields no longer could be reached. Thus, the major portion of the whole or restorable vessels probably dates exactly to the years 725-2 B.C.[611]

My study has called into question this entire line of reasoning. While Holladay correctly believed that a significant portion of the Pit *i* pottery group originated at a relatively late date, even this chronological observation bears little or no direct relationship to the state of preservation seen among the various pieces involved. As the summary of my own analysis in Table 43 shows, the majority (55.56%) of materials published from this locus seems to reflect a series of rather late developments in Iron Age II ceramic traditions, i.e., trends that arose or flourished after the Assyrian takeover of Samaria (= my *Late Group*). Yet most of these elements survive only in fragmentary form, owing largely to the thin, hard-baked ware of the majority of the classes involved (local imitations of Assyrian Palace Ware and thin-walled decanters). In fact, the largest collection of whole or near-whole vessels (33.33%) appears to predate the so-called *Pax Assyriaca*, with many of the traditions easily extending as far back as the ninth century BCE (see my *Early Group*). This clear dichotomy within the pit assemblage also offers an opposing view to Holladay's position that "no serious questions can be raised about the essential homogeneity of the group."[612] If Kenyon is correct in her belief that the house in question served the Israelite community in both BP IV and BP V/PP6,[613] many of the materials comprising my Early Group might easily derive from the first of those two occupational phases (while my Late Group might postdate *Israelite* Samaria altogether).

In order to remain in fundamental support of Kenyon's historical and chronological frameworks, Holladay presumed that the clearly late forms attributed to this pit represented post-PP 6 intrusive elements. I accept, with Holladay and Kenyon, the likelihood that such contamination would occur if the truncated top of the structure had in fact remained open for some time. Yet I must add the caveat that the excavators apparently found no stratigraphic separation of the various pottery traditions assigned to the pit; all but one item (the bowl in No. 8) came from the same local layer, Va. Working only from the published report, however, Holladay did not have this important datum at his disposal. Nor did he know of the actual retrieval of these goods from two disparate loci (recall the *122.125.19.122* vs. *122.126.19.121* dilemma) or of the somewhat ambiguous relationships between these two areas and between them and the

---

[611] Holladay, 68.

[612] Holladay, 68.

[613] As I have shown, no clear *Building Period VI* exists in this summit area. Kenyon's own theory recognized that the ceramic materials she assigned to "Period VI" simply marked the final period of use for the BP V house. Consequently, the final report does not offer a new Top Plan for that period.

PP 6: PIT i — SUMMARY

Early Group *(44.44% of overall group):*

   whole or near-whole forms
      Segment 122.125.19.121
         Bowls: Nos. 1-6
         Juglets: Nos. 21-23   **total:** 9 entries (33.33%)

   fragments
      Segment 122.125.19.121
         Jug/Decanter(?): No. 20   **total:** 1 entry (3.70%)
      Segment 122.126.19.121
         Bowls: No. 14
         Cooking Pots: No. 26   **total:** 2 entries (7.41%)

Late Group *(55.56% of overall group):*

   whole or near-whole forms
      Segment 122.125.19.121
         Bowls: Nos. 7-8
         Jugs: Nos. 15-16
         Decanters: Nos. 17   **total:** 5 entries (18.52%)
      Segment 122.126.19.121
         Juglets: No. 24
         Jars: No. 25   **total:** 2 entries (7.41%)

   fragments
      Segment 122.125.19.121
         Decanters: Nos. 18-19   **total:** 2 entries (7.41%)
      Segment 122.126.19.121
         Bowls: Nos. 9-12, 13(?)
         Cooking Pots: No. 27   **total:** 6 entries (22.22%)

The Pottery Group Ascribed to Pit i:
Summary of Analysis

Table 43

pit itself. By working mainly from the unpublished field registry and excavation records, my study has exposed these issues and, when possible, brought new data to bear on their resolution.

Based on the new information, one may now ask what evidence substantiates in the first place the function of this installation as an indoor latrine for those who occupied the house. Kenyon recorded only:

> It may have been either a rubbish pit or a latrine. No entrance was visible and since the walls were standing considerably above the level of the adjoining

rooms, it must presumably have had an aperture [sic] on an upper floor, and its identification as a latrine is very probable.[614]

The entire methodology that Kenyon and others have applied to this locus seems tendentious in nature. One must at least view the decision to base an historical reckoning of the final stages of Israelite occupation of Samaria and the Assyrian destruction of the capital city on this particular repertoire of goods as enigmatic in the extreme. Surely the excavators encountered better-stratified contexts on which to base their historical judgments relating to these important events. Due to the truncation of the mouth and upper levels of the pit, one cannot even surmise its original height. Under the circumstances, the pottery assigned to the pit can assist in providing only *one* possible period of use for the installation itself, not for the house as a whole.[615] To expand the ceramic chronology to the broader area of the house, the exact stratigraphic relationship between the pit and the house floors must receive clear definition and recording. The final report nowhere fulfills this requirement, either in the narrative or by means of section drawings, and the resultant gap now proves impossible to fill due to a lack of necessary data.

Since, according to Kenyon, no access to the pit existed in any of the surviving depositional layers relating to the ground floor levels of the house itself, it stretches the imagination to accept this installation as an upstairs latrine constructed as such a narrow shaft with containment walls that somehow ran through the entire lower house area. Without a clearer delineation of the stratigraphic links between this depository and the house, one wonders whether the two actually relate temporally at all despite their obvious close spatial proximity. At present, I can only say that this rather circumscribed feature contained the remains of a number of very stylish pottery forms, including many pieces that apparently stemmed from metal prototypes that might easily postdate the fall of the city into Assyrian hands (e.g., a number of thin-ware, Assyrian-style bowls and the oenochoe pitchers or jugs; here I may also note the presence of the latest phase of the Samaria Ware tradition, regardless of whether it harks back to metal predecessors). Beyond this fact, however, it remains impossible to establish a *terminus ante quem* for the full range of items that the pit might have contained originally. Yet, judging from the vessels that did survive, it seems clear that the functional life of the pit ran well into the seventh century BCE.

---

[614] *SS III*, 120.

[615] Holladay takes the opposite view in stating that the assemblage from Pit *i* constitutes one of "five groups of pottery datable *independent of ceramic comparisons* . . ." (*Holladay*, 69-70, emphasis added). Here he limits the dating this group to the period between 725 and 722 BCE. (He holds that the other four groups datable in this way consist in PP 1, PP 2, PP 3, and PP 5).

Pottery Period 6: Conclusions

In their reassessment of the archaeology of Tell Abu Hawām, Herrera and Balensi observed that the relationship between Megiddo IVA and Samaria V-VI stood in need of much study.[616] Though this portion of my study has proven long and sometimes tedious, it has helped us begin to address both this concern and the historical connections between Megiddo Stratum III and other, contemporary levels at multiple sites throughout the general region. In my extended Excursus at the outset of this chapter, I underscored a consistent pattern of historical development at a number of major, northern sites lying within the political and economic orbit of Samaria. Following the first substantial wave of Assyrian military engagements throughout the northern valley areas during the decade of the 730s BCE, a brief lull in any further, major activity seems to have set in until after the final collapse of Israelite control over the capital city at Samaria in the late 720s. As Table 44 shows, my examination of levels at the most important sites corroborates this position. To this list I might add the more northerly Hazor, which flourished in Stratum V during the mid-eighth century and which eventually became a substantial citadel under the Assyrians in Stratum III from the seventh century BCE; during the intermediate Stratum IV, from the final decades of the eighth century, excavations have revealed only a small, unfortified settlement. Further, my analysis of the pottery in the published PP 6 assemblage has shown that this rather heterogeneous collection might also fall into two disparate groups, an early one dating from before or just after 732 BCE, and a later group that stems from the period of Assyrian control over the site in the late eighth and early seventh centuries BCE.

	Suggested *terminus ante quem* of 732 BCE	Suggested *terminus post quem* of 720 BCE
Megiddo	IVA	III
Taʿanach	IV	V
Yoqneʿam	10	9
Tell Keisan	(gap)	5
Tell Abu Hawām	III	II

*Comparative Stratigraphy of Major Northern Sites
in and around the Samaria-Jezreel Valley Area*

Table 44

---

[616] M.-D. Herrera and J. Balensi, "More about the Greek Geometric Pottery at Tell Abu Hawam," *Levant* 18 (1986), 171.

I have shown further that, where adequate field data remain available, a much smoother transition with uninterrupted activity links the latest of these levels to the subsequent phase of activity (e.g., Megiddo III-II; Tell Keisan 5-4a,b; etc.). All these phases of occupation occurred after the fall of Samaria to the Assyrians and represent a persistent, planned organization of the most strategically significant sites by the Assyrian leadership. While the Assyrians may have gained control over the more exposed sites, such as Megiddo, sometime prior to the fall of the capital farther up in the hill country, they did very little to develop their new holdings until they controlled everything, including the royal city itself.[617] Even then, the execution of their plan evolved slowly, owing to the fact that numerous rebellions and preemptive campaigns to the far north of Israel demanded Assyria's attention and resources during the remaining reign of Sargon II (i.e., from the fall of Samaria to about 705 BCE; see Chapter VI below). Consequently, the archaeological record also attests to an acceleration in the development of the new provincial centers in Israel during the very late eighth- and the seventh-century phases at those sites, i.e., following the period of Sargon's rule (compare, for example, the planning of Megiddo III and II).

From the historian's point of view, it is important to realize that Megiddo Strata III and II have yielded the fullest body of evidence for an actual Assyrian presence and program of development. Besides the pottery itself, these data include a completely new city plan, Assyrian-style buildings, and the like. Such massive renovation came to other sites, such as Tell Keisan, only in due time (Niveau 4) during course of seventh century. Certainly, even the former capital at Samaria does not reflect this degree of Assyrian concern with its infrastructure. The Assyrians, it seems, coordinated most of their efforts from Megiddo, and reasonably so, since no site in the entire country claims a more strategic geopolitical position.

Samaria was, in fact, better situated on the seaward slopes of the Ephraimite hill country, where it faced the Mediterranean and international routes of the open trade markets, than was the former capital city at Tirzah, which lay on the leeward slopes of the hill country. Even so, I have already demonstrated that the new capital at Samaria was not conceived to be a large, international hub or depot of political and economic activity (see the Conclusion to Chapter I above). Rather, Omri's original plan aimed at providing a magnificent, *private* home for royalty and the city always retained that character. The relative sizes of ninth-century BCE Samaria and Jezreel prove this much.[618] Never in its full life did Israelite Samaria incorporate domestic housing areas for the general populace; from the beginning, it was designed for kings and, to the end, it served only them. This royal ideology spread as well to other major cities in the

---

[617] That this seems so clear in the archaeological record has prompted some scholars to suggest that Megiddo did not actually fall until Samaria itself fell (see already n. 89 above).

[618] See p. 248 for the observation that the perimeter of Jezreel enclosed approximately 17.5 acres; compare Chapter I, 170, n. 633 for a range in the size of the compound at Samaria from only 3.95 acres (with Herr) to 4.9 acres (Tappy).

POTTERY PERIOD 6: CONCLUSIONS

Northern Kingdom. Here one may note that even Solomonic (Strata VA-IVB) and Assyrian (Strata III-II) Megiddo yielded considerable tracts of space that served as domestic areas. But between these levels lies Megiddo IVA, which boasts only fortresses and other types of public infrastructure that served as the arm of the king himself; there appears little or no room for domestic quarters.[619] Though we await fuller publications of the planning and architecture at Jezreel, the same pattern seems to apply there.[620] Even compared to the likes of Solomon and the Assyrians, then, the Omride ideology allowed little place for nonroyal, private commoners. Both the ivories and the ostraca attest to the lavishness and centrism of royalty. The Omrides set forth a pattern of governance in the mid-ninth century, then, that kept the common people out of the principal royal cities and in the outlying countryside.

Though archaeologists have recovered examples of locally made Assyrian Palace Ware, a stele fragment (apparently from the time of Sargon II), and fragments from various cuneiform tablets (some apparently representing a letter to Avi-aḫi, the local governor), they have recovered precious little that might tell us about the general plan, architecture, or overall size of the Assyrian city at Samaria. Thus, while the Assyrians no doubt maintained an administrative office here (particularly after the organization of the province called *Samerina*), it appears that Megiddo quickly became the principal center and that they built it as expeditiously as possible. Levels from other key sites in and around the central the hill country corroborate this pattern.[621] As the survey of sites in my Excursus showed earlier, the Assyrians seem to have implemented the same pattern of development in the south, where they also selected only a few of the most strategic sites (such as Ekron and Gezer) for considerable investment of material resources. The Assyrian plan of occupation was selective; they rebuilt or expanded only one or two cities in each region, not every site (not even some major ones) that fell under their sway.

Finally, I return to the related subjects of comparative stratigraphy and chronology. Just as Kenyon attempted to make Samaria authoritative for establishing the early dates at all significant northern sites (i.e., she lowered Megiddo VA-IVB and Hazor X to the ninth century to link up with PP 1), she here must argue to raise the date of Megiddo III in order to link it up with the repertoire from PP 6. As noted, at many points Kenyon herself cited the close connection between the ceramic goods of Megiddo III and Samaria PP 6. In the final report, she acknowledged:

---

[619] See again the overview of these levels in my earlier *Excursus*; compare also *Megiddo*, Davies, 96-97, 101.

[620] See D. Ussishkin, "Tel Jezreel," in *OEANE* 3, 246.

[621] E.g., compare the Israelite Stratum VII at Shechem with the sparsely attested Assyrian Stratum VI; the fortified town at Tell el-Farʿah (N) in Stratum VIId with the more modest and steadily declining occupations in Strata VIIe-VIIe₁; or the administrative character of Beth-Shan Upper Stratum V during the ninth and eighth centuries BCE against the poorly built structures of the subsequent Stratum IV, which Geva dated to the years after the Assyrian conquest of the site (*contra* James; see the overview by A. Mazar—who tentatively accepts Geva's position—in "Beth-Shan," *NEAEHL*, 222); or the transition from Stratum III to Strata II-I at nearby Tel ʿAmal; and so on.

> The resemblances are thus so close that the *initial date* of Megiddo Stratum III must be close to that of Samaria VI, and is therefore *c.* 750 B.C. There are however, a considerable number of forms *later than* those found at Samaria prior to the destruction of 722 B.C. The terminal date suggested by the authors of *c.* 650 B.C. may be correct, for the material does not seem to be as late as T. Beit Mirsim Stratum A.[622]

I must add, however, that the given parallels relate mainly to the bowls, water decanters, jugs, (and chalices) that belong to my *Late* Group. In other words, the *terminus ante quem* for PP 6 relates directly to that of Megiddo III and Tell Keisan 5-4. Thus it appears that Kenyon's overall argument runs at crosscurrents with itself, since elsewhere she concluded that the PP6 materials represented those goods *in use at the destruction* of the site.[623] But in the excerpt just cited, she relates them to the *beginning* of her "Period VI." In doing so, she also abandons the basic principle of stratigraphic interpretation, which states that any given corpus of recoverable material culture largely comes from the *closing years* of a stratum's depositional history. Thus, while I must agree with the first part of her statement, namely, that there exists a clear correlation between the Megiddo III repertoire and at least part of the PP 6 assemblage from Samaria, I must also alter significantly the last part of it. A more accurate statement would read as follows: The resemblances between Megiddo III and Samaria PP 6 are so close that the *closing date* of PP 6 must lie close to that (i.e., the *closing date*) of Megiddo III, namely somewhere in the range of 700-650 BCE. While the stratigraphic detail in *Megiddo I* regarding the Stratum IVA-III transition may leave many questions and murky details, one cannot discard that evidence or rearrange its chronology solely in favor of the stratigraphic argument from Samaria "Period VI," for the latter contexts have emerged as highly dubious ones that center only on the problematic Pit *i* and some stratigraphically disconnected fill, which Kenyon presumed belonged to terrace Wall 573 but which she could not date accurately. The treatment (at least in the official report) of Pit *i* only exacerbated the confusion due to an inadequate separation of excavated segments and individual findspots and the subsequent conflation of a clearly mixed assemblage drawn from disparate loci.

In sum, the PP 6 assemblage from Samaria represents a mixed one from unreliable contexts; consequently, one cannot treat it as a single ceramic horizon, as did Holladay. If the two principal subgroups within this eclectic collection belong historically with the BP V house structure surrounding the pit, then the house appears to have served during both the late Israelite and the early Assyrian periods and to have suffered destruction only sometime well into the latter of these two occupations.

---

[622] *SS III*, 204 (emphasis added).
[623] *SS I*, 108; *SS III*, 120.

Chapter IV

POTTERY PERIOD 7

Remains of the Assyrian Siege and Destruction?

I. Introduction

To complete my study of the Israelite occupation of Samaria, I now must include a look at the architecture and objects assigned to Kenyon's "Period VII." The precise relationship between PP 6 and PP 7 remains unclear. In part, this ambiguity results from various, seemingly opposing statements made by Kenyon in her introduction of the PP 7 group. For example, she begins by asserting that the published PP 7 goods "make it quite clear that there is a sharp break between the pottery of Periods VI and VII."[1] Accordingly, evidence for this disjunction lies in the sudden predominance in PP 7 of hard-ware vessels showing a thin, burnished slip.[2] Yet her later statement that "a good deal of the Period VI wares is found in the same deposits as the new ones of VII, and would appear to have continued side by side with it"[3] seems to vitiate the supposed sharp break between these phases.[4] Moreover, Kenyon had already appealed to this very same argument (i.e., an influx of hard-ware vessels) to distinguish the goods of PP 6 from those of PP 4.[5] In addition, she invokes *SS III*, Fig. 11:22 (a bowl with rounded base, low carination, and high flaring upper sidewalls) as "the most strik-

---

[1] *SS III*, 97.

[2] To illustrate, Kenyon cites *SS III*, Fig. 11:1-7, with their thickened rims supplying another hallmark attribute.

[3] *SS III*, 98.

[4] As already demonstrated in Chapter II (PP 5) and the opening of Chapter III (PP 6), Kenyon also clearly saw the meager repertoire of pottery published to illustrate the character of BP V/PP 5 as indistinguishable from the ceramic traditions of PP 6. If, in turn, many of the attributes of the PP 6 assemblage continued to appear in the PP 7 group, then one begins to see a total breakdown in any ability to subphase the pottery that Kenyon assigned to the eighth and seventh centuries BCE at Samaria. As a result, one's ability to subphase the depositional layers that yielded this pottery also becomes hampered. At least from the perspective of the archaeology of Samaria, the net result is a very muddled view of both the ceramic industries of the north during this long time period and of the general history of the Israelite capital.

[5] *SS III*, 96, where she states that "the difference between the pottery of this period [VI] and that of IV is the appearance of a considerable quantity of hard ware, which is noticeably absent in Period IV."

ing new form"[6] in PP 7. But after relating this piece to the ceramic group known as Assyrian Palace Ware and then appealing to this general class of pottery to establish a "certain" date of 725-700 BCE for the events reflected in level VII, she concludes by asserting that, at the time of publication, 11:22 enjoyed no Assyrian parallels and suggests that this piece likely derived not from Assyria or from a locally made Assyrian imitation but from one of the foreign cultural groups transplanted in Samaria by the Assyrians.

The speculation surrounding *SS III*, Fig. 11:22 follows Kenyon's dating of the overall PP 7 group to the event of Assyria's destruction of Samaria in 722/21 BCE. In her model, PP 7 does not actually represent a new building phase, BP VII, as have most earlier pottery periods. Instead, this so-called period was defined only by "a thick layer of debris, with much burnt matter, including a considerable quantity of burnt ivory."[7] Since this debris reportedly lay over the floors of the BP V rooms, and since it supposedly separated the previous Israelite building levels from a subsequent occupational gap, Kenyon thought it "highly probable" that the PP 7 material stemmed from Assyria's sacking of the site in 722 BCE. She acknowledged a number of major deficiencies in her database, however. These deficiencies included the paltry nature of the published PP 5 corpus of pottery; the lack of a demonstrable stratigraphic connection between PP 5 and PP 6; and the fact that the putative destruction debris of PP 7 did not actually cover and seal the surviving portion of Pit *i*, which had provided the lynch pin for her chronological assessment of PP 6 and BP V.[8] These facts, together with the complex of problems bearing specifically on Pit *i* (see my previous chapter), the mixed ceramic assemblage contained therein, and the apparent inaccuracy of the field recordings relating to the pit, force the awful conclusion that the excavations at Samaria have established no direct evidence for dating any of the eighth-century BCE levels at the city, including those that might have reflected events connected with the decline of Israelite sovereignty over the erstwhile capital.

Despite some apparent misgivings, then, Kenyon's reconstruction brought her to the following three historical conclusions: the rooms of BP V represent the last phase of Israelite architecture at Samaria; the homogeneous ceramic group nicely contained in Pit *i* represents the pottery in use at the time when those buildings were laid waste;[9] and the layer containing the debris and materials of PP 7 provides secure evidence not only for the wreckage of these rooms situated north of the central courtyard but for the complete destruction[10] of the entire city by the Assyrians in 722/21 BCE.

One has seen that the new debris-layer analysis, ceramic evaluation, and historical conclusions put forward in Chapters II and III militate against the first two parts

---

[6] *SS III*, 97.

[7] *SS III*, 97.

[8] *SS III*, 97.

[9] See again *SS I*, 108.

[10] See again p. 223, n. 153.

of this proposal. In the former section, I demonstrated that the meager collection of pottery that constituted the PP 5 group came mostly from Room *hk* (Tables 19 and 25) and that it already belongs primarily to the seventh century BCE, notwithstanding two stray cooking-pot rims from earlier periods.[11] Thus, contra Kenyon,[12] seventh-century forms are not restricted to the debris of PP 7, which appeared stratigraphically later than the rooms and earlier than the .25 m-thick layer of chocolate soil assigned to "Period VIII." Unfortunately, and somewhat ironically given Kenyon's earlier principles of dating, the final report did not include any pottery found in the subfloor makeup beneath the BP V building—pottery that might have elucidated the construction date of those rooms. Two facts, then, speak to the nebulous nature of the findspots from which the excavators actually drew their PP 5 group: first, no published items came from beneath the floors, and second, the remains of PP 7, which I am about to examine, reportedly lay directly over those surfaces.

If not below or above the floors in question, where did the excavators encounter the most stratigraphically secure pottery that might help to date the final phase of Israelite architecture at the site? For Kenyon, the answer lay inside Pit/Latrine *i* (= PP 6). In her reconstruction of the archaeological remains, PP 6 dated the latest Israelite architecture while PP 7 dated an historical episode that brought an Assyrian destruction of the buildings in question. But in Chapter III, I demonstrated the heterogeneous nature of the Pit *i* assemblage and the reality of disparate findspots that bear dubious relationships to the pit. And once again, a significant portion of this corpus also claims a date in the very late eighth and early seventh centuries BCE.

The cumulative weight of these factors requires that I reconsider the PP 7 assemblage issued in support of an Assyrian destruction of Samaria. If the reported deposition of PP 7 above PP 5 (though not over PP 6 in Pit *i*) holds true, and if the repertoire of PP 7 dates no later than the period around 720 BCE, then at least the structures of BP V (but still not necessarily the pottery of PP 6) may well have seen their last functional days during that assault. My previous findings indicate that this is not the case, however. If either of the above conditions fails, then the historical reconstruction for the end of Israelite-controlled Samaria offered by the Joint Expedition will stand in need of revision. Further, a new understanding may ensue regarding the fundamental strategy by which the Assyrians implemented their expansionistic policies in the late eighth and early seventh centuries BCE. Finally, I will show that not only will the provenance data pertaining to the PP 7 goods emerge as important criteria by which to assess the historical credibility of a final devastation of the Israelite capital by the Assyrian military, but this portion of my study will complete the background necessary to placing the published ivories in their original findspots and to appraising the stratigraphic reliability of those important loci.

---

[11] See pp. 220-22.

[12] *SS I*, 108.

II. Pottery Period 7

To facilitate the stratigraphic and ceramic discussion of Kenyon's "Period VII," I have once again extracted the relevant data from Appendix A and reorganized them in Table 45 in a way that provides a complete list of the PP 7 findspots and draws together the various stratigraphic coordinates that relate to a particular architectural

	Horizontal Axis	Vertical Axis =Local Layers	Coordinates	No. of published sherds/vessels (None marked for discard)
Figure 11	Deposits *Overlying* House Floors in:			
	Room *e*	IVa, VIc	*19.51.14.20*	5
		VI	*120.121.19.126*	1
	Room *f*	IIa.f	509.126	1
		VI	120.121.19.126	1
		For possible necessary transfers to this room, see entries marked ‡ in Appendix A, PP 7		
	Room *g*	V, VI, VIw, VII, VIIe, VIII	*120.121.19.126*	12
	Room *hk*	IIIz	122.125.19.121	1
		IIIa	*125.144*	1
	Room *hq*	VIw, VII	*W of 124*	3
	Room *j*	IIa.f	509.126	1
	Room *kq*	V, VII	*120.121.19.126*	2
		IIIc, Vc	W of 124	2
	Room *l*	Va, Va.z	*504.503.509.508*	5
		IIa.f, VIII	509.126	2

Horizontal + Vertical Dimensions of PP 7 Stratigraphy
Table 45

feature (i.e., to identifiable rooms). This table also lists the number of fragments and whole or near-whole vessels that the excavators published from each locus, as well as the local stratigraphy (by layer) of the various loci.

As examination of Table 45 reveals, the collation of excavated segments and specific findspots with their associated architectural features becomes most complex here in Pottery Period 7. Though four segments bear on only a single feature, three other excavation areas ran through multiple rooms and sometimes touched on as many as four separate units. When addressing these three tracts of the excavation, I am thus prompted to adjust slightly what has become a general procedure for presenting the site's depositional history. That is, whenever possible, I have organized my stratigraphic analysis around architectural features (i.e., rooms), and I shall now maintain that approach for the single-feature segments. For the three multiple-feature segments, however, I shall incorporate all the relevant rooms under a single review of each *segment*. As it happens, each of these segments has appeared in detailed discussions of the stratigraphy from earlier historical periods. Since most of the levels recorded for those segments were treated in those discussions, I need now only review the principal deposits relating specifically to PP 7.

Before proceeding, one should note that later deposits from at least four, and possibly five, of the segments listed above (see the coordinates in bold-italics) contributed to the corpus of ivory fragments presented in *SS II*. In all except two cases, each segment yielded only one publishable fragment. The segment labeled *W of 124*, however, produced at least 18 of the ivory pieces seen in *SS II*, while Segment *19.51.14.20* added another 120 items. Together, then, these two segments contributed 77.5% of the entire collection published by the excavators. From this observation alone, one can see the significance of the so-called Room *e*, which, by all accounts, also represents the most heavily disturbed of all the rooms identified by the Joint Expedition (compare, for example, fig. 41). (For a detailed presentation of provenance data relating to the ivories, including the local layers within each segment that produced them, see Chapter V.)

Part A. Deposits Overlying House Floors in Rooms *e, f, g, hk, hq, j, kq,* and *l* (*SS I*, Fig. 50; Pl. VII — Sections EF, GH) (*SS III*, Fig. 11:1-37)

Since the official report from Samaria does not describe any new architecture for "Period VII," one should return to the BP V plan (fig. 41, which I have reproduced here as fig. 56) to aid in defining the specific parameters of the PP 7 loci. Though for the excavators the loci pertaining to PP 7 reflected a wholesale conflagration across the entire site, the findspots in question actually cover a rather circumscribed area. Based on information from *SS I*,[13] I have lightly shaded this field of excavation in fig. 56; according to that volume of the report, this tract extended precisely from 449° to 464° N and from 638° to 646° E. Such a delimited usable space resulted from serious, late (Persian-Roman) disturbances that impinged on virtually every other quarter in the surrounding areas.

---

[13] *SS I*, 110.

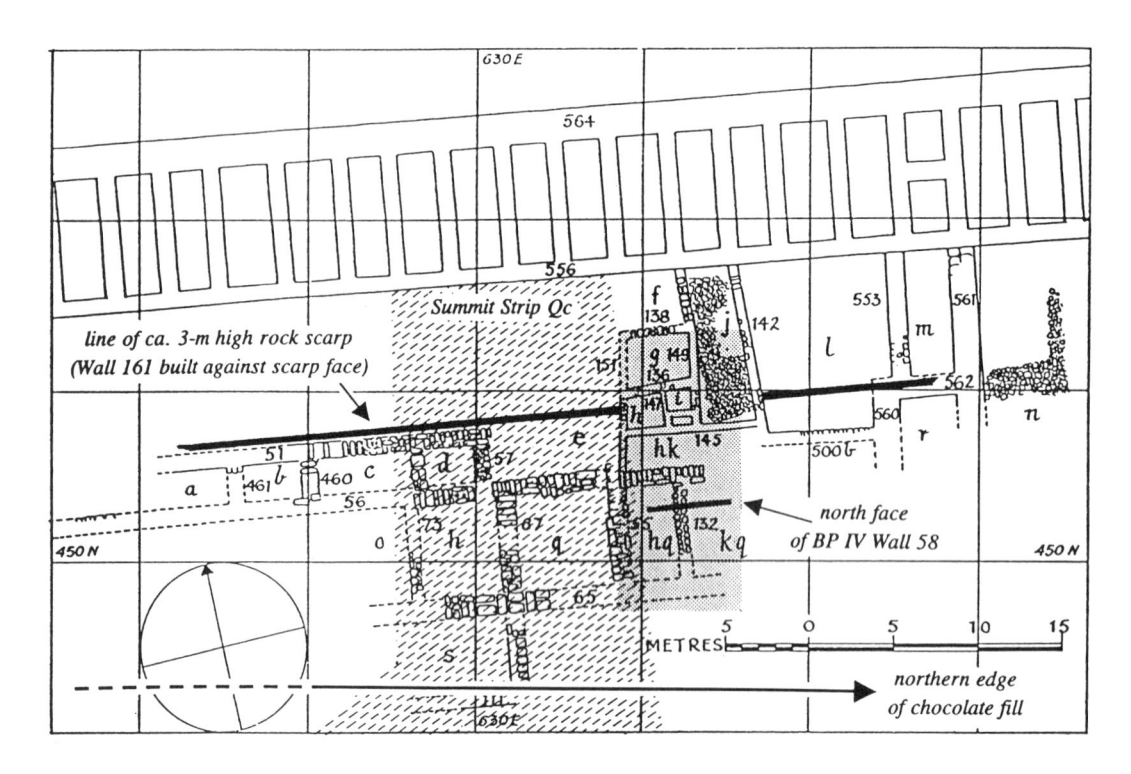

Published BP V Top Plan (including Architecture Related to PP 7)
(adapted from *SS I*, Fig. 50)

fig. 56

For example, the .25 m-thick band of sticky, chocolate colored soil that covered the entire central courtyard at some point after the Israelite period (Kenyon assigned it to her "Period VIII") revealed its northernmost edge at 443° N, where it apparently met a northern boundary wall. I have indicated the northern skirt of this deposit with a solid arrow in fig. 56. The chocolate layer is clearly visible on Published Section GH, and the onetime boundary wall seems to have existed in the space now labeled Robber Trench 98.[14] While the excavators remained uncertain of the exact east-west range of this deposit, the available evidence indicated that its western border lay somewhere between 610° and 630° E (dotted portion of arrow, fig. 56). To the east, it continued beyond the excavation area opened by the Joint Expedition.[15] Often associated with a

---

[14]*SS I*, Pl. VII. Compare also the photographic view of this layer at approximately 440° N x 640° E (10 m due south of Room *hq*) in *SS III*, Pl. XXXV:2. A similar boundary wall (No. 363?) seems to have stood in the Robber Trench now seen at the southern end of this layer (situated between RT 339 and RT 377 in Section GH).

[15]*SS I*, 113-14.

putative Persian garden, the substantial leveling and deposition involved in the making of this layer unfortunately destroyed "all the latest Israelite deposits" beneath it.[16] This situation, coupled with the fact that the entire area immediately west of 638° E had suffered from clearance to bedrock during the Hellenistic and Roman periods, kept the excavators to the north and east in their search for materials relating to the closing years of Israelite rule.

Samaria-Sebaste I provides some relatively detailed, if not always compatible, information on conditions within the excavation zone outlined in fig. 56. After reporting that only in this area were the later Israelite structures undisturbed and that "they were everywhere found covered with a layer of debris of destruction,"[17] two specific areas within this frame prove of further interest. First, the report discloses that, although this sooty deposit ran southward as far as the robber trench of Wall 65, "only a relatively small portion of the layer was undisturbed owing to the number of later walls built into it."[18] This fact alone jeopardizes the reliability of loci in the southern portion of Rooms *hq* and *kq*.

Second, one learns more about this deposit as it appeared north of the line of the earlier BP IV Wall/Robber Trench 58. A comparison of figs. 5 and 56 show that this feature ran horizontally through the central area of Rooms *hq* and *kq* at exactly the point where the BP V partition wall angles slightly to the east. Since the original north face of Wall 58 supplies an important point of reference, I have indicated its intersection with Wall 132 on fig. 56. As the debris layer ran north from that line, it "covered the top of broken wall 145" (which appears only as a Robber Trench in Kenyon's plan) before covering and lying directly on the floors of Rooms *h*, *i*, and *j*. In the first two chambers, the debris (which consisted of striations of burnt matter and hard, yellow soil) reached reported depths of over 1.5 meters. Though this may sound like an intact destruction level north of former Wall 58, I must qualify the preceding descriptions with at least two points. Though Kenyon speculated that this same situation had at one time existed in Room *k* (BP IV), she noted that the area covered by *k* now appeared "*completely disturbed* by later walls and robber trenches."[19] A review of the location of Room *k* in fig. 5 reveals that Kenyon's statement basically negates the trustworthiness of the deposit in the space between Wall 145 and the line of Wall 58 in fig. 56. One must, therefore, scrutinize closely the findspots of pottery published from Room *hk*, *hq*, and *kq*.[20] Additionally, one should recall that "Room" *i* basically represents the area of "Pit" *i* which, as I have shown, was not sealed by the spread of PP 7 debris;

---

[16] *SS I*, 110.

[17] *SS I*, 110.

[18] *SS I*, 110.

[19] *SS I*, 110 (emphasis added).

[20] Recall my earlier citations of Kenyon's own comments regarding the poor state of preservation of the surfaces running north and south of Wall 56, i.e., in the area of Rooms *hk*, *hq*, and *kq* (see my stratigraphic analyses for BP V in Chapter II).

consequently, this putative latrine(?) becomes a moot space in terms of ceramic and historical analyses.

The net result of this accounting of dubious sectors of the excavation area leaves only Rooms *h* and *j* as potentially credible portions of the overall PP 7 deposit. But the final report contained only one sherd that possibly came from Room *j* [21] and none from Room *h*. The curious choice of loci from which Kenyon drew her published repertoire further complicates one's efforts at interpretation; nearly 68% of the final group derived from Rooms *g*, *e*, and *l* (see Table 45),[22] the last two of which actually lay outside the designated excavation area. As I have already demonstrated in previous periods,[23] Kenyon tended to muster her various comparanda of late Israelite fragments from the smaller, more poorly built, and even sometimes heavily disturbed rooms situated north of the rock scarp that demarcated the central summit area and northeast of the better-constructed Rooms *a-d*, *h*, and *q*.

One must, then, exercise extreme caution regarding the potentially secondary nature of a number of findspots within the PP 7 deposit. Indeed, additional statements in the official report cast an even greater pall over the entire excavation area. For example, consider the following:

> It does not appear probable that the debris represents the actual destruction *in situ* of the objects it includes. . . .
>
> Also, it is clear that the walls were destroyed to their present height *before* the debris was spread over their broken tops. [emphasis added]
>
> In no place did the ashes look undisturbed, but were everywhere mixed with soil.
>
> What apparently took place was that the buildings were destroyed by fire, and the walls were subsequently robbed to their present level. After that the burnt debris, which had been stirred up in the process, was spread over the whole area leveling it up.[24]

Each of these remarkable statements raises greater uncertainty regarding both the integrity of the PP 7 deposit as a whole and, in turn, the precise sequence of events believed to have transpired in this area of the royal city. Since the excavators encountered the layer in a secondary (if not tertiary) context, the overall deposit assumes the basic attributes of a fill layer. As such, only the latest pottery taken from the matrix can carry some chronological value in setting the *terminus ante quem* (latest

---

[21] *SS III*, Fig. 11:26. But while *SS III*, 128, assigned this fragment to Room *j*, some confusion exists within the unpublished records as to whether it actually came from Room *j* or Room *f*.

[22] For the full pattern of spatial distribution for this group, see Pottery Analysis below.

[23] E.g., pp. 182-83 above; compare *SS I*, 107.

[24] *SS I*, 110.

possible date) of the leveling of the debris. Unfortunately, as in the case of all fills and most secondary deposits, the *terminus post quem* of the level must remain open. This reality represents one of the same methodological problems that impinged on Kenyon's interpretations in PP 1-2. Further, since the above statements reveal that Kenyon herself clearly saw the ruination of the BP V buildings and the deposition of leveling fill as temporally distinct events, a question naturally ensues as to how much time actually separates the two episodes. Even if one assigns the initial destruction of the rooms to an Assyrian invasion force, where is the evidence that this same group also bears responsibility for the subsequent leveling of the mixed debris? The answer must come from close study of the materials contained in that matrix and of the specific loci that yielded the goods.

Finally, I shall return later to a consideration of the context of the ivories. Here I shall only note Kenyon's statement that, in terms of the PP 7 debris in question, the primary concentration of ivory fragments appeared "north and south of 56, nearly as far south as 65, and on the north mainly as far as 145."[25] These parameters would place them squarely in Room *hk* and in the northern half of Rooms *hq* and *kq*. Yet in his official publication of these priceless items, Crowfoot wrote that the bulk of the ivories came from Summit Strip Qc to the west (indicated with hachures on fig. 56) and that those few, poorly preserved pieces that surfaced in Strip Qk (in the area of the PP 7 deposit) seemed principally related to Hellenistic and Roman levels.[26] In Chapter V, I shall present extensive, previously unavailable provenance data that will help to solve these ambiguities.

1a) **Stratigraphic Detail:** *Single-feature Segments*

a. Room *e*   (Published Section GH; *AIS-I*, figs. 18-22b)

[i] 19.51.14.20

While I have not had occasion to address this excavation segment in my analysis of PP 4-6, I dealt with it extensively in my earlier study of PP 3.[27] At that time, the discussion involved only the round-bottomed, "fine-ware" bowl presented in *SS III*, Fig. 4:9 (from Layer XIa), which Kenyon assigned to PP 3 but which I dated to sometime around the Iron I-Iron II transition in the tenth century BCE. Though the official report located the findspot for this piece in Room *c*,[28] I concluded that it actually derived from an area of disturbance lying farther east, in the so-called Room *e*.

---

[25] *SS I*, 110.

[26] See *SS II*, 2 and 4. Virtually all the fragments presented in this volume came from Summit Strip Qc (see p. 12, n. 1).

[27] *AIS-I*, 148-58.

[28] Compare *SS I*, Figs. 47 and 50.

This same area in Room *e* contributed to the PP 7 group five fragments from two additional local layers (IVa and VIc). As noted earlier, both the published and unpublished records also speak of an appreciable quantity of ivory fragments retrieved from this segment (139 items, or 55.6% of the entire published corpus). Since in my previous study I treated in considerable detail the problems associated with locating *19.51.14.20* on both the horizontal and the vertical planes of excavation, I need now only summarize the results of that effort. My discussion will depend mainly on fig. 56, though I shall also incorporate a few informative plans and sections from *AIS-I*.

In setting the parameters of this segment, I begin by noting that BP III Rooms *a-d* maintained only about half their original size by the time of BP V.[29] In the latter period, two walls can serve as important landmarks. Wall 56 (replacing BP III Wall 58) demarcates the southern line of these chambers, while Wall 51 defines their northern

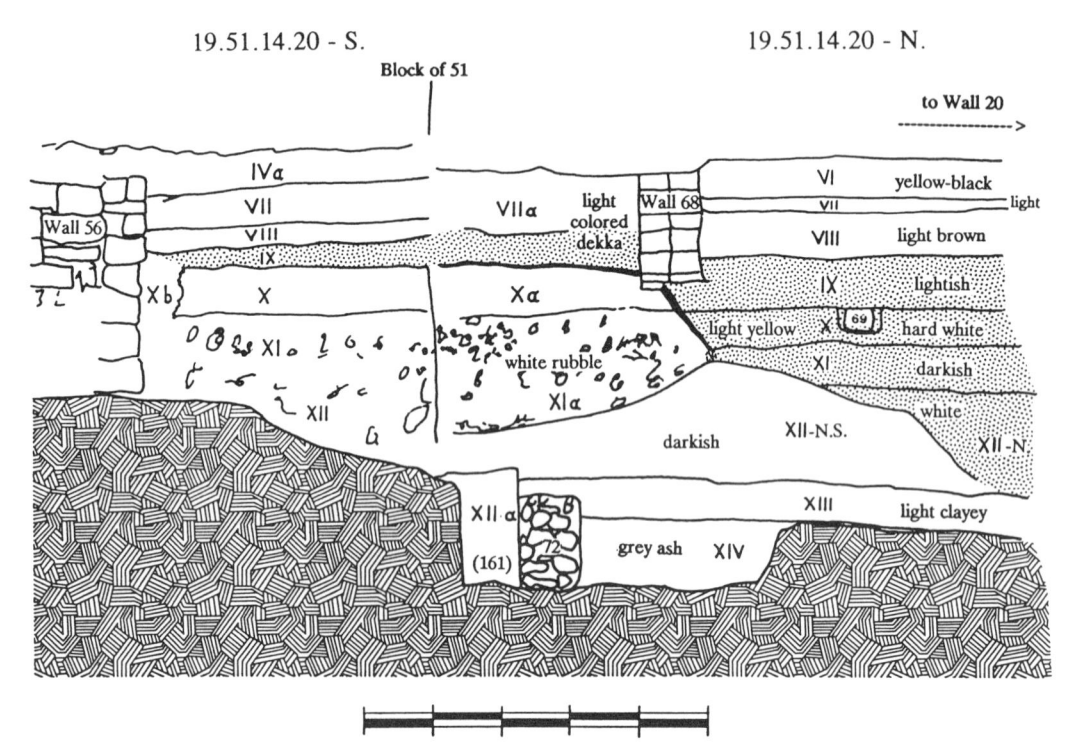

(approximate scale based on distance between Walls 56 and 161)

Segment 19.51.14.20
<— S   N —>
View toward West
fig. 57

---

[29] See again *SS I*, Figs. 47 and 50, using the ashlar that projects into Room *b* in Fig. 47 (BP III) as a reference point in Fig. 50 (BP V).

PP 7: HOUSE FLOORS — STRATIGRAPHY

border. As seen in the unpublished field section presented in fig. 57, the latter wall (51) ran along the top edge of the rock scarp that marked the northern edge of the central summit plateau. It lay immediately south of Omri's original Enclosure Wall 161, which earlier builders had set at the foot of the scarp and for which they had used the rock's vertical face as a support for the wall's foundational courses.[30] Though Wall 56 continued farther eastward (with some ostensible patching), and thereby also defined the southern limit of the bygone Room *e*, Wall 51 suffered apparent destruction on the north side of *e* and did not continue past Room *d*. Even though Kenyon recorded that the PP 7 layer of sooty debris ran as far south as the robber trench of Wall 65,[31] the features that she used to delineate this segment of excavation (Walls 14, 19, 20 and 51)[32] seem to restrict its southernmost extent to an area east of and parallel to Rooms *a-d*.[33] The published Section GH (fig. 58) shows that the Hellenistic fill south of Wall

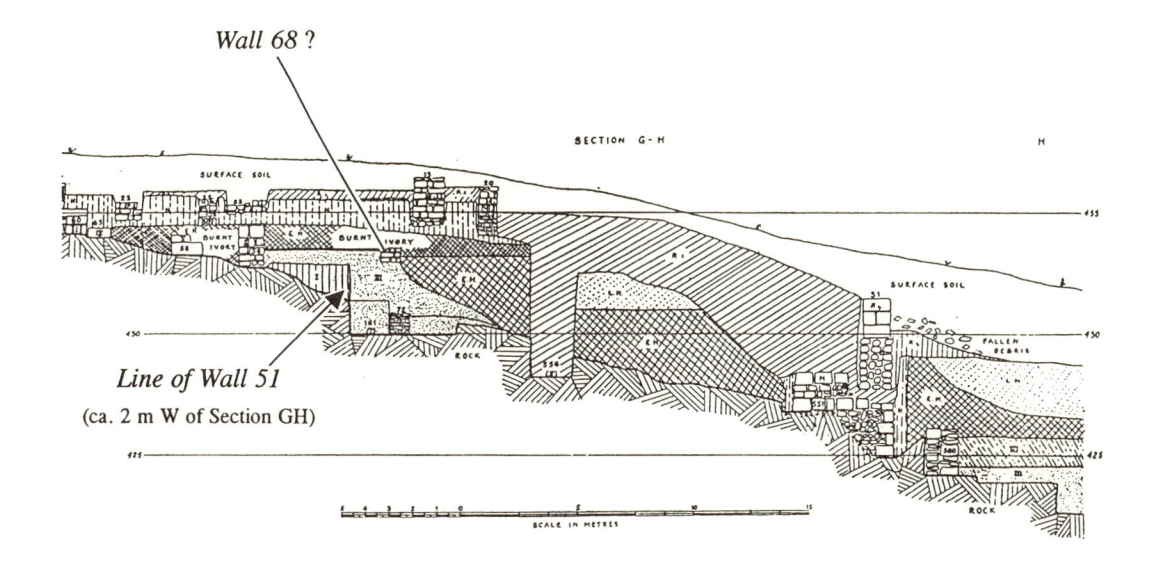

Portion of Published Section GH @ 445°-467° N
(adapted from *SS I*, Pl. VII)

fig. 58

---

[30]See also *SS I*, Pl. VII, Section GH (or fig. 58). I have indicated the line of the scarp in fig. 56 above by means of a bold solid line.

[31]*SS I*, 110.

[32]Of these, only Wall 51 actually served during the Israelite period; the others date primarily to the Herodian Period and the 1st century CE.

[33]See the shaded area in *AIS-I*, 149, fig. 18.

56 descends all the way to bedrock and therefore no traces whatsoever of Israelite levels appear in that area.[34] These observations will produce a negative impact on the chronological credibility of remains taken from Rooms *hq* and *kq* (i.e., on five specific entries in the PP 7 group).

One can see, then, that the integral portion of Segment *19.51.14.20* basically extended eastward from Wall 57 and northward from Wall 56. As a result, it might appear that any PP 7 remains assigned to Room *e* would have to come from a narrow strip of soil situated directly against the western face of Wall 151 (see Rooms *g*, *h*, and *hk*) in order to fall within the area of exposed Israelite remains outlined in *SS I* for PP 7 (449°-464° N x 638°-646° E).[35]

As demonstrated in *AIS-I*, however, Segment *19.51.14.20* actually seems to have extended farther eastward as it stretched from the northeastern corner of Room *d* (630° E) for an approximate distance of 12.5 meters and incorporated the western half of Room *hk*.[36] North of the row of chambers in *a-d*, the segment ran at least six meters more to the east, or as far as Wall 142 on the east side of Room *j*. The longitudinal axis of published Section GH reveals that *19.51.14.20* ran south over both Wall 56 and the earlier and more deeply buried Wall 58 before continuing as far as Wall 65. The debris proved quite thick here and rested directly on bedrock. To the north, this layer reached at least as far as the line of Ahab's old interior Casemate Wall 556.[37] Due to massive quantities of Roman period fill north of that line, however, I cannot say with certainty whether the deposit originally continued even further north over the declining rock surface. Only north of Wall 56, then, did the debris ascribed to PP 7 actually cover surviving Israelite layers.

More than any other single sketch, a section drawing made in the field and confined to a small area just inside the southwestern corner of "Room *e*" complements my efforts to locate the actual findspots for the PP 7 remains (fig. 59). This diagram shows that Layer IVa, which yielded several examples of thin, shallow, hard-ware bowls (*SS III*, Fig. 11:12, 15, 17), ran up against the eastern face of a surviving portion of Wall 57, which divided Rooms *d* and *e*. It appears that Layer IVa lay in close proximity to this wall, since the excavators labeled the material farther away from that point "Layer IVd."

---

[34] I noted above that Kenyon also spoke of heavy disturbance toward Wall 65 owing to numerous later walls built into this soil (*SS I*, 110).

[35] See *SS I*, 110. Kenyon appealed to these specific parameters to define the only area in which "the later Israelite buildings were undisturbed" and where "they were everywhere found covered with a layer of debris of destruction." To the south, beneath the so-called chocolate layer, "all the latest Israelite deposits had been destroyed." To the west, "clearance had been carried down to rock partly in Hellenistic times and partly in Roman." The field of excavations did not extend farther to the east (see fig. 5).

[36] The area would stop at about the hypothetical continuation of the line of Wall 132, which divides Rooms *hq* and *kq*.

[37] In *AIS-I*, I distinguished between the northern and southern sectors of this segment by referring to them as *19.51.14.20-N* and *19.51.14.20-S*, respectively (e.g., see *AIS-I*, figs. 22a-b).

PP 7: HOUSE FLOORS — STRATIGRAPHY

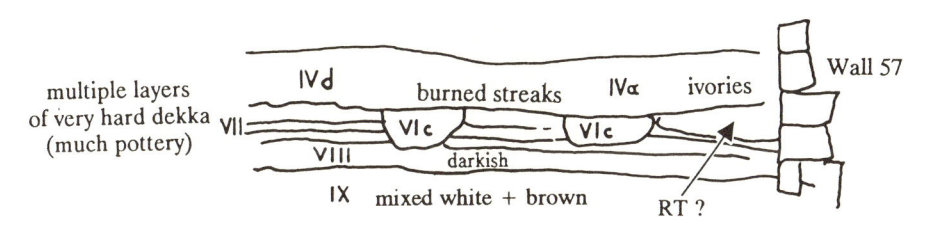

19.51.14.20–S.

[Stratigraphic section drawing with labels: "multiple layers of very hard dekka (much pottery)", "IVd", "burned streaks", "IVα", "ivories", "Wall 57", "VII", "VIc", "VIc", "VIII", "darkish", "IX", "mixed white + brown", "RT ?"]

(scale not recorded)

Segment 19.51.14.20: Southern Sector
<— E W —>
View toward South
fig. 59

At least two important observations emerge from this drawing. First, one sees that, although the lines demarcating Layer IVa do not actually touch the face of Wall 57,[38] the debris overlies a rather wide cut made into the soil immediately east of 57. I believe that this cut, though unidentified in the field drawing,[39] preserves traces of a robber trench associated with the partial plundering of Wall 57[40] and that the deposition of IVa therefore postdates the construction, use, and destruction or intentional dismantling of Feature 57. If the functional life of Wall 57 included the final days of Israelite control over Samaria, as Kenyon's published phase plan has it, then the adjacent PP 7 deposit seems to date to a later phase of activity. Second, it is clear that the combined layers in IVa-IVd cover and seal two small, pit-like loci that had, at some prior time, cut into preexisting surfaces that quite likely belonged to Wall 57 before its robbing.[41] The excavation team identified the contents of both pits (or drains?) as Layer VIc, and this matrix produced examples of a ceramic tradition (*SS III*, Fig. 11:23, 28) that differed in many respects from the finer bowls of the stratigraphically

---

[38] As a result, the exact stratigraphic relationship between this deposit and Wall 51 remains somewhat uncertain. One cannot know now whether the slight gap left between the deposit and the wall reflected the intention of the artist or simply an approximation typical of a section hastily drawn in the field.

[39] Published Section GH runs east of and parallel to Wall 57; consequently, it sheds no light on a possible explanation for this cut.

[40] Though the final, published drawing shows Wall 57 in good condition, the unpublished field section reveals that, at least around the level of Layer IVa, the feature had suffered the loss of a considerable number of ashlar blocks and consequently appeared far from complete.

[41] Though these layers undoubtedly included levels V, VI, and VII, fig. 59 shows that Kenyon actually designated only VII on her field drawing. I may also mention that she annotated the sketch with the recognition of "multiple layers of very hard dekka" that proved rich in pottery. Unhappily, none of this material reached the final stages of publication.

later IVa. Since these pits intruded into levels that likely belonged to the functional life of Wall 57 (and, by association, Wall 51), they are stratigraphically later than those surfaces. Even the materials of VIc, therefore, may easily postdate the period assigned to the principal use of both Rooms *d* and *e*.

To sum up, one can see that the precise location of the findspots related to the PP 7 group resembles in many respects the situation already witnessed in my analysis of PP 3. Besides lying quite some distance from Kenyon's alleged Room *c* deposit (to which she erroneously assigned the PP 3 fragment; see *AIS-I*), the layers of Segment *19.51.14.20* that pertain specifically to the PP 7 materials also rested an appreciable distance west of the excavation area outlined in the final report and shaded on fig. 56. In both cases, the retrieved set of goods came from very near Room *d*, but more specifically from the heavily disturbed area of "Room *e*" in Summit Strip Qc. This locational analysis also indicates, preliminarily, that the major cache of ivory fragments taken from *19.51.14.20* will derive from findspots situated either just at or even below the high rock scarp that follows roughly an east-west course through this area. Though the depositional history in this segment as a whole was poorly preserved and somewhat confused in the field records, Kenyon occasionally used it as a stratigraphic anchor by which to collate levels exposed in other segments of excavation.

In her published section, Kenyon assigned all the levels discussed here to her "Early Hellenistic Period," i.e., to a time slightly earlier than the Hellenistic Fort Wall, which she dated to the late third to early second centuries BCE. An additional though extremely convoluted notation in her unpublished fieldnotes also betrays a late date for the deposits and materials under consideration. Speaking of certain layers that ran northward from Wall 51 and the line of the scarp, she wrote:

> Levels Xa [and] XIa.S. are only found N. of the line of 51 . . . . [Therefore,] they belong to the orig. 51, [and] are post the previous Isr. wall along the bottom of the scarp.[42] X [and] XIS. w[oul]d [therefore] have to be post destruction of orig. 51. Or alternatively, orig. 51 might have turned in some place, [and] X [and] XI have run up against Isr. wall along scarp, [with] Xa [and] XIa added against them on destruct[ion] of Isr. wall. This is prob[ably] the real sequence, [since] 57 (return of 51) cuts thro[ugh] X v[ery] definitely.[43]

Despite the complexity of these details, the following conditions and sequence emerge: if Layer X is later than the original Wall 51 (= BP III?), and if Wall 57 definitely cuts Layer X, and if the PP 7 levels IVa and VIc postdate Wall 57 as they seem to do, then the PP 7 materials appear to be very late in date.

---

[42]This must refer to Omri's Enclosure Wall 161.

[43]*Fieldbook Qc-d-e-f-g-h*, 16b-17.

b. Room *hk*

Two segments of excavation entered the broad room area of Room *hk*, which, judging from fig. 41, assumed an east-west orientation immediately north of Rooms *hq* and *kq*. Once again, that each of these segments has received attention earlier in this study allows me now simply to review only the most pertinent local stratigraphy in their respective areas.

[i] 122.125.19.121
[ii] 125.144 (Published Section EF; figs. 5, 8, 10, and 12)

Consideration of these two segments of excavation takes us slightly east of the heavily disturbed area in Room *e* and back to Summit Strip Qk,[44] to the general environs of Pit *i*. I have treated each of these areas extensively in earlier sections of this study,[45] and the relevant, unpublished field records appear in *Fieldbook Qk-l-m*.[46] Despite various enigmatic features of the fieldnotes and the virtual lack of detailed information in the published report, I can locate these segments with some certainty. The collective data available on a previously presented east-west section drawing (fig. 8), a north-south section (fig. 10), and a top plan (fig. 12), direct our attention once again to the general area surrounding Room *h* and Pit *i* in fig. 56.

Wall 19 constitutes the only architectural feature shared by the identifying coordinates of the first segment (*122.125.19.121*) and those assigned to the segment just discussed in the preceding section (*19.51.14.20*). As seen on fig. 8, the robber trench associated with Wall 19 rested directly over and just to the west of a few surviving stones of the earlier Wall 151.[47] The latter feature, Wall 151, served as the western enclosure for Rooms *g*, *h*, and *hk*, and, according to the phase plan in fig. 56, the only point at which its ashlar blocks actually remained intact was in a short section of wall in Room *h*. Whereas the previous segment, *19.51.14.20*, ran from 151 westward through Room *e* and as far as Wall 57, then, Segment *122.125.19.121* extended in the opposite direction and stretched eastward from 151 at about the same latitude as *19.51.14.20*. The complete robbing of Wall 19 and the partial robbing of Wall 151 (fig. 8), however, had broken the stratigraphic connection between these two segments already in antiquity.

The field drawing in fig. 8 also confirms that, although some of the late Iron II deposits in this area ran the entire length of Room *hk*, i.e., from Wall 151 on the west

---

[44] The location on the plan in fig. 12 of three of the coordinate structures named in the segment (Walls 122, 125, and 19) confirms that this area of excavation belongs in Summit Strip Qk.

[45] For *122.125.19.121*, see pp. 40-43 (PP 4) and 299-301 (PP 6); for *125.144*, see 27-37 (PP 4) and 186-90 (PP 5).

[46] For *122.125.19.121*, see *Fieldbook Qk-l-m*, 4-5, 32-35; for *125.144*, see *Qk-l-m*, 33-35, 48-49.

[47] Notes entered in *Fieldbook Qk-l-m*, 32, corroborate this juxtaposition.

to the line of 142 on the east, the area labeled specifically *122.125.19.121* did not extend that far. Instead, it lay only in the *westernmost* portion of Room *hk*, west of where former Wall 157 (BP IV; fig. 5) had continued directly south from Pit *i*. The exposed area from 157 east to Wall 142 fell under a different segment rubric: *Between TT2-TT3*. The small, western portion of Room *hk* included as well the deposits of Segment *125.144*.

This precise horizontal placement of *122.125.19.121* concurs with my findings in PP 6, where I presented a full-length treatment aimed at clarifying the exact relationship between two curious labels — *122.125.19.121* and *122.126.19.121*. The latter numerical set represented the area from Pit *i* to the northernmost wall (138) of Room *g*. But the designation *122.125.19.121*, on the other hand, included portions of the pit and extended southward to Wall 125, which had marked the southern boundary of the combined Rooms *h* and *k* in BP V. The fact that Kenyon associated one of the PP 7 fragments taken from *122.125.19.121* with Room *hk* corroborates my decision not to restrict this segment to the pit itself but to extend it south, not north, of that feature. The excavators found the profiled jar rim presented in *SS III*, Fig. 11:25, then, in the very southwestern side of Room *hk*, quite near the inside edge of Robber Trench 151.

While the location of this fragment on the horizontal plane of excavations is now firmly established, I cannot add a great deal to what I have already presented in earlier pages concerning the overall depositional history within Segment *122.125.19.121*. The official report assigned virtually every piece of pottery thus far associated with this area to local Layer Va.[48] As indicated in Appendix A, however, both the unpublished registration books and the stratification cards ascribed the PP 7 rim fragment to Layer IIIz. I have already shown that the Joint Expedition first encountered a matrix of soil mixed with burnt material in Layer IIIa of both segments *122.125.19.121* and *125.144*, and particularly in the basal striations of that level. A thick deposit of rubble and very large stones lay immediately above this material. Sooty deposits that overran Walls 136 and 145 (formerly 153 in BP IV) correspond to III-IIIa (and their affiliated subdeposits). The fieldnotes reveal that these deposits lay immediately beneath a series of Hellenistic walls and that ancient workers had actually set one of the walls (144) in the debris itself. Thus it would appear that, in this particular zone near the northern edge of the central summit plateau, a relatively short increment of time separated the leveling of the PP 7 debris and the construction of the Hellenistic walls. An argument for the opposite case, i.e., for a substantial hiatus between the leveling and the new construction, would suggest only a nominal occupation of the site during the lengthy interim between the close of the Israelite period and the arrival of the early Greeks at Samaria.

The abstract of layers presented in the fieldnotes describes the two specific find-spots listed for *SS III*, Fig. 11:25 and 35 as follows: (1) Layer IIIz in Segment

---

[48]This group includes *SS III*, Figs. 6:12 (PP 4) and 10:1-27 (PP 6). Only one fragment, Fig. 10:8, came from the associated Layer V. Interestingly, the field notes add that "a good deal of the pottery really belonging to Va was included with IIIb" (*Fieldbook Qk-l-m*, 32).

122.125.19.121 relates to a trench that the excavators cut through the hard matrix of Layer III, which they tentatively assigned to the post-Israelite "Period VIII";[49] (2) Layer IIIa in *125.144* appears as a "sooty layer overlying III = Btw. T.T.2-T.T.3 IIIb," and reportedly comprises part of "Period VII."[50] Judging from the impressions gained by Kenyon in the field at the time of excavation, then, it would appear that she understood the deposit that produced the jar rim in Fig. 11:25 to be slightly earlier in date than the locus that yielded the jar stand seen in Fig. 11:35.

c. **Room** *l* (Published Section EF; figs. 20, 38; *AIS-I*, 23-24, 104-05)

[i] **504.503.509.508**

As I approach the last single-feature segment that yielded PP 7 goods, I move still farther east to Summit Strip *n* and the area lying within the bounds of Room *l*. The unpublished field notes describing the depositional history of *504.503.509.508* appear in the two volumes of *Fieldbooks Qn*.[51] Although these records did not include section drawings or top plans directly related to the earliest stratigraphy in this segment (PP 1-2), I addressed these local layers briefly in my earlier study by collating them with those found in Segment *509.126*.[52] Fortunately, some of the later stratigraphy did appear in both the narrative and drawings of the fieldnotes, and these resources will prove helpful at this point in my investigation.[53] In addition, the combined details of figs. 20 and 38 above will clarify the placement of this excavation area on the horizontal plane of the summit.

For the sake of convenience, I shall reproduce here the two plans seen already in figs. 20 and 38. These drawings expedite considerably the task of locating the horizontal area of Segment *504.503.509.508*. In the first, simpler drawing (fig. 60), I have shown all the coordinate features used to identify this area of the excavations and have also added Casemate Wall 556 in its proper location south of Wall 505. The area of concern must lie in the shaded portion of this sketch, since that constitutes the only place that touches upon all the coordinate walls.

The second plan (fig. 61) allows me to place this zone more precisely within the confines of Room *l*. Here one gains some indication of the area's location relative to Wall 142 on the western side of Room *l* and Wall 553 on the eastern edge of the room. One can see that the excavation segment lay more toward the western half of *l*, though

---

[49] *Fieldbook Qk-l-m*, 5a. This summary of layers correlates Layer III in *122.125.19.121* to Layer V in the segment *W of 124* and says later (p. 21a) that V is "Prob[ably] P. VIII."

[50] *Fieldbook Qk-l-m*, 48a.

[51] *Fieldbook Qn (Vol. I)*, 60-63, and *Qn (Vol. II)*, 120-21. An abstract of the local stratigraphy appears on pages 120a and 121a of *Vol. II*.

[52] See *AIS-I*, fig. 5, Table 2, and pp. 23-24, 104-05.

[53] For section drawings made in the field, see *Fieldbook Qn (Vol. II)*, 60a, 61a, 62a, 63a, and 120a and 121a.

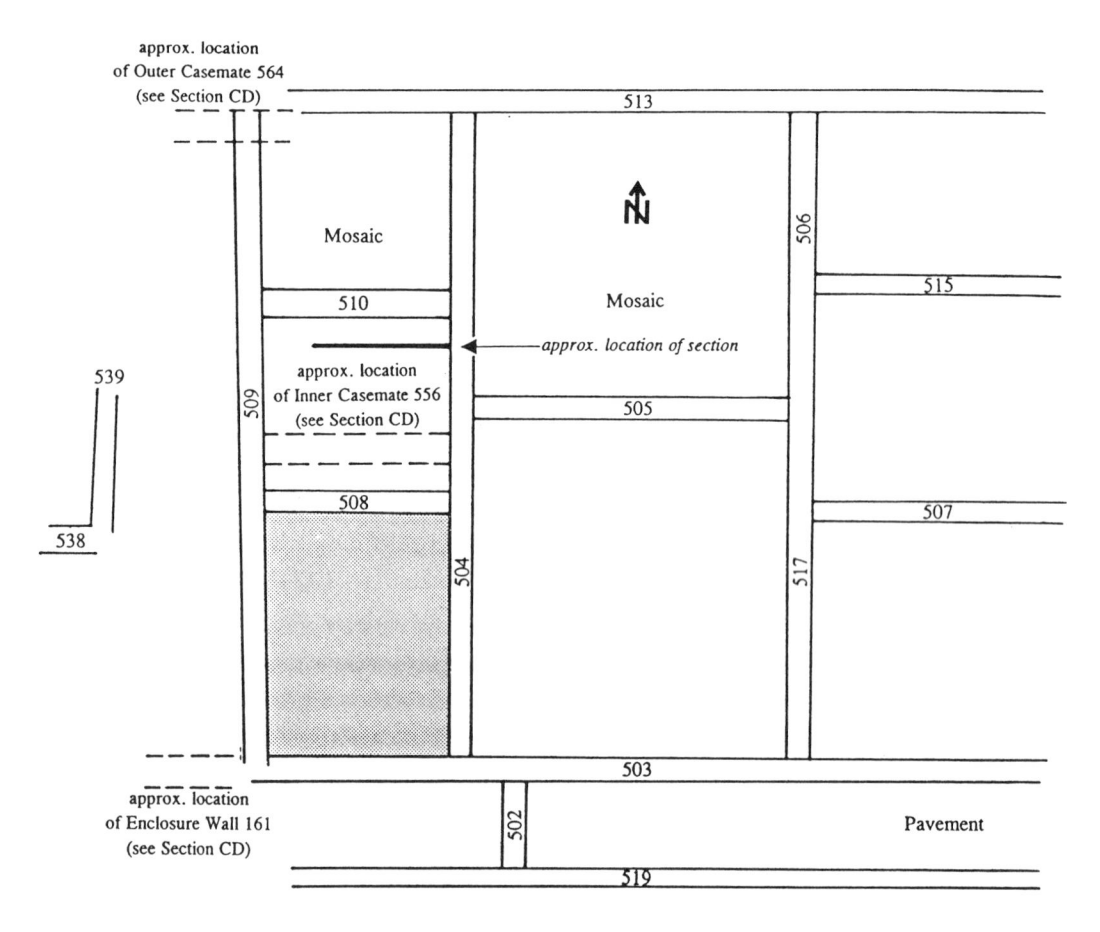

Segment 504.503.509.508 — Top Plan No. 1
(formerly fig. 38)
fig. 60

it may not have actually abutted Wall 142. While it rested not far south of the reference line established by former Casemate Wall 556, its north-south range appears to have reached neither 556 nor Wall 500b to the south. I shall demonstrate the value of this observation momentarily. Judging further from the position of Wall 138, which separated the more westerly Rooms *g-f*, one may conclude with some confidence that the excavators opened Segment *504.503.509.508* almost precisely where the wall designation "142" appears in fig. 56.

The official, published report presented a small group of five fragmentary vessels recovered from this area of Room *l*, including two bowls made of hard-ringing ware (*SS III*, Fig. 11:4, 6) and three jar rim fragments (Fig. 11:30-31, 33), with one also exhibiting a hard, thin ware and another representing a holemouth form. All except one of these pieces came from local Layer Va; only the holemouth rim surfaced in another, related sublayer, Va.z.

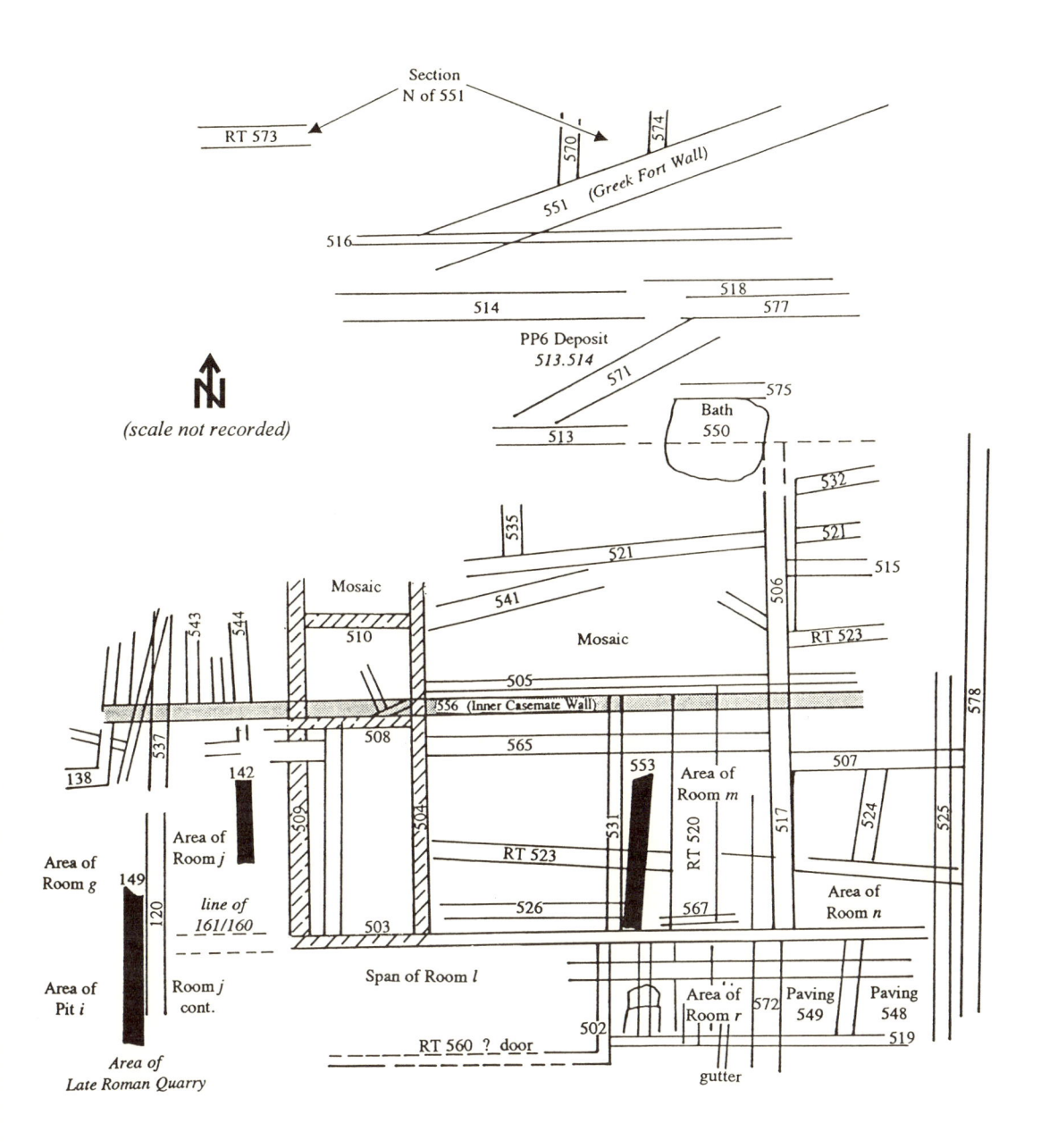

Segment 504.503.509.508 — Top Plan No. 2
(formerly fig. 20)
fig. 61

A number of field sections assist greatly one's understanding of the depositional history of this area. I believe also that they help substantiate some conclusions that have developed gradually throughout the course of this study. The first in this series of drawings presents the results of a north-south cut from Wall 508a on the north side of the segment to Wall 503a on the south side (fig. 62).[54]

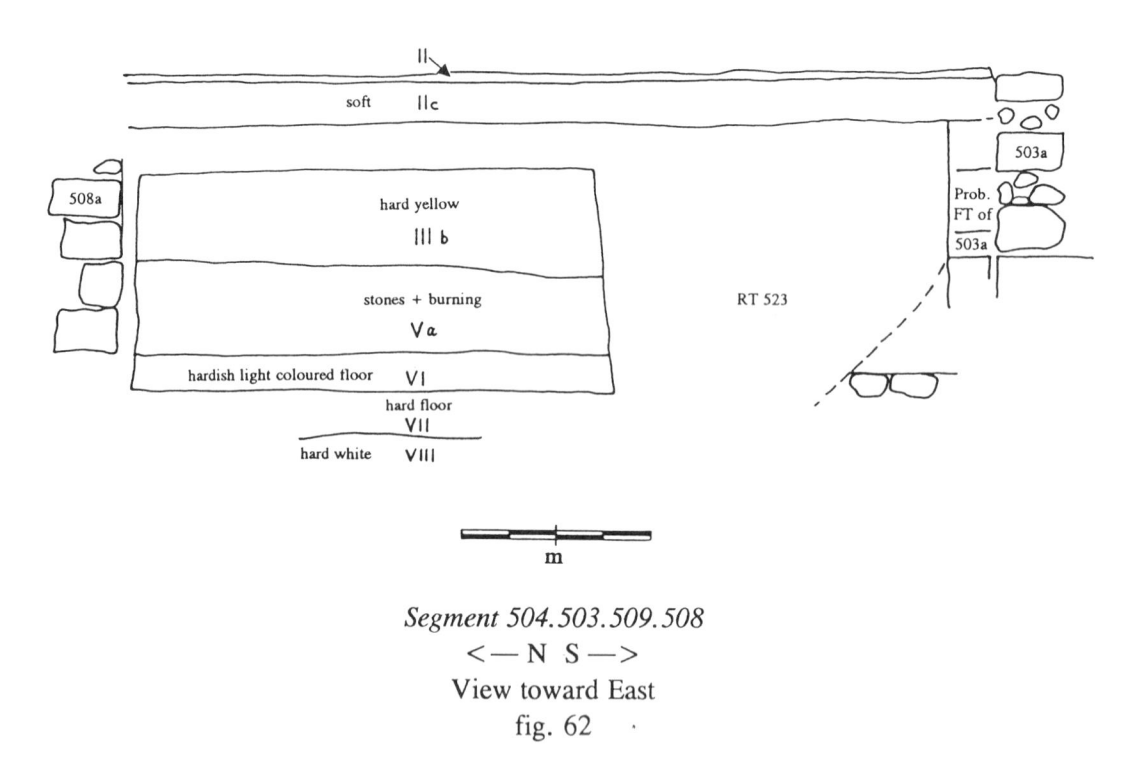

Segment 504.503.509.508
<— N   S —>
View toward East
fig. 62

Between these two features lies the westward extension of the lateral Robber Trench 523 (compare fig. 61). In this section, one sees among the earlier levels several surfaces constructed of a hard white or other light-colored matrix (Layers VIII, VII, and VI, from earliest to latest). While the stratigraphic relationship between the bottommost floor levels and Wall 508a remains unclear, certainly the wall cut through an already existing Layer VI. Above these deposits, two successive and very substantial fillings covered the segment, starting with the stones and burned debris of Layer Va (which alone yielded four of the five pieces of pottery published from this area) and continuing with the harder, yellowish soil of Layer IIIb. The massive robber trench associated with Wall 523 destroyed most of the more southerly portion of all these deposits.

Another very important, though unidentified, layer appears on this section. The space between the southern face of Wall 508a and the deposits just mentioned apparently represents the Foundation Trench of 508a, and the stratigraphic summaries

---

[54]*Fieldbook Qn (Vol. I)*, 63a.

PP 7: HOUSE FLOORS — STRATIGRAPHY 371

listed in the fieldnotes recognize this as Layer Va.z. Excavators retrieved the holemouth jar rim seen in *SS III*, Fig. 11:30 from this deposit. Since this material reflects the backfilling of the trench, and since notices in the unpublished records date Wall 508a to Kenyon's "R.4 Period," I can safely suggest a very late *terminus post quem* (depositional date) for the deposit itself in the fourth century CE; due to the secondary nature of the fill, however, the *terminus post quem* of the cultural materials (including the holemouth rim) contained therein must remain open. As a result, *SS III*, Fig. 11:30 can enter my discussion only as circumstantial evidence bearing nominal chronological value in the effort to date accurately the debris of PP 7.

The other four ceramic pieces taken from Layer Va, however, may prove more helpful in meeting my goals, but less because of the deposit's stratigraphic relationship to Wall 508a, which cut through that material, than because of another latitudinal field sketch that shows the association of Layer Va to Wall 552 (fig. 63).[55] The latter feature assumed a north-south orientation just inside the western edge of Segment *504.503.509.508*, and another unpublished section reveals that both Layers IIIb and Va

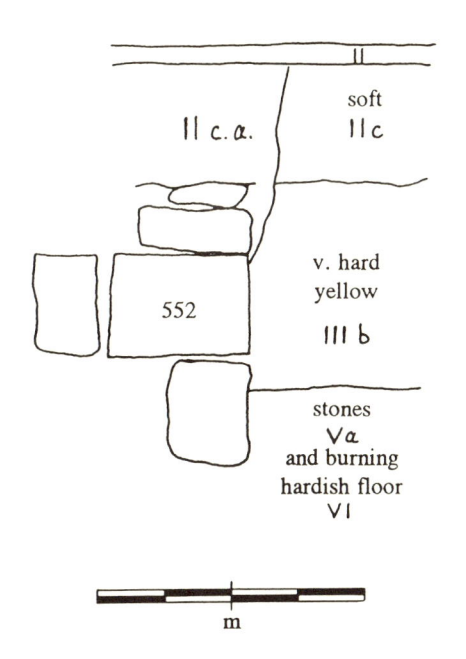

Segment 504.503.509.508: Supplement
<— W E —>
View toward North
fig. 63

---

[55] *Fieldbook Qn (Vol. I)*, 61a.

ran against the lower courses of this wall. A robber trench, which was stratigraphically earlier than the thin Layer II, cut through the softer deposit of IIc and the uppermost corner of IIIb without reaching as far down as Layer Va. In contrast to the situation in fig. 62, Kenyon posed no real distinction in this drawing between the stones and burned debris of Layer Va and the preceding, "hardish floor" of VI.

Both Layer Va and Layer VI, then, abut and belong with Wall 552. The unpublished field summaries date this architectural feature to the "R.1" period, which some miscellaneous notes describe as follows:

> Herodian building operations. The deposits included the earth ram against the north retaining wall of the temple forecourt, and the filling of the robber trenches of part of the casemate, *with material obtained by slicing off the top deposits of the adjoining area.* c. 30 B.C. [emphasis added][56]

Whereas Wall 508a cuts and therefore postdates Layer Va, Wall 552 adjoins this deposit and is contemporary with it. Not only does the notation just cited provide a dating of the deposits under consideration at this point, but the italicized excerpt helps to corroborate my earlier view that the areas lying below the rock scarp had received massive amounts of leveling fill that ancient builders had obtained from the summit plateau above the scarp.

This deduction seems to receive further confirmation from additional unpublished field sections that pertain to this general area but that fell under different segment headings. For example, in the very northwest corner of Room *l*, in Segment *509.126* (see below), a short section drawing shows the deposits lying on either side of Wall/Robber Trench 555 (fig. 64).[57] This zone clearly lay north of the hypothetical extension of the scarp line already encountered in Room *e* (see the proposed continuation of the dotted line into Room *l* in fig. 56). Here again one sees a thick matrix consisting of a mixture of light colored, sooty, and stony material stretching from both the southern and northern sides of 555. This debris lies *over* a series of hard-packed levels similar to those witnessed on earlier drawings. On the southern side, toward central Room *l*, the cutting of the robber trench has destroyed the original stratigraphic relationship between this deposit, here labeled Layer VIIc, and the original Wall 555. As indicated in fig. 64, Kenyon herself equated VIIc with Layer Va in Segment *504.503.509.508*. North of 555, however, toward the line of old Casemate Wall 556, the corresponding Layer IIa.f (also labeled "Prob. V") runs against and therefore seems contemporary with the surviving blocks of Wall 555.

Farther to the south in Room *l*, however, the stratigraphy appears significantly different from that which I have just presented. In a long sectional cut that ran nearly

---

[56]Taken from several sheets of typed notes describing "Q Area (Summit)" and stored with the Fieldbooks at the PEF.

[57]*Fieldbook Qn (Vol. II)*, 102a.

PP 7: HOUSE FLOORS — STRATIGRAPHY

Segment 509.126
<— S N —>
View toward West
fig. 64

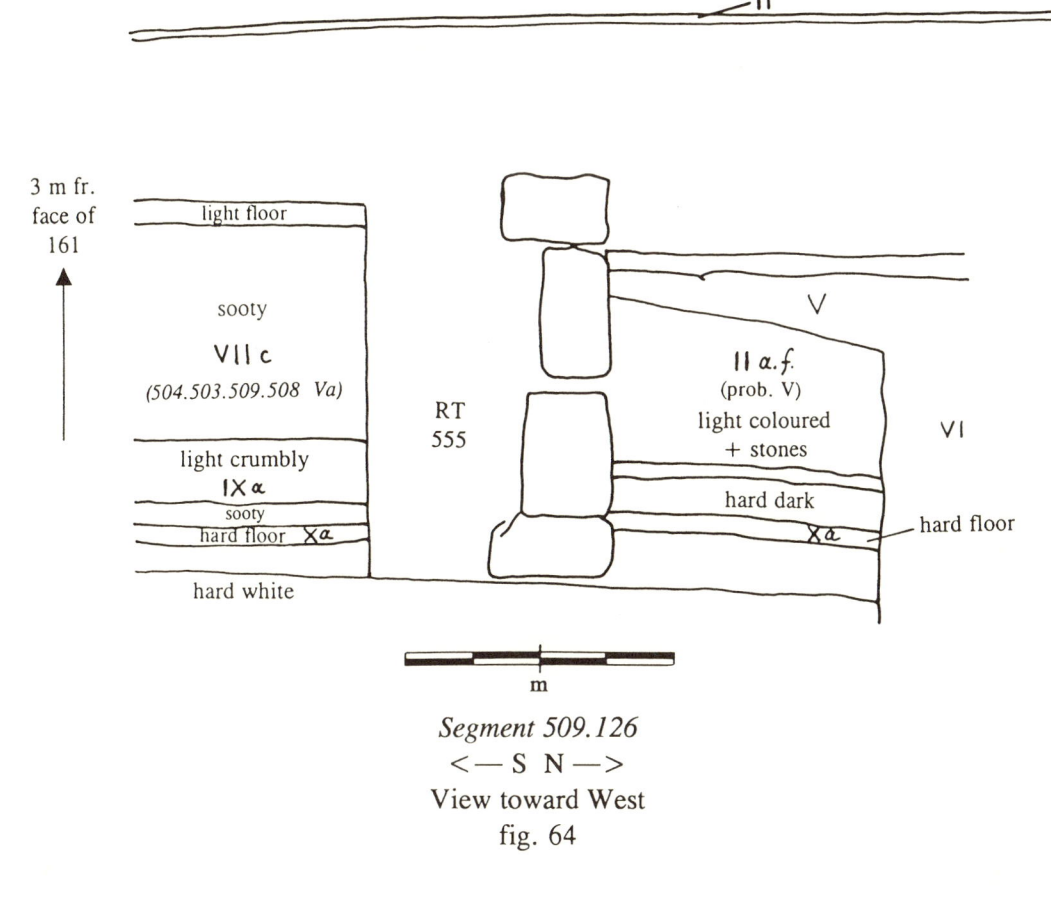

the full horizontal breadth of Room *l*, from Robber Trench 553 on the east to Wall 509-S on the west, one sees that the deepest deposits of fill seem to rest *beneath* the series of hard surfaces and to relate to earlier historical periods (fig. 65).[58] That is to say, the thick deposit of sooty fill, which purportedly covered Room *l* and which included the PP 7 ceramic repertoire and possibly one or two of the published fragments of ivory,[59] appears to have existed only in the northern portion of that room or, more specifically, in the area situated north of the rock scarp that defined the beginning of the official summit plateau to the south. Judging from another section drawn in the field (fig. 66),[60] a comparable portrait of the stratigraphy in the area between Walls 509 and 142 seems to emerge.

---

[58] *Fieldbook Qn (Vol. I)*, 11a.

[59] This last claim remains quite uncertain at this point, however, since unpublished records dealing with the ivories assign both of the pieces in question (*SS II*, Pls. XXI:7 and XXIV:8) to Room *n* even though their identifying wall coordinates (*504.503.507.508* and *501.503.504.505*, respectively) are very close to those seen here in Room *l*.

[60] *Fieldbook Qn (Vol. I)*, 32a.

374 THE ARCHAEOLOGY OF ISRAELITE SAMARIA

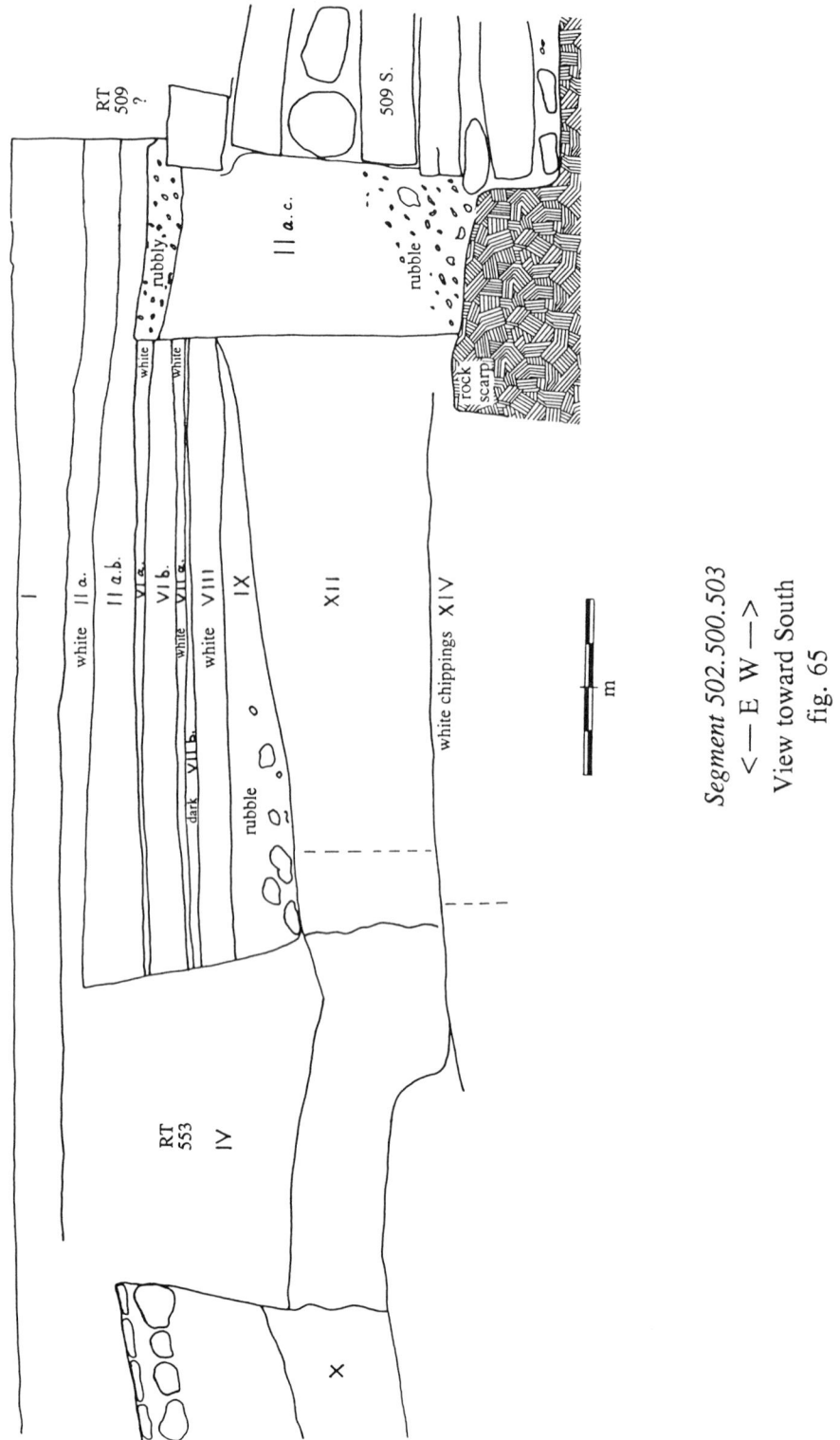

Segment 502.500.503
<— E W —>
View toward South
fig. 65

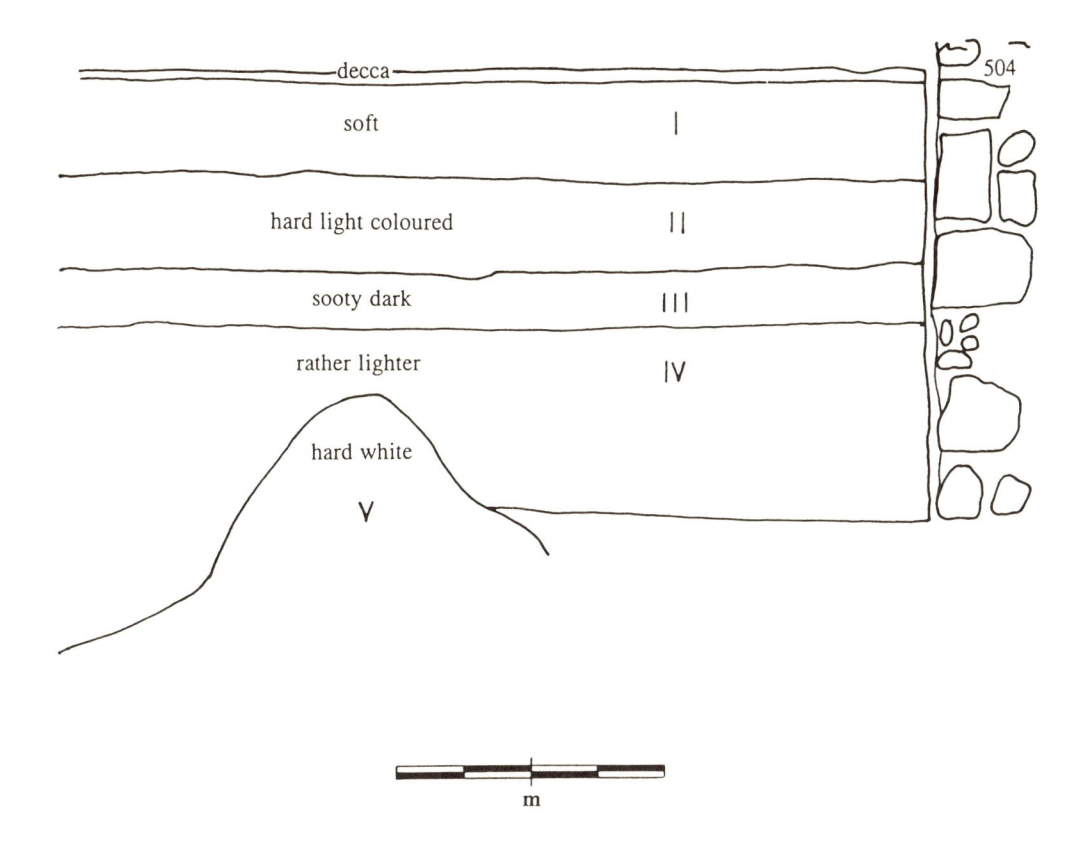

```
———decca———
    soft           I
——————————————
hard light coloured  II
——————————————
  sooty dark      III
——————————————
 rather lighter    IV

   hard white
        V
```

Segment 504.508.509.510
<— W   E —>
View toward North
fig. 66

In short, the cumulative information pertaining to Room *l* suggests that the matrix described as the PP 7 destruction debris appears confined to the more northerly portion of that room, at least somewhere north of the hypothetical extension of the scarp line discussed in relation to Room *e*. In the present sector of rooms, this rock ledge seems to lie very near the outside corner of Walls 560-562 on fig. 56. For purposes of a working plan, I have continued the established scarp line in *e* eastward at an angle that agrees with its more westerly position.

1b) Stratigraphic Detail: *Multiple-feature Segments*

Judging from the provenance data associated with three of the PP 7 segments, these strips of excavation ran through several distinct architectural units or rooms located within Summit Strips Qk and Qn. Together, these areas yielded over two-thirds (67.6%) of the published PP 7 repertoire. The first two segments focus once again on the irregularly built rooms situated north of the rock scarp that defined the central summit plateau (Rooms *e, f, g, h, j, l*; fig. 56). The final coordinate group deals with two in the series of better-constructed rooms that appear to have lined the northern perimeter of the main summit and to have enclosed the large, central courtyard area (Rooms *hq* and *kq*).

a. 120.121.19.126 (Published Section EF; *AIS-I*, figs. 5-7 and 10)

[i] Rooms *e, f, g,* and *kq*

In view of the rooms assigned to this segment in the field notes, the germane deposits appear to have been excavated in a northeasterly direction across Summit Strip Qk, starting in Room *e* and continuing through Rooms *g* and *f*. At this point, therefore, it is difficult to understand how Room *kq*, whose nearest corner lay a good six meters south of this line, figures in the layout of this area of exposure. As Table 46 shows, Kenyon retrieved most of the pottery in her PP 7 group from this segment (16 of 37 pieces = 43.2%) and, within this collection, three-quarters of the fragments came from Room *g* alone. Here the pottery derives from Layers VI-VIII and two associated subdeposits, with the heaviest concentration relating to Layer VI (6 of 12 entries). The two fragments ascribed to Rooms *e* and *f* also came from Layer VI. Thus one sees that Segment *120.121.19.126* represents a very significant excavation area by which to assess Kenyon's reconstruction of the Assyrian destruction level at the site and that, within this segment, the depositional nature of Layer VI will become a key factor to consider.

I have encountered layers associated with this segment on two previous occasions. The first came in my earlier treatment of PP 2, where 7 ceramic fragments came from Levels XII, XIII, and various subdeposits that lay between Omri's Enclosure Wall 161 and Ahab's Inner Casemate Wall 556.[61] The second encounter came earlier in the present study, in my accounting of floor levels attributed to PP 4. Though numerous problems attended the available records for that period, Kenyon assigned two ceramic pieces to various walls and another fragment to Layer IX.[62] Also, in my consideration of the putative Pit *i* deposit (PP 6), I have shown that one of the two coordinate sets ascribed to that feature, namely *122.126.19.121*, actually extended from the pit area northward into Room *g*. The close affiliation between the coordinate numbers of that strip and those in the present Segment *120.121.19.126* concurs nicely with the oblique orientation of the latter across the layers situated just north of Room *h* and Pit *i*.[63]

---

[61] *AIS-I*, 105-06, 111, 114, 118-19, 123-24. The pottery includes: *SS III*, Fig. 3:3, 11, 21, 28, 29, 35, 36.

[62] *SS III*, Fig. 6:1, 24, 39.

[63] A roughly drawn field plan available in *Fieldbook Qk-l-m*, 1a, has confirmed all these judgments (see fig. 12 in Chapter I). (When analyzing this plan in the fieldbook itself, one must note that the compass

PP 7: HOUSE FLOORS — STRATIGRAPHY

SS III Published Figure	Registry No. (* = marked for discard)	Strip	Coordinates	Feature	Local Layer
11:1	QX 117	Q(x)-k	120.121.19.126	‡Room *g*	VII
11:2	QX 120	Q(x)-k	120.121.19.126	Room *kq*	V
11:5	QX 118	Q(x)-k	120.121.19.126	Room *kq*	VII
11:7	QX 112	Q(x)-k	120.121.19.126	‡Room *g*	VII
11:9	QX 125	Q(x)-k	120.121.19.126	‡Room *g*	VIw
11:10	QX 126	Q(x)-k	120.121.19.126	Room *g*	VI
11:14	*Q 2305	Qk	120.121.19.126	‡Room *g*	VIIe
11:18	QX 128	Q(x)-k	120.121.19.126	‡Room *e*	VI
11:19	QX 129	Q(x)-k	120.121.19.126	Room *f*	VI
11:20	QX 130	Q(x)-k	120.121.19.126	‡Room *g*	VI
11:24	QX 111	Q(x)-k	120.121.19.126	Room *g*	VI
11:27	QX 110	Q(x)-k	120.121.19.126	Room *g*	VIII
11:32	QX 133	Q(x)-k	120.121.19.126	Room *g*	VI
11:34	QX 316	Q(x)-n	120.121.19.126	Room *g*	VI
11:36	QX 131	Q(x)-k	120.121.19.126	Room *g*	VII
11:37	QX 132	Q(x)-k	120.121.19.126	Room *g*	VI

‡ Room assignments corrected from Room *f* (see notation in Appendix A)

Provenance Data:
PP7 Pottery from Segment 120.121.19.126

Table 46

The excavators plotted Segment *120.121.19.126* in Summit Strip Qk just west of *North of Test Trench 2*. Rather than including section drawings of the earliest deposits in *120.121.19.126*,[64] Kenyon chose simply to correlate these layers with those found in the adjacent *N of TT2*, where she did complete field sketches of the local stratigraphy.[65] In the principal section relating to the latter area,[66] Kenyon understood Layer IX as the floor of a small Israelite room, and she assigned that level to her "Period IV" on the reasoning that it overlay the remains of BP III Wall 160 (which had, in turn, rested directly on Omri's truncated Wall 161). Beneath the floor, the darkish makeup (Layer X in *120.121.19.126*) also contained mainly PP 4 pottery and corresponded to the brown colored soil of Layer IX in *N of TT2*. Prior to this, Segment

---

orientations are reversed, with south at the top and east on the left-hand side of the drawing.)

[64]Kenyon's discussion of the local stratigraphy in *120.121.19.126* appears in *Fieldbook Qk-l-m*, 2-3, 28-31; for her stratigraphic summary, see 2a, 3a, 28a.

[65]See *AIS-I*, 105-06 and fig. 6 (p. 22).

[66]*AIS-I*, fig. 6 (= fig. 71 in the present study).

120.121.19.126 showed principally fill deposits with no sign of a clear counterpart to Kenyon's suggested "Period I" floor level in *N of TT2* (Layer XIV).[67]

While the fieldbooks did not present the earliest layers of *120.121.19.126* in section, the one drawing that did appear in those records includes the levels of principal concern to us at this point (Layers VI-VIII).[68] This lateral cut ran across Room *g*, between coordinate Walls 19 and 120,[69] both of which clearly postdate all the presently relevant deposits. On the easternmost side of the drawing there appears a row of flat paving stones that undoubtedly represent the flooring of the adjacent BP V Room *j*.

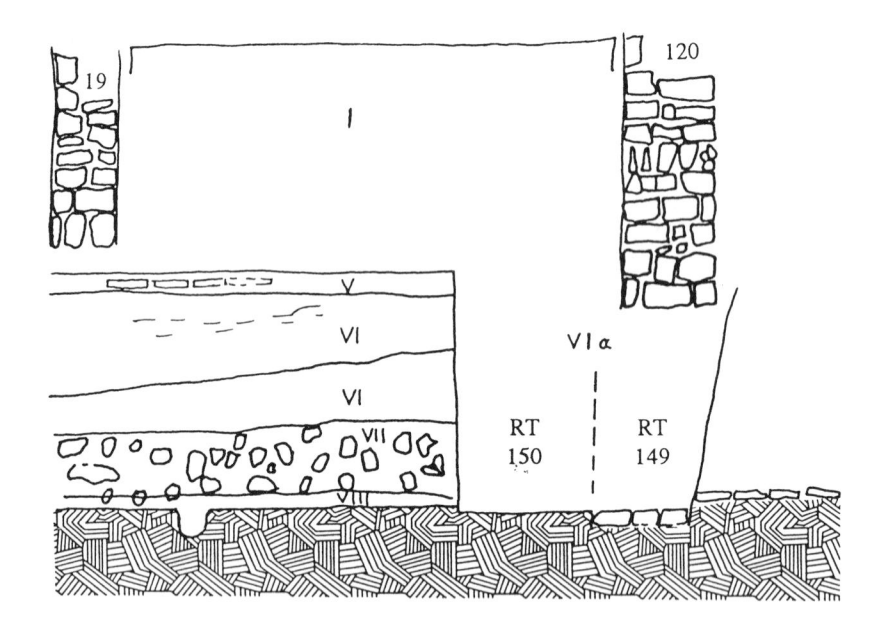

(scale not recorded)

Segment *120.121.19.126* — Room *g*
(formerly fig. 9)
< — W E — >
View toward North
fig. 67

I have already discussed the details of the local stratigraphy seen in this drawing (see pp. 20-27 in Chapter I), beginning with the scant remains (recorded as Layer IX

---

[67] I have elsewhere argued against viewing *N of TT2*, Layer XIV, as a surface of any kind (*AIS-I*, 23, 37-43, 50-52).

[68] *Fieldbook Qk-l-m*, 29a.

[69] As seen in fig. 12, coordinate Wall 126 lay north of this section, while Wall 121 undoubtedly rested to the south.

PP 7: HOUSE FLOORS — STRATIGRAPHY

but not drawn in section) of a burnt plaster floor resting beneath Layer VIII and very near the rock surface.[70] A midden-like deposit identified as Layer VIII overlay this apparent floor. The field notes indicate that this debris measured .20 m in thickness,[71] though it does not appear so in fig. 67. Workers retrieved the jar rim fragment of hard, reddish ware seen in *SS III*, Fig. 11:27 from this level. While Kenyon assigned this layer to her "Period VII," she described it as "all part of VI, Period V filling" in her abstract of levels.[72] Above this lay the rubble-filled matrix of Layer VII. As noted in my earlier discussion,[73] Kenyon wrote in her field record that she detected traces of a distinct Layer VIIa among the basal striations of VII, at a level where its larger rubble matrix showed more of the "middenish" quality of VIII. Since I found no field note reference to a subdeposit called "Layer VIIe," it seems possible that the provenance data for the red-slipped bowl rim in *SS III*, Fig. 11:14 should read VIIa instead of VIIe. This fragment embodies the only piece in the PP 7 group ascribed to VIIe, and it is the only one marked for discard in the field registries.

Two substantially thicker deposits of cleaner fill lay above VII and received the collective identification of Layer VI. These fillings provided a smooth, level, building surface for the hard floor of yellow-colored clay (Layer V),[74] which did not remain intact across the entire area of Room *g*. Importantly, Kenyon dated this surface to her "Period VIII" and added that it sealed the "walls of Period III, [and] the Period VII filling of the little rooms."[75] This sealing means that one must find the alleged destruction debris created by the full-scale Assyrian attack in the underlying deposits of VI-VIII. Judging from the presentation of these deposits in the unpublished dig records, however, they do not resemble the remains of battle. Rather, they appear as routine fillings designed simply to level up the area for the next phase of construction (reflected in Layer V), which, judging from Kenyon's field drawing, appears to have incorporated a series of flat-lying field stones similar to the style of floor in Room *j* to the east.[76]

The case also emerges that these layers disclose a sequence of varied activities — starting with the plaster floor that one should somehow relate to Layer VIII (whose "midden" may actually have included some secure occupational debris), followed by Layers VIIa, VII, and then *two* distinct episodes recorded as one in Layer VI — all of which transpired before the construction of the "BP VIII" surface in Layer V. The

---

[70]*Fieldbook Qk-l-m*, 28. Though this floor is not shown on the field section, the notes later refer to it as Layer IX.

[71]*Fieldbook Qk-l-m*, 28.

[72]*Fieldbook Qk-l-m*, 3a.

[73]See p. 26, n. 38.

[74]Recall Kenyon's method of dating a floor level by the materials found beneath it.

[75]*Fieldbook Qk-l-m*, 2a.

[76]Compare the paving sandwiched between Layers V and IVa in *N of TT2* (*AIS-I*, 22, fig. 6).

deposits presented here do not reflect a one-time distribution of now consolidated destruction debris. Even if Layer VII reflects some kind of intentional disturbance, whether local or site-wide as Kenyon would prefer, the succeeding deposits of VI look very much like the many deep fillings already witnessed in numerous other areas along the declining northern slopes of the site.

My fig. 67 also discloses that the workers found all these layers preserved only in the western portion of Room *g*. In the eastern half of that small unit, the late plundering of Walls 149 (BP V) and 150 destroyed all traces of these deposits and left only the backfill of Layer VIa,[77] which Kenyon placed in her "R.4" period (fourth century CE). Other than this subsequent event and the construction of Walls 19 and 120 during the "R.3" phase in the late second century CE, it remains difficult to assess with any confidence the deposits that came stratigraphically later than the floor level seen in Layer V. This situation prevails even though Kenyon's unpublished abstract of levels includes the following principal PP 9 accumulations, together with multiple sub-deposits: the .30 m-thick, hard Layer IV; the yellowish clay surface of Layer III; the hard but poor remains of a dekka floor in Layer II; and a "fairly g[oo]d dekka floor" in Layer I. For reasons unknown, however, she failed to delineate any of these layers (except possibly level I) in the only field section preserved in her unpublished records for Segment *120.121.19.126* (fig. 67).

I noted earlier that, if taken at face value, fig. 67 suggests that the same imported soil that filled the breaches created by Robber Trenches 149 and 150 also covered a substantial section of the floor in Layer V. Kenyon's own private observations raise further questions in this regard. Her field notes record that, "as far as can be seen, [there is] really all one level for [the] top 1.50 m, [with] sloping streaks of black."[78] Moreover, one reads that "the filling of this room is really diff[erent] on W. [and] on E. sides, [therefore] the room was apparently filled [with] the streaky soot [and] hard yellow soil *before* the E. wall was robbed (RT 149)."[79]

In short, the depositional history witnessed here seems congruent with a need to level up considerably the steep slopes that characterized the northern side of the site. Response to this need certainly seems the nature of Layer VI (and probably also VII),[80] from which most of the PP 7 assemblage derived. And while numerous robber trenches crisscross this entire area, I can anchor none of them securely to an Assyrian military invasion in 722/21 BCE. As a result of factors such as these, however, the excavators

---

[77]The field records include a number of subdeposits relating to the fill of these robber trenches, including (from earliest to latest) sub-Layers VIIp, VIy, VIh, VIa, VIS.E., Vp, IVp, IIIp, IIp, and possibly Ip, although this last matrix may have constituted part of the Foundation Trench for Wall 120, dated to the "R.3" period (late second century CE). Additional foundation trench deposits for Walls 19 and 120 were labeled Layers I-IIIr, It, Iz, I-V, IVr, and VIx (see *Fieldbook Qk-l-m*, 2a-3a).

[78]*Fieldbook Qk-l-m*, 28.

[79]*Fieldbook Qk-l-m*, 29 (emphasis added).

[80]As for the shallow bowl taken from sub-Layer VIw and presented in *SS III*, Fig. 11:9, I need note only that the field records equate this deposit with the principal Layer VI.

encountered few primary stratigraphic contexts in these roughly-built rooms situated below the north-central rock scarp and summit area.

The main PP 7 level in this area, Layer VI, represents routinely imported fill and probably also some of the makeup used in floor level V. Since that surface sealed the surviving portion of Layers VI-VIII beneath it, the latest materials found in those deposits (especially Layer VI) can assist in setting the *terminus post quem* (or construction date) for Surface V and the *terminus ante quem* (or latest use date) for the overall pottery group contained in VI-VIII. Only the *terminus post quem*, or earliest use date, of that pottery must remain open.

b. 509.126 (Published Section EF; *AIS I*, figs. 5, 8a, and Table 2)

[i] Rooms *f*, *j*, and *l*

Although *509.126* takes us once again out of Summit Strip Qk and back to the area of Room *l* in Qn, it nonetheless remains in the general precinct of service buildings situated north of and below the main summit. I shall, therefore, offer my final comments on this segment before returning to Strip Qk to complete my look at the excavation of summit Rooms *hq* and *kq*.

As indicated, the PP 7 remains assigned to Segment *509.126* reportedly came from three laterally adjoining chambers: Rooms *f*, *j*, and *l*. While there are no anomalies in this line of progression (contrast the case of Room *kq* in the previous discussion), the inclusion of Room *l* in this group merits several observations. First, this unit technically lies outside (east of) the parameters of the surviving Israelite deposits as outlined in *Samaria-Sebaste I* (449°-64° N x 638°-46° E).[81] Second, the apparent eastward extension of this segment renders it the only one thus far encountered to have spanned more than one so-called Summit Strip (in this case, Strips k and n). Third, the space identified in Kenyon's Phase Plan (fig. 56) as Room *l* appears very different in character from the "rooms" discussed in other segments. For example, it is much larger in size, it exhibits a relatively peculiar shape, and the walls that enclose it display a noticeable lack of uniformity in terms of their widths and overall construction techniques. Nearly one-fifth of the overall PP 7 pottery came from this putative room (seven of 37 pieces = 19%, with four of these fragments deriving from Segment *509.126*), and over one-third (35.1%) of the entire assemblage originated in the spaces outlined by Rooms *l* and *e*. I have already shown that Room *e* also basically lay outside the defined field of excavation and that its entire area showed signs of significant disturbance.

The depositional history of this segment has received a rather extensive review in my consideration of Pottery Periods 1, 2,[82] 4, and 5.[83] To these excerpts I may now

---

[81] *SS III*, 110.

[82] For PP 1-2, see *AIS-I*, 19-21, 104-05.

[83] For PP 4-5, see pp. 48-55 and 202-206 of the present study.

add the discussion here in PP 7 of the contiguous segment in *504.503.509.508* (see Section c.i above, figs. 60-63, 65-66).[84] These earlier probes into *509.126* raised a question as to its precise bearings (see pp. 50-52). At least some of the pottery extracted from this segment clearly bore the label "Room *j*" (as in SS III, Fig. 6:32 - PP 4). Yet the segment must have run some distance west of that room, since one of its coordinate features (Wall 126) appears on published Section EF immediately above Wall 138, which itself separates Rooms *g* and *f* (fig. 56). Yet from other descriptions found in the unpublished field records,[85] this part of the excavations also appears to have extended eastward across the entire lateral extent of the northern half of both Rooms *l* and *m* and to have reached very near Wall 561.[86]

Within this margin of uncertainty, I have found that the only notation of "Layer IIa.f," from which the excavators supposedly removed most of the PP 7 materials published from this segment, indicates that this particular level rested in the very northwestern corner of Room *l*, somewhere quite close to the edges of Segment *504.503.509.508*. Among the several sketches recorded in the *509.126* section of the field notes, only one includes a depiction of this layer, and I have presented this drawing in fig. 64 above. Judging from the location of Wall 555 within that section, Layer IIa.f. ran from the northern face of that feature toward the line of the inner Casemate Wall 556. It therefore lay at the extreme northern edge of the royal compound and virtually right against the city wall. Generally, both the presentation and position of this matrix suggests that it reflects a rather substantial deposit of secondary fill used as leveling material in this area of declining bedrock. Its overall location must resemble that of the stratigraphy portrayed at the northern end of published Section EF, where multiple layers of local accumulations received only a generic designation, "VII." All other published sections based on cuts made through strips of earth in nearby areas, e.g., Section CD, show just how extensively the later Hellenistic and Roman quarrying and leveling operations disturbed the general space north of the central summit plateau.

The final report attributed three of the PP 7 fragments from *509.126* to Layer IIa.f. (SS III, Fig. 11:16, 21, and 26), while including only one additional sherd that apparently came from Layer VIII in this segment (SS III, Fig. 11:29). That some of these forms, such as the bowls in Fig. 11:16 and 21 (probably also the holemouth jar in No. 29), appear to derive from earlier ceramic traditions than do many of the other PP 7 materials should alert us to the possibility that the matrix from which these items came will once again typify imported, secondary fill. If so, the *terminus post quem* must remain open for the assemblage of artifacts yielded by this deposit.

Besides the rather circumscribed field section in fig. 64, perhaps the most useful data in assessing the nature of the relevant local stratigraphy in *509.126* comes in the

---

[84]Pp. 367-75.

[85]Kenyon's unpublished field records pertaining to this segment appear in *Fieldbook Qn (Vol. I)*, 34-38, and *Fieldbook Qn (Vol. II)*, 102-06.

[86]See the positioning of units δ and ε (which represent Segment *509.126*) in *AIS-I*, 17, fig 4.

form of the stratigraphic correlations that Kenyon herself drew with deposits in other segments of the excavation.[87] Within this area, the field notes describe principal Layer IIa as a yellow floor that sealed the "Period VII" filling. Importantly, they continue by noting that this level should equal Layer V in Segment *120.121.19.126* (described above). At one point in the fieldnotes, the following observation occurs regarding IIa: "floor sealing IIa.f . . . apparently contains H[ellensitic] pottery, but this poss[ibly] a mistake."[88]

Layer IIa.f., in turn, represents the rubble situated beneath Floor IIa. If this surface did, in fact, contain samples of pottery from the Hellenistic period, then both it and the subfloor makeup may stem from construction activities that postdate the Israelite occupation by a considerable span of time. In her abstract of levels, Kenyon also states that IIa.f. consisted in "pure Per. VII filling" and that it contained "much VI hard ware, with poss. VII nns."[89] While the precise meaning of the last abbreviation remains impenetrable, the recognition of a certain mixture of PP 6 and 7 materials in this context militates against seeing a sharp break between the ceramic traditions of these two periods as suggested by Kenyon in the final report.

As for Layer VIII, which contributed only a single jar rim to the PP 7 group, the unpublished notes instruct us to accept a correlation with both Layer Va of Segment *504.503.509.508* and Layer IIa.f. just mentioned. I have already outlined my belief that the former deposit (Va) exemplifies a much later pouring of imported fill against the face of Wall 555 (see Section c.i above).

c. W of 124 (Published Section EF; *AIS-I*, figs. 6, 8c, and 10)

[i] Rooms *hq* and *kq*

Finally, I return to the highlighted area of Summit Strip Qk on fig. 56, but now to what I believe constituted rooms that enjoyed a more official status as part of the royal complex situated atop the rock scarp on the summit proper. The provenance data relating to the five ceramic fragments published from *W of 124*[90] indicate that this segment ran laterally through Rooms *hq* and *kq*. One may recall that, perhaps more important than the pottery found here, this locality also apparently yielded 18 publishable fragments of ivory. It is important, then, to situate as precisely as possible both the overall segment on the horizontal plane of excavations and the area's local stratigraphy

---

[87] See Kenyon's abstract of levels in *Qn (Vol. I)*, 35a, 37a, and 38a.

[88] *Fieldbook Qn (Vol. II)*, 104a.

[89] *Fieldbook Qn (Vol. I)*, 35a.

[90] The fieldnotes pertaining to the Segment *W of 124* appear in *Fieldbook Qk-l-m*, 10-11, 20-23, 44-46. Stratigraphic summaries occur in *Qk-l-m*, 10a-11a, 20a-22a. I also found section drawings made in the field in *Qk-l-m*, 10a, 23a, and 46a. The position of this area also receives some clarification in relationship to segments *N of TT2* and *Btw TT2-TT3* in another drawing on p. 41a.

within the vertical axis of cultural remains. The urgency of this effort increases now due to the fact that in my first, brief encounter in PP 5 (Chapter II) of the excavation area designated *W of 124*, I noted some confusion in records pertaining to the location of the area and to the one piece of cultural remains published from it (*SS III*, Fig. 8:1).

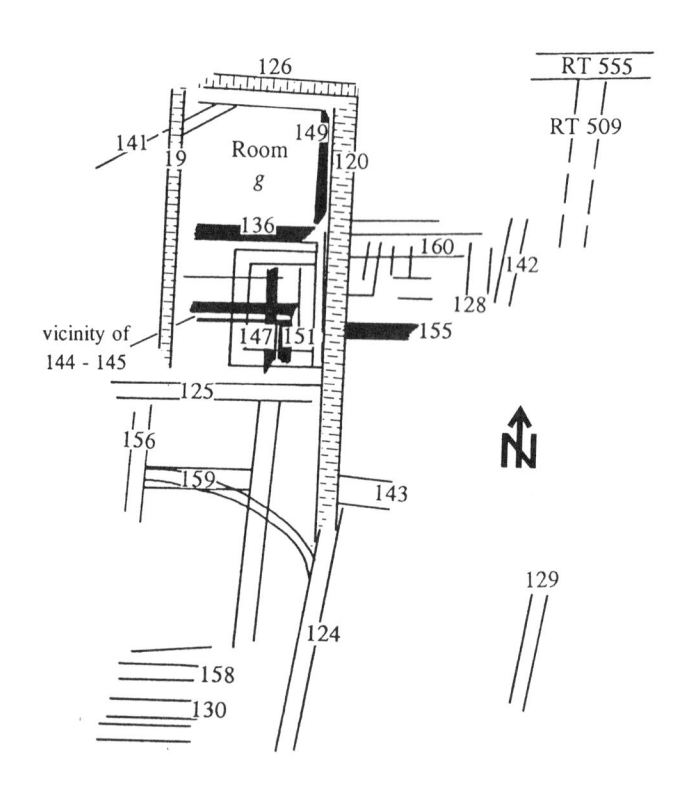

Location of Wall 124 and the Segment West of 124
(formerly fig. 12)
fig. 68

As witnessed in fig. 68,[91] the coordinate Wall 124 basically extended southward from Wall 120, which constituted an identifying feature of the first segment treated in this chapter. Wall 120, in turn, rested immediately east of Wall 149, which provided the eastern boundary of Room *g* and the Pit *i* area. As a result, I can confidently place Wall 124 and, by extension, the segment ***West of 124***, in the westernmost sector of

---

[91]*Fieldbook Qk-l-m*, 1a.

PP 7: HOUSE FLOORS — STRATIGRAPHY

original Room *kq*, not very far from the eastern face of Wall 132 (see fig. 56). Hardly any of Room *kq* actually survived the heavy Roman quarrying in the area (see fig. 70 below). One can anticipate, therefore, that the stratigraphic contexts claimed by the pottery and ivories from Room *hq* will prove more reliable than those associated with the few pieces attributed to *kq*.

Unfortunately, the local deposits in *W of 124* are not well represented among the various unpublished section drawings found in the field notebooks. The three complicated drawings that do exist relate either to Walls 125a-b, which I have shown rested above Wall 56 on the north side of Rooms *hq* and *kq*, or to Wall 132, which divides these two chambers.[92]

The first of these field sections (fig. 69) shows some of the latest layers recorded on the stratigraphic summary sheets in the notebooks. Robber Trench 130 and the remnant of Wall 133 are visible on the south side of this cut; in her field notes, Kenyon dated both features to the Late Hellenistic period. Between them and the wall series involving 125b, 125a, and 125 on the north, one sees several depositional layers

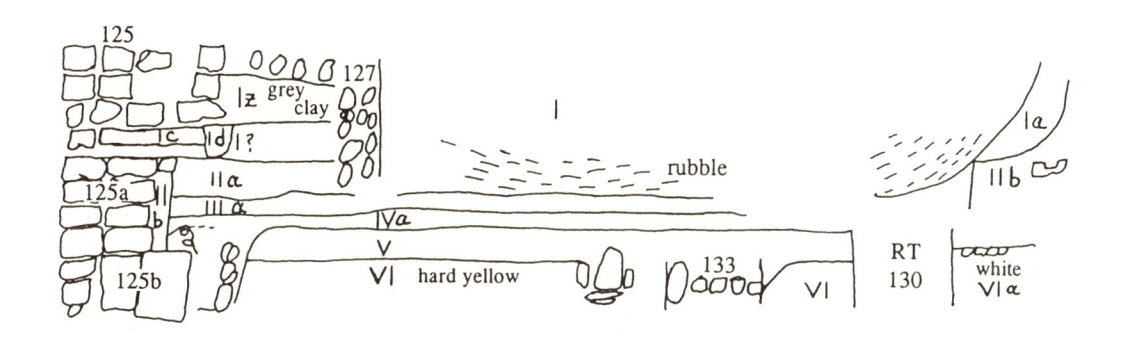

(scale not recorded)

Segment W of 124 — South of Walls 56 and the 125 Series
<— N S —>
View toward East (into Room *kq*)
fig. 69

that remain partially intact. My comments shall begin with Layer IIa, described as "hard floor, cut by 125a," though the notes also allow that the deposit may have "run up against it" at points.[93] Kenyon tentatively dated this surface to Period "VIII(?)." As

---

[92] I have based my figs. 69, 70, and 71 on these field drawings, which appear in *Fieldbook Qk-l-m*, 10a, 46a, and 41a, respectively.

[93] *Fieldbook Qk-l-m*, 11a.

depicted in this section, the Foundation Trench (IIb) of Wall 125a clearly seems to have cut level IIa. But when describing that trench, the field notes once again allow for a situation in which "IIb = F.T. of 125a (?L.H.) in IIa (poss.)."[94] Judging from fig. 69 on the preceding page, Foundation Trench IIb cut through two additional layers, IIIa and IVa. Kenyon explains the former as a "hardish level *c.* .15 m thick, beneath IIa"[95] but proposes a curious dating of "? P. IX" for both IIIa and IVa. This suggestion, of course, does not seem to correlate well with her proposed origin for IIa in "Period VIII," since Level IIa is stratigraphically later than IIIa.

Layer V consisted in a light-colored, unconsolidated matrix that included a good deal of clay.[96] Kenyon believed that it "probably" stemmed from "Period VIII." Beneath this rested Level VI, a "hard floor, .25 m below V, [which] crosses [the] broken top of 125b."[97] According to Kenyon's interpretation, this floor level belonged to "Period VII." Layer VIw, where workers found the two bowl rims in *SS III*, Fig. 11:11 and 13, represented that portion of Layer VI which may have been disturbed by the construction of the Late Hellenistic Wall 133.

A second field section (fig. 70) relevant to my investigation of the segment lying *W of 124* confirms that ancient builders set this coordinate wall parallel to and extremely close to the various phases of Wall 132, which separates Room *hq* from *kq*. It also shows that the area inside Room *kq* almost immediately succumbed to extensive quarrying activities by the Romans. Several additional layers appear to match the deposits from which excavators removed various fragments of the PP 7 ceramic group. For example, both Layers IIIc and Vc seem to rest beneath the later rebuilds of Walls 124b and 132E. Respectively, these deposits yielded the bowl rims presented in *SS III*, Fig. 11:3 and 8. The field notes report that IIIc consisted in a matrix of "mixed soot and hard yellow" that lay beneath the R.3 (late second century CE) Wall 124a.[98] Robber Trench 130 (seen in the previous section) also cut this layer, which Kenyon dated to "Period VII" though it contained samples of later ribbed-ware pottery forms. She understood Layer Vc, on the other hand, to represent a floor level beneath 132E. Importantly, she dated that surface to BP V and noted that the overall character of the pottery seemed "fairly early" and that the repertoire included some PP 4 types.[99] (In light of this observation, it is ironic that the only ceramic piece she published from this layer consists in the late [sixth-century?] bowl rim in No. 8.)

West of Wall 132W, in Room *hq* proper, one sees in fig. 70 two layers labeled VI and VIII. I have already observed that, in her summary of layers, Kenyon identified VI as a hard surface resting a quarter meter below V. She called Layer VIII another

---

[94] *Fieldbook Qk-l-m*, 20a.

[95] *Fieldbook Qk-l-m*, 20a.

[96] *Fieldbook Qk-l-m*, 21a.

[97] *Fieldbook Qk-l-m*, 21a.

[98] *Fieldbook Qk-l-m*, 20a.

[99] *Fieldbook Qk-l-m*, 21a.

PP 7: HOUSE FLOORS — STRATIGRAPHY

"decca floor" and dated it to "Period V."[100] This surface, she recorded, rested beneath Layer VII, which is not shown on her drawing. The field notes, however, call VII a deposit of "softer earth .15 m beneath VI."[101] Though it does not actually receive an identifying label in fig. 70, then, Layer VII would appear to have constituted a thin accumulation of either occupational debris associated with the putative floor of VIII[102] or a small amount of makeup connected to the basal striations of surface VI. In any event, this deposit yielded the Assyrian-style bowl published in *SS III*, Fig. 11:22, and I have already mentioned in my introduction to this chapter the importance of this particular piece to Kenyon's unequivocal interpretation of PP 7 as a thick blanket of destruction debris from the 722/21 BCE Assyrian sacking of Samaria.

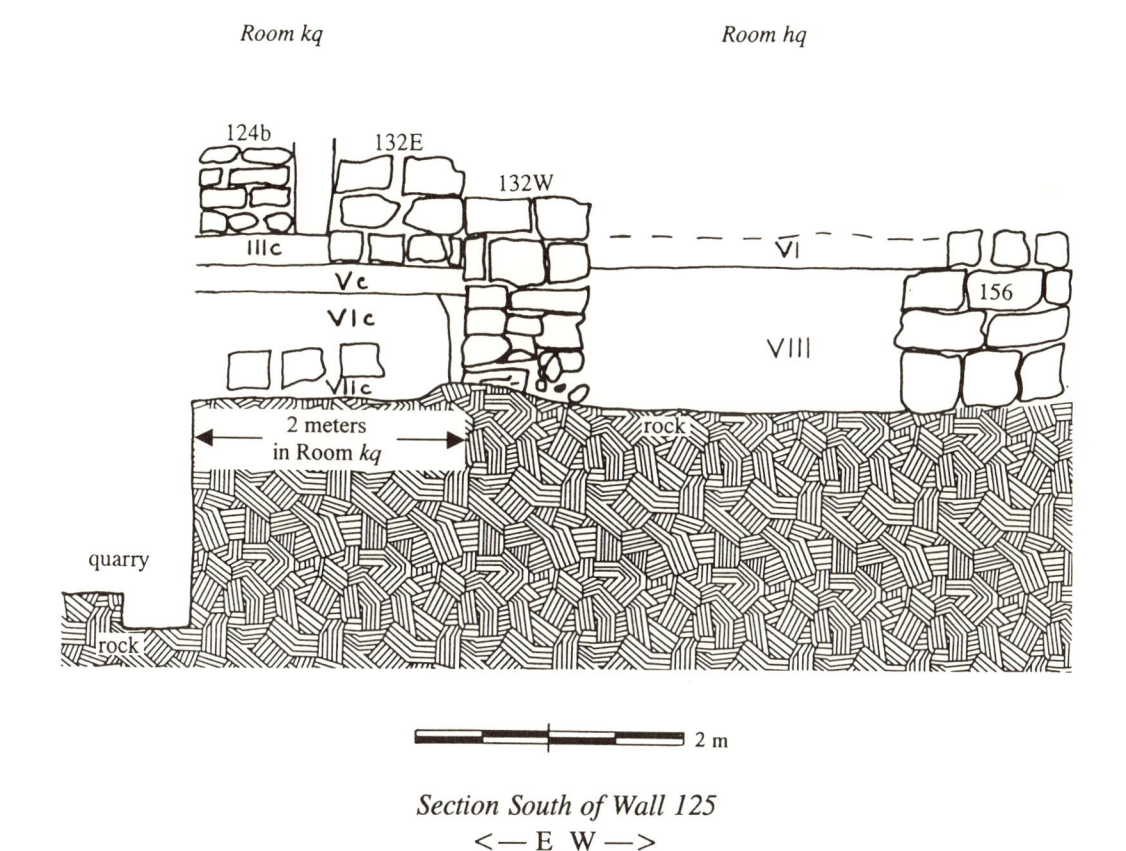

Section South of Wall 125
<— E   W —>
View toward South (mostly in Room *hq*)
fig. 70

---

[100] *Fieldbook Qk-l-m*, 22a.

[101] *Fieldbook Qk-l-m*, 22a.

[102] Judging from fig. 70, Layer VIII seems to represent a rather thick deposit of imported fill more than it does a compacted floor level.

Finally, I return to a section presented earlier, since it also speaks to certain layers in the segment *W of 124* and shows their spatial relationship to many of the deposits that I have discussed in both *AIS-I* and the present study. In this drawing (fig. 71), one can see that the bedrock declines sharply north of the line of Wall 125b and even more so north of Omri's original Enclosure Wall 161. Over the course of my two investigations, I have addressed virtually every layer presented in those two areas. Now I come to the few layers resting on the higher rock south of the 125 series of walls. These layers once again extend south as far as Robber Trench 130, which ran across at least Room *hq* and probably into the surviving strata of *kq* as well.

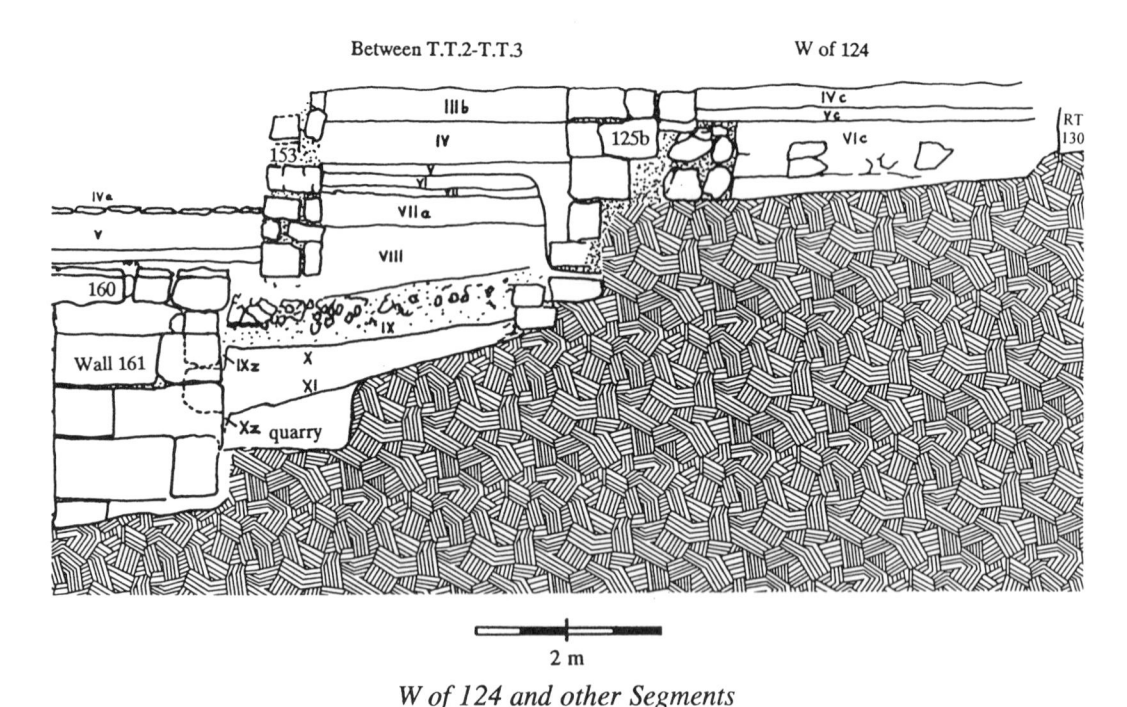

W of 124 and other Segments
<— N   S —>
View toward East
fig. 71

The field notes describe Layer IVc as the Late Hellenistic Wall 132E and the earth mixed up with it. They also note that this deposit included some fragments of ivory.[103] The floor level of Layer Vc, which I just introduced in fig. 70, runs north and actually laps up over at least one early phase of the 125 series of walls. The field notes treat Layer VIc, which rests directly on the rock in this area, as another floor beneath Vc, and they date this level tentatively to "Period IV."[104] From the depiction

---

[103] *Fieldbook Qk-l-m*, 21a.

[104] *Fieldbook Qk-l-m*, 21a.

in this drawing, however, one may question whether VIc actually constituted a floor level versus a modest deposit of rubble and fill. While another level seems to have existed beneath VIc in fig. 71, Kenyon did not identify it with a separate layer designation.

At least two conclusions follow from this survey of stratigraphy in the area *W of 124*. First, in my estimation, none of the layers that contributed pottery to the PP 7 group resembles *in situ* destruction debris that might have resulted from a single, massive conflagration. Second, whether or not they bear any relationship to a military campaign, the layers from which excavators drew the PP 7 pottery do not constitute a coherent, thick deposit that covers the entire area as Kenyon suggested. Instead, one sees a series of floor levels and their associated makeup, some possible occupational debris lying directly on other surfaces, pit fills, etc. Judging from Kenyon's own descriptions and assigned dates, a stratigraphic portrait for the segment *W of 124* emerges as follows:

Wall	Floor	Makeup	Fill	DATE
	VIc			IV
	Vc †			V
	VIII			V
		IIIc †		VII
	VI			VII
			VIw †	VII
	VII †			VII
	IIa			VIII
			V	VIII
	IIIa			IX
			IIb	L.H.
IVc				L.H.

(† = layers yielding fragments published with the PP 7 ceramic group)

Stratigraphic Summary of Layers West of 124

Table 47

This picture concurs generally with situations found in other segments of the excavation plotted along the north side of the central courtyard and then beyond the first major decline in the rock. This drop ran, perhaps somewhat erratically, between the two complexes of rooms presented in fig. 56, with the smaller, more irregularly designed and constructed chambers (*f, g, h, i, j, k, hk*) and the somewhat enigmatic *l* resting below the summit plateau, which demarcated the royal compound proper.

2) Pottery Analysis

The Pottery Period 7 assemblage concentrates on two principal categories of vessels: bowls of various types and jars. Together, these two classes of goods constitute 86.5% of the overall group of fragments published from the debris covering the floors of the BP V rooms. Once again, a methodological question emerges as to just how adequately a meager sampling of only one or two classes of goods can support the chronology and sweeping historical conclusions concerning a given period or event. The spatial distribution of each vessel type across the various rooms discussed above and presented in fig. 56 appears below.

	bowls	cooking pots	jars & jar stands	jugs	lamps	TOTAL
Service Rooms:						
Room *e*	5	-	-	1	-	6
Room *f*	2	-	-	-	-	2
Room *g*	6	1	2	1	2	12
Room *hk*	-	-	2	-	-	2
Room *j*	-	-	1	-	-	1
Room *l*	3	-	4	-	-	7
Summit Rooms:						
Room *hq*	3	-	-	-	-	3
Room *kq*	4	-	-	-	-	4
TOTAL	23	1	9	2	2	37

Distribution of PP 7 Ceramic Forms
Published from Debris Reportedly Covering the BP V House Floors

Table 48

As Table 48 shows, certain patterns of retrieval begin to appear when one catalogues the data in this way. First, nearly one-third of the entire collection came from Room *g* alone (32.4%). Excavators retrieved the majority of bowls (56.5%) from a southwest-to-northeast field of excavation that ran through Rooms *e, g,* and *f.* In a similar manner, most of the jars (77.7%) and related forms (e.g., a jar stand) stem from a parallel track of excavation that lay a bit farther east and that ran through

Rooms *hk*, *j*, and *l*. When combined, then, the segments that made up these two paths of exposure yielded 81.1% of all the goods published in support of an Assyrian military destruction of Samaria. These areas focus entirely on the smaller rooms situated below the rock scarp that defined the northern edge of the summit proper.

The only other "concentration" of published pottery consists in a group of seven bowls taken from the contiguous Rooms *hq* and *kq*. But the final report included no other vessel types from this important area. This situation is unfortunate, since these two architectural units appear to have comprised part of the official buildings of the central summit area and since *hq* seems better preserved (note its perimeter walls) than most of the other chambers discovered by the Joint Expedition. A further vexation that stems from access to such a limited ceramic repertoire from these two rooms lies in one's reduced ability to clarify with greater certainty the date of many of the ivory fragments found at the site (particularly those taken from the segment *W of 124*).

a. Bowls

The collection of PP 7 bowls presented in the final report seems somewhat eclectic in that it remains difficult to find many unifying characteristics for the overall group. The ware of the samples can occur in a grey, red, purplish-red, pinkish-red, drab or brown, light brown, buff, pale buff, or even black color fabric. Some of the wares, primarily of Nos. 1-15, exhibit a light inclusion of white, limestone grit, but this attribute seems to cross morphological lines and ultimately tells one very little. The bowls only sporadically show traces of a slip, which is often described as "drab" or simply a "self-slip." Similarly, burnishing proves relatively rare on these items, and when it does occur it generally results from a coarse, ring technique. The assemblage derives from five different segments of excavation, though most of the examples come from three of those areas. The excavators recovered a significant percentage of the group (43.5%) from Segment *120.121.19.126* alone and, within that locality, from the space inside Room *g*.[105] Various elements that derive from Assyrian or Assyrianizing traditions appear in the overall collection and play an important role in helping to establish a date for their findspots. The single trait shared by many (at least 15) of the items in the group at large, however, is the hardness of their ware, which Kenyon usually lists as a "hard ringing" or "hard thin" variety.

Despite these observations, one can organize some of these bowls into distinct morphological groups in which the specimens show only slight variations among themselves in terms of form. Kenyon herself saw this kind of relationship between entries 1-7, and that is where I shall begin my discussion of the corpus. The specific findspots for all the bowls appear in Table 49. Within that roster, I have flagged (▸) each entry for which I encountered one or more discrepancies between the various provenance data relating to that item in the unpublished records. These incongruities usually

---

[105] A summary of the distribution across segments appears as follows: *120.121.19.126* = 10 specimens; *W of 124* = 5; *19.51.14.20* = 4; *504.503.509.508* = 2; and *509.126* = 2.

involved the specific summit strip, architectural feature, or local layer to which a fragment belonged (for the exact nature of each problematic element, see Appendix A). Though the number of inconsistencies in recording remains quite high (14 of 23 entries = 60.9%), I have collated all the information contained in this table with details found on the original stratification cards managed by G. M. Crowfoot, registrar for the project, and currently stored at the Palestine Exploration Fund in London. Consequently, I currently believe all the data presented in Table 49 are correct.

SS III Published Figure	Registry No. (* = marked for discard)	Strip	Coordinates	Feature	Local Layer
▶ 11:1	QX 117	Q(x)-k	120.121.19.126	Room *g*	VII
▶ 11:2	QX 120	Q(x)-k	120.121.19.126	Room *kq*	V
11:3	QX 119	Q(x)-k	W of 124	Room *kq*	IIIc
11:4	Q 5222	Qn	504.503.509.508	Room *l*	Va
11:5	QX 118	Q(x)-k	120.121.19.126	Room *kq*	VII
11:6	Q 5221	Qn	504.503.509.508	Room *l*	Va
▶ 11:7	QX 112	Q(x)-k	120.121.19.126	Room *g*	VII
▶ 11:8	*Q 2372	Qk	W of 124	Room *kq*	Vc
▶ 11:9	QX 125	Q(x)-k	120.121.19.126	Room *g*	VIw
▶ 11:11	Q 2357a	Qk	W of 124	Room *hq*	VIw
▶ 11:12	QX 127	Q(x)-c	19.51.14.20	Room *e*	IVa
▶ 11:13	Q 2357b	Qk	W of 124	Room *hq*	VIw
▶ 11:14	*Q 2305	Qk	120.121.19.126	Room *g*	VIIe
11:15	QX 124	Q(x)-c	19.51.14.20	Room *e*	IVa
11:16	Q 5219	Qn	509.126	Room *f*	IIa.f
11:17	QX 123	Q(x)-c	19.51.14.20	Room *e*	IVa
▶ 11:18	QX 128	Q(x)-k	120.121.19.126	Room *e*	VI
11:19	QX 129	Q(x)-k	120.121.19.126	Room *f*	VI
▶ 11:20	QX 130	Q(x)-k	120.121.19.126	Room *g*	VI
▶ 11:21	Q 5235	Qn	509.126	Room *l*	IIa.f
▶ 11:22	Q 2537	Qk	W of 124	Room *hq*	VII
▶ 11:23	Q 1653	Qc	19.51.14.20	Room *e*	VIc
11:36	QX 131	Q(x)-k	120.121.19.126	Room *g*	VII

(See Appendix A for details pertaining to these recording errors)

(All information presented here now agrees with the original stratification cards)

Provenance Data:
PP7 Bowls from the Putative Destruction Debris
Covering the BP V Floors

Table 49

PP 7: HOUSE FLOORS — POTTERY

In my judgment, the published assemblage of PP 7 bowls falls into three typological subsets, with certain nuances in ware, form, and surface treatment apparent in each group. The first cluster of forms reflects a local tradition stemming from a local origin (Nos. 1-7); the second lot represents local imitations of various foreign traditions (Nos. 9, 11-15, 17, 22-23); and the third set presents a mixed collection of forms and wares, some of which reflect imitations or degenerate forms of Samaria Ware (Nos. 16, 18-21).

Kenyon described the bowls presented in *SS III*, Fig. 11:1-7 as "all near the seventh century type with thickened rim, often nearly triangular in section . . . ."[106] This subset of PP 7 vessels belongs to a rather large class of bowls that exhibit rounded sidewalls, a trait that distinguishes them from somewhat similar types with a shoulder keel (as in entry No. 1). When their bases survive, they usually assume a shallow, slightly convex ring-mode.[107] But the typology of these forms rests primarily on the construction and shape of their rims, the final forms of which often display a considerable variety in detail. Gitin has classified these attributes, when viewed in section, as oblong (Type 50A), half-moon (Type 50B), or triangular (Type 50C) in shape.[108] The last style often displays a flange on its lower outside edge.

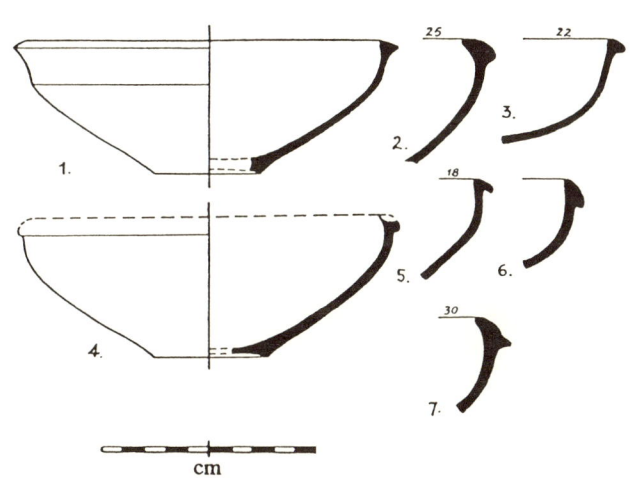

SS III, Fig. 11:1-7

Whatever nuance the final shape displays, it is generally accepted that the thickening of these rims occurred as the potter folded the upper part of the clay out and then down against the uppermost, exterior sidewall of the vessel. As a result of this technique, Wampler coined the concept "folded rim" for use with bowls that showed this rim mode at Tell en-Naṣbeh.[109] Subsequently, however, Tufnell correctly noted that one

---

[106] *SS III*, 127.

[107] This slight depression in the exterior bottom of the form proved the most durable style for use with such thin-walled construction, which required that the potter handle the vessel rather gingerly when removing it from the wheel (see Albright's comments in *TBM III*, 133, § 134).

[108] *Gezer III*, 57, 167-72. "Half-moon" is the least satisfactory of these suggested rubrics. (This classification system applies to Nos. 1-6 in the Samaria volume; for No. 7, see below.)

[109] *TN II*, 35, § 34; Pls. 57:1308-1320; 58:1321-1338. See also the sample of forms from Tell en-Naṣbeh's Cistern 370, which Wampler dated to the seventh and early sixth centuries BCE (*TN—Cistern*, 25-31; Fig. 4:x31, x24, x30, and x33).

cannot always discern the exact technique used to achieve this style without actually breaking the piece and viewing the section.[110] I should, therefore, leave open the possibility that some of these rims may have resulted from a simple thickening of the clay, not a folding of it. This seems the case with No. 1, which shows an outwardly beveled, thickened rim with flattened top. Also, I may note that not all the outwardly folded rims are pressed fully back against the side of the bowl (as in No. 5). Though all the examples presented from Samaria appeared in a hard-fired ware, Tufnell also showed that only about one-half of those found at Lachish did so.[111]

While this style bowl first appears in significant numbers in the late eighth century BCE,[112] its floruit occurs in the seventh and early sixth centuries.[113] The incipient trends toward this style of rim that appear, for example, at Hazor already in Strata VI and V always appear on much heavier bowls of thicker construction that also sometimes display a more pronounced shoulder keel.[114] Therefore, the second most important distinguishing feature of the Samaria group, perhaps even surpassing the rim formations, lies in their thin construction of hard-fired ware.[115] Some of the later, larger bowls in this class also display handles, as shown by examples from Lachish and Tell Beit Mirsim in the south and Tell-el-Farʿah in the north.[116] But at Lachish, the smaller bowls without handles appeared concentrated in Tomb 106, which Tufnell dated to the first half of the seventh century. Though none of the Samaria bowls showed the presence of handles,[117] the corpus seems to vary from smaller examples such as Nos. 4-5 (16-18 cm between the inside edges of the rim) to larger ones such as No. 7 (30 cm, assuming Kenyon's judgment of the diameter is correct).

This last example, No. 7, also distinguished itself by both the firing and color of its ware; this piece did not display the hard-ringing fabric typical of the other samples, and its ware appeared pale buff rather than red or grey in color. These characteristics may argue to place the onset of this particular tradition slightly before the turn

---

[110]*Lachish III, Text*, 277.

[111]*Lachish III, Text*, 277.

[112]Compare *Hazor I*, Pls. LIII:16; LXI:16-17; LXII:7 (Stratum V); *Hazor III-IV*, Pls. CCXXIII:14; CCXXX:6 (Stratum VB); *Beth-Shan*, James, Fig. 68:11 (Level IV).

[113]See the variant forms in *Hazor III-IV*, Pl. CCVIV:12, 13, 17 (Stratum IV); Tel Goren, in *En-Gedi*, Figs. 8:5 (Stratum V); Tell el-Farʿah (N), in *Chambon*, Pl. 56:9 (Stratum VIIe - seventh century) and 19 (Stratum VIIe-1 = sixth century).

[114]*Hazor III-IV*, Pls. CCXIV:8 (VI); CCXXII:10; CCXXIII:10-11 (VB); CCXXV:29, 36 (Stratum VA); CCXXX:6-8 (Stratum VA).

[115]As Albright noted, these attributes result from a combination of relatively good quality clay and skilled craftsmanship. "These delicate forms are also the most difficult to lift off the wheel without injury" (*TBM III*, 133, § 134).

[116]*Lachish III*, Pls. 81:109, 120-21; 82:122-23; *TBM I*, Pl. 60:1-4, 8-10 (this plate contains two No. 10s), 11-13; *TBM III*, Pl. 20:8-18 (all from Stratum A); *Chambon*, Pl. 54:8 (Stratum VIIe₁). Compare also *Bethel*, Pl. 64:1-2 (sixth century BCE), and Sinclair's discussion in *Bethel*, 71-72, § 291.

[117]In addition to the stratified group in *SS III*, Fig. 11, see also Fig. 32:6-8.

of the eighth century and perhaps even just prior to the events of 722/21 BCE, when this flanged rim-form shows a groove on the outer face of the folded clay.[118] Yet other examples from Hazor,[119] Megiddo,[120] and Gezer[121] attest to the continuation of this design well into the seventh century BCE. But since specimens like No. 7 seem related to but also different from the rest of the folded-rim group, they cannot establish a secure *terminus ante quem* of 732 BCE for the archaeological contexts in which they are found, in contrast to Rast's implication in his discussion of the Taʿanach material.[122]

The buff-colored bowl with inverted, flanged, and profiled rim in No. 7, then, actually stands over against the basic attribute set seen in the remainder of the group, which overall tends to support a later dating. For example, the apparent carelessness of the ring-burnishing[123] on mainly the interior surface and sometimes just over the outer rim area (Nos. 1, 3, 5) reflects, in my judgment, the incipient decline of that technique later in the seventh century BCE (and finally in the sixth century).[124] And while the best examples of ring-burnished bowls at other sites typically show the application of a red slip prior to the burnishing, the Samaria vessels have for the most part lost that feature as well. Yet the considerable value attached to this vessel class during its apogee becomes apparent from the fact that the ancient users often attempted to mend these particular bowls when they broke.[125]

To sum up, this family of bowls saw its predominant use during the seventh century BCE. The parallels Kenyon herself cited from Megiddo[126] in the north and

---

[118]Compare *Taʿanach*, Fig. 73:6 (Period IV); *Hazor II*, Pls. XCII:30; XCIII:1 (both = Stratum VA, though the latter displays a wheel-burnished red slip); *Hazor III-IV*, Pl. CCXXX:5 (also Stratum VA). Another similar bowl with a red-slipped interior appears in *Hazor V*, Fig. II.33:3 (described broadly as "clearly Iron II at the earliest"; found in a mixed, secondary context in Locus 673, a pit).

[119]*Hazor II*, Pl. XCVIII:16 and perhaps also 20 (Stratum IV; though with wheel burnishing on the interior).

[120]*Megiddo I*, Pl. 23:6, 8, 9 (ranging from Strata III to I, with a heavier concentration toward the later phases of that period; see 168-69, §§ 52, 56).

[121]*Gezer III*, Pl. 27:26 (Stratum VA = seventh to sixth century BCE). This style, which maintains its rounded sidewalls, corresponds to Gitin's "Type 53" at Gezer.

[122]*Taʿanach*, 43.

[123]Albright preferred the term "spiral burnishing" *TBM I*, § 117.

[124]*TBM I*, § 117; *TBM III*, §§ 134, 160.

[125]See *Megiddo I*, Pl. 23:18. Note also *TBM III*, 133, § 134, where, at the time of the publication of the Iron Age pottery from Tell Beit Mirsim, Albright said of the smaller, thin-walled bowls in this family that "apparently this was the only type of pottery that was mended."

[126]*Megiddo I*, Pl. 25:61-64. Though the excavators of Megiddo awarded minimal chronological value to these bowls (p. 169, § 59), one sees clearly that they derive mainly from Strata III-II (p. 187) at that site. For example, *M. I*, Pl. 25:62 seemed ubiquitous in Locus 1024, just as 25:64 proved abundant in Locus 1316, and both these findspots constituted part of a complex of rooms assigned to Stratum II in Area A (see *M. I*, Fig. 73, Squares P 6 and P 7). While the excavators may have taken some stray (possibly

Tell Beit Mirsim,[127] Beth-Shemesh,[128] and Lachish[129] in the south come principally from this period. At Lachish, one can now also add other examples from Stratum II.[130] According to a reported conversation between Tufnell and Kenyon, the latter concluded that this style bowl "only appeared in Period VII *after* the historic destruction of 720 B.C."[131] The appearance of this style in Niveaux 5-4 at Tell Keisan[132] and Stratum VIIe$_1$ at Tell el-Far'ah (N)[133] supports this finding. In his survey of fortresses located in the hill country of Judah, A. Mazar also found this same tradition in the latest Iron Age levels at Khirbet Abu et-Twein, and he notes similar exemplars from Beersheba II, Ramat-Rahel V, and En-Gedi V.[134] Today, Gitin's analysis of this ceramic family remains the most thorough classification of both primary and variant forms, and the numerous parallels he cites serve to corroborate my overall dating of the Samaria group.[135]

---

intrusive?) examples from Stratum IV, the earliest concentration of this type of bowl to appear at Megiddo came from Locus 539, assigned to Stratum III (*M. I*, Pl. 25:63; see the photograph in Fig. 115, Square O 4).

[127]*TBM I*, Pls. 61-62; *TBM III*, Pls. 22-23.

[128]See *SS III*, 127, for the sample cited from *APEF* II.

[129]*Lachish III*, Pl. 80:73, 75, 84, 86, although these citations take in a range of forms that spans both the shallow and deep-bowl varieties. A better sampling of the smaller sized group, such as those published from Samaria, appears in *Lachish III*, Pl. 101:626-640, 643-644. In fact, Tufnell drew a direct comparison between No. 2 in the Samaria group and Pl. 101:643 at Lachish, and between Samaria Nos. 1-6 and Lachish Pl. 101:636, 638 (see *Lachish III, Text*, 279). Forsberg has noted that Beersheba, Stratum II, actually yielded better parallels for Samaria Nos. 1-7 than did the Lachish Level III samples cited by Kenyon (*Forsberg*, 25; see also n. 134 below).

[130]Compare Bowl Types B-280 and B-530 found in Locus 3 in *Lachish V*, Pl. 47:2-3 and 11-16 (for the findspot, see Pl. 57). Aharoni seems to go too far in his statement that "the pink, spiral-burnished 'folded rim bowl'" does not appear at northern sites (*Lachish V*, 16). This observation resulted from his look at Samaria PP 6, but not PP 7.

[131]*Lachish III, Text*, 277 (emphasis added).

[132]*T. Keisan*, Pls. 40:6-6a (compare especially Samaria Nos. 3 and 5); 41:1-3, 3a-b (Niveau 5). Briend and Humbert place these bowls in a group that, for them, provides "un bon échantillonnage des formes du Fer IIC présents sur les sites de Palestine et du Liban. Qu'ils soient à lèvre à bourrelet plus ou moins marqué . . ." (*T. Keisan*, 171). From Niveau 4 in the seventh and early sixth centuries, see Pl. 30:1 (which parallels Samaria No. 2).

[133]*Chambon* Pl. 56:9, 22 (for particular comparison with Samaria Nos. 3, 4, and 6). For a possible earlier version of No. 2, with a shoulder keel, see *Chambon*, Pl. 56:20 (Stratum VIId).

[134]A. Mazar, "Iron Age Fortresses in the Judean Hills," *PEQ* July-December (1982), Fig. 13:1-6. See also his comments on p. 103. From Tel Goren, see *En-Gedi*, Fig. 8:5 (the excavators dated Stratum V between 630 and 582/81 BCE; see p. 16). From Stratum II at Beersheba, see *Beersheba I*, Pls. 59:60-62 and 68:1. To this survey, I may also add multiple examples from *Bethel*, Pl. 62 and p. 66, § 269. At another site excavated by A. Mazar, these rounded bowls appear in Stratum VII (*T. Qasîle* [2], 109, n. 1; Fig. 11-24).

[135]*Gezer III*, 57, 167-72. Compare also *Gezer II*, Pl. 37:2 (Field II, Stratum 3).

PP 7: HOUSE FLOORS — POTTERY

In Table 49, I have shown that these ring-burnished, folded-rim bowls came primarily from three local layers situated in three different segments of excavations as follows: Layer VII in Segment *120.121.19.126* (Nos. 1, 5, 7);[136] Layer IIIc in *W of 124* (No. 3); and Layer Va in Segment *504.503.509.508* (Nos. 4, 6). As demonstrated in my stratigraphic analysis, the first of these accumulations represents a routine deposit of fill, in my judgment; it seems unlikely that the deposit comprises a portion of widespread debris produced by a massive military campaign against the city. The second locus constitutes part of a matrix that was found beneath a Roman period wall and that also contained later examples of ribbed pottery. Beyond this observation, I note again that the context lay in Room *kq* and that this area proved generally much less reliable than the associated space in the adjacent *hq*. Finally, the third layer may constitute part of an actual surface, but one that abuts yet another Roman period wall (552). One may conclude, therefore, that none of these specimens derive from primary stratigraphic contexts dating to the Israelite or even early post-Israelite years.

The very shallow, thin-walled bowl presented in entry No. 8 follows the same basic motif described above, though with the thinnest wall construction of all and with a nuanced rim mode. Here the flange is pushed up to a nearly horizontal position and then tapered to a sharpened outer point. To create an opposing profile, the potter flattened (trimmed) the upper portion of the thickened rim and also drew it in to a sharp edge around the opening of the bowl. I have found only ambiguous antecedent forms that may have appeared in the far north already by Hazor VA[137] but on much thicker and heavier bowls. Adequate parallels for this appealing form remain very difficult to locate. One rim on a later and apparently rare style of bowl at Tell en-Naṣbeh mimics in some ways the nicer Samaria piece, but the upper, thickened part of the Naṣbeh rim is not tapered inward to a sharp edge as in No. 8.[138] Perhaps the most suitable comparison for this rim-type comes from a late Iron Age locus at Tel Qiri that unfortunately also yielded a mixed quantity of Roman period materials.[139] While a stricter dating of this piece awaits a more adequate corpus of parallels, I can safely suggest that it likely belongs no earlier than 700 BCE.

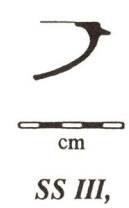

SS III, Fig. 11:8

The second subset of PP 7 bowls itself reflects two related yet distinct traditions. The entries in Nos. 9, 10 (?; see lamps, p. 430 below), 11-14, 15 and then 17, 22, and 23 represent variations within these two styles, respectively. The first group of

---

[136] The excavators found entry No. 2 in Layer V of this segment.

[137] *Hazor II*, Pl. LXXXII:2 (grey-buff ware with red burnished slip); *Hazor III-IV*, Pl. CCXXX:10. I must reiterate that these items provide only very oblique parallels, not really good ones.

[138] *TN II*, Pl. 59:1370. Wampler included this exemplar among "a miscellany of types on which there is limited formation" (p. 38, § 44).

[139] *T. Qiri*, Fig. 1:10 (from Locus 1000, dated by the excavators to Stratum VB/VI = "Iron III," though included on a plate of Roman period forms, p. 39).

forms (Nos. 9, 11-15) comprises those shallow, thin-walled vessels made of a red, brown, or grey fabric with some limestone inclusions and showing an occasional, rather drab slip but usually no burnishing. The primary diagnostic feature of this group lies in the strongly everted, flaring, or sometimes curled-out rims that result in one of the most "open" of forms (numerous reports refer to this class as "plates" rather than bowls).[140] This look can vary from a near-cyma profile to an extremely rounded form above the shoulder keel, with the latter style resulting in a deep, smooth channel around the underside of the rim-ledge (as in No. 15). In the most dramatic cases, this attribute gives the rim profile a hook-like appearance. The greater the curvature (roundness) of the rim itself, the more pronounced the shoulder keel. In nearly all instances, the outer edge of the rim represents the widest point of the entire form.

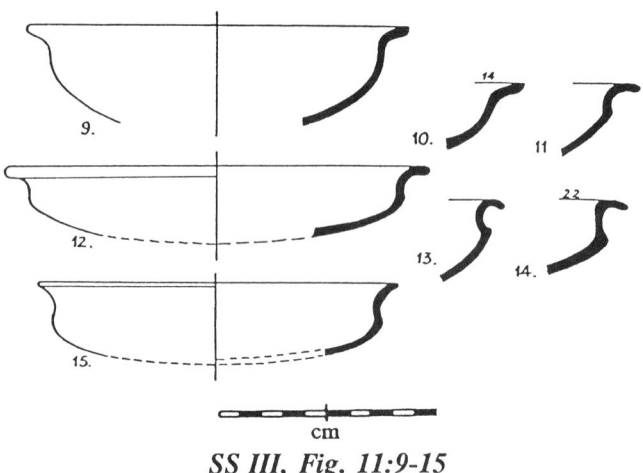

SS III, Fig. 11:9-15

Although these bowls do not generally appear in great frequency in most site reports, En-Gedi V offers adequate parallels.[141] One can see several possible examples in which the folded rims of the round-sided bowls discussed above have begun to turn toward a more outwardly curved rim in the late Iron II levels at Tell Beit Mirsim[142] and Lachish.[143] At Ta'anach, however, Rast understood this rather unusual style, with its extremely prominent rim, as a late Iron Age II descendant of a longstanding tradition of bowl-making based on the use of "flaring rims and shoulders which often have a cyma profile."[144] Though this comparison usually does not provide adequate rim parallels for the Samaria group, it may seem appropriate owing to the round bases on most of the Ta'anach examples. Though none of the bases have survived on the Samaria

---

[140]To assess the degree of "openness" for a vessel, one may compare the diameter of its mouth (at its *narrowest* point inside the rim) with the maximum width of the overall vessel (i.e., the body at its *widest* point). See *APTJ*, 37.

[141]*En-Gedi*, 26, n. 13; Figs. 8:6; 15:1-2 (Stratum V = late seventh to early sixth centuries BCE).

[142]*TBM I*, Pl. 65:20a, 25 (Stratum A).

[143]*Lachish III*, Pl. 99:603.

[144]*Ta'anach*, 32-33; compare Fig. 48:1-14 (Period IIB) for his suggested antecedent forms for *SS III*, Fig. 11:9, 11-15. If one wants to argue in favor of longstanding connections with other local traditions, it seems equally plausible to posit an historical affiliation between the less curled-out rims (as in No. 9) and the cyma-like profile frequently used in the rim modes of many chalice-bowls throughout the Iron Age period (e.g., *Chambon*, Pl. 60:9, Niveau VIIe).

bowls (including the nonstratified piece in *SS III*, Fig. 32:5 <=> Fig. 11:12), Kenyon's suggested reconstruction completes all of them in this fashion. Yet I may note that the rim comparisons drawn by authors of other site reports typically tie the Samaria exemplars to bowls with clear ring bases.

It seems to me that, rather than growing out of deep-seated local industries from tenth-century BCE Israel, this subgroup of forms differs enough from the suggested antecedents at Ta'anach to posit a later, Assyrian connection for their overall style, if not for their actual point of origin. While most reports and general studies have failed to address this affiliation,[145] the best exemplars of the style generally found in Palestine consist in the Assyrian bowls recovered through Petrie's work at Tell Jemmeh—Yurza.[146] That hundreds of fragments from these bowls surfaced there in a single grain pit located in Room DZ[147] prompted Petrie to assume a "uniform date" for the entire cache of goods.[148] His stratigraphic and ceramic analyses led him to con-

---

[145]E.g., while Forsberg noted possible form parallels for Samaria Nos. 9-14 from En-Gedi V and Beersheba, Stratum II, he failed to offer any comment on their link to Assyrian-style pottery (*Forsberg*, 25).

[146]*Gerar*, 20, § 46, Pl. XLVII:13 and pp. 23-24, § 49, Pl. LXV:11-23. Though Petrie accepted W. J. Phythian-Adams's initial identification of this site as Gerar (Phythian-Adams, "Report on Soundings at Tell Jemmeh," *PEQ* 55 [1923], 140-46, particularly 146), B. Mazar (Maisler) later argued convincingly for correlating Jemmeh with ancient Yurza based on the topographical lists of Thutmosis III and, subsequently, the Amarna letters (B. Maisler, "Yurza, The Identification of Tell Jemmeh," *PEQ* 84 [1952], 48-51). As the current head of the *Pax Assyriaca*, Esarhaddon apparently conquered this city sometime during the first half of the seventh century BCE, probably around 679 BCE (according to G. W. Van Beek, "Tel Gamma," *IEJ* 22 [1972], 246). The Assyrian later boasted, "I trod up[on Arzâ at] the 'Brook of Eg[ypt]'. I put Asuhili, its king, in fetters and took [him to Assyria]" (see the so-called "Alabaster Tablet" from Assur in *ANET*, 290 = *ARAB* II, § 710) . . . and "beside the gate ⌜inside the city of Nineveh⌝ [I kept him tied, along with, . . .] dogs and swine" (Prism S in *ARAB* II, § 515) and also possibly jackals (Prism A in *ARAB* II, § 529). Compare two additional references to "Arzani" in separate annalistic fragments (*ARAB* II, § 545; *ARAB* II, § 550 = *ANET*, 292).

[147]*Gerar*, Pl. X. Though in the narrative of the report Petrie identifies this findspot as Locus 194, it seems from the plan in Pl. X that the Assyrian pottery came from Locus 190.

[148]Following Petrie's publication of the results from Jemmeh, Albright adjusted in significant measure the proposed chronology of occupation at this site (*TBM I*, 74, § 98 [compare also § 73]; *TBM III*, 23, § 10 and 144, § 144, particularly n. 1) and extended the range of the pottery from Petrie's so-called EF Town (*Gerar*, Pl. IX) from the ninth through the eighth and even into the seventh centuries BCE. The CD Town (*Gerar*, Pl. X), in turn, belonged in the seventh century, according to Albright, with the AB Town (*Gerar*, Pl. XI) beginning only at the close of that century following Pharaoh Necho's activity in Palestine in 609 BCE. (For similar downward revisions published between the appearance of *TBM I* and *TBM III*, see G. E. Wright, "Iron: The Date of Its Introduction into Common Use in Palestine," *AJA* 43 [1939], 460. Both Albright and Wright, however, continued to associate Jemmeh with biblical Gerar.) Van Beek's renewed excavations, initiated in 1970 on behalf of the Smithsonian Institution, prompted an even further lowering of the original framework, with "substantial parts of Petrie's stratum EF and probably much of CD" falling in the seventh century and thereby moving Buildings CA-CT, DG-DH, and the rooms surrounding DT to the sixth century (G. W. Van Beek, "Tell Jemmeh," in *NEAEHL* 2, 670 and 672). This revised chronology would place Room DZ (Pl. X), mentioned above, very deep into the seventh century BCE, if not at or just after the turn of that period. According to Van Beek, then, the large, multi-room building and massive fortress of Petrie's Pl. XI stem from the Persian period in the fifth to late fourth centuries BCE.

clude further that these plates "were the table service *imported from home* by the Assyrian governor,"[149] who would likely have occupied the famous vaulted building excavated later by G. Van Beek.[150] Thereafter, this luxury class of bowls assumed the moniker "Assyrian Table Service" or "Assyrian Palace Ware."

Yet, while the general morphology of the Samaria bowls argues to link them with Assyrian traditions rather than indigenous, tenth-century BCE trends, a number of finer attributes also separate the collections from Samaria and Jemmeh. For example, the Samaria group uniformly contained thin-walled bowls, while Petrie described the Jemmeh sample as "thick plates of hard ware."[151] In fact, he points to the thickness of this set of plates to distinguish them from their thin-walled relatives recovered from the same locus but that correspond (morphologically) to Nos. 22-23 at Samaria, not to 9 or 11-15. At Samaria, the outer face of the sidewalls of these forms remained smooth except for the occasional keel of carination; at Jemmeh, Petrie noted that the presence and number of "grooves on the shoulder is the readiest means of sorting [these plates]"[152] and that "nothing like these has been found before in Palestine." The ware at Samaria appeared in shades of dark red (Nos. 11-12) or grey (Nos. 9, 15), with only two pieces showing a light red color (Nos. 13-14). The Jemmeh group varied from "creamy white, drab, pale fawn, warm fawn, to dark fawn brown" fabric. Kenyon often described the surfaces of the bowls at Samaria as having a "smooth finish" and noted only one case of apparent burnishing, while Petrie spoke of a "smooth matt surface" and added that "many are burnished, and in some the clay was a fat one which took a high polish in lines." Finally, if Kenyon's suggested restoration of round bases on the Samaria bowls proves a prudent one, then the Assyrian plates from Jemmeh once again distinguish themselves by their "sharp angular stepping at the bottom, and grooves at intervals on the flat base."[153]

---

[149] *Gerar*, 24, § 49 (emphasis added).

[150] See G. W. Van Beek, "Tel Gamma," *IEJ* 20 (1970), 230; *IEJ* 22 (1972), 245-56; *IEJ* 24 (1974), 138-39 and 274-75; *IEJ* 27 (1977), 171-76; for another series of summary reports by Van Beek, see "Tell Ğemmeh," *RB* 79 (1972), 596-99; *RB* 80 (1973), 572-76; *RB* 82 (1975), 95-97; 573-76; also idem, "Digging Up Tell Jemmeh," *Archaeology* 36/1 (1983), 12-19; idem, "Archaeological Excavations at Tell Jemmeh," *National Geographic Research Reports* 16 (1984), 675-96; and idem, "Tell Jemmeh," in *NEAEHL* 2, 667-74.

[151] All the following observations cited from Petrie appear on p. 24 of the *Gerar* volume.

[152] He added that the grooves ranged in number from zero to five.

[153] Thus far, shallow, carinated bowls with strongly everted rims and stepped bases have remained relatively scarce in the Madaba Plains area of Transjordan (*MPP-2*, 305; compare Fig. 19.9:24-25, from Integrated Phase 3 = seventh century BCE = Saʿidiyeh VII). Some authorities have regarded a similar form found in the seventh-century Stratum II at Timnah, with its grey clay and black, burnished slip, as an Ammonite import (G. L. Kelm and A. Mazar, *Timnah: A Biblical City in the Sorek Valley* [Winona Lake, IN: Eisenbrauns, 1995], 165, Fig. 8.27:4; see the comments in *MPP-2*, 305; also Kelm and Mazar, "Tel Batash [Timnah] Excavations: Second Preliminary Report," *BASOR Supplement* 23 [1985], 93-120). But see the discussion in *Amiran*, 294-97, Photo 301 and Pl. 101:1, 3 (which Amiran considers "Judaean types"), and 5 (representing an Assyrian style).

A resolution for this situation may come from a closer consideration of two late streams of ceramic tradition found within Assyria itself. First, one sees there a series of thicker-walled, moderately-deep to deep bowls whose rim typology suits very well the more dramatically curved forms in Nos. 11-14 at Samaria.[154] Almost invariably, these forms appear with ring bases, sharply carinated shoulders, strongly everted rim lips, and in well levigated, reddish ware covered with a pale wash or buff-colored slip.[155] Lines noted that "this type is at Nimrud the most common of the late Assyrian bowls. It is found at least as early as Sargon . . . ."[156] Analysts have customarily classified this group under the rubric "Ring-Based Bowls," not under Assyrian Palace Ware. In turn, they have reserved the latter designation for a second trend involving much thinner-walled, shallower plate forms that resemble closely the *body* modes of Nos. 9-17 at Samaria.[157] The rim styles attested on Palace Ware may include both the more strongly curved or bent fashion (again, Samaria Nos. 11-14)[158] or the more gracefully flared, cyma-like version (as in Nos. 9, 15, 17).[159] All these bowls, however, show some expression of the ring-base mode; round bases seem restricted to Palace Ware specimens with much higher neckwalls that simply bow outward (as in Nos. 22-23).[160] In addition, the manufacture of true Palace Ware in Assyria typically utilized a very fine, grey-green to greenish-buff clay with apparently minimal inclusions of limestone grits.[161]

The Samaria group in Nos. 9 and 11-15 (and perhaps 17, which resembles more No. 23) seems to incorporate a mixture of traits borrowed from both of the Assyrian

---

[154] E.g., J. Oates, "Late Assyrian Pottery from Fort Shalmaneser," *Iraq* 21 (1959), Pls. XXXV:9, 19, 21, 24 and XXXVI:32. See also J. Lines, "Late Assyrian Pottery from Nimrud," *Iraq* 16 (1954), Pl. XXXVII:5.

[155] See J. Oates, *Iraq* 21 (1959), 139-40. Occasionally, these bowls display a rounded vs. carinated shoulder and appear in buff- vs. red-colored ware. The following observations appear on G. M. Crowfoot's stratification card for bowl No. 13, which falls late in this series of curved rim forms: "light reddish ware—may have had a thin slip, wheel burnishing, or maybe the manner of smoothing on [a] wheel gives an appearance of burnishing."

[156] J. Lines, *Iraq* 16 (1954), 165. Oates concurs in her study (*Iraq* 21 [1959], 132).

[157] J. Oates, *Iraq* 21 (1959), 136, n. 13.

[158] See J. Oates, *Iraq* 21 (1959), Pl. XXXV:17-18 (according to Oates, these forms "occur both in Palace Ware and relatively fine ordinary ware" - p. 132); J. Lines, *Iraq* 16 (1954), Pl. XXXVII:10.

[159] Compare J. Oates, *Iraq* 21 (1959), Pl. XXXV:20 (this form belongs exclusively to the Palace-Ware group - p. 132); J. Lines, *Iraq* 16 (1954), Pl. XXXVII:9.

[160] J. Lines, *Iraq* 16 (1954), Pl. XXXVII:7-8. Importantly, Lines observed that Nimrud Type No. 8 "has, apparently, a longer occurrence than No. 7. Type 8 has been found in the Governor's Palace and [is] associated with the Burnt Palace ivories, *i.e.* probably Sargonid" (p. 166).

[161] In fact, this fabric has proved so common for these bowls that some specialists refer to the clay itself as "Palace Ware" (e.g., see J. Oates, *Iraq* 21 [1959], p. 139, annotation Nos. 17-18). The coloring of this ware "is certainly intentional, as it is consistent over too long a period for it to have been an accident of firing" (p. 136).

styles just outlined. Whereas their body-form modes tend to adhere closely to the true Palace-Ware motif, some of their rim designs and especially their wares align themselves more with the Ring-Based bowls from Assyria. While most are of a thin, even construction (like that of Palace Ware), No. 16 appears thicker and displays a coarser ware with wide ring-burnishing. In short, this hybrid set of plates seems clearly to distance itself from purely local traditions and to mimic Assyrian Palace-Ware styles, while at the same time distinguishing itself in certain key ways from the foreign templates.[162] In my judgment, therefore, the group represents locally made imitations of Assyrian originals.

None of the Assyrian pottery cited above belongs earlier than the late seventh century BCE.[163] Within Israel, adequate comparisons come from Stratum II at Beth-Shemesh[164] in the south and from Tell el-Farʿah (N), Niveau VIId.[165] While some of these potential parallels exemplify rims quite similar to No. 14 at Samaria, virtually no match exists for the graceful curvature of No. 13. Many of these forms at other sites also appear thicker and sometimes deeper than the Samaria sample. The Samaria group, then, provides one with the finest local imitations of Assyrian Palace Ware available in Israel. As such, several of these specimens also likely represent the latest such imitations (e.g., Nos. 11 and 13). On her stratification card for these two items, G. M. Crowfoot noted that the excavators found them "with some greenish ware, [dating to] the Persian Period(?)."

---

[162] A similar mixing-and-matching of traditions seems to have occurred, if on a smaller scale, in Assyria itself. For example, the Assyrians undoubtedly encountered the red slipped and wheel (ring) burnished treatment of pottery during their early campaigns to the west, including the area of Israel. Though the subsequent application of these techniques remained rare in the assemblages of Nimrud, they did appear, but most often on *native* forms, not on adopted Palestinian ones (e.g., the tripod bowls in J. Oates, *Iraq* XXI [1959], Pl. XXXV:15-16; also M. E. L. Mallowan, "The Excavations at Nimrud [Kalḫu], 1949-1950," *Iraq* 12 [1950], 183 and Pl. XXXII:1). The same holds true for the use of grey ware (seen in many of the local PP 7 traditions at Samaria) at Nimrud; though not widely popular in Assyria, this matrix again appears mainly on Type 15 Tripod Bowls (Oates, p. 137; for a discussion of the production techniques behind that color, see P. S. Rawson, "Palace Wares from Nimrud—Technical Observations on Selected Examples," *Iraq* 16 [1954], 171-72 and Pl. XLI:2). Though this style of thick but tapered straight leg does appear occasionally in Palestine (as at T. es-Saʿidiyeh, J. B. Pritchard, *Tell es-Saʿidiyeh: Excavations on the Tell, 1964-1966*. University Museum Monograph 60 [Philadelphia: University Museum/University of Pennsylvania, 1985], Fig. 17:33), the more typical form utilized three loop-handles (as in *CPP*, 28 J 5, from Tomb 227 at Tell el-Farʿah [S], *T. Farʿah-RB* [58], Fig. 4:1 from Tomb I, *Beersheba II*, Fig. 21:10 from Stratum VII and references cited there, *T. Qasîle* [BM], Fig. 5:9 from Stratum X, or the variant in *Megiddo I*, Pl. 23:3, from Stratum II). (Straight legs often occur in Palestine on stone-basalt mortars.) As these witnesses attest, this style bowl appears in the Levant in the Middle Bronze Age, and recurs somewhat in the Iron Age (see *Amiran*, 200).

[163] Lines dated her study group within a narrow range of 629-612 BCE (see *Iraq* 16 [1954], 164, n. 2). The repertoire presented by Oates revealed "a homogeneous collection" that belonged to the years following the fall of Nimrud and the destruction of the fortress there in 612 BCE, i.e., to the period immediately following the pottery seen in Lines' group (J. Oates, *Iraq* 21 [1959], 130).

[164] *AS IV*, Pl. LXVI:1-3, 26.

[165] *Chambon*, Pl. 57:1-3.

Finally, on the basis of the citations from Beth-Shemesh or Tell el-Farʿah (N), one cannot restrict these bowls to the eighth century BCE rather than the seventh. It is generally agreed that the stratigraphy of Beth-Shemesh awaits clarification from the renewed excavations currently underway there. Further, two of the three examples cited from Tell el-Farʿah appeared in contexts that contained clear Assyrian or Assyrian-style bowls. And while Chambon attributed Locus 132, which yielded the first of the plates cited in the previous note, to Niveau VIId in the drawings of the pottery (Pl. 57), he extended the chronological range of this findspot as late as Niveau VIIe$_1$ (sixth century BCE) in his list of loci.[166] Similarly, he again assigned Locus 134, from which excavators removed the third plate cited above, to Niveau VIId in the drawings of the pottery while *restricting* it to Niveaux VIIe and VIIe$_1$ (seventh and sixth centuries) in his list of loci.[167]

Therefore, it seems entirely likely that these stylish bowls entered service at Samaria in the seventh century BCE during the course of Assyrian influence over the city, its remaining Israelite inhabitants, the resettled immigrants brought here by the new government, and whatever eclectic mix of traditions the diverse residents now contributed to the cultural life of this one-time capital. Several strands of literary and archaeological evidence merge to support this dating. For example, Assyrian records confirm that Esarhaddon conquered Yurza (Arṣa), near the Brook of Egypt, in 679 BCE and that he launched successive campaigns against Egypt in 674, 671, and 669 BCE. If, as many believe, the identification of Tell Jemmeh as ancient Yurza is correct, then it seems extremely probable that Esarhaddon himself commissioned the building of the large, barrel-vaulted building to house his military governor sometime around or just following the year 679. On the late end, archaeological evidence has clearly shown that this facility was abandoned, but not destroyed, sometime very soon after 640 BCE. Thus, the structure contained "a sealed and discrete unit of material which can be narrowly dated to a time span of about 50 years, between 679 and 630 B.C."[168] and, importantly, which included the true (i.e., *imported*) Assyrian Palace Ware. While excavations have established the continued use of this luxury dinner service throughout the seventh century in the Assyrian homeland (see the work of Oates and Lines above), a tradition of locally-made imitations took hold in Palestine at sites such as Samaria. Finally, I have shown that these hybrid forms differed from their prototypes in various ways, but principally in the color and matrix of clay used to manufacture them. Since these imitations sought to emulate seventh-to-late seventh-

---

[166]*Chambon*, 104.

[167]*Chambon*, 105. One wonders about possible misrecordings in the locus list, for Locus 411 (see Pl. 57:1) is assigned to Niveau VIId in the pottery plate but to VIIc (early ninth century BCE) in the locus list (p. 131). This seems much too early a date for the "carinated plate" (Chambon's term) in question, particularly in the light of other pottery yielded by Locus 411 (compare the bowl in Pl. 56:11 and the Assyrian bowl in Pl. 61:1).

[168]G. W. Van Beek, *Archaeology* 36/1 (1983), 17.

century Assyrian templates, one should not date the Samaria bowls earlier than the second or third decade of that period.

The two bowls in Nos. 22-23 (and likely also No. 17), from a class with rounded bottoms, slightly deeper bodies, soft carination that often displays ridges on the shoulder area, and taller upper sidewalls that flare out, also clearly belong to the overall repertoire of Assyrian forms found at Samaria. This nuanced style of bowl appears more often in site reports than do the shallower plates discussed above.[169] Kenyon herself cited "exact parallels" from Tell el-Farʿah (N), Niveau 1, "which, like Samaria VII, succeeds a disastrous destruction,"[170] and similar examples from Tell Jemmeh.[171] At the time of her writing, Kenyon declared that these distinctive forms appeared only at Samaria and these two additional sites.[172] She also noted that "a considerable number of fragments of bowls of this form, carinated, with a high flaring fin occurred in Period VII deposits, *but not in any earlier or later ones*,"[173] and she concluded that the new inhabitants relocated to Samaria by the Assyrians introduced this innovative pottery to the site.[174]

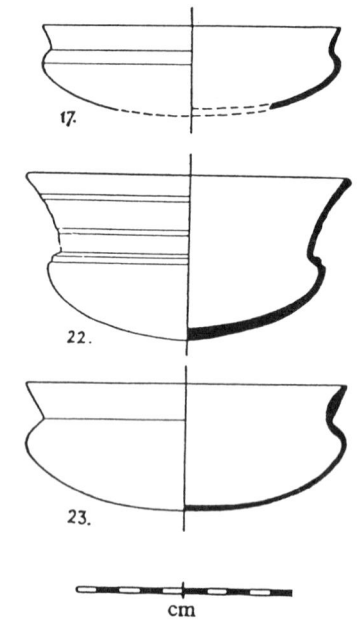

SS III, Fig. 11:17, 22-23

I may draw out a number of observations related to this discussion and in each case offer some adjustments to the conclusions reached by Kenyon. The first area of concern involves the proper dating of the ceramic traditions reflected in entries 22-23. While Kenyon's general comments limit these goods to PP 7 and to the period following the events of 722/21 BCE, her more particular statements reflect some uncertainty over the precise dating of these bowls. On the one hand, she stated that "the dating of the "Dinner Service" and thus of the Samaria, Farʿah and Gemmeh bowls associated with it at Gemmeh to the period 725-700 B.C. *is thus certain*."[175] On the other hand, she very soon added:

---

[169]Some examples of the high-flaring sidewalls do, in fact, appear on shallow, round-bottomed bowls similar to Nos. 9-17 (e.g., J. Lines, *Iraq* 16 [1954], Pl. XXXVII:7-8). Compare also L. E. Toombs and G. E. Wright, "The Fourth Campaign at Balâṭah (Shechem)," *BASOR* 169 (1963), Fig. 22:2 (Stratum VI = late eighth and seventh centuries BCE).

[170]*SS III*, 97.

[171]See *T. Farʿah-RB* [58], Fig. 12:1-4, 6; *Gerar*, Pl. LI:26w and 26x (noted in *SS III*, 128).

[172]*SS III*, 97.

[173]*SS III*, 128 (emphasis added).

[174]*SS III*, 97-98.

[175]*SS III*, 98 (emphasis added).

> As negative evidence, it may be noted that a considerable number of late seventh century forms occur in Period VIII, but are not found in VII . . . . Also, a good deal of the Period VI wares is found in the same deposits as the new ones of VII, and would appear to have continued side by side with it. It therefore appears as if *an early seventh century date would suit the deposit best*.[176]

As she reckoned with Nos. 22-23 strictly from the ceramic point of view, then, she lowered her suggested date for this tradition from the late eighth to the early seventh century BCE.

A second important consideration that Kenyon virtually never discussed for any of her published pottery addresses the specific findspots that yielded these PP 7 bowls. As my detailed stratigraphic analysis for this period has shown, item No. 22 derived from Layer VII of the excavation segment *W of 124*, which lay in Room *hq*. Using information gathered from the excavation's unpublished fieldbooks, I have shown that this deposit consisted in a thin accumulation of soft earth situated between Layer VI (which Kenyon understood as a "Period VII" floor) and Layer VIII (which she identified as a BP V surface). The second bowl, No. 23, came from Layer VIc of Segment *19.51.14.20*, situated in the stratigraphically tenuous area of the so-called "Room" *e*. As demonstrated in fig. 59, this locus actually subsumed two small pits that penetrated the layers just east of (and I believe were contemporary with) Wall 57 (see fig. 56). Sometime after the cutting of these pits, a robbing of much of Wall 57 seems to have occurred, followed by the deposition of the partially burned debris in Layer IVa, the matrix of which included some fragments of ivory. Neither provenance points to a clear destruction level, and the *terminus post quem* of the goods found in the pit fill must remain open. I might have established a *terminus ante quem* for the two pits if I knew the nature of the artifacts taken from Layer IVd, which overran and sealed them. But the final report did not include any pottery from IVd. On the basis of presently available data, then, one can only suggest that entries 22-23 appeared at this site sometime after the period of principal use of the BP V rooms.

Third, it is now certain that the *ceramic* traditions witnessed in Nos. 22-23 reflect an imitation of metal prototypes. This replication occurred even in the Assyrian homeland itself, where ceramic versions of these bowls are known to have existed at least by the last quarter of the eighth century BCE (reign of Sargon II).[177] Layard retrieved an impressive collection of nearly 150 bronze vessels of this type (some of which he referred to as "cups") from Room AB in Sargon's North-West Palace at Nineveh.[178] Following Layard's early ruminations, Kenyon considered seriously the

---

[176] *SS III*, 98 (emphasis added).

[177] See Mallowan, *Iraq* 12 (1950), 183 and Pl. XXXII:2, which he dated to ca. 700 BCE. Compare also Oates' bowl Type 59 in *Iraq* 21 (1959), Pl. XXXVII:59, and her comments and further references on p. 132, where she places the ceramic reflex of this tradition in the late seventh century BCE.

[178] A. H. Layard, *Discoveries in the Ruins of Nineveh and Babylon, Second Expedition* (New York: G. P. Putnam, 1853), 190-93 (hereafter, *Nineveh and Babylon*).

possibility that the basic morphology of this tradition originated in Palestine, not Assyria, and that diffusion into the latter area occurred during the western military campaigns of Shalmaneser V, Sargon II, or Sennacherib.[179] While she suggested further that this new style of pottery emerged from "some of the fresh settlers" whom the Assyrians relocated in Samaria and not from motifs indigenous to either Assyria or Israel, she failed to offer any evidence from a third region that might in any way support this belief. At this point, it does not appear that Assyria later imitated in metal what Israel had earlier produced in clay.[180]

Fourth, one cannot use Samaria PP 7 to restrict the functional life of these bowls to a general time frame in the late eighth or seventh century BCE. Judging from the numerous examples found in the so-called "Smithsonian Granary" at Jemmeh (late fourth century BCE),[181] traditions similar to No. 23 appear to have survived longer than any of the Assyrian motifs. But nearer to the Iron Age proper, good parallels present themselves (albeit in relatively meager quantities) from Hazor Stratum IV,[182] Tell Keisan Niveau 5,[183] Tel Qiri and Yoqneʿam in the Jezreel Valley area,[184] Tel ʿAmal Niveau II,[185] at Shechem[186] and Tell en-Naṣbeh[187] (in variant forms), the coastal sites of Tell Qasîle, Stratum VII and Ashdod, local Strata 8-7 in Area M,[188] sporadic Trans-

---

[179] *SS III*, 98. For a similar view from much earlier, see A. H. Layard, *Nineveh and Babylon*, 192-93.

[180] Layard's theory that the Assyrians did, however, obtain some of the raw materials (such as tin) necessary to the production of these bronze bowls in regions to the west ("Phoenicia") seems plausible (Layard, *Nineveh and Babylon*, 191). Yet Amiran's considered opinion that these bowls differed from Israelite traditions in ware, shape, and ceramic technique still holds today (*Amiran*, 291). My discussion has noted some of the differences between the fabric of true Palace Ware and that of the local imitations at Samaria.

[181] G. W. Van Beek, "Total Retrieval and Maximum Reconstruction of Artifacts: An Experiment in Archaeological Methodology," *Eretz-Israel* 20 (Yadin Volume, 1989), 14* and Ill. 2:285, 292, 292.1, 292.2. Compare also the reference to a similar bronze bowl found in another Persian period context at Gezer in *AS V*, 78, n. 12.

[182] *Hazor II*, Pl. XCVIII:44.

[183] *T. Keisan*, Pl. 37:11a-e.

[184] *T. Qiri*, Fig. 44:5 (noted as a likely intrusion into Stratum VII; see p. 203). Still, sparsely attested examples related to Stratum 10 at Yoqneʿam suggest the presence of these traditions in Israel around or even just prior the Assyrian conquest. For a possible later specimen from the late eighth or seventh century, see *T. Yoqneʿam* [3], Fig. 10:3 (Stratum 9).

[185] *T. ʿAmal*, 344, Fig. 7:3.

[186] L. E. Toombs and G. E. Wright, "The Fourth Campaign at Balâṭah (Shechem)," *BASOR* 169 (1963), 50, and Fig. 22:2 (Stratum VI).

[187] *TN II*, Pls. 53:1156, 1163 and 54:1192-1200. See Wampler's remarks regarding metal prototypes for these bowls and his hesitancy to offer a firm date for the class in general on pp. 33-34, § 25.

[188] *T. Qasîle* [2], Fig. 55:26-28; *Ashdod IV*, Figs. 13:1, 4 (Stratum 8); 26:1-3 (Stratum 7a). Compare also Stratum 3b-3a in Area D, *Ashdod I*, Fig. 37:1-3, and the statements concerning chronology on p. 139.

jordanian sites such as Tell el-Mazar,[189] and at least as far south as Tell el-Kheleifeh.[190] To Kenyon's citations from Tell Jemmeh, I may add other examples recovered from the same locus in Room DZ as the shallower types of Palace Ware discussed above;[191] and to supplement her parallels at Farʿah (N), see now the findings of A. Chambon.[192]

This list of citations may prompt a false impression concerning the overall numerical distribution of these Assyrian-style bowls. In fact, they remain relatively rare at most sites. Kenyon's 1957 observation basically remains intact even today: these vessels apparently saw their greatest use in only a few centers such as Samaria, Tell el-Farʿah (N), and Tell Jemmeh. Otherwise, they occur quite sporadically and in noticeably limited quantities. In this vein, the relative scarcity of Assyrian-style bowls—whether authentic or local imitations—at Gezer in the south or Megiddo in the north remains somewhat perplexing, particularly if these sites served as regional centers in the Assyrian political structure during the reorganization and reconstruction of the country in the seventh century BCE. At Gezer, Gitin related Samaria No. 22 to his Type 73, a designation for which there was only a single example attested in the entire corpus there.[193] The upper sidewalls on this form, however, appear too straight and the carination too sharp to provide an ideal parallel to the Samaria vessels. Rather, the bowls from the Israelite capital relate better to Gitin's Types 74-75, with their more rounded carination and flaring upper walls. But again, only one sample of Type 74 and two specimens of Type 75 appeared in the Gezer repertoire.[194] In commenting on both the scarcity of these bowls and the Assyrian traditions behind them, Chambon has observed that "bien que mal attesté sur les sites proprement assyriens, ce bol, ou plutôt son prototype en métal, figure couramment sur les reliefs des palais assyriens."[195]

---

[189] K. Yassine, *Tell el Mazar 1: Cemetery A* (Amman: University of Jordan, 1984), Fig. 3:3. Compare also *MPP-1*, Fig. 19.16:7 from Integrated Phase 2; *MPP-2*, Fig. 8.16:28 from Field Phase 4 = late Iron Age II.

[190] See *Amiran*, 300 and Photos 328-29 on p. 301. G. D. Pratico, "Nelson Glueck's 1938-1940 Excavations at Tell el-Kheleifeh: A Reappraisal," *BASOR* 259 (1985), Fig. 15:2-7. Elsewhere, Pratico notes that "Assyrian bowls in local imitation are ubiquitous at Tell el-Kheleifeh" (*Kheleifeh*—Pratico, 41).

[191] *Gerar*, Pl. LXV:1-3.

[192] *Chambon*, Pl. 61:2-11 (Stratum VIIe; Nos. 3-7 repeat the bowls published earlier by de Vaux and cited by Kenyon in *SS III*).

[193] *Gezer III*, Pl. 22:7 (from Stratum VB = late eighth to early seventh centuries BCE). This one example appeared sealed in the fill beneath the floor of a late eighth-century house (p. 197).

[194] *Gezer III*, Pl. 27:19-21 (Stratum VA = seventh to sixth centuries BCE). Gitin attempts to distinguish his Nos. 20-21 (Type 75) from Assyrian forms on the grounds that they display "a more open rounded carination and more vertically oriented side walls" (p. 199). Neither point is convincing, for the Assyrian forms frequently show rounded carination, and the upper walls of Gezer Fig. 27:20 flare out much more than do those of Fig. 22:7 (Type 73), which he himself understands as an Assyrian form.

[195] *Chambon*, 69.

In view of the relative scarcity of these bowls in Israel, then, an irony seems to lie in the fact that descendant forms (perhaps especially of Samaria No. 23) apparently enjoyed a very long period of use in certain instances, as in the cases of the metal bowl found in a Persian period tomb at Gezer[196] and the fourth-century granary mentioned above from Tell Jemmeh. And in view of the local origin that seems to attend most of the available sample, I may suggest that the very hard, thin, black ware and shallow, exterior ribbing on No. 22 combine to make it the best candidate for an authentic Assyrian import. Moreover, its stratigraphic situation—between tightly spaced, hard-packed floor levels dated by Kenyon to "Period V" and "Period VII," respectively—emerges as the most reliable findspot within the group thus far. Yet while the locus may relate directly to Assyrian activity at Samaria, it clearly does not on its own reflect a massive destruction event.

Finally, Van Beek observed that much of the Assyrian Palace Ware found in the vaulted building at Tell Jemmeh appears to have fallen from an upstairs room to the floor below. He currently understands this space to have served as a kitchen for the governor's residence. This conclusion lies very close to my present assessment of the so-called service rooms situated north of the rock scarp that defined the northern edge of the central summit at Samaria.

Within the third subgroup of miscellaneous bowl forms, No. 16 exhibits rounded sidewalls that are much thicker than those on the Palace Ware sample and a thickened, everted rim, which assumes a near horizontal position and displays a tapering toward a simple, outer edge. The bowl's construction and firing produced a hard but course ware of light brown color that developed a self-slip and showed an irregular ring burnishing on the interior surface. Excellent parallels for this fragment remain few in number, but the adequate ones that do exist at sites such as Hazor,[197] Tell en-Naṣbeh,[198] and Tell Beit Mirsim[199] suggest that the original bowl sat on a ring base and that the overall tradition began already during the last half of the eighth century BCE. At Gezer, Gitin considered this design "a typologically hybrid form" that fell between his Types 65 and 67.[200] The primary characteristics ascribed to this offshoot form, however, seem to relate more directly to the

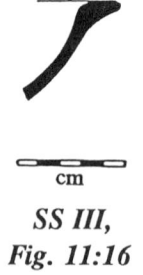

SS III, Fig. 11:16

---

[196]See E. Stern, *Material Culture of the Land of the Bible in the Persian Period, 538-332 B.C.* (Warminster: Aris and Phillips, 1982), 146, Fig. 241 (note also Stern's discussion of the evolution of metal bowls and their point of origin on pp. 144-45, Figs. 238-39). I might also point to similarities in the form of an inscribed silver bowl from the fifth century BCE found at Tell el-Maskhuta on the Nile Delta (p. xviii, Fig. 4).

[197]*Hazor II*, Pl. LXXIX:7 (Stratum VB).

[198]*TN II*, Pl. 56:1291 (late Iron Age II).

[199]*TBM III*, Pl. 21:15 (Stratum A$_2$).

[200]*Gezer III*, 191.

fragment presented in *SS III*, Fig. 19:7.[201] In my judgment, the lack of a noticeable carination on the sidewall of the Samaria piece represents its principal distinction from Gezer Type 65.[202] The closest parallel for form, ware, and surface treatment appears at Gezer in the last half of the eighth century under Type 67.[203] The combined attributes of this particular entry, then, suggest that it represents a locally made form that may well predate the group of Assyrian Palace Ware discussed above.

Entry No. 17 (pictured above with Nos. 22-23) is a shallow bowl with rounded bottom, acute but rounded carination, and short, straight upper sidewalls that flare out slightly and end in a simple rim mode. Gitin incorporates this piece under his Type 72 at Gezer,[204] but many of the traits seen on the Samaria bowl differ considerably from those witnessed at Gezer. The Gezer bowls showed a pinkish fabric (ranging from 5YR "pink" 7/4 to 7.5YR "pink" 7/4), red slip, and wheel burnishing on both the inner and outer surfaces of the vessel. By contrast, the construction of the Samaria piece involved a drab-colored matrix containing numerous orange flecks[205] and produced in a much thinner and harder fired ware than that of the Gezer bowls. Kenyon observed that this ware seemed related to similar forms discussed under PP 6 but seemed later than those pieces. While No. 17 resembles one of the principal Samaria Ware forms (as in *SS III*, Fig. 19:1), it clearly does not reflect the ware or surface treatment typical of that tradition.[206] Since other, similar forms reflect more of the basic traits of the Samaria Ware pattern, I believe that No. 17 slightly postdates Gitin's Type 72 and the parallels cited for that category of bowls.[207] This bowl retains the basic forming technique of the Samaria Ware group but reproduces the form in very different ware and lacks the surface treatment that typifies the more prestigious examples. If this entry relates at all to the Samaria Ware industry, it must fall very late in the overall tradition and likely represents a degenerate form of that group.

The bowl in No. 18 shows a very prominent keel on its lower sidewall and a relatively tall upper wall that bows slightly outward and ends in the kind of simple, everted rim that can assume various modes of construction. Similar, variant forms

---

[201] In addition to the forming tradition seen in this Samaria bowl, compare also its dark buff ware, red slip, and continuous wheel burnishing with the attributes of Gitin's Type 66.

[202] Compare *Gezer III*, Pls. 13:10; 14:18; and 15:7 (all from Stratum VIB = mid-ninth century).

[203] *Gezer III*, Pl. 20:11 (Stratum VIA). Compare also the antecedent form in Pl. 13:7 and other contemporary examples in Pl. 20:12-13 (with a stronger sidewall keel), 14, 15(?), 16-17.

[204] E.g., *Gezer III*, Pls. 22:8 (Stratum VB = late eighth and early seventh centuries BCE); 24:9 (Strata VB/VA = late eighth century and at least through the seventh century BCE).

[205] While the original stratification cards noted these flecks for this piece, Kenyon omitted mention of them in her annotation on p. 128 of *SS III*.

[206] Generally speaking, Samaria Ware shows a buff-colored fabric, red slip with buff bands left in reserve, burnishing inside and out, and often a series of closely-spaced concentric circles incised inside the buff band (see *SS III*, Fig. 19:1-4).

[207] *Gezer III*, 196-97.

showing a thicker construction appear in the north during the late eighth century at Khaldé,[208] Hazor,[209] and Tell Keisan.[210] Humbert has noted that "les parallèles provenant de Palestine couvrent tout le VIIIe s.; à Mogador et dans l'ouest méditerranéen cette forme est commune seulement au VIIe s."[211] This bowl, then, seems to represent a predominantly northern form that started in the Levant during the late eighth century BCE and that spread westward during the seventh century. Similar bowls of slightly thicker construction occurred along the southern coast of Israel during the decades of the late eighth and mid-seventh centuries.[212]

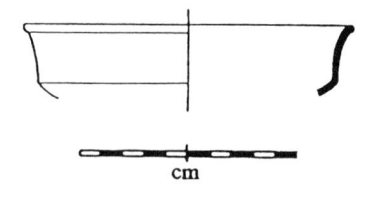

SS III, Fig. 11:18

Bowl No. 19 displays a hard grey ware and forming technique that resulted in an apparently curved lower sidewall, a point of carination, and an almost vertical upper sidewall that culminates in a nailhead-style rim. The exterior surface of the upper wall exhibits narrowly spaced grooves that give the appearance of ribbing. While close comparisons remain difficult to locate for this item, variations of the design are available and range in date from possible antecedent forms at Tell el-Farʿah (N),[213] Tell en-Naṣbeh,[214] Beth-Shemesh,[215] and also

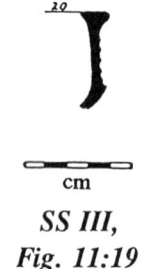

SS III, Fig. 11:19

---

[208]R. Saidah, "Fouilles de Khaldé, Rapport préliminaire sur la première et la deuxième campagnes (1961-1962)," *BMB* 19 (1966), Fig. 19:22.

[209]*Hazor II*, Pls. LXXIX:15 (Stratum VB) and XCVIII:1-3, 5, 35 (Stratum IV).

[210]*T. Keisan*, Pl. 40:7 (Niveau 5 = 720 to 700 BCE).

[211]*T. Keisan*, 170. For Mogador, see A. Jodin, *Mogador. Comptoir phénicien du Maroc atlantique. Études et travaux d'archéologie marocaine*, Vol. II: *Villes et sites du Maroc Atlantique* (Tanger, 1966), Fig. 118.

[212]E.g., *Ashdod I*, Fig. 40:2-3 (Area D, Local Stratum 2). M. Dothan and D. N. Freedman allowed that this level might have suffered destruction either at the hands of Sargon II in 712/11 BCE or by Pharaoh Psamtik I in the mid-seventh century BCE (see pp. 10-11, 141).

[213]*Chambon*, Pl. 58:9 (Niveau VIIb), for a possible early antecedent of the basic form without the exterior ribbing. A bowl with vertical upper sidewalls and some form of ribbing appeared in the early Iron II levels at Tell Jemmeh (see *Amiran*, 63:7 = *CPP*, 18 E 3). Since the artist did not present this form in section, however, it remains difficult to assess its possible links to the later tradition at Samaria. Also, the Jemmeh piece showed "two small horizontal degenerated handles," which prompted Amiran to include this bowl in her group of "debased derivation[s] from the Philistine two-handled krater"(*Amiran*, 199). While this association seems appropriate for her Pl. 63:6 and 11, it is more doubtful regarding 63:7. One may compare the Jemmeh bowl to a similar one from the Iron Age I period at Bethel (*Bethel*, Pl. 78:9) and then contrast both with *Bethel*, Pl. 63:7-8, which appear as a new developments in the course of Iron Age II.

[214]Note the krater forms in *TN II*, Pl. 1475, 1479.

[215]*AS IV*, Pl. LXI:12.

Lachish[216] to later affinities at most of those same sites.[217] But perhaps the best extant parallel comes from a single exemplar found in a late stratum at Megiddo,[218] where the excavators concluded that since this specimen "was found in Stratum I and because its distinctive peculiarities—ribbing and degree of firing—are unique, [it] appears to be a good example of a LI bowl."[219] Given the paucity of more suitable counterparts to the Samaria bowl, then, I shall for the present consider this piece as deriving from the late Iron Age II period, probably from the late eighth or perhaps early seventh century BCE.

The fragment of rim and uppermost sidewall shown in No. 20 represents a medium-to-large bowl or krater form on which the sidewalls can vary between a rounded mode and a biconical style with the keel falling near the midpoint of the body. In either body form, the upper sidewall generally slants inward and the forked rim has a wide, smooth groove placed in its top, undoubtedly to receive a lid. Depending on the posture of the rim, this groove device can appear on the exterior side of the rim's lip, as in the Samaria example. In many instances, however, the groove or channel lies in the top center portion of the rim between two equally-sized rim ridges or even toward the inside of the rim area.[220] The construction of these krater forms typically utilized a pinkish colored clay that appears buff or greyish-buff at the break. Satisfactory parallels showing the nuances in sidewall and the rim and groove designs just described suggest that this tradition began in the eighth century and continued well into the seventh century BCE. In support of this range, one may cite examples from Hazor,[221] Megiddo,[222] Gezer,[223]

SS III,
Fig. 11:20

---

[216]*Lachish III*, Pl. 100:620, 623 ("Type B.1"). Compare also Pl. 102:654, with handles and a very bowed motif on the upper sidewall. Though Tufnell's B.1 class generally shows a much thicker construction and the absence of exterior ribbing, the overall morphology of the group anticipates well the thinner and harder form of the Samaria bowl.

[217]Compare *TN II*, Pls. 56:1288, with only one ridge on the outside of the upper sidewall, and 56:1272, with exterior rilling; *AS-II*, Pl. 31:31; *AS-IV*, Pl. 66:6; Grant and Wright seemed to suggest that the general class of bowls representing this style (but without the ribbing) belonged primarily to the last phases of Stratum II (see *AS-V*, 137); and *Lachish III*, Pls. 99:604 (Tufnell's "Type B.2").

[218]*Megiddo I*, Pl. 23:2 (Stratum I). Here, however, the upper sidewall leans outward rather than inward, and the edge of the rim dips inward rather than maintaining a flat, horizontal surface as in the Samaria bowl.

[219]*Megiddo I*, 168 (LI = Late Iron period, which the Megiddo team started around 600 BCE).

[220]Compare the krater forms in *Hazor I*, Pl. XLVII:29-30; *Hazor V*, Fig. III.24:22 (Stratum VIII).

[221]Compare the sequence in *Hazor I*, Pl. LXVI:27 (Stratum VIII; compare also Nos. 25-26); *Hazor II*, Pl. LVI:7-11 (also Stratum VIII); *Hazor I*, Pl. LIV:27-29 (Stratum V); and *Hazor III-IV*, Pl. CCLV:5-6 (Stratum IV).

[222]Compare the "guttered rim" bowls represented by *Megiddo I*, Pl. 28:92 (Strata IV-II, in a brown ocher ware); see p. 169, § 65; also p. 189, where one sees that examples of this type appear concentrated in Stratum III at Megiddo.

[223]*Gezer III*, Pl. 24:20 (Stratum VB/VA).

and possibly also Lachish.[224] Variants appear in Transjordan at sites such as Tell es-Saʿidiyeh.[225] Because of the size and weight of these bowls when full, and given the apparently common use of lids, which would preclude lifting the vessels by the inside and outside portions of their rims, they often appear with large handles attached from the rim to the upper sidewall or keel area.

Finally, the complete form presented in *SS III*, Fig. 11:21 belongs to the same category of bowls as a sample assigned to Pit *i* and discussed at length earlier under PP 6 (see Fig. 10:4, including all references and parallels cited in that section). While the nascent traditions behind this style extend back to the very beginning of the Iron Age II period, the low ring base (so typical of Hazor VII) and low-riding break in the sidewall, together with the flat, incut rim, buff ware, red slip in and out, and interior ring-burnishing (described as "worn" in the unpublished notes) point to a date sometime during the eighth century BCE for this piece. To the corpus of comparisons cited in my earlier discussion, I may now add examples from Megiddo,[226] Tell Qiri,[227] Tell el-Farʿah,[228] and Beth-Shan.[229] This bowl, then, may well have originated prior to the events of 722/21 BCE, and Kenyon observed that the ware resembled closely that of other bowls from both PP 4 and PP 6.[230]

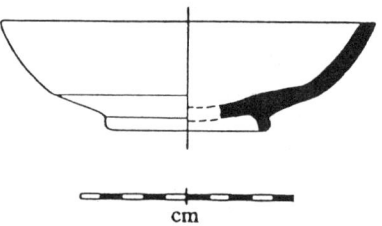

SS III, Fig. 11:21

In PP 6, I addressed the possible affinities of Type No. 21 with traditions attending the so-called Samaria Ware (see also n. 216). That several analysts, including Amiran, members of the Yoqneʿam Regional Project,[231] and others, have included a wide variety of forms in this class would seem to suggest that several additional pieces within this mixed PP 7 collection might also relate in some way to latent expressions of the Samaria Ware industry (e.g., Nos. 17, 18, 21, 23; compare even No. 7 with the

---

[224]*Lachish III*, Pl. 97:552. Tufnell placed this specimen in her "Class S.13" category of storage jars and drew a direct, though not very apt, comparison between it and *SS III*, Fig. 6:24 from PP 4.

[225]*Saʿidiyeh 1*, Fig. 7:1 (Area AA, Stratum VII).

[226]*Megiddo I*, Pl. 25:68.

[227]*T. Qiri*, Fig. 43:7 (treated in this report as a common form of Samaria Ware).

[228]*Chambon*, 67; Pl. 58:13-14 (Niveau VIId and VIIe, respectively).

[229]*Beth-Shan*, James, Fig. 63:11 (Upper Level V; in brown ware, with reddish color wash on interior, over rim, and down to the inflection of the sidewall). Note the discussion of "carinated saucer bowls" on p. 119, particularly the observation regarding the close affinities between the Beth-Shan, Level V, sample and the bowls from PP 4-6 at Samaria (James cites the unstratified examples in *SS III*, Figs. 14:8-9 and 17:4). She also adds that "the smaller, unburnished, carinated bowls with disk base, . . . (Fig. 63,10) and which are a type fossil of Beisan Level IV, do not seem to be present at all at Samaria."

[230]*SS III*, 128.

[231]*Amiran*, Pls. 66-67; *T. Qiri*, 148, 171, 201-02 and Fig. 43:1-7.

ridged style of Samaria Ware in the Qiri report). In a similar move, others appear ready to overlap certain attributes of the Samaria Ware family and the Assyrian ceramic traditions. For example, while Gitin places No. 17 in the former group,[232] Pratico views it as belonging to the latter variety.[233] In nearly all cases, it remains difficult to speak with certainty about such an assortment of bowls without the benefit of a visual inspection of the items themselves. In my judgment, the identification of true Samaria Ware involves more than finding associations with a limited number of forms; it also includes finding a specific color of matrix, slip, and surface treatment (such as concentric bands in reserve slip). While *SS III*, Figs. 4:8, 10 (PP 3), 10:4 (PP 6), 11:16, 18, 21 (PP 7), 18:5-8 (E 207), and 19:1-4 (S Tombs, E 207, and Strip Qb) may resemble Samaria Ware *forms*, all but the items presented in Fig. 19 fail to meet the other attributes specific to real Samaria Ware. This does not, however, preclude these bowls from representing imitations or traditions that are ancillary to the Samaria Ware industry.

In the PP 7 assemblage of bowls, I understand Nos. 17, 22, and 23 as clearly related to Assyrian ceramic traditions, with only No. 22 reflecting a potentially authentic import. I also include in this group *SS III*, Figs. 18:9-10 and 32:3-4 (and possibly also 5).[234] Besides the sites noted above, excavations have recovered Assyrian-style pottery from Stratum V at Ramat Raḥel[235] in Israel and from seventh-sixth century levels at a number of sites in Transjordan (including Heshbon, Adoni-Nur, Amman, Umm el-Biyara, Buṣeirah, Ghrareh, es-Sadeh, and Tell el-Kheleifeh).[236] It is important to note that many of these witnesses postdate the fall of Samaria by several decades, even though most of the regions in Transjordan had fallen under Assyrian provincial status prior to the collapse of power at Samaria. One sees here a case in which the arrival of elements from a foreign ceramic industry or the manufacture of local imitations of that industry does not necessarily occur contemporaneously with or even immediately following the military or political presence of that foreign power in a given region. The same situation appears to attend the Assyrian-style pottery at Samaria. While Kenyon's chronological and historical frameworks would pose a direct link between the putative military assault against Samaria and the presence of these bowls, there clearly seems to exist some hiatus between the events of 722/21 BCE and the appearance of these forms in significant numbers.[237] For the most part, they belong

---

[232] *Gezer III*, 197.

[233] *Kheleifeh*—Pratico, 42.

[234] See Kenyon's comments in *SS III*, 193.

[235] *Ramat Raḥel I*, Fig. 11:15.

[236] See *Kheleifeh*—Pratico, 42, for all references.

[237] In this vein, see *Holladay*, Fig. 41:G (= *SS III*, Fig. 10:8, PP 6) and his comments on p. 204; also J. S. Holladay, "Of Sherds and Strata: Contributions toward an Understanding of the Archaeology of the Divided Monarchy," pp. 253-93 in *Magnalia Dei: The Mighty Acts of God*. F. M. Cross, W. E. Lemke, and P. D. Miller, Jr., eds. (Garden City: Doubleday, 1976), 272. Note as well Amiran's comment that all imported Assyrian Ware occurs "in strata of the period following the Assyrian conquest of Samaria,

at least in the second quarter of the seventh century BCE, and therefore they call for a significant lowering of the depositional date assigned to the layers that contained them.

Finally, I may briefly note the "extremely heavy bowl" made of course red ware presented in entry No. 36. In her unpublished notes, Kenyon referred to this piece as a mortar. Most late mortars, however, possess sidewalls that angle in much more acutely toward the vessel's base.[238] Moreover, the unusually wide interior diameter (38 cm) estimated for the original vessel also militates against viewing this fragment as a late Iron II or Persian mortar form. Only one observation seems clear at this point: this specimen does not seem at home in the Iron Age. At best, it may bear some distant relationship to the series of so-called pans that appeared at certain sites, such as Tell en-Naṣbeh, late in the period.[239] But this possible connection remains uncertain. There is not a single decent parallel available anywhere in Amiran's entire catalogue of forms. Given the negligible size of the fragment and the laconic nature of Kenyon's description of it in the final report, this entry must, for the present, remain somewhat of an anomaly.

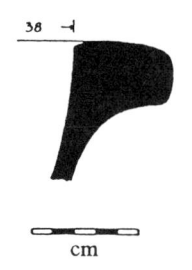

SS III, Fig. 11:36

The Joint Expedition retrieved this distinctive fragment from the same local layer as bowl Nos. 1, 5, and 7 (Room *g*, Segment *120.121.19.126*, Layer VII; fig. 67). To the excavators, this rubble-filled matrix actually appeared mixed in with the midden-like deposit of Layer VIII, which lay beneath VII. Judging from the field section, this deposit included many large boulders and exhibited an entirely different composition from the much cleaner fills that overlay it (= Layer VI).

b. Cooking Pots

The final excavation report included only one cooking-pot fragment in it PP 7 assemblage, and several apparent mistakes of recording seem to attend this entry in *SS III* (see my notes marked ▷ in Appendix A). The principal concern[240] in this regard centers on an apparent misprint in the published annotation relating to this piece. It reads: "The type with short thick ridged rim, which appears in IV, and is common in VI, continues throughout VII."[241] The reference to a "thick ridged rim" seems espe-

---

that is, after 721 B.C." (also *Amiran*, 291).

[238]E.g., *T. Keisan*, Pls. 20:15-21 (Niveau 3); 31:1-7 (Niveau 4); *Gezer III*, Pl. 30:1-17 (Stratum IV = fifth and fourth centuries BCE).

[239]*TN II*, 51, § 54; Pl. 78:1784-94, with only 1794 displaying an unusually thick, outer rim ledge as in the Samaria fragment.

[240]A more inconsequential error occurred in the published registry number, which should be QX 133 instead of QX 113. I believe my entry in Appendix A for Fig. 11:32 is correct as it appears there.

[241]*SS III*, 129.

cially inappropriate for this entry. In the handwritten draft of *SS III*, the description of a jar fragment registered as Q 5224 (= 11:26) includes the following: "rim of *cooking pot*, light red ware, with grits. *This is the type with short thick ridged rim which appears in IV, is common in VI, and continues throughout VII*" (emphasis added). Regardless of whether the italicized portion of this statement applies to the jar neck shown in Fig. 11:26, it clearly does not suit the cooking-pot rim and handle in No. 32. Consequently, one should delete that observation from the text of *SS III*; it is misleading in terms of both the morphology of No. 32 and the chronological distribution of the ware used to manufacture the form.

In general, this fragment bears certain affinities to a late Iron Age II group of deep-bodied, narrow-necked cooking pots that seem more widely attested in the south than in the north. At Tel Goren, for example, most late Iron II cooking pots/jugs show bloated bodies and more strongly everted or flaring rims (which are sometimes rilled or molded) than the one witnessed on this Samaria pot.[242] Cooking-Pot Type 100, limited to Stratum II at Lachish, closely resembles both the form and ware of the Samaria piece.[243] In the north, one can witness the basic evolution of this overall design in a series of Iron II jar forms from Megiddo,[244] though this family generally exhibits slightly taller, more erect necks and variant rim modes.[245] When compared to the ceramic corpus from Tell el-Farʿah (N), No. 32 seems to belong to a late group of Niveau VII cooking-pot forms that Chambon labeled "Type B."[246]

SS III,
Fig. 11:32

Perhaps the best parallels for No. 32 come from Tell en-Naṣbeh,[247] where numerous cooking jugs displayed a medium hard, dark grey ware with a blackish grey core that included very fine white grits plus some occasional large ones. The surfaces of this crockery were often wet-smoothed and showed evidence of smoke blackening. Mouth diameters ranged from 80-90 mm (it would be helpful to know Kenyon's

---

[242]*En-Gedi*, Figs. 8:15; 18:1-8 = Stratum V; all again with grits, and in reddish-brown to dark brown clay. Compare also *Hazor I*, Pl. LXXX:27 (Stratum II). See other examples of late Iron II cooking jars from Arad VII and VI, Lachish II, Tell Masos, Ramat Raḥel VA, and Meṣad Ḥashavyahu, in *M. & Y. Aharoni*, Fig. 8:3, 3, 3 (usually appearing in dark brown clay with grits). Note their comment that this style "appears almost exclusively in the 7th-century strata . . . . Since this common vessel does not appear in any earlier context, it is a most important type for chronology" (p. 86).

[243]*Lachish V*, Pl. 50:12. This specimen shows a hard-fired, brown-colored ware with whitish grits.

[244]*Megiddo I*, Pls. 20:115 (Stratum V); 10:38 (Stratum III); 9:33 (Strata II-I); compare *Lachish V*, Pl. 42:5 (Stratum V).

[245]Compare also the krater form in *Gezer II*, 32:4 (Field II, Stratum 6A = 9th century).

[246]*Chambon*, 61-62; Pl. 53:14. He describes these vessels as having a narrow opening ("ouverture étroite") but also a high neck ("col haut"); the latter trait fits the Samaria pot less well. Similarly, the ware of 53:14 is a "pâte rouge à dég[raissant] calcaire" (p. 210), which fits except for Samaria's distinctive *grey* coloring.

[247]*TN II*, Pl. 49:1033, 1036 (see also No. 1034 with a compatible design on a more bloated body).

estimate for the diameter of the mouth on No. 32). Wampler described this basic class as "deep-bodied and narrow-necked pots," and he noted that one subgroup of them sometimes included rilled rims (perhaps more a southern type).[248] The simple, rounded, everted rim mode of the Samaria fragment, however, fits best with his "Group 3.a," i.e., with the "plain variety," which he dated mainly to the Late Iron Age and Hellenistic periods at ʿAtlît, Tell Abu Hawām, and Samaria.[249] The entry also bears a striking morphological similarity to a type of single-handled cup known from late seventh-century levels in Nimrud,[250] and the darker color ware of No. 32 may strengthen that potential connection.

Given the stratigraphic location of this piece in Layer VI of Segment *120.121.19.126*, which I have shown represents the subfloor fill beneath a reportedly "Period VIII" surface in Layer V (fig. 67), a dating at the very end of the Iron Age II period or even slightly later still seems reasonable for this piece. While it has not totally divorced itself from previous Iron II traditions of jar and cooking-pot/jar manufacture, No. 32 seems clearly to reflect a late developing stream of tradition oriented more forward than backward in time. This fragment, then, becomes an important datum, for unless one treats it as an intrusive element in its context, the depositional date of the matrix that yielded it must fall considerably later than the initial Assyrian takeover of Samaria.

c. Jars and Jar Stands

Following the assemblage of bowls, the second largest class of vessels consists of eight fragmentary jar forms plus an intact jar stand. Though this still seems like a limited group, these entries comprise nearly a quarter of the entire PP 7 collection (24.3%). Most of them came from the large area called Room *l* (fig. 56), while Rooms *g* and *hk* contributed two pieces each. I have already noted the apparent conflation of some of the descriptions recorded for 11:26 with the annotations intended for the cooking-pot rim and handle in 11:32. Two of the jar fragments, including the stand itself, were marked as discards in some of the unpublished materials (indicated with *). Details relating to the findspots associated with these fragments appear in Table 50 (compare Appendix A).

The fragments in Nos. 24-25 reflect basic, late Iron Age II developments of the ridged-necked, profiled storage jar rim, though the two entries differ slightly in their respective wares and surface treatments and in the posture of their necks and rims. No. 24 shows a taller, more erect neck line, a rim thickened both internally and externally and beveled slightly outward, and a neck ridge that falls near a very clear juncture of the neck and shoulder. On the other hand, item No. 25 displays a shorter,

---

[248] *TN II*, 30, § 8. Compare the "low-necked cooking jar" in *T. Qiri*, Fig. 34:5.

[249] *TN II*, 30, §§ 7-10.

[250] J. Oates, *Iraq* 21 (1959), Pl. XXXVIII:92.

PP 7: HOUSE FLOORS — POTTERY

SS III Published Figure	Registry No. (* = marked for discard)	Provenance Strip	Coordinates	Feature	Local Layer
Jars:					
11:24	QX 111	Q(x)-k	120.121.19.126	Room *g*	VI
11:25	QX 115	Q(x)-k(?)	122.125.19.121	Room *hk*	IIIz
▷11:26	Q 5224	Qn	509.126	‡Room *j(f*?)	IIa.f
11:27	QX 110	Q(x)-k	120.121.19.126	Room *g*	VIII
11:29	Q 5229	Qn	509.126	Room *l*	VIII
11:30	Q 5228	Qn	504.503.509.508	Room *l*	Va.z
11:31	*Q 5218	Qn	504.503.509.508	Room *l*	Va
11:33	Q 5223	Qn	504.503.509.508	Room *l*	Va
Jar Stand:					
†11:35	*Q 2368	Qk	125.144	Room *hk*	IIIa

(See Appendix A for details pertaining to these recording errors)

(All information presented here now agrees with the original stratification cards)

Provenance Data:
PP7 Jars & Jar Stands from the Putative Destruction Debris
Covering the BP V Floors
Table 50

inwardly inclined neck, a rim that bevels more toward the inside, and an outer ridge located closer to the midpoint of the low neck. Though both bodies are missing, this style generally displayed rounded shoulders and base and a body mode that achieved maximum diameter around its midpoint. Together with Fig. 6:14 from PP 4 and 21:5 from E 207,[251] Kenyon believed No. 24 belonged to a so-called hippo jar, on which the widest diameter would fall in the lower one-third of the body, directly above the rounded base. But not enough of the sidewalls remain to establish this identification for either entry; moreover, the neck on hippo-shaped jars generally inclines inward, as in No. 25, not No. 24.[252]

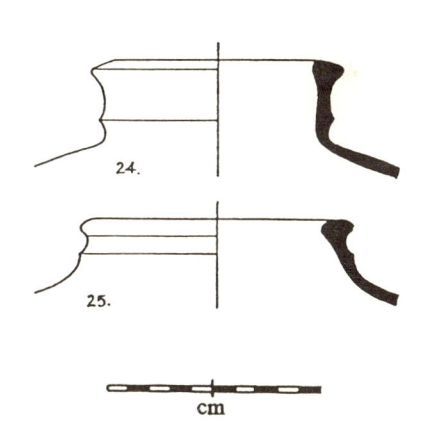

SS III, Fig. 11:24-25

---

[251] *SS III*, 163-64.

[252] See Chapter I, p. 94, n. 325. Compare also Gitin's comments in *Gezer III*, 122, regarding the misuse of "hippo-" by Crowfoot, Kenyon, and Holladay to refer to the basic oval- or ovoid-jar form.

These storage jar rims occur almost exclusively in the north, and, while their historical antecedents reach as far back as the tenth century BCE, it seems unlikely that the tradition extended much (if at all) beyond the closing quarter of the eighth century BCE. At least, these vessels do not appear in secure stratigraphic contexts after that time. The chronological spread of related variants at Hazor,[253] Megiddo,[254] Ta'anach,[255] Tell Qiri and Yoqne'am,[256] Beth-Shan,[257] and southward to the border sites of Bethel[258] and Tell en-Naṣbeh,[259] help to confirm this picture.[260] With a conspicuous absence at Tell Beit Mirsim, only a few attestations of this form occur in the south, such as those from Gibeon[261] and Lachish,[262] and these exemplars appear to represent late, declining or vestigial traces of the basic tradition (as do some of the latest rims from the north).[263] At Gezer, the best comparison comes from a mid-ninth-century BCE context, but the thickened rim is angled out much more than on the Samaria pieces.[264] Neither did this family of jars enjoy a widespread distribution in

---

[253] *Strata X-IX* — *Hazor II*, Pls. LI:18-19; LII:24; *Hazor III-IV*, Pl. CLXXIX:14 (in brown clay); **Stratum VIII** — *Hazor I*, Pl. XLVIII:12-13; *Hazor II*, Pl. LX:1-8 (mostly with necks that exhibit a vertical posture like Samaria's No. 24); **Stratum VII** — *Hazor I*, Pl. L:34, 36 (with rims that are thickened mostly on the exterior; in grey or grey-buff ware); *Hazor II*, Pl. LXV:4; *Hazor III-IV*, Pls. CLXXX:21; CCXVI:6-7; **Stratum VI** — *Hazor II*, Pl. LXXI:10, 11, 14; **Stratum V** — *Hazor I*, Pl. LXXXIV:17; *Hazor II*, Pl. LXXV:14; *Hazor III-IV*, Pls. CLXXXIX:21; CCXXIX:6-7; **Stratum IV** — *Hazor II*, Pl. CI:6.

[254] *Megiddo I*, Pls. 14:70 (Strata IV-III, but the rim shows a more bulbous and less flattened head than the Samaria pieces display); 15:76 (listed as Strata IV-II, though 77.3% of them came from IV-III); 15:77 (listed as IV-I, but the only registered piece derived once again from III). The excavators at Megiddo also classified these rims in the "hippo" jar category and forwarded the dubious suggestion that "it is fairly certain that they are the prototypes of the equally hideous Hellenistic water jars common throughout Palestine" (p. 167, § 42), such as those seen in *HES I*, Fig. 175. The ridged necked with bulbous-style rim also appears on the so-called sausage-jar forms.

[255] *Ta'anach*, 43-44; Figs. 52:1 (Period IIB, with a smoothed profiled look); 75:1, 3 (Period V, with a more sharply cut, angular profile).

[256] *T. Qiri*, Fig. 35:3, 9 (with shoulders that droop more than their Samaria counterparts).

[257] *Beth-Shan*, James, Figs. 64:12 (Upper Level V) and 70:5 (Level V; in black ware with a purplish surface).

[258] *Bethel*, Pl. 67:3, 5, 6, 11.

[259] *TN II*, Pl. 18:303-308 (see p. 137 for a description of these vessels; otherwise, they hardly receive mention in the narrative proper).

[260] Compare also similar jars at Tell el-Far'ah (N) in *Chambon*, 54; Pl. 45:6-7 (Niveau VIId).

[261] *Gibeon*, Figs. 39:25; 45:7 (Levels 4 and 1, eighth to early seventh centuries BCE).

[262] *Lachish III*, Pl. 94:481 (Level II).

[263] E.g., *Ta'anach*, Fig. 75:1 (Period V); *Hazor I*, Pls. LXXVII:30 (Stratum III); LXXVIII:25 (Strata IV-III). Rast drew a comparison between these Hazor specimens and No. 25 at Samaria, but the Hazor rims are more rounded or beveled to the outside.

[264] *Gezer III*, Pl. 14:10 (Stratum VIB). Other entries in Gitin's "Type 2" jar class show more bulbous, less flattened rims (e.g., Pls. 12:4-5, from Stratum VIB; and 18:3-4, Stratum VIA).

Transjordan, judging from the paucity of good parallels in current publications at sites such as Tell es-Saʿidiyeh, Heshbon, and others in the Madaba Plains Project.[265]

Given the relative placements of their respective neck ridges, it may seem probable that No. 25 dates to a slightly earlier phase of this tradition than does No. 24. But the taller, more vertical necks and outwardly beveled rim of No. 24 agrees well with a series of forms already attested in Niveaux III-IV at Tel ʿAmal from the mid-to-late tenth century BCE,[266] as well as at Hazor Strata X-IX[267] and Taʿanach Period IIB.[268] Moreover, a very close parallel for No. 25 comes from a reportedly sixth-century BCE context at Bethel.[269]

In sum, I may say that these jar rims may well predate the loss of Israelite control over Samaria. The secondary nature of the local stratigraphy in which each of the findspots lay certainly leaves open this possibility.

The two tall-necked jar fragments in Nos. 26-27 also bear a resemblance to each other while displaying slightly nuanced rim-form modes. They both show a hard-fired red ware that appears grey at the break and contains some white, limestone grits.[270] Generally, this class of vessels features a high, straight-sided neck that bends outwardly at the very top and ends in a rim that is thickened to varying degrees. The best parallels come from Bethel,[271] Tell en-Naṣbeh,[272] and Gezer.[273] These fragments appear to belong to a group of medium sized jar or bottle forms whose origins lie no earlier than the seventh century BCE. Gitin has suggested that, in Palestine, this class reflects "a local copy of a form common in Ammonite pottery . . . and in Neo-Assyrian pottery at Fort Shalmaneser."[274]

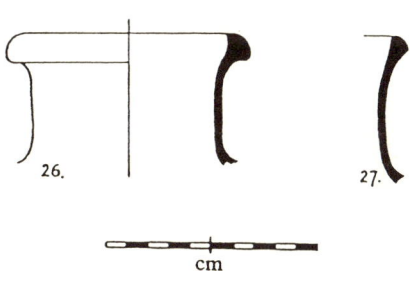

SS III, Fig. 11:26-27

---

[265] I could find only a few possible parallels, such as in *MPP-1*, Fig. 19.6:6 (Integrated Phase 3); *MPP-2*, Fig. 3.12:6-7 (Field A: Field Phase 3A); from Heshbon, see Lugenbeal and Sauer, *AUSS* 10 (1972), Pl. VIII:443-44.

[266] *T. ʿAmal*, Fig. 8:6 (IV) and 7-9 (III).

[267] See n. 253; compare *Hazor V*, Fig. III.20:13 and the transitional form in Fig. III.22:10 (Stratum X).

[268] *Taʿanach*, Figs. 33:1-2; 34:1-3.

[269] *Bethel*, Pl. 67:11. Compare also Pl. 67:1 and p. 75, § 299, n. 63.

[270] Recall my earlier comments on the recording difficulties between No. 26 and the cooking jar fragment in *SS III*, Fig. 11:32.

[271] *Bethel*, Pl. 64:19 (with a rumpled surface on the interior neckwall).

[272] *TN II*, Pl. 27:447-48; *TN—Cistern*, Fig. 2:x231 (compare also x89 as a possible variant form).

[273] *Gezer III*, Pl. 26:14 (Stratum VA).

[274] *Gezer III*, 144. Compare exemplars from the Adoni Nur Tomb in *Madeba*, Fig. 22:89, 90; from Assyria, see J. Oates, *Iraq* 21 (1959), Pls. XXXVIII:97-98; XXXIX:101, with two ridges around the midsection of the neck.

As with other local imitations, the reddish ware of the Samaria pieces helps to distinguish them from the greenish-buff clay used in the manufacture of the true Assyrian vessels.

The provenance data surrounding No. 26 perhaps remain too muddled to allow us to draw definite historical conclusions based on this fragment. I may, however, mention an important observation concerning the fact that No. 27 came from Layer VIII of Segment *120.121.19.126* in Room g. I have shown that this .20 m-thick, midden-like deposit lay very near the bedrock beneath that room. And though Kenyon did not show them in her field section (fig. 67), faint traces of a burnt plaster floor lay immediately beneath Layer VIII and the rock surface.[275] Unless this late jar rim represents an intrusive element in this context, it helps to corroborate at least a seventh-century BCE date for the succeeding levels found in this room[276]—levels that yielded much of the pottery published as a 722 BCE horizon group.

The entries in Nos. 29-30 represent typical Iron Age II holemouth rims. Because of my extended coverage of these and related forms in PP 4 (*SS III*, Fig. 6:19-24), I need not repeat the details or the corpus of parallels cited there. The best comparisons currently appear to come from Tell en-Naṣbeh.[277] Though neither of the present fragments shows a distinct shoulder, the bulging profile of their remaining sidewalls indicates that they do not belong to the class of smaller jars with cylindrically shaped bodies that drop almost straight down from the rim area;[278] rather, in each case, the widest diameter would have fallen near the midsection of the body. This single trait helps to distinguish these Samaria jars from most other late Iron Age holemouths with cylindrical bodies and, at the same time, makes good parallels difficult to locate.[279] Clearly, the more rounded body appeared less often than did its sack-like counterpart. Entry 29 exhibits a hard-ringing, variably drab ware that appears grey at the break and contains only some whitish limestone grits. The manufacture of No. 30, on the other hand, utilized a soft, buff-colored clay with a larger quantity of grit inclusions. Judging from its ware color

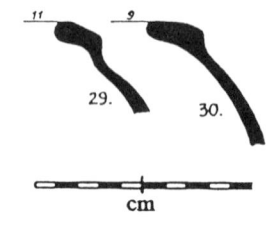

SS III, Fig. 11:29-30

---

[275]Kenyon recorded this level, Layer IX, in her unpublished fieldnotes.

[276]This includes the rubble of Layer VII, the subfloor fills/makeup of Layer VI, and the reportedly BP VIII surface in Layer V.

[277]*TN II*, Pl. 322-23, 325-26. For examples with more cylindrical bodies, see the numerous examples on Pls. 25-26. Compare Gitin's "Type 10" jar class in *Gezer III*, 130-32; Pl. 26:29-30 (Stratum VA), though the middle part of the rim is more strongly pinched in each of these examples and thereby creates a deeper groove around the exterior rim surface that accentuates the outer flange.

[278]E.g., *TBM I*, Pl. 52:1-7, 9 (Stratum A). While No. 30 shares a rim mode similar to an exemplar from Tell Qiri (*T. Qiri*, Fig. 35:15), one can detect a difference in body forms from the more cylindrical shape at Qiri to the more rounded motif on the Samaria piece.

[279]An excellent comparison for No. 30 is available from Stratum V at Tel Goren (*En-Gedi*, Fig. 21:3). Compare also *T. ʿAmal*, Fig. 7:8 (Niveau I); and *TN—Cistern*, Fig. 4:x175 (Cistern 370).

and texture, its more horizontally positioned rim, and its narrower mouth (9 cm), No. 30 may have originated slightly before the rise of No. 29; the former specimen might easily belong in the late eighth century BCE, while the latter seems better suited to seventh-century traditions.

The Joint Expedition retrieved both of these holemouth rims from the area labeled "Room *l*." But, unfortunately, Kenyon found No. 29 in a layer of Segment *509.126* that she herself correlated to known fill deposits in adjacent areas of exposure. Similarly, No. 30 came from the backfill of a foundation trench associated with a late Roman wall built during the fourth century CE (Wall 508a; Layer Va.z.; fig. 62). Due to their stratigraphic locations, then, these fragments cannot help to refine the evolution of the Iron Age II family of holemouth jars; neither can they shed any substantive light on conditions at Samaria in the late eighth century BCE. Moreover, the matrix that yielded these pieces (particularly No. 30) clearly bears no direct connection to a putative Assyrian destruction level covering all the rooms north of the courtyard area.

Like the holemouth rim in No. 30, the next two jar fragments (31, 33) also came from Segment *504.503.509.508* in Room *l*, but from Layer Va, which, as I have shown, lay primarily in the northwestern portion of that room (see figs. 60-62). And once again, as the discussion surrounding fig. 63 showed, Va represents a level of fill debris poured against the eastern face of Wall 552, which Kenyon dated to the early Herodian period. The pottery contained in that matrix, then, should not date later than that time but could conceivably include goods from any period prior to that point. Unfortunately, neither entry commands a respectable number of adequate parallels.

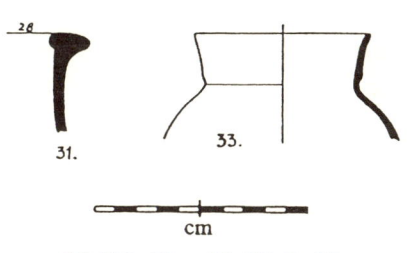

SS III, Fig. 11:31 & 33

The published description of No. 31 reads simply, "Fragment rim of jar, red brown ware."[280] As Table 50 indicates, this piece constituted one of two jar fragments marked for discard in certain unpublished field records. It shows a flat, horizontal rim that produces a kind of nailhead profile with an outside ledge rather than a collar, and its high upper sidewalls flex slightly outward as they drop away from the rim. If Kenyon's estimate of the mouth diameter is accurate, the original vessel had an unusually wide opening for a storage jar (28 cm).[281] That fact, coupled with the interior thickening of the rim, militates against seeing in this piece another fragment of an Assyrian-style, high-necked jar or goblet. These traits also distinguish it from most all established local traditions of Iron Age II store jars. Rather than claiming membership in the jar family, this rim may, in my judgment, belong to an Iron II class of kraters or

---

[280] *SS III*, 129.

[281] In a form-based paradigm of ceramic analysis, a jar basically constitutes a "closed" form, i.e., one in which the diameter of the minimal opening measures less than 50% of the maximum diameter of the overall vessel (see *APTJ*, 29, 45-46). It seems unlikely that this "jar" would have boasted an original diameter greater than 56 cm (i.e., over twice the size of the suggested mouth).

deep bowls whose antecedents reach at least as far back as the tenth century BCE[282] (and probably earlier still).[283] If, on the other hand, this fragment does belong to a class of jars, it seems best suited to a type of cooking jar that dates to the Persian period.[284] Without a fuller view of the sidewalls and a better corpus of comparative material for the rim itself, I shall, for the moment, interpret this piece as an Iron II krater form that very likely predated the fall of Samaria.[285]

If, in relation to the events of 722/21 BCE, No. 31 represents an earlier tradition of pottery making, then No. 33 seems to point in the opposite direction, toward much later motifs. Its thin construction in purplish-grey, hard ware resulted in a form with very narrow, drooping shoulders (that probably produced a bag-shaped body) and a svelte, collared neck that is tapered to a simple, slightly everted rim. The best parallels come from Hellenistic levels at Bethel,[286] though these jars usually occur in a reddish or buff-colored ware.[287] Large cylindrical-to-bag-shaped jars with rounded bases maintained a similar rim-form mode throughout the second and first centuries BCE, though the neck collar tended to lengthen as the period progressed.[288] As far as the rim mode itself goes, there also exists some resemblance to certain forms of Hellenistic cooking pots; the wide neck relative to the apparent body diameter might support such an association.[289] In any event, this rim fragment appears to us to date no earlier than the Hellenistic period.

The fact that both 31 and 33 came from the same context speaks to the heterogeneous nature of that deposit. As seen in figs. 62-63, Layer Va represents the first phase of a two- or three-part filling that ancient workers poured into the northwestern sector of Room *1* (Layers IIIb and IIc followed closely upon Va). Because of the numerous robber trenches that crisscross this room, it remains uncertain just how

---

[282] Compare *Megiddo I*, Pl. 32:167 (Stratum V); *Amiran*, Pl. 69:7 (from *Megiddo II*, Pl. 78:18, Stratum VIA); *Hazor II*, Pls. LVI:3 (Stratum VIII); LXXXIV:2 (Stratum V, also with bar handles); *Lachish V*, Pl. 39:1 (Stratum VI); *Lachish III*, Pl. 91:403 (Level III); *T. Qiri*, Fig. 39:8; *Bethel*, Pl. 63:7-8; *Lachish III*, Pl. 100:623 and *Lachish III-Text*, 268-69, Bowl "Type B.1."

[283] Compare even *Hazor III-IV*, Pl. CCLIX:19 (Area H, Stratum 3).

[284] E.g., *Gezer III*, Pl. 31:12-13 (Stratum IV).

[285] Though the upper sidewall on these kraters often assumes an oblique posture as it angles out to the point of carination, this is not always the case (compare the sidewall stance of *AS-IV*, Pl. LXIV:1 against that of 2-4).

[286] *Bethel*, Pl. 69:13-23. Compare the possibly related exemplars from Stratum II at Tel Goren (*En-Gedi*, Fig. 27:2-3). In Transjordan, see *APTJ*, p. 213, No. 300. For a similar rim mode, though with a narrower neck and a lighter color ware with more grit inclusions, see *TN II*, 10, § 51, Pl. 17:298.

[287] *Bethel*, p. 78, § 310 and p. 107.

[288] See examples from Beth-Zur, Bethany, Jerusalem, and Qumran in P. W. Lapp, *PCC*, 146-47, Type 11:D, E, F, G. See also Lapp's additional comments regarding the Bethel jars just cited in *Bethel*, 78, §§ 310-12. Subsequently, from Kenyon's pre-Herodian "Roman 1a" period, compare *SS III*, 295-96; Fig. 69:11.

[289] *Gezer III*, Pl. 42:25 (Stratum IIA).

far south or east these deposits originally extended. The field sections, however, provide clear evidence that confirms two facts: (1) Wall 508a, from the fourth century CE (Kenyon's "R.4" period), cut through the preexisting Va; (2) the early Herodian Wall 552, however, did not penetrate this fill; rather, the latter was poured against the eastern face of 552. This leveling layer, then, appears to date to the early Herodian period; therefore, it is no surprise to find both an Iron II krater rim and a Hellenistic jar rim in its matrix.

Within the category of jars or jar-related forms, I come finally to the stand presented in *SS III*, Fig. 11:35. This intact piece, also designated as a discard in the unpublished records, came from Layer IIIa in Segment *125.144* in Room *hk*, situated directly south of *l* and the *g-h-i* complex. While the Samaria report does not include a description of the ware used to make this stand,[290] its form displays matching, triangular shaped collars around both the rim and the base, which are joined by the typical concave sidewalls that create an hourglass shape and, in this case, remain plain and without any painted, incised, grooved, or ridged decorations or open fenestrations.[291] The Samaria stand belongs to the group of taller units, which seems to dominate the extant assemblage[292] and very likely functioned to support a medium-to-large size jar. Some of the shorter stands, which seem less suited to stabilizing larger jars, probably supported other vessel types, such as bowls, chalices, and the like.[293]

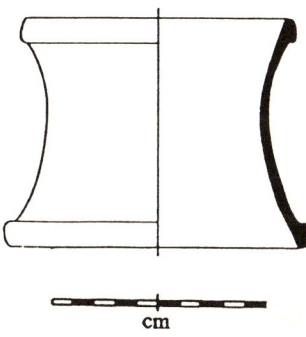

SS III, Fig. 11:35

Due to the relatively sparse attestation and the lack of distinct, diagnostic attributes of these stands, most excavation reports have considered them to hold little, if any, real chronological value.[294] Even some of the major ceramic catalogues either

---

[290] While some reports describe a drab-colored clay with grit inclusions for these items (e.g., *AS II*, Pl. XLI:24), the ringstands from Tell en-Naṣbeh display an apparently better-quality matrix that was well levigated, wet smoothed, and hard fired and that often showed signs of horizontal, vertical, or ring (spiral) burnishing (see *TN II*, 51, § 51).

[291] In contrast, compare, for example, *Hazor I*, Pl. LVII:22-23 (Stratum V); *Megiddo I*, Pl. 34:12 (Strata III-II) and 34:13 (Stratum IV); *Beth-Shan*, James, Fig. 53:14 (Level VI); G. W. Van Beek, *Eretz-Israel* 20 (Yadin Volume, 1989), Fig. III.10:249, 283. A good form parallel for the Samaria piece, but with decorative red bands bordered by black lines, appears in *Chapman*, Fig. 17:282 (also p. 161), from the site of Qrayé, near Sidon.

[292] Shorter stands were, however, attested at the site (see *SS III*, Fig. 28:6-8, from E 207; and 9-11, from Strip Zd; *HES I*, Fig. 153:13-15).

[293] See Wampler's comments in *TN II*, 51, § 49. Some studies have suggested that the shorter types succeeded the taller models and therefore claim a later date, but this hypothesis requires much further corroboration before becoming an established principle of classification. It is my opinion that the difference in height relates more to specialized functions rather than to chronological sequencing.

[294] See the comments, for example, in *Megiddo I*, 170, § 70. This sentiment echoes through many sub-

exclude any reference to stands or barely mention these items in their otherwise detailed discussions.[295] Though the use of stands extends at least back to the second millennium BCE (when more jars developed rounded or pointed vs. flattened bases),[296] their distribution in the Iron Age begins in Stratum IV at Megiddo but concentrates in Strata III and II.[297] The basic form of the Samaria stand most resembles that seen on various examples from Hazor Stratum V[298] and Niveaux 5-4 at Tell Keisan.[299] Working with materials from the latter site, Briend and Humbert categorized stands into two general types. In their system, "Type A" appears "à paroi épaisse, à lèvre à bourrelet de profil triangulaire et à base solide et épaissie," while "Type B" occurs "à paroi mince, à lèvre arrondie ou plate, ayant les bords supérieurs et inférieurs identiques."[300] The Samaria stand most resembles their Type A group, which they relate to Hazor Stratum VII, even though all but one of their citations derive from Stratum V at that site. At Tell en-Naṣbeh, a series of stands appeared with nuanced rim and base modes,[301] but Wampler placed the best parallel to No. 35 in a range between 700 and 400 BCE.[302] A similar situation emerges from Lachish, where ringstands proved common during the occupation of Level III and then trickled into each of the succeeding phases.[303] Albright placed the Tell Beit Mirsim collection securely in Stratum A2 and noted that "there is no great variation in the form of jarstands in different periods."[304]

---

sequent excavation reports.

[295] E.g., *Amiran*; Holladay drew three stands (Figs. 130:G-H; 131:B) but made no further comment in his corpus descriptions (*Holladay*, 225); *T. Qiri*; *Gezer III*; *APTJ* drew one stand (p. 185, No. 243) but offers no discussion of these forms in the narrative.

[296] *Hazor III-IV*, Pl. CCLX:14-17 (Area H, Stratum 3). Compare Pls. CCLXXVI:4-8, from Stratum 1B; *Hazor II*, Pl. CXLVII:1-2 (Area F, Stratum 1).

[297] *Megiddo I*, 193; Pls. 34:1-15; 35:16-17 (34:3 [II-I] and 11 [IV] bear the closest resemblance to the form of the Samaria stand).

[298] *Hazor III-IV*, Pl. CCXXXII:18 (No. 14 shows a similar form but with a slightly profiled neck and base collar; No. 17 represents a shorter variety, as does another specimen from Pella in Transjordan, *APTJ*, p. 185, No. 243); CCLIII:9. See also the similar but not exact parallel in *Hazor I*, Pl. LVII:23 (Stratum V, with decoration on the rim and base). This general style appears to begin at Hazor in Stratum VI (*Hazor II*, Pl. LXXIV:12). Earlier stands attested there assume an entirely different body-form mode (e.g., *Hazor II*, Pl. LXII:4-8, Stratum VIII).

[299] *T. Keisan*, Pls. 45:7-11a (Niveau 5); 32:7 (Niveau 4). Note that the sidewalls are usually not as evenly made on the Keisan stands.

[300] *T. Keisan*, 174. For Type A, see Pl. 45:9-11a; for Type B, note Pl. 45:7, 8, 12.

[301] *TN II*, Pls. 76:1757-60; 77:1761-71. *TN—Cistern*, Fig. 4:x255 (Cistern 370).

[302] *TN II*, Pl. 76:1760. See p. 51, § 50.

[303] *Lachish III*, Pl. 90:395-402; *Lachish III-Text*, 304-05. Compare *Lachish V*, Pl. 45:7 (also Stratum III).

[304] *TBM I*, 87-88, § 120; Pl. 71:7-13; for photographs, see Pl. 36:1-5. The situation at Beth-Shemesh remains somewhat muddled. While ringstands appeared there in Stratum II (*AS IV*, Pls. LXVI:42-44; LXVII:22; for photographs, see Pl. XLV:32-33), Grant and Wright noted only that they "were common

At Buṣeirah in Transjordan a stand appeared that resembled the triangular rim collar of No. 35 but that maintained a simple base (without a matching collar).[305]

Perhaps the best overall parallels for the Samaria piece, accounting for both form and height (ca. 11-12 cm), come from Niveau 1 at Tell el-Farʿah (N)[306] and, in the south, from Tell Jemmeh.[307] In Assyria, one may compare an exemplar from Fort Shalmaneser.[308] These citations would appear to suggest a mid-to-late seventh-century date for No. 35, but in her final report, Kenyon noted that "besides those listed only a few fragments [of ring stands] were found, all probably of Period VI."[309] I have demonstrated that the PP 6 group spans a long chronological range that takes in the years both before and after the fall of the city in 722/21 BCE. This stand, therefore, may have originated either in the second half of the eighth century BCE or in the post-Israelite period of the seventh century BCE. Its stratigraphic context does not help to tighten the chronology here, since it came from a deposit of leveling fill that overran Walls 136 and 145, as well as parts of Room *hk* (fig. 56), and that supported a new series of Hellenistic walls built directly on (and, in one case, set into) the mixed matrix of the fill.

d. Jugs and Juglets

The official report included in its PP 7 group two fragments belonging to the family of jugs and juglets. The information in Table 51, taken from Appendix A, provides the basic provenance data for these items and also indicates once again the presence of certain difficulties in the records relating to these two entries. For example, some of the unpublished notes include the large jug fragment of No. 28 in the group of sherds earmarked as discards. Further, the summit strip designation for No. 34 should undoubtedly read "Qk" rather than Qn, even though the usually dependable stratification cards themselves retained the erroneous Qn entry. This excavation strip (Qn) lay to the east of Room *g* (which included Segment *120.121.19.126*), in the area

---

throughout the stratum" (*AS V*, 142) and offered no further refinement of their morphological or chronological evolution. Zimhoni related the stands found at Tel ʿEton, located 11 km southeast of Lachish, to the Level III group at Lachish and to Stratum A at Tell Beit Mirsim (*T. ʿEton*, Figs. 2:6 [Stratum II]; 5:14 and 6:12 [Stratum I]; also p. 74).

[305]C.-M. Bennett, "Excavations at Buṣeirah, Southern Jordan, 1973," *Levant* 7 (1975), Fig. 7:11.

[306]*T. Farʿah-RB* [58], Fig. 12:22 (Niveau 1 = seventh century BCE), though the rim on the Farʿah specimen seems slightly narrower in relation to its base than does the Samaria rim. Compare *Chambon*, Pl. 47:1 (Niveau VIIe).

[307]*Gerar*, Pl. LXI:96m (other stands appear in Pl. LXI:96d, g, k, u, and Pl. LXII:W191 and WE). That Petrie's report lists Item 96m as coming from an elevation of 198 m in Room AG means that the stand dates to the very late Iron II period or perhaps even from the Persian period. Petrie also noted that similar ring stands for jars "are so usual in Egypt" (*Gerar*, 22, § 47).

[308]J. Oates, *Iraq* 21 (1959), 146 and Pl. XXXIX:113 (with variant forms in 110-12 and 114).

[309]*SS III*, 185.

SS III Published Figure	Registry No. (* = marked for discard)	Provenance		
		Strip	Coordinates	Feature	Local Layer
† 11:28	*Q 1667	Qc	19.51.14.20	Room *e*	VIc
11:34	QX 316	Q(x)-n	120.121.19.126	Room *g*	VI

(See Appendix A for details pertaining to these recording errors)

(All information presented here now agrees with the original stratification cards)

Provenance Data:
PP7 Jugs & Juglets from the Putative Destruction Debris
Covering the BP V Floors

Table 51

of Room *l*.[310] All the other pottery assigned to Room *g* and to *120.121.19.126* came instead from Strip Qk.

Despite their difference in overall size, both Nos. 28 and 34 display rounded shoulders and short, narrow necks that splay outward toward the top and end in a simple, outturned rim that shows either a very slight thickening (34) or a tapering toward the outside (28). Unlike the store jars in Nos. 24-27, with their inwardly leaning necks and rims that included a thickening, tapering, or interior ledge on the inside, the design of these jugs facilitated the pouring of liquids (vs. simply storing their contents). A perusal of any catalogue of pottery from ancient Israel,[311] however, will reveal that both the jug in No. 28 and the reputed juglet in 34 exhibit certain other traits that set these vessels apart from comparable forms indigenous to local industries within Israel. For example, No. 28 shows two handles drawn from the mid-neck area to the upper shoulder; jugs from Palestine rarely include double handles. The outturned rims on both pieces distinguish themselves from most local jug traditions; besides simply relating form to function (pouring, as de-

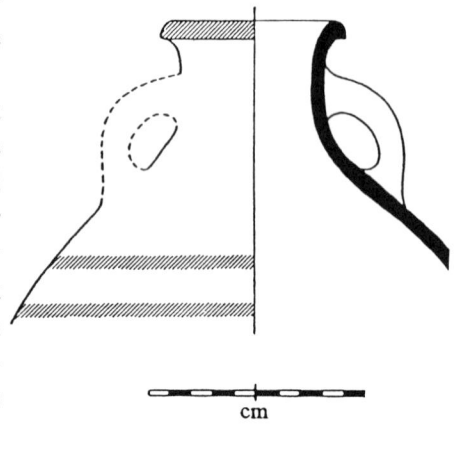

SS III, Fig. 11:28

---

[310] See *SS III*, xv, or *AIS-I*, 16, fig. 3.

[311] E.g., see *Amiran*, Pls. 86-87 for jugs and juglets of the Iron Age IIA-B period; 88-89 for the Iron II C phase.

scribed above, this attribute also connotes a different cultural industry of jug making. Further, the thick, cream-colored slip that covers the red ware of No. 28 proves rather uncommon within Israelite traditions. Finally, the painted brown bands that decorate the rim and shoulder of No. 28 and the short neck zone of No. 34 also lend a foreign flavor to these items.[312]

Once again, these attributes collectively suggest the presence of Assyrian influence in the manufacture of these two pieces and the need to reclassify No. 34 as a bottle, not a juglet. But more than helping to isolate the use of Assyrian motifs, the presence of an appreciable number of parallels (particularly for the painted bottle) at sites across the entire Assyrian empire likely indicates that these items represent actual Assyrian imports, not simply local imitations of Assyrian styles. For example, parallels to No. 34 have appeared south of Assyria in Babylon,[313] at home in Nimrud (Calah),[314] Assur,[315] and Nineveh,[316] in north Syria at Tell Ḥalaf (Gozan),[317] and in the west at Zinjirli (Samʾal)[318] and Tarsus.[319] Similarly, the geographical distribution of this form within Palestine concentrates at the major sites that lay in the path of Assyrian expansion, including (besides Samaria)[320] Megiddo,[321] Tell Qiri,[322] Tell el-Farʿah (N),[323]

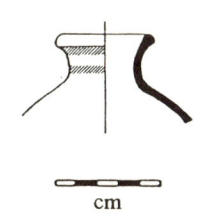

SS III, Fig. 11:34

---

[312]One may compare the painted, two-handled bottle in J. Oates, *Iraq* 21 (1959), Pl. XXXVIII:91, though she notes that this did not constitute a common form at Nimrud (p. 144).

[313]O. Reuther, "Die Innenstadt von Babylon," *Wissenschaftliche Veröffentlichung der deutschen Orient-Gessellschaft* 47 (1926), 35, Abb. 44b.

[314]J. Oates, *Iraq* 21 (1959), Pl. XXXVIII:88, 90, and the discussion on p. 134.

[315]A. Haller, "Die Gräber und Grüfte von Assur," *Wissenschaftliche Veröffentlichung der deutschen Orient-Gessellschaft* 65 (Berlin: Verlag Gebr. Mann, 1954), Tafeln 3:ap; 4:i.

[316]R. Campbell-Thompson and M. E. L. Mallowan, "The British Museum Excavations at Nineveh, 1931-1932," *AAA* 20 (1933), Pl. LXXIV:19.

[317]*T. Ḥalaf IV*, Pl. 59:111.

[318]W. Andrae, *Ausgrabungen Sendschirli V. Die Kleinfunde von Sendschirli* (Berlin, 1943), Pl. 26:f, h.

[319]*Tarsus III*, Pl. 84:1079, 1082.

[320]To the exemplar in *SS III*, one may add *HES I*, 288, Fig. 163:III-4 (plus the annotation on p. 286, which notes that Reisner found this piece with other Israelite pottery); *HES II*, Pl. 67:h. Wampler cited this specimen as the closest parallel to the base fragments presented in *TN II*, Pl. 27:463-64, which he dated no earlier than the late sixth and fifth centuries BCE (p. 13, § 67; this late dating apparently reflects the influence of Reisner's classification of the Samaria bottle in his "Babylonio-Grecian" pottery group; see my continued discussion of chronology).

[321]*Megiddo I*, Pl. 9:7 (Stratum II); a possible local imitation of the form, but now with many grits mixed into the matrix, appears in Pl. 9:6, also from Stratum II.

[322]*T. Qiri*, Fig. 44:6.

[323]*T. Farʿah-RB* [58], Fig. 12:10, 13 (Niveau 1). *Chambon*, 70, and Pl. 61:13-14 (Niveaux VIIe and VIIe-1, respectively).

Bethel,[324] Gibeon,[325] Tel Batash (Timnah),[326] Lachish,[327] Tell el-Ḥesi,[328] and many others. At Tell Keisan, the excavators noted that "contrairement aux bols carénés, [les petites bouteilles] représentent une poterie de qualité, certainement importée."[329] In Transjordan, they also appear in a number of tombs located in the Amman area,[330] as well as at Buṣeirah,[331] Meqabelain,[332] Nebo,[333] Sahab,[334] Dhiban,[335] and apparently as far south as Kheleifeh.[336]

This survey strongly recommends a date in the mid-seventh century BCE for the Assyrian bottle in No. 34.[337] The close similarity in the ware and decoration of the

---

[324] *Bethel*, 68, § 279; Pl. 79:4.

[325] See *Amiran*, 291, Photo 299.

[326] G. L. Kelm and A. Mazar, *Timnah: A Biblical City in the Sorek Valley*, 161, Fig. 8.24.

[327] *Lachish III*, Pl. 90:383-84, from Tomb 106, ca. 650 BCE.

[328] F. J. Bliss, *A Mound of Many Cities, or Tell El Hesy Excavated* (London: Committee of the PEF, by A. P. Watt & Son, 1894), 119, No. 234. Bliss described this item as "a graceful, unique specimen made of fine paste, somewhat polished, with rings of sienna, probably Greek, belonging to City V" (p. 117).

[329] *T. Keisan*, 166.

[330] E.g., G. Lankester Harding, "Two Iron Age Tombs from 'Amman," *QDAP* 11 (1945), p. 71, Nos. 21-22, with a photo of the latter shown in Pl. XVII:22; see also Pl. XVIII:55-56, 60; idem, "Two Iron Age Tombs in Amman," *ADAJ* 1 (1951), Fig. 1:12-14 (called "pointed flasks"; they show a reddish or buff colored surface and black decorative bands); idem, "Four Tomb Groups from Jordan," *APEF* 6 (1953), Fig. 22:94-99, from the Tomb of Adoni Nur and described as pointed bottles usually made of a buff colored ware and displaying a cream or buff slip with brown bands (p. 62).

[331] C.-M. Bennett, "Excavations at Buṣeirah, Southern Jordan, 1972: Preliminary Report," *Levant* 6 (1974), Fig. 16:6.

[332] G. Lankester Harding, "An Iron Age Tomb at Meqabelein," *QDAP* 14 (1950), Pl. XVI:17-18.

[333] S. J. Saller, "Iron Age Tombs at Nebo, Jordan," *LA* 16 (1966), Fig. 23:9-10.

[334] G. Lankester Harding, "An Iron Age Tomb at Sahab," *QDAP* 13 (1948), Pl. XXV:31, 35, 42, 43, and p. 98, Nos. 31-34, 35(?), 36-37. Harding noted that "the placing of the bands of decoration is curiously consistent, i.e., one or two on the neck, two on the shoulders, two about halfway down, and one near the base" (p. 95). The neck of No. 34 accords well with this observation.

[335] *Dibon*, Fig. 21:18 = Pl. XXX:1 (from Tomb J 6). Also, F. V. Winnett and W. L. Reed, *The Excavations at Dibon (Dhībân) in Moab*. AASOR XXXVI-XXXVII for 1957-1958 (New Haven: ASOR, 1964), Pls. 59:13; 77:9.

[336] *Kheleifeh*—Pratico, Pl. 27:13-14. Though he recognizes that this form represents "a type commonly designated Ammonite," Pratico presents these bottles with other clear Assyrian pottery and appears to accept Amiran's argument for an Assyrian origin for this tradition (pp. 42-43).

[337] Because of the possible earlier appearance of these forms in certain tombs in the vicinity of Amman (e.g., Lankester Harding, *ADAJ* 1 [1951], Fig. 1:12-14, from Tomb C, which he placed in the eighth century vs. the seventh century BCE), some have suggested that the tradition represents an Ammonite one. But in her comments on the pottery group from the so-called Tomb of Adoni Nur, Tufnell argued for a clear Assyrian origin for this stream of tradition (O. Tufnell, "Notes and Comparisons," *APEF* 6 [1953], 67). Most subsequent studies have accepted Tufnell's interpretation (e.g., *Amiran*, 291, 296; *T. Keisan*, 166; *T. Qiri*, 203; et passim).

larger, double-handled jug in No. 28 implies that this vessel should follow suit. Though samples of this tradition might naturally have appeared in outlying or border areas that experienced a substantial Assyrian presence long before the collapse of Israelite control over Samaria,[338] there remains no compelling reason to place their arrival in the capital prior to the period of direct Assyrian rule in the very late eighth or even the seventh century BCE. As Briend and Humbert have observed, "nous rencontrerons ces bouteilles jusqu'à la fin du Fer II C et elles dureront par le biais d'imitations jusqu'aux époques babylonienne et perse."[339] The subsequent analysis by E. Stern confirmed this chronological span; it also helped to refine the classification of these bottles into two subgroups.[340] The early group included the actual Assyrian vessels decorated with brown painted, horizontal bands and claiming a chronological range from the mid-seventh to the mid-sixth centuries BCE. The later collection involved exemplars that remained undecorated and revealed a cruder, often knife-shaven, shape. These degenerate local imitations ranged in date from the sixth to the fourth centuries BCE and, unlike the true Assyrian forms, did not appear outside Palestine.

Based on the stratigraphy at Samaria, one cannot confidently tighten the ceramic chronology for these two vessels by much. The large jug in No. 28 came from one of two pits that cut into floor levels associated with Wall 57 (see Segment *19.51.14.20*, Layer VIc, in fig. 59). This situation seems to indicate that the Assyrian jug came to rest in its ultimate findspot sometime after Room *e* and its western wall 57 fell into disuse, perhaps during the time of the partial plundering of Wall 57 (note again the apparent robber trench abutting the east face of that feature in fig. 59). Importantly, the heterogeneous matrix that included some burned debris and the majority of ivories

---

[338]E.g., note the conceivably early examples in some of the tombs near Amman in Transjordan (though I believe the dating of these deposits requires more flexibility than it provides certainty). Also, Amiran cites a bottle from Stratum V at Hazor to support the pre-722 BCE contacts between that site and Assyria (*Hazor II*, Pl. XCVII:11; *Amiran*, 291, Photo 300). But the comparison is not a totally apt one, for that form displays a much more bloated body and a rounded base mode, and it seems to represent a precursor to the more slender, carrot-shaped tradition of bottle making that succeeded it (and which I believe relates to Samaria No. 34). Similarly, Ben-Tor and Portugali want to argue that the Yoqneʿam Regional Project "provides new evidence for preconquest contact" with Assyria (*T. Qiri*, 203). The historical reality of pre-722 BCE contact with Assyria is, of course, unquestioned. But the specific issue here deals with an archaeological reality, namely, the *terminus post quem* for the morphology and surface treatment attested in Nos. 28 and 34, as well as the earliest date at which these forms arrived in Israel. The Yoqneʿam evidence to support Ben-Tor's and Portugali's position is meager and includes only a carinated bowl and a conical "jarlet." At Qiri, two bowls and a bottle were recovered. One of the bowls appeared as an intrusive element in a ninth-century context; the stratigraphic controls necessary to date the other bowl and the bottle are totally lacking.

[339]*T. Keisan*, 166.

[340]E. Stern, *Material Culture of the Land of the Bible in the Persian Period*, 125-27 (and the references cited there). As a basic outline, this scheme fits the earlier classification offered by E. Henschel-Simon in "Note on the Pottery of the ʿAmman Tombs," *QDAP* 11 (1945), 75-78, which viewed the cream-slipped, black painted bottles as the seventh-century prototypes that eventually gave way to the more crudely modelled, knife-pared imitations of the Persian and Hellenistic periods. (Harding preferred to keep the incipient tradition of painted bottles in the eighth century BCE; *QDAP* 13 [1948], 96.)

recovered from this segment overlay and sealed these pits. Consequently, that deposit must date to an even later time; its contents represent a secondary fill, not the original destruction level itself. As with many other fragments published in the final report (see Table 46), the distinctive bottle in No. 34 came from the crucial Layer VI in Room *g*. But I have shown that this level represents a two-phase filling laid down to support the presumed BP VIII surface in Layer V (fig. 67). The presence of the Assyrian painted bottle in this context, then, simply implies a construction date for this new floor level sometime in the mid-seventh century BCE or later. The context cannot clarify a *terminus post quem* for the lifespan of the bottle tradition.

Finally, I may note the strikingly heavy distribution of the bottle form in tomb contexts in Transjordan. At Samaria, however, Kenyon made no mention of the discovery of these vessels in the tombs excavated there by the Joint Expedition.

e. Lamps

Two suggested lamp fragments comprise part of the PP 7 discussion in the final report. Neither entry received the designation "discard" in the private field records, and the general provenance data appear unencumbered by other recording errors. All accounts concur in assigning the excavation segment (*120.121.19.126*) to the correct Summit Strip (Qk). As Table 52 reveals, both lamps came from the same locus as the Assyrian painted bottle just discussed in the preceding section.

SS III Published Figure	Registry No. (not marked for discard)	Provenance Strip	Coordinates	Feature	Local Layer
11:10	QX 126	Q(x)-k	120.121.19.126	Room *g*	VI
11:37	QX 132	Q(x)-k	120.121.19.126	Room *g*	VI

(See Appendix A for details pertaining to these recording errors)

(All information presented here now agrees with the original stratification cards)

Provenance Data:
PP7 Lamps from the Putative Destruction Debris
Covering the BP V Floors

Table 52

Though Kenyon placed the small fragment in entry No. 10 among the set of bowls or plates with strongly everted rims (Nos. 9-14; see pp. 397ff.), she interpreted this piece more specifically as a portion of a saucer lamp. This identification seems correct, given the noticeably smaller diameter of the original vessel. Its estimated width of 14 cm matches almost exactly that of the second lamp presented in No. 37 and proves much narrower than the width of the bowls that surround it in *SS III*, Fig. 11. The fragment of No. 10, then, represents a small section of an outturned lamp rim that was originally positioned opposite the vessel's tightly pinched wick hole. Both 10 and 37 exhibit a hard fired, red or purplish red ware that appears drab grey at the break; the rim fragment in No. 10 also shows a few limestone grit inclusions.

Iron Age lamps all seem to spring from the same basic template, and their practicality of form is reflected in their widespread geographical distribution, which takes in Israel, Phoenicia, Lebanon, Syria, Jordan, and Cyprus.[341] They are shallow, open forms, thrown originally as saucers,[342] with a single, severely pinched spout or wick holder added to one side of the vessel.[343] The flattened lip of the rim varies in width, and the base evolves from a rounded mode to a flat variety. The shallowness of the overall vessel, which provided a lower center of gravity, and the flattened base combined to promote much greater stability than the round-bottomed lamps when placed on a table, in a wall niche, or on other flat surfaces. Near the close of the eighth century BCE, lamps with disc bases appear among the general repertoire, with the distinctive bases manufactured at differing heights.[344] This style lamp gains greater prominence during the seventh century, though it does not completely replace the flat-based models.[345] While it remains somewhat risky to make definitive state-

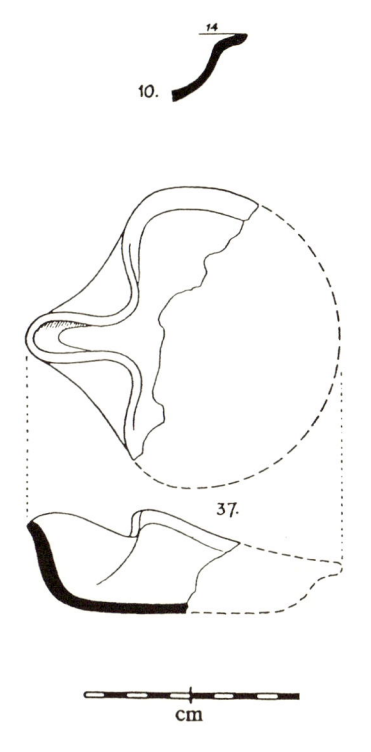

SS III, Fig. 11:10 & 37

---

[341] *Gezer III*, 227. According to Stern, "the source of this lamp is generally considered to be Phoenicia" (*Material Culture of the Land of the Bible in the Persian Period*, 128).

[342] The basic Iron Age lamp undoubtedly evolved from an ordinary household bowl or saucer and not in imitation of seashell lamps, which were, in fact, used in a few coastal Mediterranean areas such as Carthage. (See the informative article by R. Houston Smith, "The Household Lamps of Palestine in Old Testament Times," *BA* 27 [1964], 1-31.)

[343] Though this description outlines the template, variations did exist such as the bicorner or double-spouted lamps (see *HES I*, 317-18, Fig. 187:2a) and even some seven-spouted forms (*HES I*, Fig. 187:3a) also found at Samaria.

[344] See *TBM I*, Pl. 70:1-8, and the discussion on pp. 86-87, § 119. Gitin sees some typological usefulness in the heights of the bases and suggests that the examples showing a low-to-medium height originated first and date to the late eighth and seventh centuries, while the higher based varieties stem mainly from the seventh and sixth centuries BCE (*Gezer III*, 227).

[345] Rounded, flattened, and high-base models appeared together in Tomb 14 at Beth-Shemesh (*AS IV*, Pl. XLVIII:7-9). Tomb 14 represents the latest in a series of tombs found at this site (sixth century BCE).

ments regarding the chronological development of Iron Age lamps based on nuances in these attributes,[346] it appears that lamps with a low, flat body profile, flat base, and wider rim lip fall closer to the end of the period.[347] Overall, the design of No. 37 seems well suited to this late group of lamps. Citing parallels from Megiddo and Tell Jemmeh, Kenyon herself noted that this particular form "appears only in the seventh century."[348]

E. Stern's analyses of these open, flat-based, broad-rimmed lamps, first with the assemblage from En-Gedi and then in a more general study, have demonstrated that "these vessels are among the most frequently found in strata and tombs of the Persian period throughout Palestine" and, next to similarly shaped bowls, "represent the second most important hallmark of this period."[349] While acknowledging that "the typological differences do not seem to be of significance," Stern appeals to slight variations in details—such as the width of the rim and the severity of the pinched spout—to outline three subgroups within the overall collection of late Iron Age and Persian period lamps.[350] Although the fragment in No. 10 is too small to allow conclusive analysis, the lamp in No. 37 seems best suited to Stern's Group 1, for which he assigns a chronological range that spans the sixth through the fourth centuries BCE. While the currently available evidence suggests a higher *terminus post quem* for the overall group,[351] a date sometime in the seventh century would accord well with the attributes attested on No. 37.[352] This reading also suits the archaeological context that yielded these two fragments, since both pieces came from the fills and subfloor makeup that provided a bed for the hard-packed, yellowish surface Kenyon assigned to BP VIII.[353]

---

[346]See the comments in *Gezer III*, 227, including the summary statement that "unlike most other types of vessels, variations in lamp forms are not necessarily indicative of typological developments and therefore do not necessarily have chronological implications." Albright considered the variations in lamp making "a *very unsafe criterium for chronology*" (*TBM I*, 87, § 119; his emphasis).

[347]A cursory examination of the stratigraphic distribution of lamp forms presented in various catalogues and reports will corroborate this conclusion. Among others, see *Amiran*, Pl. 100; *Megiddo I*, Pls. 37-38; *T. Keisan*, Pls. 21, 32, 44, and 51; *TN II*, Pls. 70-71; *Lachish III*, Pls. 83, 103 (see also especially *Lachish III-Text*, 326); and *Chambon*, Pl. 59 (note that the close parallel in 59:11 came from Niveau VIId, late eighth century BCE).

[348]*SS III*, 129. See *Megiddo I*, Pl. 37:8, 12 (Strata III-I); *Gerar*, Pl. LXI:91n.

[349]E. Stern, *Material Culture of the Land of the Bible in the Persian Period*, 127. See Gitin's discussion of the Gezer corpus and his comparison of Gezer "Types 114A-B" and "Type 155" for differences in appearance between late Iron II open lamps and those of the Persian period (*Gezer III*, 225-27, 237).

[350]E. Stern, *Material Culture of the Land of the Bible in the Persian Period*, 127-28.

[351]I may even note, for example, *AS IV*, Pl. LXI:33-34, from Stratum III.

[352]The truly flat base of No. 37 seems to postdate all the other Iron Age examples figured in the *Gezer III* report, which themselves extend into the early seventh century (see pp. 71, 225-27; Pls. 11:8; 14:20; 19:7; and 23:10). See the good parallel for the size, shape, and ware of No. 37 from Samaria in *TN II*, Pl. 71:1624 (mislabeled "162" on the plate) and p. 45, n. 26, § 16.

[353]Note again fig. 67, *Segment 120.121.19.126*, Layer(s) VI, Room *g*, in the context of my previous discussions.

3) Evaluation and Summary

I may now elaborate on Table 48 by showing more precisely the spatial distribution of the PP 7 pottery within the local stratigraphy of the northern summit area (compare Table 53). As noted at the beginning of the pottery analysis, the majority of this collection stems from what I have called the "service rooms" that lay north of the rock scarp and the central, elevated summit plateau. Within that space below the scarp, 67.6% of the published pottery for PP 7 came from three rooms: *e, g,* and *l*. The western portion of Room *g*, Segment *120.121.19.126*, Layer VI, constituted the single most productive pottery-bearing locus (at least in terms of the items eventually published). I have demonstrated, however, that this layer actually comprised two successive deposits of leveling fill and subfloor makeup, both of which undoubtedly postdate by many years the loss of Israelite control over the site.[354] The repertoire removed from these combined levels dates almost exclusively to the seventh century BCE and later periods (with No. 24, possibly from the eighth century, representing the clearest exception).[355] Moreover, the published pottery from the rubble of Layer VII, which lay beneath VI (fig. 67), all claimed seventh-century origins (Nos. 1, 5, 7, 14). I may also mention the jar in No. 27 in this same vein, for the excavators retrieved this fragment from the .20 m-thick debris of Layer VIII that covered the poorly preserved remains of a burnt plaster floor situated very near the bedrock surface. If, as I have suggested, this piece also merits a *terminus post quem* in the seventh century BCE, then all successive layers (including VII, VI, and V) must also date to that time period or later.

My evaluation of the overall PP 7 group of goods leads me to posit the following chronological distribution based strictly on *ceramic* considerations: 18.9% of the collection might easily date to the eighth century, even prior to the events of 722 BCE;[356] 8.1% comes from the period of the eighth-seventh-century transition;[357] and 70.3% of the items belong in the heart of the seventh century or later still[358] (sometimes significantly later, as in the case of the Hellenistic jar in No. 33). Within this assemblage, I have also suggested that roughly one-third of the vessels exhibit either clear or probable ties to Assyrian pottery traditions, with most of these pieces repre-

---

[354] See my discussion on pp. 379-81 above, with special notice given to my remarks regarding the possible *terminus post quem* and *terminus ante quem* both for this and related deposits.

[355] I may also cite No. 18, from the same segment and layer in Room *e*, and No. 19, from Room *f*, as possible late eighth- or eighth-to-seventh-century forms.

[356] See Nos. 16, 18, 21, 24, 25, 29, and 31.

[357] See Nos. 19, 20, and 35.

[358] From the ***seventh century***, see Nos. 1-7, 9-15, 17, 22-23, 26-28, 30, 34, and 37 (23 of 37 total fragments = 62.2%); for the ***seventh-sixth centuries***, see No. 32 (2.7%); from the ***sixth century***, No. 8 (2.7%); and from the ***Hellenistic*** period, No. 33 (2.7%). For the present, I have left an open date for the somewhat anomalous No. 36.

	bowls	cooking pots	jars & jar stands	jugs & juglets	lamps	TOTAL
Room *e*						
19.51.14.20						
IVa	3	-	-	-	-	3
VIc	1	-	-	1	-	2
120.121.19.126						
VI	1	-	-	-	-	1
Room *f*						
509.126						
IIa.f	1	-	-	-	-	1
120.121.19.126						
VI	1	-	-	-	-	1
Room *g*						
120.121.19.126						
VI	1	1	1	1	2	6
VIw	1	-	-	-	-	1
VII	3	-	-	-	-	3
VIIe	1	-	-	-	-	1
VIII	-	-	1	-	-	1
Room *hk*						
122.125.19.121						
IIIz	-	-	1	-	-	1
125.144						
IIIa	-	-	1	-	-	1
Room *hq*						
W of 124						
VIw	2	-	-	-	-	2
VII	1	-	-	-	-	1
Room *j*						
509.126						
IIa.f	-	-	1	-	-	1
Room *kq*						
120.121.19.126						
V	1	-	-	-	-	1
VII	1	-	-	-	-	1
W of 124						
IIIc	1	-	-	-	-	1
Vc	1	-	-	-	-	1
Room *l*						
504.503.509.508						
Va	2	-	2	-	-	4
Va.z	-	-	1	-	-	1
509.126						
IIa.f	1	-	-	-	-	1
VIII	-	-	1	-	-	1
TOTAL	**23**	**1**	**9**	**2**	**2**	**37**

Distribution of PP 7 Ceramic Forms in Local Stratigraphy of House Floors
(Rooms e-g, hk, hq, j, kq, l)
Table 53

senting local imitations of their foreign counterparts[359] while a few may embody actual Assyrian imports.[360]

From a *stratigraphic* point of view, however, none of the loci that yielded these fragments can date earlier than the seventh century BCE, and on the lower end their range extends at least into the early Roman period. I must stress further that none of the layers involved reflects a wholesale conflagration spread evenly across all the rooms north of the courtyard, as Kenyon suggested. (See my conclusions below.)

Finally, on *historical* grounds, it seems reasonable to expect that some of the Assyrian-related forms described above might have appeared at sites located farther north (e.g., Hazor), along the Mediterranean coast (Jemmeh; Ashdod), and in Transjordan slightly before they entered the relatively isolated, inner-montane Samaria. My analysis seems to support this scenario, though I do not wish to undervalue the important regional and inter-regional connections enjoyed by the Israelite capital throughout its history.[361] But the former situation prevails even though Samaria served as the Israelite capital and certain other sites in the outlying, more exposed areas were not actually conquered by Assyria until after the final collapse of Israelite governance in those regions (e.g., Ashdod, which succumbed to Assyria only during the western campaign of Sargon II in 712 BCE). Most of the regions surrounding the Ephraimite hill country had become official Assyrian provinces at least a decade or so prior to the loss of sovereignty at Samaria. (See my historical discussion in Chapter VI).

Pottery Period 7: Conclusions

When one considers the various local layers that contributed pottery to the PP 7 group and allows for the separate rooms through which a single layer might have run, one encounters 23 discrete stratigraphic scenarios (i.e., segment-feature-layer combinations) whose basic characteristics are vital to understanding the overall nature of the PP 7 loci and to assessing Kenyon's historical interpretation of the late Iron II activities at Samaria. A summary overview of these levels appears in Table 54 on the following page.

The information contained in this chart clearly accents the glaring absence of a coherent, comprehensible destruction level in the rooms situated north of the main courtyard. While Kenyon acknowledged the fact that the alleged destruction debris did not appear *in situ* across the so-called "burnt house,"[362] she insisted that "the pottery

---

[359] Note the bowls in Nos. 9-15, 17(?), and 23, plus the jars in 26-27, though some relate No. 17 to the family of Samaria Ware.

[360] See the bowl in No. 22, the painted jug in 28, and the Assyrian bottle in 34.

[361] In this regard, see *AIS-I*, 10, n. 21.

[362] *SS I*, 110; *SS III*, 125.

Segment Coordinates	Architectural Feature	Local Layer	Text Figures	General Description of Layer
120.121.19.126	Room *e*	VI	58	2-phase deposit of clean, leveling fill supporting BP VIII flagstone floor
120.121.19.126	Room *f*	VI	58	(same as above)
120.121.19.126	Room *g*	VI	58	(same as above)
120.121.19.126	Room *g*	VIw	—	(?)
120.121.19.126	Room *g*	VII	58	rubble-filled matrix beneath VI
120.121.19.126	Room *g*	VIIe	—	(not mentioned in fieldnotes; poss.=VIIa)
120.121.19.126	Room *g*	VIII	58	midden-like deposit (occ. deb.?) overlying plaster floor near bedrock
120.121.19.126	Room *kq*	V	—	hard, yellowish floor (Kenyon=BP VIII)
120.121.19.126	Room *kq*	VII	—	(see Room *g* above)
W of 124	Room *kq*	IIIc	61	mixed fill beneath late 2nd Cent. CE Roman W. 124a
W of 124	Room *kq*	Vc	61-62	floor level supporting W. 132E (Kenyon's date = Per. V, with Per. IV pottery)
W of 124	Room *hq*	VIw	60-61	portion of L. VI floor disturbed in Hellensitic period
W of 124	Room *hq*	VII	p.400	thin occ.deb. on putative BPV floor L. VIII
509.126	Room *f*	IIa.f	55	subfloor fill beneath Hellenistic floor IIa; extending N toward Casemate W. 556
509.126	Room *j(f?)*	IIa.f	55	(same as above)
509.126	Room *l*	IIa.f	55	(same as above)
509.126	Room *l*	VIII	55	(same as Va in 504.503.509.508)
19.51.14.20	Room *e*	IVa	50	leveling fill (postrobbing of W. 57, btw. Rooms *d-e*)
19.51.14.20	Room *e*	VIc	50	two pit fills (postdating use of W. 57)
504.503.509.508	Room *l*	Va	53-54	substantial, mixed Herodian fill cut by W. 508a (contemporary with W. 552)
504.503.509.508	Room *l*	Va.z	53	FT for Late Roman W. 508a
122.125.19.121	Room *hk*	IIIz	6	excavation trench cut through BP VII L. III
125.144	Room *hk*	IIIa	6	sooty layer overlying L. III

Excavated Segments Relating to PP 7:
Synopsis of Local Stratigraphy

Table 54

of this period came *entirely* from deposits of debris, including much burnt material, which overlay the floors of the Period V house wherever they were intact."[363] In her subsequent studies, Kenyon wrote that, when compared to the biblical record of the catastrophic fall of Samaria,

> the archaeological record is equally eloquent of the complete destruction of the capital city. . . . Not a single element of buildings in the royal quarter survived. The walls were ruthlessly rooted out, the stones perhaps to be reused in houses on the lower slopes of the hill, where the immigrants settled by Sargon may have lived.[364]

She continues with this acknowledgement:

> The burnt debris of the actual destruction and the debris resulting from the robbing were then leveled over. In it were new pottery forms, probably to be associated with the immigrants, as well as Palestinian pottery of the types later than that associated with earlier periods, with contacts with 7th century B.C. forms. The leveling-over process therefore took place sufficiently long after Sargon's conquest for pottery brought by the newcomers, and possibly by an Assyrian garrison, which is to be presumed was present for some years, as well as the later Palestinian forms, to be lying about; a date early in the 7th century B.C. is probable.[365]

While I can agree with much of the sentiment expressed in the latter excerpt, I have shown that the diverse layers from which excavators recovered the PP 7 goods hardly present a homogeneous matrix or a depositional history centered around a single episode, whether a devastating destruction by military force or a subsequent, wholesale leveling for purposes of new construction. Rather, one witnesses a wide variety of accumulation types, including clean leveling fills, the tumble of rubble-filled matrix, pockets of possible occupational debris, hard-packed floor levels from disparate periods, at least two post-Israelite pit fills, a late foundation trench backfill, other late (Hellenistic and Roman) disturbances of earlier surfaces, and so on. In many instances, one is prompted to exercise caution against drawing firm historical conclusions from what are clearly secondary deposits.

My analysis suggests that Forsberg is entirely justified in rejecting Kenyon's quick acceptance of Assyria as the causal agent behind a widespread, thick destruction level at Samaria. Yet he does not question the presence of such a conflagration across the site, but only the view that holds Assyria responsible for it. As alternatives to this

---

[363]*SS III*, 125 (emphasis added).

[364]*RCOT*, 133.

[365]*RCOT*, 133.

historical reconstruction, he offers five options spread over the ninth, eighth, and seventh centuries BCE. First, he entertains "the possibility that the ivories were destroyed in connection with Jehu's overthrow of the Omrid dynasty in 841 B.C."[366] In this vein, he would understand the ivories as "part of the paraphernalia of the ritual banqueting known as the *marzeah*,"[367] and he would associate their desecration with the opposition to pluralism (specifically Baalism) launched by the radically orthodox circles that backed Jehu's rise to power. Forsberg's second recourse allows that the ivories "were destroyed in some outbreak of violence connected with one of the frequent *coups d'état* (e.g., 2 Kings 15:10, 25, 30) that illustrate the troubled nature of the decades following upon the reign of Jeroboam II"[368] in the eighth century BCE.

When considering the possible historical solutions dating from the seventh century BCE, Forsberg forwarded three additional scenarios that he believed offered more viable alternatives. First, the PP 7 leveling might have occurred late in the reign of Ashurbanipal when, after loosing the once firm grip on various western provinces, he thought to repopulate certain administrative centers with new peoples from foreign lands. According to Forsberg,

> The possibility that the destruction belongs in this context, that Ashurbanipal's sending new settlers to Samaria reflects Assyrian efforts to restore strength and stability there after an insurrection and that these efforts involved also the tidying up in the citadel area producing the Period VII leveling can hardly be excluded.[369]

On the other hand, according to Forsberg, a destruction and subsequent releveling of Samaria might also have taken place amidst the rapid decline of Assyrian power in this region during the 620s BCE, when the opportunistic Josiah launched his political and cultic reforms not only in Judah but also in the "cities of Samaria" (2 Kgs 23:19-20; 2 Chron 34:3-7). Forsberg believes that "such activities in the territory of Samaria presuppose the disappearance of Assyrian control there and the annexation of the former Assyrian province by Josiah."[370] Ultimately, however, Forsberg himself discounts this option on the twofold assumption that the weakening of Assyria had run its course prior to the time of Josiah and that valued items such as the ivories would not likely have survived the events associated with this political decline. He does not address the varied historical assessments (including some negative ones) of the actual extent of the Josianic reforms in the north.

---

[366]Forsberg, 33-35.

[367]Forsberg, 34.

[368]Forsberg, 35.

[369]Forsberg, 35.

[370]Forsberg, 35.

Finally, Forsberg raises one further, late seventh-century possibility, namely, a Scythian invasion of Palestine, which probably transpired in the 630s or early 620s BCE.[371] Citing a notation in Herodotus, Forsberg says that when these steppe-dwelling horsemen "ravaged their way through Palestine" only the Egyptian Psammetichus I managed to hold them at bay and turn them northward once again.[372] Nevertheless, their penetration produced the dual effect of a sudden and unexpected demise of Assyrian control and presence in the eastern Mediterranean littoral and an historical opportunity for a local ruler, Josiah, to attempt a realignment of territories on the regional level. For material evidence supporting the Scythian hypothesis, Forsberg appeals principally to the seventh-century character of the ceramic traditions attested in PP 7 and also to "a couple of interesting arrowheads" whose shape resembles a type associated with a Scythian presence at other sites in the Near East (see *SS III*, Fig. 110:13-14).[373] This last historical option seems the most appealing to Forsberg, as his final comment reveals:

> That this is the historical context in which the destruction of the ivories took place and in which the arrowheads of Scythian type appearing in Period VII fill were used . . . definitely seems an attractive possibility.[374]

My study has confirmed that Forsberg's argument enjoys a firm footing from

---

[371] *Forsberg*, 25-26 and 35-36.

[372] Herodotus, *History*, Book I, §§ 103-07. Though Psammetichus I came to power as early as 664 BCE, Forsberg cites a reference in the chronological tables of Eusebius to place the Scythian presence in Palestine during the time of Josiah. He and others have seen Jeremiah's stock descriptions of invaders from the north who threatened Judah (Jer 6:22-24) and Babylon (50:41-43) as late seventh-century BCE notices of these Scythian hordes (compare D. Stewart, "Scythian Gold," *Smithsonian* March 2000, 90).

[373] These arrowheads exhibit a triple-bladed, triangular shape and a substantial barb on their tubular or socketed shafts. The two examples in Fig. 110 received the registry numbers Q2438 and Q2439, respectively; I found two similar arrowheads in the unpublished records from Q2052, Qc, Segment 19.51.14.20, Level IVd, excavated on 6-8-32. This style was generally made of bronze (vs. iron), and seems most common during the Persian period; for the **sixth-fourth centuries**, see J. Waldbaum, *Metalwork from Sardis: The Finds through 1974* (Cambridge, MA: Harvard University Press, 1983), Pl. 3:41; N. Avigad, *Discovering Jerusalem* (Nashville: Thomas Nelson Publishers, 1980), 52-54, Figs. 32, 34; from the **fifth-fourth centuries**, see *Corinth, XII*, Pl. 91:1517-19; *Ashdod II-III*, 64, Pl. XX:10; also Z. Ilan and A. Yosef, "Ancient Settlements on the Bardawil Reef," *Qadmoniot* 10 (1977), 71-79 (Hebrew). Elsewhere in Israel, parallels occur at ʿAthlit, Yoqneʿam, Keisan, En-Gedi, Jemmeh, and Lachish, but they are rare at the last site (see *Lachish III*, 386, Pl. 60:53; *ʿAtlīt—Cemetery*, 55-56, Fig. 14c, Pl. XX:c435; also 96, Fig. 78; *Yoqneʿam I*, 218, Photo XVIII.1:1; *T. Keisan*, 323, Pl. 98:14, called "un type hellénistique commun"; *En-Gedi*, Pl. 24:7-8 [Stratum V]; *Gerar*, Pl. XXIX:1-22). Another, unstratified example came from Lachish (*Lachish V*, Pl. 36:15). An apparent seventh-century specimen appeared in the Tomb of Adoni-Nur, near Amman (G. Lankester Harding, *APEF* 6 [1953], 56, Pl. VII:30). For the Scythian use of this type, see Harding's identification in the previous reference; also W. E. McLeod, "ΤΡΙΓΛΩΧΙΣ," *AJA* 64 (1960), 370f., n. 3. But for the origin of the trilobe arrowhead in Transcaucasia and its subsequent diffusion into other regions by the Cimmerians and, later, the Scythians, see *Lachish V*, 80, and the sources cited there.

[374] *Forsberg*, 36.

the point of view of a comparative ceramic analysis. The bulk of the PP 7 pottery, including the true Assyrian or Assyrian-related forms, might easily date to the seventh century BCE, even as late as the third quarter of that era. But while his historical ruminations are interesting (even tantalizing, as in the case of the Scythian hypothesis), one can see the dangers inherent in this sort of speculation in the absence of firmer archaeological (i.e., stratigraphic) evidence to corroborate it. The mixed depositional history behind the diverse layers that relate to the PP 7 assemblage precludes one from mooring this group *en masse* to a single historical event. The two possible Scythian arrowheads notwithstanding,[375] Forsberg's position rests almost entirely on a post-722 BCE dating for the pottery (which is Israelite–Assyrian in origin, not Scythian), and his analytical work in this area, sound as it may be, proceeds without access to the local stratigraphic picture. Had he known that no single, clear level of destruction debris exists across the floors and walls of the BP V house(s), the historical scheme that he inferred from the date of the pottery might have changed dramatically.

Once again, this methodological snare serves as an emphatic statement on behalf of the importance of detailed stratigraphic analysis, that aspect of field exploration for which Kenyon became most noted but that is not found in her Samaria report. Though Forsberg handled the bulk of the PP 7 ceramic corpus correctly, he could not have known that a significant percentage of the pottery came from much later fills, disturbances, foundation trenches, and the like. One cannot repeat too often that the use of any given ceramic corpus, whether for statistical analysis or historical reconstructions, is only as secure as the context from which the excavators removed the pottery in the first place.[376] While elaborate ceramic analyses often receive a central place in archaeological reporting, that aspect of study can never displace a full-bodied stratigraphic analysis; in fact, the former depends on the latter for its ultimate credibility. A close scrutiny of a wide range of field reports reveals that allegedly firm historical conclusions too often rest on the analysis of pottery taken from mixed or very dubious stratigraphic contexts.

Ultimately, it is the lack of any stratigraphic bearings that hampers Kenyon's own reporting technique in *SS III*. As much as anything, the intent of the present study (and of *AIS-I*) has focused on filling this lacuna. In doing so, I have not encountered a blanket of destruction debris across the BP V remains at the site; rather, diverse layers dating from many time periods and extending as late as the Late Roman period have emerged. Apparently, many seventh-century pottery forms remained on or very close to the surface of the site at the time when later workers collected the matrix for these fills from areas along the northern summit. If Kenyon's Hellenistic and Roman period

---

[375] Two arrowheads alone do not provide a firm basis on which to assert either a Scythian assault against Samaria or a Scythian rebuilding of Samaria following the demise of Assyrian authority there. In addition to their limited numbers here, arrowheads often appear in a heavily corroded state and generally prove difficult to classify and date with precision.

[376] In *AIS-I*, 234-41, I noted a similar situation regarding Holladay's statistical analyses based on the Gezer Gateway assemblage.

dating for the walls and features associated with some of these layers is correct, it seems curious that one does not witness more Babylonian, Persian, and early Greek wares scattered among these deposits.

Before concluding this chapter, two final points merit attention. First, I must note the strong focus in Forsberg's general discussion on the date and circumstances of the destruction of the so-called Samaria Ivories. This focus highlights not only a general fascination with these beautiful objects but also a clear need to establish with as much certainty as possible the provenance data relating to their findspots. Once again, the reporting procedures followed by the Joint Expedition (including both Crowfoot and Kenyon) did not provide access to these data, and no archaeologist since the close of the excavations has addressed this important issue directly. Consequently, all considerations of the ivories by art historians have suffered from the lack of an archaeological backdrop against which to interpret the artifacts. Without reliable stratigraphic moorings, the ability of these objects to tell us about actual history remains severely compromised. The following chapter in my study will take up this very issue and offer a resolution to this interpretive problem.

Second, in addressing the exclusion of important data from the final reports of the work at Samaria, and by considering anew the implications of those data, I have shown again that Kenyon's archaeological chronology seems tied too directly to generally accepted historical dates (Jehu's coup) and/or presumed historical events (Assyrian military destruction of Samaria). Trends and fashions in material culture are not divorced from such significant historical events or even from regnal lists, but they ultimately establish a life of their own and, in doing so, can run at cross currents with changes on the throne, specific military campaigns, internal *coups* and rebellion, attempted political and religious reforms, and the like. In short, a direct correspondence between archaeological history and political history does not always exist.[377]

---

[377] The study by W. Y. Adams still proves relevant to the broader discussion of theories that address issues of historical causality (see W. Y. Adams, "Invasion, Diffusion, Evolution?" *Antiquity* 42 [1968], 194-215).

Chapter V

THE ARCHAEO-HISTORICAL CONTEXT OF THE SAMARIA IVORIES

A Case Study in Theory, Method, and Outcome

I. Introduction

The purpose of this chapter centers on the singular task of providing some fresh evidence relating to the findspots—both their location and overall character—of an important group of artifacts reclaimed by excavations at Samaria, namely the well-known collection of ivory carvings and glass inlays. A similar need for stratigraphic clarity has impeded all cultural-historical studies of the ostraca recovered earlier through the Harvard Expedition.[1] Both my previous study (*AIS-I*) and the present investigation, however, have dealt almost exclusively with the work of the Joint Expedition (through which the ivories appeared in the 1930s)[2] and much less so with the explorations of Schumacher and Reisner from 1908 to 1910. In the same manner, I shall now focus my attention on problems surrounding the archaeological context of the ivories, for which I have new stratigraphic data, and not on the situation of the

---

[1] As a representative sample of the literature dealing with these items, see Y. Aharoni, "The Samaria Ostraca-an Additional Note," *IEJ* 12 (1962), 67-69; F. M. Cross, "Epigraphic Notes on Hebrew Documents of the Eighth-Sixth Centuries B.C.: I. A New Reading of a Place Name in the Samaria Ostraca," *BASOR* 163 (1961), 12-14; I. T. Kaufman, "The Samaria Ostraca: A Study in Ancient Hebrew Palaeography," Text and Plates (Th.D. diss., Harvard University, 1966); idem, "The Samaria Ostraca: An Early Witness to Hebrew Writing," *BA* 45 (1982), 229-39; A. Lemaire, "Les Ostraca Hebreux de l'Epoque Royale Israelite," Text and Plates (Ph.D. diss., University of Paris, 1973); idem, *Inscriptions Hebraiques, Tome I, Les Ostraca* (Paris: Les Editions du Cerf, 1977); B. Maisler (Mazar), "The Historical Background of the Samaria Ostraca," *JPOS* 21 (1948), 117-33; A. F. Rainey, "Administration in Ugarit and the Samaria Ostraca," *IEJ* 12 (1962), 62-63; idem, "The Samaria Ostraca in the Light of Fresh Evidence," *PEQ* 99 (1967), 32-41; idem, "Semantic Parallels to the Samaria Ostraca," *PEQ* 102 (1970), 45-51; idem, "The *Sitz im Leben* of the Samaria Ostraca," *TA* 6 (1979), 91-94 (also appears in Aharoni's *Land of the Bible*, pp. 363-65); G. A. Reisner, *HES I*, 227-46; idem, *Israelite Ostraca from Samaria* (undated and unpublished, but printed by E. O. Cockayne, Boston); W. H. Shea, "The Date and Significance of the Samaria Ostraca," *IEJ* 27 (1977), 16-27; and Y. Yadin, "Recipients or Owners, a Note on the Samaria Ostraca," *IEJ* 9 (1959), 184-87; idem, "Ancient Judaean Weights and the Date of the Samaria Ostraca," *Scripta Hierosolymitana* 8 (1961), 9-25; idem, A Further Note on the Samaria Ostraca," *IEJ* 12 (1962), 64-66.

[2] For four fragments of carved ivory and several unworked pieces from the earlier excavations by Reisner, see *HES I*, 368, Section A; *HES II*, Pls. 56:c, f; 66:f-1613 and h.

ostraca, for which further primary information remains a desideratum.[3] But in neither case shall I assay these collections to any appreciable degree from a linguistic, philological, or art historical point of view; my principal concern remains, with good reason, purely archaeological. That is, I will address the artifacts and the loci that produced them primarily at their points of retrieval. Clearly, a vexing need persists to determine with far greater precision than analysts have achieved to date the original contexts in which excavators first encountered this magnificent collection of decorative carvings, plaques, and inlays. Just as my work has shown throughout with regard to attempted analyses of the pottery from Samaria, the virtually complete lack of access to the archaeological context of both the ivories and the ostraca has hampered, if not hamstrung, any who would provide a fullbodied art historical, palaeographic, or socio-economic discourse on these items.[4]

II. The Archaeo–Historical Context of the Samaria Ivories

The brief period between May 28 and June 2, 1932, must have provided a glorious week for members of the Joint Expedition. The atmosphere in camp surely crackled with electricity as the workers began to recover and clean a staggering quantity of ivory objects and decorative elements from a few excavation areas lying near the northern shoulder of Samaria's summit. The importance the directors themselves attached to these discoveries is reflected in the primacy of place they awarded them in the overall ordering of official publications. The volume presenting the ivories (1938)[5] to the scholarly world preceded the description of the architecture (1942) by four years and, ultimately, the publication of the pottery and small objects (1957) by nearly two decades.[6] Moreover, two previous articles by J. W. Crowfoot, which had appeared almost immediately after the discovery of the ivories,[7] anticipated even the

---

[3] See the brief Excursus at the end of this chapter on the spatial distribution of the ostraca.

[4] In addition to the literature by J. W. Crowfoot, R. D. Barnett, et al. contemporary to the discovery of the Samaria Ivories (see nn. 1 and 7), see I. J. Winter, "Phoenician and North Syrian Ivory Carving in Historical Context: Questions of Style and Distribution," *Iraq* 38 (1976), 1-22; E. F. Beach, "The Samaria Ivories, Marzeah, and Biblical Text," *BA* 56 (1993), 94-104; I. Jaruzelska, *Amos and the Officialdom in the Kingdom of Israel: The Socio-Economic Position of the Officials in the Light of the Biblical, the Epigraphic and Archaeological Evidence* (Poznań: Wydawnictwo Naukowe Uniwersytetu, 1998), 79-82, 164-65.

[5] The first review of this study, likewise, appeared very quickly; see R. B. Barnett's response in *PEQ* (1939), 169-73.

[6] I have noted that, despite this chronology of the publications, John and Grace Crowfoot's volume dealing with the ivories became known as *Samaria-Sebaste II*, while the description of the architecture came to be called *Samaria-Sebaste I* and the presentation of the pottery and objects became *Samaria-Sebaste III*. (See Chapter III, 296, n. 353 above.)

[7] J. W. Crowfoot, "Recent Discoveries of the Joint Expedition to Samaria," *PEFQ* (July, 1932), 132-33, Pls. I-IV; idem, "The Ivories from Samaria," *PEFQ* (January, 1933), 7-26, Pls. I-III. See also H. G. May, "Supplementary Note on the Ivory Inlays from Samaria," *PEFQ* (April, 1933), 88-89, which suggests Damascus (rather than Phoenicia or Cyprus) as the place of manufacture for the ivory-inlaid furni-

official publication of them and accompanied a number of other preliminary reports on and reactions to the progress of the excavations in general.[8] While the punctual publication of these interim accounts is commendable,[9] the haste with which the material was prepared is reflected in the fact that the provenance data for the ivory fragments published in 1932 did not appear until the 1933 follow-up article.

As a further credit to his ability to be meticulous, Crowfoot provided in his 1933 report the kind of provenance data necessary to locate precisely the findspot of each piece he published. Whenever possible, the descriptions that accompanied the plates of ivory fragments included the registration number, summit strip, architectural feature and segment designation, local layer, and date of excavation for each entry presented in the article. Unfortunately, all future publications of the Joint Expedition abandoned this detailed standard of reporting. In their official monograph on the ivories that appeared in 1938 (*SS II*), John and Grace Crowfoot failed to list any provenance data at all—not even the registration number for a single fragment included in their discussion.[10] In her much later volume dealing with the pottery and objects retrieved by the expedition, Kenyon furnished her readers with *only* the registration number for each entry—a datum that, in isolation, gives no assistance whatsoever in an attempted critical appraisal of the archaeological or historical conclusions espoused in the report.

A principal concern in my reconsideration of the reports from the Joint Expedition has centered on correcting this situation, first for the pottery and now for the published ivories. I have kept as my objective the task of bringing every published item up to the standard of reporting first pursued by Crowfoot himself in his 1933 article.

---

ture at Samaria. For a later, much more detailed, argument for Phoenician origins, see R. D. Barnett, "Phoenician and Syrian Ivory Carving," *PEQ* (1939), 4-19, Pls. I-XI.

[8] See, in chronological order: J. W. Crowfoot, "Excavations at Samaria," *PEFQ* (January, 1932), 8-34, Pls. I-VII; idem, "The Expedition to Samaria-Sebustiya. The Forum Threshing Floor Area," *PEFQ* (April, 1932), 63-70, Pls. I-VI; idem, The Samaria Excavations: The Stadium," *PEFQ* (April, 1933), 62-73, Pls. I-VI; K. Kenyon, "Excavations at Samaria. The Forecourt of the Augusteum," *PEFQ* (April, 1933), 74-87, Pls. I-XIII; J. W. Crowfoot, "Samaria: Interim Report on the Work in 1933," *PEFQ* (July, 1933), 129-36; E. L. Sukenik, "Inscribed Hebrew and Aramaic Potsherds From Samaria," *PEFQ* (July, 1933), 152-56, Pls. I-IV; idem, "Inscribed Potsherds with Biblical Names from Samaria," *PEFQ* (October, 1933), 200-04, Pls. IX-X; J. W. Crowfoot, "Report of the 1935 Samaria Excavations," *PEQ* (1935), 182-94, Pls. VII-X; E. L. Sukenik, "Potsherds from Samaria, Inscribed with the Divine Name," *PEQ* (1936), 34-37, Pls. I-II; idem, "Note on a Fragment of an Israelite Stele found at Samaria," *PEQ* (1936), 156, Pl. III; W. E. Staples, "A Note on an Inscribed Potsherd," *PEQ* (1936), 155; H. Rosenau, "Review of *Churches at Bosra and Samaria-Sebaste*, by J. W. Crowfoot," *PEQ* (1937), 212-13.

[9] One must remember, however, that the ivories constituted a set of particularly uncommon finds. Today, such discoveries still receive swift and careful treatment in the literature (e.g., note A. Biran's timely presentation of the Tel Dan Inscription).

[10] The most one gets from this volume consists in a very general discussion of the Summit Strips (e.g., Qc, Qk, etc.) that yielded ivory fragments or groups of fragments (see *SS II*, 2-4). But even then he did not relate individual pieces to specific strips, so he gave no clue from where the actual plate entries came. Instead, he deferred to Kenyon by saying that "a detailed account of the stratification will be given by Miss Kenyon, in *Samaria-Sebaste I*" (p. 4).

For the pottery assemblage, the summary of information provided in Appendix F of *AIS-I* and in Appendix A of the present study has fulfilled this goal. Though the complete absence of any provenance data from *SS II* rendered the task of locating and collating the loci that yielded the published corpus of ivory fragments extremely difficult, I have now recovered at least some information (i.e., registry number and summit strip designation) for 96.4% of the pieces and complete or near-complete details for 92% of the overall collection. Based on the data contained in Appendix B, Table 55 offers a synopsis of the distribution of ivories across the relevant excavated segments, architectural features, and local layers. I shall use this organizational scheme to guide my discussion of the archaeological context of the various ivory-bearing loci.

Part A. Spatial Distribution of Published Ivories: Overview
     (*SS I*, Fig. 50; Pl. VII — Sections EF, GH)
     (*SS II*, Pls. I-XXV)

From Table 55 alone there emerges a wealth of information concerning the corpus of ivory fragments and glass inlays published in *SS II*. Discounting the all-glass items depicted in Frontispiece 2,[11] which appear to comprise a representative sample of many similar pieces found in the same loci,[12] the Crowfoots' 1938 volume contains a total of 250 items distributed over 25 plates. This number results from the fact that, on several occasions, a single entry subsumes multiple objects (as in Pls. XXIII-XXIV) and that, at other times, what appears as a single, complete artifact in *SS II* actually consists in two or more joined fragments (e.g., Pls. II:1; III:1; IV:3). Within this overall collection, I remain unable to locate any provenance data on 20 specific fragments (or 8% of the total group). While my preliminary database, then, consists in 230 separate items, I should note further that two of these entries actually represent pottery sherds inscribed in a fashion similar to the ivory carvings and recovered from the putative shrine in E 207 (Pl. XVI:5-6).[13] Removing those two ceramic pieces from the

---

[11] It is important to note that, while the narrative of *SS II* included two plates labeled "XXIV" (pp. 44-47), only one actually appears in the collection of photographs and drawings following the text portion of the book. The first "Plate XXIV" relates to the glass insets and gold leaf items presented in Frontispiece 2. I have not included these items in my general discussion or percentage calculations, and I do not believe that doing so would alter my findings in any significant way (see the following note). One may note that the same type of items found here are repeated in the following Pl. XXIV.

[12] E.g., Frontispiece 2, No. 4 (i.e., top row, numbering from left-to-right) stems from either registered object 1903b (Qc, 19.51.14.20, Layer IVb) or 3030 (Qk, W of 124, Layer V), the latter of which I have also associated with Pl. XXIV:11m. In a similar manner, Frontispiece 2:5 = 1881 from Qc, 19.51.14.20, Layer IVb; 2:7 possibly = 2046 from Qc, 19.51.14.20, Layer IVb; 2:8 = 2017b from Qc, 19.51.14.20, Layer VI; 2:9 = 1879 from Qc, 19.51.14.20, Layer VI (sieve); 2:12 = 3028 from Qk, W of 124, Layer VIII; etc. Clearly, these items derive from the same specific contexts as the other 250 objects included in the database. My sample, therefore, is sound and would not incur substantial alteration with the addition of the elements in Frontispiece 2.

[13] Locus E 207 did not relate to a particular Summit Strip, since it lay off the summit and ca. 90 m east of Summit Strips Qc-Qk, or roughly between 470°-495° N x 1528°-1557° E (see *SS I*, Pl. I, No. 27).

Segment Coordinates	Summit Strip	Architectural Feature	Local Layer	Principal Section Nos.	TOTAL FRAGS
Principal findspots:					
19.51.14.20	Qc	Room *e*	IV	76/77	43
			IVa	59/74	7
			IVb	—	30
			IVa.b	—	1
			IVd	59	7
			V	59	2
			VI	59?/74	14
			VII	59/74	5
			VIII	59/74	1
			IX	59/74	1
			(unknown)	—	27
			(Segment total:		*138)*
49.26.25	Qc	Room *hq:* west side	II	70	54
			Beneath 26	—	1
			(unknown)	—	8
			(Segment total:		*63)*
W of 124	Qk	Rooms *hq-kq*: east side *hq*	IIIc	43/70	1
			IVc	44/71	5
			V	45	1
			Vc	43/70/71	1
			Vc.y	—	1
			VI	43/44/69	2
			VIc	70/71	2
			VIz	—	1
			VII	—	3
			(Segment total:		*17)*
Miscellaneous findspots:					
E 207 (pottery)	—	Shrine	Level C	—	2
12.27.14.13	Qc	Rooms *e-g*	V	76/77	1
19.12.20	Qc	Rooms *e-g*	IVa	76/77	1
9.21.31	Qd	N Slope fill	V-VI	81	1
N of Wall 20	Qf	N Slope fill	VII	82	1
120.121.19.126	Qk	Room *g*	VII	67	1
125.144	Qk	Room *hk*	IIIb.x	10	1
E Strip.S Half	Qk	Room *k*	IV-VII	83	1
	Qk	Room *k*	V	83	1
507.503.504.505	Qn	Casemate fill-*l*	IIIm.c	61/72	1
Hellenistic RT	Qn	Casemate fill-*l*	?	61/72	1
			(Category total:		*12)*
Unknown findspots:	—	—	—	—	20
TOTAL					**250**

Ivory-bearing Loci and Ivory Distribution

Table 55

sample leaves a working database of 228 items for which I must attempt to establish individual findspots.

As shown in Table 56, the lion's share of published ivories derives from two principal summit strips (Qc and Qk) and, within those tracts of excavation, the overwhelming majority of fragments came from Summit Strip Qc alone. Drawing from Table 55, I may summarize the horizontal distribution of ivories (and glass) as follows:

	Number of Ivory/Glass Fragments	Percentage of 228 Total
Summit Strip Qc	203	89.1
Summit Strip Qk	21	9.2
Summit Strip Qn	2	0.9
Summit Strip Qd	1	0.4
Summit Strip Qf	1	0.4

Concentrations of Ivory and Glass Fragments: Horizontal Axis

Table 56

My findings agree completely with Crowfoot's general comments on the spread of ivories across the northern summit area. He reported that "the richest haul of ivories" came from Qc, followed by Qk, and that a smaller number of examples appeared in Qn.[14] Besides those main areas, five additional outlying sectors also produced a minimal number of ivory items, including Qh which lay south of the summit, Qd and Qf on the northern slopes, and fields B and Z situated to the southeast of the summit (see fig. 72).[15] Yet "all told," wrote Crowfoot, "the pieces which we registered from these other areas do not number more than twenty whereas we registered over five hundred fragments and groups of fragments from Qc, Qk, and Qn."[16] Therefore, my data sample—based as it is on the *published* corpus—contains about one half of the total number of fragments recovered. Even within the three strips just mentioned, "the numbers dwindled steadily the farther east we travelled" from Strip Qc.[17] Table 56 not only confirms this picture but underscores a dramatic reduction in the quantity of items retrieved even within the principal recovery zone once outside the parameters of Qc.

---

[14] *SS II*, 2, 4.

[15] While at least one published item appears to have come from Strip Qd (*SS II*, Pl. XVII:3), I have not found any entry in the official report that clearly belongs to one of the other minor areas of excavation.

[16] *SS II*, 4.

[17] *SS II*, 4.

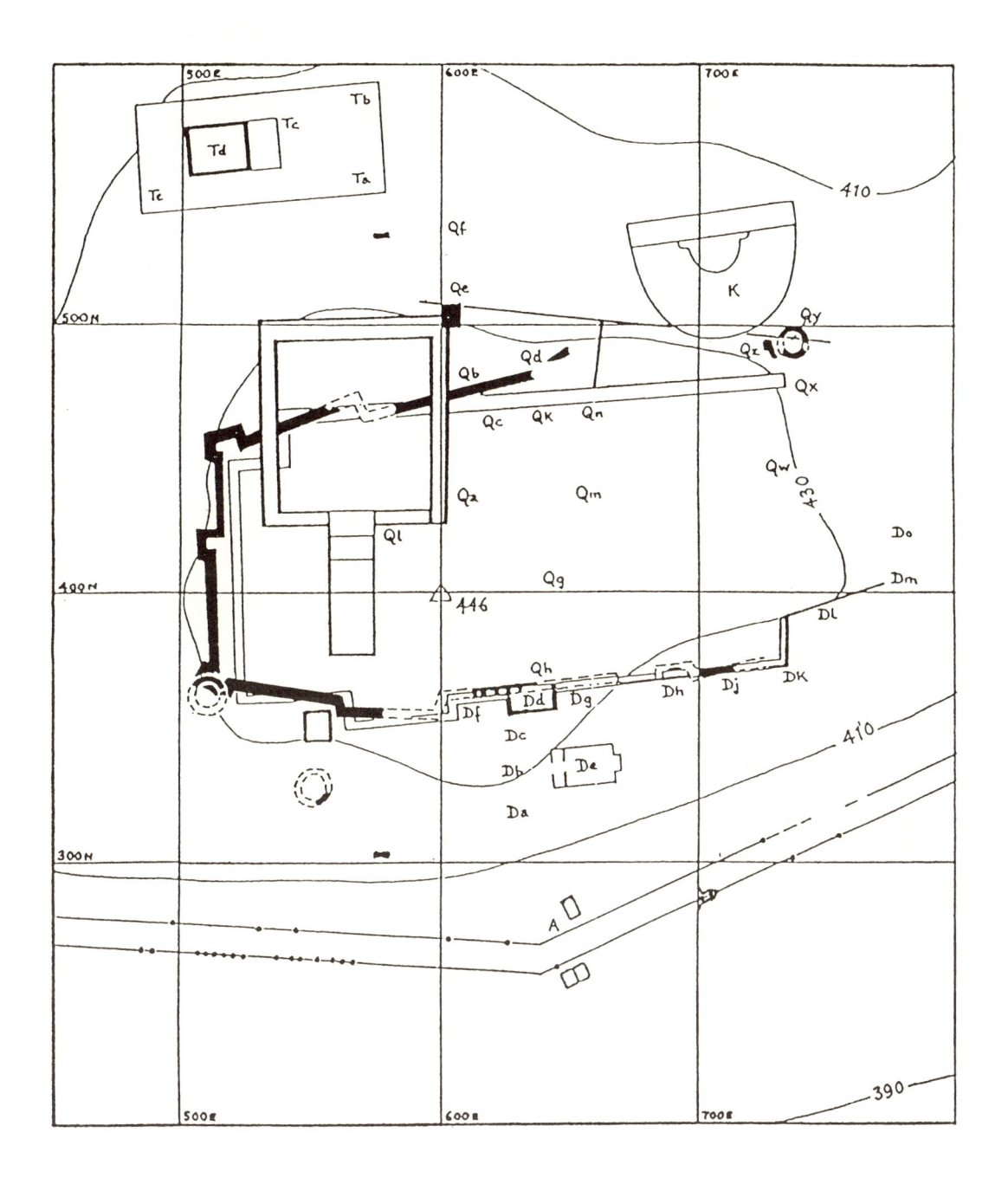

The Strip System:
Location of Principal Ivory-Bearing Areas (Qc, Qd, Qf, Qk, Qn)
(from *SS III*, xv)

fig. 72

Clearly, then, Summit Strips Qc and, to a lesser extent, Qk proffered the richest collection of ivory fragments found by the Joint Expedition. The data in Table 55 furnish two additional and very important observations concerning the distribution pattern of these artifacts. First, one sees that only three segments of the excavation yielded nearly 96% of all the entries identified in Appendix B. These include Segments *19.51.14.20* (138 of 228, or 60.5%) and *49.26.25* (27.6%) in Summit Strip Qc, plus the area lying *West of 124* (7.5%) in Qk. All the other miscellaneous loci combined yielded only 5.3% of the study sample. This means that nearly the entire corpus came from only three so-called "rooms" situated on the north side of the courtyard, Rooms *e, hq,* and *kq* (fig. 56). Unfortunately, two of these important locales constitute the most heavily disturbed spaces in the entire area (*e* and *kq*). These disturbances result from a variety of much later building projects carried out during the Hellenistic and Roman periods and do not represent a coherent destruction level dating to the age of Assyrian power. For example, quarrying activity during the Herodian period ate away nearly all the earlier, primary loci that once existed in *kq* (see *SS I*, Pl. II).

Second, one should note that within each of these three segments, two or three local layers consistently emerge as the most productive in terms of the vertical distribution of ivory and glass fragments (Table 57). For example, in Segment *19.51.14.20* the dominant levels include Layers IV, IVb, and VI, which yielded 63% of all the pieces collected from this area. In the same manner, Layer II of Segment *49.26.25* contained virtually all the now locatable ivory items retrieved there. Finally, Layers IVc, VI-VIc, and VII gave up 70.6% of the ivory published from Segment *W of 124*. Through observations such as these, it becomes clear that Layers IV-IVb and VI in Segment *19.51.14.20* and Level II in *49.26.25* constitute the pivotal ivory-bearing loci.[18] I shall review or introduce the stratigraphic reliability and overall character of these deposits in the following section.

Judging from the information assembled for the first time in these tables, then, I can determine that many of the published ivory fragments accumulated in a series of adjoining or closely situated deposits stretching laterally across the northern shoulder of the summit and just beyond the rock scarp that delineated the central royal compound area. But the situation does not reflect a totally random spreading of these erstwhile luxury items through a careless "raking" of soils and debris northward off the summit's upper shelf. On the contrary, the marked concentration of fragments in only a few layers in two segments associated with Rooms *e* (*19.51.14.20*) and *hq* (*49.26.25*) allows me to refine my conclusions regarding the depositional history of these caches. Rather than having been raked, scraped, or carelessly thrown off the central summit, these groups were poured into their final archaeological contexts, probably from large

---

[18] Of the 27 entries from *19.51.14.20* with unknown local layers, at least 12 registry numbers appear in series that seem related to Layer IV; likewise, 5 seem associated with IVb, 4 appear connected to VI, and 1 entry may have derived from IVd. I could not even venture a guess for 5 items. The fieldnotes also equate one of the miscellaneous findspots, Segment *12.27.14.13*, with *19.51.14.20* (see pp. 461-62 and n. 45 below). All 8 of the fragments from unknown deposits in *49.26.25* appear to relate to Layer II.

	Number of Ivory/Glass Fragments	Percentage of Segment Total
19.51.14.20		
IV	43	31.2
IVa	7	5.1
IVb	30	21.7
IVa.b	1	0.7
IVd	7	5.1
V	2	1.4
VI	14	10.2
VII	5	3.6
VIII	1	0.7
IX	1	0.7
(unknown)	27	19.6
49.26.25		
II	54	85.7
Beneath 26	1	1.6
(unknown)	8	12.7
W of 124		
IIIc	1	5.9
IVc	5	29.4
V	1	5.9
Vc	1	5.9
Vc.y	1	5.9
VI	2	11.7
VIc	2	11.7
VIz	1	5.9
VII	3	17.7

Concentrations of Ivory and Glass Fragments: Vertical Axis

Table 57

vessels or baskets that laborers had used to gather already somewhat mixed debris from specific spots elsewhere on the site. In other words, these clusters of goods seem to me to have moved as a group from one location to another. They do not reflect a random scattering or fanlike spray of preexisting layers and debris. But neither did they appear to the archaeologists in 1932-1933 in their original, primary ancient context; the functional life of these ivory and glass decorative elements had played itself out somewhere else on the site, most probably on the central summit plateau stretching southward from Rooms *e* and *kq* (between the longitudinal markers 630° and 650° E).

1) Stratigraphic Detail

a. Principal Findspots

[i] 19.51.14.20 (N. & S.) — Room *e* (Section GH; figs. 57-59; *AIS-I*, figs. 18-22b)

I have offered extended discussions of this segment in both my previous work and the present study.[19] For the sake of convenience, I shall reintroduce an earlier drawing and add to it a plot of published Section GH to facilitate a discussion of the depositional history in this area (fig. 73).

My studies have shown that, while Segment *19.51.14.20* may have stretched as far south as Wall 65, any possible remains from the Israelite period (however disturbed) must lie north of Wall 56 and east of Wall 57, i.e., in the area of Room *e*. Unlike Rooms *c* and *d* to the west, this feature (*e*) suffered almost total destruction

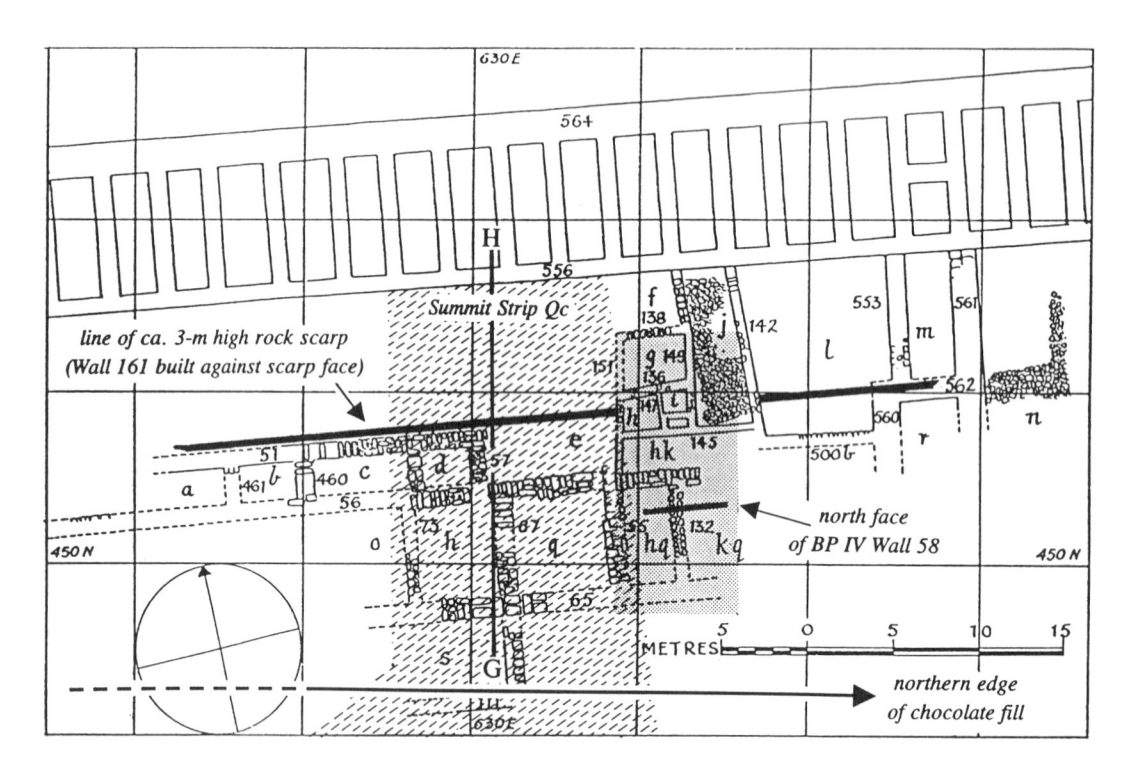

Plan of
Summit Strip Qc, Segment 19.51.14.20, and Published Section GH
(formerly fig. 56)

fig. 73

---

[19]See *AIS-I*, 150-58 (PP 3); also Chapter IV, 359-64 above (PP 7).

from 56 northward, where a noticeably thick layer of Hellenistic fill covered the earlier levels assigned to BP III. No intact Israelite remains beyond Period III appear to exist here. Moreover, Section GH attests to the fact that, south of Wall 56, this filling actually extended all the way to bedrock as it intruded upon the entire space between 56 and 65. Only a stump of BP IV Wall 58 remained buried in the midst of this deposit. This situation militates against Kenyon's published claim that the sooty debris associated with an Assyrian destruction of this area ran as far south as Wall 65.[20] North of Wall 51, which rested atop the nearly 3 m high scarp,[21] the secondary Hellenistic fill thickened as it apparently enveloped the remains of the original Casemate Wall 556 and continued on to the area of the Greek Fort Wall 551 (seen in bold print on fig. 72; compare *SS I*, Pl. IV).

It is important to note that these Hellenistic materials actually consist in at least three separate episodes of construction or leveling activity. The first, dated to Kenyon's "EH" period, which precedes the Fort Wall and belongs in the late third or early second century BCE,[22] raised the area to a level roughly even with the former BP III remains. Though this deposit appears as a single block of material in Section GH, my fig. 74 confirms that it subsumed at least four distinct layers of differing color and consistency (IX-XII). One of these levels (X) appears to depict a hard, yellowish-white floor into which a drain (69) was cut. The field notes refer to this installation as a "gutter" and note that it ran about parallel to Wall 68.[23] Importantly, then, Layer X may reflect an actual occupational phase, not a mere secondary filling as suggested in the published section and narratives. A light colored Layer IX, which yielded one of the blue glass insets presented in *SS II* (Pl. XXIV:11-*l*), overlay this possible surface and may have extended all the way to the northern face of Wall 56. It seems likely, however, that this glass item came from the portion of the deposit lying well north of Wall 51 and the rock ledge.

Sometime subsequent to this filling, a second phase of Hellenistic construction occurred in this area, indicated by the more densely hatched area in Section GH. Once again, Kenyon presented this as a unified block of material that contained quantities of burnt ivory. And again one sees from fig. 73 that the activity left multiple levels (VI-VIII north of Wall 51; IVa-VIII south of it), including another layering of light brown fill (Layer VIII) that supported a second possible floor level north of Wall 68 (Layer VII). These construction levels might also have originally extended southward to Wall 56, though one cannot be sure of this based solely on the field drawing presented in fig.

---

[20] *SS I*, 110. See also my Chapter IV, 362, n. 35.

[21] This fact is confirmed in *Fieldbook Qc-d-e-f-g-h*, 16.

[22] Note in Section GH that the Foundation Trench for Wall 551 appears to have cut through these levels of fill.

[23] *Fieldbook Qc-d-e-f-g-h*, 16. See *AIS-I*, 149, fig. 18.

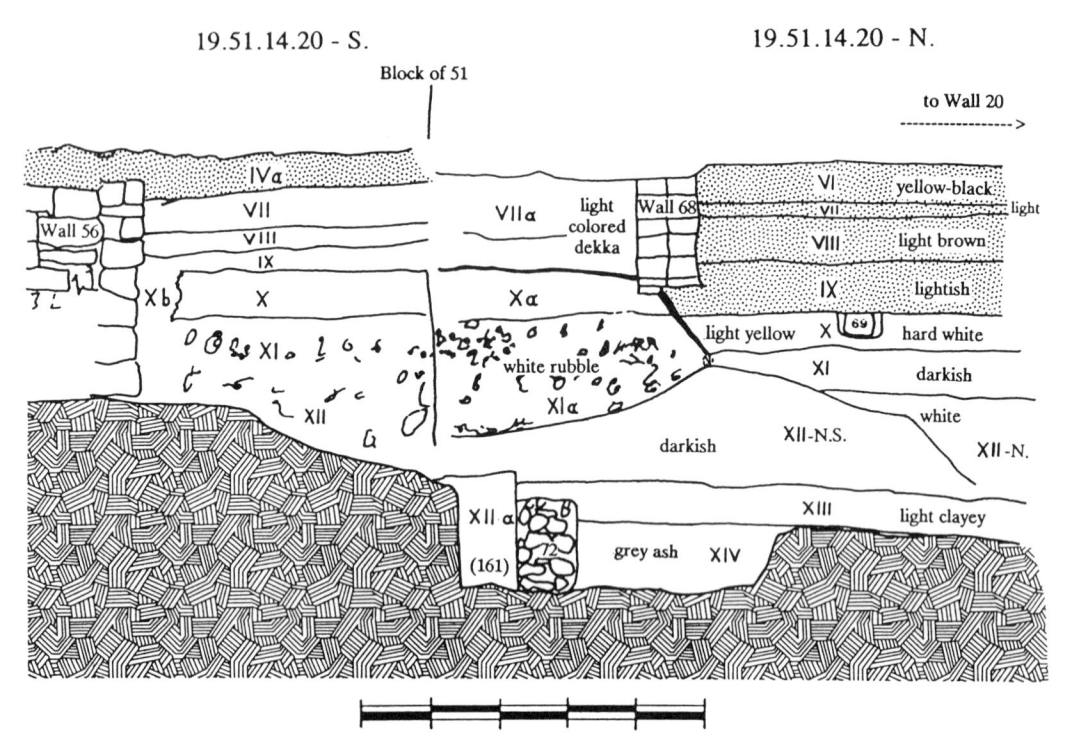

(approximate scale based on distance between Walls 56 and 161)

Segment 19.51.14.20 — North and South
(formerly fig. 57)
<— S N —>
View toward West

fig. 74

73.[24] Together, VII-VIII produced six ivory fragments deemed publishable by Crowfoot, though workers recovered two of them through sifting and not from contexts *in situ*.[25] That the original stratification card for one of these entries clearly stipulates a findspot in *19.51.14.20-North* confirms a location on the north side of fig. 74.[26]

The distinction that Kenyon drew between two separate groups of "Early Hellenistic" levels in Section GH reflects, in my judgment, the historical and stratigraphic

---

[24] To the immediate west, the close stratigraphy of possibly contemporary levels bearing the same layer numbers and running away from the east face of Wall 57 may help to corroborate this interpretation (see fig. 59).

[25] From Layer VII, see *SS III*, Pls. XII:17 (sieve); XXIII:1b; XXIV:1a-b; and XXV:3 (sieve). From Layer VIII, see Pl. XIII:4, from *19.51.14.20-N*.

[26] The distinction between *19.51.14.20 North* and *South* occurs at the line of Wall 51 or the hypothetical extension of that feature through Room *e*.

reality of two successive building phases completed in the area between the old Israelite Walls 56 and 556 (the face of the inner casemate) during the late third or early second century BCE. Later on, during the "Late Hellenistic" era (late second century BCE), workers seem to have dumped a third phase of additional fill immediately north of the line of 556.[27] Kenyon's Section GH shows that this leveling likely ran northward from the old, Israelite casemate system to the massive, new Greek Fort Wall 551, though subsequent robbing and backfilling operations during the Herodian period (= R.1) removed most of this deposit.

One of the more relevant deposits in *19.51.14.20-North* consists in the yellow-black accumulation (Layer VI) lying directly on the thinner VII. This level proved very rich in ivory fragments and contributed 14 separate items (or 10.2%) to the overall group published from this segment.[28] The field notes state that VI "def. goes right up to Wall 62, beneath 20, [without] any foundation trench at all."[29] It apparently also ran a good distance to the east, since the foundation trench for Wall 19 cut into its matrix. Kenyon observed that, to the south, the stratigraphic relationship between Layer VI and Wall 51 remained unclear. Yet she added that Wall 14a "seems to run onto top of 51, poss. joining onto it and re-using its foundations after it was partially broken down."[30] Judging from fig. 74, Layer VI did not continue south of 51 (or perhaps even 68) and in the direction of Wall 56, though the multiple striations lumped under the single designation "VII" in fig. 59 might suggest otherwise.

If, based on the unpublished field sections, Layers X and VII represent hard-packed, light-colored Hellenistic surfaces roughly situated north of 460° N on the x axis of the excavation grid,[31] then the subsequent Layers IX and VI, respectively, may well have included at least some occupational debris that went unidentified by the Joint Expedition.

I may tabulate the stratigraphic portrait and distribution of published ivories in *19.51.14.20-North* as presented in Table 58, which appears on the following page.

---

[27] Kenyon, therefore, parses out the Hellenistic stratigraphy in this area into three phases as follows: levels dating *earlier* than the so-called Greek Fort Wall (designated E.H.); deposits contemporary with the construction of this massive wall (= H.); and layers slightly later than those construction levels (compare *SS I*, Pl. IV). On Section GH, the layers labeled E.H. must represent Phase 1 of this scheme. Only FT 551, the identification of which I have added to the drawing, remains from Phase 2. The later fill of L.H. presents the best possible correlation to Phase 3, though subsequent Herodian building operations destroyed its stratigraphic connection to Wall 551.

[28] *SS III*, Pls. II:1a-b; XIII:1, 9, 12; XIV:3; XXIII:1c, 2k, 4b; and XXIV:11a, b, c, f, i.

[29] *Fieldbook Qc-d-e-f-g-h*, 4; compare the right hand side of fig. 74. See also *AIS-I*, 149, fig. 18 for the relative locations of Walls 62 and 20, which confirm the placement of this level in *19.51.14.20-North*.

[30] *Fieldbook Qc-d-e-f-g-h*, 4. Based on Kenyon's identifications in fig. 75, "14a" apparently represents the more southerly segment of Wall 14, including at least the section that extended south beyond the lateral Walls 27 and 25 (compare *AIS-I*, 149, fig. 18).

[31] For clarity of orientation, note that in my fig. 5 and also in *SS I*, Pl. II the lateral line of Omri's Enclosure Wall 161 lies directly on the 460° marker in this area (between 630° and 640° E). Both Section GH and my fig. 57, in turn, reveal that the ivory-bearing loci in question lay still north of that point.

Period and Nature of Activity	Layer and No. of Published Ivories ( )	
Phase 3: Late Hellenistic— leveling	Casemate 556 - GFW 551	
	N of 51	S of 51
Phase 2: Early Hellenistic— leveling & building	VI (14) VII (5) VIII (1)	IVa (7) — —
Phase 1: Early Hellenistic— leveling & building	IX (1) X XI XII	— — — —

Summary of Segment 19.51.14.20-North

Table 58

The situation becomes a bit murkier for those layers that are stratigraphically later than the aforementioned ones (V, IVd, IVa-IVb-IVa.b, and IV). As just noted, I can only surmise that the three layers situated between VIII and IVa/IVd in fig. 59 must in fact include Levels VII, VI, and V, even though in her field drawing Kenyon wrote only "VII" beside them. In support of this assumption, the field notes indicate that "in *19.51.14.20.S.*, IVa, V, and IVd [are] prob. all part of the same level" and that the pits labeled VIc cut through Layer VI.[32] From fig. 59, one sees that the westernmost pit actually cut V-VII, while the eastern one intruded even into Layer VIII. The notes go on to record that:

> beneath a no. of layers of v. hard cement (decca), [with] in places a gd. deal of pottery in it = VII. Beneath, a darkish level = VIII. Apparently a v. few pieces of ivory fr. it.[33]

I also concluded in my earlier stratigraphic analysis that Robber Trench 57 (for which I have added an identifying label) and the combined levels IVa-IVd followed the partial plundering of that wall. Collectively, Layers V, IVd, IVa, and IVa-b (which the field

---

[32] *Fieldbook Qc-d-e-f-g-h*, 15-16.

[33] *Fieldbook Qc-d-e-f-g-h*, 16.

notes equate with V),[34] yielded 17 artifacts of ivory.[35] It therefore appears that this second cache of ivories came from an area of late floor levels and fills situated just at the rock scarp and outside the northeastern corner of Room *d*. If so, this locus would represent the northernmost limit of *19.51.14.20-South*.

The field diaries equate the ivory-laden Layer IVb[36] with IVa. Kenyon's unpublished notes for Segment *9.27.14.13* confirm the location of both deposits in the southern portion of Room *e*, along the line of Wall 56 and east of 57.[37] The expedition removed these layers between May 31 and June 3, 1932, and the following records provide valuable provenance data for many of the more heavily burnt ivory pieces:

> 31-5-32. Work on the patch labeled IVa . . . gt. quantity of v. burnt bits found. Many burnt bits also found under a few stones (66) wh. beneath 25, and above 64, wh. removed. Labeled IVb.
>
> 1-6-32. . . . Work on IVa and IVb cont. IVa crosses line of 56, apparently where wall broken down, but poss. at its end. Consid. quantity of burnt ivory and wood, mostly completely destroyed. IVb all mixed up with rubble and ashes, beneath 66. Even more fragments than IVa.
>
> 2-6-32. Work cont. on IVa and IVb with slightly larger staff. More fragments of v. burnt ivory found.
>
> 3-6-32. Work cont. on IVa and IVb. IVb extends S. fr. line 56 in v. fine ashes and earth, mixed up with rubble. Seems to extend nearly to line of 65. . . . Beneath IVa, some stones cont. across. These partly covered by mortar, wh. prob. part of wall and nt. doorway, [since] nt. found to N. or S. of line of wall. IVa cont. [as] really all part of IVb, (..?..) N. of 56, also mixed up with rubble. Nt. nearly so much burning here. Stones of walls show no def. signs of burning.[38]

The later (post-Israelite) dating of Layer IVb receives corroboration by the recovery of a coin "in the rubble of IVb, against E. face of 58-67, 1.05 m. S. of N.E. corner," though Kenyon held open the possibility "that [the] coin drifted down fr. above, [since] stone very loosely packed." Unfortunately, she offered no more specific comments regarding the identification or possible dating of this coin. It is also important, however, to mention her observation that "the rubble on this side did nt. show much signs of soot, only occasional streaks."[39] The area in question here comprises the

---

[34]*Fieldbook Qc-d-e-f-g-h*, 15.

[35]From Layer V, see *SS II*, Pls. VII:2, 7; from IVd, see Pls. IV:1, 3b (sieve); XII:12-13; XIII:6, 10; and XV:1; from IVa and IVa-b, see Pls. XX:5; XXI:9; XXIII:3a, 4a; XXIV:3, 4, 7; and XXV:7.

[36]For specific references to the 30 fragments published in *SS II*, see Appendix B.

[37]*Fieldbook Qc-d-e-f-g-h*, 4.

[38]*Fieldbook Qc-d-e-f-g-h*, 4b (dates given in British format).

[39]All quotations taken from *Fieldbook Qc-d-e-f-g-h*, 15.

very northern edge of Room *q* in fig. 73, above the gap in Wall 67 created by the robbing of lateral BP IV Wall 58 (the original line of which I have added to this plan).[40] The ivories and the various, sometimes mixed layers that contained them lay, for the most part, north of the line of Wall 56.

I may note that the only PP 4-7 pottery published from *19.51.14.20* came from the pit fills in VIc and the overlying IVa.[41] The failure to mesh more fully the pottery-bearing loci with the ivory-bearing ones in the final, published record represents a significant shortcoming in the expedition's interpretive and reporting strategy. Though Kenyon assigned all five ceramic pieces to the putative Assyrian destruction debris of "Period VII," I have shown that, while all are related in some way to Assyrian traditions, none dates earlier than the mid-to-late seventh century BCE on ceramic grounds alone. But, from a stratigraphic point of view, it now appears that all these fragments eventually became part of much later, Hellenistic building levels.

One curious pattern of distribution emerges from a close reading of the unpublished field notes relating to these deposits. Most of the ivory recovered from Layer IVa, near Wall 57, showed signs of considerable burning (compare also the description above of pieces taken from IVb). From both the journal entries cited above and fig. 73, one sees that this deposit actually overran the truncated Wall 56 and apparently spilled down into the hollow cavity between 56 and 65 to the south—an area for which I have no further details of depositional history (compare Section GH). In the related Layer IVd, however, situated farther away from Wall 57 and toward the center of the so-called "Room *e*," the expedition found "a consid[erable] amount of unburnt ivory,"[42] including a plaque depicting some sitting lions.[43] From the records available now, I cannot tell just how far south IVd might have extended. It is indeed somewhat strange to think of Greek workers dumping load after load of debris into this area without snatching up as souvenirs the dozens of pieces of clean, complete or near-complete ivory carvings they undoubtedly saw falling out of their baskets. Perhaps as a result of their apparent apathy toward these erstwhile luxury items, we now have the pleasure of glimpsing the grandeur of old Samaria.[44]

---

[40] The field notes indicate that Level IVb ran as far south as the line of BP IV Wall 58. Though the surviving top of the wall appeared in the matrix of IVb, Kenyon stated in her field observation the feature "quite definitely underlay IVb, includ. the hard layer along 26 in IVa" (*Fieldbook Qc-d-e-f-g-h*, 15).

[41] See *SS III*, Fig. 11:12, 15, 17 (IVa) and 11:23, 28 (VIc).

[42] *Fieldbook Qc-d-e-f-g-h*, 15-16. For more on the burnt vs. unburnt collections, see p. 468.

[43] Though Crowfoot apparently did not publish this piece, it must have resembled those seen in *SS II*, Pl. IX:2-4, from Room *49.26.25*, Layer II.

[44] On the other hand, we should perhaps count our good fortune that the excavators recovered as many samples of ivory as they did, for the Greek (and Roman) workers might just as well have kept for themselves many of the most beautifully carved, best preserved items. It is not unimaginable, in this scenario, that some of these artifacts even made their way to Athens or Rome as relics of a bygone age in the exotic orient.

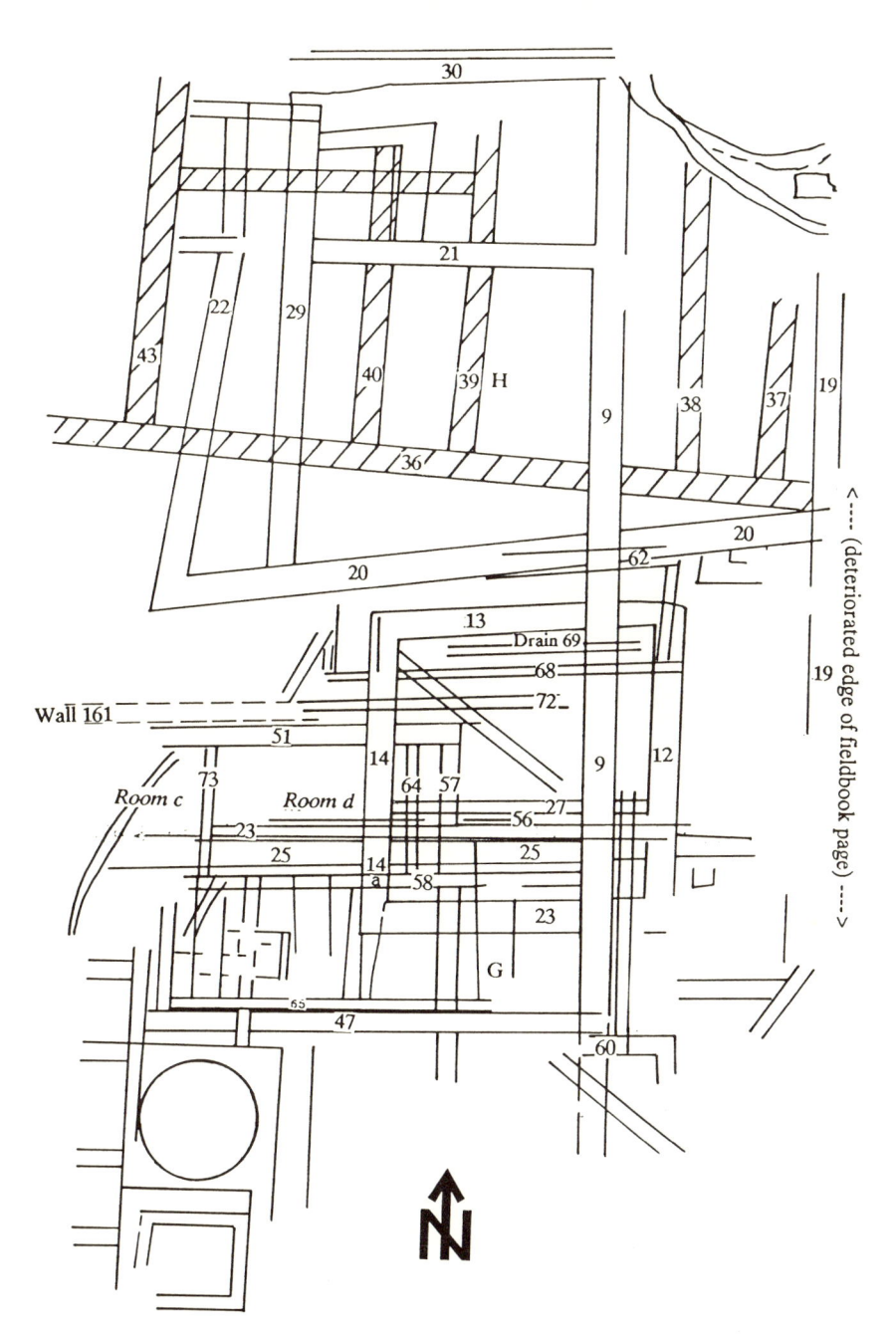

*Partial Plan of Summit Strip Qc:
Coordinate Walls 12.27.14.13 in Segment 19.51.14.20.N*

(formerly *AIS-I*, fig. 18)

fig. 75

Besides IVb, Layer IV represents perhaps the most elusive of all the ivory-bearing deposits in Segment *19.51.14.20*; as indicated in Table 55, Kenyon did not include these deposits in any of her unpublished field drawings. The irony of this lacuna lies in the prodigious nature of the layers involved. Judging from the distribution of artifacts contained in *SS II* (Table 55/Appendix B), Level IV itself yielded more decorative fragments than any other single deposit; further, IV and IVb together produced at least 73 ivory specimens, or more than half of the entire collection published from this segment of excavations (52.9%). Still, the final objects report in 1957 failed to include a single sherd of pottery taken from these layers. Though these accumulations do not appear in the drawings of this segment, one may postulate on the basis of my conclusions regarding stratigraphically earlier deposits that these layers must also stem from the Hellenistic period at the earliest. A separate document in the PEF archives labeled "Abstract of Levels, Qc" included a notation that presented Layers IVa, IVb, IVd, IVe, V, Va, VI, VIa, VIb, VIc, and VId as "levels containing ivory fragments, mostly burnt. probably deposited *c.* 3 B.C."

The only viable recourse by which to corroborate this journal entry may come from the unpublished notes concerning two additional segments, namely *12.27.14.13*

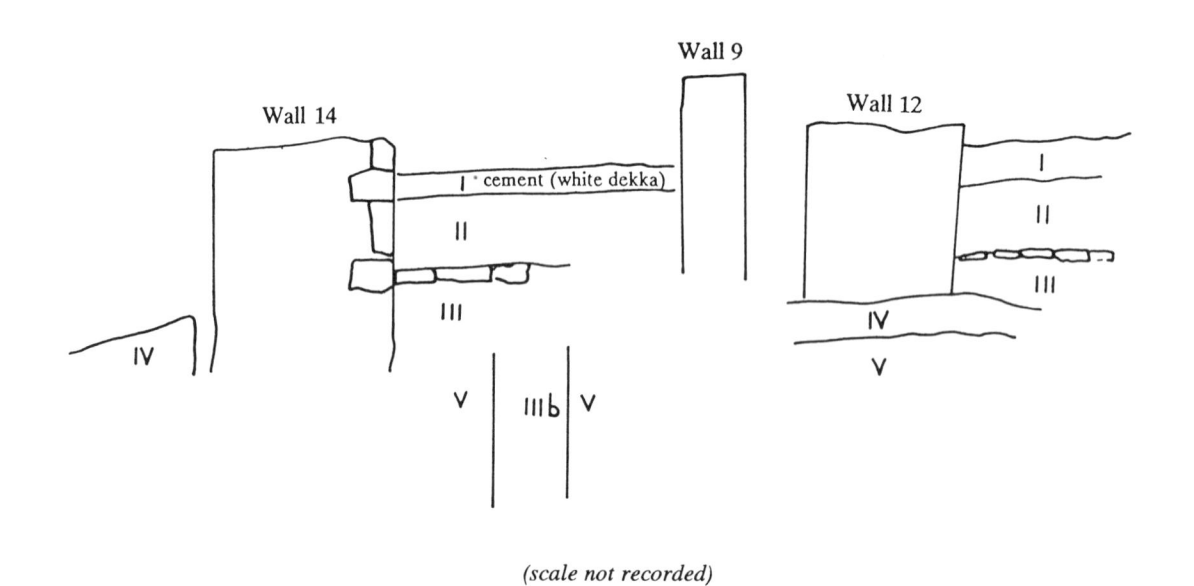

(scale not recorded)

Field Section Showing a Portion of Room *12.27.14.13*
(formerly *AIS-I*, fig. 24)
<— W   E —>
View toward North

fig. 76

plus *19.12.20*, which the field records equate with *19.51.14.20*.[45] In my previous study, I plotted these areas using a roughly sketched field plan that showed a mass of walls dating from the late Israelite through the Roman periods (reproduced here on p. 459 as fig. 75).[46] This plan, which I found attached to *Fieldbook Qc-d-e-f-g-h*, confirms the location of the room identified by the coordinates *12.27.14.13*. The drawing demonstrates that this portion of *19.51.14.20* again lay basically east of Room *d* and that it stretched from the northern half of that chamber northward to just beyond Drain 69, which itself ran parallel to and a few meters north of the lateral rock scarp and Omri's original Enclosure Wall 161.[47] This valuable information leads one again to fig. 74 above and to the realization that the important Layer IV must have rested directly above those depicted on the northern side of that section, in *19.51.14.20-N*.

Fortunately, one field section showing some of the walls and deposits in this area can assist in confirming the relative dating of at least the dominant Layer IV to the early Hellenistic period. This drawing shows a lateral view of the accumulations situated between and just outside Walls 12 and 14 (fig. 76).[48]

Segments and Layers Associated with *19.51.14.20*	Suggested Date
Room 12.27.14.13	
-I	unstratified
I	probably Herodian
II, IIb, IIIa	late Hellenistic
III	beneath Hellenistic pavement
Room 19.12.20	
I	probably Herodian
II-IV	late Hellenistic
W of 14	
I	probably Herodian
II-III	late Hellenistic
IV-VI	post-Israelite, down to early Hellenistic

Abstract of Selected Levels:
Summit Strip Qc
Table 59

---

[45]*Fieldbook Qc-d-e-f-g-h*, 4 (see n. 18 above). The aforementioned "Abstract of Levels, Qc" also included the lower levels situated *West of (Wall) 14* in this correlation.

[46]*AIS-I*, 149, fig. 18.

[47]The latter feature crossed this area at a latitude of approximately 460° N (see fig. 5).

[48]*Fieldbook Qc-d-e-f-g-h*, 4a.

The *Abstract of Levels* for Strip Qc, mentioned above, summarizes the chronology of these layers.[49] Table 59 (previous page), provides a synopsis of the data found there.

The deposits in Segment *19.12.20* refer to those that extend eastward from Wall 12 in fig. 76, while *12.27.14.13* includes the layers resting between Walls 12 and 14, and *W of 14* pertains to the Layer IV that was quite obviously cut during the construction of Wall 14. As the plans of these features reveal,[50] this Layer IV already lies well inside the area of Room *d*, which means that it lies outside (west of) the parameters of Segment *19.51.14.20* as defined by Kenyon herself. It seems, then, that one should accept the more easterly Layer IV—i.e., the one that lies directly beneath Wall 12—as the most likely correlate for the same level in *19.51.14.20*.[51] In fig. 76, there is a late Hellenistic pavement running between 14 and 12, and then on to the east from 12. The stones themselves rested .90 m below the existing height of Wall 14[52] and directly on the makeup of Layer III[53] which, in turn, overlay Layer IV (at least in the eastern portion of the section; no paving or bedding remained intact in the southwestern corner of this segment, i.e., in the area that approached the heavily disturbed Room *e*). Layer IV therefore appears to date once again to the early Hellenistic period, if not slightly later still. (Note that the abstract summary tags it as "Late Hellenistic.") In short, the crucial Layer IV (like VI-IX) belongs to the *northern* portion of Segment *19.51.14.20* and to a time frame in either Phase 2 or 3 in Table 58.

A second field drawing focuses on the layers lying just beneath and east of Wall 12 (fig. 77).[54] While it basically concurs with the picture gained already from fig. 76, it shows more explicitly that a thin strip of material ran between Layers III and IV. The field diary entries for Segment *19.12.20* recorded on May 20-24, 1932, read as follows:

> 5-20-32. Paving stones to E. of Wall 12 removed; beneath labeled Level III. The hard level found in 49.26.25 found in S.W. corner of this area, and fragments of carved ivory found in it. = IVa. Runs up against Wall 56, wh. underlies Wall

---

[49] Unpublished *Abstract*, 2 (stored in the Palestine Exploration Fund).

[50] I.e., *AIS-I*, 149, fig. 18, and fig. 75 above.

[51] In my stratigraphic analysis for PP 7, I observed that in its northernmost sector Segment *19.51.14.20* extended at least as far east as Wall 142 in fig. 56 (i.e., to the boundary between Rooms *j* and *l*).

[52] *Fieldbook Qc-d-e-f-g-h*, 4.

[53] I have noted on several occasions the failure by the authors to include in their final report any appreciable sample of pottery from these areas. The field notes indicate that near Wall 14 excavators encountered a "huge mass of pottery in [a] pit going down deep" which they identified as Layer IIIa, visible near the center of fig. 76 (*Fieldbook Qc-d-e-f-g-h*, 4). Though it remains very difficult to know with any certainty, one wonders whether this deposit might actually represent the uppermost portion, undetected at this point in the progress of excavation, of what will eventually become the Pit *i* that proceeded down through the final phases of Israelite houses in this general area.

[54] *Fieldbook Qc-d-e-f-g-h*, 7a.

26 and other fragments here, and apparently belongs to it. Earth above labeled IIIa.

5-23-32. Small portion of Level III removed. Under Wall 12. A hard yellow clay level band = IV.

5-24-32. Level IV cleared. Think layer of light yellow clay, like IV of W of 14, over darkish earth. Beneath a burnt layer = V, and a hardened lightish level = VI.[55]

The southwest corner of the plot designated by Walls 19, 12, and 20 would, by my reckoning, fall in the extreme eastern edge of Room *e* or even in the general area of the complex of Rooms *g, h,* and *i.* Judging from the two top plans mentioned above, this locus seems at any rate to lie north of the hypothetical extension of Wall 51 toward the east. That it even seems possible to associate the pottery-filled pit of Layer IIIb in fig. 76 with Pit *i* on Kenyon's phase plans (see n. 53) strengthens this placement of Layer IV.

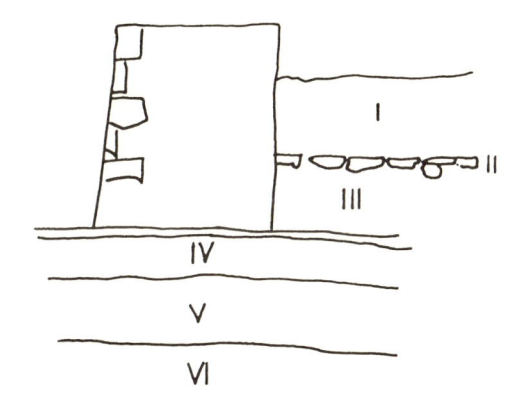

(scale not recorded)

Wall 12 from Room 12.27.14.13
<— W   E —>
View toward North

fig. 77

In summation, a number of helpful observations have emerged with regard to the ivories recovered from Segment *19.51.14.20*. First, I have shown that 138 of the 228 total pieces presented in *SS II* derived from this area of the excavations (60.5%); of these entries, I have securely located 111 items (80.4%). Generally speaking, the

---

[55] *Fieldbook Qc-d-e-f-g-h*, 7.

collection came almost entirely from the area lying north of Wall 56, and a significant percentage of the loci rested even beyond the line of Wall 51 (fig. 56). That is, they lay in levels that originated just at and mostly below the northern rock scarp and that ran from there northward at least as far as the line of the old Israelite Casemate Wall 556. I may divide the overall group more specifically between two distinct portions of the segment: *19.51.14.20-North* (mostly above 460° N; includes Layers IV and VI-IX = 64 locatable fragments, or 57.7% of 111 and 46.4% of 138) and *19.51.14.20-South* (in the portion of Room *e* lying just east of *d*; Layers IVa, IVb, IVa.b, IVd, and V = 47 specimens, or 42.3% of 111 and 34.1% of 138). Finally, the remaining 28 fragments (20%), for which neither Crowfoot nor Kenyon recorded local layers on the stratification cards or in the final register of objects, seem most often to belong to one of the three principal levels yielding the bulk of the published collection (Layers IV, IVb, and VI). Consequently, these items do not appear to have the potential to alter significantly the percentages offered here. Instead, by including them I would likely only inflate further the figures for the three already most prodigious layers in this area.

Before leaving this segment, I must note two additional areas that appear in the group of miscellaneous segments listed in Table 55, namely *12.27.14.13* and *19.12.20*. Each of these locations contributed a single fragment of ivory to the final report and I can readily situate both segments by means of the wall numbers recorded on the two plans referred to above.[56] Excavators retrieved *SS II*, Pl. X:6 from Layer V of *12.27.14.13* which, as one learns from figs. 75-76, they encountered in the space between Walls 14 and 12, if not further outside those borders. The burnt debris of V surrounded the deep pit (IIIa) containing a mass of pottery and, while it covered the rest of the sectional strip between 12 and 14, the field notes state that the hard, yellowish floor that appeared in other parts of the room did not survive above Layer V. It seems, therefore, that this deposit represents either the remaining makeup originally laid beneath that Hellenistic floor or later debris resulting from a localized disturbance of the surface.

I have already described Layer IVa of the miscellaneous segment *19.12.20* above. This level also contributed only one fragment to the final report on the ivories (see Pl. XV:4* in Appendix B).

[ii] 49.26.25 — Room *hq* (Published Sections EF, GH; fig. 75; *AIS-I*, fig. 18)

This track of excavations, which also lay in Summit Strip Qc but which has not appeared in any previous part of my study, contributed a total of 63 fragments of ivory to the Crowfoots' final report in 1938, or just over one quarter of the total published collection of 250 entries (yet *SS III* included no pottery from this area). Virtually the entire group came from a single localized deposit, Layer II. The provenance data recorded for 8 of the ivory items clearly assigned them to this segment but failed to

---

[56]*AIS-I*, 149, fig. 18 = fig. 75 above.

include the local layer from which excavators removed the items. Of all the records I have seen in the PEF relating to the collection of ivories, however, none offers a viable alternative to Layer II for any of these questionable findspots. In short, it seems safe to conclude that all the ivory and glass fragments recovered from this segment came from a single layer of earth (including *SS II*, Pl. XIII:3, which Crowfoot assigned to Layer II while adding the stipulation that workers found this piece lodged beneath Wall 26).

When considered in conjunction with fig. 75 above, various descriptive comments recorded in the field diaries help to locate at least two of the three key walls that define the parameters of this segment.[57] The meager amount of stratigraphic data available for the first wall of concern, 49, indicates that it rested directly on top of Layer II, while nearby Wall 12b actually cut through that deposit. I found no other clues that might reveal the stratigraphic or chronological relationships between Wall 49 and other architectural structures in the general area.

The second unit in the coordinates for this segment, Wall 26, also "rested on earth"[58] and ran over the top of Wall 56[59] and up against Wall 25 (see Published Section GH in fig. 58 for the relative positions of these features). This would keep 26 north of the lateral line of the BP IV Wall 58, which had earlier run through what would become the midsection of the BP V Rooms *o, h, q, hq,* and *kq* (compare my notation in fig. 56 with the actual location of 58 in fig. 5). Though Kenyon included only a portion of Wall 26 in fig. 75, the field notes confirm that it ran between Walls 9 and 12a and that it dated "prob. later than either" of those elements. I have added an identifying label to fig. 75 to show what must represent the southward extension of 26. It did not, however, survive intact as far south as that drawing makes it appear, for the notes reveal that excavators found a "gap of *c*. 3 m between it and [the] end of 47, wh. looked as if it had been broken down for it."

As shown in section in fig. 58 and in plan in fig. 75, the laterally oriented Wall 25 followed a course lying just north of 23 and 58. Once again, then, this wall relates directly to the northern half of Rooms *hq* and *kq*. The notes explain further that it survived to a length of 1.10 m east of Wall 12 (this seems to agree with the field drawing in fig. 75).

Though I do not know the precise orientation of Wall 49, then, the juncture between Walls 26 and 25 clearly lay east of the north-south Wall 9 (fig. 75), which places it at least 7 m farther east than the eastern side of Room *d*. Moreover, the 26-25 intersection rested south of the lateral Wall 56 but not south of the line of 58 (fig. 56). By this reckoning, a plot of the excavation segment labeled *49.25.26* must fall somewhere near the northwestern corner of Room *hq*, i.e., very near the eastern limit of

---

[57] Unless indicated otherwise, the primary data for the ensuing discussion of *49.26.25* came entirely from *Fieldbook Qc-d-e-f-g-h*, 14. Unfortunately, I could find information relating to this segment only in this short portion of the field diaries.

[58] I presume this means that the excavators saw no apparent foundation trench for this wall.

[59] *Fieldbook Qc-d-e-f-g-h*, 7.

Summit Strip Qc but, unlike *19.51.14.20*, on the central summit plateau and not below the rock scarp on which Wall 51 was built.

Turning to the distribution of ivory fragments down through the vertical axis of this segment, I found that the unpublished field notes address only a few distinct depositional layers in this area. This situation results from the fact that the expedition found no signs of stratification to a depth of approximately 3 meters, but only an unusually heavy overburden in this particular precinct. Consequently, the Abstract of Levels for Summit Strip Qc listed only three principal layers in its summary of the depositional history in Segment *49.26.25*: Layer I, "mainly unstratified"; Layer II, "unburnt ivory level, deposited probably c. 3 B.C." [i.e., third century BCE]; and Layer III, "Hellenistic." In other words, it seems that no intact remains from the Israelite period appeared in this area. The field records did not include a section drawing of any of these levels.

The pivotal layer, II, consisted in a hard, yellowish matrix that contained generous quantities of ivories and that extended southward to within 1.10 m of Wall 65 and the rock scarp that reportedly ran behind it. This drop in the level of the rock is not analogous to the more pronounced ledge that crossed the area at a point farther north and on which Wall 51 sat. Published Section GH shows a steady decline in the rock north of Wall 65 but not a steep scarp. Another north-south cut, Section EF,[60] which passed through the line of 65 at approximately 642° E, or about 9-10 m east of GH (at roughly 633° E),[61] provides a clearer view of both the minor scarp that buttressed the foundation courses of Wall 65 and the irregularly declining rock stretching from there to Wall 51 (which, though not shown on this section, would rest atop the ledge situated directly south of 161/160). This section (EF), therefore, ran through the area belonging to the eastern half of Room *hq*. These two field cuts show that a minor fall in the rock surface helped to define the southern boundary of this chamber just as the major drop-off defined the northern limits of Rooms *a-d (e)*.

A limited field plan,[62] which Kenyon apparently completed only to show the horizontal location of the ivory-rich Layer II, confirms that this deposit lay north of Wall 65 and the minor drop in the surface of the bedrock on the summit side of that wall (fig. 78).

Taken together, the data provided here confirm a location for Layer II of Segment *49.26.25* in the westernmost portion of Room *hq* and, more specifically, in the northwest corner of that area. The last conclusion stems from the fact that the segment lay north of the Wall 58 line and that it would have had to involve the westernmost part of the room in order to remain within the stated bounds of Strip Qc. The drawing in fig. 78, then, shows some of the remaining blocks of Wall 65, the Robber Trench 65 running further east (left) from those stones, and a perpendicular, adjoining wall which

---

[60] *SS I*, Pl. VII.

[61] See fig. 5 for a plotting of this section on the horizontal plane.

[62] *Fieldbook Qc-d-e-f-g-h*, 14a.

(to summit)

scarp   65

Level II

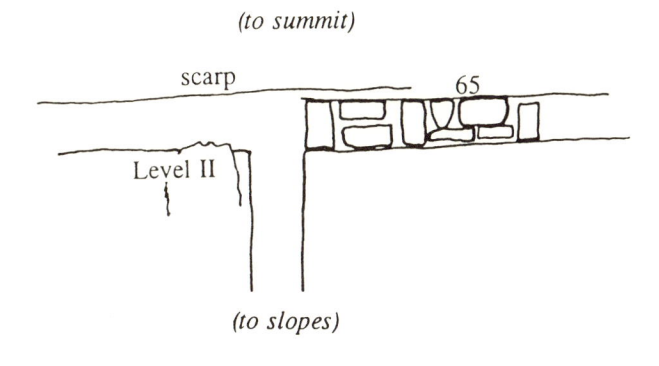

(to slopes)

(scale not recorded)

Partial Plan of Summit Strip Qc:
Segment 49.26.25, Layer II (Room hq)

fig. 78

most likely represents the line of Wall 55 (west side of Room *hq*) though Kenyon provided no label for it. A statement contained in the field journal entry for May 27, 1932, seems to corroborate this identification by juxtaposing Layer II and a section of Wall 55. Here, while recording the continuation of efforts to clear Level II, Kenyon remarked that "there may be a foundation trench of 1 cm belonging to 55a, but cert. nt. more."

I have noted the lack of clear stratigraphy in the thick level labeled Layer I, where workers encountered a "consid. mass of walls and pottery fr. below [the] level of [the] top of [. . ? . .] mass." Yet, in her personal records, Kenyon did distinguish a blanket of darkish soil, which apparently ran from the edge of the minor scarp at Wall 65 and overlapped portions or possibly all of Layer II. While the field notes indicate that this level, called Layer Ia, contained pottery (but not ivories), Kenyon did not specify the vessel types or suggested dates of the ceramic fragments. This omission is unfortunate, since knowledge of the other kinds of goods contained in Ia might have helped to establish a *terminus ante quem* for the ivory-bearing Level II which lay beneath it. Similarly, had the expedition published pottery from Layer III, which underlay Level II and at points revealed traces of a hard surface but did not yield any pieces of ivory, one might have had a better opportunity to suggest a *terminus post quem* for the crucial Layer II. In a pocket situated beneath Level III, which would have to rest on or very near the bedrock surface, the team discovered pottery dating to the Early Bronze Age.

It seems clear, then, that only Layer II produced the ivory and glass fragments in *49.26.25*. Besides Kenyon's own assessment of the date of this deposit, which she recorded in the Abstract of Levels and which I presume she based on an analysis of the unpublished pottery taken from this and contiguous layers, there remains only a single comment in the field diaries to help tie Layer II to the Hellenistic period. As I have already noted, Kenyon observed elsewhere that "the hard level found in *49.26.25* [also appeared] in the S.W. corner of this area [i.e, Segment *19.12.20*]," which lay directly north of *49.26.25*, in the general area of Rooms *g-hk*. The southwest corner of *19.12.20* would correspond to the northwest corner of *49.26.25*, and this constitutes, in my judgment, the point of discovery of the present cache of ivories.

Finally, it is important to mention that on several occasions the field notes distinguish between the *burnt* ivory remains yielded by Segment *19.51.14.20* and related areas and the *unburnt* carvings that came from Layer II of *49.26.25*. As I have demonstrated, the former, damaged collection derived mainly from areas lying north of Wall 56, in the heavily disturbed space of Room *e*, or even further north beyond the 3 m-high scarp beneath Wall 51. Even the considerable number of fragments found in Layer IVa of *19.51.14.20*, which lay only a few feet away from the present area and just across the line of Wall 56, displayed a noticeably poorer state of preservation and signs of much heavier burning than did the pieces recovered from *49.26.25*. Thus far, this more intact group of remains has stemmed almost entirely from the better-built and preserved Room *hq*, i.e., from an architectural feature relating to the central summit compound and not to the more poorly constructed service rooms that surrounded the royal quarter.

[iii] W of 124 — Rooms *hq* and *kq*   (Published Section EF; figs. 7, 42-43, 59-62)

This segment takes us east of Summit Strip Qc and into the contiguous area of Qk. The local stratigraphy of the segment labeled *W of 124* has received detailed comments at two previous points in this study, first in my look at Pottery Period 5 and then in Pottery Period 7.[63] In those discussions, I demonstrated that work in the segment focused on the area south of (not north of, contra the pottery registries) a series of superimposed, east-west walls that included Nos. 56, 125b, and 125a.[64] The course taken by Wall 56, and followed later by the others, divided the narrow northern chambers (*a-e, hk*) from the more squarish or rectangular ones to their south (*o, h, q, hq, kq*) during the late Israelite period (see fig. 56). I have shown further that the coordinate Wall 124, which Kenyon used to locate this field of excavation, extended southward from Walls 120 and 149, the latter of which provided the eastern boundary of Room *g* and the Pit *i* area. According to Kenyon's own designation, the area of concern lay *west* of Wall 124 and in the direction of a parallel feature (Wall 132) that split Room *kq* from Room *hq*. Since hardly any of Room *kq* survived the heavy Roman quarrying in this general area (fig. 70), the intact stratigraphic contexts that produced

---

[63]For PP 5, see pp. 190-97; for PP 7, see pp. 383-90.

[64]The published Section EF reveals that the north face of the 125 series lay ca. 4.25 m south of Omri's Original Enclosure Wall 161, while the north face of 56 rested a little less than 4 m south of 161.

both the pottery and the ivory taken from this segment lay right along the eastern and western sides of Wall 132.

In Table 60, I have augmented the summary of layers presented for this segment in my earlier treatment of the pottery assigned to PP 7 by adding and earmarking those levels from which excavators retrieved pieces of ivory or glass. Nearly all these layers relate more directly to the area west of Wall 132, i.e., to Room *hq*, than to the more heavily disturbed Room *kq*. My figs. 69-70 show that only Levels IIIc, Vc–Vc.y, and VIc belong to *kq* and that even these deposits lay within (Vc.y) or immediately beneath Wall 132W (and 124b/a?), not out in the open space of Room *kq* proper. In sum, then, the principal deposits of this segment rested in the easternmost part of Room *hq*, i.e., directly east of the previous area, *49.26.25*, and its Layer II.

Wall	Floor	Makeup	Fill	PERIOD
	VIc*2			IV
Vc.y*1	Vc †*1			V
				V
	VIII			V
		IIIc †*1		VII
	VI*2			VII
			VIw †	VII
	VIz*1			VII (IV?)
	VII †*3			VII
	IIa			VIII
			V*1	VIII
	IIIa			IX
			IIb	L.H.
IVc*5				L.H.

(† = layers yielding fragments published with the PP 7 ceramic group)

(* = layers yielding ivory or glass fragments published in *SS II*)

(raised numerals = no. of fragments published from each layer)

Stratigraphic Summary of Layers West of 124

Table 60

As shown in Table 55, this portion of the excavations contributed 17 ivory or glass fragments to the final report and, unlike the situation with either *19.51.14.20* or *49.26.25*, the unpublished records have permitted me to identify and describe all nine local layers from which workers removed these items (earmarked * in Table 60). Judging from this table, which reflects Kenyon's suggested phasing of the various deposits, one encounters here a series of floors and surfaces constructed during the late eighth century BCE and then caught up in the Assyrian destruction of Samaria near the close of that period (Kenyon's "Periods IV-VII"). If I were to accept this interpretation, then over half of the ivory fragments published from this area might possibly extend from more reliable stratigraphic contexts than I have hitherto encountered (9 of 17 pieces, 53%; the superscripted numerals denote the actual number of ivory fragments published from each layer). I shall group and review the relevant deposits according to the room in which they appear, starting with those belonging to the better-preserved Room *hq*.

Because a discussion of this area has gradually involved a complex of walls and rebuilds of walls, the following summary of data helps sort out Kenyon's understanding of the chronology of these features and provides a backdrop against which to suggest new interpretations.

Wall Designation	Kenyon's Suggested Date
124	R.4 (fourth century CE)
124a	R.3 (late second century CE)
125	R.4
125a	L.H. (late second century BCE)
125b	"Period V" (late Israelite)†
132	"Period V" (= 132W?)
132E	L.H.
132W	"Period V"

† *this dating now requires a downward adjustment to a time between the close of the Israelite period and the early Hellenistic period*

Summary of Walls Relating to Segment West of 124
Table 61

In their official report, the Crowfoots included ivory fragments recovered from five distinct deposits found inside or associated with Room *hq*, namely, Layers IVc, V, VI, VIz, and VII. Using fig. 56 as the basic plan of reference (compare also fig. 71), it becomes clear that these deposits rested south of the 56-125-125a-125b series of walls and just west of Wall 132. I may note, however, that none of the private field drawings cover the area thoroughly enough to show traces of the Robber Trench for former Wall

58.⁶⁵ Moreover, Wall 132 follows exactly the north-south line of former BP IV Wall 157, but none of the available section drawings (published or unpublished) take account of this by including any reference to 157. Finally, it is important to recall that, in my discussion relating to fig. 7 (= fig. 71) near the beginning of this study, I demonstrated further that Wall 125b constitutes a stratigraphically later rebuild on the remains of the older Israelite Wall 56; that is, it appears to follow the Israelite period though it may still predate the Hellenistic period.

All but one (V) of the ivory-bearing levels in Room *hq* relate in some way to a field section presented at two different points earlier in this study. For the sake of convenience, I now reintroduce this drawing, which concentrates specifically on the juncture between Rooms *hq* and *kq*. Here one sees that Wall 132E clearly represents a later structure built against the broken remains of the east face of an earlier wall, 132W, the

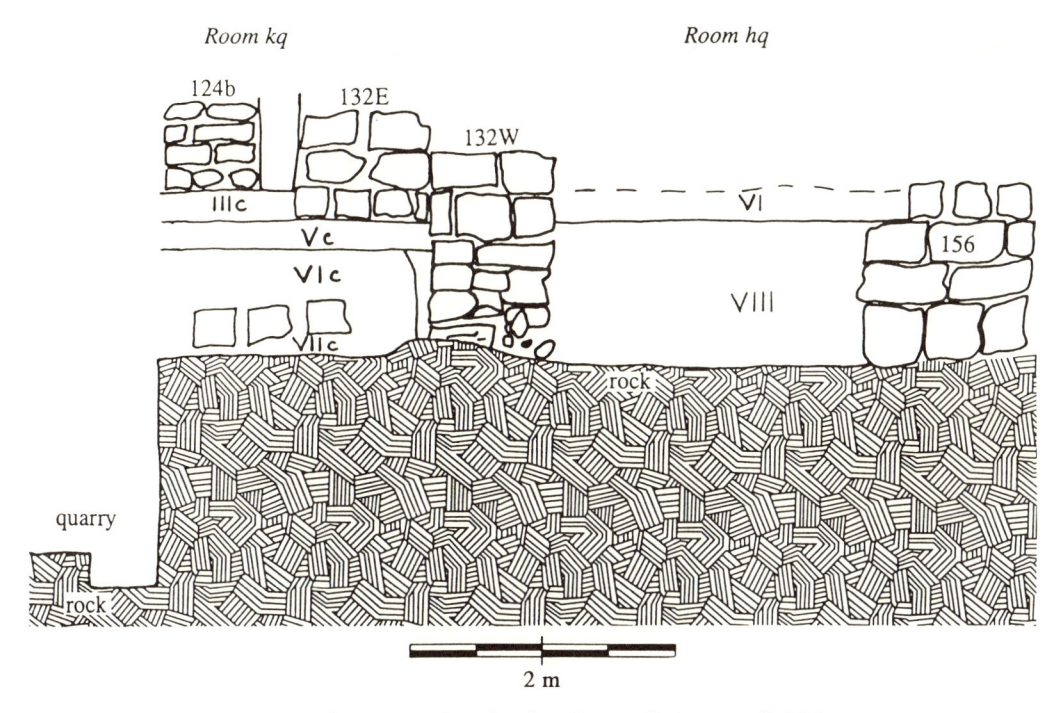

Lateral Section South of and Parallel to Wall 125
(formerly figs. 43, 70)
<— E W —>
View toward South (mostly in Room *hq*)

fig. 79

---

⁶⁵See Chapter II, 190-91, n. 54.

foundation courses of which rested directly on bedrock.[66] Since 132E stems from the late second century BCE, a similar dating for the ivory fragments assigned to Layer IVc becomes apparent from the field records, which state clearly that this designation represents "Wall 132E and earth mixed up with it, including ivories."[67] This soil and the small-size debris that it contained apparently served as packing around some of the large blocks during the construction phase of 132E. As a consequence, it does not appear in fig. 79 as a distinct layer couched between IIIc and Vc, as one might expect; rather, it reflects a different kind of deposit altogether. Importantly, this matrix contributed more fragments of ivory to *SS II* than any other single layer in the segment *W of 124* (nearly 30% of the total group; Table 55).[68] This collection, then, derives from a clearly secondary context dating to the Hellenistic period.

While the field notes pertaining to the segment *W of 124* prove considerably more extensive than they do with many other areas of excavation,[69] the reference cited above stands out as the *only* mention of Layer IVc in any of the narratives or stratigraphic summaries that describe this area. This fact, coupled with the explicit mention of ivory fragments, prompts me to accept the 132E packing as the correct point of reference for "Layer IVc" in Appendix B. Yet an uneasy question emerges concerning the precise relationship between this wall construction matrix and the horizontal layer of soil labeled "IVc" in *AIS-I*, fig. 6 and in figs. 7, 71, and 80 above. Here one witnesses a stratified soil level that overruns the remnants of Wall 56, abuts the south face of 125b, and extends southward nearly as far as the Robber Trench 130. Nowhere does it appear that Kenyon incorporated a description of this layer in her field diaries and, judging from the depositional correlates in fig. 79, it seems entirely likely that this level should actually carry the designation IIIc.[70] The discussion shall return to this and surrounding levels, and to the drawing in fig. 71, once I move eastward into the adjacent Room *kq*.

To the west of Walls 132E-W, in Room *hq* proper, one sees two rather substantial layers depicted in fig. 79 (Layers VI and VIII). These deposits extended from 132W at least as far west as Wall 156, which Kenyon assigned to "Period III" in her field records but failed to mention in her published report on this period or to include in her BP III phase plan.[71] In her unpublished notes, Kenyon described Layer VI as a hard floor resting approximately .25 m below the light-colored, unconsolidated clay of level V.[72] At a crucial point of interpretation, however, the notes betray Kenyon's con-

---

[66] Again, how shall one then account for Wall 157?

[67] *Fieldbook Qk-l-m*, 21a.

[68] *SS II*, Pls. VII:13; X:7-8; XVII:13; XXV:12.

[69] See *Fieldbook Qk-l-m*, 10-11, 20-23, and 44-46, plus associated summary sheets and field drawings.

[70] See the discussion under PP 5 in Chapter II, 194-97 above.

[71] See *SS I*, 101-103; Fig. 47.

[72] *Fieldbook Qk-l-m*, 21a.

fusion regarding the stratigraphic relationships held by Level VI. For example, in her stratigraphic summary, she states that VI "definitely crosses the broken top of 125b." But elsewhere in her narrative section, she recorded that "VI is quite def. cut by 125b and by 133 (can't be by 125b, poss. 125a)."[73] A quick review of fig. 69, which shows both the northward extension of Layers V and VI toward the 125a/125b complex and their southern approach to Robber Trenches 133 and 130,[74] indicates clearly that the construction (or possibly robbing) of 125b cut through both V and VI.

Additional records relating to these layers appear as follows:

> The grey of V only found on W. edge between R.T. 130 and 133, and also the hard level VI. E. of that point, seems to be one filling down to rock with mixed grey clay (V broken up?). This poss. connected to R.T. of 135 and wd. account for why only able to find N. edge of R.T. 130 at W. end. . . . Beneath Strip Vx [i.e., matrix that possibly included some of the trench backfill from RT 130], VI seems to cont. in E. part, up to F.T. of 132, but to W., soft dark soil. . . .
>
> The soft soil beneath Vx cleared. In it a large amphora (apparently nt. complete) lying on side, Vx.z. Obviously had orig. been set in hole surrounded by stones, most of wh. remained. . . .
>
> In level VI, besides the amphora set in stones, also a hollowed block of softish limestone, set flush with floor (see drawing [fig. 81]). The amphora of VI showed signs of fire . . .[75]

Though Kenyon, unfortunately, did not publish or comment further on the amphora in question (in fact, none of the PP 7 ceramic group came from *W of 124*, Layer VI), she sketched the worked block of limestone in her fieldbook as shown on the following page. I can supplement the remarks just cited with the observation that Kenyon presented Layer VIz as that portion of VI which lay against Wall 132; moreover, she included the comment that this particular subdeposit "shd. be pure."[76] Together, these two accumulations contributed three fragments to the final report in *SS II*,[77] while the apparently disturbed, clayey matrix of Layer V added only a single entry to that volume.[78]

---

[73]*Fieldbook Qk-l-m*, 21a and 45 for the first statement, 22 for the second position. On p. 45, Kenyon again stated that "VI definitely crosses the broken top of 125b."

[74]In the field notes, the subdeposit VIw represents that portion of VI which suffered possible disturbance during the cutting of RT 133 (*Fieldbook Qk-l-m*, 21a). In her final report on the pottery and objects, Kenyon presented two bowls from VIw that date to the mid-to-late seventh century BCE (*SS III*, Fig. 11:11, 13).

[75]*Fieldbook Qk-l-m*, 21-22.

[76]*Fieldbook Qk-l-m*, 21a.

[77]*SS II*, Pls. XII:11 (from Layer VIz); XXIII:3c, d (from VI).

[78]*SS II*, Pl. XXIV:11m.

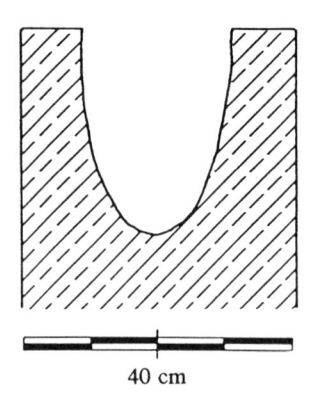

Hollowed Stone Set into W of 124, Layer VI

fig. 80

Although Layer VII does not appear in any of the field drawings cited thus far, the unpublished notes describe it as a patch of softer earth resting .25 m beneath VI.[79] This would seem to place VII in this same general vicinity of Room *hq*, particularly since the notes do stipulate that the subdeposit labeled "VIIc" represents that soil found lying beneath a "poss. Period I or II wall" and beneath VIc (see the Room *kq* portion of fig. 70).[80] Layer VII, then, apparently rested somewhere between VI and VIII in Room *hq* of fig. 70. Excavators recovered three pieces of ivory[81] and a late seventh-century BCE Assyrian bowl[82] from this level.

From this overview of Room *hq*, it might appear that three of the local deposits (VI, VIz, VII) abut the western face of Wall 132W. A closer scrutiny of fig. 79, however, reveals that only the earlier Layer VIII (which the field notes treat as a BP V "dekka floor," though it seems quite unlikely that it represents anything but a thick level of fill material) actually meets the intact portion of Walls 132W and 156. Layer VI (and presumably also VII), on the other hand, might easily belong to a later phase of activity that saw the partial plundering of those features, i.e., to a time at the end of or even after the useful life of the walls in question. It follows, therefore, that if 132W dates to the last phase of Israelite architecture at the site, as Kenyon believed, then both VII and VI may fall sometime after that period, though they are probably not as far removed from it as the Hellenistic era. From the ceramic point of view, the only available evidence seems to support this conclusion.[83] It remains difficult, however, to com-

---

[79] *Fieldbook Qk-l-m*, 22a.

[80] *Fieldbook Qk-l-m*, 22a.

[81] *SS II*, Pls. III:2; XXII:1; XXV:8.

[82] *SS III*, Fig. 11:22 (PP 7). See Chapter IV, 404-08 for my analysis of this piece.

[83] From PP 7, note again the three mid-to-late seventh-century Assyrian-style bowls in *SS III*, Fig. 11:11 and 13 (from Layer VIw) and 22 (Layer VII). From PP 5, see my discussion of the elongated, bag-shaped jar form in Fig. 8:1 (from Layer VIII, which rested directly on the rock surface).

ment with certainty on the exact depositional character of either VI or VII since Kenyon did not include the latter layer anywhere in her section drawings and since she left the precise outlines of the former level ambiguous in fig. 79. At this point, the clearest determination possible is that the construction of 132W cut a pre-existing Layer VIc in Room *kq* and that Level VIII in *hq* represents a post-construction fill designed to raise the general level inside that room to a height comparable to that in *kq*.

I may move now to the ivory-bearing loci situated in the more heavily disturbed Room *kq*. As confirmed in fig. 79, much of this space suffered destruction in the course of extensive quarrying activities carried out during the Roman period. A strip of deposits only 2 m wide remained immediately east of Wall 132W. Within this narrow band of accumulations, the field section gives record to four superimposed levels lying beneath the later Walls 132E and 124a,[84] including (in their proper stratigraphic sequence) VIIc, VIc, Vc, and IIIc.[85] The last three levels, together with the associated subdeposit called "Layer Vc.y," collectively added five fragments of ivory to the final report.[86]

I have already noted that Kenyon described Layer VIIc simply as the material that lay beneath a possible "Period I or II" wall and also beneath VIc. She wrote that "there may be a N.-S. wall running along lip of quarry scarp, sealed by VIc, but v. fragmentary. Some of this removed and clearance cont. beneath = VIIc."[87] One must still approach this potential feature with much uncertainty; fig. 79 shows only three individual blocks lying side-by-side but also separate from one another. It seems possible that these stones reflect the residue from the dismantling of an earlier wall, possibly 157 from BP IV (note my observation above that this structure ran directly through this area but that no section seems to acknowledge any trace of it; pp. 471-72, n. 66). In any event, no ivory fragments presented in *SS II* came from Layer VIIc.

Above VIIc and the three dressed blocks just mentioned lay Level VIc, which Kenyon described simply as a "floor beneath Vc" and which she tentatively dated to "? P.IV." In a similarly laconic manner, she presented Layer Vc as a "floor beneath 132E," adding only a suggested date of "Period V" even though the pottery appeared "mainly early, some IV."[88] The associated subdeposit Vc.y represented that portion of Vc which lay against Wall 132 and which, according to Kenyon, should therefore pre-

---

[84] Though the field section in fig. 79 labeled the latter wall "124b," the field notes clearly identify it as 124a, from the late second century CE.

[85] Note again that the latest level shown for the segment *W of 124* in fig. 71 should undoubtedly carry the label "Layer IIIc," not IVc. The latter identification, used in my earlier study (which did not treat this segment), may have resulted from a simple misreading of the small handwriting made in No. 2 lead pencil on both sides of translucent tracing paper in fieldbooks that are now up to 68 years old.

[86] *SS II*, Pls. VII:5 (Layer IIIc); XXIII:4c (Vc); XXII:2 and XXIII:3b (VIc). From Vc.y, see Pl. XXIV:9.

[87] *Fieldbook Qk-l-m*, 46.

[88] *Fieldbook Qk-l-m*, 21a, for all quotations (the pottery of reference was not published).

sent a pure context. The bottom courses of Wall 132E appear to have sat directly on Vc. Subsequently, Layer IIIc ran up to the lower, east face of 132E. This level of "mixed soot and hard yellow"[89] matrix lay, in turn, beneath the Roman period Wall 124a/b(?). Slightly to the south, Robber Trench 130 cut through this material. Kenyon described the ceramic assemblage from IIIc as belonging to her "Period VII" but added that it also contained examples of late, ribbed ware, which she necessarily regarded as intrusive.

The traditional interpretation, then, sees in the narrow strip surviving along the westernmost edge of Room *kq* two, or possibly three, floor levels from the Israelite period (VIIc, VIc, Vc), which were covered sometime around 722 BCE with the debris from an Assyrian destruction of the city (IIIc). Much of this interpretation seems to rest on three primary suppositions: first, Wall 132W dates to the Israelite "Period V"; second, this feature "cuts thro levels V and VI [with a] F.T. *c.* .40 m wide..";[90] and third, the limited portion of any given stratified deposit that lies against the face of a wall typically provides a "pure" context. Kenyon appealed to the last principle in her analysis of levels found in both Room *hq* (recall the relationship between VI and VIz) and in Room *kq* (Vc–Vc.y). One may, however, question the validity of this method of stratigraphic analysis, especially if universally applied. Foundation trenches, robber trenches, and various other realities of depositional history may well impinge on this very area. Such a working hypothesis, therefore, requires the presentation of a good selection of pottery from the loci that were contiguous to walls, including close statistical studies of the types and chronological range of ceramic forms found there. Kenyon did not offer such supporting evidence in her publications.

Even though Wall 132W may well date to the Israelite period as suggested, it is not clear that the construction of this feature involved cutting through both Layers Vc and VIc. On the contrary, fig. 79 clearly indicates that this effort intruded only upon level VIc. This wall did not cut Layer Vc to its east (in Room *kq*) or the heavy deposit of fill in Layer VIII to its west (Room *hq*). Kenyon's own designation of Vc.y as that soil of Vc that abuts Wall 132 militates, therefore, against her other stratigraphic interpretation. Moreover, Vc lies near the broken top of 132W and might well have served as the bedding for the construction of the late Hellenistic wall 132E, just as Layer IIIC functioned later in the same capacity for the Roman period Wall 124a. If both IIIc and Vc represent Israelite surfaces of beaten earth (and the notes nowhere indicate a different construction for these putative floors), then their .40–.50 m thicknesses seem quite remarkable for levels of this nature. In my judgment, these layers do not represent Israelite floors but successive leveling fills intended to support the architectural phases that rested on them. If this proves correct, it is important to note that the destruction-like debris (mixed soot) appears here in the stratigraphic record only in the *latest* fill poured into the area during the Roman era. The records do not indicate such a

---

[89] *Fieldbook Qk-l-m*, 20a.

[90] *Fieldbook Qk-l-m*, 20.

matrix in either the late Hellenistic level (Vc) or in the earlier, more substantial fill of VIc. From this observation, it seems quite likely that the sooty striations that streak through the yellowish matrix of IIIc originated at a time much later than the Israelite period.

In all of this, it appears that the best argument (on stratigraphic grounds) for an early, Israelite date of the corpus of ivories comes principally from Layer VIc. Accepting that Wall 132W belongs to the final phase of Israelite architecture at the site, one sees from fig. 79 that it clearly postdates the deposition of VIc. Yet I must stress that, judging from this section drawing, Layer VIc looks even less like a beaten earth surface than either Vc or IIIc above it. If these rooms, or other chambers surrounding them, belonged originally to a so-called "Ivory House" of King Ahab or anyone else, it is unlikely that such an opulent space would have presented simple floors of beaten earth in the first place. Layer VIc appears, rather, to reflect a substantial filling poured into this area during the pursuit of a building phase completed prior to the late eighth century BCE. In my studies, I have shown time and again that the *terminus post quem* for such secondary fills must remain open. This would allow the two ivory fragments taken from VIc to date to any period prior to the deposition of that level, and that period might easily fall within the years of Israelite control over their capital city.

This investigation into the segment lying *West of Wall 124* has shown that, contrary to Kenyon's published interpretation of this area, one does not see here a series of two or three Israelite floors covered ultimately by a coherent destruction level from the 722/21 BCE Assyrian assault against the city. Instead, in Room *hq* I encountered deposits with the following stratigraphic associations: Layer IVc belongs with the late second-century BCE Hellenistic Wall 132E; both Layers V and VI were cut by Wall 125b, which postdates the Israelite period by an unspecified period of time; both levels rested near the top of the broken Israelite Wall 132W and, therefore, likely also belong later than the Israelite occupation; level VII proved the most elusive accumulation, though it yielded three fragments of ivory and a very nice example of a late seventh-century BCE Assyrian bowl; finally, only the substantial fill of Layer VIII (which did not contribute any ivories to *SS II*) seems contemporary with the late Israelite Wall 132W.

A similar situation attends the rather delimited layers that survived in Room *kq*. Though Kenyon saw Vc = Vc.y as a clear Israelite floor level, I have shown that it more likely represents the leveling base for the Late Hellenistic Wall 132E. Similarly, the unconsolidated soot and clay mixture that subsequently overran this layer (IIIc) and contained fragments of late ribbed ware served as the supporting makeup for the Roman period Wall 124a/b?. Only Layer VIc appears to comprise a substantial construction fill from the Israelite period. In my judgment, then, no floors exist here and certainly no coherent, *in situ* destruction level stemming from an Assyrian attack.

In sum, one is again left with few reliable (primary) stratigraphic findspots for the corpus of published ivories in the excavation segment *W of 124*. Though Layer VIc in Room *kq* seems to represent the *earliest* deposit of reference in this area, it, too, emerges as a secondary context of imported fill. Since no drawing shows a trace of the allegedly BP IV Wall 157 (which assumed the same course as 132 from BP V), I cannot comment on the possible stratigraphic connection between VIc and 157; that is, I cannot say whether VIc was earlier than or contemporary to this feature. This portion of my study has also prompted me to ask certain questions related to the method and theory of stratigraphic interpretation. For example, can one assume that a layer of soil (whether comprising a floor or fill level) inherently becomes a more secure context as it approaches the face of a wall? But once again, the primary restriction on one's ability to arrive at a firmer chronology for the ivory-bearing loci turns on the near total lack of correlation between these findspots and those that produced the datable ceramic assemblage ultimately incorporated into the official excavation report.

This concludes my review of the three principal segments that contributed the bulk of material to *SS II*. Together they subsume 218 of the 228 units in my study sample (95.6%). I shall now comment on a minor series of excavation segments, each of which yielded only one publishable fragment of ivory or glass to the official report in 1938. Excluding the two ceramic pieces from E 207, I will group these segments according to their summit strip affiliations.

b. Miscellaneous Findspots

[i] E 207 — Shrine (or Tomb ?)

As noted earlier, the two items published from this installation actually comprise inscribed ceramic fragments, not ivory ones (*SS II*, Pl. XVI:5-6). I have, therefore, excluded them from my discussion of the corpus of published ivories. For purposes of reference, however, I have already identified the specific location of this purported shrine in the area east of the summit (see n. 13 above).

[ii] 12.27.14.13 — Room *e*   (Summit Strip Qc)
[iii] 19.12.20 — Room *e*   (Summit Strip Qc)

In an earlier section of this chapter, I relied on the unpublished field diaries to establish the equation *12.27.14.13* + *19.12.20* + the lower levels of *W of 14* = *19.51.14.20* (see the discussion under this segment, pp. 460-64). Like all the other ivory-bearing deposits relating in some way to Segment *19.51.14.20*, the relevant layers in *12.27.14.13* (Layer V)[91] and *19.12.20* (IVa)[92] seem to stem from the early Hellenistic period.

---

[91] *Fieldbook Qc-d-e-f-g-h*, 4.

[92] *Fieldbook Qc-d-e-f-g-h*, 7.

[iv] 9.21.31 — Northern Slope   (Summit Strip Qd)
[v] North of Wall 20 — Northern Slope   (Summit Strip Qf)

I come now to two segments of excavation that have not appeared earlier in my study. Records from the field refer to the first area, which yielded an ivory fragment inscribed with the letter *resh*, at two separate points—once in a journal of photographs that included it, and again on the stratification card No. 1593, which listed a number of ivory fragments engraved with palaeo-Hebrew letters. While these sources allowed me to assign this fragmentary palm base and tenon to *9.21.31*, neither instance identified the Summit Strip to which the segment belonged. A return to fig. 75 above, however, clarifies the fact that the intersection of the first two coordinate walls, Nos. 9 and 21, lay a considerable distance north of all the areas considered thus far.

Published Section GH (fig. 58) confirms further that the third feature used to name the segment, Wall 31, followed an east-west course that lay 12-13 meters north of the outer face of the old Casemate Wall 556 and 14-15 meters north of Wall 20 (compare again fig. 75). This location would conceivably place Wall 31 on a line parallel to but just south of Wall 30 at the northern end of fig. 75. Judging from Section GH, the dressed blocks of the Late Roman (R.4 = fourth century CE) Wall 31 rested directly on an earlier wall of unworked stones, which builders had constructed just above the northern edge of the mostly ruined Greek Fort Wall 551 of the mid-second century BCE. Moreover, Section GH shows that both Wall 31 and its antecedent cut through the truly massive Herodian (R.1) fill that had covered the truncated remains of the Greek Fort Wall and extended south all the way to Wall 20, while filling the huge robber trench of 556 in the process. Clearly, all remains from every occupational phase prior to the Hellenistic and Roman periods suffered total destruction in the span between Walls 20 and 31 (Section GH).

With these facts at hand, one may presume that the ivory palm base with inscribed tenon from *9.21.31* (*SS II*, Pl. XV:14) came from inside Summit Strip Qd (compare fig. 72).[93] As reported in Appendix B, excavators found the heavily damaged, formerly inlaid papyrus blossom assigned to the precinct *North of Wall 20* in Summit Strip Qf, situated "on the lower slopes north of the forecourt of the Augusteum about 90 m away from the main findspot of ivories . . ."[94] (at approximately 537° N). Because this area lay so far north of Wall 20, the segment designation seems somewhat inapt. No published section drawing extends even close to this area. Among the unpublished records, both the narratives and the sections pertaining to deposits on the northern slopes seem unusually brief and even sometimes cryptic;[95] moreover, Kenyon did not include a stratigraphic summary of any of the layers found here.

---

[93] Crowfoot acknowledged that some ivory and/or glass fragments came from Qd but said nothing of Qb immediately to the west in fig. 72 (see p. 449 above).

[94] *SS II*, 34.

[95] *Fieldbook Qc-d-e-f-g-h*, recorded in 1932, represents the first such set of field notes maintained by Kenyon. Subsequent field diaries, written from 1933 to 1935, become noticeably more organized.

If, as I have suggested, Segment *9.21.31* lay within the frame created by Walls 9, 21, 29, and 30 in fig. 75, I have in fig. 81 at least one roughly drawn field section that sheds some light on the general stratigraphy of the area in question.[96]

One must remember, as Kenyon notes, that while these levels appear somewhat horizontally aligned in this east-west section, they drop down considerably toward the north. The ivory fragment published from *9.21.31* came from Levels V-VI, which the

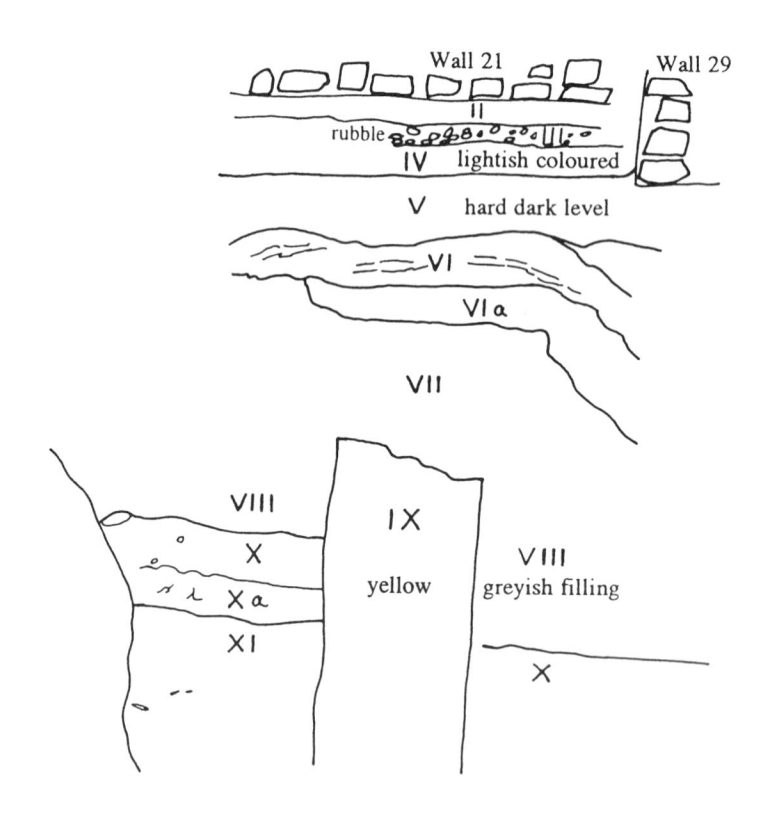

(scale not recorded)

Room 9.21.29.30 — Stratification under Wall 21
<— E   W —>
View toward South

fig. 81

---

[96] From *Fieldbook Qc-d-e-f-g-h*, 9a. A corollary section of levels beneath Wall 29 confirms this same basic stratigraphic portrait.

field notes describe as "a distinct darkish [and] hard level" (V) overlying "a light-coloured level" (VI) which was "v[ery] streaky." The preceding Layer VII revealed "a dark level [with] many specks of charcoal [and] 1 thick streak of burning." A "pillar" of yellow filling appeared under Wall 21 (labeled Layer IX) without extending further out into the room, and it was surrounded by a "greyish filling [with] many specks of charcoal" (= VIII).[97] All the remaining levels received similar descriptions: layers of dark filling containing appreciable flecks of charcoal. As a result, it once again seems clear that none of these materials lie *in situ*; rather, they represent a succession of imported fills poured down over the steep northern slope. No surfaces or floor levels appear here, though the more compacted Layer V likely served as the base for Wall 21 and the hypothetical floor that went with it. Again, judging from Section GH, all these materials claim a depositional date sometime during the Herodian period.

The same type of depositional history (substantial, irregular fills) emerges from another field section relating to one strip immediately north of Wall 20.[98] Unlike the previous section, the north-south orientation of this cut allows one to view the declining posture of the layers as they proceed northward down over the steep rock slope. Kenyon observed in her notes that she found no apparent floor level in the trench cut north of Wall 20. Layer VI presented the excavators with an unconsolidated scattering of brown soil that lay "below level of top of Wall 20" and which Kenyon interpreted as "probably" pre-Herodian in date. In contrast, the underlying level VII showed a lighter, yellowish matrix that "proved to contain Isr[aelite] sherds."[99] When the excavation process reached VII at the northern end of the trench labeled *N of 20*, Kenyon wrote that "it is clear here that there is nearly 2 metres of agricultural soil, tho' rubble level underneath having dropped steeply about on line [with] end of Wall 24."[100] At points, VII showed much disturbance as it approached the foundation trench backfill for Wall 24 (= Layer VIc, which "contain[ed] much ribbed ware") and the excavators failed to separate properly the two deposits, prompting Kenyon to note that here VII should receive the revised label VIc. The heavier rubble lying at the very bottom of VII became Layer VIII, and Kenyon observed "lines of fall from E. to W.,"[101] which apparently indicate that ancient workers had not simply raked this matrix directly off the upper slopes or the summit located to the south.

The carved papyrus blossoms, published in *SS II*, Pl. XVII:3, came from the light-colored Layer VII in the area *North of Wall 20*. Whatever interpretation one attaches to these deposits, it seems clear that they do not represent an *in situ* destruction layer covering the rooms of houses or buildings from the Israelite period. Yet while

---

[97] *Fieldbook Qc-d-e-f-g-h*, 9.

[98] *Fieldbook Qc-d-e-f-g-h*, 27a.

[99] *Fieldbook Qc-d-e-f-g-h*, 27.

[100] *Fieldbook Qc-d-e-f-g-h*, 27.

[101] *Fieldbook Qc-d-e-f-g-h*, 27b.

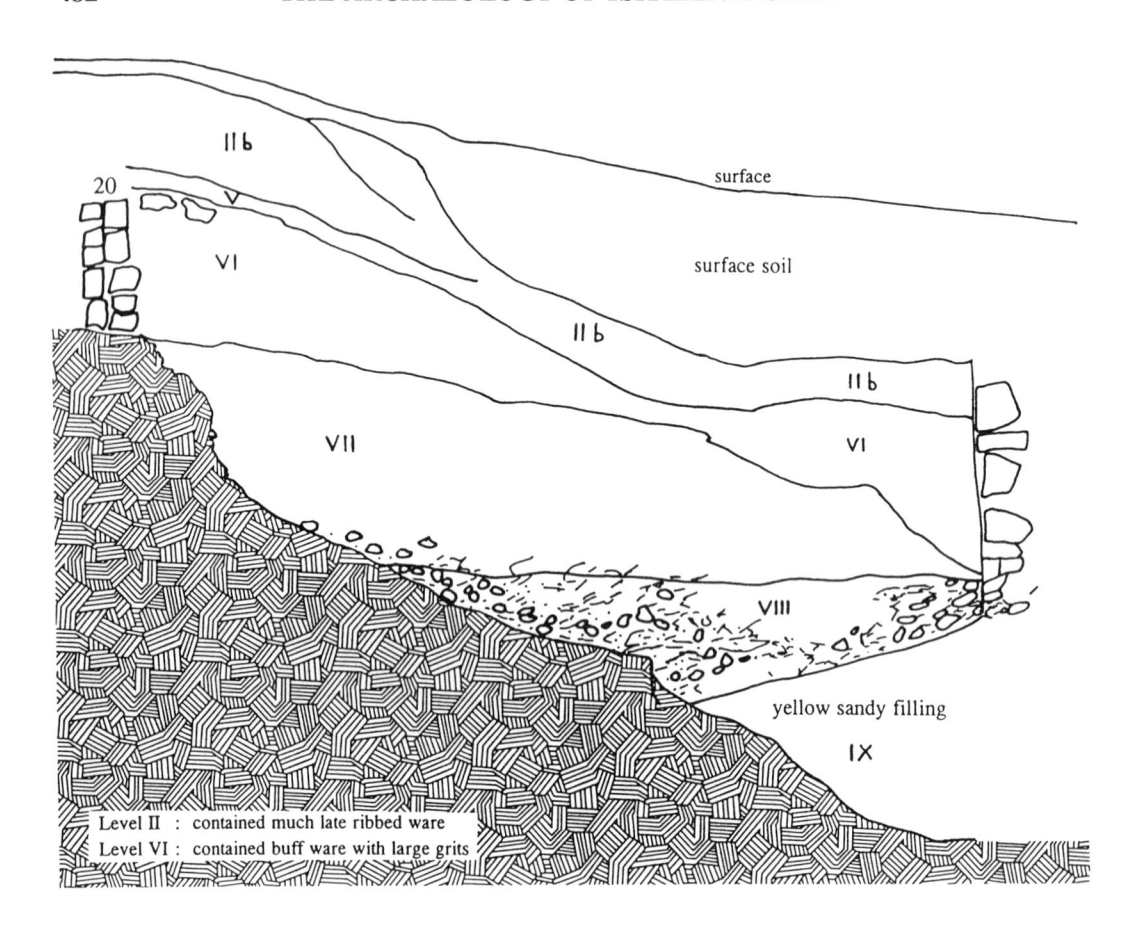

Section of Trench North of Wall 20
<— S   N —>
View toward West

(scale uncertain)

fig. 82

they represent secondary fills and dumps, the soils and materials contained in these levels very likely came originally from somewhere farther up the slopes or on the summit plateau itself. The primary context for this debris, however, now remains unrecoverable.

[vi] 120.121.19.126 — Room *g* (Summit Strip Qk)

I have addressed Segment *120.121.19.126* both in my earlier study of Pottery Period 2[102] and in the present analysis of Periods 4 and 7.[103] The richest period, in terms of the overall pottery assemblage, comes from PP 7 and I have tabulated the provenance data for these items in Chapter IV, Table 46; over 43% of that group came from this segment alone. In these previous discussions, I demonstrated that this excavation strip ran diagonally through Rooms *e, g,* and *f* in Summit Strip Qk. Besides the pottery involved, the expedition removed a small ivory fragment showing the upper back, hind quarters, and raised, forked tail of a probable Set animal from Layer VII in this segment. This deposit almost certainly lay within the confines of Room *g*, though one of the four ceramic fragments from VII received the anomalous association with Room *kq* (*SS III*, Fig. 11:5).[104]

All the relevant levels (VI-VIII) in this room survived only in the westernmost portion of the area; the eastern half of this area suffered significant disturbances as a result of Roman plundering of earlier walls located here. As discussed in connection with fig. 67 above (p. 378), Level VII lay between the limited traces of a burnt plaster floor that rested on or near the bedrock and showed a thin covering of softer material over it (Layers IX and VIII, respectively) and two successive phases of deep fillings (VI) that supported a hard yellow floor (Layer V) which Kenyon assigned to BP VIII. Most of the pottery that came from VII proved to belong to a local tradition of rounded bowls with folded, sometime even flanged, rims (*SS III*, Fig. 11:1, 5, 7). These traits, together with their thin, hard-fired ware, indicate a functional life for these vessels somewhere in the seventh to early sixth centuries BCE.[105] While the rubble of Layer VII hardly provides ample evidence to support seeing a wholesale destruction level across the entire site, these bowls strongly indicate a late- or even post-Assyrian date for the deposition of this material. The general context is clearly a secondary one, not enough of which remains to allow further judgments at this time.

[vii] 125.144 — Rooms *h/hk* (Summit Strip Qk)

This parcel of the excavations represents another tract that I have already

---

[102]*AIS-I*, 105-06. The deeper levels in this segment (mainly Layers XII-XIII and related subdeposits) yielded a somewhat mixed but generally early group of pottery: a cyma bowl (*SS III*, Fig. 3:11), various Iron I cooking pot rims (Fig. 3:21, 28, 29), a late ninth-century BCE holemouth rim (Fig. 3:35), and a short-necked store jar with simple rim and heavy, gritty ware (Fig. 3:36).

[103]For *PP 4*, see Chapter I, 20-27, 40, and 48; for *PP 7*, return to 376-81 above.

[104]The greatest pottery-producing layer in this area consisted in Layer VI, which alone contributed half of the PP 7 group assigned to *120.121.19.126*.

[105]In my formal treatment of these pieces, I allowed that the thicker, pale buff ware of No. 7 might argue for placing it slightly earlier in the sequence, perhaps later in the eighth century.

addressed in much detail in my treatments of PP 4, 5, and 7.[106] This area lay along a lateral section that the excavators cut through the northern half of the BP IV Rooms *h* and *k*, which were combined into one, elongated but narrow chamber (*hk*) in BP V. I have shown further that another segment (*Btw TT2-TT3*) related mainly to the eastern portion of this vicinity (i.e., to the former Room *k*) and that *125.144* aligned itself mainly with the more westerly space inside the previous Room *h* (compare figs. 10-11). Although Kenyon published several PP 4 ceramic fragments taken from both portions (*h* and *k*) of this area,[107] and though half of her meager PP 5 group[108] came more specifically from *125.144* in the western sector of Room *hk*, she once again failed to include any pottery from the deposit that yielded a most tantalizing ivory plaque (*SS II*, Pl. XI:1,[109] from Layer IIIb.x).

Though now quite fragmentary, the two pieces that comprise this scene depict one figure seated on a throne facing right and another figure apparently standing (?)[110] behind the throne. The standing attendant wears a tightly fitting cap, while the headdress of the seated figure exhibits a vertical ribbing and his robe shows tassels or fringing along its edges. No footwear appears on either person, and the feet of the seated figure rest directly on the ground in front of the chair/throne, not on a footstool. The armless, straight-backed throne seems stoutly built in a relatively plain, rectilinear design and displays a paneled side with vertical slats that, in some respects, resembles a double-framed window (compare the triple-framed window in Pl. XIII:2). A blanket or cushion drapes over the backrest and seat of the chair, apparently to provide greater comfort for the occupant. Lotus flowers seem to have decorated the area around the throne. The fact that so much of the center portion of this plaque is missing prevented the Crowfoots from estimating its original height. But judging both from the large-scale tenons on the top and bottom of the scene and from the letter *zayin* that appears on the upper one, this fragment seems to have "formed part of a longer composition made up of pieces which had to be assembled in the right order."[111] One cannot know now, therefore, whether a processional of sorts belongs in front of the seated figure. Without commenting further, Crowfoot drew the following conclusion concerning this piece:

> The lotus flower is not like any of the other lotus flowers in the collection, nor are the borders of the plaque, and the carving seems to us to be of a different quality. The form of the letter *zayin* is also unlike other examples of this letter

---

[106] *PP 4* = Chapter I, 27-37, 58; *PP 5* = Chapter II, 186-90; and *PP 7* = 365-67 above.

[107] *SS III*, Fig. 6:5(a), 14-15.

[108] See the jars in *SS III*, Fig. 8:2, 3, 4, 8.

[109] See Kenyon's descriptions and suggested parallels in *SS II*, 26.

[110] The entire body, from neck to ankles, is missing.

[111] *SS II*, 26.

(see pl. xxv), and *we are disposed to think that this one ivory may be of a later date*.[112]

The stratigraphic context that yielded this important artifact appears to corroborate Crowfoot's inclination to assign a late (post-Israelite) date to this plaque. As indicated in Appendix B, the expedition's stratification cards assigned these joined fragments to Layer IIIb.x. But no such layer appears in any of the unpublished section drawings, narrative discussions, or stratigraphic summaries.[113] Instead, the proper designation likely points to Layer IIIa.x. The fieldbook describes Layer IIIa as a "sooty layer overlying III = Betw. T.T.2–T.T.3 IIIb."[114] Level IIIa.x represents that portion of IIIa that actually crossed over the broken end of Wall 125b. Similarly, IIIa.z reflects, in turn, that portion of IIIa that ran against Wall 155, though elsewhere Kenyon recorded that "the sooty level IIIa [was] removed against 155, top of wh. it crosses."[115] It appears, then, that IIIa ran both against and over 155, which Kenyon dated to her "Period IVa." Yet 155 seems to have rested on the remains of the defunct BP IV Wall 153. The primary deposits and architectural features are presented in fig. 10 above (p. 33; compare also the plan in fig. 5). Moreover, I have shown at several points that Wall 125b likely postdates the Israelite period by some unknown span of time.

One sees, then, that the excavation's published as well as unpublished records leave much to be desired regarding the findspot of this unique and interesting ivory carving. Its precise location within the depositional history of Room *hk* remains indeterminate at best. In terms of what the larger plaque might have depicted, one can now only wonder whether the seated figure represents a visiting dignitary to Samaria or a local personage.

[viii] E Strip. E Half — Rooms *k/hk*   (Summit Strip Qk)

This portion of the excavations represents the only miscellaneous segment (besides E 207, which gave up two pottery sherds engraved in the style of the ivory floral carvings) to contribute more than one fragment to the official report in 1938. The small ivory plaque showing the forepart of a sphinx wearing the Egyptian double crown, wig, and a Phoenician-style folded kilt came from Layer V in this area (*SS II*, Pl. VII:6), while Crowfoot and Kenyon ascribed the asp made of blue glass and crowned with disk and horns[116] to Levels IV-VII (*SS II*, Pl. XXIV:12, represented

---

[112]*SS II*, 26 (emphasis added).

[113]For records relating to *125.144*, see *Fieldbook Qk-l-m*, 33-35, 48-49.

[114]*Fieldbook Qk-l-m*, 48a.

[115]*Fieldbook Qk-l-m* 35.

[116]Crowfoot added this further annotation: "Thickness varies, about 5 mm. Height 4 cm. A fragment is broken away at the shoulder This. [sic] piece may have been an inset, or an amulet, but there is no trace of a hole for suspension" (*SS II*, 47).

here in drawing only). The association of multiple deposits with the latter object likely reflects the poor state of its preservation and the probable fact that excavators recovered individual pieces of it from the various striations named.

This general segment lay in Summit Strip Qk[117] and, in my earlier discussions, I have encountered portions of this area that relate specifically to the segments identified as *North of TT2*[118] and *Between TT2-TT3*.[119] To the section drawings presented at those points of my investigation,[120] I may now add another, more limited view of the stratigraphy available in the field diaries relating specifically to the southern half of the so-called East Strip.[121] Together, these references show that this segment centered mainly on the space inside the BP IV Room *k*, the northern half of which combined with *h* to become Room *hk* in BP V (compare figs. 5 and 56). This new section ran north-south and lay half a meter west of Wall 129 (fig. 83). The location of this wall fragment was south and slightly east of the line of 142 (fig. 56), a fact that places this section in what would have constituted the far eastern portion of Rooms *k-hk*, had they survived the quarrying activities of the Romans throughout this area. I must, therefore, plot this section very close to the quarry itself and to the edge of the field of excavations, at roughly 455° N x 648° E (fig. 5).

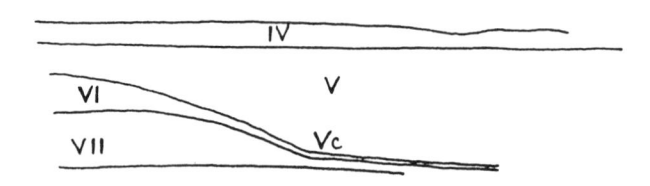

East Strip: South Half — Section .50 m West of 129
<— N   S —>
View toward East
(scale not recorded)
fig. 83

---

[117]*Fieldbook Qk-l-m*, 12-19, 36-38, 40-41; for the entries dealing specifically with the S Half of this area, see pp. 15-16 and 24-27.

[118]For the pottery relating to this part of the area, see *SS III*, Fig. 3:27 (PP 2; Layer XIIIz) and 6:35 (PP 4; Room *j*, Layer IXr). This northern section of the East Strip ran "to just south of [BP III Wall] 160," built directly over Omri's original Enclosure Wall 161 (*Fieldbook Qk-l-m*, 16a).

[119]For this pottery group, see *SS III*, Fig. 6:5b, 7, 17, 25, and 35 (PP 4; Room *k*, Layers VII-VIII), and 8:5 (PP 5; Room *hk*, Layer V).

[120]The principal drawings to review include the following: **north-south sections** — figs. 7 = 71, which runs from Wall 125b north through Rooms *k* and *g* (*Fieldbook Qk-l-m*, 41a); fig. 13, which takes in the area south of Robber Trench 153, in Room *k*, and north of that trench in Room *j* (*Fieldbook Qk-l-m*, 18a); *east-west sections* — fig. 8, extending east from Wall 157 as far as Wall 142, or through Rooms *k* and *j* (*Fieldbook Qk-l-m*, 40a). For the horizontal locations of the features named here, see the plan in fig. 5 (with comparison to figs. 41 and 56).

[121]*Fieldbook Qk-l-m*, 24a.

This section, albeit restricted in its overall range, shows the very layers in question with regard to the ivory and glass fragments in *SS II*, Pls. VII:6 and XXIV:12. From Kenyon's own judgments concerning them, these deposits all appear to represent secondary fill levels. Of this E Strip, she wrote:

> In S. half it seems prob. that the levels III, IV, V, [and] poss. VI [reflect] mainly only tip lines, [since they extend unevenly across the area], tho' IV maintains [a] fairly even level for some distance.
>
> It is clear that the stratification of the S. end of the area S. of line of 125 is diff. fr. that of N. N. of the line of 125, the v. hard dekka of *Between TT2-TT3* [Layer] III down begin (prob. broken by cont. E. of 125 a or b).
>
> In S. half what was thought to be Wall 124b prob. a rock scarp. Trench started where the whitish level VI at low level.[122]

Two further fieldbook entries merit attention. First, one reads:

> The trench started where whitish level VI lowest, found that VI nt. really here present at all, [and] that really is bottom of V, tho' labeled VI. The white level VI was cut thro', [and] found also to be a tip line, tho' pretty hard. Beneath [lay] a br[own] level, wh. may also be part of the tipping = VII. The S. cont. of the trench showed only dark soil, prob. all part of V.[123]

Finally, arriving at Kenyon's understanding regarding the date of these deposits, one learns:

> The filling of this area seems to be homogeneous at least from level IV (*c.* 1.50 m in from surface) down to rock, [and] is obviously post-quarrying. The rock E. of 129 does nt. seem to be quarried.[124]

Like so many of the fragments before them, the ivory and glass artifacts published from the *south half* of the *East Strip* clearly seem to derive from very late, secondary contexts.

[ix] 507.503.504.505 — Room *l*   (Summit Strip Qn)
[x] Hellenistic Robber Trench — Backfill/Room *l*   (Summit Strip Qn)

The final glass and ivory fragments in the study sample derive from an area situated to the east of those treated above, namely from the northern portion of Room *l*

---

[122] *Fieldbook Qk-l-m*, 15-16.

[123] *Fieldbook Qk-l-m*, 24.

[124] *Fieldbook Qk-l-m*, 26.

in Summit Strip Qn (fig. 73). To establish once again the general location of this portion of the excavations on the horizontal plane, one may recall the detailed discussion surrounding the plans in figs. 60-61 above (pp. 367-69). Moreover, the two segments that are of concern here, *507.503.504.505* and the *Hellenistic Robber Trench filling*, relate directly to a number of excavation fields addressed both in my previous study[125] and in the present investigation,[126] and a review of the many plans and sections presented at those points will also help to clarify the local, relevant stratigraphy.

The two artifacts recovered from this area include: a square inset made of green glass and white paste and showing a blue glass center (*SS II*, Pl. XXIV:8); and a carving in ivory that displays the left arm or wing of a figure facing to the right (*SS II*, Pl. IV:4). Notes relating to the former piece appeared on a stratification card that included several other items. Since the card did not, however, mention a specific findspot for the glass inset, I have extrapolated the provenance data for it from the information recorded for the other fragments mentioned on that same card.[127] In her stratigraphic summaries, Kenyon indicated that although Layer IIIm.c (of Segment *517.503.504.505*)[128] contained fragments of Israelite pottery that she assigned to "Periods VI, VII, and VIII," the matrix itself actually was "all part of [Layer] III," described as "the soft upper filling of Hell. (G.F.W.) casemate robber."[129] In fact, she later noted that IIIm.c came from a trench created by the plunder of one of the interior, north-south walls situated inside the casemate system.[130] This locus, then, lay north of Room *l* in the area of either Wall A or B on fig. 56. During the workday on May 29, 1935, Kenyon observed that "it looks now as if ivory is coming fr. blocks btw. casemates, but v. diff. to see strat. when [PN] is working!"[131] A separate sheet of notes, titled "Notes of Levels" in the Q field of the summit, explains this debris as:

---

[125]From **Pottery Period 1**, compare *AIS-I*, 23-25 (for *504.503.509.508* and *506.505.504*; *SS III*, Fig. 1:17 and 24); for **Pottery Period 2**, see pp. 105-110 (for *504.503.509.508*, *503.517.507*, and *517.503.504.505*; *SS III*, Fig. 3:1, 5-8, 13-16, 19, 23, 25-26, and 30).

[126]For **Pottery Period 4**, see pp. 148-53 above (for the Casemate filling of *504.508.509.510*; *SS III*, Fig. 7:1-9); and, finally, for **Pottery Period 7**, see pp. 367-75 (for *504.503.509.508* in Room *l*; *SS III*, Fig. 11:4, 6, 30-31, 33).

[127]These entries included the following: registered Item No. 6032, a blue glass fragment found in the Hellenistic filling of the Casemate Wall; Item No. 6033, a pale blue glass rod, elliptical in shape and flattened on one side, from *502.503*, Layer IVd; and Item No. 6034, a rod of green glass with a fragment of gold leaf still in place from *507.503.504.505*, Layer IIIm.c. Judging from the matching segment designations, both the present square glass inset (registered item No. 6031) and the rod of green glass appear to have come from the last locus mentioned in this list.

[128]This constitutes the only segment discussed in the field diaries from this area that includes a layer by this designation. In my judgment, this strip must relate directly to *501.503.504.505*, and a review of the layout of walls in fig. 60 suggests that the first coordinate wall (501) might even represent a mistake in the field records and that it should actually read *517*.

[129]*Fieldbook Qn (Vol. I)*, 20a and 29a.

[130]*Fieldbook Qn (Vol. II)*, 107.

[131]*Fieldbook Qn (Vol. II)*, 107 (I have intentionally deleted the personal name).

> deposits contemporary with the construction of the Hellenistic Fort Wall. This included the filling of the large robber trenches made by the removal of part of the casemate walls, with material obtained *by slicing off the highest deposits of the surrounding area*, including a lot of Period VIII pottery. Objects from this deposit are in some cases marked G.F.W. Mid second century B.C.[132]

Clearly, then, the first artifact came from a secondary context, the deposition of which occurred some six centuries after the close of Israelite rule over the site in the late eighth century BCE. Moreover, this is the second point at which Kenyon has acknowledged that the matrix of layers which she wants to relate to Israelite pottery- or ivory-bearing loci actually represents secondary debris raked or shaved off the summit proper. The first such notice came in my discussion of Segment *504.503.509.508*, also situated in Room *l* and immediately west of the present *507.503.504.505* (see p. 372 above; compare figs. 60-61 for the contiguous positions of these segments).

The same situation attends the second published item recovered from Summit Strip Qn. In fact, the only provenance data recorded for this piece ignores the local layer designation and reads simply "Qn. In filling of Hellenistic robber trenches of casemate walls. 1935" (taken from stratification card 5134). Crowfoot understood the fragment generally as belonging to a series of panels of winged figures adoring the child Horus, who is sitting on a lotus flower.[133] In commenting on the second item in particular, Crowfoot noted:

> In scale and technique it is more like the Arslan Tash figures than any of the above [somewhat similar entries in Pl. IV]: the feathers on the wings are outlined by ribs like the cloisons on an inlaid piece but the ivory between the ribs was not cut away: wings are treated in the same way at Arslan Tash.[134]

Both items recovered and published from Summit Strip Qn, then, appear to derive from the room or space labeled *l* on Kenyon's BP IV-V plans, or perhaps slightly farther north in the area of the old Israelite casemate system and beyond.[135] The final robbing of this once stalwart structure seems to have transpired in the Hellenistic period during the construction of the massive Greek Fort Wall, which ran obliquely through the area lying nearly 15 meters outside the casemates (figs. 60-61, 72).

---

[132] From miscellaneous summary sheets stored with the *Fieldbooks* at the Palestine Exploration Fund (emphasis added).

[133] Note the discussion in *SS II*, 18; also 19, Fig. 3.

[134] *SS II*, 18.

[135] A limited field sketch in *Fieldbook Qn (Vol. II)*, 77a, places Layers IIIm.a and IIIm.b directly beneath the basal course of Wall 505, which ran parallel to and north of the Casemate 556.

2) Evaluation and Summary

Despite the lack of precision regarding the distribution of ivories on the vertical axis, Crowfoot's report on the horizontal distribution of these artifacts across the northern summit receives confirmation from my study. I have located Segment *19.51.14.20-North* in the mixed debris stretching north from Wall 51 toward the inner casemate wall. Just south of this material rested *19.51.14.20-South*, near the northeastern corner of Room *d* and south to Wall 56, with certain layers possibly running just over that feature. These areas lay on or below the principal rock scarp that separated the central summit platform from the surrounding service rooms. Nearly all the fragments published from these two tracts of excavation emerged in a poor state of preservation, and it appeared that "they had evidently been broken and burnt before they were thus scattered."[136] Segment *49.26.25*, on the other hand, lay in the northwest corner of Room *hq* near the edge of the summit plateau and produced mainly unburnt articles from a single deposit dating to the third century BCE. The area labeled *W of 124* rested just east of this point, on and against both faces of Wall 132. Loci associated with Room *hq* yielded most of the ivories from this segment (70.6% from Layers IVc, V, VI, VIz, and VII), while those from *kq* produced only 29.4 % of the group (Layers IIIc, Vc, Vc.y, and VIc). But virtually all these findspots—and the collection of unburnt ivory that came from them—constitute late (Hellenistic or Roman) fills,[137] however, and even the best candidate for an Israelite level (VIc) has proven to represent a deposit of secondary filling. In the later publication of the pottery from Samaria, Kenyon herself acknowledged that the PP 7 deposits were not found *in situ* and that the numerous fragments of burnt ivory were

> definitely not lying as they would have fallen from the furniture to which they had been attached. Joining fragments come from widely separated spots. It is thus apparent that *objects and pottery in the debris may well have belonged to the people doing this extensive levelling up and removing of walls as well as to the last occupants of the house.*[138]

Finally, most of the "Miscellaneous Findspots" in Table 55 relate to the zone lying beyond the rock scarp.[139] Two of these loci belong either to fills inside the old

---

[136] J. W. Crowfoot and G. M. Crowfoot, "The Ivories from Samaria," *PEFQ* (January, 1933), 7.

[137] Note the authors' observation that "in the few inches that separated this mass from the rock we found several fragments of late Rhodian ware, a piece of red glazed ware, and various other Hellenistic sherds. The debris in which the ivories lay must, therefore, have been moved from elsewhere and spread about here in the Hellenistic period" (J. W. Crowfoot and G. M. Crowfoot, *PEFQ* [January, 1933], 8). It appears, then, that even the collection of unburnt ivories taken from rooms on the summit proper already lay in a secondary deposit and may not have belonged originally in those rooms.

[138] *SS III*, 125 (emphasis added).

[139] E.g., *12.27.14.13, 19.12.20, 120.121.19.126*.

casemate system of defense[140] or to similar contexts situated even farther afield in areas running down the steep northern slope.[141]

The Samaria Ivories: Conclusions

> Samaria was the capital of Israel just when the temporal power of Israel counted for most among the surrounding nations, and the massive walls are striking witnesses to the wealth and advanced civilization of the time. Very few small objects, however, were found until last week, when some splendid fragments of ivory were discovered.[142]

In this way, John Crowfoot first announced the appearance at Samaria of artifacts carved in ivory. In light of the explicit reference in the Deuteronomistic History to the "ivory house" that Ahab built (1 Kgs 22:39), the impulse to link these artifacts with the opulent capital and lifestyle of this king and to date the collection rather narrowly to the second quarter of the ninth century and the years immediately thereafter seemed natural. Because of where he discovered the cache of ivories, Crowfoot even suggested that a second Israelite palace occupied the northern area of the summit and that this structure actually stood as the primary royal building in the compound, with the large "palace" discovered to the west by the Harvard team in 1908-1910 only supplementing the main house. He wrote, "It is possible that the greatest of all the palaces, perhaps even the 'ivory house' of Ahab, lay in our region."[143] He also substantially overestimated the area covered by these purported palaces by suggesting that they took up "perhaps seven or eight acres of ground" within the "vast open court" of the summit.[144]

Five years later, in their official report on the ivory finds, the Crowfoots withdrew this entire grand reconstruction and acknowledged that the walls of the onetime "considerable building" on the north side of the summit compound actually comprised only a section of a second, inner enclosure wall (presumably Omri's Wall 161), and that the excavators ultimately could not "make a room or pavilion out of them." In fact, they had to state in 1938 that "we have not succeeded in identifying even the foundations of the house itself."[145]

---

[140] E.g., *507.503.504.505* and *Hellenistic RT*.

[141] E.g., *9.21.31* and *North of 20*. One may therefore question the Crowfoots' assertion that the few fragments published from Strips Qd and Qf derive from "uncontaminated Israelite levels" (J. W. Crowfoot and G. M. Crowfoot, *PEFQ* [January, 1933], 8).

[142] J. W. Crowfoot, "Recent Discoveries of the Joint Expedition to Samaria," *PEFQ* (July, 1932), 132.

[143] J. W. Crowfoot, *PEFQ* (July, 1932), 133.

[144] J. W. Crowfoot and G. M. Crowfoot, *PEFQ* (January, 1933), 7.

[145] *SS II*, 2.

Moreover, the Crowfoots' early description of the conditions in the area of this so-called northern palace already betrays both the secondary nature and the late date of deposition for the ivory-bearing deposits in question.

> We came upon traces of it [the presumed northern palace] in 1931 a few metres to the west of our latest excavations; this year we came upon more rock scarps and trenches connected with our former finds, but the remains of early masonry were even more scanty, only a small section of a single course was in position. It was *above* these remains, and in the space between them and the enclosure wall of the court [i.e., Casemate Wall 556] that most of the ivories were found, in a level which was covered unevenly by a black stratum and crossed by the foundations of several walls that date apparently from the late Israelite period to the Hellenistic period.[146]

From a stricter reading of Kenyon's stratigraphic notes and summaries, one finds that most of these contexts, in fact, date to the Hellenistic and Roman periods, while very few (perhaps only one) of them seem to derive from clear Israelite activities. In their preliminary articles, the authors also tended to speak of "the stratum"[147] or "a level"[148] that produced the ivory collection. My detailed analysis has shown, however, that the corpus of ivory fragments came from multiple local layers diverse in character, quality, and date. It is difficult to speak of a coherent stratum, i.e., a layer or series of related layers reflecting a single period of occupation without significant structural or cultural interruption, as the only (or even principal) context of the ivory carvings and glass inlays.

Because of this variegated stratigraphic portrait, the authors of *SS II* relied solely on external, comparative evidence to propose a date of use for the ivories and, by extrapolation, to describe their original setting. Nowhere in their preliminary articles or the official report do they appeal to the archaeological history of Samaria to support their conclusions.[149] Instead, they must resort to similar collections from the North-West Palace at Nimrud (ancient Kalḫu)[150] on the east bank of the Tigris River

---

[146] J. W. Crowfoot and G. M. Crowfoot, *PEFQ* (January, 1933), 7 (emphasis added).

[147] J. W. Crowfoot, *PEFQ* (July, 1932), 133.

[148] J. W. Crowfoot and G. M. Crowfoot, *PEFQ* (January, 1933), 7.

[149] See *SS II*, 6, where the Crowfoots list the following three criteria for dating the Samaria ivories to the first half of the ninth century BCE: "the tradition in the book of Kings that Ahab made an ivory house, the character of the letters on the backs of many of the plaques which points to this period, and the date proposed on epigraphic evidence by the French Expedition for the very similar collection from Arslan Tash."

[150] A. H. Layard, *The Monuments of Nineveh*, Volumes 1-2 (London, 1849-1853); idem, *Nineveh and its Remains* (New York: George P. Putnam, 1849); idem, *Discoveries in the Ruins of Nineveh and Babylon* (New York: G. P. Putnam and Co., 1853); (also in 1853, H. C. Rawlinson corrected the ancient identification of Nimrud from Nineveh to Kalḫu). On the composition of the Nimrud collection, see R. D. Barnett, "The Nimrud Ivories and the Art of the Phoenicians," *Iraq* 2 (1935), 179-210.

in the Assyrian homeland and at Arslan Tash (ancient Ḫadatu)[151] in northern Syria to help establish these criteria. But while the stylistic and art historical aspects of these comparisons proved plentiful and apt, neither resource could fix the date of the Samaria group within a very narrow margin. Though the palace at Nimrud was built by Assur-nasir-pal (885-860 BCE) and renovated by Sargon II (722-705 BCE), Assyrian tribute inventories speak of ivory objects at least from the reign of Tukultu-Enurta (the predecessor of Assur-nasir-pal) through that of Sennacherib (the successor of Sargon II). The Crowfoots concluded that the Nimrud ivories "were carved at different times and in different places, but [they] all must fall within the above limits."[152] Based on an ivory artifact bearing the name of Haza'el and on the tribute lists of Adad-nirari II (808-792 BCE), the Arslan Tash series might easily cover the entire second half of the ninth century BCE and may extend into the early eighth century. On the basis of these data, Crowfoot argued that "the external evidence is therefore sufficient to indicate within *wide* limits the approximate date of these [Samaria] ivories . . . ."[153] Though the team ultimately decided to link these marvelous finds with the great "Ivory House" of Ahab in the ninth century BCE, the authors also drew parallels from textual descriptions of various decorations in the temple of Solomon in the tenth century BCE.[154]

Finally, I may note that, on stylistic grounds, Crowfoot parsed the Samaria ivories into two distinct groups. The first lot was carved in low relief and displayed quite simple borders and backgrounds, but it appeared to have been so lavishly decorated with gold foil and insets of lapis lazuli "that very little of the ivory was left showing."[155] Also, strong Egyptian motifs dominate this cluster. The second group, on the other hand, displayed a deeper relief and hardly any trace of colored insets. While Egyptian elements maintained a prominent place in the art of these items, Crowfoot added that "the style is no longer Egyptian though it is not Assyrian, as a glance at the Assyrian or Assyrianising (?) ivories from Nimrud will show."[156] In terms of their respective states of preservation, the second group suffered greater damage and must therefore relate more to the burnt vs. the unburnt batches mentioned above. The differences separating these two groups led Crowfoot to distinguish between their relative places of manufacture but not their relative dates. He wrote: "at Samaria the two groups will be practically contemporaneous, the products of different hands or different workshops, not of different periods."[157] Even so, Crowfoot ultimately suggested that

---

[151] F. Thureau-Dangin, A. G. Barrois, G. Dossin, and M. Dunand, *Arslan-Tash*, 2 Vols. *Bibliothèque Archéologique et Historique*, Vol. 16 (Paris, 1931).

[152] J. W. Crowfoot and G. M. Crowfoot, *PEFQ* (January, 1933), 18.

[153] J. W. Crowfoot and G. M. Crowfoot, *PEFQ* (January, 1933), 18 (emphasis added).

[154] J. W. Crowfoot and G. M. Crowfoot, *PEFQ* (January, 1933), 23.

[155] J. W. Crowfoot and G. M. Crowfoot, *PEFQ* (January, 1933), 19-20.

[156] J. W. Crowfoot and G. M. Crowfoot, *PEFQ* (January, 1933), 21.

[157] J. W. Crowfoot and G. M. Crowfoot, *PEFQ* (January, 1933), 22.

the Arslan Tash ivories were carved in Damascus and that the Samaria ones were manufactured within Samaria itself.[158]

Whatever treatment art historians of the future will give these ivory objects and panels from Samaria, I believe that the information provided in this study will aid in their overall assessment of the collection. While anyone would appreciate the irresistibly strong temptation to connect these artifacts directly with the reign and structures of Ahab, I have shown that any such interpretation is grounded ultimately on biblical traditions alone, not on secure, primary archaeological contexts at the site itself. The broader discussion that a study of this nature spawns raises numerous issues concerning the relationship between biblical "history" and archaeological or depositional "history," neither of which is immune to the subjectivity of interpretation, whether ancient or modern. From the point of view of archaeological recording and reporting, however, the principal handicap bequeathed to us by the Joint Expedition centers on the glaring lack of any real correlation between the respective comparanda of ceramic and ivory fragments.

Despite acknowledging the numerous stratigraphic misfortunes discussed above, the leaders of the Joint Expedition ultimately clung to the association of these ivory carvings and glass inlays with the grandeur of King Ahab's court in the ninth century BCE. In the end, they rather blithely concluded by saying:

> The site is a good one. It lies in a central position on the north side of the hill sheltered from the south-west winds which are the most disagreeable winds at Samaria. In much later days the Romans built an exedra close by which looked over the broad valley to [the] north. It is a site which a king might well have chosen.[159]

Throughout the preliminary and official publications relating to the Samaria ivories, then, one feels some consanguinity but also a great deal of hermeneutical tension between the archaeological data and the story as told in the biblical texts. The situation surrounding the retrieval and publication of the these artifacts seems to represent a classic illustration of "old school" Biblical Archaeology, for while the authors may be altogether correct—however tendentious—in their historical evaluation of these items, it remains impossible to buttress their conclusions with secure, stratigraphic data. The exuberance of the excavators upon seeing these goods is entirely rational, even if their handling of the depositional history is not.

Yet one final caveat merits equal attention. In the case of the ivories from Samaria, as with many other known collections, the late archaeological context of the overall assemblage speaks only to events surrounding the final deposition of the artifacts, not to their original, primary historical context. The late date of the matrix in

---

[158] J. W. Crowfoot and G. M. Crowfoot, *PEFQ* (January, 1933), 23.

[159] *SS II*, 4.

which excavators found the ivories can no more fix the time of their functional life to the Hellenistic period than the Greek graffito and late pottery found by R. A. S. Macalister in the vicinity of the reused Gezer gateway could make that tenth-century BCE structure a Maccabean castle in its origins. In other words, these goods can provide no fodder for revisionist historians who intend to adjust the chronology of this or another site to any serious degree. As for the ivories themselves, the basic rule of stratigraphic analysis remains poignant and pivotal: secondary deposits and imported fills represent contexts that can claim only a firm *terminus ante quem*, based on the latest articles situated within them; the *terminus post quem* for such levels, and for the materials they contain, must remain open.

Excursus

A Comment on the Spatial Distribution of the Samaria Ostraca

Horizontal Axis

George Andrew Reisner recovered the first ostracon from Room 401 in Summit Strip S4, west of the Israelite palace and central summit area, on August 11, 1910. Between that day and September 26, 1910, he retrieved a total of 75 inked or inscribed fragments of pottery that, after he successfully joined several of the matching pieces, comprised a corpus of 63 ostraca (see Appendix C). All these items came from the easternmost portion of only two Summit Strips, namely S4 and, to its north, S7 (fig. 84). The spatial distribution of these items appears as follows:

	Number of Ostraca	Percentage of 75
Summit Strip S4		
Room 401	1	1.33
Room 416	1	1.33
Room 417	22	29.33
Room 417-N	12	16.00
Room 418	10	13.33
Summit Strip S7		
Room 723	1	1.33
Room 772	13	17.33
Room 772-N	1	1.33
Room 772-W	2	2.70
Room 773	8	10.66
Room 776	4	5.33

Spatial Distribution of Ostraca:
Horizontal Axis

Table 62

Most of the collection came from S4 (61.3%), and within that space virtually all the fragments lay in the two long rooms numbered 417 and 418 (95.7%, or 58.7% of the total collection). In S7, Rooms 772-773 constituted the two most productive areas (82.8% of that group; 32% of the overall corpus). It is significant, then, that on the horizontal axis none of the ostraca derive from supposed storerooms *inside* the actual

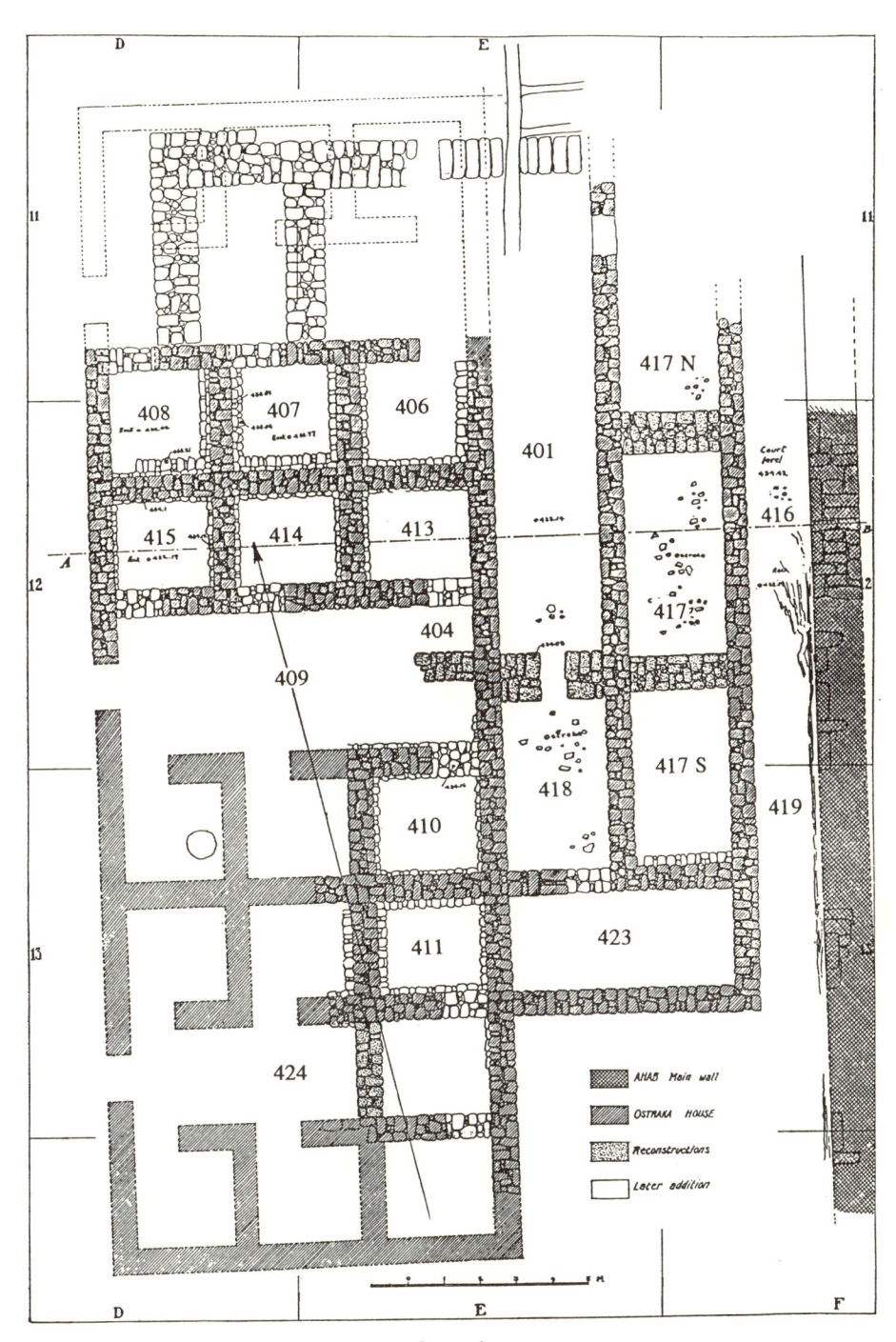

Plan of
The Ostraca House
(adapted from *HES I*, 114, Fig. 42)

fig. 84

"Ostraca House" itself.[160] Rather, they all come from levels associated with the long chambers (which probably served as stables, tethering rooms, or receiving areas) to their east. These rooms underwent at least three phases of construction and, originally, did not include any of the cross walls shown in *HES I*, 114, Fig. 42, or in Reisner's undated publication of the ostraca.[161] If Reisner's understanding that the front of the Ostraca House "faced towards the west"[162] is correct, then these receiving areas[163] ran along the entire length of the rear of the building. A long, stone-capped drain heads north from Room 401 and may have curved to the west before continuing outside the Casemate System in Reisner's Square C5. This should be expected in areas where pack animals would have stood for long periods of time as the goods they carried were loaded or unloaded.

One should also note that many of the ostraca appeared in an area that lay 30 meters north (in S7) of the surviving portions of the main building. It seems likely that the original structure extended even into this area and made the overall facility much larger than it appears on the plans of Clarence Fisher. That is, the structure generally accepted as the "Ostraca House" may well represent only the southernmost portion of the original building.[164] Judging from the ostraca that name a specific commodity, both the northern and southern clusters of rooms housed stores of wine and oil, though only a few fragments pertaining to oil appeared in S7.

But there lingers a serious question as to whether one can draw any further historical conclusions from the ostraca based on their location and distribution as recorded by Reisner's team. The recording system utilized during that phase of exploration failed

---

[160]Contra Holladay, who saw the ostraca as "peculiarly scattered . . . about *on the living floor* of several rooms of the 'Ostraca House' and the courtyard outside the building (in fine black debris!) and all sealed under the uppermost Israelite floor in the area" (*Holladay*, 67; emphasis added). This statement also assumes the preservation of several Israelite floor levels within the storehouse, a suggestion that runs counter to Reisner's own description of the local stratigraphy.

[161]*HES I*, 116-17.

[162]*HES I*, 114.

[163]I understand the ostraca to represent shipping dockets that accompanied certain commodities sent to the capital city from various outlying estates, not as a record of goods travelling the other direction. For a much earlier use in Ramesside Egypt of inscribed flint bulbs as a manifest for wares forwarded to an addressee, see A. Eran, "Weights and Weighing in the City of David: The Early Weights from the Bronze Age to the Persian Period," pp. 204-56 in *The Excavations at the City of David, 1978-1985, Volume IV: Various Reports*, D. T. Ariel and A. de Groot, eds. *Qedem* 35 (Jerusalem: The Hebrew University Institute of Archaeology, 1996), p. 209. As with the ostraca, a discussion arose around these stone objects as to whether they represented dockets forwarded to an addressee or records kept at the stores that issued the wares. Their scattered distribution among the laborers' campsites in the Valley of the Kings suggested the former use to Eran. (See Chapter VI, n. 82 below.)

[164]Reisner himself apparently accepted the possibility or even the likelihood of this proposal (see *HES I*, 117), although elsewhere he remarked, "It was not possible to determine whether the Ostraca House extended northwards into S7. The plan of the part preserved seems to require such an extension; but no trace was found of the foundations nor even of the foundation trenches. I am personally of the opinion that the Ostraca House did not extend into S7" (*HES I*, 78).

to detail specific stratigraphic relationships. Concerning the primary building levels encountered in Strip S4, Reisner wrote:

> The chief features . . . were the floor of the Ahab courtyard, several layers of Hellenistic debris, the floor of the Herodian house, and the remains of the Severan period. This unusual preservation of material was due to the protection afforded by the debris held up by the Greek Fort Wall on the west and to the absence of large buildings during all the Greek and Hellenistic periods. . . . The floor of the Ahab courtyard was about 434 m. above sea-level, while the floor of the earliest Hellenistic building was at or above 435 m. *The lower layer of debris between was disturbed yellow debris containing a great abundance of Israelite potsherds (none of them inscribed)*.[165]

Reisner noted further that the earliest phases of the Hellenistic walls sat *on* the yellow debris and *in* a black matrix that contained "Hellenistic objects." A massive, post-Herodian robber trench in the western portion of S4 had resulted in the mixing of the yellow and black debris and, in turn, the Israelite and Hellenistic fragments typical of each deposit.[166] The best preserved layers, then, rested in the eastern half of the storehouse area. But a clear correlation between the information cited here and the principal section drawing pertaining to the Ostraca House (fig. 85) remains difficult to establish.

A number of important issues emerge from this drawing. First, Reisner identifies this cut as part of Section AB but, according to *HES II*, Plan 5, that baulk line bypassed the storehouse altogether by following a north-south course that ran approximately 15 meters east of the receiving room No. 417. (Compare instead Squares D-F of the east-west Section GH in *HES II*, Plan 4, which did proceed through the Ostraca House area.) Second, the latitudinal section presented in fig. 85 includes, from east to west, Rooms 417, 401 and 414, 415. Between these two sets of chambers, the drawing shows Room 405, which nowhere appears on the published Plan 5. Instead, this space would seem to relate to Room 413. Third, the only yellow debris in this area—debris which Reisner earlier described as lying on the Ahab surface—comprises "a stratum of yellow chip debris . . . which had accumulated during the cutting and dressing of the masonry for the walls of the main palace" (labeled "o" in fig. 85).[167] This matrix rested directly on the rock surface and was cut by the later foundation walls of the Ostraca House. Fourth, the presumed level of Ahab's surface seems based solely on the height of the surviving fill in Room 417 (labeled "c"). Following Reisner's reconstruction, one should assume that Israelite builders deposited this filling here during the second quarter of the ninth century BCE, since Israelite fragments were found in it.

---

[165] *HES I*, 75 (emphasis added).

[166] *HES I*, 75-76.

[167] *HES I*, 116.

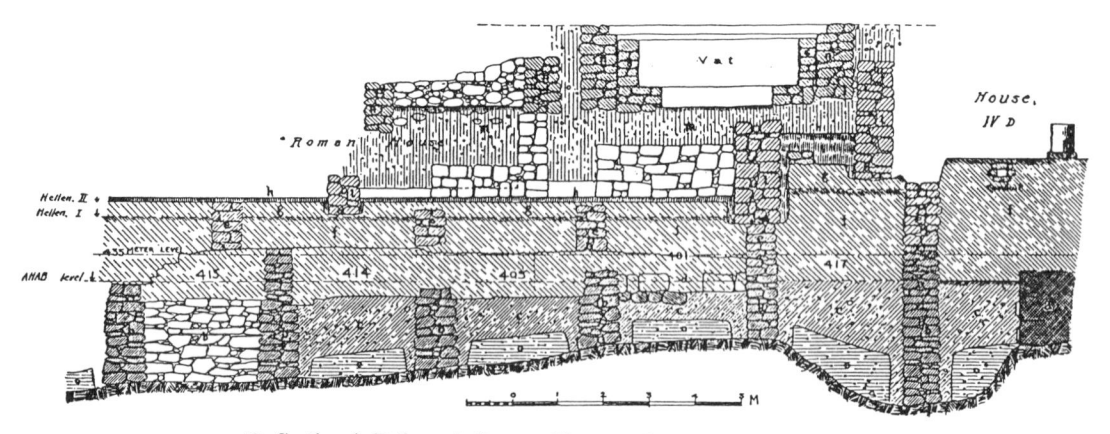

43. Section A–B through Ostraca House and superimposed strata.
- a. West wall of main Ahab building.
- bb. Foundations of Ostraca House.
- c. Filling in below floor of Ostraca House.
- o. Yellow debris above rock.
- d. Later wall.
- ee. Walls of first Greek period.
- f. Construction debris of Greek period.
- g. Second Greek period.
- h. Herodian Atrium House.
- ll. Street walls, Herodian period.
- m. Debris of the same.
- n. Severan walls.
- s. Severan walls, additions.

*Section through
The Ostraca House and Superimposed Layers*
(adapted from *HES I*, 63, 115; Figs. 14 & 43)

fig. 85

But such a conclusion requires a wider publication and much closer study of the remains recovered from that context. In fact, the presence of so much Israelite material in this secondary deposit might easily indicate a significantly later date for the original deposition of this matrix, i.e., a date sometime after the functional life of the ceramic styles contained therein.[168] Also, one sees that this substantial, subfloor filling did not survive to the theorized Israelite floor level in any of the rooms to the west (401, 405/413, 414, 415), and even in Room 417 there appears no indication that any trace of the floor itself survived. This situation suggests that most of the ostraca from Strip S4 (i.e., all those from Rooms 417 and 418, since the latter chamber was located immediately south of 401) would have derived from poorly dated, secondary leveling debris. If not from there, then Reisner's section would seem to leave only one further possibility, namely, the later Greek construction detritus labeled "f" in fig. 85. In his narrative description of the building, Reisner himself noted that none of its superstructure survived except for small sections from the northern wall of Room 406 and from the southern wall of 410, 413, and 414.[169] Moreover, both the construction (of stones that were neither dressed nor fitted and that were set in columns displaying multiple offsets of 10-20 cm in width and 80 cm to 1.0 m in height) and the quality (flat fragments of rocks with broken edges) of the storehouse walls seen in fig. 85 help to corroborate their use as subsurface support structures.[170]

The stratigraphic portrait of Summit Strip S7 to the north mirrors that just seen in S4 starting with a similarly configured rock surface covered directly by a substantial layer of yellow construction(?) debris cut by the "remains of thick walls" that appeared stratigraphically earlier than the so-called Osorkon House. Reisner concluded that "the southern wall of the Osorkon House must have been built over the northern wall of the Ostraca House, as preserved,"[171] though no direct stratigraphic connection existed between the two buildings. He dated the floor level of the Osorkon House (which rested at approximately 434.88 m above sea level) by means of an Osorkon vase and ivory uraeus found in the makeup beneath the surface. These items

> ... were either in place when the Osorkon House was built or were in the earth used in leveling the floor of that house. The layer in which they were found con-

---

[168] According to Holladay's analysis, "... it seems *quite obvious* that the reconstruction of the 'Ostraca House' (which involved the construction of a new floor over the ostraca) *probably* accompanied the larger general rebuilding [during] Period V, and this *probably* followed the general destruction involved in the assassination of Pekahiah by Pekah" (*Holladay*, 67; emphasis added). Since he dates this new phase of the storehouse to the years of the Syro-Ephraimite alliance (roughly 734-732 BCE), the ostraca would accordingly precede that time by an unspecified period owing to their discovery in secondary leveling fill.

[169] *HES I*, 115.

[170] *HES I*, 116.

[171] *HES I*, 79.

tained *only Israelite objects*, mostly potsherds, and *appeared* to be the same layer of *surface debris* as that which contained the Israelite ostraca.[172]

Without new stratigraphic and ceramic data pertaining directly to these areas of concern,[173] my opinion remains that neither the date of the Osorkon House nor of the Ostraca House can be established with certainty based on the reasoning presented in the official Harvard report. Both the Osorkon vase and the ivory uraeus represent valuable objects or heirlooms that might have been kept for many years, even decades, after the period of their manufacture or primary use. As such, they alone might fix a working *terminus post quem* (construction date) for the Osorkon House floors *only* if they clearly represent the latest items found in the subfloor makeup. If, as it appears, they were simply mixed in as part of an eclectic, heterogeneous gathering of artifacts, then they do not provide as firm a date for the superseding structure as Reisner assumed they might.

One should exercise similar caution when appealing to these two Egyptian items to assign a narrow chronological range to the Israelite ostraca. Besides the ramifications of their long-term preservation as potential heirlooms, it is apparent that Reisner could not establish a direct stratigraphic connection between the layer that contained them and the one that yielded the ostraca. He recorded only that these two deposits "appeared" to belong together. Finally, I have already observed that, judging from Reisner's published section drawings, I can detect no actual Israelite occupational ("surface") debris in the area of the Ostraca House,[174] though Reisner himself subsequently referred to the ostraca-bearing layer as "surface debris." Contra Holladay, one can hardly appeal to the clarity of provenance data and historical situation for the ostraca to affirm an absolute date for Kenyon's "Period V" remains discovered on the north side of the central summit compound.[175]

In conclusion, I may note that the same kinds of problems that hamper a critical reading of the reports from the Joint Expedition also preclude a clear understanding of the specific archaeological context of the ostraca. These limitations include the failure to publish (1) information relating to key stratigraphic relationships and (2) a statistically significant pottery sample taken from the same loci as the cache of special objects, e.g., the ivories or the ostraca. In terms of archaeological reporting, then, Kenyon's publications achieved little to no progress over those offered by Reisner thirty-three years earlier. In terms of the collection of ostraca, however, I can now suggest that, despite the disappointing state of the *archaeological* data relating to their specific

---

[172]*HES I*, 79 (emphasis added).

[173]I have not had occasion to examine closely the unpublished field records of the Harvard Expedition as I have those from the Joint Expedition.

[174]Recall my earlier notation that Holladay's reconstruction assumed the existence of several Israelite surfaces in this building.

[175]*Holladay*, 60-67.

provenance, one may perhaps hope for more positive results from future *palaeographic* studies of these items, e.g., the new effort by C. Rollston, B. Zuckerman, and I. Kaufman.[176] Also, there is now a fresh *historical* treatment of the content of the ostraca in a study by D. Schloen.[177]

---

[176] See the mention of their new efforts to render in a digital format the photographs of the ostraca now stored in the collections of the Harvard Semitic Museum in J. Greene and Ilene Springer, "The Museum's Archives: Decades Old and Still 'Going'," *Semitic Museum News* 3 (2000), 2. Unfortunately, this work is based solely on available photographs of the ostraca; the actual artifacts themselves remain in the Istanbul Museum in Turkey.

[177] J. D. Schloen, *The House of the Father as Fact and Symbol: Patrimonialism in Ugarit and the Ancient Near East*. Studies in the Archaeology and History of the Levant 2 (Winona Lake, IN: Eisenbrauns, 2001); see pp. 155-65 for a treatment of the Samaria Ostraca.

Chapter VI

ISRAEL AND ASSYRIA

A Summary of Relations during the Iron Age II

I. Introduction

From the records available today, it seems clear that no foreign power altered the history of Israelite Samaria with more devastating results than did the Neo-Assyrian Empire. Yet the gravity of the latter's influence upon Israel's royal city stands in glaring disproportion to the limited number of years during which the two states actually met in direct political and military confrontation. Prior to the second half of the eighth century BCE, Shalmaneser III was the only Assyrian monarch who encountered an Israelite king in a battle or post-battle context or who even breached the borders of the Northern Kingdom of Israel. But my elaboration below on the historical circumstances surrounding each of these occasions will underscore both the lack of meaning that the former meeting had for the inhabitants of Samaria and the relatively nonaggressive, ordinary character of the latter occurrence. Not until over a century later did another Assyrian ruler enter the land of Israel and then, in the incredibly short span of two years (734-732 BCE), Tiglath-pileser III effected the total collapse of Samaria's political machinery and made the city's ultimate fall inevitable.

Examination of the ninth- and eighth-century BCE notices regarding Samaria within the corpus of Assyrian literature (Appendix D) demonstrates how heavily Tiglath-pileser weighed in the history and destiny of the Israelite capital. He was the first Assyrian general to lead his army in battle on regional soil, the first to apply the principle of population deportation against Samaria, and the first to establish an Assyrian governor in that city. Moreover, the corpus of literature deriving from his reign contains more direct references to Samaria and Israel than do the combined records of all the prior Neo-Assyrian kings. Taken together, the historical annals and summary or display inscriptions that tell of events during the rule of Tiglath-pileser recount dealings with more Israelite kings than any other single Assyrian leader. Because, ultimately, Tiglath-pileser wielded absolute control over Israel's highest office, he stripped the kingdom of any autonomy and reduced it to a mere rump state confined to the Ephraimite hill country.

The *longue durée* of Assyria's climactic ascent to a position of dominance throughout the ancient Near East during the late eighth century BCE schematizes itself nicely into the following phases of 30-50 years each:

> A.1) initial ascent halted by internal revolt
> Shalmaneser III, ca. 859-828 BCE
>
> A.2) attempted but unsuccessful recovery and consolidation
> Shamshi-Adad V and Adad-nirari III, ca. 828-783 BCE
>
> A.3) collapse into extreme weakness and retreat
> Shalmaneser IV, Ashur-dan II, and Ashur-nirari V, ca. 783-745 BCE
>
> A.4) brilliant resurgence and rapid rise to full power
> Tiglath-pileser III, Shalmaneser V, and Sargon II, ca. 745-705 BCE

By outlining an analogous pattern, most historical studies have depicted the development and eclipse of Israelite Samaria in a strikingly similar historical trajectory during these very same years:

> S.1) foundation and growth halted by internal revolt
> Omride Dynasty to Jehu, ca. 867-842/841 BCE
>
> S.2) attempted but only moderately successful stabilization
> Jehu, ca. 842/841-815 BCE
>
> S.3) stagnation in weakness
> Jehoahaz to Jehoash (first half of reign), ca. 815-mid-790s BCE
>
> S.4) steady growth and rise to apogee of affluence and power
> Jehoash (last half of reign) to Jeroboam II, ca. 790s-746 BCE
>
> S.5) rapid decline and ultimate collapse
> Zechariah to Hoshea, ca. 746/745-721 BCE

This rather facile comparison, however, merits a methodological caveat. In both *AIS-I* and the present study, I have shown numerous occasions on which a direct correlation does not exist between the principal events in Samaria's military and political history (as outlined above) and changes that occur in the trends and motifs of its cultural history (as discussed throughout *AIS-I* and *AIS-II*). Instead, floor levels and major architectural units were often utilized by a succession of kings; both local ceramic industries and foreign imports alike sometimes changed gradually even in the face of sharp political contests within the region or between that area and an outside trading partner. In this vein, it is reasonable to believe that something of a time lag developed between the point at which the Assyrians first appeared as a military or political force in the region or city of Samaria (and perhaps even the time at which that region fell under provincial status) and the appearance of a statistically significant sample of native Assyrian pottery and goods. In fact, since the excavation reports from many sites often describe the so-called Assyrian-style pottery as locally-made imitations, a question inevitably arises as to whether these materials really tell anything about the number of Assyrians who actually occupied and resided in the land of Israel.

In short, one cannot always tie archaeological history or chronology inextricably to political history. Localized depositional layers and the individuals whose names appear on a city's king list do not necessarily point to the same aspects of historical change. The acceptance or rejection of this principle inevitably affects both one's method and theory of analysis and the interpretation that results. I addressed this subject in some detail in *AIS-I* by avoiding Kenyon's strict one-to-one correlation between the particular rulers of Samaria and the so-called Pottery Periods or Building Periods detected in the city's architectural and cultural history.

Having said this, one can see from the outlines presented above that each phase of Samaria's *political* history slightly predates the corresponding, similar period in Assyria's development (i.e., generally, S.2~A.1; S.3~A.2; etc.). Beginning only in phase A.4, with the accession of Tiglath-pileser III in 745 BCE, do Assyria's expansionistic policies take hold and relate directly and causally to the now concurrent phase of Samaria's history (S.5). The futures of the two nations converge now as never before. For Israel, the new encounters spell an ever increasing loss of autonomy; for Assyria, another important link locks into place within the imperial design to extend its borders as far as Egypt.

Relying on my new analysis of the archaeology of Samaria (including *AIS-I* and the present study), I shall now consider the reasons for Samaria's head-on clash with Assyria by tracing each power's most significant political and military activities during the course of the ninth and eighth centuries BCE. My focus will fall on the western campaigns of Tiglath-pileser III, Shalmaneser V (his son and successor), and finally on the activities of Sargon II. As a result of my archaeological analyses, I am now able to assess more accurately the impact of Assyrian policies on the physical site of Samaria.

II. Samaria's Entanglement with Assyria

Part A. Early Encounters

1) Shalmaneser III: 853, 841 BCE

Shalmaneser III's Monolith Inscription from Kurkh offers the earliest Neo-Assyrian reference to Israel or to one of its kings.[1] Relating the empire's military

---

[1] *ARAB* I.611. The principal editions and translations of texts surviving from the reign of Shalmaneser III appear as follows: (1) the **Monolith Inscription** from Kurkh, which relates the first six years of Shalmaneser's rule but omits the fifth year (*Rawlinson* III R 7-8; *ARAB* I.594-611); (2) the **Annals from Aššur**, which cover Shalmaneser's first 16 years (*ARAB* I.626-639; G. G. Cameron, "The Annals of Shalmaneser III, King of Assyria," *Sumer* 6 [1950], 6-26; E. Michel, "Ein neuentdeckter Annalen-Text Salmanassars III," *WdO* 1 [1952], 454-75; compare also idem, "Die Assur-Texte Salmanassars III. (858-824) 3. Fortsetzung," *WdO* 1 [1949], 255-71); (3) some additional **Annals from Aššur**, telling of the ruler's first 20 years (F. Safar, "A Further Text of Shalmaneser III. From Assur," *Sumer* 7 [1951], 3-21;

activities between 859 and 853 BCE, this stele outlines Shalmaneser's early attempt in 858 BCE to dominate northern Syria by militarily penetrating the numerous Aramaean states that had spread previously throughout the area south of the anti-Taurus[2] and, as a consequence, had bisected Assyrian routes westward. But after advancing to the region of Patina and the city-state of Sam'al (which commanded the Beilan and Bahçe Passes, respectively),[3] his efforts to lay open a passage from Calah to Cappadocia and points north were short-circuited by a stalwart north-Syrian confederacy.[4] In the wake of this check on Assyrian expansion, Shalmaneser hastened back to Bit Adini, subdued its king (Ahuni) and his capital city (Til Barsip = Tell Aḥmar),[5] and established firm control over the entire area between the Balikh River and the westernmost reaches of the Euphrates River. He thus secured an excellent starting position for a second attempt redirected now at southern Syria.

Anticipating this strategy, the southern peoples terminated their petty interstate feuding (see 1 Kgs 20) and organized a league of twelve kings from throughout Syria-Palestine, Arabia, and Ammon. The Monolith Inscription identifies the three principals in the following order: Hadadezer (Hadad-ʿidr) of Damascus, Irḫuleni of Hamath, and Ahab the Israelite (*A-ḫa-ab-bu māt Sir-ʾi-la-a-a*). Judging from the record of personnel and materials that each participant contributed to this cause, Damascus itself seems to have led the effort.

Though the Assyrian hammer blows against Syria began in 853 BCE and fell again in 849, 848, 845, 841, 838, and 834 (Appendix D), no extant textual evidence

---

E. Michel, "Die Assur-Texte Salmanassars III. (858-824)," *WdO* 2 [1954], 27-45); (4) the **Annals from Calah/Nimrud**, describing the first 18 years (for the text, see A. H. Layard, *Inscriptions*, 12-16 and 46-47; for the editing, see the work of Billerbeck and Delitzsch, cited in J. V. K. Wilson, "The Kurba'il Statue of Shalmaneser III," *Iraq* 24 (1962), 93, n. 11; for a translation, *ARAB* I.640-663); (5) the **Black Obelisk** from Nimrud, dealing with the first 31 years (*ARAB* I.553-593; E. Michel, "Die Assur-Texte Salmanassars III. (858-824) (Salmanassar-Obelisk bis Zeile 126)," *WdO* 2 [1955], 137-57, and "Die Assur-Texte Salmanassars III. (858-824) Salmanassar-Obelisk Zeile 126b-Zeile 190 (Ende)," *WdO* 2 [1956], 221-33); (6) the **Bronze Gates at Balawat** (*ARAB* I.612-625; E. Michel, "Die Assur-Texte Salmanassars III. (858-824) (9. Fortsetzung), 34. Text [Balawat-Inschrift]," *WdO* 2 [1958-1959], 408-15, and "Die Assur-Texte Salmanassars III. (858-824) 11. Forts.," *WdO* 4 [1967-1968], 29-37); (7) the **Berlin Statue Inscription** from Aššur (*ARAB* I.679-683); (8) another, very poorly preserved **Statue Inscription** from Nimrud (J. Laessøe, "A Statue of Shalmaneser III, from Nimrud," *Iraq* 21 [1959], 147-57); (9) the **Kurba'il Statue** of Shalmaneser, with a brief description of years 18-20 (J. V. Kinnier Wilson, *Iraq* 24 [1962], 90-115 [see above]); (10) an **annalistic text** written in poetic style and discovered among the Sultantepe tablets, *STT* I.43, Pls. LVIII-LIX (see also W. G. Lambert, "The Sultantepe Tablets [continued]. VIII. Shalmaneser in Ararat," *Anatolian Studies* 11 [1961], 143-58).

[2]*ARAB* I.366-68.

[3]See J. du Plat Taylor et al., "The Excavations at Sakce Gözü," *Iraq* 12 (1950), 68.

[4]See *ANET*, 277.

[5]Whether the prophet Amos, a century later, recalled this downfall of Bit Adini (= biblical Beth Eden) or the later deposition of the overly ambitious Assyrian governor of Bit Adini, Šamšī-ilu, remains a matter of debate (see A. Malamat, "Amos 1:5 in the Light of the Til Barsip Inscriptions," *BASOR* 129 [1953], 25-26). See also n. 10 below.

supports a case for any military involvement by Israel after the initial encounter at Qarqar in 853[6]—a conflict that occurred only a year or two prior to the death of Ahab.[7] Moreover, the significance at home of Ahab's encounter in 853 with Shalmaneser III gains sharper focus in a reevaluation of the chariot corp sent by Israel as military support.[8] Elat's belief in the authenticity of the 2,000-unit figure[9] seems untenable. In this period, Samaria's warring activities were generally confined to localized or, at most, interstate feuding with Aram, Judah, and Moab; the city's ability to maintain and field a force of 2,000 chariots (roughly equal to the number mustered by Assyria during its apogee) in distant, international conflict remains extremely dubious.[10] Furthermore, by the end of Jehu's reign roughly 25 years later, the Hebrew Bible records a corp of only ten chariots available to Jehu's successor (2 Kgs 13:7). Even subsequent to the prosperity realized under Jeroboam II, Sargon's Nineveh Prism (line 6)[11] lists only 200 chariots among the booty captured by Assyria when Samaria fell. The Monolith Inscription, then, smacks of the typical hyperbolic portrayal of the size and might of Assyria's foes by the field scribes who travelled with the Assyrian army.[12] In this light,

---

[6]Contra M. Elat, "The Campaigns of Shalmaneser III against Aram and Israel," *IEJ* 25 (1975), 25-35; M. C. Astour, "841 B.C.: The First Assyrian Invasion of Israel," *JAOS* 91 (1971), 387; A. R. Green, "Sua and Jehu: The Boundaries of Shalmaneser's Conquest," *PEQ* 111 (1979), 35.

[7]See the "Synopsis of Suggested Regnal Chronologies for the Kings of Samaria" in *AIS-I*, Appendix C, p. 255.

[8]*ARAB* I.611.

[9]Elat, *IEJ* 25 (1975), 25-35.

[10]Malamat speculates that Ahab's impressive contribution of chariots and infantry at Qarqar likely included auxiliary units from Jehoshaphat of Judah (vis à vis 1 Kgs 22:4 and 2 Kgs 3:7) and from the Samarian vassal states of Ammon and Moab (A. Malamat, "The Aramaeans," in *Peoples of Old Testament Times*, D. J. Wiseman, ed. [Oxford: Clarendon, 1973], 144). J. H. Hayes adds Edom to this list and states that Judah, Moab, and Edom represented "states subordinate to Israel at the time" (J. H. Hayes, *Amos: The Eighth Century Prophet* [Nashville, TN: Abingdon, 1988], 17, 23-24). But the number of chariots controlled by any of these regional kingdoms remains too poorly attested to confirm this argument, even though Samaria might well have exercised authority over some of these regions. Interestingly, this roster of powers begins to resemble the list of foreign nations mentioned in the oracles of Amos 1:2-2:16 (see p. 515 below). The history of interpretation of these speeches, however, proves exceedingly complex and lies beyond the scope of this study. While many scholars understand the proclamations against Judah and Edom as secondary to the original list, and others include here the oracles on Tyre and Gaza/Philistia (and, in certain cases, even the Israel declaration itself), still others have argued for the integrity and unity of the speeches (as do F. I. Andersen and D. N. Freedman, *Amos* [New York: Doubleday, 1989], 183-206; see Hayes, *Amos*, 48-119 for a full outline of the issues; also H. W. Wolff, *Joel and Amos* [Philadelphia: Fortress, 1977] for text-critical matters; and, for the alternate view that the nations cited in the speeches were once "member nations of the Davidic empire" whose rebellion against Davidic rule and subsequent atrocities against fellow members had garnered them the condemnation of the eighth-century prophet, see M. E. Polley, *Amos and the Davidic Empire: A Socio-Historical Approach* [Oxford: Oxford University Press, 1989], esp. 55-74).

[11]J. C. Gadd, "Inscribed Prisms of Sargon II from Nimrud," *Iraq* 16 (1954), 173-201.

[12]The heroic style of the Assyrian inscriptions exhibits a much greater use of hyperbole than do the more succinct *Chronicles* of Assyrian activities. For comments on some of the historiographic problems

separate suggestions by Na'aman and Rainey[13] to reduce considerably the number of chariots dispatched from Samaria (or its outlying royal cities, such as Megiddo) to Qarqar appear entirely justified.

Nevertheless, it is important to recognize the enduring influence that the three centers at Damascus, Hamath, and Samaria appear to have held over a vast portion of Syria-Palestine during the ninth and eighth centuries BCE. Roughly 130 years after the encounter with Shalamaneser III at Qarqar, when another Shalmaneser (V) had besieged and controlled Samaria, the sometimes curious turns of history would once again result in a near perfect repetition of this ninth-century BCE scenario. It appears that Damascus, Hamath, and Samaria once again led a rebellion against Assyrian rule sometime around 722 or 721 BCE.[14] Though Shalmaneser V died before he could fully address this threat in the west, his successor, Sargon II, went against the region in his second *palû* and defeated the coalition at Qarqar in 720 BCE.[15] Together, these events help establish a pattern of strategy: whenever the west managed to organize a large-scale offensive against Assyria, the participants attempted to keep the Assyrians out of south Syria and Palestine altogether by meeting them in or near the borderlands. That even this late coalition did not have to wait to defend itself until the Assyrians had entered the hinterland speaks to the fact that these regional powers, including Samaria, maintained enough control over the local scene to allow them to go to the field against Assyria without worrying about the Assyrian garrisons stationed inside the territories themselves.

In addition to the apparent Assyrian inflation of the size of Samaria's army, as well as a modern misconception regarding the city's tenure in the early anti-Assyrian league that fomented in south Syria around 853 BCE, the Hebrew Bible's silence about this important battle usually gains some attention in scholars' historical interpretations of the event. C. F. Whitley[16] suggests that, contrary to the information given by the Assyrian records themselves, the Syrian coalition posted a great victory at Qarqar, but

---

created by such exaggerations, see B. Oded, *Mass Deportations and Deportees in the Neo-Assyrian Empire* (Wiesbaden: Reichert, 1979), 6ff. See also H. Tadmor, "History and Ideology in the Assyrian Royal Inscriptions," in *Assyrian Royal Inscriptions: New Horizons*, F. M. Fales, ed. (Roma: Instituto per l'Oriente, 1981), 17-18, n. 16.

[13]N. Na'aman, "Two Notes on the Monolith Inscription of Shalmaneser III from Kurkh," *TA* 3 (1976), 89-106; see also A. F. Rainey's editorial note in Y. Aharoni, *Land of the Bible* (Philadelphia: Westminster, 1979), 336.

[14]See the discussion of the Aššur-Charter:17-28 below. One may view the Samaria–Damascus alliance during the Syro-Ephraimite War a decade or so prior to this time as a prelude to the more fully developed anti-Assyrian coalition of the 720s BCE.

[15]An annalistic fragment that appears to relate to this campaign indicates that Sargon at this time incorporated into his royal army only 50 chariots from Israel, not 200 as some have suggested elsewhere (see above).

[16]C. F. Whitley, "The Deuteronomic Presentation of the House of Omri," *VT* 2 (1952), 149-50. See also N. M. Sarna, "The Biblical Sources for the History of the Monarchy," in *WHJP*, Vol. IV/1, A. Malamat, ed. (Jerusalem: Masada Press, 1979), 3-19.

that the Deuteronomistic Historian, who wished only to criticize the northern kings, simply ignored Ahab's achievement. One must recognize, however, Shalmaneser's decisive defeat of the south Syrian states in 841 BCE, at which time he turned from Damascus, marched through Israel with no further military engagement,[17] and proceeded to Mount Carmel,[18] where he received tribute from Baal-manzer of Tyre, the Sidonians, and Jehu of Samaria (specifically, ᵐIu-ú-a DUMU ᵐḪu-um-ri-i,[19] usually translated literally as "Jehu, son of Omri" but probably to be understood as "Jehu, King of [Bīt]-Ḫumrî"[20]). This foray marks the first Assyrian incursion into Israel proper[21] and the second personal encounter between Shalmaneser and an Israelite king

---

[17] According to the Assyrian records (*ARAB* I.672), Shalmaneser first encountered Haza'el at Mount Saniru (= Seir, ca. 20 km northwest of Damascus). From there, he marched into Damascus, then on to the mountains of Hauran (*šade* MAT *Ḫa-ú-ra-ni*, ca. 100 km southeast of Damascus), and finally to Mount Carmel, undoubtedly via Beth-Shan, Jezreel, Megiddo, and Yoqneʿam. That Shalmaneser apparently did not pass through Hazor at this time places Aharoni's suggestion that he is responsible for the destruction of Stratum VIII of that city open to question. A. Negev's assignment of that same conflagration to the ongoing Aramaean battles with Israel seem equally as plausible (see Y. Aharoni, *Land of the Bible*, 341; A. Negev, *Archaeological Encyclopedia of the Holy Land* [Jerusalem: The Jerusalem Publishing House, 1972], 140).

[18] That the Assyrian Ba'li-ra'si denotes Mount Carmel rather than the cliff near the south of Nahr el-Kalb, just north of Beirut, received clarification in Safar's edition of Shalmaneser's annals published already in 1951. Whereas the previously known annalistic fragment (*ARAB* I.672) read simply, "to Mt. Ba'li-ra'si, a promontory on the sea," the material published by Safar adds, "over against/at the entrance of the land of Tyre" (rev. IV:9). That the Carmel range lay on the Israel-Tyre border during this period has been adequately demonstrated (see Aharoni, *Land of the Bible* 341, and n. 57 for further bibliography). I may, however, issue one caveat: KUR Ba'li-ra'si is not to be confused with URU Ba'ali, which appears later in Adad-nirari III's records (see n. 73 below).

[19] Many have accepted the spelling of Jehu's name as *ia-ú-a* on the Black Obelisk (*ARAB* I.590) and in an annalistic fragment from Calah/Nimrud (*ARAB* I.672; compare also J. V. Kinner Wilson, "The Kurba'il Statue of Shalmaneser III," *Iraq* 24 [1962], 94, lines 28-30, which agree with the text of Rawlinson's IIIR, Pl. 5, No. 6). In the fourth edition of the annals published by Safar, it appears as *ia-a-ú* ("A Further Text of Shalmaneser III from Assur," *Sumer* 7 [1951], 3-21). For the recent rendering *Iu-ú-a*, see N. Na'aman, "Jehu Son of Omri: Legitimizing a Loyal Vassal by his Overlord," *IEJ* 48 (1998), 236; idem, "Transcribing the Theophoric Element in North Israelite Names," *NABU* n°1, Mars (1997), 19-20. Though some have suggested reading this name as Jehoram (i.e., Joram ben-Ahab) rather than as Jehu (see P. K. McCarter, "'Yaw, son of 'Omri': A Philological Note on Israelite Chronology," *BASOR* 216 [1974], 5-7), most commentators have considered the reading "Jehu" beyond reproach. Moreover, Thiele has correctly adjusted McCarter's proposed date of 841 BCE for this event (see E. R. Thiele, "An Additional Chronological Note on 'Yaw, Son of 'Omri'," *BASOR* 222 [1976], 19-23; also M. Weippert, "Jau(a) mār Ḫumri–Joram oder Jehu von Israel?" *VT* 28 [1978], 113-18).

[20] On the expression *mār Ḫu-um-ri-i* as "King of Bīt-Ḫumrî," see H. Tadmor's early comments in "The Historical Inscriptions of Adad-nirari III," *Iraq* 35 (1973), 149, l. 12. He later accepted "Jehu, son of Omri" as a proper translation but noted that the use of *Ḫumrî* or *bīt Ḫumrî* in Akkadian generally refers specifically to the Kingdom of Israel by using the name of the ruler whom the Assyrians considered to be the state's founding figure. Thus "the designation 'son' in Assyrian texts refers to the ancestral founder of a dynastic house and not to the name of an individual's father" (M. Cogan and H. Tadmor, *II Kings* [AB 11; Garden City, NY: Doubleday, 1988], 106).

[21] On the basis of her interpretation of an Assyrian bas-relief attributed to Shalmaneser's predecessor,

(see Appendix D). Yet the Bible again does not mention these events,[22] which might have provided a biased Judahite historian with substantially negative material. Rather than giving a subtle clue as to the outcome of the fighting at Qarqar, the silence of the biblical record regarding these battles likely reflects the low priority attached to the events in Samaria itself. Moreover, the Deuteronomic editor(s) of Kings condemns nearly all the Judahite rulers in addition to those from Israel,[23] so that the exclusion of the Qarqar episode from this literature does not necessarily betray original or redactional prejudices against the north.

In a similar way, the potential relevance to the biblical historian of Jehu's later payment of tribute to Shalmaneser paled in the face of Jehu's bloody annihilation of Samaria's royal house together with his near eradication of the Judahite dynasty. When addressing the half-century following the collapse of the United Monarchy, which brought an invasion by the Egyptian Shishak and the acceleration of religious syncretism at home, internal or regional affairs captured the concerns of the biblical writers more than contacts with powers lying farther afield—powers of whom they had not yet acquired an appreciable knowledge or apprehension. One should remember that Shalmaneser encountered King Ahab in the first instance approximately 450 km north of Samaria and, twelve years later, he met the usurper Jehu in an apparently noncombative circumstance at the old cultic site of Carmel rather than at the political nerve center of Samaria. There is no evidence that Shalmaneser III ever visited the Israelite capital.

Ashur-nasir-pal II (883-859 BCE), P. Albenda has suggested that the latter ruler fought against Hazor during his reign. If so, this would present an earlier breach into Palestine by a Neo-Assyrian king (notwithstanding that the "Neo-Assyrian" period is generally dated from Shalmaneser III's reign). Her evidence, however, seems extremely speculative (e.g., the claim is based solely on the appearance in the relief of a bucket and pulley, which Albenda says may have been used in a water system similar to that known from Hazor; no cuneiform inscription accompanies the relief to confirm this connection). My present argument, therefore, remains an acceptable one. (See P. Albenda, "A Syro-Palestinian[?] City on a Ninth Century B.C. Assyrian Relief," *BASOR* 206 [1972], 42-48).

[22] I have not overlooked Hosea 10:14, which recalls that "Shalman destroyed Beth-Arbel." Astour's association of these names with Shalmaneser III and Arbela in Transjordan (listed in the district of Pella in Eusebius' *Onomasticon*) is interesting, but his assumption that this biblical notation confirms that Beth-Arbel was under the jurisdiction of Samaria rather than Damascus in 841 BCE and that the forces of Joram-Jehu were there fighting the Assyrians rather than the Aramaeans is unconvincing inasmuch as it is based on the belief that the Israel-Aram alliance of 853 continued unabated through 841 BCE, despite the limited duration of Samaria's involvement noted explicitly in 1 Kgs 22:1 and implied in the Assyrian records (see M. Astour, "841 B.C.: The First Assyrian Invasion of Israel," *JAOS* 91 [1971], 383-89). Moreover, the Assyrian accounts of 841 BCE targeted *only* Damascus. Astour should not be surprised that Hosea employed a non-Israelite example in his pronouncement of judgment (see Amos 1-2). One should also note that the identification of Shalman as Shalmaneser III has not gone uncontested (see Bartlett, "The Moabites and Edomites," in *Peoples of Old Testament Times*, D. J. Wiseman, ed. [Oxford: Clarendon, 1973], 239). Finally, that Samaria—in my judgment—no longer stood as an active member of the anti-Assyrian coalition in south Syria would not have dampened the reality of the first Assyrian presence in Israel for the reportedly biased historian.

[23] R. de Vaux, *Ancient Israel: Volume 1 — Social Institutions* (New York: McGraw Hill, 1961), 99.

The effects of Jehu's purge in 841 BCE might easily have proven disastrous for Israel.[24] Though the new king surely realized that the key to economic stability lay in the west (via Phoenicia), his personal cognizance that the rising power of Assyria would ultimately control those western resources seems to have dictated his strategy. Unhappily for Israel, Jehu's anticipation of the Assyrian ascent to dominance was premature, for following Shalmaneser's reign the struggling eastern power lapsed into over a half-century of the most troublesome years in its history (ca. 830-745 BCE). In shifting the focus of his administration's allegiance from Tyre to neophyte Assyria, Jehu leaned on a power that itself had not come fully of age and jeopardized strong economic ties in favor of dangerous political ones. Moreover, by couching this focal shift within a score of political assassinations, he surely weakened Samaria's connections to adjacent areas, such as Judah and Phoenicia. And the mutual recognition that arose between Jehu and Shalmaneser III cut strongly across the earlier anti-Assyrian activities of Israel's erstwhile ally in Damascus.

Yet this bold move neither failed utterly nor occasioned the downfall of Israel. Contrary to the opinion of H. Reviv, Samaria's relations with Judah and Phoenicia were not "severed for good" and did not leave an isolated Israel no hope of "withstanding a more formidable Aramaean kingdom."[25] Instead, both the nation of Israel and the ruler Jehu survived all threats from Damascus for decades to come. Moreover, my analysis of the Pottery Period 3 material has suggested that some level of contact with Phoenicia continued throughout the course of the ninth century BCE.[26] Again, in cases such as this one, the archaeology of Samaria may reflect better the commercial history of the site than it does the kingdom's broader political history. On the Assyrian side of the equation, one sees that Jehu ultimately stood as the only Israelite king ever referred to as *mār PN* by the Assyrians, who otherwise call Ahab (Omri's real biological son) simply "the Israelite"[27] and both Joash and Menahem "the Samarian."[28] By naming Jehu as the "King of the House/Dynasty of Omri" (*mār*

---

[24]One may detect the far-reaching effects of Jehu's actions in the fact that it prompted the only break in the Davidic dynasty in Jerusalem by creating a situation wherein the Israelite princess, Athaliah (either the daughter or step-daughter of Ahab), seized control of the Jerusalemite throne and attempted to murder all the remaining members of the Davidic line. She reigned for approximately six years before it was revealed that Joash, of Davidic descent, had been secretly saved from Athaliah's wrath by Jehoiadah. Joash was promptly proclaimed king of Judah.

[25]H. Reviv, "The Canaanite and Israelite Periods," in *A History of the Holy Land*, M. Avi-Yonah, ed. (Jerusalem: Steimatzky, 1969), 87. That Tyre, Sidon, and Samaria comprise the only three cities specifically mentioned in Assyrian annals does not support Kraeling's early suggestion that Jehu maintained the Omride tradition of fraternizing with Phoenicia (E. Kraeling, *Aram and Israel* [New York: Columbia University Press, 1918], 80). Rather, the Assyrian record merely reflects the mutual interest of these particular cities, as vassals or treaty partners of Damascus (compare the Melqart Stele), neutralizing the Damascus inroads and demands on their resources.

[26]*AIS-I*, 215, as well as the full discussion of PP 3 forms.

[27]See the Monolith Inscription, *ARAB* I.611.

[28]N. Na'aman, *IEJ* 48 (1998), 236 (for full reference, see n. 19 above).

Ḫumri), Shalmaneser sanctioned Jehu's position even though he did not belong to[29] the royal house that had originally founded the dynasty and had even assassinated its heirs.[30] Jehu clearly adopted a pro-Assyrian stance and, during his coup d'état, appears to have utilized at least some Assyrian tactics of psychological warfare (compare the "heap of heads at the entrance of the gate" in 2 Kgs 10:7-8 with Shalmaneser III's strategies[31] in many of the royal cities that he conquered). Finally, it now seems possible that the break from Damascus had already begun under the rule of Jehu's predecessor, Jehoram, and that this decision may have related in some way to the latter's fall under a punitive assault by Haza'el of Damascus.[32]

Even so, relations between Israel and the anti-Assyrian Aramaeans undoubtedly grew even more strained throughout the latter half of the ninth century BCE. Though Jehu may have regained some degree of sovereignty over certain regions in Transjordan

---

[29] Available evidence does not support the view that Jehu was actually a descendant of the "House of Omri" (contra T. Schneider, "Did King Jehu Kill his Own Family?" *BAR* 21/1 [1995], 26-33; idem, "Rethinking Jehu,"*Biblica* 77 [1996], 100-107).

[30] Elsewhere, when a local king who had usurped control of the throne stood as an enemy against Shalmaneser III, the Assyrian typically referred to him as the "son of a nobody" (Haza'el of Damascus; *ARAB* I.681), the "one without right to the throne" (Surri of Patina; *ARAB* I.585), "the usurper" (Marduk-bel-usate; *ARAB* I.622; also E. Michel, *WdO* 4 [1967-1968], 31, l. 4), or the like. In both Assyrian and various Northwest Semitic writings, the rubric "son of PN" generally refers to the historic founder of the throne in a given city, not to a given figure's biological father (besides Na'aman's article cited above, see again my n. 20 as well as A. Ungnad, "Jaua, mār Ḫumrî," *Orientalische Literaturzeitung* 9 [1906], 224-25; J. A. Brinkman, *A Political History of Post-Kassite Babylonia 1158-722 B.C.* [Rome, 1968], 247).

[31] *ARAB* I.598, 599 (2x), 605, 609(?). For another edition of Luckenbill's § 605, see W. G. Lambert, "The Sultantepe Tablets (continued). VIII. Shalmaneser in Ararat," *Anatolian Studies* 11 (1961), 146-49.

[32] The polemical discussions of the text of the Tel Dan Stele notwithstanding, I continue to accept the historical probability of Biran's original interpretation regarding the events and figures behind this monument (see A. Biran and J. Naveh, "An Aramaic Stele from Tel Dan," *IEJ* 43 [1993], 81-98; idem, "The Tel Dan Inscription: A New Fragment," *IEJ* 45 [1995], 1-18). The problem, of course, centers on the claim in 2 Kgs 9 that Jehoram of Israel was assassinated by Jehu rather than by Haza'el. Biran has suggested that perhaps "Hazael saw Jehu as his agent" (*IEJ* 45 [1995], 18). It seems equally possible that the biblical writers viewed the relationship in reverse, particularly if the anticipated rise of Jehu had already been announced in Damascus. The two notations in 2 Kgs 9:14-26 that Jehu did, in fact, conspire (presumably with another party) against Jehoram and that Jehoram received his initial wounds from the forces of Haza'el while in battle at Ramoth-gilead may provide some clues to the complexity of the Jehu-Haza'el involvement in the overthrow of the existing Israelite leadership. If, as Biran surmises, the Tel Dan Inscription was not erected until late in the reign of Haza'el, and then as a summary inscription rather than an annalistic account, one can see how Haza'el might easily have claimed full credit for a political assassination in which he had played a key role nearly four decades earlier (regardless of whether or not the wounds he inflicted on Jehoram had actually caused the death of the Israelite king). But note also the similarity between Haza'el's boast of having killed 70 kings and the record of Jehu having displayed the heads of 70 royal figures from the house of Omri, both of which acts occurred during the early stages of each king's rise to power. Once again it seems possible, in my judgment, that the (likely exaggerated) claims of these two new rulers are intertwined and may relate, at least in part, to the same set of opponents. If so, it may not prove necessary to date the Tel Dan Inscription to a time after Haza'el's reign.

(Phase S.2),[33] it appears that by the end of his reign Haza'el had reconquered Bashan and Gilead as far south as Aroer near the Arnon River (see 2 Kgs 10:32-33). And immediately following Jehu's death (in 815 or 814 BCE), Samaria was unable to deter the campaign by Damascus against Gath and Jerusalem (2 Kgs 12:18-19)[34]—an event which heralded a period of weakness and stagnation for the kingdom of Israel (Phase S.3).[35] Jehu's relatively long reign, then, fell between at least two separate incursions by Damascus. The first campaign had helped to open the way for Jehu's rise to power; the second attack closed a turbulent period that left the leadership of Samaria in a weakened state near the end of the ninth century and in the opening years of the eighth century BCE. By this time, every power once allied or subservient to Israel—including Damascus, Philistia, Tyre, Edom, Ammon, Moab, and Judah (see n. 10 above)—had rebelled or otherwise fallen away from Samaria. Undoubtedly as one result of this decline in Israelite power, Jehu's successor, Jehoahaz, inherited an emaciated army (2 Kgs 13:7; Heb. *'am*, perhaps "kinsmen" or "citizenry") and endured continued harassment from bands in Transjordan (vv. 20-21) as well as from Damascus (v. 22). These same powers would again pose a serious threat to Israel's stability during the reign of Tiglath-pileser III in the latter half of the eighth century BCE (see pp. 542ff. below).

Regarding the earliest set of Assyrian references to Samaria, then, both Ahab's military liaison with Syrian and Aramaean enterprises around 853 BCE and Jehu's relatively peaceful reception of Shalmaneser at Carmel in the wake of his violent 841 BCE coup seem to have figured minimally in the domestic political and literary scene of the Israelite capital. Consequently, neither occurrence received mention by the biblical historian(s). Herrmann's belief that the former event was, in fact, recorded in the

---

[33] Compare A. H. van Zyl, *The Moabites* (Leiden: E. J. Brill, 1960), 145-46; and J. R. Bartlett, "The Moabites and Edomites," in *Peoples of Old Testament Times*, D. J. Wiseman, ed. (Oxford: Clarendon, 1973), 238.

[34] For the synchronism of the biblical data relating to this event and the conclusion that it is best dated immediately following Jehu's death, see W. W. Hallo, "From Qarqar to Carchemish: Assyria and Israel in the Light of New Discoveries," in *Biblical Archaeologist Reader*, Vol. 2., E. F. Campbell and D. N. Freedman, eds. (Missoula: Scholars Press, 1975), 163-64 plus the bibliography on p. 164, n. 42.

[35] Aram's ability to escalate its warfare against Palestine and to strike unopposed at Gath reflects the internal weakness current in both the Samarian and Assyrian regimes. The assault on Gath undoubtedly relates to an attempt to control the southwestern trade depots (e.g., Gaza), which were handling a significant percentage of the spice and incense trade from southern Arabia. Syrian control over this southern extension of the coastal route would have proven especially desirable if the historical kernel behind 2 Kgs 7:6 points to a strengthened Samaria-Egypt relationship during this period. I should note, however, that this verse is usually emended to read "Assyrian armies" in reference to Adad-nirari III; Kraeling and, later, Gray understood *Miṣraim* as a reference to the northern "Musri"—i.e., the Cappadocians of Anatolia—as opposed to the Egyptians on grounds of the former's geographical proximity to the Hittites (Kraeling, *Aram and Israel*, 82-83; see my n. 77 below; Gray, *I and II Kings* [Philadelphia: Westminster, 1970], 268-69 and 524-2). Also, Haza'el's cognizance of the supply and value of South Arabian commodities would have been enhanced if this ruler were himself of Arabian extraction, as further proposed by Kraeling in *Aram and Israel*, 81, n. 1.

Chronicles of the Kings of Israel but later edited out for this very reason[36] is overly speculative.

2.) Adad-nirari III: 796 BCE

The long period of Assyrian weakness (Phases A.2-3) mentioned above began when Shalmaneser's two sons engaged in a power struggle for the throne in Calah during the late 830s BCE. The results proved even more protracted and disastrous for Assyria than Jehu's revolution had for Israel. Revolt broke out in 27 cities in central Assyria[37] and resulted in the death of Shalmaneser in 824 BCE (the Eponym Chronicle records *sīḫu*, "revolt,"[38] for the years 826-820 BCE). Rebellion then rippled across the entire empire, washing away Assyrian footholds everywhere. The initial attempts to regain control and move toward stability (Phase A.2) suffered yet another setback when the succeeding Shamshi-Adad V was forced to recognize formally the overlordship of Babylon in the south.[39] To the north, the opportunistic Urartean kings began to expand both east and west of Assyria, from around Lake Urumia throughout the upper Euphrates. All the territories formerly subdued by Shalmaneser III west of the Euphrates quickly shirked the Assyrian yoke so that Til Barsip (Bit Adini) once again constituted the westernmost Assyrian outpost.[40] The empire returned to virtually the same contracted borders it claimed at Shalmaneser's accession to the throne (note Shamshi-Adad's consequent record of the kingdom's shrunken parameters in *ARAB* I.716). The territorial, and therefore economic, gains of 30 years seemed suddenly negated. Crippled by this state of turmoil, the Assyrian rulers attempted no further western campaigns between 831 BCE ("to Que") and 805 BCE ("to Arpad").[41]

Toward the end of this downward cycle, sometime around 810 or 809 BCE, an empire still languishing beneath the effects of internal rebellion passed into the hands of

---

[36] S. Herrmann, *A History of Israel in Old Testament Times*, Revised Edition (Philadelphia: Fortress, 1981), 213. Kraeling's (n. 25 above) early interpretation that saw Samaria completely free of any Assyrian presence at this time seems overstated; it is predicated on the belief that Jehu travelled to Nahr el-Kalb (not to Mount Carmel) to offer his tribute at a time when none of the adjacent states (Arvad, Simyra, etc.) were forced to pay similar obeisance.

[37] *ARAB* I.715; only Calah itself remained loyal.

[38] *CAD* S, 240-41; for the Eponym Chronicle's listings, see the reference to Millard in n. 51 below.

[39] See M. Noth, "Der historische Hintergrund der Inschriften von Sefire," *ZDPV* 77 (1961), 143, n. 73.

[40] Even sites closer to Assyria (e.g., Gozan [Tell Ḥalaf] on the upper Khabur River, a later place of deportation of Samarians, 2 Kgs 17:6, 19:12) seem to have established their independence during Shamshi-Adad V's rule (see Hallo, *Biblical Archaeologist Reader*, Vol. 2 [1975], 163, n. 40 for bibliography).

[41] Though Shalmaneser III maintained a high level of activity in the west during the decade following his 841 BCE meeting with Jehu, he confined the majority of his efforts to the areas of northern Syria that had intercepted his 858 BCE advances. While the Black Obelisk (*ARAB* I.578) indicates that Shalmaneser came against Aram/Damascus in south Syria again in his twenty-first year (838 BCE), the principal series of late northern campaigns included Que (eastern Cilicia) in 839 BCE (*ARAB* I.577), Tabal (biblical Tubal) in 836 BCE (*ARAB* I.579), Melid (modern Malatya) in 835 BCE (*ARAB* I.580), and Que again in

Adad-nirari III.[42] The chronology of this king's reign continues to vex modern historians partly because all the extant primary sources represent later, summary inscriptions and not annalistic accounts contemporary with the events they describe. The Eponym Chronicle, on the other hand, appears to have received its entries at the turn of each year and to have recorded the precise location of the king and his imperial army at that time.[43] As a consequence, this source provides the most reliable chronological indicators for the late ninth century (beginning in 840 BCE) and continuing down to 649 BCE.

Inscription	Tributaries Recorded
Tell al-Rimah Stele – 1st Year[44]	Tyre; Sidon; Arvad; Samaria; Aram
Nimrud Slab[45]	Tyre; Sidon; Ḫumri-Land (Israel); Edom; Palastu; Aram
Sheik Hammad Stele[46]	Arpad
Saba'a Stele – 5th year[47]	Palaštu; Aram

Historical Inscriptions Relating to the Reign of Adad-nirari III of Assyria

Table 63

The overall paucity of written sources recovered from this administration,[48] the heated debate that the few extant inscriptions have sparked regarding the dates of its

---

833-32 BCE, when he drove as far west as Tarzi (Tarsus; *ARAB* I.582).

[42] A debate continues as to whether or not Adad-nirari was a minor at his accession and therefore ruled merely as an insignificant coregent with his famous mother Sammuramet. Though scholars early on accepted this scenario (compare *ARAB* I. 734; A. T. Olmstead, *History of Assyria* [New York: Charles Scribner's Sons, 1923], 158; Hallo, *Biblical Archaeological Reader*, Vol. 2 [1975], 164), Grayson has argued more recently that "there is no evidence for a coregency in contemporary sources nor is there any indication that Adad-nirari was particularly young at his accession" (A. K. Grayson, "Assyria: Ashurdan II to Ashur-nirari V [934-745 B.C.]," in *The Cambridge Ancient History*, Vol. III/1, Second Edition. J. Boardman et al., eds. [Cambridge: Cambridge University Press, 1982], 271-72).

[43] A. R. Millard and H. Tadmor, "Adad-nirari III in Syria: Another Stele Fragment and the Dates of His Campaigns," *Iraq* 35 (1973), 62.

[44] S. Page, "A Stele of Adad-nirari III and Nergal-Ereš from Tell al Rimah," *Iraq* 30 (1968), 139-53, Pl. XXXIX; also Tadmor, *Iraq* 35 (1973), 141-150 (for full reference, see n. 20 above).

[45] *ARAB* I.739-41; again, Tadmor, *Iraq* 35 (1973), 141-150.

[46] Millard and Tadmor, *Iraq* 35 (1973), 57-64 (see n. 43 above).

[47] *ARAB* I.733-37; H. Tadmor, "The Historical Inscriptions of Adad-nirari III," *Iraq* 35 (1973), 141-150.

[48] Grayson has noted that "not a single annalistic text is preserved" from this period (Grayson, *CAH*, Vol. III/1, Second Edition (1982), 271. For sources published prior to the ones listed here, see A. K. Grayson, *Assyrian and Babylonian Chronicles*. Texts from Cuneiform Sources 5 (Locust Valley, NY: J.

military campaigns,[49] and the lack of systematic archaeological excavations in many regions of northern Syria have combined to make a reliable historical reconstruction of the ensuing years an extremely arduous task. The best-preserved sources that tell of Adad-nirari's efforts to consolidate once again the western territories under the control of Calah/Nimrud (Phase A.2) and that contain the second set of direct references to the northern kingdom of Israel, its capital or king, appear in Table 63 above.[50] In addition, the chronologically more reliable Eponym Chronicle[51] provides the following pertinent entries:

805 BCE	a-na ^{māt}ar-pad-da	to Arpad
804 BCE	a-na ^{āl}ḫa-za-zi	to Hazazu
803 BCE	a-na ^{āl}ba-a'-li	to Ba'alu
802 BCE	a-na muḫḫi tam-tim mu-ta-nu	to the seacoast
801-797 BCE	(to various areas both north and east of Assyria)	
796 BCE	a-na man-ṣu-a-te	to Manṣuate

Historical Entries in the Eponym Chronicle

Table 64

Of the multiple, longstanding issues that have shrouded the proper chronology of the above references, at least two questions carry direct implications for my study: (1) when did Samaria proffer its tribute to Adad-nirari (see the Nimrud and Rimah inscriptions); and (2) what were the circumstances of that payment, i.e., did the Assyrians, in fact, encroach upon Israelite soil to encounter the king personally in Samaria? Since the second question requires a briefer treatment, I shall address it first.

Beginning with Unger's *editio princeps* of the Saba'a Stele,[52] scholars construed the reference to *Palaštu* as reflecting an actual penetration into Palestine by Adad-nirari

---

J. Augustin Publisher, 1970), 205-06.

[49]None of the few extant inscriptions offers an unequivocal date for any campaign (see A. R. Millard, "Adad-nirari III, Aram, and Arpad," *PEQ* 105 [1973], 161).

[50]Hamath's pro-Assyrian stance and resistance against Damascus reflected in contemporary Northwest Semitic sources (see the Zakkur Stele) militates strongly against Wiseman's assigning fragment ND.5417, which speaks of Assyrian military operations in the west including Hamath and Damascus, to Adad-nirari III. This reservation, together with the fact that the content of this fragment carries no direct import for the history of Samaria, prompts me to omit it here. For a notation of the few remaining inscriptions that can be dated to Adad-nirari with any degree of certainty, see S. Page, "A Stele of Adad-nirari III and Nergal-Ereš from Tell al Rimah," *Iraq* 30 (1968), 140.

[51]A. Millard, *The Eponyms of the Assyrian Empire, 910-612 BC*. State Archives of Assyria, Volume II (Finland: The Neo-Assyrian Text Corpus Project at the University of Helsinki, 1994), 33-35, 57. For an earlier edition of this Chronicle, see A. Ungnad, "Eponymen," pp. 412-57 in *Reallexikon der Assyriologie II*, E. Ebeling and B. Meissner, eds. (Berlin and Leipzig: Walter de Gruyter and Co., 1938); compare also A. T. Olmstead, "The Assyrian Chronicle," *JAOS* 34 (1915), 344-68.

[52]E. Unger, *Reliefstele Adadniraris III aus Saba'a und Semiramis*. Publicationen der Kaiserlich osmanischen Museen 2 (Constantinople: A.Ihsan, 1916).

III,[53] despite the peculiarity of the Nimrud Slab's clear portrayal of Israel and Palaštu as distinct entities. Tadmor emended Unger's original reading of *ana* KUR *Pa-*/erasure/*-la-áš-*[*tú*] (Saba'a Stele, line 12) to *ana māt Ḫat-te x*[*y*], i.e., "to Hatti-Land," which refers to the area of northern (and later, also central and southern) Syria, not to the southern coastal plains of Palestine.[54] The discovery and publication of the so-called Sheik Hammad Stele[55] corroborated Tadmor's correction. In the light of this new evidence, Tadmor understood the remaining "Palaštu" of the Nimrud Slab as comparable to the later Assyrian citations of *Pilista/Pilišta* and therefore as a notice that Philistia, though never actually invaded by Adad-nirari, now stood in vassalage to Damascus (here I may note again Haza'el's drive as far south as Gath following Jehu's death). Wiseman, on the other hand, interpreted the same reference as pointing to "S. Phoenicia."[56] In either case, one may now confidently state that Adad-nirari III at no time breached the borders of the Northern Kingdom of Israel.[57]

To address the first question raised above (i.e., the date of Samaria's tribute), I must deal with the fact that the Saba'a, Nimrud, and Tell al-Rimah inscriptions all portray the defeat of Damascus as one of Adad-nirari's major accomplishments, even though the Eponym Chronicle does not mention this city. Corollary questions surround the exact number and the dates of Adad-nirari's assaults against Damascus, since the Saba'a Stele refers to his fifth year while the Rimah Stele cites his first year. That Samaria and Damascus appear to have paid their tribute at the same time reveals the importance of these issues to the present study. Two solutions have been proposed.

If one takes the position that Adad-nirari's mother, Sammuramet (the Semiramis of Greek legend),[58] ruled in his stead during the first four years of the new king's reign owing to his youth (809-806 BCE), one may conclude either that Years 1 and 5 both refer to 806 BCE or that the former alone represents 806 while the latter points to 802 or 801 BCE. This approach, however, spawns the further problem of a disparity between the three Assyrian sources just mentioned and nearly all recent studies of

---

[53] Compare D. D. Luckenbill in *ARAB* I.734 and, later, A. L. Oppenheim in *ANET*, 282. A. Poebel went even further by suggesting that in 802 BCE Adad-nirari not only entered Israel but drove as far as Philistia and even into Edom (A. Poebel, "The Assyrian King List from Khorsabad—concluded," *JNES* 2 [1943], 84).

[54] H. Tadmor, "A Note on the Saba'a Stele of Adad-nirari III," *IEJ* 19 (1969), 47-48. Tadmor suggested further the possible restoration of *ana māt Ḫat-te* ⌜*rabīte*⌝, or "to the great (land of) Ḫatti." Compare also the later comments on line 12 of the Saba'a Stele in Tadmor, *Iraq* 35 (1973), 145.

[55] A. R. Millard and H. Tadmor, *Iraq* 35 (1973), 57-64.

[56] D. J. Wiseman, "Fragments of Historical Texts from Nimrud," *Iraq* 26 (1964), 119.

[57] In this light, Mallowan's inference that Adad-nirari adopted Samaria's masonry techniques (ashlar blocks in the upper courses and rusticated ones in the subterranean courses), after having observed them during an incursion into the city, is misleading (M. Mallowan, "Samaria and Calah Nimrud: Conjunctions in History and Archaeology," in *Archaeology in the Levant: Essays for Kathleen Kenyon*, R. Moorey and P. Parr, eds. [Warminster, England: Aris & Phillips, 1978], 158).

[58] See Herodotus, *History*, Book I, § 184.

Israelite chronology,[59] most of which place the accession of Joash—the tributary king from Samaria who is explicitly cited in the Rimah Stele—around 801 BCE or later. As a solution, Cody suggested that Joash's reign, in fact, began earlier than previously thought and that he also served as a coregent with his father, Jehoahaz, from 806 BCE to sometime between 801 and 798 or 797 BCE, when Joash finally assumed full control at Samaria.[60] The first approach regards the dating schema contained in the Assyrian records as basically correct, though complicated, and it adjusts the biblical data accordingly. But the fact that such a framework receives no support from the Hebrew Bible itself remains somewhat troublesome; moreover, it seems likely that the Assyrians would have cited the more established ruler, Jehoahaz, as the tributary king rather than one just recently promoted only to vice regent. An alternative solution forwarded by S. Page proposed to see three Assyrian assaults against Damascus (in 806, 802, and 798 BCE). In such a scheme, Samaria would have offered its tribute during the last of these campaigns, and the Rimah Stele would have subsequently conflated all three episodes into one account.[61] This view avoids modifying the biblical chronology, i.e., raising the accession date for the rule of Joash.

Breaking the deadlock between these two camps, the work of Millard and Tadmor has provided a more acceptable explanation. After clarifying the principle that governs the nature of the entries in the Eponym Chronicle, they showed that the specific listings in the Chronicle represent "the actual location of the king and his camp at the turn of the year"[62] rather than the major military target or conquest of that year, as others had thought (see further below). Elsewhere, when dealing with issues of Assyrian historiography, Tadmor demonstrated that the annalistic records underwent periodic rewriting, typically every five to ten years.[63] With this clarification in mind, one recognizes the likelihood that the extant royal inscriptions of Adad-nirari, though

---

[59] For a listing of suggested regnal chronologies, see *AIS-I*, 255, Appendix C. Three of the major chronological schemes forwarded for the Judahite-Israelite kings include (in order of appearance):
  (a) Albright, "The Chronology of the Divided Monarchy of Israel," *BASOR* 100 (1945), 16-22; this model places the accession of Joash around 801 BCE;
  (b) Thiele, *Mysterious Numbers of the Hebrew Kings* (Chicago: University of Chicago Press, 1951); Thiele places the rise of Joash to the throne in 798 BCE;
  (c) Tadmor, *Encyclopedia Miqra'it* 4 (Jerusalem: Bialik Institute, 1961), 261-62; repeated later in Cogan and Tadmor, *II Kings*, 341; here, the accession of Joash falls in 800 or 799 BCE.

[60] A. Cody, "A New Inscription from Tell al-Rimah and King Jehoash of Israel," *CBQ* 32 (1970), 333-37. Yeivin suggests a coregency for Joash but beginning only in 801 BCE, after which he assumed sole rights to the throne in 799 BCE (S. Yeivin, "The Divided Kingdom: Rehoboam-Ahaz/Jeroboam-Pekah," in *WHJP*, Vol. IV/1. A. Malamat, ed. [Jerusalem: Masada Press Ltd., 1979], 126-27).

[61] S. Page, *Iraq* 30 (1968), 139-52.

[62] A. R. Millard and H. Tadmor, *Iraq* 35 (1973), 62. See also H. Tadmor, *Iraq* 35 (1973), 147, where he argues strongly against seeing a four-year coregency involving Adad-nirari III and his mother, Sammuramet.

[63] H. Tadmor, "Observations on Assyrian Historiography," in *Essays on the Ancient Near East in Memory of Jacob Joel Finkelstein* (Hamden, CT: Archon Books for the Connecticut Academy of Arts & Sciences, Vol. XIX, 1977), 209-210.

admittedly few in number, present conflated accounts of the king's various western campaigns[64] set down by his scribes following the close of all the efforts in the west, i.e., sometime after 797 BCE.

On the assumption, then, that the Eponym Chronicle represents the most reliable tool by which to establish the chronology of these campaigns, the foregoing discussion leads me to conclude that Samaria rendered its tribute to Adad-nirari in 796 BCE, soon after the accession of Joash, but that the payment itself was sent by special embassy from Samaria to Damascus. During the relatively long reign of the pro-Assyrian Jehu and in the closing decades of the ninth century BCE, Samaria's posture toward Assyria had undoubtedly become somewhat ambiguous; Joash's tribute-bearing envoy to Damascus clearly reinstated Israel's link to the struggling eastern power.

From the second set of Assyrian texts examined here, then, one sees that Adad-nirari III neither entered Israel nor personally encountered King Joash, though the Rimah Stele does single out the latter's tribute and also provides the earliest mention in the existing cuneiform sources of either the region or the capital city of Samaria (^{m}Ya-$^{\jmath}a$-su ^{māt}Sa-me-ri-na-a-a).[65] Whereas Shalmaneser III had referred both to Israel and to the House of Omri, Assyrian scribes from Adad-nirari on will employ only the House of Omri and Samaria.[66]

The broader political picture that emerges from these documents portrays a reorganized Syria at the end of the ninth century BCE, whose city-states once again gravitated around the two older power centers, Arpad (Tell Rifaʿat) in the north and Damascus in the south. Whereas the former incorporated Que, ʾUmq, Gurgum, Samʾal, and Melid (see Zakkur Stele, lines 5-7),[67] the latter held sway over Phoenicia, Israel, Edom, Philistia (based on Tadmor's interpretation of the Nimrud Slab's reference to *Palaštu*),[68] and possibly even Judah (2 Kgs 12:18-19). Hamath, apparently Assyria's only sympathetic western contact, lay between these two coalitions.[69]

---

[64]This assertion takes into account the conclusions of Poebel regarding the Sabaʾa Inscription (*JNES* 2 [1943], 84) and, more recently, of Page regarding the Rimah Inscription (*Iraq* 30 [1968], 139-53) and Tadmor regarding the Nimrud Slab Inscription (see above references; also Millard, *PEQ* 105 [1973], 162; and Tadmor, *Iraq* 35 [1973], 148ff.).

[65]For a general explanation of the name *ya-ʾa-su* (or possibly *yu-ʾa-su*), see Malamat, "On the Akkadian Transcription of the Name of King Joash," *BASOR* 204 (1971), 37-39. For this name in relationship to phonetic changes occurring between West Semitic and cuneiform writing in this period, see Page, *Iraq* 30 (1968), 148-49. On the ligature sign *i + a*, see I. J. Gelb, "Comments on the Akkadian Syllabary," *Orientalia* 39 (1970), 516-46. Also, the dating of the Joash's tribute to 797 BCE receives additional support from the further work of Tadmor in *Iraq* 35 (1973), 141-50; also J. N. Postgate in *Neo-Assyrian Royal Grants and Decrees* (Rome: Pontifical Biblical Institute, 1969), 115-17.

[66]See the summary chart in M. Weippert, "Jau(a) Mār Ḥumrî — Joram oder Jehu von Israel?" *VT* 28 (1978), 114.

[67]J. C. L. Gibson, *Textbook of Syrian Semitic Inscriptions, Volume 2: Aramaic Inscriptions* (Oxford: Clarendon, 1975), 6-17.

[68]See pp. 518-19 above.

[69]See n. 50 above.

Adad-nirari's early efforts to revive an expansionistic policy in the west during the period between 805 and 802 BCE were limited to northern Syria by the following three factors: the high degree of power now wielded by the city of Arpad;[70] an arc of Urartean pressure that extended across the entire northern Near East, from Lake Urumia across the Nippur Hills due north of Assyria and throughout the mountainous country as far west as the Mediterranean and south to Aleppo;[71] and even a possible sudden outbreak of the pestilence in Syria,[72] the spread of which might easily have compromised the mobility and effectiveness of the Assyrian army. The Eponym Chronicle entries of Arpad (805 BCE) followed by Hazazu (804) and Baʾalu (803)[73] —cities just north of Aleppo—help one trace the concerted efforts of the Assyrians in northern Syria during this period. Their subsequent march "to the seacoast" (802 BCE) likely corresponds to the notice in the Rimah Stele (ll. 9-12) regarding Arvad (contra Page's suggestion of Damascus). A close text-critical analysis of this inscription has demonstrated that it represents a summary inscription and, more specifically, a conflation of two originally disparate documents.[74] The first source (ll. 3-6a) provides information related to the general assault against Hatti, while the second strand of material (ll. 6b-8), which includes the reference to Joash of Samaria, simply contains an abridged list of political entities that now paid tribute to Assyria. None of the evidence supports seeing an actual breach of the borders in any region or city named in this latter group.

Squelched by illness and increasing threats on its northern and eastern fronts, then, Assyria delayed any attempt to penetrate further south until 797-796 BCE, when

---

[70] The significant position to which this geopolitically important site was catapulted around the close of the ninth century BCE is well attested by its treatment in both the Zakkur and Sefire Stelae. Also, the so-called Sheik Hammad Stele corroborates this fact by revealing that the site of Paqarhubuna, on the Euphrates' west bank near the region of Bit Adini (see *ARAB* I.599), and not Arpad itself, was the initial target of Adad-nirari's 805 BCE efforts in the west. An unpublished stele in the Maras Museum in Turkey, alluded to by Millard in *Iraq* 35 (1973), 59, provides even further confirmation. Yet one may draw an appropriate appreciation for Arpad's current strength by noting that the Eponym Chronicle entries for 805-802 BCE indicate that Assyria confined its western activity during those years to that city and the surrounding region; Damascus was not assaulted at that time.

[71] J. du Plat Taylor, M. V. Seton Williams, and J. Waechter, "The Excavations at Sakce Gözü," *Iraq* 12 (1950), 69.

[72] Note the Eponym Chronicle entry for 802 BCE: "to the Sea; plague" (A. Millard, *The Eponyms of the Assyrian Empire*, 34, 57). For an early reference to this possibility, see A. T. Olmstead, *History of Palestine and Syria to the Macedonian Conquest* (New York: Charles Scribner's Sons, 1931), 416.

[73] One should not confuse this Chronicle listing (URU *Baʾali*, "the city of Baʾalu") with Shalmaneser III's earlier designation for Mount Carmel (KUR *Baʾali-rāʾsi*; see again n. 18 above). "The determinatives URU and KUR do indeed interchange, but that happens only when KUR stands for *mātu*, not for *šadû*" (Millard and Tadmor, *Iraq* 35 [1973], 63, n. 23). For an example of this interchange, see Tiglath-pileser's stele fragment in M. Weippert, "Die Feldzüge Adadniraris III. nach Syrien. Voraussetzungen, Verlauf, Folgen," *ZDPV* 108 (1992), 44; L. D. Levine, "Menahem and Tiglath-pileser: A New Synchronism," *BASOR* 206 (1972), 40-42. See the article by Millard and Tadmor for opposing views.

[74] Tadmor, *Iraq* 35 (1973), 142-43.

Adad-nirari returned and established a base camp at Manṣuate.[75] Strategically situated about 50 miles north of Damascus in the Beqaʿ Valley, through which ran the region's principal north-south routes, this site provided an effective blockade against the center of Aramaean resistance in southern Syria. Moreover, with the pro-Assyrian Hamath positioned between Manṣuate and Damascus, the way lay open for Adad-nirari's quick, unobstructed penetration southward. Here, in the current political posture of Hamath, one can witness perhaps the most enduring and valuable legacy of the previous military efforts in the west by Shalmaneser III. When the Assyrians besieged and conquered Damascus, Adad-nirari himself entered its palace to receive tribute,[76] whereupon the rulers of Tyre, Sidon, Samaria, Philistia, and Edom immediately surrendered payment in order to stave off further threats against their own borders.

Adad-nirari's control of Damascus loosened Aram's menacing grip on Samaria; consequently, scholars frequently identify him as the unnamed מוֹשִׁיעַ ("savior") of Israel alluded to in 2 Kgs 13:5.[77] As a result of their regained stability, both the capital and kingdom of Israel entered a new phase of development (Phase S.4). Launching no fewer than three campaigns in Transjordan, Samaria's King Joash reclaimed all the territory which his predecessors had lost to Hazaʾel and his son, Bir Hadad (2 Kgs 13:14-19, 22, 24-25). It seems clear now that the accounts of Israel's wars with the Aramaeans given in 1 Kgs 20-2 Kgs 8 actually describe events that occurred sometime during the Jehu Dynasty (most likely under King Joash), not during the earlier reigns of Omri and Ahab.[78] Damascus either gained the necessary strength or made the con-

---

[75] A question remains as to whether Manṣuate represents a city or a regional name (see Millard and Tadmor, *Iraq* 35 [1973], 63, n. 21, for a selected bibliography pertaining to each view). All occurrences of this name in Akkadian are preceded by either the determinative URU or KUR, except for the present Eponym Chronicle entry where no determinative is given. But this may not prove as unusual as first thought, given the similar omission of two URU determinatives in line 18 of the Rimah Stele (see Page, *Iraq* 30 [1968], 146). I note further that this name later served as a province name under Tiglath-pileser III, when provinces typically assumed the name of their most important city (compare the provinces of Dor, Megiddo, Gilead, Karnaim, Damascus, Hamath, and, later, Samerina; see *MBA* Nos. 148 and 151). Here, then, I take Manṣuate as a reference to a city located either in the southern end of the Beqaʿ Valley (roughly 50 miles northwest of Damascus) or in the northeastern end of that valley (approximately half the distance from Qarqar to Aleppo).

[76] *ARAB* I.740.

[77] Though I also accept Adad-nirari as the best alternative on the basis of an historical reading of the Nimrud, Sabaʾa, and Rimah inscriptions, other suggestions have included Jeroboam II (compare 2 Kgs 14:25-27), Elisha (2 Kgs 13:14-21), the Cappadocians, Hittites, and Haldians (E. Kraeling, *Aram and Israel*, 82-83), and Jehoash (Joash) himself (see Cody, *CBQ* 32 [1970], 337). To the usual list of possibilities, one might add Zakkur, king of Hamath, notwithstanding the relatively unsettled date of the Zakkur Stele (probably written sometime around 800 BCE).

[78] In fact, "there is virtually no information in the biblical sources about Damascus during the time of the Omride Dynasty" (W. Pitard, *Ancient Damascus: A Historical Study of the Syrian City-State from Earliest Times until its Fall to the Assyrian in 732 B.C.E.* [Winona Lake, IN: Eisenbrauns, 1987], 124; see pp. 114-25 for a critical review of all the texts and history relating to this matter). For a discussion of the relationship between prophecy and kingship in the Kingdom of Israel and of the place which these curious verses hold within this relationship, see F. M. Cross, *CMHE*, 222-29, particularly 226.

scious decision to pursue imperial expansion southward only under the rule of Haza'el in the second half of the ninth century BCE, perhaps in response to the now pro-Assyrian actions of Jehu and his successors (in this context, recall the Tel Dan Inscription; see n. 32 above with accompanying text). Thus Ahab's alliance with Hadad-ʿidr at Qarqar marks the end of Samaria's congenial relations with or, at times, dominance over Damascus. More than any other single factor, Israel's shift in attitude toward the rising power of Assyria seems to have prompted this enduring break with the Aramaean kingdom. Not all of Samaria's foreign contacts, however, remained so tenuous after the turmoil of the mid-ninth century. For example, while Jehu's actions may also have strained Israel's relations with Tyre early in this period, there is little evidence in the archaeology of Samaria that a total breakdown occurred in their trading (and thus treaty) agreements. Further, one learns from 2 Kgs 14:8-14 and 2 Chron 25:6-10, 13, 20-23 that, to the south, Israel also reestablished control over Judah during the early eighth-century reign of King Joash—the first to break the defenses of Jerusalem.

Most commentators have seen the prosperity of the early eighth century expressed in new phases of building activities in and around the royal quarter, and most have attributed these projects to Joash's successor, Jeroboam II.[79] They include in this recent construction a palace annex that resulted in a columned entrance court and, nearby, a large pool (33.5 ft. x 17 ft.) to enhance the beauty of the royal precinct. To underscore the luxury and opulence of Samaria's royal quarter, these writers point to the beautifully crafted ivory carvings and decorative inlays, which until now were thought to have emerged from a thick deposit of burned debris resulting from Assyria's ultimate conflagration against the city. The excavators understood an inscribed limestone stele discovered in the city to embody "the first proof that monumental stelai like those in Moab and N. Syria were erected also in Samaria,"[80] though only a single word of its broken text remains legible (the relative pronoun אֲשֶׁר). In a tightly circumscribed area around the capital city, and particularly between Samaria and the old center at Shechem,[81] great wealthy estates under the control of powerful land barons began to thrive, as attested by the Samaria Ostraca.[82]

---

[79] The assignment by both Albright and Wright of these renovations to Jeroboam II (and, I believe, already under Joash) rather than to Jehu, as Kenyon and Avigad concluded, receives support from the historical interpretation offered in this study, even if the archaeological record remains quite muddled.

[80] *SS III*, 33.

[81] See Y. Aharoni, *The Land of the Bible*, 369, Map 29; Y. Aharoni and M. Avi-Yonah, *The Macmillan Bible Atlas*, Revised Edition (New York: Macmillan, 1977), 87, Map. No. 137.

[82] These documents have sparked a great deal of debate. Points of contention surround details such as the texts' exact date, their meaning (shipping dockets or tax collection receipts), the extent and nature of Egyptian influence regarding the numerals that appear on them, the precise role of the so-called "l-men," the meaning of and relationship between -ל and אל in contexts with and without a governing verb, etc. (on the last issue, see Chapter V, n. 163 above). Also, the corpus of secondary literature pertaining to the ostraca is too extensive to cite here (see Aharoni, Cross, Kaufman, Maisler, Rainey, Reisner, Shea, and Yadin, in my bibliography; also Cross, *CMHE*, 222, n. 11). Briefly, I may say that Yadin (and more recently Shea) dates them to the later reigns of Menahem and Pekah, whereas Aharoni and Rainey prefer

It is regrettable, however, that the transition from the ninth to the eighth century BCE at Samaria, the succeeding affluence in Israel, and the events leading to Samaria's ultimate decline and loss of power and resources receive so little clarity from the archaeological work completed at the site. From my extensive review of the depositional history of the city, I have shown that the grand view of prosperity and expansion described above depends largely on the biblical record and draws very little from the excavations at the site (see the conclusions to each of the preceding chapters). While a series of well-built, royal rooms does appear on the north side of the summit compound in the expedition's plans for BP III and BP IV, for example, the excavators did not phase the surfaces or the pottery adequately enough to allow one to refine the history of the site based on the material recovered there. Kenyon's discussion of "Period IV-IVa" (which, in her chronology, should relate to the early eighth-century BCE prosperity) touched on neither the stratigraphy nor the ceramics of those rooms. Still she argued that the greatest break in ceramic tradition for the entire Israelite period falls between PP 3 and PP 4.[83] Despite the reputation for tight stratigraphic controls in their work, the Joint Expedition's historical reconstruction for this period remains tenuous at best. My analysis has, unfortunately, revealed that the extended period between the rule of the House of Omri and Building Period IV receives only sparse documentation in the final report. Finally, since there is no coherent destruction level across the entire site, as suggested by Kenyon, the nature of Israel's loss of control over the city needs serious review. Clearly, the archaeological context of the ivories proves much different from the general picture that most have drawn from the published reports. Without the use of texts (including the Hebrew Bible) and foreign parallels, such as the collection of ivories from Nimrud, the archaeological context of the Samaria ivories would allow very little detailed comment on their original historical context. Renewed excavations that use modern methods and that follow a regional research design which incorporates not only the eastern half of the summit area but also the slopes of the city and the surrounding valley areas would be essential to clarifying this and other historical periods.

Judging from the biblical record, though, it seems that Jeroboam II further exploited the easing of Aramaean pressure in 796 BCE and Joash's successes in Transjordan and Judah by reestablishing Israelite influence both toward the north and the south. In the former area, he apparently pushed out to לבוא חמת, or "to the entering/entrance of Hamath," where the Orontes Valley widens south of the Lebanese mountains (i.e., to the borders of the area controlled by Hamath, not to the very gates of the city itself).[84] In the south, traditions credit him with restoring the border of

---

an earlier date, probably during the reigns of Joash and Jeroboam II. Reisner's original suggestion to place them during Ahab's administration is now generally discarded.

[83] *SS I*, 105.

[84] For the minority view that "Lebo-Hamath" refers to an otherwise unknown "territory in Transjordania which once belonged to Israel" and not to the region controlled by the city-state of Hamath in the north, see S. Herrmann, *A History of Israel in Old Testament Times*, 229 and nn. 5-6.

Israel as far as the "Sea/Brook of the Arabah" (2 Kgs 14:25; compare Amos 6:14). While one must exercise a great deal of caution with this report, inasmuch as it may represent a mere extrapolation from the limits of the kingdom attributed to Solomon in 1 Kgs 5:1 and 8:65, it may reflect some privilege of expansion during the rule of Jeroboam II. Due to the general nature of the southern geographical reference, however, it is not certain whether this king merely hemmed in the Moabites or, in fact, conquered them. Yet the broadening of Samaria's jurisdiction during my Phase S.4 appears to have included significant sections of all the major trade routes. This development undoubtedly revitalized Samaria's close commercial contacts, if not an actual treaty relationship, with Tyre and other Phoenician city states.[85] Though prophetic traditions produced a sharply critical treatment of Samaria during this period (recall the pronouncements of Amos, Hosea, etc.), Samaria's political structure appears to have maintained its recently gained prominence for the duration of Jeroboam II's rule.

As for Assyria, the first half of the eighth century saw only the worsening of the weakened state into which the empire had lapsed (Phase A.3). Adad-nirari's few and often disputed victories in the west do not successfully disguise the general posture of retreat. After the Urarteans gained control over the entire mountainous north country, they drove to within 25 miles of Nineveh; anarchy again engulfed Babylonia; and the bubonic plague spread into Assyria proper.[86] Adad-nirari's goal of consolidating and expanding the empire proved unattainable at this time.

If the beautiful ivory carvings from Samaria belonged originally in the early eighth century BCE, then the archaeological record of Assyria's contemporary building activities sets these efforts in stark contrast to the situation in Samaria. Though the royal buildings in Assyria were erected on immense platforms requiring an enormous expenditure of labor, the buildings were blemished by a noticeable diminution of artwork. Ivory panels concealing the dull, mudbrick walls of Palace AB, for example, remained devoid of any sculptured relief and suggest severe economic decline.[87] In the ancient world, such degeneration in art likely reflects an erosion of the government's political or economic stability. As a further consequence of this weakening, unemployment in Assyria seems now to have risen sharply, so that sculptors and stonemasons abandoned their native land in search of work among the Aramaean and Neo-Hittite states of north Syria. This migration may help to account for noticeable similarities in certain art forms (e.g., ivory carving) between those areas and the Assyrian homeland.[88]

---

[85]If, in fact, some or all of the ivory artifacts stem originally from this period, one may note the Phoenician influences apparent in art from Samaria during this period (see T. C. Mitchell, "Israel and Judah from Jehu until the Period of Assyrian Domination [841-c.750 B.C.]," in *CAH*, Vol. III/1, Second Edition. J. Boardman et al., eds. [Cambridge: Cambridge University Press, 1982], 507).

[86]Olmstead, *History of Palestine and Syria*, 416.

[87]M. E. L. Mallowan, "The Excavations at Nimrud (Kalḫu), 1957," *Iraq* 20 [1958], 104.

[88]See Winter's observation that the North Syrian-style ivories generally precede the Phoenician works in

Aside from Adad-nirari's few accomplishments in the field, the failure to execute an aggressive, successful foreign policy during my Phases A.2 and A.3 left him unable to provide either the raw materials or the substance for scenes of great battle victories similar to those that lined the palace halls during previous and subsequent eras. Perhaps the most prominent phenomenon that occurred during this period of persistent internal instability consisted in the gradual usurping of power and wealth "by a few strong individuals both in the palace and in the provinces"[89] (in Israel, the Samaria Ostraca may reflect a similar situation). Because it gradually undermined monarchical authority, this development seemed particularly acute in the west. Nergal-Ereš, the Assyrian governor of Rasappa (803-775 BCE)[90] who played a vital role in the assault against Damascus in 797 BCE, either received or personally seized control over the entire area immediately west of Assyria following the 797 campaign[91] (i.e., between the Wadi Tharthar and the Khabur River, as far south as the middle Euphrates). Just west of this domain, the *tartanu* (or, "commander-in-chief") Šamšī-ilu, who served under every king from Adad-nirari III to Ashur-nirari V,[92] began inscribing his own monuments at Kar-Shalmaneser (in the Bit Adini province) in quasi-royal style[93] and thereby claimed virtual parity in Syria with the Assyrian king himself. At home in Calah/Nimrud, governor Bel-tarsi-iluma maintained his own archives and so increased in significance that he was the eponym entry for 797 BCE.[94]

Unable to organize checks against such encroachments upon their prerogatives, a succession of kings fell prey to this permanent state of internal, albeit sometimes subtle, rebellion. Excavations at Calah point to extensive domestic fighting there under

---

date and her discussion of Assyria's central role in terminating the North Syrian ivory-carving industry (largely through the deportation of the craftsmen there; I. Winter, "Phoenician and North Syrian Ivory Carving in Historical Context: Questions of Style and Distribution," *Iraq* 38 [1976], 18-22). The strong influence of North Syrian ivory carving traditions on those of the Assyrian homeland, then, arose through processes of both emigration and (sometimes forced) immigration.

[89] A. K. Grayson, "Assyria: Ashur-dan II to Ashur-nirari V (934-745 B.C.)," in *The Cambridge Ancient History*, Volume III/1, Second Edition. J. Boardman et al., eds. (Cambridge: Cambridge University Press, 1982), 276.

[90] Note the Eponym Chronicle entries for the years 803 and 775 (A. Millard, *The Eponyms of the Assyrian Empire*, 57-58).

[91] See the Saba'a Stele, ll. 23-25, in light of Tadmor's interpretation in *Iraq* 35 (1973), 147-48. In fact, Tadmor posits that Nergal-Ereš himself commissioned the erection of the Rimah, Saba'a, and the Sheikh Hammad Stelae.

[92] Grayson, *CAH*, Volume III/1, p. 278.

[93] Hallo, *Biblical Archaeologist Reader*, Vol. 2 (1975), 166. "Shamshi-ilu went so far as to omit the king's name altogether, inserting his own name, rank and official titles instead; and he inscribed an account of campaigns that he personally conducted against Urartu, embroidering the narrative with poetic hyperbole and his own bravado" (Page, *Iraq* 30 [1968], 151; see also Reade, "The Neo-Assyrian Court and Army: Evidence from the Sculptures," *Iraq* 34 [1972], 89). Compare also Page's comments regarding similar and repeated actions by Nergal-Ereš, who may himself have initiated this daring practice.

[94] A. Millard, *The Eponyms of the Assyrian Empire*, 57.

Shalmaneser IV,[95] and additional revolutions are known to have occurred in Aššur (763-762 BCE), Arrapkha (761-760 BCE), and again in Calah (746-745 BCE).[96] During this ebb of imperial strength, Shalmaneser IV's high chamberlain, Bēl-Ḫarrān-bēlu-uṣur, founded a city in the desert west of Calah, organized its separate cult, and personally exempted the city from certain taxes levied by his royal masters.[97] Between 772 and 754 BCE, only four military campaigns were directed against north Syria, but these seem to have been merely defensive actions taken by local governors or "glorified raids or border clashes," not cohesive efforts at further Assyrian expansion.[98] When Ashur-nirari V ascended the throne (755/4 BCE), he mustered his army and attempted to march once again against Arpad. The resulting treaty with Mati'-ilu of Arpad relates Ashur-nirari's heinous threats against the well-being of the city and its rulers should they fail to remain subservient to Assyria.[99] Almost as soon as the emperor departed, however, Mati'-ilu ignored what he apparently perceived as florid but hollow rhetoric and proceeded to establish treaty relations with Bar-Ga'yah of *Ktk*.[100]

Once again, the west had slipped free from the weakening grip of Assyria. Ultimately, when Sarduri I of Urartu claimed to have "conquered the land of Ashur-

---

[95]D. Oates, "Fort Shalmaneser—An Interim Report," *Iraq* 21 (1959), 126-27. I should note, however, that, judging from Goetze's overview of sites where Urartean inscriptions have been found, Shalmaneser IV may have realized some limited success in expanding Assyria's northern border against Argishti I (A. Goetze, *Kulturgeschichte Kleinasiens* [München: C. H. Beck'sche Verlagsbuchhandlung, 1957], 188-89).

[96]Olmstead speculates that the solar eclipse known to have occurred in the Near East in 763 BCE was construed by the Assyrians as a visible sign of the gods' anger against the current set of weak rulers and consequently initiated these revolts with the design to bring a new king to the throne (Olmstead, *History of Palestine and Syria*, 433; see also G. Smith, *Assyrian Discoveries* [New York: Scribner, Armstrong and Co., 1875], 11-12, who fixed a date of June 15, 763 BCE, for this event). The throne changed hands in 755/754 BCE with the accession of Ashur-Nirari V, but the desperate economic situation remained the same. This king, in turn, fell during another rebellion in 745, when the ruthless Tiglath-pileser III seized control of the government. As an aside, it is interesting to note the possible effects that this solar eclipse, together with the earthquake that occurred around this same time (destroying Hazor, Stratum VI, built by Jeroboam II; see A. Negev, *Archaeological Encyclopedia of the Holy Land* [Jerusalem: The Jerusalem Publishing House, 1972], 140-41; also W. G. Dever, "A Case-Study in Biblical Archaeology: The Earthquake of ca. 760 BCE," *Eretz-Israel* 23 [Biran Volume, 1992], 27*-35*), had on subsequent Hebrew writings, such as the language and imagery of Isaiah 5-11 (especially 8:21-9:2 and 10:33-11:1; see P. Machinist, "Assyria and Its Image in the First Isaiah," *JAOS* 103 [1983], 719-37) and the chronological reference point for the career of Amos (1:1).

[97]*ARAB* I.823ff. This figure, now listed as "palace herald," became the eponym entry for the year 741 BCE (see A. Millard, *The Eponyms of the Assyrian Empire*, 59).

[98]H. W. F. Saggs, *The Might That Was Assyria* (London: Sidgwich and Jackson, 1984), 81-82. As Kraeling observed early on, these feeble attempts served only to enhance Jeroboam II's ability to expand northward even late into his reign (E. Kraeling, *Aram and Israel*, 84).

[99]*ARAB* I.749ff.

[100]For quick reference to these treaties, see J. C. L. Gibson, *Textbook of Syrian Semitic Inscriptions*, Vol. 2, 20ff., and the bibliographies cited there. Note especially, N. Na'aman, "Looking for KTK," *WdO* 9 (1977-1978), 220-39.

nirari, king of Assyria"—construed as a probable reference to the territory near Carchemish[101]—the latter ruler was unable to respond. By 746/5 BCE, the eighth-century breakdown of Assyrian influence reached its nadir. At the core of the empire, bitter revolt claimed the life of Ashur-nirari V in 745 BCE at Calah and brought an end to the rule of the sitting royal dynasty. The possibility of restoration and even the preservation of the throne itself appeared to hang on the character and abilities of its next occupant.

The foregoing examination of the early Neo-Assyrian references to Samaria-Israel shows that as late as the mid-eighth century BCE this and other areas in Palestine, Phoenicia, and even southern Syria remained safely outside the sphere of Assyria's principal concern or influence; only Damascus felt the need to keep a wary eye eastward. The Zakkur Stele (n. 67), a Northwest Semitic source from around the turn of the century, confirms this situation. In this text, one sees all Arpad's north Syrian allies rallying together to battle the pro-Assyrian Hamath, whereas Damascus participates without the aid of a single state over which it had recently held sway in south Syria and Palestine. The archaeological record attests to the sparse evidence of any exchange in ceramic wares or motifs between the capitals at Nimrud and Samaria until well into the second half of the eighth century BCE[102]—a fact that further betrays the lack of direct contact between these two cities despite heavy Assyrian activity in the west throughout the preceding century. Finally, the distribution and nature of biblical notices regarding Assyrian engagements in Samaria or Israel help to corroborate this state of affairs. The earliest references include only a possible retrospective mention of Shalmaneser III (Hosea 10:14), who, as I have pointed out, likely spent most of his effort in Aramaean rather than Israelite territory, and a possible veiled recognition of Adad-nirari III (2 Kgs 13:5). The Bible's first explicit citation of a reigning Assyrian king does not occur until the rise of Tiglath-pileser III (2 Kgs 15:19).

Part B. The Western Campaigns and Inscriptions of Tiglath-pileser III

1) Introduction to Phases A.4 and S.5

With the death of Jeroboam II in 746 BCE, ominous cracks appeared in the façade of Israel's affluence and regional power base. The accession of Jeroboam's son, Zechariah (2 Kgs 15:8), initiated a period of malice and intrigue reminiscent of the pre-Omride years at Tirzah, and the closing thirty years of Israelite Samaria experienced a rapid succession of six kings, no fewer than three of whom seized power through political assassinations (Phase S.5; cf. Hosea 10:7 in light of the date formula in 1:1). After reigning only six months, Zechariah fell prey to the conspiring Shallum ben Jabesh (2

---

[101] H. W. F. Saggs, *The Might That Was Assyria*, 83.

[102] On the Samaria side, see my ceramic analyses presented throughout *AIS-I* and the present study. For a brief statement on the situation in Nimrud, see M. E. L. Mallowan, "Samaria and Calah Nimrud: Conjunctions in History and Archaeology," in *Archaeology in the Levant: Essays for Kathleen Kenyon*, 157.

Kgs 15:8, 10), who, in turn, was assassinated one month later by Menahem ben Gadi (2 Kgs 15:14, 17). During the latter's reign, one encounters not only the next set of Assyrian references to Samaria but also the first explicit historical notation in the Hebrew Bible regarding a specific Assyrian ruler (Appendix D; 2 Kgs 15:19, 29, notwithstanding Hosea 10:14 mentioned above).

In Assyria, the revolt of 746-745 BCE occasioned the ascension of Tiglath-pileser III,[103] who rapidly established himself as an astute administrator and shrewd military strategist. These two qualities enabled the new ruler to lead his country out of what had become a threatening military and economic decline[104] into an unparalleled era of internal economic stability through military expansion abroad. Inability to reconcile the constant tension between these two facets of executive rule had precipitated the undoing of previous regimes. The far-reaching ninth-century imperial expansion under Ashur-nasir-pal II and Shalmaneser III had placed heavy strains (economic and otherwise) on the Assyrian heartland as it attempted to fund and maintain a military capable of establishing and protecting the foreign trade networks that fed its local economy. But when the strain grew so great that open rebellion ensued, these outlying economic ties disintegrated before an army too engaged in domestic warfare to maintain the distant outposts.

To overcome this paradox, which had plagued Assyria for nearly a century, Tiglath-pileser III gave his country's foreign policy a complete overhaul. His *modus operandi* now implemented a principal strategic adjustment: future campaigns would proceed according to what one may call the "down-the-line approach," i.e., highly organized military activity designed to achieve a step-by-step reduction of autonomy in as many states as possible by staging each new aggression from the previous, nearby victory site rather than from the distant capital in Nimrud. In addition to his newly choreographed campaigns, Tiglath-pileser's field tactics now included total conquest, displacement of captive populations, and, ultimately, the organization of outlying provinces rather than mere tributary or vassal states. The stages in his improved strategy involved: 1) reduction of an area to vassalage by unleashing the full Assyrian military might on a specifically defined region; 2) subsequent (sometimes concurrent)

---

[103]The identity of Tiglath-pileser with Pul, as he is called in the biblical text, was established long ago by E. Schrader, *Die Keilinschriften und das Alte Testament* (Giessen, 1872), 124-28, with further elaboration on the point in idem, *Keilinschriften und Geschichtsforschung* (Giessen, 1878), 422-60. Notable also is an annalistic fragment recovered from Tyre that was later quoted by Josephus (*Ant.* IX, 28ff.), who referred to this monarch as πύλας (=Pul). Regarding the question of whether or not TP III was of royal extraction, see the discussion in A. S. Anspacher, *Tiglath-pileser III* (New York: AMS Press Inc., reprinted 1966), 15ff. I may note that in the reconstructed prologue to his annals (*STP*, Reliefs 46, 47, Pls. LXXII, LXXIII), this ruler traces his lineage to the nobility residing in the ancient quarter of Ashur known as Baltil. Interestingly, the Babylonian King List A offers comment on both of the foregoing issues in its reference to TP III (*Pulu*) and Shalmaneser V (*Ululai*) as comprising the dynasty of BAL.TIL (cf. Tadmor, "Introductory Remarks to a New Edition of the Annals of Tiglath-pileser III," in *Proceedings of the Israel Academy of Sciences and Humanities*, Vol. 2 [Jerusalem: I.A.S.H., 1968], 182-83).

[104]H. W. F. Saggs, "The Nimrud Letters, 1952 - Part V," *Iraq* 21 (1959), 176.

replacement of the vassal ruler by an *Assyrian-appointed* official (usually an Assyrian sympathizer discovered within the native royal dynasty); plus 3) removal of this appointee at the slightest hint of insubordination, as well as rescension of all political autonomy through the establishment of an official province under the rule of an *Assyrian* governor.[105] Inasmuch as no previous Assyrian king had attempted to apply such a stringent policy farther west than the Euphrates,[106] the new monarch's immediate interest in the broad sphere that included Israel became apparent.

With his blueprint well-defined, Tiglath-pileser III embarked upon two series of major western campaigns (743-738 and 734-732 BCE; see Phase A.4–Appendix D).[107] Though Samaria's hopes of an autonomous existence were intercepted during the second wave of Assyrian expansion, the events of the earlier campaigns carried for King Menahem a portent of the disaster to come.

2) The West: Phase I (743-738 BCE)

A synopsis of the first phase of Tiglath-pileser's western activity appears in Table 65 (p. 533). After stabilizing Assyria's domestic political scene and checking the menacing effects of the eastern side of Urartu's pincer-hold on the empire (745-744 BCE),[108] Tiglath-pileser looked immediately to the west. Cognizant of the need to

---

[105] See Donner, "The Separate States of Israel and Judah," in *Israelite and Judaean History*, John J. Hayes and J. Maxwell Miller, eds. (Philadelphia: Westminster, 1977), 419.

[106] J. D. Hawkins, "The Neo-Hittite States in Syria and Anatolia," in *CAH*, Vol. 3, Part 1, Second Edition, J. Boardman et al., eds. (Cambridge: Cambridge University Press, 1982), 409.

[107] I shall deal with each of these periods separately, while bearing in mind that an inerrant historical-chronological reconstruction of all the events remains impossible given the extensively damaged state of the slabs that contain the Annals of Tiglath-pileser III. These slabs suffered severe damage when Esarhaddon removed them from TP's palace in Calah/Nimrud and retrimmed many of the stones for use in his own palace in that same city. Some have speculated that this rare mutilation by an Assyrian king of previous annalistic records reflects a "particular hatred" for TP III by the Sargonid dynasty, which viewed him as a usurper and illegitimate heir to the throne (cf. S. Smith, "The Supremacy of Assyria," in *CAH*, Vol. 3, J. B. Bury et al., eds. [Cambridge: Cambridge University Press, 1925], 32-33). This possibility remains unproven, however (see n. 103 above). Note that one Assyrian king list refers to TP III as the son of his predecessor, Ashur-nirari V (I. J. Gelb, "Two Assyrian King Lists," *JNES* 13 [1954], 209-30), while elsewhere he is called the son of Adad-nirari III (*ARAB* I.822).

[108] Until recently, TP III's activities south of Assyria (*ARAB* I.762 = Rost, *KTP, Die Annalen*, ll. 1-7) have been misplaced at the head of the annals and ascribed to Tiglath-pileser's first *palû* in 745 BCE. The misplacement has prompted the modern notion that the Assyrian king abandoned his efforts against Babylon that year and did not return until 14 years later. Tadmor's recent work on a new edition of these annals has demonstrated convincingly that this brief section should be transferred to the year 731 BCE (Tadmor, "Introductory Remarks to a New Edition of the Annals of TP III," *Proceedings of the Israel Academy of Sciences and Humanities*, Vol. 2, No. 9 [Jerusalem, 1968], 181-82). Therefore, I have placed in hatching the data in Table 65 that allude to these events in the south (cf. Notes 187 and 192 below); the necessary correction also needs to be made when approaching other articles on this subject (e.g. Reade, "The Palace of Tiglath-pileser III," *Iraq* 30 [1968], 72). In further support of Tadmor's suggestion, I note that the Eponym Chronicle records that in 745 BCE Tiglath-pileser "marched to the territory between the rivers," a reference I take as the usual designation for the region of Bit Adini,

revitalize the work of his ninth-century predecessors in the west,[109] the new king set about the task of consolidating his political position in the western elbow of the Euphrates. Following historical precedent, he once again focused specifically on the area of Bit Adini. That these operations now proceeded according to a predetermined pace (my "down-the-line" approach), however, becomes quite apparent. Unlike Shalmaneser III who, in 858 BCE, shortsightedly rushed passed this point to meet his enemy further afield at Sam'al only to be forced back to Bit Adini to start anew, Tiglath-pileser understood the groundwork that had to precede any major effort in Syria proper or in Palestine.

Control of Bit Adini would also enable Tiglath-pileser to begin reversing the pernicious phenomenon that had developed to disastrous limits during the first half of the century, namely, the usurping of great power by local authorities in the west. The monuments of Šamšī-ilu, noted above as the ambitious ruler of the area between the Balikh and Euphrates Rivers, suffered deliberate defacement in Til Barsip and Arslan Tash by the invading Assyrians.[110] This act reflected the resolve of the new leader's policy toward such presumptuous officials, and the portentous deposing of Šamšī-ilu signaled a reviving central power. From the outset of Tiglath-pileser's reign, the name of Šamšī-ilu disappears from the Eponym Chronicle as *turtanu* of Bit Adini.[111] With the termination of his office complete, the district he once governed came unequivocally under Assyrian control.

Now that the new monarch enjoyed absolute rule over the west as far as the outer reaches of the Euphrates, he prepared to spring against the alliance that Sarduri III of Urartu had orchestrated in northern Syria. Though questions remain as to the exact configuration of this league, it seems certain that the leading indigenous power consisted once again in Arpad (note its frequent mention in the Eponym Lists).[112] In addition, the pro-Urartean and now familiar states of Melid, Gurgum, and Kummuh

---

between the Balikh and Euphrates Rivers. The reference may relate to the early deposition of Šamšī-ilu, which I discuss on p. 533 below (cf. Amos 1:5; nn. 5 above and 192 below). This sculptured relief also contains a depiction of the capture of *(āl) Ga-az-ru*, generally accepted as Gezer (cf. the later name for this city, *Gazara*, in I Macc 4:15; 9:52; 13:43-48; etc.). By transferring this relief to its appropriate chronological place, the fall of Gezer appears as it should among Tiglath-pileser's Syro-Palestinian wars rather than among the events of 745 BCE (cf. also Lance, "Gezer in the Land and in History," *BA* 30 [1967], 42-45). Interestingly, this is the first *specific* identification of an Israelite city on an Assyrian bas-relief (Albenda, *BASOR* 206 [1972], 46, n. 17).

[109] G. S. Goodspeed, *A History of the Babylonians and the Assyrians* (New York: Charles Scribner's Sons, 1902), 228.

[110] Hawkins, *CAH*, Vol. III, Part 1, 404; also, Malamat, *BASOR* 129 (1953), 25-26. (Cf. also my references to Page and Reade in n. 93 above.)

[111] Šamšī-ilu had appeared previously as the eponymate in the listings for 780, 770, and 752 BCE (see A. Millard, *The Eponyms of the Assyrian Empire*, 38, 40, 42, 58-59, and 120).

[112] See the location of the king and his army at the turn of the year in 743, 742, 741, and 740 BCE (A. Millard, *The Eponyms of the Assyrian Empire*, 59; *ARAB* II, 436).

Direction from Assyria	Source: Hebrew Bible ARAB I	Year	Region or City Targeted; Purpose of Campaign
SOUTH	§§ 762-65	745	"Aramaeans of Chaldea"; Babylonian cities to the Persian Gulf area
			Purpose: to preclude Babylonian interference in the recovery of lost territories east & west of Assyria (but see n. 108)
EAST	§§ 766-68	744	Entire area east of Assyria, south of Lake Urumia
			Purpose: to circumvent & control Urartean expansion by establishing a new Assyrian province on the empire's eastern border
WEST	Amos 1:5	late 744	Bit-Adini
			Purpose: to restore royal authority at Til Barsip/Harran; to develop a staging area from which to orchestrate later anti-Syrian/Urartean campaigns
	§ 769a	743	Melid, Gurgum, Kummuh
			Purpose: to halt Urartean penetration into Syria along the northern mountainous crescent
	§ 769a	743/42-740	Arpad (annexed in 740 BCE)
			Purpose: to extend royal authority west of the Euphrates & sytematically advance seaward (w/Arpad as a base for tribute collection)
NORTH	§§ 769 770-771 EC entry	739	Na'iri, lands of Ulluba (due north of Nimrud)
			Purpose: (main body of army returns east while TP III remains in Hatti-Land)

– – – – (broken line indicates conflated annalistic accounts for 739-738 BCE) – – – –

WEST	§§ 738	738	Tutammu of Unqi; Azriyau (of PN?); 19 districts of 770-771 Hamath (which had aligned themselves with Azriyau)
			Purpose: to quell unrest that had developed during a military absence from the West in 739 BCE by taking punitive measures against obstinate vassals
	§ 772 2 Kgs 15	738	**Summary of Tributary Western Kings** *(including Menahem of Samaria)*

(see Appendix D for primary editions & translations to accompany each ARAB § entry)

Tiglath-pileser III:
Summary and Context of Military Activities in the West (Phase I)

Table 65

participated. After establishing a base camp near Arpad in 743 BCE,[113] Tiglath-pileser utilized a somewhat surprising, yet highly systematic, approach. Rather than initially striking again at Arpad itself, which would have left a northern flank susceptible to Urartean countermeasures, he cunningly marched his troops upriver and into Kummuh, where "his unexpected arrival and sudden attack threw the army of Sarduri III into confusion."[114] One should, therefore, understand the import of the Eponym Chronicle entry for 743 BCE as "Urartu was defeated (in the land of) Arpad."[115] This ignominious routing of the Urarteans successfully squelched the agent that had instigated Assyrian defections throughout the northwest. Now the Assyrians could address the leader of the coalition, namely, Arpad. The subjection of this pivotal city would clear the approaches into central and southern Syria and bring the imperial army within striking distance of Israel.

Unhappily, none of the extant primary sources sheds light on the nature of the siege of Arpad, the particular alignment of the Syro-Hittite states during the conflict, or the eventual terms of settlement (see Appendix D re: Tiglath-pileser's IV and V *palûs*). Only by examining the listings in the Eponym Chronicle can one surmise another three-year siege against that city (742-740 BCE).[116] Despite the power it had continued to wield, however, Arpad succumbed in 740 BCE[117] and, after annexing the territory at

---

[113] The Eponym Chronicle entry *ina* āl*ar-pad-da* for 743 BCE is interesting; normally, the preposition appears as *ana* (see n. 117). The word *ina* carries a wide range of possible meanings, which include "from" and "through" as well as the obvious "in" (*CAD* I/J, 141b-142a). In my judgment, Assyria did not launch its direct assault against the city of Arpad until 742 BCE; the siege continued into 740 BCE. Accordingly, the Eponym Chronicle listing for 743 BCE may record the march of the imperial army "through" the *region* of Arpad (Bit Gusi) without its actually entering the capital city (contra A. S. Anspacher, *Tiglath-pileser III*, 36). Once in this area, the king and army established a base camp in order to stage their attack against the northern leader Sarduri III, who from the time of Tiglath-pileser's predecessor had persisted as a menace to Assyria's hold on Arpad (compare the treaties recorded in *ARAB* I.749ff. and the Sefire Inscriptions).

[114] G. S. Goodspeed, *A History of the Babylonians and the Assyrians*, 229.

[115] See Tadmor, *ITP*, 232, n.7, and 268.

[116] That Arpad continued to represent the major center of resistance in north Syria confirms the inadequacy of Ashur-nirari V's treaty threats against that city only a few years earlier (see p. 528 above); yet this treaty relationship, however weak, would have legitimized politically Tiglath-pileser's right as suzerain to enter the city/region of Arpad (see n. 113) and to orchestrate from its soil assaults farther afield.

[117] The Eponym Chronicle entries for 743-740 BCE appear as follows:
    743 BCE — *ina Arpadda*. A massacre took place in the land of Urartu.
    742 BCE — *ana Arpadda*.
    741 BCE — *ana Arpadda*. After three years it was conquered.
    740 BCE — *ana Arpadda*.
Interpreting the *ana Arpadda* of 741 BCE as "to Arpad" rather than the generally accepted "against Arpad" (i.e., with military force), Shea has argued that this city actually fell in 741 rather than in 740 BCE and assumes that the latter date represents a time when Tiglath-pileser III entered the city without combat and with the sole purpose of receiving tribute from nearby states. His translation of *ana* in this instance stands in stark contrast to the overwhelming number of occurrences in the Eponym Chronicle

large, Tiglath-pileser settled in to receive tribute from surrounding states, whose kings hastened to pay homage.[118] Most notable among the tributaries are Kummuh, Gurgum, and Carchemish, all former Urartean sympathizers, together with Tyre[119] and Que; even Damascus paid deference from southern Syria. In essence, all these states hereby submitted voluntarily to the first stage of Assyrian domination. Though lacunae exist within the Assyrian records for this event, none seems large enough to have included *Mi-ni-ḫi-im-mi (ālu) Sa-mi-ri-na-ai* ("Menahem the Samaritan") as a tribute bearer in 740 BCE.

Tiglath-pileser III was forced to send his army home to confront Ulluba in 739 BCE and to entrust its leadership to local governors in the north and east, while he himself remained in Syria.[120] In the absence of Tiglath-pileser's full military power, two wrinkles developed in Assyrian control over the western territories. First, Unqi's King Tutammu attempted to withhold tribute; second, the enigmatic Azriyau (from a

---

where this preposition clearly denotes military activity against a specified area. Moreover, the 740 BCE entry is identical to those of 742 and 741, years in which Assyrian military strikes inside the city of Arpad cannot be questioned. In 743 BCE, when the Assyrian army encamped near Arpad (or perhaps passed "through Arpad") but fought farther north against the Urarteans, the switch in prepositions to *ina* further accents, in this instance, the combative connotations of *ana*. Tadmor's suggestion that the second part of the 741 entry in fact belongs after the 742 listing and, as it stands, represents a scribal error seems as good a solution as any for the peculiar 741 BCE entry (see W. H. Shea, "Menahem and Tiglath-pileser III," *JNES* 37 [1978], 45, 47; and H. Tadmor, "Azriyau of Yaudi," in *Scripta Hierosolymitana* 8 [Jerusalem, 1961], 254).

[118] *ARAB* I.769. Tadmor, *ITP*, Annals 21 and 25; Iran Stele IIB:4' (see Appendix D, VI *palû*, for additional references).

[119] Luckenbill's reconstruction of "Hiram" as the name of Tyre's ruler at this time (740 BCE) came under question following the discovery in Iran of the only known stele belonging to Tiglath-pileser III. The text of this stele matches the tributary list of 738 BCE (Tadmor, *ITP*, 90-110; *ARAB* I.772) in most respects except that it contains 18 instead of 17 kings and it also names Tubail (equated by Katzenstein with Ethbaal II) as the king of Tyre rather than Hiram, who appears in the annals. Since the annalistic list, which includes Menahem of Samaria, appears in the chronologically arranged record immediately preceding the events of 737 BCE, it seems unlikely that either the stele or the annal text should be dated any earlier than 738 BCE (contra Thiele, who early on mistakenly suggested that the annalistic record was not arranged in chronological order). It seems possible that 738 may represent the year in which Hiram succeeded Tubail (the historical text ND 4301 + 4305, rev. lines 5-8, dating from 732 BCE, shows that Hiram followed Tubail rather than preceded him, as Levine intimates on p. 42 of his article) and that both rulers felt the effects of Assyria's aggressive foreign policy when they were forced to pay tribute to Tiglath-pileser III. Since it was likely carved before the annals were completed, the stele recorded the earlier Tyrian king while the annals name the later one. (See Levine, "Menahem and Tiglath-pileser III: A New Synchronism," *BASOR* 206 [1972], 40-42; Thiele, *Mysterious Number of the Hebrew Kings*, 90-98; Katzenstein, *The History of Tyre* [Jerusalem: The Shocken Institute for Jewish Research, 1973], 204-05).

[120] Tadmor, *ITP*, Ann. 19*:18-20 and Ann. 13*:1-3; *ARAB* I.771. Postgate has located Ulluba "at the foot of" or "behind" Mount Nal and connects it with "the wide plain in which the Lesser Khabur river flows." The sparsely attested Mount Nal, then, would belong to "the range of mountains separating this from the flat lands stretching south towards Nineveh." (See J. N. Postgate, "The Inscription of Tiglath-pileser III At Mila Mergi," *Sumer* 29 [1973], 57; compare the map in D. J. Wiseman, "A Fragmentary Inscription of Tiglath-pileser III from Nimrud," *Iraq* 18 [1956], Pl. XXI).

missing or unnamed country)[121] colluded with numerous districts in the region of Hamath in an apparent move to reject Assyrian dominion there.[122] After achieving some progress on the eastern front, Tiglath-pileser recalled the Assyrian army to Syria and personally directed it in order to deal effectively with these new rebels.[123] He successfully concluded this offensive in 738 BCE, and the gains led ultimately to an updated tribute list for that year. Both new provinces[124] and new tributaries,[125] (the latter group now including Menahem of Samaria) appear in this list.[126] So great was Tiglath-pileser's intolerance of the kind of insubordination he had squelched that he expeditiously advanced all areas participating in the insurgency from mere tributary to provincial status and bypassed completely the usual intermediate stage of vassalage.[127]

---

[121] See Tadmor, *ITP*, Ann. 19*:2. The problems that attend the identity of the enigmatic figure of Azriyau are multiple and complex. Most scholars have rejected any putative association of this name with Azariah/Uzziah of Judah in 2 Kgs 15 (e.g., N. Na'aman, "Sennacherib's 'Letter to God' on his Campaign to Judah," *BASOR* 214 [1974], 25-38; Shea, *JNES* 37 [1978], 46-47; Hawkins, *CAH*, Vol. III/1, Second Edition, 410-11; see also Oded, "The Phoenician Cities and the Assyrian Empire in the Time of Tiglath-pileser III," *ZDPV* 90 [1974], 42ff.). Na'aman's reassessment of fragment K6205, from which G. Smith originally drew the connection between Azriyau of Yaudi and Uzziah of Judah, has shown instead that this text refers to Sennacherib's 701 invasion of Judah, not to Tiglath-pileser's activities in 739-738 BCE. Though Tadmor, early on, held the Azriyau–Uzziah correlation as correct (*Scripta Hierosolymitana*, 8 [1961], 255ff; idem, "The Southern Border of Aram," *IEJ* 12 [1962], 121; see also the earlier articles in my bibliography by Haydn [1909] and Luckenbill [1925], plus Luckenbill's translation in *ARAB* I.770), he has now also abandoned the possibility of any such connection (see *ITP*, 273-74). The general context surrounding the mention of one Azriyau in the annals places him among the kings from various states in northern Syria and along the northern seacoast. Donner has suggested identifying Azriyau's base with a north Syrian state contiguous to and sometimes part of the city-state of Sam'al (Donner, in *Israelite and Judaean History*, 424). Multiple references in the Zinjirli Inscriptions (*KAI* 214; 215; commentary in Vol. 3, pp. 216ff.) and possibly in the Sefire material (*KAI* 222B:9) to a kingdom called Y'di combine with Tiglath-pileser III's inclusion of Y'di's king, Panammu (*ARAB* I.772), in the tribute list from 738 BCE to lend credence to this hypothesis. Elsewhere, Na'aman has suggested viewing this figure as a little known ruler of Hattarikka, or biblical Hadrach (Na'aman, *WdO* IX [1978], 229-39). In any event, the identity of this royal figure and his kingdom remains far from settled, and attempting a solution lies well beyond the scope of this study. I may add only that 2 Kgs 14:28 seems to have suffered too greatly in transmission to stand as incontestable proof of a contemporary Judahite expansion into the northern region of Hamath; reason requires a cautious approach, as in Cogan and Tadmor, *II Kings*, 160-64.

[122] *ARAB* I.770a; Tadmor's collation of extant primary sources has shown that the translations in *ARAB* I.770-772 relate to the activities of Tiglath-pileser up through his VIII *palû*, or 738 BCE. For fresh translations of the texts describing these events, see Tadmor, *ITP*, Annals 2, 3, 13*, 19*, 22, 26, 27, and the other publications cited there.

[123] *ARAB* I.770b; Tadmor, *ITP*, Ann. 19*:13-14.

[124] *ARAB* I.772a; Tadmor, *ITP*, Ann. 13*:1-10a.

[125] *ARAB* I.772b; Tadmor, *ITP*, Ann. 13*:10b-12.

[126] For a discussion of the political entities that appear on the tributary list for 738 BCE, see Tadmor, *ITP*, Supplementary Studies D and F, pp. 265-68 and 273-78, respectively.

[127] Na'aman (*BASOR* 214 [1974], 36-37) has concluded that we are left without any account of the Syrian wars during these years save the 738 BCE Eponym Chronicle entry, which states that "Kullani

In addition, the notice in Nimrud Letter XV (ND.2696)[128] that Tutammu and his courtiers were removed to Assyria and the annalistic record of the resettling of Hamathian citizens in Ulluba[129] both point to Tiglath-pileser's early use of population deportation as an effective strategy against the west (compare 2 Kgs 15:29, which reveals the extension of this practice to Samaria for the first time in 733-732 BCE). Though Israel had not offered tribute in 740 BCE, the gravity of Tiglath-pileser's actions in 738 BCE, even for regions that lay as far south as Israel, now prompted Samaria to pay homage to the Assyrian ruler.

Despite the complexity of the extant sources, I may reiterate the importance of the events they relate for the history of Samaria (and for all the still unconquered western regions). Besides marking the first major divergence from traditional goals of Assyrian foreign policy, these episodes underscore the abilities and intentions of the empire's new monarch and reveal a convergence, for the first time in over half a century, of Assyrian foreign policy and political developments in the Israelite capital at Samaria. I have noted that from the days of Shalmaneser III the outer rim of the Euphrates delineated the border of Assyria proper; Syrian states situated farther west remained mere vassals. With the imperial annexation of Arpad, however, Tiglath-pileser set in motion a plan for extending his kingdom as far as the Mediterranean seaboard. Toward this end, he now left no doubt regarding north and central Syria: they belonged to Assyria. The biblical account corroborates that Tiglath-pileser also made clear his interest in southern Syria and Palestine at this same time (2 Kgs 15).

---

was captured" (^{āl}kul-la-ni-i ka-$šid$). Today, many scholars (including Na'aman, Hawkins, and Tadmor) have accepted the phonetically uneasy association of Kullani with Kinalia/Kunalia, the capital of Unqi mentioned in the Assyrian annals, despite the obvious metathesis between the roots *KLN* and *KNL* (see the summary in Tadmor, *ITP*, 58-59, note on line 11'). If the association stands, the site would undoubtedly have rested somewhere near the coast, as Olmstead had it in his early *History of Assyria*, 188, and the accompanying map. Another option allows for an accurate, historical distinction between *KLN* and *KNL* wherein the former root (hence, Kullani) alone relates to the site of Calneh (Is 10:9 = כלנו; Am 6:2 = כלנה; both without the metathesis of ל and נ), which lay in the eastern section of North Syria, near the vicinity of Arpad-Aleppo, rather than along the coast (Gelb, "Calneh," *AJSL* 51 [1935], 189-91; see also *MBA*, Nos. 116, 146). In any event, Rawlinson's early attempt (in III R I, Pl. I) to read "Calneh" in Gen 10:10 and to link that name with Nippur in southern Mesopotamia became obsolete with Albright's corrected reading of the verse (W. F. Albright, "The End of Calneh in Shinar," *JNES* 3 [1944], 254-55; more recently, see R. L. Zettler, "Nippur," *OEANE* 4, 148).

[128] See Saggs, "The Nimrud Letters, 1952–Part II," *Iraq* 17 (1955), 133-34, 149. I believe that this letter reflects the events of 739-738 BCE, while Saggs dates it to 740 BCE. It is significant that Assyria's deportation system did not develop gradually but "began systematically and with great momentum in the reign of Tiglath-pileser III" (B. Oded, *Mass Deportations and Deportees in the Neo-Assyrian Empire* [Wiesbaden: Dr. Ludwig Reichert Verlag, 1979], 19). This fact receives vivid accentuation in Oded's tabulation (p. 20) of the number of deportations carried out by each of the Assyrian rulers in the ninth through the seventh centuries BCE (among whom are Shalmaneser III [8 deportations], Shamshi-Adad V [6], Adad-nirari III [1], Shalmaneser IV/Ashur-dan III/Ashur-nirari V [0!], and Tiglath-pileser III [37]).

[129] *ARAB* I.770; Tadmor, *ITP*, Ann. 19*:11-12. Since Ulluba did not fall until 739 BCE, Tiglath-pileser would not likely have organized and transferred deportees there until very late in that year or, more probably, in 738 BCE (*ITP*, 276).

By 738 BCE, the Assyrian administration of north-central Syria consisted in a quadripartite configuration of provinces. To the north, Arpad lay contiguous to Kullani while to the south Hattarikka adjoined Ṣimirra. The hypothetical line that arcs from Ṣimirra (roughly 70 km north of Byblos) through Hattarikka (about 25 km south of Aleppo)[130] and that continues on to the Euphrates south of Adini plots the southern hem of what I shall call the Assyrian "province line." This line corresponds almost exactly to the inner fringe of the well-known Fertile Crescent. But as Smith correctly noted long ago, "with Tiglath-pileser such an annexation generally entailed the sending of an expedition to overawe immediate neighbors."[131] His show of force, which signalled a revived expansionistic policy, sent shock waves that reverberated across southern Syria and Phoenicia, the whole of Palestine, through Transjordan, and into the Syro-Arabian plateau in what I may call a "pressure line." This atmosphere of tension would henceforth move well ahead of the Assyrian army and serve as a harbinger of imminent military campaigns and forthcoming provinces. As a result, each leader in the regions under pressure initiated a series of activities and local treaties designed to strengthen his own rule and ensure the preservation of his dynasty. The political divisions delineated in the 738 BCE tribute list[132] appear as follows:

Anatolian states:	Kaska (in the Taurus Mts., north of the Melid-Tabal route); Tabal, Tuhana (controlling the Cilician Gates); Tuna, Ishtunda, Hubishna (probably minor single cities)[133]
Syrian states:	(*north*) Kummuh, Melid, Gurgum, Que, Sam'al, Carchemish (*central*) Hamath (*south*) Aram-Damascus
Phoenician-Palestinian states:	Gubla (Byblos), Tyre, Samaria
Arabian states:	Zabibe, "Queen of Arabia"

Tiglath-pileser III:
Political Entities in the Tribute List from 738 BCE

Table 66

---

[130] On the location of Hattarikka, see J. Lewy, "The Old West Semitic Sun-God Hammu," *HUCA* 18 (1944), 449, n. 108. The summary inscription ND 4301 + 4305 (which dates no earlier than 733 BCE and arranges its political units *geographically*) seems to place this site somewhere between Arpad and Damascus (D. J. Wiseman, *Iraq* 18 [1956], 123, obv. ll. 24-27 and rev. ll. 1-2). The inscription has often been associated with biblical Hadrach (see Zech 9:1). Regarding the organization of provinces in 738 BCE, see K. Kessler, "Die Anzahl der assyrischen Provinzen des Jahres 738 v.Chr. in Nordsyrien," *WdO* 8 (1975-76), 49ff.

[131] S. Smith, *CAH*, Vol. III, First Edition (1925), 37.

[132] *ARAB* I.772; compare Rost, *KTP*, *Die Annalen*, ll. 150-57 (see also nn. 124-28 above).

[133] For discussions of the locations and the rulers of these cities, see Postgate, "Assyrian Texts and Fragments," *Iraq* 35 (1973), 27-32; also Hawkins, *CAH*, Vol. III/1, Second Edition, 412-13.

Though the impending danger inherent in having the imperial army so close at hand for four out of five years running may alone explain the capitulation in 738 BCE of so many rulers throughout the Mediterranean littoral, it appears that Menahem's motivation for following suit stemmed as much from internal affairs as from external ones. This Israelite king openly sought Tiglath-pileser's approval and protection for his administration (2 Kgs 15:19), and the biblical record makes it clear that the Assyrian ruler now crossed the borders of the Northern Kingdom to receive Menahem's overture in person (2 Kgs 15:19a, 20b).[134] It had become somewhat of a tradition, as I have shown, for newly installed Israelite kings to seek at least tacit approval from Assyria as a means of bolstering their own power base in Samaria. On the Assyrian side of the equation, however, the arrival of Tiglath-pileser differs markedly from the earlier operations of Shalmaneser III and Adad-nirari III, whose initial southern approaches centered primarily on Damascus and Transjordan and only secondarily, if at all, on Samaria-Israel.

Tiglath-pileser's approach to Samaria apparently coincided with a time of bitter civil strife in Israel. The near future would show the cunning ability of the Assyrian king to exploit such situations on the local scene. Since collaboration with Assyria and hostility toward Aram had characterized the administrative policies of every ruler in the previous Jehu Dynasty (841 to roughly 745 BCE), it seems unlikely that Menahem's exacting of the huge amount necessary to appease Tiglath-pileser gained acceptance through any recently popularized pro-Assyrian shift in the party platform (similar to Ahaz' soon-to-come shift in Jerusalem; Isaiah 7-11). Rather, the immediate threat of full-scale warfare between Israel and Assyria should Samaria fail to recognize Nimrud's new authority figure surely accounts for the willingness of Israel's aristocracy to gather the needed silver (2 Kgs 15:20). The decision reflects more of an interest in self-preservation and local autonomy than a vote of confidence for their own king.

The Assyrian "pressure line," then, seems to have functioned as intended. Knowledge of the nearby Assyrian network of fortresses extending into southern Syria, from Qadesh on the Orontes to Damascus (revealed in several letters from Nimrud),[135] compounded the apprehension felt by Israel's inhabitants. Therefore, despite Menahem's apparently rapid mustering of funds, one cannot presume the existence of a solid political base or constituent loyalty for him. Quite the contrary. The information in 2 Kgs 15:19b, together with the fact that the biblical record nowhere suggests that Menahem gathered any of the tribute from the temple or palace treasuries despite the great wealth reportedly amassed by Samaria's royal family during Phase S.4, betrays the king's lack of control over the governmental reins and resources.[136]

---

[134]This reading runs against Shea's opinion that the tribute was collected and forwarded to the Assyrian king in Arpad in 740 BCE (Shea, *JNES* 37 [1978], 49).

[135]B. Oded, "Two Assyrian References to the Town of Qadesh on the Orontes," *IEJ* 14 (1964), 272-73.

[136]In fact, Malamat has suggested that the Akkadian shift from *Bīt-Ḫumrî* as the official name for both Israel and its capital to the appellative "the Samaritan" [*(māt) Sa-me-ri-na-a-a*; see n. 65] when referring to Menahem may reflect the limited territory under Menahem's control, at least at the outset of his reign

In protecting their own shared interests by financing Israel's tribute in 738, the landed gentry also provided a degree of stability inside Israel proper for Menahem's administration. The principal threat to his rule now consisted in the ongoing political intrigues of various factions based across the Jordan River. Menahem's arch rival, Pekah son of Remaliahu, had sought to upset Samaria's political balance by sponsoring a revolt in Transjordan as early as 751 BCE during the reign of Jeroboam II.[137] Jeroboam's son and successor, Zechariah, soon fell prey to Shallum ben Jabesh who, in turn, ruled only one month prior to his assassination by Menahem ben Gadi. Judging from their names, both Shallum and Menahem may also have come from Transjordan and both rose to power in Samaria as usurpers. With Tiglath-pileser's official recognition of Menahem's kingship, however, the new Israelite ruler effectively neutralized Pekah, at least for the moment (Pekah later killed Menahem's son, Pekahiah, with the help of 50 *Gileadites*; 2 Kgs 15:25). Menahem's ploy had achieved a temporary political stability and set a precedent for Ahaz' reliance upon Assyrian succor in 733 BCE.

An examination of the historical backdrop to the first close encounter between Samaria's royal house and Tiglath-pileser III, then, reveals the more serious nature of its implications compared to previous Israelite-Assyrian confrontations. Though they had twice received tribute from Samaria prior to this time, the Assyrian kings had never before intervened directly in the internal political affairs of the Israelite capital. But by the very nature of his appeal to Tiglath-pileser, Menahem in essence moved his country to the intermediate stage of vassalage as he himself now stood directly accountable to the suzerain king. From other cuneiform as well as Northwest Semitic sources, one learns that this sort of intervention in the domestic politics of foreign regions became one of Tiglath-pileser's hallmarks by the time of his second western invasion in 734-732 BCE. For example, the ensuing years saw the Assyrians remove Uassurme from the throne in Tabal and replace him with Hulliu,[138] whose subsequent tribute to Tiglath-pileser included the familiar 1,000 talents of silver (compare 2 Kgs 15:19). The Panammua Inscriptions[139] attest to similar Assyrian control of its ruling house. But the

---

(Malamat, *BASOR* 204 [1971], 37-38). Due to external pressures (from Transjordan, for example), his rule may have extended over "a mere district around the city of Samaria." (Malamat makes this suggestion for both Joash and Menahem, each of whom receives this same appellative.) It may be, then, that as the wealth of the kingdom had become more or less decentralized (recall the landed gentry reflected in the Samaria Ostraca), so had the power over the kingdom. Menahem's tribute to Tiglath-pileser would emerge as a means by which to recentralize both the political and economic aspects of government.

[137] Yeivin, *WHJP*, Vol. IV/1 (1979), 167. Yeivin postulates that the earlier King Jehu was a Gileadite. If so, it appears that within 25 years of the establishment of Samaria, aspiring politicians and military figures from Transjordan sought to wield control over the new capital (note the coup in 841 BCE, which Jehu had also launched from Transjordan). Beginning with Jehu, the only confirmed non-Transjordanian king of Samaria was Hoshea, whom Tiglath-pileser III installed as a puppet king in 732 BCE. On the names Shallum and Menahem, see Cogan and Tadmor, *II Kings*, 170-71, 178-79 (see Conclusion below).

[138] Tadmor, *ITP*, 191, Summary Inscription 9:27-29; compare *ARAB* I.772 and 802; also ND 4301 + 4305, rev. ll. 27-28 (Wiseman, *Iraq* 18 [1956], 124).

[139] J. C. L. Gibson, *Textbook of Syrian Semitic Inscriptions, Volume 2: Aramaic Inscriptions*, 76-86.

Assyrian and biblical records of Menahem's tribute in 738 BCE suggest that Samaria constituted one of the earliest states to open its door voluntarily to this type of Assyrian manipulation. By the outset of Hoshea's reign in 732 BCE, as I shall show, Tiglath-pileser had wrested virtually all the power from Samaria's highest office; he himself installed the city's last king as a mere figurehead on behalf of Assyrian interests.

Due to a paucity of written sources, the events in both Israel and Judah between 738 and 734 BCE remain quite obscure. As I have demonstrated, the problematic nature of the archaeology of Samaria provides little clarity beyond the clues given in the historical sources. From the Eponym Chronicle, one learns that events unfolding closer to home, particularly in Media and Urartu, required the attention of the Assyrian army during these years.[140] However, Nimrud Letters XIV and XX, together with fragment ND.400 (line 9),[141] confirm that the empire's accomplishments in the west were closely monitored by Assyrian appointees (^{lú}šakin māti, "the governor of the land [of PN]"; see n. 210 below) seated both in Tyre, to oversee activities in south Syria and Palestine, and in Ṣimirra,[142] to manage events in north Syria. As Nimrud Letter XX further reveals, the series of substantially fortified towns mentioned above provided a stalwart defense for the so-called "province line" against any potential incursion from farther south.[143]

The last attempt by a ruling house to maintain dynastic succession in Samaria failed with the assassination of Menahem's son, Pekahiah, by the persistent Pekah (2 Kgs 15:25), who somehow had come to serve under the new young king in the official capacity of šālîš—apparently a high military (2 Sam 23:8; רֹאשׁ הַשָּׁלִשִׁי), political (2 Kgs 7:2), or judicial (2 Kgs 7:17) figure.[144] Finally, I should note before taking up Tiglath-pileser's second phase of western activity that Menahem's reign placed considerable economic strain on his constituency. As the royal treasury evaporated, Samaria felt pressured to search for ways to regain its lost stability and status. Here I may return to the sudden appearance of Zabibe of Arabia among the tributaries of 738 BCE; prior neo-Assyrian records contain no other mention of Arabs. But Zabibe had managed to

---

[140] A. Millard, *The Eponyms of the Assyrian Empire*, 59.

[141] For Nimrud Letters XIV and XX, see Saggs, *Iraq* 17 (1955), 131-32 (compare also p. 152) and 139-41 (compare pp. 153-54), respectively. Regarding ND.400, which relates the situation by 732 BCE, see D. J. Wiseman, "Two Historical Inscriptions from Nimrud," *Iraq* 13 (1951), 21-24.

[142] Early on, it was suggested that the governor in Ṣimirra who checked the events in northern Syria, where the Assyrians had fought so hard for over a century, was none other than Tiglath-pileser's son and crown prince, Shalmaneser V (Olmstead, *History of Assyria*, 188). Though, to my knowledge, there exists no firm textual basis for this position (note Borger's objections as cited by B. Oded in *ZDPV* 90 [1974], 43, n. 26), it seems (judging from their names, *Qurdi-assur-lamur*, etc.) that these overseers were Assyrians rather than people of local, West Semitic backgrounds (note also the appeal for additional *Assyrian* officials in lines 30-40 of Nimrud Letter XX).

[143] Nimrud Letter XX (lines 37ff.) shows that as many as 10 fortified towns lay in the province of Ṣupite alone (south of Hamath). (See again Saggs, *Iraq* 17 [1955], 140 [full citation in n. 127 above]).

[144] For more on the role of this official, see Thiele, "The Chronology of the Kings of Judah and Israel," *JNES* 3 (1944), 169, n. 85; also, Yeivin, *WHJP*, Vol. IV/1, 173, n. 185.

gain increased prominence through participation in the well-established desert trade network, which channeled its commodities either along the King's Highway to Damascus or through Palestine to Tyre.[145]

By seeking a more active role in this process with hopes of restabilizing its own local economy,[146] Samaria ironically became all the more valuable and vulnerable to Assyrian interests. As the tributary list of 738 BCE indicates, Tiglath-pileser III had already learned that by regulating the trade economies of the principal outlets (e.g., the Phoenician coastal cities) he in essence wielded substantial power over the entire inland network (e.g., the South Arabian production centers and Israelite depots and caravanserai) without undertaking lengthy and financially draining campaigns in those regions. During the latter half of his reign, economic manipulation through well-placed military intervention emerges fully as the cornerstone of his designs.

3) The West: Phase II (734-732 BCE)

Though the second phase of Tiglath-pileser's western exploits consumed half the time and concentrated on a smaller expanse of territory than did the first phase, no fewer problems of chronology attend the historiography of the campaigns involved. The events of this relatively brief period brought the Assyrian army into direct military confrontation with Samaria inside the kingdom of Israel for the first time, and the fate of the capital city was determined during the last two years of this cycle. The sequence of events leading to this turning point in the Samaria's history are as follows.

By 734 BCE, the political picture that emerges from Assyrian records and, even more pointedly, from the biblical literature regarding southern Syria and Palestine is one of escalating instability and intrigue on the local and regional levels. In Samaria, Menahem's act of paying tribute to Assyria in 738 BCE had by its very nature heightened the pro-Assyrian posture that the royal house there had assumed at least since the days of Jehu (841 BCE). Though the city, as a result, had averted a direct Assyrian attack in 738, its second-stage vassal relationship to Calah made stronger Assyrian management of its material resources inevitable.[147] An apparent realization of the economic impetus behind Assyria's aggressive foreign policy prompted certain local

---

[145] I. Eph'al, *The Ancient Arabs: Nomads on the Borders of the Fertile Crescent, Ninth-Fifth Centuries BC* (Jerusalem: Magnes Press—Hebrew University, 1982), 83. For notes pertaining to this well-established South Arabian trade network, see Aharoni, *The Land of the Bible*, 296; G. S. Van Beek, "Frankincense and Myrrh in Ancient South Arabia," *JAOS* 78 (1958), 141ff.; idem, "Frankincense and Myrrh," *BA* 23 (1960), 70ff.; note also 1 Kgs 9:26-10:22 (// 2 Chron 8:17-9:21). The origin of similar networks extends back at least as far as the setting of Judges 5 (see J. D. Schloen, "Caravans, Kenites, and *Casus belli*: Enmity and Alliance in the Song of Deborah," *CBQ* 55 [1993], 18-38).

[146] For historical antecedents of this goal, see the reference to Schloen in the previous note.

[147] Samaria's situation, namely of not suffering direct attack by Tiglath-pileser but falling increasingly under Assyrian control, parallels closely that of Sidon, Tyre, and other Phoenician coastal cities (see the comments of G. Herm, *The Phoenicians: The Purple Empire of the Ancient World* [London: Victor Gollancz, 1975], 146-47).

officials in Ramoth-Gilead, a major trade depot on the King's Highway that had fallen alternately under the jurisdiction of Samaria and Damascus, to renew their attempts to seize control of the throne in Samaria. Toward this end, Remaliahu's son, Pekah, had remained quite active in governmental affairs. Ultimately, he and his band of Gileadites realized their goal through a coup against Menahem's son and successor, Pekahiah (736-734 BCE; 2 Kgs 15:25), who undoubtedly had continued his father's pro-Assyrian policy with faithful annual tribute. For nearly two decades, Jerusalem and Damascus had supported, at least indirectly, such attacks on Samaria from Transjordan.[148]

As Jeroboam II attempted to guide his country through a period of prosperity, Jerusalem's long-reigning Uzziah (= Azariah) concurrently (mid-780s to mid-740s) expanded Judah's hold on Philistia and Edom in a parallel attempt to exploit the transit trade as it moved along the southern branches of both the King's Highway and Mediterranean coastal route on its way toward the Northern Kingdom. The diversion that Ramoth-Gilead created for Samaria allowed Uzziah to pursue such goals without fear of an Israelite assault similar to the one his father had faced at Beth-Shemesh (2 Kgs 14:8-14). That Damascus had continued to suffer significant territorial losses to Samaria under Jeroboam II (2 Kgs 14:25) provided ample reason for its rulers to support Transjordanian attacks against their old rival to the south. By 735/734 BCE, when Pekah succeeded in gaining control of Samaria's highest office, the Judahite throne passed into the hands of the *pro*-Assyrian Ahaz (Is 7-8). Almost immediately, an anti-Assyrian coalition sprang up between Samaria and Damascus against Jerusalem.[149] Either to seal officially their new alliance or to express gratitude for the recent Damascene support of his political aspirations, Pekah appears now to have ceded possession of Golan and Bashan (including the important trade center of Ramoth-Gilead) to control by Damascus.[150] The Assyrian scribe, at least, understood these borderlands[151] as the property of Damascus at the point of annexation in 733 BCE, and no evidence suggests

---

[148]Pekah's attempted coup of 751 BCE bears witness to the longevity of the Transjordanian political factions opposing the established order in Samaria. That Judah not only supported but encouraged the constant Gileadite pressure on the Northern Kingdom receives corroboration in the writings of the historians from the south. When addressing the length of Pekah's administration, they apparently considered his reign to have begun with his rebellion in 751 BCE even though he, in fact, did not ascend the throne in Samaria until 18 years later in 734 BCE (compare 2 Kgs 15:27; 16:1; 18:1, 9, 10). The difficult chronologies of these and other verses have been worked out in detail by, among others, Thiele, *JNES* 3 (1944), 164ff. and Yeivin, *WHJP*, Vol. IV/1, 167ff.

[149]The epilogue to the reign of Jotham (2 Kgs 15:36-38) may well indicate that the Syro-Ephraimite pressure against Jerusalem had already begun under Ahaz's predecessor.

[150]Compare the parallel texts of Nimrud inscriptions III R 10,2 (ll. 6-8), ND 4301 + 4305 (rev., ll. 3-4), and K 2649 (rev., ll. 3-4). For the full texts and translations of these excerpts, see H. Tadmor, "The Southern Border of Aram," *IEJ* 12 (1962), 114-18. See Tadmor, *ITP*, 180-91, Summary Inscription 9. For the revised collation (by P. Hulin) behind Tadmor's new edition, see R. Borger and H. Tadmor, "Zwei Beiträge zur alttestamentlichen Wissenschaft aufgrund der Inschriften Tiglatpilesers III," *ZAW* 94 (1984), 244-51.

[151]On the southern borders of Aram, see H. Tadmor, *IEJ* 12 (1962), 114-122.

an Aramaean recovery of this territory through actual wars waged against Samaria in the troubled interim between 735 and 733 BCE.

Most historians have remained content to view the Syro-Ephraimite antagonism toward Judah as the sole precipitating factor behind the Assyrian penetration into Palestine in 734 BCE.[152] The new link between Pekah of Samaria and the anti-Assyrian Rezin of Damascus certainly marks a brief departure from the longstanding Assyrian connections held by Samaria since the days of Jehu. But this position seems too shortsighted in its consideration of the following variables: (1) the mainly economic impetus underlying Assyrian imperial expansion; (2) Tiglath-pileser's calculated sequencing of each advance with the campaigns conducted before and after it. In this light, I suggest rather that the 734 BCE Assyrian appearance in Philistia itself brought to a boil the simmering discord between Samaria/Damascus on the one hand and Jerusalem on the other. By 738 BCE, Tiglath-pileser had subdued the entire northern seaboard from Que and the Gulf of Alexandretta through the regions of Unqi and northern Phoenicia and as far as Ṣimirra, Byblos, and Sidon/Tyre. These successes naturally led him to understand the advantages that control over all maritime activity conducted between Syria and the only other non-Egyptian center of sea trade, Philistia, would yield. Monopolizing the Levantine sea lanes would create a virtual blanket of dominion over the whole of Near Eastern economy, including the lucrative contacts lying around the entire Mediterranean rim to the west. Tiglath-pileser had devised a grand master plan that aimed at controlling the sea trade entering and leaving Phoenicia, goods moving to and from Egypt, and a monopoly of the caravan routes leading to the highland cultures and, deeper still, into the Arabian peninsula.[153]

As a consequence, Damascus, though representative of the core of Aramaean resistance in the hitherto unannexed but heavily fortified southern half of Syria, proved less vital on economic grounds than did Philistia. By this time, the western-oriented *port cities* served as gateways to the outside world and, from past experience in his dealings with north Phoenicia, this new-breed imperialist understood the principle whereby control of the terminus of any trade route effected control of the entire route. Firm occupation of Philistia would also yield absolute command over the major land routes in and out of the Delta region. Such control would, in turn, afford Assyria a greater chance of isolating Egypt from Syria-Palestine. An immediate result of the campaign against Philistia in 734 BCE included the establishment of a trading emporium in Gaza after Hanunu (Hanno), the city's Neo-Philistine leader, fled to seek asylum in Egypt.[154] This commercial center provided Assyria with the opportunity to

---

[152] E.g., Hallo, *Biblical Archaeology Reader*, Vol. 2, 172-73; Aharoni, *The Land of the Bible*, 371; Donner in *Israelite and Judaean History*, 426-27.

[153] See B. Becking, *The Fall of Samaria: An Historical and Archaeological Summary*. Studies in the History of the Ancient Near East, Volume II (Leiden: E. J. Brill, 1992), 9.

[154] See ND 4301 + 4305, rev., ll. 13'-16' in D. J. Wiseman, *Iraq* 18 (1956), 121, 124, 126 and, more recently, Tadmor, *ITP*, 189, Summary Inscription 9, and Excursus 4 on pp. 222-25.

exact tribute from various Arabian tribes in exchange for the right to use this new commercial center.[155] To oversee all transactions here, Tiglath-pileser appointed Idibi'ilu as the official "Gatekeeper facing Egypt"[156] and then proceeded southward to erect a commemorative stele near the Egyptian border, at the Brook of Egypt.[157]

Reasoning would indicate, then, that Tiglath-pileser never intended to attack Israel or Damascus prior to subduing Philistia.[158] Such an approach harmonizes well with the strategy he had executed earlier against the states of northern Syria. There, as I have discussed, his plan called first for a blockade of his prime target, Arpad, to prevent this city from receiving aid coming in from the larger kingdom of Urartu. In 734 BCE, Assyria's goal of gaining control over southern Syria (Damascus) after initially subjecting Philistia emerges as the mirror image of previous maneuvers against the northern states. Just as no follow-up operations were launched against Urartu from Kummuh, no Egyptian campaigns were planned immediately after the initial encounters in Philistia.[159] Of additional importance here is Nimrud Letter ND.2715,[160] which mentions certain trade restrictions leveled against Phoenician ports, including an embargo on all timber shipments to Philistia and Egypt. This text suggests that, at the time of its writing, Philistia remained independent of direct Assyrian rule but that the Empire had already incorporated the region in its overall design. The dating of this correspondence to the period just following the organization of Syria into provinces in 738

---

[155] See Rost, *KTP, Die Annalen*, 36-39, ll. 218-225; compare Tadmor, *ITP*, 200-203, Summary Inscription 13, ll. 3'-16'; also Rost, *KTP, Die Thontafelinschrift*, 70-71, rev., ll. 3'-5'; *Kleinere Inschriften* I, 82-83, ll. 27'-33'.

[156] Tadmor, *ITP*, 202-03, Summary Inscription 13, l. 16'.

[157] ND 400, l. 18'. See D. J. Wiseman, *Iraq* 13 (1951), 23, Pl. XI; Tadmor, *ITP*, 178-79, Summary Inscription 8, l. 18'. Both Wiseman and Na'aman read the initial element in the phrase *āl Na-hal Mu-ṣur* as a determinative and the remaining two words as the proper name of the city (Naḥal-muṣur = "Brook/River of Egypt") in which the Assyrians placed the monument (see N. Na'aman, "The Brook of Egypt and Assyrian Policy on the Border of Egypt," *TA* 6 [1979], 68-90; idem, "The Shihor of Egypt and Shur that is before Egypt," *TA* 7 [1980], 105).

[158] Both historical texts and recent field exploration have revealed the strong connections between the southern Palestinian and Phoenician coastal cities. Even as late as the fifth and fourth centuries BCE, much of the wealth of Palestine seems to have been concentrated in the coastal region. In this same vein, Katzenstein has noted the special position that the Phoenician and Palestinian coasts assumed in the foreign policy of Tiglath-pileser III (see *The History of Tyre*, 206). Note also that Tiglath-pileser's desire to control the Philistine ports and trade routes may have been foreshadowed by the interest that Damascus itself had shown in this area (see nn. 34-35).

[159] Contra Donner in *Israelite and Judaean History*, 425. The goals set by Tiglath-pileser seemed never to overextend the resources available to him. Note that Esarhaddon's later attempt to conquer both Lower and Upper Egypt finally exceeded the limits of natural control from Calah/Nimrud—Nineveh. Subsequently (and consequently, at least in part), "Assyria's decline and fall came with surprising rapidity" (Aharoni and Avi-Yonah, *MBA*, 101). Though for somewhat different reasons, I note Samaria's rapid decline and fall (see my Introduction, Phase S.5) as yet another parallel between the histories of that city and of Neo-Assyria generally.

[160] H. W. F. Saggs, "The Nimrud Letters, 1952–Part II," *Iraq* 17 (1955), 150; for the text of the letter, see pp. 127-28 and Pl. XXX.

BCE also serves to identify Philistia as the *predetermined* initial target for the next season of western campaigns.

Other factors converge to corroborate my view regarding the lack of any hiatus between Assyrian activities in Philistia in 734 BCE and those against Samaria–Damascus in 733-732 BCE. Assyria did not require such a delay to organize and mobilize its military against the Aramaean and Israelite kingdoms. First, to posit Calah/Nimrud as the inauguration point for an early 733 BCE assault against Damascus introduces serious logistical problems, which commentators often overlook. Briefly stated, an army composed of as many divisions fully outfitted for large scale war and equipped with siege machinery as one sees depicted in the Assyrian reliefs[161] required three to four months' marching time to complete an uninterrupted journey from its own capital to Palestine.[162] Any encounter of insurrection in established provinces, or the conquering of new cities along the way, of course increased the travel time proportionately. The generally accepted view that the Assyrians battled in Philistia during the summer of 734 BCE and then reappeared in Damascus from Calah/Nimrud early on in 733 essentially implies a nonstop march home and back again in too short a period. This wrinkle becomes even more noticeable when one considers that those who espouse this view also attempt to place Tiglath-pileser's subjection, reorganization, and annexation of northern Israel and Gilead into the provinces of *Magiddu* (Megiddo)[163] and *Gal'adi* (Gilead), respectively, prior to the main encroachment against Damascus.[164] As I have already shown, the Assyrians subdued Megiddo at this time but did not rebuild and utilize the city as a political and economic hub in the region

---

[161] For a look at the composition of the Assyrian army, see H. W. F. Saggs, "Assyrian Warfare in the Sargonid Period," *Iraq* 25 (1963), 145-54; also J. Reade, "The Neo-Assyrian Court and Army: Evidence from the Sculptures," *Iraq* 34 (1972), 87-111; idem, *Assyrian Sculpture* (Cambridge: Harvard University Press, 1999).

[162] The marching pace of the Assyrian army appears to have ranged from 15-30 km per day, depending on conditions. See: W. Mayer, "Sargons Feldzug gegen Urartu – 714 v. Chr.: Eine militärhistorische Würdigung," *MDOG* 112 (1980), 13-33; H. Kühne, "Zur Rekonstruktion der Feldzüge Adad-nīrāi II., Tukulti-Ninurta II. und Aššurnaṣirpal II. im Ḫābūr-Gebiet," *Baghdader Mitteilungen* 11 (1980), 44-70; H. F. Russell, "Shalmaneser's Campaign to Urarṭu in 856 B.C. and the Historical Geography of Eastern Anatolia according to the Assyrian Sources," *Anatolian Studies* 34 (1984), 171-201; K. Lawson Younger, Jr., "The Fall of Samaria in Light of Recent Research," *CBQ* 61 (1999), 472. Compare also Saggs' early comments on the advance of the Assyrian army, where he doubles the daily distance to 30 miles ("Assyrian Warfare in the Sargonid Period," *Iraq* 25 [1963], 147 and n. 25).

[163] The heavy amount of debris found in the destruction level at Megiddo attributed to Tiglath-pileser (Stratum IVA) attests to the fact that these operations were themselves extensive ones that required considerable time and energy.

[164] Early on, J. Begrich recognized these logistical difficulties and rightly concluded that the campaigns against Damascus and Samaria in 733-732 BCE must have originated from the Philistine coastal plain. But he erred in accepting the Philistia campaign of 734 BCE as the initial step taken by Tiglath-pileser in response to the supplication of Ahaz, which he assumed was delivered to the Assyrian capital (Begrich, "Der syrisch-ephraimitische Krieg und seine weltpolitischen Zusammenhange," *ZDMG* 83 [1929], 213-37; cf. H. Donner's discussion of this work in *Israelite and Judaean History*, 428).

until sometime later—at least not before the fall of Samaria (see the discussion and relevant notes pertaining to the Megiddo IVA-III-II transitions on pp. 242-52 above). The immediate preoccupation with Damascus and Samaria following Assyria's initial subjection of Megiddo surely helps to account for this hiatus.

Second, Wiseman's suggestion that the fragmented account of an unidentified campaign at the end of inscription ND.400 (lines 22-25) contains a reference to the Sagur River region (mentioned by Shalmaneser III as lying in the Til Barsip-Pitru districts)[165] and that this portion of the tablet delineates Tiglath-pileser's *northern* approach to Damascus in 733 BCE has not withstood close scrutiny. The Assyrians had no need to isolate Damascus from the potential Urartean aid that Wiseman posits inasmuch as their sound defeat of the Urarteans years before had sent the latter fleeing into the Ararat Mountains. Moreover, tablet ND.400 is of the summary (vs. annalistic) variety, i.e., it is arranged in geographical rather than in chronological order. The sudden reference, therefore, to a location in the extreme northeast of Syria would not coincide with the subject matter of the present text, which centers on the approach to and conquest of Philistia and the subsequent erection of a victory stele at "the Brook of Egypt." Further, the text reveals that the area in question had not humbled itself before Tiglath-pileser's predecessors in Assyria (ND 400, l. 20'). Excavations at Til Barsip, on the other hand, have supported the fact that "this citadel remained under Assyrian control throughout the period of weakness"[166] that preceded the current administration. Besides these historical observations, Tadmor has now corrected Wiseman's early reading of ND 400, l. 22', from *al(?) ru-at-ti (māt) mu-'-na-a-a*, a purported geographical reference to a city in the same northern area as the Sagur River, to ⌈m⌉(!)*Si-ru-at-ti* ᵏᵘʳ*Mu-'u-na-a+a*, i.e., as a specific mention of Siruatu the Meʿunite chieftain. This notation, therefore, represents the first extra-biblical reference to Meʿunim/Maon, i.e., the Meʿunites (2 Chron 26:7; no parallel in Kings) who dwelt in northern Sinai along the trade routes running from Edom and South Arabia through the region of Kadesh-Barnea to the coastal road at el-ʿArish.[167]

---

[165] See *ARAB* I.603.

[166] W. W. Hallo, *Biblical Archaeology Reader*, Vol. 2, 163; see also F. Thureau-Dangin and M. Dunand, *Til Barsip*. Paris: Librairie Orientaliste Paul Geuthner (1936), 141ff.

[167] Tadmor, "Philistia Under Assyrian Rule," *BA* 29 (1966), 89; idem, *ITP*, 178-79, Summary Inscription 8, l. 22' and accompanying notes. Biblical notices concerning the Menuites include 2 Chron 26:6ff., which describes the actions of Judah's Uzziah against certain peoples in the area of northern Sinai, near the Wadi el-ʿArish. Just as Wiseman's reference to the Sagurri River as located near Til Barsip seems somewhat awkward in the present geographically arranged list, so too does the RSV's translation of הָעַמּוֹנִים (2 Chron 26:8) as Ammonites. Ammon seems out of keeping with the geographical progression of the surrounding verses. Moreover, the expression commonly used by the Chronicler to refer to the Ammonites is בְּנֵי עַמּוֹן (e.g., 2 Chron 27:5). Therefore, I follow the LXX reading, wherein both הַמְּעוּנִים (v. 7) and הָעַמּוֹנִים (v. 8) are rendered οἱ Μιναῖοι, or "Menʿuites" (compare LXX in 2 Chron 20:21). For another rebuttal of Wiseman's mishandling of ND.400, see Ehpʿal, *The Ancient Arabs*, 68-69, nn. 212-213, and 91, n. 286.

Third, a new collation of the fragmentary inscriptions from Nimrud[168] demonstrates that the geographical referents listed there proceed from Mount Lebanon to Abel-Beth-Maacah to (Ramoth-)Gilead, which abutted the borders of *Beth Omri* (= Israel).[169] Because the first translation of these tablets to appear (III R 10,2)[170] spoke of these sites in relation to [*xxxxxxx*]*li rap-šu a-na si-[ḫir-ti-šá]* (". . . the widespread [land of . . .]li, in its entirety"), early commentators connected them with the text of 2 Kgs 15:29 and understood them as a delineation of Tiglath-pileser's approach to Damascus and Galilee from the north, i.e., from a starting point at Calah/Nimrud. The subsequent discovery of tablet ND 4301 + 4305 (rev., l. 3'), however, prompted the restoration of [*xxxxxxx*]*li rap-šu* as *[(māt) bīt-(m)ḫa-za-'i-i-]li*, and this resulted in a reference to "Beth Hazaʾel" (i.e., Aram) rather than to Naphtali in Israel (see *[Nap-ta-]li* in Rost, *KTP, Kleinere Inschriften* I, 78-79, l. 7).

Tadmor demonstrated further that these texts reflect the southern border of the Aramaean empire in 734-733 BCE and do not indicate the approach route of the Assyrian army. Inasmuch as the notations in 2 Kings 15:29 include cities that unquestionably lay outside the realm of Aram-Damascus (e.g., Janoah, Kedesh, Hazor), one cannot assert that this verse offers yet another record of the Aramaean-Israelite border parallel to that of the aforementioned Assyrian sources. But the nature of this biblical passage, in fact, resembles the Assyrian documents described as *summary writings*, i.e., their toponyms appear in a geographical arrangement rather than a chronological one. This verse, then, merely summarizes Tiglath-pileser's victories in Gilead and Galilee without shedding any light on the actual route of his approach to these areas.[171] In fact, Is 10:28-32 (compare Mic 1:10-15) may instead reflect an approach directly from Philistia and may reveal that the army passed through both Judah, the petitioning vassal, and Israel en route to Damascus (but see further below).

---

[168] III R 10,2 (ll. 6-8); ND 4301 + 4305 (rev., ll. 3-4); and K 2649 (rev., ll. 3-4).

[169] See ND 4301 + 4305, rev., l. 4', Tadmor, *IEJ* 12 (1962), 114ff.; also now Tadmor, *ITP*, 186-87, Summary Inscription 9, ll. 3'-4'.

[170] For the earliest translation, see G. Smith, *AD*, 284, Twelfth fragment, l. 7.

[171] Contra Aharoni and Avi-Yonah, *MBA*, No. 147. If my assertion regarding the "summary" nature of this biblical list holds true, then one must reconsider current interpretations of other similar lists in terms of their potential contribution to the reconstruction of history (e.g., Is 10:28-32 and Mic 1:10-15; if both relate to Tiglath-pileser III, I may ask whether one is summary and the other annalistic in nature). Machinist has broken new ground in exploring the possible points of direct contact between Akkadian and Hebrew literature that resulted in similarities in form, imagery, style, and the like (P. Machinist, "Assyria and Its Image in the First Isaiah," *JAOS* 103 [1983], 719-37). In fact, he argues that the evidence of Isaiah provides one with important insights into the "official Assyrian perspective" in light of the apparent access that the biblical writer had to Assyrian propaganda literature (p. 737). I would hold the opposite as also true, i.e., the Assyrians knew of and actually studied Hebrew prophetic oracles and the like (they apparently knew of Hezekiah's attempted reforms and renewed centralization of the Israelite cult [2 Kgs 18:22], prior prophetic warnings that Yhwh would deliver Israel into the hands of a foreign power [v. 25], as well as how to converse in the southern Hebrew dialect spoken in Judah [v. 26]). Significantly, one period during which the proposed contact seems especially great both "in volume and variety of reference" begins with the reign of Tiglath-pileser III (p. 721). Though this all begs fur-

Finally, I turn to the Eponym Chronicle listing for the year 734 BCE as yet another indication that the Assyrian army remained in the Philistia at the turn of the year. Millard and Tadmor have demonstrated that the Chronicle entries "recording the military engagements fall clearly into two categories: *general*, i.e., names of lands and peoples (the Medes, the land of Na'iri, the land of the Itū'a-tribe, etc.); or *specific*, i.e., the cities, cf. Hazazi, Ba'ali, Dēri."[172] As I noted above for the records of Adad-nirari III, entries of a specific nature give the actual location of the army's encampment at the turn of the year. These records likely came from field scribes who travelled with the army. Court scribes, on the other hand, recorded a general listing at the outset of a march against a certain country and then allowed it to stand as that year's entry until incoming field reports designated the specific location of the king and his troops. In the event that such a report was delayed or not dispatched, the "general entry" then became the official one for the year in question.[173] The Chronicle provides the following notations for 734-732 BCE:[174]

734 BCE *a-na* ᵐᵃᵗ*pi-liš-ta*	to/against Philistia	(general)
733 BCE *a-na* ᵐᵃᵗ*di-maš-qa*	to/against the land of Damascus	(specific)
732 BCE *a-na* ᵐᵃᵗ*di-maš-qa*	to/against the land of Damascus	(specific)

Eponym Chronicle Entries: 734-732 BCE

Table 67

One may reasonably conclude, therefore, that neither Tiglath-pileser nor any of his messengers returned to Calah/Nimrud at the close of 734 BCE, for, if they had, the victories at Ashkelon and Gaza or those along the Egyptian border would likely have constituted a "specific entry" for the year 734 BCE as well.

I need not multiply arguments corroborating the staging of Assyria's attack on Samaria–Damascus from the southern coastal plain of Palestine.[175] Modern attempts to

---

ther investigation, I may state with confidence that Is 7:18-20 does not provide proof for Tiglath-pileser's having approached Damascus from Calah/Nimrud.

[172] A. R. Millard and H. Tadmor, *Iraq* 35 (1973), 62 (italics added).

[173] Millard and Tadmor *Iraq* 35 (1973), 62, n. 19 (though the last sentence of the main text of that page implies that a specific victory could, in fact, have transpired in the field without changing the "general" listing once it was made).

[174] A. Millard, *The Eponyms of the Assyrian Empire*, 44-45, 59.

[175] For example, Wiseman infers that the . . . *ana bīt ka-a-ri ša (māt) aššur*ᵏⁱ . . . ("to Assyria's warehouse" — ND 4301 + 4305, rev., l. 16′) implies that the Assyrian army transported the spoils of war to these "merchant quarters" in their native land, from which they were gradually "infiltrated into normal economic life of the Assyrian capital" (D. J. Wiseman, *Iraq* 18 [1956], 129). But this remains open to serious question, and more recent translators have not taken it so (e.g., Tadmor, *ITP*, 188-89,

establish a hiatus between the campaigns against Philistia and Gilead–Galilee remain without textual validation. Rather, efforts to find such validation stem from a lack of awareness that Assyria's campaign against Philistia actually precipitated the Syro-Ephraimite War. Echoing the traditional view, Donner wrote that "one can scarcely believe that the coalition would have taken action at a time when the Assyrians were already in the area."[176] Only Tiglath-pileser's absence from the region, according to this understanding, could have provided for a logical inauguration of that war. Yet Oded observed that, if Tiglath-pileser had in fact withdrawn to Calah following his coastal activity, then "it is not clear why [Damascus and Samaria] should weaken themselves by a prolonged war against Jerusalem, thereby exposing their northern flank to the Assyrian forces."[177] Thus the dynamics between the Syro-Ephraimite conflict and the current foreign policy of Assyria, as well as the bearing which their relationship had on the history of Samaria, have gone unclarified.

It seems reasonable, however, to conclude that word had reached the officials in Calah, probably through the Assyrian watchman stationed in Tyre (see p. 541 above), regarding the local–regional instabilities and political reconfigurations unfolding in Aram–Palestine during the 730s BCE. Tiglath-pileser decided, in 734 BCE, to capitalize on this unstable situation by leading his army through the southernmost of the Syrian provinces (Ḫatarikka and Ṣimirra) and, after establishing Assyrian officials in several "cities of the upper sea,"[178] by continuing south to Palestine via the Sidonian coast and proceeding straightway to Philistia's two main harbor cities, Ashkelon and Gaza. The rapidity of the advance found Ashkelon's King Mitinti unable to organize a substantial defense; for him, no option remained but to surrender tribute willingly (K 3751, rev., l. 11).[179] Hanunu of Gaza suffered even greater ignominy. According to

---

Summary Inscription 9, l. 16). The Assyrians surely maintained store cities in the territories they subdued. Oded believes that the *kārum* mentioned in this line refers either to Qadesh on the Orontes or to a settlement on the Phoenician coast (Oded, *ZDPV* 90 [1974], 47, n. 50). I suggest that it might just as easily refer to Gaza itself (note Epheʿal's discussion of the broader meaning of *kārum* in Akkadian as "quay, harbor" and of Sargon II's use of the term in reference to a place in southern Philistia or on the Philistine-Egyptian border in *The Ancient Arabs*, 101ff., especially nn. 339-42, the latter of which seems to place the *kārum* in Gaza; on the meaning of "quay, harbor," see the Hurrian and Ugaritic cognates of *ka-a-ru* in a recent treatment of the polyglot vocabularies from Ugarit, J. Huehnergard, *Ugaritic Vocabulary in Syllabic Transcription*. Harvard Semitic Studies 33. Atlanta, GA: Scholars Press [1987], 83, No. 183.5). Yeivin has postulated that the חוצות (literally "streets" = RSV's "bazaars") that Damascene rulers established in Samaria (and vice versa) as early as the Omride dynasty (1 Kgs 20:34) may represent storage areas outside the city's main marketplace (Yeivin, *WHJP*, Vol. IV/1, 138). In short, it seems the Neo-Assyrian term *kārum* refers to storage or merchant quarters located in the foreign or provincial cities much as it had earlier in the Old Assyrian trading colonies in Cappadocia.

[176]H. Donner, "The Separate States of Israel and Judah," in *Israelite and Judaean History*, 429.

[177]Oded, "The Historical Background of the Syro-Ephraimite War Reconsidered," *CBQ* 34 (1972), 153.

[178]*ARAB* I.815; Tadmor, *ITP*, 138-39, Summary Inscription 4, ll. 4'-5'.

[179]For a structural analysis of this text and further comments on King Mitinti, see Epheʿal, *The Ancient Arabs*, 28-29, 84.

ND.400 (l. 14),[180] he deserted his troops and citizens sometime during the course of the sacking and fled out of fear to Egypt. As I have noted above, Tiglath-pileser both underscored his subjection of Philistia and sent a message to Egypt by erecting stelae and images of himself in the palace at Gaza and at the more southerly Brook of Egypt[181] ("the River of Egypt"—ND.400 line 19; if the two passages cited are to be equated, it would seem that Gaza itself was called Naḥal-muṣur and constituted the southernmost coastal city of Palestine at this time). In sum, the Assyrians were now entrenched deep into Palestine; cities along the very border of Bīt-Ḥumrî, "the Kingdom (lit., House[hold]) of Omri," had already succumbed to Assyrian rule.[182]

The baleful presence of the imperial army throughout the southern coastal region spawned immediate effects on the politics of Samaria. Tiglath-pileser's quickly established supremacy through Philistia to the border of Egypt activated the usual shock waves of fear, which rolled out over all surrounding territories. For Damascus and Samaria, this situation constituted a reverberation of the pressure they felt previously during Assyria's activities in north Syria in 738 BCE. Now, however, the portentous state of affairs prompted their opposition rather than submission via the offering of tribute, as King Menahem had chosen. The fragmentary tablet K 3751 (Appendix D) outlines the states that proffered tribute in 734 BCE.[183] Though the kings of Arvad, Ammon, Moab, Ashkelon, Judah, Edom, Gaza, and of two additional states lost in lacunae acquiesced at this time (rev., ll. 10′-12′), neither Samaria nor Damascus followed suit.[184] Instead, Pekah and Rezin responded to this loss of coastal lands by escalating the hostilities they had initiated earlier against Jerusalem. Their original strategy involved a relentless taunting of Judah aimed at coercing the Southern Kingdom into alignment with the anti-Assyrian policies of surrounding states by eroding public support for King Ahaz and installing their own puppet king (undoubtedly the *Transjordanian* Tabeel of Is 7:6)[185] on the Jerusalemite throne. But the unexpected and frighteningly swift accomplishments of Tiglath-pileser in Philistia cast an entirely

---

[180] D. J. Wiseman, *Iraq* 13 (1951), 23; Tadmor, *ITP*, 176-77, Summary Inscription 8, ll. 14′-18′.

[181] On the spoliation of divine images by the Neo-Assyrian army, see M. Cogan, *Imperialism and Religion: Assyria, Judah and Israel in the Eighth and Seventh Centuries B.C.E.* Society of Biblical Literature Monograph Series 19 (Missoula: Scholars Press, 1974), 40-41. Note also his interesting comments on the possible parallel practice by the Judahite army in 2 Chron 25:14-16 (pp. 116-17).

[182] *ARAB* I.815; Tadmor, *ITP*, 136-43, Summary Inscription 4.

[183] See rev., ll. 7-13; compare Rost, *KTP*, 70-73, *Die Thontafelinschrift*, rev. 7′-12′; *ARAB* I.801.

[184] See Ephʿal, *The Ancient Arabs*, 29, n. 76. Though the final names are missing from each of the lines in rev. 7-9, it would seem that the cities of Damascus and Samaria are, in fact, listed there. But a comparative analysis of this and other Neo-Assyrian tribute lists has shown that these lines were simply copied from the list of vassal kings in 738 BCE (see Rost, *KTP*, ll. 150-54; *ARAB* I.772). My claim that Samaria and Damascus chose not to render tribute in 734 BCE therefore seems a reasonable one.

[185] W. F. Albright, "The Son of Tabeel (Isaiah 7:6)," *BASOR* 140 (1955), 34-35; J. B. Curtis, "East is East . . . ," *JBL* 80 (1961), 362. I may reiterate here that Pekah himself had seized power in Samaria by leading a garrison of Gileadites against Pekahiah (2 Kgs 15:25).

defensive aura around their tactics. Their coastal and southern flanks demanded immediate securing as they found themselves suddenly exposed and vulnerable with states in both regions now under tribute to Assyria. Insufficient time remained in which to engage their southern neighbor in a war of attrition; Ahaz himself would now have to serve as pawn and his kingdom as buffer against the eventual Assyrian move north again out of Philistia. In this light, the catalyst behind the overt Syro-Ephraimite aggression against Judah even while Assyria's army remained securely garrisoned in Philistia becomes clearer. The joint conspirators were leaders of now intimidated and isolated regimes forced to take certain risks to secure their cities. For Pekah, the desire to maintain Samaria's autonomy at all costs is particularly understandable in light of the extended period of time during which he had sought the throne with no success (at least 751-734 BCE).

But the risks taken by Damascus and Samaria soon proved miscalculated. The Syro-Ephraimite plot paled when juxtaposed to other coalitions previously shattered by Tiglath-pileser (e.g., Arpad, Yaudi, Hamath), and this alliance would not hold the Assyrian army at bay on its haunches in Philistia. When Ahaz dispatched to Philistia his plea for Assyrian protection,[186] he simultaneously deepened the schism between the prophetic and royal offices in Jerusalem (note Is 7ff.) and provided the Assyrian ruler with a timely reason to take full advantage of the political instability now rampant in the hinterland, an area of secondary importance to the coastal cities. If 2 Kgs 15:29-30 presents a geographical rather than a chronological arrangement of cities, it remains difficult to ascertain whether this passage alludes to a preliminary isolation of Rezin from his allies or to various regional operations subsequent to the main siege against Damascus.[187] At any rate, the events that ensued witnessed the reduction of Israel to a mere rump state restricted to the central Ephraimite hill country and the deportation of many of the kingdom's citizens to Assyria.[188]

The Assyrians ultimately transformed the bulk of the northern kingdom into two provinces, Du'ru (= Dor) and Magiddu (= Megiddo). After a forty-five day siege

---

[186] I cannot agree with Eph'al in his intimation that ND 4301 + 4305 (rev., ll. 20'-21') contains references, albeit indirect, to the plea from King Ahaz for Assyrian assistance. Though it may be true that Ahaz had not previously "humbled himself" before Tiglath-pileser's predecessors, (ND 4301 + 4305, rev., l. 23'; ND.400, l. 20'), there is no evidence that he journeyed to Calah in his supplication for Assyrian protection (ND 4301 + 4305, rev., l. 25'). But more important, ND.400 (l. 21') makes it clear that the ruler mentioned here paid obeisance to the Assyrian king in full accord with the advice of his prophets. The biblical data (Is 7:4, 16-17; 8:4-8a; etc.) show that these references cannot refer to King Ahaz; however, they apparently do relate to a territory near Judah, as the texts' geographical ordering of the place names would imply.

[187] For the former view, see Aharoni, *The Land of the Bible*, 371-72; for the latter view, see Tadmor, *BA* 29 (1966), 89. At some point, these regional operations involved a kind of whiplash effect when the Assyrian army once again struck the coastal area because of the panic there following the defeat of Damascus (*ARAB* I.779). It is during this follow-up assault on Philistia that the conquest of Gezer seems to fit best (see n. 108 above).

[188] See the reference below to Tadmor, *ITP*, 202-03, Summary Inscription 13, ll. 17'-18'.

against the walls of Damascus,[189] the city suffered utter devastation. Curiously, the deportation of masses of people to foreign territories and the execution of the leader, Raḍyān (Rezin),[190] receives mention only in the biblical record (2 Kgs 16:9), not in any of the extant annalistic or summary/display inscriptions from Assyria. The boast of Tiglath-pileser in his annals that "591 cities of the 16 districts of Aram I destroyed like mounds of ruins after the Deluge"[191] bears a striking resemblance to the language and imagery of Is 8:5-8.[192] Though the nature and number of administrative units established at this time in the sprawling kingdom of Aram-Damascus remain enigmatic, most scholars posit that Transjordan saw a partitioning of the area into three districts, with Hauran and Qarnini contiguous to Gal'adi. Others maintain instead the existence of a single province, Gal'adi (= Gilead), with its capital at the familiar commercial center of Ramoth-Gilead.[193] In any event, it seems clear that the Assyrian network of provinces now subsumed the area across the Jordan that Pekah had restored to Raḍyān's authority. Samaria lay completely enveloped by an Assyrian political and military network[194] that wielded control over all the area's major trade routes, depots, and outlets. As for the Southern Kingdom, Ahaz himself had already implemented a suzerain-vassal relationship between Judah and Assyria by invoking the latter's protective custody; accordingly, Tiglath-pileser exacted heavy tribute from Jerusalem (2 Chron 28:20-21). In short, the entire Mediterranean littoral and hinterland had succumbed to absolute Assyrian control within the astonishingly brief span of three years.

Stripped of all the cities and territories that undergirded Samaria's economic and political stability, Pekah found himself completely vulnerable to the conspiracy of Hoshea, who, according to 2 Kgs 15:30, assassinated the reigning Israelite king.

---

[189] Tadmor, *ITP*, 78-79, Ann. 23, ll. 10'-12', and the commentary on line 11'. Compare Rost, *KTP, Die Annalen*, 34-35, l. 204. The reference is not to 45 select Assyrian soldiers, as in *ARAB* I.776-778.

[190] The spelling of this name appears as רקין in Old Aramaic sources and as רצין ("Rezin") in the Hebrew Bible. For a succinct discussion of the etymology of the name and the final years of autonomy in Damascus, see W. T. Pitard, *Ancient Damascus*, 179-89.

[191] *ARAB* I.777; Tadmor, *ITP*, 78-81, Ann. 23, l. 16'-17'.

[192] This reshuffling of Aram-Damascus into a group of Assyrian provinces effected the termination of Aramaean autonomy in both north and south Syria and prompted a shift in the focus of Aramaean history to areas in Babylon (compare Malamat, "The Aramaeans," in *Peoples of Old Testament Times*, 139 [for full bibliographic data, see n. 10 above; for the Israelite–Assyrian similarity in language, see the reference to P. Machinist in n. 171]).

[193] For the former view, see B. Oded, "Observations on Methods of Assyrian Rule in Transjordan after the Palestinian Campaign of Tiglath-pileser III," *JNES* 29 (1970), 178; Malamat in *People of Old Testament Times*, 146; Aharoni, *The Land of the Bible*, 375, map 31. For the latter view, see Cogan, *Imperialism and Religion*, 99, n. 10. Oded's study underscores our limited knowledge of this topic since he must repeatedly make statements such as, "on the basis of our present knowledge of Assyrian military-political-social organization in other conquered territories, it seems reasonable to conclude/to conjecture a similar situation in Transjordan." For Gal'adi (with Weippert) vs. Gal'aza, see Tadmor, *ITP*, 186, l. 3.

[194] ND 4301 + 4305, rev., ll. 3'-4'; Tadmor, *ITP*, 186-87, Summary Inscription 9, ll. 3'-4'; see *ARAB* I.815.

Records from Assyria[195] supplement our knowledge of this transition by crediting Tiglath-pileser himself with the actual installation of Hoshea following the demise of Pekah, both of which events resulted either from a popular revolt within Israel or from an act by the Assyrian forces (*Pa-qa-ḫa šarru-⌐šú¬-⌐nu¬ [. . .]-du-⌐x_1¬-⌐x_2¬-ma ^{m}A-úsi-'i [a-na šarru-ti i]-na muḫḫi-šú-nu áš-kun*[196] = "Peqah, their king [I/they killed] and I installed Hoshea [as king] over them."[197] Recalling Tiglath-pileser's dealings with the royal houses of northern Syria (see above), there is no sound reason to distrust the claim that he established Hoshea on the throne at Samaria. The Assyrians enacted a similar strategy even at other Palestinian cities, such as Ashkelon, where they replaced King Mitinti with Rukibtu,[198] and Gaza, where they somewhat surprisingly granted the fugitive Hanunu immunity from punishment upon his return from Egypt in exchange for faithful service to Assyria. In addition, Tiglath-pileser is known to have utilized loyal tribal groups as subordinate instruments of political control in these areas (see the references to the tribespeople of Idibi'ilu in the area south of Philistia).[199]

The biblical and Assyrian statements regarding the backdrop to this ataxic transference of power from Pekah to Hoshea in 732 BCE, then, emerge as complementary accounts that betray the appreciable degree of in-house political dissension lingering in Samaria, a situation that the Assyrians' severe truncation of the kingdom as a whole had surely exacerbated. The city's pro- and anti-Assyrian factions had never stood at greater odds; each blamed the other for the current series of devastating events. Thus, aware of the longstanding threat to Samaria from Ramoth-Gilead and the danger that the anti-Assyrian followers of Pekah represented for any future stability in the Israelite capital (see n. 137), Tiglath-pileser's design aimed at breaking Samaria's chain of Transjordanian rulers by approving (if not orchestrating) Hoshea's rise to office. This

---

[195]Tadmor, *ITP*, 140-41, Summary Inscription 4, ll. 17'-18'; *ARAB* I.816 = Rost, *KTP, Kleinere Inschriften*, 80-81, ll. 17'-18' = III R 10,2 ~ G. Smith, *AD*, 285, Twelfth fragment; also ND 4301 + 4305, rev., l. 10'.

[196]Transliteration and translation following Tadmor, *ITP*, Summary Inscription 4, ll. 17'-18'. Note especially the statement that "the possible restoration of the verb describing Peqah's fate is still a riddle." Rost's early reading used the third person masculine *plural* preterite verbal form of *skp* ("to thrust, push away; to depose") and thereby implied that Tiglath-pileser himself did not kill Pekah. But Tadmor's edition of the text now holds that "Rost's *is-ki-pu-ma* is entirely conjectural" (see the commentary on l. 17').

[197]Note that *CAD* S, 71a, takes the subject of *iskipu* to be "the Judeans" rather than the people of Samaria or of the Northern Kingdom at large. This is a very interesting position, especially in light of my following discussion, which outlines briefly Jerusalem's vested interests in the events transpiring between Samaria and Transjordan and the vacillatory relationship between Pekah in particular and the Jerusalemite rulers. But one must ultimately leave it in the realm of speculation in the absence of supporting textual evidence and in the light of my treatment of 2 Kgs 16:6 (n. 204), a verse which reveals that Jerusalem was apparently busied with problems of rebellion on its southern borders during the time of Pekah's deposition as king of Israel.

[198]*ARAB* I.779.

[199]See I. Ephʿal, *The Ancient Arabs*, 93 and Appendix A-1, pp. 215-16; compare *ARAB* I.779, 800, 819; *ANET* 282.

development certainly could not have transpired at this point against Assyrian wishes.

The Chronicler's account of the tribal genealogies sheds additional light on Tiglath-pileser's (here called *Tiglath-pilneser*) decisive handling of the Transjordanian regions by recording that he exiled the descendants of Reuben, Gad, and Manasseh to areas along the Khabur River north of the central Euphrates (1 Chron 5:26). In subsequent waves of deportation, the Assyrians resettled Israelites from *Samaria* in these same cities and regions (2 Kgs 17:6). This intentional mixture of the bitterly antagonistic Trans- and Cis-jordanian constituencies undoubtedly served to dissuade any potential collusion of these displaced factions that might have resulted in an undesired concentration of local power. (See my discussion above of Šamšī-ilu and the nature of Tiglath-pileser's war against him in the adjacent Balikh River region.)[200] When relating the exile of the Transjordanian peoples, the Chronicler makes the further point that the deportees included the political leaders (נְשִׂיאִים) who had established themselves in Transjordan (1 Chron 5:6). The transit trade that moved steadily along the King's Highway had strengthened these local eastern economies so that, by the close of Jeroboam II's reign in Samaria (note 1 Chron 5:17), these "princes" of the larger trans-river centers (e.g., Ramoth-Gilead) were able to maintain their own standing armies (1 Chron 5:18). This fact casts considerable light on the economic backdrop to the political and military pressure that Samaria constantly felt from factions across the Jordan.[201]

On a similar level, the strong ties that the Southern Kingdom claimed with its eastern neighbors (1 Chron 5:1-2) just prior to the Syro-Ephraimite War and Tiglath-pileser's incorporation of Transjordan into the Assyrian provincial system merit a brief exploration. An awareness of these relationships corroborates further my view that Jerusalem tacitly supported repeated coup attempts staged against Samaria from areas across the river. One should recall that Judah established its control over Edom by the time of Kings Amaziah (2 Kgs 14:7 // 2 Chron 25:11-12) and Uzziah (2 Kgs 14:22 // 2 Chron 26:2). At some point, probably subsequent to the death of Jeroboam II in Samaria (ca. 746/745 BCE), the Southern Kingdom appears also to have succeeded in reversing Israel's gains in the more northerly Ammonite territory (2 Kgs 14:25). Although I have issued strong warning against the widely held view that 2 Chron 26:8 contains an explicit mention of this expansion of Judah's jurisdiction over *Ammon* (see

---

[200]Note that the Assyrians employed a similar tactic of mixing various ethnic groups in Samaria itself as witnessed in the resettling of both Hamathians and Babylonians there (2 Kgs 17:24). In addition, South Arabian tribes were moved to Samaria, undoubtedly to facilitate the handling of commodities from their native lands as they passed through the city on their way to coastal ports (see the Nimrud Prism, Fragment D, column iv, 37-41, published by J. C. Gadd, "Inscribed Prisms of Sargon II from Nimrud," *Iraq* 16 [1954], 179).

[201]To help place in historical perspective a view of the political, economic, and religious influence (and sometimes pressure) that those living on the west side of the River Jordan felt from entities to the east (in this case, particularly around the area associated with the tribe of Reuben), see F. M. Cross, "Reuben, the Firstborn of Jacob: Sacral Traditions and Early Israelite History," pp. 53-70 in *From Epic to Canon: History and Literature in Ancient Israel* (Baltimore: The Johns Hopkins University Press, 1998).

n. 167), I may safely state that Jerusalemite hegemony in that region seems relatively secure by the reign of Uzziah's successor, Jotham. The latter ruler responded with heat to an attempted revolt by the Ammonite king (2 Chron 27:5), probably named *Sanip/b*, *Shanip/b*, or the like (compare the Akkadian ^{m}*Sa-ni-pu* ^{uru}*Bīt-Am-ma-na-a+-a*).[202] At some point during these events, it seems likely that one of the aforementioned Judaean kings also subdued Moab, which lay between Edom and Ammon. At the least, one sees that, by the time Ahaz rendered tribute to Tiglath-pileser (ca. 734/733 BCE),[203] the three transriver State kingdoms followed suit, perhaps even as nominal vassals rather than mere allies of Jerusalem.[204]

In short, Judahite connections with Transjordanian regions as far north as Ramoth-Gilead become quite apparent.[205] Amos 1:13 underscores vividly the vicissitudes of the Gileadite–Ammonite border in the mid-eighth century BCE. When parts of southern Gilead fell into Ammonite hands, Judah heightened its interest and participation in the events of both areas. As a corollary policy, Jerusalem leveraged its ability to maintain indirect pressure on its old nemesis, Samaria (recall the roster of Samaria's erstwhile allies/enemies as sketched in Amos 1:3-2:5). After Menahem's rule reaffirmed a pro-Assyrian posture in the north, Judah supported the anti-Assyrian factions operating adjacent to or within its Transjordanian affiliates. But when the Assyrian juggernaut pressed in upon Judah itself and prompted Ahaz's *pro*-Assyrian shift after even Gilead had become an Assyrian province, Jerusalem's old transriver cohort, Pekah, turned with bitterness on the southern capital, by which he felt betrayed.

Tiglath-pileser's actions in Transjordan effected a total dissolution of the long-standing anti-Assyrian element there. The imperial province of Gal'adi subsumed the territories formerly inhabited by the Gadites and the half-tribe of Manasseh[206] and rendered the native inhabitants who escaped deportation incapable of any further politi-

---

[202]Tadmor, *ITP*, 170, Summary Inscription 7, rev., l. 10′ = Rost, *KTP*, 72, *Die Thontafelinschrift*, rev., l. 10′, from ca. 733 BCE.

[203]The Assyrians called Ahaz by his full name, Jehoahaz. Tadmor notes that "the payment of tribute by Ahaz in 734 is not necessarily identical with the 'bribe' (שׁחד) of II Kings xvi:8, sent to Tiglath-pileser in order to secure Assyria's intervention on the side of the beleaguered Judah" (Tadmor, *ITP*, 277).

[204]*ARAB* I.801 = K 3751, rev., ll. 11′-12′ = Tadmor, *ITP*, 154, 170-71, 268, 277. Written sometime near the close of the XVII *palû* (729 BCE), this Summary Inscription contains two separate geographical rosters. The first lists the Syro-Anatolian tribute bearers of 738 BCE, and the second names the kings of Syria-Palestine, who paid tribute sometime later, most probably in 734 BCE. At least in the case of Edom, the likelihood of its existing in a vassal relationship to Judah at this time receives support from a corrected reading of 2 Kgs 16:6, which should appear as follows: "At that time, the king of Edom [MT inserted 'Rezin' from v. 5 and consequently confused the *reš* and *dalet* and read 'Aram' instead of 'Edom' to satisfy the now corrupt context] recovered Elath for Edom [MT = 'Aram'] and he drove the Judahites from Elath; then the Edomites [reading the Greek/Targum/Vulgate/qere against the MT 'Aramaeans'] entered Elath and have dwelt there until this day." The Edomites, then, took advantage of the Syro-Ephraimite aggression against Jerusalem to throw off their Judaean yoke. None of the other historical controls or textual evidence lends support to the received Masoretic reading for this verse.

[205]Note Ammon's northern border in *IDB* 1, Maps VIII-IX.

[206]See *MBA* Nos. 68 and 148.

cal tampering with the nonprovincial enclave around Samaria. Though the old tribal configuration recalled by the Chronicler (see above) may have long since dissolved, this record affords at least some insight into the complexities of the relationships between political entities on either side of the Jordan Valley, the fate of the new powers which had arisen across the river, and the relevance of each to the history of Samaria. The taxing assaults leveled against the Israelite capital by both Assyrian and Transjordanian leaders might easily have provided the background information for the later lament in Psalm 83.[207]

Inasmuch as Hoshea was elevated to kingship over virtually the only region north of the Dead Sea (both east and west of the Jordan River) that had averted provincial status, a question arises as to his official political relationship to Assyria. Postgate has shown that Nimrud Letter No. 39 (ND 2759)[208] reveals another similar situation in which an area's native king (Unqi of Que) stood in a vassal-ruler relationship to an Assyrian appointed governor who oversaw Calah's diplomatic and military interests in the subdued kingdom. Closer to home, Nimrud Letter XVI (lines 35-36)[209] relates that the major cities and regions in southern Palestine, including Gaza and Jerusalem, had already received official Assyrian emissaries (LÚ.MAḪ.MEŠ)[210] by the close of Tiglath-pileser's western campaigns in 732 BCE, even though each lay outside the established provincial network and each retained its own king. One may reasonably argue, then, that Tiglath-pileser likely assigned Samaria its first Assyrian governor concurrent with Hoshea's accession/appointment as king. Whether or not future epigraphic discoveries corroborate this suggestion, it remains clear that the political autonomy of Israel's capital city had essentially evaporated already by 732 or 731 BCE. The course of Samaria's future now seemed determined and, from a political point of view, the

---

[207] While I cite the applicability of this communal lament to Samaria's present historical situation, I recognize that form critical and other considerations have led many scholars to prefer a much later date of composition for its text (e.g., C. Westermann, *Praise and Lament in the Psalms* [Atlanta, GA: John Knox Press, 1981], 174, where he writes that "certainly it is to be considered a postexilian Psalm").

[208] J. N. Postgate, *Iraq* 35 (1973), 28.

[209] Saggs, *Iraq* 17 (1955), 134-35.

[210] LÚ.MAḪ.MEŠ = *amīlu ṣīrī*, literally, "men of first rank." The term is restricted to use in the later periods (Neo-Assyrian and Neo-Babylonian) and is commonly used to refer to foreign chieftains (*CAD* S, 210, 213). The relationship of this official to those whose titles appear in other contemporary (TP III) sources remains unclear. In Nimrud Letter XX, one reads of LÚ.GAR.UMUŠ-te (= *šākin ṭēmi*) officials as well as LÚ.GAL.URU.MEŠ-te ones; the former title derives from the Akkadian phrase *šakānu ṭēma*, "to set down a report (in writing)," and seems to describe a liaison between the Assyrian governors in the various outposts and the bureaucratic nerve center in Calah/Nimrud. In addition to other responsibilities, these men probably escorted the transport of tribute to the Assyrian capital; there was one *šākin ṭēmi* official per major city (note the *[amēl] šākin* in ND.400, line 9). On the other hand, the LÚ.GAL.URU.MEŠ-te officials consisted in the "City Rulers" who took up permanent residence in their assigned districts. That the LÚ.MAḪ.MEŠ officials appear mainly in political and administrative documents casts some doubt on their putative association with the prophetic guild—a link that some have posited on the basis of the Akkadian word *maḫû*, "to be in a frenzy." (For additional comment and bibliography, see Saggs, *Iraq* 17 [1955], 135 and 140).

Assyrians neither desired nor needed a physical destruction of the city at any point after this time. It was perhaps this comfortable position of power that helped account for the Assyrian willingness to accept a rather protracted siege against Samaria a decade later when the imperial army undoubtedly had the capacity to level a quicker, heavier blow against the rebellious town.

Part C. Israelite Sovereignty: The Final Years

1) Shalmaneser V: 727-722 BCE

The extant records from the relatively short reign of Shalmaneser V are notoriously scant. Unhappily, I know of no royal annals from this period. The single text that Luckenbill attributed to this king (*ARAB* I.829-830) appears rather to belong to Esarhaddon;[211] in any event, the badly damaged cylinder does not mention Samaria. Even the Eponym Chronicle entries from this administration suffered destruction.[212] The principal Mesopotamian source for Shalmaneser V derives from the Babylonian Chronicle,[213] and it clearly credits him with the fall of Samaria. In fact, this laconic citation records *only* that Shalmaneser ascended the throne in Assyria and Akkad (Chronicle I, Col. i:27-28), that he captured Samaria (I i:28),[214] and that he died in his fifth year of rule (I i:29-30).[215] From a fragmentary entry in the Assyrian eponym

---

[211] W. W. Hallo, *Biblical Archaeology Reader*, Vol. 2 (1975), 175, n. 95; also A. K. Grayson, *Assyrian and Babylonian Chronicles*. Texts From Cuneiform Sources, A. L. Oppenheim, ed. (Locust Valley, NY: J. J. Augustin Publisher, 1975), 242.

[212] J. D. Hawkins, *CAH*, Vol. III/1, Second Edition (1982), 415. See A. Millard, *The Eponyms of the Assyrian Empire*, 45-46, 59.

[213] A. K. Grayson, *ABC*, 15, 72-73. This text came from Babylon and dates to the twenty-second year of Darius.

[214] Following the publication of the Chronicles, an early and extended debate ensued as to whether the correct reading listed the place name ^{uru}Ŝá-ma-ra-'-in, "Samaria," or ^{uru}Ŝá-ba-ra-'-in, i.e., a reference to a city known as Sibraim, Sefarvaim, or the like. Choosing the latter reading would disconnect Shalmaneser from Samaria and resolve the identity of the conqueror of the Israelite capital *in the Assyrian sources* (though not the remaining discrepancy between these writings and the biblical record), since then only Sargon II would actually claim credit for that feat. But from 1958 to the present Tadmor's reading of "Samaria" has gained almost universal acceptance (compare the following: H. Tadmor, "The Campaigns of Sargon II of Assur: A Chronological-Historical Study," *JCS* 12 (1958), Part 1, pp. 22-40; Part 2, pp. 77-100; E. Vogt, "Samaria A. 722 et 720 AB Assyriis Capta," *Biblica* 39 [1958], 536; W. W. Hallo, "From Qarqar to Carchemish: Assyria and Israel in the Light of New Discoveries," *BA* 23 [1960], 51; A. Jepsen, "Noch einmal zur israelitisch-jüdischen chronologie," *VT* 18 [1968], 43; J. A. Brinkman, *A Political History of Post-Kassite Babylonia, 1158-722 B.C.* Analecta Orientalia 43 [Rome, 1968], 244; A. K. Grayson, *ABC* [1975], 73; I. Eph'al, "Israel: Fall and Exile," in *WHJP*, First Series, IV/1, A. Malamat, ed. [Jerusalem, 1979], 187; B. Becking, *The Fall of Samaria*, 22-23; K. Lawson Younger, Jr., *CBQ* 61 [1999], 465; among others).

[215] Besides these references, an Aramaic letter notes that Shalmaneser V conquered Bit Adini, and a fragmentary brick inscription from Apqu (Tell Abu Marya) may belong to him as well (see Grayson, *Assyrian and Babylonian Chronicles*, 242, for the relevant bibliographic data).

lists, one may establish Shalmaneser's accession year as 727 BCE.[216]

For years, the central issue relating to the declaration in both the Babylonian Chronicle and the Hebrew Bible (2 Kgs 17:3-6) that Shalmaneser V conquered Samaria focused on how to reconcile those statements with the numerous Assyrian sources in which his successor, Sargon II, claims credit for the feat. Several major studies have now clarified the military details of those two Assyrian reigns and have erased any potential conflict within the sources by showing the involvement of both Shalmaneser and Sargon in Samaria's downfall.[217] Since these studies cover the issues with remarkable clarity and detail, I need only summarize their findings here as I outline my own position.

The fall of Samaria occurred in stages[218] and as the result of at least two major campaigns against the city (723/22 and 720/19).[219] The biblical writers likely also knew of a more perfunctory Assyrian approach to the region or city of Samaria early in the reign of Shalmaneser V.[220] It appears that, after succeeding Tiglath-pileser III in 727 BCE, the new king led his army through central Syria and "came up against" Hoshea (עָלָיו עָלָה; 2 Kgs 17:3a) in a relatively benign show of force designed to preclude any dissipation of Assyrian authority in the west. Samaria willingly offered its preset, annual tribute at this time (וַיָּשֶׁב לוֹ מִנְחָה; v. 3b). If the wording of 2 Kgs 17:3 reflects a discrete historical episode, then the account of Shalmaneser's full scale assault against the capital itself begins only in v. 4.[221]

---

[216]Note the reading [-n]u-ašarēd₃ : ina [ ], in A. Millard, *The Eponyms of the Assyrian Empire*, 45, 59.

[217]The three key investigations include: H. Tadmor, *JCS* 12 (1958), Part 1, pp. 22-40; Part 2, pp. 77-100; B. Becking, *The Fall of Samaria* (1992); and K. Lawson Younger, Jr., *CBQ* 61 (1999), 461-82.

[218]Following Tadmor's seminal study in 1958 of the campaigns of Sargon II, only a few scholars held to the view that Sargon simply usurped credit for Shalmaneser V's victory at Samaria and possibly even "appropriated Shalmaneser's war illustrations" in the reliefs and sculptures from Assyria (e.g., J. E. Reade, "Sargon's Campaigns of 720, 716, and 715 B.C.: Evidence from the Sculptures," *JNES* 35 [1976], 95-104, esp. 100).

[219]Modern scholarship has reconstructed several scenarios regarding the number of battles that occurred at Samaria and whether one should credit those campaigns to Shalmaneser, Sargon, or both. The clearest reviews of all the positions appear in G. Galil, "The Last Years of the Kingdom of Israel and the Fall of Samaria," *CBQ* 57 (1995), 52-65, esp. 55-59; K. L. Younger, Jr., *CBQ* 61 (1999), 461-62, 479-82.

[220]The issue here centers on whether 2 Kgs 17:3-5 alludes to only one or to at least two distinct Assyrian actions involving Samaria. This matter asks a different question from how many sources lie behind vv. 3-6 (many writers have suggested seeing at least two parent writings here). In my judgment, these verses involve more than one event. Younger, on the other hand, sees only a single episode throughout, though he then readily admits that "the activities of a number of years have been compressed into one overarching portrayal" (K. Lawson Younger, Jr., *CBQ* 61 [1999], 478-79).

[221]Becking sees a similar division of the text, though he groups vv. 3-4 together and ascribes the traditions contained in them to the Archives of Israel, while viewing both 17:5-6 and 18:9-11 as deriving from a separate source, the Archives of Judah. All three writings, he believes, list the events they describe in their proper chronological order (Becking, *The Fall of Samaria*, 49-53). Yet he also sees both of these traditions as alluding to only one conquest (p. 39), and it is here that one should exercise caution

At least by the spring of 725 BCE, some obscure factor prompted Hoshea to violate his allegiance to Assyria. In addition to withholding annual tribute, he conspired with the king of Egypt (2 Kgs 17:4). Without hesitation, Shalmaneser returned to the region, deposed and deported Hoshea, and invaded (עלה) the outlying areas of Samaria (v. 5; וַיַּעַל מֶלֶךְ־אַשּׁוּר בְּכָל־הָאָרֶץ וַיַּעַל שֹׁמְרוֹן). Ultimately, he came up against Samaria itself and initiated a direct though protracted siege against the capital in the seventh year of Hoshea's rule (2 Kgs 18:9; see 17:5b; עָלָה שַׁלְמַנְאֶסֶר מֶלֶךְ־ אַשּׁוּר עַל־שֹׁמְרוֹן וַיָּצַר עָלֶיהָ). Not until Hoshea's ninth year, however, did Shalmaneser succeed in capturing the city, and the Hebrew verb now changes to indicate this action (from Hebrew עלה to לכד, 2 Kgs 17:6 and 18:10; compare the Akkadian *ḥepû*, "to break").

The two places at which the biblical texts describe the fall of Samaria, then, seem to agree in all major aspects: they hint at an ongoing series of annoyances between Samaria and Assyria during the last three years of Hoshea's rule and conclude that Shalmaneser V was, in fact, the initial conqueror of the city as a result of a major campaign there (2 Kgs 17:3-6 and 18:9-11). Assyria's protracted offensive against Samaria attests to the city's stalwart defense systems, which still included the strong Casemate Wall designed and built by King Ahab over one and a quarter centuries earlier.

One important question that remains centers on the precise dating of these events. Though the principal source is a fragmentary one, it appears that Hoshea (or, more likely, a representative) offered the new king's tribute (perhaps for the first time) to Tiglath-pileser in Sarrabani, a site in the distant region of Bit Shilani in southern Babylon.[222] This city and its king, Nabû-ushabshi, undoubtedly fell to the Assyrians only in 731 BCE, sometime during the siege of Shapiya.[223] That Hoshea's diplomatic corp travelled so far to see Tiglath-pileser remains a truly astonishing fact and suggests that Israel viewed the contact as somehow vital to its own interests. Besides sending suitable tribute with his emissaries, Hoshea may well have sought continued Assyrian support to help bolster his claim to the throne in the wake of an uneasy transition from the previous ruler from Transjordan. In this case, it hardly seems likely that the new Israelite king himself would have ventured so far from home, especially if his nascent rule was proving a shaky one on the local scene in Samaria. In any event, the Assyrian sources just cited touch upon issues relating to two crucial aspects of the chronology of

---

regarding his interpretation. Becking acknowledges his indebtedness to many scholars who have preceded him on this interpretive path, including H. Winckler, M. Noth, J. Gray, R. D. Nelson, J. C. Trebolle, and G. H. Jones (see *The Fall of Samaria*, 49, n. 8). More recently, M. Z. Brettler has also seen disparate sources behind 2 Kgs 17:1-6, but he believes that, while vv. 1-2 stem from a Deuteronomistic writing in Hebrew, vv. 3-4 and 5-6 actually come from two separate Assyrian records (see M. Z. Brettler, *The Creation of History in Ancient Israel* [London/New York: Routledge, 1995], 112-34, 208-17).

[222]Tadmor, *ITP*, 188-89, Summary Inscription 9, rev., ll. 10-11.

[223]Compare Tadmor, *ITP*, 160-63, Summary Inscription 7, obv., ll. 15-17, and the eponym entry for 731 in Millard, *The Eponyms of the Assyrian Empire*, 45, 59.

the fall of Samaria, though one must recognize these writings as summary (geographically arranged) rather than annalistic (chronologically presented) texts.

First, it appears that new troubles in Chaldea necessitated the departure of the Assyrian army and its leader from the Damascus–Samaria arena almost immediately following the 733/32 BCE destruction of the former and the installation of Hoshea as puppet king in the latter. Whatever role Tiglath-pileser may have played in Hoshea's rise to power, the Assyrian monarch did not remain in Israel to ensure local compliance with the new regime. Moreover, these new concerns in the east further explain the apparent time lapse between the point at which Assyria first controlled various Israelite centers such as Megiddo and the time when it transformed them into regional seats of imperial political and economic activity (see pp. 546-47). Second, the sources make it clear that Hoshea had assumed the throne in Samaria already by 731 BCE, when he reestablished ties with the Assyrian leader in southern Babylonia. Therefore, a reckoning of 732-731 BCE as Hoshea's first year as king produces, in turn, dates of 726-725 for his seventh year, when Shalmaneser V first laid siege to Samaria (2 Kgs 18:9), and 724-723 for his ninth year, when the city finally succumbed to its attackers (2 Kgs 17:6; 18:10). Tadmor appeals to the last set of dates to mark both the outset of Shalmaneser's assault against Samaria and the arrest and deportation of Hoshea; both episodes relate, he says, to the information recorded in 2 Kgs 17:4. According to this view, then, the city ultimately fell "two years later in the winter of 722/21."[224]

After a close analysis of the regnal chronologies for both Hoshea of Israel and Hezekiah of Judah (2 Kgs 18), Becking has concluded that the fall of Samaria actually occurred slightly earlier, sometime between the spring of 723 and the spring of 722 BCE.[225] The question turns on which season in Hoshea's seventh year Shalmaneser launched his siege against Samaria: autumn/winter of 726 BCE or spring of 725 BCE. The addition of a three-year siege to the former starting date would place the final collapse of Israelite sovereignty in 723 BCE (with Becking), while extending the aggression from 725 would result in a 722 BCE conquest date (with Tadmor).[226] In considering these options, however, one must also allow that the report in 2 Kgs 17:5 of a three-year offensive may very well reflect a span of time rounded to the nearest year. Even if Shalmaneser began his efforts in the spring of 725 BCE and eventually realized his goals in the late autumn or winter of 723, it seems entirely likely that the biblical writers might naturally have counted the siege period as three years. In short, I can only say that, judging from the evidence currently available, the city of Samaria fell from Israelite control sometime in the late autumn of 723 BCE or the winter or early spring of 722 BCE. It is noteworthy that Shalmaneser himself became the eponymate

---

[224] Tadmor, *ITP*, 278.

[225] Becking, *The Fall of Samaria*, 47-56.

[226] Na'aman offers a different understanding of the chronology of these events (N. Na'aman, *VT* 36 [1986], 71-74; idem, "The Historical Background to the Conquest of Samaria [720 BC]," *Biblica* 71 [1990], 206-25).

for the year 723 BCE, or the period during which he realized his greatest successes in the west.[227] Sometime after this, he died of unknown causes (though possibly natural ones),[228] and Sargon II succeeded him on the throne of Assyria.[229]

The second issue introduced above deals with the nature of the transition from Israelite to Assyrian hegemony over Samaria: how much violence and destruction attended the Assyrian takeover? Since divergent interpretations of the Akkadian verb ḫepû have only complicated the answer to this question, it behooves one ultimately to weigh those opinions against the archaeology of Samaria (see Conclusions). Na'aman has suggested that ḫepû generally designates military operations within a larger region rather than against a specific city.[230] Moreover, he prefers to translate the word as "to plunder or ravage" and to refrain from reading into it a physical destruction of walls and buildings that might result from a direct military attack against a particular target. In other words, this verb expresses control over and exploitation of Assyria's quarry, not necessarily the physical destruction of it. Others have disagreed with both points by noting that ḫepû might just as easily refer to an assault against a certain city (in this case, Samaria) as to the surrounding countryside and that the verb often denotes the partial or complete ruination of a site following the campaign.[231]

But besides a meaning of "to break, ruin, or scatter," the conceptual range of this term clearly carries a more generic meaning of "to capture,"[232] with the sense of "to control or subdue." In my judgment, it is the latter nuance that suits well the Hebrew verb לכד, though the Assyrians also frequently used kašādu to render this same basic meaning.[233] While all those commentators mentioned here agree that Shalmaneser surely "captured" Samaria, my detailed analysis of the actual depositional history of the site has demonstrated the lack of a coherent destruction level that might date to Tiglath-pileser III, Shalmaneser V, or Sargon II. In short, I understand the Babylonian Chronicle to refer to Shalmaneser's attack specifically against the city of

---

[227] See A. Millard, *The Eponyms of the Assyrian Empire*, 46, 59. In a similar way, Tiglath-pileser III's name appears on the list during his campaigns at Arpad in northern Syria in 743 BCE.

[228] On the understanding of NAM.MEŠ (*šīmāti*) as indicating a death of natural causes, see: B. Becking, *The Fall of Samaria*, 22, n.6; G. W. Vera Chamaza, "Sargon II's Ascent to the Throne: The Political Situation," *State Archives of Assyria Bulletin* 6 (1992), 21-33; Na'aman seems to intimate the same belief in *Biblica* 71 (1990), 218, 224. In the case of a natural death for Shalmaneser V, Sargon II would not have seized the throne as a usurper. For a contrasting view, see H. Tadmor, "History and Ideology in the Assyrian Royal Inscriptions," in *Assyrian Royal Inscriptions: New Horizons in Literary, Ideological and Historical Analysis*. F. M. Fales, ed. Orientis Antiqui Collectio 17 (Rome: Instituto per l'Oriente, Centro per le Antichità e la Storia dell'Arte del Vicino Oriente, 1981), 26-29.

[229] The Babylonian Chronicle I i:27-31 reports that Shalmaneser died in the month Tebeth and that Sargon rose to the throne on the twelfth day of Tebeth (A. K. Grayson, *ABC*, 73).

[230] N. Na'aman, *Biblica* 71 (1990), 211, 215-16.

[231] See Becking, *The Fall of Samaria*, 24-25; K. L. Younger, Jr, *CBQ* 61 (1999), 465-66.

[232] *CAD* Ḫ, 170-74.

[233] *CAD* K, 271-84.

Samaria (contra Na'aman). Yet the archaeology of the site certainly precludes me from also allowing that single witness to suggest that I should expect such an episode to have produced clear signs of conflagration, whether surgical or complete in nature, somewhere inside the walls of the capital. My extended treatment of the remains from the area of the royal compound, then, confirms Na'aman's skepticism regarding the presence of a wholesale destruction of the site at any time by Neo-Assyrian forces.[234]

Theory does not necessarily alter reality. No matter what one concludes about the semantic range of the Akkadian verb *ḫepû*, then, it cannot transform what one finds (or fails to find) in the actual remains from the site itself. In fact, the latter can (and perhaps must) inform the former. The archaeology of Samaria speaks for itself and proves no more vulnerable to the woes of interpretation and manipulation than do the textual and lexical studies that most have used to drive their reconstructions of Israelite history.

2) Sargon II: 720, 716 BCE

Events leading up to the accession of Sargon II in Assyria had sealed the fate of the kingdom of Israel and its capital city at Samaria. Yet these areas gave one final gasp, and, through the sometimes ironic turns of history, their last attempt to shake off Assyrian governance would echo a political scenario from 133 years earlier. As before, the Assyrian answer would come at Qarqar. Unlike the situation with Shalmaneser V, however, Sargon and fate have bequeathed to us at least eight textual witnesses relating to these and other activities in and around Samaria (see Appendix D).[235] As a prelude to my discussion of the events, I may draw six immediate observations pertaining to the sources themselves.

First, all but the annals appear as "summary inscriptions," i.e., they follow a geographical rather than a chronological ordering of events. Second, and as a consequence of the previous point, these inscriptions do little to help narrow the date of Sargon's approach to Samaria, even though, in certain instances, the reference to Samaria appears alongside another site for which the date of attack is more certain. For example, the Small Display Inscription (*Kleine Prunkinschrift*) mentions Samaria in

---

[234] Na'aman may overstate his position, however, by suggesting that the apparent disjuncture between the archaeology of Samaria and the Assyrian texts that speak of the fall of the city stands in stark contrast to the situations found at all other sites conquered by the Assyrians. That is, the thrust of his thesis holds that, except for Samaria, whenever the Assyrians say they conquered a city, one can find a destruction level there (see my Conclusions below).

[235] It appears that Assyrian scribes recorded most of these sources only in the second half of Sargon's reign. For example, the Cylinder Inscription and the Pavement Inscription both mention aspects related to the construction of Sargon's new capital at Dur Sharrukin, where workers laid the foundations for the palace in 717 BCE, dedicated the temple in 707, and inaugurated the city in 706 BCE. Tadmor places the Cylinder Inscription "a short time after 713." He dates another principal source, the Display Inscription, "not earlier than . . . 707" (Tadmor, *JCS* 12 [1958], 36). The earliest source from Sargon, the so-called Nimrud Inscription (*ARAB* II.136-138), dates to shortly after 716 BCE and mentions Judah but not Samaria.

context with Šinuḫtu, a site in Cilicia that fell to Sargon in 718 BCE. But such a conflation of disparate episodes provides only a *terminus ante quem* for Sargon's control over Samaria; it does not yield a firm date for his actual assault against the erstwhile Israelite capital. (Thus a similar theory of interpretation must attend both battle itineraries of the "summary" type and archaeological layers of imported fill.) Third, the fragmentary nature of the annalistic record dealing with Samaria has compelled most analysts to restore the crucial lines by means of the best preserved summary inscriptions available, particularly Nimrud Prism IV and the *Prunkinschrift*, or Great Display Inscription. Fourth, all items except one within this corpus of evidence mention an entity of Samerina directly by name; only the Cylinder Inscription fails to cite Samaria and uses only the broader term "Bīt-Ḫumrî." Fifth, two texts (Annals-*ARAB* II.4 and Nimrud Prism IV) speak directly of the citizenry of Samaria by writing the gentilic lú.uru*Sa-me-ri-na-a-a* rather than the standard uru*Sa-me-ri-na* to reference the city or region. The Prism text, in particular, makes the distinction clear, since it includes both designations just mentioned within a single paragraph. Sixth, at least four of the passages relating to Israel attest to the amazing longevity of the rubric KUR(*māt*) É(*bīt*)-*Ḫu-um-ri-a*, or "the land belonging to the House(hold)/Dynasty/ Kingdom of Omri." By this period, Assyrian scribes consistently complement this reference with the descriptive KUR, i.e., "land of" (*Kleine Prunkinschrift* plus the Bull, Palace Door, and Cylinder Inscriptions). One cannot, therefore, restrict political and geographical identifications based on the name of Samaria's founding king to the years during or even immediately following the Omride rule (i.e., to Jehu, Shalmaneser III, and the Black Obelisk).

The use of both Samerina (with the city determinative, URU) and Bīt-Ḫumrî (with a designation for land, KUR) raises a question regarding the proper name of this hill country province. If uru*Samerina* itself refers to the province, what does kur*Bīt-Ḫumrî* imply, particularly when both appear in the same text? Surely the Assyrians drew some distinction between these two designations. I may note again that the Cylinder Inscription uses only the latter title to name the area of the former Northern Kingdom and omits any mention of Samerina. In my judgment, Bīt-Ḫumrî may, at times, have represented the actual name of the province. Otherwise, one must establish some viable criteria by which to determine when Samerina means the city of Samaria and when it points to the province as a whole. Toward this end, Becking has observed that the Assyrians appear to have used É-*Ḫu-um-ri-a-a* as a designation for the entire Israelite kingdom until 720 BCE, after which time they called only Samaria by that name when relating reports of the fall of the city.[236] At any rate, the problem is not dissimilar to the use of "Samaria" in the Hebrew Bible as a reference both to the capital city and to the entire Ephraimite hill country (see pp. 4-5 above).

Besides the royal annals themselves, the Nimrud Prism IV text and the Great Display Inscription offer the two most detailed accounts of Sargon's specific liaison

---

[236] Becking, *The Fall of Samaria*, 109.

with Samaria in the early years of his reign.[237] Two problems arise quickly, however, in one's examination of these sources. First, a disparity of one year exists between the chronology of events as presented in the annalistic record (and followed by the Aššur Charter) and the time line used in parallel accounts such as the prism texts. This discrepancy between the sources stems from the fact that Sargon did not undertake a military expedition outside the Assyrian heartland during his first regnal year (721 BCE). Thus the annals from Khorsabad place his first credible expedition, which began only after the spring of 720 BCE and included an assault against Samaria, in "Year 2." The prisms, on the other hand, treat the episode as part of Sargon's "first" *palû*.[238] Appealing to other extant Mesopotamian sources, such as the Babylonian Chronicle and Aššur Charter, early foundational studies have established a firm *terminus post quem* for the new king's first feasible contact with Samaria.[239] The question that lingers involves the latest possible date to which his confrontations in Syria, Israel, and Philistia might have extended (see below).

Second, the poor state of preservation seen in Prism IV:25-28 (lines that begin the discussion of the campaign that included Samaria) has prompted various proposed restorations and historical interpretations. The broken lines[240] appear as follows:

25 [lú.uru*Sa-*]*me-ri-na-a-a ša it-ti* LUGAL
26 [. . .]-*ia a-na la e-peš ar-du-ti*
27 [*ù la na-*]*še bil-ti*
28 [. . .]*š ig-me-lu-ma e-pu-šu ta-ḫa-zu*

25 [The Sa]marians who agreed with a king
26 [. . .] me not to continue their servitude
27 [and not to de]liver tribute
28 [   ] did battle

Analysts have generally agreed on the above restoration of lines 25 and 27. The principal historical problem centers on the gap at the beginning of l. 26 and what relationship that lost portion of text held to the anonymous king mentioned at the end of l. 25. In the mid-1950s, Gadd proposed to mend the lacuna with [*na-ki-ri(?)*]-*ia*, and Tadmor basically agreed by suggesting [LÚ.KÚR]-*ia*.[241] Both readings focus on an unnamed

---

[237]The so-called Aššur Charter mentions Samaria but concentrates on the anti-Assyrian coalition headed by Ilu-bi'di of Hamath.

[238]Tadmor and Becking have disagreed on the motives behind the two counting systems (compare Tadmor, *JCS* 12 [1958], 26-33 and Becking, *The Fall of Samaria*, 45).

[239]Compare A. T. Olmstead, *Western Asia in the Days of Sargon of Assyria, 722-705 B.C.* Cornell Studies in History and Political Science, Vol. II (1908), 8-11, and H. Tadmor, *JCS* 12 (1958), 22-33.

[240]Compare the Annals, ll. 11-12, in Tadmor, *JCS* 12 (1958), 34.

[241]C. J. Gadd, "Inscribed Prisms of Sargon II from Nimrud," *Iraq* 16 (1954), 179; H. Tadmor, *JCS* 12 (1958), 34.

ruler who acted with hostility (*nakru*) toward Sargon.[242] Those who accept this interpretation generally see Ilu-bi'di of Hamath (sometimes written Yaubi'di) as the most probable reference, particularly since the Aššur Charter makes it clear that he led the anti-Assyrian coalition (at least in the north) in 720 BCE. Objections on the grounds that Sargon's hatred for Ilu-bi'di ran so deep that he would never have allowed an Assyrian document to recognize him under the official title "king"[243] lack adequate persuasion, in my judgment. The Assyrian disdain for this western ruler manifests itself here in the fact that the scribe employed *šarru* (LUGAL) in a generic manner without an explicit mention of Ilu-bi'di's personal name.

Alternately, Borger recommended [IGI.DU]-*ia*, i.e., [*ālik pān*]-*ia*, as the preferred reconstruction of l. 26, which means essentially "the king my [predecessor]/the one going before me" and would point specifically to Shalmaneser V.[244] Under this reading, Sargon II launched his first military campaign in the west in 720 in order to quell a rebellion that had erupted there already in the days of Shalmaneser V two years earlier. This view became a central component in Na'aman's reconstruction of events for this period.[245] "Would Sargon's scribe," he asks, "have linked a rebellion started during the reign of Shalmaneser with the conquest of the rebellious city by his lord, if the rebellion was suppressed and the city conquered by the previous king [i.e., by Shalmaneser]?"[246] One might pose the question another way: Would any ablebodied Assyrian ruler, given the empire's current level of commitment in the west, have allowed illicit anarchy to fester there for at least two years before addressing it directly and forcefully? A positive reply seems unlikely. In my judgment, then, the reading of Nimrud Prism IV suggested by Gadd and Tadmor makes the best historical sense of the situation described therein;[247] moreover, none of the other Assyrian sources appears to provide any corroboration for the alternative Borger–Na'aman–Dalley proposal. I also accept Ilu-bi'di of Hamath as the proper identity of the hostile king in Prism IV:25-26 with whom Samaria and others had conspired by 720 BCE.[248]

---

[242] Both Becking and Younger have accepted this basic reading (Becking, *The Fall of Samaria*, 28-29; Younger, *CBQ* 61 [1999], 469-70).

[243] S. Dalley, "Foreign Chariotry and Cavalry in the Armies of Tiglath-pileser III and Sargon II," *Iraq* 47 (1985), 36.

[244] R. Borger, *Textbuch zur Geschichte Israels*, K. Galling, ed. (Tübingen, 1968), No. 30; idem, *Texte aus der Umwelt des Alten Testaments*, 1/4, O. Kaiser, ed. (Gütersloh, 1984), 382; also H. Spieckermann, *Juda unter Assur in der Sargonidenzeit*. FRLANT 129, (Göttingen, 1982), 349-50. Both Na'aman and Dalley have followed this restoration (Na'aman, *Biblica* 71 [1990], 209-10; S. Dalley, *Iraq* 47 [1985], 36).

[245] E.g., N. Na'aman, *Biblica* 71 (1990), 206-25, esp. 209-10.

[246] N. Na'aman, *Biblica* 71 (1990), 210.

[247] Becking has also noted grammatical problems with the Borger–Na'aman–Dalley restoration (B. Becking, *The Fall of Samaria*, 30).

[248] The attempt by Hayes and Kuan to see an unnamed, native Israelite king here—one who ruled after Hoshea without ever receiving notice in the Bible—also remains unconvincing (see J. H. Hayes and J. K.

The unrest and rebellion that may well have begun by the end of Shalmaneser's reign and that preoccupied Sargon at the outset of his rule actually came from within the Assyrian homeland itself and in the region of Elam to the southeast. From the Borowski Stele[249] and the Aššur Charter[250] one learns that Sargon both restored and granted new privileges to the city of Aššur as a means of reviving local trust following the institution of corvée, heavy taxation, and cultic indifference under Shalmaneser V.[251] One sees as well that, with the transition of rulers in Assyria, the territory of Elam assisted Marduk-alpa-ìddina (= Merodach-baladan; Is 39:1) in reclaiming the throne of Babylon, over which Tiglath-pileser III had established Assyrian control in 729 BCE. Rather than attacking Babylon directly, Sargon moved in his second year against Humban-nigaš, King of Elam, and boasted of a "smashing" victory there.[252] The Babylonian Chronicle records, however, that although the forces of Merodach-baladan did not reach the battle front in time to help engage Sargon, the army of Humban-nigaš alone defeated the Assyrians and coerced them into retreat.[253]

Within only a short while, news of this military success against Assyria in the east likely emboldened the powers of the west to shirk the imperial authority there.[254] The Assyrian hold on those regional states that Shalmaneser V had established crumbled quickly following his death, when Sargon's army found itself so preoccupied with events at home and in the east. A new anti-Assyrian coalition arose headed in the north by Ilu-bi'di of Hamath and in the south by Hanunu of Gaza, whose rule had somewhat miraculously survived under Tiglath-pileser following his (Hanunu's) flight to and return from Egypt in 734 BCE.[255] Virtually all the old alliance partners from both north and south Syria and Israel who had managed to survive under Assyrian pressure since the days of Shalmaneser III allied themselves to the renewed effort, includ-

---

Kuan, "The Final Years of Samaria [730-720 BC]," *Biblica* 72 [1991], 174). Tadmor, who himself originated this possibility, rejected it for good reason already in 1958 (Tadmor, *JCA* 12 [1958], 37).

[249] See W. G. Lambert, *Ladders to Heaven: Art Treasures from Lands of the Bible*, O. W. Muscarella, ed. (Toronto: McClelland and Stewart, 1981), 125.

[250] H. W. F. Saggs, "Historical Texts and Fragments of Sargon II of Assyria: I. The 'Aššur Charter'," *Iraq* 37 (1975), 11-20, esp. "Classification as 'Charter'" on p. 12-13.

[251] Together with the fragmentary opening lines (ll. 1-4) of the Charter, ll. 30-40 suggest that the hardships levied against the native Assyrians by Shalmaneser V had led to the desecration of various sanctuaries in Assyria. For a similar view, see Saggs's citation of Tallqvist's work in *Iraq* 37 (1975), 16, notes accompanying line 2 of the Aššur Charter.

[252] Aššur Charter, ll. 16-17.

[253] Grayson, *ABC*, 73-74, Chronicle I i:33-37.

[254] Galil correctly notes that, while it seems unlikely that the entire Assyrian army had withdrawn from their western garrisons following the death of Shalmaneser and the rise of Sargon, the Assyrian contingent that remained encamped at or near Samaria "was probably of limited scope" (G. Galil, *CBQ* 57 [1995], 60).

[255] See again Tadmor, *ITP*, 176-79, Summary Inscription 8, ll. 14'-19'.

ing at least Hamath, Arpad, Ṣimirra, Damascus, Ḥatarikka, and Samaria.[256] Following the defense strategy of their predecessors against Shalmaneser III in the mid-ninth century BCE, the allied powers went north to meet the Assyrians at Qarqar. But though the battle results from 853 BCE may remain somewhat uncertain, those of Sargon's assault in 720 seem perfectly clear. The Assyrians defeated the coalition, captured and publicly flayed Ilu-bi'di,[257] and then sped south to confront and punish participants there.

Citing Is 10:27-32, Younger believes that Sargon now struck even inside Judah as he moved south;[258] others have related this text either to Tiglath-pileser III or Sennacherib. In any event, Sargon then moved against the southern coastal area, defeated an Egyptian contingent south of Gaza, captured and destroyed Raphia near the border of Egypt, organized and deported 9,033 citizens from that area, subdued and returned Gaza to Assyrian control, and arrested Hanunu, whom he finally deported to Assyria as a common prisoner. Somewhere amidst this flurry of activity, Sargon also firmly reestablished Assyrian rule in Samaria. Hayes and Kuan believe that this occurred only at the end of the sequence just outlined[259] (Samaria does appear last in the lists relating these events), while Younger places the strike against Samaria soon after the one at Qarqar and prior to the one against Judah.[260] If Is 10:27-32 describes the route taken by Sargon through the hill country of Ephraim/Judah, then Younger's view may prove correct. Micah 1:10-16, on the other hand, outlines a southern approach to Jerusalem from the plain of Philistia. (It remains uncertain, however, whether these specific oracles relate to Tiglath-pileser III or to Sargon's actions around 720 BCE; see p. 548.)

The logistical challenges of Sargon's military activity in 720 are staggering. Even if the battle against Babylon/Elam occurred near the outset of Sargon's second *palû* in the spring of 720 BCE, the time which that event consumed coupled with the required marching time from Assyria to Qarqar and on to the Egyptian frontier would almost surely have left precious few weeks in that year (and certainly before the onset of winter) during which all the events in the west might have unfolded. Allowances for

---

[256] For a list of sources related to this revived alliance, see Becking, *The Fall of Samaria*, 36, n. 70.

[257] The depiction of this event appears on a relief from the reign of Sargon in P. E. Botta and M. E. Flandin, *Monument de Ninive* (Paris: Imprimerie Nationale, 1949-1950), Vol. 2, Pl. 120 and Vol. 4, Pl. 181-No. 2.

[258] K. L. Younger, Jr., *CBQ* 61 (1999), 472. Also M. A. Sweeney, "Sargon's Threat against Jerusalem in Isaiah 10,27-32," *Biblica* 75 (1994), 457-70; K. L. Younger, Jr., "Sargon's Campaign against Jerusalem—A Further Note," *Biblica* 77 (1996), 108-10; N. Na'aman, "The Historical Portion of Sargon II's Nimrud Inscription," *State Archives of Assyria Bulletin* 8 (1994), 17-20. Sweeney and Younger differ in their understanding of Sargon's self-description in the Nimrud Inscription (*ARAB* II.137) as "subduer of the Land of Judah." Sweeney sees Sargon's threat against Jerusalem as symbolic in nature, i.e., a passing show of force designed to intimidate the people without planning an actual military operation against the city. Younger, on the other hand, leaves open the possibility that Sargon undertook some direct, though perhaps small scale, action against Jerusalem in 720 BCE.

[259] J. H. Hayes and J. K. Kuan, *Biblica* 72 (1991), 178.

[260] K. L. Younger, Jr., *CBQ* 61 (1999), 471; also M. Sweeney, *Biblica* 75 (1994), 465, 469.

the likelihood of the Assyrian army having to reorganize and marshal both its material and human resources following the setback at Der before undertaking even a straight march, unfettered by interruptions of any kind, from Babylon or Elam to Qarqar only exacerbate the problem immensely.[261] Younger's solution that the siege and conquest of Qarqar, Samaria, Judah, Gaza, and Raphia, plus the assembling and deporting of captives from these cities and regions, embodied a *Blitzkrieg* through already severely weakened western states that could throw up little defense against Sargon's strength may prove partially correct but falls short of entirely answering the problem.[262] It seems highly unlikely that all the events in the record from Elam to Egypt could have transpired within the limited time span between the spring and the close of 720 BCE. Hayes and Kuan, as a consequence, believe that the forays in the west extended well into the year 719.[263] For reasons of mere practicality, one must accept the plausibility of this position. Sargon could not have launched successive field campaigns against Babylon/Elam and then Hamath/Egypt before the spring of 720 BCE. While the Small Display Inscription shows that he had subdued Samaria certainly by 718 BCE,[264] the Aššur Charter suggests a date before that point. Judging from the best calculations, then, the second and final "fall" of Samaria occurred sometime between spring 720 and spring 719,[265] and the Assyrian scribes responsible for the Prism texts counted this as part of Sargon's "first *palû*," while those who produced the annalistic accounts reckoned it as his "Year 2," or second *palû* (see above).

Even though there may be up to four battle scenes from Samaria preserved in the reliefs found in Sargon's palace at Dur Sharrukin,[266] precious few details telling of the actual confrontation at the Israelite capital remain available otherwise. One Neo-Assyrian letter (*CT* 53, 458 = *SAA* I, No. 255) may speak of the attempt to control the water supply at Samaria. Curiously, this text mentions a "river in front of Samaria" and appears to note the presence of (only?) one cistern in the vicinity of the city. Given the very fragmentary condition of this letter, however, it remains quite difficult to draw much reliable historical information from it or even to date it with any precision.[267]

---

[261] Recall the discussion under Tiglath-pileser above concerning estimated daily marching distances for the fully equipped, battle-ready Assyrian army (see n. 162).

[262] K. L. Younger, Jr., *CBQ* 61 (1999), 471-73.

[263] J. H. Hayes and J. K. Kuan, *Biblica* 72 (1991), 170-71.

[264] Fuchs, *Sargons II*, 76 and 308 (l. 15). See pp. 563-64 above for the notice that Samaria appears in this text beside a site in Cilicia that Sargon conquered during his fourth *palû*, or in 718 BCE.

[265] Tadmor, *JCS* 12 (1958), 31.

[266] N. Franklin, "The Room V Reliefs at Dur-Sharrukin and Sargon II's Western Campaigns," *TA* 21 (1994), 258-59, 264, 271-72; also the Upper Registers on slabs presented in Figs. 4-7. Interestingly, the curved swords used by the defenders of Samaria in these reliefs have parallels only in the booty taken slightly later from Lachish in the south by Sennacherib.

[267] Becking notes that it likely derives from the period of Sargon II or Sennacherib (Becking, *The Fall of Samaria*, 109-110).

The report from the Joint Expedition's work at Samaria states that "the nearest good springs are a mile away on the far side of a deep valley and they would have been cut off whenever the city was closely beleaguered; the cisterns inside the walls could not have been sufficient for many thousand inhabitants plus their horses and donkeys."[268]

It seems more certain that both the citizens and the spoils of war from Samaria found themselves deported to various cities in the east. In two Assyrian sources, Nimrud Prism IV:31 and the Great Display Inscription (l. 24), the scribes of Sargon recorded similar figures of 27,280 and 27,290 deportees from Samaria. Though, as I just noted, the excavators of Samaria realized that, judging from the water supply alone, the city could not have accommodated "many thousand inhabitants," they later allow for a population of between 25,000 and 40,000 people.[269] The figures included in 1 Kgs 20:13-15, however, may suggest a substantially lower estimate. In his investigation into possible West Semitic personal names appearing in cuneiform sources from Sargon, Becking has collected references to no more than about 50 individuals.[270] But he also correctly notes that not every deported Israelite would appear in Assyrian writings and that the low number of those who did might merely reflect a rapid assimilation into a foreign culture in which children naturally received local, Assyrian names.

Both 2 Kgs 17:24, 30-31[271] and the Assyrian royal annals[272] indicate a two-way deportation of peoples that involved the resettling of citizens from the northern and eastern areas of the empire in Samaria.[273] The traditions of 2 Kgs 17:6 and 18:11 say that the deportations began already under Shalmaneser V, who sent those Samarians to Halah, to Gozan on the upper reaches of the River Khabur, and to various cities belonging to the Medes. While Becking's detailed analysis of these lists has demonstrated both their historicity and the fact that other Israelites went to core cities in the Assyrian heartland (such as Dur Sharruken, Calah/Nimrud, and Nineveh),[274]

---

[268] *SS I*, 1. See also further comments on the water supply at Samaria on p. 4.

[269] Compare *SS I*, 2, 4. Estimates of Samaria's population vary rather widely in the excavation report.

[270] Becking, *The Fall of Samaria*, 92-93.

[271] See G. R. Driver, "Geographical Problems," *Eretz-Israel* 5 (Mazar Volume, 1959), 18*-20*; also R. Zadok, "Geographical and Onomastic Notes," *JANES* 8 (1976), 113-24. Na'aman and Zadok relate these references to Sargon's campaigns in 710-709 BCE (N. Na'aman and R. Zadok, "Sargon II's Deportations to Israel and Philistia," *JCS* 40 [1988], 44-45).

[272] See Annals, ll. 15-17, in Tadmor, *JCS* 12 (1958), 34; Fuchs, *Sargons II*, 87-88; 313-14, II:3,2—II:3,4.

[273] Two ostraca from the late eighth to mid-seventh centuries BCE at Tell Jemmeh possibly relate to these incoming deportees and suggest that the Assyrians transferred captives from the Zagros Mountains in the easternmost empire to the southwest borders near Egypt. The name lists on these inscriptions also show the effects of assimilation (or at least acculturation) even on the first generation of descendants, who already received Semitic names despite the (pre-)Iranian and Kassite patronyms of their deported fathers (see Na'aman and Zadok, *JCS* 40 [1988], 36-42).

[274] Becking, *The Fall of Samaria*, 62-73, 78-90. B. Oded has shown that these three principal cities, in fact, received a full 85% of the deportees recorded during the life of the Neo-Assyrian empire (B. Oded, *Mass Deportations and Deportees in the Neo-Assyrian Empire*, 28).

Na'aman and Zadok have shown that deportations to the hill country of Samaria and to the southern coast of Philistia did not occur until the period between 716 and 708 BCE.[275] Once again, this agrees with my view that Assyria only gradually developed the territories conquered here (including Megiddo). Sargon incorporated elements from the eastern empire among the first newcomers to sites near the Egyptian border at the Brook Besor. In turn, he moved various peoples from a block of Arabian tribes that had held connections with Gaza and other southwestern regions to Samaria and the surrounding hill country area.[276] According to the Annals, this act occurred during Sargon's seventh *palû* in spring 716–spring 715 BCE.[277]

The Assyrians also appear to have conscripted a number of Israelite chariots or charioteers[278] for service in the imperial army. The exact number of units involved here remains subject to debate. Both the Great Display Inscription (l. 24) and a fragment from the Khorsabad annals[279] record a figure of 50 chariots taken from the Samarians. Nimrud Prism IV:33, on the other hand, appears to calculate the number at 200.[280] In addition, the Assyrians also confiscated and removed various cultic images from Samaria.[281] The spoilation of venerated items such as these promoted the idea of divine abandonment in the minds of the captive population.[282]

The city of Samaria thus became the center of a new province, *Samerina*, and various taxes, including a corn tax,[283] were imposed on it.[284] Deportations served, as

---

[275] N. Na'aman and R. Zadok, *JCS* 40 (1988), 42-46.

[276] Cylinder Inscription, ll. 19-20. I. Eph'al tempers this report by noting that a true deportation generally placed a greater distance between the homeland and the ultimate destination of an uprooted group. He suggests (1) that the Assyrian scribes have exaggerated Sargon's claim to have conquered these Arabian tribes, and (2) that the arrival of Arabs in Samaria emerged from a strictly economic arrangement made between Sargon and seminomadic groups in the area of Midian. The purpose, he says, involved a mutually beneficial arrangement in which native personnel processed the Arab trade through the Ephraimite hill country on its route to port depots, such as Tyre. See I. Eph'al, *The Ancient Arabs*, 105-07.

[277] Annals, ll. 120-23 (Fuchs, *Sargons II*, 110 and 320; II:11,3—II:11,6); see also Tadmor, *JCS* 12 (1958), 78; compare *ARAB* II.17.

[278] Dalley *Iraq* 47 (1985), 31-43, has suggested that one should understand such references as pointing to human resources, i.e., the charioteers, rather than restricting it to material resources, i.e., actual chariots. At least one legal document dealing with the sale of slaves in 709 BCE mentions an apparent Israelite as a chariot driver (see Becking, *The Fall of Samaria*, 65-66 and 77-78).

[279] *ARAB* II.4; *ANET*, 284.

[280] See Becking, *The Fall of Samaria*, 41-42, for the various numbers (always rounded) of chariots captured from different sites.

[281] Nimrud Prism IV:32.

[282] M. Cogan, *Imperialism and Religion: Assyria, Judah and Israel in the Eighth and Seventh Centuries B.C.E.* SBL Monograph Series 19 (Missoula, MT: Scholars Press, 1974), 22-41, 120.

[283] ABL 1201 = SAA I, No. 220, ll. 4-5. This letter also shows clearly that Samaria often proved delinquent in its payment of such taxes.

[284] In light of such taxes and the military and cultic spoilation just mentioned, Hayes and Kuan seem

most everything else, Assyria's economic strategies, and one text that contains Semitic names indicates that at least those Samarians who were resettled in the Khabur River region worked on royal estates that produced food and other basic commodities for the political center in Assyria.[285] Unfortunately, hardly any textual documentation has survived that deals directly with Samaria following the city's final submission to Assyria in 720 BCE. Though the name ⁱ*ᵘ*Sa-mì-ri-na appears alongside its adjacent provinces, Du'ru and Magiddu, in two (perhaps three)[286] province lists, it remains difficult to know with certainty how long the Assyrians managed to keep it under official provincial status. The general region, however, remained part of the *Pax Assyriaca* at least until the reigns of Esarhaddon and Ashurbanipal, and the eponym lists cite *Nabû-kēnu-uṣur* and *Nabû-šar-aḫḫēšu* as "governors" of Samaria in 690 and 646, respectively.[287] The mention of this high office in connection with this city indicates that it served as an administrative center within the new province. Archaeologists from the two major expeditions to Samaria, however, have recovered only a few remains from the Assyrian occupation there, including an inscribed bulla with a royal Assyrian seal,[288] a tantalizing stele fragment (possibly from the time of Sargon II),[289] a late-Assyrian cylinder seal,[290] which may indicate that teachers of cuneiform script now lived in Samaria,[291] and, as I have already shown, good examples of the famous Palace Ware (much of which undoubtedly represents local imitations of Assyrian originals).

It is important to remember that the repopulation and restructuring of Samaria by Assyria did not take place immediately following Sargon's final subjection of the city. In 719 BCE, after his sortie into the Ephraimite hill country, circumstances called for his hasty return to Mannai and Zikitu, areas around Lake Urumia northeast of the Assyrian homeland, to undertake punitive campaigns against the rebellious cities of

---

incorrect in their assertion that, during and after the fall of Samaria, "no special penalties were imposed on the people and no reference is made to any special booty taken" (J. H. Hayes and J. H. Kuan, *Biblica* 72 [1991], 178). Franklin's new, detailed analysis of the Room V reliefs at Dur Sharrukin has suggested plausibly that the Upper Registers in Slabs 4 and 5 may actually depict the removal of Samarian booty by Assyrian soldiers (N. Franklin, *TA* 21 [1994], 264, Figs. 4-5).

[285]See Becking, *The Fall of Samaria*, 69 and nn. 51-52. Based on the content and historical backdrop of the Samaria Ostraca, one can assume that these northern Israelites were chosen not only because of their agricultural skills but as a result of their previous knowledge of and experience with an estate system that served a central capital.

[286]See K. 152, K. 276, and K. 14252 in Becking, *The Fall of Samaria*, 106-07.

[287]Compare A. Millard, *The Eponyms of the Assyrian Empire*, 50 and 61, for the former listing, and M. Falkner, "Die Eponymen der spätassyrischen Zeit," *AfO* 17 (1954-56), 104 and 118, for both entries.

[288]*HES I*, 247, Pl. 56a.

[289]*SS III*, 35 and Pl. IV, Nos. 2-3.

[290]See O. Gurney's reading in *SS III*, 87, No. 18, as well as the impression and photograph in Pl. XV:18a-b.

[291]Becking, *The Fall of Samaria*, 114.

Shuandahul and Durdukka.[292] The ensuing period, from 719 to 716 BCE or later, most likely represents the time during which Sargon eventually placed certain segments of deported Samarians in the cities of the Medes (again, 2 Kgs 17:6, 18:11). A potential gap of as much as a decade, therefore, exists between the point at which he first removed elements of Samaria's native population and the time when he completely replaced them with foreign ethnic groups (see n. 275).

Finally, the interpretation of one written source relates to the question raised earlier regarding the supposed extent to which the Assyrians destroyed the city of Samaria. Traditional readings of the notation in Nimrud Prism IV:37-38 and a parallel annalistic fragment[293] seem to spring from the assumption that the city needed rebuilding following the devastation leveled against it by Sargon II. More recently, however, Dalley's understanding of the prism text calls for replacing the first Assyrian verb, *târu* ("to return, restore"),[294] with a form of *atāru* ("to augment in number or size")[295] and emending the transliteration *ú-še-me* to *ú-še-šib*. These changes result in "a common hendiadys, *uttir . . . ušēšib*" meaning simply "I made the population greater [than it was before]."[296] The statement, therefore, refers only to the importation of foreign citizenry to Samaria, not to a physical reconstruction of the site.[297] In concluding her argument, Dalley notes:

> none of the Assyrian sources says that Samaria was burnt or rebuilt; we only have the Chronicle account saying that Shalmaneser "broke" Samaria city, a usage which may have its origins in the successful culmination of a siege, in the breaching of walls or of national frontiers.[298]

---

[292] *ARAB* II.6 (Fuchs, *Sargons II*, 90-92, 315 [II:6,6—II:7,2]). Sargon had to return to this area yet again in 716 BCE (*ARAB* II.12).

[293] For the Prism text, see Tadmor, *JCS* 12 (1958), 34; compare the Annals, l. 16 in Fuchs, *Sargons II*, 88 and 314, II:3,3. The traditional transliteration of the lines in question appears as follows: (37) uru*Sa-ma-ri-na ú-tir-ma eli šá pa-ni* (38) *ú-še-me/mì* UN.MEŠ*(nišī)* KUR.KUR*(mātāti) ki-šit-ti* ŠU*(qātī)-ia* (39) *i-na lib-bi ú-še-rib* . . . . Tadmor's translation reads: "37. The city of Samaria I resettled and made it greater than before. 38. People of the lands conquered by my own hands (= by myself) 39. I brought there."

[294] *AHw* 3, 1332-36.

[295] *CAD* A 1.II, 487-92.

[296] Dalley, *Iraq* 47 (1985), 36. Becking confusingly accepts Dalley's basic reading (*The Fall of Samaria*, 29-30 and 31, n. 42) yet also reads too much into the text by listing as one of the five important details given by the Nimrud Prism the fact that "after the conquest the city was rebuilt" (p. 31).

[297] Hayes and Kuan accept Dalley's interpretation (J. H. Hayes and J. K. Kuan, *Biblica* 72 [1991], 178). I have already discussed Na'aman's view that the citadel of Samaria suffered little, if any, destruction during the confrontation with Sargon. Becking follows Tadmor's transliteration exactly but accepts Dalley's translation (Becking, *The Fall of Samaria*, 28-29).

[298] Dalley, *Iraq* 47 (1985), 36.

I have shown in considerable detail that the archaeology of the site lends little support either to a massive restoration of broken walls or to a large scale construction of new buildings around the beginning of the last quarter of the eighth century BCE. Yet one very valuable, though fragmentary, letter from the reign of Sargon reports that Arpad, Samaria, and Megiddo each received shipments of 40,000 bricks.[299] Becking has suggested that the Assyrians sent these building materials to the capital cities of their western provinces so that workers might construct administrative centers there.[300] In light of the Assyrian-style buildings excavated at Megiddo, this conclusion might well fit that site, but not Samaria. Though the latter city appears to have served as an administrative center within its province, I have found there no credible architectural remains from a newly established administration building or governor's palace.

There exists another option, however, for the use of the bricks in Samaria. Rather than restoring a devastated summit, these materials may well have gone to the construction (for the first time) of the perimeter Wall 576 that enclosed at least the northern slopes of the city. Earlier in this study, I discussed in some detail this wall, the heavy backfills that ran up to it, and the pottery groups recovered from those imported fillings. Though Kenyon vacillated on her preferred dating for this structure, she allowed that it might easily belong to the postfall construction activities of Sargon II.[301] As I have shown, much of the pottery taken from the layers associated with Wall 573 belongs in the seventh century BCE. In light of the gradual nature of Assyria's reorganization and repopulating of sites such as Megiddo and Samaria, it is not impossible to think that the bricks that reached Samaria near the end of Sargon's rule were only incorporated into Wall 573 (and perhaps other unexcavated features) during subsequent reigns. In any event, it seems clear that the Assyrians undertook more new phases of construction at the strategically-located Megiddo than they did at the more insulated Samaria. At these and other sites, however, a certain hiatus seems to have separated the first Assyrian presence in the city from its ultimate political fall through a variety of military means (not always involving a frontal assault). Even more time passed between the final collapse of local authority and the reorganization, potential rebuilding, and official utilization of the city by the Assyrian government.

Assyria's new administrative apparatus did not materialize immediately, then, even in its provincial capitals. To understand the reasons behind this fact, one must try to view Samaria as Sargon did, not as modern biblical commentators for whom Israel (vs. Assyria) constitutes the focal point. The prominent place that Sargon awarded this city in the layout of reliefs depicting his western military campaigns in Room V of the palace at Dur Sharrukin (Khorsabad)[302] likely stems from Samaria's role as a principal to the seditious coalition in 722-720 BCE and from the fact that it constituted one of the

---

[299] *CT* 53, 38 = *SAA* V, No. 291.

[300] Becking, *The Fall of Samaria*, 111-12.

[301] *SS I*, 108.

[302] See N. Franklin, *TA* 21 (1994), 258-59, 271-72.

first of the rebel states to fall once again into Assyrian hands during Sargon's very first expedition to the west. In terms of the economics that drove the Empire's war machine, Samaria's distinction in the line-up of wall slabs seems a somewhat dubious one. As important as this capital became within Israel, Samaria was not likely considered the hub of the Assyrian empire in the west. Had that been the case, the city would have fallen into foreign hands long before it did.

Israel and Assyria: Conclusions

In this chapter, I have attempted to follow the development of Samaria's relations with the foreign power that ultimately undercut its autonomy and possessed it, namely Assyria. The picture that emerged has proved rather a clear one in the most fundamental aspects: until the reign of Tiglath-pileser III, the Assyrians did nothing that seriously threatened the existence or even the special interests of Samaria, despite oftentimes heavy fighting by the imperial army in both northern and southern Syria. Prior to 738 BCE, only one Assyrian king had actually entered the land of Israel, and he did so without a military operation or serious economic and political manipulation of the kingdom. Assyrian activities in the area between 734 and 732 BCE, however, rapidly isolated the city, crippled its economy, and left its leadership in the hands of a puppet king and perhaps an Assyrian official of high rank stationed in Samaria.

In considering the impetus behind this dramatic transformation in the life of Samaria, I have suggested mainly economic motivations for both the regional and the international wars in which the Israelite kingdom and capital became embroiled.[303] I have also proposed that the role assumed by Transjordan powers in the labyrinth of political intrigues during the ninth and eighth centuries BCE appears more complex and vital to an accurate understanding of these events than many have recognized. As the history of the city progressed, individuals, factions, and trade economies from centers located in the area of Gilead played an increasingly important part in Samaria's politics from the mid-ninth century on.

The role that Jehu's revolt played in shifting the balance of power to this region has not received adequate attention. Though the earliest leaders of the nascent Kingdom of Israel came from within the hill-country tribe of Ephraim (the "House of Jeroboam I" = Jeroboam and his son Nadab), an early conspiracy transferred the new state's leadership base to the area of Issachar even while the capital was still at Tirzah (see 1 Kgs 15:27-29; the "House of Baasha" = Baasha and his son Elah). Despite a brief interregnum, during which a second coup went awry and a subsequent pretender to the

---

[303]Examples of articles that in essence pass over completely the importance of economics in the war efforts and political strategies of the ninth and eighth centuries BCE include T. C. Mitchel's "Israel and Judah until the Revolt of Jehu" and "Israel and Judah from Jehu until the Period of Assyrian Domination" in *CAH*, Vol. III/1, Second Edition. J. Boardman et al., eds. (Cambridge: Cambridge University Press, 1982), 442-87 and 488-510, respectively. Note, however, the excellence of H. Tadmor's work in this area, just as I have noted the same in so many areas throughout this discussion.

throne failed,[304] the rise of the "House of Omri" held the power base in Issachar (and extended it to roughly 65 out of the first 88 years of Israel's history; see p. 4, n. 4). Not until the violent rise of Jehu did a rival from outside Issachar succeed in breaking the influence of leaders from that tribe and in opening the way to greater political control over Samaria from Transjordan. Perhaps recognizing Jehu's plot as another attempt to fracture the control of the ruling houses of Issachar (assuming Zimri did not come from that tribe; see n. 304), the Phoenician immigrant Queen Jezebel boldly linked his actions to those of Zimri in sarcastically addressing Jehu by that name (2 Kgs 9:31). As noted earlier (n. 137), the ancestral history of the so-called House of Jehu (a title used only in Hosea 1:4)[305] may have had its roots in Gilead. If so, one sees that from Jehu on every claimant to the throne of Israel seems to have come from some transriver area and faction—a situation that continued from the mid-ninth century down to the last, Assyrian-appointed ruler, Hoshea, whose home town remains unknown. Following the establishment of Israel in the early Iron Age II period, then, the three principal conspirators included Baasha, Zimri, and Jehu. The first figure brought power to Issachar; the second attempted but failed to subvert that power (either by claiming it for a rival lineage within Issachar or by moving it outside that area); and the third succeeded in transferring the political authority to a different region altogether.

Thus the years following the dynasty of Omri posed serious challenges to the achievement of his original goals to distance the new capital from its eastern ties, shirk its old enemies there, and reorient it toward Phoenicia and the Mediterranean world at large. Threats and overt interference from the east increased almost in direct line with the arrival of Assyria in the last half of the eighth century BCE. Ultimately, the new seat of power in Transjordan itself proved an unstable one as competing leaders, such

---

[304] For the attempted conspiracy, see the story of Zimri, who managed to rule for only seven days (1 Kgs 16:9-20). It remains uncertain whether Zimri himself hailed from Issachar and represented a rival faction there or whether he came from somewhere outside Issachar. In any event, following Zimri's death Tibni posed a temporary challenge to Omri's claim to the throne at Samaria (1 Kgs 16:21-22).

[305] In fact, the biblical writers never again use the designation "House of /royal name/" as a reference to any of the northern kings. This marks a change in Israelite historiography that parallels the Assyrian use of the old rubric "House of *Omri*" (but never a subsequent king) throughout the remaining history of Israelite Samaria (see n. 20 above). The only possible exception in the biblical record comes with the mention of the "House of Jeroboam" in the vision of Am 7:9, which most commentators understand as a reference to the contemporary dynasty established by Jeroboam II (e.g., J. H. Hayes, *Amos*, 206-07). But I believe it is just as likely that, in describing this vision, the words of the speaker (or writer) carry an intentional double meaning, i.e., they were meant literally to recall the condemnation of the "House of Jeroboam I"—a curse that carries a familiar refrain in other biblical accounts (e.g., 1 Kgs 13:34; 2 Kgs 13:6; et passim)—and yet to include Jeroboam II in the same pronouncement of judgment. The king's informer, Amaziah, certainly took the bait (Am 7:10). By using the name of Israel's first successful dynast (Jeroboam I), then, the vision in Amos relates to and anticipates the fall of the entire kingdom, not merely the dynasty or "House" of the reigning Jeroboam II. Finally, the frequent use of *mār/Bīt-Ḫumrî* by the Assyrians from the time of Jehu on may stem not only from the fact that they knew Omri as founder of Samaria (see n. 20 above) but also from their knowledge that all leaders subsequent to the Omride Dynasty came, in fact, from Transjordan. In their own political organization, the Assyrians always seem to have kept this region (*Galʾadi*) distinct from Israel proper (*Samerina*).

as Shallum, Menahem, his son Pekahiah, and finally Pekah, plotted against each other for control over Israel. The political intrigues that resulted made inevitable Samaria's ties to lands just across the Jordan from old Issachar and rendered the city's relations with other regional powers, such as Damascus and Jerusalem, precarious at best.

Within this context, one must consider the reasons for Tiglath-pileser's having allowed the enclave around Samaria to retain its nonprovincial status—particularly since he had already incorporated virtually every other area north of the Sorek River system on the coast west of Israel and toward the Dead Sea on the east (including territories on both sides of the Jordan River) into the Assyrian network of provinces. At least part of the answer surely raises very practical issues: the Assyrians, as shown in their reliefs and sculptures, relied heavily on chariot-corp warfare. Damascus had discovered earlier that chariots proved cumbersome at best and most often useless in mountainous terrain such as that which surrounded Samaria (1 Kgs 20, especially vv. 23-25). The Assyrians surely made the same discovery during their difficult and protracted struggle against the Urarteans. But beyond this basic factor, the more substantive reason again focuses primarily on the economic strategy of Assyria. The main north-south artery running along the Mediterranean coast, though only 10 or so miles west of Samaria, now lay inside the new province of Du'ru, while Gal'adi and Magiddu controlled, respectively, the King's Highway and the most direct lateral route connecting the coastal areas to the hinterland—a route that bypassed Samaria to the north. Moreover, the increasingly unpredictable power base in Transjordan had become part of Gal'adi, while Magiddu appears to have taken in the area of older networks in Issachar. These developments stripped the economic strategists in the Israelite capital, now isolated on the seaward slopes of Ephraim, of access to the lucrative transit trade flowing through and around Palestine. The ultimate subjection of Samaria and its organization as a province would hold mainly symbolic gains for Assyria's master plan in the west, not impressive economic ones. By the conclusion of Tiglath-pileser's western activities in 732 BCE, the Assyrian grip on all surrounding commercial centers, particularly the terminal ports and trade outlets, combined with the concomitant reduction of autonomy within the northern kingdom itself, had strangled the capital city economically and therefore had determined its bleak political destiny.

Yet to the end Samaria remained true to the overall purpose and design envisioned by its founders, Omri and Ahab. The new city served primarily as a royal compound, a home to the ruling elite of Israel. As such, it never functioned as a commercial center in its own right; its charter called only for the production of a certain royal ideology. The city's reputation never survived on its economic or cultic status, but only on the fame of the potentates who ruled from within its walls. As a result, Samaria represented an even greater conglomerate of consumers, proportionately speaking, than did Jerusalem to the south. In time, a network of private estates grew up in the Ephraimite hill country around the city to support their representatives in the court.[306] And unlike Jerusalem, this capital appears always to have remained a city closed to the

---

[306] See the spatial distribution of sites named in the Samaria Ostraca in *MBA*, 87, No. 137.

prophets of Israel and to any others who would oppose its goals. To posit that the biblical traditions have suppressed all accounts that revealed any access which these orthodox religious figures might have had to the northern capital seems unrealistic. The Deuteronomistic Historians, in fact, showed much greater interest in recording the details of prophetic activity in the Israel than they did in Judah. Even when political change occurred with the help of such factions (as in the case of Jehu and Elijah/Elisha), the prophets themselves never seem to have gained entry inside the gates of Samaria. While many have assumed that the city planning included one or more Israelite-Canaanite temples, archaeology remains quite inconclusive concerning such a structure. In the biblical record, neither does one hear of great cultic pageantry at Samaria.

In short, if Jerusalem embodied a "regal-ritual city"[307] that served mainly ideological functions and thereby became economically dependent on its rural environs, Samaria evolved in much the same manner, economically speaking, yet the city appears to have focused its efforts more on the regal business of kingship than on the strictures of kinship or the ritual of cult. Unlike Jerusalem, Samaria left its cultic aspect to previously designated, outlying centers near the borders of the kingdom (e.g., Dan in the north, Bethel in the south), while the most orthodox Yahwists continued to promote their cause at former cult sites, such as Gilgal, Shechem, Shiloh, and Mount Carmel. Prophets working in the north generally had to speak in these places and either summon the king to the site (Ahab at Carmel) or depend on governmental lackeys to carry the word to the court at Samaria (Amos vs. Amaziah at Bethel). Neither did the rulers of Samaria replicate the city's plan or central power structure in the outlying countryside, and in this they deviated from another of Fox's noted attributes of the true regal-ritual city. While the centers at Megiddo and Hazor may have satisfied in certain ways the criterion of self-duplication, one must remember that Samaria itself did not establish those store cities but inherited them as previous creations of Jerusalem/Judah (assuming a tenth-century BCE date for certain key strata at both of the northern sites mentioned). In any event, as grand as the capital of Israel might have appeared at its zenith, it always lacked a quantitative urban aspect and served primarily as the private habitation of the kingdom's secular leaders, who found that their access to positions of authority depended more on active achievement than on mere heredity (as with the House[hold] of David in Jerusalem). The throne in Samaria never fully incorporated the concept of ascribed kingship.

Finally, I must reiterate one point regarding the archaeology of Samaria in the age of Assyria. Virtually every recent investigation into the history of this period has

---

[307]This rubric comes from an insightful study of urban centers presented in R. G. Fox, *Urban Anthropology: Cities in their Cultural Settings* (Englewood Cliffs, NJ: Prentice-Hall, Inc., 1977), 39-57. Nearly all recent studies of the character and function of the political and spiritual capitals in the ancient Near East continue to overlook this very helpful model (e.g., see the essays in J. G. Westenholz, ed., *Capital Cities: Urban Planning and Spiritual Dimensions*. Bible Lands Museum Jerusalem Publications No. 2 (Jerusalem: Bible Lands Museum, 1998).

asserted that the empirical record at Samaria appears unestablished or, at best, difficult to interpret and that any appeal to it must receive support from "all the other available evidence,"[308] which I take to mean the written texts. I value the expediency of a holistic approach to any historical problem and recommend taking under consideration every relevant source of information. To assist in this pursuit, my principal goal has aimed at outlining and evaluating each stratified deposit that yielded some portion of the published corpus of pottery that Kenyon used in support of her historical reconstruction. One result of this effort shows that, mainly for the reasons cited above, the foreign takeover of Samaria did not involve a wholesale or even formidable destruction of the city. In fact, though the Assyrians did utilize the former Israelite capital within a larger plan, the official report from the Joint Expedition to Samaria leaves one with the impression that traces of their empire are few in number there.

---

[308] K. L. Younger, Jr., *CBQ* 61 (1999), 473-75.

Chapter VII

CONCLUDING REMARKS

The City and Region of Samaria beyond the Iron Age

*Our knowledge of the past is made up
from its sweepings and rubbish-pits.
We could do with more of them.*

R. D. Barnett, *PEQ* 1939, 172

According to biblical traditions, the region of Samaria experienced three successive models of social, economic, and political organization during the Iron Age I-II periods: (1) locally controlled tribal allotments under Joshua in the days of the judges (Josh 16-17; 19:49-50); (2) centrally controlled administrative districts under Solomon (1 Kgs 4:7-19); and (3) a foreign controlled imperial province, beginning with Assyrian hegemony in the second half of the eighth century BCE (2 Kgs 17:24ff.). This study has focused on the last of these historical phases.

Though in Phase 1 the region embodied the "cradle of Israelite civilization," it attained its greatest prominence following Omri's rise to power in the early ninth century BCE. Quickly transferring the country's political center from Tirzah to Samaria (1 Kgs 16:21-24), Omri and his successors—particularly his son Ahab—transformed this one-time family estate into a relatively small but cosmopolitan royal city. So impressive appeared the fortification walls, palace, large courtyards with rectangular pools, public buildings, and storerooms, that writers spoke of Samaria as the undisputed "head of Ephraim" (Is 7:9), or as Jerusalem's "*elder* sister" who ruled and influenced numerous "daughters" (outlying villages) of her own (Ezek 16:46, 53, 55, 61; 23:4-5). Bountiful archaeological discoveries of ivory fragments and furnishings spanning the period from Ahab to Jeroboam II correlate well with later biblical memories of opulent, ivory-appointed houses and royal banquets in the capital (1 Kgs 22:39; Am 3:15, 6:4; Ps 45:9 [MT]). That the city now gave its name to the larger region bespeaks the power that emanated from this new, stately center. Even the villagers themselves sometimes came to be known as "Samaritans" rather than Israelites (2 Kgs 17:29).

Omri's new economic orientation toward the open markets of the Mediterranean brought the entire region of Samaria into greater contact with foreign cultures. With Ahab's politically motivated marriage to Jezebel, Samaria gained access to Phoenician wealth and also exposure to religious beliefs and customs there. As it became increasingly syncretistic under this influence, the political leadership incurred the scorn of Elijah and the orthodox religious establishment generally (1 Kgs 17-19). Ultraconservative factions with both religious and political aspirations arose. With backing from the prophetic leadership, conservative social groups, such as the Rechabites, and zealous segments of the military, the populist Jehu seized the throne of Samaria in 842 BCE (2 Kgs 9-10). Yet even in the late eighth century BCE the Assyrians continued referring to this region under the name *Bît Ḫu-um-ri-ia*, or "the House(hold)/Kingdom of Omri." Until the capital city itself fell ultimately to Sargon II in 720 BCE, Assyrian scribes sometimes used the designations "The House of Omri" and "Samaria" (*Sa-me-ri-na-a-a*) interchangeably, much as the contemporary Hebrew prophets themselves employed Samaria in reference both to the specific city and to the entire Ephraimite hill country.

From ca. 884-722/21 BCE, fourteen Israelite kings ruled from the city of Samaria. But the regional and even international prominence they brought to the area also presented its capital and religious centers (e.g., Bethel) as the clearest and most dangerous symbols of opposition to the Southern Kingdom of Judah and its cult at Jerusalem. This deeply rooted north-south schism and the Judahite perspective taken in the final Deuteronomistic History produced a critical treatment of the rulers and activities at Samaria in the Hebrew Bible, while extrabiblical sources (Mesha Stele; Assyrian annals) often pointed to the capital's political, military, and economic successes, despite periods of severe drought and famine (1 Kgs 17:1, 7; 18:2).

By the late eighth century BCE, the Assyrian provinces of Dor, Megiddo, and Gilead (compare Is 9:1) encompassed the Ephraimite hill country on the west, north, and east, respectively. In 722/21 BCE, armies led by Shalmaneser V and Sargon II penetrated the highlands, besieged and occupied the city of Samaria, deported large numbers of Israelites, and resettled the city primarily with captives from distant Syro-Mesopotamian locations as well as from southern Arabia (2 Kgs 17:24; the Display, Bull, Khorsabad Pavement, and Cylinder inscriptions of Sargon). If it has any historical credibility, the large number of deportees from Samaria (variously reported in Mesopotamian sources as 27,280 or 27,290 individuals) must surely have come from the "land of Samaria," a political concept that resembles the "land of Urushalimum" in the Amarna letters from the Late Bronze Age. The Assyrians came to identify virtually the entire Ephraimite hill country with the leading administrative center there and, in this manner, effectually transformed the highland region into the province of *Samerina*. Though its southern border remained fixed between Bethel and Mizpah (2 Kgs 17:28), Samerina appears now to have subsumed the coastal district of Dor, inasmuch as no governor's name appears for the latter in Assyrian Eponym Lists and a battle itinerary from Esarhaddon's tenth campaign in 671 BCE records Aphek, in the southern Sharon Plain, as part of the "land of Samerina." Though now an official part of Samaria's political structure, this important site had served the economic interests of the area throughout Iron Age II before becoming part of the Dor district.

Following the decline of Assyrian influence at home and abroad after 633 BCE, Josiah attempted to reannex to Judah at least the southern extent of Samerina, as far as Bethel (2 Kgs 23:4), and perhaps the province in full measure (2 Kgs 23:29-30 // 2 Chron 35:20-24). His political and religious reforms led him to desecrate local shrines in the north and to execute their priests (1 Kgs 13:1-2; 2 Kgs 23:15-20), while merely closing the high places of the south and recalling local priests to Jerusalem. After the fall of Jerusalem to Nebuchadnezzar in 587/86 BCE, the Babylonian-appointed governor of Judah, Gedaliah, established his administrative center at Mizpah rather than in Jerusalem (Jer 41:1). This decision may belie the south's orientation toward Samaria more than Jerusalem at this time, possibly because those who survived the scourge of Judah needed the stores of grain, honey, and oil that remained available in the region of Samaria (Jer 41:4-8). Some have suggested that the Babylonians now officially considered the ravaged south part of Samaria.

When Persia conquered Babylon in 539 BCE, Cyrus and his successors retained Samaria as the administrative center in the "Province Beyond the River [Euphrates]" and placed it under the governorship of Sanballat. Excavators have discovered a large garden area (.25 m-thick; 45 x 50 m) that surrounded the district governor's palace there. A fifth-century Athenian coin, three Sidonian coins from the reign of Abdastart I (370-358 BCE), fourteen Aramaic ostraca, plus significant quantities of pottery imported from Aegean centers during the late sixth to late fourth centuries BCE (e.g., Black- and Red-Figured, White-Ground, and Black-Burnished Wares) all attest to the solvency of the Ephraimite economy, which Persia apparently underwrote (Ez 4:14). It seems likely that the economic dependence of Judah upon Samaria increased during this period (compare Neh 5:1-5). As a result, northern leaders viewed efforts to revitalize Jerusalem as a fortified center of activity late in this period as an act of sedition against Samaria and the Persian empire alike (Ez 4; Neh 2, 4, 6; 1 Esd 2).

The local and international economies of the north continued to flourish throughout most of the turbulent Hellenistic Period, as witnessed in thousands of Rhodian stamped jar fragments recovered from the city of Samaria. In the late fourth century BCE, when locals assassinated Andromachus, a Greek general whom Alexander the Great had installed as prefect of Syria, Samaria incurred Alexander's full wrath. Citizens who could fled eastward with numerous legal and administrative documents written in Aramaic (the Samaria Papyri), only to have Alexander's army overtake and execute them in a cave in the precipitous Wadi ed-Daliyeh. As the city they abandoned became more fully Greek in character, the center of Samaritan activity shifted to the old political and cultic base at Shechem. A series of beautifully built round towers at Samaria (8.5 m in height; 13 to 14.7 m in diameter) and a subsequent massive defense wall (4 m thick) with square towers bear witness to the current political vicissitudes, as the successors of Alexander the Great, the Ptolemies and Seleucids, competed for control over the region. The greatest setback to Samaria, however, emerged more locally. Late in this period (ca. 108/107 BCE), the Hasmonean priest John Hyrcanus gained de facto independence in Judea following the death of the

Seleucid ruler Antiochus VII in 128 BCE and planned a frontal assault on the region and city of Samaria. Following the capture of Shechem and the burning of the Samaritan temple on Mount Gerizim, a year-long siege against the city of Samaria destroyed much of the Fortress Wall and brought the entire region temporarily under Judean control (Josephus, *Antiquities* XIII.275-281; *Wars* I.64-66).

The Roman conquest of Palestine by Pompey in 63 BCE set the stage for the climactic resurgence of Samaria, beginning with the tenure of Gabinius (57-55 BCE) as provincial governor. He rebuilt the city walls, created new residential areas, and constructed a forum with an adjoining basilica northeast of the summit. Soon after the earthquake in 31 BCE, Herod the Great expanded the city's fortifications (the perimeter wall stretched for nearly 3 km in circumference and enclosed an area of roughly 160 acres), apportioned both city and territorial properties among his former allies in war (Josephus recorded a figure of 6,000 colonists), offered them special constitutional rights, and consequently considered Samaria "a third rampart against the entire nation," behind only his own palace in Jerusalem and the fortress Antonia, which protected the temple there (Josephus, *Antiquities* XV.292-98; *Wars* I.403). Even the 12.5-meter-wide street that led into the city became a thriving bazaar, and additional temples and altars as well as a stadium and theater adorned the summit and slopes of the city. To honor Emperor Augustus, Herod renamed this magnificent place *Sebaste*. It became a center of celebration, ceremony, and magic (compare Acts 8:9). Perhaps for these reasons, and because of the Samaritan–Jewish schism, natives of Judea generally circumnavigated the entire region when travelling to and from Jerusalem (Matt 19:1; Luke 17:11; compare John 4:4-9), and the followers of Jesus treated it as a virtual foreign territory in their early missionary and church planting efforts (Acts 1:8; Acts 8:1-25; 9:31; 15:3).

Following the Roman period, the grandeur of Samaria-Sebaste gradually faded during the Byzantine era. Archaeologists have recovered few remains from the site that date to this period.

APPENDIXES

Appendix A: *Findspots for Published Stratified Pottery (Periods 4-7)*

Appendix B: *Findspots for Published Stratified Fragments of Ivory*

Appendix C: *Findspots for Published Stratified Israelite Ostraca*

Appendix D: *Neo-Assyrian Literary References to the Northern Kingdom of Israel*

Appendix E: *Published Stratified Pottery Representing Periods 4-7*

APPENDIX A

FINDSPOTS FOR PUBLISHED STRATIFIED POTTERY (PERIODS 4-7)

(data collected from field registry *Sabastya Qn, 1935*, Rockefeller Museum, Jerusalem;
cross referenced and corrected according to G. M. Crowfoot's handwritten stratification cards, PEF, London)

SS III Published Figure	Registry No. (* = marked for discard)	Strip	Provenance Coordinates	Feature	Local Layer	Principal Section Drawings	Date Excavated	Rockefeller Museum Ref. No.
Pottery Period 4								
6:1	Q 5271	Qk	120.121.19.126	Room *g*	Wall 136	9/67	—	—
6:2	QX 53	Q(x)-k	147.145.151.136	Room *h*	IX	—	—	—
6:3	QX 61	Q(x)-k	Between TT2-TT3	Room *k*	VIII	7/8/10	—	—
6:4	Q 4571	Qn	502.503	Room *n*	XII	22/23/65	5-22-35	—
6:5	*Q 2373 (base)	Qk	125.144	Room *k* (*h*?)	IVa.y	8/10/11	6-19-33	33.3147
	*Q 2374 (rim)	Qk	▶ Between TT2-TT3	Room *k*	VII, VIII	7/8/10	6-6/7-33	33.3383-84
6:6	QX 55	Q(x)-k	Between TT2-TT3	Room *k*	VII	7/8/10	—	—
6:7	*Q 2548d	Qk	▶ Between TT2-TT3	Room *k*	VII	7/8/10	6-6-33(?)	—
6:8	QX 44	Q(x)-k	North of TT2	Room *j*	IX	7/13-16	—	—
6:9	QX 30	Q(x)-c	▷ 86.2.88.E	N Courtyard	VIe	25-27	—	—
6:10	QX 43	Q(x)-c	86.2.88	N Courtyard	IV	25-27	—	—
6:11	QX 40	Q(x)-c	86.2.88.W	N Courtyard	IVh	25-27	—	—
6:12	QX 42	Q(x)-k	122.125.19.121	Room *h* (?)	Va	8	(1935)	—
6:13	QX 46	Q(x)-c	86.2.88.E, W of 104	N Courtyard	V	25-27	—	—
†6:14	QX 76	Q(x)-k	125.144	Room *h*	IVx.z	8/10/11	—	—
6:15	QX 45	Q(x)-k	125.144	Room *h*	IVa	8/10/11	—	—
6:16	QX 41	Q(x)-k	North of TT2	Room *j*	IX	7/13-16	—	—
6:17	*Q 2328c	Qk	▶ Between TT2-TT3	Room *k*	VII	7/8/10	6-7-33	—
6:18	*Q 2377	Qk	155.151.136.147	Room *h* (*l*?)	IX	—	6-16-33	—
6:19	*Q 2267	Qg	325.304	Courtyard	IX	30-32/37	5-20-33	—
6:20	*Q 5213	Qn	502.503	Room *n*	XII	22/23/65	6-16-33	—
6:21	*QX 54	Q(x)-k	120.121.19.126	Room *g* (*n*?)	IXb	9/67	—	—
6:22	?Q 5214	Qn	502.503	Room *n*	XIa	22/23/65	—	—
6:23	?Q 5212	Qn	502.503	Room *n* (*g*?)	XIIa.b	22/23/65	—	—
6:24	?Q 5211	Qn	502.503	Room *n*	XIa	22/23/65	—	—
6:25	*Q 2328a	Qk	▶ Between TT2-TT3	Room *k*	VII	7/8/10	6-7-33	—
6:26	Q 5058	Qn	502.503	Room *n*	XIa.b	22/23/65	—	—
6:27	Q 5061	Qn	502.503	Room *n*	XIa	22/23/65	—	—
6:28	Q 5059	Qn	502.503	Room *n*	XII	22/23/65	—	—
6:29	Q 5060	Qn	502.503	Room *n*	Xa	22/23/65	—	—
6:30	Q 5054	Qn	502.503	Room *n*	Xa	22/23/65	—	—
6:31	QX 32	Q(x)-c	86.2.88.E	N Courtyard	VIe	25-27	—	—
6:32	Q 5066a	Qn	509.126	Room *j*	X	19/64	(1935)	—
6:33	*Q 2532	Qk	∗ N of TT2	Room *j*	IXr	7/13-16	6-26-33	—
6:34	Q 5056	Qn	502.503	Room *n*	XI	22/23/65	—	—
6:35	*Q 2328b	Qk	▶ Between TT2-TT3	Room *k*	VII	7/8/10	6-7-33	—
6:36	Q 5055	Qn	502.503	Room *n*	Xa	22/23/65	—	—
6:37	Q 5065	Qn	502.503	Room *n*	XI	22/23/65	(1935)	—
6:38	Q 5057	Qn	502.503	Room *n*	XI	22/23/65	—	—
6:39	Q 5062	Qk	120.121.19.126	Room *h*	Wall 157	9/67	(1935)	—
6:40	Q 5063	Qn	502.503	Room *n*	XIa	22/23/65	(1935)	—

† = the only fragment published in support of Kenyon's "Period IVa" (see *SS III*, 113f.)
▶ = recorded as *E Strip, Between TT2-TT3* in field notebook *Sabastya Qn*, Rockefeller Museum, Jerusalem
▷ = recorded as *86.2.88* in field notebook *Sabastya Qn*, Rockefeller Museum, Jerusalem
∗ = recorded as *E Strip, N or TT2* in field notebook *Sabastya Qn*, Rockefeller Museum, Jerusalem

Pottery Period 4

7:1	Q 4881	Qn	504.508.509.510	Casemate	V	39/66	6-5-35	——
7:2	Q 4876	Qn	504.508.509.510	Casemate	V	39/66	6-5-35	——
7:3	Q 5254	Qn	504.508.509.510	Casemate	V	39/66	6-5-35	——
7:4	Q 5255	Qn	504.508.509.510	Casemate	V	39/66	6-5-35	——
7:5	[no registry number in the published report; this rim likely came from the same locus as the other fragments in this group]							
7:6	Q 5257	Qn	504.508.509.510	Casemate	V(?)	39/66	(1935)	——
7:7	Q 4880	Qn	504.508.509.510	Casemate	V	39/66	6-5-35	——
7:8	Q 5256	Qn	504.508.509.510	Casemate	V(?)	39/66	(1935)	——
7:9	Q 4927	Qn	504.508.509.510	Casemate	V	39/66	6-5-35	——

Pottery Period 5

8:1	Q 2535	Qk	W of 124	Room (hk?) hq	VIII	7/42-44	6-15-33	33.3406
8:2	QX 104	Q(x)-n	125.144	Room hk	III	8/10/11	——	——
8:3	QX 90	Q(x)-n	125.144	Room hk	IIIo	8/10/11	——	——
8:4	*Q 2327	Qk	E Strip, Btw TT2-TT3	Room hk	V	7/8/10	6-6-33	——
8:5	QX 91	Q(x)-n	125.144	Room hk	III	8/10/11	——	——
8:6	Q 5215	Qn	502.503	Room n	IX	22/23/65	——	——
8:7	Q 5216	Qn	509.126	Room j (n?)	IX	19/64	——	——
8:8	QX 97	Q(x)-n	125.144	Room hk	IIIo	8/10/11	——	——

Pottery Period 6

9:1 †	Q 4978	Qn	513.514 (N of 551?)	leveling	VI (V?)	50/53-54	6-15-35	——
9:2 †	Q 4976	Qn	North of 551	leveling	V	50-52	6-15-35	35.3623
9:3	Q 5227	Qn	North of 551	leveling	Va	50-52	——	——
9:4 †	Q 5028	Qn	North of 551	leveling	V	50-52	6-15-35	——
9:5	Q 5225	Qn	North of 551	leveling	Va	50-52	——	——
9:6	Q 5226	Qn	North of 551	leveling	Va	50-52	——	——
9:7 †	Q 4977	Qn	North of 551	leveling	V	50-52	6-15-35	——
9:8 †	Q 4979b	Qn	North of 551	leveling	V	50-52	6-15-35	——
9:9 ††	Q 4979a	Qn	North of 551	leveling	V	50-52	6-15-35	——
9:10	Q 5238	Qn	North of 551	leveling	V	50-52	——	——
9:11	Q 5236	Qn	North of 551	leveling	Va	50-52	——	——
9:12	Q 5237	Qn	North of 551	leveling	V	50-52	——	——
9:13	Q 5231	Qn	North of 551	leveling	V	50-52	——	——
9:14	Q 5239	Qn	North of 551	leveling	Va	50-52	——	——
9:15	Q 5233	Qn	North of 551	leveling	V	50-52	——	——
9:16	Q 5232	Qn	North of 551	leveling	Va	50-52	——	——
9:17	Q 5230	Qn	North of 551	leveling	Va	50-52	——	——
9:18 ††	Q 4912	Qn	North of 551	leveling	Va	50-52	6-7-35	——

† = field register Qn lists only the published registry number; other data derived from the more primary stratification cards
†† = field register Qn contains no record of these two fragments; provenance data derived from the stratification cards

Pottery Period 6

10:1	Q 2471	Qk	122.125.19.121	Pit i	Va	8	6-8-33	33.3392
10:2	Q 2472	Qk	122.125.19.121	Pit i	Va	8	6-8-33	——
10:3	Q 2473	Qk	122.125.19.121	Pit i	Va	8	6-8-33	——
10:4	Q 2450	Qk	122.125.19.121	Pit i	Va	8	6-8-33	33.3389
10:5	Q 2478	Qk	122.125.19.121	Pit i	Va	8	6-8-33	33.3395
10:6	Q 2479	Qk	122.125.19.121	Pit i	Va	8	6-8-33	——
10:7	Q 2475	Qk	122.125.19.121	Pit i	Va	8	6-8-33	——
10:8	Q 2365	Qk	122.125.19.121	Pit i	V	8	6-8-33	33.3382
10:9	Q 2511	Qk	122.126.19.121	Pit i	Va	8	6-8-33	——

APPENDIX A — POTTERY

Pottery Period 6, cont.

10:10	Q 2512	Qk	122.126.19.121	Pit *i*	Va	8	6-8-33	——
10:11	Q 2514	Qk	122.126(?).19.121	Pit *i*	Va	8	6-8-33	——
10:12	Q 2513	Qk	122.126(?).19.121	Pit *i*	Va	8	6-8-33	——
10:13	Q 2515	Qk	122.126(?).19.121	Pit *i*	Va	8	6-8-33	——
10:14	Q 2516	Qk	122.126(?).19.121	Pit *i*	Va	8	6-8-33	——
10:15	Q 2481	Qk	122.125.19.121	Pit *i*	Va	8	6-8-33	——
10:16	Q 2483	Qk	122.125.19.121	Pit *i*	Va	8	6-8-33	33.3397
10:17	Q 2480	Qk	122.125.19.121	Pit *i*	Va	8	6-8-33	33.3396
10:18	Q 2485	Qk	122.125.19.121	Pit *i*	Va	8	6-8-33	1/47-1203
10:19	Q 2484	Qk	122.125.19.121	Pit *i*	Va	8	6-8-33	——
10:20	Q 2486	Qk	122.125.19.121	Pit *i*	Va	8	6-8-33	——
10:21	Q 2489	Qk	122.125.19.121	Pit *i*	Va	8	6-8-33	——
10:22	Q 2487	Qk	122.125.19.121	Pit *i*	Va	8	6-8-33	33.3398
10:23	Q 2488	Qk	122.125.19.121	Pit *i*	Va	8	6-8-33	33.3399
10:24	Q 2508	Qk	122.126.19.121	Pit *i*	Va	8	6-8-33	——
10:25	Q 2536	Qk	122.126.19.121	Pit *i*	Va	8	6-8-33	——
10:26	Q 2509a	Qk	122.126.19.121	Pit *i*	Va	8	6-8-33	33.3403
10:27	Q 2509b	Qk	122.126.19.121	Pit *i*	Va	8	6-8-33	33.3403

Field register *Qn* lists only the published registry numbers with no additional identifying data for any fragment listed in Fig. 10. The information given above appeared on G. M. Crowfoot's handwritten stratification cards.

This entire group was removed from *Pit i* in Kenyon's "Period V House." This pit cut into the middle of Wall 157 which, together with other associated walls, remained "standing considerably above the level of the adjoining rooms." In the final report, Kenyon concluded that *Pit i* served as a latrine for an upstairs room in the house. This unsealed pit "was full of midden-like rubbish, which contained a large amount of pottery" (*SS III*, 119-20). Kenyon's comments in *SS III*, 120, are convoluted and completely ambiguous as to whether this pit served Period IV, V, VI or VII, or throughout all of these phases (see also *SS I*, 105).

Pottery Period 7

▶ 11:1	QX 117	Q(x)-k	120.121.19.126	‡Room *g*	VII	9/67	——	——
▶ 11:2	QX 120	Q(x)-k	120.121.19.126	Room *kq*	V	9/67	——	——
11:3	QX 119	Q(x)-k	W of 124	Room *kq*	IIIc	7/42-44	——	——
11:4	Q 5222	Qn	504.503.509.508	Room *l*	Va	60-63	——	——
11:5	QX 118	Q(x)-k	120.121.19.126	Room *kq*	VII	9/67	——	——
11:6	Q 5221	Qn	504.503.509.508	Room *l*	Va	60-63	——	——
▶ 11:7	QX 112	Q(x)-k	120.121.19.126	‡Room *g*	VII	9/67	——	——
11:8	*Q 2372	Qk	W of 124	Room *kq*	Vc	7/42-44	6-20-33	——
11:9	QX 125	Q(x)-k	120.121.19.126	‡Room *g*	VIw	9/67	——	——
11:10	QX 126	Q(x)-k	120.121.19.126	Room *g*	VI	9/67	——	——
11:11	Q 2357a	Qk	W of 124	Room *hq*	VIw	7/42-44	6-15-33	——
▶ 11:12	QX 127	Q(x)-c	19.51.14.20	Room *e*	IVa	57/59	——	——
11:13	Q 2357b	Qk	W of 124	Room *hq*	VIw	7/42-44	6-15-33	——
11:14	*Q 2305	Qk	120.121.19.126	‡Room *g*	VIIe	9/67	5-31-33	——
11:15	QX 124	Q(x)-c	19.51.14.20	Room *e*	IVa	57/59	——	——
11:16	Q 5219	Qn	509.126	Room *f*	IIa.f	19/64	——	——
11:17	QX 123	Q(x)-c	19.51.14.20	Room *e*	IVa	57/59	——	——
11:18	QX 128	Q(x)-k	120.121.19.126	‡Room *e*	VI	9/67	——	——
11:19	QX 129	Q(x)-k	120.121.19.126	Room *f*	VI	9/67	——	——
11:20	QX 130	Q(x)-k	120.121.19.126	‡Room *g*	VI	9/67	——	——
▶ 11:21	Q 5235	Qn	509.126	Room *l*	IIa.f	19/64	——	——
11:22	Q 2537	Qk	W of 124	Room *hq*	VII	7/42-44	6-14-33	35.3720
11:23	Q 1653	Qc	19.51.14.20	Room *e*	VIc	57/59	6-8-33	——
11:24	QX 111	Q(x)-k	120.121.19.126	Room *g*	VI	9/67	——	——
11:25	QX 115	Q(x)-k(?)	122.125.19.121	Room *hk*	IIIz	8	——	——
▷ 11:26	Q 5224	Qn	509.126	‡Room *j (f?)*	IIa.f	19/64	——	——

Pottery Period 7, cont.

11:27	QX 110	Q(x)-k	120.121.19.126	Room g	VIII	9/67	———	———
11:28	*Q 1667	Qc	19.51.14.20	Room e	VIc	57/59	6-8-32	———
11:29	Q 5229	Qn	509.126	Room l	VIII	19/64	———	———
11:30	Q 5228	Qn	504.503.509.508	Room l	Va.z	60-63	———	———
11:31	*Q 5218	Qn	504.503.509.508	Room l	Va	60-63	———	———
▷ 11:32	QX 133	Q(x)-k	120.121.19.126	Room g	VI	9/67	———	———
11:33	Q 5223	Qn	504.503.509.508	Room l	Va	60-63	———	———
11:34	QX 316	Q(x)-n	120.121.19.126	Room g	VI	9/67	———	———
11:35	*Q 2368	Qk	125.144	Room hk	IIIa	8/10/11	6-19-33	———
11:36	QX 131	Q(x)-k	120.121.19.126	Room g	VII	9/67	———	———
11:37	QX 132	Q(x)-k	120.121.19.126	Room g	VI	9/67	———	———

▶ Note the following discrepancies:
   11:1 = Layer VI, according to Kenyon's handwritten draft of *SS III*
   11:2 = *W of 124*, Layer VIw, according to Kenyon's handwritten draft of *SS III*
   11:7 = QX 122, Layer V, according to Kenyon's handwritten draft of *SS III*
   11:12 = Layer IV c (or e?; illegible), according to Kenyon's handwritten draft of *SS III*
   11:21 = *504.503.509.508*, Layer Va, according to Kenyon's handwritten draft of *SS III*

▷ The entry for Q 5224 (11:26) in the handwritten draft of *SS III* reads as follows: *Rim of cooking pot, light red ware, with grits. This is the type with short thick ridged rim which appears in IV, is common in VI, and continues throughout VII.* The latter statement matches that actually published in *SS III* under Fig. 11:32, QX 113. This exact statement also appears in the PEF records under fragment QX 133, which is marked for publication as Fig. 11:32 (which, in turn, mistakenly printed the registry number as 113). The typescript notes in field registry *Sabastya Qn, 1935* (Rockefeller Museum, Jerusalem) describes Q 5224 as *Frag. jar rim, red to gray hard ware, rare white limestone grits*, and assigns it to Qn, *509.126*, IIaf. The PEF record concurs but assigns the fragment to Room *f*, while *SS III* (Fig. 11:26) eventually placed it in Room *j*. In sum, I believe the data entered above for 11:32 are correct; too many questions surround the jar rim described in 11:26, however, to allow certainty regarding its provenance; it shares the same coordinates and local layer designations as 11:21 (which, alas, has recording difficulties of its own–see previous note), and thereby may even belong to Room *l*.

* Vessel/fragment marked for discard in field registry *Sabastya, Qn, 1935*, Rockefeller Museum.

‡ Kenyon's handwritten draft of *SS III*, Fig. 11, corrected these room assignments from Room *f* to the room shown above (usually to Room *g*, which was contiguous to *f* on the south). For, 11:18, these notes also altered Room *f* to Room *g*; yet it appeared finally in the published report under Room *e*. Since field registry *Sabastya, Qn* (Rockefeller Museum) did not include room designations, I could not cross-reference these entries.

NB: *Despite all the notations and glosses that clutter the entries in PP 7, I have now confirmed the provenance data for every item against the information recorded on the Stratification Cards recorded and maintained by Ms. Grace M. Crowfoot and now stored in the Palestine Exploration Fund, London. As a result, the provenance data shown above are, in our judgment, reliable.*

(The reader may wish to refer to the notes which follow Appendix F in our earlier work, *AIS-I*, 260. Although those remarks apply here as well, I will not repeat them for the sake of brevity.)

APPENDIX B

FINDSPOTS FOR PUBLISHED STRATIFIED FRAGMENTS OF IVORY

(data collected and collated from the *Q* field registries recorded by G. M. Crowfoot
and stored in the Palestine Exploration Fund, London)

SS II Published Figure	Unpublished Registry No.	Strip	Coordinates	Feature	Local Layer	Principal Section Drawing #	Date Excavated	Brief Description
SS II, Pl. I								
1	1580	Qc	49.26.25	Room *hq*	II	70	5-27-32	Horus medallion in relief
2	1544	Qc	49.26.25	Room *hq*	II	70	5-20-32	Horus plaque in relief
3	1542	Qc	49.26.25	Room *hq*	II	70	5-18-32	Horus plaque/medallion (?)
SS II, Pl. II								
1a	1595	Qc	19.51.14.20	Room *e*	VI	59?/74	5-23-32	Headless figure: top frag.
b	1596	Qc	19.51.14.20	Room *e*	VI	59?/74	5-24-32	Headless figure: bottom frag.
2	1543	Qc	49.26.25	Room *hq*	II	70	5-19-32	Hah figure plaque
SS II, Pl. III								
1a	1546	Qc	49.26.25	Room *hq*	II	70	5-19-32	Isis & Nephthys: left side
b	1592	Qc	49.26.25	Room *hq*	II	70	5-25-32	Isis & Nephthys: right side
2	3018	Qk	W of 124	Rooms *hq-kq*	VII	——	6-14-33	The Eyes of Horus
SS II, Pl. IV								
1	1978	Qc	19.51.14.20	Room *e*	IVd	59	6-9-32	Figure facing right
2	1995	Qc	19.51.14.20	Room *e*	IVb	——	6-6-32	Arm-wing of figure facing left
3a	1995	Qc	19.51.14.20	Room *e*	IVb	——	6-6-32	Arms-wing (Frag. 1: Upper part)
b	1995	Qc	19.51.14.20	Room *e*	IVd-sift	——	6-9-32	Legs-garment (Frag. 2: Lower part
4	5134	Qn	(in filling of Hellenistic RT of casemate walls)			61/72	1935	Arm-wing of fig. facing right
5	1970	Qc	19.51.14.20	Room *e*	IVb	——	6-3-32	Wing-hand grasping flower

* associated with No. 3 in the photography journal at the PEF, and subsumed under the same Registry No.

SS II, Pl. V								
1	1577	Qc	49.26.25	Room *hq*	II	70	5-27-32	Sphinx in lotus thicket
2	1584	Qc	19.51.14.20	Room *e*	IV	43	5-25-32	Frag. similar to No. 1
3	1582	Qc	49.26.25	Room *hq*	?	70	5-27-32	Frag. sphinx on solid plaque
SS II, Pl. VI								
1	1632	Qc	19.51.14.20	Room *e*	?	——	5-25-32	Fragmentary sphinx
2	1799	Qc	19.(51.14.20)	Room *e*	?	——	5-25-32	Ram-heads, sphinx bodies, & double crowns
SS II, Pl. VII								
1	1843	Qc	(provenance data not available)*		——	——	5-31-32	Wing w/blue and red inlay
2	1930	Qc	19.51.14.20	Room *e*	V	59	6-2-32	Frag. head (of sphinx?)
3	2034	Qc	19.51.14.20	Room *e*	IVb	——	6-1-32	Frag. body, wings, tail
4	1586	Qc	19.51.14.20	Room *e*	IV	76/77	5-27-32	Sphinx wing & palmette
5	3007	Qk	W of 124	Rooms *hq-kq*	IIIc	43/70	6-13-33	Hindquarters-wing tips of sphinx
6	3006	Qk	E Strip.S Half	Room *k*	V	83	5-31-33	Forepart of sphinx
7	1600	Qc	19.51.14.20	Room *e*	V	59	5-25-32	Sphinx similar to No. 6
8	1997a	Qc	19.51.14.20	Room *e*	IVb	——	6-1-32	Chest of ram (?)

9	1944b.2	Qc	19.51.14.20	Room e	IV	76/77	1932	Frag. of feathering
10	1944b.3	Qc	19.51.14.20	Room e	IV	76/77	1932	Frag. of feathering
11	1944b.6	Qc	19.51.14.20	Room e	IV	76/77	1932	Feathering or bushy tail
12	1941	Qc	19.51.14.20	Room e	IV	76/77	6-6-32	Kilt with chevron pattern
13	3001	Qk	W of 124	Wall 132E	IVc	44/71	6-17-33	Double crown & sacred tree
14	1787c	Qc	19.51.14.20 (?)	Room e	?	——	5-25-32	Frag. kilt w/chevron pattern

* it is amazing that the provenance data were not recorded for unusual pieces like this one; compare similar fragments in No. 1892, taken from Qc, *19.51.14.20*, Layer IVb, 6-1-32

SS II, Pl. VIII

1	1823	Qc	19.51.14.20	Room e	IVb	——	6-1-32	Battling lion & griffin (?)
2	2033	Qc	19.51.14.20	Room e	IVb	——	6-1-32	Fragment of lion*
3	2033	Qc	19.51.14.20	Room e	IVb	——	6-1-32	Fragment of lion
4	2036	Qc	19.51.14.20	Room e	IV	76/77	6-2-32	Additional frag. from No. 1
5	2033	Qc	19.51.14.20	Room e	IVb	——	6-1-32	Leg of bull

* Nos. 2-5 reportedly represent fragments from the same plaque as No. 1 (or one quite similar to it) and Crowfoot noted that "all were found close together" (*SS II*, 22)

SS II, Pl. IX

1a	1553	Qc	49.26.25	Room hq	II	70	5-20-32	Two lions:
b	1554	Qc	49.26.25	Room hq	II	70	5-20-32	carved in the round
2	1574	Qc	49.26.25	Room hq	II	70	5-28-32	Lion on plaque in relief
3	1762	Qc	(unavailable; compared to 1573-74, from 49.26.25, II)				6-9-32	Lion on plaque in relief
4	1573	Qc	49.26.25	Room hq	II	70	5-20-32	Lion on plaque in relief

SS II, Pl. X

1	1545	Qc	49.26.25	Room hq	II	70	5-19-32	Lion grappling with bull
2	1572	Qc	49.26.25	Room hq	II (?)*	70	5-20-32	Lion-Bull plaque
3	1637b	Qc	49.26.25 (?)	Room hq	?	70?	6-1-32	Lion trampling human victim
4	1754	Qc	19.51.14.20	Room e	IVb	——	6-1-32	Scene resembling Nos. 3 & 5
5	1637a	Qc	(notes say photographed with No. 1827b = Pl. XXIII:5)				5-29-32	Lion trampling human victim
6	1776a	Qc	12.27.14.13	Rooms e-g	V	76/77	5-24-32	Hoofed animal, hindlegs (horse?)
7	3005	Qk	W of 124	Wall 132E	IVc	44/71	6-19-33	Hindlegs & udder of cow
8	3004	Qk	W of 124	Wall 132E	IVc	44/71	6-19-33	Plaque of grazing/drinking deer

* published originally in *PEFQ* January (1933), Pl. II:3, with all provenance data *except* a local layer designation, which is also absent from the stratification cards; this seems to confirm the failure to record this datum at the point of excavation

SS II, Pl. XI

1	3008	Qk	125.144	Room hk	IIIb.x	10	6-24-33	Throned figure w/attendant
2	1802a	Qc	(provenance data not available)				5-25-32	Lower face w/beard
3	——	——	——	——	——	——	——	Profile of face (inlaid eye)
4	1932	Qc	19.51.14.20	Room e	IV	76/77	6-4-32	Frag. of face w/crown (inlaid eye)
5	1751a*	Qc	19.51.14.20	Room e	IVb	——	6-1-32	Face w/hair & inlaid eye**
6	1753	Qc	19.51.14.20	Room e	IVb	——	6-3-32	Head crowned w/disk

* a duplication of this registration number occurred with a pale blue faience amulet, Qc, *19.51.14.20*, Layer VIc
** a handwritten note on the stratification card indicates that this item "can't be found"

SS II, Pl. XII

1	1601	Qc	19.51.14.20	Room e	?	——	6-1-32	Man w/right hand raised
2	1603	Qc	19.51.14.20	Room e	?	——	5-25-32	Human-headed figure (sphinx?)
3	1604	Qc	19.51.14.20	Room e	?	——	5-25-32	Human-headed figure (sphinx?)
4	1919	Qc	19.51.14.20	Room e	IV	76/77	6-2-32	Ear & back of human head
5	1844c	Qc	19.51.14.20	Room e	?	——	5-31-32	Top of head w/frag. of uraeus

APPENDIX B — IVORIES

6	1599	Qc	19.51.14.20	Room e	?	——	5-31-32	Man's head w/conical cap w/tassel
7	1752	Q	(provenance data not available)		——	——	——	Frag. of head (sphinx?)
8	1918	Qc	19.51.14.20	Room e	IV	76/77	6-2-32	Head of a man
9	1913	Qc	19.51.14.20	Room e	IV	76/77	6-1-32	Man w/right arm extended
10	1558	Qc	19.12.(51.14).20	Room e	IV*	76/77	5-18-32	Frag. leg of striding figure
11	3010	Qk	W of 124	Rooms hq-kq	VIz	——	6-15-33	Crown, 2 ostrich feathers, & disk
12	1961	Qc	19.51.14.20	Room e	IVd	59	6-9-32	Hand grasping an object
13	1968	Qc	19.51.14.20	Room e	IVd	59	6-8-32	Human foot w/toes (from plaque)
14	1940	Qc	19.51.14.20	Room e	IV	76/77	6-6-32	Left arm & shoulder of figure
15	1817a	Qc	19.51.14.20	Room e	IV	76/77	6-1-32	Outer robe of figure moving left
16	1948	Qc	19.51.14.20	Room e	IV	76/77	6-2-32	Phrygian cap
17	2023	Qc	19.51.14.20	Room e	VII-sift	59/74	6-13-32	Phrygian cap
18	1817b	Qc	19.51.14.20	Room e	IV	76/77	6-1-32	Frag. of kneeling figure
19	1874	Qc	19.51.14.20	Room e	IV	76/77	6-1-32	Frag. leg of figure striding right

* According to *SS II*, 28, "the piece was found in Qc in the same disturbed stratum as the finer, less damaged, fragments"; thus, Qc, *19.51.14.20*, Layer IV, seems to offer the most likely findspot for this entry. The sharpening of this fragment occurred subsequent to its breakage and therefore seems intentional (suggested by both the stratification card notes and the annotated entry in *SS II*)

SS II, Pl. XIII

1	1602	Qc	19.51.14.20	Room e	VI	59?/74	5-28-32	Two rows of hieroglyphs
2	1588	Qc	19.51.14.20	Room e	?*	——	5-29-32	Woman at the window
3	1775	Qc	49.26.25	Beneath 26	II	70	5-24-32	Fish
4	1635	Qc	14(19).51.14.20.N	Room e	VIII	59/74	6-14-32	Winged uraeus on papyrus flower
5	1598	Qc	49.26.25	Room hq	?	70	5-28-32	Uraeus crowned w/disk
6	1810	Qc	19.51.14.20**	Room e	IVd	59	5-28-32	Goat on hind legs
7	1923	Qc	19.51.14.20	Room e	IV	76/77	6-1-32	Bear or small lion
8	2043	Qc	19.51.14.20	Room e	IV	76/77	6-1-32	Hawk's head w/frag. crown
9	1815	Qc	19.51.14.20***	Room e	VI	59?/74	5-28-32	Ibis head of Thoth
10	1958	Qc	19.51.14.20	Room e	IVd	59	6-9-32	Frag. from a replica of No. 6
11	3022	Qk	120.121.19.126	Room g	VII	59/74	5-31-33	Hindquarters of (Set?) animal
12	1813	Qc	19.51.14.20***	Room e	VI	59?/74	5-28-32	Head of an ibex
13	1912	Qc	19.51.14.20	Room e	IVb-sift	——	6-1-32	Hand w/*neb*-bowl; eye of Horus

* The famous ivory showing "The Lady at the Window" attests clearly to the fact that the excavators failed to record all local layer designations in their provenance data; when Crowfoot initially published this piece in *PEFQ* January (1933), Pl. III:3, he was able to cite summit strip, segment, and date of excavation, but not the layer from which the workers had retrieved this piece.

** While only "Qc, 5-28-32" appeared on the stratification card for No. 1810, the card referred us to Q1958, from which I gathered the provenance data given here.

*** provenance data not available on stratification card; verified through the photography journal

SS II, Pl. XIV

1	1979	Qc	19.51.14.20	Room e	IV	76/77	6-2-32	Pharaoh smiting an enemy
2	1980	Qc	19.51.14.20	Room e	IV	76/77	6-2-32	Winged human fig. holding lilies
3	1822	Qc	19.51.14.20	Room e	VI	59?/74	5-28-32	Sphinx, lily, and lion
4	1982	Qc	19.51.14.20	Room e	IV	76/77	6-2-32	Bird-headed sphinx
5	1981	Qc	19.51.14.20	Room e	IV	76/77	6-2-32	Winged sphinx, double crown, kilt
6	1983	Qc	19.51.14.20	Room e	IV	76/77	6-2-32	Frag. similar to No. 5
7	1984	Qc	19.51.14.20	Room e	IV	76/77	6-2-32	Kilted sphinx w/captive
8	1985c	Qc	19.51.14.20	Room e	IV	76/77	6-2-32	Winged figure facing right
9	1985b	Qc	19.51.14.20	Room e	IV	76/77	6-2-32	Figure approaching sacred tree
10	1985d	Qc	19.51.14.20	Room e	IV	76/77	6-2-32	Figure advancing left
11	1985a	Qc	19.51.14.20	Room e	IV	76/77	6-2-32	Frag. figure w/one hand raised

SS II, Pl. XV

1	1847	Qc	19.51.14.20	Room *e*	IVd	59	6-3-32	Two lotus flowers & lily
2	1988a	Qc	19.51.14.20	Room *e*	IV	76/77	6-1/2-32	Row of lotus (w/glass)
3	1988b	Qc	19.51.14.20	Room *e*	IV	76/77	6-1/2-32	Chain of lotus & bud
4	1988d.1	Qc	19.51.14.20	Room *e*	IV	76/77	6-1/2-32	Chain of palmettes & buds
4*	1770d	Qc	19.12.20	Rooms *e-g*	IVa	59/74	5-23-32	
5	1758	Qc	19.51.14.20	Room *e*	?	——	6-7-32	Row of lotus & bud
6	1988c	Qc	19.51.14.20	Room *e*	IV	76/77	6-1/2-32	Row/chain of palmettes
7	1988d.2	Qc	19.51.14.20	Room *e*	IV	76/77	6-1/2-32	From a winged figure holding lily
8	(reconstructed *drawing* to illustrate No. 6; same Registry No. - 1988)							
9	(reconstructed *drawing* to illustrate No. 7; same Registry No. - 1988)							

* as indicated, this plate of fragments contains two entries labelled "No. 4"

SS II, Pl. XVI

1	1547	Qc	49.26.45	Room *hq*	II	70	5-20-32	Lotus and bud chain
2	1541	Qc	49.26.45	Room *hq*	II	70	5-18-32	Lotus and bud chain*
3	1971	Qc	19.51.14.20	Room *e*	IVb	——	6-3-32	Lotus and palmette chain
4	1821b	Qc	(provenance data not recorded on registry card)				——	5-28-32 Chain resembling No. 3
5	1208	E 207	Level C	Shrine(?)	Level C	——	5-?-33	Sherd incised w/lotus, bud
6	1207	E 207	Level C	Shrine(?)	Level C	——	5-?-33	Sherd incised w/lotus, bud
7a	1769	Qc	49.26.25	Room *hq*	II	70	5-19-32	(restoration drawing similar
b**	1853	Qc	19.51.14.20	Room *e*	IVb	——	5-31-32	to Nos. 1-2)

* for Nos. 1-2, compare Nos. 2038-40, from Qc, *19.51.14.20*, Layers IV and IVb, 6-1/2-32
**No. 7 reflects "a restoration made up from a number of small fragments . . ." (*SS II*, 33); I have selected two pertinent fragments to represent this entry

SS II, Pl. XVII

1	1576	Qc	49.26.25	Room *hq*	II	70	5-25-32	Plaque w/frame & tenon
2	1575	Qc	49.26.25	Room *hq*	II	70	5-20-32	Lilies from lower plaque*
3	920	Qf	N of Wall 20	N Slope fill	VII	82	4-13-32	Papyrus blossoms (inlaid)
4	1585	Qc	19.51.14.20	Room *e*	IV	76/77	5-25-32	Palmette tree w/double volutes
5	1829	Qc	49.26.25	Room *hq*	?	70	5-19/20-32	Lotus
6	1811a	Qc	(provenance data unavailable)				5-28-32	Plaque w/incurving volutes
7	1783	——	(provenance data unavailable; cf. 2060a from Summit Strip Qh)					Frag. of inlaid plaque
8	1624	Qc	(provenance data unavailable)		——	——	5-25/28-32	Frag. inlaid border w/flowers
9	1901	Qc	19.51.14.20	Room *e*	IVb	——	6-1-32	Lily
10	1788	Qc	(provenance data uncertain)**		——	——	5-25-32	Palmette
11	1864	Qc	19.51.14.20	Room *e*	IVb	——	6-1-32	Alternate palmettes & buds
12	——	——	(provenance data unavailable)***		——	——	——	Palmette
13	3061	Qk	W of 124	Wall 132E	IVc	44/71	6-19-33	Papyrus head
14	1862	Qc	19.51.14.20	Room *e*	IVb	——	6-1-32	Palmette

* fragment of upper left stems, with lillies on them
** but compare No. 2000, from Qc, *19.51.14.20*, Layer IVb, 6-2-32; and 2060a from Qh, Room *211.259.201.261*, Layer IIIa, 5-21-32
*** compare No. 1863 from Qc, *19.51.14.20*, Layer IVb, 6-1-32

SS II, Pl. XVIII

1a	1597	Qc	49.26.25	Room *hq*	II(?)	70	5-25-32	Palm: base + bottom left frond
b		Qc	49(19).51.14.20	Room *e*	IV	76/77	6-3-32	Palm: upper section
2	1567	Qc	49.26.25	Room *hq*	II	70	5-19/20-32	Palm
3	1568(?)	Qc	49.26.25	Room *hq*	II	70	5-19/20-32	Palm

APPENDIX B — IVORIES

SS II, Pl. XIX

1	1998*	Qc	19.51.14.20	Room *e*	IV	76/77	6-1-32	Palm w/dates
2	1568**	Qc	49.26.25	Room *hq*	II	70	5-19/20-32	Palm
3	1999	Qc	19.51.14.20	Room *e*	IV	76/77	6-1-32	Palm w/dates

* provenance data for Nos. 1 and 3 assigned in agreement with data contained in the photograph journal stored at the PEF; judging from the stratification cards, however, the two entries may be transposed

**for the upper part, compare No. 1875

SS II, Pl. XX

1	1569	Qc	49.26.25	Room *hq*	II	70	5-21-32	Palm
2	1570	Qc	19.51.14.20	Room *e*	?	——	5-27-32	Palm
3	1755	Qc	19.51.14.20	Room *e*	IVb	——	5-31-32	Palm
4	1927	Qc	19.51.14.20	Room *e*	IV	76/77	6-1-32	Palm
5	2024	Qc	19.51.14.20	Room *e*	IVa	59/74	6-1-32	Palm

Note: for other drooping palms, see also Nos. 1567-68, 1770, 1755, 1782, 1824, 1906, 2001, 2009, 2025-26, 3033-34, 3039, 3049, 3054, 3080, et passim

SS II, Pl. XXI

1	1566	Qc	49.26.25	Room *hq*	II	70	5-21-32	Border w/fan-shaped palmettes
2	1583	Qc	19.51.14.20	Room *e*	IV	76/77	5-25-32	Phoenician palmette on sacred tree
3	1571	Qc	49.26.25	Room *hq*	II	70	5-19-32	Unfinished border
4	1818	Qc	19.51.14.20	Room *e*	IVb	——	6-1-32	Thin panel of Phoenician palmettes
5	1819	Qc	19.51.14.20	Room *e*	IVb	——	6-1-32	Smaller strip similar to No. 4
6	1564	Qc	49.26.25	Room *hq*	II	70	5-19/21-32	Row of 8-petalled daisies
7**	1638b	Qc	19.51.14.20	Room *e*	?	——	5-27/28-32	Enclosed twist or cable border
8	1868	Qc	19.51.14.20	Room *e*	IVb	——	6-1-32	Multiple frags. similar to No. 4*
9	1942a	Qc	19.51.14.20	Room *e*	IVa.b	——	6-1/2-32	Border w/lattice of rhombs
10	1578	Qc	19.51.14.20	Room *e*	IV	76/77	5-28-32	Border w/lattice of squares

* see also No. 1605 from Qc, *19.51.14.20* (layer unknown)

**for other, selected examples, see No. 1804c from Qc, *49.26.25*, Layer II, 5-27-32; No. 3041 from Qk, *W of 124*, Layer IVc, 6-17-33; No. 5132 from Qn, *504.503.507.508*, Layer IIy, 4-22-35; these all show a single inner circle; for a double inner circle, see No. 1539 from Summit Strip Qd, (segment unknown), Level VI, 5-31-32; compare also *SS II*, 41, fig. 12a

SS II, Pl. XXII

1	3036	Qk	W of 124	Rooms *hq-kq*	VII	——	6-14-33	Fragments of ivory capital
2	3016	Qk	W of 124	Rooms *hq-kq*	VIc	70/71	6-20-33	Asp or Uraeus carved in round
3	1891	Qc	19.51.14.20	Room *e*	IVb	——	5-24-32	Large frag. of unworked tusk*

* compare also No. 1842 from Qc, *19.51.14.20*, layer unknown, 5-27-32

SS II, Pl. XXIII

1a	1591(?)	Qc	19.51.14.20	Room *e*	?	——	6-25-32	Carved/perforated (spindle?) whorl
b	1634(?)	Qc	19.50(51).14.20	Room *e*	VII	59/74	6-11-32	Frag.: daisy w/rounded petals
c	1622	Qc	19.51.14.20	Room *e*	VI	59?/74	6-1-32	Carved/perforated (spindle?) whorl
d	1589	Qc	19.51.14.20	Room *e*	?	——	6-25-32	Carved/perforated (spindle?) whorl
2a	1555	Qc	49.26.25	Room *hq*	II	70	5-20-32	Eleven daisies w/8 or 12 petals*
b	1556	Qc	49.26.25	Room *hq*	II	70	5-20-32	
c	1561	Qc	49.26.25	Room *hq*	II	70	5-21-32	
d	1562	Qc	49.26.25	Room *hq*	II	70	5-21-32	
e	1563	Qc	49.26.25	Room *hq*	II	70	5-21-32	

f	1626a	Qc	(While the stratification cards recorded			70	all exca-	
g	1626b	Qc	only the Summit Strip for this set, it			70	vated	
h	1626c	Qc	seems likely that they derive from the			70	between	
i	1626d	Qc	same layer as the previous ones, in			70	May 25-28	
j	1626e	Qc	Segment 49.26.25)			70	1932	
k	1828	Qc	19.51.14.20	Room *e*	VI	59?/74	5-28-32	
3a	1887	Qc	19.51.14.20	Room *e*	IVa	59/74	6-1-32	Four
b	3017	Qk	W of 124	Rooms *hq-kq*	VIc	70/71	6-1-32	plain
c	3042b	Qk	W of 124	Rooms *hq-kq*	VI	43/44/69	6-1-32	hemispherical
d	3042a	Qk	W of 124	Rooms *hq-kq*	VI	43/44/69	6-1-32	knobs**
4a	1888	Qc	19.51.14.20	Room *e*	IVa	59/74	6-1-32	Ivory studs w/head (parts of pins)
b	2013	Qc	19.51.14.20	Room *e*	VI	59?/74	6-13-32	
c	3080	Qk	W of 124	Rooms *hq-kq*	Vc	43/70/71	6-27-33	
5	1827b	Q	(no data recorded; photographed w/1637a = Pl. X:5)				5-28-32	Ivory frag. w/peg
6a	—	—	(provenance data unavailable)		—	—	—	Scoring on plaques (reverse)
b	—	—	(provenance data unavailable)		—	—	—	
c	1773	Qc	49.26.24	Room *hq*	Beneath 26	70	5-24-32 (frag. burnt; surface polish	
d	—	—	(provenance data unavailable)		—	—	—	
e	1550	Qc	49.26.25	Room *hq*	II	70	5-20-32	(one end broken; other slanted)
f	—	—	(provenance data unavailable)		—	—	—	
g	1549	Qc	49.26.25	Room *hq*	II	70	5-18-32	(not exact shape as 6g)

* see also Nos. 1623a-b (no provenance data recorded) and 1633-34 from Qc, *19.50(51).14.20*, Layer VII, 6-11-32
**see also Nos. 1789b, 1805, 1807, 1828, et passim

SS II, Pl. XXIV (and Frontispiece 2)

1	Lotus petal in blue glass
2	Triangle in green glass
3	Papyrus/lotus head in blue glass
4	Human leg in red-greenish glass
5	(While the narrative portion of *SS II* includes references to two plates labeled "XXIV" [pp. 44-45], only one such plate actually appears in the book. The other Plate XXIV relates to the glass insets or gold leaf items depicted in the colored painting of Frontispiece 2. This omission precludes any attempt to collate the provenance data for these artifacts, which are excluded from my database sample. (See further p. 446, n. 11.))
	Daisy inset in dark blue glass
6	Triangle in green glass
7	Round blue glass inset
8	Long inset in blue glass (frag.)
9	Scale in blue glass
10	Circular daisy inset in blue glass
11	Eye (?) inset in three colors
12	Flower petal, blue glass

SS II, Pl. XXIV (See No. 1834 for information re: abbreviated references to "49 etc.")

1a	1830a	Qc	19.51.14.20	Room *e*	VII	59/74	6-11-32	Gold leaf (frag.) on ivory disk
b	1830	Qc	19.51.14.20	Room *e*	VII	59/74	6-11-32	Fragment of circular gold leaf
c*	1551	Qc	49.26.25	Room *hq*	II	70	5-19-32	Scale in decayed white glass
d	1551	Qc	49.26.25	Room *hq*	II	70	5-19-32	Gold scale (placed over entry *c*)
e	1551	Qc	49.26.25	Room *hq*	II	70	5-19-32	Scale in gold leaf
f	1551	Qc	49.26.25	Room *hq*	II	70	5-19-32	Scale in gold leaf
g	1551	Qc	49.26.25	Room *hq*	II	70	5-19-32	Scale in gold leaf
h	1551	Qc	49.26.25	Room *hq*	II	70	5-19-32	Scale in gold leaf
i	1551	Qc	49.26.25	Room *hq*	II	70	5-19-32	Scale in gold leaf
j	1551	Qc	49.26.25	Room *hq*	II	70	5-19-32	Scale in gold leaf
k	1551	Qc	49.26.25	Room *hq*	II	70	5-19-32	Scale in decayed white glass
l	1551	Qc	49.26.25	Room *hq*	II	70	5-19-32	Gold scale (placed over entry *k*)
2a*	1627a	Qc	19.31(51).14.20	Room *e*	?	—	5-19-32	Daisy in blue gl. & wh. paste
b	1627c	Qc	19.31(51).14.20	Room *e*	?	—	?	Daisy in blue gl. & wh. paste
c	1627d	Qc	19.31(51).14.20	Room *e*	?	—	6-7-32	Daisy in blue gl. & wh. paste
d	1628	Qc	19.31(51).14.20	Room *e*	?	—	5-25-32	Square inset, bird in blk./wh.

APPENDIX B — IVORIES

e	1627b.2	Qc	19.31(51).14.20	Room *e*	?	——	5-24-32	Daisy in blue gl. w/wh. petals
f	1631	Qc	19.31(51).14.20	Room *e*	?	——	6-1-32	Traingle in green glass
g	1627b.1	Qc	19.31(51).14.20	Room *e*	?	——	5-24-32	Frag: daisy in bl.gl./wh.paste
h	1552	Qc	49.26.25	Room *hq*	II	70	5-19-32	Rod in green glass w/ red spot
i	1552	Qc	49.26.25	Room *hq*	II	70	5-19-32	Traingle in green glass
j	1552	Qc	49.26.25	Room *hq*	II	70	5-19-32	Triangle in greenish glass
k	1630-lft.	Qc	19.31(51).14.20	Room *e*	?	——	5-25-32	Eye, bl. gl./brown-white paste
l	1630-rt.	Qc	19.31(51).14.20	Room *e*	?	——	5-25-32	Eye, bl. gl./brown-white paste
3	5109a	Qc	19.51.14.20	Room *e*	IVa	59/74	6-1-32	(enlargement of No. 2d)**
4	5109b	Qc	19.51.14.20	Room *e*	IVa	59/74	6-1-32	(drawing, inset in blue glass)**
5	1631b	Qc	19.31(51).14.20	Room *e*	?	——	6-1-32	Ivory disk w/green glass center
6	1629*****	Qc	19.31(51).14.20	Room *e*	IV	76/77	5-31-32	Grape cluster, bl.glass-bronze stem
7	1606***	Qc	19.51.14.20	Room *e*	IVa	59/74	5-27-32(?)	Sun/moon inset inside gold ring
8	6031	Qn	507.503.504.505	RT fill-*l*	IIIm.c	61/72	5-31-35	(drawing: square in green glass)
9	3015a	Qk	W of 124	Rooms *hq-kq*	Vc.y	——	7-1-33	(drawing: rhomb in gr.-red glass)
10	——	——	(provenance data unavailable)		VI	——	——	(drawing: square blue glass frame)
11a	1835	Qc	19.51.14.20	Room *e*	VI	59?/74	5-28-32	Blue & green glass****
b	1835	Qc	19.51.14.20	Room *e*	VI	59?/74	5-28-32	Blue glass
c	1835	Qc	19.51.14.20	Room *e*	VI	59?/74	5-28-32	Blue glass
d	——	——	(provenance data unavailable)		——	——	——	
11e	1831b	Qc	49.26.25	Room *hq*	?	70	5-18/19-32	
f	1877a^	Qc	19.51.14.20	Room *e*	VI	59?/74	6-1-32	
g	1903c	Qc	19.51.14.20	Room *e*	IVb	——	6-3-32	Green glass
h	1831a	Qc	49.26.25	Room *hq*	?	70	5-18/19-32	
i	1835	Qc	19.51.14.20	Room *e*	VI	59?/74	5-28-32	Blue glass
j	——	——	(provenance data unavailable)		——	——	——	
k	1831b	Qc	49.26.25	Room *hq*	?	70	5-18/19-32	
l	2017b(?)	Qc	19.51.14.20	Room *e*	IX	59/74	6-14-32	Blue glass inset
m	3030	Qk	W of 124	Rooms *hq-kq*	V	45	5-27-33	Leg (or arm?)
12	3009	Qk	E Strip.S Half	Room *k*	IV-VII	83	6-8-33	(drawing: asp w/disk & horns)

* see also Nos. 1832a from Qc, *49.26.25*, Layer II; 1876/1879 and 1956 from Qc, *19.51.14.20*, Layers VI (sift) and VIe, respective
** nos. 3-4 presented dual entries: for 3, see also No. 1628 (same provenance data); for 4, compare 3015b, Qk, *W of 124*, Vc.y, 7-4-
*** see also No. 3014a-b from Qk, *W of 124*, Layer VI, 6-15-33
**** see also No. 1937 from Qc, *19.51.14.20*, Layer IVb, 6-6-32
***** compare No. 1865 from Qc, *19.51.14.20*, Layer IV, 5-31-32
^ compare No. 2016a, from Qc, *19.51.14.20-N*, Layer VIII, 6-14-32

SS II, Pl. XXV

1	1593	Qc	19.51.14.20	Room *e*	?	——	?	Letter: aleph
2	1908	Qc	19.51.14.20	Room *e*	IVb	——	6-3-32	Letter: beth
3	1917c	Qc	19.51.14.20	Room *e*	VII-sift	59/74	6-13-32	Letter: gimel
4	1909	Qc	19.51.14.20	Room *e*	IVb	——	6-3-32	Letter: daleth
5	1593	Qc	19.51.14.20	Room *e*	?	——	5-31-32	Letter: waw
6	1593	Qc	49.26.25	Room *hq*	?	70	?	Letter: zayin
7	2025	Qc	19.51.14.20	Room *e*	IVa	59/74	6-1-32	Letter: zayin*
8	3000	Qk	W of 124	Rooms *hq-kq*	VII	——	6-14-33	Letter: heth
9	1593	Qc	19.51.14.20	Room *e*	IVb	——	6-3-32	Letter: teth
10	1917b	Qc	19.51.14.20	Room *e*	IVb	——	6-2-32	Letter: yod
11	1593	Qc	19.51.14.20	Room *e*	?	——	5-25-32	Letter: nun
12	3070	Qk	W of 124	Wall 132E	IVc	44/71	6-19-33	Letter: samekh
13	1917a	Qc	19.51.14.20	Room *e*	IVb	——	6-4-32	Letter: pe
14	874	Qd(?)	9.21.31	N Slope fill	V-VI	81	4-12-32	Letter: resh**
15	1545/1593	Qc	49.26.25	Room *hq*	II	70	5-19-32	Letter: taw
16	1907a	Qc	19.51.14.20	Room *e*	IVb	——	6-1-32	Letters: aleph, taw
17	1564	Qc	49.26.25	Room *hq*	II	70	5-19/21-32	Letter: teth***
18	1986(No.5)	Qc	19.51.14.20	Room *e*	IV	76/77	6-2-32	Letter: waw

* this letter appeared on the lower fragment of a palm tree plaque; see also the *zayin* on the upper, originally concealed tenon of the plaque in Pl. XI:1.

** this fragment constitutes the base of a palm and therefore appears upside down in *SS II*; if Crowfoot's reading of a *resh* is correct, then this letter was inscribed only after the palm passed out of use; turning the piece upright, however, may yielded a rather unshapely ʾ*aleph*, in which case it may reflect a marking made on the palm even when the latter was still in use

*** this letter appeared on the back of small panel with daisy designs and incised lines on the front

---

If excavation dates or provenance data appeared at the bottom of a stratification card bearing multiple entries (but not under each specific entry), I have assumed that this information applies to all items shown on that card.

APPENDIX C
FINDSPOTS FOR PUBLISHED STRATIFIED ISRAELITE OSTRACA

(data collected and collated from G. A. Reisner, *HES I*, 232-38)

SS II Published Figure	Unpublished Registry No.	Strip	Coordinates	Feature	Local Layer	Date Excavated	Commodity
1	4075	S4	417	N sub	(data on pre-	8-23	wine
2	4583	S7	776	sub	cise local	9-20	—
3	4614	S7	772	sub	stratigraphy	9-22	wine
4	3855	S4	401	sub	do not appear	8-11	wine
5	3863	S4	418	sub	in Reisner's	8-12	wine
6	3997	S4	417	N	published re-	8-19	wine
7	4578	S7	772	—	ports)	9-20	wine
8	3957	S4	416	—		8-17	wine
9	4524	S7	772	—		9-16	wine
10	4580	S7	773	—		9-20	wine
11	4526	S7	772	—		9-16	wine
12	4525	S7	772	—		9-16	wine
13a	4030	S4	417	N		8-22	wine
b	4032	(same . . .)					
14	4608	S7	772	—		9-22	wine
15	4607	S7	772	—		9-21	—
16a	3891	S4	417	—		8-15	oil
b	3898	S4	418	—		8-15	—
17a	3894	S4	417	—		8-15	oil
b	3899	S4	418	—		8-15	oil
18	3931	S4	417	—		8-16	oil
19	4031	S4	417	N		8-22	oil
20	3995	S4	417	N		8-19	oil
21	3889	S4	417	—		8-15	oil
22	3932	S4	417	—		8-16	—
23	3917	S4	417	—		8-15	—
24a	3865	S4	418	—		8-12	—
b	3866	(same . . .)					
25a	4079	S4	417	N		8-23	—
b	4080	(same . . .)					
26	3873	S4	418	—		8-13	—
27	4553	S7	773	—		8-19	—
28	4552	S7	773	—		9-19	—
29a	4555	S7	773	—		9-19	—
b	4556	(same . . .)					
c	4579	(same . . .)					
30	3900	S4	417	—		8-15	—
31a	3895	S4	417	—		8-15	—
b	3992	(same ??)				8-16	—
32	3916	S4	417	—		8-15	—
33	3909	S4	417	—		8-15	—
34a	3903	S4	417	—		8-15/16	—
b	3933	(same . . .)					
35a	3913	S4	417	—		8-15	—
b	3914	(same . . .)					

36a	3902	S4	417	—		8-15	wine
b	3906	(same . . .)					
37	4551	S7	773	—		9-19	——
38	3993	S4	417	—		8-19	——
39	4619	S7	772	—		9-22	——
40	4527	S7	772	—		9-16	——
41	4550	S7	776	—		9-19	——
42	3994	S4	417	N		8-19	——
43	3875	S4	418	—		8-12	——
44	3867	S4	418	—		8-13	wine
45	3896	S4	417	—		8-15	——
46	3915	S4	417	—		8-15	——
47	4616	S7	772	—		9-22	——
48a	3897	S4	418	—		8-15	——
b	3990 B	S4	417	N		8-19	——
49	3990 A	S4	417	N		8-19	——
50	4630	S7	772	N		9-23	——
51	4661	S7	772	W		9-26	——
52	4629	S7	772	—		9-23	——
53	3890	S4	417	—		8-15	wine/oil
54	4171	S7	723	—		9-1	wine/oil
55	4660	S7	772	W		9-26	oil
56	4617	S7	772	—		9-22	——
57	4582	S7	776	—		9-20	——
58	4554	S7	773	—		9-19	——
59	4581	S7	776	—		9-20	oil
60	4627	S7	772	—		9-23	——
61	3864	S4	418	—		8-12	——
62	3934	S4	417	—		8-16	wine
63	3991	S4	417	N		8-19	——

compare also:

64	2854	surface find on southern slope of the hill	6-18-10	——
65	4925	S11 9 (in disturbed yellow debris in front of cave mouth)	10-22-10	
66	1825	cuneiform tablet with Israelite seal impression		
67	??	(ten large building stones bearing Israelite letters/quarry marks)		

APPENDIX D

NEO-ASSYRIAN LITERARY REFERENCES TO THE NORTHERN KINGDOM OF ISRAEL

(a roster of texts collated from the historical annals, summary/display inscriptions, and eponym lists
of the Assyrian Empire and from the Assyrian and Babylonian Chronicles)

SHALMANESER III — Mid-Ninth Century BCE

Primary Sources:

853 BCE	6th Year	Aram, Hamath, 12 kings of the seacoast	a) Bull Inscription --E. Michel, *WdO* I/6 (1952), 465, ll. 27-28 --G. G. Cameron, *Sumer* VI/1 (1950), 13, 21; obv. II:27-28 --J. Læssøe, *Iraq* XXI/2 (1959), 151-52, l. 32 --*ARAB* I.647
			b) Bronze Gates (Band IX) --*ARAB* I. 613-14 (for another reference to "the kings of the seacoast," see *ARAB* I.618 and E. Michel, *WdO*, II/5-6 (1958-1959), 413, l. 4)
		Aram, Hamath, kings of Hatti and the seacoast	c) Black Obelisk --E. Michel, *WdO* II/1 (1954), 33, ll. 17-19 --E. Michel, *WdO* II/2 (1955), 149, ll. 59-61 --*ARAB* I.563
		Hadad-ezer of Aram, Irhuleni of Hamath, Ahab the Israelite, 12 kings total	d) Monolith Inscription --*ARAB* I.610-11

---

849 BCE	10th Year	Aram, Hamath, 12 kings of the seacoast	a) Bull Inscription --E. Michel, *WdO* I/6 (1952), 467, ll. 61-62 --G. G. Cameron, *Sumer* VI/1 (1950), 14, 22; obv. II:60-62 --*ARAB* I.652
			b) Assur annalistic fragment --*ARAB* I.667
			c) Bronze Gates (Band XIII) --*ARAB* I.613-14

---

848 BCE	11th Year	Aram, Hamath, 12 kings of the seacoast	a) Bull Inscription --E. Michel, *WdO* I/6 (1952), 469, ll. 3-5 --E. Michel, *WdO* II/1 (1954), 36, ll. 1-2 --G. G. Cameron, *Sumer* VI/1 (1950), 15, 22; rev. III:3-5 --*ARAB* I.654

		Hamath, Aram, 12 kings of land of Hatti	b) Black Obelisk --E. Michel, *WdO* II/2 (1955), 151, ll. 87-89 --*ARAB* I.568
845 BCE	14th Year	Aram, Hamath, 12 kings of the seacoast	a) Bull Inscription --E. Michel, *WdO* I/6 (1952), 469, ll. 27-29 --E. Michel, *WdO* II/1 (1954), 37, ll. 17-19 --G. G. Cameron, *Sumer* VI/1 (1950), 15, 23; rev. III:27-28 --*ARAB* I.659
		12 kings (a likely reference to the Syrian coalition)	b) Black Obelisk --E. Michel, *WdO* II/1 (1954), 37, ll. 17-19 --E. Michel, *WdO* II/2 (1955), 153, ll. 91-92 --*ARAB* I.571
841 BCE	18th Year	Aram (Hazael)	a) Bull Inscription --E. Michel, *WdO* II/1 (1954), 39, l. 46 --*ARAB* I. 663
			b) Black Obelisk --E. Michel, *WdO* II/1 (1954), 39, ll. 46 --E. Michel, *WdO* II/2 (1955), 153, ll. 97-99 --*ARAB* I.575
		Hazael of Damascus, Jehu, son of Omri	c) Assur annalistic fragment --E. Michel, *WdO* I/4 (1949), 266-67, Text No. 22, ll. 2, 25-26, plus commentary on pp. 267-68 --E. Michel, *WdO* II/1 (1954), 39, l. 11 --*ARAB* I.672
			d) Nimrud Statue --Wilson, *Iraq* XXIV (1962), 93-96
			e) Black Obelisk --E. Michel, *WdO* I/4 (1949), 266-67, ll. 2, 25-26, plus commentary on pp. 267-68, n. 9 --E. Michel, *WdO* II/2 (1955), 141, B[B$_1$-B$_4$] --*ARAB* I.590
			f) E. Michel, *WdO* II/2 (1955), 141, B, plus commentary on pp. 138-39
			g) F. Safar, *Sumer* VII (1951), 3-21

APPENDIX D — ASSYRIAN LITERARY REFERENCES

838 BCE	21st Year	Hazael of Aram	a) Black Obelisk --E. Michel, *WdO* II/2 (1955), 155, ll. 102-03 --*ARAB* I.578
		Hazael of Damascus	b) Cylinder Seal --E. Michel, *WdO* I/4 (1949), No. 24, ll. 3-4
			c) compare J. Læssøe, *Iraq* XXI/2 (1959), 154-55, l. 12
834 BCE	25th Year	tribute from kings of Hatti	a) Black Obelisk --E. Michel, *WdO* II/3 (1956), 221, l. 127 --*ARAB* I.582

Shalmaneser III:
Summary of References Relating Directly to Samaria

1) "Ahab, the Israelite" — participation at Qarqar
    a) Monolith Inscription (*ARAB* I.611)

2) "Jehu, son of Omri" — payment of tribute at Mt. Carmel in 841 BCE
    a) Black Obelisk, written above the relief (*ARAB* I.590; E. Michel, *WdO* II/2 (1955), 141)
    b) Nimrud Statue (Wilson, *Iraq* XXIV (1962), 93-96)
    c) Assur annalistic fragment (*ARAB* I.672)
    d) Fourth Edition of the Annals of Shalmaneser III (Safar, *Sumer* VII [1951], 3-21)

ADAD-NIRARI III — Late Ninth and Early Eighth Centuries BCE

Primary Sources:[†]

| †† 806/805 to 802 BCE and again in ‡ 796 BCE | (precise regnal years are not indicated in these inscriptions) | Land of Hatti; Land of Damascus; Joash of Samaria

Land of Omri; Edom; Philistia; Aram/Damascus

Land of Hatti | a) Tell al-Rimah Stele
--S. Page, *Iraq* XXX (1968), 139-53
--H. Tadmor, *Iraq* XXXV (1973), 141-44

b) Nimrud Slab Inscription
--H. Tadmor, *Iraq* XXXV (1973), 148-50
--*ARAB* I.738-741

c) Sheik Hammad Stele
--A. R. Millard and H. Tadmor, *Iraq* XXXV (1973), 57-64 |

| 806/805 BCE | 5th Year | Land of Hatti; Damascus | d) Sab'a Stele
--H. Tadmor, *IEJ* 19 (1969), 46-48
--H. Tadmor, *Iraq* XXXV (1973), 144-48
--*ARAB* I.732-737 |

---

† For the difficulties involved in the establishing the dates of these stelae and of the campaigns to which they refer, see the full discussions in the secondary sources cited above

†† For actions concentrating in **North Syria**; based on the following Eponym Chronicle entries: 805 = Arpad; 804 = Hazazu; 803 = Ba'alu; 802 = to the [Mediterranean?] Sea

‡ For actions involving **South Syria** and **Palestine**; Eponym Chronicle entry, 796 = Mansuate

Adad-nirari III:
Summary of References Relating Directly to Samaria

1) "the Kingdom (Land) of Omri" — payment of tax and tribute, 797 BCE
   a) Nimrud Slab Inscription, line 12

2) "Joash the Samarian" — payment of tribute in Damascus, 796 BCE
   a) Tell al-Rimah Stele, lines 8-9

TIGLATH-PILESER — Mid-Eighth Century BCE

Primary Sources: The West — Phase I

743 BCE	III *palû*	(*ina*) Arpad Melid Gurgum Kummuk (?)	**Annalistic :: Series C** a) Tadmor, *ITP*, Ann. 17, pp. 32, 50-53, Pls. XIII-XIV b) Layard, *ICC*, 71a + 71b + 72a c) Smith, *AD*, 272-73, frag. 5 d) Rost, *KTP*, 12-14, ll. 58-73, Pl. XIX e) *ARAB* I.769
742-741 BCE	IV-V *palûs*	(*ana*) Arpad	{a large gap in extant primary sources pertaining to the siege of Arpad and conquest of North Syria; this section is completely missing from the Calah recension of the Annals}
740 BCE	VI *palû*	(*ana*) Arpad Rezin [of Damascus] Kummuh Tyre	**Annalistic :: Series C** a) Tadmor, *ITP*, Ann. 21, pp. 34 and 54-55, Pl. XIX (appears on same slab as Ann. 20 below)

APPENDIX D — ASSYRIAN LITERARY REFERENCES

			Que Carchemish Gurgum	b) Layard, *ICC*, 45b-2 c) Smith, *AD*, 274, frag. 6:9-16 d) Rost, *KTP*, 14-16, ll. 82-89, Pl. XIII e) *ARAB* I.769
			Unqi	f) Tadmor, *ITP*, Ann. 25, pp. 34-35 and 56-59, Pl. XXIV g) Rawlinson, III R 9,1 (squeeze No. 123) h) Smith, *AD*, 274-75, frag. 6:16-27 i) Rost, *KTP*, 16-18, ll. 90-101, Pl. XIV j) *ARAB* I.769
739 BCE	VII *palû*		Ulluba	**Annalistic :: Series C** a) Tadmor, *ITP*, Ann. 20, pp. 33 and 54-55, Pl. XVIII (appears on same slab as Ann. 21 above) b) Layard, *ICC*, 45b-1 c) Smith, *AD*, 274, frag. 6:1-8 d) Rost, *KTP*, 14, ll. 74-81, Pl. XIII e) The Mila Merga Rock Relief, ll. 16-46; Tadmor, *ITP*, 112-15 f) J. N. Postgate, *Sumer* XXIX/1-2 (1973), 47-59, Figs. 1-7 g) *ARAB* I.769 (compare § 785)
738 BCE	VIII *palû*		Hatti Unqi	**Annalistic :: Series A** a) Tadmor, *ITP*, Ann. 2, pp. 30, 86, Pl. II (ll. 1-7 = Ann. 13:3-8) (appears on same slab as Ann. 3 below) b) Layard, *ICC*, 69b-1 c) Rost, *KTP*, 24, ll. 143-48, Pl. III
			Rezin of Damascus Menahem of Samaria Hiram of Tyre Eni-il of Hamath (plus Kummuh, Byblos, Que, Carchemish, Sam'al, Gurgum, Melid, and others)	d) Tadmor, *ITP*, Ann. 3, pp. 30, 87, Pl. II (ll. 1-7 = Ann. 13:8-14:3) (appears on same slab as Ann. 2 above) e) Layard, *ICC*, 69b-2 + 69a-1 f) Rost, *KTP*, 24-26, ll. 148-55, Pls. IV-V **Miscellaneous Stele Text** g) The Iran Stele IIB:4' (Tadmor, *ITP*, 90-110, Fig. 6; 106-07, Frag. 1, Col. III A:5; compare Levine, *Two Neo-Assyrian Stelae from Iran* (1972a), 11ff.; idem., *BASOR* 206 (1972b), 40-41; and Weippert, *ZDPV* 89 (1973), 26-53, text on pp. 29-30) **Annalistic :: Series B** h) Tadmor, *ITP*, Ann. 13*, pp. 31 and 66-69, Pl. IX (restored from Anns. 2, 3, 27)

i) Layard, *ICC*, 50a
  (= Rost, *KTP*, ll. 141-52, Pl. IV)
j) Rawlinson, III R 9, 3, ll.41-52 (Smith copy)
k) Rost, *KTP*, 24-26, ll. 141-52, Pl. XV
l) Barnett and Falkner, *STP*, Reliefs 31 and 33; Pls. LXXXV and LXXXI
m) *ARAB* I.771-772

(*note*: for the continuation of Ann. 13* above, see Ann. 14* = Layard, *ICC*, 50b + 67a = Rost, *KTP*, 26-28, ll. 153-57, Pl. XVI; Tadmor, *ITP*, Ann. 4 = Layard, *ICC*, 69a-2 + 68b = Rost, *KTP*, ll. 155-57, Pls. VI-VII helps to restore Ann. 14*:3-10)

19 districts of Hamath

Hattarikka (and its king Azriyau?)

Annalistic :: Series C
n) Tadmor, *ITP*, Ann. 19*, pp. 32-33 and 58-65, Pls. XVI-XVIII
  (for restoration, note duplicate texts: Series C, Anns. 22, 26, and 27 in *ITP*, 34-35, 88-89; also 36, Fig. 5; compare Gadd, *Stones of Assyria* (1936), 154-55 = original publication of BM 118899 and 118900; also Barnett and Falkner, *STP*, Reliefs 25 and 26; Pls. XCVII and XCVIII)
o) Layard, *ICC*, 65
p) Rawlinson, III R 9, 3, ll. 22-41 (Smith copy)
q) Smith, *AD*, 276-77, frag. 8:1-20
r) Rost, *KTP*, 20-24, ll. 123-141, PL. XXI
s) *ARAB* I.770-771

Tiglath-pileser III (West, Phase I):
Summary of References Relating Directly to Samaria

1) "Menahem the Samarian" — payment of tribute, 738 BCE
   a) Nimrud Slab Inscription, line 12
   b) fragmentary stele text (Levine, *BASOR* 206 [1972], 40-41; Weippert, *ZDPV* 89 [1973], 29-30)
   c) regarding "Menahem(?)" in *ARAB* I.815, see Saggs, *Iraq* XVII (1955), 147, n. 7

2) "(Province of) Samerina" — <too fragmentary to ascertain exact historical context>
   a) Nimrud Annals (*ARAB* I.779)

APPENDIX D — ASSYRIAN LITERARY REFERENCES

Primary Sources: The West — Phase II

734 BCE	XII *palû*	Philistia (?)	**Annalistic** {gap in extant primary sources; this section is completely missing from the Calah recension of the Annals; but note the Eponym Chronicle listing *a-na* māt*pi-lis-ta*}

---

733 BCE   XIII
palû
(first
Damascus
campaign)

Bit-Humria
Mutinti & Rukibtu
  of Ashkelon
Rezin [of Damascus]

Annalistic :: Series C
a) Tadmor, *ITP*, Ann. 18, pp. 32 and 80-83, Pls. XV, XXIII
b) Layard, *ICC*, 29b (fragmentary)
c) Smith, *AD*, 283-84, frag. 11
d) Rost, *KTP*, 38-40, ll. 229-40, Pl. XVIIIb
e) *ARAB* I.779

Rezin of Damascus
[...]hadara (birthplace
  of Rezin)
Samsi, Queen of the Arabs

f) Tadmor, *ITP*, Ann. 23, pp. 34 and 78-81, Pls. XX-XXII
(appears on same slab as Ann. 24 below)
g) Layard, *ICC*, 72b + 73a
h) Smith, *AD*, 282-83, frag. 10:1-16
i) Rost, *KTP*, 34-36, ll. 195-210, Pl. XXII
j) *ARAB* I.776-778

(*note:* Rost, *KTP*, Pl. XVIIIa; Tadmor, *ITP*, Ann. 24, pp. 34, 80-83, and 285; this presents a duplicate of the text in Ann. 18:2ff. and has helped to restore portions of Ann. 18; the text appears on the same slab as Ann. 23 above)

border of Bit-Humria
Dynasty of Hazael
Hanunu of Gaza
Land of Bit-Humria
Pekah and Hoshea
Samsi, Queen of the Arabs
Idibi'ilu the Gatekeeper

Summary Inscriptions
a) Tadmor, *ITP*, Summary 4 (on stone slab), pp. 136-43, Pls. XLIX-LI
b) Rawlinson, III R 10,2, Pl. 10
c) Smith, *AD*, 253, 284-85, frag. 12:1-23
d) Rost *KTP*, I, p. 78:6 and II, Pls. XXV-XXVI
e) *ARAB* I.815-819

Bit-Agusi (Arpad)
Unqi
Dynasty of Hazael
Border of Bit-Humria
Hiram of Tyre
Rezin [of Damascus]

f) Tadmor, *ITP*, Summary 9 (on clay tablet), pp. 180-91, ll. 9'-10'
g) ND 4301 + 4305
  --Wiseman, *Iraq* XVIII (1956), 117-29, Pls. XXII-XXIII
  --Tadmor, *IEJ* 12 (1962), 114-18, ll. 1'-8'

		Land of Bit-Humria Hoshea Hanunu of Gaza Samsi, Queen of the Arabs	h) ND 5422 --Wiseman, *Iraq* XXVI (1964), 119-21, Pl. XXVI i) *ARAB* I.815-817 (= Summ. 9, Rev., ll. 1-22) j) *ANET*, 283-84

732 BCE	XIV
	palû
	
	(second
	Damascus
	campaign)
	
	(completely missing from the Calah
	recension of the Annals, although
	Rost, Luckenbill, Oppenheim, *et
	al.*, published the texts to the
	right as annalistic ones)
		Idibi'ilu the Gatekeeper
		Land of Bit-Humria
		
		Samerina
		Pekah
			Summary Inscriptions
			a) Tadmor, *ITP*, Summary 13 (on stone slab),
			    pp. 198-203, Pls. LIX-LX, ll. 17'-18'
			b) Layard, *ICC*, 66
			c) Smith, *AD*, 285-86
			d) Rost, *KTP*, 36-38, ll. 211-28, Pl. XXIII
			e) *ARAB* I.778-779
			f) *ANET*, 283
			
			note: compare again ND 4301 + 4305
			    (see references in Year 733 above)

		poss. reference to
		  Tyre or Israel (?)
		Hanunu of Gaza
		Brook of Egypt
		Samsi, Queen of the Arabs
			Summary Inscriptions
			a) Tadmor, *ITP*, Summary 8 (on clay tablet),
			    pp. 156 and 176-79, ll. 10'-13', Pl. LVI
			b) ND 400
			    --Wiseman, *Iraq* XIII (1951), 21-24,
			    Pl. XI

731 BCE	(taken up with military campaigns in central and southern Babylon)		
730 BCE	(Eponym Chronicle: "in the land" — king remained in Assyria; no annalistic account preserved)		

729 BCE	XVII
	palû
		lines 7'-13' contain
		a summary of the vassal
		areas and kings in the west:
		  Kummuh
		  Que
		  Byblos
		  Tyre
		  Carchemish
		  Hamath
		  Sam'al
		  Gurgum
		  Melid
		  Kashka
		  Tabal
		  Tuna
		  Tuhana
			Summary Inscriptions
			a) Tadmor, *ITP*, Summary 7 (on clay tablet),
			    pp. 154-75, 268, Pls. LIV-LV (text com-
			    posed in 729 or 728 BCE)
			b) Smith, *AD*, 256-65 (= K 3751)
			c) Rost, *KTP*, Die Thontafelinschrift,
			    Avers. 54-69; Revers. 70-77
			d) *ARAB* I.787-804
			
			(*note*: once again, no records currently exist
			for this year from the Calah recension of the
			Annals)

APPENDIX D — ASSYRIAN LITERARY REFERENCES

        Ishtunda
        Hubishna
        Arvad
        Ammon
        Moab
        Ashkelon
        Jehoahaz of Judah
        Edom
        [..?..]
        Gaza

Tiglath-pileser III (West, Phase II):
Summary of References Relating Directly to Samaria

4) "The Kingdom/Dynasty of Omri" — parts of Israel annexed, 733 BCE;
                                        all surrounding areas receive Assyrian governor
    a) fragmentary display inscription (*ARAB* I.815)
    b) ND 4301 + 4305, reverse, lines 3-4

5) "The Kingdom/Dynasty of Omri" — Israel incurs some deportation, 732 BCE
    a) fragmentary display inscription (*ARAB* I.816)

6) "Pekah" — deposed as king, 732 BCE
    a) fragmentary display inscription (*ARAB* I.816)

7) "Hoshea" — installed as puppet king; payment of tribute; 732 BCE
    a) fragmentary display inscription (*ARAB* I.816)
    b) ND 4301 + 4305, reverse, lines 9-11

8) (note also the reference to "Jehoahaz of Judah" in Summary Inscription 7; see the references in Tadmor, *ITP*, 154 to K3751 = II R,67; translated in *ANET* 282, ll. 56-63 & *ARAB* I.801)

SHALMANESER V — Third Quarter of Eighth Century BCE

Primary Sources:

(general entry with   Samaria   a) Babylonian Chronicle I i:27-30
undated campaign)   --A. K. Grayson (1975), 72-73

Shalmaneser V:
Summary of References Relating Directly to Samaria

1) "Samarin" — conquered
    a) Bab. Chronicle I i:28

SARGON II — Late Eighth Century BCE

Primary Sources:

720 BCE	2nd Year	Samaria	

Annalistic Records:

a) Annalistic fragments from Khorsabad
 --Fuchs, *Sargons II*, 82-188 (text only)
 --*ARAB* II.4 (Fuchs, *Sargons II*, 87-88; II:2,11-II:3,3)
 --*ANET*, 284 (Fuchs, *Sargons II*, 110; II:11,16)

Other Annalistic Fragments from Sargon's Second and Seventh Years:

Hamath
Arpad
Ṣimirra
Damascus
Samaria
Hanunu [of Gaza]
Raphia
So. Arabian tribes

--*ARAB* II.5 (Fuchs, *Sargons II*, 89; II:3,12)
--*ARAB* II.17 (Fuchs, *Sargons II*, 110, 320; II:11,3-II:11,6)

Summary Inscriptions:

Samaria

b) The Great Display (Summary) Inscription: *Prunkinschrift*, ll. 23-25
 --Becking, *The Fall of Samaria*, 26
 --Fuchs, *Sargons II*, 197 (text only)
 --*ARAB* II.55

Samarians
Samaria

c) The Nimrud Prism, Col. IV:25-41, on both Text D (ND 2601 + 3401 + 3417), and Text E (ND 3400 + 3408 + 3409)
 --C. J. Gadd, *Iraq* XVI (1954), 179-82, Pls. XLV-XLVI (text only)
 --Becking, *The Fall of Samaria*, 28-30

Hamath
Arpad
Samaria

d) The Aššur Charter
 --Saggs, *Iraq* XXXVII (1975), 11-20, Pl. IX
 --*ARAB* II.133-135

Samaria
Bit-Humri

e) The Palace Door Inscription, IV:31-32
 --Becking, *The Fall of Samaria*, 27
 --Fuchs, *Sargon II*, 261
 --*ARAB* II.99

APPENDIX D — ASSYRIAN LITERARY REFERENCES

	Samaria Bit-Humri	f) The Bull Inscription, l. 21 --Becking, *The Fall of Samaria*, 33 --Fuchs, *Sargons II*, 63 --*ARAB* II.92
718+ BCE	Samaria Bit-Humri	g) The Small Display (Summary) Inscription: *Kleine Prunkinschrift*, l. 15 --Becking, *The Fall of Samaria*, 27-28 --Fuchs, *Sargons II*, 76 --*ARAB* II.80 --*ANET*, 285
715+ BCE	Bit-Humri (2x) Raphia Gaza So. Arabian tribes	h) The Cylinder Inscription, ll. 19-20 --Becking, *The Fall of Samaria*, 32 --Fuchs, *Sargons II*, 34

Sargon II:
Summary of References Relating Directly to Samaria

1) The Wide/Extensive Land of Bit-Humri (the province)
    a) Cylinder Inscription (*ARAB* II.118)

2) Samerina (the city)
   — in league with Damascus, Arpad, Hamath, and Ṣimirra
    a) Annals from Khorsabad (*ARAB* II.5)
    b) Great Display (Summary) Inscription (*ARAB* II.55)
    c) Aššur Charter (*ARAB* II.134)
   — resettled with South Arabian desert tribes
    a) Annals (*ARAB* II.17)

3) Samerina (the city) and the Entire Land of Bit-Humri (the province) — plundered
    a) Small Display (Summary) Inscription (*ARAB* II.80)
    b) Bull Inscription (*ARAB* II.92)
    c) Palace Door Plaster Inscription IV (*ARAB* II.99)

4) Samerinai, "(The People of) Samaria" — incur heavy deportations and conscription of 50 chariots
    a) Annals from Khorsabad (*ARAB* II.4)
    b) The Nimrud Prism IV

Post-Sargon II — Early Seventh Century BCE

1) "(the province of) Samerina" —record of the *limmu* of Nabû-kēnu-uṣur, Assyrian governor of Samaria
    (note the Eponym Chronicle listing for the year 690 BCE)

APPENDIX E
PUBLISHED STRATIFIED POTTERY REPRESENTING PERIODS 4-7

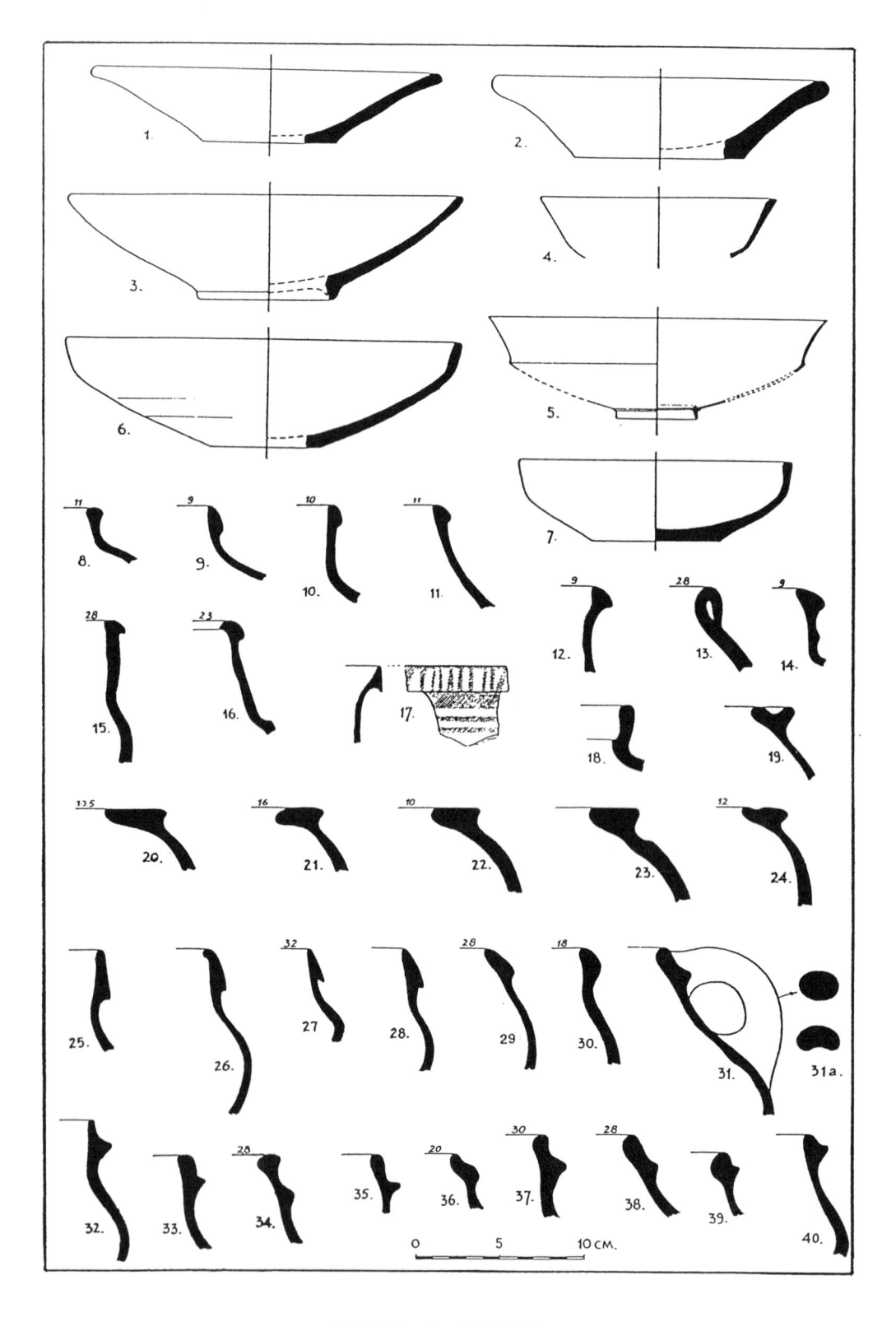

SS III, Fig. 6.   Period IV

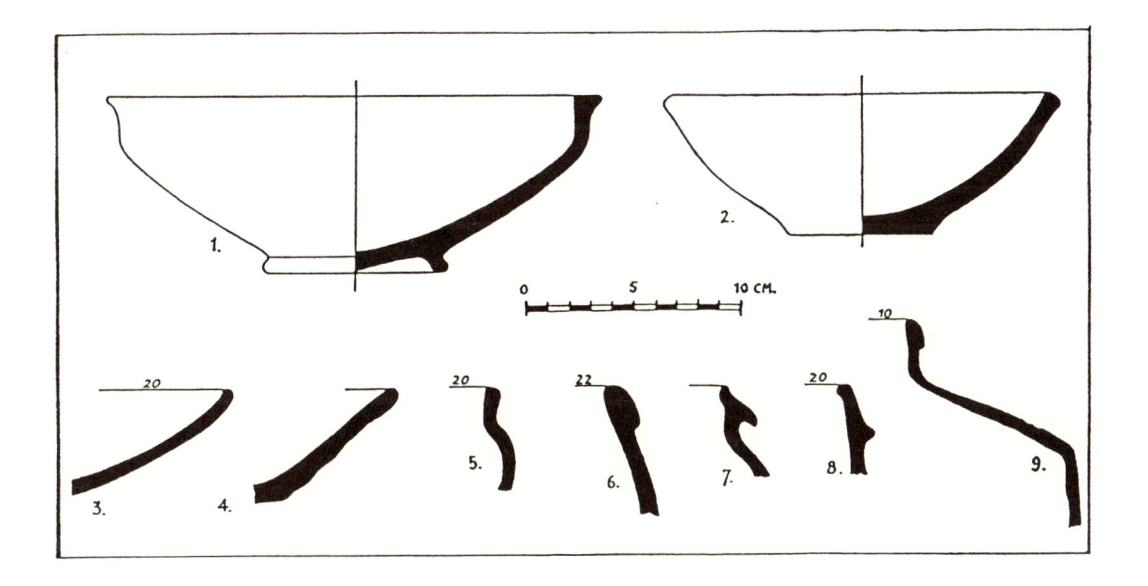

SS III, Fig. 7.   Period IV

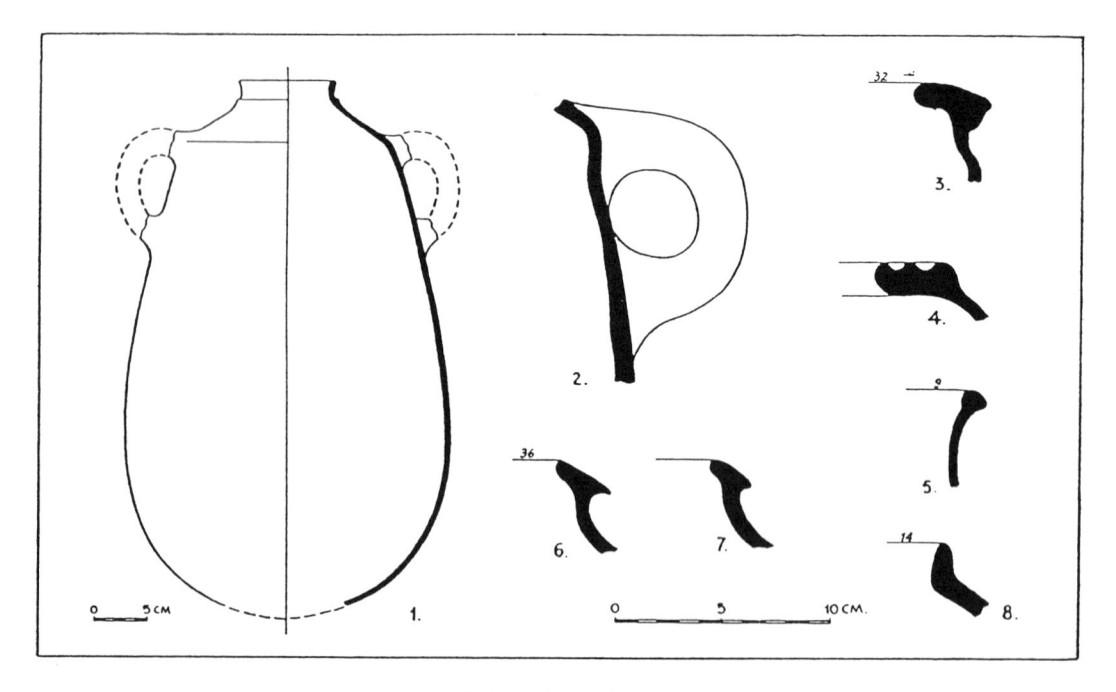

SS III, Fig. 8.   Period V

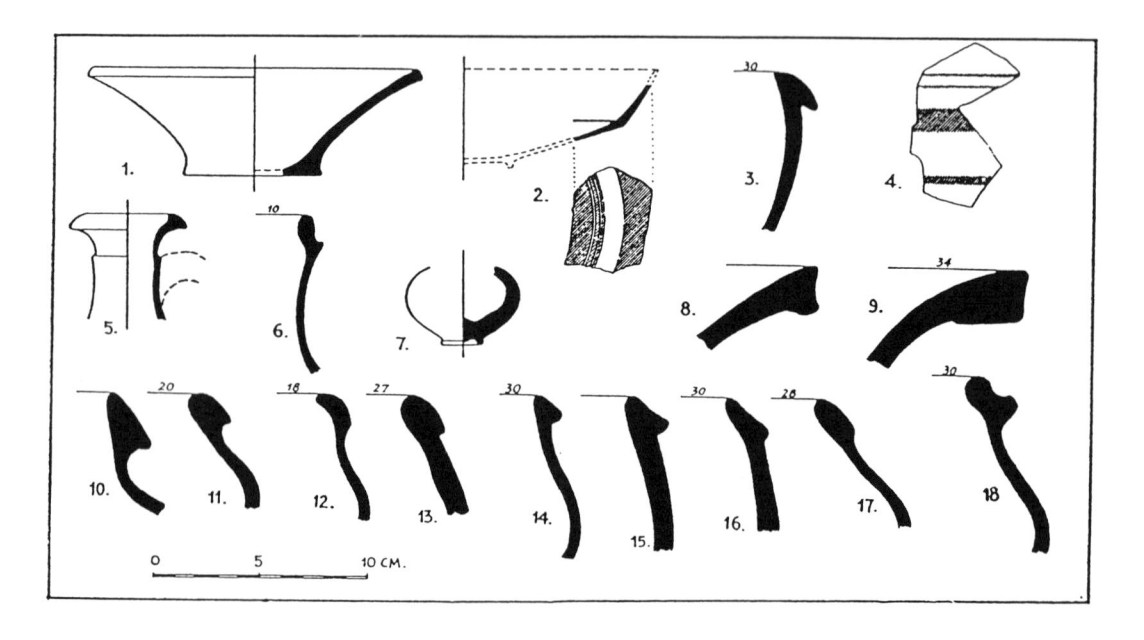

SS III, Fig. 9.   Period VI

APPENDIX E — PUBLISHED STRATIFIED POTTERY 615

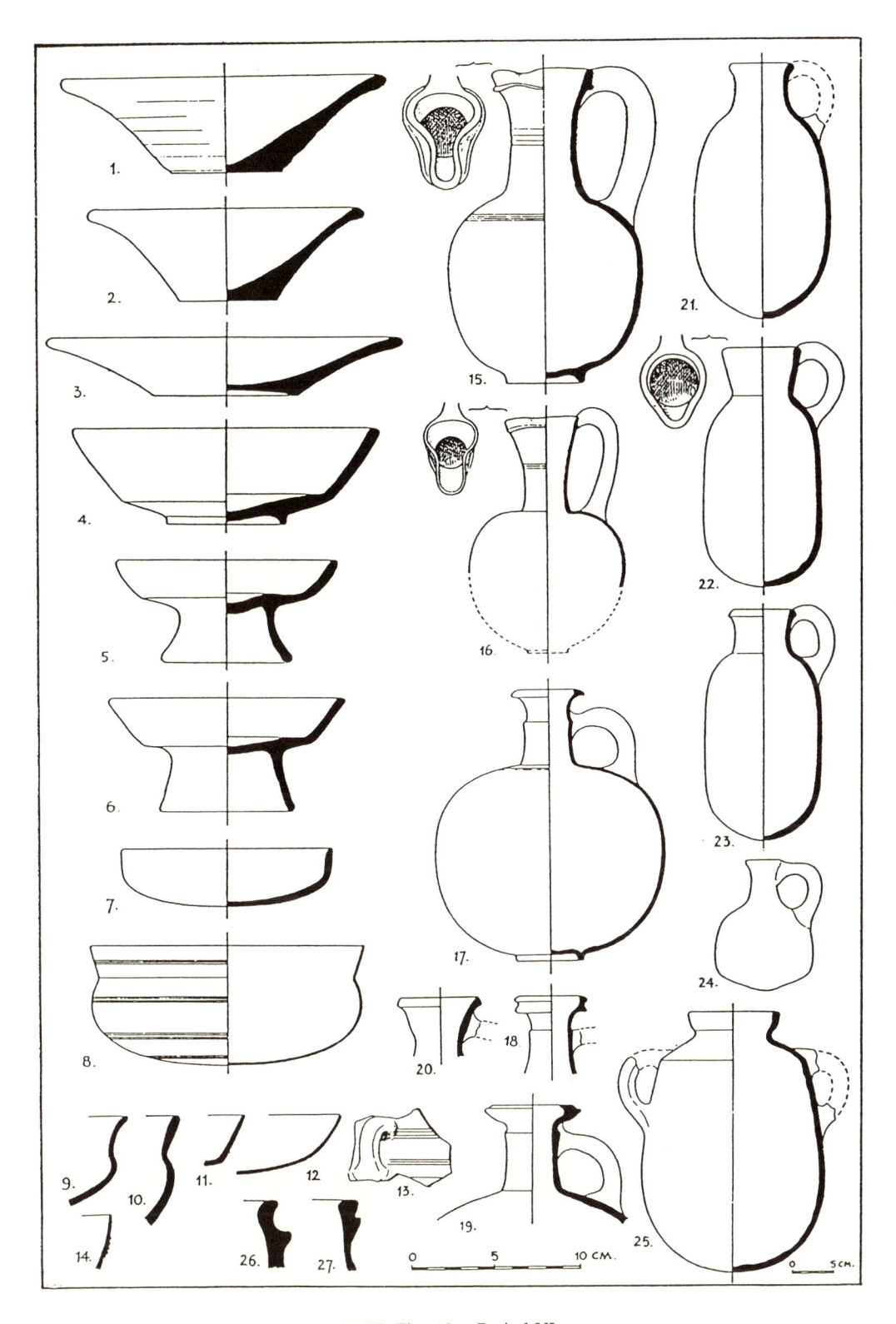

SS III, Fig. 10. Period VI

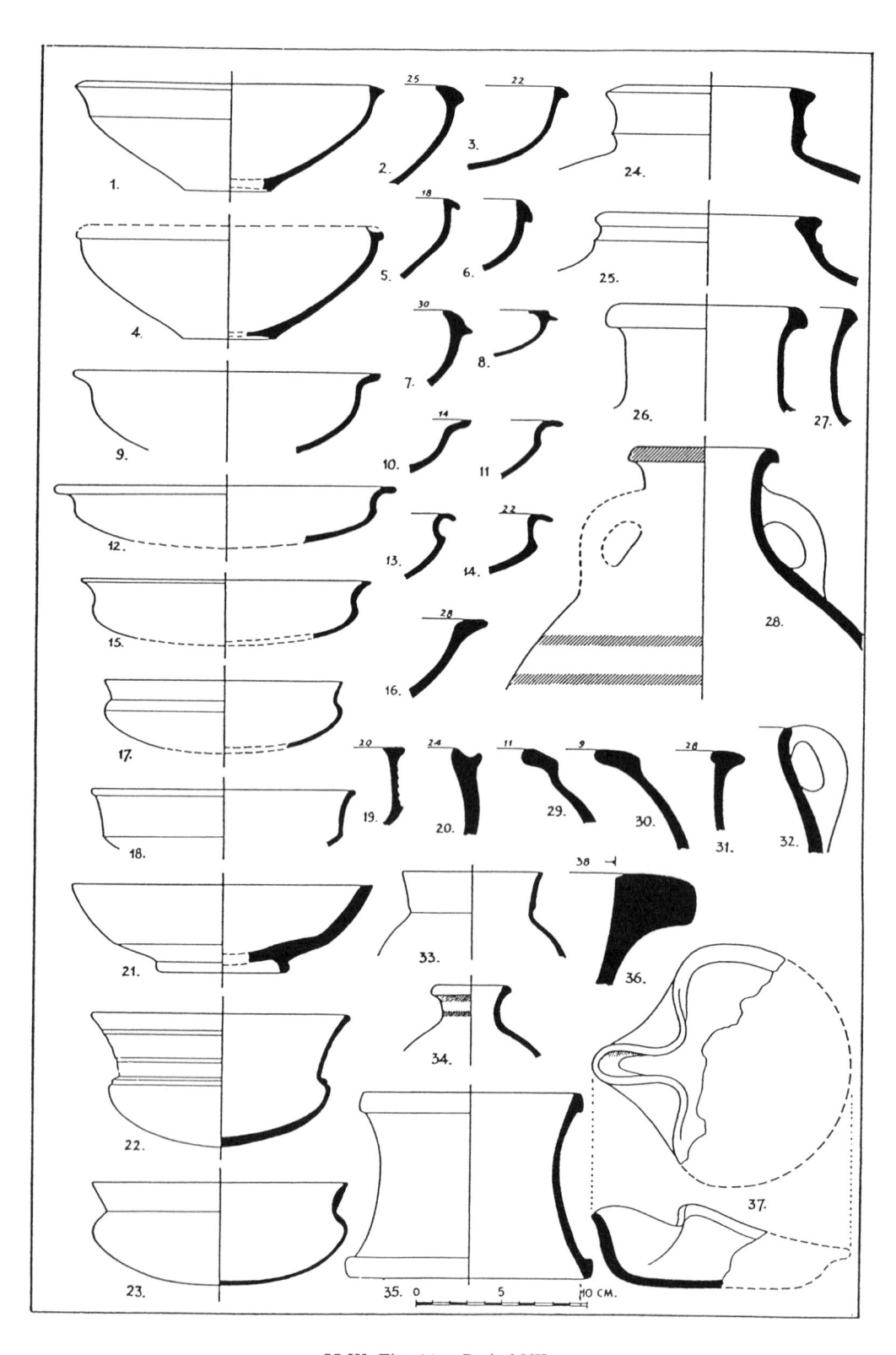

SS III, Fig. 11. Period VII

BIBLIOGRAPHY

Adams, W. Y.
    1968   "Invasion, Diffusion, Evolution?" *Antiquity* 42:194-215.

Aharoni, M. and Y. Aharoni
    1976   "The Stratification of Judahite Sites in the 8th and 7th Centuries B.C.E.," *BASOR* 224:73-90.

Aharoni, Y.
    1962   "The Samaria Ostraca—an Additional Note," *IEJ* 12:67-69.
    1975a   *Investigations at Lachish: The Sanctuary and the Residency* (Tel Aviv: Gateway).
    1975b   "Excavations at Tel Beer-Sheba, Preliminary Report of the Fifth and Sixth Seasons, 1973-1974," *TA* 2 (1975), 146-68.
    1979   *The Land of the Bible: A Historical Geography*. Rev. and enl. ed. (Philadelphia: Westminster).

Aharoni, Y., ed.
    1973   *Beer-Sheba I. Excavations at Tel Beer-Sheba, 1969-1971 Seasons* (Tel Aviv: Tel Aviv University, Institute of Archaeology).

Aharoni, Y. and R. Amiran
    1958   "A New Scheme for the Sub-Division of the Iron Age in Palestine," *IEJ* 8:171-84.

Aharoni, Y. and M. Avi-Yonah
    1977   *The Macmillan Bible Atlas*. Rev. ed. (New York: Macmillan).

Aharoni, Y. et al.
    1962a   *Excavations at Ramat Raḥel I. Seasons 1959 and 1960* (Roma: Università degli studi, Centro di studi semitici).
    1962b   *Excavations at Ramat Raḥel II. Seasons 1961 and 1962* (Roma: Università degli studi, Centro di studi semitici).

Albenda, P.
    1972   "A Syro-Palestinian(?) City on a Ninth Century B.C. Assyrian Relief," *BASOR* 206:42-48.

Albright, W. F.
    1932   *The Excavation of Tell Beit Mirsim, Vol. I: The Pottery of the First Three Campaigns*, AASOR 12 (New Haven: American Schools of Oriental Research).
    1940   "Review of *Megiddo I: Seasons of 1925-1934, Strata I-V*," *AJA* 44:546-50.
    1943   *The Excavation of Tell Beit Mirsim, Vol. III: The Iron Age*, AASOR 21-22 (New Haven: American Schools of Orienta Research).
    1944   "The End of Calneh in Shinar," *JNES* 3:254-55.
    1945   "The Chronology of the Divided Monarchy of Israel," *BASOR* 100:16-22.

1955	"The Son of Tabeel (Isaiah 7:6)," *BASOR* 140:34-35.
1958	"Recent Progress in Palestinian Archaeology: Samaria–Sebaste III and Hazor I," *BASOR* 150:21-25.
1960	*The Archaeology of Palestine*. Rev. ed. (Baltimore: Penguin Books).

Alexandre, Y.
1995	"The 'Hippo' Jar and Other Storage Jars at Hurvat Rosh Zayit," *TA* 22:77-88.

Amiran, R.
1969	*Ancient Pottery of the Holy Land* (Ramat Gan: Biyalik Institute; Jerusalem: Masada).

Andersen, F. I. and D. N. Freedman
1989	*Amos* (Anchor 24A; New York: Doubleday).

Andrae, W.
1943	*Ausgrabungen Sendschirli V. Die Kleinfunde von Sendschirli* (Berlin: W. Spemann).

Anspacher, A. S.
1966	*Tiglath-pileser III* (New York: Columbia University Press, 1912. Repr., New York: AMS).

Astour, M. C.
1971	"841 B.C.: The First Assyrian Invasion of Israel," *JAOS* 91:383-89.

Avigad, N.
1972	"Two Hebrew Inscriptions on Wine-Jars," *IEJ* 22:1-9.
1978	"Samaria," pp. 1032-50 in *Encyclopedia of Archaeological Excavations in the Holy Land*, Vol. 4. M. Avi-Yonah and E. Stern, eds. (Jerusalem: Israel Exploration Society and Massada).
1980	*Discovering Jerusalem* (Nashville: Thomas Nelson Publishers).

Avi-Yonah, M. and E. Stern, eds.
1975-1978	*Encyclopedia of Archaeological Excavations in the Holy Land*, Vols. 1-4 (Jerusalem: Israel Exploration Society and Massada).

Badè, W. F.
1931	*Some Tombs of Tell en-Naṣbeh Discovered in 1929* (Berkeley: The Palestine Institute of Pacific School of Religion).

Balensi, J.
1980	"Les fouilles de R. W. Hamilton à Tell Abu Hawam, Niveaux IV et V: Dossier sur l'histoire d'un port Méditerranéen durant les Ages du Bronze et du Fer (?1600-950 av. J.C.)." Ph.D. diss., University of Strasbourg.
1985	"Revising Tell Abu Hawam," *BASOR* 257:65-74.

Balensi, J. and M.-D. Herrera
1985	"Tell Abou Hawam 1983-1984. Rapport préliminaire (Planches V-

VI)," *RB* 92:82-128.

Balensi, J., M.-D. Herrera, and M. Artzy
   1993   "Abu Hawam, Tell," pp. 7-14 in *The New Encyclopedia of Archaeological Excavations in the Holy Land*, Vol. 1. E. Stern, ed. (Jerusalem: Israel Exploration Society).

Barkay, G.
   1992   "The Iron Age II-III," pp. 302-73 in *The Archaeology of Ancient Israel*, A. Ben-Tor, ed. (New Haven: Yale University Press).

Barnett, R. D.
   1935   "The Nimrud Ivories and the Art of the Phoenicians," *Iraq* 2:179-210.
   1939a   "Phoenician and Syrian Ivory Carving," *PEQ*:4-19.
   1939b   "Review of *Samaria-Sebaste 2. Early Ivories from Samaria*," *PEQ*:169-73.

Barnett, R. D. and M. Falkner
   1962   *The Sculptures of Assur-naṣir-pal II (883-859 B.C.), Tiglath-pileser III (745-727 B.C.), Esarhaddon (681-669 B.C.), from the Central and South-West Palaces at Nimrud* (London: Trustees of the British Museum).

Barth, H.
   1977   *Die Jesaja-Worte in der Josiazeit* (Neukirchen-Vluyn).

Bartlett, J. R.
   1973   "The Moabites and Edomites," pp. 229-58 in *People of Old Testament Times*, D. J. Wiseman, ed. (Oxford: Clarendon).

Beach, E. F.
   1993   "The Samaria Ivories, Marzeah, and Biblical Text," *BA* 56:94-104.

Becking, B.
   1992   *The Fall of Samaria: An Historical and Archaeological Summary*. Studies in the History of the Ancient Near East, Volume 2 (Leiden: E. J. Brill).

Begrich, J.
   1929   "Der syrisch-ephraimitische Krieg und seine weltpolitischen Zusammenhange," *ZDMG* 83:213-37.

Bennett, C.-M.
   1974   "Excavations at Buṣeirah, Southern Jordan, 1972: Preliminary Report," *Levant* 6:1-24, Figs. 1-16, Pls. I-VI.
   1975   "Excavations at Buṣeirah, Southern Jordan, 1973," *Levant* 7:1-19.

Ben-Tor, A., M. Avissar, and Y. Portugali
   1996   *Yoqneʿam I: The Late Periods* (Jerusalem: The Institute of Archaeology at Hebrew University and the Israel Exploration Society).

Ben-Tor, A., R. Bonfil, Y. Garfinkel, R. Greenberg, A. Maeir, and A. Mazar
    1997   *Hazor V: An Account of the Fifth Season of Excavation, 1968* (Jerusalem: The Israel Exploration Society and the Hebrew University of Jerusalem).

Ben-Tor, A. and Y. Portugali
    1987   *Tell Qiri: A Village in the Jezreel Valley, Report of the Archaeological Excavations, 1975-77.* Qedem 24 (Jerusalem: The Hebrew University of Jerusalem, Institute of Archaeology).

Ben-Tor, A., Y. Portugali, and M. Avissar
    1979   "The Second Season of Excavations at Tel Yoqneʿam, 1978: Preliminary Report," *IEJ* 29:65-83.
    1983   "The Third and Fourth Seasons of Excavations at Tel Yoqneʿam, 1979 and 1981: Preliminary Report," *IEJ* 33:30-54.

Ben-Tor, A. and R. Rosenthal
    1978   "The First Season of Excavations at Tel Yoqneʿam, 1977: Preliminary Report," *IEJ* 28:57-82.

Bienkowski, P.
    1997   "Buṣeirah," pp. 387-90 in *The Oxford Encyclopedia of Archaeology in the Near East*, Vol. 1. E. M. Meyers, ed. (Oxford/New York: Oxford University Press).

Bikai, P. M.
    1978a   "The Late Phoenician Pottery Complex and Chronology," *BASOR* 229:47-56.
    1978b   *The Pottery of Tyre* (Warminster, England: Aris & Phillips).

Biran, A.
    1994   *Biblical Dan* (Jerusalem: Israel Exploration Society and Hebrew Union College—Jewish Institute of Religion).

Biran, A. and J. Naveh
    1993   "An Aramaic Stele from Tel Dan," *IEJ* 43:81-98.
    1995   "The Tel Dan Inscription: A New Fragment," *IEJ* 45:1-18.

Bliss, F. J.
    1894   *A Mound of Many Cities, or Tell El Hesy Excavated* (London: Committee of the PEF, by A. P. Watt & Son).

Borger, R.
    1968   *Textbuch zur Geschichte Israels*, K. Galling, ed. (Tübingen: Mohr Siebeck).
    1984   *Texte aus der Umwelt des Alten Testaments*, 1/4, O. Kaiser, ed. (Gütersloh: G. Mohn).

Borger, R. and H. Tadmor
    1984   "Zwei Beiträge zur alttestamentlichen Wissenschaft aufgrund der

Inschriften Tiglatpilesers III," *ZAW* 94:244-51.

Botta, P. E. and M. E. Flandin
1949-1950   *Monument de Ninive* (Paris: Imprimerie Nationale).

Brandl, B. and R. Reich
1985   "Gezer Under Assyrian Rule," *PEQ* 117:41-54.

Braudel, F.
1958   "La longue durée," *Annales Economies Sociétés Civilisations* 13:725-53.
1980   "History and the Social Sciences: The *Longue Durée*," pp. 25-54 in *On History*. Trans. by S. Matthews (Chicago: University of Chicago Press).

Brettler, M. Z.
1995   *The Creation of History in Ancient Israel* (London/New York: Routledge).

Briend, J. and J. B. Humbert
1980   *Tell Keisan (1971-1976): Une Cité Phénicienne en Galilée* (Paris: J. Gabalda).

Brinkman, J. A.
1968   *A Political History of Post-Kassite Babylonia, 1158-722 B.C.* Analecta Orientalia 43 (Roma: Pontificium Institutum Biblicum).

Bunimovitz, S. and Z. Lederman
1993   "Beth-Shemesh," pp. 249-53 in *The New Encyclopedia of Archaeological Excavations in the Holy Land*, Vol. 1. E. Stern, ed. (Jerusalem: Israel Exploration Society).

Butterick, G. A.
1962   *The Interpreter's Dictionary of the Bible*, Vol. 1 (Nashville: Abingdon).

Callaway, J. A.
1969   "The 1966 ʿAi (et-Tell) Excavations," *BASOR* 196:2-16.

Cameron, G. G.
1950   "The Annals of Shalmaneser III, King of Assyria," *Sumer* 6:6-26.

Campbell-Thompson, R. and M. E. L. Mallowan
1933   "The British Museum Excavations at Nineveh, 1931-1932," *AAA* 20:71-186, Pls. XXXV-CVI.

Chambon, A.
1984   *Tell el-Farʿah I: L'Âge du Fer* (Paris: Editions Recherche sur les Civilisations).
1993   "Farʿah, Tell el- [North]: Late Bronze Age to the Roman Period," pp. 439-40 in *The New Encyclopedia of Archaeological Excavations in the Holy Land*, Vol. 2. E. Stern, ed. (Jerusalem: Israel Exploration

Society).

Chapman, S. V.
1972 "A Catalogue of Iron Age Pottery from the Cemeteries of Khirbet Silm, Joya, Qraye' and Qasmieh of South Lebanon," *Berytus* 21:55-194.

Chicago Epigraphic Survey
1954 Chicago Epigraphic Survey — *Reliefs and Inscriptions at Karnak*, III, *The Babastite Portal*. H. H. Nelson, field director (Chicago: University of Chicago Press, Oriental Institute).

Cody, A.
1970 "A New Inscription from Tell al-Rimah and King Jehoash of Israel," *CBQ* 32:333-37.

Cogan, M.
1974 *Imperialism and Religion: Assyria, Judah and Israel in the Eighth and Seventh Centuries B.C.E.* Society of Biblical Literature Monograph Series 19 (Missoula: Scholars Press).

Cogan, M. and H. Tadmor
1988 *II Kings*. Anchor Bible 11 (Garden City, NY: Doubleday).

Coldstream, J. N.
1968 *Greek Geometric Pottery: A Survey of Ten Local Styles and Their Chronology* (London: Barnes and Noble).

Contenau, G.
1920 "Mission archéologique à Sidon (1914)," *Syria* 1:108-54.

Cross, F. M., Jr.
1961 "Epigraphic Notes on Hebrew Documents of the Eighth-Sixth Centuries B.C.: I. A New Reading of a Place Name in the Samaria Ostraca," *BASOR* 163:12-14.
1968 "Jar Inscriptions from Shiqmona," *IEJ* 18:226-33.
1973 *Canaanite Myth and Hebrew Epic* (Cambridge, MA: Harvard University Press).
1998 "Reuben, the Firstborn of Jacob: Sacral Traditions and Early Israelite History," pp. 53-70 in *From Epic to Canon: History and Literature in Ancient Israel* (Baltimore: The Johns Hopkins University Press).

Crowfoot, G. M.
1932 "Pots, Ancient and Modern," *PEQ* October:179-87.

Crowfoot, J. W.
1932a "Excavations at Samaria, 1931" *PEFQS* January:8-34, Pls. I-VII.
1932b "The Expedition to Samaria–Sebustiya. The Forum Threshing Floor Area," *PEFQS* April:63-70, Pls. I-VI.
1932c "Recent Discoveries of the Joint Expedition to Samaria," *PEFQS*

	July:132-33, Pls. I-IV.
1933a	"The Samaria Excavations: The Stadium," *PEFQS* April:62-73, Pls. I-VI.
1933b	"Samaria: Interim Report on the Work in 1933," *PEFQS* July:129-36.
1935	"Report of the 1935 Samaria Excavations," *PEFQS*:182-94, Pls. VII-X.

Crowfoot, J. W. and G. M. Crowfoot
1933	"The Ivories from Samaria," *PEFQS* January:7-26, Pls. I-III.
1938	*Samaria-Sebaste 2: Early Ivories from Samaria* (London: Palestine Exploration Fund).

Crowfoot, J. W., G. M. Crowfoot, and K. M. Kenyon
1957	*Samaria-Sebaste III: The Objects* (London: Palestine Exploration Fund).

Crowfoot, J. W., K. M. Kenyon, and E. L. Sukenik
1942	*The Buildings at Samaria* (London: Palestine Exploration Fund).

Culican, W.
1968	"Quelques aperçus sur les ateliers phéniciens," *Syria* 45:275-93.

Curtis, J. B.
1961	"East is East . . . ," *JBL* 80:355-63.

Dalley, S.
1985	"Foreign Chariotry and Cavalry in the Armies of Tiglath-pileser III and Sargon II," *Iraq* 47:31-48.

Davidson, G. R.
1952	*Corinth, XII: The Minor Objects* (Princeton: American School of Classical Studies at Athens).

Davies, G. I.
1986	*Megiddo* (Cambridge, Eng.: Lutterworth).
1988	"Solomonic Stables at Megiddo After All?" *PEQ* 120:130-41.
1994	"King Solomon's Stables—Still at Megiddo?" *BAR* 20/1:44-49.

Demsky, A.
1972	"'Dark Wine' from Judah," *IEJ* 22:233-34.

Dever, W. G.
1992	"A Case-Study in Biblical Archaeology: The Earthquake of ca. 760 BCE," *Eretz-Israel* 23 (Biran Volume):27*-35*.
1997	"Tell Keisan," pp. 278-79 in *The Oxford Encyclopedia of Archaeology in the Near East*, Vol. 3. E. M. Meyers, ed. (Oxford/New York: Oxford University Press).

Dever, W. G., ed.
1974	*Gezer II* (Jerusalem: Hebrew Union College/Nelson Glueck School of

1986	Biblical Archaeology). *Gezer IV*, Part 1, Text; Part 2, Plates, Plans (Jerusalem: Nelson Gleuck School of Biblical Archaeology).

Dever, W. G., H. D. Lance, and G. E. Wright
1970	*Gezer I* (Jerusalem: Hebrew Union College Biblical and Archaeological School).

Donner, H.
1977	"The Separate States of Israel and Judah," pp. 381-434 in *Israelite and Judaean History*, J. H. Hayes and J. M. Miller, eds. (Philadelphia: Westminster).

Donner, H. and W. Röllig
1962-1964	*Kanaanäische und Aramäische Inschriften*, 3 vols. (Wiesbaden: Otto Harrassowitz).

Dorsey, D. A.
1991	*The Roads and Highways of Ancient Israel* (Baltimore: The Johns Hopkins University Press).

Dothan, M.
1955	"Excavations at ʿAfula," *ʿAtîqôt* 1:19-70 (English series).
1971	*Ashdod II-III: The Second and Third Seasons of Excavations, 1963, 1965, Soundings in 1967 (Text; Figures and Plates)*, ʿAtîqôt 9-10 (Jerusalem: The Department of Antiquities and Museums, Ministry of Education and Culture).
1982	*Ashdod IV*, ʿAtiqot 15 (Jerusalem: The Department of Antiquities and Museums, Ministry of Education and Culture).

Dothan, M. and D. N. Freedman
1967	*Ashdod I: The First Season of Excavations, 1962*, ʿAtîqôt 7 (Jerusalem: The Department of Antiquities and Museums, Ministry of Education and Culture, Holy Land Exhibition Fund, Ashdod Expedition).

Dothan, T.
1982	*The Philistines and Their Material Culture* (New Haven: Yale University Press).

Driver, G. R.
1959	"Geographical Problems," *Eretz-Israel* 5 (Mazar Volume):18*-20*.

Dunand, M.
1954	*Fouilles de Byblos, Tome I and Tome II, 1933-1938* (Paris: Librairie d'Amérique et d'Orient Adrien Maisonneuve).

Duncan, J. G.
1930	*Corpus of Dated Palestinian Pottery* (London: British School of Archaeology in Egypt).

1931	*Digging up Biblical History*, Vol. II (London: Society for Promoting Christian Knowledge).
Eitan, A.	
1974	"Notes and News: Megiddo," *IEJ* 24:275-76.
Elat, M.	
1975	"The Campaigns of Shalmaneser III against Aram and Israel," *IEJ* 25:25-35.
Eph'al, I.	
1979a	"Israel: Fall and Exile," pp. 180-91, 341-43 in *The World History of the Jewish People*, Vol. IV–Part 1 (Jerusalem: Massada).
1979b	"Assyrian Dominion in Palestine," pp. 276-89, 364-68 in *The World History of the Jewish People*, Vol. IV–Part 1 (Jerusalem: Massada).
1982	*The Ancient Arabs: Nomads on the Borders of the Fertile Crescent, Ninth-Fifth Centuries BC* (Jerusalem: Magnes–The Hebrew University).
Eran, A.	
1996	"Weights and Weighing in the City of David: The Early Weights from the Bronze Age to the Persian Period," pp. 204-56 in *The Excavations at the City of David, 1978-1985, Volume IV: Various Reports*, D. T. Ariel and A. de Groot, eds. Qedem 35 (Jerusalem: The Hebrew University Institute of Archaeology).
Esse, D.	
1992	"The Collared Pithos at Megiddo: Ceramic Distribution and Ethnicity," *JNES* 51:81-103.
Falkner, M.	
1954-1956	"Die Eponymen der spätassyrischen Zeit," *AfO* 17:100-120.
Fargo, V. M.	
1983	"Is the Solomonic City Gate at Megiddo Really Solomonic?" *BAR* 9:8-13.
Finkelstein, I.	
1994	"The Emergence of Israel: A Phase in the Cyclic History of Canaan in the Third and Second Millennia BCE," pp. 150-78 in *From Nomadism to Monarchy: Archaeological and Historical Aspects of Early Israel*. I. Finkelstein and N. Na'aman, eds. (Jerusalem: Israel Exploration Society).
1996	"The Archaeology of the United Monarchy: an Alternative View," *Levant* XXVIII:177-87.
Fitzgerald, G. M.	
1930	*The Four Canaanite Temples of Beth Shean, Part II: The Pottery*, Vol. II/2 (Philadelphia: University of Pennsylvania Press).

Forsberg, S.
- 1995 *Near Eastern Destruction Datings as Sources for Greek and Near Eastern Iron Age Chronology: Archaeological and Historical Studies, The Cases of Samaria (722 B.C.) and Tarsus (696 B.C.)*. Uppsala Studies in Ancient Mediterranean and Near Eastern Civilizations 19 (Uppsala: Acta Universitatis Upsaliensis).

Fox, R. G.
- 1977 *Urban Anthropology: Cities in Their Cultural Settings* (Englewood Cliffs, NJ: Prentice-Hall).

Franken, H. J.
- 1969 *Excavations at Tell Deir ʿAllā: I* (Leiden: E. J. Brill).

Franklin, N.
- 1994 "The Room V Reliefs at Dur-Sharrukin and Sargon II's Western Campaigns," *TA* 21:255-75.

Fritz, W. and A. Kempinski
- 1983 *Ergebnisse der Ausgrabungen auf der Ḥirbet el Masas (Tel Masos), 1972-1975* (Wiesbaden: Harrassowitz).

Fuchs, A.
- 1994 *Die Inschriften Sargons II. aus Khorsabad* (Göttingen: Cuvillier Verlag) [based on Fuchs' Ph.D. diss., Göttingen University, 1993].

Gadd, C. J.
- 1936 *The Stones of Assyria* (London: Chatto and Windus).
- 1954 "Inscribed Prisms of Sargon II from Nimrud," *Iraq* 16:173-201.

Galil, G.
- 1995 "The Last Years of the Kingdom of Israel and the Fall of Samaria," *CBQ* 57:52-65.

Gelb, I. J.
- 1935 "Calneh," *AJSL* 51:189-91.
- 1954 "Two Assyrian King Lists," *JNES* 13:209-30.
- 1970 "Comments on the Akkadian Syllabary," *Orientalia* 39:516-46.

Geraty, L. T., L. G. Herr, Ø. S. LaBianca, and R. W. Younker, eds.
- 1989 *Madaba Plains Project 1: The 1984 Season at Tell el-ʿUmeiri and Vicinity and Subsequent Studies* (Berrien Springs, MI: Andrews University).

Geva, S.
- 1982 "Archaeological Evidence for the Trade Between Israel and Tyre?" *BASOR* 248:69-72.

Gibson, J. C. L.
- 1975 *Textbook of Syrian Semitic Inscriptions, Volume 2: Aramaic Inscriptions* (Oxford: Clarendon).

Gill, D.
1996 "The Geology of the City of David and its Ancient Subterranean Water Works," pp. 1-28 in *City of David Excavations, 1978-1985, Vol. IV: Various Reports*, D. T. Ariel and A. de Groot, eds. Qedem 35 (Jerusalem: The Hebrew University of Jerusalem, Institute of Archaeology).

Gitin, S.
1979 "An Abstract of 'A Ceramic Typology of the Late Iron II, Persian, and Hellenistic Periods at Tell Gezer'." Ph.D. diss., Hebrew Union College, Cincinnati.
1990 *Gezer III, A Ceramic Typology of the Late Iron II, Persian and Hellenistic Periods at Tell Gezer* (Jerusalem: Hebrew Union College/Nelson Gleuck School of Biblical Archaeology).

Gjerstad, E.
1948 *The Swedish Cyprus Expedition*, Vol. IV. Part 2 (Stockholm: The Swedish Cyprus Expedition).

Glueck, N.
1993 "Tell el-Kheleifeh," pp. 867-69 in *The New Encyclopedia of Archaeological Excavations in the Holy Land*, Vol. 3 (Jerusalem: Israel Exploration Society).

Godley, A. D., trans.
1946 *Herodotus*. The Loeb Classical Library (Cambridge, MA: Harvard University Press).

Goetze, A.
1957 *Kulturgeschichte Kleinasiens* (München: C. H. Beck'sche Verlagsbuchhandlung, 1957).

Goldman, H., ed.
1963 *Excavations at Gözlü Kule, Tarsus, Volume III: The Iron Age, Text and Plates* (Princeton: Princeton University Press).

Goodspeed, G. S.
1902 *A History of the Babylonians and the Assyrians* (New York: Charles Scribner's Sons).

Grant, E.
1932 *ʿAin Shems Excavations, 1928-1929-1930-1931, Part II* (Haverford: Haverford College).

Grant, E. and G. E. Wright
1938 *ʿAin Shems Excavations, Part IV: The Pottery (plates)* (Haverford: Haverford College).
1939 *ʿAin Shems Excavations, Part V (text)* (Haverford: Haverford College).

Gray, J.
　1970　　　*I and II Kings: A Commentary.* 2d rev. ed. (Philadelphia: Westminster).

Grayson, A. K.
　1975　　　*Assyrian and Babylonian Chronicles.* Texts from Cuneiform Sources, Volume V (Locust Valley, NY: J. J. Augustin Publisher; reprinted Winona Lake, IN: Eisenbrauns, 2000).
　1982　　　"Assyria: Ashur-dan II to Ashur-nirari V (934-745 B.C.)," pp. 238-81 in *The Cambridge Ancient History*, Vol. III/1, 2d ed. J. Boardman et al., eds. (Cambridge, Eng.: Cambridge University Press).

Green, A. R.
　1979　　　"Sua and Jehu: The Boundaries of Shalmaneser's Conquest," *PEQ* 111:35-39.

Greene, J. and I. Springer
　2000　　　"The Museum's Archives: Decades Old and Still 'Going'," *Semitic Museum News* 3:2.

Gurney, O. R. and J. J. Finkelstein
　1957　　　*The Sultantepe Tablets I.* Occasional Publications of the British Institute of Archaeology at Ankara No. 3 (London: British Institute of Archaeology at Ankara).

Gurney, O. R. and P. Hulin
　1964　　　*The Sultantepe Tablets II.* Occasional Publications of the British Institute of Archaeology at Ankara No. 7 (London: British Institute of Archaeology at Ankara).

Guy, P. L. O.
　1924　　　"Mt. Carmel, An Early Iron Age Cemetery Near Haifa, Excavated September 1922," *BBSAJ* 5:47-55.
　1938　　　*Megiddo Tombs* (Chicago: University of Chicago Press).

Haller, A.
　1954　　　*Die Gräber und Grüfte von Assur*, Wissenschaftliche Veröffentlichung der deutschen Orient-Gessellschaft 65 (Berlin: Gebr. Mann).

Hallo, W. W.
　1960　　　"From Qarqar to Carchemish: Assyria and Israel in the Light of New Discoveries," *BA* 23:34-61.
　1975　　　"From Qarqar to Carchemish: Assyria and Israel in the Light of New Discoveries," pp. 152-88 in *Biblical Archaeologist Reader*, Vol. 2., E. F. Campbell and D. N. Freedman, eds. (Missoula: Scholars Press).

Hamilton, R. W.
　1934　　　"Tell Abu Hawam. Interim Report," *QDAP* 3:74-80.

1935 "Excavations at Tell Abu Hawām," *QDAP* 4:1-69.

Harding, G. L.
1945 "Two Iron Age Tombs from ʿAmman," *QDAP* 11:67-74.
1948 "An Iron Age Tomb at Saḥab," *QDAP* 13:92-102.
1950 "An Iron Age Tomb at Meqabelein," *QDAP* 14:44-48, Pls. XIII-XVII.
1951 "Two Iron Age Tombs in Amman," *ADAJ* 1:37-40.
1953a *Four Tomb Groups from Jordan*. Palestine Exploration Fund Annual = *APEF* 6 (London: Palestine Exploration Fund).
1953b "An Early Iron Age Tomb at Madeba," pp. 27-47 in *Four Tomb Groups from Jordan*. Palestine Exploration Fund Annual = *APEF* 6 (London: Palestine Exploration Fund).

Harding, G. L. and O. Tufnell
1953 "The Tomb of Adoni-Nur," pp. 48-75 in *Four Tomb Groups from Jordan*. Palestine Exploration Fund Annual = *APEF* 6 (London: Palestine Exploration Fund).

Harper, R. F.
1892-1914 *Assyrian and Babylonian Letters* (Chicago: The University of Chicago Press).

Hawkins, J. D.
1982 "The Neo-Hittite States in Syria and Anatolia," pp. 372-441 in *The Cambridge Ancient History*, Vol. III, Part 1, 2d ed. J. Boardman et al., eds. (Cambridge, Eng.: Cambridge University Press).

Haydn, H. M.
1909 "Azariah of Judah and Tiglath-pileser III," *JBL* 28:182-99.

Hayes, J. H.
1988 *Amos: The Eighth Century Prophet* (Nashville, TN: Abingdon).

Hayes, J. H. and J. K. Kuan
1991 "The Final Years of Samaria (730-720 BC)," *Biblica* 72:153-81.

Hendrix, R. E., P. R. Drey, and J. Bjørnar Storfjell
1996 *Ancient Pottery of Transjordan: An Introduction Utilizing Published Whole Forms, Late Neolithic through Late Islamic* (Berrien Springs, MI: Institute of Archaeology/Horn Archaeological Museum, Andrews University).

Henschel-Simon, E.
1945 "Note on the Pottery of the ʿAmman Tombs," *QDAP* 11:75-80.

Herm, G.
1975 *The Phoenicians: The Purple Empire of the Ancient World* (London: Victor Gollancz).

Herr, L. G.
1997 "The Iron Age II Period: Emerging Nations," *BA* 60:114-83.

Herr, L. G., L. T. Geraty, Ø. S. LaBianca, and R. W. Younker, eds.
1991 *Madaba Plains Project 2: The 1987 Season at Tell el-ʿUmeiri and Vicinity and Subsequent Studies* (Berrien Springs, MI: Andrews University).

Herrera, M.-D.
1990 "Las Excavaciones de R. W. Hamilton en Tell Abu Hawam, Haifa. El Stratum III, Historia del Puerto Fenicio durante los Siglos X-VIII a. de C." Ph.D. diss., Cantabria.

Herrera, M.-D. and J. Balensi
1986 "More about the Greek Geometric Pottery at Tell Abu Hawam," *Levant* 18:169-71.

Herrmann, S.
1981 *A History of Israel in Old Testament Times*. Rev. ed. (Philadelphia: Fortress).

Herzog, Z.
1984 *Beer-Sheba II: The Early Iron Age Settlements* (Tel Aviv: Tel Aviv University, Institute of Archaeology).
1993 "Tel Beersheba," pp. 167-73 in *The New Encyclopedia of Archaeological Excavations in the Holy Land*, Vol. 1. E. Stern, ed. (Jerusalem: The Israel Exploration Society and Carta).
1997 "Fortifications," pp. 319-26 in *The Oxford Encyclopedia of Archaeology in the Near East*, Vol. 2. E. M. Meyers, ed. (Oxford/New York: Oxford University Press).

Hodder, I.
1987 "The Contribution of the Long Term," pp. 1-8 in *Archaeology as Long Term History* (Cambridge, Eng.: Cambridge University Press).

Holladay, J. S., Jr.
1966 "Ninth and Eighth Century Pottery from Northern Palestine." Th.D. diss., Harvard University.
1976 "Of Sherds and Strata: Contributions toward an Understanding of the Archaeology of the Divided Monarchy," pp. 253-93 in *Magnalia Dei: The Mighty Acts of God*. F. M. Cross, W. E. Lemke, and P. D. Miller, Jr., eds. (Garden City, NY: Doubleday).

Huehnergard, J.
1987 *Ugaritic Vocabulary in Syllabic Transcription*. Harvard Semitic Studies 33 (Atlanta, GA: Scholars Press).

Humbert, J.-B.
1993 "Tell Keisan," pp. 862-67 in *The New Encyclopedia of Archaeological Excavations in the Holy Land*, Vol. 3. E. Stern, ed. (Jerusalem: The Israel Exploration Society and Carta).

Ilan, Z. and A. Yosef
    1977   "Ancient Settlements on the Bardawil Reef," *Qadmoniot* 10:71-79 (Hebrew).

James, F. W.
    1966   *The Iron Age at Beth-Shan: A Study of Levels VI-IV*, in *University Museum Monographs*, No. 28. (Philadelphia: University Museum of University of Pennsylvania).

Jaruzelska, I.
    1998   *Amos and the Officialdom in the Kingdom of Israel: The Socio-Economic Position of the Officials in the Light of the Biblical, the Epigraphic and Archaeological Evidence* (Poznań: Wydawnictwo Naukowe Uniwersytetu).

Jepsen, A.
    1968   "Noch einmal zur israelitisch-jüdischen chronologie," *VT* 18:31-46.

Jodin, A.
    1966   *Mogador. Comptoir phénicien du Maroc atlantique. Études et travaux d'archéologie marocaine, Vol. 2: Villes et sites du Maroc Atlantique* (Tanger: Éditions marocaines et internationales).

Johns, C. N.
    1933   "Excavations at ʿAtlīt (1930-1931): The South-Eastern Cemetery," *QDAP* 2 (1933) 41-104, Pls. XIV-XXXVII.
    1937   "Excavations at Pilgrims' Castle, ʿAtlīt (1933): Cremated Burials of Phoenician Origin," *QDAP* 6:121-52.

Katzenstein, H. J.
    1973   *The History of Tyre: From the Beginning of the Second Millennium B.C.E. until the Fall of the Neo-Babylonian Empire in 538 B.C.E.* (Jerusalem: The Schocken Institute for Jewish Research).

Kaufman, I. T.
    1966   "The Samaria Ostraca: A Study in Ancient Hebrew Palaeography," Text and Plates. Th.D. diss., Harvard Univerity.
    1982   "The Samaria Ostraca: An Early Witness to Hebrew Writing," *BA* 45:229-39.

Kelm, G. L. and A. Mazar
    1985   "Tel Batash (Timnah) Excavations: Second Preliminary Report," *BASOR* Supplement 23:93-120.
    1995   *Timnah: A Biblical City in the Sorek Valley* (Winona Lake, IN: Eisenbrauns).

Kelso, J. L.
    1968   *The Excavation of Bethel (1934-1960)*, in *AASOR* 39 (Cambridge, MA: ASOR).

Kenyon, K. M.
    unpublished *Abstract of Levels* for Summit Strip Qc. Ms. in the Palestine Exploration Fund, London.
    unpublished *Fieldbook Qc-d-e-f-g-h*, Notes from the 1932 Season of Excavation. Ms. in the Palestine Exploration Fund, London.
    unpublished *Fieldbook Qc-g*. Notes from the 1933 Season of Excavation. Ms. in the Palestine Exploration Fund, London.
    unpublished *Fieldbook Qk-l-m*, Notes from the 1933 Season of Excavation. Ms. in the Palestine Exploration Fund, London.
    unpublished *Fieldbook Qn (Vol I)*. Notes from the 1935 Season of Excavation. Ms. in the Palestine Exploration Fund, London.
    unpublished *Fieldbook Qn (Vol. II)*. Notes from the 1935 Season of Excavation. Ms. in the Palestine Exploration Fund, London.
    unpublished *Sabastya Qn, 1935*. General Field Registry stored in the Rockefeller Museum, Jerusalem, Israel.
    1933 "Excavations at Samaria. The Forecourt of the Augusteum," *PEFQ* April:74-87, Pls. I-XIII.
    1964 "Megiddo, Hazor, Samaria and Chronology," *BIA* (University of London) 4:143-56.
    1971 *Royal Cities of the Old Testament* (New York: Schocken).

Kenyon, K. M. et al.
    1965 *Excavations at Jericho II. The Tombs Excavated in 1955-8* (London: British School of Archaeology in Jerusalem).

Kessler, K.
    1975-1976 "Die Anzahl der assyrischen Provinzen des Jahres 738 v.Chr. in Nordsyrien," *WdO* 8:49-63.

Kitchen, K. A.
    1973 *The Third Intermediate Period in Egypt* (London: Warminster).

Kochavi, M.
    1969 "Excavations at Tel Esdar," *ʿAtîqôt* 5:14-48 [Hebrew series].
    1974 "Khirbet Rabûd = Debir," *TA* 1:2-32.

Kraeling, E.
    1918 *Aram and Israel* (New York: Columbia University Press).

Kühne, H.
    1980 "Zur Rekonstruktion der Feldzüge Adad-nīrāi II., Tukulti-Ninurta II. und Aššurnaṣirpal II. im Ḫābūr-Gebiet," *Baghdader Mitteilungen* 11:44-70.

Læssøe, J.
    1959 "A Statue of Shalmaneser III, from Nimrud," *Iraq* 21:147-57.

Lambert, W. G.
    1961 "The Sultantepe Tablets (continued). VIII. Shalmaneser in Ararat,"

Anatolian Studies 11:146-49.
- 1981 *Ladders to Heaven: Art Treasures from Lands of the Bible*, O. W. Muscarella, ed. (Toronto: McClelland and Stewart).

Lamon, R. S. and G. M. Shipton
- 1939 *Megiddo I, Seasons of 1925-1934, Strata I-V* (Chicago: University of Chicago Press).

Lance, H. D.
- 1967 "Gezer in the Land and in History," *BA* 30:34-47.

Lapp, P. W.
- 1961 *Palestinian Ceramic Chronology, 200 B.C.-A.D. 70*. ASOR Publications of the Jerusalem School, Archaeology, Volume 3 (New Haven: American Schools of Oriental Research).
- 1964 "The 1963 Excavation at Ta'annek," *BASOR* 173:4-44.
- 1967 "The 1966 Excavations at Tell Ta'annek," *BASOR* 185:2-39.
- 1969 "The 1968 Excavations at Tell Ta'annek," *BASOR* 195:2-49.

Lapp, P. W. and N. Lapp
- 1968 "Iron II—Hellenistic Pottery Groups," pp. 54-89 in *The 1957 Excavation at Beth-Zur*, by O. R. Sellers, R. W. Funk, J. L. McKenzie, P. and N. Lapp. *AASOR* 38.

Lawlor, J. I.
- 1991 "Field A: The Ammonite Citadel," pp. 15-52 in *MPP-2*, L. G. Herr et al., eds. (Berrien Springs, MI: Institute of Archaeology/Andrews University Press).

Layard, A. H.
- 1849 *Nineveh and its Remains*, Volumes 1-2 (New York: George P. Putnam).
- 1849-1853 *The Monuments of Nineveh from Drawings Made on the Spot*, Volumes 1-2 (London: J. Murray).
- 1851 *Inscriptions in the Cuneiform Character, from Assyrian Monuments* (London: British Museum).
- 1853 *Discoveries in the Ruins of Nineveh and Babylon, Second Expedition* (New York: G. P. Putnam).

Lemaire, A.
- 1973 "Les Ostraca Hebreux de l'Epoque Royale Israelite," Text and Plates. Ph.D. diss., University of Paris.
- 1977 *Inscriptions Hebraiques, Tome I, Les Ostraca* (Paris: Les Editions du Cerf).

Levine, L. D.
- 1972a *Two Neo-Assyrian Stelae from Iran*. Occasional Paper 23, Art and Archaeology, Royal Ontario Museum (Toronto: Royal Ontario Museum).

1972b   "Menahem and Tiglath-pileser III: A New Synchronism," *BASOR* 206:40-42.

Levy, S. and G. Edelstein
1972   "Cinq années de fouilles à Tel ʿAmal (Nir David)," *RB* 79:325-67.

Lewy, J.
1944   "The Old West Semitic Sun-God Ḥammu," *HUCA* 18:429-81.

Lines, J.
1954   "Late Assyrian Pottery from Nimrud," *Iraq* 16:164-167.

Loud, G.
1948   *Megiddo II* (Chicago: University of Chicago Press).

Luckenbill, D. D.
1925   "Azariah of Judah," *AJSL* 41:217-32.
1926   *Ancient Records of Assyria and Babylonia*, Vols I-II (Chicago: The University of Chicago Press).

Lugenbeal, E. N. and J. A. Sauer
1972   "Seventh-Sixth Century B.C. Pottery from Area B at Heshbon," *AUSS* 10:21-69, Pls. A-C, I-XI.

Machinist, P.
1983   "Assyria and Its Image in the First Isaiah," *JAOS* 103:719-37.

Mackenzie, D.
1912-1913   "The Excavations at ʿAin Shems (Beth-Shemesh)," *APEF* 2 (London: Palestine Exploration Fund).

Maeir, A. M.
2001   "The Philistine Culture in Transformation: A Current Perspective Based on the Results of the First Seasons of Excavations at Tell es-Safi/Gath," pp. 111-29 in *Settlement, Civilization and Culture: Proceedings of the Conference in Memory of David Alon*, A. M. Maeir and E. Baruch, eds. (Ramat-Gan: Bar-Ilan University, 2001).

Maisler (Mazar), B.
1948   "The Historical Background of the Samaria Ostraca," *JPOS* 21:117-33.
1951a   "The Stratification of Tell Abū Huwâm on the Bay of Acre," *BASOR* 124:21-25.
1951b   "The Excavations at Tell Qasîle, Preliminary Report," *IEJ* 1:61-76; 125-40; 194-218.
1952   "Yurza, The Identification of Tell Jemmeh," *PEQ* 84:48-51.

Malamat, A.
1953   "Amos 1:5 in the Light of the Til Barsip Inscriptions," *BASOR* 129:25-26.
1971   "On the Akkadian Transcription of the Name of King Joash," *BASOR*

204:37-39.
1973 "The Aramaeans," in *Peoples of Old Testament Times*, D. J. Wiseman, ed. (Oxford: Clarendon).

Mallowan, M. E. L.
1950 "The Excavations at Nimrud, 1949-1950," *Iraq* 12:147-83, Pls. XXVI-XXXII.
1958 "The Excavations at Nimrud (Kalḫu), 1957," *Iraq* 20:101-108.
1978 "Samaria and Calah Nimrud: Conjunctions in History and Archaeology," pp. 155-63 in *Archaeology in the Levant: Essays for Kathleen Kenyon*, R. Moorey and P. Parr, eds. (Warminster, England: Aris & Phillips).

Marcus, R., trans.
1943 *Josephus, Jewish Antiquities*, Vol. VII. The Loeb Classical Library (Cambridge, MA: Harvard University Press).

Marcus, R. and A. Wikgren, trans.
1963 *Josephus, Jewish Antiquities*, Vol. VIII. The Loeb Classical Library (Cambridge, MA: Harvard University Press).

Marquet-Krause, J.
1949 *La Résurrection d'une Grande Cité Biblique: Les Fouilles de 'Ay (Et-Tell), 1933-1935, Texte et Atlas*. Institut Français Archéologie de Beyrouth, Bibliothèque Archéologique et Historique, Tome 45 (Paris: Librairie Orientaliste Paul Geuthner).

May, H. G.
1933 "Supplementary Note on the Ivory Inlays from Samaria," *PEFQ* April:88-89.
1935 *Material Remains of the Megiddo Cult* (Chicago: University of Chicago Press).
1944 "A Review of *The Excavation of Tell Beit Mirsim, Vol. III: The Iron Age*," *JBL* 63:191-95.

Mayer, W.
1980 "Sargons Feldzug gegen Urartu — 714 v. Chr.: Eine militähistorische Würdigung," *MDOG* 112:13-33.

Mazar, A.
1980 *Excavations at Tell Qasile, Part One, The Philistine Sanctuary: Architecture and Cult Objects*, Qedem 12 (Jerusalem: The Hebrew University of Jerusalem, Institute of Archaeology).
1982 "Iron Age Fortresses in the Judaean Hills," *PEQ* (July-December):87-109.
1985 *Excavations at Tell Qasile, Part Two, The Philistine Sanctuary: Various Finds, the Pottery, Conclusions, Appendixes*, Qedem 20 (Jerusalem: The Hebrew University of Jerusalem, Institute of

Archaeology).
1993 "Beth-Shean," pp. 214-23 in *The New Encyclopedia of Archaeological Excavations in the Holy Land*, Vol. 1. E. Stern, ed. (Jerusalem: Israel Exploration Society).
1994 "The Northern Shephelah in the Iron Age: Some Issues in Biblical History and Archaeology," pp. 247-67 in *Scripture and Other Artifacts: Essays on the Bible and Archaeology in Honor of Philip J. King*, eds. M. D. Coogan, J. C. Exum, and L. E. Stager (Louisville: Westminster/John Knox).
1997 "Iron Age Chronology: A Reply to I. Finkelstein," *Levant* 29:157-67.

Mazar, B.
1989 "The House of Omri," *Eretz-Israel* 20 (Yadin Volume):215-19 (Hebrew).

Mazar, B., A. Biran, M. Dothan, and I. Dunayevsky
1964 "ʿEin Gev Excavations in 1961," *IEJ* 14:1-49.

Mazar, B., T. Dothan, and I. Dunayevsky
1966 *En-Gedi, The First and Second Seasons of Excavations, 1961-1962*. ʿAtiqot 5 (Jerusalem: Department of Antiquities and Culture in the Ministry of Education and Culture/Department of Archaeology, Hebrew University/Israel Exploration Society).

Mazar, E.
1989 "Royal Gateway to Ancient Jerusalem Uncovered," *BAR* 15:38-51.

McCarter, P. K.
1974 "ʿYaw, son of 'Omri': A Philological Note on Israelite Chronology," *BASOR* 216:5-7.

McLeod, W. E.
1960 "ΤΡΙΓΛΩΧΙΣ," *AJA* 64:370-71.

Meyers, E. M., ed.
1997 *The Oxford Encyclopedia of Archaeology in the Near East*, Vols. 1-5. E. M. Meyers, ed. (New York/Oxford: Oxford University Press).

Michel, E.
1949 "Die Assur-Texte Salmanassars III. (858-824) 3. Fortsetzung," *WdO* 1:255-71.
1952 "Ein neuentdeckter Annalen-Text Salmanassars III," *WdO* 1:454-75.
1954 "Die Assur-Texte Salmanassars III. (858-824)," *WdO* 2:27-45.
1955 "Die Assur-Texte Salmanassars III. (858-824) (Salmanassar-Obelisk bis Zeile 126)," *WdO* 2:137-57.
1956 "Die Assur-Texte Salmanassars III. (858-824) Salmanassar-Obelisk, Zeile 126b-Zeile 190 (Ende)," *WdO* 2:221-33.
1958-1959 "Die Assur-Texte Salmanassars III. (858-824) (9. Fortsetzung), 34, Text [Balawat-Inschrift]," *WdO* 2:408-15.

1967-1968   "Die Assur-Texte Salmanassars III. (858-824) 11. Forts," *WdO* 4:29-37.

Millard, A.
1973   "Adad-nirari III, Aram, and Arpad," *PEQ* 105:161-64.
1994   *The Eponyms of the Assyrian Empire, 910-612 BC*. State Archives of Assyria, Volume 2 (Finland: The Neo-Assyrian Text Corpus Project at the University of Helsinki).

Millard, A. R. and H. Tadmor
1973   "Adad-nirari III in Syria: Another Stele Fragment and the Dates of His Campaign," *Iraq* 35:57-64.

Mitchell, T. C.
1982a   "Israel and Judah from Jehu until the Period of Assyrian Domination (841-*c.*750 B.C.)," pp. 488-510 in *The Cambridge Ancient History*, Vol. III/1, 2d ed. J. Boardman et al., eds. (Cambridge, Eng.: Cambridge University Press).
1982b   "Israel and Judah until the Revolt of Jehu," pp. 442-87 in *The Cambridge Ancient History*, Vol. III/1, 2d ed. J. Boardman et al., eds. (Cambridge, Eng.: Cambridge University Press).

Na'aman, N.
1974   "Sennacherib's 'Letter to God' on his Campaign to Judah," *BASOR* 214:25-38.
1976   "Two Notes on the Monolith Inscription of Shalmaneser III from Kurkh," *TA* 3:89-106.
1977-1978   "Looking for KTK," *WdO* 9:220-39.
1979   "The Brook of Egypt and Assyrian Policy on the Border of Egypt," *TA* 6:68-90.
1980   "The Shihor of Egypt and Shur that is before Egypt," *TA* 7:95-109.
1986   "Historical and Chronological Notes on the Kingdoms of Israel and Judah in the Eighth Century B.C.," *VT* 36:71-92.
1990   "The Historical Background to the Conquest of Samaria (720 BC)," *Biblica* 71:206-25.
1994   "The Historical Portion of Sargon II's Nimrud Inscription," *State Archives of Assyria Bulletin* 8:17-20.
1997   "Transcribing the Theophoric Element in North Israelite Names," *NABU* 1 (Mars):19-20.
1998   "Jehu Son of Omri: Legitimizing a Loyal Vassal by his Overlord," *IEJ* 48:236-38.

Na'aman, N. and R. Zadok
1988   "Sargon II's Deportations to Israel and Philistia," *JCS* 40:36-46.

Negev, A.
1972   *Archaeological Encyclopedia of the Holy Land* (Jerusalem: The

Jerusalem Publishing House).

Noth, M.
1961 "Der historische Hintergrund der Inschriften von Sefîre," *ZDPV* 77:118-72.

Oates, D.
1959 "Fort Shalmaneser—An Interim Report," *Iraq* 21:98-129.

Oates, J.
1959 "Late Assyrian Pottery from Fort Shalmaneser," *Iraq* 21:130-46, Pls. XXXIV-XXXIX.

Oded, B.
1964 "Two Assyrian References to the Town of Qadesh on the Orontes," *IEJ* 14:272-73.
1970 "Observations on Methods of Assyrian Rule in Transjordan after the Palestinian Campaign of Tiglath-pileser III," *JNES* 29:177-86.
1972 "The Historical Background of the Syro-Ephraimite War Reconsidered," *CBQ* 34:153-65.
1974 "The Phoenician Cities and the Assyrian Empire in the Time of Tiglath-pileser III," *ZDPV* 90:38-49.
1979 *Mass Deportations and Deportees in the Neo-Assyrian Empire* (Wiesbaden: Reichert).

Olmstead, A. T.
1908 *Western Asia in the Days of Sargon of Assyria, 722-705 B.C.* Cornell Studies in History and Political Science, Vol. 2 (New York: Henry Holt).
1915 "The Assyrian Chronicle," *JAOS* 34:344-68.
1923 *History of Assyria* (New York: Charles Scribner's Sons).
1931 *History of Palestine and Syria to the Macedonian Conquest* (New York: Charles Scribner's Sons).

von Oppenheim, M. F. and B. Hrouda
1962 *Tell Halaf IV: Die Kleinfunde aus historischer Zeit* (Berlin: De Gruyter).

Orni, E. and E. Efrat
1976 *Geography of Israel*. 3d rev. ed. (Jerusalem: Israel Universities Press).

Page, S.
1968 "A Stele of Adad-nirari III and Nergal-Ereš from Tell al Rimah," *Iraq* 30:139-53.

Petrie, W. M. F.
1928 *Gerar* (London: British School of Archaeology in Egypt/Quaritch).

Phythian-Adams, W. J.
1923 "Report on Soundings at Tell Jemmeh," *PEQ* 55:140-46.

Pitard, W. T.
1987 *Ancient Damascus: A Historical Study of the Syrian City-State From Earliest Times until its Fall to the Assyrians in 732 B.C.E.* (Winona Lake, IN: Eisenbrauns).

du Plat-Taylor, J.
1959 "The Cypriot and Syrian Pottery from Al-Mina, Syria," *Iraq* 21:62-92.

du Plat-Taylor, J., M. V. Seton Williams, and J. Waechter
1950 "The Excavations at Sakce Gözü," *Iraq* 12:53-138, Figs. 1-38, Pl. XXV.

Poebel, A.
1943 "The Assyrian King List from Khorsabad—concluded," *JNES* 2:56-90.

Polley, M. E.
1989 *Amos and the Davidic Empire: A Socio-Historical Approach* (Oxford: Oxford University Press).

Postgate, J. N.
1969 *Neo-Assyrian Royal Grants and Decrees* (Rome: Pontifical Biblical Institute).
1973a "Assyrian Texts and Fragments," *Iraq* 35:13-36.
1973b "The Inscription of Tiglath-pileser III at Mila Mergi," *Sumer* 29:47-59, Figs. 1-7.

Pratico, G. D.
1985 "Nelson's Glueck's 1938-1940 Excavations at Tell el-Kheleifeh: A Reappraisal," *BASOR* 259:1-32.
1993 *Nelson's Glueck's 1938-1940 Excavations at Tell el-Kheleifeh: A Reappraisal.* American Schools of Oriental Research Archaeological Reports No. 3 (Atlanta, GA: Scholars Press).

Pritchard, J. B.
1985 *Tell es-Saʿidiyeh: Excavations on the Tell, 1964-1966.* University Museum Monograph 60 (Philadelphia: University Museum/University of Pennsylvania).
1964 *Winery, Defenses, and Soundings at Gibeon* (Philadelphia: The University Museum, University of Pennsylvania).
1969 *Ancient Near Eastern Texts Relating to the Old Testament* (Princeton, NJ: Princeton University Press).
1975 *Sarepta: A Preliminary Report on the Iron Age* (Philadelphia: The University Museum, The University of Pennsylvania).

Raban, A. and I. Galanti
1987 "Notes and News: Tell Abu Hawam, 1985," *IEJ* 37:179-81.

Rainey, A. F.
1962 "Administration in Ugarit and the Samaria Ostraca," *IEJ* 12:62-63.
1967 "The Samaria Ostraca in the Light of Fresh Evidence," *PEQ* 99:32-41.
1970 "Semantic Parallels to the Samaria Ostraca," *PEQ* 102:45-51.
1979 "The *Sitz im Leben* of the Samaria Ostraca," *TA* 6:91-94.

Rast, W. E.
1978 *Taanach I, Studies in the Iron Age Pottery* (Cambridge, MA: American Schools of Oriental Research).

Rawlinson, Sir Henry
1870 *Cuneiform Inscriptions of Western Asia* (London: British Museum, Department of Egyptian and Assyrian Antiquities).

Rawson, P. S.
1954 "Palace Wares from Nimrud—Technical Observations on Selected Examples," *Iraq* 16:168-72.

Reade, J. E.
1968 "The Palace of Tiglath-pileser III," *Iraq* 30:69-73.
1972 "The Neo-Assyrian Court and Army: Evidence from the Sculptures," *Iraq* 34:87-112, Pls. XXXIII-XL.
1976 "Sargon's Campaigns of 720, 716, and 715 B.C.: Evidence from the Sculptures," *JNES* 35:95-104.
1999 *Assyrian Sculpture* (Cambridge, MA: Harvard University Press).

Reisner, G. A.
undated *Israelite Ostraca from Samaria* (undated and unpublished, but printed by E. O. Cockayne, Boston).

Reisner, G. A., C. S. Fisher, and D. G. Lyon
1924a *Harvard Excavations at Samaria, 1908-1910*, Volume I. Text. Harvard Semitic Series (Cambridge, MA: Harvard University Press).
1924b *Harvard Excavations at Samaria, 1908-1910*, Volume II. Plans and Plates. Harvard Semitic Series (Cambridge, MA: Harvard University Press).

Reuther, O.
1926 "Die Innenstadt von Babylon (Merkes)," *Wissenschaftliche Veröffentlichung der deutschen Orient-Gessellschaft* 47 (Leipzig: J. C. Hinrichs'sche Buchhandlung).

Reviv, H.
1969 "The Canaanite and Israelite Periods," pp. 35-108 in *A History of the Holy Land*, M. Avi-Yonah, ed. (Jerusalem: Steimatzky).

Riis, P. J.
1970 *Sūkās I: The North-East Sanctuary and the First Settling of Greeks in Syria and Palestine*. Publications of the Carlsberg Expedition to

Phoenicia 1 (København: Kommissionær, Munksgaard).

Rosenau, H.
1937 "Review of *Churches at Bosra and Samaria-Sebaste*, by J. W. Crowfoot," *PEQ*:212-13.

Rost, P.
1893 *Keilschrifttexte Tiglath-pilesers III, I: Einleitung, Transscription und Ubersetzung, Worterverzeichnis mit Commentar*; *II: Autographierte Texte* (Leipzig: Verlag von Eduard Pfeiffer).

Rowe, A.
1936 *A Catalogue of Egyptian Scarabs, Scaraboids, Seals and Amulets in the Palestine Archaeological Museum* (Cairo: Imprimerie de L'Institut Français D'Archéologie Orientale).

Rowton, M.
1976 "Dimorphic Structure and Topology," *Oriens Antiquus* 15:17-31.

Russell, H. F.
1984 "Shalmaneser's Campaign to Urarṭu in 856 B.C. and the Historical Geography of Eastern Anatolia according to the Assyrian Sources," *Anatolian Studies* 34:171-201.

Safar, F.
1951 "A Further Text of Shalmaneser III from Assur," *Sumer* 7:3-21.

Saggs, H. W. F.
1955 "The Nimrud Letters, 1952 – Part II," *Iraq* 17:126-54.
1959 "The Nimrud Letters, 1952 – Part V," *Iraq* 21:158-79.
1963 "Assyrian Warfare in the Sargonid Period," *Iraq* 25:145-54.
1975 "Historical Texts and Fragments of Sargon II of Assyria: I. The 'Aššur Charter'," *Iraq* 37:11-20.
1984 *The Might That Was Assyria* (London: Sidgwich and Jackson).

Saidah, R.
1966 "Fouilles de Khaldé, Rapport préliminaire sur la première et la deuxième campagnes (1961-1962)," *BMB* 19:51-90.

Saller, S. J.
1966 "Iron Age Tombs at Nebo, Jordan," *Liber Annuus* 16:165-298.

Sarna, N. M.
1979 "The Biblical Sources for the History of the Monarchy," pp. 3-19 in *The World History of the Jewish People*, Vol. 4/1, A. Malamat, ed. (Jerusalem: Massada).

Schloen, J. D.
1993 "Caravans, Kenites, and *Casus belli*: Enmity and Alliance in the Song of Deborah," *CBQ* 55:18-38.
2001 *The House of the Father as Fact and Symbol: Patrimonialism in*

Schneider, T.
- 1995 "Did King Jehu Kill his Own Family?" *BAR* 21:26-33.
- 1996 "Rethinking Jehu," *Biblica* 77:100-107.

Schrader, E.
- 1872 *Die Keilinschriften und das Alte Testament* (Giessen: J. Ricker).
- 1878 *Keilinschriften und Geschichtsforschung* (Giessen: J. Ricker).

Sellin, E.
- 1904 *Tell Ta'annek*. Denkschriften der Kaiserlichen Akademie der Wissenschaften in Wien, Philosophisch-historische Klasse 50 (Wien: Carl Gerold's Sohn).

Shea, W. H.
- 1977 "The Date and Significance of the Samaria Ostraca," *IEJ* 27:16-27.
- 1978 "Menahem and Tiglath-pileser III," *JNES* 37:43-49.

Shiloh, Y.
- 1978 "Elements in the Development of Town Planning in the Israelite City," *IEJ* 28:46-49.
- 1980 "Solomon's Gate at Megiddo as Recorded by Its Excavator, R. Lamon, Chicago," *Levant* 12:69-76.

Shiloh, Y., and A. Horowitz
- 1975 "Ashlar Quarries of the Iron Age in the Hill Country of Israel," *BASOR* 217:37-48.

Sinclair, L. A.
- 1960 "An Archaeological Study of Gibeah (Tell el-Fûl)," *AASOR* 34-35:5-52.

Smith, G.
- 1875 *Assyrian Discoveries* (New York: Scribner, Armstrong).

Smith, R. H.
- 1964 "The Household Lamps of Palestine in Old Testament Times," *BA* 27:1-31.

Smith, S.
- 1925 "The Supremacy of Assyria," pp. 32-60 in *The Cambridge Ancient History*, Vol. III, J. B. Bury et al., eds. (Cambridge, Eng.: Cambridge University Press).

Spieckermann, H.
- 1982 *Juda unter Assur in der Sargonidenzeit*. FRLANT 129 (Göttingen: Vandenhoeck and Ruprecht).

Stager, L. E.
- 1990 "Shemer's Estate," *BASOR* 277/278:93-107.

Staples, W. E.
1936 "A Note on an Inscribed Potsherd," *PEQ*:155.

Stern, E.
1982 *Material Culture of the Land of the Bible in the Persian Period, 538-332 B.C.* (Warminster: Aris & Phillips).

Stern, E., ed.
1993 *The New Encyclopedia of Archaeological Excavations in the Holy Land,* Vols. 1-4 (Jerusalem: The Israel Exploration Society/Carta).

Stewart, D.
2000 "Scythian Gold," *Smithsonian* 30/12:88-96.

Sukenik, E. L.
1933a "Inscribed Hebrew and Aramaic Potsherds from Samaria," *PEFQ* July:152-56, Pls. I-IV.
1933b "Inscribed Potsherds with Biblical Names from Samaria," *PEFQ* October:200-04, Pls. IX-X.
1936a "Potsherds from Samaria, Inscribed with the Divine Name," *PEQ*:34-37, Pls. I-II.
1936b "Note on a Fragment of an Israelite Stele found at Samaria," *PEQ*:156, Pl. III.

Sweeney, M. A.
1994 "Sargon's Threat against Jerusalem in Isaiah 10,27-32," *Biblica* 75:457-70.

Tadmor, H.
1958 "The Campaigns of Sargon II of Assur: A Chronological-Historical Study," *JCS* 12:(Part 1), 22-40; (Part 2), 77-100.
1961a *Encyclopedia Miqra'it* 4 (Jerusalem: Bialik Institute), 261-62.
1961b "Azriyau of Yaudi," in *Scripta Hierosolymitana* 8:232-71.
1962 "The Southern Border of Aram," *IEJ* 12:114-22.
1966 "Philistia Under Assyrian Rule," *BA* 29:86-102.
1968 "Introductory Remarks to a New Edition of the Annals of Tiglath-pileser III," pp. 168-87 in *Proceedings of the Israel Academy of Sciences and Humanities*, Vol. 2 (Jerusalem: The Israel Academy of Sciences and Humanities).
1969 "A Note on the Saba'a Stele of Adad-nirari III," *IEJ* 19:47-48.
1973 "The Historical Inscriptions of Adad-nirari III," *Iraq* 35:141-150.
1977 "Observations on Assyrian Historiography," pp. 209-213 in *Essays on the Ancient Near East in Memory of Jacob Joel Finkelstein* (Hamden, CT: Archon Books for the Connecticut Academy of Arts & Sciences, Vol. XIX).
1981 "History and Ideology in the Assyrian Royal Inscriptions," pp. 13-33 in *Assyrian Royal Inscriptions: New Horizons in Literary, Ideological,*

and Historical Analysis. F. M. Fales, ed. Orientis Antiqui Collectio 17 (Rome: Instituto per l'Oriente, Centro per le Antichità e la Storia dell'Arte del Vicino Oriente).

1983   "Some Aspects of the History of Samaria during the Biblical Period," pp. 1-11 in *The Jerusalem Cathedra 3*, L. I. Levine, Y. Izḥak, eds. (Jerusalem: Ben-Zvi Institute).

1994   *The Inscriptions of Tiglath-pileser III King of Assyria, Critical Editions, with Introductions, Translations and Commentary* (Jerusalem: The Israel Academy of Sciences and Humanities).

Tappy, R. E.
1990   "Studies in the History and Archaeology of Israelite Samaria." Ph.D. diss., Harvard University.
1992   *The Archaeology of Israelite Samaria, Volume I: Early Iron Age through the Ninth Century BCE.* Harvard Semitic Studies 44 (Atlanta, GA: Scholars Press).
2000   "Samaria," pp. 1155-59 in *Eerdman's Dictionary of the Bible.* D. N. Freedman, A. C. Myers, and A. B. Beck, eds. (Grand Rapids, MI: Eerdmans).

Thackery, H. St. J., trans.
1997   *Josephus, The Jewish War*, Books I-II. The Loeb Classical Library (Cambridge, MA: Harvard University Press).

Thiele, E. R.
1944   "The Chronology of the Kings of Judah and Israel," *JNES* 3:137-86.
1965   *The Mysterious Numbers of the Hebrew Kings: Reconstruction of the Chronology of the Kingdoms of Israel and Judah* (Grand Rapids: Eerdmans [also 1951, University of Chicago Press]).
1976   "An Additional Chronological Note on 'Yaw, Son of 'Omri'," *BASOR* 222:19-23.

Thureau-Dangin, F., A. G. Barrois, G. Dossin, and M. Dunand
1931   *Arslan-Tash*, 2 vols. Bibliothèque Archéologique et Historique, Vol. 16 (Paris: Paul Geuthner).

Thureau-Dangin, F. and M. Dunand
1936   *Til Barsip* (Paris: Paul Geuthner).

Toombs, L. E. and G. E. Wright
1963   "The Fourth Campaign at Balâṭah (Shechem)," *BASOR* 169:1-60.

Tubb, J. N.
1988   "Tell es-Saʿidiyeh: Preliminary Report on the First Three Seasons of Renewed Excavations," *Levant* 20:23-88.
1990   "Preliminary Report on the Fourth Season of Excavations at Tell es-Saʿidiyeh in the Jordan Valley," *Levant* 22:21-42.

Tufnell, O.
   1953a   *Lachish III, The Iron Age*, Text and Plates (London: Oxford University Press).
   1953b   "Notes and Comparisons," pp. 66-75 in *Four Tomb Groups from Jordan*, by G. L. Harding. Palestine Exploration Fund Annual = *APEF* 6 (London: Palestine Exploration Fund).
   1959   "Hazor, Samaria, and Lachish," *PEQ* 91:90-105.

Tushingham, A. D.
   1972   "The Excavations at Dibon (Dhībân) in Moab, The Third Campaign 1952-53," *AASOR* 40 (Cambridge, MA: American Schools of Oriental Research).
   1992   "New Evidence Bearing on the Two-Winged *LMLK* Stamp," *BASOR* 287:61-65.

Unger, E.
   1916   *Reliefstele Adadniraris III aus Saba'a und Semiramis*. Publicationen der Kaiserlich osmanischen Museen 2 (Constantinople: A. Ihsan).

Ungnad, A.
   1906   "Jaua, mār Ḫumrî," *Orientalische Literaturzeitung* 9:224-25.
   1938   "Eponymen," pp. 412-57 in *Reallexikon der Assyriologie* 2, E. Ebeling and B. Meissner, eds. (Berlin and Leipzig: Walter de Gruyter).

Ussishkin, D.
   1976   "Royal Judean Storage Jars and Private Seal Impressions," *BASOR* 223:1-13.
   1977   "The Destruction of Lachish by Sennacherib and the Dating of the Royal Judean Storage Jars," *TA* 4:28-60.
   1978   "Excavations at Tel Lachish—1973-1977, Preliminary Report," *TA* 5:1-97, Pls. 1-33.
   1980   "Was the 'Solomonic' City Gate at Megiddo Built by King Solomon?" *BASOR* 239:1-18.
   1983   "Excavations at Tel Lachish 1978-1983: Second Preliminary Report," *TA* 10:97-175, Pls. 1-44.
   1997a   "Megiddo," pp. 460-69 in *The Oxford Encyclopedia of Archaeology in the Near East*, Vol. 3. E. M. Meyers, ed. (Oxford/New York: Oxford University Press).
   1997b   "Tel Jezreel," pp. 246-47 in *The Oxford Encyclopedia of Archaeology in the Near East*, Vol. 3. E. M. Meyers, ed. (Oxford/New York: Oxford University Press).

Ussishkin, D. and J. Woodhead
   1992   "Excavations at Tel Jezreel 1990-1991: Preliminary Report," *TA* 19:3-56.

1994	"Excavations at Tel Jezreel 1992-1993: Second Preliminary Report," *Levant* 26:1-48.

Van Beek, G. W.
1955	"The Date of Tell Abu Hawam, Stratum III," *BASOR* 138:34-38.
1958	"Frankincense and Myrrh in Ancient South Arabia," *JAOS* 78:141-52.
1960	"Frankincense and Myrrh," *BA* 23:70-95.
1970	"Tel Gamma," *IEJ* 20:230.
1972a	"Tell Ğemmeh," *RB* 79:596-99.
1972b	"Tel Gamma," *IEJ* 22:245-46.
1973	"Tell Ğemmeh," *RB* 80:572-76.
1974	"Tel Gamma," *IEJ* 24:138-39; 274-75.
1975	"Tell Jemmeh," *RB* 82:95-97; 573-76.
1977	"Tel Gamma, 1975-1976," *IEJ* 27:171-76.
1983	"Digging Up Tell Jemmeh," *Archaeology* 36/1:12-19.
1984	"Archaeological Excavations at Tell Jemmeh," *National Geographic Research Reports* 16:675-96.
1989	"Total Retrieval and Maximum Reconstruction of Artifacts: An Experiment in Archaeological Methodology," *Eretz-Israel* 20 (Yadin Volume):12*-29*.
1993	"Tell Jemmeh," pp. 667-74 in *The New Encyclopedia of Archaeological Excavations in the Holy Land*, Vol. 2. E. Stern, ed. (Jerusalem: Israel Exploration Society).

Van Zyl, A. H.
1960	*The Moabites* (Leiden: E. J. Brill).

de Vaux, R.
1951	"La troisième campagne de fouilles à Tell el-Farʿah, près Naplouse," *RB* 58:393-430; 566-90.
1952	"La quatrième campagne de fouilles à Tell el-Farʿah, près Naplouse," *RB* 59:551-83.
1955	"Les fouilles de Tell el-Farʿah, près Naplouse, cinquième campagne," *RB* 62:541-89.
1957	"Les fouilles de Tell el-Farʿah, près Naplouse, sixième campagne," *RB* 64:552-80.
1961	*Ancient Israel: Its Life and Institutions* (New York: McGraw-Hill).

de Vaux, R. and A. M. Stève
1947	"La première campagne de fouilles à Tell el-Farʿah, près Naplouse," *RB* 54:394-433; 573-89.

Vera Chamaza, G. W.
1992	"Sargon II's Ascent to the Throne: The Political Situation," *State Archives of Assyria Bulletin* 6:21-33.

Vilders, M. M. E.
1993 "Some Remarks on the Production of Cooking Pots in the Jordan Valley," *PEQ* 125:149-56.

Vogt, E.
1958 "Samaria A. 722 et 720 AB Assyriis Capta," *Biblica* 39:535-41.

Waldbaum, J.
1983 *Metalwork from Sardis: The Finds through 1974* (Cambridge, MA: Harvard University Press).

Walker, A.
1982 "Principles of Excavation," pp. 2-22 in *A Manual of Field Excavation: Handbook for Field Archaeologists*, W. G. Dever and H. D. Lance, eds. (New York: Hebrew Union College and the Jewish Institute of Religion).

Wampler, J. C.
1941 "Three Cistern Groups from Tell en-Naṣbeh," *BASOR* 82:25-43.
1947 *Tell en-Naṣbeh II: The Pottery* (Berkeley: American Schools of Oriental Research).

Weippert, M.
1973 "Menahem von Israel und seine Zeitgenossen in einer Steleninschrift des assyrischen Königs Tiglathpileser III. aus dem Iran," *ZDPV* 89:26-53.
1978 "Jau(a) mār Humri–Joram oder Jehu von Israel?" *VT* 28:113-18.
1992 "Die Feldzüge Adadniraris III. nach Syrien. Voraussetzungen, Verlauf, Folgen," *ZDPV* 108:42-67.

Westenholz, J. G., ed.
1998 *Capital Cities: Urban Planning and Spiritual Dimensions*. Proceedings of the Symposium Held on May 27-29, 1996, Jerusalem, Israel. Bible Lands Museum Jerusalem Publications 2 (Jerusalem: Bible Lands Museum).

Westermann, C.
1981 *Praise and Lament in the Psalms* (Atlanta, GA: John Knox).

Whitley, C. F.
1952 "The Deuteronomic Presentation of the House of Omri," *VT* 2:149-50.

Wightman, G. J.
1985 "Megiddo VIA-III: Associated Structures and Chronology," *Levant* 17:117-29.
1990 "The Myth of Solomon," *BASOR* 277/278:5-22.

Wilson, J. V. Kinnier
1962 "The Kurbaʾil Statue of Shalmaneser III," *Iraq* 24:90-115.

Winnett, F. V. and W. L. Reed
    1964   *The Excavations at Dibon (Dhībân) in Moab. AASOR* 36-37 for 1957-1958 (New Haven: ASOR).

Winter, I. J.
    1976   "Phoenician and North Syrian Ivory Carving in Historical Context: Questions of Style and Distribution," *Iraq* 38:1-22.

Wiseman, D. J.
    1951   "Two Historical Inscriptions from Nimrud," *Iraq* 13:21-26.
    1956   "A Fragmentary Inscription of Tiglath-pileser III from Nimrud," *Iraq* 18:117-29, Pls. XXI-XXIII.
    1964   "Fragments of Historical Texts from Nimrud," *Iraq* 26:118-24.

Wolff, H. W.
    1977   *Joel and Amos* (Hermeneia; Philadelphia: Fortress).

Wright, G. E.
    1939   "Iron: The Date of Its Introduction into Common Use in Palestine," *AJA* 43:458-63.
    1950a   "Review of *Megiddo II: Seasons 1935-1939*," *JAOS* 70:56-60.
    1950b   "The Discoveries at Megiddo," *BA* 13:28-46.
    1959a   "Israelite Samaria and Iron Age Chronology," *BASOR* 155:13-29.
    1959b   "Samaria," *BA* 22:67-78.
    1961   "The Archaeology of Palestine," pp. 73-112 in *The Bible and the Ancient Near East: Essays in Honor of William Foxwell Albright*, G. E. Wright, ed. (Garden City, NY: Doubleday).
    1962   "Archaeological Fills and Strata," *BA* 25:34-40.

Yadin, Y.
    1959   "Recipients or Owners: A Note on the Samaria Ostraca," *IEJ* 9:184-87.
    1961   "Ancient Judean Weights and the Date of the Samaria Ostraca," *Scripta Hierosolymitana* 8:9-25.
    1962   "A Further Note on the Samaria Ostraca," *IEJ* 12:64-66.
    1966   "Megiddo," *IEJ* 16:278-80.
    1967   "Megiddo," *IEJ* 17:119-21.
    1970   "Megiddo of the Kings of Israel," *BA* 33:66-96.
    1980   "A Rejoinder," *BASOR* 239:19-23.

Yadin, Y. et al.
    1958   *Hazor I: An Account of the First Season of Excavations, 1955* (Jerusalem: Magnes–The Hebrew University).
    1960   *Hazor II: An Account of the Second Season of Excavations, 1956* (Jerusalem: Magnes–The Hebrew University).
    1961   *Hazor III-IV: An Account of the Third and Fourth Seasons of Excavations, 1957-1958* (Jerusalem: Magnes–The Hebrew University).

1972	"Megiddo," *IEJ* 22:161-164.

Yassine, K.
| 1984 | *Tell el Mazar I: Cemetary A* (Amman: University of Jordan). |

Yeivin, S.
| 1979 | "The Divided Kingdom: Rehoboam–Ahaz/Jerobaom–Pekah," pp. 126-79 in *The World History of the Jewish People*, Vol. 4/1. A. Malamat, ed. (Jerusalem: Massada). |

Younger, Jr., K. L.
| 1996 | "Sargon's Campaign against Jerusalem—A Further Note," *Biblica* 77:108-10. |
| 1999 | "The Fall of Samaria in Light of Recent Research," *CBQ* 61:461-82. |

Zadok, R.
| 1976 | "Geographical and Onomastic Notes," *JANES* 8:113-24. |

Zarzeki-Peleg, A.
| 1997 | "Hazor, Jokneam and Megiddo in the Tenth Century B.C.E.," *TA* 24:258-88. |

Zayadine, F.
| 1967 | "Samaria-Sebaste. Clearance and Excavations (October 1965-June 1967)," *ADAJ* 12:77-80. |
| 1968 | "Une Tombe du Fer II a Samarie-Sébaste," *RB* 75:562-85. |

Zettler, R. L.
| 1997 | "Nippur," pp. 148-52 in *The Oxford Encyclopedia of Archaeology in the Near East*, Vol. 4. E. M. Meyers, ed. (Oxford/New York: Oxford University Press). |

Zimhoni, O.
1985	"The Iron Age Pottery of Tel ʿEton and Its Relation to the Lachish, Tell Beit Mirsim and Arad Assemblages," *TA* 12:63-90.
1990	"Two Ceramic Assemblages from Lachish Levels III and II," *TA* 17:3-52.
1992	"The Iron Age Pottery from Tel Jezreel—An Interim Report," *TA* 19:57-70.
1997	*Studies in the Iron Age Pottery of Israel: Typological, Archaeological and Chronological Aspects* (Tel Aviv: Tel Aviv University, Institute of Archaeology).

INDEX

BIBLICAL REFERENCES

Genesis
  10:10, 537
  48:14, 5

Joshua
  16-17, 581
  16:1-4, 4
  16:5-10, 5, 9
  17:7-10, 5
  17:14-18, 7
  19:49-50, 581

Judges
  4-5, 231
  5, 542
  10:1, 4

2 Samuel
  8:3-12, 233
  23:8, 541

1 Kings
  4:7-8, 9
  4:7-19, 581
  5:1, 526
  8:65, 526
  9:26-10:22, 542
  13:1-2, 583
  13:32, 5
  13:34, 576
  14:30, 4
  15:27, 4
  15:27-29, 575
  16:8, 4
  16:9-20, 576
  16:21-22, 576
  16:21-24, 581
  16:24, 1, 3-4, 9, 137
  17-19, 582
  17:1, 582
  17:7, 582
  18:2, 582
  20, 508, 576
  20-2 Kgs 8, 523
  20:13-15, 570
  20:15, 169-70
  20:23-25, 577
  20:34, 550

22:4, 509
22:39, 491, 581

2 Kings
  3:7, 509
  7:2, 541
  7:6, 515
  7:17, 541
  9, 514
  9-10, 582
  9:14-26, 514
  9:31, 576
  10:7-8, 514
  10:32-33, 515
  12:18-19, 515, 521
  13:3-7, 243
  13:5, 523, 529
  13:6, 576
  13:7, 509, 515
  13:14-19, 523
  13:20-22, 515
  13:22, 523
  13:24-25, 523
  14:7, 555
  14:8-14, 524, 543
  14:22, 555
  14:25, 526, 543, 555
  14:28, 536
  15, 536-37
  15:8, 529-30
  15:8-31, 177
  15:10, 438, 530
  15:14, 530
  15:17, 530
  15:19, 529-30, 540
  15:19-20, 539
  15:20, 539
  15:25, 438, 540-41, 543, 551
  15:27, 543
  15:29, 236, 243, 530, 537, 548
  15:29-30, 552
  15:30, 438, 553
  15:36-38, 543
  16:1, 543
  16:5-6, 556
  16:6, 554

16:8, 556
16:9, 553
17:1-6, 560
17:3-6, 559-61
17:6, 516, 555, 570, 573
17:17, 96
17:23-24, 222
17:24, 555, 570, 581-82
17:28, 582
17:29, 581
17:30-31, 570
18, 561
18:1, 9-10, 543
18:9-11, 559-61
18:11, 570, 573
18:22, 548
18:25-26, 548
19:12, 516
23:4, 583
23:15-20, 583
23:19-20, 438
23:29-30, 583

1 Chronicles
  5:1-2, 555
  5:6, 555
  5:17-18, 555
  5:26, 555

2 Chronicles
  8:17-9:21, 542
  13:19, 4
  20:21, 547
  25:6-10, 524
  25:11-12, 555
  25:13, 524
  25:14-16, 551
  25:20-23, 524
  26:2, 555
  26:6-8, 547
  26:8, 555
  27:5, 547, 556
  28:20-21, 553
  34:3-7, 438
  35:20-24, 583

Ezra
  4, 583
  4:14, 583

Nehemiah
  2, 4, 6, 583
  5:1-5, 583

Psalms
  45:9, 581
  78:56-67, 7
  83, 557

Isaiah
  5-11, 528
  7-8, 543, 552
  7-11, 539
  7:4, 552
  7:6, 551
  7:9, 5, 581
  7:16-17, 552
  8:4-8a, 552
  8:5-8, 553
  8:21-9:2, 528
  9:1, 582
  9:8-9, 5
  10:9, 537
  10:27-32, 568
  10:28-32, 548
  10:33-11:1, 528
  39:1, 567

Jeremiah
  6:22-24, 439
  7:12-15, 7
  26:4-5, 7
  41:1, 583
  41:4-8, 583
  50:41-43, 439

Ezekiel
  16:46, 581
  16:53, 581
  16:55, 581
  16:61, 581
  23:4-5, 581

Hosea
  1:1, 529
  1:4, 576
  10:7, 529
  10:14, 512, 529-30

Amos
  1-2, 512
  1:1, 528
  1:2-2:16, 509
  1:3-2:5, 556
  1:5, 532
  1:13, 556
  3:12, 5
  3:15, 581
  6:1, 5
  6:2, 537
  6:4, 581
  6:6, 5
  6:14, 526
  7:9, 576
  7:10, 576

Micah
  1:5, 5
  1:10-15, 548
  1:10-16, 568

Zechariah
  9:1, 538

Matthew
  19:1, 584

Luke
  17:11, 584

John
  4:4-9, 584

Acts
  1:8, 584
  8:1-25, 584
  8:9, 584
  9:31, 584
  15:3, 584

APOCRYPHA

1 Esdras
  2, 583

1 Maccabees
  4:15, 532
  9:52, 532
  13:43-48, 532

GENERAL INDEX

Abdastart I, 583
Abel-Beth-Maacah, 548
Adad-nirari II, 493
Adad-nirari III, 506, 511, 515-29, 531, 537, 539, 549
Adam, 7
Adams, W. Y., 441
Adoni-Nur, 92, 413, 419, 428, 439
'Afula, 78, 83, 233
Ahab, 36, 47, 52, 54, 57, 110-12, 115, 123, 129-31, 169-71, 202, 204, 225, 228-29, 234, 248, 362, 376, 477, 491-94, 499, 508-09, 511-13, 515, 523-25, 560, 577-78, 581
Aharoni, M., 85, 127, 160, 163, 218, 335, 337, 415
Aharoni, Y., 4, 9, 79, 81, 85, 127, 160, 163, 181, 218, 234-35, 247, 249, 270, 308, 320, 335, 337, 396, 415, 443, 511, 524, 542, 544-45, 548, 552-53
Ahaz (also *Jehoahaz*), 539-40, 543, 546, 551-53, 556
Ahuni, 508
'Ai, 83
Akhziv, 99, 329
Akkad, 558
Akko, 246
Alabaster Tablet, 399
Albenda, P., 512, 532
Albright, W. F., 98, 105, 126, 176, 181, 238, 240-41, 243-45, 287-89, 335-37, 393-95, 399, 424, 432, 520, 524, 537, 551
Aleppo, 522-23, 537-38
Alexander the Great, 583
Alexandre, Y., 88-89, 93, 213
Al-Mina (Syria), 74, 163, 246, 311, 317, 329
Amarna Letters, 399, 582
Amaziah (king), 555
Amaziah (prophet), 576, 578
Amiran, R., 79, 81, 84, 92, 96, 99, 106, 161, 181, 234-35, 247, 270, 286, 288, 291, 308, 313-14, 320, 325, 328, 330, 334-35, 400, 402, 406-07, 410, 412-14, 422, 424, 426, 428-29, 432
Amman, 92, 329, 413, 428-29
Ammon (-ite/s), 92, 329, 419, 428, 508-09, 515, 547, 551, 555-56
Amos, 508, 526, 578
amphoriskos (-i), 286
Anatolia, 152, 515
Andersen, F. I., 509

Andrae, W., 427
Andromachus, 583
Anspacher, A. S., 530, 534
Antiochus VII, 584
Antonia (fortress), 584
Aphek, 9, 582
Apqu, see *Tell Abu Marya*
Aqaba (region), 312
Arabah, 526
Arad, 160, 248, 335, 337, 415
Aram (Aramaeans), 236, 242-43, 509, 512-17, 523-26, 529, 533, 538-39, 543-44, 546, 548, 550, 553
Ararat Mts., 547
Arbela, 512
Argishti I, 528
Arnon River, 515
Aroer, 515
Arpad (see also *Tell Rifa'at*), 516-18, 521-22, 528-29, 532-35, 537-39, 545, 552, 562, 568, 574
Arrapkha, 528
arrowhead(s), 439-40
Arslan Tash, 489, 492-94, 532
Artzy, M., 249
Arvad, 516-17, 522, 551
Arzâ/Arṣa/Arzani (see also Yurza/T. Jemmeh), 399, 403
'Ashan, 291
Ashdod, 79, 80, 99-100, 163, 215, 217, 226, 291, 313, 406, 410, 435, 439
Asher, 4
Ashkelon, 549-51, 554
Ashurbanipal, 438, 572
Ashur-dan II, 506
Ashur-dan III, 537
Ashur-nasir-pal, 493
Ashur-nasir-pal II, 512, 530
Ashur-nirari V, 506, 527-29, 531, 534, 537
Aššur (Ashur), 399, 427, 508, 528, 530, 567
Aššur Charter, 510, 565-67, 569
Assyrian Courtyard Building(s), 244
Assyrian Table/Dinner Service, see *Palace Ware*
Astour, M. C., 509, 512
Asuhili, 399
Athaliah, 513
Athens, 458
'Atlīt, 306, 316, 325-27, 329, 416, 439
Attic Middle Geometric II, 175-76
Augusteum, see *Samaria*

Augustus, 584
Avi-aḥi, 349
Avigad, N., 291, 439, 524
Avi-Yonah, M., 9, 524, 545, 548
Azriyau, 533, 535-36

Baal-manzer, 511
Ba'alu/i, 518, 522, 549
Baasha, 4, 575-76
Babylon (-ia/n), 427, 439, 516, 526, 531, 533, 553, 555, 560-61, 567-69, 583
Babylonian Chronicle, 558-59, 562, 565, 567
Babylonian King List A, 530
Badè, W. F., 154
Bahçe Pass, 508
Balata, see *Shechem*
Balawat, 508
Balensi, J., 233, 239, 242, 249-51, 272, 347
Balikh River, 508, 532, 555
Ba'li-rā'si, 511, 522
Baltil, 530
Bar-Ga'yah, 528
Barkay, G., 170, 244
Barnett, R. D., 444-45, 492, 581
Barrois, A. G., 493
Barth, H., 243
Bartlett, J. R., 512, 515
Baruch, E., 127
battleship curve, 225
Bashan, 543
Beach, E. F., 444
Becking, B., 544, 558-62, 564-66, 568-74
Beersheba, 90, 97, 172, 218, 226, 242, 307, 332, 335, 396, 399, 402
Begrich, J., 546
Beilan Pass, 508
Beirut, 511
Bēl-Ḥarrān-bēlu-uṣur, 528
Bet-tarsi-iluma, 527
Bennett, C.-M., 314, 425, 428
Ben-Tor, A., 96, 229, 314, 321, 330, 429
Beqaʿ Valley, 523
Berlin Statue Inscription, 508
Besor Brook, 571
Bethany, 422
Beth-Arbel, 512
Beth Eden, 508
Beth-Shan, 74-75, 78, 81, 84, 86, 90, 92-94, 97-98, 102, 105, 125-26, 160, 163, 210, 226, 267, 276, 280, 284, 286, 289-90, 306, 315-16, 324, 326, 338-39, 341, 349, 394, 412, 418, 423, 511; *valley*, 4, 249, 313

Bethel, 93, 215, 226, 285, 394, 396, 410, 418-19, 422, 428, 578, 582-83
Beth-Shemesh, 72, 75, 78, 81, 83, 86-87, 92, 97, 126, 155, 158, 160, 210, 218, 226, 233, 238, 276, 279, 284, 309, 326, 330, 334-35, 337, 340-41, 396, 402-03, 410-11, 424, 431; *Cistern 25*, 326; *Tomb 14*, 337, 431
Beth-Zur, 422
Beyond the River (province), 583
Bichrome Ware, 99
Bieber, Jr., A. M., 164
Bienkowski, P., 314
Bikai, P., 100, 161-64, 270-72, 294, 317-18, 328-29
Biran, A., 115, 445, 514
Bir Hadad, 523
Bit Adini, 508, 516, 522, 527, 531-33, 538, 558
Bit Gusi, 534
bīt hilāni, 241
Bīt Ḥumrî(a) (see also *House of Omri*), 511, 539, 551, 564, 576, 582
Bit Shilani, 560
Black-Burnished Ware, 583
Black-Figured Ware, 583
Black-Glazed Ware, 64
Black Juglet(s), 304, 322, 324, 329-30, 333-37
Black Obelisk, 508, 511, 516, 564
Bliss, F. J., 428
Borger, R., 541, 543, 566
Borowski Stele, 567
Botta, P. E., 568
bottles, 246-47, 419, 427-30, 435
bowl(s), 67-76, 127, 153-58, 161, 204, 216, 248, 266-77, 295, 301-19, 343, 346, 350, 368, 379-80, 386-87, 390-414, 422-23, 430, 435, 483; *bar-handled bowls*, 74; *cyma*, 72, 74, 145, 157-58, 398, 401, 483; *folded-rim bowls*, 393-95, 398; *plates/platters*, 70, 75, 156, 398; *Ring-Based Bowls*, 401-02; *saucer bowls*, 75, 156, 264, 302, 412, 431
Bozrah, 314
Brandl, B., 291
Braudel, F., 7
brazier(s), 291-95, 343
Brettler, M. Z., 560
Briend, J., 313, 316, 396, 424, 429
Brinkman, J. A., 514, 558
British School of Archaeology, 248
Bronze Gates (also *Balawat*), 508
Brook of Egypt, 399, 403, 545, 547, 551
Bull Inscription, 564, 582
Bunimovitz, S., 337

INDEX

Buṣeirah, 314, 413, 425, 428
Byblos, 163, 538, 544
Calah, see *Nimrud*
Calneh, 537
Cameron, G. G., 507
Campbell-Thompson, R., 427
Cappadocia(-n), 508, 515, 523, 550
Carchemish, 529, 535, 538
Carthage, 316, 431
Cave 6024, see *Lachish*
Chaldea, 561
chalice(s), 398, 423
Chambon, A., 71-72, 85-86, 96, 103, 105, 267, 276, 286, 306, 310-11, 313, 315-16, 318, 320, 327, 333, 335, 394, 396, 398, 402-03, 407, 410, 412, 415, 418, 423, 425, 427, 432
Chapman, S. V., 99-100, 268, 270, 306, 325-26, 329
child sacrifice, 96
chocolate layer (Persian garden?), 356-57, 362
Cilicia, 516, 564
Cilician Gates, 538
Cimmerians, 439
Cistern 3, see *Samaria*
Cistern 7, see *Samaria*
Cistern 25, see *Beth-Shemesh*
Cistern 69, see *Taʿanach*
Cistern 74, see *Taʿanach*
Cistern 361, see *Tell el-Farʿah (N)*
Cistern 370, see *Tell en-Naṣbeh*
Cody, A., 520, 523
Cogan, M., 511, 536, 540, 551, 553, 571
Coldstream, J. N., 176
collared-rim store jar, see *jar(s)*
conical jar(s), see *jar(s)*
Contenau, G., 164
cooking pots, 67, 77-88, 113, 117, 123-24, 159-61, 172, 182, 206-12, 216-17, 220, 246, 248, 250-51, 265, 277-81, 295, 319-22, 343, 353, 414-16, 422, 483; *cooking jug(s)/jar(s)*, 84, 422; *Early Shallow Type*, 79, 81, 235, 251, 278, 320; *Late Shallow Type*, 82, 109, 113, 161, 278, 283, 320
Corinth, 439
Corridor *o*, see *Samaria*
Cross, Jr., F. M., 291, 443, 523-24, 555
Crowfoot, G. M., 11, 28, 68-69, 78, 102, 142, 159, 162, 176, 212, 261, 282-83, 285, 289, 292, 305, 309, 392, 401-02, 444-46, 464, 470, 484, 490-94
Crowfoot, J. W., 1, 170, 175, 299, 359, 417, 441, 444-46, 448, 454, 458, 464-65, 470, 479, 484- 85, 489-94
Culican, W., 328
Cultic Structure, see *Taʿanach*
Curtis, J. B., 551
cyma (rims), 283-85
Cylinder Inscription, 563-64, 571, 582
Cyrus, 583
Cuneiform Tablet Building, see *Taʿanach*
Cypriote Bichrome II, 96
Cypriote Red-on-Black I (III) Ware, 100
Cypro-Archaic Period I-II, 164
Cypro-Geometric II Ware, 96
Cypro-Phoenician, 16, 96, 316
Cyprus (Cypriot), 66, 164, 246, 268, 306, 316, 330, 336, 338, 431, 444

Dalley, S., 566, 571, 573
Damascus, 9, 444, 494, 508, 51-16, 518-24, 527, 529, 535, 538-39, 542-53, 561, 568, 577
Dan, see *Tel Dan*
David (-ic), 231, 233, 239-40, 509, 513, 578
Davies, G. I., 239, 241-43, 246, 349
decanters, 180, 226, 247, 287-91, 295, 297, 302, 315, 327-28, 337-41, 343-44, 350
Deir ʿAllā, 78, 233, 235
Demsky, A., 291
Der, 569
Dēri, 549
Deuteronomistic History/Historian(s), 491, 511, 578, 582
Dever, W. G., 233, 239, 528
Dhiban/Dibon, 284, 428
Dinner Service, see *Palace Ware*
Display Inscription, 582
Donner, H., 531, 536, 544-46, 550
Dor (or Province of Duʾru), 250, 523, 552, 572, 577, 582
Dorsey, D., 6
Dossin, G., 493
Dothan, 10
Dothan, M., 410
Dothan, T., 239
Drain 69, see *Samaria*
Drainpipe Structure, see *Taʿanach*
Driver, G. R., 570
Dunand, M., 493, 547
Duncan, J. G., 12
Durdukka, 573
Dur Sharrukin, 563, 569-70, 572, 574

E 207 (shrine?), see *Samaria*
earthquake(s), 235-36, 239, 528, 584

Eastern Terra Sigillata I, 157
eclipse, 528
Edelstein, G., 313
Edom, 314, 509, 515, 517, 519, 521, 523, 543, 547, 551, 555, 556
Efrat, E., 8
Egypt (-ian), 515, 524, 544-45, 549-51, 560, 567-71
Eitan, A., 245
Ekron, 349
Elah, 4, 575
Elam, 567-69
Elat, M., 509
el-ʿArish, 547
Elijah, 578, 582
Elisha, 523, 578
el-Mahruq, 7
ʿEn-Gedi, 107, 307, 337, 394, 396, 398-99, 415, 420, 422, 432, 439
ʿEn Gev, 97, 125, 284, 321
Ephʿal, I., 243-44, 542, 547, 550-52, 554, 558, 541
Eponym Chronicle, 516-23, 527, 531-32, 534, 536, 541, 549, 558
Eran, A., 12, 498
Esarhaddon, 399, 403, 531, 545, 558, 572, 582
Esse, D., 234
Ethbaal II (see also *Tubail*), 535
Euphrates River, 508, 516, 522, 527, 531-33, 537-38, 555
Eusebius, 439, 512

Falkner, M., 572
Fargo, V. M., 239
Fertile Crescent, 538
Fine Ware Plates, see *Tyre*
Finkelstein, I., 7, 227-29, 232-33, 240-42, 248-49
Fisher, C., 1, 498
Flandin, M. E., 568
flask(s), 287
folded-rim bowls, see *bowls*
Fort Shalmaneser, 92, 419, 425
Forsberg, S., 174, 178, 180-82, 221, 224-26, 227-29, 242, 244-45, 247, 254, 328, 340-41, 396, 399, 437-41
Foundation Trench 55a, see *Samaria*
Foundation Trench 120, see *Samaria*
Foundation Trench 125a, see *Samaria*
Foundation Trench 132, see *Samaria*
Foundation Trench 503a, see *Samaria*
Foundation Trench 508a, see *Samaria*
Foundation Trench 551, see *Samaria*

Foundation Trench 574, see *Samaria*
Fox, R., 578
Franklin, N., 569, 572, 574
Freedman, D. N., 410, 509
Fuchs, A., 569-71, 573

Gabinius, 584
Gad (-ites), 555-56
Gadd, J. C., 509, 555, 565-66
Galanti, I., 250
Galil, G., 559, 567
Galilee, 548, 550
Gath, 515, 519
Gaza, 509, 515, 544, 549-51, 554, 557, 567-69, 571
Gedaliah, 583
Gelb, I. J., 521, 531, 537
Gerar, 213, 313, 399-400, 404, 407, 425
Geva, S., 161-62, 164, 237, 349
Gezer, 72, 78, 80, 83-84, 90-93, 95, 97-99, 101-02, 106-07, 124, 128, 144, 155, 157-58, 162-63, 210, 212-14, 216-18, 226, 233, 267-68, 275-76, 279-81, 283-85, 289, 291-92, 306, 308, 310-11, 313-16, 325, 331-32, 340, 349, 373, 395-96, 406-09, 411, 414-15, 418-19, 422, 424, 431-32, 440, 495, 532, 552
Ghrareh, 413
Gibeah, see *Tell el-Fûl*
Gibeon, 93, 97, 107, 285, 418, 428
Gibson, J. C. L., 521, 528, 540
Gilead (-ite/s), 515, 540, 543, 546, 548, 550-51, 556, 575-76
Gilead (Province of *Gal'adi*), 523, 546, 553, 556, 577, 582
Gilgal, 578
Gill, D., 204-05
Gitin, S., 72, 91-94, 96-97, 101-02, 104-05, 107, 124-26, 128, 144, 155, 158, 212-13, 216, 267, 271, 276, 283-84, 288-91, 307-11, 313, 315-17, 325, 331-32, 339-40, 393, 395-96, 407-09, 413, 417-18, 420, 431
Glueck, N., 314
Goetze, A., 528
Golan, 543
Goodspeed, G. S., 532, 534
Gozan (Guzana), see *Tell Halaf*
Grant, E., 155, 315, 334, 411, 424
Gray, J., 515, 560
Grayson, A. K., 517, 527, 558, 562, 567
Great Display Inscription, 564, 570-71
Greek/Hellenistic Fort Wall, see *Wall 551*
Green, A. R., 509

INDEX

Greene, J., 503
Gubla, see *Byblos*
Gulf of Alexandretta, 544
Gurgum, 521, 532-33, 535, 538
Gurney, O., 572
Gutter (Drain) 359, see *Samaria*
Gutter (Drain) 376, see *Samaria*
Guy, P. L. O., 100

Hadadezer (Hadad-ʿidr), 508, 524
Ḥadatu, 493
Hadrach, see *Ḥattarikka*
Halah, 570
Haldians, 523
Haller, A., 427
Hallo, W. W., 515-17, 527, 544, 547, 558
Hamath (-ians), 508, 510, 518, 521, 523, 525, 529, 533, 536-38, 541, 552, 555, 565-69
Hamilton, R. W., 249-50, 272
Hanunu (Hanno), 544, 550, 554, 567-68
Harding, G. L., 328-29, 428-29, 439
Harran, 533
Harvard Semitic Museum, 503
Ḥattarikka, 536, 538, 550, 568
Hatti (-Land), 519, 522, 533
Hauran, 511, 553
Hawkins, J. D., 531-32, 536-38, 558
Haydn, H. M., 536
Hayes, J. H., 509, 566-69, 571-73, 576
Hazaʾel, 493, 511, 514-15, 519, 523-24
Hazazu/i, 518, 522, 549
Hazor, 9, 70-71, 75, 78-80, 82, 84-87, 89-93, 95, 97, 99-101, 105, 125-26, 129, 154-56, 160-64, 172, 210, 212, 214-16, 226, 233, 235-37, 240, 242, 248, 251, 267, 270, 272, 276, 279-81, 284, 286-87, 289, 306, 308-10, 313-14, 317, 319-20, 325, 327, 334, 339, 347, 349, 394-95, 397, 406, 408, 410-12, 415, 418-19, 422-24, 429, 435, 511-12, 528, 548, 578
header-stretcher masonry, 185-86
Hellenistic/Greek Fort Wall, see *Wall 551*
Henschel-Simon, E., 429
Herodotus, 439, 519
Herm, G., 542
Herod the Great, 584
Herr, L. G., 170, 186, 348
Herrera, M.-D., 242, 249-51, 272, 347
Herrmann, S., 515-16, 525
Herzog, Z., 152, 335
Heshbon, 280, 413, 419
Hezekiah, 548, 561
hippo jars, see *jars*

Hiram, 535
Hittite(-s), 515, 523, 526, 534
Hodder, I., 7
"hogback" handles, 323
holemouth jars, see *jars*
Holladay, Jr., J. S., 69-72, 74-75, 80, 82-83, 85, 89, 93, 102, 105, 107, 109, 125-26, 155-56, 176-78, 181, 187, 211-12, 214, 217, 221-22, 225, 228, 232-33, 235, 242, 252-53, 301, 304-06, 308, 310-12, 314, 316, 318-19, 321, 323, 325, 329, 336-37, 340, 343-44, 346, 350, 413, 417, 424, 440, 498, 501-02
Horowitz, A., 204-05
Horus, 489
Hosea, 512, 526
Hoshea, 221, 252, 506, 540-41, 553-54, 557, 559, 560-61, 576
House of Omri (Beth Omri), 521, 525, 548, 575-76, 582
House of Hazaʾel (Beth Hazaʾel), 548
Hubishna, 538
Huehnergard, J., 550
Humbert, J.-B., 246-47, 313, 316, 326, 396, 410, 424, 429
Hulin, P., 543
Hulliu, 540
Humban-nigaš, 567
Ḥumri-Land, 517
Hunt, M., 330
Hurrian(-s), 550
Hyrcanus, John, 583

Idibiʾilu, 545, 554
Ilan, Z., 439
Ilu-biʾdi (Yaubiʾdi), 565-68
Iran Stele, 535
Irḫuleni, 508
Isaiah, 548
Ishtunda, 538
Issachar, 4, 575-77
Istanbul Museum, 503
istikans, 92
Itti-Adad-aninu, 244
Itūʾa, 549
ivory (-ies), 31, 36, 43-44, 48, 55-56, 69, 114, 119, 152, 172-73, 182-84, 186, 188-90, 196-97, 206, 216, 220, 224, 260-61, 264, 295, 299, 349, 352-53, 355, 359-60, 364, 373, 383, 385, 388, 391, 401, 405, 429, 438-39, 441, 443-95, 501-02, 524-27, 581
Ivory House, 149, 173, 299, 477, 491-93

James, F., 74-75, 78, 81, 84, 86, 90, 94, 97-98, 102, 105, 125-26, 160, 163, 210, 267, 276, 280, 284, 286, 289-90, 306, 315-16, 324, 338-39, 341, 349, 394, 412, 418, 423
Janoah, 9, 548
jar(s), 88-102, 123, 144, 161-64, 182, 187, 189, 191, 208, 211-17, 221, 246, 248, 265, 302, 322-24, 368, 379, 383, 390, 415, 416-25, 433, 435, 483-84; *collared-rim*, 234; *conical*, 300; *hippo jars*, 31, 88, 93, 126, 163, 212-13, 215, 246, 417-18; *holemouth jars*, 48, 67, 102-107, 113, 117, 132, 138, 144-45, 160, 172, 182, 189, 197, 207, 212, 217-220, 227, 280, 368, 371, 382, 420-21, 483; *LMLK jars*, 97-98, 126-27, 216, 337; *Rhodian stamped jars*, 583; *sausage jars*, 93, 161, 163-65, 214, 216-17, 237, 246, 418; *stands*, 246, 423-25
Jaruzelska, I., 444
Jeba, 78
Jehoahaz, 506, 515, 520
Jehoash, 1, 506, 523
Jehoiadah, 513
Jehoram, 511-12, 514
Jehoshaphat, 509
Jehu, 38, 54, 57-58, 123, 206, 228, 234, 236, 438, 441, 506, 509, 511-16, 519, 521, 524, 540, 542, 544, 564, 575-76, 578, 582
Jehu Dynasty, 532, 531
Jepsen, A., 558
Jeremiah, 439
Jericho, 285, 287, 307
Jeroboam I, 575-76
Jeroboam II, 1, 114, 176, 236, 243, 438, 506, 509, 523-26, 528-29, 540, 543, 555, 576, 581
Jerusalem, 12, 40, 79, 127, 186, 245, 252, 273, 422, 515, 524, 543-44, 550-57, 568, 577-78, 581-84
Jesus, 582
Jezebel, 576, 581
Jezreel, *site*, 5, 229, 248-49, 320, 323, 348-49, 511; *valley*, 9, 74, 81, 94, 96, 155, 213, 216, 237, 245, 247, 249, 250, 313-14, 334, 347, 406
Joash, 513, 520-25, 540
Jodin, A., 410
Johns, C. N., 316, 326
Jones, G. H., 560
Josephus, 530, 584
Joshua, 581
Josiah, 245, 438-39, 583
Jotham, 543, 556
Joya, 99, 100, 268
Judah (Judeans), 509, 513, 515, 521, 524-25, 536, 541, 543, 547-48, 551-52, 554-56, 561, 563, 568-69, 578, 582-83
jug(s)/juglet(s), 180, 226, 246, 281-87, 295, 302, 324-37, 339, 342, 346, 350, 425-30, 435; *oenochoe jug(s)*, 316, 325-26, 328, 340, 346

Kadesh-Barnea, 547
Kalḫu, see *Nimrud*
Karnaim (province), 523
Karnak, 232
Kar-Shalmaneser, 527
kārum, 550
Kaska, 538
Katzenstein, H. J., 273, 535, 545
Kaufman, I. T., 443, 503, 524
Kedesh, 548
Kelm, G. L., 400, 428
Kelso, J. L., 329, 335
Kenyon, K. M., 1, 3, 4-5, 16-17, 19-20, 22-23, 26, 28, 30-32, 35-36, 47, 52, 54, 57-58, 60-61, 63-64, 68-69, 73, 75-76, 79, 87-88, 90, 95, 97-98, 100-01, 104, 106, 110-14, 117, 120, 122-23, 125, 128, 132, 137, 141-43, 145-47, 150-52, 154, 156-59, 164-65, 167, 169, 171-82, 184-85, 187-97, 200, 202, 204, 206-10, 212-14, 216, 219, 221-23, 227-28, 232, 239, 241-42, 246, 249, 251-52, 254, 256-57, 261, 267-69, 276, 278-80, 282-83, 287, 291-94, 296-99, 305-06, 308-09, 316-18, 320-22, 336, 338-46, 349-51, 357-58, 361-64, 367, 372, 377, 379-81, 383, 385-86, 389, 391-92, 394-96, 399-400, 404-05, 407-09, 412-14, 417, 420-22, 425, 430, 432, 435, 437, 440-41, 445, 453-58, 460, 462, 464-68, 470, 472-77, 480-81, 483-85, 487-89, 492, 502, 507, 524-25, 574, 579
Kessler, K., 538
Khabur River, 92, 516, 527, 535, 555, 570, 572
Khaldé, 306, 329, 410
Kheleifeh, see *Tell el-Kheleifeh*
Khirbet Abu et-Twein, 396
Khirbet ed-Duweir, 9
Khirbet el-Babariya, 9
Khirbet Kabuba, 9
Khirbet Kusein es-Sahel, 9
Khirbet Qarqaf, 9
Khirbet Silm, 99, 100, 306
Khirbet Yanum, 9
Khorsabad/Khorsabad Annals, 565, 571, 574
Khorsabad Pavement Inscription, 563, 582
Khu-Sebek Inscription, 5
Kinalia/Kunalia, 537
King's Highway, 314, 542-43, 555, 577

INDEX

Kitchen, K. A., 232
Koḥel, 291
Kraeling, E., 513, 515-16, 523, 528
krater(s), 129-30, 145, 160, 248, 279-80, 410-11, 421-23
Kuan, J. K., 566-69, 571-73
Kufr Lebbad, 78
Kühne, H., 546
Kullani, 536-38
Kummuh, 532-35, 538, 545
Kurba'il Statue, 508

Laessøe, J., 508
Lachish, 72-73, 78, 81, 83, 86, 90, 93, 97, 101, 107, 126-27, 154, 160, 163, 186, 213, 215, 217-19, 226, 252, 274, 276, 280-81, 284, 286, 289-91, 294, 307, 309, 316-17, 323, 326-27, 329-30, 334-35, 341, 394, 396, 398, 411-12, 415, 418, 422, 424-25, 428, 432, 439, 569; *Cave 6024*, 294; *Tomb 106*, 316, 335, 394, 428; *Tomb 116*, 326; *Tomb 1002*, 284
Lake Urumia, 516, 522, 533, 572
Lambert, W. G., 508, 514, 567
lamp(s), 397, 430-32
Lance, H. D., 532
Land of Urushalimum, 582
Lapp, N., 321
Lapp, P. W., 230, 232, 321, 422
Late Shallow Type, see *cooking pots*
Lawlor, J. I., 287
Layard, A. H., 315, 405-06, 492, 508
Lederman, Z., 337
Lemaire, A., 443
Levine, L. D., 522, 535
Levy, S., 313
Lewy, J., 538
Lines, J., 92, 95, 313, 401-04
LMLK Jars, see *jars*
Luckenbill, D. D., 514, 519, 535-36, 558
Lugenbeal, E. N., 74, 280, 419

Macalister, R. A. S., 12, 495
Machinist, P., 528, 548, 553
Machir, 4
Madaba Plains (Project), 400, 419
Maeir, A. M., 127
Magiddu (province), 244
Maisler (Mazar), B., 238, 250, 399, 443, 524
Malamat, A., 508-09, 521, 532, 539-40, 553, 558
Mallowan, M. E. L., 315, 402, 405, 427, 519, 526, 529
Manasseh (tribe), 4, 555-56

Mannai, 572
Maon, 547
Maras Museum, 522
Maṣṣuate, 518, 523
Marduk-alpa-iddina, 567
Marduk-bel-usate, 514
marzeaḥ, 438
Mati'-ilu, 528
May, H. G., 238, 240, 444
Mayer, W., 546
Mazar, A., 93, 97, 158, 217, 225, 227-29, 234, 238, 243, 325, 331, 349, 396, 400, 428
Mazar, B. (see also *Maisler*), 4
Mazar, E., 186
McCarter, P. K., 511
McClellan, T. L., 225
McLeod, W. E., 439
Medes, 549, 570, 573
Media, 541
Megiddo, 71-72, 78-80, 83-85, 90-93, 96, 99-101, 103, 105-07, 126, 129, 155, 157-58, 162-63, 172, 179-81, 212-16, 218, 226-52, 267, 272, 276, 279-80, 282, 284-90, 292, 295, 306-07, 309-12, 316-17, 320, 326-29, 334, 337-40, 347-50, 395, 402, 407, 411-12, 415, 418, 422-24, 427, 422, 510-11, 546-47, 561, 571, 574, 578; *Tomb 80C*, 273
Megiddo (province *Magidu*), 523, 546, 552, 572, 577, 582
Melid (Malatya), 516, 521, 532-33, 538
Melos, 294
Melqart Stele, 513
Menahem (ben Gadi), 513, 524, 530-31, 533, 535-36, 539-43, 551, 556, 577
Meqabelain, 428
Merodach-baladan, see *Marduk-alpa-iddina*
Meṣad Ḥashavyahu, 337, 415
Mesha Stele, 582
Meʿunite(-s/-im), 547
Michel, E., 507-08, 514
Midian, 571
Millard, A. R., 516-23, 527-28, 532, 541, 549, 558-60, 562, 572
Mitchell, T. C., 526, 575
Mitinti, 550, 554
Mizpah (see also Tell en-Naṣbeh), 582-83
Moab (-ites), 509, 515, 524, 526, 551, 556
Mogador, 410
Monolith Inscription, 507-09, 513
mortar (mortaria), 292, 414
Mount Carmel, 4, 100, 511-12, 515-16, 522, 578
Mount Ebal, 5

Mount Gerizim, 5, 584
Mount Gilboa, 4
Mount Lebanon, 548
Mount Nal, 535
Mount Saniru, 511
Munshara, 92, 294, 309, 327, 333, 337
Musri, 515
Mycenaean Ware, 268

Na'aman, N., 510-11, 513-14, 528, 536-37, 545, 561-63, 566, 568, 570-71, 573
Nabataean Temple Podium, 284
Nablus, 78, 273
Nabû-kēnu-uṣur, 572
Nabû-šar-aḫḫešu, 572
Nabû-ushabshi, 560
Nadab, 575
Nahal Kanah, 9
Nahal-muṣur, 545, 551
Nahal Shechem, 9
Nahr el-Kalb, 511, 516
Na'iri, 533, 549
Naphtali, 548
nari (limestone), 204
Naveh, J., 514
Nebo, 428
Nebuchadnezzar, 583
Neck-Decorated Ware, 99
Neco (Pharaoh), 399
Negev, A., 511, 528
Negevite Ware(s), 314
Nelson, H. H., 232
Nelson, R. D., 560
Nergal-Eriš, 527
Neutron Activation Analysis, 163
New Kingdom Egypt, 98
Nimrud, 92, 401-02, 416, 427, 492-93, 508, 511, 516, 518, 525, 527-29, 530-31, 533, 539, 542, 545-46, 548-50, 552, 557, 570
Nimrud Prism (Texts), 555, 563-66, 569-71, 573
Nimrud Slab/Inscription, 517, 519, 521, 523
Nineveh, 315, 399, 405, 427, 492, 526, 535, 545, 570
Nineveh Prism, 509
Nippur, 537
Nippur Hills, 522
Northeast Outwork, see *Ta'anach*
North-West Palace (Nineveh), 315, 405, 492
Noth, M., 516, 560

Oates, D., 528
Oates, J., 92, 95, 312-13, 315, 401-03, 405, 416, 419, 425, 427
Oded, B., 510, 536-37, 539, 541, 550, 553, 570
oenochoe jug(s), see *jugs*
Olmstead, A. T., 517-18, 522, 526, 528, 537, 541, 565
Omri (Omride), 1, 4, 9-10, 15, 18, 20, 32, 36, 38-39, 43, 45, 47, 52, 60, 64, 87, 100-01, 110, 113, 115, 119, 123, 129-31, 142-45, 147, 152, 166, 170-71, 173-75, 186-87, 204, 225, 234, 248-49, 257, 260, 265, 348-49, 361, 364, 376-77, 388, 438, 455, 461, 468, 486, 491, 506, 511, 513-14, 523, 529, 550-51, 564, 577, 581
Oppenheim, A. L., 519
Orni, E., 8
Orontes River, 539, 550
Orontes Valley, 525
Osorkon House, 501-02
Ostraca House, 1, 115, 167-71, 177-79, 226, 268, 286, 497-502
ostraca (Samaria/Israelite), see *Samaria Ostraca*

Page, S., 517-18, 520-23, 527, 532
Palace AB, 526
Palace Door Inscription, 564
Palace Ware, 92, 312-13, 344, 349, 352, 400-04, 406-09, 572
Palastu (Palaštu), 517-19, 521
Palestine Exploration Fund, 12, 68, 79-80, 103, 193, 372, 392, 460, 462, 464, 489
pan(s), 414
Panammu (king), 536
Panammua Inscriptions, 540
Paqarhubuna, 522
Patina, 508, 514
Pavement/Paving (at Samaria), *248*, 61, 64; *249*, 61, 64, 87; *249a*, 63-64; *545*, 61, 63; *548*, 60, 62-64, 107, 206-07; *549*, 60, 62-64, 107, 206-07, 211; *549a*, 64, 206
Pax Assyriaca, 291, 314, 344, 399, 572
Pekah, 177, 221, 501, 524, 540-41, 543-44, 551-54, 556, 577
Pekahiah, 177, 501, 540-41, 543, 551, 577
Pella, 424, 512
Persia, 583
pestilence (or plague), 522, 526
Petrie, Sir Flinders, 213, 312, 399-400, 425
Philistia, 509, 515, 519, 521, 523, 543-46, 548-52, 565, 568, 570
Phoenicia (-n), 161, 163, 226, 241, 247, 250, 271, 311, 316, 318, 326, 329, 336, 431, 444-45, 485, 513, 521, 526, 529, 538, 542, 544-45,

550, 576, 581-82
Phoenician Ware, 284
Phythian-Adams, W. J., 399
Pit *i*, see *Samaria*
Pitard, W., 523, 553
Pitru, 547
Plain White IV/V/VI Ware, 164
plates/platters, see *bowls*
du Plat-Taylor, J., 74, 163, 311, 317, 508
Poebel, A., 519, 521
Polley, M. E., 509
Pompey, 584
Pool 621, see *Samaria*
Portugali, Y., 97, 321, 429
Postgate, J. N., 521, 535, 538, 557
Pratico, G., 312, 314, 407, 413, 428
Prism A, 399
Prism S, 399
Pritchard, J. B., 402
Psamtik/Psammetichus I (Pharaoh), 410, 439
Ptolemies, 583
Pul, 530

Qadesh, 539, 550
Qarnini, 553
Qarqar, 509-10, 512, 523-24, 563, 568-69
Qashish, 250
quarry (-ies; quarrying), 31, 35, 43-44, 55-56, 69, 76, 135, 149, 169, 173, 195, 204, 382, 385-86, 450, 468, 475, 486-87
Que, 516, 521, 535, 538, 544, 557
Qumran, 422
Qurdi-assur-lamur, 541
Qrayé, 423

Raban, A., 250
Rabud, 97
Rainey, A. F., 443, 510, 524
Ramat Hashofet, 250
Ramat Raḥel, 307, 337, 396, 413, 415
Ramoth-gilead, 514, 543, 548, 553-56
Raphia, 568-69
Raqefet Cave, 250
Rasappa, 527
Rast, W., 129, 229-37, 240, 247, 250, 310, 395, 398, 418
Rawlinson, H. C., 492, 507, 511, 537
Rawson, P. S., 95, 402
Reade, J., 527, 531-32, 546, 559
Rechabites, 582
Red-Figured Ware, 95, 583
Red-on-Black I [III], see *Cypriote R-o-B*

Red-Painted Ware, 99
Reed, W. L., 428
regal-ritual city, 578
Reich, R., 291
Reisner, G. A., 1, 58, 71, 95, 115, 166-71, 177, 185, 204, 207, 286, 309, 427, 443, 496, 498-99, 501-02, 524-25
Reuben, 555
Reuther, O., 427
Reviv, H., 513
Rezin (Raḍyān), 544, 551-53, 556
Rhodian Ware, 490
Riis, P. J., 175-76, 225
Rimah (Tell al-) Stele/Inscription, 518-23, 527
Ring-Based Bowls, see *bowls*
Robber Trench *57*, 455; *58*, 357, 470-71; *65*, 466; *89*, 122; *95*, 119; *98*, 119, 356; *105*, 118, 121-23, 131; *107*, 118, 121, 129, 131; *130*, 190, 385-86, 388, 472-73, 476; *133*, 473; *135*, 473; *149*, 26, 27, 44, 380; *150*, 27, 47, 380; *151*, 366; *152*, 44; *153*, 29, 44, 55-56, 219, 486; *161*, 40, 63, 87; *333*, 132, 135, 137-38, 140-41; *339*, 135, 356; *362*, 141; *363*, 132, 137, 141, 143, 225; *371*, 132, 135, 140; *372*, 132, 135, 137-38, 140; *376*, 132, 137, 141, 143; *377*, 132, 137, 141-43, 225, 356; *523*, 370; *541*, 295; *553*, 50, 64, 373; *555*, 54, 372; *556*, 52, 54, 479; *573*, 257-58; *578*, 257-58, 260
Rockefeller Museum, 12, 40, 68-69, 79-80, 103, 322
Rollston, C., 503
Rome, 458
Room *a*, 16-17, 44, 55, 76, 112, 114-15, 119, 170-71, 173-74, 185-86, 224, 358, 360-62; *b*, 16-17, 44, 55, 76, 112, 114-15, 119, 170-71, 173-74, 185-86, 224, 358, 360-62; *c*, 16-17, 44, 55, 76, 112, 114-15, 119, 170-71, 173-74, 185-86, 224, 358-63; *d*, 16-17, 44, 55, 76, 112, 114-15, 119, 170-71, 173-74, 185-86, 224, 358, 360-63; *e*, 16-17, 27, 44, 55, 115, 170-71, 173-74, 185, 224, 354, 358, 359-64, 365, 372, 375, 376-81, 390, 392, 405, 429, 433-34; *f*, 17-18, 22-23, 29-30, 43, 67, 87, 115, 184, 296, 354, 358, 368, 376-81, 381-83, 390, 392, 417, 433-34; *g*, 11, 14-15, 17-20, 22-23, 25, 30, 32, 37, 43, 48, 60, 66-68, 71, 76-78, 87-89, 103, 107-09, 111-12, 114-15, 123, 130, 147, 171-72, 174, 184, 192, 224, 296, 298, 303, 305, 341, 354, 358, 362, 365-66, 368, 376-81, 382, 384, 390-92, 414, 416-17, 420, 423, 425-26, 430, 432-34; *h*, 11, 14-15, 17-20, 22-25, 27, 29-31, 37, 40, 56, 66-68, 71, 76-80, 87-89, 91, 96, 102, 107-12,

114-15, 123, 130, 152, 171-72, 174, 182, 184-88, 192, 208, 224, 296, 300, 357-58, 362, 365-66, 376, 390, 423; *j*, 11, 15-20, 22-23, 25-26, 30, 35, 38, 43-55, 57-58, 60, 66-67, 77, 80, 87, 90, 107-09, 111-12, 114-15, 130, 147, 171-72, 174, 182, 184-85, 192, 200, 202-06, 208, 211, 220, 224, 296, 354, 357-58, 362, 376, 378-79, 381-83, 390-91, 434; *k*, 15-20, 22, 25-31, 44, 55-58, 66-68, 76-78, 81-82, 87-89, 101, 107-15, 119, 130, 152, 171-72, 174, 182, 185-87, 192, 197, 200, 208, 296, 357, 366, 390; *l*, 11, 16-17, 38, 50-52, 54, 60, 80, 89, 115, 119, 153, 202, 354, 358, 367-75, 376, 381-83, 390-92, 416-17, 421-23, 426, 433-34; *m*, 16-17, 38, 50, 60, 64, 115, 119, 382; *n*, 11, 16-18, 38, 48, 58-68, 77-78, 82, 84, 87, 103, 107-09, 113-15, 119, 124, 147, 182, 184-85, 207-09, 211, 220, 224, 322, 373; *o*, 17, 44, 55, 171, 182, 185, 224; *p*, 16-17, 44, 55, 171; *q*, 17, 22, 27, 44, 55, 171, 182,185, 224, 358; *r*, 16-17, 61, 63, 115; *s*, 182, 185; *hk*, 18-19, 25, 27, 31-32, 35, 41, 44, 58, 182-87, 189-92, 195, 197, 200-01, 208, 211-14, 218-20, 222, 224, 341, 354, 357, 359, 362, 365-67, 390-91, 416-17, 423, 425, 434; *hq*, 182, 185-86, 190-92, 195, 200-01, 208, 211, 213, 219-22, 224, 354, 357, 359, 362, 365, 376, 381, 383-90, 391-92, 397, 405, 434; *kq*, 182, 185, 191-92, 195, 200-01, 219, 224, 354, 357, 359, 362, 365, 376-81, 383-90, 391-92, 397, 434; *13*, 171; *81*, 171; *82*, 171; *83*, 171; *117*, 286; *138*, 306; *404*, 268; *620*, 170-71; *622*, 170-71; *623*, 170-71
Rosenau, H., 445
Rost, P., 531, 538, 545, 548, 551, 553, 554, 556
Rowe, A., 246
Rowton, M., 7
Rukibtu, 554
Russell, H. F., 546

Sabaʾa Stele, 517-19, 521, 523, 527
es-Sadeh, 413
Safar, F., 507, 511
Saggs, H. W. F., 528-30, 537, 541, 545-46, 557, 567
Sagur (Sagurri) River, 547
Sahab, 329, 428
Saidah, R., 410
šālîš, 541
Saller, S. J., 428
Samʾal, see *Zinjirli*
Samaria, *Augustuem*, 479; *Cistern 3 (HES)*, 309; *Cistern 7 (HES)*, 94-95; *Corridor o*, 16; *Drain 69*, 453, 461; *E 207 (shrine?)*, 158, 246, 286, 293, 310, 316, 318, 321, 323, 328, 333, 413, 417, 423, 446, 478, 485; *Foundation Trench 55a*, 467; *132*, 473; *120*, 380; *125a*, 386; *503a*, 63; *508a*, 370; *551*, 453, 455; *574*, 260; *Gutter/Drain 359*, 140; *Gutter/Drain 376*, 143; *Pit i (room/latrine?)*, 17, 22, 24, 29, 32, 34-35, 37-43, 60, 92, 111, 146, 175, 177-81, 184-85, 190, 208, 215, 220, 223-24, 226, 253, 267, 289, 296-346, 350, 352-53, 357, 365-66, 376, 384, 390, 412, 423, 462-63, 468; *Pool 621*, 171; *Z Deep Pit*, 98, 100, 268, 271, 293, 328, 333, 341 (see also *Pavement/Paving*; *Robber Trench*; *Room*; *Segments*; *S Tombs*; *Summit Strip*; *walls*)
Samaria Ostraca (ostraca), 1, 9, 172, 177-78, 182, 286, 349, 443-44, 496-503, 524, 527, 540, 572, 577; *Aramaic ostraca*, 583
Samaria Papyri, 583
Samaria Ware, 155, 250, 268-75, 295, 302-03, 310-11, 315-16, 318-19, 346, 409, 412-13
Samaritans, 581
Samerina/Samirina (province), 244, 349, 523, 564, 571, 576, 582-83
Sammuramet, 517, 519-20
Šamšī-ilu, 508, 527, 532, 555
Sanballat, 583
Sanip/b (Shanip/b), 556
Sardinia, 316
Sarduri I, 528
Sarduri III, 532, 534
Sarepta, 163, 250, 306
Sargon II, 181, 221, 223, 246, 254, 327, 348-49, 401, 405-06, 410, 435, 437, 493, 506-07, 509-10, 550, 558-59, 562-75, 582
Sarna, N. M., 510
Sarrabani, 560
saucer bowls, see *bowls*
Sauer, J. E., 74, 280, 419
Saul, 231
sausage jars, see *jars*
scarab(s), 299
Schloen, J. D., 503, 542
Schneider, T., 514
Schrader, E., 530
Schumacher, G., 1, 241, 443
Scythian(s), 439-40
Sefarvaim, 558
Sefire Stelae/Inscriptions, 522, 534, 536
Segment (excavated at Samaria):
 9.21.31, 447, 479-82, 491
 9.27.14.13, 457
 12.27.14.13, 447, 450, 459-64, 478, 490

19.12.20, 447, 461-62, 464, 468, 478, 490
19.51.14.20 (N./S.), 354-55, 359-65, 391, 405, 426, 429, 435, 439, 446-47, 450-51, 452-64, 466, 468, 470, 478, 490
49.26.25, 447, 450-51, 458, 462, 464-68, 469-70, 490
86.2.88..., 117-25, 130, 322
104.109.107, 122-23
105.107, 122-23
120.121.19.126, 14, 15, 20-27, 34, 37, 40-42, 48, 52, 56, 68, 77, 103, 109-10, 300, 354, 376-81, 383, 391, 397, 414, 416-17, 420, 425-26, 430, 432-33, 436, 447, 483, 490
122.125.19.121, 24, 40-44, 89, 92, 110, 253, 296, 299-301, 305, 311-12, 319, 324, 330, 338, 341-42, 344-45, 354, 365-67, 436
122.126.19.121, 253, 296, 299-301, 305, 319, 322, 324, 341-42, 344-45, 376
125.144, 15, 20, 24, 27-37, 39, 42, 44, 56-57, 68, 89, 96, 109-10, 183, 186-88, 191, 194, 200, 202, 211-12, 214-15, 217-19, 300, 354, 365-67, 417, 423, 436, 447, 483-85
147.136.150.155, 29
147.145.151.136, 37-40, 44, 68
147.155.151.136(156?), 37, 110
150.155.147.136, 37
155.151.136.147, 37-40, 44, 89, 102, 110
302.304, 139
313.306, 139, 141-43, 145
325.304, 103, 131-32, 134-45
364.337.363, 139
501.503.504.505, 373, 488
502.503, 48, 58-66, 68, 77, 82, 87, 103, 107, 113, 209, 211, 488
502.500.503, 374
503.517.507, 488
504.503.507.508, 373
504.503.509.508, 52, 354, 367-75, 382-83, 391, 397, 417, 421, 436, 488-89
504.505(503?).509.508, 52
504.508.509.510, 146-53, 159, 161, 165, 375, 488
504.510.509, 151-52
506.505.504, 146, 152, 488
507.503.504.505, 447, 487-89, 491
509.126, 20, 48-55, 60, 77, 80, 183, 202-06, 209, 211, 225, 354, 367, 372, 378, 381-83, 391, 417, 421, 436
513.514, 253-56, 261-66, 295
517.503.504.505, 488
558.556.557.559, 152
558.559.564.557, 152

Between 509 and 544, 52
(E Strip), Btw TT 2–TT 3, 11, 15, 18, 20-21, 24, 28-30, 32, 35, 39, 42, 44, 55-58, 68, 77, 81, 89, 101, 112, 183, 187-89, 191, 197-202, 212, 218-20, 300, 366-67, 383, 484-87
E Strip.S Half, 447, 485-87
(E Strip), North of TT 2, 18-23, 27, 31, 43-48, 52, 54-57, 77, 89-90, 97, 111, 205-06, 225, 377-79, 383, 486
Hellenistic Robber Trench, 447, 487-89, 491
N of 105, 122
N of 155, 52
N of 161, 48-50
N of 551, 253-61, 266, 277, 281-82, 287-88, 291-92, 295
N of Wall 20, 447, 479-82, 491
W of 14, 461-62, 478
W of 124, 182-83, 189-97, 199-202, 211, 213, 220, 354-55, 367, 383-91, 397, 405, 436, 446-47, 450-51, 468-78, 490
W of 318, 142
W of 537, 52
Seir (Mt. Saniru), 511
Seleucid(-s), 583-84
Sellin, E., 230
Semiramis, see *Sammuramet*
Sennacherib, 238, 246, 252, 406, 493, 536, 568-69
Shabaka (Pharaoh), 246
Shallum (ben Jabesh), 529, 540, 577
Shalman (Shalmaneser III), 512
Shalmaneser III, 505-16, 521-23, 529-30, 532, 537, 539, 547, 564, 567-68
Shalmaneser IV, 506, 528, 537
Shalmaneser V, 181, 221, 406, 506-07, 510, 528, 530, 541, 558-63, 566-67, 570, 582
Shamshi-Adad V, 506, 516, 537
Shapiya, 560
Sharon Plain, 81, 250, 582
Shea, W. H., 443, 524, 534-36, 539
Shechem (Balata), 5, 9-10, 72, 78, 82-83, 93, 270, 311, 313, 318, 323, 349, 406, 524, 578, 583-84
Sheik Hammad Stele, 517, 519, 522, 527
Shemer, 4, 9, 25-26, 137
Shikmona, 250
Shiloh, 7, 9, 578
Shiloh, Y., 204-05
Shishak (Shoshenq), 74, 93, 228, 232-34, 241-42, 249, 512
Shuandahul, 573
Shunem, 249
Sibraim, 558
Sicily, 316

Sidon (-ians), 164, 423, 511, 513, 517, 523, 542, 544, 550
Ṣimirra, 538, 541, 544, 550, 568
Simyra, 516
Sinclair, L. A., 394
Sinjil, 78
Šinuḫtu, 564
Siruatu, 547
sleeper wall, 151
Small Display Inscription, 563, 569
Smith, G., 528, 536, 548, 554
Smith, R. H., 431
Smith, S., 531, 538
Smithsonian Granary, 406
Smithsonian Institution, 399
Socoh, 9, 249
Solomon (-ic), 9, 80, 238-39, 242, 250, 349, 493, 526, 581
Sorek River/Drainage System, 577
Spain, 329
Spieckermann, H., 566
Springer, I., 503
Stager, L. E., 5, 26, 152
stands, see *jar(s)*
Staples, W. E., 445
Statue Inscription, 508
Stern, E., 408, 429, 431-32
Stewart, D., 439
S Tombs (Samaria), 413; **101**, 273; **103**, 156, 158, 212, 323; **104**, 323; **107**, 71, 308; **110**, 333
Sukas, 176, 225
Sukenik, E. L., 269, 445
Sultantepe (tablets), 508
Summit Strips (at Samaria):
  Dg, 293, 333
  Qb, 413, 479
  Qc, 117, 119, 124, 131, 184, 321-22, 359, 364, 426, 439, 445-50, 452, 459-62, 464, 466-68
  Qd, 293, 333, 447-49, 479, 491
  Qf, 447-49, 479, 491
  Qg, 131-32, 139
  Qh, 448
  Qk, 20, 28, 40-41, 48, 72, 175, 184, 187, 253, 293, 296, 300, 324, 359, 365, 376-77, 381, 383, 425-26, 430, 445-50, 468, 483-87
  Qm, 41
  Qn, 48, 58, 60, 175, 253, 286, 293, 367, 376, 381, 425-26, 447-49, 487-89
  Zd, 423
  Strip 1 (Harvard), 94, 207
  Strip 2 (Harvard), 207

Strip 3 (Harvard), 207
Strip 4 (Harvard), 207, 268, 286, 496, 499, 501
Strip 7 (Harvard), 496, 498, 501
Ṣupite, 541
Surri, 514
Sweeney, M. A., 568
Syro-Ephraimite Alliance/War/Conflict, 177, 221, 501, 510, 544, 550, 552, 555

Taʿanach, 72-73, 78-79, 82-84, 90-91, 93, 98, 106, 126, 128-29, 155, 157, 160, 210, 217, 226, 229-38, 240, 247-50, 279-80, 282, 284, 309-11, 315, 317, 320-21, 323, 327, 334, 347, 395, 398-99, 418-19; *Cuneiform Tablet Building*, 78, 128, 210, 230-31, 323; *Cultic Structure*, 78, 82, 84, 231-33, 240, 279, 309, 317, 327, 334; *Cistern 69*, 82, 232, 315; *Cistern 74*, 78, 82, 232, 282, 323; *Drainpipe Structure*, 78, 231; *Northeast Outwork (NEO)*, 235-36; *Twelfth-Century House*, 128, 231
Tabal (Tubal), 516, 538, 540
Tabeel, 551
tabûn (-im), 31, 36, 37, 66-67, 172, 190, 217, 231, 299
Tadmor, H., 510-11, 517, 519-21, 523, 527, 530-31, 534-37, 540, 543-45, 547-54, 556, 558-63, 565-67, 569, 71, 573, 575
Tappuah, 10
Tappy, R. E. (*AIS-I*), 3-4, 16, 20, 22, 26, 28, 30, 32, 47-48, 50, 52, 70-75, 78, 81, 84-85, 89, 96, 100, 103, 106, 111, 114-15, 117, 121-24, 130, 132, 137-38, 143, 146, 151-52, 157, 163, 172-76, 181, 190, 201-02, 204, 230, 232-33, 239, 252-53, 260, 265, 294, 308, 311, 317, 320, 326, 330, 348, 359-63, 367, 376-79, 381-82, 388, 426, 435, 440, 443, 446, 452-53, 455, 459-62, 464, 472, 483, 488, 506-07, 509, 513, 520, 529
Tarsus (Tarzi), 427, 517
tartanu, 527, 532
Taurus Mountains, 538
Tel Batash, 410, 428
Tel Dan, 115, 578
Tel Dan Inscription, 445, 514, 524
Tel ʿEton, 337
Tel Goren, 394, 396, 415, 420, 422
Tell Abu Hawām, 78, 84, 100, 229, 233, 241, 249-51, 272, 315, 334, 347, 416
Tell Abu Marya, 558
Tell Aḥmar, see *Til Barsip*
Tell al-Rimah, 517

INDEX

Tell ʿAmal, 83-84, 91-94, 216, 226, 294, 313-14, 316, 326, 334, 349, 406, 419-20
Tell Beit Mirsim, 72, 78, 86, 92, 98, 104, 126-27, 158, 160, 163, 215, 217-18, 226, 232, 238, 276-77, 284-85, 287-89, 292, 307, 309, 329-30, 333, 335-37, 340, 350, 393-94, 396, 398, 408, 418, 420, 424-25, 431
Tell el-Farʿah (N), 7, 9-10, 71-72, 81, 85, 87, 92, 96, 106, 130, 160, 232, 249, 267, 270, 276, 286, 306, 309-10, 313-16, 318-20, 326-27, 333-34, 338, 340, 348-49, 394, 396, 402-04, 407, 410, 412, 415, 418, 425, 427, 529, 575; *Cistern 361*, 315, 581
Tell el-Farʿah (S), 92, 402
Tell el-Fûl, 78, 107, 276
Tell el-Ḥesi, 428
Tell el-Kheleifeh, 312, 314, 407, 413, 428
Tell el-Maskhuta, 408
Tell el-Mazar, 407
Tell el-ʿUmeiri, 287
Tell en-Naṣbeh, 4, 71-72, 75, 86, 90-91, 93-96, 98-100, 107, 126, 129, 154, 156-58, 160, 163, 213, 216, 218, 226, 267, 276, 280, 284, 286-87, 289-90, 294, 302, 307, 314, 326-27, 334-35, 393, 397, 406, 408, 410, 414-16, 418-20, 422-24; *Cistern 370*, 216, 218, 392
Tell Esdar, 84
Tell es-Saʿidiyeh, 81, 85, 102, 284, 400, 402, 412, 419
Tell Ḥalaf (Gozan/Guzana), 92, 427, 516, 570
Tell Jemmeh (*Yurza*), 213, 226, 246, 312, 399-400, 403-04, 406-08, 410, 425, 432, 435, 439, 570
Tell Keisan, 78, 82-83, 91, 95, 126, 155, 157, 160, 210, 216-17, 226, 229, 233, 237, 242, 246-47, 250-52, 276, 279, 292-93, 307, 311, 313-14, 319, 326, 347-48, 350, 396, 406, 410, 414, 424, 428-29, 432, 439
Tell Masos, 79, 83, 337, 415
Tell Miska, 7
Tell Qasîle, 78-80, 82-85, 90-91, 93, 95-96, 107, 125, 158, 160, 210, 217-19, 226, 233, 240, 242, 276, 279-80, 290, 313-14, 325, 330-31, 402, 406
Tell Qiri, 74, 81, 84, 86, 90, 93-98, 126, 129, 155, 210, 216, 226, 229, 237, 247-48, 250-51, 270, 272, 281-82, 284, 308, 310, 314, 321, 329-30, 334, 397, 406, 412-13, 416, 418, 420, 422, 424, 427-29
Tell Rifaʿat, 521
Tell Yoqneʿam, 71, 79-81, 84, 87, 91, 93-94, 102-04, 106, 129, 155, 213, 226, 229, 237, 247, 250-51, 265, 267, 272, 284, 300, 313-14, 321, 330, 334, 347, 406, 418, 429, 439, 511
Tel Mevorakh, 78, 250
Terra Sigillata Ware, 268
Test Trench 2, 44, 57
Thiele, E. R., 511, 520, 535, 541, 543
Thorley, J. P., 329, 335
Thureau-Dangin, F., 493, 547
Thutmosis III (Pharaoh), 399
Tiglath-pileser III, 164, 181, 221, 236, 242-44, 505-07, 515, 522-23, 528-60, 562, 567-69, 575, 577
Til Barsip (Tell Aḥmar), 508, 516, 532-33, 547
Timnah, see *Tel Batash*
Tirzah, see *Tell el-Farʿah (N)*
Tola, 4
Tomb 14, see *Beth-Shemesh*
Tomb 80C, see *Megiddo*
Tomb 106, see *Lachish*
Tomb 116, see *Lachish*
Tomb 1002, see *Lachish*
Toombs, L. E., 313, 404, 406
Trebolle, J. C., 560
Tubail, 535
Tubal, see *Tabal*
Tubas, 10
Tufnell, O., 127, 155, 176, 215, 218-19, 274, 276, 284, 290, 294, 307, 316-17, 323, 326-30, 393-94, 396, 411-12, 428
Tuhana, 538
Tukultu-Enurta, 493
Tuna, 538
Turkey, 503, 522
Tushingham, A. D., 127
Tutammu, 533, 535, 537
Twelfth-Century House, see *Taʿanach*
Tyre, 99-100, 161-65, 246, 250, 270-71, 276, 279, 294, 306, 311, 316-18, 325, 328-30, 509, 511-13, 515, 517, 523-24, 526, 530, 535, 538, 541-42, 544, 550, 571; *Fine Ware Plates (FWP)*, 270-72, 274, 317, 359

Uassurme, 540
Ugarit, 550
Ulluba, 533, 535, 537
Umm el-Biyara, 413
ʾUmq, 521
Unger, E., 518-19
Ungnad, A., 514, 518
Unqi, 533, 535, 538, 544, 557
Urartu (-ean/s), 516, 522, 526-28, 531-35, 541, 545, 547, 577

Ussishkin, D., 127-28, 239, 241, 245, 248, 337, 349
Uzziah, 536, 543, 547, 555-56

Valley of the Kings, 498
Van Beek, G. W., 250, 399, 400, 403, 406, 408, 423, 542
Van Zyl, A. H., 515
de Vaux, R., 407, 512
Vera Chamaza, G. W., 562
Vilders, M. E., 78
Vogt, E., 558

Wadi Beidan, 7
Wadi ed-Daliyeh, 583
Wadi Farʿa, 7
Wadi Tharthar, 527
Waldbaum, J., 439
Walker, A., 266
walls (at Samaria):
  9, 465, 479-80
  12, 461-65
  12a, 465
  12b, 465
  14, 361, 455, 461-64
  14a, 455
  19, 20, 37, 40-41, 300, 361, 365, 378, 380, 455, 463
  20, 361, 455, 463, 479, 481
  21, 479-81
  23, 465
  24, 481
  25, 455, 457, 465
  26, 458, 463, 465
  27, 455
  29, 480
  30, 479, 480
  31, 479
  47, 465
  49, 465
  51, 173, 360-64, 453-56, 463-64, 466, 468, 490
  55, 467
  55a, 467
  56, 22-23, 32, 34-35, 37, 172-73, 185-86, 190-91, 193, 196-97, 200-02, 213-14, 219, 221-22, 357, 360-62, 385, 452-53, 455, 457-58, 462, 464-65, 468, 470-72, 490
  57, 29, 173, 362-65, 405, 429, 452, 454, 457-58
  58, 22, 26, 29, 34, 119, 173, 186, 190, 201, 214, 224, 357, 360, 362, 453, 457-58, 465-66
  60, 16-17, 29, 115, 119, 186
  62, 455
  64, 457
  65, 16-17, 22, 115, 131, 185-86, 195, 208, 223, 357, 361-62, 452-53, 457-58, 466
  66, 457
  67, 457-58
  68, 453, 455
  73, 29
  95, 120, 122
  98, 119
  105, 117, 119, 122-24, 129, 131
  107, 117, 122-23, 129, 131
  120, 20, 25, 41, 45, 378, 380, 384, 468
  121, 20, 378
  122, 40, 300, 365
  123, 41
  124, 190, 197, 384, 468, 470
  124a, 190, 386, 469-70, 475-77
  124b, 190, 386, 469, 475-77, 487
  125, 32, 40-41, 190, 192-93, 196, 296, 300, 303, 341, 365-66, 385, 387-88, 470-71, 487
  125a, 190, 193-94, 385-86, 468, 470, 473, 487
  125b, 29-32, 34-37, 43, 56-57, 101, 188, 190-91, 193-94, 196-97, 200-02, 208, 214-15, 219-22, 385-86, 388, 468, 470-73, 477, 485-87
  126, 20, 50, 296, 303, 305, 341, 378, 382
  129, 31, 43, 486-87
  130, 190-91
  132, 192, 195, 357, 362, 385-86, 468, 469-71, 473, 475-77, 490
  132E, 190, 195-96, 386, 388, 470-72, 475-77
  132W, 190, 195-96, 386, 469-71, 474-77
  133, 190-91, 385-86, 473
  134, 41-42
  136, 20, 22-23, 27, 34, 37, 39-40, 42, 44-45, 76, 109, 111, 123, 298, 301, 366, 425
  137, 56
  138, 22-23, 58, 296, 303, 366, 368, 382
  140, 45
  142, 22, 25, 28, 38, 40, 50, 54, 56, 58, 60, 101, 186-87, 189, 202, 215, 219-220, 363, 366-68, 373, 462, 486
  144, 32, 34, 42, 301, 366
  145, 37, 184, 200, 206, 219, 357, 366, 425
  146, 41
  147, 29, 34, 40, 42, 300
  148, 45, 56
  149, 22, 25, 45, 58, 60, 380, 384, 468
  150, 26, 36, 189, 380

151, 25, 28, 34, 37, 40, 79, 109, 186, 189, 202, 215, 219-20, 362, 365
152, 45
153, 22-24, 26, 28-29, 34-35, 40, 42, 44, 47, 55-57, 101, 112, 184-85, 197, 200-01, 206, 219-20, 298, 366, 485
155, 22-23, 28-29, 32, 34-35, 37, 39-40, 110, 188-89, 298, 301, 485
156, 190, 472, 474
157, 17, 22, 25, 28-31, 37, 39-40, 79, 101, 109, 112-13, 187, 297, 366, 471-72, 475, 477, 486
159, 34
160, 18, 22-23, 28, 38, 48, 54-55, 57-58, 63-64, 170, 206, 377, 466, 486
161 (Omri's Enclosure), 15, 18, 20, 22-24, 32, 38-40, 43, 45, 47-48, 52, 55-56, 60, 62, 64, 87, 110, 113, 119, 129-30, 147, 149, 152, 169-71, 173, 186-87, 202, 204-05, 265, 361, 364, 376-77, 388, 455, 461, 466, 468, 486, 491
197, 25
304, 134
316, 132, 135
322, 134
323, 132, 135
324, 132, 135
325, 132, 134-35, 137
332, 138
336, 137
352, 140
363, 356
460, 29
461, 29
500, 147
500b, 17, 28-29, 368
501, 488
502, 146
503, 50, 60-61, 147
503a, 370
504, 146-47, 149-50, 255
505, 146-47, 367, 489
508a, 370-72, 421, 423
509, 146, 373
509–S, 373
510, 151
511, 50
512, 50
513, 146-47, 256, 261, 263
514, 261, 263, 265
516, 261
517, 60, 146, 488

519, 146
523, 370
536, 22-23, 50, 146-47
537, 50
538, 50
541, 263
551 (Greek/Hellenistic Fort Wall), 50, 61-62, 151, 172, 253, 256-57, 260-61, 263, 295, 364, 453, 455-56, 479, 488-89, 499, 584
552, 371-72, 397, 421, 423
553, 58, 60, 62-63, 367
555, 372, 382, 383
556 (Inner Casemate), 14, 22-23, 50, 52, 54, 130, 146-47, 149, 151-52, 169, 204, 211, 362, 367-68, 372, 376, 382, 453, 455-56, 464, 479, 488-89, 492, 560
560, 114, 170, 375
561, 58, 60, 63-64, 114-15, 170, 206, 382
562, 60, 114-15, 170, 375
564 (Outer Casmate), 147, 153, 204, 253, 255-56, 261, 294
568, 146
570, 254, 260
573, 169, 179-81, 205, 208, 223-24, 226, 252-66, 277, 281, 288, 291-92, 294-96, 302, 338, 343, 350
576, 265, 574
574, 169, 254, 260
577, 169, 254-56, 261, 265
578, 169, 254, 256-57, 260
639, 50
Wall A, 488
Wall B, 488
Wall C, 180
Wampler, J. C., 94-95, 98, 213, 274, 307, 334-35, 393, 397, 406, 416, 423-24, 427
Weippert, M., 511, 521-22
Westenholz, J. G., 578
Westermann, C., 557
Wheeler, Sir Mortimer, 1, 3
White-Ground Ware, 583
Whitley, C. F., 510
Wightman, G. I., 239, 241, 244
Wilson, J. V. K., 508, 511
Winckler, H., 560
Winnett, F. V., 428
Winter, I. J., 444, 526-27
Wiseman, D. J., 518-19, 535, 538, 540-41, 544-45, 547, 549, 551
Wolff, H. W., 509
Wright, G. E., 70, 82, 155, 176, 225, 238-40, 242-43, 250, 270-72, 313, 315, 334, 399, 404,

406, 411, 424, 524

Yadin, Y., 176, 238-41, 308, 327, 335, 443, 524
Yaḥzeyahu, 291
Yassıne, K., 407
Yaubi'di, see *Ilu-bi'di*
Yaudi, 552
Yeivin, S., 520, 540-41, 543, 550
Yoqneʿam, see *Tell Yoqneʿam*
Yoqneʿam Regional Project (YRP), 94, 96, 247, 250-51, 272, 279-81, 284, 308, 314, 321, 412, 429
Yosef, A., 439
Younger, Jr., K. L., 546, 558-59, 562, 566, 568-69, 579
Yurza, see *Tell Jemmeh*

Zabibe, 538, 541
Zadok, R., 570-71
Zagros Mountains, 570
Zakkur (king), 523
Zakkur Stele, 518, 521-23, 529
Zarzeki-Peleg, A., 227
Zayadine, F., 2, 179-80, 254, 309, 327, 333
Z Deep Pit, see *Samaria*
Zechariah, 506, 529, 540
Zettler, R. L., 537
Zikitu, 572
Zimhoni, O., 126-27, 219, 248-49, 289-91, 320, 323, 337, 425
Zimri, 576
Zinjirli, 427, 508, 521, 532, 536, 538
Zinjirli Inscriptions, 536
Zuckerman, B., 503